lonely planet

Coastal California

North Coast & Redwoods p212

Napa & Sonoma Wine Country p153

San Francisco p58

Marin County & the Bay Area p102

Central Coast p268

Santa Barbara County p335

Los Angeles p378

Disneyland & Orange County p416

San Diego & Around p448

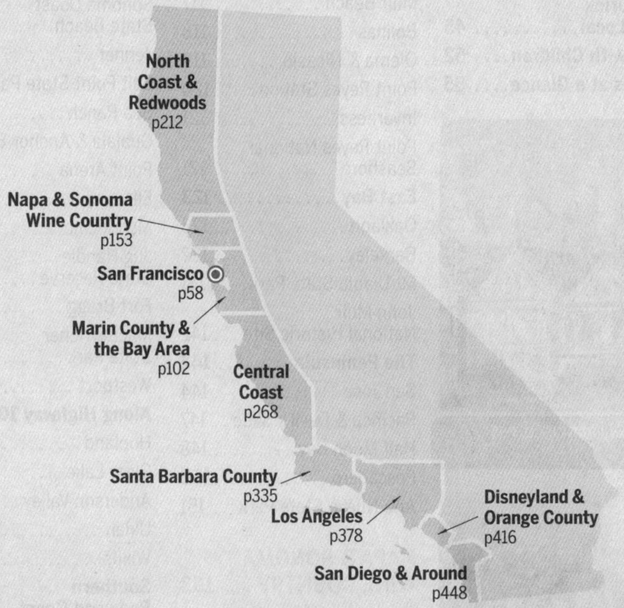

Nate Cavalieri,
Brett Atkinson, Andrew Bender, Sara Benson, Alison Bing, Cristian Bonetto,
Jade Bremner, Ashley Harrell, Josephine Quintero, John A Vlahides, Clifton Wilkinson

PLAN YOUR TRIP

CANADASTOCK/SHUTTERSTOCK ©

SAN FRANCISCO, P58

YINYANG/GETTY IMAGES ©

NAPA VALLEY P156

ON THE ROAD

Contents

Welcome to Coastal California

From towering redwoods in foggy Northern California to the perfect sun-kissed surf beaches of Southern California, this slice of Pacific Coast is a knockout beauty.

Beaches & Outdoor Fun

In all of your California dreaming, palm trees, golden sands and Pacific sunsets beckon, right? In coastal California, those cinematic fantasies really do come true. You can learn to surf, play a game of pickup volleyball or light an oceanfront bonfire on cool nights. Sunny beach towns from Santa Cruz south to San Diego, each with its own idiosyncratic personality, give you perfect excuses to go play outside. Heading north of San Francisco, dramatically windswept sands have inspired generations of poets and painters, offering miles of oceanfront for beachcombing and tramping in solitude.

Big Cities, Small Towns

No less astoundingly diverse than the landscapes are the people who have staked their fortunes here. Start out exploring San Francisco's one-of-a-kind neighborhoods, from beatnik North Beach to historic Chinatown, before going celebrity-spotting and people-watching in LA. In between, hang with radical tree-sitting lefties in Garberville, live the very good life in California's Wine Country, get groovy with new-age gurus in San Diego's North County, or talk fishing with salty dogs in port towns like Eureka, Bodega Bay and Monterey.

Food & Drink

Maybe your coastal sojourn will be an epicurean quest. Finding the most-killer fish tacos in San Diego alone could take days or even weeks. San Francisco and Los Angeles are both culinary capitals, where citizens passionately argue about the best sushi bar or food truck. LA is also a melting pot of multicultural cooking, from Thai Town to the tamale shops of East LA. Outside the cities, follow your nose and let it lead you serendipitously up and down California's coastal highways, stopping at seafood shacks, rollicking breweries and bountiful farmers markets and vineyards.

Creative Culture

From the mid-19th-century gold rush to the dot-com bubble, California has survived extreme booms and busts, often getting by on its wits. Today Hollywood still makes most of the world's movies and TV shows, fed by a vibrant performing-arts scene on stages across the state. In California the hottest trends are usually kick-started not by moguls in offices, but by motley crowds of surfers, artists and coastal dreamers concocting the out-there ideas behind everything from skateboarding to biotechnology. If you linger long enough, you might actually see the future evolving here.

Why I Love Coastal California

By Sara Benson, Writer

Like almost half of the people who live here, California wasn't where I was born, but it's where I've chosen to make my home. I never tire of road-tripping along the Golden State's coastal highways, seeking out hidden beaches and waterfalls, spots to paddle a canoe or kayak and craggy peaks to climb. Wildly beautiful Marin County is a quick drive away from my San Francisco base via the bridges over San Francisco Bay, tempting me to play truant on any given weekday. For weekend escapes, I head south to sunny Santa Cruz or north to the misty, verdant Redwood Coast.

For more about our writers, see p544

Above: Surfing in San Diego (p455)

Coastal California

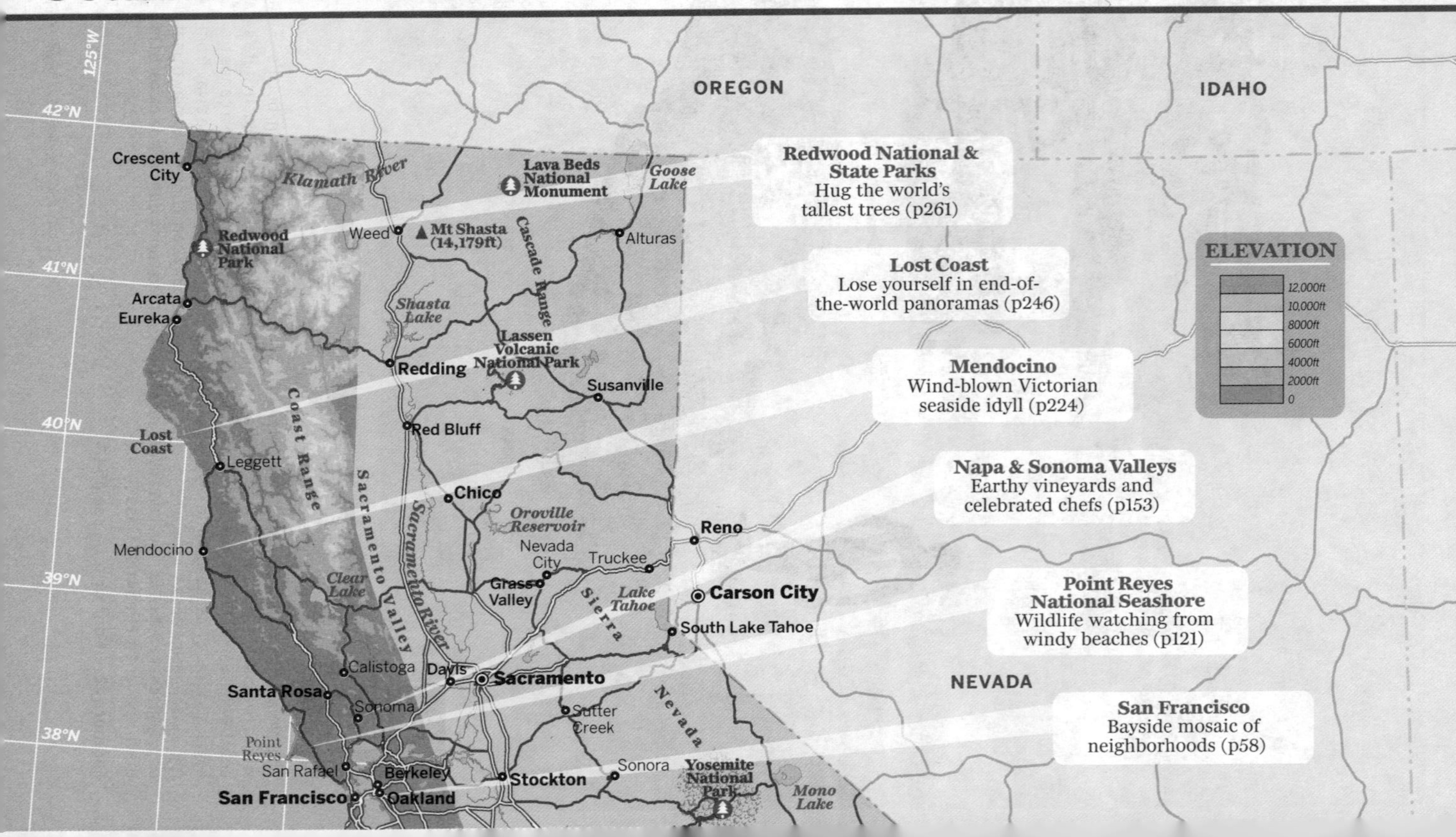

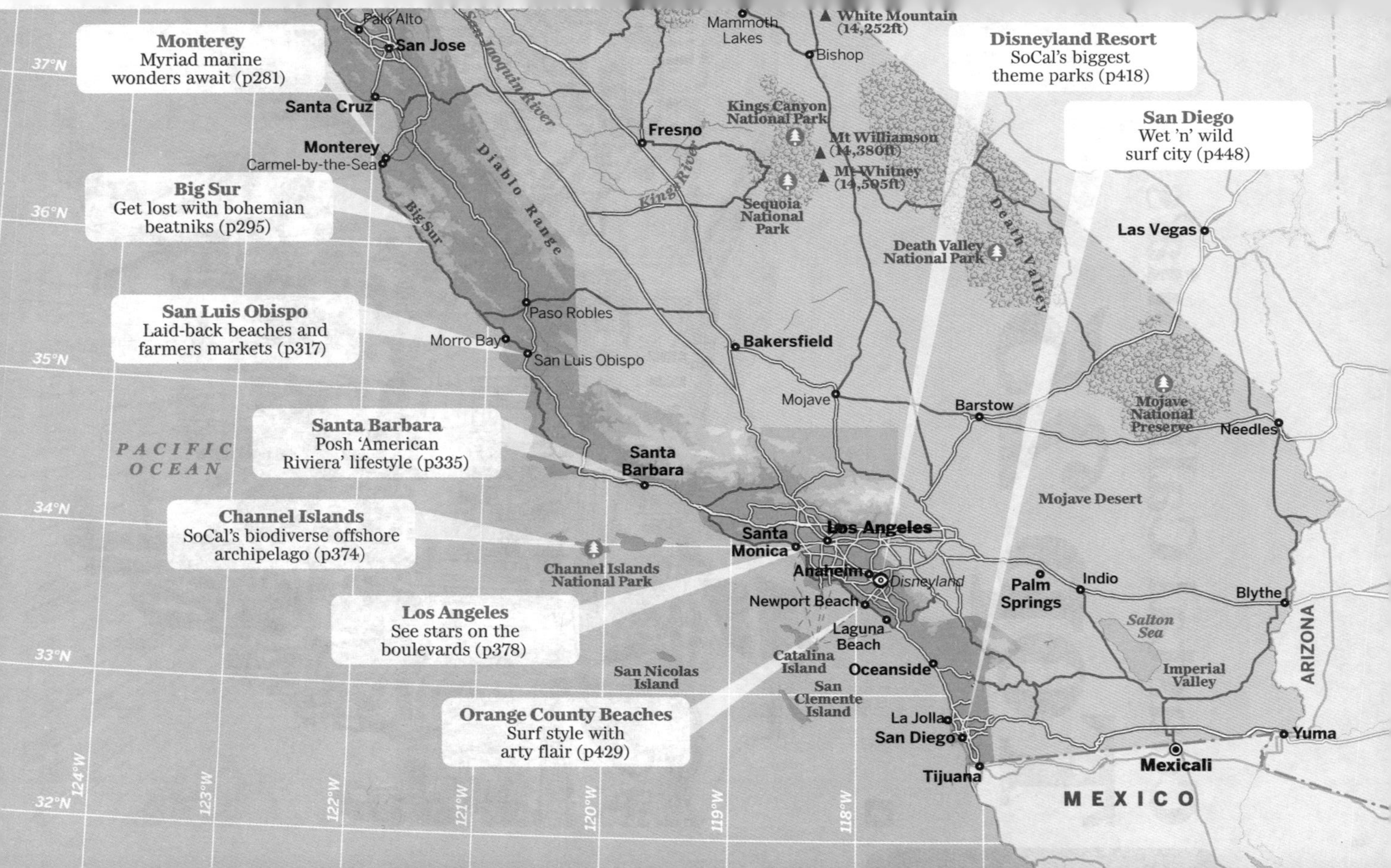

Monterey
Myriad marine wonders await (p281)
Big Sur
Get lost with bohemian beatniks (p295)
San Luis Obispo
Laid-back beaches and farmers markets (p317)
Santa Barbara
Posh 'American Riviera' lifestyle (p335)
Channel Islands
SoCal's biodiverse offshore archipelago (p374)
Los Angeles
See stars on the boulevards (p378)
Orange County Beaches
Surf style with arty flair (p429)
Disneyland Resort
SoCal's biggest theme parks (p418)
San Diego
Wet 'n' wild surf city (p448)
Palo Alto
San Jose
Santa Cruz
Monterey
Carmel-by-the-Sea
Big Sur
Diablo Range
San Joaquin River
Fresno
Kings River
Mammoth Lakes
Bishop
White Mountain (14,252ft)
Kings Canyon National Park
Mt Williamson (14,380ft)
Mt Whitney (14,505ft)
Sequoia National Park
Death Valley National Park
Death Valley
Las Vegas
Paso Robles
Morro Bay
San Luis Obispo
Bakersfield
Mojave
Barstow
Mojave National Preserve
Needles
PACIFIC OCEAN
Santa Barbara
Mojave Desert
Santa Monica
Los Angeles
Anaheim
Disneyland
Channel Islands National Park
Newport Beach
Laguna Beach
Palm Springs
Indio
Blythe
Salton Sea
ARIZONA
San Nicolas Island
Catalina Island
San Clemente Island
Oceanside
Imperial Valley
La Jolla
San Diego
Tijuana
Mexicali
Yuma
MEXICO
37°N
36°N
35°N
34°N
33°N
32°N
124°W
123°W
122°W
121°W
120°W
119°W
118°W

Coastal California's Top 25

1

San Francisco's Neighborhoods

1 As anyone who has ever clung to the side of a cable car can tell you, this city (p58) gives you a heck of a ride, from the Marina's chic waterfront to the edgy Mission District. And just when you think you have a grasp on the 'Paris of the West,' you turn another corner to find a brightly painted alleyway mural, a filigreed Victorian roofline or a hidden stairway leading up to bay-view panoramas that will entirely change your outlook. Below left: Pier 39 (p70)

Driving Big Sur

2 Nestled up against mossy, mysterious-looking redwood forests, the rocky Big Sur (p295) coast is a secretive place. Get to know it like the locals do, especially if you want to find hidden hot springs and beaches where the sand is tinged purple or where giant jade has washed ashore. Time your visit for May, when waterfalls peak, or after summer vacation crowds have left but sunny skies still rule. Crane your neck skyward to catch sight of endangered California condors taking wing above the cliffs.

BLUEBEAT76/GETTY IMAGES ©

2

PAUL M O'CONNELL/GETTY IMAGES ©

Exploring the City of Angels

3 LA (p378) runs deeper than its beaches, bottle-blond celebutantes and reality-TV entourages might lead you to believe. True, she has spawned tons of pop culture, from skateboarding to gangsta rap, while popularizing silicone implants and spandex. But the City of Angels has also nurtured artists, architects, writers, performers and film directors alongside yogis and alternative-health gurus. Ultimately, it's LA's ethnic diversity and vibrant immigrant cultures that make the biggest impression. Below: Griffith Observatory (p382)

Theme Parks

4 California is theme-park heaven, bringing Hollywood movie magic, Disney and roller coasters galore. Universal Studios Hollywood (p383) features movie-themed action rides, special-effects shows and the Wizarding World of Harry Potter. Disneyland Park (p418) and neighboring Disney California Adventure are SoCal's most visited tourist attraction: beloved cartoon characters waltz arm in arm down Main Street, U.S.A., and fireworks explode over Sleeping Beauty Castle. Knott's Berry Farm (p427) was SoCal's original theme park. Bottom: The Simpsons Ride, Universal Studios

3

CHRIS PRITCHARD/GETTY IMAGES ©

4

THE WORLD IN HDR/SHUTTERSTOCK ©

5
JORDAN SIEMENS/GETTY IMAGES ©

6
STEVE HEAP/SHUTTERSTOCK ©

7
DAVID LIU/GETTY IMAGES ©

Redwood National & State Parks

5 Ditch the cell phone and hug a tree, dude. And why not start with the world's tallest, the coast redwood? California's towering giants grow along much of the coast, from Big Sur south of San Francisco all the way north into Oregon. It's possible to cruise past these trees – or even drive right through them at old-fashioned tourist traps – but nothing compares to the awe you'll feel while walking among the ancient ones protected by interlocking Redwood National and State Parks (p261).

Malibu Escape

6 What, you didn't see any stars in Hollywood? We're so not surprised. Big-wig producers and A-list stars hide out in beachy Malibu (p387), a quick drive up the Pacific Coast Hwy from LA. Whoever said Malibu is a state of mind more than a place was right though: there's no real center here (apart from shopping malls), just miles of white-sand beaches and rolling Pacific waves backed by million-dollar oceanfront mansions. Luckily, those beautiful beaches are publicly accessible up to the high-tide line – any paparazzo can tell you that. Top right: El Matador State Beach (p387)

San Diego

7 San Diego's breezy confidence and sunny countenance are irresistible. The only problem with 'America's Finest City' (p448) is that with 70 miles of coastline and a near-perfect climate, it's tough to decide where to start. When in doubt, do as locals do: grab a fish taco and a surfboard, then hit the beach. Beautiful Balboa Park is where San Diegans come to play when they're not at the beach: you could spend the whole day at its famous zoo or immersed in any of a dozen art, cultural and science museums.

8

9

10

Hearst Castle

8 A monument to William Randolph Hearst's maniacal obsession with Old World treasures collected from Europe, Hearst Castle (p304) is the biggest showboat attraction on the Central Coast, not far south of Big Sur. Take a spin around Hearst's hilltop retreat with its sparkling outdoor Neptune Pool, interiors lavishly decorated in antiquities and jewels, and jaw-dropping coastal sunsets viewed from the balcony. Evening living-history tours will bring you back to the castle's 1930s heyday, when Hollywood celebrities hobnobbed with heads of state. Above: Doges Suite Sitting Room, Hearst Castle

Napa & Sonoma Wine Country

9 As winemaking in the Napa Valley grows evermore dizzyingly upscale, the neighboring Sonoma Valley's sun-dappled vineyards are still surrounded by pastoral ranchlands. Yet they share a common passion for the uniqueness of terroir. Here in California's best-known Wine Country (p153), you can take a tour of biodynamic vineyards, shake hands with famous winemakers or sample new vintages from the barrel in naturally cooled underground cellars, then crack open a bottle in the fields outside. Who cares if it's not noon? This is California: conventions need not apply.

Santa Barbara

10 Locals call it the 'American Riviera,' and honestly that's not too much of a stretch: Santa Barbara (p337) is so picturesque, you just have to sigh. Waving palm trees, sugar-sand beaches, boats bobbing by the harbor – it'd be a travel cliché if it wasn't the plain truth. California's 'Queen of the Missions' (Mission Santa Barbara) is a beauty, as are downtown's red-roofed, whitewashed adobe buildings, all rebuilt in harmonious Mission Revival style after a devastating earthquake in 1925. Come aspire to the breezy, rich-and-famous lifestyle over a long, lazy weekend.

Mission San Juan Capistrano

11 When you visit SoCal, you can't help but follow in at least a few of the footsteps of early Spanish conquistadors and Catholic priests. Mission San Juan Capistrano (p445), nicknamed the 'Jewel of the Missions,' was founded by peripatetic priest Junípero Serra in 1776. Authentically restored, the mission today deserves its nickname, with gorgeous gardens, stone arcades and fountains, and a chapel adorned with spiritual frescoes. In mid-March the whole town celebrates the swallows' famous return from South America to nest in the mission's walls.

Santa Cruz

12 Nowhere else can you get in touch with Northern California's countercultural roots faster than in flower-powered, surf-happy Santa Cruz (p270). White sandy beaches for wetsuit-wearing, board-riding dudes and chicks? Check. A carnivalesque downtown flush with crunchy cafes, one-of-a-kind shops and eccentric personalities? Yup. Tree-hugger hippie camps and outsider artists' cabins in the redwood forests? Uh-huh. Left-of-liberal politics, Rastafarian dreadlocks and new-age crystal readings? Of course, man.

Bottom: Hula hoopers, Steamer Lane (p273)

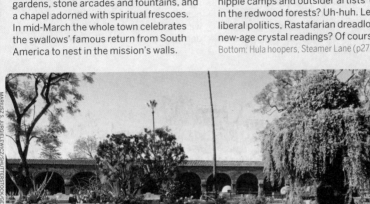

11

12

Orange County Beaches

13 In Orange County (p429), there are beaches for all. Huntington draws the hang-loose, trust-fund surfer crowd, while biker rebels, bodacious babes and anti-establishment types hit Sunset Beach. Families with younger kids gravitate toward old-fashioned Seal Beach and its pier, but glamorous teens, trophy wives and yachties cavort in the fantasyland of Newport Beach. Furthest south, Laguna Beach beckons with its sophisticated blend of money and culture. Startlingly beautiful seascapes inspired an artists colony to take root there. Below: Thousand Steps Beach (p441)

Monterey

14 Often foggy and wind-tossed, the peninsular fishing village of Monterey (p281) calls to mind John Steinbeck and his gritty novels of American realism. Hop aboard a whale-watching cruise out into the bay's national marine sanctuary, some of whose aquatic denizens also swim in Cannery Row's eco-conscious, family-friendly aquarium. Soak up more authentic maritime atmosphere at the West Coast's oldest lighthouse in Pacific Grove, then wander downtown Monterey's hidden gardens and historic adobe-walled buildings.

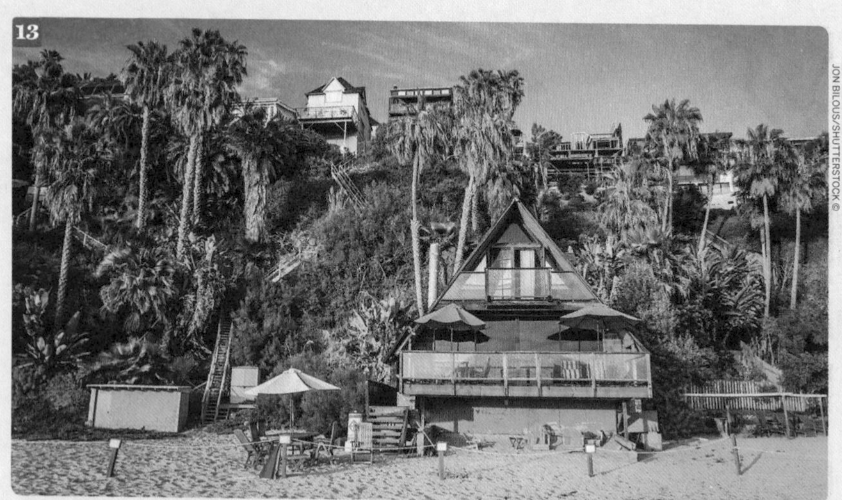

13

JON BILOUS/SHUTTERSTOCK ©

14

MARK SMITH NSB/SHUTTERSTOCK ©

KENEVA PHOTOGRAPHY/SHUTTERSTOCK ©

MMPHOTOS/GETTY IMAGES ©

COREY RICH/GETTY IMAGES ©

Point Reyes National Seashore

15 If just one park could encapsulate Northern California, Point Reyes (p121) would get our vote. Step across the jagged gash of the San Andreas Fault, then stand out by the lighthouse at what truly feels like land's end. Peer through binoculars at migratory whales, or witness the raucous birthing and mating antics of endangered elephant seals at Chimney Rock. Then go hiking among herds of tule elk and drive out to more remote, windswept beaches, where the horizon stretches toward infinity.

Above: Peregrine falcon

Mendocino

16 Originally a 19th-century port built by New Englanders, Mendocino (p224) today belongs to bohemians who would scoff at the puritanical virtues of early settlers, instead favoring art and nature's outdoor temple for their modern religions. In summer fragrant bursts of lavender and jasmine drift on fog-laden winds over the town's unique redwood water towers, while at any time of year nothing restores the soul like a ramble out onto the craggy headland cliffs here. Churning surf is never out of earshot, and driftwood-littered beaches are potent reminders of the sea's power.

Lost Coast

17 Hellloooo? Anyone out there? This is the coast that time has just about forgotten. Buoyed by the wilderness peaks of the Kings Range and speckled by wild beaches of volcanic origin, the Lost Coast (p246) makes you earn the right to see its natural wonders. Time your multiday backpacking trek to match the flow of the tides and camp out by the crashing surf on a deserted beach along the Lost Coast Trail, or drive yourself to the last outpost of civilization, tiny Shelter Cove.

Santa Barbara Wine Country

18 Southern California's answer to Napa and Sonoma is the Santa Ynez and Santa Maria Valleys, aka *Sideways* Wine Country (p357). Less than an hour's drive from Santa Barbara, you can wander through fields of grapes, tipple soft Pinot Noir and sample the sun-drenched good life. Start in dandified Los Olivos, where the streets are packed with wine-tasting rooms and bistros. Then slowly wind north along the Foxen Canyon Wine Trail, a two-lane country road where famous-name wineries and boutique winemakers are neighbors. Below: Vineyards, Los Olivos (p362)

La Jolla

19 On the most beautiful stretch of San Diego's coastline, La Jolla (p427) is definitely not just another So-Cal beach town. Sitting pretty atop rocky bluffs just a whisper's breath from the sea, La Jolla's richly adorned downtown is crowded with fashion-forward boutiques, chic cafes and posh hotels. But what's right on the shoreline is even more of a treasure, especially the all-natural fishbowl of La Jolla Cove, and windswept Torrey Pines State Natural Reserve (p473), further north along the ribbon of coastal highway, where hang-gliders fly. Right: Brown pelican

19

SARAH JESSUP/SHUTTERSTOCK ©

20

COREY JENKINS/GETTY IMAGES ©

21

CHASE DEKKER/SHUTTERSTOCK ©

San Luis Obispo

20 Almost exactly between San Francisco and Los Angeles, San Luis Obispo (p317) is often overlooked, but its collection of organic farms, vineyards and ranchlands is refreshingly down to earth. Detour here for uncrowded beach towns, spectacular hiking and camping at state parks and beaches, and, most of all, locavorian bounty sold at more than a dozen farmers markets. You won't even need a car – arrive in style on Amtrak's *Pacific Surfliner* or *Coast Starlight* trains, which chug past unforgettable coastal scenery.

Whale-Watching

21 Thar she blows! All up and down the coast, and no matter what the season, you can spot migratory whales offshore from California. During summer and fall, blue and humpback whales cruise by. But the biggest parades happen every winter and spring when gray whales make their annual migrations between the arctic waters of Alaska and balmy breeding and birthing lagoons in the Gulf of Mexico. Jump aboard a whale-watching boat tour – Monterey (p281) is a good place to start – to observe these majestic marine mammals up close and personal. Above: Humpback whale tail

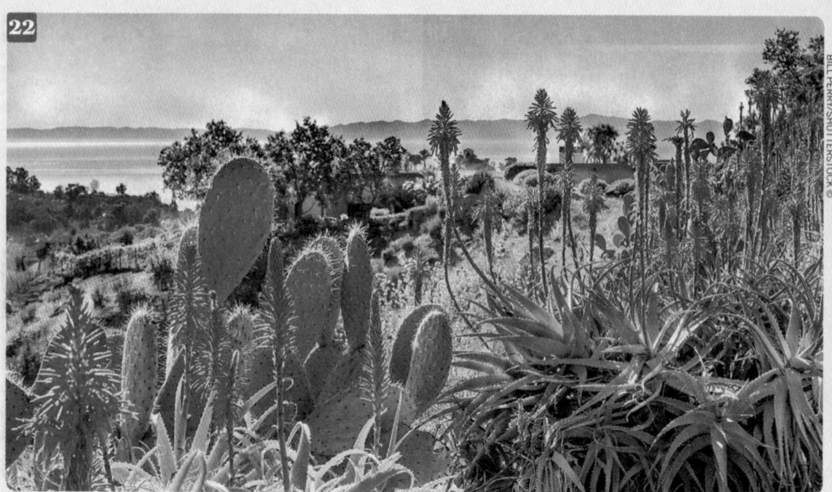

BILL PERRY/SHUTTERSTOCK ©

GIANPAOLO_PHOTO/SHUTTERSTOCK ©

Channel Islands National Park

22 The Channel Islands are SoCal's answer to the Galapagos. Centuries ago, seafaring Chumash tribespeople established villages on remote rocks. Today the islands support an abundance of marine life, from coral-reef creatures to giant colonies of pinnipeds. Get back to nature in Channel Islands National Park (p374), a wildlife haven with sea-kayaking and snorkeling opportunities, as well as challenging hiking trails and rustic campgrounds.

Venice

23 New-agey bohemians, muscled bodybuilders, goth punks, hippie tribal drummers and genuine freaks all gravitate toward the beach city of Venice (p388) and and its infamous Ocean Front Walk (aka Venice Boardwalk). It's the place where the crazy side of SoCal really lets it all hang out. Imagine an outdoor carnival in which audience participation is practically required. Strap on those in-line skates, hop on a beach cruiser or just strut in your bikini down the sunny beachfront boardwalk.

Above: Venice Skatepark (p388)

JEREMY BORKAT/SHUTTERSTOCK ©

CHAMELEONSEYE/SHUTTERSTOCK ©

Bolinas

24 Locals keep taking down the highway signs to prevent you from discovering this paradisaical hamlet (p118) by the sea in Marin County, but once you finally find it, the rewards justify the effort. Take time out to go beachcombing along Agate Beach (p119), paddle around the placid waters of Bass Lake, or gin up your courage enough to talk politics with the grizzled old fishers and baby boomers at a saloon while slurping down oyster shooters and an icy beer or two. Top: Alamere Falls (p119), Bolinas

Sausalito

25 It's not just seabirds and seals – travelers also flock to this little fishing and houseboat community (p106) on San Francisco Bay, just north of the iconic Golden Gate Bridge. Cruise Sausalito's little downtown on a bicycle, then walk around the bohemian houseboat docks. Feast on fresh sushi or grilled seafood before hopping on a ferry back across the bay, letting the salty maritime breezes lick your lips.

Need to Know

For more information, see Survival Guide (p517)

Currency
US dollar ($)

Language
English and Spanish

Visas
Generally not required for stays of 90 days or less for citizens of Visa Waiver Program (VWP) countries with ESTA approval (apply online at least 72 hours in advance).

Money
ATMs are widely available. Credit cards are usually required for reservations. Traveler's checks (US dollars) are rarely accepted. Tipping is customary, not optional.

Cell Phones
The only foreign phones that will work in the USA are GSM multiband models. Buy prepaid SIM cards locally. Coverage can be spotty in remote areas.

Time
Pacific Standard Time (GMT/UTC minus eight hours)

When to Go

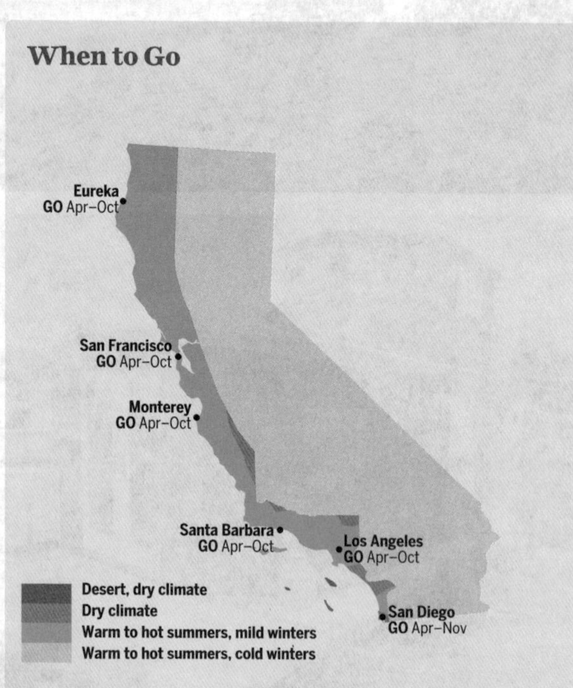

High Season (Jun–Aug)

➡ Cost of accommodations up 50–100%.

➡ Major holidays are even busier and more expensive.

➡ Thick clouds may blanket the coast during 'June gloom,' which can last into July.

Shoulder (Apr, May, Sep & Oct)

➡ Crowds and prices drop off almost everywhere along the coast.

➡ Mild temperatures, with many sunny, cloudless days.

➡ Weather typically wetter in spring, drier in autumn.

Low Season (Nov–Mar)

➡ Fewest crowds and lowest lodging rates, except sometimes in cities and around holidays and spring break.

➡ Chilly temperatures bring more frequent rainstorms throughout winter.

Useful Websites

California Travel and Tourism Commission (www.visitcalifornia.com) Multilingual trip-planning guides.

Lonely Planet (www.lonelyplanet.com/usa/california) Destination information, hotel bookings, traveler forums and more.

LA Times (www.latimes.com/travel/california) Travel news, deals and weekend escapes.

Sunset (www.sunset.com/travel/california) Savvy local and insider travel tips.

California State Parks (www.parks.ca.gov) Outdoor activities, camping and more.

Important Numbers

All phone numbers have a three-digit area code followed by a seven-digit local number. For long-distance and toll-free calls, dial ☎1 plus all 10 digits.

Country code	☎1
International dialing code	☎011
Operator	☎0
Emergency (ambulance, fire & police)	☎911
Directory assistance (local)	☎411

Exchange Rates

Australia	A$1	$0.77
Canada	C$1	$0.76
China	Y10	$1.46
Euro zone	€1	$1.05
Japan	¥100	$0.89
Mexico	MXN10	$0.50
New Zealand	NZ$1	$0.72
UK	£1	$1.25

For current exchange rates see www.xe.com.

Daily Costs

Budget: Less than $100

- Hostel dorm bed: $25–60
- Take-out meal: $8–12
- Beach parking: free–$15

Midrange: $100–250

- Two-star inland motel or hotel double room: $75–200
- Sit-down meal in casual restaurant: $20–50
- Rental car per day, excluding insurance and gas: $30–70

Top end: More than $250

- Three-star coastal hotel or beach resort room: $150–300
- Three-course meal excluding drinks in a top restaurant: $75–125

Opening Hours

Businesses, restaurants and shops may close earlier and on additional days during the winter off-season (November to March). Otherwise, standard opening hours are as follows:

Banks 9am–6pm Monday to Friday, some 9am–1pm or later Saturday

Bars 5pm–2am

Business hours (general) 9am–5pm Monday to Friday

Nightclubs 10pm–4am Thursday to Saturday

Post offices 8:30am–5pm Monday to Friday, some 8:30am–noon or later Saturday

Restaurants 7:30am–10am, 11:30am–2pm and 5pm–9pm, some open later Friday and Saturday

Shops 10am–6pm Monday to Saturday, noon–5pm Sunday (malls open later)

Supermarkets 8am–9pm or 10pm, some 24 hours

Arriving in Coastal California

Los Angeles International Airport Taxis to most city destinations ($30 to $50) take 30 minutes to one hour. Door-to-door shuttles ($15 to $20) operate 24 hours. FlyAway bus ($9.75) runs to downtown LA. Free shuttles connect with LAX City Bus Center & Metro Rail station.

San Francisco International Airport Taxis into the city ($45 to $65) take 25 to 50 minutes. Door-to-door shuttles (around $17) operate 24 hours. BART trains ($8.95, 30 minutes) serve the airport, running from 5:30am (later on weekends) to midnight daily.

Getting Around

Most people drive themselves around California. You can also fly (it's expensive) or take cheaper long-distance buses or scenic trains. In cities, when distances are too far to walk, hop aboard buses, trains, streetcars, cable cars or trolleys, or grab a taxi.

Car Metro-area traffic can be nightmarish, especially during weekday commuter rush hours (roughly 6am to 10am and 3pm to 7pm). City parking is often an expensive hassle.

Bus Usually the cheapest and slowest option, but with extensive metro-area networks. Inter-city, regional and long-distance Greyhound routes are limited and more expensive.

Train The fastest way to get around the San Francisco Bay Area and LA, but lines don't go everywhere. Pricier regional and long-distance Amtrak trains connect some destinations.

For much more on **getting around**, see p526

If You Like...

Wine

Napa and Sonoma are ultrafamous, but California's other wine regions more than hold their own. Crack open a bottle from these sun-kissed rural valleys – you'll be a believer.

Napa Valley Pay your respects to California's legendary big-name producers in this premier wine-growing region. (p156)

Sonoma Valley Shake hands with independent-minded boutique winemakers in sun-dappled biodynamic vineyards. (p179)

Russian River Valley Tipple at woodsy wineries after a lazy day of canoeing on the river. (p191)

Santa Barbara Wine Country Pastoral country roads wind past famous vintners and smaller family-owned estate wineries. (p357)

Paso Robles Dozens of down-to-earth vineyards produce rich, earthy Zinfandels, with olive-oil farms nearby. (p314)

Anderson Valley Mendocino County's rural valley, where apple orchards abound, hides petite wineries worth a detour. (p237)

National Parks & Nature Reserves

All along the coast, a chain of public parks protects an astonishing diversity of life zones, extending offshore to marine sanctuaries and wind-tossed islands. Just inland, misty redwood forests beckon.

Redwood National & State Parks Get lost ambling among ancient groves of the world's tallest trees on the foggy North Coast. (p261)

Channel Islands National Park Escape civilization on SoCal's far-flung islands, nicknamed 'California's Galapagos.' (p374)

Point Reyes National Seashore Step on the San Andreas Fault, hike to end-of-the-world beaches and spy wildlife. (p121)

Monterey Bay National Marine Sanctuary Cruise above an undersea canyon on a whale-watching boat, then kayak Elkhorn Slough. (p281)

Big Sur's state parks Find waterfalls in redwood forests and walk along sea cliffs, above which California condors soar. (p297)

Crystal Cove State Park Go scuba diving or tide pooling along gorgeously undeveloped beaches in Orange County. (p439)

Hot Springs & Spas

Get nekkid and soak in natural hot-springs pools, rent your own private redwood hot tub under the stars, or get pampered at a Wine Country spa.

Calistoga Volcanic mud baths are just what the doctor ordered before a day of wine tasting. (p174)

Big Sur Take an oceanfront sea-cliff dip at Esalen or trek to wilderness Sykes Hot Springs. (p295)

North Coast Find holistic health cures, soak in naturally carbonated springs or go bohemian hot-tubbing. (p212)

Avila Beach At a mineral-springs spa, book a hillside hot tub just for two. (p321)

RARENA/SHUTTERSTOCK ©

TERENCE/SHUTTERSTOCK ©

Top: Mission San Juan Capistrano (p444)

Bottom: Sea otter, Elkhorn Slough National Estuarine Research Reserve (p281)

Hiking

Oceanside rambles, panorama-view mountain summits and verdant forest idylls await.

North Coast & Redwoods Hardy backpackers challenge the remote Lost Coast Trail, while families ramble among tall trees. (p212)

Marin County Tawny headlands and wild, windblown Point Reyes tempt hikers across the Golden Gate Bridge. (p104)

Central Coast Seek out Big Sur's secret waterfalls and climb volcanic peaks around San Luis Obispo. (p268)

Los Angeles Run around LA's Griffith Park, or head up into the untamed Santa Monica Mountains. (p387)

Fabulous Food

Flavored by immigrant cultures for more than 200 years, California cuisine is all about creatively mixing it up, from kimchi tacos to vegan soul food.

Chez Panisse Berkeley chef Alice Waters revolutionized California cuisine with seasonal, locavorian cooking. (p138)

French Laundry This high-flying kitchen mastered by Thomas Keller is a gastronomic highlight of Napa's Wine Country. (p168)

Ferry Building Drop by the farmers market, or duck inside for San Francisco Bay Area artisanal food vendors. (p61)

LA's food trucks They're everywhere now, but LA sparked the mobile foodie revolution, with over 200 chefs-on-wheels. (p49)

Marin County Shuck fresh oysters by the sea, taste gourmet cheeses and stop at roadside farms. (p104)

Small Towns

When you tire of California's never-ending freeway traffic, make your escape to these in-between spots, whether by the beach or just down the road from vineyards.

Ferndale The North Coast's most charming Victorian farm town, filled with 'butterfat mansions.' (p250)

Bolinas This end-of-the-road hamlet in Marin County isn't exactly a secret anymore. (p118)

Seal Beach Orange County surf spot with an old-fashioned main street and wooden pier. (p430)

Ojai Catch a 'pink moment' at sunset over this sleepy, arty little Shangri-la outside LA. (p369)

Mendocino North Coast seaside village perches on ocean bluffs, where landscape painters set up their easels. (p224)

Scenic Drives

Drop the convertible top and step on it! California's coastal routes deliver surreally beautiful ocean vistas and serpentine cliffside stretches.

Orange County Coast SoCal's famous stretch of Hwy 1, aka the Pacific Coast Highway, hopscotches between beach towns in SoCal. (p331)

Avenue of the Giants Roll through ancient groves of redwood trees in NorCal's Humboldt Redwoods State Park. (p248)

Carmel-by-the-Sea Postcard Pacific vistas beckon all along the 17-Mile Drive, a private toll road around the Monterey Peninsula. (p291)

Big Sur Twist and turn atop dizzying sea cliffs along Hwy 1 on the peaceful Central Coast. (p295)

Aquariums & Zoos

California is chockablock with futuristic theme parks and other family-friendly attractions to keep kids entertained for days, but for many, it's the local wildlife that are the real stars.

Monterey Bay Aquarium Watch otters play at feeding time, touch tide-pool critters and get chills as sharks swim by. (p281)

San Diego Zoo In leafy Balboa Park, California's best zoo exhibits 800 different animal species from around the world. (p450)

San Diego Zoo Safari Park Take a safari-style tram tour through an 'open-range' zoo where giraffes and lions roam. (p479)

Aquarium of the Pacific Meet coastal California's denizens of the deep at Long Beach, just south of LA. (p388)

Los Angeles Zoo & Botanical Gardens Originally a refuge for retired circus animals, this conservation-minded zoo is inside Griffith Park. (p382)

History

Native American tribes, Spanish-colonial presidios (forts) and Catholic missions and Mexican pueblos (towns) have all left traces here for you to find.

Mission San Juan Capistrano A painstakingly restored jewel along 'El Camino Real,' California's mission trail. (p445)

Old Town San Diego State Historic Park Time travel back to the late 19th century at California's first civilian Spanish pueblo. (p453)

Monterey State Historic Park Beautifully preserved brick and adobe buildings from California's Spanish, Mexican and American periods. (p282)

Hearst Castle A fantastical hilltop mansion filled with priceless art and antiquities on the Central Coast. (p304)

Film & TV Locations

All California's a sound stage, it sometimes seems. To witness the magic in action, join a live studio audience or tour a movie studio in LA.

Los Angeles Hollywood was born here. You can't throw a director's megaphone without hitting a movie location. (p502)

San Francisco Bay Area Relive film-noir classics like *The Maltese Falcon* and Hitchcock's thrillers *Vertigo* and *The Birds*. (p501)

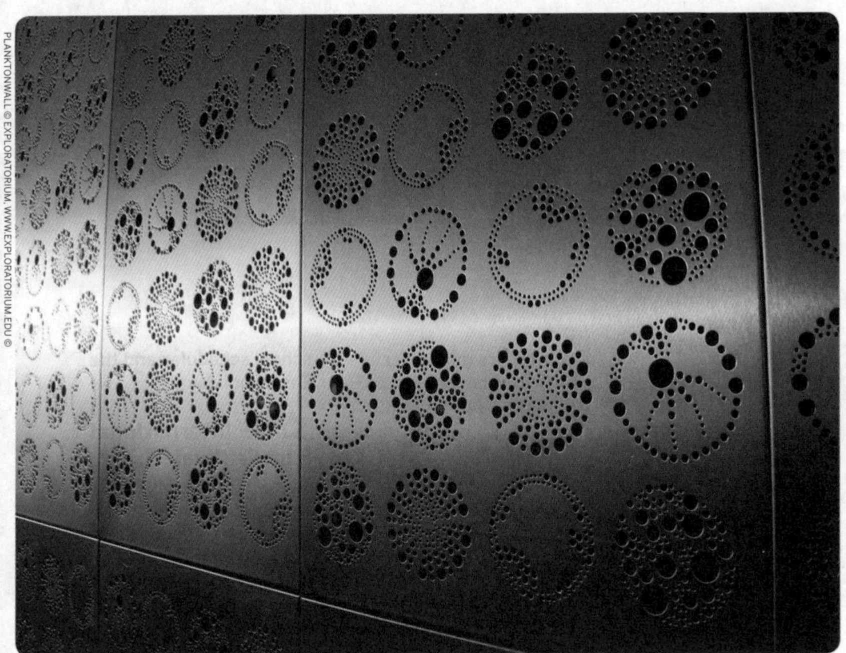

PLANKTONWALL © EXPLORATORIUM, WWW.EXPLORATORIUM.EDU ©

Planktonwall ©, Exploratorium (p69), San Francisco

Mendocino For over a century, this tiny North Coast town has starred in dozens of movies. (p224)

Santa Barbara Idyllic 'American Riviera' sets the scene for zany rom-coms such as *Sideways* and *It's Complicated*. (p337)

Museums

Who says coastal California only has pop culture? You could spend most of your trip viewing multi-million-dollar art galleries, high-tech science exhibits, out-of-this-world planetariums and more.

Balboa Park Spend all day hopping between San Diego's top-notch art, history and science museums. (p450)

Getty Center LA art museum that is as beautiful as its elevated setting and ocean views. (p385)

California Academy of Sciences Natural-history museum in SF's Golden Gate Park breathes 'green' with a living roof. (p72)

Los Angeles County Museum of Art More than 150,000 works of art span the ages and cross all borders. (p383)

Griffith Observatory There's no better place to see stars in Hollywood than at this hilltop planetarium. (p382)

Exploratorium Even adults love the interactive science fun at this indoor/outdoor landmark on San Francisco Bay. (p69)

Month by Month

TOP EVENTS

Tournament of Roses, January

Kinetic Grand Championship, May

Pageant of the Masters, July

Fleet Week, September

Tall Ships Festival, September

January

Typically the wettest and coldest month in coastal California, January is a slow time for coastal travel, except over the Martin Luther King Jr Day holiday weekend.

Tournament of Roses

Held before the Rose Bowl college football game, this famous New Year's parade of flower-festooned floats, marching bands and prancing equestrians draws more than 700,000 spectators to Pasadena, a suburb of LA.

Chinese New Year

Firecrackers, parades, lion dances and street food accompany the Lunar New Year, falling in late January or early February. Some of California's most colorful festivities happen in San Francisco and LA. (p82)

March

Mendocino Coast Whale Festivals

As the northbound winter migration of gray whales peaks, Mendocino, Fort Bragg and nearby towns celebrate with food and wine tastings, art shows and naturalist-guided walks and talks over multiple weekends in March. (p226)

Festival of the Swallows

After wintering in South America, the famous swallows return to Orange County's Mission San Juan Capistrano around March 19. The historic mission town honors its Spanish and Mexican heritage with events all month long.

April

Shoulder season all along California's coast means lower prices, especially on accommodations, except during spring break (exact dates vary, depending on school schedules and the Easter holiday).

SF International Film Festival

One of the Americas' longest-running film festivals has been lighting up San Francisco since 1957, with a slate of independent-minded films, including international premieres. (p82)

May

California's weather starts to heat up, although some coastal areas remain blanketed by fog (nicknamed 'May gray'). Travel peaks over the Memorial Day holiday weekend.

Cinco de Mayo

¡Viva México! Margaritas, music and merriment commemorate the victory of Mexican forces at the Battle of Puebla on May 5, 1862. LA and San Diego do it in style.

Kinetic Grand Championship

Over Memorial Day weekend, this 'triathlon of the art world' involves a three-day race from Arcata to Ferndale on the North Coast. Competitors outdo each other in inventing human-powered, self-propelled and sculptural contraptions. (p256)

June

Once school lets out for the summer, nearly everywhere in California gets busy, even though fog ('June gloom') lingers in some coastal areas, particularly in Northern California.

Pride

Out and proud since 1970, many of California's LGBTQ pride events take place throughout June, with costumed parades, coming-out parties, live music, DJs and more, especially in San Francisco and LA. San Diego celebrates in mid-July. (p82)

July

Beach season gets into full swing, especially in Southern California, where theme parks are mobbed by families. The July 4th holiday is summer's busiest travel weekend.

Pageant of the Masters

Exhibits by hundreds of artists and a pageant of masterpiece paintings 're-created' by actors keep Orange County's Laguna Beach extremely busy during July and August. (p442)

Reggae on the River

Come party with the 'Humboldt Nation' of hippies, Rastafarians, tree huggers and other fun NorCal freaks for four days of live reggae bands, arts and crafts, barbecue, juggling, unicycling, camping and swimming. (p246)

August

Sunny weather and warm water temperatures keep beaches packed. Students go back to school, but everywhere along the coast stays busy at least through the Labor Day holiday weekend.

Old Spanish Days Fiesta

Santa Barbara revives its early Spanish, Mexican and American heritage with flashy parades, cowboy rodeo events, arts-and-crafts shows, live music and dancing. (p345)

September

Officially summer's last hurrah is the Labor Day holiday weekend, when everywhere is extremely crowded. Afterward, the beaches and cities begin to see fewer visitors.

Fleet Week

San Diego's military pride is on display during this week (more like a month) of parades, concerts, shipboard tours and the USA's largest air show in late September or early October. (p458)

October

Despite beautifully sunny and balmy weather, coastal travel starts slowing down. Shoulder-season deals abound at beaches and in cities as temperatures begin to cool off.

Vineyard Festivals

All month long under sunny skies, California's wine countries bring in the harvest with gourmet food-and-wine shindigs, grape-stomping 'crush' parties and barrel tastings.

November

Día de los Muertos

Mexican communities honor deceased ancestors on November 2 with costumed parades, sugar skulls, graveyard picnics, candlelight processions and fabulous altars, including in San Francisco, LA and San Diego. (p84)

December

Winter rains start to drench coastal California, greening the hills. Christmas and New Year's Eve are extremely busy times, with a short-lived lull in travel between them.

Boat Parades of Lights

Spicing up the Christmas holiday season with nautical cheer, brightly bedecked and illuminated boats float through many coastal California harbors, most famously at Newport Beach and San Diego. (p435)

Itineraries

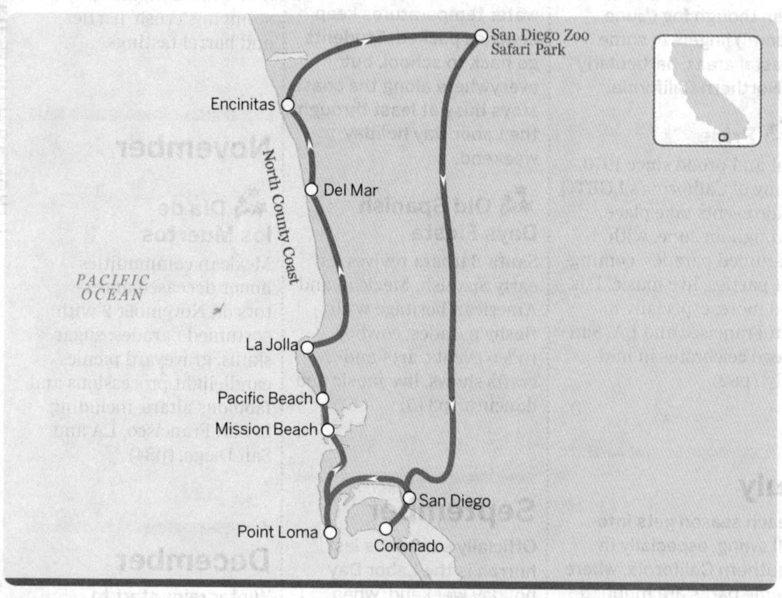

San Diego & North County

The best part about San Diego? It's almost always around 68°F (20°C) and sunny. Add insanely good Mexican food, beaches of all stripes, historic sites and one of the best zoos in the world (plus an open-range safari park). Are you sold yet?

Spend a couple of days at **San Diego**'s pearl-like beaches, stretching all the way up the North County Coast. But before you head northward, drive out to **Point Loma** for sweeping views, or take a ferry over to old-fashioned **Coronado**, with its famous Hotel del Coronado. Ride the Giant Dipper roller coaster at family-friendly **Mission Beach** and join the funky surfers at **Pacific Beach**, dive or snorkel in gorgeous **La Jolla**, soar in a hot-air balloon at **Del Mar** and get new-agey in **Encinitas**.

On day three, if you have kids, make a beeline to the suburban **San Diego Zoo Safari Park**, where giraffes, lions and zebras roam. Otherwise, head back to San Diego to explore the zoo at museum-loaded Balboa Park and the atmospheric Spanish-Mexican Old Town. End your trip with a wild night out in the city's Gaslamp Quarter downtown.

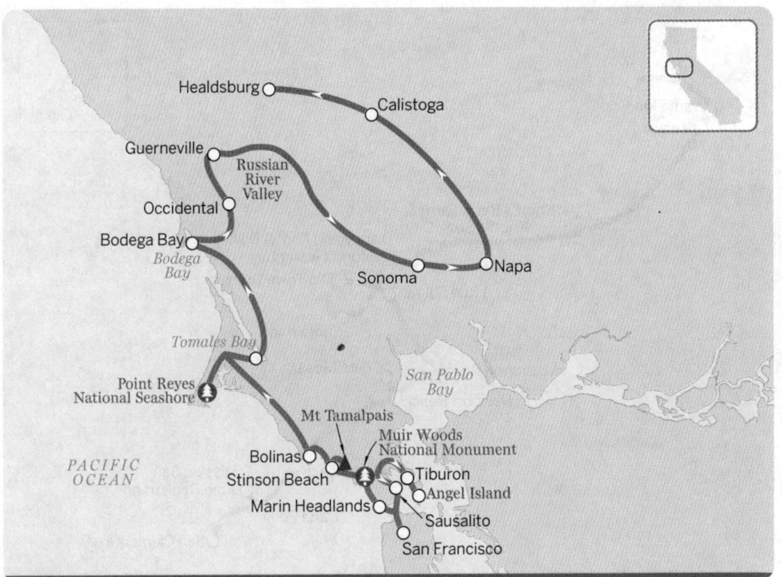

San Francisco, Marin County & Wine Country

Clamber around the hilly 7-sq-mile peninsula that is dashing, innovative San Francisco. Then soak up the natural beauty of Marin County before indulging in a wine-splashed weekend in Napa and Sonoma Wine Country.

Start with a full day in **San Francisco** spent uncovering the alleyways of Chinatown, wandering the mural-adorned Mission district and climbing Coit Tower above beatnik North Beach. Then brave the fog on a cruise over to Alcatraz from Fisherman's Wharf, or lose yourself on a sunny day in Golden Gate Park, stopping to smell the flowers where hippies danced during 1967's 'Summer of Love.' Wherever you roam, eat everything in sight – especially at the waterfront Ferry Building on the Embarcadero.

Escape the city on day two via the landmark Golden Gate Bridge, which you can trek, cycle or drive across. On the far side of the bay, photograph the floating houseboats of picturesque **Sausalito**, or go hiking and mountain-biking across the **Marin Headlands**, where a swinging footbridge leads to historic Point Bonita Lighthouse. To really get away from it all, hop aboard the ferry from **Tiburon** over to **Angel Island**, within view of San Francisco's skyscrapers.

Meander north along the Marin County coast on day three, passing the tall redwood trees of **Muir Woods National Monument**, crescent-shaped **Stinson Beach** and the turnoff to quirky small-town **Bolinas**. Veer inland to conquer **Mt Tamalpais** or make your way to wildly beautiful **Point Reyes National Seashore**, where end-of-the-world beaches lead to long rambles, and you can spy whales in winter from the historic lighthouse. Save time for sea kayaking at nearby **Tomales Bay**.

Finish with two days in Wine Country. From **Bodega Bay**, country roads wind inland to charming **Occidental** and the vineyards of the **Russian River Valley**. Paddle a canoe downriver to **Guerneville**, with its redwood cottages and swimming at the beach in summer. Truck east across Hwy 101, then head south into Northern California's Wine Country, orbiting stylish **Napa** and its countrified but still-chic cousin **Sonoma**. Soak your road-weary bones in a volcanic mud bath at a hot-springs spa in **Calistoga** before winding down in posh **Healdsburg**.

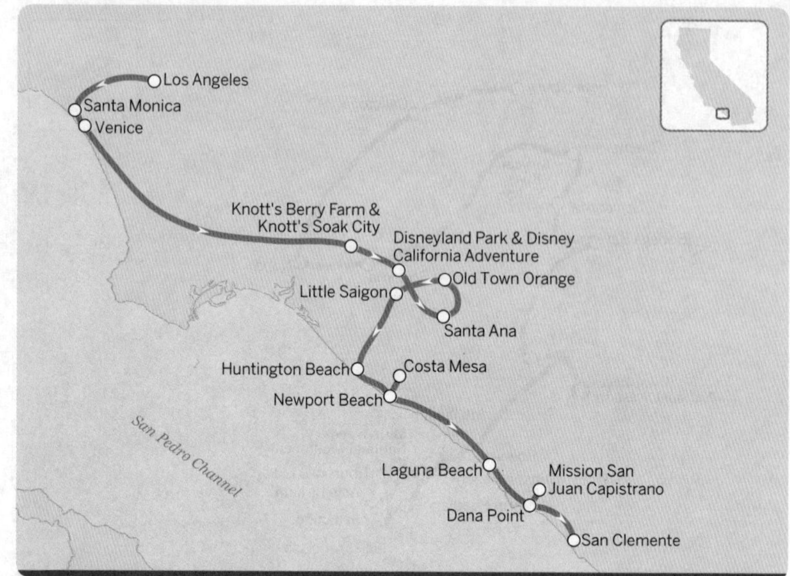

Los Angeles, Disneyland & Orange County

Kick things off in Los Angeles, where top-notch attractions, miles of beaches and tasty food form an irresistible trifecta, before tripping through Orange County's theme parks and sunny beaches.

On your first two days in **Los Angeles**, traipse along the star-studded sidewalks of clubby Hollywood, dive into the arts and cultural scenes Downtown, browse museums in Mid-City and catch sunset from the hilltop Getty Center in West LA. Out at the Pacific's edge, sophisticated **Santa Monica** beckons with a carnival seaside pier and creative restaurants, while alternative **Venice** lives and breathes beachy boho-chic style.

Heading inland on day three, make a date with Mickey at perfectly 'imagineered' **Disneyland Park** and neighboring **Disney California Adventure**, a theme park celebrating the Golden State. Both are in Anaheim, and not far from **Knott's Berry Farm**, America's oldest theme park, which pairs Old West cowboy themes with high-tech roller coasters that appeal most to teenaged speed freaks. If it's too darn hot, cool off at **Knott's Soak City** water park next door.

In **Santa Ana**, drop by the discovery cube, an interactive, family-friendly science-oriented museum, or peruse the art galleries of the Bowers Museum. Catch your breath in time-warped **Old Town Orange**, where antiques stores cluster, or **Little Saigon**, where you can trade theme-park hot dogs for a steaming bowl of Vietnamese pho.

On day four, motor west toward the ocean. In **Huntington Beach**, aka 'Surf City USA,' rent a board, play beach volleyball and build a bonfire after sunset. Hit **Newport Beach** for soap-opera worthy people-watching by the piers. Make a quick stop for power shopping in **Costa Mesa**, then roll south to **Laguna Beach**, a former artists colony with more than two dozen public beaches to spoil you, plus fashionable boutiques.

Slingshot back toward the I-5 on your last day, stopping off at **Mission San Juan Capistrano** for a glimpse of Spanish-colonial and Mexican history. Or keep up the beach-bum attitude by slacking south to **Dana Point**, with its yacht-filled harbor and beach, and retro **San Clemente**, near Trestles, a year-round surf break.

Top: Santa Monica (p387)

Right: Point Reyes National Seashore (p121)

ALICE CAHILL/GETTY IMAGES ©

Plan Your Trip

Beaches, Swimming & Surfing

Beach life and surf culture define California's freewheeling lifestyle, so consider permission granted to play hooky and hit the waves. Southern California is where you'll find the sunniest swimming beaches, while Northern California's misty cliffs and blustery strands beckon romantics and hardcore surfers.

Best Beaches

San Diego
Coronado, Mission Beach, Pacific Beach, La Jolla

Orange County
Newport Beach, Laguna Beach, Crystal Cove State Park, Doheny State Beach

Los Angeles
Santa Monica, Venice, South Bay, Malibu

Santa Barbara
East Beach, El Capitán State Beach, Refugio State Beach, Carpinteria State Beach

Central Coast
Main Beach (Santa Cruz), Moonstone Beach, Cayucos, Pismo State Beach

San Francisco Bay Area
Stinson Beach, Point Reyes National Seashore, Pacifica State Beach

North Coast
Sonoma Coast State Beach, Lost Coast, Trinidad State Beach

Swimming

If your California dream vacation means bronzing on the beach and paddling in the Pacific, head directly to Southern California (SoCal). With mile after mile of wide, sandy beaches between Santa Barbara and San Diego, you can be living the dream at least six months out of the year. Ocean temperatures in SoCal are tolerable by May or June, peaking in July and August.

Northern California (NorCal) beaches are blustery and dramatic, with high swells crashing into rocky bluffs – not great for casual swimmers but perfect for big-wave surfing. NorCal beaches remain chilly year-round, so bring a windbreaker – and if you're going to brave these waters, bring or rent a wetsuit.

Safety Tips

➡ Most California beaches have flags to distinguish between surfer-only sections and sections for swimmers. Flags also alert beachgoers to dangerous water conditions – and even seasoned California surfers know these warnings need to be taken seriously.

➡ Popular beaches in Southern California have lifeguards, but can still be dangerous places to swim. Obey all posted warning signs and ask about local conditions before venturing out.

➡ Stay out of the ocean for at least three days after a major rainstorm, while dangerously high levels of pollutants flush out through storm drains.

➡ Water quality varies from beach to beach and day to day. For current water-safety conditions and beach closures, check the Beach Report Card issued by the nonprofit organization Heal the Bay (http://brc.healthebay.org).

Best Family-Friendly Beaches

➡ **Silver Strand State Beach** (Map p452; ☎619-435-5184; www.parks.ca.gov; 5000 Hwy 75, Coronado; per car $10, RV camping from $50; ⌚7am-sunset; Ⓟ) Coronado

➡ **Santa Monica State Beach** (p388) Los Angeles

➡ **Leo Carrillo State Park** (☎310-457-8143; www.parks.ca.gov; 35000 W Pacific Coast Hwy, Malibu; per car $12; ⌚8am-10pm; Ⓟ) Malibu

➡ **Balboa Peninsula** (p434) Newport Beach

➡ **Carpinteria State Beach** (p368) Santa Barbara County

➡ **Arroyo Burro Beach County Park** (p339) Santa Barbara

➡ **Avila Beach** (p321) San Luis Obispo County

➡ **Natural Bridges State Beach** (p271) Santa Cruz

➡ **Stinson Beach** (p118) Marin County

➡ **Trinidad State Beach** (p259) North Coast

Best Beaches for Bonfires

➡ **Huntington City Beach** (p431) Orange County

➡ **Main Beach** (p439) Orange County

➡ **Mission Beach** (p454) San Diego

➡ **Carmel Beach City Park** (p292) Central Coast

➡ **Ocean Beach** (☎415-561-4323; www.parksconservancy.org; Great Hwy; ⌚sunrise-sunset; Ⓟ; 🚌5, 18, 31, Ⓜ N) San Francisco

Books & Maps

The outstanding *California Coastal Access Guide* (University of California Press, 2014) has comprehensive maps of every public beach, reef, harbor, cover, overlook and coastal campground, with valuable information about parking, hiking trails, facilities and wheelchair access. It's especially helpful for finding secret pockets of uncrowded sand.

Surfing

Surf's up! Are you down? Even if you've never set foot on a board, there's no denying the influence of surfing on California life, from street clothing to slang. Surfing is an obsession up and down the coast, particularly in Santa Cruz, San Diego and Orange County.

The most powerful ocean swells arrive along California's coast during late fall and winter. May and June are generally the flattest months. Speaking of temperature, don't expect to ride in a bikini; without a wetsuit, you'll freeze your butt off except at the height of summer – especially anywhere north of Santa Barbara.

Crowds can be a problem at many surf spots, as can overly territorial surfers. Befriend a local surfer for an introduction before hitting Cali's most famous waves, such as notoriously agro Windansea Beach and Malibu Surfrider Beach.

Sharks do inhabit California waters, but attacks are rare and take place in the so-called 'Red Triangle' between Monterey on the Central Coast, Tomales Bay north of San Francisco and the offshore Farallon Islands.

Rentals & Lessons

You'll find board rentals on just about every patch of beach where surfing is possible. Expect to pay about $25 per half-day for a board, with wetsuit rental costing another $10 or so.

Two-hour group lessons for beginners start at around $100 per person, while private, two-hour instruction easily costs over $125. If you've got bigger ambitions and deeper pockets, many surf schools offer weekend surf clinics and weeklong 'surfari' camps.

Best Surf Breaks for Beginners

The best spots to learn to surf are long, shallow bays where waves are small and rolling. Popular places for beginners and surf schools dot the California coast from San Diego to Santa Cruz, including:

➡ **San Diego Mission Beach** (Map p464; ☎858-483-8837; www.missionsurf.com; 4320 Mission Blvd, Pacific Beach; surfboard rentals from $10 (softtop) $20 (hardboard); ⏲10am-7pm), **Pacific Beach** (Map p464; ☎858-373-1138; www.pbsurfshop.com; 4150 Mission Blvd; group surfing lessons from $75; ⏲store 9am-6pm winter, 9am-7pm summer), **La Jolla** (Map p452; ☎858-454-8273; www.surfdiva.com; 2160 Avenida de la Playa; ⏲store 8:30am-5pm, lesson hours vary from season to season), Oceanside (p484)

➡ **Orange County** Seal Beach (p430), Huntington Beach (p432), Newport Beach (p434), **Laguna Beach** (Map p441; ☎949-497-1423; www.casurfshop.com; 695 S Coast Hwy; lessons group/private $75/95; ⏲8am-9pm most days)

➡ **Los Angeles Santa Monica** (☎310-663-2479; www.learntosurfla.com; group lesson per person from $85), **Malibu** (☎310-456-8508; www.malibusurfshack.com; 22935 Pacific Coast Hwy, Malibu; s kayaks per day $35, surfboards per day $25-35, SUP per 2hr/overnight $45/75, wetsuits per day $10-15, surf/SUP lessons per person $125/100; ⏲10am-6pm)

➡ **Santa Barbara County** Leadbetter Beach (p339), Carpinteria (p368)

➡ **Central Coast** Santa Cruz (p274), Cayucos (p307)

Top Surf Spots for Pros

California's coastline is dotted with easily accessible world-class surf beaches, especially in SoCal. Topping every pro surfer's bucket list are these California hot spots:

➡ **Huntington Beach** (p431) Located in Orange County, it may have the West Coast's most consistent waves, with miles of breaks centered on the pier.

➡ **Trestles** (p446) The OC's premier summer spot, with big but forgiving waves, a fast ride and both right and left breaks.

➡ **Windansea Beach** (Map p452) This San Diego spot has a powerful reef break, while nearby **Big Rock** (Map p452) churns out gnarly tubes.

➡ **Malibu Lagoon State Beach** (Surfrider Beach; ☎310-305-9503, 310-457-8143; www.parks.ca.gov; 3999 Cross Creek Rd, Malibu; per car $12; ⏲8am-sunset; Ⓟ) A clean right break in Malibu that just gets better with bigger waves.

➡ **Santa Monica** (p387) Once strictly locals only, this tough urban break by the pier is where renegades became champions and made surfing cool in the 1970s.

➡ **Carpinteria** (p368) Rincon Point is another perfect right point break that peels forever.

➡ **Steamer Lane** (p273) The 1960s surfer-girl icon Gidget made Santa Cruz a TV-legendary surf destination – especially Steamer Lane, with its glassy point breaks and rocky reef breaks. Between sessions, get to know Gidget and other surf pioneers in the tiny cliffside lighthouse housing the Santa Cruz Surfing Museum (p271).

➡ **Half Moon Bay** World-famous big-wave surfers hit this spot each winter for the **Titans of Mavericks** (http://titansofmavericks.com/event) FREE, taking on dangerous swells towering some 60ft high at this annual competition.

Online Resources

➡ Browse the comprehensive atlas, live webcams and surf reports at Surfline (www.surfline.com), and get the lowdown on the best swells from San Diego to Humboldt County on the North Coast.

➡ Orange County–based *Surfer* magazine's website (www.surfermag.com) has travel reports, gear reviews, newsy blogs, forums and totally gnarly videos.

➡ Surfers have led California's coastal conservation efforts for 40 years, and you can join their ongoing efforts through the nonprofit Surfrider Foundation (www.surfrider.org).

➡ If you're a kook, bone up on surf-speak so brahs don't go agro and give you stinkeye. For translations, use the Riptionary (www.riptionary.com).

Books & Maps

➡ Water-resistant *Surfer Magazine's Guide to Southern California Surf Spots* (Chronicle Books, 2006) and *Surfer Magazine's Guide to Northern and Central California Surf Spots* (Chronicle Books, 2006) are jam-packed with expert reviews, information, maps and photos.

DAVID M. SCHRADER/SHUTTERSTOCK ©

SEBASTIEN BUREL/SHUTTERSTOCK ©

Top: Leo Carrillo State Park (p33), Malibu

Right: Windansea Beach, San Diego

Plan Your Trip

California Camping & Outdoors

California is an all-seasons outdoor playground. Here you can go hiking among wildflowers in spring, swimming in the Pacific warmed by summer sunshine, mountain biking among fall foliage and whale-watching in winter. For bigger thrills, launch a glider off ocean bluffs or don a wet suit to dive into underwater sanctuaries.

Planning for the Outdoors

Backpacking Northern California's Lost Coast Trail (April–October)

Cycling Coastal Hwy 1 through Big Sur (April–October)

Hiking Redwood National & State Parks (April–October)

Mountain biking Marin County, especially Mt Tamalpais (April–October)

Kayaking Channel Islands National Park (July–October)

Snorkeling and scuba diving La Jolla in San Diego County (July–October)

Whale-watching Monterey Bay National Marine Sanctuary (January–March)

Windsurfing San Diego's Mission Bay (September–November)

Kayaking

Whether you're looking for an adventure exploring sea caves or just a serene float past coastal bluffs or along inland rivers, kayaking opportunities abound in coastal California. Few water-based sports are as accessible and fun for the whole family, and most people manage to get paddling along quickly with minimal instruction.

Best Places to Kayak

- Sea kayaking is fabulous in Channel Islands National Park (p374), offshore from Ventura and Santa Barbara, and Catalina Island (p413), closer to Los Angeles and Orange County. Both are ideal overnight getaways for experienced paddlers.
- Further south, beginners can paddle around the calm, protected waters of San Diego's Mission Bay (p455) or at Dana Point (p446) in Orange County.
- You can explore sea caves while floating above kelp forests and reefs of San Diego-La Jolla Underwater Park (p475).
- You'll find more coastal kayaking in Malibu (p387), among the coves of Orange County's

Laguna Beach (p441) and around Gaviota near Santa Barbara (p337).

➡ Beginners can take a spin around Morro Bay, whose waters are protected by a 4-mile sand spit, or float inland for wildlife-watching at Elkhorn Slough National Estuarine Research Reserve (p281) between Monterey and Santa Cruz.

➡ In Northern California, brave the choppy waters of San Francisco Bay, or head for more sheltered Richardson Bay in Sausalito, Tomales Bay near Point Reyes, Bodega Bay (p215) further north, or Pillar Point Harbor near Half Moon Bay south along Hwy 1.

➡ In Sonoma's wine country, the Russian River is a pretty place to paddle a kayak or canoe, with put-ins at Guerneville, Jenner and Healdsburg.

➡ Just outside Mendocino, the Big River tidal estuary is a peaceful kayak or canoe trip for families.

➡ All along the North Coast (p212), you'll find challenging put-in points for experienced sea kayakers, as well as gentler lagoons, coves and bays for beginners.

Rentals, Lessons & Tours

Most outfitters offer a choice between sit-upon (open) kayaks and sit-in (closed-hull) ones; the latter are slightly more difficult to keep balanced and upright. Kayak rentals average $30 to $60 for a half-day, and you'll usually have a choice between single or tandem. Whatever kind of kayak you get, a reputable outfitter will make sure you're aware of the tide schedule and wind conditions for your proposed route.

Many kayaking outfitters give lessons and lead guided tours (from $50), including sunrise, sunset and full-moon paddles. There's nothing quite like seeing the reflection of the moon and stars glittering on the water and hearing the gentle splash of water on your kayak's hull. Small-group tours led by guides with natural-history knowledge are best.

Whether you're taking a tour or renting kayaks, try to make reservations at least a day or two in advance

Resources

For dozens of links to local kayaking outfitters, schools and organizations, plus helpful advice, see: Kayak Online (www.kayakonline.com/california.html)

Camping

Camping is a popular way to enjoy the outdoors; no five-star-hotel views can compare to the kind of scenery on display. If you can't get a campsite reservation, plan to show up at the campground between 10am and noon, when the previous night's campers may be leaving. Don't be too choosy, or you may end up with no site at all – especially on holidays or summer weekends. Park rangers, visitor centers and campground hosts can often tell you where spaces may still be available, if there are any. Otherwise, ask about overflow camping and dispersed camping nearby. For more information on rates and reservations, see p519.

Scuba Diving & Snorkeling

All along the California coast, rock reefs, shipwrecks and kelp beds teem with sea creatures ready for their close-up. Underwater playgrounds are suited to all skill and experience levels. Ocean waters are warmest in Southern California and between July and September, but wet suits are recommended for divers year-round.

Best Scuba Diving & Snorekling Spots

➡ **San Diego-La Jolla Underwater Park** (p475) is a great place for beginning divers, while La Jolla Cove attracts snorkelers.

➡ More experienced divers steer towards Orange County's Crystal Cove State Park (p439), just south of Newport Beach; Divers Cove (p442) in Laguna Beach; and Wreck Alley near San Diego's Mission Bay (p455).

➡ Some popular dive spots are also good for snorkeling, for example offshore Channel Islands National Park (p374) and Catalina Island (p413). Boats depart from Los Angeles, Orange County and Ventura County, south of Santa Barbara.

➡ With its national marine sanctuary, Monterey Bay offers world-renowned diving and snorkeling, but it's chilly – you'll need a thick wet suit.

Camping in Coastal California

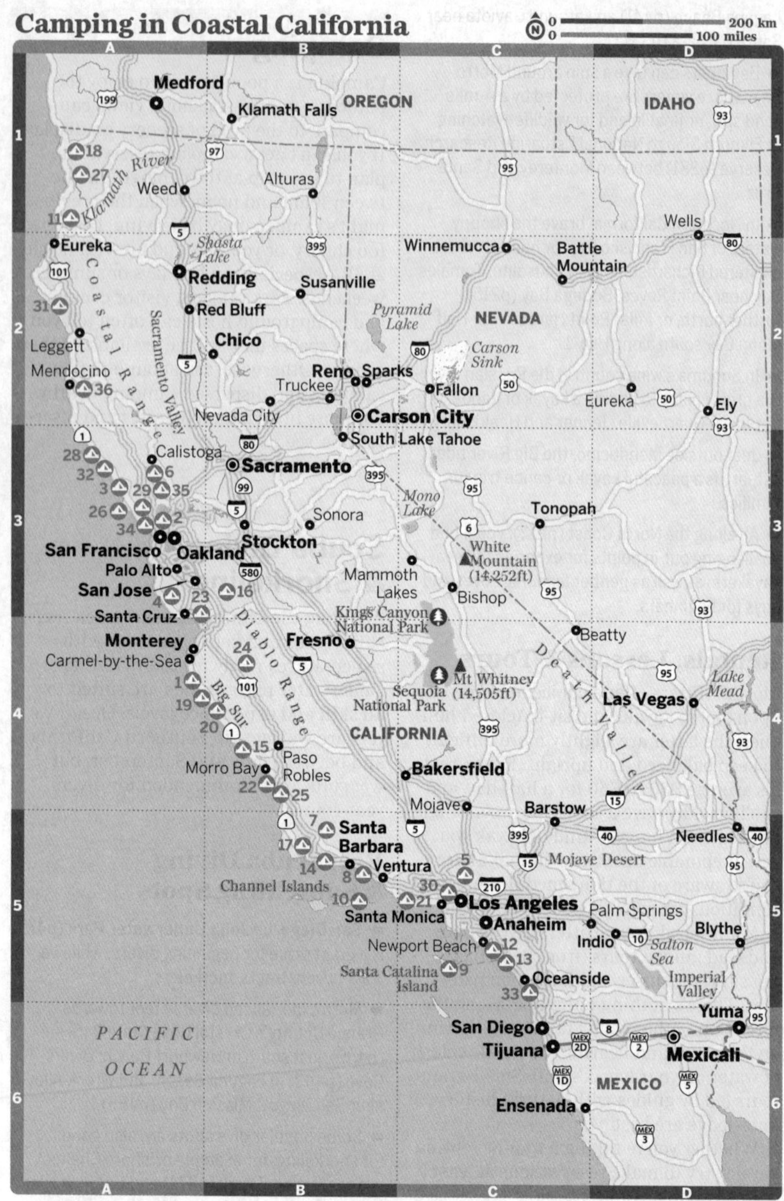

➡ Just south of Monterey, Point Lobos State Natural Reserve (p292) is another gem for divers and snorkelers (permit reservations required on weekdays).

Rentals, Lessons & Tours

Local dive shops are your best resource for equipment, guides, instructors and boat trips. If you already have your Professional Association of Diving Instruc-

Camping in Coastal California

Sleeping

No.	Name	Map
1	Andrew Molera State Park	A4
2	Angel Island State Park	A3
3	Austin Creek State Recreation Area	A3
4	Big Basin Redwoods State Park	A3
5	Big Bear Lake	C5
6	Bothe-Napa Valley State Park	A3
7	Cachuma Lake Recreation Area	B5
8	Carpinteria State Beach	B5
	Casini Ranch	(see 3)
9	Catalina Island	C5
10	Channel Islands National Park	B5
11	Clam Beach County Park	A1
12	Crystal Cove State Park	C5
13	Doheny State Beach	C5
14	El Capitán State Beach	B5
15	Hearst San Simeon State Park	B4
	Henry Cowell Redwoods State Park	(see 4)
16	Henry W Coe State Park	B3
17	Jalama Beach County Park	B5
18	Jedediah Smith Redwoods State Park	A1
19	Julia Pfeiffer Burns State Park	A4
20	Kirk Creek	B4
21	Leo Carrillo State Beach	C5
	Limekiln State Park	(see 1)
	Los Padres National Forest	(see 7)
	Marin Headlands	(see 34)
	Montaña de Oro State Park	(see 22)
22	Morro Bay State Park	B4
23	New Brighton State Beach	A3
	Pfeiffer Big Sur State Park	(see 1)
24	Pinnacles National Monument	B4
25	Pismo State Beach	B4
	Plaskett Creek	(see 20)
26	Point Reyes National Seashore	A3
27	Prairie Creek Redwoods State Park	A1
	Refugio State Beach	(see 14)
28	Salt Point State Park	A3
29	Samuel P Taylor State Park	A3
30	Santa Monica Mountains National Recreation Area	C5
31	Sinkyone Wilderness State Park	A2
32	Sonoma Coast State Beach	A3
33	South Carlsbad State Beach	C5
34	Steep Ravine Environmental Campground	A3
35	Sugarloaf Ridge State Park	A3
36	Van Damme State Park	A2

tors (PADI) certification, you can book a one-tank boat dive for $65 to $155; reserve at least a day in advance. To dabble in diving, ask about beginner scuba courses that include basic instruction, followed by a shallow beach or boat dive, from around $120. A multiday Open Water certificate course costs anywhere from $300 to $600.

Snorkel kits (including mask, snorkel, fins and maybe a wet suit) can be rented from beach concessionaires and many dive shops from about $20 per day. If you're going to be taking the plunge more than once or twice, it's probably worth buying your own mask and fins. Remember not to touch anything while you're out snorkeling, don't snorkel alone and always wear a T-shirt or sunblock on your back.

Resources

Lonely Planet's *Diving & Snorkeling Southern California & the Channel Islands* is David Krival's hands-on guide to happy encounters with coastal California's marine critters.

Scuba Diving (www.scubadiving.com) and *Sport Diver* (www.sportdiver.com) published by PADI, are magazines with comprehensive websites dedicated to underwater adventures.

Windsurfing & Kiteboarding

Experienced windsurfers tear up the waves along the coast, while newbies or those who want a mellower ride skim along calm bays and protected beaches. There's almost always a breeze, but the best winds blow from September through November. Wet suits are a good idea year-round, especially in Northern California.

Best Places to Windsurf & Kiteboard

Usually any place that has good windsurfing also has good kiteboarding. Look for the people doing aerial acrobatics as their parachute-like kites yank them from the water. In wide-open spaces devoid of obstacles like piers and power lines, you won't have to worry about unexpected flights that could slam you into concrete.

- In San Diego, novices should check out Santa Clara Point in Mission Bay (p455).
- Santa Barbara's Leadbetter Beach (p339) is another good spot for beginners to learn.
- In LA County, you'll see lots of action off **Belmont Shores** (Long Beach; Red

Passport) near Long Beach and Point Fermin (p389) near San Pedro.

➡ Offshore from San Francisco's Crissy Field (p69) is a favorite spot for experienced boarders. The wind literally howls as it squeezes into the bay.

Rentals & Lessons

The learning curve in windsurfing is steeper than other board sports – imagine balancing on a fast-moving plank through choppy waters while trying to read the wind and angle the sail just so. At most windsurfing hot spots, a half-day introductory lesson costs $100 to $150.

Although it's harder to get started kiteboarding, experts say it's easier to advance quickly once the basics are down. Beginner kiteboarding lessons start at $175 to $225, and usually take place over a few days. The first lesson is spent learning kite control on the beach and the second lesson gets you into the water.

Windsurfing gear rentals cost about $50 to $75 per day for a beginner's board and harness. Most windsurfing shops usually won't rent kite gear to people who aren't also taking kiteboarding lessons.

Resources

iKitesurf (http://wx.ikitesurf.com) Primo locations, wind reports and more for aspiring and experienced kiteboarders.

iWindsurf (http://wx.iwindsurf.com) Wind reports, weather forecasts, pro favorites and active discussion forums.

Whale-Watching

During their annual migration, gray whales can be spotted off the California coast from December to April, while blue, humpback and sperm whales pass by in summer and fall. Just about every port town worth its sea salt along the coast offers whale-watching boat excursions, especially during winter. You can try your luck whale-watching while staying shore-bound (eg from lighthouses) – it's free, but you're less likely to see any whales and you'll be removed from all the action.

Half-day whale-watching boat trips (usually $30 to $70 per adult, up to 50% off per child) last from 2½ to four hours, and sometimes include snacks and drinks. Make reservations at minimum a day or two in advance. Better boats limit the number of people and have a trained naturalist on board. Some companies will let you go out again for free if you don't spot any whales on your first cruise.

Bring binoculars and dress in warm, waterproof layers. Choppy seas can be nauseating. To avoid seasickness, sit outside on the boat's second level – but not too close to the diesel fumes in back.

Hiking & Backpacking

No matter where you find yourself in coastal California, you're never far from a trail, even in busy metropolitan areas. The best trails are often amid the jaw-dropping scenery of national and state parks, forests, recreation areas and other public lands. Take your pick of a staggering variety of routes, from easy strolls negotiable by wheelchairs and baby strollers to multiday backpacking treks through the wilderness. Don't miss a ramble among the world's tallest trees, coast redwoods, or California's spring wildflowers that bloom with all the colors of a painter's palette.

Best Places to Hike

North Coast Redwood National & State Parks (p261) and Humboldt Redwoods State Park (p248) offer misty walks through groves of old-growth coast redwoods, or you can discover remote beaches and lighthouses along the challenging Lost Coast Trail (p247).

San Francisco Bay Area The Marin Headlands (p104), Muir Woods (p117), Mt Tamalpais (p115) and Point Reyes National Seashore (p121), all within a 90-minute drive of San Francisco, are crisscrossed by dozens of superb trails.

Central Coast & Santa Barbara Santa Cruz (p279) and Big Sur (p297) state parks abound with redwood-forest trails, while Point Lobos State Natural Reserve (p292) and Channel Islands National Park (p374) offer ocean-view treks and wildlife-watching. In Santa Barbara County, the Santa Ynez Mountains and **Los Padres National Forest** (☎805-967-3481; www.fs.usda.gov/lpnf; 3505 Paradise Rd; daily pass per car $5;

Humpback whale, Moneterey Bay (p283)

⏲8am-4:30pm Mon-Fri, also 8am-4:30pm Sat late May–early Sep) 🍃 beckon.

Los Angeles Ditch your car in urban Griffith Park (p382) and the wild Santa Monica Mountains. Offshore, day hikers and backpackers trek Catalina Island (p413).

Fees & Wilderness Permits

➡ Many of coastal California's national parks, including Redwood National Park, Point Reyes National Seashore and Channel Islands National Park, are free for entry.

➡ Most California state parks charge a daily parking fee of $3 to $15. There's often no charge for pedestrians or cyclists. Don't park your car just outside the gate and then walk in – California's state parks are chronically underfunded and need your support.

➡ For unlimited admission to national parks, national forests and other federal recreation lands, buy an 'America the Beautiful' annual pass ($80) from national park visitor centers and entrance stations and at some United States Forest Service (USFS) ranger stations and visitor centers.

➡ Otherwise, you'll need a National Forest Adventure Pass (per day $5, annual pass $30) to park in some recreational areas of Southern California's San Bernardino, Cleveland, Angeles and Los Padres National Forests. Buy these passes on the spot from USFS ranger stations and authorized local vendors (eg sporting-goods stores), or order them online or by phone or mail in advance.

➡ Often required for overnight backpacking trips, wilderness permits (fee usually $5 to $20 or more, sometimes free) are issued at ranger stations and park visitor centers. Daily quotas may be in effect during peak periods, usually from late spring through early fall. Some permits can be reserved ahead of time, and permits for popular trails may sell out months in advance.

Resources

California Coastal Trail Association (http://coastwalk.org) Helping build a 1200-mile trail along California's shoreline – it's already half finished.

Leave No Trace Center for Outdoor Ethics (www.lnt.org) Learn how to minimize your impact on the environment while hiking and camping.

BEWARE: POISON OAK!

Watch out for western poison oak throughout coastal California, especially in forests and foothills below 5000ft in elevation. This poisonous shrub is most easily identified by its shiny reddish-green tripartite leaves (remember the rhyme 'Leaves of three, let it be!'), which turn crimson in the fall, and its white berries. In winter, when the plant has no leaves, it looks brown and twiggy, but can still cause a serious allergic reaction if even one billionth of a gram of urushiol oil touches your skin. If you brush against poison oak, scrub the affected area immediately with soap and water or an over-the-counter remedy such as Tecnu, a soap specially formulated to remove the plant's itchy urushiol oils.

Cycling & Mountain Biking

California is outstanding cycling territory, no matter whether you're off for a leisurely spin along the beach, an adrenaline-fueled mountain ride or a coastal road tour along Hwy 1. Southern California's cycling season runs year-round, although late summer can be blazing hot and coastal fog may rob you of views in winter and early summer. Late spring through early fall is prime time for pedaling around Northern California, where winters are generally cold, rainy and not ideal for cycling.

Road Rules

➡ In national and state parks, bicycles are usually limited to paved and dirt roads and not allowed on trails or in designated wilderness.

➡ Most national forests and Bureau of Land Management (BLM) areas are open to mountain bikers. Stay on already established tracks and always yield to hikers and horseback riders.

Best Places for Cycling

➡ Even the heavily trafficked urban areas of Southern California may sport some good cycling turf. Take, for example, the beachside South Bay Bicycle Trail (p388) in Los Angeles or oceanfront recreational paths in Orange County's Newport Beach (p434) and Huntington Beach (p431) and in Santa Barbara (p337) and Ventura (p372).

➡ In Northern California's bike-friendly San Francisco (p58), you can cruise through Golden Gate Park (p72) and over the Golden Gate Bridge (p65), then hop on a ferry back across the bay from Sausalito (p4). In the middle of the bay, Angel Island (p114) is another great bike-and-ferry combo.

➡ On the Central Coast, the waterfront Monterey Peninsula Recreational Trail is an easy pedal for the whole family, while the scenic 17-Mile Drive entices more skilled riders. For long-distance cyclists, nothing surpasses coastal Hwy 1, especially the dizzying stretch through Big Sur (p295).

➡ Many of California's Wine Countries, including both Napa Valley (p156) and Sonoma Valley (p179), offer beautiful guided and DIY bike tours that take you past vineyards, farms and small towns.

Best Places for Mountain Biking

➡ North of San Francisco, the Marin Headlands (p104) offer a bonanza of trails for fat-tire fans, while Mt Tamalpais State Park (p115) lays claim to being the sport's birthplace. Even Point Reyes National Seashore (p121) has some single-track.

➡ You'll find miles of backcountry roads and trails for mountain biking in the Santa Monica Mountains (p44), located north of Los Angeles.

➡ A day trip from LA, Big Bear Lake is another fat-tire playground, with national forest trails and a ski-resort chairlift that serves mountain bikers in summer.

➡ Coastal state parks that are especially popular with mountain bikers include Orange County's Crystal Cove State Park (p439), NorCal's **Prairie Creek Redwoods State Park** (☎707-488-2039; www.parks.ca.gov; Newton B Drury Scenic Pkwy; ⏰9am-5pm May-Sep, to 4pm Wed-Sun Oct-Apr), and Montaña de Oro State Park (p310), located on the Central Coast.

➡ Inland from Monterey (p281), Fort Ord National Monument has over 80 miles of dirt single-track and fire roads open to mountain bikers.

CHRISTOPHER KIMMEL/GETTY IMAGES ©

JENNIFER WAN/SHUTTERSTOCK ©

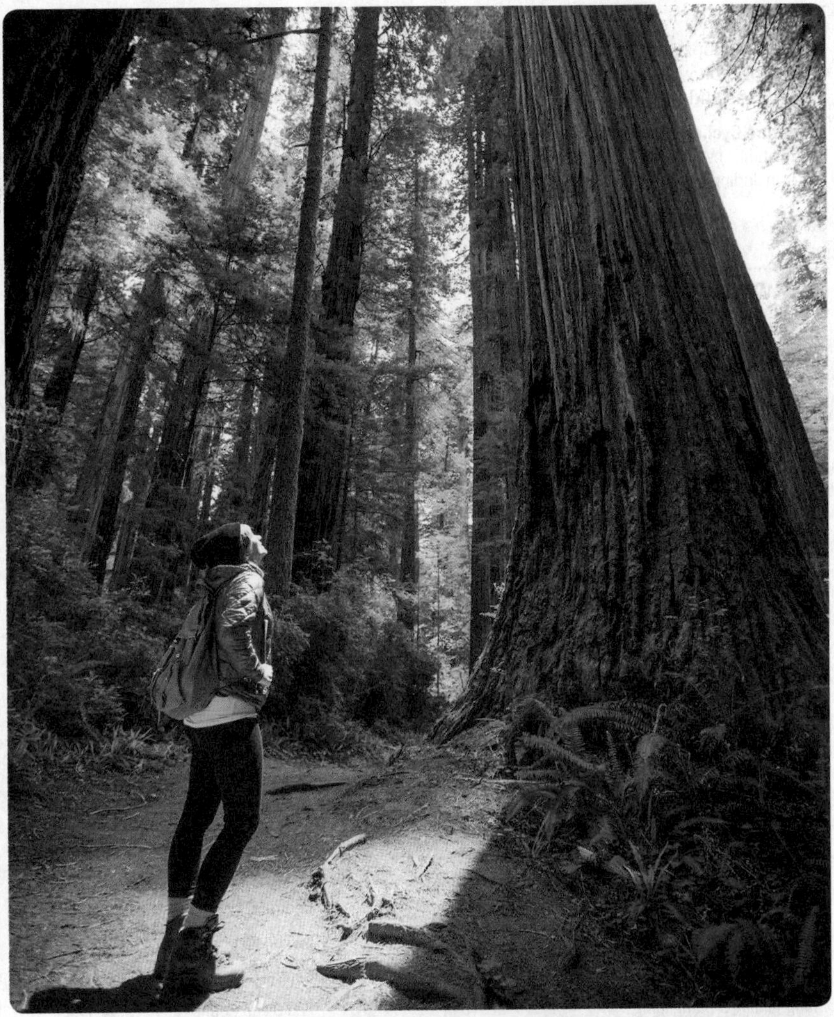

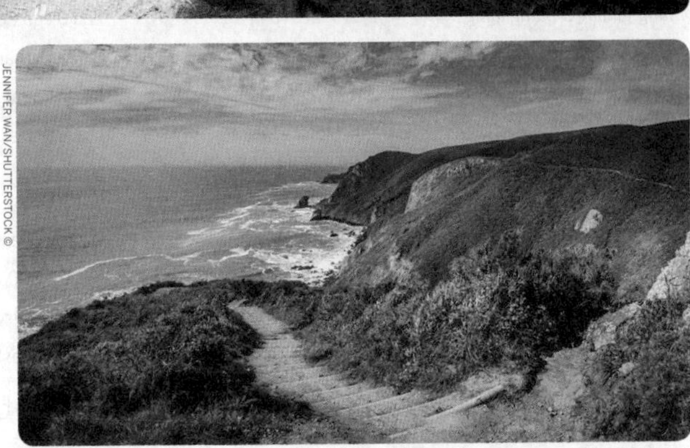

Top: Stout Grove, Jedediah Smith Redwoods State Park (p263)
Right: Hiking trail, Marin Headlands (p104)

Resources

Local bike shops and some visitor centers can supply you with more cycling-route ideas, maps and advice.

Adventure Cycling Association (p528) Sells long-distance cycling route guides and touring maps, including for the entire Pacific Coast.

California Bicycle Coalition (www.calbike.org) Links to free online cycling maps and suggested touring routes.

League of American Bicyclists (www.bikeleague.org) Find bicycle specialty shops, local cycling clubs, group rides and special events.

MTBR.com (www.mtbr.com) and **SoCal Trail Riders** (www.socaltrailriders.org) Online forums and reviews of mountain-biking trails.

BUT WAIT, THERE'S MORE!

ACTIVITY	LOCATION	REGION
Bird-watching	Channel Islands National Park (p44)	Santa Barbara County
	Elkhorn Slough (p44)	Central Coast
	Point Reyes National Seashore (p44)	Marin County
	Martin Griffin Preserve (p44)	Marin County
	Point Lobos State Natural Reserve (p44)	Central Coast
	Humboldt Bay National Wildlife Refuge (p44)	North Coast
	Lake Earl Wildlife Area (p44)	North Coast
	Clear Lake (p44)	North Coast
Caving	Pinnacles National Park (p44)	Central Coast
Fishing*	Point Loma & Mission Bay	San Diego
	Bodega Bay	North Coast
	Monterey Bay (p44)	Central Coast
	Dana Point (p44)	Orange County
Golf	Pebble Beach	Central Coast
	Torrey Pines	San Diego County
	Pacific Grove (p44)	Central Coast
Hang-gliding & paragliding	Torrey Pines (p44)	San Diego County
	Santa Barbara	Santa Barbara County
Horseback riding	Point Reyes National Seashore	Marin County
	Santa Monica Mountains (www.nps.gov/samo/index.htm)	Los Angeles
	Bodega Bay	North Coast
	Big Sur	Central Coast
Hot-air ballooning	Del Mar	San Diego County
	Napa Valley	Wine Country
Rock climbing	Pinnacles National Park (p44)	Central Coast

* For fishing licenses, regulations and location information, consult the California Department of Fish & Wildlife (www.wildlife.ca.gov).

ED FREEMAN/GETTY IMAGES ©

Santa Barbara Wine Country (p357)

Plan Your Trip

Eat & Drink Like a Local

As you graze the Golden State, you'll often want to compliment the chef – and that chef will pass it on to the local farmers, fishers, ranchers, winemakers and artisan food producers that make their menu possible. California cuisine is a team effort that changes with every season – and it's changed the way the world eats.

Best Food & Drink Festivals

Arcata Bay Oyster Festival (p256)
Get yours raw or Rockefeller on the North Coast in mid-June.

California Avocado Festival (p368)
Guacamole for days in Santa Barbara County in early October.

Castroville Artichoke Food & Wine Festival (p284)
Master tricky pairings near Monterey in May or June.

Eat Real Fest
Oakland celebrates sustainable, local food in late September (http://eatrealfest.com).

Gilroy Garlic Festival (p311)
Tons of garlic fries and zero vampires in late July.

Gravenstein Apple Fair (p196)
Pie galore in Sonoma County in mid-August.

Mendocino Wine & Mushroom Festival (p226)
Morels and pinot make perfect Mendo pairings in early November.

San Diego Beer Week (p458)
Craft brews flow citywide in early November.

HERMAN AU PHOTOGRAPHY/GETTY IMAGES ©

Ramen

California Cuisine: Then & Now

'Let the ingredients speak for themselves!' is the rallying cry of California cuisine. With fruit, vegetables, meats and seafood this fresh, heavy French sauces and fussy molecular-gastronomy foams aren't required to make meals memorable. So when New York chefs David Chang and Anthony Bourdain mocked California cuisine as merely putting an organic fig on a plate, Californian chefs retorted that New Yorkers shouldn't knock it until they tried real Mission figs – one of hundreds of rare California heirloom produce varietals cultivated here since the late 18th century for their unique flavor, not their refrigerator shelf life. In California, even fast food gets the California-fresh treatment: one grass-fed burger with heirloom-tomato ketchup, coming right up!

California's 20th Century Food Revolution

Seasonal, locavore eating has become mainstream, but California started the movement more than 40 years ago. As the turbulent 1960s wound down, many disillusioned idealists concluded that the revolution was not about to be delivered on a platter – but California's pioneering organic farmers weren't about to give up.

In 1971 Alice Waters opened her now-legendary restaurant Chez Panisse (p138) in a converted house in Berkeley with the then-radical notion of making the most of

Gilroy Garlic Festival (p311)

California's organically farmed, sustainably sourced bounty. Waters combined rustic French finesse with California's seasonal flavors, and diners tasted the difference.

Waters' call for 'good, clean, fair food' was heard around the world, inspiring Italy's Carlo Petrini to cofound the worldwide Slow Food movement in the 1980s. Meanwhile in California, crowds flock year-round to 800 certified California farmers markets across the state, stocking up on farm-fresh ingredients direct from 2500 local producers.

California's Regional Specialties

Calculate the distance between your tomato's origin and your fork: chances are it's shorter than you might think in California. So what are your best bets on local menus? That depends where you are and the time of year. Winter may be slim pickings for salad in the fertile Central Valley, but ideal for Southern California citrus.

San Francisco Bay Area

For miners converging here for the gold rush, San Francisco offered an unrivaled variety of novelties and cuisines, from cheap Chinese street food to French fine dining for those who struck it rich. Today, San Francisco's adventurous eaters support the most restaurants per capita of any US city – five times more than NYC, ahem – and farmers markets every day of the week, year-round.

Some of San Francisco's novelty dishes have extraordinary staying power, including chocolate bars (invented by the Ghirardelli family as power bars for miners), ever-popular cioppino (seafood stew), and sourdough bread, with original gold-rush era mother dough still yielding local loaves with a distinctive tang. To sample SF classics and the latest local inventions, stop by San Francisco's monument to food: the Ferry Building (p61).

Today no Bay Area star chef's tasting menu would be complete without a few foraged ingredients – including wild chanterelles found beneath California oaks, miner's lettuce from Berkeley hillsides,

PAUL_BRIGHTON/SHUTTERSTOCK ©

Fish tacos

and edible nasturtium flowers from SF backyards. But some pioneering San Francisco chefs are taking local a step further, growing herbs and hosting beehives right on their restaurant rooftops. Don't laugh: urban farming may be coming soon to a green roof near you.

Napa & Sonoma Wine Country

With international acclaim for Napa and Sonoma wines in the 1970s came woozy Wine Country visitors in need of food, and local cheese-makers and restaurateurs graciously obliged. In 1994 chef Thomas Keller transformed a 1900s Yountville saloon into an international foodie landmark called French Laundry (p168), showcasing garden-grown organic produce and casual elegance in multicourse feasts. Other chefs eager to make their names and fortunes among free-spending wine tasters descended on this 30-mile valley – and now the night skies over Napa are crowded with 11 Michelin stars. To sample the artisan food scene, stop by Napa's Oxbow Public Market (p163).

North Coast

San Francisco hippies headed back to the land here in the 1960s to find a more self-sufficient lifestyle, reviving traditions of making breads and cheeses from scratch and growing their own *everything*. Early adopters of pesticide-free farming, these hippie homesteaders innovated hearty, organic cuisine that was health-minded – yet still satisfied pot-smoking munchies.

On the North Coast today, you can taste the influence of Ohlone and Miwok traditions. Alongside traditional shellfish collection, sustainable oyster farms have sprung up. Nature has been kind to this landscape, yielding bonanzas of wildflower honey and berries. Fearless foragers have identified every edible plant from wood sorrel to Mendocino sea vegetables – though key spots for wild mushrooms remain closely guarded local secrets. To try wild Mendo morels at their peak, don't miss the Mendocino WIne & Mushroom Festival (p226).

Central Valley & Central Coast

Over on the Central Coast, some of California's freshest seafood is harvested from

Beer

Monterey Bay. For help choosing the most sustainable catch on restaurant menus, check out the handy report card of the Monterey Bay Aquarium at www.seafoodwatch.org. Excellent wine tasting awaits in the fog-kissed Santa Cruz Mountains, the sun-drenched hills around Paso Robles and the lush valleys north of Santa Barbara.

Southern California

Follow authenticity-seeking Angelenos to Koreatown for flavor-bursting *kalbi* (marinated, grilled beef short ribs), East LA for tacos *al pastor* (marinated, fried pork), Torrance for ramen noodles made fresh daily, and the San Gabriel Valley for Chinese dim sum. Further south, San Diego and Orange County surfers cruise from Ocean Beach to Huntington Beach in search of epic waves, but also for the ultimate Cal-Mex fish taco.

As with Hollywood blockbusters, trendy LA restaurants don't always live up to the hype though – for brutally honest opinions, read reviews by respected food critic Jonathan Gold in the Los Angeles Times, or follow him on Twitter (@thejgold).

True Californian foodies insist that immortality isn't achieved with a star in a Michelin guide or on the Hollywood Walk of Fame, but by having a dish named in your honor. Bob Cobb was the celebrity owner of Hollywood's Brown Derby Restaurant, and his legend lives on with his namesake salad: lettuce, tomato, avocado, egg, chicken and blue cheese. First concocted in the 1930s, it's been ordered by countless starlets since.

When salads fail to satisfy, make late-night raids on local food trucks – fleets are standing by in LA and San Diego. In Hollywood, barflies hit diners that have survived since the 1950s with only minor remodeling – more than you can say for some celebrities around here.

Food Trucks & Pop-Up Restaurants

Weekday lunches may last only 30 minutes for Californians, and every minute counts. California's legendary food trucks deliver gourmet options on the go, from Indian curry-and-naan wraps to Chinese buns packed with roast duck and fresh mango. One way to find trucks coming soon to a curb near you is by searching for 'food truck' and your location on Twitter. Come prepared with cash and sunblock: most trucks don't accept plastic cards, and lines can be long.

Dinner has recently also been popping up in unexpected urban spaces, including art galleries, warehouses and storefronts. Chefs at pop-up restaurants prepare wildly creative meals around a theme, like all-chocolate meals or winemakers' dinners. Foodies seek out these overnight taste sensations via Twitter and websites like www.eater.com. Bring cash and arrive early, as popular dishes run out fast.

Wine, Beer & Beyond

Powerful drink explains a lot about California. Mission vineyards planted in the 18th century gave California a taste for wine, and the mid-19th-century gold rush brought a rush on the bar. By 1850 San Francisco had one woman per 100 men, but 500 saloons shilling hooch for consolation. Today California's traditions of wine, beer and cocktails are being reinvented by cult winemakers, craft brewers and microdistillers.

JUDY BELLAH/GETTY IMAGES ©

SUPANNEE_HICKMAN/SHUTTERSTOCK ©

Top: Food store in the Ferry Building (p61), San Francisco

Left: Food trucks (p49), Los Angeles

Wine

During the gold rush, when imported French wine was slow to arrive in California via Australia, three brothers from Bohemia named Korbel started making their own bubbly in 1882. Today, the Russian River winery they founded has become the biggest US maker of sparkling wines.

Many California vines survived federal scrutiny during Prohibition (1920–33) with a flimsy alibi: the grapes were needed for sacramental wines back east. The authorities bought this story, or at least the bribes that came with it. The ensuing bootlegging bonanza kept West Coast speakeasies well supplied, and saved old vinestock from being torn out by the authorities.

By 1976 California had an established reputation for mass-market plonk and bottled wine spritzers, when upstart Napa Valley and Santa Cruz Mountains wineries suddenly gained international status. At a landmark blind tasting by international critics, their Cabernet Sauvignon and Chardonnay beat venerable French wines to take top honors. This event became known as the Judgment of Paris, as amusingly retold in the movie *Bottle Shock* (2008).

During the internet bubble of the late 1990s, owning a vineyard became the ultimate Silicon Valley status symbol. It seemed like a comparatively solid investment – until a phylloxera blight made a catastrophic comeback, and acres of infected vines across the state had to be dug out from the roots. But disaster brought breakthroughs: winemakers rethought their approach, using organic and biodynamic methods to keep the soil healthy and pests at bay. So whether you order a red, white or pink small-production California vintage, chances are your wine is green.

Beer

Some 400 craft breweries are based in California – more than any other US state. Even the most laid-back surfer here geeks out over Belgian tripels, and will passionately debate optimum hoppiness levels. You won't get attitude for ordering beer with fancy food here, and many sommeliers are happy to suggest beer pairings with your five-star meal.

Any self-respecting California city has at least one brewery or brewpub of note, serving quality small-batch brews you won't find elsewhere. The well-established craft-beer scenes in San Diego and on the North Coast will spoil you for choice – but you'll also find memorable microbrews around the San Francisco Bay Area and along the Central Coast, especially around Santa Cruz and Santa Barbara.

Cocktails

Cocktails have been shaken in Northern California since San Francisco's Barbary Coast days, when they were used to sedate men in order to deliver them onto outbound ships in need of crews. Now hip bartenders across the state are researching old recipes and inventing new cocktail traditions, aided and abetted by local distillers. Don't be surprised to see NorCal's own St George absinthe poured into cordial glasses of Sazerac, or holiday eggnog spiked with Sonoma County Distilling rye and organic orange peel.

Legend has it that the martini was invented when a boozehound walked into an SF bar and demanded something to tide him over until he reached Martinez across the bay – a likely story, but we'll drink to that. The original was made with vermouth, gin, bitters, lemon, maraschino cherry and ice, although by the days of Sinatra's Rat Pack, the recipe was reduced to gin with vermouth vapors and an olive or two.

Beach weather calls for tropical drinks, and California obliges at legendary tiki bars such as Trader Sam's Enchanted Tiki Lounge (p425) in Disneyland and San Francisco's Tonga Room (p95). The mai tai (with rum, orgeat, curaçao and lime juice) is another cocktail allegedly invented in the Bay Area, at Trader Vic's tiki bar in Oakland in the 1940s – and you can try another original version with Chinese *baijiu* (white lightning) in San Francisco Chinatown's historic Li Po (p94). For those who like their cocktails less sweet and sometimes downright mean, margaritas (made with tequila, lime, Cointreau, ice and salt) have been SoCal's poolside drink of choice since the 1940s.

Plan Your Trip

Travel with Children

Coastal California is a tailor-made destination for traveling with kids. The kids will already be begging to go to Southern California's theme parks. Get those over with (you might enjoy them too) and then introduce them to the great outdoors, from sunny southern beaches to magical northern redwood forests.

Best Regions for Kids

Los Angeles

See stars in Hollywood and movie magic at Universal Studios, then hit the beaches and Griffith Park for fun in the sun. What, it's raining? Dive into LA's kid-friendly museums instead.

Orange County & San Diego

Think beaches and theme parks galore: Disneyland, Knott's Berry Farm, the San Diego Zoo & Safari Park, Legoland and more.

San Francisco

Explore hands-on science museums, hear the barking sea lions at Pier 39, traipse through Golden Gate Park and ride the famous cable cars.

Central Coast & Santa Barbara County

Santa Cruz' beach boardwalk, Monterey's whale-watching boats and giant aquarium, Big Sur's forests and riverside campgrounds, and laid-back beach towns all attract families.

North Coast & Redwoods

Go tide-pooling at NorCal's rocky beaches and coves, then let your kids stand next to the world's tallest trees, protected by state and national parks.

Coastal California for Kids

There's not too much to worry about when traveling in coastal California with your kids, as long as you keep them covered in sunblock.

Children's discounts are available for everything from museum admission and movie tickets to bus fares and motel stays. The definition of a 'child' varies from 'under 18' to age six and under. At amusement parks, some rides may have minimum-height requirements – let younger kids know in advance to avoid disappointment and tears.

It's fine to bring kids along to most restaurants, except top-end places. Casual restaurants usually have high chairs and children's menus and break out paper place mats and crayons for drawing. Generally, dining earlier (say, before 6pm) is better for families with young ones. At theme parks, pack a cooler in the car and have a picnic in the parking lot to save money. On the road, many supermarkets have wholesome, ready-to-eat takeout dishes.

Baby food, infant formula, disposable diapers (nappies) and other necessities are widely sold at supermarkets and pharmacies. Many public toilets have a baby-changing table, while private gender-neutral 'family' bathrooms may be available at airports, museums etc.

Children's Highlights

It's easy to keep kids entertained no matter where you travel in coastal California. At national and state parks, ask at visitor centers about family-friendly, ranger-led activities and self-guided 'Junior Ranger' programs, in which kids earn themselves a badge after completing an activity booklet.

Theme Parks

Disneyland Park (p418) and Disney California Adventure (p422) Kids of all ages, even teens, and the young at heart adore the 'Magic Kingdom.'

Knott's Berry Farm (p427) Near Disneyland, SoCal's original theme park offers thrills-a-minute, especially on spooky haunted Halloween nights.

Universal Studios Hollywood (p383) Movie-themed action rides, special-effects shows, the Wizarding World of Harry Potter and a working studio backlot tram tour entertain tweens and teens.

Legoland California Resort (p481) In San Diego's North County, this fantasyland of building blocks is made for tots and youngsters.

Aquariums & Zoos

San Diego Zoo (p450) and Safari Park (p479) Journey around the world with exotic wildlife at California's best and biggest zoo, then go on safari in the suburbs.

Monterey Bay Aquarium (p281) Get acquainted with coastal California's aquatic citizens, next door to the Central Coast's biggest marine sanctuary.

Aquarium of the Pacific (p388) Long Beach's aquarium houses critters from balmy Baja California to the chilly north Pacific, including a shark lagoon.

Seymour Marine Discovery Center (p270) Santa Cruz' university-run aquarium makes interactive science fun, with tide pools for exploring by the beach.

Birch Aquarium at Scripps (p473) La Jolla's kids zone is as entertaining as it is educational, thanks to the super Scripps Institution of Oceanography.

Beaches

Los Angeles (p389) Have carnival fun on Santa Monica Pier, drop by the Manhattan Beach beach volleyball courts, or drive up Hwy 1 to perfect beaches in Malibu.

Orange County (p429) Take your pick of Newport Beach's beautiful pier-side strands, Laguna Beach's miles of million-dollar sands, surf at Huntington Beach (aka 'Surf City, USA'), or old-fashioned Seal Beach.

San Diego (p448) Head over to Coronado's idyllic Silver Strand, play in Mission Bay by SeaWorld, lap up La Jolla or unwind in a half-dozen surf-style beach towns in North County.

Santa Barbara County (p335) and **Central Coast** (p268) Laze on Santa Barbara's unmatched beaches, then roll north to Santa Cruz' famous boardwalk and pier.

San Francisco Bay Area (p102) Travel north up to Marin County for crescent-shaped Stinson Beach and wilder Point Reyes National Seashore, or south along Hwy 1 to Half Moon Bay.

Parks

Redwood National & State Parks (p261) On the fog-laden North Coast, a string of nature preserves protects magnificent wildlife, beaches and the tallest trees on earth.

Griffith Park (p382) Bigger than NYC's Central Park, this LA green space has tons of fun for younger kids, from miniature-train rides and a merry-go-round to planetarium shows.

Balboa Park (p450) Spend all day at the San Diego Zoo and museums, taking time out for the puppet theater. Plazas, fountains and gardens offer plenty of space for younger kids to let off steam.

Golden Gate Park (p72) With kids in tow, wander through the indoor rainforest at the California Academy of Sciences, tour the Japanese Tea Garden and spy on the bison herd.

Channel Islands National Park (p374) Sail across to California's version of the Galapagos for wildlife-watching, sea kayaking, hiking and camping adventure; best for teens.

Museums

San Francisco (p58) and **East Bay** (p123) San Francisco is a mind-bending classroom for kids, with the interactive Exploratorium, eco-conscious California Academy of Sciences and whimsical

Musée Mecanique. Then head over to Oakland's Chabot Space & Science Center.

Los Angeles (p378) See stars (the real ones) at the Griffith Observatory, and dinosaur bones at the Natural History Museum and the La Brea Tar Pits & Museum, then get hands-on at the energetic California Science Center, home of the retired space shuttle *Endeavour*.

San Diego (p448) Balboa Park is jam-packed with museums such as the San Diego Air & Space Museum. Downtown, take younger kids to the engaging New Children's Museum and let tweens and teens clamber aboard the USS Midway Museum.

Orange County (p416) Bring budding lab geeks to the Discovery Cube and get a pint-sized dose of arts and culture at the Kidseum at the Bowers Museum, all near Disneyland Resort.

Planning

Don't pack your schedule too tightly. When navigating metro areas such as LA, San Diego and San Francisco, allow extra time for traffic jams, parking and getting lost.

Accommodations & Child Care

Rule one: if you're traveling with kids, always mention it when making reservations. At a few places, such as B&Bs, children may not be allowed.

Motels and hotels typically have rooms with two beds or an extra sofa bed. They also may have rollaway beds or cots, usually available for a surcharge (request these when making reservations). Some offer 'kids stay free' promotions, which may apply only if no extra bedding is required.

Resorts may offer daytime activity programs for kids and child-care services. At other hotels, front-desk staff or a concierge might help with babysitting arrangements.

Transportation

Airlines usually allow infants (up to age two) to fly for free – bring proof of age – while older children require a seat of their own and don't usually qualify for reduced fares. Children receive substantial discounts on most trains and buses.

While driving in California, any child under age eight who is less than 4ft, 9in tall must be buckled up in the back seat of the car in a child or infant safety seat. Most car-rental agencies rent these for about $10 to $15 per day, but you must specifically book them in advance.

On the road, rest stops are few and far between, and gas stations and fast-food bathrooms tend to be icky. However, you're usually never far from a shopping mall, which generally have well-kept restrooms.

Regions at a Glance

Coastal California's cities have more flavors than a jar of jelly beans. Start in San Francisco, equal parts earth mother and geek chic, or Los Angeles, where dozens of independent cities roll into one multicultural mosaic. Later, kick back in surf-style San Diego.

Calling you away from California's metro areas are misty redwood forests on the North Coast, country lanes winding past vineyards in Napa and Sonoma wine country, wildlife spotting on the Central Coast, and the cinematic beaches of Orange County and Santa Barbara.

On sunny days, when the coastal fog lifts, more than 800 miles of Pacific beaches await.

San Francisco

Food
Culture
Museums

California's 'Left Coast' reputation rests on SF, where DIY self-expression, sustainability and spontaneity are the highest virtues. Obsessive foodies, innovative techies, groundbreaking arts scenes and top-tier museums are all in the creative mix.

p58

Marin County & the Bay Area

Outdoor Sports
Ecotourism
Food

Outdoors nuts adore Marin County and Hwy 1 for beaches, kayaking, and hiking and mountain-biking trails. Taste and tour organic farms that inspire chefs all around the Bay, including in multicultural Oakland and free-thinking Berkeley.

p102

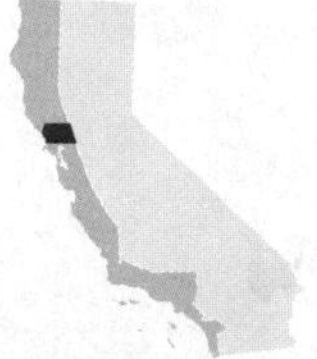

Napa & Sonoma Wine Country

Wineries
Food
Cycling

Amid fruit orchards and ranch lands, sunny valleys blanketed by cool coastal fog have made the Napa, Sonoma and Russian River Valleys into California's premier wine-growing region and a showcase for bountiful farm-to-table cuisine.

p153

North Coast & Redwoods

Hiking
Scenic Drives
Wildlife

Primeval redwood forests are the prize along NorCal's foggy, rocky coastline. Let loose your inner hippie or Rastafarian in Humboldt County, or explore bootstrap fishing villages and wind-tossed beaches from Bodega Bay to Eureka.

p212

Central Coast

Scenic Drives
Beaches
Wildlife

Surf south from hippie-dippie Santa Cruz to collegiate San Luis Obispo, stopping to hop aboard a whale-watching boat at Monterey Bay and to camp and hike in Big Sur's cool redwood forests, where waterfalls flow.

p268

Santa Barbara County

Beaches
Wineries
Water Sports

Spanish-colonial Santa Barbara prettily presides over white-sand beaches, with fruitful vineyards less than an hour's drive away. Then go snorkeling, diving and sea kayaking in treasured Channel Islands National Park, just offshore.

p335

Los Angeles

Beaches
Food
Culture

There's more to life in La La Land than just sunny beaches and air-kissing celebs. Get a dose of art and history Downtown, then dive into LA's diverse neighborhoods, from Little Tokyo to red-carpeted Hollywood.

p378

Disneyland & Orange County

Theme Parks
Beaches
Surfing

The OC's beaches are packed bronze-shoulder-to-shoulder with blond surfers, beach-volleyball fans and soap opera–esque beauties. Inland, take the kids – heck, load up the whole minivan – to Disney's Magic Kingdom.

p416

San Diego & Around

Beaches
Mexican Food
Museums

Enjoying an idyllic climate, lucky residents of California's southernmost city always seem to be chilling out. Take a permanent vacation in laid-back beach towns while devouring fish tacos, or wander Balboa Park's museums and famous zoo.

p448

On the Road

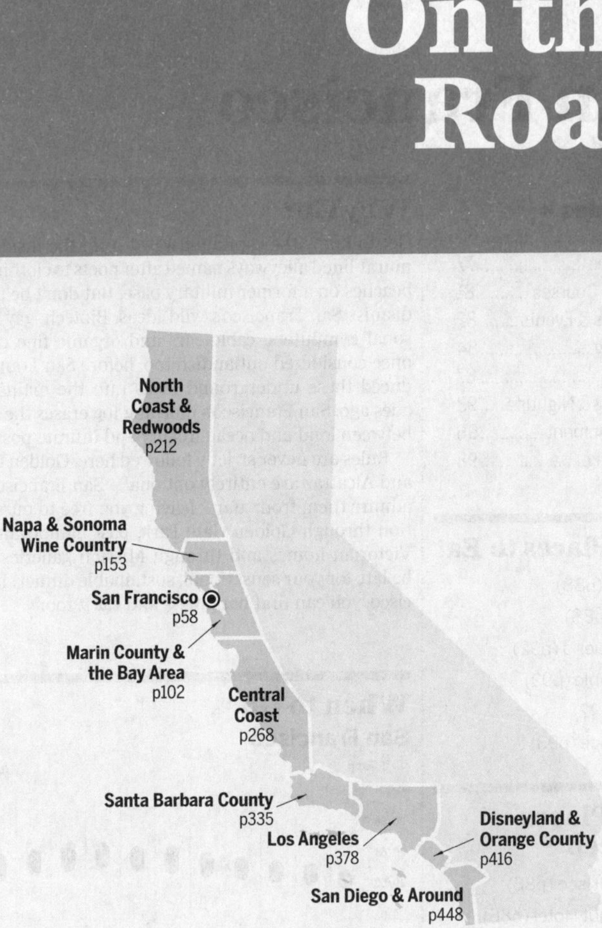

San Francisco

POP 870,887

Includes ➡

Best Places to Eat

- In Situ (p88)
- Benu (p88)
- La Taqueria (p92)
- Rich Table (p92)
- Cala (p92)
- Al's Place (p93)

Best Places to Sleep

- Hotel Drisco (p86)
- Argonaut Hotel (p86)
- Hotel Vitale (p84)
- Inn at the Presidio (p85)
- Hotel Bohème (p85)

Why Go?

Get to know the capital of weird from the inside out, from mural-lined alleyways named after poets to clothing-optional beaches on a former military base. But don't be too quick to dismiss San Francisco's wild ideas. Biotech, gay rights, personal computers, cable cars and organic fine dining were once considered outlandish too, before San Francisco introduced these underground ideas into the mainstream decades ago. San Francisco's morning fog erases the boundaries between land and ocean, reality and infinite possibility.

Rules are never strictly followed here. Golden Gate Bridge and Alcatraz are entirely optional – San Franciscans mostly admire them from afar – leaving you free to pursue inspiration through Golden Gate Park, past flamboyantly painted Victorian homes and through Mission galleries. Just don't be late for your sensational, sustainable dinner: in San Francisco, you can find happiness and eat it too.

When to Go

San Francisco

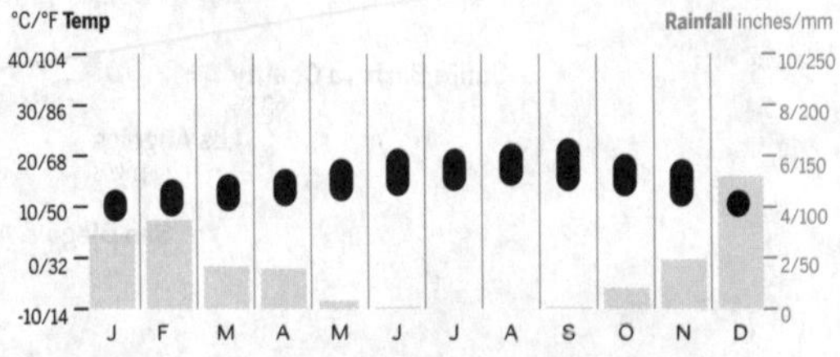

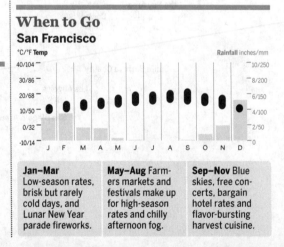

Jan–Mar Low-season rates, brisk but rarely cold days, and Lunar New Year parade fireworks.

May–Aug Farmers markets and festivals make up for high-season rates and chilly afternoon fog.

Sep–Nov Blue skies, free concerts, bargain hotel rates and flavor-bursting harvest cuisine.

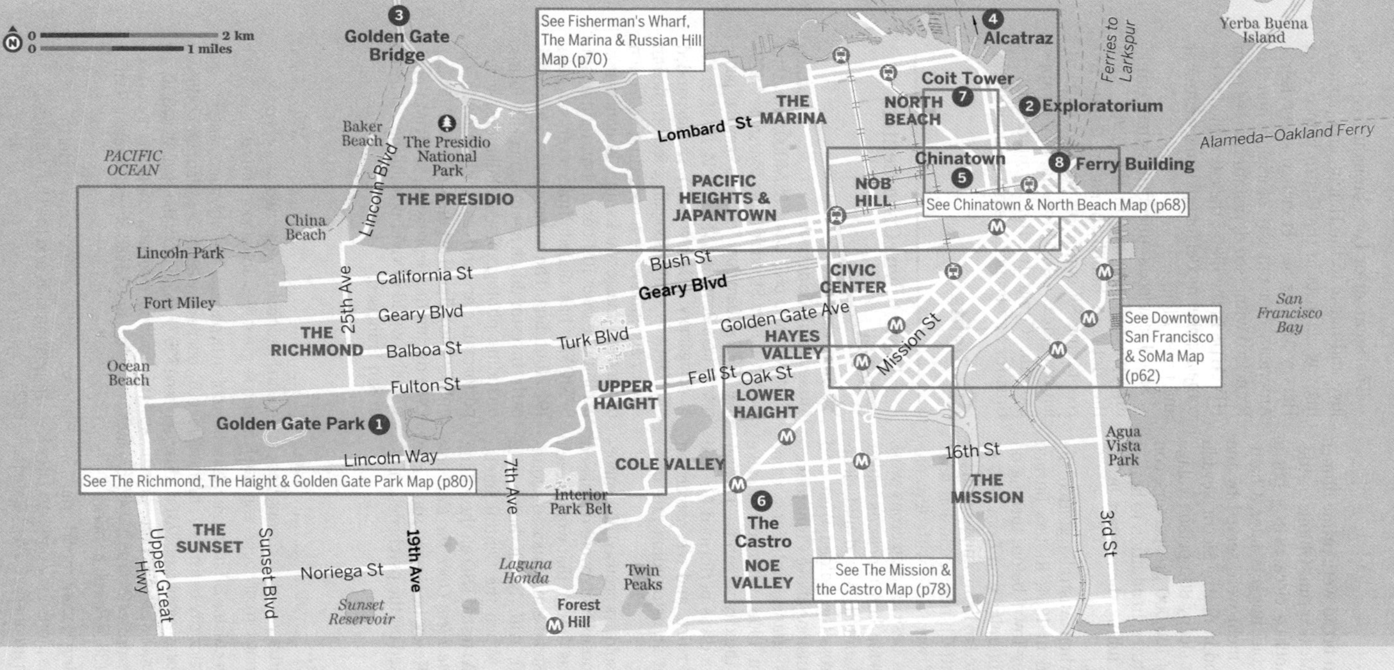

San Francisco Highlights

1 Following your bliss through SF's mile-wide wild streak: **Golden Gate Park** (p72).

2 Seeing how real life is cooler than science fiction at the **Exploratorium** (p69).

3 Watching fog dance atop the deco towers of the **Golden Gate Bridge** (p65).

4 Plotting your escape from **Alcatraz** (p65), SF's notorious island prison.

5 Wandering through 150 years of California history in **Chinatown** (p64).

6 Coming out and celebrating LGBTQ history in **The Castro** (p76), the center of the gay universe.

7 Climbing **Coit Tower** (p65), taking in the murals as you go before gazing at the panoramic views.

8 Grazing at **Ferry Building** (p61), SF's local, sustainable-food destination.

History

Oysters and acorn bread were prime dinner options in the Mexico-run Ohlone settlement of San Francisco circa 1848 – but a year and some gold nuggets later, Champagne and chow mein were served by the bucket. Gold found in nearby Sierra Nevada foothills turned a sleepy 800-person village into a port city of 100,000 prospectors, con artists and prostitutes, in addition to honest folk – good luck telling them apart in the city's 200 saloons.

Panic struck when Australia glutted the market with gold in 1854. Rioters burned waterfront 'Sydney-Town' before turning on SF's Chinese community, who from 1877 to 1945 were restricted to living and working in Chinatown by anti-Chinese exclusion laws. Chinese laborers were left with few employment options besides dangerous work building railroads for San Francisco's robber barons, who dynamited, mined and clear-cut their way across the Golden West, and built Nob Hill mansions above Chinatown.

But the city's grand ambitions came crashing down in 1906, when earthquake and fire reduced the city to rubble. Theater troupes and opera divas performed for free amid smoldering ruins, and reconstruction hummed along at an astounding rate of 15 buildings per day.

During WWII, soldiers accused of insubordination and homosexuality were dismissed in San Francisco, as though that would teach them a lesson. Instead San Francisco's counterculture thrived, with North Beach jazz and Beat poetry. When the Central Intelligence Agency (CIA) tested LSD on the willing volunteer and *One Flew Over the Cuckoo's Nest* author Ken Kesey, he slipped some into Kool-Aid and kicked off the psychedelic '60s.

The Summer of Love brought free food, love and music to the Haight, and pioneering gay activists in the Castro helped elect Harvey Milk as San Francisco supervisor – America's first out gay official. When San Francisco witnessed devastating losses from HIV/AIDS in the 1980s, the city rallied to become a global model for epidemic treatment and prevention.

San Francisco's unconventional thinking spawned the web in the 1990s, until the dot-com bubble burst in 2000. But risk-taking SF continues to float outlandish new ideas – social media, mobile apps, biotech. Congratulations: you're just in time for San Francisco's next wild ride.

Sights

Downtown, Civic Center & SoMa

★San Francisco Museum of Modern Art MUSEUM

(SFMOMA; Map p62; 415-357-4000; www.sfmoma.org; 151 3rd St; adult/under 18yr/student $25/free/$19; 10am-5pm Fri-Tue, to 9pm Thu, public spaces from 9am; ; 5, 6, 7, 14, 19, 21, 31, 38, M Montgomery, B Montgomery) The expanded SFMOMA is a mind-boggling feat, tripled in size to accommodate a sprawling collection of modern masterworks and 19 concurrent exhibitions over 10 floors – but, then again, SFMOMA has defied limits ever since its 1935 founding. The museum was a visionary early investor in then-emerging art forms, including photography, installations, video, performance art, and (as befits a global technology hub) digital art and industrial design. Even during the Depression, SFMOMA envisioned a world of vivid possibilities, starting in San Francisco.

DON'T MISS...

Saloons The Barbary Coast is roaring back to life with historically researched whiskey cocktails and staggering gin concoctions in San Francisco's great Western-saloon revival.

Rooftop-garden cuisine SF chefs are raising the roof on hyperlocal fare with ingredients raised right upstairs: city-bee honey at Jardinière (p91), edible pansies at **Coi** (Map p68; 415-393-9000; www.coirestaurant.com; 373 Broadway; set menu $250; 5:30-10pm Thu-Mon; P; 8, 10, 12, 30, 41, 45, Powell-Mason), herbs at farm:table (p87) and salad greens to feed the homeless at **Glide Memorial** (Map p62; 415-674-6090; www.glide.org; 330 Ellis St; celebrations 9am & 11am Sun; ; 38, M Powell, B Powell).

Green everything Recent reports rank San Francisco as the greenest city in North America, with its pioneering parklets, citywide composting laws and the USA's biggest stretch of urban greenery: Golden Gate Park (p72).

★ **Asian Art Museum** MUSEUM

(Map p62; ☎415-581-3500; www.asianart.org; 200 Larkin St; adult/student/child $15/10/free, 1st Sun of month free; ⏲10am-5pm Tue, Wed & Fri-Sun, to 9pm Thu; 👪; Ⓜ Civic Center, Ⓑ Civic Center) Imaginations race from ancient Persian miniatures to cutting-edge Japanese minimalism across three floors spanning 6000 years of Asian art. Besides the largest collection outside Asia – 18,000 works – the museum offers excellent programs for all ages, from shadow-puppet shows and tea tastings with star chefs to mixers with cross-cultural DJ mash-ups.

★ **Contemporary Jewish Museum** MUSEUM

(Map p62; ☎415-344-8800; www.thecjm.org; 736 Mission St; adult/student/child $14/12/free; after 5pm Thu $5; ⏲11am-5pm Mon, Tue & Fri-Sun, to 8pm Thu; 👪; 🚌14, 30, 45, Ⓑ Montgomery, Ⓜ Montgomery) That upended blue-steel box miraculously balancing on one corner isn't sculpture but the Yerba Buena Lane entry to the Contemporary Jewish Museum – an institution that upends conventional ideas about art and religion. Exhibits here are compelling explorations of Jewish ideals and visionaries, including writer Gertrude Stein, rock promoter Bill Graham, cartoonist Roz Chast and filmmaker Stanley Kubrick.

★ **Luggage Store Gallery** GALLERY

(Map p62; ☎415-255-5971; www.luggagestoregallery.org; 1007 Market St; ⏲noon-5pm Wed-Sat; 🚌5, 6, 7, 21, 31, Ⓜ Civic Center, Ⓑ Civic Center) Like a dandelion pushing through sidewalk cracks, this plucky nonprofit gallery has brought signs of life to one of the Tenderloin's toughest blocks for two decades. By giving SF street artists a gallery platform, the Luggage Store helped launch graffiti-art star Barry McGee, muralist Rigo and street photographer Cheryl Dunn. Find the graffitied door and climb to the 2nd-floor gallery, which rises above the street without losing sight of it.

★ **SF Camerawork** GALLERY

(Map p62; ☎415-487-1011; www.sfcamerawork.org; 1011 Market St, 2nd fl; ⏲noon-6pm Tue-Sat; 🚌6, 7, 9, 21, Ⓑ Civic Center, Ⓜ Civic Center) FREE Since 1974, this nonprofit art organization has championed experimental photo-based imagery beyond classic B&W prints and casual digital snapshots. Since moving into this spacious new Market St gallery, Camerawork's far-reaching exhibitions have examined memories of love and war in Southeast Asia, taken imaginary holidays with slide shows of vacation snapshots scavenged from the San Francisco Dump and showcased SF-based artist Sanaz Mazinani's mesmerizing Islamic-inspired photo montages made of tiny Trumps.

BEFORE YOU GO

- Make reservations at top San Francisco restaurants – some accept early/late walk-ins, but not all do.
- Reserve Alcatraz tickets two to four weeks ahead, especially for popular night tours.
- Download SF-invented apps for ride sharing (Lyft, Uber), home sharing (Airbnb), restaurant booking (Yelp) and audio walking tours (Detour) – all widely used here.

★ **Ferry Building** LANDMARK

(Map p62; ☎415-983-8030; www.ferrybuildingmarketplace.com; cnr Market St & the Embarcadero; ⏲10am-7pm Mon-Fri, 8am-6pm Sat, 11am-5pm Sun; 👪; 🚌2, 6, 9, 14, 21, 31, Ⓜ Embarcadero, Ⓑ Embarcadero) Hedonism is alive and well at this transit hub turned gourmet emporium, where foodies happily miss their ferries over Sonoma oysters and bubbly, SF craft beer and Marin-raised beef burgers, or locally roasted coffee and just-baked cupcakes. Star chefs are frequently spotted at the farmers market (p89) that wraps around the building all year.

Diego Rivera's Allegory of California Fresco PUBLIC ART

(Map p62; www.sfcityguides.org/desc.html?tour=96; 155 Sansome St; tours free; ⏲tours by reservation with SF City Guides 3pm 1st & 3rd Mon of month; Ⓑ Montgomery, Ⓜ Montgomery) FREE Hidden inside San Francisco's Stock Exchange tower is a priceless treasure: Diego Rivera's 1930–31 *Allegory of California* fresco. Spanning a two-story stairwell between the 10th and 11th floors, the fresco shows California as a giant golden goddess offering farm-fresh produce, while gold miners toil beneath her and oil refineries loom on the horizon. Rivera's *Allegory* is glorious, but cautionary – while Californian workers, inventors and dreamers go about their business, the pressure gauge in the left-hand corner is entering the red zone.

Downtown San Francisco & SoMa

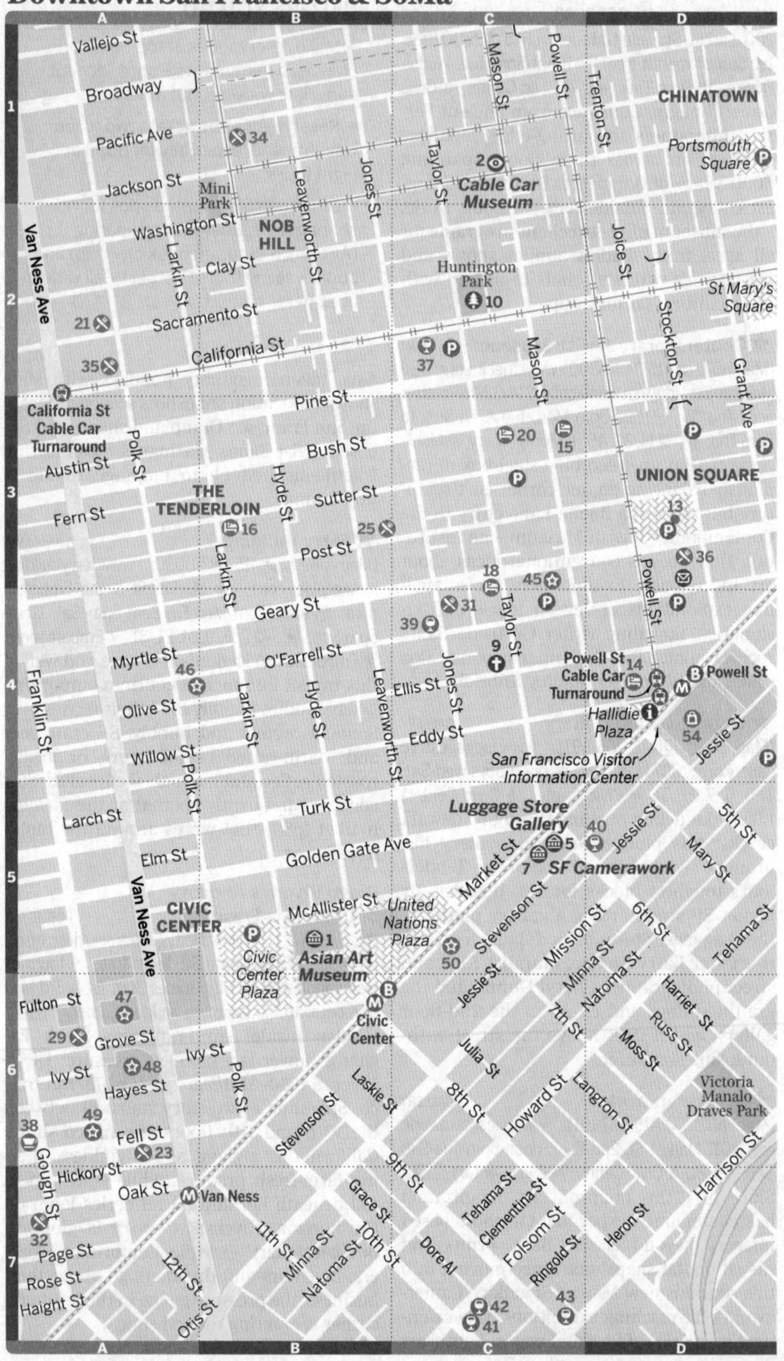

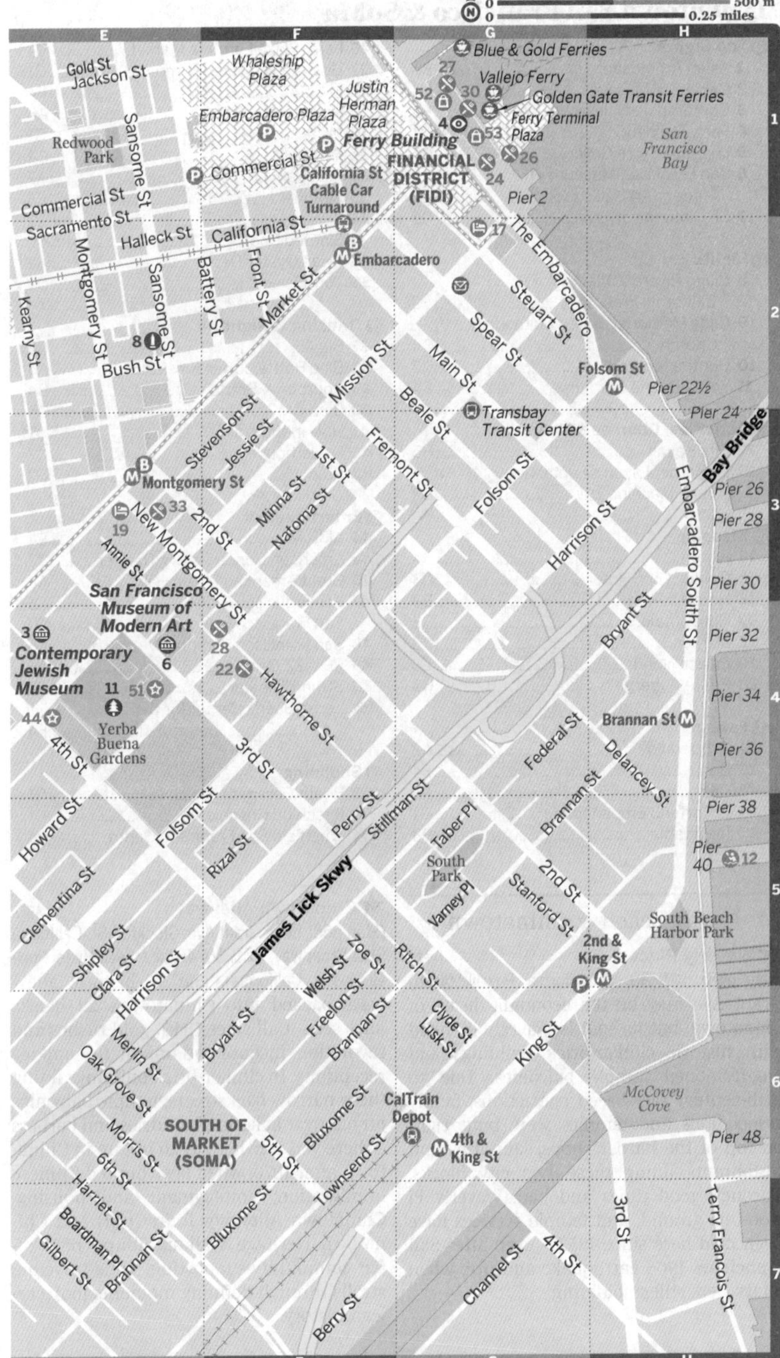

500 m
0.25 miles
Blue & Gold Ferries
Vallejo Ferry
Golden Gate Transit Ferries
Ferry Terminal Plaza
Whaleship Plaza
Justin Herman Plaza
Embarcadero Plaza
Ferry Building
FINANCIAL DISTRICT (FIDI)
California St Cable Car Turnaround
San Francisco Bay
Pier 2
Redwood Park
Embarcadero
Transbay Transit Center
Folsom St
Pier 22½
Pier 24
Bay Bridge
Montgomery St
Pier 26
Pier 28
Pier 30
Pier 32
Pier 34
Pier 36
Pier 38
Pier 40
San Francisco Museum of Modern Art
Contemporary Jewish Museum
Yerba Buena Gardens
Brannan St
South Park
South Beach Harbor Park
2nd & King St
James Lick Skwy
CalTrain Depot
4th & King St
McCovey Cove
Pier 48
SOUTH OF MARKET (SOMA)

Downtown San Francisco & SoMa

Top Sights
1 Asian Art Museum ... B5
2 Cable Car Museum ... C1
3 Contemporary Jewish Museum ... E4
4 Ferry Building ... G1
5 Luggage Store Gallery ... C5
6 San Francisco Museum of Modern Art ... E4
7 SF Camerawork ... C5

Sights
8 Diego Rivera's Allegory of California Fresco ... E2
9 Glide Memorial United Methodist Church ... C4
10 Huntington Park ... C2
11 Yerba Buena Gardens ... E4

Activities, Courses & Tours
12 City Kayak ... H5
13 Emperor Norton's Fantastic Time Machine ... D3

Sleeping
14 Axiom ... D4
15 Golden Gate Hotel ... C3
16 Hotel Carlton ... B3
17 Hotel Vitale ... G2
18 Marker ... C3
19 Palace Hotel ... E3
20 Petite Auberge ... C3

Eating
21 Acquerello ... A2
22 Benu ... F4
23 Cala ... A6
24 El Porteño Empanadas ... G1
25 farm:table ... B3
26 Ferry Plaza Farmers Market ... G1
27 Hog Island Oyster Company ... G1
28 In Situ ... F4
29 Jardinière ... A6
30 Mijita ... G1
31 Red Chilli ... C4
32 Rich Table ... A7
33 Sentinel ... E3
34 Seven Hills ... B1
Slanted Door ... (see 27)
35 Swan Oyster Depot ... A2
36 Tout Sweet ... D3

Drinking & Nightlife
37 Big 4 ... C2
38 Blue Bottle Coffee Kiosk ... A6
39 Bourbon & Branch ... C4
40 Club OMG ... D5
41 Hole in the Wall ... C7
42 Powerhouse ... C7
43 Stud ... C7

Entertainment
44 AMC Metreon 16 ... E4
45 American Conservatory Theater ... C3
46 Great American Music Hall ... A4
47 San Francisco Ballet ... A6
San Francisco Opera ... (see 47)
48 San Francisco Symphony ... A6
49 SFJAZZ Center ... A6
50 Strand Theater ... C5
51 Yerba Buena Center for the Arts ... E4

Shopping
52 Heath Ceramics ... G1
53 Recchiuti Chocolates ... G1
54 Westfield San Francisco Centre ... D4

North Beach & Chinatown

★Waverly Place
STREET

(Map p68; 1, 30, California, Powell-Mason) Grant Ave may be the economic heart of Chinatown, but its soul is Waverly Pl, lined with historic clinker-brick buildings and flag-festooned temple balconies. Due to 19th-century race-based restrictions, family associations and temples were built right on top of the barber shops, laundries and restaurants lining these two city blocks. Through good times and bad, Waverly Pl stood its ground, and temple services have been held here since 1852 – even after San Francisco's 1906 earthquake and fire, when altars were still smoldering.

★Chinatown Alleyways
AREA

(Map p68; btwn Grant Ave, Stockton St, California St & Broadway; 1, 30, 45, Powell-Hyde, Powell-Mason, California) The 41 historic alleyways packed into Chinatown's 22 blocks have seen it all since 1849: gold rushes and revolution, incense and opium, fire and icy receptions. In clinker-brick buildings lining these narrow backstreets, temple balconies jut out over bakeries, laundries and barbers – there was nowhere to go but up in Chinatown after 1870, when laws limited Chinese immigration, employment and housing. Chinatown Alleyway Tours (p81) and Chinatown Heritage Walking Tours (p82) offer community-supporting, time-traveling strolls through defining moments in American history.

★City Lights Books CULTURAL CENTER

(Map p68; ☎415-362-8193; www.citylights.com; 261 Columbus Ave; ⏰10am-midnight; 👪; 🚌8, 10, 12, 30, 41, 45, 🚋Powell-Mason, Powell-Hyde) Free speech and free spirits have flourished here since 1957, when City Lights founder and poet Lawrence Ferlinghetti and manager Shigeyoshi Murao won a landmark ruling defending their right to publish Allen Ginsberg's magnificent epic poem *Howl*. Celebrate your freedom to read freely in the designated Poet's Chair upstairs overlooking Jack Kerouac Alley, load up on 'zines on the mezzanine and entertain radical ideas downstairs in the new Pedagogies of Resistance section.

★Coit Tower PUBLIC ART

(Map p68; ☎415-249-0995; www.sfrecpark.org; Telegraph Hill Blvd; nonresident elevator fee adult/child $8/5; ⏰10am-6pm Apr-Oct, to 5pm Nov-Mar; 🚌39) The exclamation mark on San Francisco's skyline is Coit Tower, with 360-degree views of downtown and wraparound 1930s Works Progress Administration (WPA) murals glorifying SF workers. Initially denounced as communist, the murals are now a national landmark. For a wild-parrot's panoramic view of San Francisco 210ft above the city, take the elevator to the tower's open-air platform. To glimpse seven recently restored murals up a hidden stairwell on the 2nd floor, join the 11am tour Wednesday or Saturday (free; donations welcome).

Beat Museum MUSEUM

(Map p68; ☎800-537-6822; www.kerouac.com; 540 Broadway; adult/student $8/5, walking tours $25; ⏰museum 10am-7pm, walking tours 2-4pm Sat; 🚌8, 10, 12, 30, 41, 45, 🚋Powell-Mason) The closest you can get to the complete Beat experience without breaking a law. The 1000-plus artifacts in this museum's literary-ephemera collection include the sublime (the banned edition of Ginsberg's *Howl*, with the author's own annotations) and the ridiculous (those Kerouac bobblehead dolls are definite head-shakers). Downstairs, watch Beat-era films in ramshackle theater seats redolent with the odors of literary giants, pets and pot. Upstairs, pay your respects at shrines to individual Beat writers.

Chinese Historical Society of America MUSEUM

(CHSA; Map p68; ☎415-391-1188; www.chsa.org; 965 Clay St; adult/student/child $15/10/free; ⏰noon-5pm Tue-Fri, 10am-4pm Sat & Sun; 👪; 🚌1, 8, 30, 45, 🚋California, Powell-Mason, Powell-Hyde) FREE Picture what it was like to be Chinese in America during the gold rush, transcontinental railroad construction or Beat heyday in this 1932 landmark, built as Chinatown's YWCA by Julia Morgan (chief architect of Hearst Castle). CHSA historians unearth fascinating artifacts, from 1920s silk *qipao* dresses to Chinatown miniatures created by set designer Frank Wong. Exhibits reveal once-popular views of Chinatown, including the sensationalist opium-den exhibit at San Francisco's 1915 Panama-Pacific International Expo inviting fairgoers to 'Go Slumming' in Chinatown.

The Marina, Fisherman's Wharf & the Piers

★Alcatraz HISTORIC SITE

(☎Alcatraz Cruises 415-981-7625; www.nps.gov/alcatraz; tours adult/child 5-11yr day $37.25/23, night $44.25/26.50; ⏰call center 8am-7pm, ferries depart Pier 33 half-hourly 8:45am-3:50pm, night tours 5:55pm & 6:30pm; 👪) Alcatraz: for over 150 years, the name has given the innocent chills and the guilty cold sweats. Over the decades, it's been the nation's first military prison, a forbidding maximum-security penitentiary and disputed territory between Native American activists and the FBI. No wonder that first step you take onto 'the Rock' seems to cue ominous music: dunh-dunh-dunnnnh!

★Maritime National Historical Park HISTORIC SITE

(Map p70; ☎415-447-5000; www.nps.gov/safr; 499 Jefferson St, Hyde St Pier; 7-day ticket adult/child $10/free; ⏰9:30am-5pm Oct-May, to 5:30pm Jun-Sep; 👪; 🚌19, 30, 47, 🚋Powell-Hyde, ⓂF) Four historic ships are floating museums

DON'T MISS

GOLDEN GATE BRIDGE

Hard to believe the Navy almost nixed SF's signature art-deco **landmark** (www.goldengatebridge.org/visitors; Hwy 1; northbound free, southbound $6.50-7.50; 🚌28, all Golden Gate Transit buses) by architects Gertrude and Irving Murrow and engineer Joseph B Strauss. Photographers, take your cue from Hitchcock: seen from **Fort Point** (p71), the 1937 bridge induces a thrilling case of vertigo. Fog aficionados prefer Marin's Vista Point, watching gusts billow through bridge cables. For the full effect, hike or bike the 2-mile span.

Alcatraz

A HALF-DAY TOUR

Book a ferry from Pier 33 and ride 1.5 miles across the bay to explore America's most notorious former prison. The trip itself is worth the money, providing stunning views of the city skyline. Once you've landed at the ❶ **Ferry Dock & Pier**, you begin the 580-yard walk to the top of the island and prison; if you need assistance to reach the top, there's a twice-hourly tram.

As you climb toward the ❷ **Guardhouse**, notice the island's steep slope; before it was a prison, Alcatraz was a fort. In the 1850s, the military quarried the rocky shores into near-vertical cliffs. Ships could then only dock at a single port, separated from the main buildings by a sally port (a drawbridge and moat in what became the guardhouse). Inside, peer through floor grates to see Alcatraz' original prison.

Volunteers tend the brilliant ❸ **Officer's Row Gardens** an orderly counterpoint to the overgrown rose bushes surrounding the burned-out shell of the ❹ **Warden's House**. At the top of the hill, by the front door of the ❺ **Main Cellhouse**, beautiful shots unfurl all around, including a view of the ❻ **Golden Gate Bridge**. Above the main door of the administration building, notice the ❼ **historic signs & graffiti**, before you step inside the dank, cold prison to find the ❽ **Frank Morris cell**, former home to Alcatraz' most notorious jail-breaker.

TOP TIPS

➡ Book at least one month prior for self-guided daytime visits, longer for ranger-led night tours. For info on garden tours, see www.alcatraz gardens.org.

➡ Be prepared to hike; a steep path ascends from the ferry landing to the cell block. Most people spend two to three hours on the island. You need only reserve for the outbound ferry; take any ferry back.

➡ There's no food (just water) but you can bring your own; picnicking is allowed at the ferry dock only. Dress in layers as weather changes fast and it's usually windy.

ADRIEN_G/SHUTTERSTOCK ©

Historic Signs & Graffiti
During their 1969–71 occupation, Native Americans graffitied the water tower: 'Home of the Free Indian Land.' Above the cellhouse door, examine the eagle-and-flag crest to see how the red-and-white stripes were changed to spell 'Free.'

DOPTIS/SHUTTERSTOCK ©

Warden's House
Fires destroyed the warden's house and other structures during the Indian Occupation. The government blamed the Native Americans; the Native Americans blamed agents provocateurs acting on behalf of the Nixon Administration to undermine public sympathy.

Parade Grounds

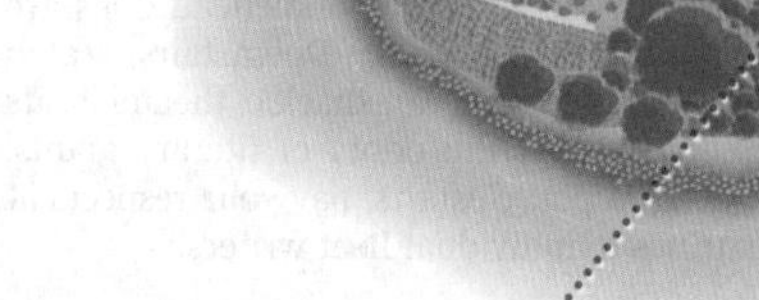

Officer's Row Gardens
In the 19th century soldiers imported topsoil to beautify the island with gardens. Well-trusted prisoners later gardened – Elliott Michener said it kept him sane. Historians, ornithologists and archaeologists choose today's plants.

Main Cellhouse
During the mid-20th century, the maximum-security prison housed the day's most notorious troublemakers, including Al Capone and Robert Stroud, the 'Birdman of Alcatraz' (who actually conducted his ornithology studies at Leavenworth).

View of Golden Gate Bridge
The Golden Gate Bridge stretches wide on the horizon. Best views are from atop the island at Eagle Plaza, near the cellhouse entrance, and at water level along the Agave Trail (September to January only).

Guardhouse
Alcatraz' oldest building dates to 1857 and retains remnants of the original drawbridge and moat. During the Civil War the basement was transformed into a military dungeon – the genesis of Alcatraz as prison.

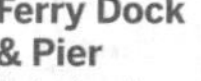

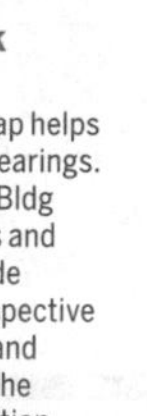

Frank Morris Cell
Peer into cell 138 on B-Block to see a recreation of the dummy's head that Frank Morris left in his bed as a decoy to aid his notorious – and successful – 1962 escape from Alcatraz.

Ferry Dock & Pier
A giant wall map helps you get your bearings. Inside nearby Bldg 64, short films and exhibits provide historical perspective on the prison and details about the Indian Occupation.

Chinatown & North Beach

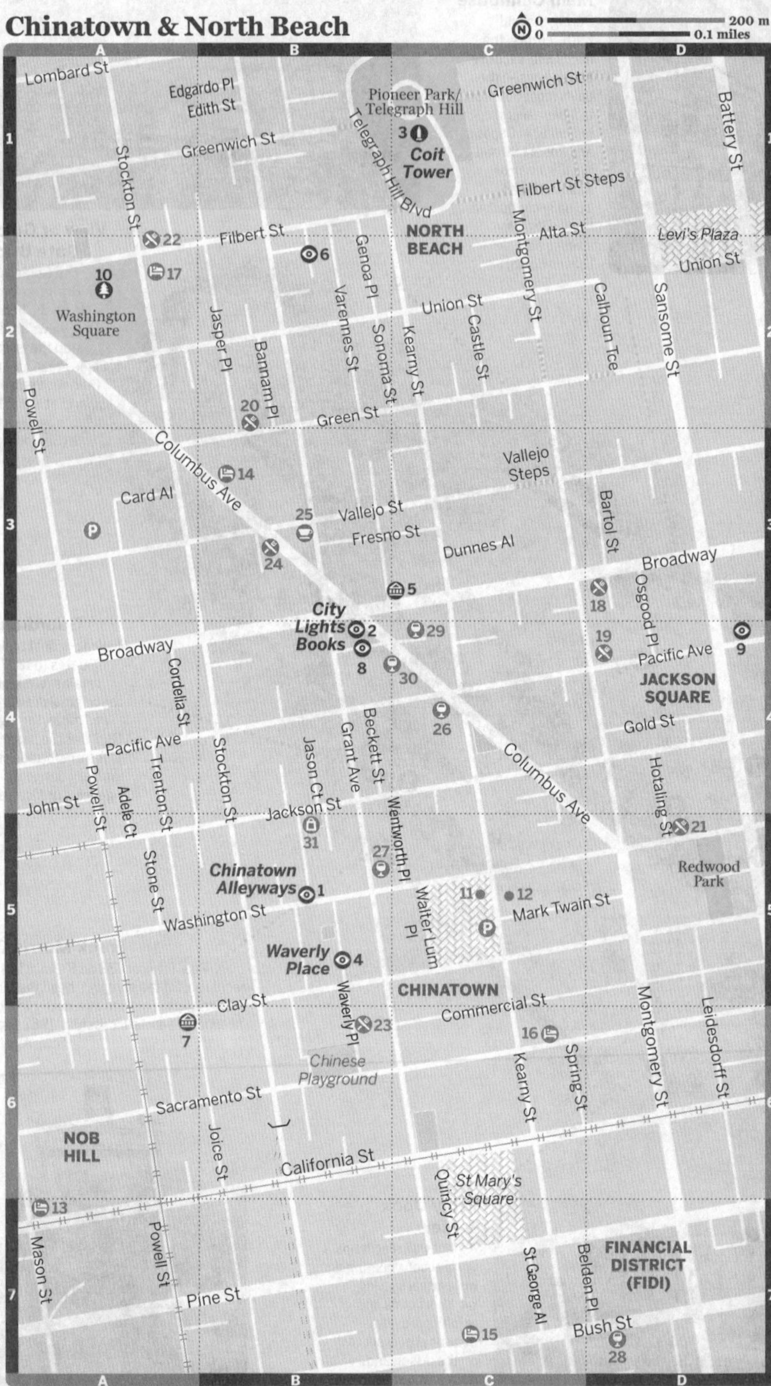

Chinatown & North Beach

Top Sights
1 Chinatown Alleyways B5
2 City Lights Books B4
3 Coit Tower C1
4 Waverly Place B5

Sights
5 Beat Museum C3
6 Bob Kaufman Alley B2
7 Chinese Historical Society of America A6
8 Jack Kerouac Alley B4
9 Jackson Square D4
10 Washington Square A2

Activities, Courses & Tours
11 Chinatown Alleyway Tours C5
12 Chinatown Heritage Walking Tours C5

Sleeping
13 Fairmont San Francisco A7
14 Hotel Bohème B3
15 Orchard Garden Hotel C7
16 Pacific Tradewinds Hostel C6
17 Washington Square Inn A2

Eating
18 Coi D3
19 Cotogna D4
20 Golden Boy B2
21 Kusakabe D5
22 Liguria Bakery A2
23 Mister Jiu's B6
24 Molinari B3

Drinking & Nightlife
25 Caffe Trieste B3
26 Comstock Saloon C4
27 Li Po B5
28 Pagan Idol D7
29 Specs C4
Tonga Room (see 13)
30 Vesuvio C4

Shopping
31 Golden Gate Fortune Cookie Company B5

at this maritime national park, Fisherman's Wharf's most authentic attraction. Moored along Hyde St Pier, standouts include the 1891 schooner *Alma*, which hosts guided sailing trips in summer; 1890 steamboat *Eureka*; paddlewheel tugboat *Eppleton Hall*; and iron-hulled *Balclutha*, which brought coal to San Francisco. It's free to walk the pier; pay only to board ships.

★ Baker Beach BEACH

(Map p80; 10am-5pm 415-561-4323; www.nps.gov/prsf; sunrise-sunset; P; 29, PresidiGo Shuttle) Picnic amid wind-sculpted pines, fish from craggy rocks or frolic nude at mile-long Baker Beach, with spectacular views of the Golden Gate. Crowds come weekends, especially on fog-free days; arrive early. For nude sunbathing (mostly straight girls and gay boys), head to the north. Families in clothing stick to the south, nearer parking. Mind the currents and the c-c-cold water.

★ Musée Mécanique AMUSEMENT PARK

(Map p70; 415-346-2000; www.museemechanique.org; Pier 45, Shed A; 10am-8pm; ; 47, Powell-Mason, Powell-Hyde, M E, F) A flashback to penny arcades, the Musée Mécanique houses a mind-blowing collection of vintage mechanical amusements. Sinister, freckle-faced Laughing Sal has creeped out kids for over a century, but don't let this manic mannequin deter you from the best arcade west of Coney Island. A quarter lets you start brawls in Wild West saloons, peep at belly dancers through a vintage Mutoscope and even learn a cautionary tale about smoking opium.

★ Exploratorium MUSEUM

(Map p70; 415-528-4444; www.exploratorium.edu; Pier 15; adult/child $30/20, 6-10pm Thu $15; 10am-5pm Tue-Sun, over 18yr only 6-10pm Thu; P; M E, F) Is there a science to skateboarding? Do toilets really flush counterclockwise in Australia? Find out things you'll wish you learned in school at San Francisco's hands-on science museum. Combining science with art and investigating human perception, the Exploratorium nudges you to question how you perceive the world around you. The setting is thrilling: a 9-acre, glass-walled pier jutting straight into San Francisco Bay, with large outdoor portions you can explore free of charge, 24 hours a day.

★ Crissy Field PARK

(Map p70; 415-561-4700; www.crissyfield.org; 1199 East Beach; P; 30, PresidiGo Shuttle) War is for the birds at Crissy Field, a military airstrip turned waterfront nature preserve with knockout Golden Gate views. Where military aircraft once zoomed in for landings, bird-watchers now huddle in the silent rushes of a reclaimed tidal marsh. Joggers pound beachside trails and the only security

Fisherman's Wharf, The Marina & Russian Hill

Fisherman's Wharf, The Marina & Russian Hill

Top Sights

1 Crissy Field........A2
2 Exploratorium........H2
3 Lombard Street........E2
4 Maritime National Historical Park........E1
5 Musée Mécanique........F1
6 Sea Lions at Pier 39........F1

Sights

7 Diego Rivera Gallery........F2
8 Fort Mason Center........D1
9 Ina Coolbrith Park........F3
10 USS Pampanito........F1
11 Vallejo Street Steps........F3

Activities, Courses & Tours

12 Alcatraz Cruises........G1
13 Basically Free Bike Rentals........F2
Blazing Saddles........(see 28)
14 Oceanic Society Expeditions........C1

Sleeping

15 Argonaut Hotel........E1
16 HI San Francisco Fisherman's Wharf........D1
17 Hotel del Sol........D2
18 Hotel Drisco........C4
19 Hotel Zephyr........F1
20 Inn at the Presidio........A3
21 Queen Anne Hotel........E4

Eating

22 Gary Danko........E1
23 Greens........D1
24 La Folie........E3
25 Lucca Delicatessen........C2
26 Off the Grid........D2
27 Out the Door........D4

Drinking & Nightlife

28 Buena Vista Cafe........E1
29 Interval Bar & Cafe........D1

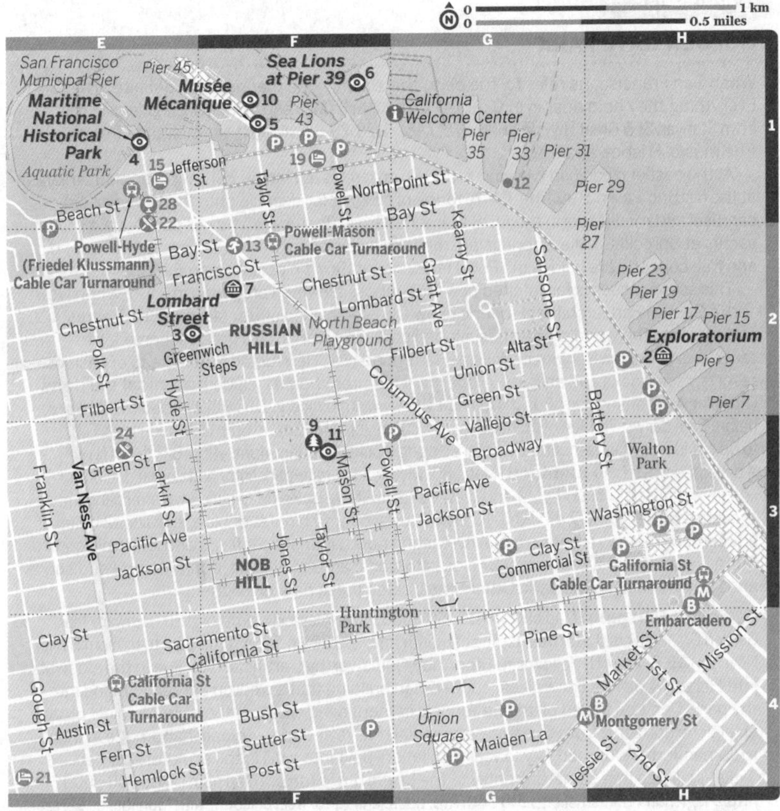

alerts are raised by puppies suspiciously sniffing surfers. On foggy days, stop by the certified-green **Warming Hut** (Map p108; ☎415-561-3042; www.parksconservancy.org/visit/eat/warming-hut.html; 983 Marine Dr; items $4-9; ⊙9am-5pm; P 👪; 🚌PresidiGo shuttle) 🌿 to browse regional-nature books and warm up with fair-trade coffee.

Fort Mason Center AREA

(Map p70; ☎415-345-7500; www.fortmason.org; cnr Marina Blvd & Laguna St; P; 🚌22, 28, 30, 43, 47, 49) San Francisco takes subversive glee in turning military installations into venues for nature, fine dining and out-there experimental art. Evidence: Fort Mason, once a shipyard and embarkation point for WWII troops, now a vast cultural center and gathering place for events, drinking and eating. Wander the waterfront, keeping your eyes peeled for fascinating outdoor art-and-science installations designed by the Exploratorium (p69).

Fort Point HISTORIC SITE

(Map p108; ☎415-556-1693; www.nps.gov/fopo; Marine Dr; ⊙10am-5pm Fri-Sun; P; 🚌28) FREE This triple-decker, brick-walled US military fortress was completed in 1861, with 126 cannons, to protect the bay against certain invasion during the Civil War…or not, as it turned out. Without a single shot having been fired, Fort Point was abandoned in 1900. Alfred Hitchcock made it famous in his 1956 film *Vertigo* – this is where Kim Novak jumped into the bay. Now the fort showcases Civil War displays and knockout panoramic viewing decks of the bridge's underside.

Pier 39 PIER

(Map p70; ☎415-705-5500; www.pier39.com; cnr Beach St & the Embarcadero; P 👪; 🚌47, 🚋Powell-Mason, ⓂE, F) The focal point of Fisherman's Wharf isn't the waning fishing fleet but the carousel, carnival-like attractions, shops and restaurants of Pier 39 – and, of course, the

DON'T MISS

GOLDEN GATE PARK

When San Franciscans refer to 'the park,' there's only one that gets the definite article. Everything they hold dear is in **Golden Gate Park** (Map p80; www.golden-gate-park.com; btwn Stanyan St & Great Hwy; P; 5, 7, 18, 21, 28, 29, 33, 44, MN), including free spirits, free music, Frisbee and bison.

At the east end you can join year-round drum circles at **Hippie Hill**, sweater-clad athletes at the historic **Lawn Bowling Club**, toddlers clinging for dear life onto the 100-year-old carousel and meditators in the AIDS Memorial Grove. To the west, turtles paddle past model yachts at Spreckels Lake, offerings are made at pagan altars behind the baseball diamond and free concerts are held in the Polo Fields, site of 1967's hippie Human Be-In.

This scenery seems far-fetched now, but impossible when proposed in 1866. When New York's Central Park architect Frederick Law Olmsted balked at transforming 1017 acres of dunes into the world's largest developed park, San Francisco's green scheme fell to tenacious young civil engineer William Hammond Hall. He insisted that instead of casinos, resorts, race tracks and an igloo village, park features should include **botanical gardens** (Strybing Arboretum; Map p80; 415-661-1316; www.strybing.org; 1199 9th Ave; adult/child $8/2, before 9am daily & 2nd Tue of month free; 7:30am-7pm Mar-Sep, to 6pm Oct–mid-Nov & Feb, to 5pm mid-Nov–Jan, last entry 1hr before closing, bookstore 10am-4pm; 6, 7, 44, MN), a dedicated **buffalo paddock** (Map p80; www.golden-gate-park.com/buffalo-paddock.html; sunrise-sunset; 5, 21) FREE and waterfalls at **Stow Lake** (Map p80; www.sfrecpark.org; sunrise-sunset; 7, 44, MN). Today the park offers 7.5 miles of bicycle trails, 12 miles of equestrian trails, an archery range, fly-casting pools, four soccer fields and 21 tennis courts. Sundays, when John F Kennedy Dr closes to traffic around 9th Ave, don't miss roller disco and lindy-hopping in the park. Other times, catch these park highlights:

de Young Museum (Map p80; 415-750-3600; http://deyoung.famsf.org; 50 Hagiwara Tea Garden Dr; adult/child $15/free, 1st Tue of month free; 9:30am-5:15pm Tue-Sun, to 8:45pm Fri Apr-Nov; 5, 7, 44, MN) Follow sculptor Andy Goldsworthy's artificial fault line in the sidewalk into Herzog & de Meuron's sleek, copper-clad building that's oxidizing green to blend into the park. Don't be fooled by the de Young's camouflaged exterior: shows here boldly broaden artistic horizons, from Oceanic ceremonial masks and trippy-hippie handmade fashion to James Turrell's domed *Skyspace* installation, built into a hill in the sculpture garden. Ticket includes free same-day entry to the **Legion of Honor** (Map p80; 415-750-3600; http://legionofhonor.famsf.org; 100 34th Ave; adult/child $15/free, discount with Muni ticket $2, 1st Tue of month free; 9:30am-5:15pm Tue-Sun; 1, 2, 18, 38); $2 discount with Muni ticket.

California Academy of Sciences (Map p80; 415-379-8000; www.calacademy.org; 55 Music Concourse Dr; adult/student/child $35/30/25; 9:30am-5pm Mon-Sat, from 11am Sun; P; 5, 6, 7, 21, 31, 33, 44, MN) Architect Renzo Piano's 2008 landmark LEED-certified green building houses 40,000 weird and wonderful animals in a four-story rainforest, split-level aquarium and planetarium all under a 'living roof' of California wildflowers. After the penguins nod off to sleep, the wild rumpus starts at the kids-only Penguins+Pajamas Sleepovers ($109 including snack and breakfast; ages five to 17, plus adult chaperones; 6pm to 8am) and the over-21 NightLife Thursdays ($15; 6pm to 10pm), when rainforest-themed cocktails encourage strange mating rituals among shy internet daters.

Japanese Tea Garden (Map p80; 415-752-1171; www.japaneseteagardensf.com; 75 Hagiwara Tea Garden Dr; adult/child $8/2, before 10am Mon, Wed & Fri free; 9am-6pm Mar-Oct, to 4:45pm Nov-Feb; P; 5, 7, 44, MN) Since 1894, this picturesque 5-acre garden has blushed with cherry blossoms in spring, flamed red with maple leaves in fall, and induced visitors to lose track of time in its meditative Zen Garden. The bonsai grove was cultivated by the Hagiwara family, who returned from WWII Japanese American internment camps to discover that many of their prized miniature evergreens had been sold – they spent decades recovering them. Visit the Tea House for tea and fortune cookies, introduced to the US right here.

Conservatory of Flowers (Map p80; info 415-831-2090; www.conservatoryofflowers.org; 100 John F Kennedy Dr; adult/student/child $8/6/2, 1st Tue of month free; 10am-4pm Tue-Sun; 5, 7, 21, 33, MN) Flower power is alive and well at San Francisco's Conservatory of Flowers. This gloriously restored 1878 Victorian greenhouse is home to freaky outer-space orchids, contemplative floating lilies and creepy carnivorous plants gulping down insect lunches.

famous **sea lions** (Map p70; www.pier39.com; Pier 39, cnr Beach St & the Embarcadero; 24hr; ; 15, 37, 49, E, F). Developed in the 1970s to revitalize tourism, the pier draws thousands of tourists daily, but it's really just a big outdoor shopping mall. On the plus side, its visitors center rents strollers, stores luggage and has free phone-charging stations.

USS Pampanito HISTORIC SITE
(Map p70; 415-775-1943, tickets 855-384-6410; www.maritime.org/pamphome.htm; Pier 45; adult/child/family $20/10/45; 9am-8pm Thu-Tue, to 6pm Wed; ; 19, 30, 47, Powell-Hyde, E, F) Explore a restored WWII submarine that survived six tours of duty while you listen to submariners' tales of stealth mode and sudden attacks in a riveting audio tour that makes surfacing afterwards a relief (caution, claustrophobes).

Nob Hill, Russian Hill & Fillmore

★Lombard Street STREET
(Map p70; Powell-Hyde) You've seen the eight switchbacks of Lombard St's 900 block in a thousand photographs. The tourist board has dubbed it 'the world's crookedest street,' which is factually incorrect: Vermont St in Potrero Hill deserves that award, but Lombard is much more scenic, with its redbrick pavement and lovingly tended flowerbeds. It wasn't always so bent; before the arrival of the car it lunged straight down the hill.

★Cable Car Museum HISTORIC SITE
(Map p62; 415-474-1887; www.cablecarmuseum.org; 1201 Mason St; donations appreciated; 10am-6pm Apr-Sep, to 5pm Oct-Mar; ; Powell-Mason, Powell-Hyde) FREE Hear that whirring beneath the cable-car tracks? That's the sound of the cables that pull the cars, and they all connect inside the city's long-functioning cable-car barn. Grips, engines, braking mechanisms…if these warm your gearhead heart, you'll be besotted with the Cable Car Museum.

Huntington Park PARK
(Map p62; http://sfrecpark.org; California St, btwn Mason & Taylor Sts; ; 1, California) San Francisco's poshest park, Huntington's 1.3 acres mark the crest of Nob Hill. At the center rises the four-sided 'Fountain of the Tortoises,' a century-old recreation of a 400-year-old limestone fountain in Rome. If you're staying down the hill and don't have a lot of time to explore, the park makes a perfect picnic destination – especially with kids, who love the little playground, kitted out with spongy-soft ground cover.

Vallejo Street Steps ARCHITECTURE
(Map p70; Vallejo St, btwn Mason & Jones Sts; Powell-Mason, Powell-Hyde) This glorious high staircase connects North Beach with Russian Hill – ideal for working off a pasta dinner. Ascend Vallejo toward Mason St; stairs rise toward Jones St, passing **Ina Coolbrith Park** (Map p70; cnr Vallejo & Taylor Sts; 10, 12, Powell-Mason). Sit at the top for brilliant views of the Bay Bridge lights, then continue west to Polk St for nightlife.

Diego Rivera Gallery GALLERY
(Map p70; 415-771-7020; www.sfai.edu; 800 Chestnut St; 9am-7pm; 30, Powell-Mason) FREE Diego Rivera's 1931 *The Making of a Fresco Showing the Building of a City* is a trompe l'oeil fresco within a fresco, showing the artist himself, pausing to admire his work, as well as the work in progress that is San Francisco. The fresco covers an entire wall in the Diego Rivera Gallery at the San Francisco Art Institute. For a memorable San Francisco aspect, head to the terrace cafe for espresso and panoramic bay views.

The Haight & Hayes Valley

Haight & Ashbury LANDMARK
(Map p80; 6, 7, 33, 37, 43) This legendary intersection was the epicenter of the psychedelic '60s, and 'Hashbury' remains a counterculture magnet. On average Saturdays here you can sign Green Party petitions, commission a poem and hear Hare Krishna on keyboards and Bob Dylan on banjo. The clock overhead always reads 4:20 – better known in herbal circles as International Bong-Hit Time. A local clockmaker recently fixed the clock; within a week it was stuck again at 4:20.

Zen Center HISTORIC BUILDING
(Map p78; 415-863-3136; http://sfzc.org; 300 Page St; 9:30am-12:30pm & 1:30-4pm Mon-Fri, 8:30am-noon Sat; 6, 7, 21, 22) With its sunny courtyard and generous cased windows, this uplifting 1922 building is an interfaith landmark. Since 1969 it's been home to the largest Buddhist community outside Asia. Before she built Hearst Castle, Julia Morgan (California's first licensed woman architect) designed this Italianate brick structure to house the Emanu-El Sisterhood, a residence for low-income Jewish working women –

POWELL & MAS
13
SAN FRAN

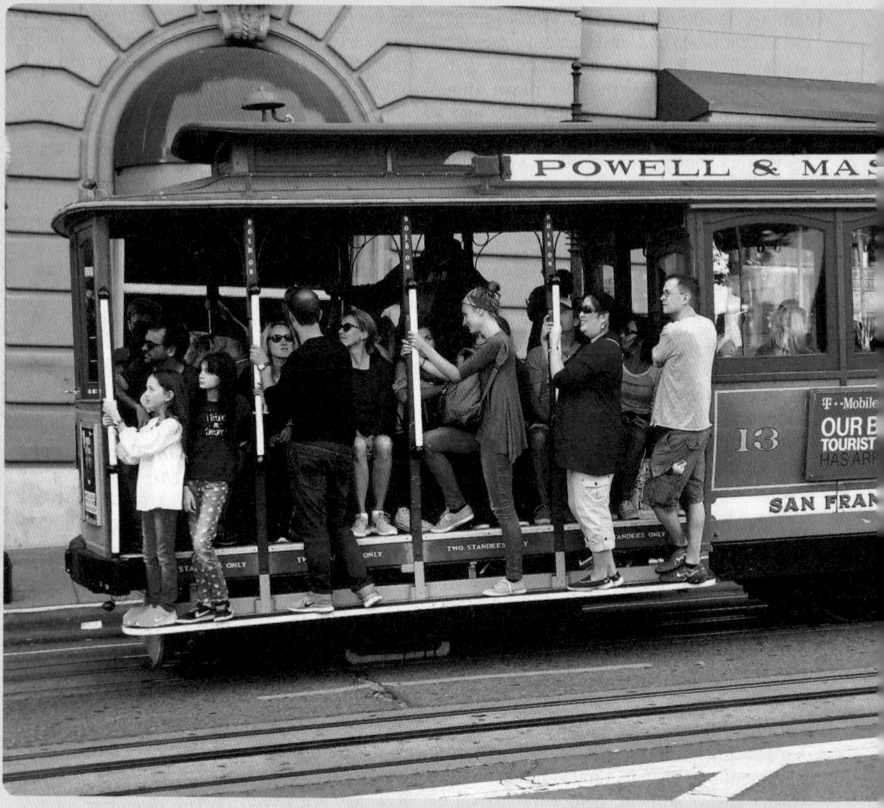

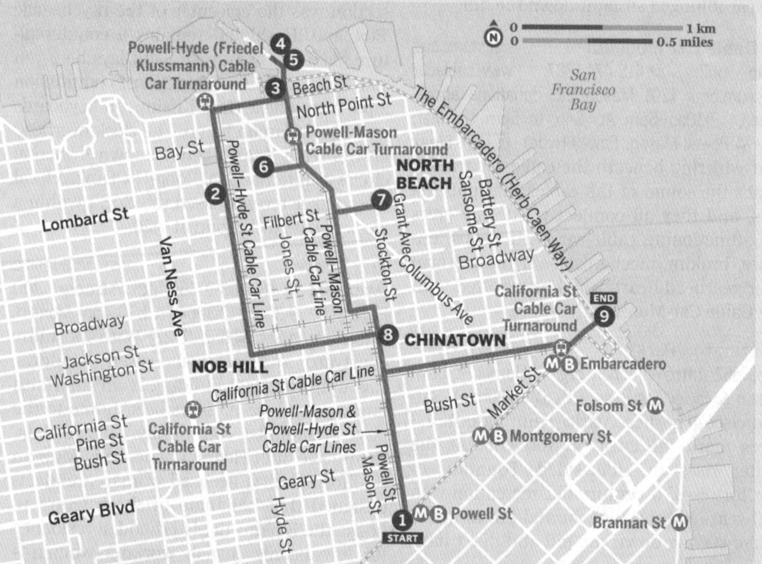

0 1 km
0 0.5 miles
San Francisco Bay
Powell-Hyde (Friedel Klussmann) Cable Car Turnaround
4
5
3
Beach St
North Point St
The Embarcadero (Herb Caen Way)
Powell-Mason Cable Car Turnaround
Bay St
Powell-Hyde St Cable Car Line
6
NORTH BEACH
2
7
Grant Ave
Sansome St
Battery St
Lombard St
Filbert St
Jones St
Powell-Mason Cable Car Line
Stockton St
Columbus Ave
Broadway
Van Ness Ave
California St Cable Car Turnaround
END
9
Broadway
8
CHINATOWN
Jackson St
Washington St
NOB HILL
Embarcadero
California St Cable Car Line
Market St
Bush St
Folsom St
California St
Pine St
Bush St
California St Cable Car Turnaround
Powell-Mason & Powell-Hyde St Cable Car Lines
Montgomery St
Geary St
Powell St
Mason St
Geary Blvd
Hyde St
1
START
Powell St
Brannan St

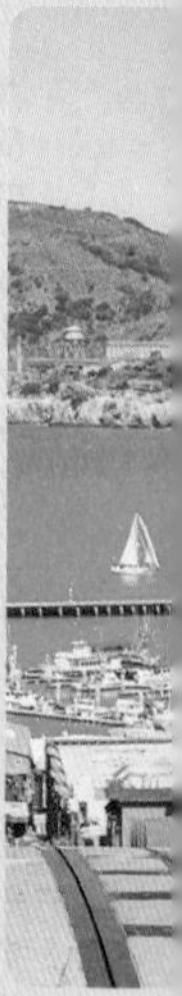

Top: Powell-Mason cable car
Bottom: Powell-Hyde cable car

San Francisco by Cable Car

Carnival rides can't compare to cable cars, San Francisco's vintage public transit. Novices slide into strangers' laps – cable cars were invented in 1873, long before seat belts – but regular commuters just grip the leather hand straps, lean back and enjoy the ride. On this trip, you'll master the San Francisco stance, and conquer SF hills without breaking a sweat.

At the **1 Powell St Cable Car Turnaround** operators turn the car atop a revolving wooden platform and there's a vintage kiosk where you can buy an all-day Muni Passport for $21, instead of paying $7 per ride. Board the red-signed Powell-Hyde cable car, and begin your 338ft ascent up Nob Hill.

Nineteenth-century city planners were skeptical of inventor Andrew Hallidie's 'wire-rope railway' – but after more than a century of near-continuous operation, his wire-and-hemp cables have seldom broken.

On the **2 Powell-Hyde car**, you'll enjoy Bay views as you careen past flower-lined Lombard Street toward **3 Fisherman's Wharf**. At the wharf you can see SF as sailors did, as you emerge from the submarine **4 USS Pampanito** (p73). Witness Western saloon brawls in vintage arcade games at the **5 Musée Mécanique** (p69) before hitching the Powell-Mason cable car to North Beach. Hop off to see Diego Rivera's 1931 cityscape in the **6 Diego Rivera Gallery** (p73) at the San Francisco Art Institute, or follow your rumbling stomach directly to **7 Liguria Bakery** (p88). Stroll through North Beach and Chinatown alleyways, or take the Powell-Mason line to time-travel through the **8 Chinese Historical Society of America** (p65). Nearby, catch a ride on the city's oldest line: the California St cable car. The terminus is near the **9 Ferry Building** (p61), where champagne-and-oyster happy hour awaits.

note the ironwork Stars of David on the 1st-floor loggia.

Today the Zen Center opens to the public for visits, meditation (see the website for a schedule), introductions to Zen practice (8:45am Saturdays) and other Zen workshops.

Alamo Square Park PARK

(Map p78; www.sfparksalliance.org/our-parks/parks/alamo-square; cnr Hayes & Steiner Sts; sunrise-sunset; ; 5, 21, 22, 24) Hippie communes and Victorian bordellos, jazz greats and opera stars, earthquakes and Church of Satan services: these genteel **'Painted Lady' Victorian mansions** have hosted them all since 1857, and survived elegantly intact. Pastel Postcard Row mansions along Alamo Sq's eastern side pale in comparison with the colorful characters along the northwestern end of this hilltop park. The northern side features Barbary Coast baroque mansions at their most bombastic, bedecked with fish-scale shingles and gingerbread trim dripping from peaked roofs.

The Castro & Noe Valley

★Castro Theatre THEATER

(Map p78; 415-621-6120; www.castrotheatre.com; 429 Castro St; Tue-Sun; M Castro St) The city's grandest movie palace opened in 1922. The Spanish-Moorish exterior yields to mishmash styles inside, from Italianate to Oriental. Ask nicely and staff may let you take a peek, or come for the nightly cult or classic films (p98), or one of the many film festivals – check calendars online. At evening shows, arrive early to hear the organist play before the curtain rises.

Barbie-Doll Window PUBLIC ART

(Map p78; 4099 19th St; 24, M Castro) No first-time loop through the Castro would be complete without a peek at the Barbie-Doll Window – better called the Billy-Doll Window, a gay spin-off of Barbie, notable for its shockingly huge penis. Dolls are dressed – well, some of them – in outrageous costumes and arranged in miniature protest lines, complete with signs. One of them says it best: 'It's Castro, Bitch.'

Harvey Milk & Jane Warner Plazas SQUARE

(Map p78; cnr Market & Castro Sts; M Castro St) A huge rainbow flag flaps above Castro and Market Sts, officially Harvey Milk Plaza. Look closer and spot a plaque honoring the man whose legacy is gay civic pride and political clout. Across Castro, by the F-train terminus, is Jane Warner Plaza, where ragtag oddballs and kids too young for the bars congregate at public tables and chairs.

The Mission, Dogpatch & Potrero Hill

★Anglim Gilbert Gallery GALLERY

(415-528-7258; http://anglimgilbertgallery.com; 1275 Minnesota St, 2nd fl; 11am-6pm Tue-Sat; 48, T) FREE The Bay Area hits the big time here, with gallerist Ed Gilbert continuing Anglim's 30-year legacy of launching art movements from Beat assemblage to Bay Area conceptualists. Major gallery artists range from political provocateur Enrique Chagoya to sublime sculptor Deborah Butterfield, yet shows here maintain a hair-raising edge, such as an upraised fist pushed through gallery walls in David Huffman's *Panther*. Check the website for concurrent Anglim Gilbert shows at the gallery's downtown location at 14 Geary St.

★826 Valencia CULTURAL CENTER

(Map p78; 415-642-5905; www.826valencia.org; 826 Valencia St; noon-6pm; ; 14, 33, 49, B 16th St Mission, M J) Avast, ye scurvy scalawags! If ye be shipwrecked without yer eye patch or McSweeney's literary anthology, lay down ye doubloons and claim yer booty at this here nonprofit Pirate Store. Below decks, kids be writing tall tales for dark nights a'sea, and ye can study writing movies and science fiction and suchlike, if that be yer dastardly inclination. Arrrr!

★Dolores Park PARK

(Map p78; http://sfrecpark.org/destination/mission-dolores-park; Dolores St, btwn 18th & 20th Sts; 6am-10pm; ; 14, 33, 49, B 16th St Mission, M J) Semiprofessional tanning and taco picnics: welcome to San Francisco's sunny side. Dolores Park has something for everyone, from street ball and tennis to the Mayan-pyramid playground (sorry, kids: no blood sacrifices allowed). Political protests and other favorite local sports happen year-round, and there are free movie nights and mime troupe performances in summer. Climb to the upper southwestern corner for superb views of downtown, framed by palm trees.

★Balmy Alley PUBLIC ART
(Map p78; ☎415-285-2287; www.precitaeyes.org; btwn 24th & 25th Sts; 🚌10, 12, 14, 27, 48, Ⓑ24th St Mission) Inspired by Diego Rivera's 1930s San Francisco murals and provoked by US foreign policy in Central America, 1970s Mission *muralistas* (muralists) led by Mia Gonzalez set out to transform the political landscape, one mural-covered garage door at a time. Today, Balmy Alley murals span three decades, from an early memorial for El Salvador activist Archbishop Óscar Romero to a homage to Frida Kahlo, Georgia O'Keeffe and other trailblazing female modern artists.

★Creativity Explored GALLERY
(Map p78; ☎415-863-2108; www.creativityexplored.org; 3245 16th St; donations welcome; ⏰10am-3pm Mon-Wed & Fri, to 7pm Thu, noon-5pm Sat & Sun; 👪; 🚌14, 22, 33, 49, Ⓑ16th St Mission, ⓂJ) Brave new worlds are captured in celebrated artworks destined for museum retrospectives, international shows, and even Marc Jacobs handbags and CB2 pillowcases – all by local artists with developmental disabilities, who create at this nonprofit center. Intriguing themes range from monsters to Morse code, and openings are joyous celebrations with the artists, their families and rock-star fan base.

★Galería de la Raza GALLERY
(Map p78; ☎415-826-8009; www.galeriadelaraza.org; 2857 24th St; donations welcome; ⏰during exhibitions noon-6pm Wed-Sat; 👪; 🚌10, 14, 33, 48, 49, Ⓑ24th St Mission) Art never forgets its roots at this nonprofit that has showcased Latino art since 1970. Culture and community are constantly being redefined here, from contemporary Mexican photography and group shows exploring Latin gay culture to performances capturing community responses to Mission gentrification. Outside is the Digital Mural Project, where, in place of the usual cigarette advertisements, a billboard features slogans like 'Abolish borders!' in English, Arabic and Spanish.

Activities

Cycling & Skating

Basically Free Bike Rentals CYCLING
(Map p70; ☎415-741-1196; www.sportsbasement.com/annex; 1196 Columbus Ave; half-/full-day bike rentals adult from $24/32, child $15/20; ⏰9am-7pm Mon-Fri, 8am-7pm Sat & Sun; 👪; 🚌F, 30, 47, 🚋Powell-Mason, Powell-Hyde) This quality bike-rental shop cleverly gives you the choice of paying for your rental or taking the cost as credit for purchases (valid for 72 hours) at sporting-goods store **Sports Basement** (☎415-437-0100; www.sportsbasement.com; 610 Old Mason St; ⏰9am-9pm Mon-Fri, 8am-8pm Sat & Sun; 🚌30, 43, PresidiGo Shuttle), in the Presidio en route to the Golden Gate Bridge. (If you buy too much to carry, Sports Basement staff will mount panniers or mail your stuff home.)

Blazing Saddles CYCLING
(Map p70; ☎415-202-8888; www.blazingsaddles.com/san-francisco; 2715 Hyde St; bicycle rental per hour $8-15, per day $32-88, electric bikes per day $48-88; ⏰8am-8pm; 👪; 🚋Powell-Hyde) Blazing Saddles is tailored to visitors, with a main shop on Hyde St and six rental stands around Fisherman's Wharf, convenient for biking the Embarcadero or to the Golden Gate Bridge. It also rents electric bikes and offers a 24-hour return service – a big plus. Reserve online for a 20% discount; rental includes all extras (bungee cords, packs etc).

BAY BRIDGE

San Francisco's other landmark bridge was inspired by a madman. Joshua Norton lost his shirt and his mind in the Gold Rush before proclaiming himself 'Emperor of these United States and Protector of Mexico,' and ordering construction of a trans-bay bridge in 1872. Taxpayers took some convincing: the Bay Bridge was completed in 1936. But the eastern span collapsed in the 1989 Loma Prieta earthquake, taking 12 years and $6.4 billion to repair.

Emperor Norton's idea seemed not quite so bright anymore – until artist Leo Villareal installed 25,000 LED lights along the western span, mesmerizing commuters with a 1.8-mile-long light show that shimmers and pulses in patterns that never repeat. The show ran from dusk until 2am nightly from March 2013 through to March 2015 – but a crowdfunding campaign in collaboration with the State of California brought the installation back in January 2016, and now the lights are now set to twinkle indefinitely. For more, see www.thebaylights.org.

The Mission & The Castro

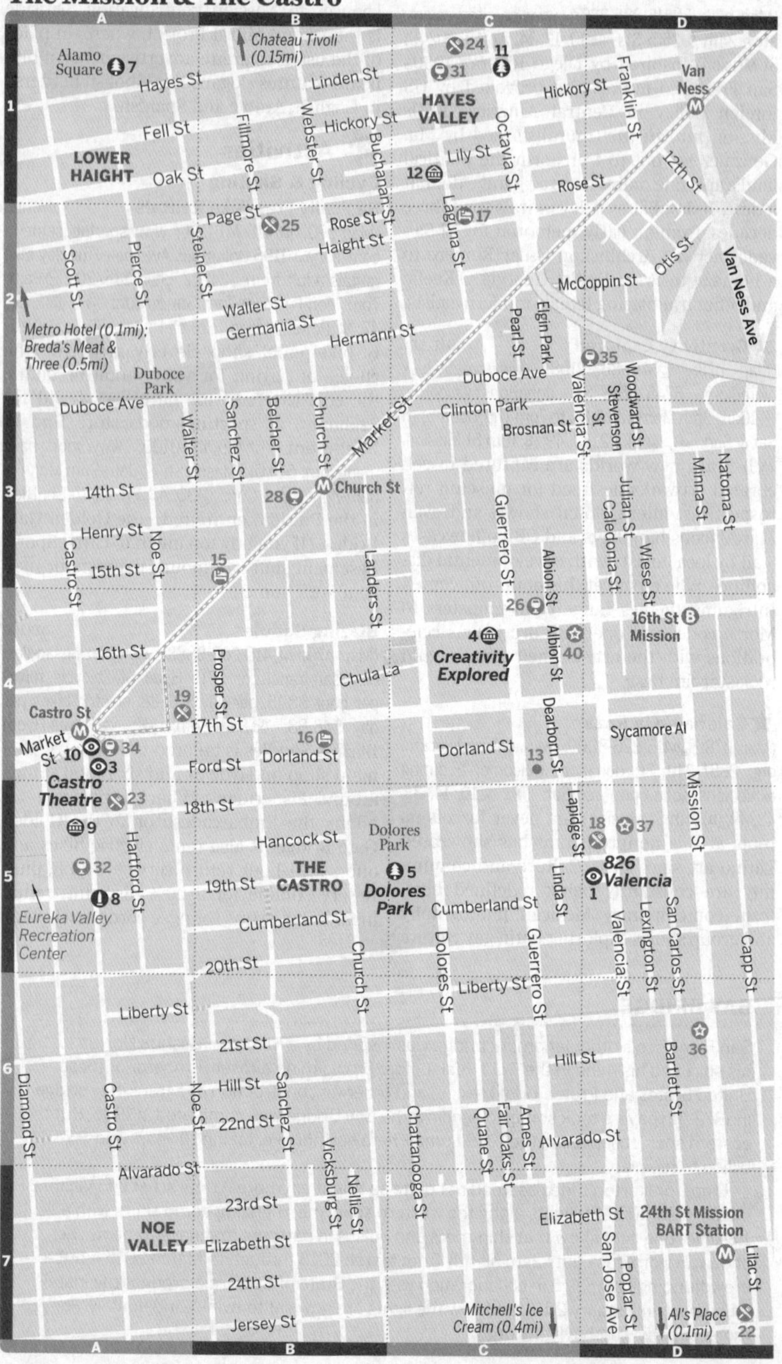

Chateau Tivoli (0.15mi)
Alamo Square
Hayes St
Linden St
HAYES VALLEY
Hickory St
Van Ness
Fell St
Fillmore St
Webster St
Hickory St
Buchanan St
Octavia St
Franklin St
LOWER HAIGHT
Oak St
Lily St
Rose St
12th St
Page St
Rose St
Haight St
Laguna St
Scott St
Pierce St
Steiner St
Otis St
Van Ness Ave
McCoppin St
Waller St
Germania St
Hermann St
Pearl St
Elgin Park
Metro Hotel (0.1mi); Breda's Meat & Three (0.5mi)
Duboce Park
Duboce Ave
Duboce Ave
Clinton Park
Brosnan St
Valencia St
Woodward St
Stevenson St
Walter St
Sanchez St
Belcher St
Church St
Market St
14th St
Church St
Julian St
Caledonia St
Minna St
Natoma St
Henry St
Noe St
Castro St
15th St
Landers St
Guerrero St
Albion St
Wiese St
16th St
16th St Mission
Albion St
Creativity Explored
Prosper St
Chula La
Castro St
17th St
Market St
Dearborn St
Sycamore Al
Dorland St
Dorland St
Ford St
Castro Theatre
18th St
Lapidge St
Mission St
Hancock St
Dolores Park
Hartford St
THE CASTRO
826 Valencia
19th St
Dolores Park
Cumberland St
Linda St
Eureka Valley Recreation Center
Cumberland St
Valencia St
Lexington St
San Carlos St
Capp St
20th St
Church St
Dolores St
Liberty St
Guerrero St
Liberty St
21st St
Hill St
Hill St
Bartlett St
Diamond St
Castro St
Noe St
Sanchez St
22nd St
Chattanooga St
Quane St
Fair Oaks St
Ames St
Alvarado St
Alvarado St
Vicksburg St
Nellie St
23rd St
Elizabeth St
24th St Mission BART Station
NOE VALLEY
Elizabeth St
San Jose Ave
Lilac St
24th St
Poplar St
Mitchell's Ice Cream (0.4mi)
Al's Place (0.1mi)
Jersey St

0 400 m
0 0.2 miles

E F

Mission St
9th St
Howard St
8th St
10th St
Folsom St
SOUTH OF MARKET (SOMA)
Kissling St
Juniper St
Harrison St
30
38 27
12th St
Norfolk St
11th St
29
13th St
Central Fwy
Erie St
14th St
Florida St
Bryant St
Shotwell St
Folsom St
15th St
Harrison St
Bottom of the Hill (0.6mi); Anglim Gilbert Gallery (2mi)
16th St
Treat Ave
17th St
39
Mariposa St
18th St
18th St
19th St
19th St
Mistral St
33
20th St
S Van Ness Ave
Shotwell St
Folsom St
Treat Ave
Harrison St
Alabama St
Florida St
Bryant St
21st St
THE MISSION
22nd St
23rd St
20
21
6 Galería de la Raza
24th St
14
2 Balmy Alley
Lucky St
25th St
Garfield Square

1 2 3 4 5 6 7

E F

The Mission & The Castro

Top Sights

1 826 Valencia D5
2 Balmy Alley F7
3 Castro Theatre A4
4 Creativity Explored C4
5 Dolores Park C5
6 Galería de la Raza F7

Sights

7 Alamo Square Park A1
8 Barbie-Doll Window A5
9 GLBT History Museum A5
10 Harvey Milk & Jane Warner Plazas A4
11 Patricia's Green C1
12 Zen Center C1

Activities, Courses & Tours

13 18 Reasons C4
14 Precita Eyes Mission Mural Tours F7

Sleeping

15 Beck's Motor Lodge B3
16 Parker Guest House B4
17 Parsonage C2

Eating

18 Craftsman & Wolves D5
Foreign Cinema .... (see 36)
19 Frances A4
20 Humphry Slocombe F7
21 La Palma Mexicatessen F7
22 La Taqueria D7
23 Poesia A5
24 Souvla C1
25 Three Twins Ice Cream B2

Drinking & Nightlife

26 %ABV C4
27 Bar Agricole E2
28 Blackbird B3
29 Eagle Tavern E2
30 Lone Star Saloon F2
31 Riddler C1
32 Swirl A5
33 Trick Dog F5
34 Twin Peaks Tavern A4
35 Zeitgeist D2

Entertainment

36 Alamo Drafthouse Cinema D6
Castro Theatre .... (see 3)
37 Chapel D5
38 Oasis E2
39 Oberlin Dance Collective E4
40 Roxie Cinema C4

The Richmond, The Haight & Golden Gate Park

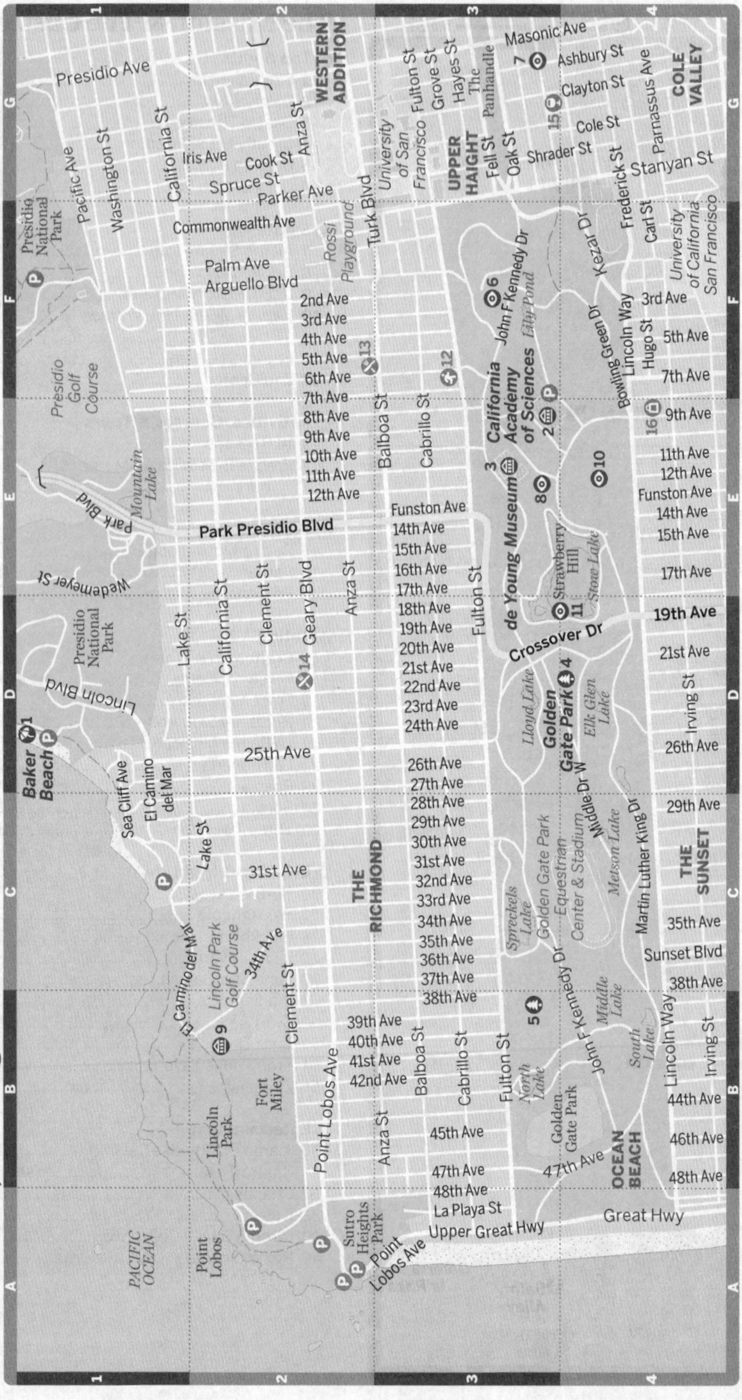

0 — 1 km
0 — 0.5 miles

A B C D E F G
1 2 3 4

PACIFIC OCEAN
Point Lobos
Lincoln Park
Fort Miley
Lincoln Park Golf Course
9
El Camino del Mar
34th Ave
Clement St
Point Lobos Ave
Sutro Heights Park
Point Lobos Ave
Upper Great Hwy
Great Hwy
Baker Beach
1
Sea Cliff Ave
El Camino del Mar
Lake St
Lincoln Blvd
Presidio National Park
Wedemeyer St
Park Blvd
Mountain Lake
Presidio Golf Course
Presidio National Park
Pacific Ave
Washington St
Presidio Ave
California St
Lake St
California St
Clement St
Geary Blvd
14
Park Presidio Blvd
31st Ave
25th Ave
Anza St
THE RICHMOND
Anza St
39th Ave
40th Ave
41st Ave
42nd Ave
Balboa St
Cabrillo St
Fulton St
45th Ave
47th Ave
48th Ave
La Playa St
38th Ave
37th Ave
36th Ave
35th Ave
34th Ave
33rd Ave
32nd Ave
31st Ave
30th Ave
29th Ave
28th Ave
27th Ave
26th Ave
24th Ave
23rd Ave
22nd Ave
21st Ave
20th Ave
19th Ave
18th Ave
17th Ave
16th Ave
15th Ave
14th Ave
Funston Ave
12th Ave
11th Ave
10th Ave
9th Ave
8th Ave
7th Ave
6th Ave
5th Ave
4th Ave
3rd Ave
2nd Ave
Arguello Blvd
Palm Ave
Commonwealth Ave
Parker Ave
Spruce St
Cook St
Iris Ave
Anza St
Rossi Playground
Turk Blvd
Balboa St
13
Cabrillo St
12
WESTERN ADDITION
University of San Francisco
Fulton St
Grove St
Hayes St
The Panhandle
UPPER HAIGHT
Fell St
Oak St
Masonic Ave
7
Shrader St
Cole St
Clayton St
Ashbury St
15
Fulton St
Spreckels Lake
North Lake
5
Golden Gate Park
Golden Gate Park Equestrian Center & Stadium
John F Kennedy Dr
47th Ave
Middle Lake
South Lake
OCEAN BEACH
Metson Lake
Middle Dr W
Lloyd Lake
Golden Gate Park
4
Elk Glen Lake
Crossover Dr
de Young Museum
3
Strawberry Hill
11
Stow Lake
8
10
California Academy of Sciences
2
6
John F Kennedy Dr
Lily Pond
Kezar Dr
Bowling Green Dr
Lincoln Way
Hugo St
16
Frederick St
Carl St
Stanyan St
Parnassus Ave
University of California San Francisco
COLE VALLEY
Martin Luther King Dr
Lincoln Way
Irving St
48th Ave
46th Ave
44th Ave
38th Ave
Sunset Blvd
35th Ave
THE SUNSET
29th Ave
26th Ave
Irving St
21st Ave
19th Ave
17th Ave
15th Ave
14th Ave
Funston Ave
12th Ave
11th Ave
9th Ave
7th Ave
5th Ave
3rd Ave

The Richmond, The Haight & Golden Gate Park

Top Sights
1 Baker Beach D1
2 California Academy of Sciences E3
3 de Young Museum E3
4 Golden Gate Park D4

Sights
5 Buffalo Paddock B3
6 Conservatory of Flowers F3
7 Haight & Ashbury G3
8 Japanese Tea Garden E3
9 Legion of Honor B2
10 San Francisco Botanical Garden E4
11 Stow Lake D4

Activities, Courses & Tours
12 Golden Gate Park Bike & Skate F3

Eating
13 Cinderella Russian Bakery F2
14 Dragon Beaux D2
Revenge Pies .... (see 16)

Drinking & Nightlife
15 Aub Zam Zam G3

Shopping
16 San Franpsycho E4

Golden Gate Park Bike & Skate CYCLING
(Map p80; ☎415-668-1117; www.goldengatepark bikeandskate.com; 3038 Fulton St; skates per hour $5-6, per day $20-24, bikes per hour $3-5, per day $15-25, tandem bikes per hour/day $15/75, discs $6/25; ⏱10am-6pm Mon-Fri, to 7pm Sat & Sun; 👪; 🚌5, 21, 31, 44) Besides bikes (for kids and adults) and skates (four-wheeled and inline), this rental shop just outside Golden Gate Park rents disc putters and drivers for the park's free Frisbee golf course. Bargain rates; helmets included with rentals. Call ahead to confirm it's open if the weather looks iffy.

Kayaking & Whale-Watching

★**Oceanic Society Expeditions** CRUISE
(Map p70; ☎415-256-9604; www.oceanicsociety.org; 3950 Scott St; whale-watching trips per person $128; ⏱office 9am-5pm Mon-Fri, to 2pm Sat; 🚌30) The Oceanic Society runs top-notch, naturalist-led, ocean-going weekend boat trips – sometimes to the Farallon Islands – during both whale-migration seasons. Cruises depart from the yacht harbor and last all day. Kids must be 10 years or older. Reservations required.

City Kayak KAYAKING
(Map p62; ☎415-294-1050, 888-966-0953; www.citykayak.com; Pier 40, South Beach Harbor; kayak rentals per hour $35-125, 3hr lesson & rental $49, tours $59-75; ⏱rentals noon-3pm, return by 5pm Thu-Mon; 🚌30, 45, Ⓜ N, T) You haven't seen San Francisco until you've seen it from the water. Newbies to kayaking can take lessons and paddle calm waters near the Bay Bridge; experienced paddlers can rent kayaks to brave currents near the Golden Gate (conditions permitting; get advice first). Sporty romantics: twilight tours past the Bay Bridge lights are ideal for proposals. Check website for details.

Spas

★**Kabuki Springs & Spa** SPA
(☎415-922-6000; www.kabukisprings.com; 1750 Geary Blvd; adult $25; ⏱10am-9:45pm, co-ed Tue, women only Wed, Fri & Sun, men only Mon, Thu & Sat; 🚌22, 38) This favorite urban retreat recreates communal, clothing-optional Japanese baths. Salt-scrub in the steam room, soak in the hot pool, then cold-plunge and reheat in the sauna. Rinse and repeat. Silence is mandatory, fostering a meditative mood – if you hear the gong, it means Shh-hh! Men and women alternate days, except on co-ed Tuesdays (bathing suits required Tuesdays).

The look befits the location – slightly dated Japanese modern, with vaulted lacquered-wood ceilings, tile mosaics and low lighting. Plan on two hours minimum, plus a 30- to 60-minute wait at peak times (add your name to the waiting list, then go next door to slurp noodles or shop; they'll text you when your key is ready). Communal bathing is discounted with massage appointments; book ahead and come on the gender-appropriate day.

Tours & Courses

★**Chinatown Alleyway Tours** WALKING
(Map p68; ☎415-984-1478; www.chinatownalleywaytours.org; Portsmouth Sq; adult/student $26/16; ⏱tours 11am Sat; 👪; 🚌1, 8, 10, 12, 30, 41, 45, 🚋California, Powell-Mason, Powell-Hyde) Teenage Chinatown residents guide you on two-hour tours through backstreets that have seen it all – Sun Yat-sen plotting China's revolution, forty-niners squandering fortunes on opium, services held in temple ruins after the 1906 earthquake. Your presence here helps the community remember its history and shape its future – Chinatown Alleyway

Tours is a nonprofit youth-led program of the Chinatown Community Development Center.

Chinatown Heritage Walking Tours WALKING
(Map p68; 415-986-1822; www.cccsf.us; Chinese Culture Center, Hilton Hotel, 3rd fl, 750 Kearny St; group tour adult $25-30, student $15-20, private tour (1-4 people) $60; tours 10am, noon & 2pm Tue-Sat; ; 1, 8, 10, 12, 30, 41, 45, California, Powell-Mason, Powell-Hyde) These local-led tours pack discoveries into a kid-friendly, school-accredited program. One-hour Public Art walks explore Chinatown's history through its murals – including new Wentworth Alley murals. Two-hour Democracy Walks reveal Chinatown's role in US civil rights and international human-rights movements. Proceeds support the nonprofit Chinese Culture Center; book online or by phone three days ahead.

★**Precita Eyes Mission Mural Tours** WALKING
(Map p78; 415-285-2287; www.precitaeyes.org; 2981 24th St; adult $15-20, child $3; ; 12, 14, 48, 49, B 24th St Mission) Muralists lead weekend walking tours covering 60 to 70 Mission murals within a six- to 10-block radius of mural-bedecked Balmy Alley (p77). Tours last 90 minutes to two hours and 15 minutes (for the more in-depth Classic Mural Walk). Proceeds fund mural upkeep at this community arts nonprofit.

★**Emperor Norton's Fantastic Time Machine** WALKING
(Map p62; 415-644-8513; www.emperornortontour.com; $20; 11am & 2:30pm Thu & Sat, 11am Sun; 30, 38, B Powell St, M Powell St, Powell-Mason, Powell-Hyde) Huzzah, San Francisco invented time-travel contraptions! They're called shoes, and you wear them to follow the self-appointed Emperor Norton (aka historian Joseph Amster) across 2 miles of the most dastardly, scheming, uplifting and urban-legendary terrain on Earth…or at least west of Berkeley. Sunday waterfront tours depart from the Ferry Building; all others depart from Union Sq's Dewey Monument. Cash only.

★**18 Reasons** COOKING
(Map p78; 415-568-2710; www.18reasons.org; 3674 18th St; classes & dining events $12-125; ; 22, 33, M J) Go gourmet at this Bi-Rite–affiliated community food nonprofit offering deliciously educational events: wine tastings, knife-skills and cheese-making workshops, and chef-led classes. Mingle with fellow foodies at family-friendly, $12 community suppers and multicourse winemaker dinners ($95 to $125). Check the website for bargain guest-chef pop-ups and low-cost classes with cookbook authors. Spots fill quickly for excellent hands-on cooking classes – book early.

Festivals & Events

Lunar New Year CULTURAL
(www.chineseparade.com; Feb) Chase the 200ft dragon, legions of lion dancers and frozen-smile runners-up for the Miss Chinatown title during Lunar New Year celebrations. Firecrackers and fierce troops of tiny-tot martial artists make this parade the highlight of San Francisco winters.

SF International Film Festival FILM
(www.sffs.org; Apr) The nation's oldest film festival is still looking stellar, featuring hundreds of films and directors, and plenty of star-studded premieres. Plan ahead for two weeks of screenings citywide, including showcases at the Castro Theatre (p98), Alamo Drafthouse (p98) and Roxie Cinema (p98).

SF Pride Celebration LGBT
(Jun) A day isn't enough to do SF proud: June begins with the San Francisco LGBTQ Film Festival and goes out in style over the last weekend with Saturday's **Dyke March** (www.thedykemarch.org) to the Castro's Pink Party and the joyous, million-strong **Pride Parade** (www.sfpride.org; last Sun Jun) on Sunday.

Bay to Breakers SPORTS
(www.baytobreakers.com; race registration from $65; 3rd Sun May) Run costumed or in not much at all from the Embarcadero to Ocean Beach; joggers dressed as salmon run upstream.

San Francisco LGBTQ Film Festival FILM
(www.frameline.org; tickets $10-35; Jun) Here, queer and ready for a premiere since 1976, the San Francisco LGBTQ Film Festival is the oldest, biggest lesbian/gay/bisexual/transgender/queer film fest anywhere. Binge-watch up to 300 films from 30 countries over two weeks. If you can afford a festival pass, get one: pass holders can show up at the last minute and avoid the ubiquitous lines.

AIDS Walk San Francisco SPORTS
(http://sf.aidswalk.net/; 3rd Sun Jul) Until AIDS takes a hike, you can: this 10km fundraiser

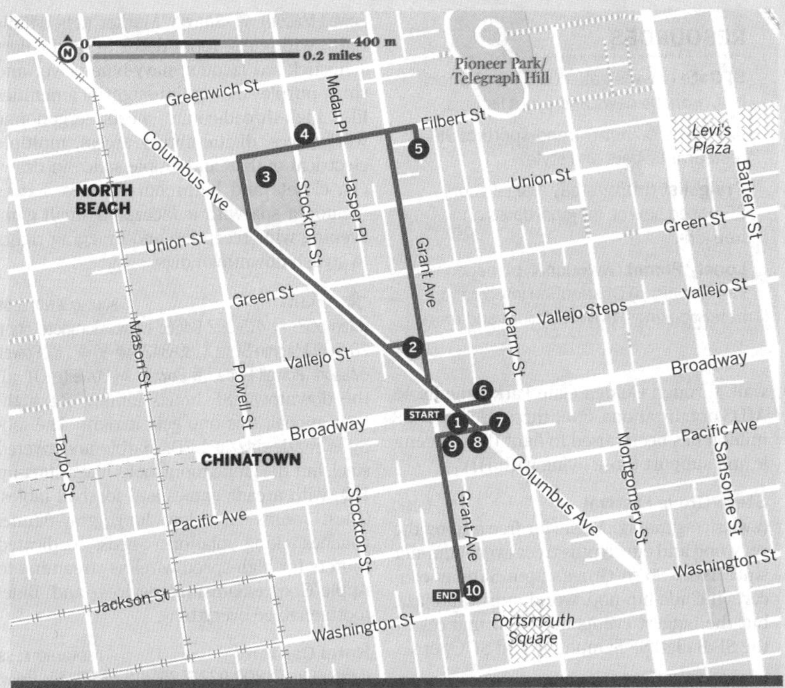

City Walk
North Beach Beat

START CITY LIGHTS BOOKS
END LI PO
LENGTH 1.5 MILES; TWO HOURS

At ❶ **City Lights Books** (p65), home of Beat poetry and free speech, pick up something to inspire your journey into literary North Beach – Ferlinghetti's *San Francisco Poems* and Ginsberg's *Howl* make excellent company.

Head to ❷ **Caffe Trieste** (p94) for opera on the jukebox and potent espresso in the back booth, where Francis Ford Coppola allegedly drafted *The Godfather* screenplay.

At ❸ **Washington Square**, you'll spot parrots in the treetops and octogenarians in tai chi tiger stances on the lawn – pure poetry in motion. At the corner, ❹ **Liguria Bakery** (p88) will give you something to write home about: focaccia hot from a 100-year-old oven.

Peaceful ❺ **Bob Kaufman Alley** was named for the legendary street-corner poet, who broke a 12-year vow of silence that lasted until the Vietnam War ended, whereupon he finally walked into a North Beach cafe and recited his poem 'All Those Ships That Never Sailed': 'Today I bring them back/Huge and transitory/And let them sail/Forever.'

Dylan jam sessions erupt in the bookshop, Allen Ginsberg spouts poetry nude in backroom documentary screenings, and onlookers grin beatifically at it all. Welcome to the ❻ **Beat Museum** (p65), where visitors are all (to quote Ginsberg's *Howl*) 'angelheaded hipsters burning for the ancient heavenly connection.'

The obligatory literary bar crawl begins at ❼ **Specs** (p94) amid merchant-marine memorabilia, tall tales and pitchers of Anchor Steam. *On the Road* author Jack Kerouac once blew off Henry Miller to go on a bender across the street at ❽ **Vesuvio** (p94), until bartenders ejected him into the street now named for him: ❾ **Jack Kerouac Alley**. Note the words of Chinese poet Li Po embedded in the alley: 'In the company of friends, there is never enough wine.'

Follow the lead of Kerouac and Ginsberg and end your night under the laughing Buddha at ❿ **Li Po** (p94) – there may not be enough wine, but there's plenty of beer.

RESOURCES

SFGate (www.sfgate.com) *San Francisco Chronicle* news and event listings.

7x7 (www.7x7.com) Trend-spotting SF restaurants, bars and style.

Craigslist (http://sfbay.craigslist.org) SF-based source for jobs, dates and free junk.

Lonely Planet (www.lonelyplanet.com/san-francisco) Destination information, hotel bookings, traveler forum and more.

walk through Golden Gate Park benefits 43 AIDS organizations. Over three decades, $88 million has been raised to fight the pandemic and support those living with HIV.

Stern Grove Festival MUSIC
(www.sterngrove.org) Music for free among the redwood and eucalyptus trees every summer since 1938. Stern Grove's 2pm Sunday concerts include hip-hop, world music and jazz, but the biggest events are performances by the SF Ballet, SF Symphony and SF Opera.

Hardly Strictly Bluegrass MUSIC
(www.hardlystrictlybluegrass.com; ⌚Oct) The West goes wild for free bluegrass at Golden Gate Park, with three days of concerts by 100-plus bands and seven stages of headliners.

Litquake LITERATURE
(www.litquake.org; ⌚2nd week Oct) Stranger-than-fiction literary events take place during SF's outlandish literary festival, with authors leading lunchtime story sessions and spilling trade secrets over drinks at the legendary Lit Crawl.

Día de los Muertos FESTIVAL
(Day of the Dead; www.dayofthedeadsf.org; ⌚2 Nov) Zombie brides and Aztec dancers in feather regalia party to wake the dead on Día de los Muertos, paying their respects to the dead at altars along the Mission processional route.

Sleeping

Downtown, Civic Center & SoMa

★Marker BOUTIQUE HOTEL $$
(Map p62; ☎844-736-2753, 415-292-0100; http://themarkersanfrancisco.com; 501 Geary St; r from $209; ; 38, Powell-Hyde, Powell-Mason) Snazzy Marker gets details right, with guest-room decor in bold colors – lipstick-red lacquer, navy-blue velvet and shiny purple silk – and thoughtful amenities like high-thread-count sheets, ergonomic workspaces, digital-library access, multiple electrical outlets and ample space in drawers, closets and bathroom vanities. Extras include a spa with a Jacuzzi, a small gym, evening wine reception and bragging rights to stylish downtown digs.

★Axiom BOUTIQUE HOTEL $$
(Map p62; ☎415-392-9466; www.axiomhotel.com; 28 Cyril Magnin St; d $189-342; ; Powell-Mason, Powell-Hyde, B Powell, M Powell) Of all the downtown SF hotels aiming for high-tech appeal, this one gets it right. The lobby is razzle-dazzle LED, marble and riveted steel, but the game room looks like a start-up HQ, with arcade games and foosball tables. Guest rooms have low-slung, gray-flannel couches, king platform beds, dedicated routers for high-speed wireless streaming to Apple/Google/Samsung devices, and Bluetooth-enabled everything.

Hotel Carlton DESIGN HOTEL $$
(Map p62; ☎800-922-7586, 415-673-0242; www.hotelcarltonsf.com; 1075 Sutter St; r $269-309; ; 2, 3, 19, 38, 47, 49) World travelers feel right at home at the Carlton amid Moroccan tea tables, Indian bedspreads, West African wax-print throw pillows and carbon-offsetting, LEED-certified initiatives (note the rooftop solar panels). It's not the most convenient location – 10 minutes from Union Sq – but offers good value for colorful, spotlessly clean rooms. The quietest rooms are those with the suffix -08 to -19.

★Hotel Vitale BOUTIQUE HOTEL $$$
(Map p62; ☎415-278-3700, 888-890-8688; www.hotelvitale.com; 8 Mission St; r $385-675; ; M Embarcadero, B Embarcadero) When your love interest or executive recruiter books you into the waterfront Vitale, you know it's serious. The office-tower exterior disguises a snazzy hotel with sleek, up-to-the-minute luxuries. Beds are dressed with silky-soft, 450-thread-count sheets, and there's an excellent on-site spa with two rooftop hot tubs. Rooms facing the bay offer spectacular Bay Bridge views, and Ferry Building dining awaits across the street.

★Palace Hotel HOTEL $$$
(Map p62; ☎415-512-1111; www.sfpalace.com; 2 New Montgomery St; r from $300; ;

M Montgomery, B Montgomery) The 1906 landmark Palace remains a monument to turn-of-the-century grandeur, with 100-year-old Austrian-crystal chandeliers and Maxfield Parrish paintings. Cushy (if staid) accommodations cater to expense-account travelers, but prices drop at weekends. Even if you're not staying here, visit the opulent Garden Court to sip tea beneath a translucent glass ceiling. There's also a spa; kids love the big pool.

North Beach & Chinatown

Pacific Tradewinds Hostel HOSTEL **$**
(Map p68; 415-433-7970; www.san-francisco-hostel.com; 680 Sacramento St; dm $35-45; front desk 8am-midnight; @; 1, California, B Montgomery) San Francisco's smartest all-dorm hostel has a blue-and-white nautical theme, a fully equipped kitchen (free peanut butter and jelly sandwiches all day!), spotless glass-brick showers, a laundry (free sock wash!), luggage storage and no lockout time. Bunks are bolted to the wall, so there's no bed-shaking when bunkmates roll. No elevator means hauling bags up three flights – but it's worth it. Great service; fun staff.

★**Hotel Bohème** BOUTIQUE HOTEL **$$**
(Map p68; 415-433-9111; www.hotelboheme.com; 444 Columbus Ave; r $235-295; @; 10, 12, 30, 41, 45) Eclectic, historic and unabashedly poetic, this quintessential North Beach boutique hotel has jazz-era color schemes, pagoda-print upholstery and photos from the Beat years on the walls. The vintage rooms are smallish, some face noisy Columbus Ave (quieter rooms are in back) and bathrooms are teensy, but novels beg to be written here – especially after bar crawls. No elevator or parking lot.

★**Orchard Garden Hotel** BOUTIQUE HOTEL **$$**
(Map p68; 415-399-9807, 888-717-2881; www.theorchardgardenhotel.com; 466 Bush St; r $207–390; P@; 2, 3, 30, 45, B Montgomery) San Francisco's original LEED-certified, all-green-practices hotel uses sustainably grown wood, chemical-free cleaning products and recycled fabrics in its soothingly quiet rooms. Don't think you'll be trading comfort for conscience: rooms have unexpectedly luxe touches, like high-end down pillows, Egyptian-cotton sheets and organic bath products. Don't miss the sunny rooftop terrace – a sweet spot at day's end.

Washington Square Inn B&B **$$**
(Map p68; 415-981-4220, 800-388-0220; www.wsisf.com; 1660 Stockton St; r $209-359; @; 30, 41, 45, Powell-Mason) On leafy, sun-dappled Washington Sq, this restored 1910 inn offers European style, complete with wine-and-cheese receptions and continental breakfasts in bed. The tasteful rooms are styled with a few choice antiques, including carved wooden armoires. The least-expensive rooms don't leave much room for North Beach shopping, but this is a stellar location for people-watching, dining and exploring. No elevator.

The Marina, Fisherman's Wharf & the Piers

★**HI San Francisco Fisherman's Wharf** HOSTEL **$**
(Map p70; 415-771-7277; www.sfhostels.com; Fort Mason, Bldg 240; dm $30-53, r $116-134; P@; 28, 30, 47, 49) Trading downtown convenience for a glorious park-like setting with million-dollar waterfront views, this hostel occupies a former army-hospital building, with bargain-priced private rooms and dorms (some co-ed) with four to 22 beds (avoid bunks one and two – they're by doorways). Huge kitchen. No curfew, but no heat during daytime: bring warm clothes. Limited free parking.

★**Inn at the Presidio** HOTEL **$$**
(Map p70; 415-800-7356; www.innatthepresidio.com; 42 Moraga Ave; r $295-380; P@; 43, PresidiGo Shuttle) Built in 1903 as bachelor quarters for army officers, this three-story, redbrick building in the Presidio was transformed in 2012 into a spiffy national-park lodge, styled with leather, linen and wood. Oversized rooms are plush, including feather beds with Egyptian-cotton sheets. Suites have gas fireplaces. Nature surrounds you, with hiking trailheads out back, but taxis downtown cost $25. Free parking.

Hotel Zephyr DESIGN HOTEL **$$**
(Map p70; 844-617-6555, 415-617-6565; www.hotelzephyrsf.com; 250 Beach St; r $250-400; P@; 8, 39, 47, Powell-Mason, M E, F) Completely revamped in 2015, this vintage-1960s hotel surrounds a vast courtyard with fire pits and lounge chairs, modern art from nautical junk, and games like table tennis in a tube – reminders you're here to play, not work. Rooms are fresh and spiffy, with

up-to-date amenities, including smart TVs that link with your devices. Best rooms face the water. Parking costs $57.

Hotel del Sol MOTEL $$

(Map p70; ☎877-433-5765, 415-921-5520; www.jdvhotels.com; 3100 Webster St; d $259-359; P ❄ @ 🛜 🏊 🐾; 🚌22, 28, 30, 43) 🌿 The spiffy, kid-friendly Marina District Hotel del Sol is a riot of color, with tropical-themed decor. This is a quiet, revamped 1950s motor lodge with a palm-lined central courtyard, and is one of the few San Francisco hotels with a heated outdoor pool. Family suites have trundle beds and board games. Free parking.

★**Hotel Drisco** BOUTIQUE HOTEL $$$

(Map p70; ☎800-634-7277, 415-346-2880; www.hoteldrisco.com; 2901 Pacific Ave; r $338-475; @ 🛜; 🚌3, 24) The only hotel in Pacific Heights, a stately 1903 apartment-hotel tucked between mansions, stands high on the ridgeline. It's notable for its architecture, attentive service and chic rooms, with their elegantly austere decor, but the high-on-a-hill location is convenient only to the Marina; anywhere else requires a bus or taxi. Still, for a real boutique hotel, it's tops.

★**Argonaut Hotel** BOUTIQUE HOTEL $$$

(Map p70; ☎800-790-1415, 415-563-0800; www.argonauthotel.com; 495 Jefferson St; r from $389; P ⊖ ❄ 🛜 🐾; 🚌19, 47, 49, 🚋Powell-Hyde) 🌿 Fisherman's Wharf's top hotel was built as a cannery in 1908 and has century-old wooden beams and exposed-brick walls. Rooms sport an over-the-top nautical theme, with port-hole-shaped mirrors and plush, deep-blue carpets. Though all rooms have the amenities of an upper-end hotel – ultra-comfy beds, iPod docks – some are tiny with limited sunlight. Parking is $59.

Nob Hill, Russian Hill & Fillmore

Golden Gate Hotel HOTEL $$

(Map p62; ☎800-835-1118, 415-392-3702; www.goldengatehotel.com; 775 Bush St; r $215, without bath $145; @ 🛜; 🚌2, 3, 🚋Powell-Hyde, Powell-Mason) Like an old-fashioned *pension*, the Golden Gate has kindly owners and simple rooms with mismatched furniture, in a 1913 Edwardian hotel safely up the hill from the Tenderloin. Rooms are small, clean and comfortable, and most have private bathrooms (some with antique claw-foot bathtubs). Enormous croissants, homemade cookies and a resident cat provide TLC after long days of sightseeing.

Petite Auberge BOUTIQUE HOTEL $$

(Map p62; ☎800-365-3004, 415-928-6000; www.petiteaubergesf.com; 863 Bush St; r $270-410; 🛜; 🚌2, 3, 27) Petite Auberge feels like a French country inn, with floral-print fabrics, sunny-yellow colors and in-room gas fireplaces – it's among central SF's most charming midprice stays. Alas, several rooms are dark (especially tiny 22) and face an alley where rubbish collectors rattle cans early (request a quiet room). Breakfast and afternoon wine are served fireside in the cozy salon.

Queen Anne Hotel B&B $$

(Map p70; ☎415-441-2828, 800-227-3970; www.queenanne.com; 1590 Sutter St; r $210-350; @ 🛜; 🚌2, 3) The Queen Anne occupies a lovely 1890 Victorian mansion, formerly a girls' boarding school, long on character and architectural charm. Though the chintz decor borders on twee, it matches the stately house. Rooms are comfy (some are tiny) and have a mishmash of antiques; some have romantic wood-burning fireplaces.

★**Fairmont San Francisco** HOTEL $$$

(Map p68; ☎800-441-1414, 415-772-5000; www.fairmont.com; 950 Mason St; r from $329; P ❄ @ 🛜 🐾; 🚋California) Heads of state choose the Fairmont, whose magnificent lobby is decked out with crystal chandeliers, marble floors and towering yellow-marble columns. Notwithstanding the opulent presidential suite, rooms have traditional business-class furnishings and lack the finer details of top-end luxury hotels. Still, few addresses compare. For old-fashioned character, reserve in the original 1906 building; for jaw-dropping views, go for the tower.

The Castro & Noe Valley

★**Parker Guest House** B&B $$

(Map p78; ☎888-520-7275, 415-621-3222; www.parkerguesthouse.com; 520 Church St; r $219-279, without bath $179-99; @ 🛜; 🚌33, Ⓜ J) The Castro's stateliest gay digs occupy two side-by-side Edwardian mansions. Details are elegant and formal, never froufrou. Rooms feel like they belong more to a swanky hotel than to a B&B, with super-comfortable beds and down duvets. Bathroom fixtures gleam. The garden is ideal for lovers' tryst – as is the steam room. No elevator.

Beck's Motor Lodge MOTEL $$
(Map p78; ☎415-621-8212; www.becksmotorlodge.com; 2222 Market St; r $189-279; P❄📶; Ⓜ Castro St) This three-story motor-lodge motel got a makeover in 2016 and its rooms look colorful, sharp and clean. Though technically not gay oriented, its placement at the center of the Castro makes it a de facto gay favorite. Bringing kids isn't recommended, especially during big gay events, when rooms book out months ahead.

The Haight & Hayes Valley

Metro Hotel HOTEL $
(☎415-861-5364; www.metrohotelsf.com; 319 Divisadero St; r $107; @📶; 🚌6, 24, 71) Trendy Divisadero St offers boutiques and restaurants galore, and the Metro Hotel has a prime position – some rooms overlook the garden patio of top-notch Ragazza Pizzeria. Rooms are cheap and clean, if bland – if possible, get the one with the SF mural. Some have two double beds; one room sleeps six ($150). The hotel's handy to the Haight and has 24-hour reception; no elevator.

★**Chateau Tivoli** B&B $$
(☎415-776-5462, 800-228-1647; www.chateautivoli.com; 1057 Steiner St; r $195-300, without bath $150-200; 📶; 🚌5, 22) The source of neighborhood gossip since 1892, this gilded and turreted mansion once hosted Isadora Duncan, Mark Twain and (rumor has it) the ghost of a Victorian opera diva – and now you can be the Chateau Tivoli's guest. Nine antique-filled rooms and suites set the scene for romance; most have claw-foot bathtubs, though two share a bathroom. No elevator; no TVs.

Parsonage B&B $$
(Map p78; ☎415-863-3699; www.theparsonage.com; 198 Haight St; r $220-280; @📶; 🚌6, 71, Ⓜ F) With rooms named for San Francisco's grand dames, this 23-room 1883 Italianate Victorian retains gorgeous original details, including rose-brass chandeliers and Carrara-marble fireplaces. Spacious, airy rooms offer antique beds with cushy SF-made McRoskey mattresses; some rooms have wood-burning fireplaces. Take breakfast in the formal dining room, and brandy and chocolates before bed. Charming owners. There's even an elevator.

Eating

Downtown, Civic Center & SoMa

★**farm:table** AMERICAN $
(Map p62; ☎415-292-7089; www.farmtablesf.com; 754 Post St; dishes $6-9; ⏰7:30am-2pm Tue-Fri, 8am-3pm Sat & Sun; 🌱; 🚌2, 3, 27, 38) 🍃 A ray of sunshine in the concrete heart of the city, this plucky little storefront showcases seasonal California organics in just-baked breakfasts and farmstead-fresh lunches. Check the menu on Twitter (@farmtable) for today's homemade cereals, savory tarts and game-changing toast – mmmm, ginger peach and mascarpone on whole-wheat sourdough. Tiny space, but immaculate kitchen and great coffee. Cash only.

Red Chilli NEPALI $
(Map p62; ☎415-931-3529; www.redchillisf.com; 522 Jones St; mains $8-11; ⏰11:30am-10:30pm; 🚌2, 3, 27, 38) Mt Everest is for amateurs – gourmet adventurers brave the Tenderloin's mean streets for Red Chilli's bargain butter chicken, Kathmandu rolls (naan wraps) and pickle-spice lamb *achar*. Can't decide? Get rice-plate combos, but don't skip the *momos* (Nepalese dumplings). This family-run storefront diner is welcoming, charmingly kitschy and convenient before/after Bourbon & Branch (p93) cocktails – otherwise, get delivery.

El Porteño Empanadas ARGENTINE $
(Map p62; ☎415-513-4529; www.elportenosf.com; 1 Ferry Bldg, cnr Market St & the Embarcadero; empanadas $4.50; ⏰9am-7pm Mon-Sat, 10am-5pm Sun; 🌱👪; Ⓑ Embarcadero, Ⓜ Embarcadero) 🍃 Pocket change left over from farmers-market shopping scores Argentine pocket pastries packed with local flavor at El Porteño. Vegetarian versions like *acelga* (organic Swiss chard and Gruyère) and *humita* (Brentwood sweet corn and caramelized onions) are just as mouthwatering as classic *jamon y queso* (prosciutto and fontina). Save room for *dulce de leche alfajores* (cookies with gooey caramel centers).

Sentinel SANDWICHES $
(Map p62; ☎415-284-9960; www.thesentinelsf.com; 37 New Montgomery St; sandwiches $9-12; ⏰7:30am-2:30pm Mon-Fri; 🚌12, 14, Ⓜ Montgomery, Ⓑ Montgomery) Rebel SF chef Dennis Leary revolutionizes the humble sandwich

with top-notch seasonal ingredients: lamb gyros get radical with pesto and eggplant, and corned beef crosses borders with Swiss cheese and housemade Russian dressing. Check the website for daily menus and call in your order, or expect a 10-minute wait – sandwiches are made to order. Enjoy in nearby **Yerba Buena Gardens** (cnr 3rd & Mission Sts).

★Cotogna ITALIAN **$$**
(Map p68; ☎415-775-8508; www.cotognasf.com; 490 Pacific Ave; mains $19-35; ⊙11:30am-10:30pm Mon-Thu, to 11pm Fri & Sat, 5-9:30pm Sun; ; 10, 12) Chef-owner Michael Tusk racks up James Beard Awards for a quintessentially Italian culinary balancing act: he strikes ideal proportions among a few pristine flavors in rustic pastas, wood-fired pizzas and salt-crusted branzino. Reserve, especially for bargain $55 four-course Sunday suppers with $35 wine pairings – or plan a walk-in late lunch/early dinner. Top-value Italian wine list (most bottles are $55).

★In Situ CALIFORNIAN, INTERNATIONAL **$$**
(Map p62; ☎415-941-6050; http://insitu.sfmoma.org; SFMOMA, 151 3rd St; mains $14-34; ⊙11am-3:30pm Mon & Tue, 11am-3:30pm & 5-9pm Thu-Sun; 5, 6, 7, 14, 19, 21, 31, 38, B Montgomery, M Montgomery) The landmark gallery of modern cuisine attached to SFMOMA also showcases avant-garde masterpieces – but these ones you'll lick clean. Chef Corey Lee collaborates with star chefs worldwide, scrupulously recreating their signature dishes with California-grown ingredients so that you can enjoy Harald Wohlfahrt's impeccable anise-marinated salmon, Hiroshi Sasaki's decadent chicken thighs and Albert Adrià's gravity-defying cocoa-bubble cake in one unforgettable sitting.

★Benu CALIFORNIAN, FUSION **$$$**
(Map p62; ☎415-685-4860; www.benusf.com; 22 Hawthorne St; tasting menu $285; ⊙6-9pm seatings Tue-Sat; 10, 12, 14, 30, 45) SF has pioneered Asian fusion cuisine for 150 years, but the pan-Pacific innovation chef-owner Corey Lee brings to the plate is gasp-inducing: foie-gras soup dumplings – what?! Dungeness crab and truffle custard pack such outsize flavor into Lee's faux-shark's fin soup, you'll swear Jaws is in there. Benu dinners are investments, but don't miss star sommelier Yoon Ha's ingenious pairings ($185).

★Kusakabe SUSHI, JAPANESE **$$$**
(Map p68; ☎415-757-0155; http://kusakabe-sf.com; 584 Washington St; prix fixe $95; ⊙5-10pm, last seating 8:30pm; 8, 10, 12, 41) Trust chef Mitsunori Kusakabe's *omakase* (tasting menu). Sit at the counter while the chef adds a herbal hint to fatty tuna with the *inside* of a *shiso* leaf. After you devour the menu – mostly with your hands, 'to release flavors' – you can special-order Hokkaido sea urchin, which the chef perfumes with the *outside* of the *shiso* leaf. Soy sauce isn't provided – or missed.

North Beach & Chinatown

★Golden Boy PIZZA **$**
(Map p68; ☎415-982-9738; www.goldenboypizza.com; 542 Green St; slices $2.75-3.75; ⊙11:30am-11:30pm Sun-Thu, to 2:30am Fri & Sat; 8, 30, 39, 41, 45, Powell-Mason) Looking for the ultimate post-bar-crawl or morning-after slice? Here you're golden. Since 1978, second-generation Sodini family *pizzaioli* (pizza makers) have perfected Genovese-style focaccia-crust pizza, achieving that mystical balance between chewy and crunchy with the ideal amount of olive oil. Go for toppings like clam and garlic or pesto, and bliss out with hot slices and draft beer at the tin-shed counter.

★Liguria Bakery BAKERY **$**
(Map p68; ☎415-421-3786; 1700 Stockton St; focaccia $4-6; ⊙8am-1pm Tue-Fri, from 7am Sat; ; 8, 30, 39, 41, 45, Powell-Mason) Bleary-eyed art students and Italian grandmothers are in line by 8am for cinnamon-raisin focaccia hot out of the 100-year-old oven, leaving 9am dawdlers a choice of tomato or classic rosemary and garlic, and 11am stragglers out of luck. Take yours in waxed paper or boxed for picnics – but don't kid yourself that you're going to save some for later. Cash only.

★Molinari DELI **$**
(Map p68; ☎415-421-2337; www.molinarisalame.com; 373 Columbus Ave; sandwiches $10-13.50; ⊙9am-6pm Mon-Fri, to 5:30pm Sat; 8, 10, 12, 30, 39, 41, 45, Powell-Mason) Observe quasi-religious North Beach noontime rituals: enter Molinari, and grab a number and a crusty roll. When your number's called, wisecracking staff pile your roll with heavenly fixings: milky buffalo mozzarella, tangy sun-dried tomatoes, translucent

THE FERRY BUILDING

San Francisco's monument to food, the Ferry Building (p61) still doubles as a trans-bay transit hub – but with dining options like these, you may never leave.

Ferry Plaza Farmers Market (Map p62; 415-291-3276; www.cuesa.org; street food $3-12; 10am-2pm Tue & Thu, from 8am Sat;) The pride and joy of SF foodies, the Ferry Building market showcases 50 to 100 prime purveyors of California-grown, organic produce, pasture-raised meats and gourmet prepared foods at accessible prices. On Saturdays, join top chefs early for prime browsing, and stay for eclectic bayside picnics of Namu Korean tacos, RoliRoti porchetta, Dirty Girl tomatoes, Nicasio cheese samples, and Frog Hollow fruit turnovers.

Slanted Door (Map p62; 415-861-8032; www.slanteddoor.com; mains $18-42; 11am-4:30pm & 5:30-10pm Mon-Sat, 11:30am-10pm Sun) Live the dream at this bayfront bistro, where California-fresh, Vietnamese-inspired dishes are served with sparkling waterfront views. Chinatown-raised chef-owner Charles Phan is a James Beard Award winner and a local hero for championing California-grown ingredients in signature dishes like garlicky grass-fed 'shaking beef' and Dungeness crab heaped atop cellophane noodles. Book weeks ahead, or settle for Out the Door takeout.

Hog Island Oyster Company (Map p62; 415-391-7117; www.hogislandoysters.com; 4 oysters $14; 11am-9pm) Slurp the bounty of the North Bay with East Bay views at this local, sustainable oyster bar. Get them raw, grilled with chipotle-bourbon butter, or Rockefeller (cooked with spinach, Pernod and cream). Not the cheapest oysters in town, but consistently the best – with excellent wines. Stop by Hog Island's farmers-market stall 8am to 2pm Saturday for $2 oysters.

Mijita (Map p62; 415-399-0814; www.mijitasf.com; dishes $4-10; 10am-7pm Mon-Thu, to 8pm Fri, 9am-8pm Sat, 9am-3pm Sun;) Jealous seagulls circle above your outdoor bayside table, eyeing your sustainable fish tacos and tangy jicama and grapefruit salad. James Beard Award–winning chef Traci Des Jardins honors her Mexican grandmother's cooking at this sunny taqueria – the Mexico City–style quesadilla is laced with *epazote* (Mayan herbs) and the *agua fresca* (fruit punch) is made from just-squeezed juice.

sheets of prosciutto di Parma, slabs of legendary house-cured salami, drizzles of olive oil and balsamic. Enjoy hot from the panini press at sidewalk tables.

★**Mister Jiu's** CHINESE $$

(Map p68; 415-857-9688; http://misterjius.com; 28 Waverly Pl; mains $14-45; 5:30-10:30pm Tue-Sat; 30, California) Ever since the gold rush, San Francisco has craved Chinese food, powerful cocktails and hyperlocal specialties – and Mister Jiu's satisfies on all counts. Build your own banquet of Chinese classics with California twists: chanterelle chow mein, Dungeness-crab rice noodles, quail and Mission-fig sticky rice. Cocktail pairings are equally inspired – try the jasmine-infused-gin Happiness ($13) with tea-smoked Sonoma-duck confit.

The Marina, Fisherman's Wharf & the Piers

★**Off the Grid** FOOD TRUCK $

(Map p70; www.offthegridsf.com; Fort Mason Center, 2 Marina Blvd; items $6-14; 5-10pm Fri Apr-Oct; ; 22, 28) Spring through fall, some 30 food trucks circle their wagons at SF's largest mobile-gourmet hootenannies on Friday night at Fort Mason Center, and 11am to 4pm Sunday for **Picnic at the Presidio** on the Main Post lawn. Arrive early for the best selection and to minimize waits. Cash only.

Lucca Delicatessen DELI $

(Map p70; 415-921-7873; www.luccadeli.com; 2120 Chestnut St; sandwiches $9-12; 9am-6pm; 28, 30, 43) Open since 1929, this classic Italian deli is an ideal spot to assemble picnics for Marina Green. Besides perfect prosciutto and salami, nutty cheeses and fruity

Chiantis, expect made-to-order sandwiches on fresh-baked Acme bread, including yummy meatball subs. There's hot homemade soup from 11am to 3pm.

★**Greens** VEGETARIAN, CALIFORNIAN $$
(Map p108; ☎415-771-6222; www.greensrestaurant.com; Fort Mason Center, 2 Marina Blvd, Bldg A; mains lunch $16-19, dinner $20-28; ⏲11:45am-2:30pm & 5:30-9pm; ; 22, 28, 30, 43, 47, 49) Career carnivores won't realize there's zero meat in the hearty black-bean chili, or in Greens' other flavor-packed vegetarian dishes, made using ingredients from a Zen farm in Marin. And, oh, what views! The Golden Gate rises just outside the window-lined dining room. The on-site cafe serves to-go lunches, but for sit-down meals, including Sunday brunch, reservations are essential.

★**Gary Danko** CALIFORNIAN $$$
(Map p70; ☎415-749-2060; www.garydanko.com; 800 North Point St; 3-/5-course menu $86/124; ⏲5:30-10pm; 19, 30, 47, Powell-Hyde) Gary Danko wins James Beard Awards for his impeccable Californian *haute cuisine*. Smoked-glass windows prevent passersby from tripping over their tongues at the exquisite presentations – roasted lobster with blood oranges, blushing duck breast with port-roasted grapes, lavish cheeses and trios of crèmes brûlées. Reservations a must.

Nob Hill, Russian Hill & Fillmore

★**Swan Oyster Depot** SEAFOOD $$
(Map p62; ☎415-673-1101; 1517 Polk St; dishes $10-25; ⏲10:30am-5:30pm Mon-Sat; 1, 19, 47, 49, California) Superior flavor without the superior attitude of typical seafood restaurants – Swan's downside is an inevitable wait for the few stools at its vintage lunch counter, but the upside of high turnover is incredibly fresh seafood.

Out the Door VIETNAMESE $$
(Map p70; ☎415-923 9575; www.outthedoors.com; 2232 Bush St; mains lunch $14-22, dinner $20-36; ⏲11am-2:30pm & 5:30-9:30pm Mon-Fri, 9am-2:30pm & 5:30-9:30pm Sat & Sun; 2, 3, 22) Offshoot of the famous Slanted Door (p89), this casual outpost jump-starts afternoon shopping with stellar Dungeness-crab noodles, five-spice chicken and rice plates and Vietnamese coffee. At dinner, rice plates

SAN FRANCISCO TREATS

Life is sweet in San Francisco, where chocolate bars were invented in the gold rush and velvet ropes keep ice-cream lines from getting ugly. Before you dismiss dessert, consider these temptations.

Tout Sweet (Map p62; ☎415-385-1679; www.toutsweetsf.com; Macy's, 3rd fl, cnr Geary & Stockton Sts; baked goods $2-8; ⏲11am-6pm Sun-Wed, to 8pm Thu-Sat; ; 2, 38, Powell-Mason, Powell-Hyde, B Powell) Mango with Thai chili or peanut butter and jelly? Choosing your favorite California-French macaron isn't easy at Tout Sweet, where *Top Chef Just Desserts* champion Yigit Pura keeps outdoing his own inventions – he's like the love child of Julia Child and Steve Jobs. Chef Pura's sweet retreat on Macy's 3rd floor offers unbeatable views overlooking Union Sq, excellent teas and free wi-fi.

Craftsman & Wolves (Map p78; ☎415-913-7713; http://craftsman-wolves.com; 746 Valencia St; pastries $3-8; ⏲7am-6pm Mon-Fri, from 8am Sat & Sun; 14, 22, 33, 49, B 16th St Mission, M J) Breakfast routines are made to be broken by the infamous Rebel Within: a sausage-spiked Asiago-cheese muffin with a silken soft-boiled egg baked inside. SF's surest pick-me-up is a Highwire macchiato with *matcha* (green tea) cookies; a Thai coconut-curry scone enjoyed with pea soup and rosé is lunch perfected. Exquisite hazelnut cube-cakes and vanilla-violet cheesecakes are ideal for celebrating unbirthdays and imaginary holidays.

Humphry Slocombe (Map p78; ☎415-550-6971; www.humphryslocombe.com; 2790 Harrison St; ice creams $4-6; ⏲1-11pm Mon-Fri, from noon Sat & Sun; ; 12, 14, 49, B 24th St Mission) Indie-rock organic ice cream may permanently spoil you for Top 40 flavors. Once 'Elvis: The Fat Years' (banana and peanut butter) and 'Hibiscus Beet Sorbet' have rocked your taste buds, cookie dough seems so basic – and ordinary sundaes can't compare to 'Secret Breakfast' (bourbon and cornflakes) and 'Blue Bottle Vietnamese Coffee' drizzled with hot fudge, California olive oil and sea salt.

and noodles are replaced with savory claypot meats and fish – an evening you won't soon forget. Make reservations.

★**La Folie** FRENCH **$$$**
(Map p70; ☎415-776-5577; www.lafolie.com; 2316 Polk St; 3-/4-/5-course menu $100/120/140; ⏱5:30-10pm Tue-Sat; 🚌19, 41, 45, 47) Casually sophisticated La Folie remains one of SF's top tables – even after 30 years. Its success lies in the French-born chef-owner's uncanny ability to balance formal and playful. He's a true artist, whose cooking references classical tradition but also nods to California sensibilities. The colorful flourishes on the plate are mirrored in the *très professionnel* staff. Book a week ahead.

★**Acquerello** CALIFORNIAN, ITALIAN **$$$**
(Map p62; ☎415-567-5432; www.acquerello.com; 1722 Sacramento St; 3-/4-/5-course menu $95/120/140; ⏱5:30-9:30pm Tue-Sat; 🚌1, 19, 47, 49, 🚋California) A converted chapel is a fitting location for a meal that'll turn Italian culinary purists into true believers in Cal-Italian cuisine. Chef Suzette Gresham's generous pastas and ingenious seasonal meat dishes include heavenly quail salad, devilish lobster *panzerotti* and venison loin chops. Suave *maître d'hôtel* Giancarlo Paterlini indulges every whim, even providing black-linen napkins if you're worried about lint.

★**Seven Hills** ITALIAN **$$$**
(Map p62; ☎415-775-1550; www.sevenhillssf.com; 1550 Hyde St; mains $19-31; ⏱5:30-9:30pm Sun-Thu, to 10pm Fri & Sat; 🚌10, 12, 🚋Powell-Hyde) Anthony Florian has studied with some of the great chefs of California and Italy, and he's an expert at taking several seasonal ingredients and making them shine. His short, market-driven menu features house-made pastas with elements such as rabbit and house-cured pancetta. The four mains showcase quality California meats. Tables are close in the elegant little storefront, but brilliant sound-canceling technology eliminates noise. Stellar service, too.

★**State Bird Provisions** CALIFORNIAN **$$$**
(☎415-795-1272; http://statebirdsf.com; 1529 Fillmore St; dishes $9-30; ⏱5:30-10pm Sun-Thu, to 11pm Fri & Sat; 🚌22, 38) Even before winning back-to-back James Beard Awards, State Bird attracted lines for 5:30pm seatings not seen since the Dead played neighboring Fillmore Auditorium. The draw is a thrilling play on dim sum, wildly inventive with seasonal-regional ingredients and esoteric flavors, like fennel pollen and garum. Plan to order multiple dishes. Book exactly 60 days ahead. The staff couldn't be lovelier.

The Haight & Hayes Valley

★**Souvla** GREEK **$**
(Map p78; ☎415-400-5458; www.souvlasf.com; 517 Hayes St; sandwiches & salads $11-14; ⏱11am-10pm; 🚌5, 21, 47, 49, Ⓜ Van Ness) Ancient Greek philosophers didn't think too hard about lunch, and neither should you at Souvla. Get in line and make no-fail choices: pita or salad, wine or not. Instead of go-to gyros, try roast lamb atop kale with yogurt dressing, or tangy chicken salad with pickled onion and *mizithra* cheese. Go early/late for skylit communal seating, or head to **Patricia's Green** (Map p78; http://proxysf.net; cnr Octavia Blvd & Fell St; 🚌5, 21) with takeout.

★**Brenda's Meat & Three** SOUTHERN US **$**
(☎415-926-8657; http://brendasmeatandthree.com; 919 Divisadero St; mains $8-15; ⏱8am-10pm Wed-Mon; 🚌5, 21, 24, 38) The name means one meaty main course plus three sides – though only superheroes finish ham steak with Creole red-eye gravy and exemplary grits, let alone cream biscuits and eggs. Chef Brenda Buenviaje's portions are defiantly Southern, which explains brunch lines of marathoners and partiers who forgot to eat last night. Arrive early, share sweet-potato pancakes, and pray for crawfish specials.

Three Twins Ice Cream ICE CREAM **$**
(Map p78; ☎415-487-8946; www.threetwinsicecream.com; 254 Fillmore St; cones $3-5.75; ⏱3-10pm Mon, 2-10pm Tue-Thu, 2-11pm Fri, 1-11pm Sat, 1-10pm Sun; 👪; 🚌6, 7, 22, Ⓜ N) 🌿 For local flavor, join the motley crowd of Lower Haighters lining up for extra-creamy organic ice cream in seasonal flavors. To guess who gets what, here's a cheat sheet: Wiggle bikers brake for dad's cardamom, foodie babies coo over lemon cookie, and stoned skaters feast on California clichés (two scoops, pistachios, olive oil, sea salt, caramel and whipped cream).

★**Jardinière** CALIFORNIAN **$$**
(Map p62; ☎415-861-5555; www.jardiniere.com; 300 Grove St; mains $20-36; ⏱5-9pm Sun-Thu, to 10:30pm Fri & Sat; 🚌5, 21, 47, 49, Ⓜ Van Ness) 🌿 *Iron Chef* winner, *Top Chef Masters* finalist and James Beard Award–winner Traci Des Jardins champions sustainable, salacious California cuisine. She has a way

with California's organic produce, sustainable meats, and seafood, slathering sturgeon with buttery chanterelles and lavishing root vegetables with truffles and honey from Jardinière's rooftop hives. Mondays bring $55 three-course dinners with wine pairings.

★Rich Table CALIFORNIAN **$$**
(Map p62; ☎415-355-9085; http://richtablesf.com; 199 Gough St; mains $17-36; ⊙5:30-10pm Sun-Thu, to 10:30pm Fri & Sat; 🚌5, 6, 7, 21, 47, 49, Ⓜ Van Ness) Impossible cravings begin at Rich Table, inventor of porcini doughnuts, miso-marrow-stuffed pasta and fried-chicken madeleines with caviar. Married co-chefs and owners Sarah and Evan Rich playfully riff on seasonal California fare, freestyling with whimsical off-menu amuse-bouches like trippy beet marshmallows or the Dirty Hippie: nutty hemp atop silky goat-buttermilk *pannacotta*, as offbeat and entrancing as Hippie Hill drum circles.

★Cala MEXICAN, CALIFORNIAN **$$$**
(Map p62; ☎415-660-7701; www.calarestaurant.com; 149 Fell St; ⊙5-10pm Mon-Wed, to 11pm Thu-Sat, 11am-3pm Sun, taco bar 11am-2pm Mon-Fri; 🚌6, 7, 21, 47, 49, Ⓜ Van Ness) Like discovering a long-lost twin, Cala's Mexico Norte cuisine is a revelation. San Francisco's Mexican-rancher roots are deeply honored here: silky bone-marrow salsa and fragrant heritage-corn tortillas grace a sweet potato slow-cooked in ashes. Brace yourself with mezcal margaritas for the ultimate California surf and turf: sea urchin with beef tongue. Original and unforgettable, even before Mayan-chocolate gelato with amaranth brittle.

The Castro & Noe Valley

★Poesia ITALIAN **$$**
(Map p78; ☎415-252-9325; http://poesiasf.com; 4072 18th St; mains $19-31; ⊙5-10:30pm Mon-Sat, to 10pm Sun; Ⓜ Castro St) An all-Italian staff flirts with diners at this unpretentious 2nd-floor bistro with a sunny yellow interior and comfy banquettes good for lingering long after a hearty dinner. Expect dishes you don't typically see at American-Italian restaurants, with standout housemade pastas and a stellar *branzino* (sea bass) cooked in parchment. Fun fact: this is where Oprah ate when she visited the Castro.

★Frances CALIFORNIAN **$$$**
(Map p78; ☎415-621-3870; www.frances-sf.com; 3870 17th St; mains $26-34; ⊙5-10pm Sun & Tue-Thu, to 10:30pm Fri & Sat; Ⓜ Castro St) Chef-owner Melissa Perello earned a Michelin star for fine dining, then ditched downtown to start this market-inspired neighborhood bistro. Daily menus showcase bright, seasonal flavors and luxurious textures: cloud-like sheep's-milk ricotta gnocchi with crunchy breadcrumbs and broccolini, grilled calamari with preserved Meyer lemon, and artisan wine served by the ounce, directly from Wine Country.

The Mission, Dogpatch & Potrero Hill

★La Taqueria MEXICAN **$**
(Map p78; ☎415-285-7117; 2889 Mission St; items $3-11; ⊙11am-9pm Mon-Sat, to 8pm Sun; 👪; 🚌12, 14, 48, 49, Ⓑ 24th St Mission) SF's definitive burrito has no saffron rice, spinach tortilla or mango salsa – just perfectly grilled meats, slow-cooked beans and tomatillo or mesquite salsa wrapped in a flour tortilla. They're purists at James Beard Award-winning La Taqueria. You'll pay extra to go without beans, because they add more meat – but spicy pickles and *crema* (sour cream) bring burrito bliss. Worth the wait, always.

★Mitchell's Ice Cream ICE CREAM **$**
(☎415-648-2300; www.mitchellsicecream.com; 688 San Jose Ave; ice cream $3.50-6; ⊙11am-11pm; 👪; 🚌14, 49, Ⓑ 24th St Mission, Ⓜ J) When you see happy dances break out on Mission sidewalks, you must be getting close to Mitchell's. One glance at the day's flavors induces gleeful gluttony: classic Kahlua mocha cream, exotic tropical *macapuno* (young coconut)… or *both*?! Avocado and *ube* (purple yam) are acquired tastes, but they've been local favorites for generations – Mitchell's has kept fans coming back for seconds since 1953.

★La Palma Mexicatessen MEXICAN **$**
(Map p78; ☎415-647-1500; www.lapalmasf.com; 2884 24th St; tamales, tacos & huarache $3-5; ⊙8am-6pm Mon-Sat, to 5pm Sun; 🌶👪; 🚌12, 14, 27, 48, Ⓑ 24th St Mission) Follow the applause: that's the sound of organic tortilla-making in progress at La Palma. You've found the Mission mother lode of handmade tamales, *pupusas* (tortilla pockets) with potato and *chicharones* (pork crackling), *carnitas* (slow-roasted pork), *cotija* (Oaxacan cheese) and La Palma's own tangy tomatillo sauce. Get takeout, or bring a small army to finish that massive meal at sunny sidewalk tables.

★ **Al's Place** CALIFORNIAN $$

(415-416-6136; www.alsplacesf.com; 1499 Valencia St; share plates $15-19; 5:30-10pm Wed-Sun; ; 12, 14, 49, J, 24th St Mission) The Golden State dazzles on Al's plates, featuring homegrown heirloom ingredients, pristine Pacific seafood, and grass-fed meat on the side. Painstaking preparation yields sun-drenched flavors and exquisite textures: crispy-skin cod with frothy preserved-lime dip, grilled peach melting into velvety foie gras. Dishes are half the size but thrice the flavor of mains elsewhere – get two or three, and you'll be California dreaming.

Foreign Cinema CALIFORNIAN $$$

(Map p78; 415-648-7600; www.foreigncinema.com; 2534 Mission St; mains $22-33; 5:30-10pm Sun-Wed, to 11pm Thu-Sat, brunch 11am-2:30pm Sat & Sun; 12, 14, 33, 48, 49, 24th St Mission) Chef Gayle Pirie's acclaimed California classics such as velvety Pacific *poke* (marinated tuna) and crisp sesame fried chicken are the star attractions here – but subtitled films by Luis Buñuel and François Truffaut screening in the courtyard are mighty handy when conversation lags with first dates or in-laws. Get the red-carpet treatment with valet parking ($15) and a well-stocked oyster bar.

Golden Gate Park & the Avenues

★ **Cinderella Russian Bakery** RUSSIAN $

(Map p80; 415-751-6723; www.cinderellabakery.com; 436 Balboa St; pastries $1.50-3.50, mains $7-13; 7am-7pm; ; 5, 21, 31, 33) Fog banks and cold wars are no match for the heartwarming powers of the Cinderella, serving treats like your *baba* used to make since 1953. Join SF's Russian community in Cinderella's new parklet near Golden Gate Park for scrumptious, just-baked egg-and-green-onion piroshki, hearty borscht and decadent dumplings – all at neighborly prices.

Revenge Pies DESSERTS $

(Map p80; www.revengepies.com; 1248 9th Ave; pies $5-8, picecreams $3-6; 9am-9pm; ; 6, 7, 43, 44, N) Living well is only the second-best revenge – a face full of pecan Revenge Pie is far more satisfying. Here's the compensation for every skimpy à la mode serving you've endured: picecream (homemade frozen custard with flakes of buttery pie crust). The chocolate-almond Revenge Pie is a crowd-pleaser – but the key-lime picecream could make, break and remake friendships. Inside San Franpsycho.

★ **Dragon Beaux** DIM SUM $

(Map p80; 415-333-8899; www.dragonbeaux.com; 5700 Geary Blvd; dumplings $4-9; 11:30am-2:30pm & 5:30-10pm Mon-Thu, to 10:30pm Fri, 10am-3pm & 5:30-10pm Sat & Sun; ; 2, 38) Hong Kong meets Vegas at SF's most glamorous, decadent Cantonese restaurant. Say yes to cartloads of succulent roast meats – hello, duck and pork belly – and creative dumplings, especially XO dumplings with plump, brandy-laced shrimp in spinach wrappers. Expect premium teas, sharp service and impeccable Cantonese standards, including Chinese doughnuts, *har gow* (shrimp dumplings) and Chinese broccoli in oyster sauce.

Drinking & Nightlife

No matter what you're having, SF bars, cafes and clubs are here to oblige. But why stick to your usual, when there are California wines, Bay spirits, microbrews and local roasts to try? Adventurous drinking is abetted by local bartenders, who've been making good on gold-rush-saloon history. SF baristas take their cappuccino-foam drawings seriously and, around here, DJs invent their own software.

Downtown, Civic Center & SoMa

★ **Pagan Idol** LOUNGE

(Map p68; 415-985-6375; www.paganidol.com; 375 Bush St; 4pm-1am Mon-Fri, 6pm-1:30am Sat; Montgomery, F, J, K, L, M) Volcanoes erupt inside Pagan Idol every half hour, or until there's a virgin sacrifice...what, no takers? Then order your island cocktail and brace for impact – these tiki drinks are no joke. Flirt with disaster over a Hemingway is Dead: rum, bitters and grapefruit, served in a skull. Book online to nab a hut for groups of four to six.

★ **Bourbon & Branch** BAR

(Map p62; 415-346-1735; www.bourbonandbranch.com; 501 Jones St; 6pm-2am; 27, 38) 'Don't even think of asking for a cosmo' read the House Rules at this Prohibition-era speakeasy, recognizable by its deliciously misleading Anti-Saloon League sign. For award-winning cocktails in the liquored-up library, whisper the password ('books') to be ushered through the bookcase secret passageway. Reservations required for front-room booths and Wilson & Wilson Detective Agency, the noir-themed speakeasy-within-a-speakeasy (password supplied with reservations).

★Bar Agricole BAR

(Map p78; ☎415-355-9400; www.baragricole.com; 355 11th St; ⏰5-11pm Mon-Thu, 5pm-12am Fri & Sat, 10am-2pm & 6-9pm Sun; 🚌9, 12, 27, 47) 🌿 Drink your way to a history degree with well-researched cocktails: Whiz Bang with house bitters, whiskey, vermouth and absinthe scores high, but El Presidente with white rum, farmhouse curaçao and California-pomegranate grenadine takes top honors. This overachiever wins James Beard Award nods for spirits and eco-savvy design, plus popular acclaim for $1 oysters and $5 aperitifs during happy hour (5pm to 6pm, Monday to Sunday).

North Beach & Chinatown

★Comstock Saloon BAR

(Map p68; ☎415-617-0071; www.comstocksaloon.com; 155 Columbus Ave; ⏰4pm-midnight Sun-Mon, to 2am Tue-Thu & Sat, noon-2am Fri; 🚌8, 10, 12, 30, 45, 🚋Powell-Mason) Relieving yourself in the marble trough below the bar is no longer advisable – Emperor Norton is watching from above – but otherwise this 1907 Victorian saloon brings back the Barbary Coast's glory days with authentic pisco punch and martini-precursor Martinez (gin, vermouth, bitters, maraschino liqueur). Reserve booths or back-parlor seating to hear on nights when ragtime-jazz bands play.

★Li Po BAR

(Map p68; ☎415-982-0072; www.lipolounge.com; 916 Grant Ave; ⏰2pm-2am; 🚌8, 30, 45, 🚋Powell-Mason, Powell-Hyde) Beat a hasty retreat to red-vinyl booths where Allen Ginsberg and Jack Kerouac debated the meaning of life under a golden Buddha. Enter the 1937 faux-grotto doorway and dodge red lanterns to place your order: Tsingtao beer or a sweet, sneaky-strong Chinese mai tai made with *baijiu* (rice liquor). Brusque bartenders, basement bathrooms, cash only – a world-class dive bar.

★Specs BAR

(Specs Twelve Adler Museum Cafe; Map p68; ☎415-421-4112; 12 William Saroyan Pl; ⏰5pm-2am; 🚌8, 10, 12, 30, 41, 45, 🚋Powell-Mason) The walls here are plastered with merchant-marine memorabilia, and you'll be plastered too if you try to keep up with the salty characters holding court in back. Surrounded by seafaring mementos – including walrus genitalia over the bar – your order seems obvious: pitcher of Anchor Steam, coming right up. Cash only.

★Caffe Trieste CAFE

(Map p68; ☎415-392-6739; www.caffetrieste.com; 601 Vallejo St; ⏰6:30am-10pm Sun-Thu, to 11pm Fri & Sat; 📶; 🚌8, 10, 12, 30, 41, 45) Poetry on bathroom walls, opera on the jukebox, live accordion jams and sightings of Beat poet-laureate Lawrence Ferlinghetti: this is North Beach at its best, since the 1950s. Linger over legendary espresso and scribble your screenplay under the Sardinian fishing mural just as young Francis Ford Coppola did. Perhaps you've heard of the movie: *The Godfather*. Cash only.

★Vesuvio BAR

(Map p68; ☎415-362-3370; www.vesuvio.com; 255 Columbus Ave; ⏰8am-2am; 🚌8, 10, 12, 30, 41, 45, 🚋Powell-Mason) Guy walks into a bar, roars and leaves. Without missing a beat, the bartender says to the next customer, 'Welcome to Vesuvio, honey – what can I get you?' Jack Kerouac blew off Henry Miller to go on a bender here and, after you've joined neighborhood characters on the stained-glass mezzanine for microbrews or Kerouacs (rum, tequila and OJ), you'll see why.

The Marina, Fisherman's Wharf & the Piers

★Interval Bar & Cafe BAR

(Map p70; www.theinterval.org; 2 Marina Blvd, Fort Mason Center, Bldg A; ⏰10am-midnight; 🚌10, 22, 28, 30, 47, 49) Designed to stimulate discussion of philosophy and art, the Interval is a favorite spot in the Marina for cocktails and conversation. It's inside the Long Now Foundation, with floor-to-ceiling bookshelves, which contain the canon of Western lit, rising above a glorious 10,000-year clock – a fitting backdrop for a daiquiri, gimlet or aged Tom Collins, or single-origin coffee, tea and snacks.

★Buena Vista Cafe BAR

(Map p70; ☎415-474-5044; www.thebuenavista.com; 2765 Hyde St; ⏰9am-2am Mon-Fri, 8am-2am Sat & Sun; 📶; 🚌19, 47, 🚋Powell-Hyde) Warm your cockles with a prim little goblet of bitter-creamy Irish coffee, introduced to America at this destination bar that once served sailors and cannery workers. That old Victorian floor manages to hold up carousers and families alike, served community-style

SOMA GAY BARS

Sailors have cruised Polk St and Tenderloin gay/trans joints since the 1940s, Castro bars boomed in the 1970s and women into women have been hitting Mission dives since the '60s – but SoMa warehouses have been the biggest weekend gay scene for decades now. From leather bars and drag cabarets to full-time LGBTQ clubs, SoMa has it all. True, internet cruising has thinned the herd, many women still prefer the Mission and some nights are slow starters – but the following fixtures on the gay drinking scene pack at weekends.

Eagle Tavern (Map p78; www.sf-eagle.com; 398 12th St; $5-10; 2pm-2am Mon-Fri, from noon Sat & Sun; 9, 12, 27, 47) Legendary leather bar with Sunday beer busts.

Oasis (Map p78; 415-795-3180; www.sfoasis.com; 298 11th St; tickets $15-35; 9, 12, 14, 47, M Van Ness) SF's dedicated drag cabaret mounts outrageous shows, sometimes literally.

Lone Star Saloon (Map p78; 415-863-9999; http://lonestarsf.com; 1354 Harrison St; 4pm-2am Mon-Thu, from 2pm Fri, from noon Sat & Sun; 9, 12, 27, 47) The original bear bar makes manly men warm and fuzzy at happy hour.

Stud (Map p62; www.studsf.com; 399 9th St; $5-8; noon-2am Tue, 5pm-3am Thu-Sat, 5pm-midnight Sun; 12, 19, 27, 47) The freaks come out at night for surreal, only-in-SF theme events.

Powerhouse (Map p62; 415-522-8689; www.powerhouse-sf.com; 1347 Folsom St; free-$10; 4pm-2am; 9, 12, 27, 47) Major men-only back-patio action.

Hole in the Wall (Map p62; 415-431-4695; www.holeinthewallsaloon.com; 1369 Folsom St; 2pm-2am Mon-Fri, noon-2am Sat & Sun; 9, 12, 47) Spiritual home to gay bikers and loudmouth punks.

Club OMG (Map p62; 415-896-6473; www.clubomgsf.com; 43 6th St; free-$10; 5pm-2am Tue-Fri & Sun, 7pm-2am Sat; M Powell, B Powell) Dance in your skivvies on Skid Row.

at round tables overlooking the cable-car turnaround at Victoria Park.

Nob Hill, Russian Hill & Fillmore

★Tonga Room LOUNGE

(Map p68; reservations 415-772-5278; www.tongaroom.com; Fairmont San Francisco, 950 Mason St; cover $5-7; 5-11:30pm Sun, Wed & Thu, to 12:30am Fri & Sat; 1, California, Powell-Mason, Powell-Hyde) Tonight's San Francisco weather: 100% chance of tropical rainstorms every 20 minutes, but only on the top-40 band playing on the island in the middle of the indoor pool – you're safe in your grass hut. For a more powerful hurricane, order one in a plastic coconut. Who said tiki bars were dead? Come before 8pm to beat the cover charge.

Big 4 BAR

(Map p62; www.big4restaurant.com; 1075 California St; 11:30am-midnight; ; 1, California) A classic for swank cocktails, the Big 4 is named for the railroad barons who once dominated Nob Hill society, and its decor pays tribute with opulence – oak-paneled walls, studded green leather and a big mahogany bar where you can order great martinis. Service isn't fab, but the room's lovely. Live piano on weekend evenings.

The Haight & Hayes Valley

★Blue Bottle Coffee Kiosk CAFE

(Map p62; www.bluebottlecoffee.net; 315 Linden St; 7am-6pm Mon-Sat, from 8am Sun; ; 5, 21, 47, 49, M Van Ness) Don't mock SF's coffee geekery until you've tried the elixir emerging from this back-alley garage-door kiosk. The Bay Area's Blue Bottle built its reputation with microroasted organic coffee – especially Blue Bottle–invented, off-the-menu Gibraltar, the barista-favorite drink with foam and espresso poured together into the eponymous short glass. Expect a (short) wait and seats outside on creatively repurposed traffic curbs.

★Riddler WINE BAR

(Map p78; www.theriddlersf.com; 528 Laguna St; 4-10pm Tue-Thu & Sun, to 11pm Fri & Sat; 5, 6, 7, 21) Riddle me this: how can you ever thank the women in your life? As the Riddler's all-women sommelier-chef-investor team points out, champagne makes a fine start. Bubbles begin at $12 and include Veuve

Clicquot, the brand named after the woman who invented riddling, the process that gives champagne its unclouded sparkle.

★Aub Zam Zam BAR
(Map p80; ☎415-861-2545; 1633 Haight St; ⏰3pm-2am Mon-Fri, 1pm-2am Sat & Sun; 🚌6, 7, 22, 33, 43, Ⓜ N) Persian arches, *One Thousand and One Nights* murals, 1930s jazz on the jukebox and top-shelf cocktails at low-shelf prices have brought Bohemian bliss to Haight St since 1941. Legendary founder Bruno used to throw people out for ordering a vodka martini, but he was a softie in the end, bequeathing his beloved bar to regulars who had become friends. Cash only.

The Castro & Noe Valley

Swirl WINE BAR
(Map p78; ☎415-864-2262; www.swirloncastro.com; 572 Castro St; ⏰2-8pm Mon-Thu, 1-9pm Fri, noon-9pm Sat, to 8pm Sun; 🚌33, 🚋F, Ⓜ K, L, M) Other Castro bars are niche driven, but this wine shop–bar has universal appeal: reliably delicious wine at fair prices in friendly company. Come as you are – pinstripes or leather, gay, straight or whatever – to toast freedom with sublime bubbly, or find liquid courage for sing-alongs at the Castro Theatre in flights of bold reds.

Blackbird GAY
(Map p78; ☎415-503-0630; www.blackbirdbar.com; 2124 Market St; ⏰3pm-2am Mon-Fri, from 2pm Sat & Sun; Ⓜ Church St) The Castro's first-choice lounge-bar draws an unpretentious mix of guys in tight T-shirts and their gal pals for seasonally changing cocktails made with bitters and tinctures, good wine and craft beer by the glass, billiards and – everyone's favorite bar amenity – the photo booth. Ideal on a Castro pub crawl, but crowded – and earsplittingly loud – at weekends.

Twin Peaks Tavern GAY
(Map p78; ☎415-864-9470; www.twinpeakstavern.com; 401 Castro St; ⏰noon-2am Mon-Fri, from 8am Sat & Sun; Ⓜ Castro St) Don't call it the glass coffin. Show some respect: Twin Peaks was the world's first gay bar with windows open to the street. The jovial crowd skews (way) over 40, but they're not chicken hawks (or they wouldn't hang here) and they love it when happy kids show up to join the party.

The Mission, Dogpatch & Potrero Hill

★%ABV COCKTAIL BAR
(Map p78; ☎415-400-4748; www.abvsf.com; 3174 16th St; ⏰2pm-2am; 🚌14, 22, Ⓑ 16th St Mission, Ⓜ J) As kindred spirits will deduce from the name (the abbreviation for 'percent alcohol by volume'), this bar is backed by cocktail crafters who know their Rittenhouse rye from their Japanese malt whisky. Top-notch hooch is served promptly and without pretension, including excellent Cali wine and beer on tap and original historically inspired cocktails like the Sutro Swizzle (Armagnac, grapefruit shrub, maraschino liqueur).

★Trick Dog BAR
(Map p78; ☎415-471-2999; www.trickdogbar.com; 3010 20th St; ⏰3pm-2am; 🚌12, 14, 49) Drink adventurously with ingenious cocktails inspired by local obsessions: San Francisco muralists, Chinese diners or conspiracy theories. Every six months, Trick Dog adopts a new theme and the entire menu changes – proof that you can teach an old dog new tricks, and improve on classics like the Manhattan. Arrive early for bar stools or hit the mood-lit loft for high-concept bar bites.

★Zeitgeist BAR
(Map p78; ☎415-255-7505; www.zeitgeistsf.com; 199 Valencia St; ⏰9am-2am; 🚌14, 22, 49, Ⓑ 16th St Mission) You've got two seconds flat to order from tough-gal barkeeps used to putting macho bikers in their place – but with 48 beers on draft, you're spoiled for choice. Epic afternoons unfold in the graveled beer garden, with folks hanging out and smoking at long picnic tables. SF's longest happy hour lasts 9am to 8pm weekdays. Cash only; no photos (read: no evidence).

☆ Entertainment

Live Music

★SFJAZZ Center JAZZ
(Map p62; ☎866-920-5299; www.sfjazz.org; 201 Franklin St; tickets $25-120; 👪; 🚌5, 6, 7, 21, 47, 49, Ⓜ Van Ness) 🌿 Jazz legends and singular talents from Argentina to Yemen are showcased at North America's newest, largest jazz center. Hear fresh takes on classic jazz albums and poets riffing with jazz combos in the downstairs Joe Henderson Lab, and witness extraordinary main-stage collaborations ranging from Afro-Cuban All Stars

to roots legends Emmylou Harris, Rosanne Cash and Lucinda Williams.

★**Chapel** LIVE MUSIC
(Map p78; ☎415-551-5157; www.thechapelsf.com; 777 Valencia St; cover $15-40; ⊙bar 7pm-2am; 🚌14, 33, Ⓜ J, Ⓑ16th St Mission) Musical prayers are answered in a 1914 California arts-and-crafts landmark with heavenly acoustics. The 40ft roof is regularly raised by shows by New Orleans brass bands, folk-YEAH! Americana groups, legendary rockers like Peter Murphy and hip-hop icons such as Prince Paul. Many shows are all ages, except when comedians like W Kamau Bell test edgy material.

★**Bottom of the Hill** LIVE MUSIC
(☎415-621-4455; www.bottomofthehill.com; 1233 17th St; $5-20; ⊙shows generally 9pm Tue-Sat; 🚌10, 19, 22) The bottom of Potrero Hill tops the list for rocking out with punk legends the Avengers, Pansy Division and Nerf Herder and newcomers worth checking out for their names alone (Summer Salt, the Regrettes, Sorority Noise). The smokers' patio is covered in handbills and ruled by a cat that prefers music to people – totally punk rock. Anchor Steam on tap; cash-only bar.

★**Great American Music Hall** LIVE MUSIC
(Map p62; ☎415-885-0750; www.gamh.com; 859 O'Farrell St; shows $20-45; ⊙box office 10:30am-6pm Mon-Fri & show nights; 🚸; 🚌19, 38, 47, 49) Everyone busts out their best sets at this opulent 1907 bordello turned all-ages venue – indie rockers like the Band Perry throw down, international legends such as Salif Keita grace the stage, and John Waters hosts Christmas extravaganzas. Pay $25 extra for dinner with prime balcony seating to watch shows comfortably, or rock out with the standing-room scrum downstairs.

Fillmore Auditorium LIVE MUSIC
(☎415-346-6000; http://thefillmore.com; 1805 Geary Blvd; tickets from $20; ⊙box office 10am-3pm Sun, plus 30min before doors open to 10pm show nights; 🚌22, 38) Jimi Hendrix, Janis Joplin, the Doors – they all played the Fillmore. Now you might catch the Indigo Girls, Willie Nelson or Tracy Chapman in the historic 1250-capacity, standing-room-only theater (if you're polite and lead with the hip, you might squeeze up to the stage). Don't miss the priceless collection of psychedelic posters in the upstairs gallery.

Classical Music & Dance

★**San Francisco Symphony** CLASSICAL MUSIC
(Map p62; ☎box office 415-864-6000, rush-ticket hotline 415-503-5577; www.sfsymphony.org; Grove St, btwn Franklin St & Van Ness Ave; tickets $20-150; 🚌21, 45, 47, Ⓜ Van Ness, Ⓑ Civic Center) From the moment conductor Michael Tilson Thomas bounces up on his toes and raises his baton, the audience is on the edge of their seats for another thunderous performance by the Grammy-winning SF Symphony. Don't miss signature concerts of Beethoven and Mahler, live symphony performances with such films as *Star Trek*, and creative collaborations with artists from Elvis Costello to Metallica.

★**San Francisco Opera** OPERA
(Map p62; ☎415-864-3330; www.sfopera.com; War Memorial Opera House, 301 Van Ness Ave; tickets $10-350; 🚌21, 45, 47, 49, Ⓑ Civic Center, Ⓜ Van Ness) Opera was SF's gold-rush soundtrack – and SF Opera rivals the Met, with world premieres of original works ranging from Stephen King's *Dolores Claiborne* to *Girls of the Golden West*, filmmaker Peter Sellars' collaboration with composer John Adams. Expect haute couture costumes and radical sets by painter David Hockney. Score $10 same-day standing-room tickets at 10am; check website for Opera Lab pop-ups.

San Francisco Ballet DANCE
(Map p62; ☎tickets 415-865-2000; www.sfballet.org; War Memorial Opera House, 301 Van Ness Ave; tickets $22-141; ⊙ticket sales 10am-4pm Mon-Fri; 🚌5, 21, 47, 49, Ⓜ Van Ness, Ⓑ Civic Center) The USA's oldest ballet company is looking sharp in more than 100 shows annually, from *The Nutcracker* (the US premiere was here) to modern originals. Performances are mostly at the War Memorial Opera House from January to May, and occasionally at the Yerba Buena Center for the Arts. Score $15-to-$20 same-day standing-room tickets at the box office (from noon Tuesday to Friday, 10am weekends).

Theater & Performing Arts

★**American Conservatory Theater** THEATER
(ACT; Map p62; ☎415-749-2228; www.act-sf.org; 405 Geary St; ⊙box office 10am-6pm Mon, to curtain Tue-Sun; 🚌8, 30, 38, 45, 🚋Powell-Mason, Powell-Hyde, Ⓑ Powell, Ⓜ Powell) Breakthrough shows launch at this turn-of-the-century landmark, which has hosted ACT's productions of Tony Kushner's *Angels in America*

and Robert Wilson's *Black Rider*, with William S Burroughs' libretto and music by Tom Waits. Major playwrights like Tom Stoppard, Dustin Lance Black, Eve Ensler and David Mamet premiere work here, while the ACT's new **Strand Theater** (Map p62; 415-749-2228; www.act-sf.org/home/box_office/strand.html; 1127 Market St; F, B Civic Center, M Civic Center) stages experimental works.

★Oberlin Dance Collective DANCE
(ODC; Map p78; box office 415-863-9834, classes 415-549-8519; www.odctheater.org; 3153 17th St; drop-in classes from $15, shows $20-50; 12, 14, 22, 33, 49, B 16th St Mission) For 45 years, ODC has been redefining dance with risky, raw performances and the sheer joy of movement. ODC's season runs from September to December, but its stage presents year-round shows featuring local and international artists. ODC Dance Commons is a hub and hangout for the dance community, offering 200-plus classes a week, from flamenco to vogue; all ages and skill levels welcome.

Yerba Buena Center for the Arts PERFORMING ARTS
(YBCA; Map p62; 415-978-2700; www.ybca.org; 700 Howard St; tickets free-$35; box office noon-6pm Sun, Tue & Wed, to 8pm Thu-Sat, galleries closed Mon & Tue; ; 14, M Powell, B Powell) Rock stars would be jealous of art stars at YBCA openings, which draw overflow crowds of art-school groupies with shows ranging from cyberpunk video art to hip-hop showdowns and Indian kathak–American tap-dance fusion freestyle. Most touring dance and jazz companies perform at YBCA's main theater (across the sidewalk from the gallery).

Cinema

★Castro Theatre CINEMA
(Map p78; 415-621-6120; www.castrotheatre.com; 429 Castro St; adult/child $11/8.50; M Castro St) The Mighty Wurlitzer organ rises from the orchestra pit before evening performances and the audience cheers for the Great American Songbook, ending with: 'San Francisco open your Golden Gate/You let no stranger wait outside your door...' If there's a cult classic on the bill – say, *Whatever Happened to Baby Jane?* – expect participation. Otherwise, crowds are well behaved and rapt.

★Alamo Drafthouse Cinema CINEMA
(Map p78; 415-549-5959; https://drafthouse.com/sf; 2550 Mission St; tickets $9-20; ; 14, B 24th St Mission) The landmark 1932 New Mission cinema, now restored to its original Timothy Pfleuger–designed art-deco glory, has a new mission: to upgrade dinner-and-a-movie dates. Staff deliver microbrews and tasty fare to plush banquette seats, so you don't miss a moment of the premieres, cult revivals (especially Music Mondays) or SF favorites from *Mrs Doubtfire* to *Dirty Harry* – often with filmmaker Q&As.

★Roxie Cinema CINEMA
(Map p78; 415-863-1087; www.roxie.com; 3117 16th St; regular screening/matinee $11/8; 14, 22, 33, 49, B 16th St Mission) This vintage 1909 cinema is a neighborhood nonprofit with an international reputation for distributing documentaries and showing controversial films banned elsewhere. Tickets to film-festival premieres, rare revivals and raucous Oscars telecasts sell out – get tickets online – but if the main show's packed, discover riveting documentaries in teensy next-door Little Roxy instead. No ads, plus personal introductions to every film.

Shopping

Union Square is the city's principal shopping district, with flagship stores and department stores, including international chains. Downtown shopping-district borders are (roughly) Powell St (west), Sutter St (north), Kearny St (east) and Market St (south), where the **Westfield mall** (Map p62; www.westfield.com/sanfrancisco; 865 Market St; 10am-8:30pm Mon-Sat, 11am-7pm Sun; ; Powell-Mason, Powell-Hyde, M Powell, B Powell) sprawls. The epicenter of the Union Square shopping area is around Post St, near Grant Ave. Stockton St crosses Market St and becomes 4th St, flanked by flagship stores and **Metreon cinema and mall** (Map p62; 415-369-6201; www.amctheatres.com; 101 4th St; adult/child $14.49/11.49; 14, M Powell, B Powell). For boutique offerings, head toward **Jackson Sq** (Map p68; www.jacksonsquaresf.com; around Jackson & Montgomery Sts; M Embarcadero, B Embarcadero) and along Commercial St.

★Recchiuti Chocolates FOOD & DRINKS
(Map p62; 415-834-9494; www.recchiuticonfections.com; 1 Ferry Bldg, cnr Market St & the Embarcadero; 10am-7pm Mon-Fri, 8am-6pm Sat, 10am-5pm Sun; M Embarcadero, B Embarcadero) No San Franciscan can resist award-winning Recchiuti: Pacific Heights parts with old money for its *fleur de sel* caramels; Noe Valley's foodie kids prefer S'more Bites to the

campground variety; North Beach toasts to the red-wine-pairing chocolate box; and the Mission approves SF-landmark chocolates designed by Creativity Explored – proceeds benefit the Mission arts-education nonprofit for artists with developmental disabilities.

★**Heath Ceramics** HOMEWARES
(Map p62; ☎415-399-9284; www.heathceramics.com; 1 Ferry Bldg, cnr Market St & the Embarcadero; ⏰10am-7pm Mon-Fri, 8am-6pm Sat, 11am-5pm Sun; Ⓜ Embarcadero, Ⓑ Embarcadero) Odds are your favorite SF meal was served on Heath Ceramics, Bay Area chefs' tableware of choice ever since Alice Waters started using Heath's modern, hand-thrown dishes at Chez Panisse. Heath's muted colors and streamlined, mid-century designs stay true to Edith Heath's originals c 1948. Pieces are priced for fine dining, except studio seconds, sold here at weekends.

★**Golden Gate Fortune Cookie Company** FOOD & DRINKS
(Map p68; ☎415-781-3956; 56 Ross Alley; ⏰9am-6pm; 🚌8, 30, 45, 🚋Powell-Mason, Powell-Hyde) Make a fortune at this bakery, where cookies are stamped from vintage presses – just as they were in 1909, when fortune cookies were invented for SF's Japanese Tea Garden (p72). Write your own fortunes for custom cookies (50¢ each), or get cookies with regular or risqué fortunes (pro tip: add 'in bed' to regular ones). Cash only; 50¢ tip for photos.

ℹ Information

DANGERS & ANNOYANCES

Keep your city smarts and wits about you, especially at night in the Tenderloin, South of Market (SoMa) and the Mission.

➡ Avoid using your smart phone unnecessarily on the street – phone-snatching is a crime of opportunity and a problem in SF.

➡ The Bayview–Hunters Point neighborhood (south of Potrero Hill, along the water) is plagued by crime and violence and isn't suitable for wandering tourists.

➡ After dark, Mission Dolores Park, Buena Vista Park and the entry to Golden Gate Park at Haight and Stanyan Sts are used for drug deals and casual sex hookups.

EMERGENCY & MEDICAL SERVICES

Before traveling, contact your health-insurance provider to learn what medical care they will cover outside your hometown (or home country). Overseas visitors should acquire travel insurance that covers medical situations in the US, where nonemergency care for uninsured patients can be very expensive.

For nonemergency appointments at hospitals, you'll need proof of insurance, or credit card or cash. Even with insurance, you'll most likely have to pay up front for nonemergency care and then wrangle afterward with your insurance company to get reimbursed. San Francisco has excellent medical facilities, plus alternative medical practices and herbal apothecaries.

San Francisco General Hopsital (Zuckerberg San Francisco General Hospital and Trauma Center; ☎emergency 415-206-8111, main hospital 415-206-8000; www.sfdph.org; 1001 Potrero Ave; ⏰24hr; 🚌9, 10, 33, 48) Best for serious trauma. Provides care to uninsured patients, including psychiatric care; no documentation required beyond ID.

University of California San Francisco Medical Center (☎415-476-1000; www.ucsfhealth.org; 505 Parnassus Ave; ⏰24hr; 🚌6, 7, 43, Ⓜ N) ER at leading university hospital.

Haight-Ashbury Free Clinic (HealthRIGHT 360; ☎415-746-1950; www.healthright360.org; 558 Clayton St; ⏰by appointment 8:45am-noon & 1-5pm; 🚌6, 7, 33, 37, 43, Ⓜ N) Provides substance abuse and mental health services by appointment.

San Francisco City Clinic (☎415-487-5500; www.sfcityclinic.org; 356 7th St; ⏰8am-4pm Mon, Wed & Fri, 1-6pm Tue, 1-4pm Thu) Low-cost treatment for sexually transmitted diseases (STDs), including emergency contraception and post-exposure prevention (PEP) for HIV.

Drug & Alcohol Emergency Info Line (☎415-362-3400; www.sfsuicide.org)

Trauma Recovery & Rape Treatment Center (☎24hr hotline 415-206-8125, business hours 415-437-3000; www.traumarecoverycenter.org)

INTERNET ACCESS

Apple Store (☎415-392-0202; www.apple.com/retail/sanfrancisco; 300 Post St; ⏰9am-9pm Mon-Sat, 10am-8pm Sun; 📶; 🚌38, 🚋Powell-Mason, Powell-Hyde, Ⓜ Powell) Free wi-fi and internet-terminal usage.

San Francisco Main Library (☎415-557-4400; www.sfpl.org; 100 Larkin St; ⏰10am-6pm Mon & Sat, 9am-8pm Tue-Thu, noon-6pm Fri, noon-5pm Sun; 📶; Ⓜ Civic Center) Free 30-minute internet-terminal usage; spotty wi-fi access.

POST

Rincon Center Post Office (Map p62; ☎800-275-8777; www.usps.gov; 180 Steuart St; ⏰7:30am-5pm Mon-Fri, 9am-2pm Sat; Ⓜ Embarcadero, Ⓑ Embarcadero) Postal services plus historic murals.

US Post Office (Map p62; ☎800-275-8777; www.usps.gov; Macy's, 170 O'Farrell St; ⌚10am-5pm Mon-Sat; Powell-Mason, Powell-Hyde, M Powell, B Powell) Inside Macy's department store.

TOURIST INFORMATION

California Welcome Center (Map p70; ☎415-981-1280; www.visitcwc.com; Pier 39, 2nd fl; ⌚9am-7pm; 47, Powell-Mason, M E, F) Handy resource for stroller and wheelchair rental, plus luggage storage, phone charging, and ideas for broader California travel.

San Francisco Visitor Information Center (Map p62; ☎415-391-2000; www.sftravel.com/visitor-information-center; lower level, Hallidie Plaza, cnr Market & Powell Sts; ⌚9am-5pm Mon-Fri, to 3pm Sat & Sun, closed Sun Nov-Apr; Powell-Mason, Powell-Hyde, M Powell, B Powell) Provides practical multilingual information, sells transportation passes, publishes glossy maps and booklets, and provides interactive touch screens.

Getting There & Away

If you've unlimited time, consider taking the train, instead of driving or flying, to avoid traffic hassles and excess carbon emissions.

Flights, cars and tours can be booked online at lonelyplanet.com/bookings.

AIR

The Bay Area has three international airports: **San Francisco** (SFO; www.flysfo.com; S McDonnell Rd), **Oakland (OAK**; p131) and **San Jose (SJC**; p147). Direct flights from Los Angeles take 60 minutes; Chicago, four hours; Atlanta, five hours; New York, six hours. Factor in additional transit time – and cost – to reach San Francisco proper from Oakland or San Jose, and note that what you save in airfare you may wind up spending on ground transportation. However, if schedule is most important, note that SFO has more weather-related delays than OAK.

BUS

San Francisco's intercity hub is the Transbay Transit Center. From here you can catch the following buses:

AC Transit (p131) Buses to the East Bay.

Greyhound (☎800-231-2222; www.greyhound.com) Buses leave daily for Los Angeles ($39 to $90, eight to 12 hours), Truckee near Lake Tahoe ($35 to $46, 5½ hours) and other major destinations.

Megabus (p147) Low-cost bus service to San Francisco from Los Angeles, Sacramento and Reno.

SamTrans Southbound buses to Palo Alto and the Pacific coast.

TRAIN

Easy on the eyes and light on carbon emissions, train travel is a good way to visit the Bay Area and beyond.

Caltrain (www.caltrain.com; cnr 4th & King Sts) connects San Francisco with Silicon Valley hubs and San Jose.

Amtrak (☎800-872-7245; www.amtrakcalifornia.com) serves San Francisco via stations in Oakland and Emeryville (near Oakland), with free shuttle-bus connections to San Francisco's Ferry Building and Caltrain station, and Oakland's Jack London Sq. Amtrak offers rail passes good for seven days of travel in California within a 21-day period (from $159).

CAR & MOTORCYCLE

Major car-rental operators have offices at airports and downtown.

Getting Around

When San Franciscans aren't pressed for time, most walk, bike or ride Muni instead of taking a car or cab. Traffic is notoriously bad at rush hour, and parking is next to impossible in center-city neighborhoods. Avoid driving until it's time to leave town – or drive during off-peak hours.

For Bay Area transit options, departures and arrivals, call ☎511 or check www.511.org. A detailed *Muni Street & Transit Map* is available free online.

BART High-speed transit to East Bay, Mission St, SF airport and Millbrae, where it connects with Caltrain.

Cable cars Frequent, slow and scenic, from 6am to 12:30am daily. Single rides cost $7; for frequent use, get a Muni Passport ($21 per day).

Muni streetcar and bus Reasonably fast, but schedules vary wildly by line; infrequent after 9pm. Fares are $2.50.

Taxi Fares are about $2.75 per mile; meters start at $3.50. Add 15% to the fare as a tip ($1 minimum). For quickest service in San Francisco, download the Flywheel app for smart phones, which dispatches the nearest taxi.

TO/FROM THE AIRPORT

SamTrans (☎800-660-4287; www.samtrans.com) Express bus KX takes about 30 to 45 minutes to run from San Francisco International Airport to SF's **Transbay Transit Center** (Map p62; cnr Howard & Main Sts; 5,38,41,71), and makes two stops in downtown SF (the last at the Transbay Transit Center).

Airport Express (☎800-327-2024; www.airportexpressinc.com) Runs a scheduled shuttle every hour from 5:30am to 12:30am between San Francisco International Airport and Sonoma ($34) and Marin ($26) counties.

BART

The fastest link between downtown and the Mission District also offers transit to SF airport (SFO; $8.95), Oakland ($3.45) and Berkeley ($4). Four of the system's five lines pass through SF before terminating at Daly City or SFO. Within SF, one-way fares start at $1.95.

BICYCLE

Contact the San Francisco Bicycle Coalition (p106) for maps, information and legal matters regarding bicyclists. Bike sharing is new in SF: racks for **Bay Area Bike Share** (☎855-480-2453; www.bayareabikeshare.com; 30-day membership $30) are located east of Van Ness Ave, and in the SoMa area; however, bikes come without helmets, and biking downtown without proper protection can be particularly dangerous. Bicycles can be taken on BART, but not aboard crowded trains, and never in the first car, nor in the first three cars during weekday rush hours; folded bikes are allowed in all cars at all times. On Amtrak, bikes can be checked as baggage for $5.

BOAT

With the revival of the Embarcadero and the reinvention of the Ferry Building as a gourmet dining destination, commuters and tourists alike are taking the scenic ferry across the bay.

Alcatraz

Alcatraz Cruises (Map p70; ☎415-981-7625; www.alcatrazcruises.com; tours day adult/child/family $37.25/23/112.75, night adult/child $44.25/26.50; Ⓜ E, F) has ferries (reservations essential) departing Pier 33 for Alcatraz every half-hour from 8:45am to 3:50pm and at 5:55pm and 6:30pm for night tours.

East Bay

Blue & Gold Fleet Ferries (Map p62; ☎415-705-8200; www.blueandgoldfleet.com) operates from the Ferry Building, Pier 39 and Pier 41 at Fisherman's Wharf to Jack London Sq in Oakland (one way $6.65). During baseball season, a Giants ferry service runs directly from the landing at AT&T Park's Seals Plaza entrance to Oakland and Alameda. Ticket booths are located at the Ferry Building and Piers 39 and 41.

San Francisco Bay Ferry (p131) operates from both Pier 41 and the Ferry Building to Oakland/Alameda. Fares are $6.60.

Marin County

Golden Gate Transit Ferries (Map p62; ☎415-455-2000; www.goldengateferry.org; ⏲6am-9:30pm Mon-Fri, 10am-6pm Sat & Sun) runs regular ferry services from the Ferry Building to Larkspur and Sausalito (one way $11.75). Transfers are available to Muni bus services and bicycles are permitted. Blue & Gold Fleet Ferries also operate to Tiburon or Sausalito (one way $11.50) from Pier 41.

Napa Valley

Get to Napa car free (weekdays only) via the **Vallejo Ferry** (Map p62; ☎707-643-3779, 877-643-3779; http://sanfranciscobayferry.com), with departures from the Ferry Building docks about every hour from 6:30am to 7pm weekdays and roughly every 90 minutes from 10am to 9pm on weekends; bikes are permitted. However, the connecting bus from the Vallejo Ferry Terminal – Napa Valley Vine bus 29 to downtown Napa, Yountville, St Helena or Calistoga – operates only on weekdays. Fares are $13.80.

CAR

If you can, avoid driving in San Francisco: heavy traffic is a given, street parking is harder to find than true love, and meter readers are ruthless.

MUNI

Muni (Municipal Transit Agency; ☎511; www.sfmta.com) Operates bus, streetcar and cable-car lines. Buses and streetcars are referred to interchangeably as Muni, but when streetcars run underground beneath Market St, they're called the Muni Metro. Some areas are better connected than others, but Muni spares you the costly hassle of driving and parking – and it's often faster than driving, especially along metro-streetcar lines J, K/T, L, M and N.

Muni stops are indicated by a street sign and/or a yellow-painted stripe on the nearest lamppost, with route numbers stamped on the yellow stripe; if there is no street sign or lamppost, look on the pavement for a yellow bar with a route number painted on it. Ignore yellow circles and Xs on the pavement, or bars that do not also have route numbers; these other markings tell electric-trolley drivers when to engage or disengage the throttle; they do not indicate bus stops.

TAXI

DeSoto Cab (☎415-970-1300; http://flywheeltaxi.com/)

Green Cab (☎415-626-4733; www.greencabsf.com) Fuel-efficient hybrids; worker-owned collective.

Homobiles (☎415-574-5023; www.homobiles.org) Get home safely with secure, reliable, donation-based transport for the GLBT community: drivers provide 24/7 taxi service – text for fastest service.

Luxor (☎415-282-4141; www.luxorcab.com)

Yellow Cab (☎415-333-3333; www.yellowcabsf.com)

Marin County & the Bay Area

Includes ➡

Best Places to Eat

- ➡ Chez Panisse (p138)
- ➡ Fish (p110)
- ➡ Hog Island Oyster Company (p120)
- ➡ Sunday Marin Farmers Market (p113)
- ➡ Commis (p127)

Best Places to Sleep

- ➡ Cavallo Point (p105)
- ➡ Mountain Home Inn (p115)
- ➡ HI Pigeon Point Lighthouse (p151)
- ➡ Steep Ravine (p116)

Why Go?

The San Francisco Bay Area encompasses a bonanza of natural vistas and wildlife. Cross the Golden Gate Bridge into Marin County and visit wizened ancient redwoods body-blocking the sun and herds of elegant tule elk prancing along the bluffs of Tomales Bay. Gray whales show some fluke off the cape of the wind-scoured Point Reyes peninsula, while hawks surf the skies in the shaggy hills of the Marin Headlands.

On the cutting edge of intellectual thought, Stanford University – near the tech powerhouse of Silicon Valley and the University of California, Berkeley in the East Bay – draws academics and students from around the world. The city of Berkeley sparked the state's locavore food movement and continues to be at the forefront of environmental and left-leaning political causes. South of Sahn Francisco, Hwy 1 traces miles of undeveloped coastline and sandy pocket beaches as it slowly winds south to Santa Cruz.

When to Go

Berkeley

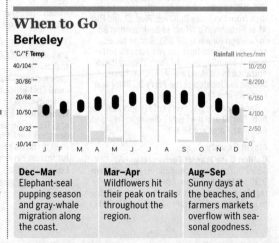

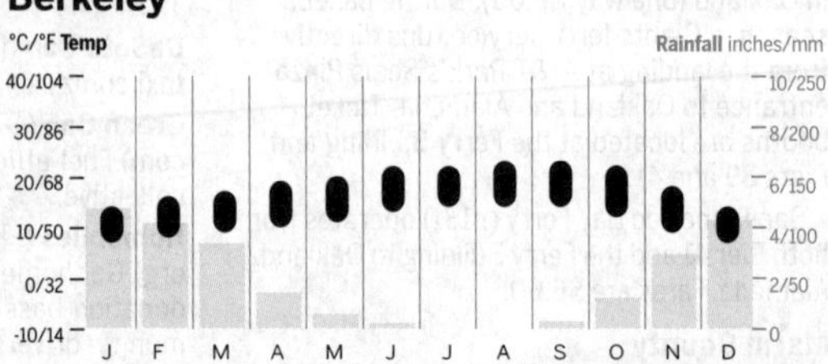

Dec–Mar
Elephant-seal pupping season and gray-whale migration along the coast.

Mar–Apr
Wildflowers hit their peak on trails throughout the region.

Aug–Sep
Sunny days at the beaches, and farmers markets overflow with seasonal goodness.

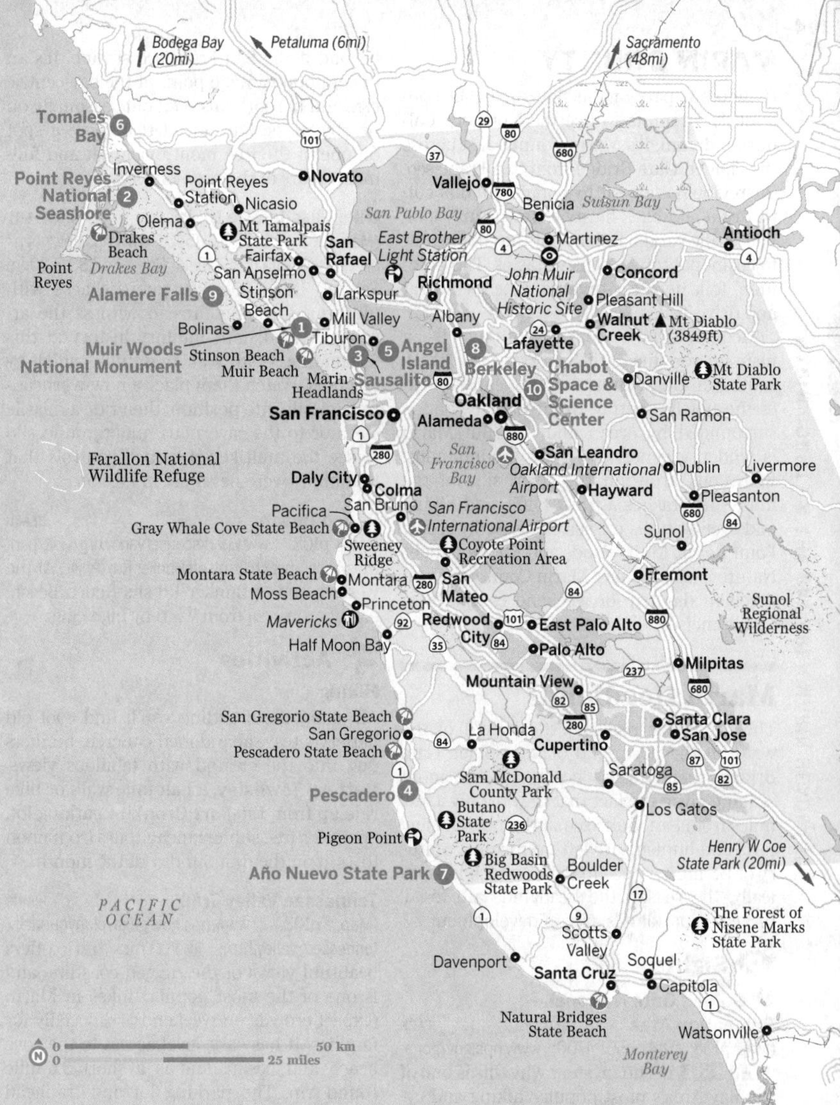

Marin County & the Bay Area Highlights

1. Gazing up at a majestic redwood canopy at **Muir Woods National Monument** (p117).
2. Spotting gray whales from the lighthouse at **Point Reyes National Seashore** (p121).
3. Ferrying over from San Francisco to bohemian **Sausalito** (p106) houseboats bobbing in the bay.
4. Touring the coastline along Hwy 1 to **Pescadero** (p150).
5. Hiking or cycling the **Angel Island** (p114) perimeter.
6. Kayaking past harbor seals in **Tomales Bay** (p121).
7. Spying on noisy elephant seals in **Año Nuevo State Park** (p151).
8. Hanging with hippies, students and passionate foodies in **Berkeley** (p132).
9. Cooling off at blissful Bass Lake, then trekking to **Alamere Falls** (p119).
10. Heading into the Oakland Hills to marvel at stars and planets in the **Chabot Space & Science Center** (p126).

MARIN COUNTY

If there's a part of the Bay Area that consciously attempts to live the Northern California dream, it's Marin County. Just across the Golden Gate Bridge from San Francisco, the region has a wealthy population that cultivates a laid-back lifestyle. Towns may look like idyllic rural hamlets, but the shops cater to cosmopolitan, expensive tastes. The 'common' folk here eat organic, vote Democrat and drive Teslas.

Geographically, Marin County is a near mirror image of San Francisco. It's a south-pointing peninsula that nearly touches the north-pointing tip of the city, and is surrounded by ocean and bay. But Marin is wilder, greener and more mountainous. Redwoods grow on the coast side of the hills, surf crashes against cliffs, and hiking and cycling trails crisscross blessedly scenic Point Reyes, Muir Woods and Mt Tamalpais. Nature is what makes Marin County such an excellent day trip or weekend escape from San Francisco.

Marin Headlands

The headlands rise majestically out of the water at the north end of the Golden Gate Bridge, their rugged beauty all the more striking given the fact that they're only a few miles from San Francisco's urban core. A few forts and bunkers are left over from a century of US military occupation – which is, ironically, the reason the headlands are today protected parklands, free of development.

Sights

★Golden Gate National Recreation Area PARK
(Map p108; ☎415-561-4700; www.nps.gov/goga; P 👪) FREE It's no mystery why this is one of the Bay Area's most popular hiking and cycling destinations. As the trails wind beside the Pacific Ocean and San Francisco Bay and through the Marin Headlands, they afford stunning views of the sea, the Golden Gate Bridge and the city of San Francisco.

★Point Bonita Lighthouse LIGHTHOUSE
(Map p108; ☎415-331-1540; www.nps.gov/goga/pobo.htm; ⌚12:30-3:30pm Sat-Mon; P) FREE This historical lighthouse is a breathtaking half-mile walk from a small parking area off Field Rd. From the tip of Point Bonita, you can see the distant Golden Gate Bridge and beyond it the San Francisco skyline. It's an uncommon vantage point of the bay-centric city, and harbor seals haul out seasonally on nearby rocks. Call ahead to reserve a spot on one of the free monthly sunset and full-moon tours of the promontory.

Nike Missile Site SF-88 HISTORIC SITE
(Map p108; ☎415-331-1540; www.nps.gov/goga/nike-missile-site.htm; Field Rd; ⌚12:30-3:30pm Sat; P) FREE File past guard shacks with uniformed mannequins to witness the area's not-too-distant military history at this fascinating Cold War museum staffed by veterans. Watch them place a now-warhead-free missile into position, then ride a missile elevator to the cavernous underground silo to see the multikeyed launch controls that thankfully were never set in motion.

Rodeo Beach BEACH
(Map p108; www.parksconservancy.org/visit/park sites/rodeo-beach.html; off Bunker Rd; P 👪) At the western end of Bunker Rd sits Rodeo Beach, partly protected from wind by high cliffs.

Activities

Hiking

All along the coastline you'll find cool old battery sites – abandoned concrete bunkers dug into the ground with fabulous views. **Battery Townsley**, a half-mile walk or bike ride up from the **Fort Cronkite** parking lot, opens for free subterranean tours from noon to 4pm on the first Sunday of the month.

Tennessee Valley Trail HIKING
(Map p108; www.nps.gov/goga/planyourvisit/tennessee_valley.htm; 👪) This trail offers beautiful views of the rugged coastline and is one of the most popular hikes in Marin (expect crowds on weekends), especially for families. It has easy, level access to the cove beach and ocean, and is a short 3.5-mile round-trip. The parking lot and trailhead are at the end of Tennessee Valley Rd. From Hwy 101, take the Mill Valley/Stinson Beach/Hwy 1 exit, follow Shoreline Hwy and turn left on to Tennessee Valley Rd.

Coastal Trail HIKING
(Map p108; www.nps.gov/goga/planyourvisit/hiking.htm) From nearby Rodeo Beach, the Coastal Trail meanders 3.5 miles inland, past abandoned military bunkers, to intersect the Tennessee Valley Trail. It then continues almost 3 miles along the blustery headlands all the way to Muir Beach (p117).

WHY IS IT SO FOGGY?

When the summer sun's rays warm the air over the chilly Pacific, fog forms and hovers offshore. To grasp how it moves inland requires an understanding of California's geography. The vast agricultural region in the state's interior, the Central Valley, is ringed by mountains like a giant bathtub. The only substantial sea-level break in these mountains occurs at the Golden Gate to the west, which happens to be the direction from which prevailing winds blow. As the inland valley heats up and the warm air rises, it creates a deficit of air at surface level, generating wind that gets sucked through the only opening it can find: the Golden Gate. It happens fast and it's unpredictable. Gusty wind is the only indication that the fog is about to roll in. But even this is inconsistent: there can be fog at the beaches south of the Golden Gate and sun a mile to the north. Hills block fog – especially at times of high atmospheric pressure, as often happens in summer. Because of this, weather forecasters speak of the Bay Area's 'microclimates.' In July it's not uncommon for inland areas to top 100°F (38°C), while the mercury at the coast barely reaches 70°F (21°C).

Mountain Biking

The Marin Headlands have some excellent mountain-biking routes and it's an exhilarating ride across the Golden Gate Bridge to reach them.

For a good 12-mile dirt loop, choose the **Coastal Trail** west from the fork of Conzelman and McCullough Rds, bumping and winding down to Bunker Rd where it meets **Bobcat Trail**, which joins **Marincello Trail** and descends steeply into the Tennessee Valley parking area. The **Old Springs Trail** and the **Miwok Trail** take you back to Bunker Rd a bit more gently than the Bobcat Trail, though any attempt to avoid at least a couple of hefty climbs is futile.

Sleeping

There's one deluxe lodge, a cozy youth hostel and four campgrounds in the headlands. **Hawk Camp**, **Bicentennial** and **Haypress** campgrounds are inland, with free camping; sites must be reserved through the Marin Headlands Visitor Center (p106). None have water available and two campgrounds require hiking (or cycling) in from the nearest parking lot.

Kirby Cove Campground CAMPGROUND $

(Map p108; reservations 877-444-6777; www.recreation.gov; Kirby Cove Rd; tent sites $25; Apr-Nov; P) In a spectacular shady nook near the entrance to the bay, there's a small beach with the Golden Gate Bridge arching over the rocks nearby. At night you can watch the phantom shadows of cargo ships passing by (and sometimes be lulled to sleep by the dirge of a fog horn). Reserve far ahead.

HI Marin Headlands HOSTEL $

(Map p108; 415-331-2777; www.norcalhostels.org/marin; Fort Barry, Bldg 941; r with shared bath $105-135, dm $31-40; reception 7:30am-11:30pm; P) Wake up to grazing deer and dew on the ground at this Spartan 1907 military compound snuggled in the woods. It has comfortable beds and two well-stocked kitchens, and guests can gather round a fireplace in the common room, shoot pool or play Ping-Pong. Hiking trails beckon outside.

Cavallo Point LODGE $$$

(Map p108; 415-339-4700; www.cavallopoint.com; 601 Murray Circle; r from $399; P) Spread over 45 acres of the Bay Area's most scenic parkland, Cavallo Point lodge flaunts an eco-conscious focus with a full-service spa, restaurant and bar, and easy access to outdoor activities. Choose from richly renovated rooms in the landmark Fort Baker officers' quarters or contemporary, stylish 'green' accommodations with exquisite bay views (including a turret of the Golden Gate Bridge).

Eating

Bring a picnic lunch, trail snacks and enough water with you, since there's nowhere to eat in the Marin Headlands except at Cavallo Point lodge and the children's museum, near Sausalito.

Murray Circle MODERN AMERICAN $$$

(Map p108; 415-339-4750; www.cavallopoint.com; 601 Murray Circle; dinner mains $25-36; 7-11am & 11:30am-2pm Mon-Fri, 7am-2:30pm Sat & Sun, 5:30-9pm Sun-Thu, 5:30-10pm Fri & Sat;) At Cavallo Point lodge, dine on locally sourced

DON'T MISS

HIKING & CYCLING THE GOLDEN GATE BRIDGE

Walking or cycling across the Golden Gate Bridge to Sausalito is a fun way to avoid traffic, get some great ocean views and fresh air. Getting to Sausalito is a relatively easy journey, mostly flat or downhill when heading north from San Francisco. Cycling back isn't nearly as fun. The return trip involves a big climb out of Sausalito. Unless you want a work out, simply hop on a ferry back to SF.

The trip is about 4 miles from the south end of the bridge and takes less than an hour. Pedestrians have access to the bridge's east walkway between 5am and 9pm daily (until 6pm in winter). Cyclists generally use the west side, except on weekdays between 5am and 3:30pm, when they share the east side with pedestrians (who have the right-of-way). After 9pm (6pm in winter), cyclists can still cross the bridge on the east side through a security gate. Check the bridge website for changes.

For more ambitious cyclists, the Cal Park Hill Tunnel is a safe subterranean passage from Larkspur (another ferry terminus) to San Rafael.

More information and resources are available at the websites of the **San Francisco Bicycle Coalition** (☎415-431-2453; www.sfbike.org) and the **Marin County Bicycle Coalition** (MCBC; ☎415-456-3469; www.marinbike.org).

meats, seafood and produce – perhaps grass-fed organic beef burgers or Dungeness-crab BLT sandwiches – in a clubby dining room topped by a pressed-tin ceiling. Reservations recommended for dinner and weekend brunch.

Information

Information is available from the **Golden Gate National Recreation Area** (p104) and the **Marin Headlands Visitors Center** (Map p108; ☎415-331-1540; www.nps.gov/goga/marin-headlands.htm; Bunker Rd, Fort Barry; ⊙9:30am-4:30pm), in an old chapel off Bunker Rd near Fort Barry.

Getting There & Away

By car, take the Alexander Ave exit just after crossing north over the Golden Gate Bridge and dip left under the freeway. Conzelman Rd, to the right, takes you up along the bluffs; you can also take Bunker Rd, which leads to the headlands through a one-way tunnel. Arrive before 2pm on weekends to avoid traffic and parking congestion, or cycle over the bridge instead.

On Saturday, Sunday and holidays, **MUNI** (☎511, 415-701-2311; www.sfmta.com) bus 76X runs every 60 to 90 minutes from San Francisco's Financial District to the Marin Headlands Visitors Center, Rodeo Beach and the Nike missile site. Buses are equipped with bicycle racks.

Sausalito

Perfectly arranged on a secure little harbor on the bay, Sausalito is undeniably lovely. Named for the tiny willows that once populated the banks of its creeks, it's famous for its colorful houseboats bobbing in the bay. Much of the well-heeled downtown has uninterrupted views of San Francisco and Angel Island, and due to the ridgeline at its back, fog generally skips it.

Sausalito is understandably a major tourist trap, jam-packed with souvenir shops and costly boutiques. It's the first town you encounter after crossing the Golden Gate Bridge from San Francisco, so daytime crowds turn up in droves and make parking difficult. Ferrying over from San Francisco makes for a more relaxing excursion.

The town sits on Richardson Bay, a smaller bay within San Francisco Bay. The commercial district is mainly one street, Bridgeway Blvd, which runs alongside the waterfront.

Sights

★**Sausalito Houseboats** ARCHITECTURE

(Map p108) Bohemia still thrives along the shoreline of Richardson Bay, where free spirits inhabit hundreds of quirky homes that bobble in the waves among the seabirds and seals. Structures range from psychedelic mural-splashed castles to dilapidated salt-sprayed shacks and immaculate three-story floating mansions. You can poke around the houseboat docks located off Bridgeway Blvd between Gate 5 and Gate 6½ Rds.

It's a tight-knit community, where residents tend sprawling dockside gardens and stop to chat on the creaky wooden boardwalks as they wheel their groceries home.

Etiquette tips for visitors: no smoking, no pets, no bicycles and no loud noise.

Bay Model Visitors Center MUSEUM
(Map p108; ☎415-332-3871; www.spn.usace.army.mil/missions/recreation/baymodelvisitorcenter.aspx; 2100 Bridgeway Blvd; ⏰9am-4pm Tue-Sat, extended summer hours 10am-5pm Sat & Sun; P 👪) FREE One of the coolest things in town, fascinating to both kids and adults, is the Army Corps of Engineers' solar-powered visitor center. Housed in one of the old (and cold!) Marinship warehouses, it's a 1.5-acre hydraulic model of San Francisco Bay and the delta region. Self-guided tours take you over and around it as the water flows.

Bay Area Discovery Museum MUSEUM
(Map p108; ☎415-339-3900; www.baykidsmuseum.org; 557 McReynolds Rd; $14, 1st Wed each month free; ⏰9am-4pm Tue-Fri, to 5pm Sat & Sun, also 9am-4pm some Mon; P 👪) Below the north tower of the Golden Gate Bridge, at Fort Baker, this excellent hands-on activity museum is designed for children. Multilingual exhibits include a wave workshop, a small underwater tunnel and a large outdoor play area with a shipwreck to romp around. The museum's **Bean Sprouts Café** has healthy nibbles.

Activities

Sausalito is great for **bicycling**, whether for a leisurely ride around town, a trip across the Golden Gate Bridge or a longer-haul journey. From the ferry terminal, an easy option is to head south on Bridgeway Blvd, veering left on to East Rd toward the Bay Area Discovery Museum. Another nice route heads north along Bridgeway Blvd, then crosses under Hwy 101 to Mill Valley. At Blithedale Ave, you can veer east to Tiburon; a bike path parallels parts of Tiburon Blvd.

Sea Trek KAYAKING, SUP
(Map p108; ☎415-332-8494; www.seatrek.com; 2100 Bridgeway; kayak or SUP set per hour from $25, tours from $75; ⏰9am-5pm Mon-Fri, 8:30am-5pm Sat & Sun Apr-Oct, 9am-4pm daily Nov-Mar) On a sunny day, Richardson Bay is irresistible. Kayaks and stand up paddleboard (SUP) sets can be rented here. No experience is necessary, and lessons and group outings are also available. Guided kayaking excursions include full-moon and starlight tours and an adventurous crossing to Angel Island. May through October is the best time to paddle.

Sausalito Bike Rentals BICYCLE RENTAL
(☎415-331-2453, 415-332-8815; www.sausalitobikerentals.com; 34a Princess St; bicycle rental per hour from $15; ⏰9:30am-6:30pm; 👪) Rents road, mountain, hybrid, tandem and electric bicycles by the hour or the day to explore the area.

Sleeping

Most of the lodgings in town charge a pretty penny, with a two-night minimum on weekends. On the outskirts of town, midrange chain motels and hotels line the Hwy 101 corridor.

Hotel Sausalito HISTORIC HOTEL **$$**
(Map p108; ☎415-332-0700; www.hotelsausalito.com; 16 El Portal St; r from $175; P ⊖ ❄ 📶) Steps away from the ferry in the middle of downtown, this grand 1915 hotel has loads of period charm, paired with modern touches such as satellite TV, DVD player and MP3-player docking station. Each guest room is decorated in Mediterranean hues and some enjoy partial bay views. Parking is $20.

Inn Above Tide BOUTIQUE HOTEL **$$$**
(Map p108; ☎415-332-9535; www.innabovetide.com; 30 El Portal; r $405-695; P ⊖ ❄ @ 📶) Next to the ferry terminal, ensconce yourself in one of 31 modern and spacious rooms – most with private deck and wood-burning fireplace – that practically levitate over the water. There are envy-inducing bay views from your window; scan the horizon with the in-room binoculars. Free parking and loaner bicycles.

Gables Inn INN **$$$**
(Map p108; ☎415-289-1100; www.gablesinnsausalito.com; 62 Princess St; r $190-545; P ⊖ @ 📶) Tranquil and inviting, this inn has nine guest rooms in a historic 1869 home and six in a newer building. The more expensive rooms have Jacuzzi, fireplace and balcony with spectacular views, but even the smaller, cheaper rooms are stylish and tranquil. Evening wine and cheese included. Parking is $20.

Eating

Bridgeway Blvd is packed with moderately priced cafes, a few casual budget-priced options and many more expensive bay-view seafood restaurants.

Marin County

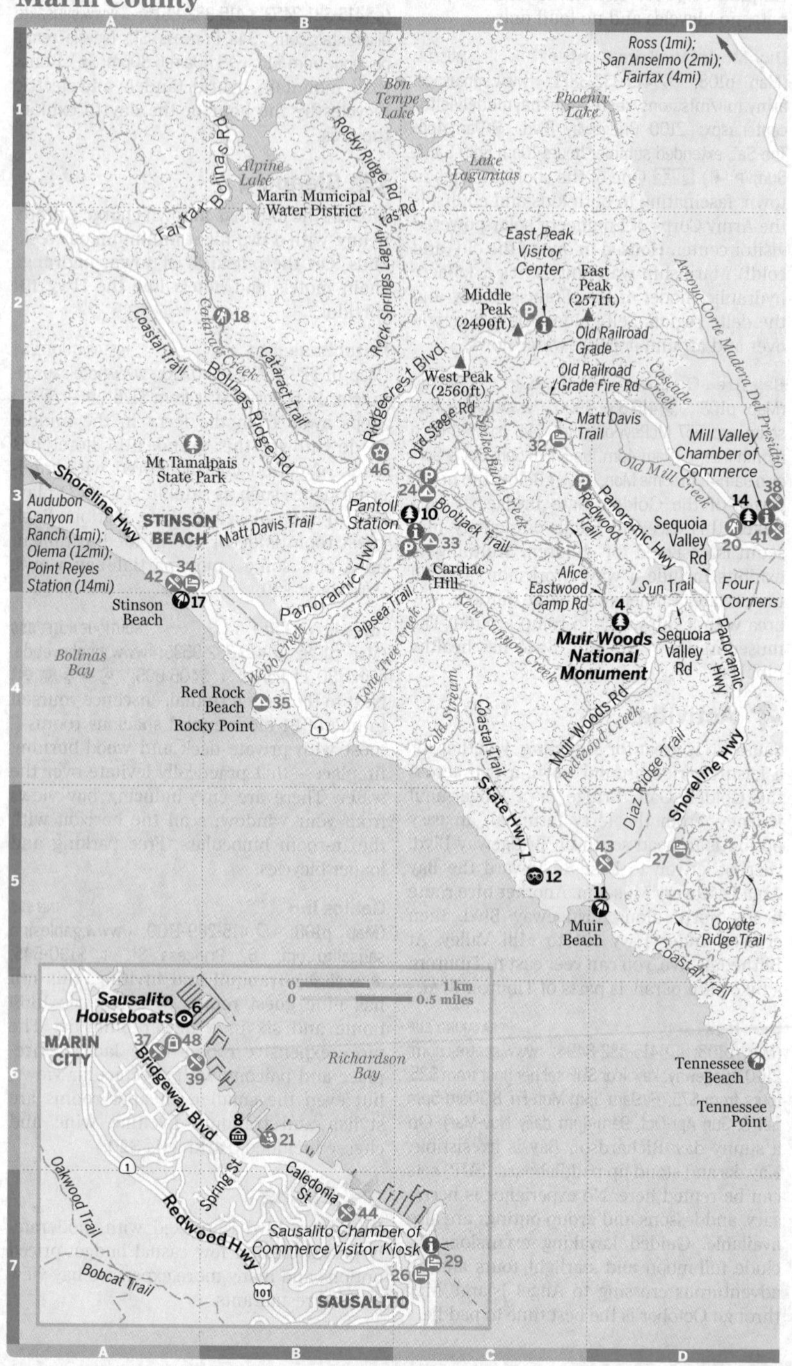

MARIN COUNTY & THE BAY AREA

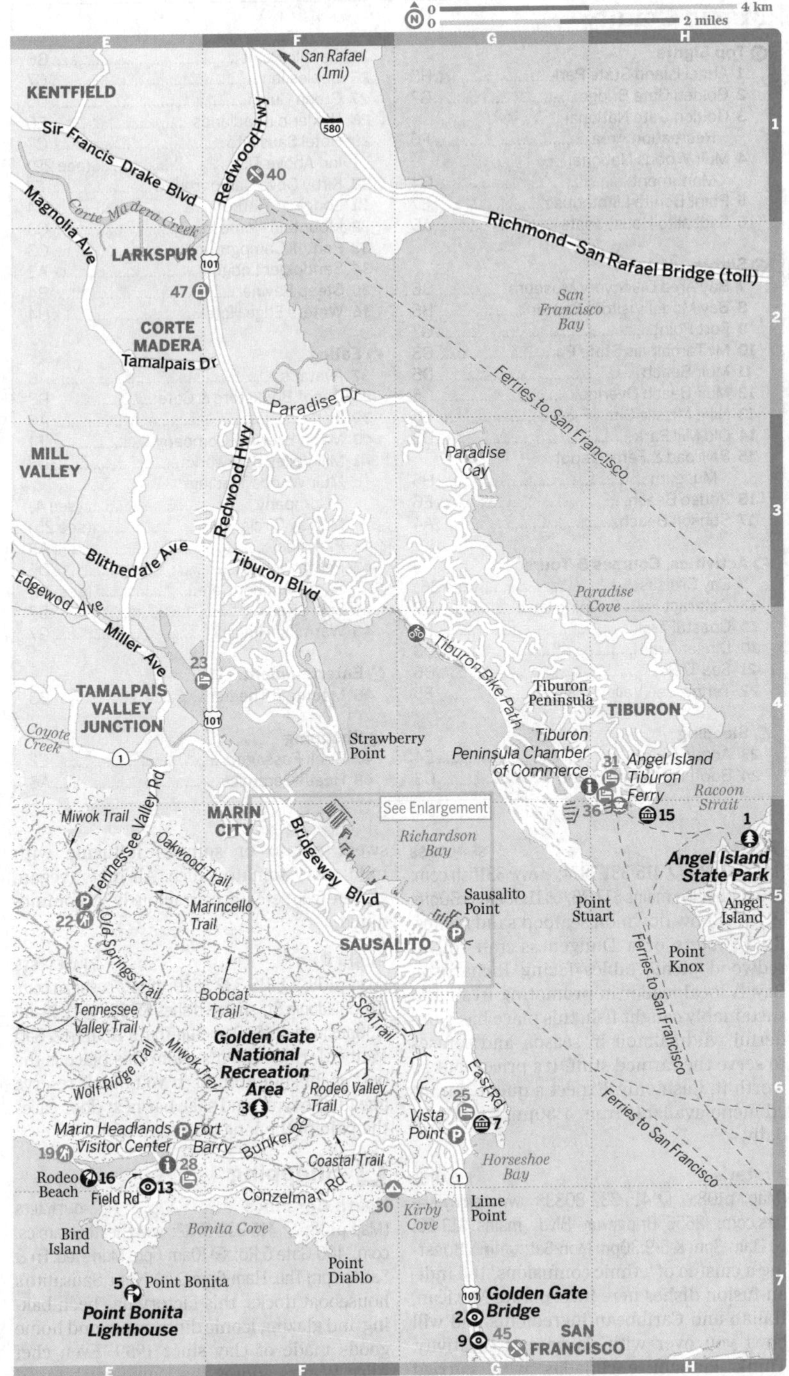
0 4 km
0 2 miles
San Rafael (1mi)
KENTFIELD
Sir Francis Drake Blvd
Redwood Hwy
580
40
Magnolia Ave
Corte Madera Creek
Richmond–San Rafael Bridge (toll)
LARKSPUR
101
47
San Francisco Bay
CORTE MADERA
Tamalpais Dr
Ferries to San Francisco
Paradise Dr
MILL VALLEY
Paradise Cay
Blithedale Ave
Tiburon Blvd
Edgewod Ave
Paradise Cove
Miller Ave
Tiburon Bike Path
23
TAMALPAIS VALLEY JUNCTION
Tiburon Peninsula
TIBURON
Coyote Creek
Strawberry Point
Tiburon Peninsula Chamber of Commerce
31
Angel Island Tiburon Ferry
Racoon Strait
36
15
Miwok Trail
Tennessee Valley Rd
MARIN CITY
See Enlargement
1
Oakwood Trail
Bridgeway Blvd
Richardson Bay
Angel Island State Park
22
Marincello Trail
Sausalito Point
Point Stuart
Angel Island
Old Springs Trail
SAUSALITO
Point Knox
Bobcat Trail
Tennessee Valley Trail
SCA Trail
Golden Gate National Recreation Area
Miwok Trail
Wolf Ridge Trail
East Rd
Rodeo Valley Trail
3
25
Vista Point
7
Marin Headlands Visitor Center
Fort Barry
Bunker Rd
19
Coastal Trail
Horseshoe Bay
Rodeo Beach
16
28
Field Rd
13
Conzelman Rd
30
Kirby Cove
Lime Point
Bonita Cove
Bird Island
Point Diablo
5
Point Bonita
Point Bonita Lighthouse
Golden Gate Bridge
2
9
45
SAN FRANCISCO
E
F
G
H
1
2
3
4
5
6
7

Marin County

Top Sights
1 Angel Island State Park H5
2 Golden Gate Bridge G7
3 Golden Gate National Recreation Area F6
4 Muir Woods National Monument D4
5 Point Bonita Lighthouse E7
6 Sausalito Houseboats A6

Sights
7 Bay Area Discovery Museum G6
8 Bay Model Visitors Center B6
9 Fort Point G7
10 Mt Tamalpais State Park C3
11 Muir Beach D5
12 Muir Beach Overlook C5
13 Nike Missile Site SF-88 .... E6
14 Old Mill Park D3
15 Railroad & Ferry Depot Museum H5
16 Rodeo Beach E6
17 Stinson Beach A4

Activities, Courses & Tours
Bay Cruises .... (see 36)
18 Cataract Falls & Alpine Lake B2
19 Coastal Trail E6
20 Dipsea Trail D3
21 Sea Trek B6
22 Tennessee Valley Trail E5

Sleeping
23 Acqua Hotel E4
24 Bootjack Campground C3
25 Cavallo Point G6
26 Gables Inn C7
27 Green Gulch D5
28 HI Marin Headlands E6
29 Hotel Sausalito C7
Inn Above Tide .... (see 29)
30 Kirby Cove Campground F7
31 Lodge at Tiburon H4
32 Mountain Home Inn C3
33 Pantoll Campground C3
34 Sandpiper Lodging A3
35 Steep Ravine B4
36 Waters Edge Hotel H4

Eating
37 Avatar's A6
38 Depot Bookstore & Cafe D3
39 Fish A6
40 Marin Brewing Company F1
41 Mill Valley Beerworks D3
Muir Woods Trading Company .... (see 4)
Murray Circle .... (see 25)
42 Parkside A3
43 Pelican Inn D5
Sam's Anchor Cafe .... (see 36)
44 Sushi Ran B7
45 Warming Hut G7

Entertainment
46 Mountain Theater B3

Shopping
47 Book Passage E2
48 Heath Ceramics A6

★Fish SEAFOOD $$
(Map p108; 415-331-3474; www.331fish.com; 350 Harbor Dr; mains $17-36; 11:30am-8:30pm;) Chow down on seafood sandwiches, BBQ oysters or a Dungeness-crab roll at redwood picnic tables facing Richardson Bay. A local leader in promoting fresh and sustainably caught fish, this place has wonderful wild salmon in season and refuses to serve the farmed stuff. It's pricey, but so worth it. Cash only. Expect a queue. Limited menu available from 4:30pm to 5:30pm daily.

Avatar's INDIAN $$
(Map p108; 415-332-8083; www.enjoyavatars.com; 2656 Bridgeway Blvd; mains $13-20; 11am-3pm & 5-9:30pm Mon-Sat;) Boasting a cuisine of 'ethnic confusions,' the Indian-fusion dishes here incorporate Mexican, Italian and Caribbean ingredients and will bowl you over with flavor and creativity. Think Punjabi enchiladas with curried sweet potato or spinach fettucine with mild-curry tomato sauce. All diets (vegan, gluten-free etc) are graciously accommodated.

Sushi Ran JAPANESE $$$
(Map p108; 415-332-3620; http://sushiran.com; 107 Caledonia St; shared dishes $5-38; 11:45am-2:30pm Mon-Fri, 5-10pm Sun-Thu, 5-11pm Fri & Sat) Many Marin residents claim this place is the best sushi spot around. If you didn't reserve ahead, the wine and sake bar next door eases the pain of the long wait for a table.

Shopping

Heath Ceramics HOMEWARES
(Map p108; 415-332-3732; www.heathceramics.com; 400 Gate 5 Rd; 10am-6pm Mon-Wed, Fri & Sat, to 7pm Thu, 11am-6pm Sun) Near Sausalito's houseboat docks, this factory has been baking and glazing iconic dinnerware and home goods made of clay since 1959. Even chef Alice Waters adores the iconic earth-toned

place settings, which show arts-and-crafts styling. The showroom discounts overstock and seconds. Reserve ahead for free factory tours on Fridays, Saturdays and Sundays.

Information

Sausalito Chamber of Commerce (Map p108; 415-331-1093; www.sausalito.org; foot of El Portal St; 10am-4pm) offers local information at a visitor kiosk by the ferry terminal.

Getting There & Away

Driving to Sausalito from San Francisco, take the Alexander Ave exit (the first exit after the Golden Gate Bridge) and follow the signs into downtown. There are five municipal parking lots in town, each charging varying rates; you can get three hours of free parking in the lot at the foot of Locust St, off Bridgeway Blvd. Street parking (metered or free, but time-limited) is difficult to find.

The ferry is a fun and easy way to travel to Sausalito. **Golden Gate Ferry** (415-455-2000, 511; http://goldengateferry.org) operates to and from San Francisco's Ferry Building ($11.75, 25 to 30 minutes) several times daily. **Blue & Gold Fleet** (415-705-8200; www.blueandgoldfleet.com) sails to Sausalito several times daily from the Fisherman's Wharf area in San Francisco ($11.50, 30 to 55 minutes). Both ferries operate year-round and transport bicycles for no additional charge.

Golden Gate Transit (415-455-2000, 511; www.goldengatetransit.org) bus 30 runs hourly to Sausalito from downtown San Francisco ($4.75, 40 to 55 minutes). On weekends and holidays, **West Marin Stagecoach** (415-226-0825; www.marintransit.org/stage.html) route 61 ($2) extends to Sausalito, with at least a few departures for Pantoll Station in Mt Tamalpais State Park, Stinson Beach and Bolinas. The seasonal **Muir Woods Shuttle** (Route 66F; www.marintransit.org; round-trip adult/child $5/free) connects with San Francisco ferries arriving in Sausalito before 3pm.

Tiburon

At the end of a small peninsula pointing out into the center of the bay, Tiburon is blessed with gorgeous views. The name comes from the Spanish Punta de Tiburon (Shark Point). Take the ferry from San Francisco, browse the shops on Main St, grab a bite to eat and you've seen Tiburon. The town is also a jumping-off point for nearby Angel Island.

The central part of town is comprised of Tiburon Blvd, Juanita Lane and charming Main St. Main St, which is also known as Ark Row, is where the old houseboats have taken root on dry land and metamorphosed into classy shops and boutiques.

Sights & Activities

Railroad & Ferry Depot Museum MUSEUM
(Map p108; 415-435-1853; http://landmarkssociety.com; 1920 Paradise Dr; suggested donation $5; 1-4pm Wed-Sun Apr-Oct) Formerly the terminus for a 3000-person ferry to San Francisco and a railroad that once reached north to Ukiah, this late 19th-century building showcases a scale model of Tiburon's commercial hub, c 1900. The restored stationmaster's quarters can be visited upstairs.

Bay Cruises CRUISE
(Map p108; 415-435-2131; http://angelislandferry.com; 21 Main St; 90min cruise adult/child $20/10; usually 6:30-8pm Fri & Sat mid-May–mid-Oct) The Angel Island Tiburon Ferry (p112) runs San Francisco Bay sunset cruises on weekend evenings in summer and fall. Reserve ahead and bring your own picnic dinner to enjoy outside on the deck.

Sleeping

Tiburon has only a couple of places to stay downtown. Midrange motels and chain hotels line Hwy 101.

Lodge at Tiburon HOTEL $$
(Map p108; 415-435-3133; www.lodgeattiburon.com; 1651 Tiburon Blvd; r from $225;) Now a stylish and comfortable contemporary hotel, concrete hallways and staircases testify to the more basic motel it once was. The best value in town, it's a short stroll to anywhere – including the ferry – and there's a pool, DVD library, tavern, rental bikes, free parking and a rooftop deck with fireplace and heady Mt Tamalpais views.

Waters Edge Hotel BOUTIQUE HOTEL $$$
(Map p108; 415-789-5999; www.watersedgehotel.com; 25 Main St; r from $269;) At this hotel, with its deck extending over the bay, tasteful rooms have an elegant minimalism that combines comfort and style. Rooms with rustic, high wood ceilings are quite romantic and all afford bay views. Complimentary bicycles and evening wine and cheese included. Parking is $15.

Eating

Downtown, Tiburon Blvd and Main St offer several cafes and restaurants, mostly pricey and unsatisfying.

Sam's Anchor Cafe SEAFOOD $$
(Map p108; ☎415-435-4527; www.samscafe.com; 27 Main St; mains $13-25; ⏰11am-9:30pm Mon-Fri, from 9:30am Sat & Sun; 🚸) Sam's has been slinging seafood and burgers since 1920, and though the entrance looks like a shambling little shack, the area out back has fantastic waterfront views. On a warm afternoon, you can't beat a cocktail or a tasty plate of sautéed prawns on the deck.

Information

Tiburon Peninsula Chamber of Commerce (Map p108; ☎415-435-5633; www.tiburonchamber.org; 96b Main St) provides area information.

Getting There & Away

On Hwy 101, look for the off-ramp for Tiburon Blvd/E Blithedale Ave/Hwy 131. Drive about 4 miles east to downtown, where Tiburon Blvd intersects Main St.

Golden Gate Transit (p111) commuter bus 8 runs direct between San Francisco and Tiburon ($5.50, 60 to 80 minutes) once or twice on weekdays.

Blue & Gold Fleet (p111) sails several times daily from San Francisco's Pier 41 or 39 to Tiburon ($11.50, 30 to 50 minutes). Golden Gate Ferry (p111) connects San Francisco's Ferry Building with Tiburon ($11.50, 30 minutes) during weekday commuter hours only. You can transport bicycles for free on both ferry services.

In downtown Tiburon, the smaller **Angel Island Tiburon Ferry** (Map p108; ☎415-435-2131; http://angelislandferry.com; 21 Main St; round-trip adult/child/bicycle $15/13/1; 🚸) departs from a nearby dock.

Sir Francis Drake Boulevard & Around

The towns along and nearby the Sir Francis Drake Blvd corridor – including Larkspur, Corte Madera, Ross, San Anselmo and Fairfax – evoke charmed small-town life, even though things get busy around Hwy 101.

Starting from the eastern section in **Larkspur**, window-shop along Magnolia Ave or explore the redwoods in nearby **Baltimore Canyon**. On the east side of the freeway is the hulking mass of **San Quentin State Penitentiary**, California's oldest and most notorious prison, founded in 1852.

Take the bicycle and pedestrian bridge from the ferry terminal across the road to the **Marin Country Mart**, a shopping center with a excellent eateries and outdoor seating. One favorite is the **Marin Brewing Company** (Map p108; ☎415-461-4677; www.marinbrewing.com; 1809 Larkspur Landing Cirle, Larkspur; mains $11-15; ⏰11:30am-midnight Sun-Thu, to 1am Fri & Sat; 📶🚸) brewpub, where you can see the glassed-in kettles behind the bar. The head brewer, Arne Johnson, has won many awards, and the Mt Tam Pale Ale complements the menu of pizza, burgers and hearty sandwiches.

Just south, **Corte Madera** is home to one of the Bay Area's best bookstores, **Book Passage** (Map p108; ☎415-927-0960; www.bookpassage.com; 51 Tamal Vista Blvd; ⏰9am-9pm; 📶), in the Marketplace shopping center. It has a strong travel section, and frequent readings.

West along Sir Francis Drake, **San Anselmo** is a cute downtown area along San Anselmo Ave. The attractive center of neighboring **Fairfax** has ample dining and shopping options, and cyclists congregate at **Gestalt Haus Fairfax** (☎415-721-7895; https://gestalthausoffairfax.com; 28 Bolinas Rd, Fairfax; ⏰11:30am-10pm Mon, to 11pm Tue, to midnight Wed & Thu, to 2am Fri & Sat, to 9pm Sun) for the indoor bicycle parking, board games, European draft beers and sausages.

Six miles east of Olema on Sir Francis Drake Blvd, **Samuel P Taylor State Park** (☎415-488-9897; www.parks.ca.gov; 8889 Sir Francis Drake Blvd, Lagunitas; per car $8; ⏰8am-sunset; 🅿🚸) has beautiful, secluded campsites in redwood groves and a coveted handful of new five-person cabins with electricity and wood stoves. The park's also located on the paved **Cross Marin Trail**, with miles of creekside landscape to explore along a former railroad grade.

San Rafael

The oldest and largest town in Marin, San Rafael is slightly less upscale than most of its neighbors but doesn't lack atmosphere. It's a common stop for travelers on their way to Point Reyes. Two blocks south of the 19th-century Spanish Catholic mission that gives the town its name, San Rafael's main drag, 4th St, is lined with cafes and shops. If you follow it west out of downtown San Rafael, it meets Sir Francis Drake Blvd and continues west to the coast. Just north of San Rafael, Lucas Valley Rd heads west toward Nicasio, passing George Lucas' Skywalker Ranch.

Sights

Marin County Civic Center ARCHITECTURE
(415-473-3762; www.marincounty.org/depts/cu/tours; 3501 Civic Center Dr; tour adult/child $10/5; 10am-6pm Mon-Fri, guided tour 10:30am Wed; P) Although he didn't live to see it built, this was architect Frank Lloyd Wright's final commission. He designed the horizontal hilltop buildings to flow with the natural beauty of the county's landscape, with sky-blue roofs and sand-colored walls. Show up on Wednesday morning for a one-hour guided tour or access the prerecorded audioguide and self-guiding tour brochure online anytime.

China Camp State Park PARK
(415-456-0766; https://friendsofchinacamp.org; San Pedro Rd; per car $5; 8am-sunset; P) About 6 miles northeast of San Rafael, this is a pleasant place to stop for a picnic or short hike. From Hwy 101, take the N San Pedro Rd exit and continue east. A Chinese shrimp-fishing village once stood here and a small museum exhibits interesting artifacts from the 19th-century settlement.

Sleeping

Midrange motels and hotels hug Hwy 101 on the outskirts of town.

China Camp State Park Campground CAMPGROUND $
(reservations 800-444-7275; www.reserveamerica.com; 730 N San Pedro Rd; tent sites $35; P) Pretty waterfront park with 31 walk-in campsites. It has pleasant shade and coin-op hot showers.

Eating

Downtown overflows with restaurants and cafes, all within walking distance of each other. Start exploring along 4th St.

★ **Sunday Marin Farmers Market** MARKET $
(415-472-6100; http://agriculturalinstitute.org; 3501 Civic Center Dr; 8am-1pm Sun; P) Nowhere else in Marin County do as many farmers, ranchers, fishers and gourmet-food makers gather than at this Sunday-morning farmers market, happening rain or shine at the Marin Civic Center off Hwy 101. Browse the season's most luscious fruit, freshest vegetables, richest honey and cheeses, aromatic breads, colorful flowers and even handmade art, jewelry and crafts. With almost 200 vendors, it's the third-largest farmers market in California.

Sol Food PUERTO RICAN $$
(415-451-4765; www.solfoodrestaurant.com; 903 Lincoln Ave; mains $8-17; 9am-midnight Sun-Thu, to 1am Fri & Sat) Lazy ceiling fans, tropical plants and the pulse of Latin rhythms create a soothing atmosphere for delicious dishes such as a *jíbaro* sandwich with thinly sliced steak and other island-inspired meals concocted with plantains, organic veggies and free-range meats.

State Room CALIFORNIAN $$
(415-295-7929; http://stateroombrewery.com; 1132 4th St; mains $15-25; 11:30am-10pm Sun & Tue-Wed, to midnight Thu-Sat) Wood-fired pizzas, fresh market salads and create-your-own burgers stacked hands high will sate your grumbling stomach at this downtown brewery, bar and kitchen. Serious cocktails and draft beers, ciders and barley wine on tap.

Entertainment

Smith Rafael Film Center CINEMA
(415-454-1222; http://rafaelfilm.cafilm.org; 1118 4th St; tickets $8.50-11.25) Innovative art-house programming on three screens in state-of-the-art surroundings in a restored cinema.

Information

Marin Convention & Visitors Bureau (415-925-2060; www.visitmarin.org; 1 Mitchell Blvd; 9am-5pm Mon-Fri) Provides tourist information for the entire county.

Getting There & Away

Several Golden Gate Transit (p111) buses operate between San Francisco and the San Rafael Transit Center at 3rd and Hetherton Sts ($6.75, one hour). From the transit center, local buses ($2) run by Golden Gate Transit and **Marin Transit** (415-455-2000, 511; www.marintransit.org) fan out across the county.

For ambitious cyclists, the Cal Park Hill Tunnel is a safe subterranean passage from Larkspur – a terminus for Golden Gate Ferry (p111) services from San Francisco – to San Rafael.

Mill Valley

Nestled under the redwoods at the base of Mt Tamalpais, tiny Mill Valley is one of the Bay Area's most picturesque hamlets. Mill

WORTH A TRIP

ANGEL ISLAND

Angel Island (Map p108; ☎415-435-5390; www.parks.ca.gov; 👪) FREE, in San Francisco Bay, has a mild climate with fresh bay breezes, which makes it pleasant for hiking and cycling. For a unique treat, picnic in a protected cove overlooking the surrounding cities. The island history is apparent in its unique buildings – it was a hunting and fishing ground for the Miwok people, served as a military base, an immigration station, a WWII Japanese internment camp and a Nike missile site. There are 12 miles of roads and trails around the island, including a hike to the summit of 781ft **Mt Livermore** (no bicycles) and a 5-mile perimeter trail.

The **Immigration Station** (USIS; ☎415-435-5537; www.aiisf.org/visit; adult/child $5/3, incl tour $7/5, cash only; ⏰11am-3pm Wed-Sun), which operated from 1910 to 1940, was the Ellis Island of the West Coast. But this facility was primarily a screening and detention center for Chinese immigrants, who were at that time restricted from entering the US under the **Chinese Exclusion Act**. Many detainees were cruelly held for long periods before ultimately being sent home. The mournful Chinese poetry etched into the barrack walls is a heartbreaking testament to their trials. The site is now a museum with excellent interpretive exhibits; tours include admission fees and can be reserved ahead or purchased on-site.

Sea Trek (p107) runs kayaking excursions around the island. You can rent bicycles (per hour/day $12.50/40) at **Ayala Cove**, and there are **tram tours** ($15) around the island. Tour schedules vary seasonally; go to www.angelisland.com for information.

You can camp on the island, and when the last ferry sails for the night, the place is your own – except for the very persistent raccoons. The dozen hike-, bicycle- or kayak-in **campsites** (☎reservations 800-444-7275; www.reserveamerica.com; tent sites from $30) are usually reserved months in advance. Near the ferry dock, there's a cafe serving sandwiches and snacks.

Getting There & Away

All ferry tickets are sold on a first-come, first-served basis.

From San Francisco's Pier 41, take a **Blue & Gold Fleet** (p111) ferry (one-way adult/child $9/4.75). There are at least three or four daily sailings year-round.

From Tiburon, take the **Angel Island Tiburon Ferry** (p112), which runs daily from April to September (weekends only November to March). As you board, pay fares (one-way adult/child $9/4.75) by cash or check only.

Valley was originally a logging town, its name stemming from an 1830s sawmill – the first in the Bay Area to provide lumber. Though the 1892 Mill Valley Lumber Company still greets motorists on Miller Ave, the town is a vastly different place today, packed with wildly expensive homes, luxury cars and pricey boutiques.

Mill Valley once served as the starting point for the scenic railway that carried visitors up Mt Tamalpais. The tracks were removed in 1940 and today the Depot Bookstore & Cafe occupies the former rail station.

Activities

★Dipsea Trail HIKING

(Map p108; www.dipsea.org) A beloved though demanding hike, the 7-mile Dipsea Trail climbs over the coastal range and down to Stinson Beach, cutting through a corner of Muir Woods (p117). This classic trail starts at **Old Mill Park** (Map p108; ☎415-383-1370; www.cityofmillvalley.org; Throckmorton Ave & Cascade Dr; ⏰dawn-dusk; 👪) with a climb up 676 steps in three separate flights, and includes a few more ups and downs before reaching the ocean.

The few slaloms between staircases aren't well-signed, but locals can point the way. West Marin Stagecoach (p111) route-61 buses run from Stinson Beach back to Mill Valley at least a few times every day, making it a doable one-way day hike. You can refill water bottles and grab a snack at **Muir Woods Trading Company** (Map p108; ☎415-388-7059; www.muirwoodstradingcompany.com; 1 Muir Woods Rd, Mill Valley; items $2-11; ⏰8am-5pm; 👪) 🍃 cafe, about a 2-mile hike from Mill Valley, or start or end the trail there instead.

Festivals & Events

Mill Valley Film Festival FILM

(☎415-383-5256; www.mvff.com; adult/child per film $15/10; ⌚Oct) In October look for an innovative, internationally regarded program of independent films screened in Mill Valley and San Rafael.

Sleeping

Lackluster midrange motels stand beside Hwy 101. Boutique hotels and inns shelter by the waterfront and on the forested hillsides around Mt Tamalpais.

Acqua Hotel BOUTIQUE HOTEL $$

(Map p108; ☎415-380-0400; www.marinhotels.com; 555 Redwood Hwy; r from $229; P ⊖ ❄ @ 🛜 🐾) With views of the bay and Mt Tamalpais, and a lobby with a welcoming fireplace, this boutique hotel doesn't lack for eye candy. Contemporary rooms are sleekly designed with beautiful fabrics and aromatherapy bath products. Perks include free loaner bikes for guests and a morning espresso bar and evening wine service.

Mountain Home Inn INN $$$

(Map p108; ☎415-381-9000; www.mtnhomeinn.com; 810 Panoramic Hwy; r $195-345; ⊖ 🛜) Set amid redwood, spruce and pine trees on a ridge of Mt Tamalpais, this retreat is both modern and rustic. The larger (more expensive) rooms are rugged beauties, with unfinished timbers forming columns from floor to ceiling, as though the forest is shooting up through the floor. Smaller rooms are cozy dens for two. The positioning of a good local trail map on each dresser makes it clear that it's a place to breathe and unwind. West Marin Stagecoach (p111) route 61 stops at the inn.

Eating

You'll find a handful of cafes and restaurants downtown.

Depot Bookstore & Cafe CAFE $

(Map p108; ☎415-383-2665; http://depotbookstore.com; 87 Throckmorton Ave; mains $5-10; ⌚cafe 7am-7pm, bookstore from 8am; 🛜) Smack in the town center, Depot serves coffee and espresso drinks, sandwiches, soups and baked goods. The bookstore sells lots of local publications, including trail guides.

Mill Valley Beerworks GASTROPUB $$

(Map p108; ☎415-888-8218; www.millvalleybeerworks.com; 173 Throckmorton Ave; dinner mains $18-30; ⌚5:30-9pm Sun & Mon, to 9:30pm Tue-Thu, to 10:30pm Fri & Sat, also 11:30am-3pm Sat & Sun) With hard-to-find bottled brews and a few of its own (from Fort Point Beer Company in San Francisco) among the dozen or so on tap, here beer-lovers can pair their favorites with the kitchen's delicious farm-to-table cooking. The unsigned seating is stark and stylish, with a pressed-tin wall and chalkboards above the bar.

Information

Mill Valley Chamber of Commerce (Map p108; ☎415-388-9700; www.enjoymillvalley.com; 85 Throckmorton Ave; ⌚10am-4pm Tue-Sat) Offers tourist information and maps.

Getting There & Away

From San Francisco or Sausalito, take Hwy 101 north to the Mill Valley/Stinson Beach/Hwy 1 exit. Follow Hwy 1/Shoreline Hwy to Almonte Blvd (which becomes Miller Ave), then follow Miller Ave into downtown Mill Valley.

From the north, take the E Blithedale Ave exit from Hwy 101, then head west into downtown Mill Valley.

Golden Gate Transit (p111) bus 4 runs directly from San Francisco to Mill Valley ($4.75, one hour, every 20 to 60 minutes) on weekdays. Marin Transit (p113) route 17 ($2, 30 minutes, every 30 to 60 minutes) connects Mill Valley with the Sausalito ferry terminal daily.

Mt Tamalpais State Park

Standing guard over Marin County, majestic Mt Tamalpais (Mt Tam) has breathtaking 360-degree views of ocean, bay and hills rolling into the distance. The rich, natural beauty of the 2572ft mountain and its surrounding area is inspiring – especially considering it lies within an hour's drive from one of the state's largest metropolitan areas.

Mt Tamalpais State Park (Map p108; ☎415-388-2070; www.parks.ca.gov; per car $8; ⌚7am-sunset; P 🚻) was formed in 1930, partly from land donated by congressman and naturalist William Kent (who also donated the land that became Muir Woods National Monument in 1907). Its 6300 acres are home to deer, foxes, bobcats and 60 miles of hiking and mountain-biking trails.

Mt Tam was a sacred place to the Coast Miwok people for thousands of years before the arrival of European and American settlers. By the late 19th century, San Franciscans were escaping the bustle of the city with all-day outings on the mountain, and in 1896 the 'world's crookedest railroad' (281 turns) was completed from Mill Valley to the summit. Though the railroad was closed in 1930, Old Railroad Grade is today one of Mt Tam's most popular and scenic hiking and cycling paths.

Activities

Panoramic Hwy climbs from Mill Valley through the park to Stinson Beach. From Pantoll Station, it's 4.2 miles by car to **East Peak Summit**; take Pantoll Rd and then panoramic Ridgecrest Blvd to the top. A 10-minute hike leads to a fire lookout at the very top and awesome sea-to-bay views.

Mountain Biking

Cyclists must stay on the fire roads (and off the single-track trails) and keep to speeds under 15mph. Rangers are prickly about these rules and a ticket can result in a steep fine.

The most popular ride is the Old Railroad Grade from Mill Valley to Mt Tam's East Peak. Alternatively, from just west of Pantoll Station, cyclists can take either the **Deer Park Fire Road**, which runs close to the Dipsea Trail through giant redwoods to the main entrance of Muir Woods, or the aptly named **Coast View Trail**, which joins Hwy 1 north of Muir Beach Overlook. Both options require a return to Mill Valley via Frank Valley/Muir Woods Rd, which climbs steadily (800ft) to Panoramic Hwy, then becomes Sequoia Valley Rd as it drops toward Mill Valley.

For more information on bicycle routes and rules, contact the Marin County Bicycle Coalition (p106); its *Marin Bicycle Map* ($10) is the gold standard for local cycling.

Old Railroad Grade MOUNTAIN BIKING

For a sweaty, 6-mile, 2500ft climb, start in Mill Valley at the end of W Blithedale Ave and cycle up to East Peak. For a head start, begin part way up at the Mountain Home Inn instead and follow Gravity Car Rd to the Old Railroad Grade, an easy half-hour ride to the summit.

Hiking

The park map is a smart investment as there are a dozen worthwhile hiking trails, including to Cataract Falls.

From Pantoll Station, the **Steep Ravine Trail** follows a wooded creek on to the coast (about 2.1 miles each way). For a longer hike, veer right (northwest) after 1.5 miles on to the Dipsea Trail (p114), which meanders through trees for 1 mile before ending at Stinson Beach. Grab some lunch, then walk north through town and follow signs for the **Matt Davis Trail**, which leads 2.7 miles back to Pantoll Station, making a good loop. The Matt Davis Trail continues on beyond Pantoll Station, wrapping gently around the mountain with superb views.

Cataract Falls & Alpine Lake HIKING

(Map p108) A worthy hiking option on Mt Tam is the **Cataract Trail**, which runs along Cataract Creek. From the trailhead along Pantoll Rd, it's less than 3 miles to Alpine Lake. The last mile or so is a spectacular rooty staircase that descends alongside Cataract Falls, at its prettiest immediately after winter or spring rainfall.

Sleeping

★ Steep Ravine CAMPGROUND, CABIN $

(Map p38; ☎reservations 800-444-7275; www.reserveamerica.com; tent sites $25, cabins $100; ⏲Nov-Sep; P) Just off Hwy 1, about 1 mile south of Stinson Beach, this jewel has seven primitive beachfront campsites and nine rustic five-person cabins with woodstoves overlooking the ocean. Both options book up far in advance; reservations can be made up to seven months ahead.

Bootjack Campground CAMPGROUND $

(Map p108; ☎info 415-388-2070; www.parks.ca.gov; Panoramic Hwy; tent sites $25; P🐾) The 15 first-come, first-served walk-in campsites are right on two of the park's best hiking trails and adjacent to Redwood Creek, with open vistas to the south. It's 0.3 miles northeast of Pantoll Station.

Pantoll Campground CAMPGROUND $

(Map p108; ☎info 415-388-2070; www.parks.ca.gov; Panoramic Hwy; tent sites $25; P🐾) From the parking lot it's only a 100yd walk or cycle to the campground, with 16 first-come, first-served woodsy tent sites, fire pits, picnic tables and potable water, but no showers.

Entertainment

Mountain Theater THEATER

(Cushing Memorial Amphitheater; Map p108; ☎415-383-1100; www.mountainplay.org; off Pantoll Rd; adult/child $40/25; ⏲late May–mid-Jun; 👪) Built by the Civilian Conservation Corps in the 1930s, the park's natural-stone, 3750-seat theater hosts the annual 'Mountain Play' series on weekend afternoons in late spring and early summer. Free shuttles run from Mill Valley; otherwise, parking is $15 to $20.

Information

Pantoll Station (Map p108; ☎415-388-2070; www.parks.ca.gov; 801 Panoramic Hwy; ⊙hours vary;) The park headquarters. Detailed park maps are sold here.

East Peak Visitor Center (Map p108; www.friendsofmttam.org; off Ridgecrest Blvd; ⊙11am-4pm Sat & Sun) Small center with nature and historical exhibits and a gift shop.

Getting There & Away

To reach Pantoll Station by car, take Hwy 1 to the Panoramic Hwy and look for the signs. Panoramic Hwy climbs from Mill Valley through the park, then winds downhill to Stinson Beach.

West Marin Stagecoach (p111) route 61 runs a few times daily on weekdays from Marin City via Mill Valley (more frequent weekend and holiday service from the Sausalito ferry terminal) to Pantoll Station ($2, 55 minutes).

Muir Woods National Monument

Walking through an awesome stand of the world's tallest trees is an experience to be had only in Northern California and a small part of southern Oregon. The old-growth redwoods at **Muir Woods** (Map p108; ☎415-388-2595; www.nps.gov/muwo; 1 Muir Woods Rd, Mill Valley; adult/child $10/free; ⊙8am-8pm mid-Mar–mid-Sep, to 7pm mid-Sep–early Oct, to 6pm Feb–mid-Mar & early Oct-early Nov, to 5pm early Nov-Jan; P) , just 12 miles north of the Golden Gate Bridge, make up the closest redwood stand to San Francisco. The trees were initially eyed by loggers, and Redwood Creek, as the area was known, seemed ideal for a dam. Those plans were halted when congressman and naturalist William Kent bought a section of Redwood Creek and, in 1907, donated 295 acres to the federal government. President Theodore Roosevelt made the site a national monument in 1908, the name honoring John Muir, naturalist and founder of environmental organization the Sierra Club.

Muir Woods can become quite crowded, especially on weekends. Try to come midweek, early in the morning or late in the afternoon, when tour buses are less of a problem. Even at busy times, a short hike will get you out of the densest crowds and onto trails with huge trees and stunning vistas. A lovely cafe, **Muir Woods Trading Company** (Map p108; ☎415-388-7059; www.muirwoodstradingcompany.com; 1 Muir Woods Rd, Mill Valley; items $2-11; ⊙8am-5pm;) serves local and organic goodies and hot drinks that hit the spot on foggy days.

Activities

The 1-mile Main Trail Loop is a gentle walk alongside Redwood Creek to the 1000-year-old trees at **Cathedral Grove**; it returns via **Bohemian Grove**, where the tallest tree in the park stands 254ft high. The **Dipsea Trail** is a good 2-mile hike up to the top of aptly named Cardiac Hill.

You can also walk down into Muir Woods by taking trails from the Panoramic Hwy, such as the **Bootjack Trail** from the Bootjack picnic area, or from Mt Tamalpais' Pantoll Station campground, along the **Ben Johnson Trail**.

Getting There & Away

The parking lot is insanely full during busy periods, so consider taking the seasonal **Muir Woods Shuttle** (p111) from Sausalito, where ferries from San Francisco arrive.

To get there by car, drive north on Hwy 101, exit at Hwy 1 and continue north along Hwy 1/Shoreline Hwy to the Panoramic Hwy (a right-hand fork). Follow that for about 1 mile to Four Corners, where you turn left on to Muir Woods Rd (there are plenty of signs).

Muir Beach

Muir Beach is a quiet hamlet with a pretty beach and superb views up and down the coast from an overlook just north of town. For visitors, it's a quick stop between visiting Muir Woods and Stinson Beach.

Sights

Muir Beach Overlook VIEWPOINT
(Map p108; www.nps.gov/goga/planyourvisit/muirbeach.htm; Shoreline Hwy; P) Just over a mile north of Pelican Inn (p118) along Hwy 1, there are superb coastal views from this overlook. During WWII scouts kept watch from the surrounding concrete lookouts for invading Japanese ships.

Muir Beach BEACH
(Map p108; www.nps.gov/goga/planyourvisit/muirbeach.htm; off Pacific Way; P) Restored wetlands, creeks, lagoons and sand dunes provide habitat for birds, California red-legged frogs and coho salmon. In winter you might spot monarch butterflies roosting in

a small grove of Monterey pines and migratory whales swimming offshore. The turnoff from Hwy 1 is next to the coast's longest row of mailboxes at Mile 5.7, just before Pelican Inn.

Sleeping & Eating

Most people visit Muir Beach on a day trip from San Francisco.

Green Gulch LODGE $$

(Map p108; ☎415-383-3134; www.sfzc.org/greengulch; 1601 Shoreline Hwy; s $100-175, d $175-250, incl all meals; P ⊖ @ ☎) In the hills above Muir Beach, this Zen Buddhist retreat center's contemporary accommodations are restful. Delicious buffet-style vegetarian meals are included.

Pelican Inn PUB FOOD $$$

(Map p108; ☎415-383-6000; www.pelicaninn.com; 10 Pacific Way; dinner mains $18-36; ⊙8-11am Sat & Sun, 11:30am-3pm & 5:30-9pm daily;) The oh-so-English Pelican Inn is Muir Beach's only commercial establishment. Hikers, cyclists and families come for pub lunches inside its timbered restaurant and cozy bar, perfect for a pint, a game of darts and warming up beside the open fire. The food is nothing mind-blowing and the service is hit or miss, but the setting is magical. Upstairs are seven cozy rooms (from $225) with half-canopy beds.

Stinson Beach

Just 5 miles north of Muir Beach, Stinson Beach is positively buzzing on warm weekends. The town flanks Hwy 1 for about three blocks and is densely packed with galleries, shops, eateries and B&Bs. The beach is often blanketed with fog, and when the sun's shining it's blanketed with surfers, families and gawkers. There are views of Point Reyes and San Francisco on clear days, and the beach is long enough for an invigorating stroll.

Sights

Stinson Beach BEACH

(Map p108; ☎415-868-0942; www.nps.gov/goga; off Hwy 1; ⊙from 9am daily, closing time varies seasonally; P) Three-mile-long Stinson Beach is a popular surf spot, with swimming advised from late May to mid-September only. For updated weather and surf conditions call ☎415-868-1922. The beach is one block west of Hwy 1. There's free parking but the lot often fills up before noon on sunny days.

Martin Griffin Preserve WILDLIFE RESERVE

(☎415-868-9244; www.egret.org; 4900 Shoreline Hwy; suggested donation $20; ⊙hours vary; P) One of four regional Audubon Canyon Ranch preserves hides in the hills above Bolinas Lagoon. It's a major nesting ground for great blue herons and great egrets; viewing scopes are set up behind blinds where you can watch these magnificent birds congregate to nest and hatch their chicks in tall redwoods. At low tide, harbor seals often doze on sandbars in the lagoon. Confirm hours, which vary seasonally, before visiting. It's 3 miles north of Stinson Beach on Hwy 1.

Sleeping & Eating

Sandpiper Lodging MOTEL, CABIN $$

(Map p108; ☎415-868-1632; www.sandpiperstinsonbeach.com; 1 Marine Way; r $165-180, cabins $220-250, cottages $350; P ⊖ ☎) Just off Hwy 1 and a quick stroll to the beach, these nine comfortable rooms, cabins and cottage all have gas fireplace and kitchenette, and are ensconced in a lush garden and picnic area. Two-night minimum stay on weekends and holidays between April and October.

Parkside AMERICAN, BAKERY $$

(Map p108; ☎415-868-1272; www.parksidecafe.com; 43 Arenal Ave; mains $9-28; ⊙7:30am-9pm, coffee bar from 6am;) Famous for its hearty breakfasts and lunches, this cozy eatery next to the beach serves wood-fired pizzas and excellent coastal cuisine such as Tomales Bay oysters and king salmon at dinner, when reservations are recommended. Popular with beachgoers, hikers and cyclists, Parkside's outdoor snack bar serves burgers, fruit smoothies, baked goods and ice cream.

Getting There & Away

By car from San Francisco, it's nearly an hour's drive, though on weekends plan for toe-tapping traffic delays.

West Marin Stagecoach (p111) route 61 runs a few daily minibuses ($2) from Marin City (one hour), with more frequent weekend and holiday services connecting with Sausalito ferries (75 minutes).

Bolinas

For a town that is so famously unexcited about tourism, Bolinas offers some fairly tempting attractions for the visitor. Known as Jugville during the gold-rush days, the sleepy beachside community is home to writers, musicians and fisherfolk, and deliberately hard to find. The highway department used to put signs up at the turnoff from Hwy 1; locals kept taking them down, so the highway department finally gave up.

Sights & Activities

Palomarin Field Station NATURE CENTER
(415-868-0655; www.pointblue.org; 999 Mesa Rd; sunrise-sunset;) FREE Formerly Point Reyes Bird Observatory, Point Blue's Palomarin Field Station has bird-banding and netting demonstrations, an unstaffed visitor center and a nature trail. Banding demonstrations are held in the morning Tuesday to Sunday from May through late November, and on Wednesday, Saturday and Sunday the rest of the year. Show up between 8am and 11am for the best bird-watching.

★ **Bass Lake & Alamere Falls Trail** HIKING
(www.nps.gov/pore) At the end of Mesa Rd, the Palomarin parking lot accesses various hiking trails in the southern part of Point Reyes National Seashore (p121), including the easy (and popular) 3-mile trail to lovely **Bass Lake**. Continuing another 1.5 miles northwest, you'll reach an unmaintained trail to **Alamere Falls**, a fantastic flume plunging 50ft off a cliff and on to the beach.

A sweet inland spot buffered by tall trees, small Bass Lake is perfect for a swim on a toasty day. You can dive in wearing your birthday suit (or not), bring an inner tube to float about, or do a long lap all the way across.

Approaching Alamere Falls, sketchy beach access may make it more enjoyable to hike another 1.5 miles along the trail to Wildcat Beach, then backtrack a mile south on sand.

2 Mile Surf Shop SURFING
(415-868-0264, surf report 415-868-2412; www.2milesurf.com; 22 Brighton Ave; 9am-6pm May-Oct, 10am-5pm Nov-Apr, closed Wed Jan-Mar) Surfing's popular in these parts, and this shop behind the post office rents boards and wet suits and also gives lessons.

Agate Beach County Park BEACH
(www.marincounty.org; end of Elm Rd; dawn-dusk) Meander by tide pools along the coastline at Agate Beach, around the end of Duxbury Point. Collecting rocks, shells or marine life is prohibited.

Sleeping & Eating

Smiley's Saloon & Hotel INN $$
(415-868-1311; http://smileyssaloon.com; 41 Wharf Rd; r $135-225;) A crusty old place dating to 1851, Smiley's has simple but decent rooms (no TV or phone), and last-minute weekday rates can be a bargain. The bar, which serves some food, has live bands on weekends and is frequented by plenty of salty dogs and grizzled deadheads.

Coast Cafe AMERICAN $$
(415-868-2298; www.coastcafebolinas.com; 46 Wharf Rd; dinner mains $15-32; 11:30am-3pm & 5-8pm Tue-Thu, to 9pm Fri, 8am-3pm & 5-9pm Sat, to 8pm Sun;) The only 'real' restaurant in town. Everyone jockeys for outdoor seats among the flower boxes for fish-and-chips, barbecued oysters, or buttermilk pancakes with damn good coffee. Live music on Thursday and Sunday nights.

Getting There & Away

By car, follow Hwy 1 north from Stinson Beach and turn west for Bolinas at the first road north of the lagoon. At the first stop sign, take another left on to Olema–Bolinas Rd and follow it 2 miles to town.

West Marin Stagecoach (p111) route 61 travels a few times daily from the Marin City transit hub (more frequent weekend and holiday service connects with the Sausalito ferry) to downtown Bolinas ($2).

Olema & Nicasio

Near the junction of Hwy 1 and Sir Francis Drake Blvd, Olema was the main settlement in west Marin in the 1860s. Back then, there was stagecoach service to San Rafael and *six* saloons. In 1875, when the railroad was built through Point Reyes Station instead of Olema, the town's importance began to fade.

About a 15-minute drive inland from Olema, at the geographic center of Marin County, is Nicasio, a tiny town with a low-key rural flavor.

The **Bolinas Ridge Trail** (www.nps.gov/goga/planyourvisit/bolinas.htm), a 12-mile series of ups and downs for hikers or bikers, starts about 1 mile west of Olema, on Sir Francis Drake Blvd. It has great views.

In the former Olema Inn, a creaky 1876 building, hyper-local **Sir & Star** (415-663-

1034; www.sirandstar.com; 10000 Sir Francis Drake Blvd, Olema; mains $20, Sat prix-fixe menu $85; ⏲5-9pm Wed-Sun; 📶) restaurant delights with Marin-sourced seasonal bounty such as Tomales Bay oysters, Dungeness crab and duck 'faux' gras. Reservations recommended.

A few minutes away in Nicasio, check out the **Nicasio Valley Cheese Company** (☎415-662-6200; http://nicasiocheese.com; 5300 Nicasio Valley Rd; ⏲10am-5pm), where you can get free tastings at one of Marin County's renowned cheese-making shops. Crafted on a ranch started by a Swiss immigrant family, these wheels of soft cheeses – such as the award-winning Foggy Morning *fromage blanc* – appear on chef's menus and at farmers markets around the Bay Area.

You can get a dose of local flavor at the tiny town's music venue, **Rancho Nicasio** (☎415-662-2219; www.ranchonicasio.com; 1 Old Rancheria Rd, Nicasio; tickets free-$25; ⏲show schedules vary), a rustic saloon that regularly attracts local and national blues, rock and country performers.

Getting There & Away

Olema is about 13 miles northwest of Stinson Beach via Hwy 1. Nicasio is at the west end of Lucas Valley Rd, 10 miles from Hwy 101.

West Marin Stagecoach (p111) Route 68 runs several times daily to Olema from the San Rafael Transit Center, stopping at Samuel P Taylor State Park.

Point Reyes Station

Though the railroad stopped coming through in 1933 and the town is small, Point Reyes Station is nevertheless the hub of western Marin County. Dominated by dairies and ranches, the region was invaded by artists in the 1960s. Today Main St is a diverting blend of art galleries, tourist shops, restaurants and cafes. The town has a rowdy saloon and the occasional smell of cattle on the afternoon breeze.

Sleeping & Eating

Cute little cottages, cabins and B&Bs are plentiful in and around Point Reyes. The **West Marin Chamber of Commerce** (☎415-663-9232; www.pointreyes.org) and the Point Reyes Lodging Association (www.ptreyes.com) have additional listings.

Windsong Cottage Guest Yurt YURT **$$**
(☎415-663-9695; www.windsongcottage.com; 25 McDonald Lane; d $195-230; P ⊖ 📶) A wood-burning stove, private outdoor hot tub, comfy king bed and kitchen stocked with breakfast supplies make this round skylighted abode a slice of rural heaven.

Nick's Cove COTTAGE **$$$**
(☎415-663-1033; http://nickscove.com; 23240 Hwy 1, Marshall; cottages $250-850; P ⊖ 📶 🐾) Fronting a peaceful cove at Tomales Bay, these water-view and waterfront vacation cottages are expensive, but oh-so romantic. Some have wood-burning fireplace, deep soaking tub, private deck and plasma TV. Two-night minimum stay on weekends and holidays. It's about a 20-minute drive north of Point Reyes Station.

★ **Hog Island Oyster Company** SEAFOOD **$**
(☎415-663-9218; https://hogislandoysters.com; 20215 Hwy 1, Marshall; 12 oysters $13-16, picnic per person $5; ⏲shop 9am-5pm daily, picnic area from 10am, cafe 11am-5pm Fri-Mon) Ten miles north of Point Reyes Station you'll find the salty turnout for Hog Island Oyster Company. There's not much to see: just some picnic tables and BBQ grills, an outdoor cafe and a window selling the famously silky oysters and a few other provisions. A picnic at the farm is an unforgettable lunch – and popular, so make reservations (required).

Cowgirl Creamery at Tomales Bay Foods DELI **$**
(☎415-663-9335; www.cowgirlcreamery.com; 80 4th St; deli items $3-10; ⏲10am-6pm Wed-Sun; 🖋 👪) An indoor deli and marketplace in an old barn sells farm-fresh picnic items, including gourmet cheeses and organic produce. Reserve in advance for an artisanal cheese-maker's demonstration and tasting ($5); watch the curd-making and cutting; then sample a half-dozen fresh and aged cheeses. The milk is local and organic, with vegetarian rennet in soft cheeses.

Bovine Bakery BAKERY **$**
(☎415-663-9420; www.bovinebakeryptreyes.com; 11315 Hwy 1; most items $2-6; ⏲6:30am-5pm Mon-Fri, 7am-5pm Sat, 7am-4pm Sun; 🖋 👪) Don't leave town without sampling something buttery from this beloved country bakery. A sweet bear-claw pastry and organic coffee are a good way to kick off your morning.

Marshall Store SEAFOOD **$$**
(☎415-663-1339; www.themarshallstore.com; 19225 Hwy 1, Marshall; mains $11-20; ⏲10am-5pm Mon-Fri, to 6pm Sat & Sun, closes 1hr earlier Oct-Apr; 👪) Catapulted to fame by peripatetic chef and

TV host Anthony Bourdain, this ramshackle country store lets you slurp down BBQ oysters at tables as your legs practically dangle in Tomales Bay. Smoked seafood plates and sandwiches aren't half bad either. It's a 15-minute drive north of Point Reyes Station.

Getting There & Away

From Hwy 101 and San Rafael, it's about a 45-minute drive to Point Reyes Station. Driving the coast, it's less than 30 minutes from Bolinas. Hwy 1 becomes Main St in town, running right through the center.

West Marin Stagecoach (p111) route 68 runs to Point Reyes Station several times daily from the San Rafael Transit Center ($2, 75 minutes) via Bear Valley Visitor Center at Point Reyes National Seashore.

Inverness

The last outpost on your journey westward toward the tip of Point Reyes, this tiny town stretches out along the west side of Tomales Bay. Several great beaches are only a short drive away.

Activities

★Blue Waters Kayaking KAYAKING
(415-669-2600; www.bluewaterskayaking.com; 12944 Sir Francis Drake Blvd; rentals/tours from $60/68; usually 9am-5pm, last rental 2pm;) Long-running outfit guides tours of Tomales Bay, or you can rent a kayak and paddle to secluded beaches and rocky crevices on your own; no experience necessary. Book ahead for full-moon and bioluminescence excursions.

Sleeping

Dancing Coyote Beach Cottages COTTAGE $$$
(415-669-7200; www.dancingcoyotebeach.com; 12794 Sir Francis Drake Blvd; cottages $200-295;) Serene and comfortable, these four modern cottages back right on to Tomales Bay, with skylights and decks extending the views in all directions. Full kitchens contain locally sourced breakfast foods, and fireplaces are stocked with firewood for foggy nights.

Cottages at Point Reyes Seashore COTTAGE $$
(415-669-7250; www.cottagespointreyes.com; 13275 Sir Francis Drake Blvd; r $129-269;) Hidden in the woods, this family-friendly place offers contemporary kitchenette rooms in A-frame structures and a tennis court, hot tub, croquet, horseshoe pitches, barbecue grills and saltwater pool. There's also a large garden and private nature trail.

Getting There & Away

From Hwy 1, Sir Francis Drake Blvd heads northwest straight into Inverness. West Marin Stagecoach (p111) route 68 from San Rafael ($2) makes several daily runs here via Olema and Point Reyes Station.

Point Reyes National Seashore

Windswept Point Reyes peninsula is a rough-hewn beauty that has always lured marine mammals and migratory birds as well as scores of shipwrecks. It was here in 1579 that Sir Francis Drake landed to repair his ship, the *Golden Hind*. During his five-week stay he mounted a brass plaque near the shore claiming this land for England. In 1595 the first of scores of ships lost in these waters went down. The *San Augustine* was a Spanish treasure ship out of Manila, laden with luxury goods – to this day bits of its cargo still wash up on shore. Despite modern navigatiosan, the dangerous waters here continue to claim the odd boat.

Point Reyes National Seashore (Map p38; 415-654-5100; www.nps.gov/pore;) FREE protects 110 sq miles of pristine ocean beaches and coastal wilderness and has excellent hiking and camping opportunities. Be sure to bring warm clothing, as even the sunniest days can quickly turn cold and foggy.

Sights & Activities

For a curious view, follow the 0.6-mile **Earthquake Trail** from the picnic area opposite Bear Valley Visitor Center. The trail reaches a 16ft gap between the two halves of a once-connected fence line, a lasting testimonial to the power of the 1906 earthquake that was centered in this area. Another 0.8-mile trail leads from the visitor center around **Kule Loklo**, a reproduction of a Coast Miwok village.

Limantour Rd, off Bear Valley Rd about 1 mile north of Bear Valley Visitor Center, leads to **Limantour Beach**, where a 2-mile trail runs along Limantour Spit with Estero de Limantour on one side and Drakes

Bay on the other. The **Inverness Ridge Trail** heads from Limantour Rd for around 3 miles up to Mt Vision (1282ft), affording spectacular views of the entire national seashore. You can drive almost to the top of Mt Vision from the other side.

Northwest of the town of Inverness, Pierce Point Rd splits off to the right from Sir Francis Drake Blvd. The road lets you access two swimming beaches on Tomales Bay: seductively named **Heart's Desire**, in **Tomales Bay State Park** (☎415-669-1140; www.parks.ca.gov; 1100 Pierce Point Rd, Inverness; per car $8; ⏰8am-sunset; P 👪), is accessible by car, while **Marshall Beach** requires a 1.2-mile hike from the parking area at the end of the road.

Pierce Point Rd continues to the huge windswept sand dunes at **Abbotts Lagoon**, full of peeping killdeer and other shorebirds. At the end of the road is historical Pierce Point Ranch, the trailhead for the 9.4-mile round-trip **Tomales Point Trail** through the **Tule Elk Reserve**. The plentiful elk are an amazing sight, standing with their big horns against the backdrop of Tomales Point, with Bodega Bay to the north, Tomales Bay to the east and the Pacific Ocean to the west.

Point Reyes Lighthouse LIGHTHOUSE
(☎415-669-1534; www.nps.gov/pore; end of Sir Francis Drake Blvd; ⏰10am-4:30pm Fri-Mon, lens room 2:30-4pm Fri-Mon; P 👪) FREE With wild terrain and ferocious winds, this spot feels like the end of the earth and offers the best whale-watching along the coast. The lighthouse sits below the headlands; to reach it you need to descend more than 300 stairs.

Five Brooks Ranch HORSEBACK RIDING
(☎415-663-1570; www.fivebrooks.com; 8001 Shoreline Hwy, Olema; trail rides $40-180; 👪) Explore the Point Reyes landscape on horseback with a trail ride. Take a slow amble through a pasture or ascend Inverness Ridge for views of the Olema Valley. If you can stay in the saddle for six hours, ride along the coastline to Alamere Falls (p119) via Wildcat Beach.

Chimney Rock HIKING
(www.nps.gov/pore; off Sir Francis Drake Blvd) Not far from the lighthouse, Chimney Rock is a fine short hike, especially in spring when wildflowers are blossoming. During winter, a viewing area allows you to spy on an elephant-seal colony hauled out below the cliffs.

Sleeping

Wake up to deer nibbling under a blanket of fog at one of Point Reyes' very popular **backcountry campgrounds** (☎reservations 877-444-6777; www.recreation.gov; tent sites $20), or stay at the pastoral youth hostel. More inns, motels and B&Bs are found in nearby Inverness, off Sir Francis Drake Blvd.

HI Point Reyes HOSTEL $
(☎415-663-8811; www.norcalhostels.org/reyes; 1390 Limantour Spit Rd; r with shared bath $105-130, dm $29-38; ⏰reception 7:30-10:30am & 4:30-10pm; P 🚭 @) Just off Limantour Rd, this rustic hostel has bunkhouses with warm and cozy front rooms, big-view windows and outdoor areas with hill vistas. A newer building with Leadership in Energy and Environmental Design (LEED) certification has four private rooms (two-night minimum stay on weekends) and a modern kitchen. It's in a beautiful secluded valley 2 miles from the ocean and surrounded by lovely hiking trails.

Information

At park headquarters, a mile west of Olema, **Bear Valley Visitor Center** (☎415-464-5100; www.nps.gov/pore; 1 Bear Valley Rd, Point Reyes Station; ⏰10am-5pm Mon-Fri, 9am-5pm Sat & Sun; 👪) has information and maps. You can also get information at the Point Reyes Lighthouse and the **Kenneth Patrick Center** (☎415-669-1250; www.nps.gov/pore; 1 Drakes Beach Rd; ⏰9:30am-4:30pm Sat, Sun & holidays late Dec-late Mar or early Apr) at Drakes Beach.

Getting There & Away

By car you can get to Point Reyes a few different ways. The curviest is along Hwy 1, through Stinson Beach and Olema. More direct is to exit Hwy 101 in San Rafael and follow Sir Francis Drake Blvd all the way to the tip of Point Reyes. By either route, it's less than 1½ hours to Olema from San Francisco barring weekend and rush-hour traffic jams.

Just north of Olema, where Hwy 1 and Sir Francis Drake Blvd come together, is Bear Valley Rd; turn left to reach Bear Valley Visitor Center. If you're heading to the outermost reaches of Point Reyes, follow Sir Francis Drake Blvd north toward Point Reyes Station, turning left and heading out on to the peninsula (at least a 45-minute drive).

West Marin Stagecoach (p111) route 68 from San Rafael stops several times daily at the Bear Valley Visitor Center ($2, 70 minutes) before continuing to the town of Point Reyes Station.

EAST BAY

Berkeley and Oakland are what most San Franciscans think of as the East Bay, though the area includes numerous other suburbs that swoop up from the bayside flats into exclusive enclaves in the hills. Many residents of the 'West Bay' would like to think they needn't ever cross the Bay Bridge or take a Bay Area Rapid Transit (BART) train through an underwater tunnel. But a wealth of museums and historical sites, a world-famous university, excellent restaurants and bars, a creative arts scene, offbeat shopping, woodsy parks and better weather are just some of the attractions that lure travelers from San Francisco over to the sunny side of the Bay.

Oakland

Named for the grand oak trees that once lined its streets, Oakland is to San Francisco what Brooklyn is to Manhattan. To some degree a less expensive alternative to 'the city' across the Bay, this is often where people have moved to escape skyrocketing San Francisco housing costs. An ethnically diverse city, Oakland has a strong African American community and a long labor-union history. Urban farmers raise chickens in their backyard or occupy abandoned lots to start community gardens; families find more room to stretch out; and self-satisfied residents thumb their noses at San Francisco's fog while basking in sunny weather. For visitors, the city offers a handful of diverting museums and historical sites, a vibrant arts scene, innovative restaurants and bars, vintage and boutique shops, and outdoor recreation galore – down by the waterfront, around Lake Merritt and up in the forested hills.

Sights & Activities

Oakland is full of historic buildings and a growing number of colorful businesses. With such easy access from San Francisco via BART or ferry, it's worth spending part of a day exploring here on foot or by bicycle.

Downtown, Chinatown & Waterfront

Pedestrianized **City Center**, between Broadway and Clay St, 12th and 14th Sts, forms the heart of downtown Oakland. Nearby **City Hall** (Map p124; ☎510-444-2489; www.oaklandnet.com; Frank H Ogawa Plaza; ⏰9am-6pm Mon-Fri; Ⓑ12th St Oakland City Center) is a beautifully refurbished 1914 beaux-arts building.

Old Oakland, west of Broadway between 8th and 10th Sts, is lined with restored historic buildings dating from the late 19th century. The area has a lively restaurant and after-work scene, and a farmers market every Friday from 8am until 2pm.

East of Broadway and bustling with commerce, Oakland's Chinatown centers on Franklin and Webster Sts, as it has since the 1850s. Jack London Sq is on the waterfront further south.

Oakland Museum of California MUSEUM
(OMCA; Map p124; ☎510-318-8400; http://museumca.org; 1000 Oak St; adult/child $16/7, 1st Sun each month free; ⏰11am-5pm Wed-Thu, to 9pm Fri, 10am-6pm Sat & Sun; Ⓟ🚻; ⒷLake Merritt) Near the southern end of Lake Merritt, this museum has rotating exhibitions on artistic and scientific themes, and permanent galleries dedicated to the state's diverse ecology and history, as well as California art. Admission is steeply discounted on Friday nights (after 5pm), when DJs, food trucks and free art workshops for kids make it a fun hangout.

Uptown & Lake Merritt

North of downtown Oakland, the Uptown district contains many of the city's art-deco beauties, such as the Fox Theater (p129) and Paramount Theatre (p130), and a proliferating arts, restaurant and nightlife scene. The area stretches roughly between Telegraph and Broadway, bounded by Grand Ave to the north.

Follow Grand Ave east of Broadway and you'll run into the shores of Lake Merritt. Grand Ave (north of the lake) and Lakeshore Ave (east of the lake) are pedestrian-friendly streets for local shops, restaurants, cafes and bars.

Lake Merritt LAKE
(Map p124; ☎510-238-7275; www.oaklandnet.com; Ⓟ🚻; ⒷLake Merritt) 🍃 An urban respite, Lake Merritt is a popular place to stroll or go running (a 3.5-mile paved path circles the lake), with bonsai and botanical gardens, a children's amusement park (p125), bird sanctuary, **boathouse** (Map p124; ☎510-238-2196; www.oaklandnet.com; 568 Bellevue Ave; boat rentals per hour $12-24, cash only; ⏰daily Mar-Oct, Sat & Sun only Nov-Feb; 🚻; 🚌AC Transit 12) and **gondola rides** (Map p124; ☎510-663-6603;

Central Oakland

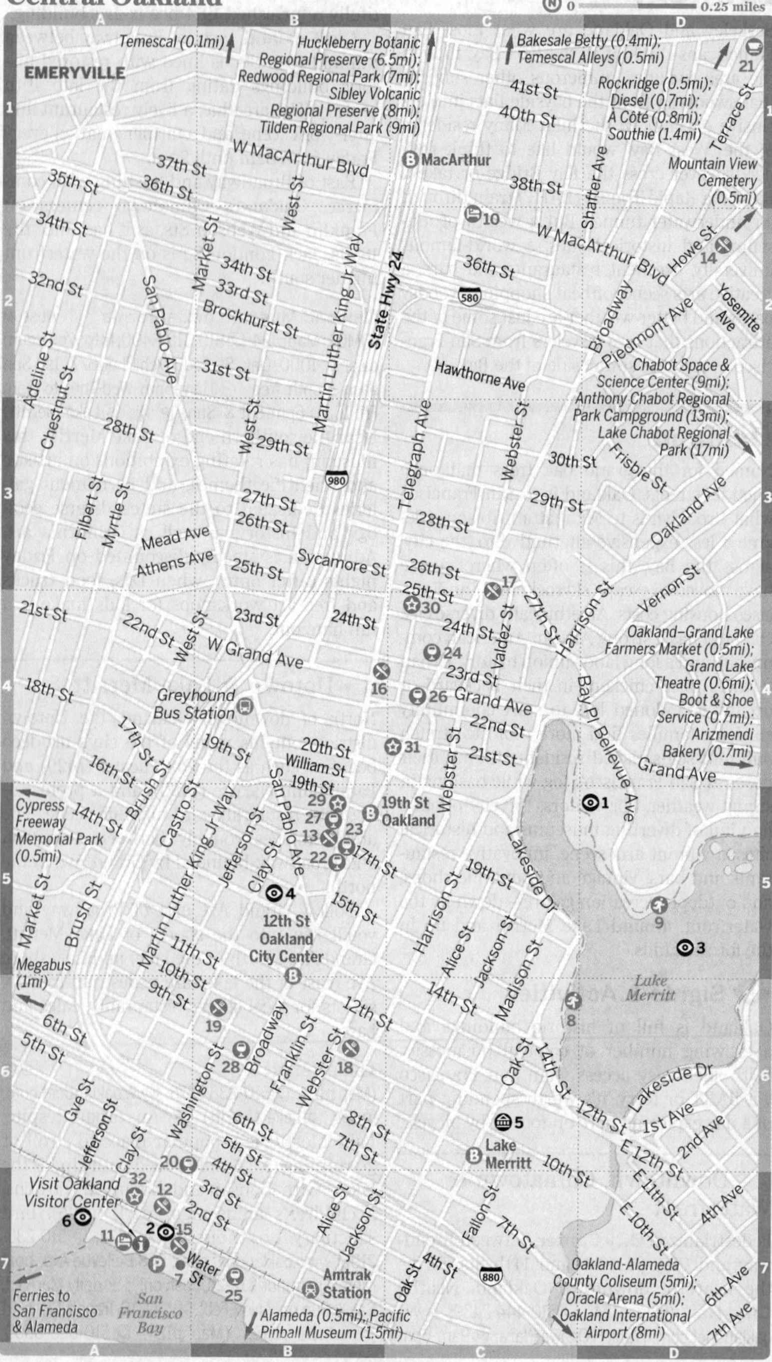

Central Oakland

Sights

1 Children's Fairyland D5
2 Jack London Square A7
3 Lake Merritt D5
4 Oakland City Hall B5
5 Oakland Museum of California C6
6 USS Potomac A7

Activities, Courses & Tours

7 California Canoe & Kayak A7
8 Gondola Servizio C6
9 Lake Merritt Boating Center D5

Sleeping

10 Inn at Temescal C2
11 Waterfront Hotel A7

Eating

12 Authentic Bagel Co A7
13 Camber Uptown B5
14 Commis D2
15 Jack London Square Farmers Market A7
16 Kingston 11 .... B4
17 Mua C3
18 Shandong Restaurant B6
19 Swan's Market B6

Drinking & Nightlife

20 Beer Revolution A6
21 Blue Bottle Coffee Company D1
22 Café Van Kleef B5
23 Dogwood B5
24 Drake's Dealership C4
25 Heinold's First & Last Chance Saloon B7
26 Luka's Taproom & Lounge C4
27 Make Westing B5
28 Trappist B6

Entertainment

29 Fox Theater B5
30 New Parkway Theater C4
31 Paramount Theatre C4
32 Yoshi's A7

http://gondolaservizio.com; 1520 Lakeside Dr; 30/50min cruise $60/85; B Lake Merritt). The two main commercial streets skirting Lake Merritt are Grand Ave, running along the north shore, and Lakeshore Ave on the eastern edge of the lake.

Children's Fairyland AMUSEMENT PARK
(Map p124; 510-452-2259; http://fairyland.org; 699 Bellevue Ave; $10, child under 1yr free; 10am-4pm Mon-Fri, to 5pm Sat & Sun Jun-Aug, off-season hours vary; P; AC Transit 12) Lakeside Park, on the northern side of Lake Merritt, includes this 10-acre kiddie attraction, which dates from 1950 and has a charming fairy-tale-themed train, carousel and mini Ferris wheel.

Jack London Square

Jack London Square SQUARE
(Map p124; 510-645-9292; www.jacklondonsquare.com; Broadway & Embarcadero; 24hr, shop, restaurant & bar hours vary; P; Broadway Shuttle) The area where writer and adventurer Jack London once raised hell now bears his name. The pretty waterfront location is worth a stroll, especially when the Sunday **farmers market** (Map p124; 415-291-3276; www.cuesa.org; Jack London Sq; 10am-3pm Sun;) takes over, or get off your feet and kayak around the harbor. Contemporary redevelopment has added a cinema complex, condo development and popular restaurants and bars. A replica of Jack London's Yukon **cabin** stands at the eastern end of the square. Oddly, people throw coins inside as if it's a fountain.

Another interesting historical stop, adjacent to the tiny cabin, is Heinold's First & Last Chance Saloon (p129). Catch a ferry from San Francisco – a worthwhile excursion in itself – and you'll land just paces away.

USS Potomac SHIP
(Map p124; 510-627-1215; www.usspotomac.org; 540 Water St; adult/child $10/free; tours 11am-2:30pm Wed, Fri & Sun; Broadway Shuttle) Franklin D Roosevelt's 'floating White House,' the 165ft USS *Potomac*, is moored at Clay and Water Sts by the ferry dock, and is open for dockside tours. Two-hour cruises (adult/child $55/35) are scheduled several times a month from April through November (book far ahead).

Piedmont Ave, Temescal & Rockridge

North of downtown Oakland, Broadway becomes a lengthy strip of car dealerships called Auto Row. Detour a couple of blocks east to Piedmont Ave, wall-to-wall with vintage-clothing stores, coffeehouses, restaurants and an art-house cinema.

A half-dozen or so long blocks west of Broadway, Temescal wins the prize for being Oakland's artiest, hippest neighborhood.

Find unique shops, creative restaurants and happening bars on Telegraph Ave north of 40th St.

Rockridge, a lively, upscale neighborhood, is further north between Broadway and Telegraph Ave. College Ave is lined with upscale boutiques, a bookstore, pubs and cafes and quite a few fancy restaurants.

Mountain View Cemetery CEMETERY
(510-658-2588; www.mountainviewcemetery.org; 5000 Piedmont Ave; 6:30am-7:30pm; P; AC Transit 12) At the northern end of Piedmont Ave, this is perhaps the most serene and lovely artificial landscape in the East Bay. Designed by Frederick Law Olmstead (the landscape architect of New York City's Central Park), it's great for walking and the views are stupendous.

Oakland Hills

The large parks of the Oakland Hills are ideal for day hiking and challenging cycling, and the **East Bay Regional Parks** (888-327-2757; www.ebparks.org; per car free-$6; hours vary;) manages more than 1200 miles of trails in 65 regional parks, preserves and recreation areas in the Alameda and Contra Costa Counties.

Off Hwy 24, **Robert Sibley Volcanic Regional Preserve** is the northernmost of the Oakland Hills parks. It has great views of the Bay Area from its **Round Top Peak** (1761ft). From Sibley, Skyline Blvd runs south past **Redwood Regional Park** and adjacent **Joaquin Miller Park** to **Anthony Chabot Regional Park**. A hike or mountain-bike ride through the groves and along the hilltops of any of these sizable parks will make you forget you're in an urban area. At the southern end of Chabot Park is the enormous **Lake Chabot**, with an easy trail along its shore, and canoes, kayaks and other boats for rent from the **Lake Chabot Marina** (510-247-2526; www.lakechabotrecreation.com; 17936 Lake Chabot Rd, Castro Valley; rentals/tours from $23/45; 6am-6pm Mon-Thu, to 7pm Fri-Sun May-early Sep, off-season hours vary;).

★ **Chabot Space & Science Center** MUSEUM
(510-336-7300; www.chabotspace.org; 10000 Skyline Blvd; adult/child $18/14; 10am-5pm Wed-Sun, also Tue Jun-Aug; P; AC Transit 339) Stargazers will go gaga over this kid-oriented science and technology center in the Oakland Hills with loads of exhibits on subjects such as space travel and eclipses, as well as cool planetarium shows. When the weather's good, check out the free Friday and Saturday evening viewings (7:30pm to 10:30pm) using a 20in refractor telescope.

Admission is just $5 on the first Friday evening of each month (6pm to 10pm), when the museum organizes hands-on activities, science demonstrations, movies and night hikes.

Festivals & Events

Oakland First Fridays STREET CARNIVAL
(510-361-0615; http://oaklandfirstfridays.org; Telegraph Ave; entry by donation; 5-9:30pm 1st Fri each month; ; B 19th St Oakland) A kinetic street festival takes place on the first Friday of the month, when a five-block stretch of Telegraph Ave closes to car traffic. Thousands of people turn out for food vendors, live music and performances.

Sleeping

Oakland has surprisingly few places to stay, apart from chain motels and hotels off the freeways, downtown and near the airport.

Anthony Chabot Regional Park CAMPGROUND $
(reservations 888-327-2757; www.reserveamerica.com; end of Marciel Rd, Castro Valley; tent sites $25, RV sites with hookups $25-35; P) In the East Bay's forested hills, this 5000-acre park has 75 campsites open year-round and hot showers.

Inn at Temescal MOTEL $$
(Map p124; 510-652-9800; www.innattemescal.com; 3720 Telegraph Ave; r from $129; P; B MacArthur) Though the location isn't lovely, it's a short walk to BART or Temescal's main strip. Recently renovated, the motel has exterior doors painted in avocado green and sunset orange. Clean-lined rooms come with pillow-top mattresses, wall-sized historic photos and retro accents. Expect some street noise.

Waterfront Hotel BOUTIQUE HOTEL $$$
(Map p124; 510-836-3800; www.waterfronthoteloakland.com; 10 Washington St; r from $299; P@) Paddle-printed wallpaper and lamps fashioned from faux lanterns round out the playful nautical theme of this cheerful harborside hotel. A huge brass-topped fireplace warms the foyer, and comfy rooms include iPod docking stations and coffeemakers. Unless you're an avid

train-spotter, water-view rooms are preferred, as trains rattle by on the city side. Complimentary wine-and-cheese reception on weekdays. Parking is $30.

Eating

Oakland's diverse eateries nearly rival those of foodie neighbor San Francisco. Take your pick of sophisticated restaurants run by top Bay Area chefs, neighborhood cafes, international kitchens or pop-up food trucks. Downtown, Old Oakland and Chinatown abound with budget-friendly local favorites. Uptown, Temescal and Rockridge attract culinary trend-spotters. West Oakland does soul food, while East Oakland has authentic taquerias.

Uptown, Downtown & Jack London Square

Swan's Market FOOD HALL $

(Map p124; 510-287-5353; http://swansmarket.com; 510 9th St; most mains $8-15; 9am-10pm Mon-Sat; ; 12th St Oakland City Center) Old Oakland's 100-year-old marketplace has been given new life with a gourmet food court, where the wooden tables are always full, day and night. Stop at Cosecha for Mexican fare, AS B-Dama for udon noodles and Japanese fried chicken, Delage sushi bar, the Cook & Her Farmer oyster bar and cafe, Rosamunde Sausage Grill or Miss Ollie's for Caribbean food.

Shandong Restaurant CHINESE $

(Map p124; 510-839-2299; http://shandongoakland.com; 328 10th St; mains $7-13; 11am-3pm & 4-9pm Sun-Thu, to 9:30pm Fri & Sat; ; 12th St Oakland City Center) Not everything tastes so amazing at this crowded, family-friendly Chinatown restaurant, but that's OK because you're only here for two things: handmade sesame noodles and from-scratch pork dumplings. Expect a wait for a table.

Authentic Bagel Co BAKERY, DELI $

(Map p124; 510-459-1201; www.abagelcompany.com; 463 2nd St; sandwiches $3-10; 7am-3pm;) Once upon a time two Jewish guys from Rhode Island set up shop near Jack London Sq. Today they make the Bay Area's best East Coast–style bagels while blasting Beastie Boys albums. Chow down on a 'Lox Monsta' (pumpernickel bagel with bacon, lox, avocado and cilantro curry) at sunny sidewalk tables.

Kingston 11 CARIBBEAN $$

(Map p124; 510-465-2558; http://kingston11eats.com; 2270 Telegraph Ave; mains $13-20; 11am-2pm & 5-10pm Tue-Fri, 5-10pm Sat, 11am-4pm Sun; ; 19th St Oakland) The wait will be worth it at this raucous Caribbean bar with a groovy soundtrack, where oxtail stew, salt-fish fritters, fried plantains and goat curry are succulent delights. Swing by for 'Irie Hour' (5pm to 7pm Tuesday through Friday) to sip out-of-this-world cocktails such as the Rise Up (cold-brew coffee, coconut milk, spiced rum and Angostura bitters). Reservations recommended.

Mua CALIFORNIAN $$

(Map p124; 510-238-1100; https://muaoakland.com; 2442a Webster St; shared plates $7-15, mains $21-35; 5:30-11pm Mon-Thu, to midnight Fri & Sat, 5-10pm Sun; ; 19th St Oakland) A warehouse-sized space in Uptown, this social gathering spot is just as good for date night as it is for groups getting ready for a night out. Peruse the long, long menu of creative shared plates like quinoa-arugula salad with nectarines and goat's cheese or beef bone-marrow toast, with a 'Stormy Oaktown' cocktail or rosemary martini in hand. Reservations recommended.

Camber Uptown THAI, LAOTIAN $$

(Map p124; 510-663-4560; http://camberoakland.com; 1707 Telegraph Ave; mains $10-20; 11:30am-2:30pm & 5-9:30pm Mon-Thu, 11:30am-11:30pm Fri, 5-11:30pm Sat; ; 19th St Oakland) While you might find cheaper and more authentic Southeast Asian kitchens in Oakland's Chinatown, Camber can't be beaten for proximity to Uptown nightlife. Fusion dishes such as the 'bouncing beef' stir-fry and garlic-basil fish with sliced jalapeño peppers are popular with the young crowd sidling up to the bar.

Piedmont Ave, Temescal & Rockridge

★ **Commis** CALIFORNIAN $$$

(Map p124; 510-653-3902; http://commisrestaurant.com; 3859 Piedmont Ave; 8-course dinner $149, with wine & beer pairings $229; 5:30-9:30pm Wed-Sat, 5-9pm Sun; AC Transit 51A) The East Bay's only Michelin-starred restaurant, the signless and discreet dining room counts a minimalist decor and some coveted counter real estate where patrons can watch chef James Syhabout and his team piece together creative and innovative dishes,

SUMMONING ALL PINBALL WIZARDS

Put down that video-game console, cast aside your latest phone app, and return to the bygone days of pinball play. Lose yourself in bells and flashing lights at **Pacific Pinball Museum** (☎510-769-1349; http://pacificpinball.org; 1510 Webster St, Alameda; all-day pass adult/child $20/10; ⏰11am-9pm Tue-Thu & Sun, to 10pm Fri & Sat; 👪; 🚌AC Transit 51A), a pinball parlor with almost 100 games dating from the 1930s to the present, and vintage jukeboxes playing hits from the past. Take AC Transit bus 51A from downtown Oakland.

maybe Monterey Bay abalone, soy-milk custard with chanterelles or a perfectly ripe peach topped with oats, beeswax creme and marigolds. Reservations essential.

Bakesale Betty SANDWICHES, BAKERY **$**
(☎510-985-1213; www.bakesalebetty.com; 5098 Telegraph Ave; sandwiches $9; ⏰11am-2pm Tue-Sat; 🚌AC Transit 6) Aussie expat Alison Barakat has patrons licking their lips and lining up out the door and down the block for heavenly strawberry shortcake and scrumptious fried-chicken sandwiches. Rolling pins dangle from the ceiling and blissed-out locals sit down at ironing-board sidewalk tables.

Southie SANDWICHES **$**
(☎510-654-0100; http://southieoakland.com; 6311 College Ave; mains $9-18; ⏰9am-9pm Mon-Sat, to 3pm Sun; Ⓑ Rockridge) Wood Tavern's side venture steals the show with its gobstopping meatball and pork-belly sandwiches. This busy storefront eatery has only a few tightly squeezed-together tables, with a half-dozen wines and craft beers on tap. Finish off with passion-fruit–buttermilk *panna cotta* or a brownie ice-cream sandwich.

Lake Merritt

★Oakland–Grand Lake Farmers Market MARKET **$**
(☎415-472-6100; https://agriculturalinstitute.org; Lake Park Ave, at Grand Ave; ⏰9am-2pm Sat; 🖉👪; 🚌AC Transit 12) 🍃 A rival to San Francisco's Ferry Plaza Farmers Market, this bountiful weekly market hauls in bushels of fresh fruit, vegetables, seafood, ranched meats, artisanal cheese and baked goods from as far away as Marin County and the Central Valley. The northern side of the market is cheek-to-jowl with food trucks and hot-food vendors – don't skip the dim-sum tent.

Arizmendi Bakery BAKERY **$**
(☎510-268-8849; http://arizmendilakeshore.com; 3265 Lakeshore Ave; pizza slices $2.50; ⏰7am-8pm Tue-Sun; 🖉; 🚌AC Transit 12) 🍃 Great for breakfast or lunch but beware: this bakery co-op is not for the weak-willed. Gourmet vegetarian pizza, chewy breads and gigantic scones, all baked fresh, are addictive.

Boot & Shoe Service PIZZA **$$**
(☎510-763-2668; www.bootandshoeservice.com; 3308 Grand Ave; pizzas $14-22; ⏰7am-noon & 5:30-10pm Tue-Thu, 7am-noon & 5-10:30pm Fri,10am-2pm & 5-10:30pm Sat, 10am-2pm & 5-10pm Sun; 🖉; 🚌AC Transit 12) 🍃 The name plays off its former identity as a cobbler's shop, but the current patrons pack this brick-walled place for its wood-fired pizzas, original cocktails and creative antipasti made from sustainably sourced fresh ingredients.

Camino CALIFORNIAN **$$$**
(☎510-547-5035; www.caminorestaurant.com; 3917 Grand Ave; dinner mains $32-42; ⏰5:30-9:30pm Mon, Wed & Thu, to 10pm Fri, 10am-2pm & 5:30-10pm Sat, to 9:30pm Sun; 🖉; 🚌AC Transit 12) 🍃 From the culinary imagination of chef Russell Moore (a Chez Panisse alum), Camino's short daily-changing menu showcases the best of local organic produce and meats, most cooked over an open fire in slow-food-meets-California-now style. The tables are of recycled old-growth redwood and the place buzzes with bon vivants buzzed on craft cocktails and European and California wines. Reservations essential.

🍷 Drinking & Nightlife

Oakland's busiest and hippest bars are in the Uptown district, just north of downtown and a short stumble from BART. You'll find eclectic watering holes near Jack London Sq and in Old Oakland. Students hang out in Rockridge, while a mix of locals gravitate to bars around Lake Merritt, along Piedmont Ave and on Temescal's main drag.

★Blue Bottle Coffee Company CAFE
(Map p124; ☎510-653-3394; http://bluebottlecoffee.com; 4270 Broadway; ⏰7am-6pm; 🚌AC Transit 51A) 🍃 Blue Bottle's roomier cafe is inside the beautiful WC Morse Building, a 1920s truck showroom. Communal tables, lofty ceilings and minimalist white decor in-

vite sipping a Gibraltar – similar to a cortado (espresso with a dash of milk), but made with more milk – or a cold-brew iced coffee.

Drake's Dealership BEER GARDEN

(Map p124; ☎510-568-2739; http://drinkdrakes.com/visit/dealership; 2325 Broadway; ⊙11:30am-11pm Sun-Wed, to 1am Thu-Sat; ; B19th St Oakland) East Bay craft brewer Drake's Brewing Company has transformed a humdrum Dodge dealership into a lively restaurant, bar and outdoor beer garden with fire pits that crackle on foggy nights. Order a pint of Black Robusto porter or Hopocalypse double IPA with a wood-oven-fired pizza. DJs spin Thursday to Saturday. Book ahead online for complimentary tours of the actual brewery, a short bus ride from San Leandro BART station.

Dogwood COCKTAIL BAR

(Map p124; ☎510-444-6669; www.bardogwood.com; 1644 Telegraph Ave; ⊙4pm-2am; B19th St Oakland) A hip, tattooed young crowd hobnobs inside this red-brick-walled bar on a busy corner of Uptown. Order a creative house cocktail or classic concoction such as the Brooklyn from mixologists behind the bar. Simple sandwiches and meat-and-cheese plates keep stomachs from growling.

Make Westing COCKTAIL BAR

(Map p124; ☎510-251-1400; www.makewesting.com; 1741 Telegraph Ave; ⊙4pm-2am; B19th St Oakland) On weekends, people pack this Uptown hot spot, named for a Jack London short story, for its indoor bocce courts and eclectic cocktails. Toss back a 'Garden Gimlet' (gin, cucumber, basil and lime) and satiate the munchies with cilantro-and-habañero-infused popcorn or a mason jar of homemade pickled beets.

Trappist PUB

(Map p124; ☎510-238-8900; www.thetrappist.com; 460 8th St; ⊙noon-12:30am Sun-Thu, to 1:30am Fri & Sat; B Oakland 12th St City Center) Busting out of its original brick-and-wood-paneled shoe box into a second storefront and outdoor back patio, this place specialises in Belgian ales. Two dozen drafts rotate through the taps, and tasty charcuterie and cheese boards, salads and grilled cheese sandwiches make it easy to linger.

Heinold's First & Last Chance Saloon BAR

(Map p124; ☎510-839-6761; www.heinoldsfirstandlastchance.com; 48 Webster St; ⊙noon-11pm Sun-Thu, to 1am Fri & Sat; Broadway Shuttle) At this 1883 bar constructed from wood scavenged from an old whaling ship, you really have to hold on to your beer. Keeled to a severe slant during the 1906 earthquake, the building's tilt might make you feel self-conscious about stumbling before you even order. Its big claim to fame is that adventure writer Jack London was a regular patron.

Café Van Kleef BAR

(Map p124; ☎510-763-7711; http://cafevankleef.com; 1621 Telegraph Ave; ⊙4pm-2am Mon, from noon Tue-Fri, from 6pm Sat, from 7pm Sun; B19th St Oakland) Order a greyhound (with freshly squeezed grapefruit juice) and take a gander at the profusion of antique musical instruments, fake taxidermy heads, sprawling formal chandeliers and bizarro ephemera clinging to every surface possible. Quirky even *before* you get lit, it features live blues, jazz and the occasional rock band on weekends.

Luka's Taproom & Lounge LOUNGE

(Map p124; ☎510-451-4677; www.lukasoakland.com; 2221 Broadway; ⊙5:30-11pm Sun-Wed, to 1am Thu, to 2am Fri & Sat; B19th St Oakland) Go Uptown to get down. At this long-running restaurant and lounge, DJs spin a soulful mix of hip-hop, R&B and Latin grooves Thursday to Sunday nights (cover charge $5 to $10).

Beer Revolution BAR

(Map p124; http://beer-revolution.com; 464 3rd St; ⊙noon-11pm Sun-Thu, to midnight Fri & Sat; Broadway Shuttle) With 50 beers on tap and hundreds more in bottles, there's a lifetime of discovery ahead, so kick back on the sunny deck or park yourself at that barrel table embedded with bottle caps. Bonuses include a punk-rock soundtrack played at conversation-friendly levels.

☆ Entertainment

Professional sports teams play at Oakland–Alameda County Coliseum and Oracle Arena off I-880 including Golden State Warriors (p130) (NBA basketball; moving to San Francisco in 2019), Oakland Raiders (p130) (NFL football; headed to Las Vegas in 2020) or Oakland A's (p130) (American League baseball; not leaving, phew). See www.coliseum.com for upcoming concerts and events. Most of Oakland's smaller live-music and performing-arts venues are Uptown.

★Fox Theater THEATER

(Map p124; ☎510-302-2250, tickets 800-745-3000; http://thefoxoakland.com; 1807 Telegraph

Ave; tickets from $35; ⏲hours vary; B 19th St Oakland) A phoenix arisen from the urban ashes, this restored 1928 art-deco stunner adds dazzle and neon lights to Telegraph Ave, where it's a cornerstone of the happening Uptown theater and nightlife district. Once a movie house, it's now a popular concert venue for edgy and independent Californian, national and international music acts. Buy tickets early, since many shows sell out.

★ **Golden State Warriors** BASKETBALL

(☎ tickets 888-479-4667; www.nba.com/warriors; 7000 Coliseum Way; tickets from $55; ⏲Oct-Apr; ; B Coliseum) If it's hoops you must have, then it's the Warriors for you. Originally from Philadelphia, this team moved across the bay from San Francisco in 1971. Today they play at Oracle Arena (next to the Coliseum). The Warriors caused quite a commotion when they won the National Basketball Association (NBA) championship playoffs in 2015. Alas, they're moving back to San Francisco in 2019.

Paramount Theatre THEATER, CINEMA

(Map p124; ☎510-465-6400; www.paramounttheatre.com; 2025 Broadway; movie/concert tickets from $7/25; ⏲hours vary; 19th St Oakland) This massive 1931 art-deco masterpiece shows classic films a few times each month and is also home to the Oakland Symphony (www.oaklandsymphony.org) and Oakland Ballet (http://oaklandballet.org). It periodically books big-name concerts and screens classic flicks. Guided tours ($5) are given at 10am on the first and third Saturdays of the month (no reservations).

Yoshi's JAZZ

(Map p124; ☎510-238-9200; www.yoshis.com; 510 Embarcadero W; from $20; ⏲hours vary; Broadway Shuttle) Yoshi's has a solid jazz calendar, with talent from around the world passing through on a near-nightly basis. It's also a Japanese restaurant, so if you enjoy a sushi dinner before the show, you'll be rewarded with reserved cabaret-style seating. Otherwise, resign yourself to limited high-top tables squeezed along the back walls of this intimate club.

Grand Lake Theatre CINEMA

(☎510-452-3556; www.renaissancerialto.com; 3200 Grand Ave; tickets $5-12.50; ⏲hours vary; ; AC Transit 12) Once a vaudeville theater and silent-movie house, this 1926 beauty near Lake Merritt lures you in with its huge corner marquee (which sometimes displays left-leaning political messages) and keeps you coming with a fun balcony and a Wurlitzer organ playing on weekends.

New Parkway Theater CINEMA

(Map p124; ☎510-658-7900; www.thenewparkway.com; 474 24th St; tickets $5-10; ⏲hours vary; AC Transit 6) This laid-back movie house, pub and community-events space shows second-run and throwback indie films. Reasonably priced beer, wine, sandwiches and pizza are delivered to your couch seat.

Oakland A's BASEBALL

(☎510-568-5600, tickets 877-493-2255; http://oakland.athletics.mlb.com; 7000 Coliseum Way; tickets from $15; ⏲Apr-Sep; ; B Coliseum) When the San Francisco Giants are away, the Oakland A's are usually home, which expands the possibilities for those desperate for a summer baseball fix. The A's most recent World Series pennant came at the Giants' expense in the quake-addled 1989 series, and they remain contenders. If you want to catch them in interleague play, get tickets early.

Oakland Raiders FOOTBALL

(☎510-864-5022, tickets 800-724-3377; www.raiders.com; 7000 Coliseum Way; tickets from $40; ⏲Sep-Jan; B Coliseum) With three Super Bowl championships, the notorious bad boys of the National Footbal League (NFL) have had ups and downs over the years, but they still have the staunchest, rowdiest fans in the western US. The team ungratefully moved to Los Angeles for 12 years, but returned in 1995 to Oakland's open arms. They're leaving again for Las Vegas in 2020.

ℹ Information

MEDIA

Oakland's daily newspaper is the *Oakland Tribune* (www.insidebayarea.com/oaklandtribune). The free weekly *East Bay Express* (www.eastbayexpress.com) has good Oakland and Berkeley listings.

TOURIST INFORMATION

Visit Oakland Visitor Center (Map p124; ☎510-839-9000; www.visitoakland.com; 481 Water St; ⏲9am-5pm Mon-Fri, 10am-4pm Sat & Sun) At Jack London Sq.

ℹ Getting There & Away

AIR

Oakland International Airport is less crowded and sometimes cheaper to fly into than San Francisco International Airport (SFO) across the bay. OAK airport is connected to Oakland, Berkeley and San Francisco by frequent BART trains.

BART

Within the Bay Area, the most convenient way to get to Oakland and back is by BART (Bay Area Rapid Transit; www.bart.gov). Trains run on a set schedule approximately every 10 to 20 minutes from around 4:30am to midnight on weekdays, 6am to midnight on Saturday and 8am to midnight on Sunday.

Downtown BART stations are on Broadway at 12th and 19th Sts; other Oakland stations are on the south side of Lake Merritt, close to Chinatown; near Temescal (MacArthur station) and in Rockridge.

To get to downtown Oakland, catch a Richmond or Pittsburg/Bay Point train. The fare to Oakland's 12th or 19th St stations from any BART station in downtown San Francisco is $3.45. Rockridge is on the Pittsburg/Bay Point line, while all Berkeley stops are on the Richmond line. To Lake Merritt or the Coliseum (for connections to Oakland's airport), catch a BART train heading toward Fremont or Dublin/Pleasanton.

BUS

AC Transit (☎510-891-4777; www.actransit.org) runs convenient buses from San Francisco's Transbay Transit Center to downtown Oakland ($4.20, or $2.10 with purchase of $5 day pass valid on local East Bay buses). Scores of Transbay buses run during commute hours, but only the 'O' line runs both ways all day and on weekends.

After BART trains stop, late-night transportation between downtown San Francisco and downtown Oakland is with the AC Transit bus 800 line ($4.20), which runs hourly on weekdays and every 20 minutes on weekends.

Between downtown Berkeley and downtown Oakland, take fast and frequent AC Transit bus 6 along Telegraph Ave. Alternatively, take AC Transit bus 18 via Martin Luther King Jr Way and Shattuck Ave. The one way local bus fare for either is $2.10.

Greyhound (p527) operates direct buses from Oakland, including to Vallejo, San Jose, Santa Rosa, Sacramento and Los Angeles; its **bus station** (Map p124; ☎510-832-4730; 2103 San Pablo Ave; Ⓑ19th St Oakland) in downtown Oakland is seedy. Discount carrier **Megabus** (☎877-462-6342; http://us.megabus.com) has daily service to LA, Burbank and Anaheim, departing from outside the West Oakland BART station.

CAR & MOTORCYCLE

From San Francisco by car, cross the Bay Bridge and enter Oakland via one of two ways: I-580, which leads to I-980 heading to downtown Oakland; or I-880, which curves through West Oakland and lets you off near the south end of Broadway. I-880 then continues to the Coliseum, Oakland International Airport and, eventually, San Jose. Driving back westbound from the East Bay to San Francisco, the bridge toll is $4 to $6, depending on the time and day of the week.

FERRY

From San Francisco's Ferry Building and Pier 41, **San Francisco Bay Ferry** (☎415-705-8291; http://sanfranciscobayferry.com) sails to Jack London Sq (one-way $6.60, 30 to 45 minutes) more frequently on weekdays than on weekends. Ferry tickets include a free transfer, which you can use on AC Transit buses.

TRAIN

Oakland is a regular stop for Amtrak (p527) trains operating up and down the coast. From Oakland's **Amtrak station** (245 2nd St; 🚌Broadway Shuttle) at Jack London Sq, catch AC Transit bus 12 or the free Broadway Shuttle to downtown Oakland, or take a ferry across the bay to San Francisco.

Amtrak passengers with reservations on to San Francisco disembark at the **Emeryville Amtrak station** (5885 Horton St), one stop north of Oakland. From there, an Amtrak bus shuttles you to San Francisco's Ferry Building stop. Emeryville is also the terminus for Amtrak's daily California Zephyr train service to/from Chicago. The free **Emery Go Round** (☎510-451-3862; www.emerygoround.com) shuttle runs a weekday circuit including the Emeryville Amtrak and MacArthur BART stations.

ℹ Getting Around

The best way to get around much of central Oakland is to walk, cycle or take public buses.

TO/FROM THE AIRPORT

Flying into **Oakland International Airport** (OAK; www.oaklandairport.com; 1 Airport Dr; 📶; Ⓑ Oakland International Airport), car rentals are available from all the major agencies. Outside the terminal, free shuttle buses depart every 10 minutes for the airport's rental-car center.

BART is the easiest public transportation option. Opposite the terminal, catch a BART shuttle train to Coliseum Station, where you'll paymin the fare to your final destination when changing trains. BART trains run on weekdays between 4:30am until after midnight daily (from 6am on Saturday, 8am on Sunday).

SuperShuttle (☎800-258-3826; www.supershuttle.com) is one of many door-to-door shuttle services operating out of Oakland International Airport. One-way service to San Francisco destinations starts at around $60 for up to four people. East Bay service destinations are also served. Reserve ahead.

A taxi from Oakland International Airport to downtown Oakland costs about $40; to downtown San Francisco about $70.

BUS

AC Transit (p131) has a comprehensive bus network within Oakland. Local bus fares are $2.10; pay with cash (bring exact change) or a Clipper card (www.clippercard.com).

The free **Broadway Shuttle** (www.meetdowntownoak.com/shuttle.php; 7am-10pm Mon-Thu, to 1am Fri, 6pm-1am Sat) runs along Broadway between Jack London Sq and Lake Merritt, stopping at Old Oakland/Chinatown, downtown BART stations and the Uptown district. The lime-green buses arrive every 10 to 15 minutes.

Berkeley

Berkeley – the birthplace of the free-speech and disability-rights movements, and the home of the hallowed halls of the University of California, Berkeley (aka 'Cal') – is no bashful wallflower. A national hot spot of (mostly left-of-center) intellectual discourse and with one of the most vocal activist populations in the country, this infamous college town has an interesting mix of graying progressives and idealistic undergrads. It's easy to stereotype 'Beserkeley' for some of its recycle-or-else PC crankiness, but the city is often on the forefront of environmental and political issues that eventually go mainstream.

Berkeley is also home to a large South Asian community, as evidenced by an abundance of sari shops on University Ave and an unusually large number of Indian, Pakistani and Nepalese restaurants.

Sights & Activities

University of California, Berkeley

The Berkeley campus of the University of California (UCB, called 'Cal' by both students and locals) is the oldest university in the state. The decision to found the college was made in 1866, and the first students arrived in 1873. Today UCB has more than 35,000 students, more than 1500 professors and more Nobel laureates than you could point a particle accelerator at.

From Telegraph Ave, enter the campus via Sproul Plaza and Sather Gate, a center for people-watching, soapbox oration and pseudotribal drumming. Or you can enter from Center St and Oxford Lane, near the downtown BART station.

Campanile LANDMARK

(Sather Tower; Map p134; 510-642-6000; http://campanile.berkeley.edu; adult/child $3/2; 10am-3:45pm Mon-Fri, 10am-4:45pm Sat, to 1:30pm & 3-4:45pm Sun; ; B Downtown Berkeley) Officially called Sather Tower, the Campanile was modeled on St Mark's Basilica in Venice. The 307ft spire offers fine views of the Bay Area, and at the top you can stare up into the carillon of 61 bells, ranging from the size of a cereal bowl to that of a Volkswagen. Recitals take place on weekdays at 7:50am and at noon and 6pm Monday to Saturday, with a longer piece performed at 2pm on Sunday.

Sather Gate GATE

(Map p134; 510-642-6000; www.berkeley.edu; Sather Rd; 24hr; AC Transit 6, 51B) The frenetic energy buzzing from the university's Sather Gate on any given day is a mixture of youthful posthippies reminiscing about days before their time and fashion-conscious hipsters and punk rockers who sneer at tie-dyed nostalgia. Political activists still hand out leaflets here at the south entrance to campus.

Bancroft Library LIBRARY

(Map p134; 510-642-3781; www.lib.berkeley.edu/libraries/bancroft-library; University Dr; archives 10am-4pm or 5pm Mon-Fri; B Downtown Berkeley) FREE The Bancroft houses, among other gems, the papers of Mark Twain, a copy of Shakespeare's folios and a diary from the Donner Party. Its small public exhibits of historical Californiana include the surprisingly small gold nugget that sparked the 1849 gold rush. Rotating temporary exhibits spotlight history and art, with pieces from the library's own collections. To register to use the library, you must present a current government or academic-issued photo ID. The registration desk is on your way in.

UC Berkeley Art Museum MUSEUM

(BAMPFA; Map p134; 510-642-0808; www.bampfa.berkeley.edu; 2155 Center St; adult/child $12/free; 11am-7pm Sun, Wed & Thu, to 9pm Fri & Sat; B Downtown Berkeley) With a stainless-steel exterior wrapping around a 1930s printing plant, the museum's new location holds multiple galleries showcasing a limited number of artworks, from ancient Chinese to cutting-edge contemporary. The complex also houses a bookstore, cafe and the much-loved Pacific Film Archive (p140).

Phoebe A Hearst Museum of Anthropology MUSEUM
(Map p134; ☎510-642-3682; http://hearstmuseum.berkeley.edu; Bancroft Way, at College Ave; adult/child $6/free; ⏰11am-5pm Sun-Wed & Fri, to 8pm Thu, 10am-6pm Sat; 🚌AC Transit 6, 51B) South of the Campanile in Kroeber Hall, this small museum includes exhibits from indigenous cultures around the world, including ancient Peruvian, Egyptian and African items. There's also a large collection highlighting Native Californian cultures.

UC Museum of Paleontology MUSEUM
(Map p134; ☎510-642-1821; www.ucmp.berkeley.edu; Campanile Way; ⏰8am-10pm Mon-Thu, 8am-5pm Fri, 10am-5pm Sat, 1-10pm Sun; Ⓑ Downtown Berkeley) FREE Housed in the ornate Valley Life Sciences Building (and primarily a research facility that's closed to the public), this museum has a number of fossil exhibits in the atrium, including a *Tyrannosaurus rex* skeleton.

South of Campus

South of campus along College Ave is the **Elmwood District**, a charming nook of shops and restaurants that offers a calming alternative to the frenetic buzz around Telegraph Ave. Continue further south and you'll be in Rockridge, in the neighboring city of Oakland.

Telegraph Avenue STREET
(Map p134; ⏰shop & restaurant hours vary; Ⓟ; 🚌AC Transit 6) Telegraph Ave has traditionally been the throbbing heart of studentville in Berkeley, the sidewalks crowded with undergrads, postdocs and youthful shoppers squeezing their way past throngs of vendors, buskers and panhandlers. Street stalls hawk everything from crystals to bumper stickers to self-published tracts. Several cafes and budget eateries cater to students.

First Church of Christ, Scientist CHURCH
(Map p134; ☎510-845-7199; www.friendsoffirstchurch.org; 2619 Dwight Way; ⏰tour 12:15pm 1st Sun each month; Ⓟ; 🚌AC Transit 6) FREE Bernard Maybeck's impressive 1910 church uses concrete and wood in its blend of arts-and-crafts, Asian and Gothic influences. Maybeck was a professor of architecture at UC Berkeley and designed San Francisco's Palace of Fine Arts, plus many landmark homes in the Berkeley Hills.

Free 45-minute guided tours are given on the first Sunday of every month.

Julia Morgan Theater THEATER
(Map p134; ☎510-845-8542; http://tickets.berkeleyplayhouse.org; 2640 College Ave; ⏰not open to the public, except for performances; 🚌AC Transit 51B) A beautifully understated, redwood-paneled 1910 theater, this performance space (formerly a church) was created by Bay Area architect Julia Morgan. She designed several landmark Bay Area buildings and, most famously, Hearst Castle on the Central Coast.

People's Park PARK
(Map p134; 2556 Haste St; ⏰24hr; 🚌AC Transit 6) This park, just east of Telegraph Ave, is a marker in local history as a political battleground between residents and the city and state government in the late 1960s. Occasional festivals do still happen here, but it's rather run-down and serves mostly as a gathering spot for Berkeley's homeless.

There's talk of redeveloping the park into university-student housing.

Downtown

Berkeley's downtown, centered on Shattuck Ave between University Ave and Dwight Way, has few traces of the city's tie-dyed reputation. Today it abounds with shops, restaurants and restored public buildings.

The nearby **arts district** revolves around the acclaimed thespian stomping grounds of the Berkeley Repertory Theatre and Aurora Theatre Company and live music at the historic Freight & Salvage Coffeehouse, all on Addison St.

North Berkeley & Albany

Not too far north of the university campus, North Berkeley is a neighborhood filled with lovely garden-front homes and parks. The popular **Gourmet Ghetto** stretches along Shattuck Ave north of University Ave for several blocks, anchored by acclaimed restaurant Chez Panisse (p138). Further northwest, **Solano Avenue**, which crosses from Berkeley into Albany, is lined with funky shops and family-friendly restaurants.

Berkeley Rose Garden GARDENS
(☎510-981-6700; www.ci.berkeley.ca.us; 1200 Euclid Ave; ⏰dawn-dusk; 🚌AC Transit 65) FREE In North Berkeley discover the Berkeley Rose Garden, with its eight terraces of colorful explosions. Here you'll find quiet benches and a plethora of almost perpetually blooming roses arranged by hue. Across the street,

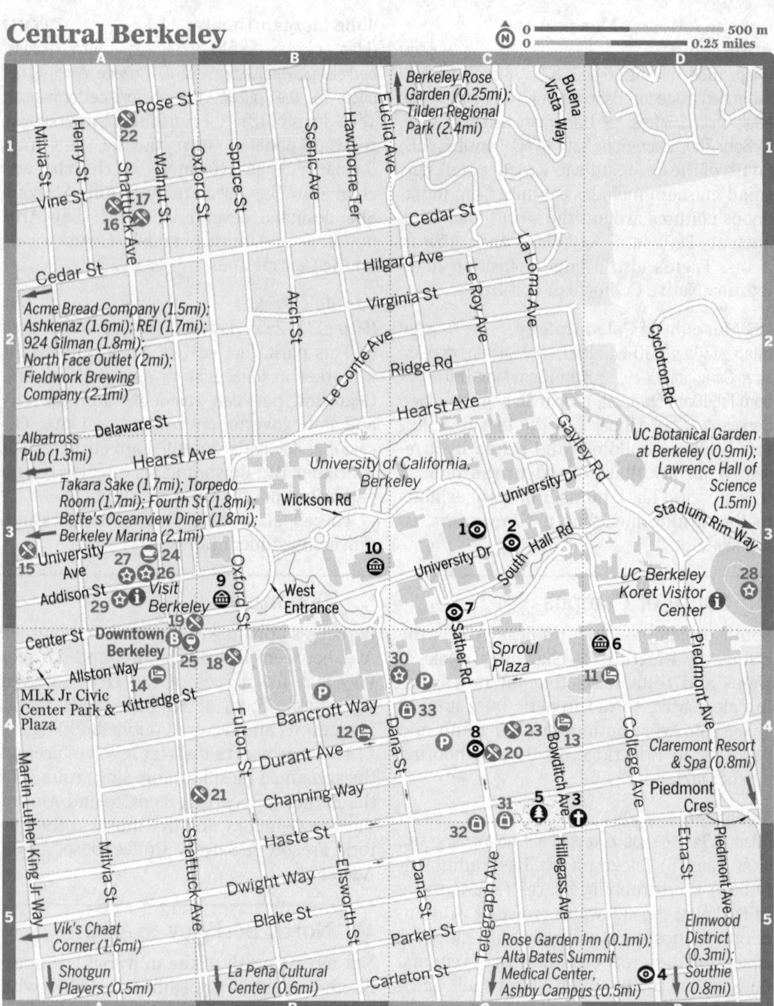

Cordornices Park has a children's playground with a very fun concrete slide, about 40ft long.

The Berkeley Hills

★Tilden Regional Park PARK

(☎510-544-2747; www.ebparks.org/parks/tilden; ⏰5am-10pm; P; AC Transit 67) FREE This 2079-acre park, up in the hills east of town, is Berkeley's best. It has nearly 40 miles of hiking and multiuse trails of varying difficulty, from paved paths to hilly scrambles, including part of the magnificent Bay Area Ridge Trail. There's also a miniature steam train ($3), a children's farm and environmental education center, a wonderfully wild-looking botanical garden and an 18-hole golf course. Lake Anza is good for picnics and from spring through fall you can swim ($3.50).

AC Transit bus 67 runs to the park on weekends and holidays from Downtown Berkeley BART station, but only stops at the park entrance on weekdays.

Central Berkeley

Sights

1 Bancroft Library ... C3
2 Campanile ... C3
3 First Church of Christ, Scientist ... C4
4 Julia Morgan Theater ... D5
5 People's Park ... C4
6 Phoebe A Hearst Museum of Anthropology ... D4
7 Sather Gate ... C3
8 Telegraph Avenue ... C4
9 UC Berkeley Art Museum ... B3
10 UC Museum of Paleontology ... B3

Sleeping

11 Bancroft Hotel ... D4
12 Berkeley City Club ... B4
13 Graduate Berkeley ... C4
14 Hotel Shattuck Plaza ... A4

Eating

15 Butcher's Son ... A3
16 Cheese Board Collective ... A1
17 Chez Panisse ... A1
Cream ... (see 20)
18 Gather ... B4
19 Ippuku ... A3
20 KoJa Kitchen ... C4
21 La Note ... B4
22 North Berkeley Farmers Market ... A1
23 Smoke's Poutinerie ... C4

Drinking & Nightlife

24 Asha Tea House ... A3
Caffe Strada ... (see 11)
25 Jupiter ... A4

Entertainment

26 Aurora Theatre Company ... A3
27 Berkeley Repertory Theatre ... A3
28 California Memorial Stadium ... D3
29 Freight & Salvage Coffeehouse ... A3
Pacific Film Archive ... (see 9)
30 Zellerbach Hall ... C4

Shopping

31 Amoeba Music ... C4
32 Moe's Books ... C5
33 University Press Books ... C4

UC Botanical Garden at Berkeley GARDENS
(☎510-643-2755; http://botanicalgarden.berkeley.edu; 200 Centennial Dr; adult/child $10/2; ⊙9am-5pm, last entry 4:30pm, closed 1st Tue each month; P ♿; Bear Transit H) With 34 acres and more than 10,000 types of plants, this garden in the hills above campus has one of the most varied collections in the USA. Flora from every continent except Antarctica are lovingly tended here, with special emphasis on Mediterranean species that grow in California, the Americas, the Mediterranean and southern Africa.

On weekdays, catch the university's Bear Transit H Line shuttle ($1) from campus. Limited parking across the street from the garden costs $1 per hour.

A nearby **fire trail** makes a woodsy walking loop around Strawberry Canyon, offering great views of town and the off-limits Lawrence Berkeley National Laboratory. Find the trailhead on the east side of Centennial Dr just southwest of the botanical garden; you'll emerge near the Lawrence Hall of Science.

Lawrence Hall of Science MUSEUM
(☎510-642-5132; www.lawrencehallofscience.org; 1 Centennial Dr; adult/child $12/10; ⊙10am-5pm Wed-Sun, daily mid-Jun–early Sep; P ♿; AC Transit 65) Near Grizzly Peak Blvd, this science hall is named after Ernest Lawrence, who won the Nobel Prize for his invention of the cyclotron particle accelerator. He was a key member of the WWII Manhattan Project, and he's also the name behind the Lawrence Berkeley and Lawrence Livermore national laboratories. The museum has interactive but dated exhibits for kids and adults (many closed weekdays) on subjects ranging from earthquakes to nanotechnology. Outside there's a 60ft model of a DNA molecule.

From Downtown Berkeley BART station, take AC Transit bus 65. From campus, catch the university's Bear Transit H Line shuttle ($1). On-site parking costs $1 per hour.

West Berkeley

Adventure Playground PARK
(☎510-981-6720; www.cityofberkeley.info/adventureplayground; 160 University Ave; ⊙11am-5pm mid-Jun–mid-Aug, Sat & Sun only rest of year; P ♿; AC Transit 81) FREE At the Berkeley Marina, this is one of the coolest play spaces in the Bay Area – a free outdoor park encouraging creativity and cooperation where supervised kids of any age can help build and paint their own structures. There's an awesome zipline too. Dress the tykes in play clothes, because they *will* get dirty.

Berkeley Marina MARINA
(☎510-981-6740; www.ci.berkeley.ca.us; 201 University Ave; ⊙6am-10pm; P ♿ 🐾; AC Transit

81) At the west end of University Ave is the marina, frequented by squawking seagulls, silent types fishing from the pier and, especially on windy weekends, families flying colorful kites. It offers sweeping waterfront views from paved walking, cycling and running paths.

The marina was originally built in the late 19th century, then replaced by a ferry pier in the 1920s (its unusual length dictated by the bay's extreme shallowness).

Takara Sake MUSEUM

(☎510-540-8250; www.takarasake.com; 708 Addison St; tasting fee $5-10; ⏰noon-6pm, last tasting 5:30pm; 🚌AC Transit 51B) Stop in to see the traditional wooden tools used for making sake and a short video of the brewing process. Tours of the factory aren't offered, but you can view elements of modern production and bottling through a window. Sake flights are poured in a spacious tasting room constructed with reclaimed wood and floor tiles fashioned from recycled glass.

Sleeping

Lodging rates spike during special university events such as graduation (mid-May) and home football games. A number of older, less expensive motels along University Ave can be handy during peak demand, as can chain motels and hotels off I-80 in Emeryville or Vallejo.

Graduate Berkeley BOUTIQUE HOTEL $$

(Map p134; ☎510-845-8981; http://graduateberkeley.com; 2600 Durant Ave; r from $160; P ⊖ ❄ @ ᯤ 🐾; 🚌AC Transit 51B) Located a block from campus, this classic 1928 hotel has been cheekily renovated to highlight the connection to the university. The lobby is adorned with embarrassing yearbook photos and a ceiling mobile of exam books, and smallish rooms have dictionary-covered shower curtains and bongs repurposed into bedside lamps. Parking is $20.

Berkeley City Club HISTORIC HOTEL $$

(Map p134; ☎510-848-7800; www.berkeleycityclub.com; 2315 Durant Ave; r/ste from $215; P ⊖ @ ᯤ 🏊; 🚌AC Transit 51B) Designed by Julia Morgan (the architect of Hearst Castle), the 35 rooms and dazzling common areas of this refurbished 1929 historic landmark building (which is also a private club) feel like a glorious time warp into a more refined era. The hotel contains lush and serene Italianate courtyards, gardens and terraces and a stunning indoor pool. Parking is $20.

Elegant Old World rooms contain no TV, and those with numbers ending in 4 and 8 have to-die-for views of the bay and the Golden Gate Bridge.

Hotel Shattuck Plaza HOTEL $$

(Map p134; ☎510-845-7300; www.hotelshattuckplaza.com; 2086 Allston Way; r from $200; P ⊖ ❄ @ ᯤ; B Downtown Berkeley) Following a $15-million renovation and greening of this 100-year-old downtown jewel, a foyer of red Italian glass lighting, flocked Victorian-style wallpaper – and yes, a peace sign tiled into the floor – leads to comfortable rooms with down comforters and an airy, columned restaurant serving all meals. Accommodations off Shattuck Ave are quietest, while cityscape rooms boast bay views.

Bancroft Hotel HISTORIC HOTEL $$

(Map p134; ☎510-549-1000; http://bancrofthotel.com; 2680 Bancroft Way; r $125-230; P ⊖ @ ᯤ; 🚌AC Transit 51B) 🍃 A gorgeous 1928 arts-and-crafts building that was originally a women's club, the Bancroft is just across the street from campus and two blocks from Telegraph Ave (p133). It has 22 small, simply furnished rooms (some with lovely balconies) and a spectacular bay-view rooftop, though no elevator. Limited parking.

★**Claremont Resort & Spa** RESORT $$$

(☎510-843-3000; www.fairmont.com/claremont-berkeley; 41 Tunnel Rd; r from $240; P ⊖ ❄ @ ᯤ 🏊 🐾) The East Bay's classy crème de la crème, this Fairmont-owned historic hotel is a glamorous white 1915 building with elegant restaurants, a fitness center, swimming pools, tennis courts and a full-service spa. The bay-view rooms are superb. It's located at the foot of the Berkeley Hills, off Hwy 13 (Tunnel Rd) near the Oakland border. Parking is $30.

Eating

Telegraph Ave is packed with cafes, pizza counters and cheap restaurants, and Berkeley's Little India runs along the University Ave corridor. Many more restaurants can be found along Shattuck Ave near the Downtown Berkeley BART station. The section of Shattuck Ave north of University Ave, nicknamed the 'Gourmet Ghetto,' is home to excellent restaurants and cafes for all budgets.

Downtown & Around Campus

KoJa Kitchen FUSION $

(Map p134; ☎510-962-5652; www.kojakitchen.com; 2395 Telegraph Ave; items $4-10; ⏰11am-10pm; 🚌AC Transit 51B) From food truck to a brick-and-mortar shop, this Korean-Japanese fusion eatery makes addictive short-rib and braised-pork sandwiches out of garlicky fried-rice buns, with kimchi-spiked waffle fries on the side. Order ahead, or expect a wait.

Smoke's Poutinerie FAST FOOD $

(Map p134; ☎510-540-7500; http://smokespoutinerie.com; 2518 Durant Ave; items $3-13; ⏰11am-4am; 🚌AC Transit 51B) Since California legalized recreational marijuana use, demand has only increased at this Canadian poutine shop, open till the wee hours. Get the classic Quebecois taste of cheese curds and gravy, or a wilder combination such as jerk chicken or veggie nacho.

Butcher's Son VEGAN, DELI $

(Map p134; ☎510-984-0818; www.thebutchersveganson.com; 1941 University Ave; mains $8-13; ⏰11am-8pm Mon & Thu-Fri, to 3pm Tue & Wed, 9am-5pm Sat & Sun; 🌱; Ⓑ Downtown Berkeley) What could be more in tune with Berkeley's granola-crunchy, latter-day-hippie vibe than a vegan deli? Gorge yourself on imitation deli meats and cheeses that will scratch that itch for a fried mozzarella and meatball sandwich or hot turkey and roast beef on rye, all made without any animal products.

Cream ICE CREAM $

(Map p134; ☎510-649-1000; http://creamnation.com; 2399 Telegraph Ave; items $2-4; ⏰noon-11pm Sun-Thu, to midnight Fri & Sat; 🌱👪; 🚌AC Transit 51B) With a line out the door, this corner shop smooshes together ice-cream sandwiches with creative flavors and freshly baked cookies. Otherwise, get an ice-cream sundae in a less exciting cup or cone.

North Berkeley Farmers Market MARKET $

(Map p134; ☎510-548-3333; www.ecologycenter.org; Shattuck Ave, at Rose St; ⏰3-7pm Thu; 🌱👪; 🚌AC Transit 79) 🍃 Pick up some organic produce or tasty prepared food at North Berkeley's weekly farmers market, operating year-round.

Ippuku JAPANESE $$

(Map p134; ☎510-665-1969; www.ippukuberkeley.com; 2130 Center St; shared plates $5-20; ⏰5-10pm Tue-Thu, to 11pm Fri & Sat; Ⓑ Downtown Berkeley) Japanese expats gush that Ippuku reminds them of *izakaya* (Japanese gastropubs) back in Tokyo. Choose from a menu of yakitori (skewered meats and vegetables) and handmade soba noodles as you settle in at one of the traditional tatami tables (no

WATERSPORTS ON THE BAY

As well as making for a lovely postcard or iconic snapshot, San Francisco Bay offers plenty of options for getting out on the water. Myriad outfitters provide equipment, lessons and guided tours.

California Canoe & Kayak (Map p124; ☎510-893-7833; www.calkayak.com; 409 Water St; kayak & SUP rentals per hour $25-50, tours from $50; ⏰10am-6pm Mon-Fri, 9am-6pm Sat, 9am-5pm Sun; 🚌Broadway Shuttle) Rents kayaks and stand up paddleboard (SUP) sets at Oakland's Jack London Sq. Book ahead for moonlight paddles along the waterfront.

Cal Adventures (☎510-642-4000, recorded info 510-642-7707; http://recsports.berkeley.edu/cal-adventures; 124 University Ave; rentals/classes from $20/45; ⏰hours vary; 🚌AC Transit 81) Run by the UC Aquatic Center at Berkeley Marina, it organizes sailing, windsurfing, SUP and sea-kayaking classes and rentals.

Cal Sailing Club (www.cal-sailing.org; 124 University Ave; 3-month membership $99; ⏰noon-sunset Mon-Fri, from 9am Sat & Sun; 🚌AC Transit 81) Membership-based, volunteer-run nonprofit that runs sailing and windsurfing programs at Berkeley Marina.

Boardsports California (☎415-385-1224; https://boardsportscalifornia.com; rentals/lessons from $25/49; ⏰hours vary) Offers lessons and rentals for kiteboarding, windsurfing, SUP and kayaking, with locations at Alameda in the East Bay and Coyote Point Recreation Area in San Mateo, near San Francisco International Airport.

Sea Trek (p107) In Sausalito, this long-running outfitter has kayaks and SUP sets for rent and a fabulous array of tours, including bay crossings to Angel Island.

shoes, please) or cozy booth perches. Order *shōchū,* a distilled alcohol usually made from rice or barley. Reservations essential.

La Note FRENCH **$$**
(Map p134; ☎510-843-1525; www.lanoterestaurant.com; 2377 Shattuck Ave; mains $10-25; ⏲breakfast & lunch 8am-2:30pm Mon-Fri, to 3pm Sat & Sun, dinner 6-10pm Thu-Sat; Ⓑ Downtown Berkeley) A rustic country-French bistro downtown, La Note serves excellent breakfasts. Wake up to a big bowl of café au lait, paired with brioche *pain perdu* or lemon-gingerbread pancakes with poached pears. Anticipate a wait on weekends.

Gather CALIFORNIAN **$$**
(Map p134; ☎510-809-0400; www.gatherrestaurant.com; 2200 Oxford St; dinner mains $16-30; ⏲11:30am-2pm & 5-9pm Mon-Thu, 11:30-2pm & 5-10pm Fri, 10am-2pm & 5-10pm Sat, 10am-2pm & 5-9pm Sun; ; Ⓑ Downtown Berkeley) When vegan foodies and passionate farm-to-table types dine out together, they often end up here. Inside a salvaged-wood interior punctuated by green vines streaking down over an open kitchen, dishes are created from locally sourced ingredients and sustainably raised meats. Reservations recommended.

North Berkeley

Cheese Board Collective PIZZA **$**
(Map p134; ☎510-549-3055; www.cheeseboardcollective.coop; 1504 & 1512 Shattuck Ave; slices/half-pizzas $2.75/11; ⏲shop 7am-1pm Mon, to 6pm Tue-Fri, to 5pm Sat, pizzeria 11:30am-3pm & 4:30-8pm Tue-Sat; ; AC Transit 7) Stop in to take stock of more than 300 cheeses available at this worker-owned business and scoop up some fresh bread to make a picnic lunch. Or sit down for a slice of the crispy veggie pizza just next door, where live music's often featured.

★**Chez Panisse** CALIFORNIAN **$$$**
(Map p134; ☎cafe 510-548-5049, restaurant 510-548-5525; www.chezpanisse.com; 1517 Shattuck Ave; cafe dinner mains $22-35, restaurant prix-fixe dinner $75-125; ⏲cafe 11:30am-2:45pm & 5-10:30pm Mon-Thu, 11:30am-3pm & 5-11:30pm Fri & Sat, restaurant seatings 5:30pm & 8pm Mon-Sat; ; AC Transit 7) Foodies come to worship here at the church of Alice Waters, inventor of California cuisine. It's in a lovely arts-and-crafts house in Berkeley's 'Gourmet Ghetto,' and you can choose to pull out all the stops with a prix-fixe meal downstairs, or go less expensive and a tad less formal in the upstairs cafe. Reservations accepted one month ahead. The restaurant is as good and popular as it ever was, and despite its fame, the place has retained a welcoming atmosphere.

West Berkeley

Vik's Chaat Corner INDIAN **$**
(☎510-644-4412; www.vikschaatcorner.com; 2390 4th St; mains $6-12; ⏲11am-6pm Mon-Thu, to 8pm Fri-Sun; ; AC Transit 80) Off in West Berkeley, this longtime, popular *chaat* house gets mobbed at lunchtime by regulars that include equal numbers of hungry office workers, students and Indian families. Order samosas or a puffy *bhature* (flatbread) with *chole* (chickpea curry), an *uttapam* (savory pancake) or one of many filling *dosas* (savory crepes). Colorful Indian sweets, sold by the piece or pound, are irresistible.

Bette's Oceanview Diner AMERICAN **$$**
(☎510-644-3230; www.bettesdiner.com; 1807 4th St; mains $7-16; ⏲6:30am-2:30pm Mon-Fri, to 4pm Sat & Sun; ; AC Transit 51B) This is a buzzing breakfast spot, especially on the weekends. It dishes up baked soufflé pancakes and German-style potato pancakes with applesauce, plus eggs and sandwiches. From-scratch baked goods and a nifty diner interior make it worth the wait.

Drinking & Nightlife

You'll never come up short of places to imbibe in Berkeley. Join students at bars and pubs scattered around downtown, on side streets near the university campus or along College Ave in Elmwood. Detour to industrial areas of West Berkeley to discover craft beers and a sake distillery (p136).

Fieldwork Brewing Company BREWERY
(☎510-898-1203; http://fieldworkbrewing.com; 1160 6th St; ⏲11am-10pm Sun-Thu, to 11pm Fri & Sat; AC Transit 12) Come to this industrial brewery taproom at the edge of town for outstanding craft beer and sit down on the outdoor patio with a tasting flight of IPAs or a glass of rich Mexican hot chocolate stout. It's dog-friendly, and there are racks to hang your bicycle inside the front door. There's a short menu of Mexican-Californian food too.

Asha Tea House CAFE
(Map p134; www.ashateahouse.com; 2086 University Ave; ⏲11am-10pm Mon-Sat, to 8pm Sun; ; Ⓑ Downtown Berkeley) Find your bliss in this industrial-modern tea shop, where acrylic prints of verdant tea plantations

overhang the bar. Handcrafted Indian chai, Japanese matcha and Hong Kong–style milk tea star on a connoisseur's drinks menu.

Torpedo Room BAR
(510-647-3439; www.sierranevada.com/brewery/california/torpedoroom; 2031 4th St; noon-9pm Tue-Fri, from 11am Sat, noon-7pm Sun; AC Transit 51B) Sample a flight of tasting pours or order a pint from the 16 rotating drafts (including some rare small-batch beers) on tap at Sierra Nevada brewery's tasting room in West Berkeley.

Albatross PUB
(510-843-2473; www.albatrosspub.com; 1822 San Pablo Ave; 6pm-2am Sun-Tue, from 4:30pm Wed-Sat; AC Transit 51B) Berkeley's oldest pub is one of the most inviting and friendly in the city. Some serious darts are played here and board games get played around many of the worn-out tables. Sunday is trivia quiz night.

Jupiter PUB
(Map p134; 510-843-8277; www.jupiterbeer.com; 2181 Shattuck Ave; 11:30am-12:30am Mon-Thu, to 1:30am Fri, noon-1:30am Sat, noon-11:30pm Sun; B Downtown Berkeley) This downtown pub has loads of regional microbrews, a beer garden, decent pizza and live bands most nights. Sit upstairs for a bird's-eye view of bustling Shattuck Ave.

Caffe Strada CAFE
(Map p134; 510-843-5282; 2300 College Ave; 6am-midnight; ; AC Transit 51B) At this popular, student-saturated hangout with an inviting shaded patio, try the strong espressos or a sweet white-chocolate mocha.

☆ Entertainment

Berkeley's arts district, centered on Addison St between Milvia St and Shattuck Ave, anchors downtown's performing-arts scene.

Berkeley also has plenty of intimate live-music venues. Cover charges usually range from $5 to $20, and several venues are all-ages or 18-and-over.

Freight & Salvage Coffeehouse LIVE MUSIC
(Map p134; 510-644-2020; www.thefreight.org; 2020 Addison St; tickets $5-45; shows daily; ; B Downtown Berkeley) This legendary club has almost 50 years of history and is conveniently located in the downtown arts district. It features great traditional folk, country, bluegrass and world music and welcomes all ages, with half-price tickets for patrons under 21.

924 Gilman LIVE MUSIC
(510-524-8180; www.924gilman.org; 924 Gilman St; tickets from $10; Sat & Sun; AC Transit 12) This volunteer-run and booze-free all-ages space is a West Coast punk-rock institution. Check the online calendar for upcoming shows on weekend nights.

Ashkenaz WORLD MUSIC, DANCE
(510-525-5054; www.ashkenaz.com; 1317 San Pablo Ave; free-$20; hours vary; ; AC Transit 52) Ashkenaz is a 'music and dance community center' attracting activists, hippies and fans of folk, swing, world music and more who love to dance (lessons offered).

La Peña Cultural Center WORLD MUSIC
(510-849-2568; www.lapena.org; 3105 Shattuck Ave; free-$16; hours vary; B Ashby) This fun-loving, warmhearted community center presents dynamic dance classes and musical and visual arts events with a peace and justice bent. Look for a vibrant mural outside and the on-site Mexican cafe, perfect for grabbing drinks and a preshow bite.

Berkeley Repertory Theatre THEATER
(Map p134; 510-647-2949; www.berkeleyrep.org; 2025 Addison St; tickets $40-100; box office noon-7pm Tue-Sun; B Downtown Berkeley) This highly respected company has produced bold versions of classical and modern plays since 1968. Most shows have half-price tickets for patrons under 30.

California Shakespeare Theater THEATER
(510-548-9666; www.calshakes.org; 701 Heinz Ave; tickets $21-56; late May-early Oct) Headquartered in Berkeley, with the fantastic outdoor Bruns Amphitheater east of the Berkeley Hills in Orinda, 'Cal Shakes' is a warm-weather tradition of alfresco Shakespeare and other classic productions.

Zellerbach Hall PERFORMING ARTS
(Map p134; 510-642-9988; https://calperformances.org; off Bancroft Way; tickets from $10; ticket office usually noon-5:30pm Tue-Fri, 1-5pm Sat & Sun; AC Transit 51B) At the south end of campus near Bancroft Way and Dana St, Zellerbach Hall features dance events, musical concerts and performances of all types by national and international touring artists. The on-site Cal Performances Ticket Office sells tickets.

Shotgun Players THEATER
(510-841-6500; www.shotgunplayers.org; 1901 Ashby Ave; tickets $20-50; hours vary; B Downtown Berkeley) Berkeley's solar-powered

WORTH A TRIP

EAST BROTHER LIGHT STATION

Most Bay Area residents have never heard of this speck of an island off the East Bay city of Richmond, and even fewer know that the **East Brother Light Station** (510-233-2385; www.ebls.org; 1900 Stenmark Dr, Richmond; d incl breakfast & dinner $295-415; Thu-Sun;) is a five-room Victorian B&B. Spend the night in the romantic lighthouse or fog-signal building (the foghorn blares from October 1 to April 1). Access is by boat; reserve ahead.

Resident innkeepers serve afternoon hors d'oeuvres and champagne, and after dinner you can stroll around the breezy 0.75-acre islet and rummage through historical photos and artifacts.

theater company stages exciting and provocative works in an intimate space.

Aurora Theatre Company THEATER
(Map p134; 510-843-4822; www.auroratheatre.org; 2081 Addison St; tickets from $25; box office usually 1-4pm Tue-Fri; Downtown Berkeley) Intimate downtown theater performs contemporary, thought-provoking plays staged with subtle aesthetics.

Pacific Film Archive CINEMA
(PFA; Map p134; 510-642-5249; www.bampfa.berkeley.edu; 2155 Center St; adult/child from $12/8; hours vary; ; Downtown Berkeley) A world-renowned film center with an ever-changing schedule of international and classic films – cineastes should seek out this place. The spacious theater has seats comfy enough for hours-long movie marathons. Movie tickets include same-day admission to the UC Berkeley Art Museum (p132).

Shopping

Heading south of the university campus, Telegraph Ave caters mostly to students, hawking a steady dose of urban hippie gear, handmade sidewalk-vendor jewelry and head-shop paraphernalia. Audiophiles will swoon over the music stores.

Berkeley's other shopping corridors include College Ave in the Elmwood District (on the Oakland border), 4th St (north of University Ave) and Solano Ave (heading into Albany).

Amoeba Music MUSIC
(Map p134; 510-549-1125; www.amoeba.com; 2455 Telegraph Ave; 11am-8pm Sun-Thu, to 10pm Fri & Sat; AC Transit 51B) If you're a music junkie, you might plan on spending a few hours at the original Berkeley branch of Amoeba Music, packed with massive quantities of new and used CDs, DVDs, tapes and records (yes, lots of vinyl).

Down Home Music MUSIC
(510-525-2129; www.downhomemusic.com; 10341 San Pablo Ave, El Cerrito; 11am-7pm Tue-Sun; AC Transit 72) North of Berkeley, this world-class store for roots, blues, folk, country, jazz and world music is affiliated with the Arhoolie record label, which has been issuing landmark recordings since the early 1960s.

University Press Books BOOKS
(Map p134; 510-548-0585; www.universitypressbooks.com; 2430 Bancroft Way; 11am-7pm Mon-Fri, to 6pm Sat, noon-5pm Sun; AC Transit 51B) Across the street from campus, this academic and scholarly bookstore stocks works by UC Berkeley professors and other academic and museum publishers, with frequent author appearances.

REI SPORTS & OUTDOORS
(510-527-4140; www.rei.com; 1338 San Pablo Ave; 10am-9pm Mon-Fri, to 8pm Sat, to 7pm Sun; ; AC Transit 52) This large and busy co-op lures in active folks for camping and mountaineering rentals, sports clothing and all kinds of nifty outdoor gear.

North Face Outlet SPORTS & OUTDOORS
(510-526-3530; www.thenorthface.com; 1238 5th St; 10am-7pm Mon-Sat, 11am-5pm Sun; AC Transit 12) Discount store for the Bay Area–based brand of outdoor gear is just off Gilman St.

Fourth Street HOMEWARES, FASHION
(510-644-3002; www.fourthstreet.com; store hours vary; AC Transit 51B) Hidden within an industrial section near I-80, this three-block area offers shaded sidewalks for upscale shopping or just strolling, and a few good restaurants.

Moe's Books BOOKS
(Map p134; 510-849-2087; www.moesbooks.com; 2476 Telegraph Ave; 10am-10pm; AC Transit 51B) A long-standing local favorite, Moe's offers four floors of new, used and remaindered books for hours of browsing.

Information

MEDICAL SERVICES

Alta Bates Summit Medical Center, Ashby Campus (☎510-204-4444; www.sutterhealth.org; 2450 Ashby Ave; ⏱24hr; 🚌AC Transit 6) offers 24-hour emergency services.

TOURIST INFORMATION

UC Berkeley Koret Visitor Center (Map p134; ☎510-642-5215; http://visit.berkeley.edu; 2227 Piedmont Ave; ⏱8:30am-4:30pm Mon-Fri, 9am-1pm Sat & Sun; 🚌AC Transit 36) Campus maps anad information available at the new visitor center on Goldman Plaza at California Memorial Stadium (Map p134; ☎510-642-2730; www.californiamemorialstadium.com; 2227 Piedmont Ave; ⏱hours vary; 👪; 🚌AC Transit 52). Free 90-minute campus walking tours usually start at 10am daily (advance reservations required).

Visit Berkeley (Map p134; ☎510-549-7040; www.visitberkeley.com; 2030 Addison St; ⏱9am-1pm & 2-5pm Mon-Fri; Ⓑ Downtown Berkeley) The helpful Berkeley Convention & Visitors Bureau prints a free visitors guide, also available online.

Getting There & Away

BART

To get to Berkeley, catch a Richmond-bound train to one of three BART (p131) stations: Ashby, Downtown Berkeley or North Berkeley. Fares between Berkeley and San Francisco cost $4.10 to $4.40, between Berkeley and downtown Oakland $1.95. After 8pm on weekdays, 6pm on Saturday and all day Sunday, there is no direct train service operating from San Francisco to Berkeley; instead, catch a Pittsburg/Bay Point train, then transfer at 19th St station in Oakland.

BUS

On AC Transit (p131), the F line leaves from the Transbay Transit Center in San Francisco for downtown Berkeley and the university campus approximately every half-hour ($4.20, 40 minutes). The Transbay bus fare is discounted to $2.10 if you also purchase a day pass ($5) valid on AC Transit's local East Bay bus routes.

Between downtown Berkeley and downtown Oakland, take fast and frequent AC Transit bus 6 along Telegraph Ave. Alternatively, take bus 18 via Martin Luther King Jr Way and Shattuck Ave. Bus 51B travels along University Ave past Downtown Berkeley BART station to the Berkeley Marina. All one-way local bus fares on AC Transit are $2.10.

CAR & MOTORCYCLE

From San Francisco, drive over the Bay Bridge and then follow either I-80 (for University Ave, Berkeley Marina, downtown Berkeley and the university campus) or Hwy 24 (for College Ave and the Berkeley Hills).

TRAIN

Amtrak does stop in Berkeley, but the platform is not staffed and direct connections are few. More convenient is Emeryville Amtrak station (p131), about 2 miles south.

To reach the Emeryville station from downtown Berkeley, take AC Transit bus F ($4.20) or ride BART to the MacArthur station ($1.95, five minutes) and then catch the free Emery Go Round (p131) shuttle bus.

Getting Around

Local buses, cycling and walking are the best ways to get around Berkeley.

BICYCLE

By Downtown Berkeley BART station, **Bike Station** (☎510-548-7433; http://bikehub.com/bartbikestation; 2208 Shattuck Ave; per day/week/month $35/95/200; ⏱7am-9pm Mon-Fri, 11am-7pm Sat) rents bicycles with a helmet and U-lock.

BUS

AC Transit (p131) operates local public buses in and around Berkeley. The one-way fare is $2.10; pay with cash (exact change required) or a Clipper card (www.clippercard.com).

The university's **Bear Transit** (☎510-643-7701; http://pt.berkeley.edu) runs a shuttle from Downtown Berkeley BART station to various points on campus. From Bear Transit's on-campus stop at Hearst Mining Circle, the H Line runs along Centennial Dr to the upper parts of the campus. For visitors, each ride costs $1 (bring cash).

CAR & MOTORCYCLE

Drivers should note that numerous barriers have been set up to prevent car traffic from traversing residential streets at high speeds, so zigzagging is necessary in some neighborhoods.

Downtown and near the university campus, pay-parking lots are well signed. Metered street-parking spots are rarely empty.

Mt Diablo State Park

Collecting a light dusting of snowflakes on the coldest days of winter, Mt Diablo (3849ft) is over 1200ft higher than Mt Tamalpais in Marin County. On a clear day (early on a winter morning is a good bet) the views from Diablo's summit are vast and sweeping. To the west you can see over the bay and out to the Farallon Islands; to the east you can look out over the Central Valley to the Sierra Nevada.

Most easily accessed from Danville or Walnut Creek, the **park** (☎925-837-2525; www.mdia.org; per vehicle $6-10; ⏰8am-sunset) is threaded by over 50 miles of hiking trails. You can also drive to the summit, where there's a visitor center.

Sleeping

Mt Diablo State Park Campgrounds CAMPGROUND $
(☎reservations 800-444-7275; www.reserveamerica.com; tent & RV sites $30) Of the park's three drive-in campgrounds, Juniper and Live Oak have showers. All campgrounds may be closed during high fire danger and water may be turned off throughout the park if water restrictions are in effect.

Information

Summit Visitor Center (www.parks.ca.gov; ⏰10am-4pm) Mt Diablo State Park's small main visitor center.

John Muir National Historic Site

Naturalist John Muir's **former residence** (☎925-228-8860; www.nps.gov/jomu; 4202 Alhambra Ave, Martinez; ⏰Muir Home 10am-5pm, Mt Wanda sunrise-sunset) FREE sits in a pastoral patch of farmland in bustling, modern Martinez. Though Muir wrote of sauntering the Sierra Nevada with a sack of tea and bread, it may be a shock for those familiar with the iconic Sierra Club founder's ascetic weather-beaten appearance that this house (built by his father-in-law) is a model of Victorian Italianate refinement, with a tower cupola, a daintily upholstered parlor and splashes of white lace.

Muir's 'scribble den' has been left as it was during his life, with crumbled papers overflowing from wire wastebaskets and dried-bread balls – his preferred snack – resting on the mantelpiece.

Acres of the family's fruit orchards still stand, and visitors can enjoy seasonal samples. The grounds include the 1849 Martinez Adobe, part of the ranch on which the house was built, and oak-speckled hiking trails on nearby Mt Wanda, named for one of Muir's daughters. Check the website for special campfire programs, wildflower walks and full-moon hikes. The park is just north of Hwy 4. **County Connection** (☎925-676-7500; https://countyconnection.com) buses 16 and 98X from nearby Amtrak and BART stations stop here.

THE PENINSULA

South of San Francisco, squeezed tightly between the bay and the coastal foothills, a vast swath of suburbia continues toward San Jose. Dotted inside this area are Palo Alto, home of Stanford University, and Silicon Valley, the epicenter of the Bay Area's tech industry.

Don't bother looking for Silicon Valley on the map – you won't find it. Because silicon chips form the basis of modern microcomputers, and the Santa Clara Valley – stretching from Palo Alto through Mountain View, Sunnyvale and Cupertino to San Jose – is thought of as the birthplace of the microcomputer, it's nicknamed 'Silicon Valley.' It's hard to imagine that even after WWII this was still a wide expanse of orchards and farms.

Further west, the 70-mile stretch of coastal Hwy 1 from San Francisco to Santa Cruz is one of California's most bewitching ocean-side drives. For the most part, it's winding, two-lane blacktop, passing beach after beach.

San Francisco to San Jose

South of the San Francisco peninsula, I-280 is the dividing line between the densely populated South Bay area and the rugged and lightly populated Pacific Coast. With sweeping views of hills and reservoirs, I-280 is a more scenic choice than Hwy 101, which runs through business parks. Unfortunately, these parallel north–south arteries are often both clogged with traffic.

A historic site where European explorers first set eyes on San Francisco Bay, **Sweeney Ridge** (www.nps.gov/goga/sweeney.htm; end of Sneath Lane, San Bruno) straddles a prime spot between Pacifica and San Bruno, and offers hikers unparalleled ocean and bay views. From I-280, exit at Sneath Lane and follow it 2 miles west until it dead ends at the trailhead.

Right on the bay at the northern edge of San Mateo, 4 miles south of San Francisco International Airport, is **Coyote Point Recreation Area** (☎650-573-2592; http://parks.smcgov.org; 1701 Coyote Point Dr, San Mateo; per car $6; ⏰8am-8pm Apr-Aug, to 6pm or 7pm Sep-

Mar; P), a popular park and windsurfing destination. The main attraction – formerly known as the Coyote Point Museum – is **CuriOdyssey** (650-342-7755; http://curiodyssey.org; adult/child $11/8; 10am-5pm Tue-Sun; P), with innovative exhibits highlighting science and wildlife. Exit Hwy 101 at Coyote Point Dr.

Stanford University

Sprawled over 8200 leafy acres in Palo Alto, Stanford University (www.stanford.edu) was founded by Leland Stanford, one of the Central Pacific Railroad's 'Big Four' founders and a former governor of California. When the Stanfords' only child died of typhoid during a European tour in 1884, they decided to build a university in his memory. The campus was built on the site of the Stanfords' horse-breeding farm and, as a result, Stanford is still known as 'The Farm.'

Sights

Main Quad PLAZA

(650-723-2560; http://visit.stanford.edu/plan/guides/visit.html; off Palm Dr) Auguste Rodin's *Burghers of Calais* bronze sculpture marks the entrance to Stanford University's Main Quad, an open plaza where the original 12 campus buildings, a mix of Romanesque and Mission Revival styles, were joined by Memorial Church in 1903. The church is noted for its beautiful mosaic-tiled frontage, stained-glass windows and five organs with more than 8000 pipes. Free guided tours of 'MemChu' are given at 2pm every Friday and 11:15am on the first Sunday of the month.

Hoover Tower TOWER

(650-723-2560; http://visit.stanford.edu/plan/guides/hoover.html; adult/child $4/3; 10am-4pm, last entry 3:30pm) A campus landmark at the east of the Main Quad, the 285ft-high Hoover Tower offers superb views. The tower houses a university library, offices and part of the right-wing Hoover Institution on War, Revolution & Peace (where Donald Rumsfeld caused a university-wide stir by accepting a position after he resigned as Secretary of Defense).

Cantor Arts Center MUSEUM

(650-498-1480; http://museum.stanford.edu; 328 Lomita Dr; 11am-5pm Wed & Fri-Mon, to 8pm Thu; P) FREE The Cantor Center for Visual Arts is a large museum originally dating from 1894. Its collection spans works from ancient civilizations to contemporary art, sculpture and photography, and rotating exhibits are eclectic in scope. Step outside into the Rodin and Papua New Guinea sculpture gardens.

Information

Stanford Visitor Center (650-723-2560; http://visit.stanford.edu; 295 Galvez St; 8:30am-5pm Mon-Fri, 10am-5pm Sat & Sun) Offers free 70-minute walking tours of the campus at 11am and 3:15pm daily, except during academic breaks and some holidays. Special-interest tours also available.

NERD'S NIRVANA

Touted as the largest computer-history exhibition in the world, the **Computer History Museum** (650-810-1010; www.computerhistory.org; 1401 N Shoreline Blvd, Mountain View; adult $17.50, student & senior $13.50; 10am-5pm Wed-Sun, to 8pm Fri; P) has rotating exhibits drawn from its 100,000-item collection. Artifacts range from the abacus to the iPod, including Cray-1 supercomputers, a Babbage Difference Engine (a Victorian-era automatic computing engine) and the first Google server.

Though there are no tours of the **Googleplex** (650-214-3308; www.google.com/about/company/facts/locations; 1600 Amphitheatre Pkwy, Mountain View; store 10am-6:30pm Mon-Fri; P), visitors can stroll the campus and gawk at the public art on the leafy grounds, where scads of Googlers zoom about on primary-colored bicycles. Don't miss the 'dessert yard' outside Building 44, with lawn sculptures of Android operating systems (a cupcake! a donut! a robot!), and across the street, a toothy Tyrannosaurus rex festooned in pink flamingos next to the volleyball court.

At the Intel headquarters, the **Intel Museum** (408-765-5050; www.intel.com/museum; 2200 Mission College Blvd, Santa Clara; usually 9am-6pm Mon-Fri, 10am-5pm Sat; P) FREE has displays on the birth and growth of the computer industry with special emphasis, not surprisingly, on microchips and Intel's involvement. Reserve ahead if you want to schedule a tour.

Getting There & Away

Stanford University's free public shuttle, **Marguerite** (650-723-9362; http://transportation.stanford.edu/marguerite), provides service from Caltrain's Palo Alto and California Ave stations to the campus, and has bicycle racks. Parking on campus is expensive and trying.

San Jose

Though culturally diverse and historic, San Jose has always been in San Francisco's shadow, awash in Silicon Valley's suburbia. Founded in 1777 as El Pueblo de San José de Guadalupe, San Jose is California's oldest Spanish civilian settlement. Its downtown is small and scarcely used for a city of its size, though it does bustle with 20-something clubgoers on weekends. Industrial parks, high-tech computer firms and look-alike housing developments have sprawled across the city's landscape, taking over where farms, ranches and open spaces once spread between the bay and the surrounding hills.

Sights

History Park HISTORIC BUILDING
(408-287-2290; http://historysanjose.org; 1650 Senter Rd; noon-5pm Mon-Fri, 11am-5pm Sat & Sun, last entry 4:30pm; P) FREE Historic buildings from all over San Jose have been brought together in this open-air history museum, southeast of the city center in Kelley Park. The centerpiece is a scaled-down replica of the 1881 **Electric Light Tower**. Other buildings include the 1880 **Pacific Hotel**, which has rotating art exhibits inside (closed Monday). The **Trolley Barn** restores historic trolley cars to operate on San Jose's light-rail line; on weekends you can ride a trolley along the park's own short line.

Tech Museum of Innovation MUSEUM
(The Tech; 408-294-8324; www.thetech.org; 201 S Market St; adult/child $24/19, incl IMAX movie $29/23; 10am-5pm;) Opposite Plaza de Cesar Chavez, San Jose's excellent technology museum examines subjects from robotics to space exploration, and genetics to virtual reality. The museum also includes an IMAX dome theater, which screens newly released films throughout the day.

MACLA GALLERY
(Movimiento de Arte y Cultura Latino Americana; 408-998-2783; http://maclaarte.org; 510 S 1st St; noon-7pm Wed & Thu, to 5pm Fri & Sat) FREE A cutting-edge gallery highlighting themes by both established and emerging Latino artists, MACLA is one of the Bay Area's best community arts spaces, with open-mike performances, live-music shows, experimental theater and well-curated, thought-provoking visual-arts exhibits.

Rosicrucian Egyptian Museum MUSEUM
(408-947-3635; www.egyptianmuseum.org; 1660 Park Ave; adult/child $9/5; 9am-5pm Wed-Fri, 10am-6pm Sat & Sun; P) West of downtown, this unusual and educational Egyptian museum is one of San Jose's more unusual attractions. Its extensive collection includes statues, household items and mummies; there's even a two-room, walk-through reproduction of an ancient subterranean tomb.

San Jose Museum of Art MUSEUM
(408-271-6840; http://sjmusart.org; 110 S Market St; adult/child $10/5; 11am-5pm Tue-Sun) With a permanent collection of 20th-century works and imaginative changing exhibits, the city's central art museum is worth a quick look. The main building started life as the post office in 1892, was damaged by the 1906 earthquake and became an art gallery in 1933. A modern wing was added in 1991.

Sleeping

Budget and midrange motels and hotels cluster near freeways, especially Hwy 101 from south of San Francisco International Airport to San Jose. Upmarket hotels and motels and atmospheric lodges and inns cluster off Hwy 1 near the beaches, especially around Half Moon Bay. Off Hwy 1 is also where you'll find charming lighthouse hostels, campgrounds and cabins.

Hotel De Anza HISTORIC HOTEL $$
(408-286-1000; www.destinationhotels.com/hotel-de-anza; 233 W Santa Clara St; r from $149; @) Opened during the Jazz Age, this downtown hotel is a restored art-deco beauty that pays homage to the property's history. Guest rooms offer plush comforts (those facing south are a tad larger) and there's full concierge service. Complimentary midnight snacks, in-room espresso makers and a 24-hour fitness center seal the deal.

Hotel Valencia BOUTIQUE HOTEL $$
(408-551-0010; www.hotelvalencia-santanarow.com; 355 Santana Row; r from $189; P@

WINCHESTER MYSTERY HOUSE

An odd structure purposefully commissioned to be so by the heir to the Winchester rifle fortune, this ridiculous Victorian **mansion** (408-247-2101; www.winchestermysteryhouse.com; 525 S Winchester Blvd; adult/child $36/26; 9am-7pm, to 5pm early Sep-late May; P) is filled with 160 rooms of various sizes and little utility, with dead-end hallways and a staircase that runs up to a ceiling all jammed together like a toddler playing architect. The standard hour-long guided mansion tour includes a self-guided romp through the gardens plus entry to an exhibition of guns and rifles.

Apparently, Sarah Winchester spent 38 years constructing this mammoth white elephant because the spirits of the people killed by Winchester rifles told her to. No expense was spared in the construction, the extreme results of which sprawl over 4 acres.

The house is west of central San Jose and just north of I-280, incongruously across the street from **Santana Row** (p145), a shopping center.

) A burbling lobby fountain and deep-red corridor carpeting set the tone for this tranquil 212-room contemporary hotel in the **Santana Row** (408-551-4611; www.santanarow.com; 377 Santana Row; 10am-9pm Mon-Sat, 11am-7pm Sun;) shopping complex. In-room minibars and bathrobes and an outdoor pool and hot tub create a stylish oasis of contemporary design. Parking is $24.

Westin San Jose HISTORIC HOTEL **$$**
(408-295-2000; www.westinsanjose.com; 302 S Market St; r from $149; P) Formerly the Sainte Claire, this atmospheric 1926 landmark hotel overlooking Plaza de Cesar Chavez has a gorgeous lobby with stretched-leather ceilings. Guest rooms are smallish, but have been remodeled. Parking is $39.

Eating

San Jose is no culinary hub, but you'll find plenty of thronged restaurants downtown. Budget-friendly cafes are further east near the SJSU campus. For a more memorable meal, visit San Jose's historic Japantown, spread out along Jackson St east of 1st St, north of downtown.

Hukilau FUSION **$**
(408-279-4888; www.dahukilau.com/sanjose; 230 Jackson St; mains $10-18; 11am-2pm & 5-9pm Mon-Thu & Sun, 11am-2pm & 5-10pm Fri, 11am-2.30pm & 5-10pm Sat;) Incongruously located in San Jose's tiny Japantown, this fun Hawaii-themed bar puts together incredibly filling island-style plate meals (sesame chicken is da best) and *pupus* (snacks or appetizers) such as Spam *musubi* (block of rice with a slice of fried Spam on top, wrapped with a strip of nori) and bowls of *ahi poke* (raw-fish salad). Live Hawaiian music some weekend evenings.

San Pedro Square Market FOOD HALL **$**
(www.sanpedrosquaremarket.com; 87 N San Pedro St; most mains $6-20; usually 7am to 10pm-1am;) Always busy, this indoor/outdoor marketplace downtown showcases a few shining local food stars such as Bray Butcher Block and Bistro, Pizza Bocca Lupo, Konjoe Burger Bar and Treatbot ice cream. All seating is first-come, first-served. Live music every Friday and Saturday evening and Sunday afternoon. Some vendors validate parking in the adjacent garage.

Tofoo Com Chay VEGETARIAN, VIETNAMESE **$**
(408-286-6335; 388 E Santa Clara St; mains from $6.50; 9am-9pm Mon-Fri, 10am-6pm Sat;) Conveniently located on the border of the San Jose State University campus. Students and vegetarians queue for the Vietnamese dishes such as the fake-meat pho and the heaped combo plates.

Back A Yard CARIBBEAN **$$**
(408-294-8626; www.backayard.net/sanjose; 80 N Market St; mains $8-16; 11am-2:30pm & 4:30-8:30pm Mon-Thu, 11am-9pm Fri, from noon Sat) Jamaican-jerk chicken, pork, salmon and tofu are the house specialties of this Caribbean-barbecue kitchen, which also fries catfish, snapper and shrimp, all hot and spicy. Look for beef oxtail and curried goat on the daily specials menu, and tropically colored murals on the red-brick walls.

Original Joe's ITALIAN **$$**
(408-292-7030; www.originaljoes.com; 301 S 1st St; mains $10-33; 11am-midnight) Waiters in bow ties flit about this busy 1950s San Jose landmark, serving standard Italian dishes to locals and conventioneers. The dining room is a curious but tasteful hodgepodge of '50s

brick, contemporary wood paneling and tall Asian vases. Expect a wait.

Arcadia STEAK, SEAFOOD $$$
(408-278-4555; www.michaelmina.net/restaurants; 100 W San Carlos St; mains lunch $15-23, dinner $34-64; 6:30am-2pm daily, 5:30-10pm Mon-Sat) This New American steakhouse restaurant in the Marriott Hotel is run by chef Michael Mina, one of San Francisco's celebrity chefs. It's not the daring, cutting-edge style Mina is known for, but it's slick, expensive and reasonably good.

Drinking & Nightlife

Original Gravity Public House CRAFT BEER
(408-915-2337; www.originalgravitypub.com; 66 S 1st St; 11:30am-10:30pm Sun-Wed, to midnight Thu-Sat) Squeeze inside this crowded yet friendly pub for beer geeks and the 'craft curious.' With nearly three dozen rotating taps of brews, including ciders and meads, as well as scores of bottles, you'll be confounded by choice. Consider your options while you nosh on housemade sausage, a grilled cheese sandwich or duck-fat poutine.

Paper Plane COCKTAIL BAR
(408-713-2625; www.paperplanesj.com; 72 S 1st St; 4:30pm-midnight Sun-Tue, to 2am Wed-Sat) Downtown at this industrial-chic watering hole with wall-sized, backlit shelves of liquor, tattooed bartenders willingly customize your drink if nothing on the menu of old-school classics and imaginative modern mixology tempts. Share a punch bowl and appetizers with friends.

B2 Coffee COFFEE
(www.bellanocoffee.com; 170 W St John St; 7am-7pm Mon-Fri, 8am-7pm Sat & Sun) Haute coffee-roaster Bellano has opened a branch inside downtown's San Pedro Square Market (p145), serving the same rich pour-over coffee, nitro cold brew and iced almond-milk lattes mixed with from-scratch vanilla syrup.

Haberdasher COCKTAIL BAR
(408-792-7356; www.haberdashersj.com; 43 W San Salvador St; 5pm-midnight Sun, Tue & Wed, to 1am Thu-Sat) A cool basement lounge, where sharply dressed bartenders artfully mix cocktails (including 'House Fittings' options), with some recipes dating to before Prohibition. It's a justifiably popular place but you can (and should) book ahead for a table Friday and Saturday nights to guarantee your spot.

Hedley Club LOUNGE
(408-286-1000; www.destinationhotels.com/hotel-de-anza/dining/hedley-club-lounge; 233 W Santa Clara St; hours vary) Inside the elegant 1931 Hotel De Anza, the Hedley Club is a good place for a quiet drink in swanky art-deco surroundings. Jazz combos play most nights.

☆ Entertainment

Avaya Stadium SPECTATOR SPORT
(1123 Coleman Rd; hours vary) Located near San Jose's airport, this is the home of the **San Jose Earthquakes** (408-556-7700; www.sjearthquakes.com), the city's professional soccer team (season runs from February through October).

SAN JOSE FOR CHILDREN

Children's Discovery Museum (408-298-5437; www.cdm.org; 180 Woz Way; $13, child under 1yr free; 10am-5pm Tue-Sat, noon-5pm Sun;) Downtown, this science and creativity museum has hands-on displays incorporating art, technology and the environment, with plenty of toys and cool play-and-learn areas for tots to school-aged children. The museum is on Woz Way, named after Steve Wozniak, cofounder of Apple.

California's Great America (408-988-1776; www.cagreatamerica.com; 4701 Great America Pkwy, Santa Clara; adult/child under 4ft $69/48; Apr-Oct, hours vary;) If you can handle the shameless product placements, kids love the roller coasters and other thrill rides. Online tickets cost much less than walk-up prices. Parking is $15 to $25, but the park is also accessible by public transportation.

Raging Waters (408-238-9900; www.rwsplash.com; 2333 S White Rd; adult/child under 4ft $39/29; May-Sep, hours vary;) A water park inside Lake Cunningham Regional Park, Raging Waters has fast waterslides, a wave pool and a nifty Pirate's Cove. Buy tickets online for discounts. Parking is $6 to $10.

SAP Center STADIUM

(☎408-287-9200; www.sapcenteratsanjose.com; 525 W Santa Clara St) The fanatically popular **San Jose Sharks** (☎800-559-2333; www.nhl.com/sharks), the city's professional hockey team, plays at this massive glass-and-metal stadium (formerly the HP Pavilion) from September through April. Megaconcerts by touring acts go on stage year-round.

California Theatre THEATER

(☎408-792-4111; http://sanjosetheaters.org/theaters/california-theatre; 345 S 1st St; ⊙hours vary) The absolutely stunning Spanish Colonial interior of this landmark entertainment venue is cathedral-worthy. The theater is home to Opera San Jose and Symphony Silicon Valley.

Information

San Jose Convention & Visitors Bureau (☎408-792-4511; www.sanjose.org; 408 Almaden Blvd; ⊙9am-5pm Mon-Fri) Free visitor information guides and maps online.

Santa Clara Valley Medical Center (☎408-885-5000; www.scvmc.org; 751 S Bascom Ave; ⊙24hr) 24-hour emergency services.

Getting There & Away

AIR

Four miles northwest of downtown between Hwy 101 and I-880, **Mineta San Jose International Airport** (SJC; ☎408-392-3600; www.flysanjose.com; 1701 Airport Blvd) has free wi-fi and mostly domestic US flights from two terminals.

BART

To access the BART (p131) system in the East Bay, VTA (p147) bus 181 runs between downtown San Jose and the Fremont BART station ($4, 35 to 45 minutes, every 15 to 20 minutes).

BUS

Greyhound (p527) buses to Los Angeles ($21 to $84, 6½ to 10½ hours) leave from San Jose's **Diridon Station** (Diridon Transit Center; 65 Cahill St). Discount carrier **Megabus** (☎877-462-6342; http://us.megabus.com) offers daily service between San Jose and Burbank, Los Angeles or Anaheim ($5 to $44, six to seven hours), with departures outside Diridon Station.

The **Santa Clara Valley Transportation Authority** (VTA; ☎408-321-2300, 800-894-9908; www.vta.org) Hwy 17 Express bus plies a handy route between Diridon Station and Santa Cruz ($7, 55 minutes, hourly).

CAR & MOTORCYCLE

San Jose is at the southern end of the San Francisco Bay, about 40 miles from Oakland (via I-880) or 50 miles from San Francisco (via Hwy 101 or I-280). Expect lots of traffic at all times of day on Hwy 101 from San Francisco; although I-280 is slightly longer, it's much prettier and usually less congested. Heading south, Hwy 17 leads over the mountains to Santa Cruz.

TRAIN

A double-decker commuter rail service operating up and down the peninsula, **Caltrain** (☎800-660-4287; www.caltrain.com) runs between San Jose and San Francisco ($9.75, 65 to 85 minutes). Trains run hourly on weekends and more frequently on weekdays. Bicycles may be brought on designated cars only. San Jose's terminal, **Diridon Station**, is just south of the Alameda.

Diridon Station also is the terminal for Amtrak (p527) trains serving Seattle, Los Angeles and Sacramento, as well as **Altamont Commuter Express** (ACE; ☎800-411-7245; www.acerail.com) trains, which run to Great America, Livermore and Stockton.

VTA runs a free weekday shuttle (known as the Downtown Area Shuttle or DASH) from Diridon Station to downtown San Jose.

Getting Around

VTA buses run all over Silicon Valley. Fares for VTA buses (except express lines) and light-rail trains are $2 for a single ride (day pass $6).

From the airport, free VTA Airport Flyer shuttles (route 10) run every 10 to 15 minutes to the Metro/Airport Light Rail station, where you can catch light rail to downtown San Jose; shuttles also go to the Santa Clara Caltrain station.

The main San Jose light-rail line runs north–south from the city center. Heading south gets you as far as Almaden and Santa Teresa. The northern route runs to Japantown, the airport and Tasman, where it connects with another line that heads west past Great America to downtown Mountain View.

In San Jose, many downtown retailers offer two-hour parking validation. Otherwise, city-owned lots and garages downtown charge a $5 flat rate after 6pm on weekdays and all day on weekends. Check www.sjdowntownparking.com for details.

Pacifica & Devil's Slide

One of the real surprises of the Bay Area is how fast the cityscape disappears along the rugged and largely undeveloped coast. The lazy beach town of Pacifica, just 15 miles from downtown San Francisco, signals the end of the urban sprawl. Most beaches along Hwy 1 are buffeted by wild and unpredictable surf, making them better suited to sunbathing (weather permitting) than swimming. Immediately south of Pacifica is the Devil's Slide, a gorgeous coastal cliff area now bypassed by a car tunnel.

Pacifica State Beach BEACH
(Linda Mar Beach; ☎650-738-7381; www.parks.ca.gov; 5000 Pacific Coast Hwy; per car $5-9; ⏲5am-dusk; P 🚻) In Pacifica, collecting a suntan or catching a wave are the main attractions at popular Pacifica State Beach, as well as Rockaway Beach just north.

Nor-Cal Surf Shop SURFING
(☎650-738-9283; 5440 Coast Hwy, Pedro Point Shopping Center; ⏲9am-6pm Sun-Thu, to 7pm Fri, 8am-7pm Sat) Rents surfboards ($19 per day), wet suits ($16.50) and SUP sets ($45) next to Pacifica State Beach. Book ahead for surf lessons (from $95).

Devil's Slide Trail HIKING
(☎650-355-8289; http://parks.smcgov.org/devils-slide-trail; Hwy 1; ⏲8am-8pm Apr-Aug, closes earlier Sep-Mar; 🚻) Hikers and cyclists cruise along the Devil's Slide Coastal Trail, a paved 1.3-mile section of the old highway. Heading south or north on Hwy 1, turn off before entering the tunnels into the trailhead parking lots.

Pacifica to Half Moon Bay

Other than a string of gorgeous, wild beaches along Hwy 1, there's little to stop for on the short, but distractingly scenic drive between Pacifica and Half Moon Bay. South of historic Point Montara Lighthouse, a hidden marine reserve protects natural tide pools and harbor seals.

Montara State Beach STATE PARK
(☎650-726-8819; www.parks.ca.gov; Hwy 1; ⏲8am-sunset; P 🚻) FREE About 5 miles south of the town of Pacifica, this wide-open crescent is a local favorite for its pristine sand. Inland the park encompasses **McNee Ranch**, which has hiking and cycling trails aplenty, including a strenuous ascent to a panoramic viewpoint atop **Montara Mountain** (1898ft), a 7.6-mile round-trip from Hwy 1.

Ranch Corral de Tierra PARK
(www.nps.gov/goga/rcdt.htm; off Hwy 1) FREE From the town of Montara, about 20 miles from San Francisco, trails climb from Montara State Beach to access the undeveloped 4000-acre park of Ranch Corral de Tierra, part of Golden Gate National Recreation Area.

Fitzgerald Marine Reserve NATURE RESERVE
(☎650-728-3584; www.fitzgeraldreserve.org; 200 Nevada Ave, Moss Beach; ⏲8am-8pm Apr-Aug, closes earlier Sep-Mar; P 🚻) FREE At Moss Beach, this marine reserve protects tide pools teeming with sea life. Walk out among the pools at low tide – wearing shoes that you can get wet – and explore the myriad crabs, sea stars, mollusks and rainbow-colored sea anemone. Note that it's illegal to remove any creatures, shells or even rocks from the marine reserve.

From Hwy 1, turn west on to Vermont Ave, which becomes Lake St and intersects Nevada Ave. SamTrans (p151) bus 17 stops along Hwy 1, only a five-minute walk or so from the reserve.

HI Point Montara Lighthouse HOSTEL $
(☎650-728-7177; www.norcalhostels.org/montara; cnr Hwy 1 & 16th St, Montara; r with shared bath $83-128, dm $33-39; ⏲reception 7:30am-10:30pm; P ⊖ @ ᯤ) Starting life as a fog station in 1875, Point Montara Lighthouse Hostel is adjacent to the current lighthouse, which dates from 1928. This very popular hostel has a living room, kitchen facilities and an international clientele. There are a few private rooms for couples or families. Reservations are a good idea anytime, but especially on weekends and in summer.

If you're not staying at the hostel, you can visit the lighthouse grounds between 9am and sunset daily (but check in at the front desk first). SamTrans bus 17 stops across the highway from the hostel.

Moss Beach Distillery BAR
(☎650-728-5595; www.mossbeachdistillery.com; 140 Beach Way, Moss Beach; ⏲noon-9pm Mon-Sat, 11am-9pm Sun) Overlooking the cove where bootleggers used to unload Prohibition-era liquor, the restaurant's heated ocean-view deck is perfectly positioned to catch sunset. In fair weather it's the best place for miles around to have a leisurely cocktail, but head elsewhere for a meal if you're hungry.

Half Moon Bay

With its long coastline and mild weather, this area has always been prime real estate. When Spanish missionaries set up shop along the coast in the late 1700s, this had been indigenous Ohlone territory for thousands of years. Developed as a beach resort in the early 1900s, Half Moon Bay today is the main coastal town between San Francisco

SCENIC DRIVE: HIGHWAY 84

Inland from the Pacific, vast stretches of the peninsula's hills are protected in a patchwork of parks that, just like the coast, remain remarkably untouched despite huge urban populations only a short drive away.

Heading east from Hwy 1, about 10 miles south of Half Moon Bay (p148), Hwy 84 winds its way upward through thick stands of redwood trees, passing local and state parks and open-space preserves with hiking and mountain-biking opportunities. Allow at least an hour to make the 25-mile drive to Palo Alto without stopping.

A mile in from **San Gregorio State Beach** (650-726-8819; www.parks.ca.gov; Hwy 1, San Gregorio; per car $8; 8am-sunset) on Hwy 1, kick off your shoes and stomp your feet to live bluegrass, Celtic and folk music on the weekends at the **San Gregorio General Store** (650-726-0565; www.sangregoriostore.com; 7615 Stage Rd, San Gregorio; store 10:30am-6pm Sun-Thu, to 7pm Fri, 10am-7pm Sat, to 6pm Sun). Check out the wooden bar singed by area branding irons.

Eight miles further east is the tiny township of **La Honda**, former home to *One Flew Over the Cuckoo's Nest* author Ken Kesey and the launching spot for his 1964 psychedelic bus trip immortalized in Tom Wolfe's *The Electric Kool-Aid Acid Test*. Housed in a 19th-century blacksmith's shop, **Apple Jack's** (650-747-0331; 8790 Hwy 84; noon-2am) is a rustic, down-home country-and-western bar with motorcycles lined up in a row outside.

To stretch your legs in the redwoods, **Sam McDonald County Park** (650-879-0238; http://parks.smcgov.org/sam-mcdonald-park; 13435 Pescadero Creek Rd, Loma Mar; per car $6; 8am-8pm Apr-Aug, closes earlier Sep-Mar; P), 2 miles south of La Honda, has forested hiking trails and a secluded hike-to **cabin** (650-390-8411; www.sierraclub.org/loma-prieta/hikers-hut; per night adult $20-30, child $10;). From the park, it's a 20-minute winding drive downhill along Pescadero Creek Rd to visit the tiny farm town of Pescadero (p150), just inland from the coast.

Otherwise, backtrack to La Honda and continue north on Hwy 84, passing more nature preserves and viewpoints over Silicon Valley. Turn left on to Skyline Blvd to eat at **Alice's Restaurant** (650-851-0303; www.alicesrestaurant.com; 17288 Skyline Blvd, Woodside; mains $9-14; 8am-8pm Sun-Thu, to 9pm Fri-Sat) inside an early 20th-century general store. It's not the same diner made famous by 1960s folk singer Arlo Guthrie, but it's still a popular stop for bikers, cyclists and Sunday drivers, especially for weekend brunch.

Keep following Hwy 84 as it corkscrews downhill, turning right on to Sand Hill Rd, which leads east to Stanford University (p143) and downtown Palo Alto.

(29 miles north) and Santa Cruz (49 miles south). Its long stretches of beach still attract rambling weekenders and die-hard surfers.

Half Moon Bay spreads out along Hwy 1/Cabrillo Hwy, but despite development, it's still relatively small. Downtown, the main drag is a five-block stretch of Main St lined with art galleries, antiques shops, cafes and restaurants. For aquatic pursuits and seafood restaurants, detour to Pillar Point Harbor, about 4 miles northwest of downtown, off Hwy 1.

Sea Horse Ranch HORSEBACK RIDING
(650-726-9903; http://seahorseranch.org; 1828 Cabrillo Hwy; trail ride $60-90; hours vary;) Just over a mile north of the Hwy 92 junction, Sea Horse Ranch offers daily horseback rides along the beach. Minimum age for riders is seven years; weight limits and clothing restrictions apply. Book ahead.

Half Moon Bay Kayak Co WATER SPORTS, CYCLING
(650-773-6101; www.hmbkayak.com; 2 Johnson Pier; kayak or SUP set rental per hour/day $25/75, bicycle rental $25/50; 9am-5pm Wed-Mon;) When the bay is calm, get out on the water with Half Moon Bay Kayak Co, which rents kayaks, stand up paddle surfing (SUP) sets and bicycles too. Book ahead for harbor, sunset or full-moon tours or an adventurous kayak-fishing trip. Last walk-up rental is at 3:30pm.

Mavericks SURFING

At the western end of Pillar Point is Mavericks, a serious surf break that attracts pro big-wave riders to battle its huge, steep and very dangerous waves. The invitational **Titans of Mavericks** (http://titansofmavericks.com/event) FREE surf contest, called on a few days' notice when the swells get huge, is held annually between November and March.

Half Moon Bay Art & Pumpkin Festival FOOD, CULTURAL

(☎650-726-9652; www.pumpkinfest.miramarevents.com; Main St; ⊙mid-Oct;) FREE Pumpkins are a major deal around Half Moon Bay and the pre-Halloween harvest is celebrated with this annual festival. It kicks off with the World Championship Pumpkin Weigh-Off, where some bulbous beasts bust the scales at nearly 2000lb.

Half Moon Bay Brewing Company PUB FOOD $$

(☎650-728-2739; www.hmbbrewingco.com; 390 Capistrano Rd; mains $12-25; ⊙11:30am-9pm Mon-Thu, to 10pm Fri, 10am-10pm Sat, to 9pm Sun;) Chomp on seafood and burgers while you swill pints from a respectable menu of local brews and gaze out at the bay from a sheltered, heated outdoor patio. Live music some weekends.

Getting There & Away

SamTrans bus 294 operates hourly between the Caltrain (p147) Hillsdale station in San Mateo and Half Moon Bay ($2.25, 45 minutes). From Half Moon Bay, SamTrans bus 17 heads up the coast to Moss Beach, Montara and Pacifica ($2.25, one hour) every hour or two daily, with limited weekday service south to Pescadero ($2.25, 25 minutes).

Pescadero

A foggy speck of coastal crossroads between Half Moon Bay and Santa Cruz, 160-year-old Pescadero is a close-knit rural town of sugar-lending neighbors and community pancake breakfasts. But on weekends the tiny downtown strains its seams with long-distance cyclists panting for carbohydrates and day-trippers dive-bombing in from the oceanfront highway. They're all drawn to the winter vistas of emerald-green hills parched to burlap brown in summer, the wild Pacific beaches populated by seals and pelicans, and the unbelievably fresh food from local farms and ranches. With its cornucopia of tide-pool coves and parks of sky-blotting redwood canopy, city dwellers come here to slow down and smell the sea breeze wafting over fields of bushy artichokes.

Sights

Pigeon Point Light Station State Historic Park LIGHTHOUSE

(☎650-879-2120; www.parks.ca.gov; 210 Pigeon Point Rd; ⊙8am-sunset, visitor center 10am-4pm Thu-Mon; P) A half-dozen miles south of Pescadero along the coast, the 115ft light station is one of the tallest lighthouses on the West Coast. The 1872 landmark had to close access to the upper tower when chunks of its cornice began to rain from the sky (future restorations are planned), but the beam still flashes brightly and the bluff is a prime though blustery spot to scan for breaching gray whales in winter. Half-hour guided history walks of the lighthouse grounds leave at 1pm (weather permitting) from the visitor center and bookstore.

Bean Hollow State Beach BEACH

(☎650-726-8819; www.parks.ca.gov; off Hwy 1; ⊙8am-sunset; P) FREE Pretty sand beaches speckle the coast, though one of the most interesting places to stop is Pebble Beach, a jewel less than 2 miles south of Pescadero Creek Rd (and part of Bean Hollow State Beach). The shore is awash with bite-sized eye candy of agate, jade and carnelian, and sandstone troughs are pockmarked by groovy honeycombed formations called tafoni.

Butano State Park STATE PARK

(☎650-879-2040; www.parks.ca.gov; 1500 Cloverdale Rd; per car $10; ⊙sunrise-sunset; P) Five miles south of Pescadero, bobcats and coyotes reside discreetly in this pretty park's 4600 acres of dense redwood canyon and uplands laced with hiking and mountain-biking trails and shady campsites. From Pescadero Creek Rd in downtown Pescadero, follow Cloverdale Rd south for 4 miles to the turnoff.

To take the scenic route back to Hwy 1, continue south on Cloverdale Rd, turning right on to Gazos Creek Rd and winding 2 more miles to the coast.

Pescadero State Beach & Marsh Natural Preserve STATE PARK

(☎650-726-8819; www.parks.ca.gov; off Hwy 1; per car $8; ⊙8am-sunset; P) Fifteen miles south of Half Moon Bay, this state beach and marshland preserve attract beachcombers and birders. Pull over and get out of the car to explore the marine-life-rich coastal tide pools on rocky outcroppings.

Sleeping & Eating

HI Pigeon Point Lighthouse HOSTEL $
(☎650-879-0633; www.norcalhostels.org/pigeon; 210 Pigeon Point Rd; r with shared bath from $82-186, dm $26-32; ⏰reception 7:30am-10:30pm; P ⊜ @ 🛜) Not your workaday youth hostel, this highly coveted coastside lodging is all about location. Book ahead and check in early to snag a spot in the outdoor hot tub ($8 per person per 30 minutes) and contemplate roaring waves as the lighthouse beacon races through a starburst sky. It's about 6 miles south of Pescadero.

Butano State Park Campground CAMPGROUND $
(☎reservations 800-444-7275; www.reserveamerica.com; 1500 Cloverdale Rd; tent & RV sites $35; P 🐾) Shady campsites have picnic tables and fire pits, but the most serene spots are the walk-in, tent-only sites tucked back into the forest.

Costanoa CABIN, LODGE $$
(☎650-879-1100; www.costanoa.com; 2001 Rossi Rd; tent/cabin with shared bath from $100/200, lodge r from $200; P ⊜ 🛜) Even though this coastal resort, about 10 miles south of Pescadero, includes a **campground** (☎650-879-7302; http://koa.com/campgrounds/santa-cruz-north; tent/RV sites with hookups from $36/85; P 🛜 🐾), no one can pull a straight face and declare they're actually roughing it here. Down bedding swaddles guests in canvas-sided tent bungalows and hard-sided Douglas-fir cabins. Chill-averse folks can use communal 'comfort stations' with 24-hour dry saunas, fireside patio seating, heated floors and hot showers.

Bland lodge rooms with private fireplaces and hot-tub access cater to those without such Spartan delusions. There's an expensive restaurant, bar and spa on-site. Bicycle rentals, yoga classes, horseback rides and guided bird-watching are available to guests only.

Pescadero Creek Inn INN $$
(☎650-879-1898; www.pescaderocreekinn.com; 393 Stage Rd; d $175-250; P ⊜ 🛜) Unwind in the private two-room cottage or one of the spotless Victorian rooms in a restored 100-year-old farmhouse with a tranquil creekside garden.

Duarte's Tavern AMERICAN $$
(☎650-879-0464; www.duartestavern.com; 202 Stage Rd; mains $8-39; ⏰7am-8pm; 👪) You'll rub shoulders with fancy-pants foodies, spandex-swathed cyclists and dusty cowboys at this casual, surprisingly unpretentious fourth-generation family restaurant. Duarte's is this town's culinary magnet, though some critics say it's resting on its laurels. Feast on crab cioppino and a half-and-half split of cream of artichoke and green-chili soups, then bring it home with a wedge of olallieberry pie. Except for the unfortunate lull of Prohibition, the wood-paneled bar has been hosting the locals and their honored guests since 1894. Reservations strongly recommended.

Getting There & Away

By car, the town is 3 miles east of Hwy 1 on Pescadero Creek Rd, leading inland from Pescadero State Beach. On weekdays, **SamTrans** (☎511, 800-660-4287; www.samtrans.com) bus 17 runs twice a day to and from Half Moon Bay ($2.25, 25 minutes).

Año Nuevo State Park

Just over a dozen miles southeast of Pescadero State Beach, **Año Nuevo State Park** (☎park office 650-879-2025, recorded info 650-879-0227, tour reservations 800-444-4445; www.parks.ca.gov; 1 New Years Creek Rd; per car $10, 2½hr tour per person $7; ⏰8:30am-sunset Apr-Nov, tours only Dec 15–Mar 31; P 👪) is home to the world's largest mainland breeding colonies of northern elephant seals. More raucous than a full-moon beach rave, thousands of boisterous animals party year-round on the dunes of Año Nuevo Point, their squeals and barks reaching fever pitch during the winter pupping season.

Northern elephant seals were just as fearless two centuries ago as they are today, but unfortunately, seal trappers were not as friendly as today's tourists. During the 19th century, northern elephant seals were driven to the edge of extinction. Only a handful survived around the Guadalupe Islands off the Mexican state of Baja California. With the availability of substitutes for seal oil and the conservationist attitudes of more recent times, northern elephant seals have come back, reappearing on the Southern

THE CULINARY COAST

Pescadero is renowned for Duarte's Tavern (p151), but loads of other tidbits are close by.

Arcangeli Grocery Company (Norm's Market; ☎650-879-0147; www.normsmarket.com; 287 Stage Rd; sandwiches $7-10; ⊙10am-6pm;) Create a picnic with made-to-order deli sandwiches, homemade artichoke salsa and a chilled bottle of California wine. Don't go breezing out the door without nabbing a crusty loaf of the famous artichoke garlic herb bread, baked fresh almost hourly.

Harley Farms Goat Dairy (☎650-879-0480; http://harleyfarms.com; 250 North St; ⊙10am-5pm Thu-Mon Apr-Dec, 11am-4pm Fri-Sun Jan-Mar; P) Another local food treasure, here the split-level farm shop sells creamy artisanal goat's cheeses festooned with fruit, nuts and a rainbow of edible flowers, as well as goat's-milk bath and body products. Show up anytime to pat the heads of the goats out back, or reserve ahead for a weekend farm tour ($30) or dinner ($150) in the Victorian-era barn. The farm is less than a mile east of downtown: follow the cool wooden cutouts of the goat and the Wellington-shod girl with the faraway eyes.

Pie Ranch (☎650-879-9281; www.pieranch.org; 2080 Cabrillo Hwy; ⊙noon-5pm Mon-Fri, 10am-5pm Sat & Sun;) Hit the brakes for this roadside farm stand in a wooden barn to pick up fresh produce, eggs and coffee, plus amazing fruit pies (which sell out fast). The historic pie-slice-shaped farm is a nonprofit dedicated to leadership development and food education for urban youth. Check the website for volunteer work days, farm tours, potluck dinners and barn dances. It's around 11 miles south of Pescadero Creek Rd.

Swanton Berry Farm Stand & U-Pick (☎650-469-8804; www.swantonberryfarm.com; 25 Swanton Rd, Davenport; ⊙8am-8pm late May-early Sep, closes earlier rest of year; P) Roll up your shirtsleeves and harvest some fruit at this organic pick-your-own farm south of Año Nuevo. It's a union outfit (operated by Cesar Chavez's United Farm Workers), with buckets of seasonal strawberries, olallieberries, blackberries and even kiwis ripe for the plucking. The farm stand sells baskets of ripe berries and berry shortcakes, pies and jams.

Bonnie Doon Vineyard Tasting Room (☎831-471-8031; www.bonnydoonvineyard.com; 450 Hwy 1, Davenport; tasting fee $10-20; ⊙11am-5pm, to 6pm Fri & Sat late May-early Sep, closed Wed early Sep-Feb; P) In the sleepy village of Davenport, round out your palate with a wine flight in the roadside tasting room of Randall Grahm's acclaimed winery, where Edison lights and rough-hewed wooden tables entice you to sample Le Cigare Volant (yes, that's a flying cigar), a Rhône-style red blend and other bottles made with lesser-known grape varietals. The tasting room is about 10 miles northwest of Santa Cruz on Hwy 1.

California coast during the 1920s. They returned to Año Nuevo Beach in 1955.

In peak season, during the mating and birthing time from mid-December to end of March, visitors are only permitted access to the reserve on guided tours. For the busiest period, from mid-January to mid-February, it's recommended you book two months ahead. Although the park office can answer general questions, tours must be arranged through ReserveAmerica (http://anonuevo.reserveamerica.com).

The rest of the year, advance reservations aren't necessary, but visitor permits from the entrance station are required; arrive before 3pm in September, October or November or 3:30pm April to August. From the ranger station it's a 3- to 5-mile round-trip hike on sand; allow two to three hours. Dogs are not allowed on-site and no visitors are permitted during the first two weeks of December.

The park is less than 7 miles southeast of Pigeon Point or over 20 miles northwest of Santa Cruz.

Napa & Sonoma Wine Country

Includes ➡

Best Places to Eat

- ➡ Handline (p196)
- ➡ Oxbow Public Market (p163)
- ➡ Fremont Diner (p186)
- ➡ SingleThread (p210)
- ➡ Shed (p209)

Best Places to Sleep

- ➡ El Bonita (p170)
- ➡ Shanti Permaculture Farm (p198)
- ➡ Hotel Healdsburg (p208)
- ➡ Windhaven Cottage (p185)
- ➡ Brannan Cottage Inn (p176)

Why Go?

America's premier viticulture region has earned its reputation among the world's best. Despite hype about Wine Country style, it's from the land that all Wine Country lore springs. Rolling hills, dotted with century-old oaks, turn the color of lion's fur under the summer sun and swaths of vineyards carpet hillsides as far as the eye can see. Where they end, redwood forests follow serpentine rivers to the sea.

There are over 900 wineries in Napa and Sonoma Counties, but it's quality, not quantity, that distinguishes the region – especially in Napa, which competes with France and doubles as an outpost of San Francisco's top-end culinary scene. Sonoma prides itself on agricultural diversity, with goat's-cheese farms, you-pick-'em orchards and roadside fruit stands. Plan to get lost on back roads, and, as you picnic atop sun-dappled hillsides, grab a hunk of earth and know firsthand the thing of greatest meaning in Wine Country.

When to Go

Napa

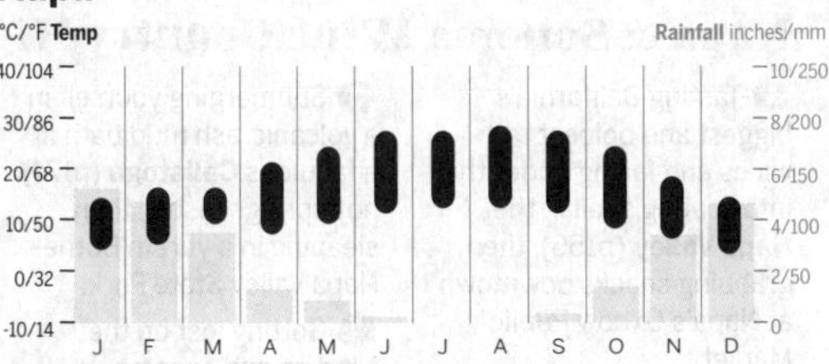

Jan Bright-yellow flowers carpet the valleys during the off-season; room rates plummet.

Apr–May Before summer holidays is the perfect time for touring, with long days and warm sun.

Sep–Oct 'Crush' time is peak season, when winemaking operations are in full force.

Getting There & Getting Away

Napa and Sonoma Counties each have an eponymous city and valley. So Sonoma town is in Sonoma County, at the southern end of Sonoma Valley. The same goes for the city, county and valley of Napa.

From San Francisco, public transportation gets you to the valleys, but it's insufficient for vineyard-hopping. For public-transit information, dial ☎ 511, or look online at www.transit.511.org.

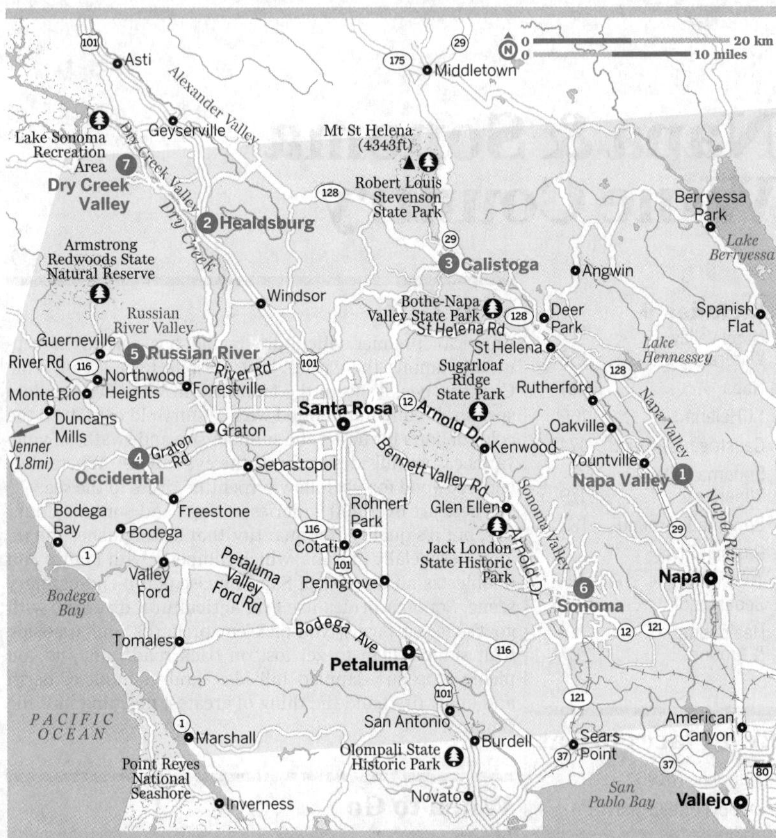

Napa & Sonoma Wine Country Highlights

1 Tasting California's biggest and boldest red wines and falling under their intoxicating spell in the **Napa Valley** (p156), then grabbing snacks downtown at Napa's Oxbow Public Market.

2 Feasting in Northern California's greatest food town, **Healdsburg** (p207). Then, wallet permitting, hitting up exciting new restaurant, SingleThread.

3 Submerging yourself in a volcanic-ash mud bath at a fabulous **Calistoga** (p174) hot-springs resort, then sleeping in a yurt in Bothe-Napa Valley State Park.

4 Getting lost on the winding and spectacular Coleman Valley Rd before arriving in the region's wackiest town, **Occidental** (p197) .

5 Floating in a canoe, kayak or tube down NorCal's natural lazy **Russian River** (p19; put-ins available at Guerneville and Healdsburg), then hopping out and drinking some wine.

6 Picnicking in sun-dappled grass on the state's largest historic town square, **Sonoma Plaza** (p182)

7 Pedaling between wineries along pastoral and undulating West Dry Creek Rd in **Dry Creek Valley** (p193).

Both valleys are a 90-minute drive from San Francisco. Napa, further inland, has about 500 wineries and attracts the most visitors (expect heavy traffic on summer weekends). Sonoma County has more than 425 wineries and around 40 in Sonoma Valley, which is less commercial and less congested than Napa. If you have time to visit only one, for ease go with Sonoma.

AIR

Visitors fly into either **San Francisco International Airport** (☎650-821-8211; www.flysfo.com; 780 S Airport Blvd) or **Sacramento International Airport** (☎916-929-5411; http://sacramento.aero/smf; 6900 Airport Blvd); the drive from either to Napa Valley takes about 1½ hours. San Francisco is a more attractive destination but its airport is also far busier and more crowded than Sacramento's.

BOAT

Baylink Ferry (☎877-643-3779; www.sanfranciscobayferry.com) Downtown San Francisco to Vallejo (adult/child $13.80/6.90, 60 minutes); connect with Napa Valley Vine bus 29 (weekdays) or bus 11 (daily).

BUS

Evans Transportation (☎707-255-1559; www.evanstransportation.com) Shuttles ($40) to Napa from San Francisco and Oakland airports.

Golden Gate Transit (p111) Bus from San Francisco to Petaluma (adult/youth $11.75/5.75) and Santa Rosa (adult/youth $13/6.50); board at 1st and Mission Sts. Connects with Sonoma County Transit buses.

Greyhound (☎800-231-2222; www.greyhound.com) Buses run from San Francisco to Santa Rosa ($21 to $38).

Napa Valley Vine Operates local bus 10 daily from downtown Napa to Calistoga ($1.60); express bus 29 Monday to Friday from the Vallejo Ferry Terminal ($3.25) and El Cerrito del Norte Bay Area Rapid Transit (BART) station via Napa to Calistoga ($5.50); and local bus 11 daily from the Vallejo Ferry Terminal to downtown Napa ($1.60).

Sonoma County Airport Express (☎800-327-2024, 707-837-8700; www.airportexpressinc.com) Shuttles ($34) between Sonoma County Airport (Santa Rosa) and San Francisco and Oakland airports.

CAR & MOTORCYCLE

From San Francisco, take Hwy 101 north over the Golden Gate Bridge, then Hwy 37 east to Hwy 121 north; continue to the junction of Hwy 12/121. For Sonoma Valley, take Hwy 12 north; for Napa Valley, take Hwy 12/121 east. Plan 70 minutes in light traffic, two hours during the weekday commute.

Hwy 12/121 splits south of Napa: Hwy 121 turns north and joins with Hwy 29/St Helena Hwy; Hwy 12 merges with southbound Hwy 29 toward Vallejo. Hwy 29 backs up weekdays 3pm to 7pm, slowing returns to San Francisco.

From the East Bay (or downtown San Francisco), take I-80 east to Hwy 37 west (north of Vallejo), then northbound Hwy 29.

From Santa Rosa, take Hwy 12 east to access the northern end of Sonoma Valley. From Petaluma and Hwy 101, take Hwy 116 east.

TRAIN

Amtrak (☎800-872-7245; www.amtrak.com) trains travel to Martinez (south of Vallejo), with connecting buses to Napa (45 minutes), Santa Rosa (1¼ hours) and Healdsburg (1¾ hours). From San Francisco, **BART Trains** (☎415-989-2278; www.bart.gov) connecting to Richmond station can deliver you to Amtrak.

BART also runs from San Francisco to El Cerrito del Norte ($4.45, 30 minutes). **Napa Valley Vine** bus 29 runs weekdays from that same BART stop to Calistoga, via Napa ($5.50); on Saturdays take **SolTrans** (☎707-648-4666; www.soltransride.com; adult/youth $5/4) from BART to Vallejo ($5, 30 minutes), then connect with Napa Valley Vine bus 11 to Napa and Calistoga ($1.60); on Sundays, there's no connecting bus service from BART.

ℹ Getting Around

You'll need a car or bike to winery-hop. Alternatively visit tasting rooms in downtown Napa or downtown Sonoma. For more information on touring Napa and Sonoma Wine Country by bicycle, see page p157.

BICYCLE

Touring Wine Country by bicycle is a fantastic experience. The majority of trails between wineries are flat and very approachable for beginners, however crossing between the Napa and Sonoma valleys is challenging with steep roads. It's best to stick to back roads, and we particularly recommend West Dry Creek Rd.

BUS

Sonoma County Transit (☎800-345-7433, 707-576-7433; http://sctransit.com) buses travel around Santa Rosa, Healdsburg, Sebastopol, Petaluma, Kenwood, Glen Ellen, Russian River towns, Sonoma Valley and Geyserville. Prices range from $1.50 to $4.80 depending on how many zones you pass through on your journey. Youth prices range from $1.25 to $4.55.

Napa Valley Vine (☎800-696-6443, 707-251-2800; www.ridethevine.com) local bus 10 runs daily from downtown Napa to Calistoga (adult/youth $1.60/1.10).

CAR & MOTORCYCLE

Napa Valley is 30 miles long and 5 miles across at its widest point (city of Napa) and 1 mile at its narrowest (Calistoga). Two roads run north–south: Hwy 29/St Helena Hwy and the more scenic Silverado Trail, a mile east. Drive up one, down the other.

The American Automobile Association ranks Napa Valley among America's most congested rural vacation destinations. Summer and fall weekend traffic is unbearable, especially on Hwy 29 between Napa and St Helena. Plan accordingly.

Cross-valley roads linking Silverado Trail with Hwy 29 – including Yountville, Oakville and Rutherford crossroads – are bucolic and get less traffic. For scenery, the Oakville Grade and rural Trinity Rd (which leads southwest to Hwy 12 in Sonoma Valley) are narrow, curvy and beautiful – but treacherous in rainstorms. Mt Veeder Rd leads through pristine countryside west of Yountville.

Note: police watch like hawks for traffic violators. *Don't drink and drive.*

There are a number of shortcuts between the Napa and Sonoma Valleys: from Oakville, take Oakville Grade to Trinity Rd; from St Helena, take Spring Mountain Rd into Calistoga Rd; from Calistoga, take Petrified Forest Rd to Calistoga Rd.

TRAIN

The **Napa Valley Wine Train** (p161) can take you from Napa to St Helena and back in a comfy, vintage dining car. An additional winery tour is optional. Trains depart from **Napa Valley Wine Train Depot** (http://winetrain.com/getting-here; 1275 McKinstry St) on McKinstry St near 1st St.

NAPA VALLEY

The birthplace of modern-day Wine Country is famous for regal Cabernet Sauvignons, château-like wineries and fabulous food. It attracts more than three million visitors a year, many planning to wine and dine themselves into a stupor, maybe get a massage, and sleep somewhere swell with fine linens and a heated pool.

The city of Napa anchors the valley, but the real work happens up-valley. And while Napa may not be as scenic as other stops, it has some noteworthy sights, among them Oxbow Public Market and the new cooking-school campus, CIA at Copia. The prettiest towns include St Helena, Yountville and Calistoga – the latter more famous for mud and water than wine.

History

A few decades ago, Napa was a quiet agricultural valley dense with orchards, its 5-by-35-mile strip peppered with stagecoach stops. Grapes had grown here since the gold rush, but juice-sucking phylloxera bugs, Prohibition and the Great Depression reduced 140 wineries in the 1890s to around 25 by the 1960s.

In 1968 Napa was declared the 'Napa Valley Agricultural Preserve,' effectively blocking future valley development for non-ag purposes. The law prohibited the subdivision of valley-floor land under 40 acres, which helped preserve the valley's natural beauty. But when Napa wines earned top honors at a 1976 blind tasting in Paris, the wine-drinking world noticed, land values skyrocketed and only the very rich could afford to build – hence so many architecturally jaw-dropping wineries. Independent, family-owned wineries still exist – we highlight a number of them – but much of Napa Valley is now owned by global conglomerates.

Napa Valley Wineries

Cab is king in Napa. No varietal captures imaginations like the fruit of the Cabernet Sauvignon vine – Bordeaux is the French equivalent – and no wine fetches a higher price. Napa farmers can't afford *not* to grow Cabernet, and Chardonnay, which flourishes in the calcium-rich soil of cooler areas of the valley, is second. Other varietals such as Merlot and Zinfandel also thrive here.

Napa's wines merit their reputation among the world's finest – complex, with luxurious finishes. Napa wineries sell many 'buy-and-hold' wines, versus Sonoma's 'drink-now' wines.

★ Hess Collection WINERY, GALLERY

(☎707-255-1144; www.hesscollection.com; 4411 Redwood Rd, Napa; museum free, tasting $25 & $35, tours free; ⏱10am-5:30pm, last tasting 5pm)

Art-lovers: don't miss Hess Collection, whose galleries display mixed-media and large-canvas works, including pieces by Francis Bacon and Robert Motherwell. In the elegant stone-walled tasting room, find well-known Cabernet Sauvignon and Chardonnay, but also try the Viognier. There's garden service in the warmer months, which is lovely, as Hess overlooks the valley. Make reservations and be prepared to drive a winding road. Bottles are $30 to $100. Public tour 10:30am.

TOURING NAPA & SONOMA WINE COUNTRY

Touring Wine Country by bicycle is unforgettable. Stick to back roads. We love pastoral West Dry Creek Rd, northwest of Healdsburg, in Sonoma County. Through Sonoma Valley, take Arnold Dr instead of Hwy 12; through Napa Valley, take the Silverado Trail instead of Hwy 29. Cycling between wineries isn't demanding – the valleys are mostly flat – but crossing between the Napa and Sonoma Valleys is intense, particularly via steep Oakville Grade and Trinity Rd (between Oakville and Glen Ellen). Bicycles, in boxes, can be checked on Greyhound buses (p155) for $30 to $40; bike boxes cost $10 (call ahead). You can transport bicycles on Golden Gate Transit (p111) buses.

Bicycle Tours & Rentals

Guided tours start around $90 per day including bikes, tastings and lunch. Daily rentals cost $25 to $85; make reservations.

Getaway Adventures (☎800-499-2453, 707-568-3040; http://getawayadventures.com; 5½hr tour $139-175) These great guided cycling tours visit wineries and other attractions, and include a picnic lunch. They depart from Napa and Calistoga.

Backroads (☎800-462-2848; www.backroads.com) All-inclusive, multiday guided biking and walking.

Calistoga Bike Shop (Map p172; ☎707-942-9687; http://calistogabikeshop.com; 1318 Lincoln Ave; bicycle rental from $28, guided tours from $149; ⊙10am-6pm) Rents full-suspension mountain bikes, hybrids, road bikes and tandem models and provides reliable trail information. DIY touring packages ($110 per day) include free tastings and wine pickup.

Napa River Velo (☎707-258-8729; www.napariververlo.com; 680 Main St, Napa; rentals per day $40-90; ⊙10am-7pm Mon-Fri, 9am-6pm Sat, to 5pm Sun) Hourly, daily and weekly rentals in downtown Napa; reservations recommended.

Spoke Folk Cyclery (☎707-433-7171; www.spokefolk.com; 201 Center St; hybrid bicycle rental per hour/day from $14/38; ⊙10am-6pm Mon-Fri, to 5pm Sat & Sun) Rents touring, racing and tandem bicycles that come with locks and helmets. Great service.

Sonoma Adventures (☎707-938-2080; www.sonoma-adventures.com; bicycle rental per day $30-65, tours $129-189, segway tours $129) Bicycle rentals and guided cycling tours of Sonoma Valley, Dry Creek Valley and Carneros. There's a minimum of two people for the Sonoma tours, four people for the Dry Creek Valley and Carneros tours.

Wine Country Bikes (Map p192; ☎707-473-0610; www.winecountrybikes.com; 61 Front St; rentals per day from $39, guided tours from $139; ⊙9am-5pm) Rents bikes in downtown Healdsburg and guides multiday Sonoma County tours.

Napa Valley Bike Tours (Map p167; ☎707-944-2953; www.napavalleybiketours.com; 6500 Washington St, Yountville; bicycle rental per day $45-75, tours $109-124; ⊙8:30am-5pm) Two-hour and daily rentals, as well as easy and moderately difficult tours starting in Yountville. Second location at the foot of the Vine Trail at 3259 California Blvd, you can rent in one location and drop off in the other for $10 extra.

Other Tours

Platypus Wine Tours (☎707-253-2723; www.platypustours.com; join-in tour per person $110) Billed as the anti-wine-snob tour, Platypus specializes in backroad vineyards and family-owned operations. There's a daily 'join-in' tour that takes in four wineries and a picnic lunch, and private tours with a dedicated driver. The Napa tours are the most popular, but Platypus also takes people to Sonoma, Russian River and Dry Creek Valleys.

Beyond the Label (☎707-363-4023; www.btlnv.com; per couple from $995) Personalized tours, including lunch at home with a vintner, guided by a knowledgeable Napa native.

Beau Wine Tours (Map p162; ☎707-938-8001, 800-387-2328; www.beauwinetours.com) Winery tours in sedans and stretch limos; charges a base rate of $65 to $205 per hour (four- to six-hour minimum), but expect to pay more for gas, tax and tip.

Magnum Tours (☎707-753-0088; www.magnumwinetours.com) Sedans and specialty limousines from $65 to $110 per hour (four-hour minimum, five hours Saturdays).

★Robert Sinskey Vineyards WINERY

(Map p167; ☎707-944-9090; www.robertsinskey.com; 6320 Silverado Trail, Napa; bar tasting $40, seated food & wine pairings $70-175; ⊙10am-4:30pm; P) The fabulous hillside tasting room, constructed of stone, redwood and teak, resembles a small cathedral – fitting, given the sacred status here bestowed upon food and wine. It specializes in bright-acid organic Pinot Noir, plus exceptional aromatic white varietals, dry rosé and Bordeaux varietals such as Merlot and Cab Franc, all crafted for the dinner table.

Small bites accompany bar tastings, and seated food and wine experiences are curated by chef Maria Sinskey herself. Reserve ahead for sit-down tastings and culinary tours. Bottles $22 to $100.

★Frog's Leap WINERY

(Map p167; ☎707-963-4704; www.frogsleap.com; 8815 Conn Creek Rd, Rutherford; tasting $20-25, incl tour $25; ⊙10am-4pm by appointment only; P) Meandering paths wind through magical gardens and fruit-bearing orchards surrounding an 1884 barn and farmstead with cats and chickens. The vibe is casual, with a major emphasis on *fun*. Sauvignon Blanc is its best-known wine but the Merlot merits attention. There's also a dry, restrained Cabernet, atypical of Napa.All grapes are organically farmed. Bottles cost $20 to $55.

★Tres Sabores WINERY

(Map p167; ☎707-967-8027; www.tressabores.com; 1620 South Whitehall Lane, St Helena; tour & tasting $40; ⊙10:30am-3pm, by appointment;) At the valley's westernmost edge, where sloping vineyards meet wooded hillsides, Tres Sabores is a portal to old Napa – no fancy tasting room, no snobbery, just great wine in a spectacular setting. Bucking the Cabernet custom, Tres Sabores crafts elegantly structured, Burgundian-style Zinfandel and spritely Sauvignon Blanc, which the *New York Times* dubbed a top 10 of its kind in California. Reservations are essential.

Pride Mountain WINERY

(☎707-963-4949; www.pridewines.com; 4026 Spring Mountain Rd, St Helena; tasting & tour $20-30, summit experience $75; ⊙by appointment only) High atop Spring Mountain, cult-favorite Pride straddles the Napa–Sonoma border and bottles vintages under both appellations. The well-structured Cabernet and heavy-hitting Merlot are the best-known wines but there's also an elegant Viognier (perfect with oysters) and standout Cab Franc, available only here. Picnicking is spectacular: choose Viewpoint for drop-dead vistas, or Ghost Winery for shade and the historic ruins of a 19th-century winery, but you must first reserve a tasting. Bottles cost $42 to $70.

Artesa WINERY

(☎707-254-2126; www.artesawinery.com; 1345 Henry Rd, Napa; tastings from $35, tour/glass $45/15; ⊙10am-5pm, last pour 4:30pm) Begin or end the day with a glass of bubbly or Pinot at Artesa, southwest of Napa. Built into a mountainside, the ultramodern Barcelona-style ar-

NAPA OR SONOMA?

Napa and Sonoma Valleys run parallel, separated by the narrow, imposing Mayacamas Mountains. The two couldn't be more different. It's easy to mock aggressively sophisticated Napa, its monuments to ego, trophy homes and trophy wives, $1000-a-night inns, $50-plus tastings and wine-snob visitors. Sonoma residents refer to Napa as 'the dark side'; still, its wines are some of the world's best. Constrained by geography, Napa stretches along a single valley, making it easy to visit. Drawbacks are high prices and heavy traffic, but there are more than 500 wineries, nearly side by side. And the valley is gorgeous.

There are three Sonomas: Sonoma town is in Sonoma Valley, which is in Sonoma County. Think of them as Russian dolls. Sonoma County is much more down-to-earth and politically left-leaning. Though it's becoming gentrified, Sonoma lacks Napa's chic factor (Healdsburg notwithstanding) and locals like it that way. The wines are more approachable, but the county's 400 or so wineries are spread out. If you're here on a weekend, head to Sonoma (County or Valley), which gets less traffic, but on a weekday, see Napa too. Ideally schedule two to four days: one for each valley and one or two additional days for western Sonoma County.

Spring and fall are the best times to visit. Summers are hot, dusty and crowded. Fall brings fine weather, harvest time and the 'crush,' the pressing of the grapes, but lodging prices skyrocket.

chitecture is stunning and you can't beat the top-of-the-world vistas over San Pablo Bay. Tours run at 11am and 2pm. Recent changes include a new winemaker and increased focus on wine and food pairings. Reservations recommended. Bottles cost $28 to $85.

Cade WINERY

(Map p172; ☎707-965-2746; www.cadewinery.com; 360 Howell Mountain Rd S, Angwin; tasting & tour $80; ⊙by appointment only) Ascend Mt Veeder for drop-dead vistas, 1800ft above the valley, at Napa's oh-so-swank, first-ever organically farmed, Leadership in Energy and Environmental Design (LEED) gold-certified winery, partly owned by former San Francisco mayor Gavin Newsom. Hawks ride thermals at eye level as you sample bright Sauvignon Blanc and luscious Cabernet Sauvignon that's more Bordelaise in style than Californian. Reservations required. Bottles cost $44 to $80.

Vincent Arroyo WINERY

(Map p172; ☎707-942-6995; www.vincentarroyo.com; 2361 Greenwood Ave, Calistoga; ⊙by appointment) FREE The tasting room is a garage, where you may even meet Mr Arroyo, known for his all-estate-grown Petite Sirah and Cabernet Sauvignon. They're distributed nowhere else and are so consistently good that 75% of production is sold before it's bottled. Tastings are free, but appointments are required. Bottles are $21 to $65.

Long Meadow Ranch FARM

(Map p172; ☎707-963-4555; www.longmeadowranch.com; 738 Main St, St Helena; tasting $25-40, chef's table $145; ⊙11am-6pm) Long Meadow stands out for olive-oil tastings ($5), plus good estate-grown Cabernet, Sauvignon Blanc, Chardonnay and Pinot Noir, served inside an 1874 farmhouse surrounded by lovely gardens. It also has a whiskey flight for $30; sells housemade products such as preserves, BBQ sauce; and hosts chef's tables (four- to five-course food and wine experiences) at lunch and dinner daily. Reservations for chef's table required. Bottles $20 to $50.

Twenty Rows WINERY

(Map p167; ☎707-265-7750; www.twentyrows.com; 880 Vallejo St, Napa; tasting $20, glass $10; ⊙11am-6pm Wed-Mon, by appointment Tue) This long-standing downtown winery crafts light-on-the-palate Cabernet Sauvignon ($32 a bottle). Taste in a chilly garage with fun dudes who know their wines, or sip on the newly constructed back patio.

BOOKING APPOINTMENTS AT WINERIES

Because of strict county zoning laws, many Napa wineries cannot legally receive drop-in visitors; unless you've come strictly to buy, you'll have to call ahead. This is *not* the case with all wineries. We recommend booking one tasting, plus a lunch or dinner reservation, and planning your day around those appointments.

Hall WINERY

(Map p172; ☎707-967-2626; www.hallwines.com; 401 St Helena Hwy, St Helena; tasting & tour from $40; ⊙10am-5:30pm; P) Co-owned by Bill Clinton's former ambassador to Austria, Hall specializes in Cabernet Sauvignon, Sauvignon Blanc and Merlot, crafted in big-fruit California style. Its dramatic tasting room has a stand-up bar with 180-degree views of vineyards and mountains through floor-to-ceiling glass, and the glorious art collection includes a giant chrome rabbit leaping over the vines. Bottles cost $24 to $170.

Schramsberg WINERY

(Map p172; ☎707-942-2414, 800-877-3623; www.schramsberg.com; 1400 Schramsberg Rd, off Peterson Dr; tour & tasting $70, tour & sparkling-wine tasting $95, reserve wine & cheese pairing $125; ⊙by appointment at 9:30am, 10am, 10:30am, 11:30am, noon, 1:30pm, & 2:30pm) Napa's second-oldest winery, Schramsberg makes some of California's best brut sparkling wines, and in 1972 was the first domestic wine served at the White House. Blanc de Blancs is the signature. The appointment-only tasting and tour (book well ahead) is expensive, but you'll sample all the *tête de cuvées,* not just the low-end wines. Tours include a walk through the caves; bring a sweater. Bottles cost $24 to $150.

Titus WINERY

(Map p172; ☎707-963-3235; www.titusvineyards.com; 2971 Silverado Trail N, St Helena; tasting $20; ⊙by appointment) Formerly modest Titus has gone fancy of late, opening a modern tasting facility with windows for days, surrounded by 40 acres of vineyards. It's best to call ahead to sample the winery's good-value, Cabernet Sauvignon and old-vine Zinfandel – rare in Napa. Afterward, take your glass outside, and relax on the expansive patio. The tasting fee is waived with a purchase; bottles are $20 to $70.

ℹ HIGH SEASON VS LOW SEASON

Many Wine Country restaurants and hotels diminish operations in winter. Make reservations, especially in summertime, or you may not eat. Hotel rates jump during the most popular time – September and October's grape-crushing season.

Castello di Amorosa WINERY, CASTLE

(Map p172; ☎707-967-6272; www.castellodiamorosa.com; 4045 Hwy 29, Calistoga; entry & tasting $25-35, incl guided tour $40-85; ⏱9:30am-6pm Mar-Oct, to 5pm Nov-Feb; P ♿) It took 14 years to build this perfectly replicated, 13th-century Italian castle, complete with moat, hand-cut stone walls, ceiling frescoes by Italian artisans, Roman-style cross-vault brick catacombs, and a torture chamber with period equipment. You can taste without an appointment, but this is one tour worth taking. Oh, the wine? Some respectable Italian varietals, including a velvety Tuscan blend and a Merlot that goes great with pizza. Bottles are $20 to $98.

Darioush WINERY

(Map p167; ☎707-257-2345; www.darioush.com; 4240 Silverado Trail, Napa; tasting from $40; ⏱10:30am-5pm; P) Like a modern-day Persian palace, Darioush ranks high on the fabulosity scale, with towering columns, Persian rugs and travertine walls. Though known for Cabernet Sauvignon, Darioush also bottles Chardonnay, Merlot and Shiraz, all made with 100% of their respective varietals. Call about wine-and-cheese pairings ($75). Bottles cost $40 to $95.

Mumm Napa WINERY, GALLERY

(Map p167: ☎800-686-6272; www.mummnapa.com; 8445 Silverado Trail, Rutherford; tasting $20-50, tour $30, glass $12-15; ⏱10am-6pm; P) Valley views are spectacular at Mumm, which makes respectable sparkling wines you can sample by the glass beneath a vineyard-side pergola or seated on a vineyard-view terrace – ideal if you want to impress conservative parents-in-law. Dodge crowds by coming early, or paying $50 for the reserve-tasting Oak Terrace (reservations required). There's also a fabulous photography gallery featuring the work of Ansel Adams. Last seating is at 5:45pm.

Regusci WINERY

(Map p167; ☎707-254-0403; www.reguscawinery.com; 5584 Silverado Trail, Napa; tasting $50, incl tour $60; ⏱10am-5pm; P) One of Napa's oldest, Regusci dates to the late 1800s, with 160 acres of vineyards unfurling around a century-old stone winery that makes Bordeaux-style blends on the valley's quieter eastern side – good when traffic up-valley is bad. There's a lovely oak-shaded picnic area. Reservations required; tasting fee is waived with a purchase of $80 or more. Bottles cost $55 to $120.

Elizabeth Spencer WINERY

(Map p167; ☎707-963-6067; www.elizabethspencerwinery.com; 1165 Rutherford Rd, Rutherford; tasting $25-60; ⏱10am-6pm, last tasting 5:30pm) Check in at this 1872 former post-office building and indulge in tastings tableside in the outdoor garden courtyard at this inviting small winery. Featured are monster-sized Pinot Noir, a range of white-wine varietals including Sauvignon Blanc and Chenan Blanc, structured light-body Grenache and an array of Cabernet. Tastings are a relaxed affair; allow an hour for the alfresco experience. Bottles cost $35 to $250.

Robert Mondavi WINERY

(Map p167: ☎707-226-1395, 888-766-6328; www.robertmondaviwinery.com; 7801 Hwy 29, Oakville; tasting/tour from $5/25; ⏱10am-5pm, store to 6pm; P ♿) 🍃 Tour buses flock to this corporate-owned winery, but if you know nothing

CALIFORNIA WILDFIRES

In October 2017 a series of wildfires burned throughout Northern California including Mendocino, Napa and Sonoma Counties. For 19 days the wildfires burned killing at least 42 people, destroying thousands of homes and prompting 100,000 people to evacuate.

The research for this book was conducted before the fires hit and the content was sent to print soon afterward, when long term effects of the fires were still unknown. This area of California is heavily reliant on tourism and most businesses were already announcing they were open for guests. Still, the state parks remained closed until further notice and many businesses and historic sites were uncertain when they would be back on their feet. Those planning to travel to Napa & Sonoma Wine Country should check official websites for the latest information.

about wine and can cope with crowds, the worthwhile tours provide good insight into winemaking. Definitely skip the charcuterie plate, but do consider attending one of the glorious outdoor summer **concerts**; call for schedules. Bottles cost $35 to $165.

Napa

The valley's workaday hub was once a nothing-special city of storefronts, Victorian cottages and riverfront warehouses, but booming real-estate values caused an influx of new money that's transforming downtown into a hub of arts and food.

Napa lies between Silverado Trail and St Helena Hwy/Hwy 29. For downtown, exit Hwy 29 at 1st St and drive east. Napa's main drag, 1st St, is lined with shops and restaurants.

Sights

★di Rosa ARTS CENTER

(707-226-5991; www.dirosaart.org; 5200 Hwy 121; $5, tours $12-15; 10am-4pm Wed-Sun; P) West of downtown, scrap-metal sculptures dot Carneros vineyards at the 217-acre di Rosa Art + Nature Preserve, a stunning collection of Northern California art, displayed indoors in galleries and outdoors in gardens by a giant lake. Reservations recommended for tours.

★Oxbow Public Market MARKET

(Map p162; 707-226-6529; www.oxbowpublicmarket.com; 610 & 644 1st St; 9am-9pm; P) Showcasing all things culinary (produce stalls, kitchen shops and everywhere something to taste), Oxbow is foodie central with an emphasis on seasonal eating and sustainability. Some vendors and restaurants open early or close late. Come hungry.

CIA at Copia CENTER

(Map p162; 707-967-2500; www.ciaatcopia.com; 500 1st St; 10:30am-9pm) The former food museum beside Napa's famous Oxbow Public Market has been revived as a center of all things edible by the prestigious Culinary Institute of America. In its new life as Copia, the 80,000-sq-ft campus offers wine tastings, interactive cooking demos, an innovative restaurant, a massive fork statue (composed of many thousands of smaller forks) and more food-related features.

The eponymous **Restaurant at CIA Copia** takes a new approach to food service, with cart-and-tray dishes traveling around the dining room and chefs similarly on the move, answering questions from curious guests.

Tours

Napa Valley Wine Train TOURS

(Map p162; 800-427-4124, 707-253-2111; http://winetrain.com; 1275 McKinstry St; ticket incl dining from $146) A cushy, if touristy, way to see Wine Country, the Wine Train offers three-hour daily trips in vintage Pullman dining cars, from Napa to St Helena and back, with optional winery tours. It also offers six-hour journeys visiting multiple wineries with Napa Valley cuisine served between visits.

Sleeping

The digs here are decent, ranging from high-end spa resorts to quiet inns to comfy chain hotels but prices are high. On weekends and over summer, when rates skyrocket, consider staying in Calistoga. Archer Hotel (https://archerhotel.com/napa) and its Charlie Palmer Steakhouse are new to downtown, and everybody is talking about them.

★Carneros Resort & Spa RESORT $$$

(888-400-9000, 707-299-4900; www.thecarnerosresort.com; 4048 Sonoma Hwy; r from $500;) Carneros Resort & Spa's contemporary aesthetic and retro small-town agricultural theme shatter the predictable Wine Country mold. The semidetached, corrugated-metal cottages look like itinerant housing, but inside they're snappy and chic, with cherry-wood floors, ultrasuede headboards, wood-burning fireplaces, heated-tile bathroom floors, giant tubs and indoor-outdoor showers.

CUTTING COSTS IN NAPA

To avoid overspending on tasting fees, it's perfectly acceptable to pay for one tasting to share between two people. Ask in advance if fees are applicable to purchase (they usually aren't). Tour fees cannot be split. Ask at your hotel, or at visitor centers, for free- or discounted-tasting coupons, or download from www.napatouristguide.com. If you can't afford the hotels, try western Sonoma County, but if you want to be closer to Napa, try the suburban towns of Vallejo and American Canyon, about 20 minutes from downtown Napa. Both have motels for $75 to $125 in high season. Also find chains 30 minutes away in Fairfield, off I-80 exits 41 (Pittman Rd) and 45 (Travis Blvd).

Napa

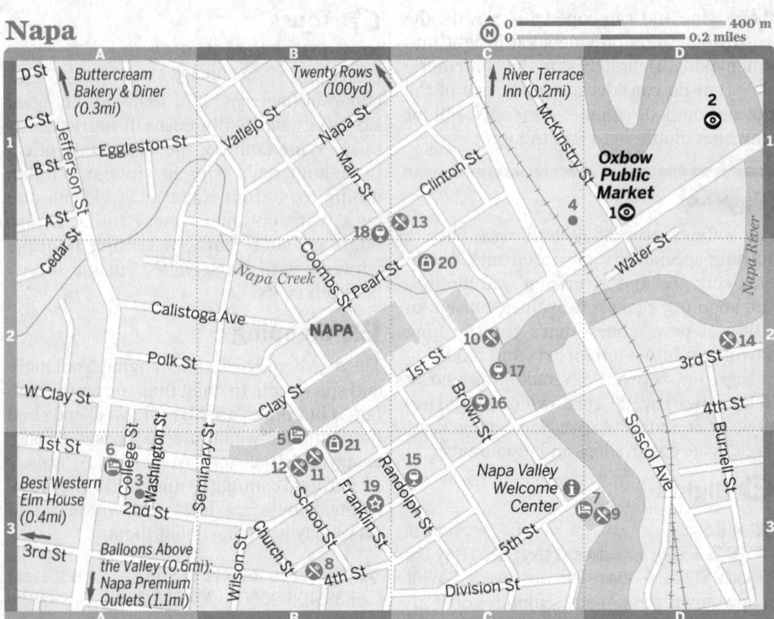

Napa

Top Sights
1 Oxbow Public Market D1

Sights
2 CIA at Copia D1

Activities, Courses & Tours
3 Beau Wine Tours A3
4 Napa Valley Wine Train C1

Sleeping
5 Andaz Napa B3
6 Blackbird Inn A3
7 Napa River Inn D3

Eating
8 Alexis Baking Company & Cafe B3
9 Angèle D3
10 Bounty Hunter Wine Bar & Smokin' BBQ C2
11 Norman Rose Tavern B3
12 Oenotri B3
Oxbow Public Market .... (see 1)
13 Pizza Azzuro C1
14 Taqueria Maria D2
Torc .... (see 20)

Drinking & Nightlife
15 Billco's Billiards & Darts C3
16 Carpe Diem Wine Bar C2
17 Downtown Joe's C2
18 Vintners' Collective B1

Entertainment
Silo's Jazz Club .... (see 7)
19 Uptown Theatre B3

Shopping
20 Betty's Girl C2
Napa General Store .... (see 7)
21 Napa Valley Olive Oil Mfg Co B3

Andaz Napa HOTEL $$$
(Map p162; ☎707-687-1234; www.andaznapa.com; 1450 1st St; r from $270; P ⊖ ✻ @ ☎) Smack downtown, the Andaz was constructed in 2009 and feels like a big-city hotel, with business-class-fancy rooms styled in sexy contemporary style. It's walking distance to restaurants and bars. There's an on-site terrace bar with fire pits and guests have access to an adjacent health club with indoor lap pool, sauna and gym.

Cottages of Napa Valley BUNGALOW $$$
(Map p167; ☎707-252-7810; www.napacottages.com; 1012 Darns Lane; cottages $350-600; ✻ ☎) Eight pristine cottages of quality construction – made

for romantic hideaways, with extralong soaking tubs, indoor gas fireplaces and outdoor campfire pits – surround a big garden shaded by towering pines. Cottages 4 and 8 have private porches and swinging chairs. The only drawback is noise from traffic, but interiors are quiet.

Milliken Creek Inn INN $$$
(Map p167; 707-255-1197; www.millikencreekinn.com; 1815 Silverado Trail; r $295-750;) Understatedly elegant Milliken Creek combines small-inn charm, fine-hotel service and B&B intimacy. Rooms are impeccably styled in English-colonial style and higher-end rooms have top-flight amenities, fireplace and ultrahigh-thread-count linen. Breakfast is delivered. Book a river-view room.

Blackbird Inn B&B $$$
(Map p162; 707-226-2450, 888-567-9811; www.blackbirdinnnapa.com; 1755 1st St; r $250-285;) Gorgeous, eight-room arts-and-crafts-style B&B. Anticipate street noise.

Napa River Inn HOTEL $$$
(Map p162; 707-251-8500, 877-251-8500; www.napariverinn.com; 500 Main St; r $300-600;) Beside the river in the 1884 Hatt Building, the inn has top-end rooms, Victoriana to modern, in three satellite buildings. Walkable distance to restaurants and bars. Dogs get special treatment.

Napa Winery Inn HOTEL $$$
(Map p167; 707-257-7220; www.napawineryinn.com; 1998 Trower Ave; r Mon-Fri $179-279, Sat & Sun $229-350;) Request a remodeled room at this good-value hotel, north of downtown, decorated with generic Colonial-style furniture. It has a hot tub and good service. There are complimentary wine receptions each night: weekdays 5:30pm to 6:30pm, to 7pm weekends.

River Terrace Inn HOTEL $$$
(Map p167; 707-320-9000; www.riverterraceinn.com; 1600 Soscol Ave; r $189-360;) Upmarket, business-class, chain-style hotel with shopping-mall-bland architecture fronting on the Napa River. The entire property was recently renovated, including a new restaurant and bar.

Eating

Deliciousness abounds, but it's going to cost you. Make reservations whenever possible, and cut costs by grabbing sandwiches from Soda Canyon Store for a picnic lunch.

★ **Oxbow Public Market** MARKET $
(Map p162; 707-226-6529; www.oxbowpublicmarket.com; 610 & 644 1st St; items from $3; 9am-9pm;) Graze at this gourmet market and plug into the Northern California food scene. Standouts: **Hog Island Oyster Co**; comfort cooking at celeb-chef Todd Humphries' **Kitchen Door**; great Cal-Mexican tacos at **C Casa & Taco Lounge**; the India pale ales (IPAs) and sour beers at **Fieldwork Brewing Company**; espresso from **Ritual Coffee**; and **Three Twins** certified-organic ice cream.

Tuesday is locals' night (5pm to 8pm), with many discounts. Some stalls remain open to 9pm, even on Sundays, but many close earlier and some vendors open early in the morning.

Alexis Baking Company & Cafe CAFE $
(Map p162; 707-258-1827; www.abcnapa.com; 1517 3rd St; mains $9-17; 7am-3pm Mon-Fri, 7:30am-3pm Sat, 8am-2pm Sun;) Our fave spot for quality egg scrambles, granola, focaccia sandwiches, big cups of joe and boxed lunches to go.

Taqueria Maria MEXICAN $
(Map p162; 707-257-6925; www.taqueriamariannapa1.com; 640 3rd St; mains $8-15; 8am-9pm Sun-Thu, to 9:30pm Fri & Sat;) Reliably good Mexican cooking that won't break the bank. Also serves breakfast.

Buttercream Bakery & Diner DINER $
(Map p167; 707-255-6700; www.buttercreambakery.com; 2297 Jefferson St; breakfast $5-10, cakes $15-25; bakery 5:30am-6pm Mon-Sat, to 4pm Sun, diner 5:30am-3pm Mon-Sat, to 2:30pm Sun) This retro flashback pink-striped diner, favored by Napa's little old ladies, has all-day breakfasts and white-bread lunches, served by matrons in heavy eye shadow. Also famous for its champagne cakes.

Soda Canyon Store DELI $
(Map p167; 707-252-0285; www.sodacanyonstore.com; 4006 Silverado Trail; 6am-6pm Mon-Sat, 7am-5pm Sun) This roadside deli with shaded picnic area makes an easy stop while winery-hopping north of town.

Oenotri ITALIAN $$
(Map p162; 707-252-1022; www.oenotri.com; 1425 1st St; brunch $13-15, dinner mains $18-34; brunch 10am-3pm Sat & Sun, 5:30-9pm Sun-Thu, to 10pm Fri & Sat) Housemade *salumi* (cured meat) and pastas, and wood-fired Naples-style pizzas are the stars at always-busy Oenotri,

which draws crowds for daily-changing, locally sourced, rustic-Italian cooking, served in a cavernous brick-walled space.

Pizza Azzuro PIZZA **$$**

(Map p162; ☎707-255-5552; www.azzurropizzeria.com; 1260 Main St; mains $15-18; ⊙11:30am-9:30pm Sun-Thu, to 10pm Fri & Sat;) This Napa classic gets deafeningly loud, but it's worth bearing for tender-crusted pizzas, salad-topped 'manciata' bread, good Caesar salads and pastas.

Norman Rose Tavern PUB FOOD **$$**

(Map p162; ☎707-258-1516; www.normanrosenapa.com; 1401 1st St; mains $10-24; ⊙11:30am-9pm Sun-Thu, to 10pm Fri & Sat;) This happening gastropub, styled with reclaimed wood and tufted-leather banquettes, is good for a burger and beer. Great fries and plenty of seasonal favorites. Full bar.

Bounty Hunter Wine Bar & Smokin' BBQ BARBECUE **$$**

(Map p162; ☎707-226-3976; www.bountyhunterwinebar.com; 975 1st St; mains $14-28; ⊙11am-10pm Sun-Thu, to midnight Fri & Sat;) Inside an 1888 grocery store, Bounty Hunter has an Old West vibe and superb barbecue, made with house-smoked meats. The standout 'beer-can chicken' is a whole chicken roasted over a can of Tecate. Libations include 40 local beers, 60 whiskeys and 400 wines (40 by the glass).

Angèle FRENCH **$$$**

(Map p162; ☎707-252-8115; www.angelerestaurant.com; 540 Main St; lunch mains $14-27, dinner $26-30; ⊙11:30am-4pm & 5-9pm Sun-Thu, to 10pm Sat & Sun) Stalwart Angèle serves reliable provincial-French cooking – French onion soup, Nicoise salads and *croques messieurs* (gourmet toasted ham and cheese sandwiches) at lunch, cassoulet with duck confit at dinner – on a river-view deck or in the cozy dining room, both perfect for lingering with a good bottle of wine.

Bistro Don Giovanni ITALIAN **$$$**

(Map p167; ☎707-224-3300; www.bistrodongiovanni.com; 4110 Howard Lane; mains $16-34; ⊙11:30am-10pm Sun-Thu, to 11pm Fri & Sat) This long-running favorite roadhouse serves modern-Italian pastas, crispy pizzas and wood-roasted meats. Reservations essential. Weekends get packed – and loud. Request a vineyard-view table (good luck).

Torc CALIFORNIAN **$$$**

(Map p162; ☎707-252-3292; www.torcnapa.com; 1140 Main St; mains $28-46, prix-fixe menu $46; ⊙5-9:30pm Wed-Mon) Wildly popular Torc plays off the seasons with dynamic combinations of farm-fresh ingredients such as pork belly with satsuma-imo potato and choy raab, or artichoke velouté with wild mushrooms. Well-arranged for people-watching, the big stone dining room has an open-truss ceiling and pinewood tables that downplay formality. Reservations essential.

A LOVELY SPOT FOR A PICNIC

Unlike Sonoma, there aren't many places to picnic legally in Napa. Here's a short list, in south–north order, but call ahead and remember to buy a bottle (or glass, if available) of your host's wine. If you don't finish it, California law forbids driving with an uncorked bottle in the car (keep it in the trunk).

➡ Regusci (p160)

➡ Napa Valley Museum (p166)

➡ Pride Mountain (p158)

➡ Casa Nuestra (p160)

Drinking & Nightlife

There is no shortage of drinking establishments in the downtown area, including breweries, sports bars and wine-tasting rooms, which have proliferated in recent years.

Vintners' Collective WINE BAR

(Map p162; ☎707-255-7150; www.vintnerscollective.com; 1245 Main St; tastings $10-40, private tastings $75 & $95; ⊙11am-7pm) Ditch the car and chill in downtown Napa at this tasting bar inside a former 20th-century brothel. It represents 20-plus high-end boutique wineries that are too small to have their own tasting rooms. There are around 140 wines to try, and the pricier the tasting, the more sought-after the wine. The $75 and $95 tastings include artisanal cheese and charcuterie.

Tannery Bend Beerworks BREWERY

(Map p167; ☎707-681-5774; http://tannerybendbeerworks.com; 101 S Coombs St; ⊙noon-8pm Wed-Sun) What do you call a brewery smaller than micro? A Napa brewery stepped up to answer that question in 2017 and this nanobrewery produces just 15 gallons of beer per batch. The teeny tiny booze biz is a collaboration between a chef, a brewer and a restaurateur (same one who owns the fabulous Oenotri, p163).

With their powers combined, they've created a few delicious and locally sourced Saisons and IPAs, in addition to a rotating menu of food pairings featuring things such as grilled blue crab and deviled eggs.

Carpe Diem Wine Bar WINE BAR
(Map p162; ☎707-224-0800; www.carpediemwinebar.com; 1001 2nd St; ⊙4-9pm Mon-Thu, to 10pm Fri & Sat) This busy storefront wine bar and restaurant (mains $22–$48) makes inventive, flavorful small plates, from simple skewers and flatbreads to elaborate ostrich burgers, salumi platters and – wait for it – duck confit 'quack and cheese.'

Downtown Joe's SPORTS BAR, BREWERY
(Map p162; ☎707-258-2337; www.downtownjoes.com; 902 Main St, at 2nd St; ⊙8am-1am Mon & Tue, to 2am Wed-Sun; 📶) Live music Thursday to Sunday, TV sports nightly and a pet-friendly, riverfront patio. Often packed, usually messy.

Billco's Billiards & Darts SPORTS BAR
(Map p162; www.billcos.com; 1234 3rd St; ⊙noon-2am Mon-Sat, to midnight Sun) Dudes with beards swill craft beers and throw darts inside this lively pool hall.

☆ Entertainment

Silo's Jazz Club LIVE MUSIC
(Map p162; ☎707-251-5833; www.silosnapa.com; 530 Main St; cover varies; ⊙4-10pm Wed, 5-10pm Thu, 7-11pm Fri & Sat, varied hours Sun) A cabaret-style wine-and-beer bar, Silo's hosts free jazz on Wednesday, and varied music acts on Friday and Saturday nights. On Thursday it's good for drinks. Buy tickets ahead of time on weekends.

Uptown Theatre THEATER
(Map p162; ☎707-259-0123, ext 6; www.uptowntheatrenapa.com; 1350 3rd St) Big-name acts play this restored 1937 theater.

Shopping

Napa Valley Olive Oil Mfg Co FOOD
(Map p162; ☎707-265-6866; 1331 1st St; ⊙10am-5:30pm) Sample 40 varieties of fine olive oil and vinegar at this downtown specialty-food boutique, which also carries fancy salts and local jam.

Betty's Girl WOMEN'S CLOTHING, VINTAGE
(Map p162; ☎707-254-7560; www.bettysgirlnapa.com; 968 Pearl St; ⊙by appointment) Expert couturier Kim Northrup fits women with fabulous vintage cocktail dresses and custom-made designs, altering and shipping for no additional charge. She also has an annex at 1320 2nd St.

SHIPPING IT HOME

Bodega Shipping Co (☎Napa 707-968-5462, Sonoma 707-343-1656; www.bodegashippingco.com) picks up wine in Napa and Sonoma Valleys, packages it, and ships nationwide via UPS and FedEx, with no hidden fees. Also ships to some international destinations, including the UK, Australia, Hong Kong and some countries in South America. For a case (12 bottles) budget $38 to $73; in summer add $10 to $20 for temperature-controlled shipping; for international shipments, budget a few hundred dollars, depending on destination. Call for a quote.

Napa General Store GIFTS & SOUVENIRS
(Map p162; ☎707-259-0762; www.napageneralstore.com; 540 Main St; ⊙8am-6pm) Finally, cutesy Wine Country souvenirs reasonably priced. The on-site **wine bar** is convenient for nonshopping spouses.

Information

INTERNET

Napa Library (☎707-253-4241; www.countyofnapa.org/library; 580 Coombs St; ⊙10am-9pm Mon-Thu, to 6pm Fri & Sat; 📶) Free internet access.

TOURIST INFORMATION

Napa Valley Welcome Center (Map p162; ☎707-251-5895, 855-847-6272; www.visitnapavalley.com; 600 Main St; ⊙9am-5pm; 👪) Lodging assistance (call ☎707-251-9188 or ☎855-333-6272), wine-tasting passes, spa deals and comprehensive winery maps.

Getting There & Away

From San Francisco, public transportation can get you to Napa, but it's insufficient for vineyard-hopping. For public-transit information, dial ☎511, or look online at www.transit.511.org.

Downtown Napa is about an 80-minute drive from San Francisco.

Getting Around

Pedicabs park outside downtown restaurants – especially at the foot of Main St, near the Napa Valley Welcome Center – in summer. Car-sharing service Uber (www.uber.com) operates in Napa, but plans to hire an Uber can go awry in some areas due to spotty cell reception.

Yountville

This onetime stagecoach stop, 9 miles north of Napa, is now a fine-food destination playing to the haute bourgeoisie, with more Michelin stars per capita than any other American town. A stay in Yountville means drinking at dinner without having to drive afterward, as the town is walkable, but Napa and Calistoga make for livelier bases. Most businesses are on Washington St.

Sights

Ma(i)sonry GALLERY, WINERY

(Map p167; 707-944-0889; www.maisonry.com; 6711 Washington St; 10:30am-4:30pm Sun-Thu, to 5:30pm Fri & Sat; P) Ma(i)sonry occupies a free-to-browse 1904 stone house and garden, transformed into a fussy winery-collective and gallery of pricey rustic-modern *meubles* (furniture) and art, some quite cool. Reservations recommended for wine tastings.

Napa Valley Museum MUSEUM

(Map p167; 707-944-0500; www.napavalleymuseum.org; 55 Presidents Circle; adult/child $7/2.50; 11am-4pm Wed-Sun; P) Yountville's modernist 40,000-sq-ft museum chronicles cultural history and showcases local paintings. From town, it's across Hwy 29. Second Saturdays of the month are free.

Yountville Park PARK

(Map p167; cnr Washington & Madison Sts; 6am-8pm) Good park for a picnic.

Sleeping

There are some lovely inns here and many are walking distance from the restaurants and shops. Budget travelers will not find suitable accommodations though.

Poetry Inn INN $$$

(Map p167; 707-944-0646; www.poetryinn.com; 6380 Silverado Trail; r $1100-1975;) There's no better valley view than from this contemporary five-room inn, high on the hills east of Yountville. Decorated with posh restraint, rooms have private balcony, wood-burning fireplace, 1000-thread-count linen and enormous bath with indoor-outdoor shower.

Petit Logis INN $$$

(Map p167; 877-944-2332, 707-944-2332; www.petitlogis.com; 6527 Yount St; r $145-325;) Simple, cozy and comfortable, this cedar-sided inn has five uniquely adorned rooms, each with jetted tub and gas fireplace.

Eating

Make reservations or you may not eat. Yountville Park has picnic tables and barbecue grills. Find groceries across from the post office. There's a great taco truck parked in town.

Bouchon Bakery BAKERY $

(Map p167; 707-944-2253; www.bouchonbakery.com; 6528 Washington St; items from $3; 7am-7pm;) Bouchon makes as-good-as-in-Paris French pastries and strong coffee. There's always a line and rarely a seat: get it to go.

Ottimo ITALIAN $

(Map p167; 707-944-0102; www.ottimo-nv.com; 6525 Washington St; pizzas $14, crescintines $8; 7am-6pm) Chef Michael Chiarello opened this Italian market, cafe and *mozzeria* in Yountville's V Marketplace across from his popular farm-to-table establishment Bottega in early 2017, and it quietly became a prime spot for industry folks and in-the-know tourists. Most delicious are the brick-oven pizzas and crescentines (panini-like sandwiches), along with samples of preserves (from Chiarello's family recipes) in the shop. Grab a table on the sunny outdoor patio.

Tacos Garcia FAST FOOD $

(Map p167; 707-980-4896; 6764 Washington St; tacos $1.50; 11am-9pm) This beloved taco truck operates out of the parking lot in front of the dive bar Pancha's (p168), offering delicious tacos with fillings such as beef cheeks, *tripa* (fried intestine) and fried pork double-wrapped in a corn tortilla and topped with onion and cilantro.

Redd Wood ITALIAN $$

(Map p167; 707-299-5030; www.redd-wood.com; 6755 Washington St; pizzas $16-19, most mains $17-28; 11:30am-10pm Sun-Thu, to 11pm Fri & Sat) Celeb-chef Richard Reddington's casual Italian trattoria serves outstanding homemade pastas, *salumi* and tender-to-the-tooth pizzas from a wood-fired oven.

Addendum SOUTHERN US $$

(Map p167; 707-944-1565; www.adhocrestaurant.com/addendum; 6476 Washington St; box lunch $16.50; 11am-2pm Thu-Sat;) An offspring of parent restaurant Ad Hoc (p168), Thomas Keller's Addendum provides boxed lunches of finger-lickin' buttermilk-fried chicken, BBQ pork ribs and pulled-pork sandwiches, accompanied by Southern-style sides to go. It's simple and delicious.

Napa Valley South

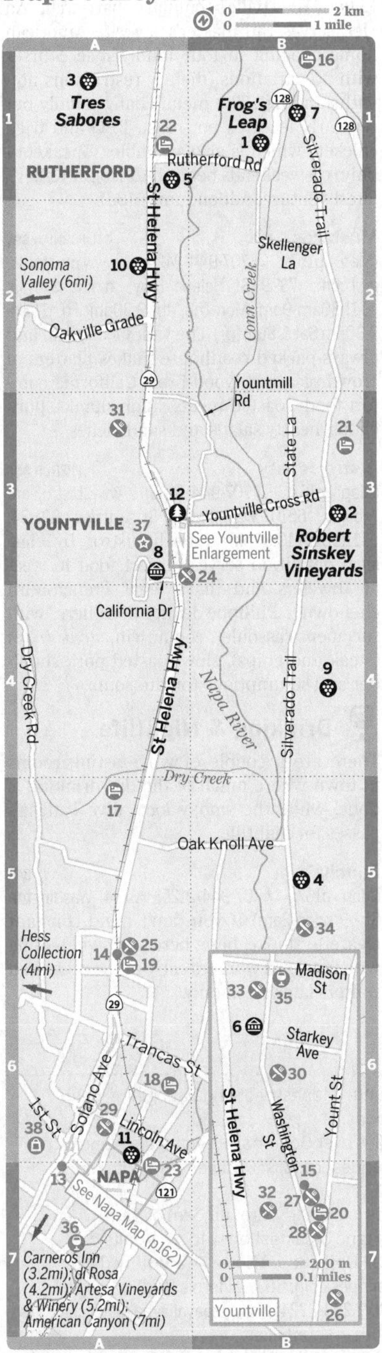

0 — 2 km
0 — 1 mile

Napa Valley South

Top Sights
1 Frog's Leap B1
2 Robert Sinskey Vineyards B3
3 Tres Sabores A1

Sights
4 Darioush B5
5 Elizabeth Spencer A1
6 Ma(i)sonry B6
7 Mumm Napa B1
8 Napa Valley Museum A3
9 Regusci B4
10 Robert Mondavi A2
11 Twenty Rows A6
12 Yountville Park A3

Activities, Courses & Tours
13 Balloons Above the Valley A7
14 Napa Valley Balloons A5
15 Napa Valley Bike Tours B7

Sleeping
16 Auberge du Soleil B1
17 Cottages of Napa Valley A5
18 Milliken Creek Inn A6
19 Napa Winery Inn A5
20 Petit Logis B7
21 Poetry Inn B3
22 Rancho Caymus A1
23 River Terrace Inn A7

Eating
Ad Hoc .... (see 24)
24 Addendum A3
25 Bistro Don Giovanni A5
26 Bistro Jeanty B7
27 Bouchon B7
28 Bouchon Bakery B7
29 Buttercream Bakery & Diner A6
Ciccio .... (see 35)
30 French Laundry B6
31 Mustards Grill A3
32 Ottimo B7
33 Redd Wood B6
Rutherford Grill .... (see 22)
34 Soda Canyon Store B5
Tacos Garcia .... (see 35)

Drinking & Nightlife
35 Pancha's B6
36 Tannery Bend Beerworks A7

Entertainment
37 Lincoln Theater A3

Shopping
Finesse, the Store .... (see 15)
38 Napa Premium Outlets A6

★ **French Laundry** CALIFORNIAN $$$

(Map p167; ☎707-944-2380; www.thomaskeller.com/tfl; 6640 Washington St; prix-fixe dinner $310; ⊙seatings 11am-12:30pm Fri-Sun, 5-9pm daily) The pinnacle of California dining, Thomas Keller's French Laundry is epic, a high-wattage culinary experience on par with the world's best. Book one month ahead on the online app Tock, where tickets are released in groupings. This is the meal you can brag about.

★ **Ciccio** ITALIAN $$$

(Map p167; ☎707-945-1000; www.ciccionapavalley.com; 6770 Washington St; mains $25-32; ⊙5-9pm Wed-Sun) The small, frequently changing menu at this family-owned Italian place is dependent on the season and likely to include just a couple of veggies, pastas, meat options and four to six wood-fired pizzas. But wow! You cannot go wrong, especially if you're lucky enough to show up when whole sea bass and garlicky pea tendrils are available. There's a negroni bar and many delicious wines from the owner's Altamura Ranch, along with a prix-fixe chef's dinner (by limited reservation) that includes menu and off-menu favorites for visitors to choose from.

Bouchon FRENCH $$$

(Map p167; ☎707-944-8037; www.thomaskeller.com; 6354 Washington St; mains $19-59; ⊙11am-midnight Mon-Fri, from 10am Sat & Sun) Details at celeb-chef Thomas Keller's French brasserie are so impeccable – zinc bar to white-aproned waiters – you'd swear you were in Paris. Only the Bermuda-shorts-clad Americans look out of place. On the menu: oysters, onion soup, roasted chicken, trout with almonds, runny cheeses and perfect profiteroles.

Ad Hoc CALIFORNIAN $$$

(Map p167; ☎707-944-2487; www.adhocrestaurant.com; 6476 Washington St; prix-fixe dinner from $55; ⊙5-10pm Thu-Sat & Mon, 9am-1:30pm & 5-10pm Sun) A winning formula by Thomas Keller, Yountville's culinary patriarch, Ad Hoc serves the master's favorite American home cooking in four family-style courses with no variations (dietary restrictions notwithstanding). The menu changes daily but regularly features pot roast, BBQ and fried chicken, which is also available (for takeout only) on weekends behind Ad Hoc at Keller's latest venture, Addendum (p166).

Mustards Grill CALIFORNIAN $$$

(Map p167; ☎707-944-2424; www.mustardsgrill.com; 7399 St Helena Hwy; mains $16-33; ⊙11:30am-9pm Mon-Thu, to 9:30pm Fri, 11am-9:30pm Sat & Sun; 👪) The valley's original and always-packed roadhouse makes platters of crowd-pleasing, wood-fired, California comfort food: roasted meats, lamb shanks, pork chops, hearty salads and sandwiches.

Bistro Jeanty FRENCH $$$

(Map p167; ☎707-944-0103; www.bistrojeanty.com; 6510 Washington St; mains $21-34; ⊙11:30am-10:30pm) French bistros by classical definition serve comfort food to weary travelers and that's what French-born chef-owner Philippe Jeanty does here, with succulent cassoulet, coq au vin, *steak frites* (steak and chips), slow-roasted pork shoulder and scrumptious tomato soup.

Drinking & Nightlife

There are a couple of wine-tasting rooms in town where much of the day-drinking is done, while the smoky local dive Pancha's passes for nightlife.

Pancha's BAR

(Map p167; ☎707-944-2125; 6764 Washington St; ⊙noon-2am) If you don't mind constant cigarette smoke, hang here and swill tequila with vineyard workers early in the night and waiters later. Cash only.

FLYING & BALLOONING

Wine Country is stunning from the air – a multihued tapestry of undulating hills, deep valleys and rambling vineyards. Make reservations.

The **Vintage Aircraft Company** (p185) flies over Sonoma in a vintage biplane with an awesome pilot who'll do loop-de-loops on request (add $50). Twenty-minute tours cost $175/270 for one/two adults.

Napa Valley's signature hot-air balloon flights leave early, around 6am or 7am, when the air is coolest; they usually include a champagne breakfast on landing. Adults pay about $200 to $250, and kids $150 to $175. Call **Balloons Above the Valley** (Map p167; ☎707-253-2222, 800-464-6824; www.balloonrides.com; 603 California Blvd) or **Napa Valley Balloons** (Map p167; ☎707-944-0228, 800-253-2224; www.napavalleyballoons.com; per person $239, 2-person private flight $2200), both in Yountville.

Entertainment

Lincoln Theater THEATER

(Map p167; box office 707-949-9900; www.lincolntheater.org; 100 California Dr) Various artists, including Napa Valley Symphony, play this 1200-seat theater.

Shopping

Finesse, the Store GIFTS & SOUVENIRS

(Map p167; 707-363-9552; www.finessethestore.com; 6540 Washington St; 11am-6pm Thu-Mon) Thomas Keller disciples and fanatics can finally take a piece of the action home. The culinary guru's new gift and souvenir shop features items such as cookbooks, cookware, aprons and sauces.

Getting There & Away

For public-transit information, dial 511, or look online at www.transit.511.org. Yountville is about an 80-minute drive from San Francisco.

Oakville & Rutherford

It'd be easy to drive through Oakville and never know you'd missed it. Vineyards sprawl everywhere. Rutherford is slightly more conspicuous.

Sleeping & Eating

There aren't many places to stay here and those on a budget should steer clear. North in Calistoga and south in downtown Napa there are far more choices.

The two tiny towns have between them a couple of good markets and the lip-smacking Rutherford Grill, which is essentially a Houston's.

★ **Auberge du Soleil** LUXURY HOTEL $$$

(Map p167; 800-348-5406, 707-963-1211; www.aubergedusoleil.com; 180 Rutherford Hill Rd, Rutherford; r $795-1500, ste $1525-5300;) The top splurge for a no-holds-barred romantic weekend, Auberge's hillside cottages, some of which are brand new, are second to none. A meal in its **dining room** (breakfast mains $33, lunch $31 to $42, three-/four-/six-course prix-fixe dinner $115/130/150) is an iconic Napa experience: come for a fancy breakfast, lazy lunch or will-you-wear-my-ring dinner; valley views are mesmerizing – *don't* sit inside. Make reservations; arrive before sunset.

Rancho Caymus HOTEL $$$

(Map p167; 800-845-1777, 707-963-1777; www.ranchocaymus.com; 1140 Rutherford Rd, Rutherford; r $400-800;) Styled after California's missions, this hacienda-like inn was closed for years before a recent comeback. The restored hotel features 25 large suites with oak-beamed wood ceilings, gas fireplaces and secluded patios. The steeper price reflects work put in to refurbish the entire property, including the relaxing spa, leafy courtyard and plunge pool.

Rutherford Grill AMERICAN $$

(Map p167; 707-963-1792; www.rutherfordgrill.com; 1180 Rutherford Rd, Rutherford; mains $15-38; 11:30am-9:30pm Mon-Thu, to 10pm Fri, 11am-10pm Sat, to 9:30pm Sun) Yes, it's part of a chain (Houston's), but its bar at lunchtime provides a chance to rub shoulders with winemakers. The food is consistent – ribs, rotisserie chicken, good grilled artichokes – and there's no corkage, so bring that bottle you just bought.

St Helena

You'll know you're here when traffic halts. St Helena (ha-*lee*-na) is the Rodeo Dr of Napa. Fancy boutiques line the historic downtown's Main St (Hwy 29) and provide excellent window-shopping. Parking, however, is next-to-impossible on summer weekends. Tip: look behind the visitor center (p174).

Sights

Robert Louis Stevenson Museum MUSEUM

(Map p172; 707-963-3757; http://stevensonmuseum.org; 1490 Library Lane; noon-4pm Tue-Sat; P) FREE This museum contains the largest displayed collection of Robert Louis Stevenson's belongings in the world. In 1880 the author – then sick, penniless and unknown – stayed in an abandoned bunkhouse at the old Silverado Mine on Mt St Helena with his wife, Fanny Osbourne; his novel the *Silverado Squatters* is based on his time there. Turn east off Hwy 29 at the Adams St traffic light and cross the railroad tracks.

Farmers Market MARKET

(Map p172; 707-486-2662; www.sthelenafarmersmkt.org; 7:30am-noon Fri May-Oct) Meets at Crane Park, half a mile south of downtown.

Courses

Culinary Institute of America at Greystone COOKING

(Map p172; 707-967-1100; www.ciachef.edu/california; 2555 Main St;) Inside an 1889 stone château, this culinary-school campus houses a new restaurant, a gadget- and cookbook-filled culinary shop, a bakery-cafe, weekend cooking demonstrations and wine-tasting classes. Cooking demonstrations are $25 and take place at 1:30pm Saturday and Sunday. Classes start at $95.

Sleeping

Most options in St Helena are pricey, particularly on weekends and during high season. The one reasonable option is El Bonita, but it fills up fast.

★ El Bonita MOTEL $$

(Map p172; ☎800-541-3284, 707-963-3216; www.elbonita.com; 195 Main St; r $140-325; P ⊖ ❄ @ 🛜 ≋ 🐾) Book in advance to secure this sought-after motel, with up-to-date rooms (quietest are in back), attractive grounds, a heated pool, hot tub and sauna.

Las Alcobas BOUTIQUE HOTEL $$$

(Map p172; ☎707-963-7000; www.lasalcobasnapavalley.com; 1915 Main St; r from $600-2500; ❄ 🛜 ≋) A newcomer with a sister property in Mexico City, this boutique has already secured its place among Napa Valley's finest stays. The plush, modern rooms offer both vineyard vista and proximity to some of the region's best dining, shopping and wine tasting. That's if you attempt to pry yourself from the delicious hotel-restaurant Acacia, heated pool and relaxing spa.

Meadowood RESORT $$$

(Map p172; ☎707-963-3646, 877-963-3646; www.meadowood.com; 900 Meadowood Lane; r from $850; P ⊖ ❄ @ 🛜 ≋) Hidden in a wooded dell with towering pines and miles of hiking, Napa's grandest resort has cottages and rooms in satellite buildings surrounding a croquet lawn. We most like the hillside fireplace suites; lawn-view rooms lack privacy but are good for families. The vibe is Republican country club: wear linen and play *Great Gatsby*. Kids love the mammoth pool and there's also an adult pool.

Harvest Inn by Charlie Palmer INN $$$

(Map p172; ☎800-950-8466, 707-963-9463; www.harvestinn.com; 1 Main St; r $449-899; ❄ @ 🛜 ≋ 🐾) 🍃 A former estate, this 78-room resort has rooms in satellite buildings on sprawling manicured grounds. The reception and rooms were recently repainted and redecorated; vineyard-view rooms are loveliest (each has private hot tub). The grounds contain two heated pools and two hot tubs. The Harvest Table restaurant is delish, with ostentatious flaming cocktails and locally sourced, expertly prepared New American cuisine.

Wydown Hotel BOUTIQUE HOTEL $$$

(Map p172; ☎707-963-5100; www.wydownhotel.com; 1424 Main St; r Sun-Thu $320-370, Fri & Sat $500-550; ❄ 🛜) Opened in 2012, this fashion-forward boutique hotel, with good service, sits smack downtown, its 12 oversized rooms smartly decorated with tufted velvet, distressed leather, subway-tile baths and California-king beds with white-on-white high-thread-count linens.

Eating

St Helena is packed with fabulous restaurants where you'll need reservations; alternatively, self-cater at the local market Sunshine Foods.

Napa Valley Olive Oil Mfg Co MARKET $

(Map p172; ☎707-963-4173; www.oliveoilsainthelena.com; 835 Charter Oak Ave; ⏲8am-5:30pm) Before the advent of fancy-food stores, this ramshackle market introduced Napa to Italian delicacies: prosciutto and salami, olives, fresh bread, nutty cheeses and, of course, olive oil. Ask nicely and the owner will lend you a knife and a board to picnic at the rickety tables in the grass outside. Cash only.

Sunshine Foods MARKET, DELI $

(Map p172; ☎707-963-7070; www.sunshinefoodsmarket.com; 1115 Main St; ⏲7:30am-8:30pm) Town's best grocery store; excellent deli.

Model Bakery CAFE $

(Map p172; ☎707-963-8192; www.themodelbakery.com; 1357 Main St; dishes $8-10; ⏲6:30am-5pm Mon-Sat, 7am-5pm Sun) Good bakery with muffins, salads, pizzas, sandwiches and exceptional coffee.

Cook St. Helena ITALIAN $$

(Map p172; ☎707-963-7088; www.cooksthelena.com; 1310 Main St; lunch $14-23, dinner $18-26; ⏲11:30am-10pm Mon-Sat, 4-9pm Sun) Locals crowd this tiny storefront bistro, beloved for its earthy Cal-Italian cooking: homemade pasta and risotto, crispy sole and soft polenta. Expect a wait, even with reservations. Next door, the pizzeria Cook Tavern is under the same ownership and also a good choice.

Cindy's Backstreet Kitchen MODERN AMERICAN $$

(Map p172; ☎707-963-1200; www.cindysbackstreetkitchen.com; 1327 Railroad Ave; mains $17-29; ⏲11:30am-9pm) 🍃 The inviting retro decor complements the Cal-American comfort

WINE TASTING

The best way to discover the real Wine Country is to avoid factory wineries and visit family-owned boutique houses (producing fewer than 20,000 annual cases) and midsized houses (20,000 to 60,000 annual cases). Why does it matter? Think of it. If you were to attend two dinner parties, one for 10 people, one for 1000, which would have the better food? Small wineries maintain tighter control. Also, you won't easily find these wines elsewhere.

Tastings are called 'flights' and include four to six different wines. Napa wineries charge around $10 to $50. In Sonoma Valley, tastings cost about $5 to $20, often refundable with purchase. In Sonoma County, tastings are free or $5 to $10. You must be 21 to taste.

Do not drink and drive. The curvy roads are dangerous and police monitor traffic, especially on Napa's Hwy 29.

To avoid burnout, visit no more than three wineries per day. Most open daily 10am or 11am to 4pm or 5pm, but call ahead if your heart's set, or you absolutely want a tour, especially in Napa, where law requires that some wineries accept visitors only by appointment. If you're buying, ask if there's a wine club, which is free to join and provides discounts, but you'll have to agree to buy a certain amount annually.

food, such as avocado-and-papaya salad, a Chinatown duck burger and sautéed petrale sole. The bar makes a mean mojito.

Gott's Roadside AMERICAN **$$**
(Map p172; 707-963-3486; http://gotts.com; 933 Main St; mains $8-16; 10am-10pm May-Sep, to 9pm Oct-Apr;) Wiggle your toes in the grass and feast on quality burgers – beef, turkey, ahi or veggie – plus Cobb salads and fish tacos at this roadside drive-in. Avoid weekend waits by phoning ahead or ordering online. There's another at Oxbow Public Market (p163).

Market MODERN AMERICAN **$$**
(Map p172; 707-963-3799; www.marketsthelena.com; 1347 Main St; mains $14-22; 11:30am-9pm Mon-Thu, to 10pm Fri & Sat, 10am-9pm Sun) We love Market's big portions of simple, fresh American cooking, including hearty salads of local produce and soul-satisfying mains such as buttermilk-fried chicken. The stone-walled dining room dates to the 19th century, as does the ornate backbar, where cocktails get muddled to order. Free corkage.

Restaurant at Meadowood CALIFORNIAN **$$$**
(Map p172; 707-967-1205; www.meadowood.com; 900 Meadowood Lane; 12-course menu $275; 5:30-9:30pm Tue-Sat) If you couldn't score reservations at French Laundry, fear not: Meadowood – the valley's only other three-Michelin-star restaurant – has a slightly more sensibly priced menu, unfussy dining room and lavish haute cuisine. Auberge (p169) has better views, but Meadowood's food and service far surpass it.

Farmstead MODERN AMERICAN **$$$**
(Map p172; 707-963-4555; www.longmeadowranch.com; 738 Main St; mains $22-31; 11:30am-9:30pm Mon-Thu, to 10pm Fri & Sat, 11am-9:30pm Sun;) An enormous open-truss barn with big leather booths and rocking-chair porch, Farmstead draws an all-ages crowd and farms many of its own ingredients – including grass-fed beef and lamb – for an earthy menu highlighting wood-fired cooking.

Terra CALIFORNIAN **$$$**
(Map p172; 707-963-8931; www.terrarestaurant.com; 1345 Railroad Ave; 4-/5-/6-course menu $78/93/105; 6-9pm Thu-Mon) Seamlessly blending Japanese, French and Italian culinary styles, Terra is one of Wine Country's top tables – the signature meal is broiled sake-marinated black cod with shrimp dumplings in shiso broth. The adjoining bar serves small bites without reservations, but the dining room's the thing.

Archetype FUSION **$$$**
(Map p172; 707-968-9200; http://archetypenapa.com; 1429 Main St; dinner mains $25-37; 11am-2:30pm Wed & Thu, 9am-2:30pm Sat & Sun, 5:30-9pm Wed-Sun) In an architect-designed dining room that breaks the Wine Country mold, Archetype effortlessly melds Asian and Mediterranean techniques with the best of California farms and foraging. Savor anything from the oak wood-burning oven and grill, or show up for sweet weekend brunch on the sunny back patio. Happy-hour drinks and bites are a steal (from just $5).

Napa Valley North

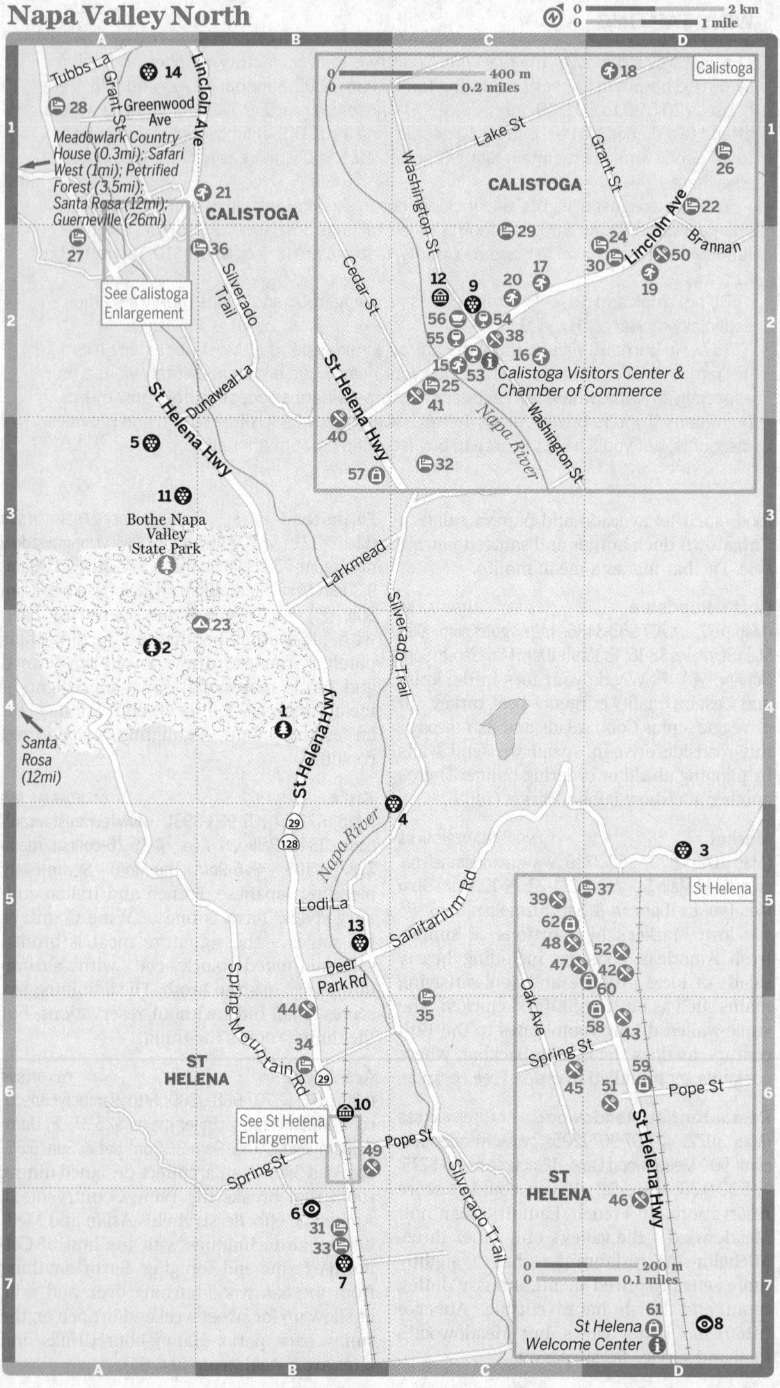

0 2 km
0 1 mile

Tubbs La
14
Grant St
Lincoln Ave
28
Greenwood Ave
Meadowlark Country House (0.3mi); Safari West (1mi); Petrified Forest (3.5mi); Santa Rosa (12mi); Guerneville (26mi)
21
CALISTOGA
27
36
Silverado Trail
See Calistoga Enlargement
Dunaweal La
St Helena Hwy
5
11
Bothe Napa Valley State Park
Larkmead
23
2
Silverado Trail
1
Santa Rosa (12mi)
St Helena Hwy
4
Napa River
29
128
3
Sanitarium Rd
Lodi La
13
Deer Park Rd
35
Spring Mountain Rd
44
34
ST HELENA
29
10
See St Helena Enlargement
Pope St
49
Spring St
Silverado Trail
6
31
33
7

Calistoga
0 400 m
0 0.2 miles
18
Lake St
Washington St
Grant St
26
CALISTOGA
22
Lincoln Ave
Brannan
29
24
30
50
Cedar St
12
9
20
17
19
56
54
55
38
16
15
53
Calistoga Visitors Center & Chamber of Commerce
St Helena Hwy
25
41
Napa River
Washington St
40
57
32

St Helena
37
39
62
48
52
47
42
60
Oak Ave
58
43
Spring St
59
45
51
Pope St
St Helena Hwy
ST HELENA
46
0 200 m
0 0.1 miles
61
8
St Helena Welcome Center

Napa Valley North

Sights

1 Bale Grist Mill State Historic Park......B4
2 Bothe-Napa Valley State Park......A4
3 Cade......D5
4 Casa Nuestra......C5
5 Castello di Amorosa......A3
6 Farmers Market......B7
7 Hall......B7
8 Long Meadow Ranch......D7
9 Olabisi Wines......C2
10 Robert Louis Stevenson Museum......B6
11 Schramsberg......A3
12 Sharpsteen Museum......C2
13 Titus......B5
14 Vincent Arroyo......A1

Activities, Courses & Tours

15 Calistoga Bike Shop......C2
16 Calistoga Spa Hot Springs......C2
Culinary Institute of America at Greystone......(see 44)
17 Dr Wilkinson's Hot Springs Resort......C2
18 Golden Haven Hot Springs......D1
19 Indian Springs Spa......D2
20 Mount View Spa......C2
21 Oat Hill Mine Trail......B1
Spa Solage......(see 36)

Sleeping

Aurora Park Cottages......(see 27)
22 Best Western Plus Stevenson Manor......D1
23 Bothe-Napa Valley State Park Campground......B4
24 Brannan Cottage Inn......D2
25 Calistoga Inn......C2
26 Calistoga Motor Lodge & Spa......D1
Calistoga Spa Hot Springs......(see 16)
27 Chanric......A2
28 Chateau De Vie......A1
29 Chelsea Garden Inn......C2
30 Cottage Grove Inn......D2
Dr Wilkinson's Motel & Hideaway Cottages......(see 17)
31 El Bonita......B7
32 EuroSpa & Inn......C3
33 Harvest Inn by Charlie Palmer......B7
Indian Springs Resort......(see 19)
34 Las Alcobas......B6
35 Meadowood......C6
Mount View Hotel & Spa......(see 20)
36 Solage......B2
37 Wydown Hotel......D5

Eating

38 All Seasons Bistro......C2
39 Archetype......C5
40 Buster's Southern BBQ......B3
Calistoga Inn & Brewery......(see 25)
41 Calistoga Kitchen......C2
42 Cindy's Backstreet Kitchen......D5
43 Cook St. Helena......D6
Farmstead......(see 8)
44 Gatehouse Restaurant......B6
45 Goose & Gander......C6
46 Gott's Roadside......D7
47 Market......C5
48 Model Bakery......C5
49 Napa Valley Olive Oil Mfg Co......B6
Restaurant at Meadowood......(see 35)
50 Sam's Social Club......D2
Solbar......(see 36)
51 Sunshine Foods......D6
52 Terra......D5

Drinking & Nightlife

53 Brannan's Grill......C2
54 Hydro Grill......C2
Solbar......(see 36)
55 Susie's Bar......C2
56 Yo El Rey......C2

Shopping

57 Calistoga Pottery......B3
Coperfield's Books......(see 15)
58 Footcandy......D6
59 Lolo's Consignment......D6
60 Main Street Books......D5
61 Napa Soap Company......D7
Rabbit Rabbit Fair Trade......(see 47)
62 Woodhouse Chocolates......C5

Goose & Gander MODERN AMERICAN **$$$**

(Map p172; ☎707-967-8779; www.goosegander.com; 1245 Spring St; mains $19-39; ⊙11:30am-11pm Sun-Thu, to midnight Fri & Sat) Inside a converted arts-and-crafts house with cathedral ceiling and gorgeous woodwork, Goose & Gander has a clubby vibe conducive to drinking, excellent craft cocktails and an imaginative (sometimes heavy) menu with standouts such as the G&G burger. Consider the garden, although hard-drinking locals favor the basement pub.

Gatehouse Restaurant CALIFORNIAN **$$$**

(Map p172; ☎707-967-1010; www.ciarestaurantgroup.com/gatehouse-restaurant; 2555 Main St; 3-/4-course lunch $32/$42, dinner $39/$49; ⊙11:30am-1pm & 6-8:30pm Tue-Sat) Testing skills and knowledge they've picked up in culinary school, students serve prix-fixe meals at this elegant restaurant on the Culinary Institute of America's Greystone campus. Ingredients for many dishes come from CIA's farm and herb gardens.

Drinking & Nightlife

There's not a whole lot going on here after hours. Calistoga to the north offers a more vibrant bar scene.

Shopping

Main St is lined with high-end boutiques (think $100 socks), but some mom-and-pop shops remain.

Woodhouse Chocolates FOOD
(Map p172; www.woodhousechocolate.com; 1367 Main St; ⌚11am-5:30pm) Woodhouse looks more like Tiffany than a candy shop, with housemade chocolates similarly priced, but their quality is beyond reproach.

Rabbit Rabbit Fair Trade HOMEWARES
(Map p172; ☎707-968-9182; www.rabbitrabbitfairtrade.com; 1327 Main St; ⌚11am-5pm Sun & Mon, 10am-5pm Tue-Thu, to 6pm Fri & Sat) Handcrafted fair-trade goods including gifts, cards, toys, household items, accessories and other items.

Footcandy SHOES
(Map p172; ☎707-963-2040; www.footcandyshoes.com/info/about; 1239 Main St; Manolo Blahnik pairs up to $1245; ⌚10am-6pm Mon-Sat, 10:30am-6pm Sun) A boutique shoe store that feels more like high-heel museum, with designer pairs from Christian Louboutin and Manolo Blahnik.

Napa Soap Company COSMETICS
(Map p172; ☎707-963-5010; www.napasoap.com; 655 Main St; ⌚10am-5:30pm) Ecofriendly bath products, locally produced.

Lolo's Consignment VINTAGE
(Map p172; ☎707-963-7972; www.lolosconsignment.com; 1120 Main St; ⌚10am-4pm Mon, to 5:30pm Tue-Sat, 11am-4pm Sun) Groovy cheap dresses and cast-off cashmere.

Main Street Books BOOKS
(Map p172; ☎707-963-1338; 1315 Main St; ⌚10am-5:30pm Mon-Sat, 11am-3pm Sun) Good used books.

Information

St Helena Welcome Center (☎707-963-4456; www.sthelena.com; 657 Main St; ⌚9am-5pm Mon-Fri, 10am-4pm Sat, 11am-5pm Sun) The visitor center has information and lodging assistance.

Getting There & Away

For public-transit information, dial ☎511, or look online at www.transit.511.org. St Helena is an 80-minute drive from San Francisco.

Calistoga & Around

Famed 19th-century author Robert Louis Stevenson said of Calistoga: 'the whole neighborhood of Mt St Helena is full of sulfur and boiling springs…Calistoga itself seems to repose on a mere film above a boiling, subterranean lake.' And indeed, it does. Calistoga is synonymous with mineral water bearing its name, bottled here since 1924, and its springs and geysers have earned it an appropriate nickname: 'Hot springs of the West.'

The least gentrified town in Napa Valley feels refreshingly simple, with an old-fashioned main street lined with quirky shops and diverse characters wandering the sidewalks. Bad hair? No problem. Fancy-pants St Helena couldn't feel further away. Many don't go this far north, but you should, if only for a spa visit to indulge in the local specialty: hot-mud baths, made with volcanic ash from nearby Mt St Helena.

Sights

Safari West ZOO
(☎707-579-2551; www.safariwest.com; 3115 Porter Creek Rd; adult/child 4-12yr from $83/45; ⌚tours at 9am, 10am, 1pm, 2pm & 4pm; P) Giraffes in Wine Country? Whadya know. Safari West sprawls over 400 acres and protects wildebeests, zebras, cheetahs and other exotic animals, which mostly roam free. See them and some recently born giraffe and wildebeest babies on a guided 2½-hour safari in open-sided jeeps, which also includes a 30-minute hike; reservations required, no kids under four (unless you book a private wagon). Those feeling adventurous can stay overnight in nifty canvas-sided **tent cabins** (including breakfast $260 to $475) inside the preserve.

Bale Grist Mill State Historic Park PARK
(Map p172; ☎707-963-2236; 3369 St Helena Hwy; adult/child $5/2; ⌚10am-4pm Sat & Sun) This park features a 36ft-high water-powered mill wheel dating to 1846 – the largest still operating in North America; on Saturdays and Sundays (and sometimes Fridays, rarely Mondays) from 10am to 4pm, it grinds flour. In early October, look for living-history festival Old Mill Days.

Robert Louis Stevenson State Park STATE PARK
(☎707-942-4575; www.parks.ca.gov; 3801 Hwy 29; ⌚sunrise-sunset; P) FREE At this undeveloped state park 8 miles north of Calistoga,

NAPA & SONOMA WINE COUNTRY CALISTOGA & AROUND

the long-extinct volcanic cone of Mt St Helena marks Napa Valley's end and often gets snow in winter. It's a strenuous 5-mile climb to the peak's 4343ft summit, but what a view – 200 miles on a clear winter's day. Check conditions before setting out. Also consider 2.2-mile one-way **Table Rock Trail** (go south from the summit trailhead parking area) for drop-dead valley views. No dogs allowed.

Olabisi Wines WINERY
(Map p172; ☎707-942-4472; www.olabisiwines.com; 1226 Washington St; tasting $25; ⊙11am-6pm) In downtown Calistoga, this newer tasting room run by a long-time winemaker specializes in small-production wines produced with wild yeast. The big Cabs, floral Pinots and dry whites often sell out quickly, with the winery producing less than 1000 cases a year. Bottles cost $38 to $125. Tasting fee is waived with a purchase of three bottles.

Bothe-Napa Valley State Park STATE PARK
(Map p172; ☎707-942-4575; 3801 St Helena Hwy; parking $8; ⊙8am-sunset; 👪) A mile-long trail leads from Bale Grist Mill State Historic Park to adjacent Bothe-Napa Valley State Park, where there's a swimming pool ($5) and camping, plus hiking through redwood groves. If you're two or more adults, go first to Bothe and pay $8, instead of the per-head charge at Bale Grist.

Sharpsteen Museum MUSEUM
(Map p172; ☎707-942-5911; www.sharpsteenmuseum.org; 1311 Washington St; suggested donation $3; ⊙11am-4pm; 👪) FREE Across from the picturesque 1902 City Hall (originally an opera house), the Sharpsteen Museum was created by an ex-Disney animator (whose Oscar is on display) and houses a fantastic diorama of town in the 1860s, big Victorian dollhouse, full-size horse-drawn carriage and a restored cottage from entrepreneur Samuel Brannan's original resort. (The only Brannan cottage still at its original site is at 109 Wappo Ave).

Petrified Forest FOREST
(☎707-942-6667; www.petrifiedforest.org; 4100 Petrified Forest Rd; adult/child 6-11yr/child 12-18yr $12/6/8; ⊙10am-7pm late May-early Sep, to 6pm Apr-late May & early Sep-Oct, to 5pm Nov-Mar; P 👪) Three million years ago at this now roadside-Americana attraction, a volcanic eruption at Mt St Helena blew down a stand of redwoods. The trees fell in the same direction, away from the blast, and over the millennia the mighty giants' trunks turned to stone. Discover them on short trails through the woods and stop by the monument that marks Robert Louis Stevenson's 1880 visit, which he described in the *Silverado Squatters*. Guided tours go at 11am, 1pm and 3pm.

Activities

Find biking information and rentals at Calistoga Bike Shop (p157).

Oat Hill Mine Trail CYCLING, HIKING
(Map p172; 2082 Oat Hill Mine Rd) One of Northern California's most technically challenging trails, this draws hard-core mountain bikers and hikers. Less experienced walkers take heart: a moderately strenuous half-mile up from town, there's a bench with incredible valley views. The trailhead is at the intersection of Hwy 29 and Silverado Trail.

Spas

Calistoga is famous for hot-spring spas and mud-bath emporiums, where you're buried in hot mud and emerge feeling supple, detoxified and enlivened. (The mud is made with volcanic ash and peat; the higher the ash content, the better the bath.)

Packages take 60 to 90 minutes and cost $90 to $100. You start semisubmerged in hot mud, then soak in hot mineral water – a steam bath and blanket-wrap follow. A massage increases the cost to $130 or more.

Baths can be taken solo or, at some spas, as couples. Variations include thin, painted-on clay-mud wraps (called 'fango' baths, good for those uncomfortable sitting in mud), herbal wraps, seaweed baths and various massage treatments. Discount coupons are sometimes available from the visitors center (p179). Book ahead, especially on summer weekends. Reservations are essential everywhere. Most spas offer multitreatment packages. Some offer discounted spa-lodging packages.

★**Indian Springs Spa** SPA
(Map p172; ☎707-709-2449; www.indianspringscalistoga.com; 1712 Lincoln Ave; ⊙by appointment 9am-9pm) California's longest continually operating spa, and original Calistoga resort, has concrete mud tubs and mines its own ash. Treatments include use of the huge, hot-spring-fed pool. Great cucumber body lotion.

Dr Wilkinson's Hot Springs Resort SPA
(Map p172; ☎707-942-4102; www.drwilkinson.com; 1507 Lincoln Ave; mud bath from $94; ⊙by appointment 8:30am-3:45pm) For more than 60 years running, 'the doc' uses more peat in its mud.

Spa Solage SPA
(Map p172; 707-266-0825; www.solage.aubergeresorts.com/spa; 755 Silverado Trail; by appointment 8am-8pm) Chichi, austere, top-end spa, with couples' rooms and a fango-mud bar for DIY paint-on treatments. Also has zero-gravity chairs for blanket wraps and sex-segregated clothing-optional mineral pools.

Golden Haven Hot Springs SPA
(Map p172; 707-942-8000; www.goldenhaven.com; 1713 Lake St; mud bath $99; by appointment 8am-8pm) Old-school and unfussy; offers couples' mud baths and massage.

Calistoga Spa Hot Springs SPA
(Map p172; 707-942-6269, 866-822-5772; www.calistogaspa.com; 1006 Washington St; mud bath $99; by appointment 9am-4pm Mon-Thu, to 7pm Fri-Sun) Traditional mud baths and massage at a complex with two huge swimming pools.

Mount View Spa SPA
(Map p172; 707-942-1500; www.mountviewhotel.com; 1457 Lincoln Ave; single/couple mud bath $90/110; by appointment 8:30am-7pm) Traditional full-service, five-room spa, good for clean-hands gals who prefer a mineral bath infused with lighter mud.

Sleeping

From upscale hot-springs resorts to quaint country cottages, there must be a dozen good options in and around Calistoga. Budget travelers will love the yurts and campsites in Bothe-Napa Valley State Park.

Bothe-Napa Valley State Park Campground CAMPGROUND $
(Map p172; 800-444-7275; www.reserveamerica.com; 3801 Hwy 128; camping & RV sites $35, yurts $55-70, cabins $150-225;) Three miles south of Calistoga, Bothe has shady camping near redwoods, coin-operated showers, and gorgeous hiking (p175). Sites 28 to 36 are most secluded.

EuroSpa & Inn MOTEL $$
(Map p172; 707-942-6829; www.eurospa.com; 1202 Pine St; r $169-325;) Immaculate single-story motel on a quiet side street, with extras such as gas-burning fireplaces, afternoon refreshments and small on-site spa. Excellent service, but tiny pool.

Dr Wilkinson's Motel & Hideaway Cottages MOTEL, COTTAGES $$
(Map p172; 707-942-4102; www.drwilkinson.com; 1507 Lincoln Ave; r $165-275, cottage $175-280;) This good-value vintage-1950s motel has well-kept rooms facing a swimming-pool courtyard with hot tub, three pools (one indoors) and mud baths. Also rents simple, great-value stand-alone cottages with kitchen at the affiliated Hideaway Cottages, also with pool and hot tub.

Best Western Plus Stevenson Manor HOTEL $$
(Map p172; 800-528-1234, 707-942-1112; www.stevensonmanor.com; 1830 Lincoln Ave; r weekday $179-209, weekend $299-329;) This entry-level business-class hotel feels generic, but has good extras, including full hot breakfast. Upstairs rooms are quietest. New elevator and exercise room.

Calistoga Spa Hot Springs MOTEL $$
(Map p172; 866-822-5772, 707-942-6269; www.calistogaspa.com; 1006 Washington St; r $197-267;) Great for families who jam the place on weekends, this motel-resort has slightly scuffed generic rooms (request one that's been remodeled) with kitchenette, and fantastic pools: two full size, a kiddie pool with miniwaterfall and a huge adults-only Jacuzzi. Outside are barbecues and a snack bar.

Calistoga Inn INN $$
(Map p172; 707-942-4101; www.calistogainn.com; 1250 Lincoln Ave; r with shared bath $169-229, cottages $229-289;) Upstairs from a busy bar, this inn has 17 clean, basic rooms with shared bath, ideal for no-fuss bargain hunters. No TV and no elevator. Bring earplugs. A newer cottage contains its own bathroom, air-conditioning and TV.

★**Brannan Cottage Inn** BOUTIQUE HOTEL $$$
(Map p172; 707-942-4200; https://brannancottageinn.com; 109 Wappo Ave; r from $309;) Adorable, gingerbread-style Victorian cottage amid lush grounds that in the 1860s belonged to the town's favorite entrepreneur Samuel Brannan. Recently restored to preserve its old-timey character, the cottage is listed in the National Register of Historic Places and offers six uniquely adorned rooms featuring comfy, pillow-top mattresses and modern amenities. A concierge will help plan your trip.

Solage RESORT $$$
(Map p172; 707-226-0800, 866-942-7442; www.solage.aubergeresorts.com; 755 Silverado Trail; r $530-675, ste $835-1275;) Calistoga's top spa-hotel ups the style factor, with

Cali-chic semidetached cottages and a glam pool surrounded by palm trees. Rooms are austere, with vaulted ceilings, zillion-thread-count linens and pebble-floor showers. Cruiser bikes included.

Indian Springs Resort RESORT $$$
(Map p172; ☎707-942-4913; www.indiansprings calistoga.com; 1712 Lincoln Ave; r/cottages from $269/349;) The definitive old-school Calistoga resort, Indian Springs has cottages facing a central lawn with palm trees, shuffleboard, bocce and hammocks – not unlike a vintage Florida resort. There are also top-end, motel-style lodge rooms (adults only). Huge hot-springs-fed swimming pool. Also has Sam's Social Club (p178).

Meadowlark Country House B&B $$$
(☎707-942-5651; www.meadowlarkinn.com; 601 Petrified Forest Rd; r $245-450, ste $310-355;) About a mile west of Calistoga, sitting on 20 lush acres, Meadowlark has homey rooms decorated in contemporary style, most with deck and Jacuzzi. Outside there's a hot tub, sauna and clothing-optional pool. The truth-telling innkeeper lives elsewhere, offers helpful advice, then vanishes when you want privacy. There's a fabulous cottage costing $450 for two and $640 for four. Gay friendly.

Cottage Grove Inn BUNGALOW $$$
(Map p172; ☎707-942-8400; www.cottagegrove.com; 1711 Lincoln Ave; cottages $275-450;) Romantic cottages for over-40s, with wood-burning fireplaces, two-person Jacuzzis and rocking-chair front porches.

Chelsea Garden Inn B&B $$$
(Map p172; ☎707-942-0948; www.chelseagarden-inn.com; 1443 2nd St; r $195-350;) On a quiet side street, this single-story inn has five floral-print rooms with private entrances, facing pretty gardens. Never mind the pool's rust spots.

Chateau De Vie B&B $$$
(Map p172; ☎707-942-6446, 877-558-2513; www.cdvnapavalley.com; 3250 Hwy 128; r $269-469;) Surrounded by vineyards, with gorgeous views of Mt St Helena, CDV has five modern, elegantly decorated B&B rooms with top-end amenities and zero froufrou. Charming owners serve wine on the sun-dappled patio, then leave you alone. Hot tub, big pool. Gay friendly.

Chanric B&B $$$
(Map p172; ☎707-942-4535; www.thechanric.com; 1805 Foothill Blvd; r from $690;) A converted Victorian near the road, this cushy B&B has small but smartly furnished rooms, plus many free extras including champagne on arrival and lavish three-course breakfasts. Gay friendly. No elevator.

Aurora Park Cottages COTTAGE $$$
(Map p172; ☎707-942-6733, 877-942-7700; www.aurorapark.com; 1807 Foothill Blvd; cottages $269-349, houses $399-899;) Six immaculately kept, sunny-yellow cottages – with polished-wood floors, feather beds and sundeck – stand in a row beside flowering gardens. There's also a pricier rental home with a full kitchen. Though close to the road, everything's quiet by night and the innkeeper couldn't be nicer.

Mount View Hotel & Spa HISTORIC HOTEL $$$
(Map p172; ☎707-942-6877; www.mountviewhotel.com; 1457 Lincoln Ave; r Mon-Fri $209-429, Sat & Sun $279-459;) Smack in the middle of town, this 1917 Mission Revival hotel is decorated in vaguely mod-Italian style at odds with the vintage building – rooms are clean and fresh-looking nonetheless. Gleaming bathrooms, spa, year-round heated pool.

Calistoga Motor Lodge & Spa MOTEL $$$
(Map p172; ☎707-942-0991; www.thesunburstcalistoga.com; 1880 Lincoln Ave; r $229-469; @) This single-story 1950s motor lodge got a makeover in 2017, with mid-century-modern-led aesthetics, but it's basically still a drive-to-the-door motel with upscale furnishings and thin walls.

Eating

The dining scene in Calistoga isn't as uppity as the rest of the valley, but you can certainly procure a high-class meal at Calistoga Kitchen (p178), Solbar (p178) and the newly opened Sam's Social Club (p178). Many decent and affordable restaurants line Lincoln Ave.

Buster's Southern BBQ BARBECUE $
(Map p172; ☎707-942-5605; www.busterssouthernbbq.com; 1207 Foothill Blvd; dishes $8-12; 10am-8pm Mon-Sat, to 7pm Sun;) The sheriff dines at this indoor-outdoor barbecue joint, which serves smoky ribs, chicken, tri-tip steak and burgers, plus beer and wine. It closes early at dinnertime.

★Calistoga Kitchen CALIFORNIAN $$$
(Map p172; ☎707-942-6500; www.calistogakitchen.com; 1107 Cedar St; mains lunch $12-18, dinner $20-36; ⌚5:30pm-close Thu, 11:30am-3pm & 5:30pm-close Fri & Sat, 9:30am-3pm Sun) A sparsely decorated cottage surrounded by a white picket fence, Calistoga Kitchen is especially good for lunch in the garden. The chef-owner favors simplicity, focusing on quality ingredients in a half-dozen changing dishes, such as a delicious braised rabbit. Reservations advised, especially for the patio.

Solbar CALIFORNIAN $$$
(Map p172; ☎707-226-0860; www.solage.aubergeresorts.com; 755 Silverado Trail N, Calistoga; lounge menu dishes $4-16, dinner mains $26-38; ⌚7am-11:30am, 11:45am-3pm & 5:30-9pm, to 9:30pm Fri & Sat) We like the Spartan ag-chic look of this Michelin-starred resort restaurant, the menu of which writing maximizes seasonal produce in elegant dishes, playfully composed. A chef from Italy had just been hired, but the crispy petrale sole tacos were as delectable as ever. The menu remains split for calorie-counters into light and hearty dishes. Reservations essential.

All Seasons Bistro MODERN AMERICAN $$$
(Map p172; ☎707-942-9111; www.allseasonsnapavalley.net; 1400 Lincoln Ave; mains lunch $12-18, dinner $16-27; ⌚11:30am-2:30pm & 5:30-9pm, hours vary) It looks like a white-tablecloth soda fountain, but All Seasons makes very fine meals, from a simple lasagna to composed dishes such as scallop, prawn, mussel and clam risotto. The salads are fresh and totally organic.

Sam's Social Club AMERICAN $$$
(Map p172; ☎707-942-4969; http://samssocialclub.com; 1712 Lincoln Ave; dinner mains $17-38; ⌚7:30am-9pm Mon-Wed, to 9:30pm Thu-Sun) Housed in the Indian Springs Resort (p177), this is Calistoga's fancy American restaurant that also brews its own beer. Colorful and expertly prepared dishes feature the freshest local ingredients, and the bacon-wrapped, Point Reyes Farmstead blue-cheese-stuffed dates are otherworldly. There's outdoor patio seating and a bright, comfortable dining room and bar. It's perfect for a relaxing feast post mud bath.

Calistoga Inn & Brewery AMERICAN $$$
(Map p172; ☎707-942-4101; www.calistogainn.com; 1250 Lincoln Ave; dinner mains $15-38; ⌚11:30am-9:30pm Mon-Fri, from 11am Sat & Sun) Locals crowd the outdoor beer garden on Sundays. Midweek we prefer the country dining room's big oakwood tables – a homey spot for simple American cooking. Live music on summer weekends.

Drinking & Nightlife

There are a few hoppin' bars along Lincoln Ave and they'll often have live music on weekends.

Brannan's Grill BAR
(Map p172; ☎707-942-2233; www.brannanscalistoga.com; 1374 Lincoln Ave; ⌚11:30am-9pm) The mahogany bar at Calistoga's handsomest restaurant is great for martinis and microbrews, especially 7pm to 10pm Friday and Saturday, when there's live jazz.

Yo El Rey CAFE
(Map p172; www.yoelreyroasting.com; 1217 Washington St; ⌚6:30am-5:30pm) Hip kids favor this microroastery, which serves stellar small-batch, organic, fair-trade coffee.

Susie's Bar BAR
(Map p172; ☎707-942-6710; 1365 Lincoln Ave; ⌚noon-2am Mon-Fri, 10am-2am Sat & Sun) Turn your baseball cap sideways, swill beer and shoot pool to a soundtrack of classic rock.

Solbar BAR
(Map p172; ☎707-226-0860; www.solage.aubergeresorts.com; 755 Silverado Trail; ⌚11am-9pm, to 9:30pm Fri & Sat) Sip craft cocktails beside outdoor fireplaces and a pool surrounded with palm trees at this Napa-swank resort bar.

Hydro Grill BAR
(Map p172; ☎707-942-9777; 1403 Lincoln Ave; ⌚8:30am-10:30pm Mon-Thu, to 11:30pm Fri-Sun) Live music plays on Sundays and one Saturday a month at this hoppin' bar-restaurant.

Shopping

Calistoga Pottery CERAMICS
(Map p172; ☎707-942-0216; www.calistogapottery.com; 1001 Foothill Blvd; ⌚9am-5pm Mon-Sat) Artisanal pottery, hand-thrown on-site. Ask about the pots glazed with local grapevine ash.

Coperfield's Books BOOKS
(Map p172; ☎707-942-1616; 1330 Lincoln Ave; ⌚10am-7pm Sun-Thu, to 8pm Fri & Sat) Indie bookshop, with local maps and guides.

Information

Calistoga Visitors Center & Chamber of Commerce (707-942-6333; www.visitcalistoga.com; 1133 Washington St; 9am-5pm) Lodging info, maps, pamphlets etc.

Getting There & Away

From San Francisco, public transportation can get you to Calistoga, though it's better to have your own wheels. For public-transit information, dial 511, or look online at www.transit.511.org.

Calistoga is about a 100-minute drive from San Francisco.

Getting Around

Hwys 128 and 29 split in Calistoga, where Hwy 29 turns east and becomes Lincoln Ave, continuing across Silverado Trail, toward Clear Lake. Hwy 128 continues north as Foothill Blvd.

OUTLET SHOPPING

Max out your credit cards on last season's closeouts.

Napa Premium Outlets (Map p167; 707-226-9876; www.premiumoutlets.com; 629 Factory Stores Dr; 10am-8pm Mon-Thu, to 9pm Fri & Sat, to 7pm Sun) A large shopping center with fifty storeswest of downtown Napa..

Petaluma Village Premium Outlets (707-778-9300; www.premiumoutlets.com; 2200 Petaluma Blvd N, Petaluma; 10am-9pm) Sixty stores, Sonoma County.

Vacaville Premium Outlets (707-447-5755; www.premiumoutlets.com/vacaville; 321 Nut Tree Rd, Vacaville; 10am-9pm) One hundred and twenty stores, northeast of Wine Country on I-80.

SONOMA VALLEY

We have a soft spot for Sonoma's folksy ways. Unlike fancy Napa, nobody cares if you drive a clunker and vote Green. Locals call it 'Slow-noma.' Anchoring the bucolic 17-mile-long valley, the town of Sonoma makes a great jumping-off point for exploring Wine Country – it's an hour from San Francisco – and has a marvelous sense of place, with storied 19th-century historical sights surrounding the state's largest town square.

Halfway up-valley, tiny Glen Ellen (p188) is straight from a Norman Rockwell painting – in stark contrast to the valley's northernmost town, Santa Rosa (p204), the workaday urban center best known for traffic. If you have more than a day, explore Sonoma's quiet, rustic western side along the Russian River Valley, and continue to the sea.

Sonoma Valley Wineries

Rolling grass-covered hills rise from Sonoma Valley. Its 40-some wineries get less attention than Napa's, but many are equally good. If you love Zinfandel and Syrah, you're in for a treat.

Picnicking is allowed at Sonoma wineries. Get maps and discount coupons in the town of Sonoma or, if you're approaching from the south, the Sonoma Valley Visitors Bureau (p185) at Cornerstone Gardens.

Plan at least five hours to visit the valley from bottom to top.

★Gundlach-Bundschu Winery WINERY
(Map p180; 707-938-5277; www.gunbun.com; 2000 Denmark St, Sonoma; tasting $20-30, incl tour $30-60; 11am-5:30pm May-Oct, to 4:30pm Nov-Apr; P) California's oldest family-run winery looks like a castle but has a down-to-earth vibe. Founded in 1858 by a Bavarian immigrant, its signatures are Gewürztraminer and Pinot Noir, but 'Gun-Bun' was the first American winery to produce 100% Merlot. Down a winding lane, it's a terrific bike-to winery with picnicking, hiking, a lake and frequent concerts, including a two-day folk-music festival in June. Tour the 1800-barrel cave by reservation only. Bottles are $20 to $50.

★Bartholomew Park Winery WINERY
(Map p180; 707-939-3026; www.bartpark.com; 1000 Vineyard Lane, Sonoma; tasting $15; 11am-4:30pm; P) A great bike-to winery, Bartholomew Park occupies a 375-acre nature preserve with oak-shaded picnicking and valley-view hiking. The vineyards were originally cultivated in 1857 and now yield certified-organic, citrusy Sauvignon Blanc, Cabernet Sauvignon softer in style than Napa and lush Zinfandel. There's also a new collection of reserve wines and a new private tasting experience. Bottles are $27 to $48. Tasting fee is waived with bottle purchase.

St Francis Winery & Vineyards WINERY
(Map p180; 707-538-9463; www.stfranciswinery.com; 100 Pythian Rd at Hwy 12, Santa Rosa; tasting $15, wine & cheese pairing $25, wine & food pairing

$68; 10am-5pm) The vineyards are scenic and all, but the real reason to visit St Francis is the much-lauded food-pairing experience. The mouthwatering, multicourse affair is hosted by amiable and informative wine experts and includes things such as braised Kurobuta pork with Okinawan sweet potatoes paired with Cab Franc, and American Wagyu strip loin and chanterelles paired with an old-vine Zin. Seatings at 11am, 1pm and 3pm, Thursday to Monday. Spots fill fast; book well in advance.

Robledo WINERY

(Map p180; 707-939-6903; www.robledofamilywinery.com; 21901 Bonness Rd, off Hwy 116; tasting $15-25; 10am-5pm Mon-Sat, 11am-4pm Sun) Sonoma Valley's feel-good winery, Robledo was founded by a former migrant worker from Mexico who worked his way up to vineyard manager, then land owner, now vintner. His kids run the place. The wines – served at hand-carved Mexican furniture in a barn – include a nonoaked Sauvignon Blanc, spicy Cabernet and bright, fruit-forward Pinot Noir. Bottles cost $20 to $60. Appointments recommended for groups of six or more.

Little Vineyards WINERY

(Map p180; 707-996-2750; www.littlevineyards.com; 15188 Sonoma Hwy, Glen Ellen; tasting $15; 11am-4:30pm Thu-Mon;) The name fits at this family-owned small-scale winery surrounded by grapes, with a lazy dog to greet you and a weathered, old-timey wooden bar, at which Jack London formerly drank (before it moved here). The big reds include Syrah, Petite Sirah, Zin, Cab and several delish blends. It also has a rosé and a Pinot Blanc. There's good picnicking on the vineyard-view terrace. Also rents a cottage in the vines. Bottles cost $20 to $50.

Homewood WINERY

(Map p180; 707-996-6353; www.homewoodwinery.com; 23120 Burndale Rd, Sonoma; tasting $10; 10am-4pm; P) Barn cats dart about at this down-home winery with several different tasting areas and a $20 wine and chocolate pairing. The winemaker crafts standout Chardonnays and Roussannes, and an array of other whites, reds and late-harvest dessert wines. Bottles are $22 to $36; tasting fee waived with purchase.

Hawkes TASTING ROOM

(Map p184; 707-938-7620; www.hawkeswine.com; 383 1st St W, Sonoma; tasting $15; 11am-6pm Thu-Mon) When you're in downtown

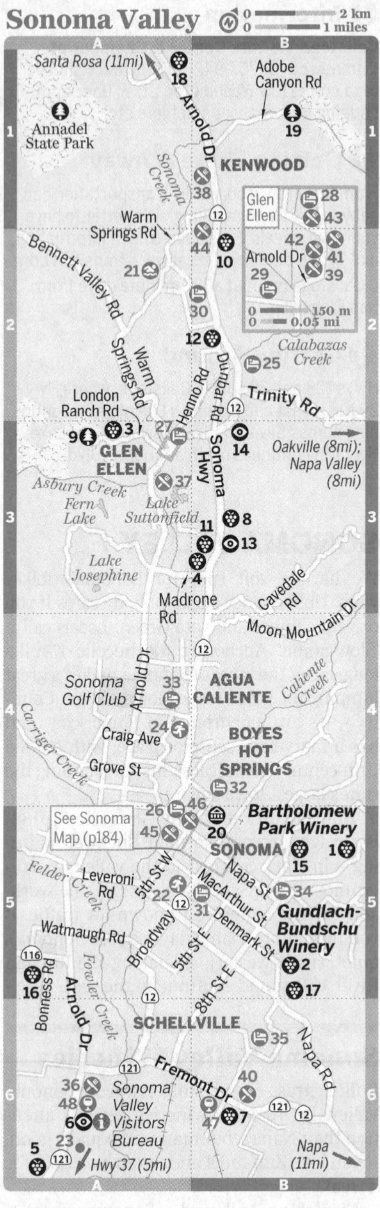

Sonoma and don't feel like fighting traffic, Hawke's refreshingly unfussy tasting room showcases meaty Cabernet Sauvignon from family-owned vineyards in Alexander Valley, never blended with other varietals. Bottles are $30 to $70; the tasting fee is waived with a purchase over $40.

Sonoma Valley

Top Sights
1 Bartholomew Park Winery B5
2 Gundlach-Bundschu Winery B5

Sights
Bartholomew Park .... (see 1)
3 Benziger A3
4 BR Cohn B3
5 Cline Cellars A6
6 Cornerstone Sonoma A6
7 Homewood B6
8 Imagery Estate B3
9 Jack London State Historic Park A3
10 Kunde B2
11 Little Vineyards B3
12 Loxton B2
13 Oak Hill Farm B3
14 Quarryhill Botanical Garden B3
15 Ravenswood Winery B5
16 Robledo A5
17 Scribe B5
18 St Francis Winery & Vineyards A1
19 Sugarloaf Ridge State Park B1
20 Vallejo's Home B5

Activities, Courses & Tours
21 Morton's Warm Springs A2
22 Sonoma Valley Cyclery A5
Triple Creek Horse Outfit .... (see 9)
23 Vintage Aircraft Company A6
24 Willow Stream Spa at Sonoma Mission Inn A4

Sleeping
25 Beltane Ranch B2
26 El Pueblo Inn A5
27 Gaige House Inn A3
28 Glen Ellen Cottages B1
29 Jack London Lodge B2
30 Kenwood Inn & Spa B2
31 MacArthur Place B5
32 Sonoma Chalet B4
33 Sonoma Creek Inn A4
34 Sonoma's Best Guest Cottages B5
Sugarloaf Ridge State Park .... (see 19)
35 Windhaven Cottage B6

Eating
36 Angelo's Wine Country Deli A6
37 Aventine A3
38 Cafe Citti B1
39 Fig Cafe & Winebar B2
40 Fremont Diner B6
41 Garden Court Cafe & Bakery B2
42 Glen Ellen Inn B2
43 Glen Ellen Star B1
44 Mayo Winery Reserve B2
45 Pearl's Diner A5
46 Sonoma Market A5

Drinking & Nightlife
47 Carneros Brewing Company B6
48 Prohibition Spirits Distillery A6

Benziger WINERY

(Map p180; ☎888-490-2739, 707-935-3000; www.benziger.com; 1883 London Ranch Rd, Glen Ellen; tasting $20-40, tours $25-50; ⏰10am-5pm; P 🚻) If you're new to wine, make Benziger your first stop for Sonoma's best crash course in winemaking. The worthwhile tour (11am–3:30pm; reservations recommended) includes an open-air tram ride (weather permitting) through biodynamic vineyards and a five-wine tasting. Great picnicking, excellent for families. The large-production wine is OK (head for the reserves); the tour's the thing. Bottles are $20 to $80.

Marimar Estate WINERY

(☎707-823-4365; www.marimarestate.com; 11400 Graton Rd, Sebastopol; tasting $15; ⏰11am-5pm by appointment only; 🐾) Middle-of-nowhere Marimar Estates specializes in all-organic Pinot – seven different kinds – and Spanish varietals. The hilltop tasting room has a knockout vineyard-view terrace, good for picnics. Also consider the guided tour, which includes a bottle ($95). Bottles are $49 to $59.

Cline Cellars WINERY

(Map p180; ☎707-940-4030; www.clinecellars.com; 24737 Arnold Dr, Hwy 121; tasting free-$20; ⏰tasting room 10am-6pm, museum to 4pm) Balmy days are for pondside picnics and rainy ones for fireside tastings of old-vine Zinfandel and Mourvèdre inside an 1850s farmhouse. Stroll out back to the **California Mission Museum**, housing 1930s miniature replicas of California's original 21 Spanish Colonial missions.

Kunde WINERY

(Map p180; ☎707-833-5501; www.kunde.com; 9825 Hwy 12, Kenwood; tasting $15-50, cave tours free; ⏰10:30am-5pm; P) This family-owned winery on a historic ranch has vineyards that are more than a century old. It offers mountaintop tastings with impressive valley views and seasonal guided hikes (advance reservations recommended), though you can also just stop for a tasting and a tour. Elegant, 100% estate-grown wines include crisp Chardonnay and unfussy red blends, all made sustainably. Bottles $17 to $100.

Loxton WINERY

(Map p180; ☎707-935-7221; www.loxtonwines.com; 11466 Dunbar Rd, Glen Ellen; tasting $10-20, walking tour $25; ⏲11am-5pm) Say g'day to Chris the Aussie winemaker at Loxton, a no-frills winery with million-dollar views of the grapes you'll actually be tasting. The tasting room contains a small warehouse where racing cars were once designed, and there you can sample wonderful Syrah and Zinfandel; nonoaky, fruit-forward Chardonnay; and good port. Bottles cost $17 to $32.

Ravenswood Winery WINERY

(Map p180; ☎707-933-2332; www.ravenswoodwinery.com; 18701 Gehricke Rd, Sonoma; tasting $20-60, incl tour $25; ⏲10am-4:30pm) With the slogan 'no wimpy wines,' this buzzing winery pours a full slate of estate Zinfandels. Novices welcome. Tours at 10:30am daily; reservations recommended.

Scribe WINERY

(Map p180; ☎707-939-1858; http://scribewinery.com; 2100 Denmark St, Sonoma; tasting $35, food pairing $65; ⏲11:30am-4pm Thu-Mon, by appointment only) With Scribe, a new generation has found its place in Wine Country. Bantering groups of bespectacled, high-waisted-jeans-wearing millennials frequent this hip winery designed to resemble a French château, and at outdoor picnic tables they hold forth on the terroir-driven rosé of Pinot, the skin-fermented Chardonnay and the bold Cab. The food pairing is hit and miss.

BR Cohn WINERY

(Map p180; ☎707-938-4064, 800-330-4064; www.brcohn.com; 15000 Sonoma Hwy, Glen Ellen; tasting indoors $20, weekend patio tasting $30; ⏲10am-5pm) Picnic like a rock star at always-busy BR Cohn. Its founder managed '70s super-band the Doobie Brothers before moving on to make outstanding organic olive oils and fine wines. Although the winery has changed hands, it's still an excellent spot for tasting wine, slurping oysters (weekends only) and sampling olive oil in the gourmet shop. Bottles are $16 to $56.

Imagery Estate WINERY

(Map p180; ☎707-935-4515, 800-989-8890; www.imagerywinery.com; 14335 Sonoma Hwy, Glen Ellen; tasting $15; ⏲10am-4:30pm Mon-Fri, to 5:30pm Sat & Sun; P 👪) Imagery produces lesser-known varietals such as Legrain and Tannat, biodynamically grown, that you often can't buy anywhere else. Each bottle sports an artist-designed label, with originals on display in the on-site gallery. Lovely gardens include a grassy picnic area with horseshoes, cornhole and bocce. Limited picnic supplies available. Bottles are $27 to $65. Kid and dog-friendly.

Sonoma & Around

Fancy boutiques may lately be replacing hardware stores, but Sonoma still retains an old-fashioned charm, thanks to the plaza – California's largest town square – and its surrounding frozen-in-time historic buildings. You can legally drink on the plaza – a rarity in California parks – but only between 11:30am and sunset.

Sonoma has a rich history. In 1846 it was the site of a second American revolution, this time against Mexico, when General Mariano Guadalupe Vallejo deported all foreigners from California, prompting outraged frontiersmen to occupy the Sonoma Presidio and declare independence. They dubbed California the Bear Flag Republic after the battle flag they'd fashioned.

The republic was short-lived. The Mexican-American War broke out a month later, and California was annexed by the US. The revolt gave California its flag, which remains emblazoned with the words 'California Republic' beneath a muscular brown bear. Vallejo was initially imprisoned but ultimately returned to Sonoma to play a major role in its development.

Sights

★Sonoma Plaza SQUARE

(Map p184; btwn Napa, Spain & 1st Sts) Smack in the center of the plaza, the Mission Revival–style city hall, built 1906–08, has identical facades on four sides, reportedly because plaza businesses all demanded City Hall face their direction. At the plaza's northeast corner, the **Bear Flag Monument** (Map p184; Sonoma Plaza) marks Sonoma's moment of revolutionary glory. The **weekly farmers market** (5:30-8pm Tues Apr-Oct) showcases Sonoma's incredible produce.

Sonoma State Historic Park HISTORIC SITE

(Map p184; ☎707-938-9560; www.parks.ca.gov; adult/child $3/2; ⏲10am-5pm) This park in Sonoma is comprised of multiple sites, most side by side. Founded in 1823, Mission San Francisco Solano anchors the plaza, and was the final California mission. Sonoma Barracks houses exhibits on 19th-century life.

A WINE COUNTRY PRIMER

When people talk about Sonoma, they're referring to the *whole* county, which unlike Napa, is huge. It extends all the way from the coast, up the Russian River Valley, into Sonoma Valley and eastward to Napa Valley; in the south it stretches from San Pablo Bay (an extension of San Francisco Bay) to Healdsburg in the north. It's essential to break Sonoma down by district.

West County refers to everything west of Hwy 101 and includes the Russian River Valley and the coast. Sonoma Valley stretches north–south along Hwy 12. In northern Sonoma County, Alexander Valley lies east of Healdsburg, and Dry Creek Valley lies north of Healdsburg. In the south, Carneros straddles the Sonoma–Napa border, north of San Pablo Bay. Each region has its own particular wines; what grows where depends upon the weather.

Inland valleys get hot; coastal regions stay cool. In West County and Carneros, nighttime fog blankets the vineyards. Burgundy-style wines do best, particularly Pinot Noir and Chardonnay. Further inland, Alexander, Sonoma and much of Dry Creek Valleys (as well as Napa Valley) are protected from fog. Here Bordeaux-style wines thrive, especially Cabernet Sauvignon, Sauvignon Blanc, Merlot and other heat-loving varieties. For California's famous Cabernets, head to Napa. Zinfandel and Rhône-style varieties such as Syrah and Viognier grow in both regions, warm and cool. In cooler climes, wines are lighter and more elegant; in warmer areas they are heavier and more rustic. As you explore, notice the bases of grapevines: the fatter they are, the older. 'Old vine' grapes yield color and complexity not found in grapes from younger vines.

Some basics: wineries and vineyards aren't the same. Grapes grow in a vineyard then get fermented at a winery. Wineries that grow their own grapes are called estates, as in 'estate-grown' or 'estate-bottled,' but estates also ferment grapes from other vineyards. When vintners speak of 'single-vineyard' or 'vineyard-designate' wines, they mean the grapes all originated from the same vineyard; this allows for tighter quality control. 'Single varietal' means all the grapes are the same variety (such as 100% Merlot) but may come from different vineyards. Reserves are the vintner's limited-production wines; they're usually available only at the winery.

Don't be afraid to ask questions. Vintners love to talk. If you don't know how to taste wine, or what to look for, ask the person behind the counter to help you discover what you like. Just remember to spit out the wine; the slightest buzz will diminish your capacity to taste.

For a handy-dandy reference on the road, pick up a copy of Karen MacNeil's *The Wine Bible* (2015, Workman Publishing) or Jancis Robinson's *The Oxford Companion to Wine* (2015, Oxford University Press) to carry in the car.

The 1886 Toscano Hotel lobby is beautifully preserved – peek inside. The 1852 Vallejo's Home (p185) lies a half-mile northwest. One ticket allows same-day admission to all, including **Petaluma Adobe State Park** (☎707-762-4871; www.petalumaadobe.com; 3325 Adobe Rd, Petaluma; adult/child $3/2; ⏰10am-5pm; P) at General Vallejo's former ranch, 15 miles away.

Mission San Francisco Solano HISTORIC BUILDING
(Map p184; ☎707-938-9560; www.parks.ca.gov; 114 E Spain St; adult/child $3/2; ⏰10am-5pm) At Sonoma Plaza's northeast corner, the mission was built in 1823, partly to forestall Russians at Fort Ross from moving inland. This was the 21st and final California mission – the northernmost point on El Camino Real – and the only one built during the Mexican period (the rest were founded during the Spanish Colonial era). Five original rooms remain. The not-to-be-missed **chapel** dates to 1840.

Toscano Hotel HISTORIC BUILDING
(Map p184; ☎707-938-9560; www.parks.ca.gov; 20 E Spain St; adult/child $3/2; ⏰10am-5pm) Toscano Hotel opened as a store and library in the 1850s, then became a hotel in 1886. Peek into the lobby and, except for the traffic outside, you'd swear you were peering back in time. Tours 1pm–4pm Saturday and Sunday.

Sonoma Barracks HISTORIC BUILDING
(Map p184; ☎707-939-9420; www.parks.ca.gov; 20 E Spain St; adult/child $3/2; ⏰10am-5pm) The adobe Sonoma Barracks was built by Vallejo between 1834 and 1841 to house Mexican troops. Today, interpretive displays describe life during the Mexican and

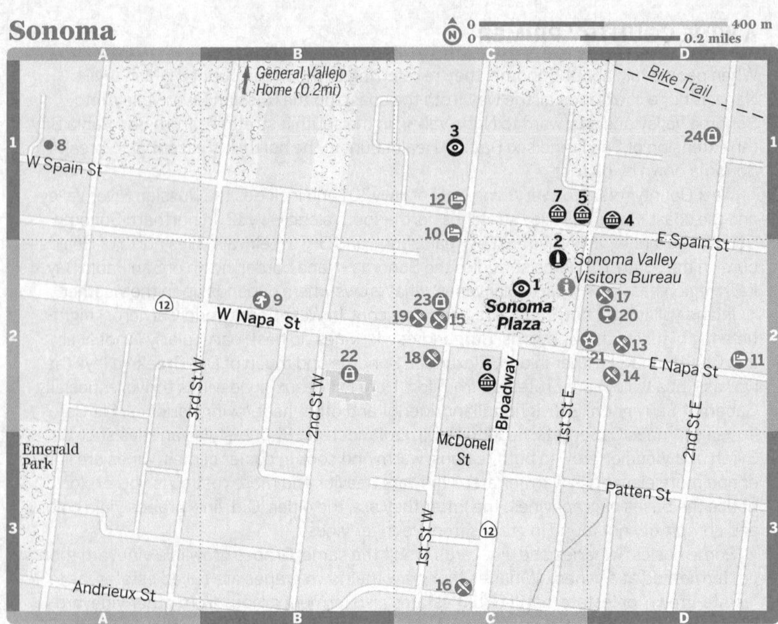

Sonoma

Top Sights
1 Sonoma Plaza C2

Sights
2 Bear Flag Monument C2
3 Hawkes C1
4 Mission San Francisco Solano D1
5 Sonoma Barracks C1
Sonoma State Historic Park .... (see 4)
6 Sonoma Valley Museum of Art C2
7 Toscano Hotel C1

Activities, Courses & Tours
8 Ramekins Sonoma Valley Culinary School A1
9 Wine Country Cyclery B2

Sleeping
10 El Dorado Hotel C1
11 Hidden Oak Inn D2
12 Sonoma Hotel C1

Eating
13 Cafe La Haye D2
14 Della Santina's D2
El Dorado Kitchen .... (see 10)
Girl & the Fig .... (see 12)
15 Harvest Moon Cafe C2
16 Hopmonk Tavern C3
17 La Salette D2
18 Red Grape C2
19 Tasca Tasca C2
Taste of the Himalayas .... (see 20)

Drinking & Nightlife
20 Murphy's Irish Pub D2
Steiner's .... (see 15)

Entertainment
21 Sebastiani Theatre D2

Shopping
22 Chateau Sonoma B2
23 Figone's Olive Oil C2
Tiddle E Winks .... (see 14)
24 Vella Cheese Co D1

American periods. The barracks became the capital of a rogue nation on June 9, 1846, when American settlers of varying sobriety surprised guards and declared an independent 'California Republc' [sic] with a homemade flag featuring a blotchy bear.

Bartholomew Park PARK
(Map p180; ☎707-938-2244; www.bartholomewpark.org; 1000 Vineyard Lane; ⏲10am-4:30pm; P 👪) FREE The top near-town outdoors destination is 375-acre Bartholomew Park, off Castle Rd, where you can picnic beneath gi-

ant oaks and hike 2 miles of trails, with hilltop vistas to San Francisco. The **Palladian Villa**, at the park's entrance, is a re-creation of Count Haraszthy's original Pompeian residence, open noon to 3pm Saturdays and Sundays. There's also a good **winery**, independently operated. Last entry is at 4:30pm.

Vallejo's Home HISTORIC BUILDING
(Map p180; ☎707-938-9559; 363 3rd St W; adult/child $3/2; ⏰10am-5pm) A half-mile from the plaza, this lovely historical estate, also known as Lachryma Montis (Latin for 'Tears of the Mountain'), was built in the 1850s for General Vallejo and named for the on-site spring, which the Vallejo family made good money from by piping water to town. The Gothic-style American-Victorian home remained in the family until 1933, when the state of California purchased it, along with its original furnishings. A bicycle path leads to the house from downtown. Tours 1pm, 2pm and 3pm Saturday and Sunday.

Sonoma Valley Museum of Art MUSEUM
(Map p184; ☎707-939-7862; www.svma.org; 551 Broadway; adult/child 14-17yr/family $10/5/15; ⏰11am-5pm Wed-Sun) The 8000-sq-ft modern- and contemporary-art museum presents changing exhibitions by international and local artists, and focuses on building community around art.

Cornerstone Sonoma GARDENS
(Map p180; ☎707-933-3010; www.cornerstonesonoma.com; 23570 Arnold Dr; ⏰10am-5pm, gardens to 4pm; 🅿👪) FREE This roadside, Wine Country marketplace showcases 25 walk-through (in some cases edible) gardens, along with a bunch of innovative and adorable shops, wine-tasting parlors and on-site **Sonoma Valley Visitors Bureau** (Map p180; ☎707-996-1090; www.sonomavalley.com; 23570 Hwy 121, Cornerstone Gardens; ⏰10am-4pm). There's a good, if pricey, cafe, and an outdoor 'test kitchen.' Look for the enormous orange Adirondack chair at road's edge.

Activities

Many local inns provide bicycles.

Willow Stream Spa at Sonoma Mission Inn SPA
(Map p180; ☎707-938-9000; www.fairmont.com/sonoma; 100 Boyes Blvd; ⏰9am-6pm Mon-Thu, to 8pm Fri-Sun) Few Wine Country spas compare with glitzy Sonoma Mission Inn. Purchasing a treatment or paying $89 (make reservations) allows use of three outdoor and two indoor mineral pools, gym, sauna and herbal steam room at the Romanesque bathhouse. No under 18s.

Wine Country Cyclery CYCLING
(Map p184; ☎707-966-6800; www.winecountrycyclery.com; 262 W Napa St; bicycle rental per day $30-75; ⏰10am-6pm) Offers hybrids, electric bikes, road bikes and even tandem bikes. Book ahead.

Sonoma Valley Cyclery CYCLING
(Map p180; ☎707-935-3377; www.sonomacyclery.com; 20091 Broadway/Hwy 12; bikes per day from $30; ⏰10am-6pm Mon-Sat, to 4pm Sun; 👪) Sonoma is ideal for cycling – not too hilly – with multiple wineries near downtown. This place rents mountain bikes, road bikes and hybrids. Book ahead for weekends.

Vintage Aircraft Company SCENIC FLIGHTS
(Map p180; ☎707-938-2444; www.vintageaircraft.com; 23982 Arnold Dr, Sonoma; 20min flight 1/2 people $175/270) Scenic flights in biplanes, with an option to add aerobatic maneuvers.

Courses

Ramekins Sonoma Valley Culinary School COOKING
(Map p184; ☎707-933-0450; www.ramekins.com; 450 W Spain St; 👪) Offers excellent demonstrations and hands-on classes for home chefs, covering things such as hors d'oeuvres and cheese-and-wine pairings. The school also hosts culinary tours of local farms and dinners with vintners and chefs.

Sleeping

There are lots of historic inns and romantic cottages suitable for a midrange budget, but those counting pennies will have better luck in Santa Rosa. Off-season rates plummet. Reserve ahead and ask about parking; some inns don't have lots.

★**Windhaven Cottage** COTTAGE $$
(Map p180; ☎707-938-2175, 707-483-1856; www.windhavencottage.com; 21700 Pearson Ave; cottages $165-175; ❄📶) Great-bargain Windhaven has two units: a hideaway cottage with vaulted wooden ceilings and fireplace, and a handsome 800-sq-ft studio. We prefer the romantic cottage. Both have hot tubs. Bicycles and barbecues sweeten the deal.

Sonoma Chalet B&B $$
(Map p180; ☎800-938-3129, 707-938-3129; www.sonomachalet.com; 18935 5th St W; r $160-190, r with shared bath $150, cottages $210-235; 🅿🚭) On

a historic farmstead surrounded by rolling hills, rooms in this Swiss-chalet-style house are adorned with little balconies and country-style bric-a-brac. We love the garden hot tub and the freestanding cottages; Laura's has a wood-burning fireplace. Breakfast is served on a deck overlooking a nature preserve. No air-conditioning in rooms with shared bath. No phone, no internet.

Sonoma Creek Inn MOTEL $$
(Map p180; ☎707-939-9463; www.sonomacreekinn.com; 239 Boyes Blvd; r Sun-Thu $155-195, Fri & Sat $205-240;) This cute-as-a-button motel has spotless, cheery, retro-Americana rooms, but it's not downtown. Valley wineries are a short drive. When available, last-minute bookings cost just $89.

Sonoma Hotel HISTORIC HOTEL $$
(Map p184; ☎707-996-2996, 800-468-6016; www.sonomahotel.com; 110 W Spain St; r weekday $160-248, weekend $225-248, ste $308;) Long on charm, this good-value, vintage hotel was built in 1872 and is decorated with country-style willow-wood furnishings. It sits right on the plaza and its double-pane glass blocks the noise, but there's no elevator or parking lot.

El Dorado Hotel BOUTIQUE HOTEL $$$
(Map p184; ☎707-996-3030; www.eldoradosonoma.com; 405 1st St W; r Sun-Thu $225-330, Fri & Sat $385-500;) Stylish touches, such as high-end linens, justify rates and compensate for the rooms' compact size, as do private balconies, which overlook the plaza or rear courtyard (we prefer the plaza view, despite noise). No elevator.

El Pueblo Inn MOTEL $$$
(Map p180; ☎707-996-3651, 800-900-8844; www.elpuebloinn.com; 896 W Napa St; r $189-384;) One mile west of downtown, family-owned El Pueblo has surprisingly cushy rooms with great beds. The big lawns and heated pool are perfect for kids; parents appreciate the 24-hour hot tub. Check the website for discounts.

Hidden Oak Inn B&B $$$
(Map p184; ☎707-996-9863; www.hiddenoakinn.com; 214 E Napa St; r $255-315;) Three-room, 1914 arts-and-crafts B&B with lovely service.

MacArthur Place INN $$$
(Map p180; ☎707-938-2929, 800-722-1866; www.macarthurplace.com; 29 E MacArthur St; r/ste from $399/555;) Sonoma's top full-service inn occupies a former estate with century-old gardens. There's also an attached steakhouse, spa, giant chess set on the lawn and a complimentary wine-and-cheese reception each night.

Sonoma's Best Guest Cottages COTTAGE $$$
(Map p180; ☎707-933-0340; www.sonomasbestcottages.com; 1190 E Napa St; cottages $199-349, q $279-395;) Each of these four colorful, inviting cottages has a bedroom, living room, kitchen and barbecue, with comfy furniture, stereo, DVDs and bicycles. It's 1 mile east of the plaza, just behind a general store under the same ownership, featuring a deli, an espresso bar and a wine-tasting room.

Eating

Sonoma takes a culinary backseat to many towns in Napa Valley and Healdsburg to the north, but has some decent restaurants on the plaza plus Fremont Diner, the best diner in Wine Country.

Angelo's Wine Country Deli DELI $
(Map p180; ☎707-938-3688; 23400 Arnold Dr; sandwiches $7; 9am-5pm) Look for the cow on the roof of this roadside deli south of town, a fave for fat sandwiches and homemade turkey and beef jerky (free samples!).

Pearl's Diner DINER $
(Map p180; ☎707-996-1783; 561 5th St W; mains $7-10; 7am-2:30pm;) Across from Safeway's west-facing wall, greasy-spoon Pearl's serves giant American breakfasts, including standout bacon and waffles with batter enriched by melted vanilla ice cream. More of a locals joint than a tourist spot.

Sonoma Market DELI $
(Map p180; ☎707-996-3411; https://sonomamarket.net; 500 W Napa St; sandwiches from $6; 5am-9:30pm) Sonoma's best groceries and deli sandwiches.

★**Fremont Diner** AMERICAN, SOUTHERN $$
(Map p180; ☎707-938-7370; www.thefremontdiner.com; 2698 Fremont Dr; mains $9-22; 8am-3pm Mon-Wed, to 9pm Thu-Sun;) Lines snake out the door at peak times at this farm-to-table roadside diner. We prefer the indoor tables but will happily accept a picnic table to feast on buttermilk pancakes with homemade cinnamon-vanilla syrup, chicken and waffles, oyster po'boys, finger-licking barbecue and skillet-baked cornbread.Arrive early or late to beat queues, or call ahead within

an hour of your arrival to put your name on the wait list.

Della Santina's ITALIAN **$$**
(Map p184; ☎707-935-0576; www.dellasantinas.com; 133 E Napa St; mains $14-26; ⊙11:30am-3pm & 5-9:30pm) The waiters have been here forever and the 'specials' rarely change, but Della Santina's Italian-American cooking – linguini pesto, veal parmigiana, rotisserie chickens – is consistently good and the brick courtyard is inviting on warm evenings.

Hopmonk Tavern PUB FOOD **$$**
(Map p184; ☎707-935-9100; www.hopmonk.com; 691 Broadway; mains $11-23; ⊙11:30am-9pm Sun-Thu, to 10pm Fri & Sat) This happening gastropub and beer garden takes its brews seriously with over a dozen of its own and guest beers on tap, served in type-appropriate glassware. Live music Friday through Sunday, open mike on Wednesday starting at 8pm.

Taste of the Himalayas INDIAN, NEPALESE **$$**
(Map p184; ☎707-996-1161; 464 1st St E; mains $10-20; ⊙11am-2:30 Tue-Sun, 5-10pm daily) Spicy curries, luscious lentil soup and sizzle-platter meats make a refreshing break from the usual French-Italian Wine Country fare.

Red Grape ITALIAN **$$**
(Map p184; ☎707-996-4103; http://theredgrape.com; 529 1st St W; mains $12-20; ⊙11:30am-9pm; 👪) A reliable spot for an easy meal, Red Grape serves good thin-crust pizzas and big salads in a cavernous, echoey space. Good for takeout too.

★**Cafe La Haye** CALIFORNIAN **$$$**
(Map p184; ☎707-935-5994; www.cafelahaye.com; 140 E Napa St; mains $19-25; ⊙5:30-9pm Tue-Sat) 🌿 One of Sonoma's top tables for earthy New American cooking, La Haye only uses produce sourced from within 60 miles. Its dining room gets packed cheek-by-jowl and service can border on perfunctory, but the clean simplicity and flavor-packed cooking make it many foodies' first choice. Reserve well ahead.

Girl & the Fig FRENCH **$$$**
(Map p184; ☎707-938-3634; www.thegirlandthefig.com; 110 W Spain St; mains $20-32; ⊙11:30am-10pm Mon-Thu, 11am-11pm Fri, 8am-11pm Sat, 10am-10pm Sun) For a festive evening, book a garden table at this French-provincial bistro, with good small plates ($14 to $16), including steamed mussels with matchstick fries or duck confit with lentils. Weekday three-course prix fixe costs $42; add $12 for wine. Stellar cheeses. Reservations essential.

La Salette PORTUGUESE **$$$**
(Map p184; ☎707-938-1927; www.lasalette-restaurant.com; 452 1st St E; mains lunch $12-25, dinner $22-32; ⊙11:30am-2:30pm & 5:30-9pm Mon-Fri, 11:30am-9pm Sat & Sun) 🌿 Contemporary Portuguese cuisine is the focus at this just-off-the-plaza restaurant that serves excellent-value, proper sit-down meals, including a standout fisherman's stew. Make reservations.

El Dorado Kitchen CALIFORNIAN **$$$**
(Map p184; ☎707-996-3030; http://eldoradosonoma.com/restaurant; 405 1st St W; mains lunch $15-24, dinner $21-31; ⊙8-11am, 11:30am-2:30pm & 5:30-9pm Mon-Thu, to 10pm Fri & Sat) 🌿 The swank plazaside choice for contemporary California-Mediterranean cooking, El Dorado showcases seasonal-regional ingredients in dishes such as seafood paella, ahi tartare and housemade pasta, served in a see-and-be-seen dining room with a big community table at its center. The happening lounge serves good small plates ($11 to $22) and craft cocktails. Make reservations.

Harvest Moon Cafe MODERN AMERICAN **$$$**
(Map p184; ☎707-933-8160; www.harvestmooncafesonoma.com; 487 1st St W; mains $19-29; ⊙5:30-9pm Sun-Mon & Wed-Thu, to 9:30pm Sat & Sun) 🌿 Inside a cozy 1836 adobe, this casual bistro uses local ingredients in its changing menu, with simple soul-satisfying dishes such as grilled Liberty Farm duck breast with dried cherry farro, cauliflower and saba sauce. Book the patio in warm weather.

🍷 Drinking & Nightlife

There's more of a late-night scene here than in other Sonoma Valley towns; **Steiner's** (Map p184; ☎707-996-3812; www.steinerstavern.com; 465 1st St W; ⊙6am-2am; 📶) is pretty much the social hub.

Carneros Brewing Company MICROBREWERY
(Map p180; ☎707-938-1880; www.carnerosbrewing.com; 22985 Burndale Rd; ⊙noon-5:30pm Wed-Mon) A family-owned microbrewery with seasonal craft beers and a mission-inspired tap room halfway between downtown Sonoma and Napa. On weekend afternoons the beer garden is a lively scene.

Prohibition Spirits Distillery DISTILLERY
(Map p180; ☎707-933-7507; www.prohibition-spirits.com; 23570 Arnold Dr, Sunset Gardens at Cornerstone; ⊙10am-5pm) New at Cornerstone, this

WHAT'S CRUSH?

Crush is autumn harvest, the most atmospheric time of year, when the vine's leaves turn brilliant colors and you can smell fermenting fruit on the breeze. Farmers throw big parties for the vineyard workers to celebrate their work. Everyone wants to be here and room rates skyrocket. If you can afford it, visit in autumn. To score party invitations, join your favorite winery's wine club.

hip tasting room offers sips of a California version of Italian aperitifs limoncello, orangecello and grappa, along with tasty gins made with things such as cantaloupe and elderflower, and brandy distilled from prickly pear cacti.

Murphy's Irish Pub PUB
(Map p184; ☎707-935-0660; www.sonomapub.com; 464 1st St E; ⏲11am-9pm) Don't ask for Bud – there are only *real* brews here. Good hand-cut fries and shepherd's pie. Live music Friday and Saturday evenings.

☆ Entertainment

Free jazz concerts happen on the plaza every second Tuesday of the month, June to September, 6pm to 8:30pm; arrive early and bring a picnic.

Sebastiani Theatre CINEMA
(Map p184; ☎707-996-2020; www.sebastianitheatre.com; 476 1st St E) The plaza's gorgeous 1934 Mission Revival cinema screens art-house and revival films, and sometimes live theater.

Shopping

Chateau Sonoma HOMEWARES
(Map p184; ☎707-935-8553; www.chateausonoma.com; 23588 Arnold Dr; ⏲10am-5pm) France meets Sonoma in one-of-a-kind gifts and arty home-decor store, which recently relocated to Cornerstone Sonoma.

Figone's Olive Oil FOOD
(Map p184; ☎707-282-9092; www.figoneoliveoil.com; 483 1st St W; ⏲10am-6pm Sun-Thu, to 7pm Fri & Sat) Figone's presses its own extra-virgin olive oil and infuses some with flavors such as Meyer lemon, all free to sample.

Vella Cheese Co FOOD
(Map p184; ☎707-938-3232; www.vellacheese.com; 315 2nd St E; ⏲9:30am-6pm Mon-Fri, to 5pm Sat) Known for its jacks (made here since the 1930s), Vella specializes in dry-jack with a cocoa-powder-dusted rind. Also try Mezzo Secco, a cheese you can only find here. Staff will vacuum-pack for shipping.

Tiddle E Winks TOYS
(Map p184; ☎707-939-6933; www.tiddleewinks.com; 115 E Napa St; ⏲10:30am-5:30pm Mon-Sat, 11am-5pm Sun; 👪) Vintage five-and-dime, with classic mid-20th-century toys.

ℹ Information

Sonoma Valley Visitors Bureau (Map p184; ☎866-966-1090; www.sonomavalley.com; 453 1st St E; ⏲9am-5pm Mon-Sat, 10am-5pm Sun) Offers guides, maps, pamphlets, merchandise information on deals and events, and more. There's another at Cornerstone Sonoma (p185).

ℹ Getting There & Away

Public transport is not a great idea but it can be done. Find out by dialing ☎511 or looking online at www.transit.511.org. Sonoma Valley is a 90-minute drive from San Francisco.

ℹ Getting Around

Sonoma Hwy/Hwy 12 is lined with wineries and runs from Sonoma to Santa Rosa, then to western Sonoma County; Arnold Dr has less traffic (but few wineries) and runs parallel up the valley's western side to Glen Ellen. Plan at least five hours to visit the valley from bottom to top.

Glen Ellen & Kenwood

Sleepy Glen Ellen is a snapshot of old Sonoma, with white picket fences and tiny cottages beside a poplar-lined creek. When downtown Sonoma is jammed, you can wander quiet Glen Ellen and feel far away. It's ideal for a leg-stretching stopover between wineries or a romantic overnight – the nighttime sky blazes with stars. Glen Ellen's biggest daytime attractions are Jack London State Historic Park and Benziger winery (p181).

Sights & Activites

Jack London State Historic Park PARK
(Map p180; ☎707-938-5216; www.jacklondonpark.com; 2400 London Ranch Rd, Glen Ellen; per car $10, cottage adult/child $4/2; ⏲9:30am-5pm; 🅿👪) 🍃 Napa has Robert Louis Stevenson, but Sonoma has Jack London. This 1400-acre park frames that author's last years; don't miss the excellent on-site museum. Miles of **hiking trails** (some open to mountain bikes)

weave through oak-dotted woodlands, between 600ft and 2300ft elevations; an easy 2-mile loop meanders to **London Lake**, great for picnicking. On select summer evenings, the park transforms into a theater for 'Broadway Under the Stars.' Be alert for poison oak.

Changing occupations from Oakland fisher-man to Alaska gold prospector to Pacific yachtsman (and novelist on the side) London (1876–1916) ultimately took up farming. He bought 'Beauty Ranch' in 1905 and moved here in 1911. With his second wife, Charmian, he lived and wrote in a small cottage while his mansion, **Wolf House**, was under construction. On the eve of its completion in 1913, it burned down. The disaster devastated London, and although he toyed with rebuilding, he died before construction got underway. His widow, Charmian, built the **House of Happy Walls**, which has been preserved as a **museum** (open 10am to 5pm). It's a half-mile walk from there to the remains of Wolf House, passing London's grave along the way. Other paths wind around the farm to the cottage, open noon to 4pm, where he lived and worked.

Quarryhill Botanical Garden GARDENS

(Map p180; ☎707-996-3166; www.quarryhillbg.org; 12841 Hwy 12; adult/child 13-17yr $12/8; ⏲9am-4pm) Just when you thought the vineyards would stretch as far as the eye could see, out of nowhere comes a world-renowned botanical garden specializing in the flora of Asia. It's a treat to stroll the trails, observing specimens collected on yearly expeditions to countries throughout the Far East, and to relax near the pond, contemplating the artfully created woodland landscape.

Sugarloaf Ridge State Park PARK

(Map p180; ☎707-833-5712; www.sugarloafpark.org; 2605 Adobe Canyon Rd, Kenwood; per car $8; P) There are 30 miles of fantastic hiking – when it's not blazingly hot. On clear days, **Bald Mountain** has drop-dead views to the sea, while the **Brushy Peaks Trail** peers into Napa Valley. Both are moderately strenuous; plan on a three-hour round-trip. Bikes and horses can use perimeter trails seasonally. There's a small but well-stocked visitor center.

Oak Hill Farm FARM

(Map p180; ☎707-996-6643; www.oakhillfarm.net; 15101 Sonoma Hwy, Glen Ellen; ⏲9am-3pm Sat May-Dec; P) At the southern end of Glen Ellen, Oak Hill Farm contains acres upon acres of organic flowers and produce, hemmed in by lovely steep oak and manzanita woodland. The farm's **Red Barn Store** is a historic dairy barn filled with handmade wreaths, herbs and organic goods reaped from the surrounding fields. Try the heirloom tomatoes, pumpkins and blue plums.

Triple Creek Horse Outfit HORSEBACK RIDING

(Map p180; ☎707-887-8700; www.triplecreekhorseoutfit.com; 2400 London Ranch Rd; 60/90min rides $80/100; ⏲9am-5pm Mon-Sat) Explore Jack London State Park by horseback for vistas over Sonoma Valley. Reservations required.

Morton's Warm Springs SWIMMING

(Map p180; ☎707-833-5511; www.mortonswarmsprings.com; 1651 Warm Springs Rd, Glen Ellen; adult/child $12/6; ⏲10am-6pm Tue-Sun Jun-Aug, Sat, Sun & holidays May & Sep;) This old-fashioned spring-fed geothermal-pool complex and family-friendly gathering place has two mineral pools, limited hiking, volleyball and BBQ facilities. From Sonoma Hwy in Kenwood, turn west on Warm Springs Rd.

Sleeping

Couples will not regret staying in the romantic cottages and inns of Glen Ellen. Kenwood has one high-end resort and an excellent campground.

Sugarloaf Ridge State Park CAMPGROUND $

(Map p38; ☎707-833-6084, 800-444-7275; www.reserveamerica.com; 2605 Adobe Canyon Rd, Kenwood; tent & RV sites $35;) Sonoma's nearest camping is north of Kenwood at this lovely hilltop park, with 48 drive-in sites, clean coin-operated showers and great hiking.

Beltane Ranch B&B $$

(Map p180; ☎707-833-4233; www.beltaneranch.com; 11775 Hwy 12, Glen Ellen; d $185-375; P) Surrounded by horse pastures and vineyards, Beltane is a throwback to 19th-century Sonoma. The cheerful 1890s ranch house has double porches lined with swinging chairs and white wicker. Though it's technically a B&B, each country-Americana-style room and the cottage has a private entrance – nobody will make you pet the cat. No phone or TV means zero distraction from pastoral bliss.

Glen Ellen Cottages BUNGALOW $$

(☎707-996-1174; www.glenelleninn.com; 13670 Arnold Dr, Glen Ellen; cottages Sun-Thu $149-175, Fri & Sat $219-275;) Hidden behind Glen Ellen Inn (p190), these five creekside cottages are designed for romance, with oversized jetted tub, steam shower and gas fireplace.

Jack London Lodge MOTEL **$$**
(707-938-8510; www.jacklondonlodge.com; 13740 Arnold Dr, Glen Ellen; r Mon-Fri $134, Sat & Sun $205;) An old-fashioned wood-sided motel with well-kept rooms decorated with antique repros, this is a weekday bargain. Outside there's a pool and hot tub; next door, a saloon. Two-night minimum during high-season weekends.

Gaige House Inn INN **$$$**
(707-935-0237; www.gaige.com; 13540 Arnold Dr, Glen Ellen; d/ste from $275/345;) Among the valley's most chic inns, Gaige has 23 rooms, five inside an 1890 house decked out in Euro-Asian style. Best are the Japanese-style 'Zen suites,' with requisite high-end bells and whistles, including freestanding tubs made from hollowed-out granite boulders. Fabulous.

Kenwood Inn & Spa INN **$$$**
(Map p180; 707-833-1293, 800-353-6966; www.kenwoodinn.com; 10400 Sonoma Hwy, Kenwood; r $450-825;) Lush gardens surround ivy-covered bungalows at this sexy 30-room inn, designed to resemble a Mediterranean château. Two hot tubs (one with a waterfall) and an on-site spa make it ideal for lovers, boring for singles. No kids. Book an upstairs balcony room.

Eating

Italian and French establishments dominate the scene, but there are also a couple of good bakeries and a market for self-caterers. Jack London Village has some good options.

Garden Court Cafe & Bakery CAFE **$**
(707-935-1565; www.gardencourtcafe.com; 13647 Arnold Dr, Glen Ellen; mains $9-12; 8:30am-2pm Wed, Thu & Mon, 8am-2pm Sat & Sun) Basic breakfasts, sandwiches and salads.

Fig Cafe & Winebar FRENCH, CALIFORNIAN **$$**
(707-938-2130; www.thefigcafe.com; 13690 Arnold Dr, Glen Ellen; mains $12-24, 3-course dinner $36; 10am-2:30pm Sat & Sun, 5-9pm Sun-Thu, 5-9:30pm Fri & Sat) The earthy California-Provençal comfort food includes flash-fried calamari with spicy lemon aioli, fig and arugula salad and *steak frites*. Good wine prices and weekend brunch give reason to return. No reservations; complimentary corkage.

Mayo Winery Reserve WINERY **$$**
(Map p180; 707-833-5504; www.mayofamilywinery.com; 9200 Sonoma Hwy, Kenwood; 7-course menu $50; by appointment 10:30am-6:30pm) Feast on a seven-course small-plates menu paired with seven wines for $50 at this roadside wine-tasting room.

Cafe Citti ITALIAN **$$**
(Map p180; 707-833-2690; www.cafecitti.com; 9049 Sonoma Hwy, Kenwood; mains $8-15; 11am-3:30pm & 5-8:30pm Sun-Thu, to 9pm Fri & Sat;) Locals favor this order-at-the-counter Italian-American deli, with standout roast chicken, and homemade gnocchi and ravioli. At lunchtime there's pizza and house-baked focaccia sandwiches.

Glen Ellen Inn AMERICAN **$$**
(707-996-6409; www.glenelleninn.com; 13670 Arnold Dr, Glen Ellen; mains $16-25; 11:30am-9pm Thu-Tue, 5:30-9pm Wed) Oysters, martinis and grilled steaks. Lovely garden, full bar.

Glen Ellen Star CALIFORNIAN, ITALIAN **$$$**
(707-343-1384; http://glenellenstar.com; 13648 Arnold Dr, Glen Ellen; pizzas $15-20, mains $24-50; 5:30-9pm Sun-Thu, to 9:30pm Fri & Sat;) Helmed by chef Ari Weiswasser, who once worked at Thomas Keller's French Laundry (p168), this petite Glen Ellen bistro shines a light on the best of Sonoma farms and ranches. Local, organic and seasonal ingredients star in dishes such as spring-lamb ragù, whole roasted fish with broccoli di cicco or golden beets with harissa crumble. Reservations recommended. Wednesdays are neighborhood nights, which means no corkage fee and a $35 two-course menu.

Aventine ITALIAN **$$$**
(Map p180; 707-934-8911; http://glenellen.aventinehospitality.com; 14301 Arnold Dr, Glen Ellen; mains $14-28; 4:30-10pm Wed-Fri, 11am-10pm Sat & Sun) The Sonoma outpost of the popular San Francisco restaurant occupies an atmospheric former grist mill with a sun-dappled outdoor patio. It serves Italian-derived dishes, including house-special Aventino: mozzarella-stuffed meatball with pesto over polenta. Make reservations.

Getting There & Away

Glen Ellen is an hour's drive north from San Francisco.

RUSSIAN RIVER AREA

Lesser-known western Sonoma County was formerly famous for its apple farms and vacation cottages. Lately vineyards are replacing orchards and the Russian River has taken its place among California's important wine appellations, especially for Pinot Noir.

'The River,' as locals call it, has long been a summer-weekend destination for Northern Californians who come to canoe, wander country lanes, taste wine, hike redwood forests and live at a lazy pace. In winter the river floods, and nobody's here. The Russian River begins in the mountains north of Ukiah, in Mendocino County, but the most visited sections lie southwest of Healdsburg, where the river cuts a serpentine course toward the sea.

Russian River Wineries

Sonoma County's wine-growing regions encompass several diverse areas, each famous for different reasons. Pick up the free, useful *Russian River Wine Road* map (www.wineroad.com) from tourist-brochure racks.

Russian River Valley

Nighttime coastal fog drifts up the Russian River Valley, then usually clears by midday. Pinot Noir does beautifully, as does Chardonnay, which also grows in hotter regions, but prefers the longer 'hang time' of cooler climes. The highest concentration of wineries is along Westside Rd, between Guerneville and Healdsburg.

★Macrostie WINERY

(Map p192; ☎707-473-9303; www.macrostiewinery.com; 4605 Westside Rd; tasting $20-25, with tour $55; ⏲11am-5pm Mon-Thu, 10am-5pm Fri-Sun) For its creamy and crisp Chardonnays and earthy Pinots, along with top-notch service and an elegant tasting room, Macrostie is the talk of Wine Country. The sit-down tastings are relaxed and highly personal, with gorgeous views of the vineyard. Visionary winemaker Heidi Bridenhagen holds the distinction of being the youngest female on the job in Sonoma Valley. Pair your tasting with a delicious charcuterie plate that includes three local cheeses, prosciutto, olives, almonds and dried fruit.

Hartford WINERY

(Map p192; ☎800-588-0234; www.hartfordwines.com; 8075 Martinelli Rd, Forestville; tasting $15; ⏲10am-4:30pm) Surprisingly upscale for West County, Hartford sits in a pastoral valley surrounded by redwood-forested hills, on one of the area's prettiest back roads. It specializes in fine single-vineyard Pinot (13 kinds), Chardonnay and Zinfandel from old-vine fruit. Umbrella-shaded picnic tables dot the garden. Bottles are $30 to $100; the tasting fee is waived with purchase.

J Winery WINERY

(Map p192; ☎707-431-3646, 707-431-5430; www.jwine.com; 11447 Old Redwood Hwy; tasting/tour $20/30; ⏲11am-5pm) J crafts crisp sparkling wines, among Sonoma's best, but it's pricey. Make an appointment and splurge on one of the seated food-and-wine-pairing experiences. The decadent 'bubble room' tasting includes five wines paired with five locally sourced dishes prepared by chef Carl Shelton ($110 per person). The alfresco 'terrace' tasting (April to November) is also a winner, with four wines paired with four small appetizers ($55). Bottles cost $24 to $75.

De La Montanya WINERY

(Map p192; ☎707-433-3711; www.dlmwine.com; 999 Foreman Lane, Healdsburg; tasting $10; ⏲11am-4:30pm; 🐾) This tiny winery, tucked amid vineyards, is known for 17 small-batch varieties made with estate-grown fruit. Viognier, Primitivo, Pinot and Cabernet are signatures; the 'summer white' and Gewürztraminer are great back-porch wines. Apple-shaded picnic area, bocce ball and horseshoes add to the fun. Bottles are $20 to $60 and the tasting fee is refundable with a purchase. Appointments suggested.

Landmark Vineyards at Hop Kiln Estate WINERY

(Map p192; ☎707-433-6491; www.landmarkwine.com; 6050 Westside Rd; tasting $20; ⏲10am-5pm) This photogenic historic landmark has a busy tasting room inside a former hop kiln; we especially like the Flocchini Chardonnay. You can build your own picnic with meats, cheeses and crackers for $40, and the winery provides wine glasses, baskets, blankets and cheese boards with knives.

Porter Creek WINERY

(Map p192; ☎707-433-6321; www.portercreekvineyards.com; 8735 Westside Rd; tasting $15; ⏲10:30am-4:30pm; Ⓟ) Inside a vintage-1920s garage, Porter Creek's tasting bar is a former bowling-alley lane. Porter is old-school Northern California, an early

Russian River Area

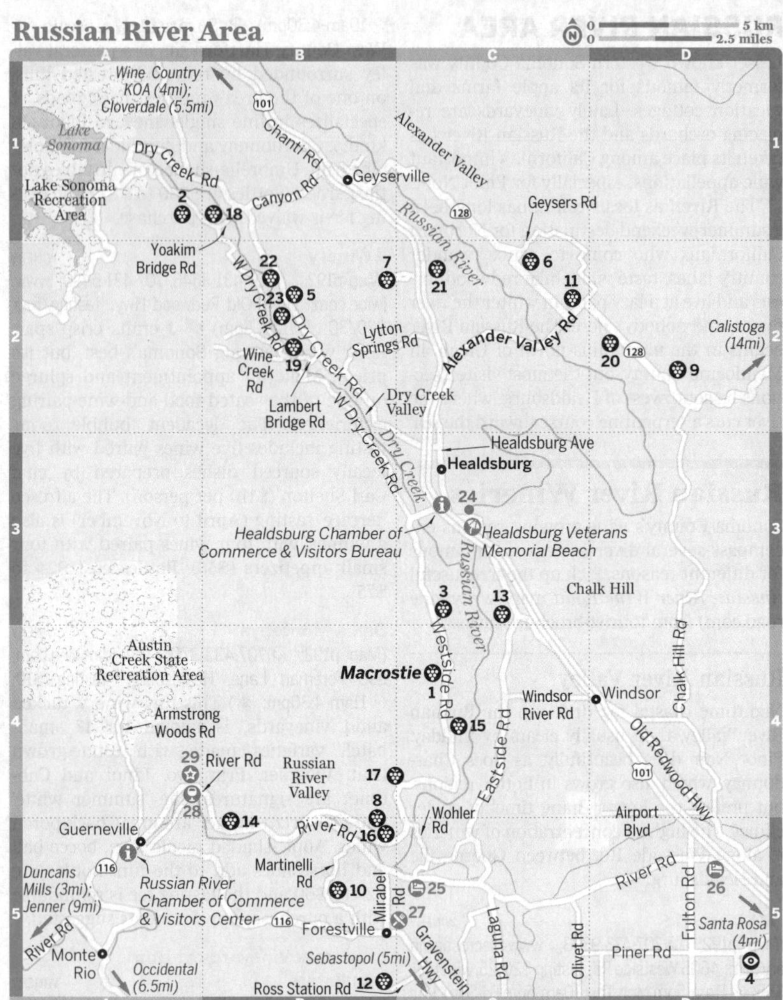

pioneer in biodynamic farming. High-acid, food-friendly Pinot Noir and Chardonnay are specialties, but there's old-vine Zinfandel and other Burgundian- and Rhône-style wines too. Tasting fee waived with purchase. Bottles cost $24 to $72.

Moshin WINERY

(Map p192; ☎707-433-5499; www.moshinvineyards.com; 10295 Westside Rd; tasting $15, private tour & tasting by appointment only $30; ⏰11am-4:30pm; P) Pinot Noir is a finicky grape that withers in sun and mildews in fog, yet it thrives in Russian River Valley, including at solar-powered Moshin Vineyards. The winery also specializes in small-production Pinot Noir, Sauvignon Blanc, Chardonnay, Merlot, Petite Sirah and Zinfandel. Tasting fee waived with purchase.

Iron Horse WINERY

(Map p192; ☎707-887-1507; www.ironhorsevineyards.com; 9786 Ross Station Rd, off Hwy 116, Sebastopol; tasting $25, incl tour $50; ⏰10am-4:30pm, last tasting 4pm; P) Atop a hill with drop-dead views over the county, Iron Horse is known for sparkling wines, which the White House often pours. The outdoor

Russian River Area

Top Sights

1 Macrostie C4

Sights

2 Bella A1
3 De La Montanya C3
4 Epicenter D5
5 Family Wineries B2
6 Foley Sonoma C2
7 Francis Ford Coppola Winery B2
8 Gary Farrell B4
9 Hanna D2
10 Hartford B5
11 Hawkes C2
12 Iron Horse B5
13 J Winery C3
14 Korbel B5
15 Landmark Vineyards at Hop Kiln Estate C4
16 Moshin B5
17 Porter Creek B4
18 Preston B1
19 Quivira B2
20 Soda Rock Winery D2
21 Trentadue C2
22 Truett Hurst B2
23 Unti Vineyards B2

Activities, Courses & Tours

Francis Ford Coppola Winery Swimming Pools .... (see 7)
24 Wine Country Bikes C3

Sleeping

25 Farmhouse Inn C5
26 Vintners Inn D5

Eating

27 Canneti Roadhouse C5

Drinking & Nightlife

28 Stumptown Brewery A4

Entertainment

29 Rio Nido Roadhouse A4

tasting room is refreshingly unfussy; when you're done with your wine, pour it in the grass. On Sundays from noon to 4pm, April through October, oysters, cheese and olive oil are served. Bottles cost $30 to $110. Reservations strongly recommended.

Korbel WINERY

(Map p192; 707-824-7000; www.korbel.com; 13250 River Rd, Guerneville; 10am-5pm; P) FREE Gorgeous rose gardens (April to October) and a stellar on-site deli make Korbel worth a stop for a free tasting, but the sparkling wine's just OK. Try the sparkling wine you can't get elsewhere; the rouge is particularly good.

Gary Farrell WINERY

(Map p192; 707-473-2909; www.garyfarrellwines.com; 10701 Westside Rd; tasting $35-75; 10am-3pm Mon-Fri, by appointment; P) High on a hilltop overlooking the Russian River, Gary Farrell's tasting room sits perched among second-growth redwoods. The elegant Chardonnay and long-finish Pinot Noir, made by a big-name winemaker, score high marks for consistency. Bottles are $35 to $75.

Dry Creek Valley

Hemmed in by 2000ft-high mountains, Dry Creek Valley is relatively warm, ideal for Sauvignon Blanc and Zinfandel, and in some places Cabernet Sauvignon. It's west of Hwy 101, between Healdsburg and Lake Sonoma. Dry Creek Rd is the fast-moving main thoroughfare. Parallel-running West Dry Creek Road is an undulating country lane with no center stripe – one of Sonoma's great back roads, ideal for cycling.

Bella WINERY

(Map p192; 707-473-9171; www.bellawinery.com; 9711 W Dry Creek Rd; tasting $15; 11am-4:30pm; P) Atop the valley's north end, always-fun Bella has cool caves built into the hillside. The estate-grown grapes include 112-year-old vines from Alexander Valley. The focus is on big reds – Zinfandel and Syrah – but there's terrific rosé (good for barbecues) and late-harvest Zinfandel (great with brownies). The wonderful vibe and dynamic staff make Bella special. Bottles are $25 to $55.

Preston WINERY

(Map p192; 707-433-3372; www.prestonvineyards.com; 9282 W Dry Creek Rd; tasting/tours $10/25; 11am-4:30pm; P) An early leader in organics and recently certified biodynamic, Lou Preston's 19th-century farm is old Sonoma. Weathered picket fencing frames the tasting room, with candy-colored walls and tongue-in-groove ceilings setting a country mood. The signature is citrusy Sauvignon Blanc, but try the Rhône varietals and small-lot wines: Carignane, Viognier, Cinsault and cult-favorite Barbera. Preston also bakes good bread and cold-presses its own olive oil; picnic in the shade of a walnut tree. Bottles are $22 to $40. Tours by appointment.Monday to Friday, there's bocce and a new farm store sells seasonal produce adjacent to the tasting room.

Family Wineries WINERY
(Map p192; ☎888-433-6555; www.familywines.com; 4791 Dry Creek Rd; tasting $10; ⏲10:30am-4:30pm Mar-Dec, Thu-Mon Jan-Feb) Sample multiple varietals at this cooperative, which showcases six boutique wineries too small to have their own tasting rooms. Tasting fee is refundable with a purchase.

Truett Hurst WINERY
(Map p192; ☎707-433-9545; www.truetthurst.com; 5610 Dry Creek Rd; tasting $10; ⏲10am-5pm; P) Pull up an Adirondack chair and picnic creekside at Truett Hurst, one of Dry Creek's biodynamic wineries. Sample terrific old-vine Zinfandel, standout Petite Sirah and Russian River Pinot Noir at the handsome contemporary tasting room, then meander through fragrant fruit and gardens to the creek, where salmon spawn in autumn. Another good winery, VML, now shares tasting-room space with Truett Hurst. Bottles are $20 to $53.

Unti Vineyards WINERY
(Map p192; ☎707-433-5590; www.untivineyards.com; 4202 Dry Creek Rd; tasting $10; ⏲10am-4pm by appointment only; 🐾) Inside a vineyard-view tasting room, Unti pours all estate-grown varietals – Châteauneuf-du-Pape–style Grenache, compelling Syrah and superb Sangiovese – favored by oenophiles for their structured tannins and concentrated fruit. If you love small-batch wines, don't miss Unti. Bottles are $20 to $50 and the tasting fee is refundable with a purchase.

Quivira WINERY
(Map p192; ☎707-431-8333, 800-292-8339; www.quivirawine.com; 4900 W Dry Creek Rd; tasting $15-30, incl tour $40, tour & estate tasting by reservation only; ⏲11am-4pm, 10am-4:30pm Apr-Oct; P 👪 🐾) Sunflowers, lavender, beehives and crowing roosters greet your arrival at this winery and biodynamic farm, with self-guided garden tours and a redwood grove beside the vines. Kids can giggle with pigs and chickens while you sample Rhône varietals, unusual blends and lip-smacking, award-winning Sauvignon Blanc. Bottles are $24 to $55.

Alexander Valley

Bucolic Alexander Valley flanks the Mayacamas Mountains, with postcard-perfect vistas and wide-open vineyards. Summers are hot, ideal for Cabernet Sauvignon, Merlot and warm-weather Chardonnays, but there are also fine Sauvignon Blancs and Zinfandels. For events info visit www.alexandervalley.org.

Hawkes WINERY
(Map p192; ☎707-433-4295; www.hawkeswine.com; 6734 Hwy 128; tasting $15, barrel/vineyard tour $45/45; ⏲10am-5pm; P 🐾) Hawkes makes an easy stopover while you're exploring the valley, and offers private barrel tastings in which guests sample straight from the oak and order 'futures' from a new vintage before the wine is bottled or released to the market. The single-vineyard Cabernet Sauvignon is damn good, as is the Merlot; there's also a clean-and-crisp Chardonnay. Bottles are $30 to $75.

Francis Ford Coppola Winery WINERY, MUSEUM
(Map p192; ☎707-857-1471; www.francisfordcoppolawinery.com; 300 Via Archimedes, Geyserville; tasting $18-25; ⏲11am-6pm; P 👪) The famous movie director's vineyard estate is a self-described 'wine wonderland.' Taking over historic Chateau Souverain, this hillside winery has a bit of everything: wine-tasting flights, a free museum of moviemaking memorabilia, a shameless gift shop and two modern Italian-American restaurants. Outside you'll find bocce courts by two **swimming pools** (Map p192; day pass adult/child $35/15; ⏲11am-6pm daily Jun-Sep, Fri-Sun Apr, May & Oct; 👪). The most satisfying tasting is the reserve flight ($25) upstairs. Bottles are $12 to $90. From 5pm to 9pm on Tuesdays, there's A Tavola, a multiple-course, family-style meal served by staff in elaborate costumes ($45).

Hanna WINERY
(Map p192; ☎707-431-4310, 800-854-3987; www.hannawinery.com; 9280 Hwy 128; tasting $20-40; ⏲10am-4pm; P) Abutting oak-studded hills, Hanna's tasting room has lovely vineyard views and good picnicking. At the bar, find estate-grown Sauvignon Blanc, Malbec, Cabernet Sauvignon, Chardonnay and big-fruit Zinfandel. Sit-down wine-and-cheese tastings ($40) are available with advance reservations. Bottles cost $19 to $68.

Soda Rock Winery WINERY
(Map p192; ☎707-433-3303; www.sodarockwinery.com; 8015 CA 128; tasting $15; ⏲11am-5pm) Come to Soda Rock to behold Lord Snort, a 20,000lb metal boar sculpture displayed out front, and stay for the big Bordeaux varietals, including Cabernet Savignon, Cab Franc and Petit Verdot, along with a rare and juicy Primitivo. With a sky-high ceiling and dignified brick, the lovingly restored tasting room is a former general store that now doubles as an elegant event space. Bottles cost $18 to $41. Tasting fee waived with one bottle purchase.

Trentadue WINERY
(Map p192; ☎707-433-3104, 888-332-3032; www.trentadue.com; 19170 Geyserville Ave, Geyserville; tasting $10-15, tour $25; ⊙10am-5pm; 🐾) Specializes in ports (ruby, not tawny); the chocolate port makes a great gift. The tour is good fun and includes tastes of sparkling and still wine as guests are towed through the vineyards by a tractor. Tasting fee waived with four-bottle purchase or wine-club sign-up. Bottles $15 to $38.

Foley Sonoma WINERY
(Map p192; ☎707-433-1944; www.foleysonoma.com; 5110 Hwy 128; tasting $20, incl tour $40; ⊙10am-5pm; P) Wow, what a view from the hilltop concrete-and-glass tasting room at Foley Sonoma. Winemaker Courtney Foley specializes in Bordeaux varietals and blends, along with Zinfandels and Pinots. An hour-long tour takes guests through the crush pad, barrel room and vineyard and finishes with a tasting. Bottles are $30 to $80.

Sebastopol

Grapes have replaced apples as the new cash crop, but Sebastopol's farm-town identity remains rooted in the apple – evidenced by the much-heralded summertime Gravenstein Apple Fair. The town center feels suburban because of traffic, but a hippie tinge gives it color. This is the refreshingly laid-back side of Wine Country and makes a good-value base for exploring the area.

Sights

Around Sebastopol, look for family-friendly farms, gardens, animal sanctuaries and pick-your-own orchards. For a countywide list, check out the Sonoma County Farm Trails Guide (www.farmtrails.org).

★**Patrick Amiot Junk Art** GALLERY
(www.patrickamiot.com; Florence Ave; P) Prepare to gawk and giggle at the wacky Patrick Amiot sculptures gracing front yards along Florence Ave. Fashioned from recycled materials, a hot-rodding rat, a hectic waitress and a witch in midflight are a few of the oversized and demented lawn ornaments parading along the street. Keep an eye out and you'll notice more of these scattered throughout Sebastopol.

California Carnivores GARDENS
(☎707-824-0433; www.californiacarnivores.com; 2833 Old Gravenstein Hwy S; ⊙10am-4pm Thu-Mon) Even vegans can't help admiring these incredible carnivorous plants (the largest collection in the US), including specimens from around the globe. Owner Peter D'Amato encourages visitors to BYOB (bring your own bugs) and watch as the plants devour them. He's also written a book with a perfect name, *The Savage Garden*.

Spirit Works Distillery DISTILLERY
(☎707-634-4793; www.spiritworksdistillery.com; 6790 McKinley St, 100, Barlow; tasting/tour $18/20; ⊙11am-5pm Wed-Sun) A bracing alternative to wine tasting, Spirit Works crafts superb small-batch spirits – vodka, gin, sloe gin and (soon) whiskey – from organic California red-winter wheat. The distillery abides by a 'grain-to-glass' philosophy, with milling, mashing, fermenting and distilling all done on-site. Sample and buy in the warehouse. Tours (by reservation) happen Friday to Sunday at 5pm and finish with a tasting. Bottles are $27 to $36.

Barlow MARKET
(☎707-824-5600; www.thebarlow.net; cnr Sebastopol & Morris Sts; ⊙hours vary; P) The Barlow occupies a former apple-processing plant, repurposed into a 12-acre village of food producers, artists, winemakers, coffee roasters, spirits distillers and indie restaurateurs, who showcase West County's culinary and artistic diversity. Wander shed to shed, sample everything from house-brewed beer to ice cream flash-frozen with liquid nitrogen and meet artisans in their workshops. Usually on Thursdays 4pm to 8pm, from May to October, the Barlow hosts a 'street fair,' with live music and local vendors.

Farmers Market MARKET
(www.sebastopolfarmmarket.org; cnr Petaluma & McKinley Aves; ⊙10am-1:30pm Sun) Meets at the downtown plaza.

Festivals & Events

Apple Blossom Festival CULTURAL
(www.appleblossomfest.com; ⊙Apr) Live music, food, drink, wine, a parade and exhibits.

Gravenstein Apple Fair FOOD & DRINK
(www.gravensteinapplefair.com; ⊙Aug) Arts, crafts, food, wine, brews, games, live entertainment and farm-life activities.

Sleeping

There are only a couple of hotels in Sebastopol, but staying here is convenient to Russian River Valley, the coast and Sonoma Valley.

Sebastopol Inn MOTEL $$
(800-653-1082, 707-829-2500; www.sebastopolinn.com; 6751 Sebastopol Ave; r $119-388;) We like this independent, *non*-cookie-cutter motel for its quiet, off-street location, usually reasonable rates and good-looking if basic rooms. Outside are grassy areas for kids and a hot tub.

Eating

Sebastopol is a town of artists and locavores, and while its restaurant scene reflects those predilections, there are plenty of international options as well. Above all, the local produce and seafood is top-notch.

★Handline CALIFORNIAN $
(707-827-3744; www.handline.com; 935 Gravenstein Ave; mains $9-21; 11am-10pm) Housed in a former Foster's Freeze, this highly anticipated seafood restaurant is over-the-counter casual but undeniably elegant. The stylish interior is defined by reclaimed wood and shoji-style paneling that opens to a tree-shaded patio. In a room designated the *tortilleria,* corn tortillas are hand-molded each day and topped with battered and fried rockfish, pickled onion and roasted summer squash. The oysters and ceviche are divine, and in a nod to the previous tenant there's organic Straus soft serve for dessert.

Slice of Life VEGETARIAN $
(707-829-6627; www.thesliceoflife.com; 6970 McKinley St; mains under $10; 11am-9pm Tue-Fri, 9am-9pm Sat & Sun;) This good vegan-vegetarian kitchen doubles as a pizzeria and also offers plenty of Mexican dishes. Breakfast all day. Great smoothies.

Mom's Apple Pie DESSERTS $
(707-823-8330; www.momsapplepieusa.com; 4550 Gravenstein Hwy N; whole pies $7-17; 10am-6pm;) Pie's the thing at this roadside bakery – and yum, that flaky crust. Apple is predictably good, especially in autumn, but the blueberry is our fave, made better with vanilla ice cream.

Screamin' Mimi ICE CREAM $
(707-823-5902; www.screaminmimisicecream.com; 6902 Sebastopol Ave; 11am-10pm) Delish homemade ice cream.

Pacific Market MARKET $
(Pacific Market; 707-823-9735; www.pacificmkt.com; 550 Gravenstein Hwy N; 7am-9pm Mon-Sat, 8am-8pm Sun) Excellent for groceries and picnics; north of downtown.

Hopmonk Tavern PUB FOOD $$
(707-829-7300; www.hopmonk.com; 230 Petaluma Ave; mains $12-23; 11:30am-9pm Mon-Thu, to 10pm Fri, 11am-10pm Sat & Sun;) Inside a converted 1903 railroad station, Hopmonk's serves 76 varieties of beer – served in type-specific glassware – that pair with a good menu of burgers, fried calamari, charcuterie platters and salads.

Zazu Kitchen & Farm AMERICAN $$$
(707-523-4814; http://zazukitchen.com; 6770 McKinley St, 150, Barlow; mains lunch $13-18, dinner $24-29; 5-10pm Mon & Wed, 3-10pm Thu, 11:30am-midnight Fri & Sat, 9am-10pm Sun) We love the farm-to-table ethos of Zazu – it grows its own pigs and sources everything locally – but some dishes miss and the industrial-style space gets crazy loud. Still, it does excellent pizzas, salads, housemade *salumi*, pork and bacon. Good breakfasts too.

K&L Bistro FRENCH $$$
(707-823-6614; www.klbistro.com; 119 S Main St; lunch $14-20, dinner $19-29; 11am-11pm) K&L serves earthy provincial Cal-French bistro cooking in a convivial bar-and-grill space with sidewalk patio. Expect classics such as mussels and french fries, and grilled steaks with red-wine reduction. Reservations essential.

Drinking & Nightlife

Nightlife isn't Sebastopol's strong suit, but there are a couple of great breweries and tastings rooms at the Barlow (p195).

Woodfour Brewing Co BREWERY
(707-823-3144; www.woodfourbrewing.com; 6780 Depot St, Barlow; noon-7pm Wed & Thu, to 8pm Fri & Sat, 11am-6pm Sun) Woodfour's solar-powered brewery serves about a dozen housemade beers, light on alcohol and hops, plus several sours (high-acid beer). It also has an exceptionally good menu of small plates (designed to pair with beer), from simple snacks to refined, technique-driven dishes better than any we've had at a California brewery.

Taylor Maid Farms CAFE
(707-634-7129; www.taylormaidfarms.com; 6790 McKinley St, Barlow; 6:30am-6pm Sun-Thu, to 7pm Fri, 7am-7pm Sat) Choose your brew method (drip, press etc) at this third-wave coffeehouse that roasts its own organic beans. Seasonal drinks include lavender lattes.

Hardcore Espresso CAFE
(707-823-7588; 81 Bloomfield Rd; 5am-7pm Mon-Fri, 6am-7pm Sat & Sun;) Meet local hippies and artists over coffee and smoothies at this classic NorCal, off-the-grid, indoor-outdoor coffeehouse, south of downtown, that's essentially a corrugated-metal-roofed shack surrounded by umbrella tables.

Shopping

Antique shops line Gravenstein Hwy S toward Hwy 101.

Funk & Flash CLOTHING
(707-829-1142; www.funkandflash.com; 228 S Main St; 11am-7pm) Disco-glam party clothes, inspired by Burning Man.

Midgley's Country Flea Market MARKET
(707-823-7874; www.mfleamarket.com; 2200 Gravenstein Hwy S; 7:30am-4:30pm Sat, 6:30am-5:30pm Sun) The region's largest flea market.

Copperfield's Books BOOKS
(707-823-2618; www.copperfields.net; 138 N Main St; 10am-7pm Mon-Sat, to 6pm Sun) Indie bookshop with literary events.

Beekind FOOD, HOMEWARES
(707-824-2905; www.beekind.com; 921 Gravenstein Hwy S; 10am-6pm Mon-Sat, to 4pm Sun) Local honey and beeswax candles.

Antique Society ANTIQUES
(707-829-1733; www.antiquesociety.com; 2661 Gravenstein Hwy S; 10am-5pm) More than 125 antiques vendors under one roof.

Aubergine VINTAGE
(707-827-3460; www.auberginevintageemporium.com; 755 Petaluma Ave; 10:30am-6pm) Vast vintage emporium, specializing in cast-off European thrift-shop clothing.

Sumbody COSMETICS
(707-823-2053; www.sumbody.com; 118 N Main St; 10am-7pm Mon-Fri, to 8pm Sat, to 6pm Sun) Ecofriendly bath products made with all-natural ingredients. Also offers facials ($79) and massages ($80) at its small on-site spa.

Toyworks TOYS
(707-829-2003; www.sonomatoyworks.com; 6940 Sebastopol Ave; 10am-6pm Mon-Sat, 11am-5pm Sun;) Indie toy seller with phenomenal selection of quality games for kids.

Information

Sebastopol Area Chamber of Commerce & Visitors Center (877-828-4748, 707-823-3032; www.sebastopol.org; 265 S Main St; 10am-5pm Mon-Fri) Maps, information and exhibits.

Getting There & Away

For public-transit information, dial 511, or look online at www.transit.511.org.

Sebastopol is about an 80-minute drive north from San Francisco. Hwy 116 splits downtown; southbound traffic uses Main St, northbound traffic Petaluma Ave. North of town, it's called Gravenstein Hwy N and continues toward Guerneville; south of downtown, it's Gravenstein Hwy S, which heads toward Hwy 101 and Sonoma.

Occidental & Around

Our favorite West County town is a haven of artists, back-to-the-landers and counter-culturalists. Historic 19th-century buildings line a single main street, easy to explore in an hour; continue north by car and you'll hit the Russian River in Monte Rio. At Christmas-time, Bay Area families flock to Occidental to buy trees. The town decorates to the nines and there's weekend cookie-decorating and caroling at the Union Hotel's Bocce Ballroom.

Sights & Activities

Grove of the Old Trees FOREST
(707-544-7284; www.landpaths.org; 17599 Fitzpatrick Lane; dawn-dusk) FREE Outside Occidental and up on a ridge off Fitzpatrick Lane, Grove of the Old Trees is a peaceful, 28-acre forest of old-growth redwoods. The forest and its trails are managed by a local nonprofit.

Bohème Wines WINERY
(707-874-3218; www.bohemewines.com; 3625 Main St; 3-5pm Thu & Fri, noon-6pm Sat & Sun) Drop in to this little tasting room in downtown Occidental for free swigs of dry Chardonnay, earthy Pinots and a big Syrah, all from the cooler climes. Bottles from $39 to $49.

Occidental Bohemian Farmers Market MARKET
(707-874-8478; www.occidentalfarmersmarket.com; 3611 Bohemian Hwy; 4pm-dusk Fri Jun-Oct;) Meet the whole community at Occidental's detour-worthy farmers market, with musicians, craftspeople and – the star attraction – Gerard's Paella (www.gerardspaella.com) of Food Network TV fame.

Osmosis SPA

(707-823-8231; www.osmosis.com; 209 Bohemian Hwy, Freestone; packages from $219; by appointment 9am-8pm) Tranquility prevails at this Japanese-inspired spa, which indulges patrons with dry-enzyme baths of aromatic cedar fibers paired with other treatments including outdoor massages and facials. The tea-and-meditation gardens are lovely. Make reservations.

Sonoma Canopy Tours OUTDOORS

(888-494-7868; www.sonomacanopytours.com; 6250 Bohemian Hwy; adult $99-109, child $69) North of town, fly through the redwood canopy on seven interconnected ziplines, ending with an 80ft-rappel descent; reservations required.

Sleeping

Occidental offers a couple of historic inns and one fantastic farmstay.

★**Shanti Permaculture Farm** FARMSTAY $$

(707-874-2001; www.shantioccidental.com; Coleman Valley Rd; tent & RV sites $75, cottages & yurts $199-225) Tucked back in the redwoods on scenic Coleman Valley Rd, this is the ultimate NorCal farmstay. The knowledgeable Oregonian owner educates guests about ecofriendly agricultural concepts such as biochar and hugelkultur, and shows off her chickens, ducks, goats and enormous llama. While the operation feels somewhat rustic, it is impressively MacGyvered and the one-bedroom cottage is surprisingly posh.

Near the top of the 6-acre property, a wonderfully homey yurt offers comfort and seclusion, though the llama has been known to wander up the hill to stare through a window at sleeping guests. Continuing down the hill, private campsites are ensconced in the trees, and RVs are also welcome at the bottom of the hill, where a hookup is available for a fee. Delicious farm-to-table meals are available for $15 to $20.

Valley Ford Hotel INN $$

(707-876-1983; www.vfordhotel.com; r $115-175) Surrounded by pastureland 8 miles southeast in Valley Ford, this 19th-century, seven-room inn has good beds, great rates and a terrific roadhouse bar and restaurant.

Inn at Occidental INN $$$

(800-522-6324, 707-874-1047; www.innatoccidental.com; 3657 Church St; r $259-399;) One of Sonoma's finest, this beautifully restored 18-room Victorian inn is filled with collectible antiques; rooms have gas fireplaces and cozy feather beds.

Eating & Drinking

Delicious meals and snacks abound for every budget, all in close proximity.

Wild Flour Bread BAKERY $

(707-874-2938; www.wildflourbread.com; 140 Bohemian Hwy, Freestone; items from $3; 8:30am-6:30pm Fri-Mon;) Organic brick-oven artisan breads, giant sticky buns and good coffee.

Howard Station Cafe AMERICAN $

(707-874-2838; www.howardstationcafe.com; 3611 Bohemian Hwy; mains $8-14; 7am-2:30pm Mon-Fri, to 3pm Sat & Sun;) Big plates of comfort-food cooking and freshly squeezed juices. Cash only.

Bohemian Market DELI $

(707-874-3312; 3633 Main St; 8am-9pm, 7am-9pm Sat & Sun) Occidental's best grocery store has a good deli which prepares sandwiches from 10am to 7pm. There's also a coffee bar open daily until 1pm.

Hazel CALIFORNIAN $$

(707-874-6003; www.restauranthazel.com; 3782 Bohemian Hwy; mains $15-32; 5-9pm Wed-Sat, 10am-2pm & 5-9pm Sun) Occidental's newest restaurant is small, unassuming and serves absolutely delectable food. The menu only features a few starters, pizzas and mains but you cannot go wrong, particularly with the scallop ceviche (fresh mango, radishes, a delightful medley of oils and spices, delicate morsels of mollusk). Also great: fried brussels sprouts, braised pot roast and the strawberry-rhubarb crisp with vanilla ice cream.

Union Hotel ITALIAN $$

(707-874-3555; www.unionhoteloccidental.com; 3703 Bohemian Hwy; meals $15-26; 11am-9pm, bar to 2am;) Occidental has two old-school American-Italian restaurants that serve family-style meals. The Union is slightly better and serves a delicious, complimentary bruschetta with the purchase of any main. Monday nights mean $5 pizza or pasta in-house (adults only). On a sunny day you can't beat the patio for lunch, and there's also a bakery with freshly baked cookies for $1.

Barley & Hops PUB

(707-874-9037; www.barleynhops.com; 3688 Bohemian Hwy; 4-9pm Mon-Thu, 1-9:30pm Fri-Sun) Serving around 40 beers, sandwiches, burgers, giant salads and amazing bacon-cheddar fries. Mains $10-15.

Shopping

Hand Goods CERAMICS

(☎707-874-2161; www.handgoods.net; 3627 Main St; ⊙10am-6pm) Collective of ceramicists, potters, jewelers, fine artists and more.

Getting There & Away

Occidental is about a two-hour drive from San Francisco. There's no good way to get here via public transportation.

Guerneville & Around

The Russian River's biggest vacation-resort town, Guerneville gets busy over summer weekends with party-hardy gay boys, sun-worshiping lesbians and long-haired, beer-drinking Harley riders, earning it the nickname 'Groin-ville.' Though the town is slowly gentrifying, it hasn't lost its honky-tonk vibe – fun-seeking crowds still come to canoe, hike and hammer cocktails poolside.

Downriver, some areas are sketchy (due to drugs). The local chamber of commerce has chased most of the tweakers from Main St in Guerneville, but if some off-the-beaten-path areas feel creepy – especially campgrounds – they probably are.

Four miles downriver, tiny Monte Rio has a sign over Hwy 116 declaring it 'Vacation Wonderland' – an overstatement, but the dog-friendly beach is a hit with families. Further west, idyllic Duncans Mills is home to a few dozen souls and has picture-ready historic buildings converted into cute shops. Upriver, east of Guerneville, Forestville is where farm country resumes.

Sights & Activies

Look for sandy beaches and swimming holes along the river; there's good river access east of town at Sunset Beach. Fishing and watercraft outfitters operate mid-May to early October, after which winter rains dangerously swell the river. A **farmers market** (16290 5th St) meets downtown on Wednesdays, May through September, from 3pm to 7pm. On summer Saturdays, there's also one at **Monte Rio Beach**, 11am to 2pm.

Armstrong Redwoods State Natural Reserve FOREST

(☎info 707-869-2015, visitor center 707-869-2958; www.parks.ca.gov; 17000 Armstrong Woods Rd; per car $8; ⊙8am-1hr after sunset; P 👪) A magnificent redwood forest 2 miles north of Guerneville, this 805-acre reserve was saved from the saw by a 19th-century lumber magnate. Short interpretive trails lead into magical forests, with old-growth redwoods 30 stories high. Beyond lie 20 miles of back-country trails through oak woodlands in adjoining **Austin Creek State Recreation Area**, one of Sonoma County's last remaining wilderness areas. Walk or cycle in for free; pay only to park.

Sunset Beach BEACH

(☎707-433-1625; www.sonoma-county.org/parks; 11060 River Rd, Forestville; per car $7; ⊙7am-sunset) Nice park on the water featuring paddle sports and picnicking.

Burke's Canoe Trips CANOEING

(☎707-887-1222; www.burkescanoetrips.com; 8600 River Rd, Forestville; canoe/kayak rental incl shuttle $68/$45, cash only) You can't beat Burke's for a day on the river. Self-guided canoe and kayak trips include shuttle back to your car. Make reservations; plan for four hours. Camping in the riverside redwood grove is $10 per person.

Johnson's Beach WATER SPORTS

(☎707-869-2022; www.johnsonsbeach.com; 16215 &16217 First St; kayak & canoe rental per hour/day $15/40; ⊙10am-6pm summer only; 👪) FREE Canoe, kayak and paddleboat rental available. Beer, wine, hot dogs and burgers are for sale. Beach admission is free though it's $5 to park and closed in poor weather. You can camp (p200) here.

R3 Hotel Pool SWIMMING

(Triple R; ☎707-869-8399; www.ther3hotel.com; 16390 4th St; ⊙9am-close) FREE The gay, adults-only, party-scene swimming pool at the R3 Hotel (p200) is free, provided you buy drinks. Bring your own towel. Bathing suits are mandatory, but only because state liquor-license laws require them.

Pee Wee Golf & Arcade GOLF, CYCLING

(☎707-869-9321; 16155 Drake Rd, at Hwy 116; 18/36 holes $8/12; ⊙11am-10pm Jun-Aug, to 5pm Sat & Sun May & Sep; 👪) Flash back to 1948 at this impeccably kept retro-kitsch 36-hole miniature golf course, just south of the Hwy 116 bridge, with brilliantly painted obstacles, including T Rex and Yogi Bear. Bring your own cocktails. It also rents gas barbecue grills.

King's Sport & Tackle OUTDOORS

(☎707-869-2156; www.kingsrussianriver.com; 16258 Main St; ⊙8am-6pm May-Oct, hours vary Nov-Apr) *The* local source for fishing and river-condition information. Also rents kayaks

($45 to $65), stand up paddleboards (from $60) and fishing gear.

River Rider CYCLING
(☎707-887-2453; www.riverridersrentals.com; half-/full-day rental from $35/45, delivery $20; ⏰7am-7pm) Delivers bicycles, along with wine-tasting passes on request; there are discounts for multiday rentals.

Festivals & Events

Naughty Nuns Bingo LGBT
(www.rrsisters.org/bingo.html; 16255 1st St; 2 bingo cards & 5 raffle tickets $20; ⏰doors 5:30pm, 2nd Sat of month) These fabulous themed bingo nights are put on by the Russian River Sisters of Perpetual Indulgence, an activist group of gender-bending performance artists who dress as ostentatious nuns.

Monte Rio Variety Show MUSIC
(www.monterioshow.org; adult/child $30/15; ⏰Jul) Members of the elite, secretive Bohemian Grove (Google it) perform publicly, sometimes showcasing unannounced celebrities.

Lazy Bear Weekend LGBT
(www.lazybearweekend.com; ⏰Aug) Read: heavy, furry gay men.

Russian River Jazz & Blues Festival MUSIC
(www.russianriverfestivals.com; ⏰Sep) A day of jazz, followed by a day of blues, with occasional luminaries such as BB King.

Sleeping

Guerneville has lovely resorts, inns and cottages, but few budget sleeps apart from campgrounds; prices drop midweek. For weekends and holidays, book ahead. Also, because the river sometimes floods, some lodgings have cold linoleum floors: pack slippers.

Guerneville

Bullfrog Pond Campground CAMPGROUND $
(☎707-869-2015; www.stewardscr.org; sites reserved/nonreserved $35/25; 🐾) Reached via a steep road from Armstrong Redwoods State Natural Reserve (p199), 4 miles from the entrance kiosk, Bullfrog Pond has forested campsites with cold water and primitive hike-in and equestrian backcountry campsites. Reserve via www.hipcamp.com or by phone.

Johnson's Beach Resort CABIN, CAMPGROUND $
(☎707-869-2022; www.johnsonsbeach.com; 16241 1st St; tent sites $40, cabins $145-165) On the river in Guerneville, Johnson's (p199) has rustic but clean, thin-walled cabins on stilts; all have kitchen. There's camping too, but no RVs. Credit card only.

Schoolhouse Canyon Campground CAMPGROUND $
(☎707-869-2311; www.schoolhousecanyon.com; 12600 River Rd; tent sites for 2 people & a car $40; 🐾) Two miles east of Guerneville, Schoolhouse's well-tended sites lie beneath tall trees across the main road from the river. Coin-operated hot showers, clean bathrooms, quiet by night. Cash only.

Guerneville Lodge CAMPGROUND $
(☎707-869-0102; www.guernevillelodge.com; 15905 River Rd; tent sites $40) The prettiest place to camp in downtown Guerneville is behind this retreat-center lodge on sprawling grassy lawns fronting the river. Amenities: hot clean showers, big campsites, refrigerator access, fire pits with grills. When available, lodge rooms cost $199.

R3 Hotel RESORT $$
(Triple R; ☎707-869-8399; www.ther3hotel.com; 16390 4th St; r $125-299; 📶🏊) Ground zero for party-hardy gay lads and lesbians, Triple R (as it's known) has plain-Jane, motel-style rooms surrounding a bar and pool deck that get so crowded on summer weekends that management won't allow guests to bring pets because 'they get hurt' (actual quote). Come for the scene, not for quiet (light sleepers: bring earplugs). Midweek it's mellow, wintertime dead.

Boon Hotel + Spa BOUTIQUE HOTEL $$
(☎707-869-2721; www.boonhotels.com; 14711 Armstrong Woods Rd; tents $175-225, r $225-425; P🚭📶🏊🐾) 🍃 Rooms surround a swimming-pool courtyard (with Jacuzzi) at this 14-room adults-only resort, gussied up in minimalist modern style. The look is austere but fresh, with organic-cotton linens and spacious rooms; most have wood-burning fireplaces. Between Memorial Day and Labor Day, 'glamping tents' and an Airstream trailer are also available. It's a 15-minute walk north of downtown.

Highlands Resort CABIN, CAMPGROUND $$
(☎707-869-0333; www.highlandsresort.com; 14000 Woodland Dr; tent sites $40-60, r $95-180, cabins $130-215; 📶🏊🐾) Guerneville's mellowest gay (and straight-friendly) resort sits on a wooded hillside, walkable distance to town, and has simply furnished rooms, little

WORTH A TRIP

SCENIC DRIVE: COLEMAN VALLEY ROAD

Wine Country's most scenic drive isn't through the grapes, but along these 10 miles of winding West County byway, from Occidental to the sea. It's best late morning, after the fog has cleared. Drive west, not east, with the sun behind you and the ocean ahead. First you'll pass through redwood forests and lush valleys where Douglas firs stand draped in sphagnum moss – an eerie sight in the fog. The real beauty shots lie further ahead, when the road ascends 1000ft hills, dotted with gnarled oaks and craggy rock formations, with the vast blue Pacific unfurling below. The road ends at coastal Hwy 1, where you can explore Sonoma Coast State Beach (p217), then turn left and find your way to the tiny town of Bodega (not Bodega Bay) to see locales where Hitchcock shot his 1963 classic, *The Birds*.

cottages with porches and good camping. The large pool is clothing-optional (weekday/weekend day use $10/15).

Fern Grove Cottages CABIN $$
(707-869-8105; www.ferngrove.com; 16650 River Rd; cabins $159-249, with kitchen $229-299;) Downtown Guerneville's cheeriest resort, Fern Grove has vintage-1930s pine-paneled cabins tucked beneath redwoods and surrounded by lush flowering gardens. Some have Jacuzzi and fireplace. The pool uses salt, not chlorine; there are concierge services and breakfast includes homemade granola.

★ **Applewood Inn** INN $$$
(707-869-9093; www.applewoodinn.com; 13555 Hwy 116; r $250-500;) A hideaway estate on a wooded hilltop south of town, cushy Applewood has marvelous 1920s-era detail, with dark wood and heavy furniture that echo the forest. Some rooms have Jacuzzi and couples' shower; some have fireplace. Amenities include a small spa and two heated pools, but the best perk is the coupon for complimentary tastings at more than 100 wineries. At the time of writing, the hotel's new Italian restaurant was about to open.

Santa Nella House B&B $$$
(707-869-9488; www.santanellahouse.com; 12130 Hwy 116; r $205-249;) All five spotless rooms at this 1871 Victorian, south of town, have wood-burning fireplace and frilly Victorian furnishings. Upstairs rooms are biggest. Outside there's a hot tub and sauna. Best for travelers who appreciate the B&B aesthetic.

Forestville

Farmhouse Inn INN $$$
(Map p192; 707-887-3300, 800-464-6642; www.farmhouseinn.com; 7871 River Rd; r $695-1495;) Think love nest. The area's premier inn was recently renovated and offers spacious rooms and cottages, styled with cushy amenities such as saunas, steam showers and wood-burning fireplaces. Small on-site spa and top-notch restaurant (Farmhouse Inn restaurant on p202). Check in early to maximize time.

Raford Inn B&B $$$
(707-887-9573, 800-887-9503; http://rafordinn.com; 10630 Wohler Rd; r $225-275;) We love this 1880 Victorian B&B's secluded hilltop location, surrounded by tall palms and rambling vineyards. Rooms are big and airy, with lace and antiques; some have fireplace. And wow, those sunset views.

Monte Rio

Village Inn INN $$
(707-865-2304; www.villageinn-ca.com; 20822 River Blvd; r $145-250;) This cute, old-fashioned, 11-room inn perches beneath towering trees, right on the river. Some rooms have river views; all have fridge and microwave. No elevator.

Rio Villa Beach Resort INN $$
(707-865-1143, 877-746-8455; www.riovilla.com; 20292 Hwy 116; r with kitchen $190-205, without $160-165;) Landscaping is lush at this small riverside resort with excellent sun exposure (you see redwoods, but you're not under them). Rooms are well-kept but simple (request a quiet room, not by the road); the emphasis is on the outdoors, evident by the large riverside terrace, outdoor fireplace and barbecues. Some air-conditioning.

Highland Dell INN $$
(707-865-2300; www.highlanddell.com; 21050 River Blvd; r $109-179; Apr-Nov;) Built in 1906 in grand lodge style, redone in 2007, the inn fronts right on to the river. Above the giant dining room are 12 bright, fresh-looking

rooms with comfy beds. No elevator. Doubles as an event center.

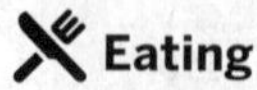

Eating

Staying downtown means you can walk to restaurants and bars. From deli sandwiches to farm-to-table feasts to Korean-diner grub, there are plenty of good options.

Guerneville

Big Bottom Market MARKET, CAFE $
(707-604-7295; www.bigbottommarket.com; 16228 Main St; sandwiches $11-15; 8am-5pm Wed-Mon) Gourmet deli and wine shop with coffee, delicious pastries and grab-and-go picnic supplies. Supposedly the home of Oprah's favorite biscuit.

Taqueria La Tapatia MEXICAN $
(707-869-1821; 16632 Main St; mains $7-14; 4-9pm Tue-Sun) Reasonable choice for traditional Mexican.

Garden Grill BARBECUE $
(707-869-3922; www.gardengrillbbq.com; 17132 Hwy 116, Guernewood Park; mains $6-12; 8am-3pm) One mile west of Guerneville, this roadhouse barbecue joint, with redwood-shaded patio, serves good house-smoked meats but the fries could be better.

Food for Humans MARKET $
(707-869-3612; 16385 1st St; 9am-8pm;) Organic groceries; better alternative than neighboring Safeway.

Dick Blomster's Korean Diner KOREAN, AMERICAN $$
(707-896-8006; 16236 Main St; mains breakfast & lunch $8.50-12.50, dinner $15-20; 8am-2pm & 5-9pm Sun-Thu, to 10pm Fri & Sat) By day a vintage-1940s coffee shop, by night a Korean-American diner with full bar, Dick Blomster's serves playfully tongue-in-cheek dishes, including fried peanut butter and jelly sandwiches and 'the other KFC – Korean fried crack': fried chicken with sugary-sweet brown sauce, which sure hits the spot after a night of drinking.

Seaside Metal Oyster Bar SEAFOOD $$
(707-604-7250; http://seasidemetal.com; 16222 Main St; dishes $8-18; 5-9pm Wed, Thu & Sun, to 10pm Fri & Sat) Unexpectedly urban for Guerneville, this storefront raw bar is an offshoot of San Francisco's Bar Crudo – one of the city's best – and showcases oysters, clams, shrimp and exquisitely prepared raw-fish dishes. There's limited hot food, but it's overwrought: stick to raw. Reservations recommended.

Boon Eat + Drink CALIFORNIAN $$$
(707-869-0780; http://eatatboon.com; 16248 Main St; mains lunch $15-18, dinner $15-26; 11am-3pm Thu-Tue, 5-9pm Sun-Thu, to 10pm Fri & Sat;) Locally sourced ingredients inform the seasonal, Cali-smart cooking at this tiny, always-packed, New American bistro, with cheek-by-jowl tables that fill every night. Serves local wine and craft beer. Show up early or expect to wait.

Forestville

Canneti Roadhouse ITALIAN $$
(Map p192; 707-887-2232; http://cannetirestaurant.com; 6675 Front St; mains lunch $12-24, dinner $16-38; 5:30-9pm Tue-Wed, 11:30am-3pm & 5:30-9pm Thu-Sat, 11am-8:30pm Sun) A Tuscan-born chef makes bona fide *cucina Italiana* using quality ingredients from local farms at this austere restaurant in downtown Forestville, worth the 15-minute drive from Guerneville. The menu ranges from simple brick-oven pizzas to an all-Tuscan, five-course tasting menu ($65, dinner only). When it's warm, sit on the patio beneath a giant redwood. Make reservations. Thursdays, three-course dinners cost $40.

★Backyard CALIFORNIAN $$$
(707-820-8445; www.backyardforestville.com; 6566 Front St; mains lunch & brunch $10-22, dinner mains $21-28; 11am-9pm Mon & Thu, to 9:30pm Fri, 9am-9:30pm Sat, to 8:30pm Sun) This relaxing, alfresco spot gets every fruit, vegetable and animal from local farmers or fishers and the chef knows just what to do with all of it. California-inspired dishes are simple and delicious; the steak, piquillo-pepper and duck-egg hash was perhaps the world's most perfect brunch. The coffee and artisanal doughnut holes are winners.

Oh, and don't start a meal with anything other than the house pickle plate, which comes with the most delightful array of pickled, seasonal vegetables (often including cauliflower and asparagus) and house-fermented kimchi.

Farmhouse Inn MODERN AMERICAN $$$
(707-695-1495; www.farmhouseinn.com; 7871 River Rd; 3-/4-course dinner $99/115; 5:30-8:30pm Thu-Mon) Special-occasion worthy, Michelin-starred Farmhouse changes its seasonal Euro-Cal menu daily, using locally

raised, organic ingredients such as Sonoma lamb, wild halibut and rabbit – the latter is the house specialty. The wine pairings are exquisite, but detractors call the whole thing precious. Reservations required.

Monte Rio

Rio Café FAST FOOD $
(☎707-865-4190; www.riocafetake2.com; 20396 Bohemian Hwy; sandwiches $4-12; ⏰8am-8pm Wed-Sun summer, noon-7pm Fri-Sun winter;) Gourmet burgers, hot dogs and grilled sandwiches, along with breakfast options and lots of veggie choices, behind the Rio Theater. Beer and wine also served.

Village Inn AMERICAN $$$
(☎707-865-2304; www.villageinn-ca.com; 20822 River Blvd; mains $19-26; ⏰5-8pm Wed-Sun) The straightforward steaks-and-seafood menu is basic American and doesn't distract from the wonderful river views. Great local wine list, full bar.

Duncans Mills

Cape Fear Cafe AMERICAN $$
(☎707-865-9246; 25191 Main St; mains lunch $9-15, dinner $15-25; ⏰10am-9pm Mon-Fri, to 9pm Sat & Sun) A country-Americana diner in a 19th-century grange, Cape Fear is visually charming, but it's erratic – except at weekend brunch when the kitchen makes excellent Benedicts. Good stopover en route to the coast.

Drinking & Nightlife

Stumptown Brewery is the town's after-hours social hub, but there are plenty of good opportunities for day-drinking – particularly at the wineries and while floating down the river in summer.

Rainbow Cattle Company GAY
(www.queersteer.com; 16220 Main St; ⏰noon-2am) This stalwart gay watering hole has pinball and shuffleboard. Tuesdays are big, with a donation-based buffet, silent auction, raffle and a percentage of sales going to various causes.

Sophie's Cellars WINE BAR
(☎707-865-1122; www.sophiescellars.com; 25179 Main St/Hwy 116; glasses $7-15; ⏰11am-5pm Thu, Sat & Sun, to 7pm Fri) The perfect stopover between river and coast, Sophie's rural wine bar pours glasses and tastes of local wine, and carries cheese, salami and a well-curated selection of bottles. Friday's 'locals happy hour' (4pm to 7pm) brings hors d'oeuvres, drink specials and a big crowd.

Stumptown Brewery BREWERY
(Map p192; www.stumptown.com; 15045 River Rd; ⏰11am-midnight Sun-Thu, to 2am Fri & Sat) Guerneville's best straight bar, 1 mile east of downtown, is gay friendly and has a foot-stompin' jukebox, billiards, riverside beer garden and several homemade brews. Pretty good pub grub includes house-smoked barbecue.

Entertainment

Rio Nido Roadhouse LIVE MUSIC
(Map p192; ☎707-869-0821; www.rionidoroadhouse.com; 14540 Canyon Two, off River Rd, Rio Nido) Raucous roadhouse bar, 4 miles east of Guerneville, with eclectic lineup of live bands. Shows start 6pm Saturday and sometimes Friday and Sunday too; check website. There's also a pool open 11am to 6pm daily, to 5pm on Saturday and water aerobics is offered. The pool was being renovated at the time of writing.

Rio Theater CINEMA
(☎707-865-0913, 707-520-4075; www.riotheater.com; 20396 Bohemian Hwy, Monte Rio; $10-12;) Dinner and a movie take on new meaning at this vintage-WWII Quonset hut converted to a cinema in 1950. In 2014 they finally added heat, but still supply blankets. Only in Monte Rio. Shows nightly (and sometimes Sunday afternoons), but call ahead, especially off-season.

Main Street Bistro CABARET
(☎707-869-0501; www.mainststation.com; 16280 Main St; ⏰4-11pm Mon-Thu, noon-11pm Fri-Sun;) Hosts live acoustic-only jazz, blues and cabaret nightly in summer (weekends in winter). Families are welcome as the cabaret doubles as an American-Italian restaurant (stick to pizza).

Shopping

Eight miles west of Guerneville, tiny Duncans Mills has good shopping in a handful of side-by-side businesses within weathered 19th-century cottages.

★**Guerneville Bank Club** FOOD
(☎707- 666-9411; www.guernevillebankclub.com; 16290 Main St; ⏰11am-9pm Sun-Thu, to 10pm Fri & Sat) After 30 years of abandonment, this beautifully restored 1921 bank building now contains stuff more valuable than money:

art, wine, ice cream and pie. The new collective retail and art-gallery space houses small businesses such as Chile Pies Banking Company (go for the Mexican Chocolate Pecan) and Nimble Finn's Ice Cream, which sells organic dairy products, jams, cakes etc. There's a small wine-tasting room and the old vault has been converted into a photo booth adorned in murals.

Pig Alley JEWELRY
(☎707-865-2698; www.pigalleyshop.com; 25193 Main St; ⏲10am-5pm Mon-Fri, 9:30am-5:30pm Sat & Sun) Vast selection of hand-crafted American-made jewelry, notable for gorgeous earrings.

Mr Trombly's Tea & Table FOOD & DRINKS
(☎707-865-9610; www.mrtromblystea.com; 25185 Main St; ⏲10am-5pm Sun-Thu, to 5:30pm Fri & Sat) Different kinds of tea and teapots, plus quality kitchen gadgets and well-priced tableware.

Information

Russian River Chamber of Commerce & Visitors Center (Map p192; ☎707-869-9000; www.russianriver.com; 16209 1st St; ⏲10am-5pm Mon-Sat, plus to 3pm Sun May-Oct) Information and lodging referrals.

Getting There & Away

Public transit isn't a great option, but to check bus routes dial ☎511, or look online at www.transit.511.org. The drive from San Francisco takes about two hours.

Santa Rosa

Wine Country's biggest city and the Sonoma County seat, Santa Rosa claims two famous native sons – a world-renowned cartoonist and a celebrated horticulturalist – whose legacies include museums and gardens that'll keep you busy for an afternoon. Otherwise, there isn't much to do, unless you need your car fixed or you're here in July during the **Sonoma County Fair** (www.sonomacountyfair.com), at the fairgrounds on Bennett Valley Rd.

Beyond that, Santa Rosa is mostly known for traffic and suburban sprawl, though the downtown's redwood trees make for some impressive landscaping.

Orientation

The main shopping stretch is 4th St, which abruptly ends at Hwy 101, but reemerges across the freeway at historic Railroad Sq. Downtown parking garages (75¢ per hour, $8 maximum) are cheaper than street parking. East of town, 4th St becomes Hwy 12 into Sonoma Valley.

Sights & Activities

Charles M Schulz Museum MUSEUM
(☎707-579-4452; www.schulzmuseum.org; 2301 Hardies Lane; adult/child $12/5; ⏲11am-5pm Mon & Wed-Fri, 10am-5pm Sat & Sun; P 👪) Charles Schulz, creator of *Peanuts* cartoons and Santa Rosa resident, was born in 1922, published his first drawing in 1937, introduced Snoopy and Charlie Brown in 1950 and produced *Peanuts* cartoons until his death in 2000. This modern museum honors his legacy with a Snoopy labyrinth, *Peanuts*-related art and a re-creation of Schulz' studio. Skip Snoopy's Gallery gift shop; the museum has the good stuff.

Farmers Market MARKET
(www.wednesdaynightmarket.org; Old Courthouse Sq; ⏲5-8:30pm Wed mid-May–Aug) Sonoma County's largest farmers market. A second smaller market meets year-round, 9am to 1pm, Wednesdays and Saturdays at Santa Rosa Veterans Building.

Luther Burbank Home & Gardens GARDENS
(☎707-524-5445; www.lutherburbank.org; 204 Santa Rosa Ave; grounds free, tour adult/child $10/5; ⏲gardens 8am-dusk, museum 10am-4pm Tue-Sun Apr-Oct) Pioneering horticulturist Luther Burbank (1849–1926) developed many hybrid plant species, including the Shasta daisy, here at his 19th-century, Greek-revival home. Guided tours 10am-3:30pm Tuesday-Sunday April-October. The extensive gardens are lovely. The house and adjacent **Carriage Museum** have displays on Burbank's life and work, or you can take a self-guided cell-phone tour of the grounds for free.

Epicenter CENTER
(Map p192; ☎707-708-3742; www.visitepicenter.com; 3215 Coffey Lane; ⏲11am-midnight Sun-Thu, to 2am Fri & Sat) An entertainment complex with restaurants, bars, bowling, an arcade and a trampoline park.

Children's Museum of Sonoma County SCIENCE CENTER
(☎707-546-4069; www.cmosc.org; 1835 Steele Lane; $12; ⏲9am-4pm Mon & Wed-Sat, 11am-4pm Sun; 👪) Geared to children 10 and under, this happy learning center inspires discovery, exploration and creativity with hands-on indoor

and outdoor exhibits focused on nature and science. Picnicking welcome. No adults without kids.

Redwood Empire Ice Arena SKATING
(707-546-7147; www.snoopyshomeice.com; 1667 West Steele Lane; incl skates $5-13; hours vary;) This skating rink was formerly owned and deeply loved by *Peanuts* cartoon creator Charles Schulz. It's open most afternoons (call for schedules). Bring a sweater.

Sleeping

Chain hotels abound, in addition to a couple of historic inns and a decent campground. In general, Santa Rosa offers reasonably priced accommodations and easy access to Sonoma County and Valley.

Spring Lake Park CAMPGROUND $
(707-539-8092, reservations 707-565-2267; www.sonomacountyparks.org; 5585 Newanga Ave; sites $32; campground May-Sep, weekends only Oct-Apr;) Lovely lakeside park, 4 miles from downtown; make reservations online ($8.50 fee) or by phone 10am to 3pm weekdays. The park is open year-round, with lake swimming (complete with a floating playground) in summer. Take 4th St eastbound, turn right on Farmer's Lane, pass the first Hoen St and turn left on the second Hoen St, then left on Newanga Ave.

Hillside Inn MOTEL $
(707-546-9353; www.hillside-inn.com; 2901 4th St; s/d $78/86;) Santa Rosa's best-value motel, Hillside is close to Sonoma Valley; add $4 for kitchens. Furnishings are dated and service peculiar, but everything is scrupulously maintained. Adjoins an excellent breakfast cafe.

Sandman INN $$
(707-293-2100; www.sandmansantarosa.com; 3421 Cleveland Ave; r $120-300;) Once Santa Rosa's best budget choice, Sandman has been revamped by new owners to feature a Southwestern aesthetic, quirky vintage furnishings and a hot bar replete with bamboo sofas and poolside cocktail window. The pool's heated and there's a hot tub.

Hotel La Rose HISTORIC HOTEL $$
(707-579-3200; www.hotellarose.com; 308 Wilson St; r Mon-Fri $149-199, Sat & Sun $209-269;) At Railroad Sq, Hotel La Rose has rooms in a well-kept historic 1907 brick hotel and across the street in a 1980s-built 'carriage house,' which feels like a small condo complex with boxy, spacious rooms. All are decorated in out-of-fashion pastels but have excellent beds with quality linens and down duvets; some have jetted tubs.

Vintners Inn INN $$$
(Map p192; 707-575-7350, 800-421-2584; www.vintnersinn.com; 4350 Barnes Rd; r $245-495;) Surrounded by 92 acres of vineyards north of town (near River Rd), Vintner's Inn caters to the gated-community crowd with business-class amenities. Complimentary wine tastings in the lobby at 5pm on Fridays. Check for last-minute specials.

Flamingo Conference Resort & Spa HOTEL $$
(707-545-8530, 800-848-8300; www.flamingoresort.com; 2777 4th St; r $179-299;) Sprawling over 11 acres, this mid-century modern hotel doubles as a conference center. Rooms are business-class generic, but the pool is gigantic – and kept at 82ºF (28ºC) year-round. Kids love it. On-site health club and gym. Prices double on summer weekends.

Best Western Garden Inn MOTEL $$
(707-546-4031; www.thegardeninn.com; 1500 Santa Rosa Ave; r Mon-Fri $119-139, Sat & Sun $199-229;) Recently renovated motel, south of downtown, with two pools and a hot tub. Rear rooms open to grassy gardens, but you may hear kids in the pool; book up front for quiet. The street gets seedy by night but the hotel is secure, clean and comfortable.

Best Western Wine Country Inn & Suites HOTEL $$
(707-545-9000; www.winecountryhotel.com; 870 Hopper Ave; r Sun-Thu $135-140, Sat & Sun $180-220;) Pretty standard midrange chain hotel, off Cleveland Ave. There's a pool and some rooms have Jacuzzi.

Eating

Santa Rosa's culinary star is on the rise, with a solid selection of long-time international and farm-to-table restaurants and plenty of ambitious openings to keep things interesting.

Criminal Baking Co BAKERY $
(707-888-3546; www.criminalbaking.com; 463 Sebastopol Ave; baked goods $1-5; 7:30am-4pm Mon-Fri, 8am-4pm Sat & Sun) A superior Santa Rosa bakery, with delicious vegan banana-walnut cookies, three-cheese knishes and supernutritious lunches such as the

'warrior bowl,' which comes with spinach, quinoa, potatoes, artichokes, bacon and goat's cheese. Don't miss the lavender lemonade.

Taqueria Las Palmas MEXICAN $
(707-546-3091; 415 Santa Rosa Ave; dishes $4-11; 9am-9pm;) For Mexican, this is the real deal, with standout *carnitas* (barbecued pork), homemade salsas and veggie burritos.

Jeffrey's Hillside Cafe AMERICAN $
(707-546-6317; www.jeffreyshillsidecafe.com; 2901 4th St; dishes $9-13; 7am-2pm;) East of downtown, near Sonoma Valley, chef-owned Jeffrey's is excellent for breakfast or brunch before wine tasting.

Tasca Tasca TAPAS $$
(Map p184; 707-996-8272; www.tascatasca.com; 122 W Napa St; 3/5/7 items $15/24/32; noon-midnight) Specializing in Portuguese and Mediterranean fare, this new tapas tavern in food-obsessed downtown Sonoma holds its own. Try the authentic *caldo verde* (Portugal's national soup), along with one of the fabulous cheeses and the inventive Dungeness-crab empanadas with chipotle mayo. Wash everything down with the house-red sangria, made with passion fruit.

Yeti NEPALI $$
(707-521-9608; www.yeticuisine.com; 190 Farmers Lane; mains lunch $12-17, dinner $18-25; 11:30am-2pm & 5-9:30pm) This places serves up spectacular Indian and Nepali dishes, and offers a brunch smorgasbord every Saturday and Sunday with spicy curries, *saag paneer* (spinach and paneer curry) and tikka masala (with both meat and veggie options).

OLIVE-OIL TASTING

When you weary of wine tasting, pop by one of the following olive-oil makers and dip some crusty bread – it's free. Harvest and pressing happen in November.

- BR Cohn (p182)
- Napa Valley Olive Oil Mfg Co (p165)
- Long Meadow Ranch (p159)
- Figone's Olive Oil (p188)

Naked Pig CAFE $$
(707-978-3231; 435 Santa Rosa Ave; mains $11-14; 8am-3pm Wed-Sun) This tiny cafe in a former bus depot makes everything from scratch and serves simple-delicious, farm-to-table breakfasts and lunches at communal tables.

Rosso Pizzeria & Wine Bar PIZZA $$
(707-546-6317; www.rossopizzeria.com; 53 Montgomery Dr, Creekside Shopping Center; pizzas $13-17; 11:30am-10pm;) Fantastic wood-fired pizzas, inventive salads and standout wines make Rosso worth seeking out.

★ Flower + Bone INTERNATIONAL $$$
(707-708-8529; www.flowerandbonerestaurant.com; 640 5th St; mezes $11-18, 6-course prix fixe $67; 11am-3pm Wed, 6-9pm Thu-Sat) From the foraging, pickling, preserving Santa Rosa couple behind the Naked Pig comes Flower + Bone. The cuisine is inspired by ancient cooking techniques, including bone broths, pasture-raised meat and housemade hooch. The prix-fixe menu, also known as 'the full story,' is epic, with everything from foraged weeds to Polish dumplings. Dessert involves a gold-dusted truffle.

Spinster Sisters CALIFORNIAN $$$
(707-528-7100; www.thespinstersisters.com; 401 South A St; mains lunch $10-16, dinner $23-26; 8am-2:30pm Mon, to 9pm Tue-Thu, to 10pm Fri, 9am-10pm Sat, to 2:30pm Sun) At Santa Rosa's culinary vanguard, this casual market-driven restaurant makes its own bagels, cheese and charcuterie meats. The diverse tapas-like small plates ($7 to $14) pair well with the extensive wine list.

Drinking & Nightlife

There are a few decent pubs and bars around town, but Russian River Brewing Co is the social hub of Santa Rosa, drawing visitors from all over Northern California for its double IPA.

★ Russian River Brewing Co BREWERY
(707-545-2337; www.russianriverbrewing.com; 729 4th St; 11am-midnight) Santa Rosa's justly famous brewery crafts a wildly popular double IPA called Pliny the Elder, plus top-grade sour beer aged in wine barrels. Good pizza and pub grub too.

A'Roma Roasters CAFE
(707-576-7765; www.aromaroasters.com; 95 5th St, Railroad Sq; 6am-11pm Mon-Thu, to midnight

Fri, 7am-midnight Sat, to 10pm Sun;) Town's hippest cafe serves no booze, but hosts acoustic music Saturday evenings.

Information

MEDICAL SERVICES

Santa Rosa Memorial Hospital (707-525-5300; www.stjoesonoma.org; 1165 Montgomery Dr; 24hr) Wide range of health services; houses the region's trauma center.

TOURIST INFORMATION

California Welcome Center & Santa Rosa Visitors Bureau (707-577-8674, 800-404-7673; www.visitsantarosa.com; 9 4th St; 9am-5pm) Same-day lodging assistance. At Railroad Sq, west of Hwy 101; take downtown exit from Hwy 12 or 101.

Getting There & Away

Sonoma County Airport Express (p155) runs shuttles ($34) between Sonoma County Airport (Santa Rosa) and San Francisco and Oakland airports.

Golden Gate Transit (p111) buses run between San Francisco and Santa Rosa (adult/youth $13/6.50); board at 1st and Mission Sts in San Fran.

Greyhound (p155) buses run from San Francisco to Santa Rosa ($21 to $38).

Healdsburg & Around

Once a sleepy ag town best known for its Future Farmers of America parade, Healdsburg has emerged as northern Sonoma County's culinary capital. Foodie-scenester restaurants and cafes, wine-tasting rooms and fancy boutiques line Healdsburg Plaza, the town's sun-dappled central square (bordered by Healdsburg Ave and Center, Matheson and Plaza Sts).

Traffic grinds to a halt on summer weekends, when second-home-owners and tourists jam downtown. Old-timers aren't happy with the Napa-style gentrification but at least Healdsburg retains its historic look, if not its once-quiet summers. It's best visited weekdays – stroll tree-lined streets, sample locavore cooking and soak up the NorCal flavor.

Sights

Tasting rooms surround the plaza.

Saturday Market MARKET
(www.healdsburgfarmersmarket.org; 9am-noon Sat May-Dec) Healdsburg's downtown farmers market.

Wednesday Market MARKET
(707-824-8717; cnr Vine & North Sts; 3:30-6pm Wed Jun-Nov) Healdsburg's weekday farmers market.

Locals Tasting Room TASTING ROOM
(707-857-4900; www.tastelocalwines.com; Geyserville Ave & Hwy 128; 11am-6pm) FREE Eight miles north of Healdsburg, tiny Geyserville is home to this indie tasting room, which represents 10 small-production wineries with free tastings.

Healdsburg Public Library LIBRARY
(707-433-3772; www.sonomalibrary.org; cnr Piper & Center Sts; 10am-9pm Mon & Wed, to 6pm Tue, Thu & Fri, to 4pm Sat) Wine Country's leading oenology-reference library.

Healdsburg Veterans Memorial Beach BEACH
(Map p192; 707-433-1625; www.sonomacountyparks.org; 13839 Old Redwood Hwy; per car $7; 7am-30min before sunset; P) You can swim at this in-town beach between July and early September – lifeguards are on duty summer weekends. The fastidious can confirm current water quality online (www.sonoma-county.org/health/services/freshwater.asp).

Healdsburg Museum MUSEUM
(707-431-3325; www.healdsburgmuseum.org; 221 Matheson St; donation requested; 11am-4pm Wed-Sun) Rotating exhibits include compelling installations on northern Sonoma County history, with an emphasis on Healdsburg. Pick up the walking-tour pamphlet.

Activities

After you've walked around the plaza, there isn't much to do in town. Go wine tasting in Dry Creek Valley or Russian River Valley. Bicycling on winding W Dry Creek Rd is brilliant, as is paddling the Russian River, which runs through town. Rent bikes from Spoke Folk Cyclery (p157).

River's Edge Kayak & Canoe Trips KAYAKING, CANOEING
(707-433-7247; www.riversedgekayakandcanoe.com; 13840 Healdsburg Ave; kayak/canoe rental & shuttle from $50/100) Rents hard-sided canoes and kayaks (single and double) for self-guided river tours that include a shuttle.

Russian River Adventures CANOEING
(707-433-5599, 800-280-7627; www.russianriveradventures.com; 20 Healdsburg Ave; half-day

canoe rental & shuttle adult/child from $45/25;) Paddle a secluded stretch of river in quiet inflatable canoes, stopping for rope swings, swimming holes, beaches and bird-watching. This ecotourism outfit points you in the right direction and shuttles you back at day's end. Or they'll guide your kids downriver while you go wine tasting (guides $125 per day). Reservations required.

Tours

Getaway Adventures CYCLING, KAYAKING
(800-499-2453; www.getawayadventures.com; tours 1-day $139-175, multiday $899-2500) Guides a variety of hiking, biking and kayaking tours in Dry Creek Valley, varying in length and difficulty. For example, a one-day tour might include spectacular morning vineyard cycling in Dry Creek Valley, followed by lunch and optional kayaking on Russian River.

Courses

Relish Culinary Adventures COOKING
(707-431-9999; www.relishculinary.com; 14 Matheson St; by appointment) Plug into the locavore food scene with culinary day trips, demo-kitchen classes or winemaker dinners.

Festivals & Events

Russian River Wine Road Barrel Tasting WINE
(www.wineroad.com; Mar) Sample wine, directly from the cask, before it's bottled or released for sale.

Future Farmers Parade CULTURAL
(www.healdsburgfair.org; May) The whole town shows up for this classic-Americana farm parade, which kicks off a country fair.

Wine & Food Affair FOOD & DRINK
(www.wineroad.com/events/wine-food-affair; Nov) Special food and wine pairings at over 100 wineries.

Sleeping

Healdsburg is expensive: demand exceeds supply. Rates drop winter to spring, but not significantly. Guerneville is much less expensive and just 20 minutes away. Most Healdsburg inns are within walking distance of the plaza; several B&Bs are in surrounding countryside. Find motels at Hwy 101's Dry Creek exit.

Cloverdale Wine Country KOA CAMPGROUND $
(707-894-3337, 800-562-4042; www.winecountrykoa.com; 1166 Asti Ridge Rd, Cloverdale; tent/RV sites from $50/65, 1-/2-bedroom cabins $85/95;) Six miles from central Cloverdale (exit 520) off Hwy 101; hot showers, pool, hot tub, laundry, paddleboats and bicycles.

L&M Motel MOTEL $$
(707-433-6528; www.landmmotel.com; 70 Healdsburg Ave; r $175-195; P) This simple, clean, old-fashioned motel with big lawns and barbecue grills is great for families. There's an indoor swimming pool, Jacuzzi and dry cedar sauna too. Breakfast included. Winter rates plummet.

Geyserville Inn MOTEL $$
(877-857-4343, 707-857-4343; www.geyservilleinn.com; 21714 Geyserville Ave, Geyserville; r Mon-Fri $160-205, Sat & Sun $269-315; P) Eight miles north of Healdsburg, this immaculately kept upmarket motel is surrounded by vineyards. Rooms have unexpectedly smart furnishings and quality extras such as feather pillows. Request a remodeled room. There's a solar-heated pool and a hot tub.

Best Western Dry Creek MOTEL $$
(707-433-0300; www.drycreekinn.com; 198 Dry Creek Rd; r Mon-Wed $143-198, Thu-Sun $187-239; @) This generic midrange motel has good service and an outdoor hot tub. New rooms have jetted tubs and gas fireplaces.

★ **Hotel Healdsburg** HOTEL $$$
(707-431-2800; www.hotelhealdsburg.com; 25 Matheson St; r from $499; @) Smack on the plaza, the fashion-forward HH has a coolly minimalist style of concrete and velvet, with requisite top-end amenities, including sumptuous beds and extradeep tubs. There's a full-service spa. The restaurant, **Dry Creek Kitchen**, is run by celeb-chef Charlie Palmer.

Madrona Manor HISTORIC HOTEL $$$
(800-258-4003, 707-433-4231; www.madronamanor.com; 1001 Westside Rd; r Mon-Fri $255-655;) The first choice of lovers of country inns and stately manor homes, the regal 1881 Madrona Manor exudes Victorian elegance. Surrounded by 8 acres of woods and gorgeous century-old gardens, the hilltop mansion is decked out with many original

furnishings. A mile west of downtown, it's convenient to Westside Rd wineries.

Belle de Jour Inn B&B $$$
(707-431-9777; www.belledejourinn.com; 16276 Healdsburg Ave; r $225-295, ste $355;) Charming Belle de Jour's sunny, uncluttered rooms have American-country furnishings, with extras such as private entrances, sun-dried sheets and jetted tubs. The manicured gardens are ready-made for a moonlight tryst.

Camellia Inn B&B $$$
(707-433-8182, 800-727-8182; www.camelliainn.com; 211 North St; r $159-395;) Elegantly furnished 1869 mansion, with (among others) a rare-for-Healdsburg budget room ($159), plus a two-bed family room ($269). There are no TVs, but iPads are provided. Also, the innkeeper is really nice.

Healdsburg Inn on the Plaza INN $$$
(800-431-8663, 707-433-6991; www.healdsburginn.com; 112 Matheson St; r $295-460;) The spiffy, clean-lined rooms, conservatively styled in khaki and beige, feel bourgeois summer-house casual, with fine linen and gas fireplace; some have jetted double tub. The plaza-front location explains the price.

H2 Hotel HOTEL $$$
(707-431-2202; www.h2hotel.com; 219 Healdsburg Ave; r Mon-Fri $269-389, Sat & Sun $399-699; P@) Little sister to Hotel Healdsburg, H2 has the same angular concrete style, but was built LEED-gold-certified from the ground up, with a living roof, reclaimed everything and fresh-looking rooms with bamboo floors and organic-cotton linens. Also has a heated saltwater pool and free bikes. Waters, snacks and espresso are complimentary.

Haydon Street Inn B&B $$$
(707-433-5228; www.haydon.com; 321 Haydon St; r $210-350, cottages $425-450;) Two-story Queen Anne with big front porch and separate cottage.

Honor Mansion INN $$$
(707-433-4277, 800-554-4667; www.honormansion.com; 891 Grove St; r $450-695;) Elegant 1883 Victorian mansion with spectacular resort-like grounds, cushy rooms and great service.

Eating

Healdsburg is the gastronomic capital of Sonoma County. Your hardest decision will be choosing where to eat. Reservations essential.

★Shed CAFE $$
(707-431-7433; www.healdsburgshed.com; 25 North St; dinner mains $15-30; 8am-9pm Wed-Mon, to 6pm Tue;) At the vanguard of locavore eating, the Shed integrates food at all stages of production, milling its own locally sourced grain flours, fermenting vinegars and kombucha from local fruit and growing its own produce. It comprises a cafe with wood-fired dishes, a fermentation bar with homegrown shrubs, a coffee bar with stellar pastries and a market with prepared-to-go foods.

Reason enough to visit Healdsburg, the Shed is not a restaurant per se, but a dynamic multiuse culinary center, like a modern-day grange built of glass, nudging diners to see through what they're eating and take an active role in the future of food. Events, such as movie nights, biodynamic cannabis panel discussions and sushi-making workshops, are held upstairs.

Costeaux French Bakery & Cafe CAFE $$
(707-433-1913; www.costeaux.com; 417 Healdsburg Ave; mains $10-13; cafe 7am-3pm Mon-Sat, to 1pm Sun, bakery to 4pm Mon-Thu, to 5pm Sat & Sun;) This cavernous bakery-cafe is good for an easy lunch of salads and sandwiches on house-baked bread, plus all-day breakfast dishes including omelets and scrambles.

Diavola ITALIAN, CALIFORNIAN $$
(707-814-0111; www.diavolapizzera.com; 21021 Geyserville Ave, Geyserville; mains $16-29; 11:30am-9pm;) Ideal for lunch while wine tasting in Alexander Valley, Diavola makes outstanding *salumi* and thin-crust pizzas, served in an Old West, brick-walled space, loud enough to drown out the kids.

Healdsburg Bar & Grill PUB FOOD $$
(707-433-3333; www.healdsburgbarandgrill.com; 245 Healdsburg Ave; mains $11-23; 11am-9pm Mon-Fri, 9am-9pm Sat & Sun) *Top Chef Masters* winner Doug Keane's gastropub is perfect when you're famished but don't want to fuss. Expect simple classics – mac 'n' cheese, pulled-pork sandwiches, top-end burgers and truffle-parmesan fries. At breakfast, look for homemade waffles and English

muffins fresh from Costeaux Bakery. Sit in the garden.

★Madrona Manor CALIFORNIAN **$$$**
(☎707-433-4231, 800-258-4003; www.madronamanor.com; 1001 Westside Rd; 11-course menu $165; ⊙6-9pm Wed-Sun) You'd be hard-pressed to find a lovelier place to propose than this retro-formal Victorian mansion's garden-view verandah – though there's nothing old-fashioned about the artful haute cuisine: the kitchen churns its own butter, each course comes with a different variety of just-baked bread, courses include items such as Monterey abalone and Hokkaido-scallop crudo, and there's frozen lemon verbena for dessert. Reserve a presunset table.

★SingleThread Farm-Restaurant-Inn JAPANESE **$$$**
(☎707-723-4646; www.singlethreadfarms.com; 131 North St; tasting menu per person $293; ⊙5:30-11pm Tue-Sun) The most ambitious project in Northern California is SingleThread, a world-class restaurant and, secondarily, an inn, where *omotenashi* (warm hospitality in Japanese) reigns and dishes from an 11-course tasting menu are prepared in handmade Japanese *donabe* (earthenware pots). The cuisine is California-Japanese and guests book tickets in advance, offering up their preferences and dietary restrictions, and the chef abides.

On arrival, guests are taken to a roof to enjoy sparkling wine, canapes and 360-degree views of the countryside before sitting down to feast. The sleek space features its own fermentation tank, which local winemakers use to craft a new vintage each year, along with a boutique **hotel** offering five sumptuous rooms starting at $800 a night. Down the road, the owners have a 5-acre organic garden where they farm specialized Japanese produce, hens and flowers.

Valette CALIFORNIAN **$$$**
(☎707-473-0946; www.valettehealdsburg.com; 344 Center St; 'trust me' tasting menu per course $15, minimum 4 courses; ⊙5:30-9:30pm) If you're looking to impress somebody, Healdsburg residents suggest Valette. The sleek American restaurant is regularly packed with suits and fancy ladies making a show of swirling their local wine (corkage fee is only $20) and ordering the multicourse 'trust me' tasting menu, where the gifted chef asks what you're into then decides what to feed you.

The scallop dish, which is baked within a squid-inked puffy pastry and bathed in caviar-studded champagne beurre blanc, is otherworldly.

Barndiva CALIFORNIAN **$$$**
(☎707-431-0100; www.barndiva.com; 231 Center St; mains lunch $16-24, dinner $28-38; ⊙noon-2:30pm & 5:30-9pm Wed-Sat, from 11am Sun) Impeccable seasonal-regional cooking, happening bar, beautiful garden, but service sometimes misses.

Bravas Bar de Tapas TAPAS **$$$**
(☎707-433-7700; www.starkrestaurants.com/stark-restaurant/bravas-bar-de-tapas; 420 Center St; tapas $7-16, family-style large plates $28-74; ⊙11:30am-9pm Sun-Thu, to 10pm Fri & Sat) This beloved tapas restaurant is part of the distinguished Stark restaurant chain and serves up Spanish cuisine, including the ever-popular paella, on small and large plates to share. The back patio is particularly lovely on a warm evening and the vast menu includes everything from crispy pig ears to duck-meatball sliders. Good sangria too.

Mateo's Cocina Latina FUSION **$$$**
(☎707-433-1520; www.mateoscocinalatina.com; 214 Healdsburg Ave; mains lunch $12-19, dinner $14-35; ⊙11am-9pm Wed-Sun) Here the upmarket Yucatan-inspired cooking at lunch and the California-French fusion dishes in the evening integrate fine technique and all-local ingredients for standout dishes, such as daily beef cuts and *cochinita pibil* (a pork dish cooked with annatto seed), whose subtle flavors shine through the spice. The full bar showcases rare tequilas and mescals. Make reservations; request a garden table.

Self-Catering

Downtown Bakery & Creamery BAKERY **$**
(☎707-431-2719; 308a Center St; ⊙6am-5:30pm Mon-Fri, 7am-5:30pm Sat, 7am-4pm Sun) Healdsburg's classic bakery makes perfect breakfast pastries and specialty breads.

Noble Folk Ice Cream & Pie Bar DESSERTS **$**
(☎707-395-4426; www.thenoblefolk.com; 116 Matheson St; items $3-6; ⊙noon-9pm;) Hand-crafted ice cream and classic American pie, made with top-quality, all-local ingredients.

Moustache Baked Goods BAKERY **$**
(☎707-395-4111; www.moustachebakedgoods.com; 381 Healdsburg Ave; cupcakes $3.50;

(⏰11am-7pm) 🍃 Incredible locavore small-batch sweets (some gluten-free), including scrumptious cupcakes in unusual combos such as maple-bacon (available seasonally).

Shelton's Natural Foods Market MARKET, DELI **$**
(☎707-431-0530; www.sheltonsmarket.com; 428 Center St; ⏰8am-8pm) 🍃 Indie alternative for groceries and picnic supplies; reasonably priced.

Jimtown Store DELI, MARKET **$$**
(☎707-433-1212; www.jimtown.com; 6706 Hwy 128; sandwiches $8-13; ⏰7am-3pm Sun, Mon & Wed-Fri, 7:30am-4pm Sat) One of our favorite Alexander Valley stopovers, Jimtown is great for picnic supplies and sandwiches spread with housemade condiments.

Oakville Grocery DELI **$$**
(☎707-433-3200; www.oakvillegrocery.com; 124 Matheson St; sandwiches $10-15; ⏰5am-5pm) Fancy sandwiches and grab-and-go gourmet picnics. It's pricey, but the plaza-view fireside terrace is ever so fun for scouting Botox blonds, while nibbling cheese and sipping vino.

Drinking & Nightlife

Healdsburg is not a party town, but there are some good craft breweries and a new cocktail bar that stays open on weekends till (gasp!) 2am.

Bear Republic Brewing Company BREWERY
(☎707-433-2337; www.bearrepublic.com; 345 Healdsburg Ave; ⏰11am-9:30pm Sun-Thu, to 10pm Fri & Sat) Bear Republic features hand-crafted award-winning ales, non-award-winning pub grub, weekly trivia and monthly comedy nights.

Duke's Spirited Cocktails COCKTAIL BAR
(☎707-431-1060; www.healdsburgcottages.com; 111 Plaza St; ⏰4pm-midnight Sun-Thu, 4pm-2am Fri, 2pm-2am Sat) The town's new cocktail bar is as popular for its crafty libations as it is for staying open beyond midnight on weekends, which is pretty much unheard of in Healdsburg. Also the drinks have really cute names such as 'Unicorn Tears' and 'Mr Bojangles.'

Flying Goat Coffee CAFE
(www.flyinggoatcoffee.com; 324 Center St; ⏰7am-7pm) 🍃 See ya later, Starbucks. Flying Goat is what coffee should be – fair-trade and house-roasted – and locals line up for it every morning.

Entertainment

In summer free summer concerts take place each Tuesday afternoon in the plaza.

Raven Performing Arts Theater THEATER
(☎707-433-6335; www.ravenfilmcenter.com; 115 North St) Hosts concerts, events and first-run art-house films.

Shopping

One World GIFTS & SOUVENIRS
(☎707-473-0880; www.oneworldfairtrade.net; 104 Matheson St; ⏰10am-6pm, to 5:30pm Sun) 🍃 Household goods with a global outlook: alpaca shawls to Vietnamese trivets to cashmere shawls from Tibet, sourced from fair-trade collectives in 58 countries.

Copperfield's Books BOOKS
(☎707-433-9270; www.copperfieldsbooks.com; 104 Matheson St; ⏰9am-7pm Sun-Thu, to 8pm Fri & Sat) Good general-interest books.

Options Gallery CRAFTS, JEWELRY
(☎707-431-8861; www.optionsgallery.com; 126 Matheson St; ⏰10:30am-5:30pm Mon-Sat, 11am-4pm Sun) Gifts, crafts and jewelry by local artists, including lovely earrings.

Gardener GARDENS
(☎707-431-1063; www.thegardener.com; 516 Dry Creek Rd; ⏰10am-5pm) 🍃 Garden-shop lovers: don't miss this rural beauty.

Levin & Company BOOKS, MUSIC
(☎707-433-1118; 306 Center St; ⏰9am-9pm Mon-Sat, 10am-6pm Sun) Fiction and CDs; co-op art gallery.

Information

Healdsburg Chamber of Commerce & Visitors Bureau (Map p192; ☎800-648-9922, 707-433-6935; www.healdsburg.com; 217 Healdsburg Ave; ⏰10am-4pm Mon-Fri, to 3pm Sat & Sun) A block south of the plaza. Has winery maps and information on ballooning, golf, tennis, spas and nearby farms; 24-hour walk-up booth.

Getting There & Away

Sonoma County Transit (p155) buses travel around Healdsburg and connect it to neighboring cities, with prices ranging from $1.50 to $4.80 depending on how many zones you pass through on your journey. Youth prices range from $1.25 to $4.55.

Healdsburg is about an 80-minute drive north from San Francisco.

North Coast & Redwoods

Includes ➡

Best Places to Eat

- ➡ Saw Shop Bistro (p236)
- ➡ Brick & Fire (p253)
- ➡ Saucy Ukiah (p240)
- ➡ Taka's Japanese Grill (p231)
- ➡ Fishetarian Fish Market (p216)

Best Places to Sleep

- ➡ Alegria (p227)
- ➡ Philo Apple Farm Guest Cottages (p239)
- ➡ Bay Hill Mansion (p216)
- ➡ Elk Cove Inn & Spa (p224)
- ➡ Didjeridoo Dreamtime Inn (p226)

Why Go?

This is not the legendary California of the Beach Boys' song – there are no palm-flanked beaches and very few surfboards. The jagged edge of the continent is wild, scenic and even slightly foreboding, where spectral fog and an outsider spirit have fostered the world's tallest trees, most potent weed and a string of idiosyncratic two-stoplight towns. Explore hidden coves with a blanket and a bottle of local wine, scan the horizon for migrating whales and retreat at night to fire-warmed Victorians. As you travel further north, find valleys of redwood, wide rivers and mossy, overgrown forests. Expect cooler, damper weather too. Befitting this dramatic clash of land and water are its unlikely mélange of residents: timber barons and tree huggers, pot farmers and radicals of every political persuasion.

When to Go

Eureka

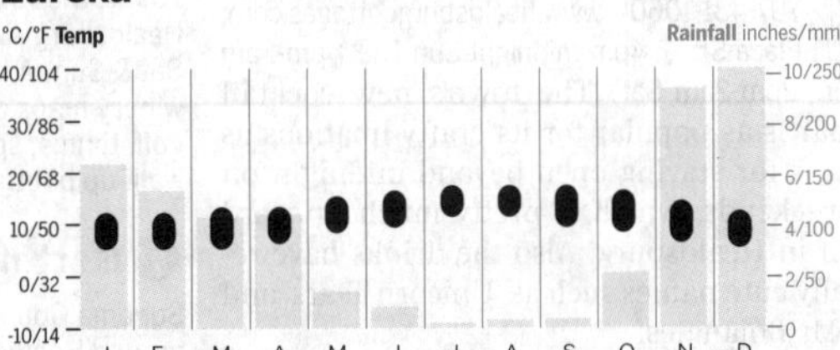

Jun–Jul The driest season in the Redwoods is spectacular for day hikes and big views.

Aug–Oct Warm weather and clear skies are the best for hiking the Lost Coast.

Dec–Apr Whales migrate off the coast. In early spring look for mothers and calves.

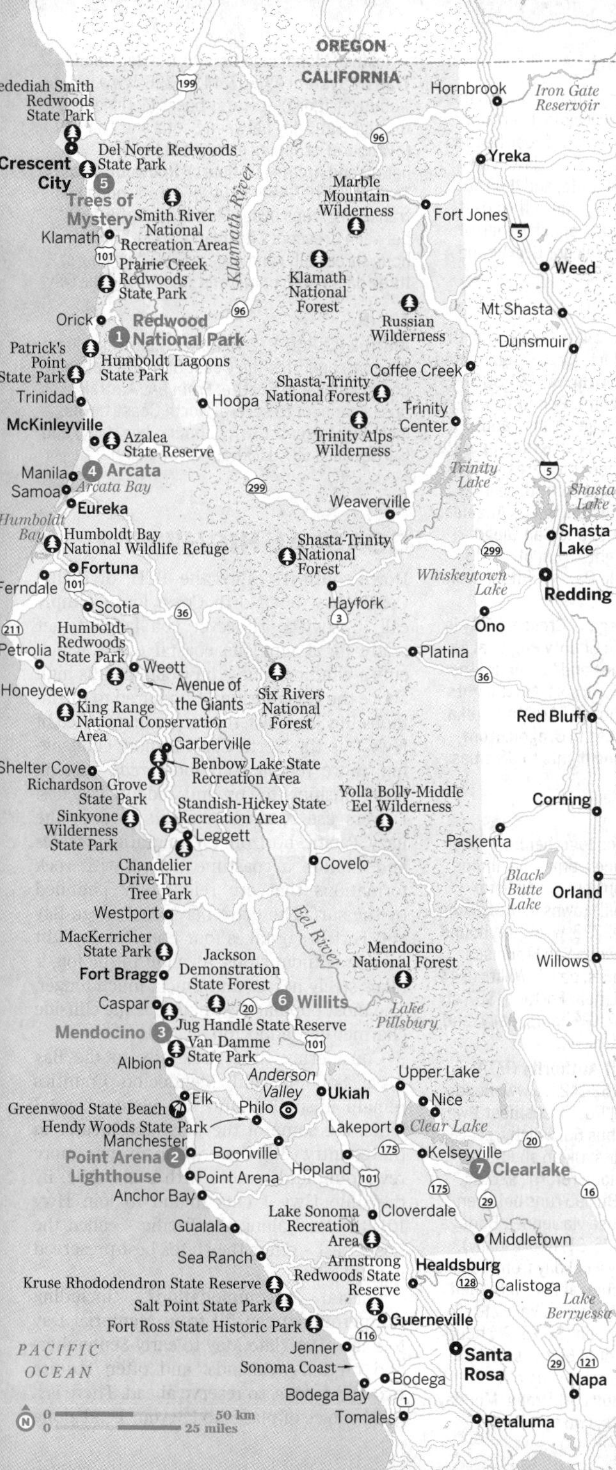

North Coast & Redwoods Highlights

1. Hiking along meandering trails of **Redwood National Park** (p261), flanked by virgin redwood forests that will give you a crick in your neck.
2. Climbing to the top of historic **Point Arena Lighthouse** (p222) for sweeping views over the extraordinary coastline.
3. Admiring the dazzle of plants and flowers at the coast-side **Mendocino Coast Botanical Gardens** (p230).
4. Sipping the samplers at brewpub **Six Rivers Brewery** (p257) near Arcata; one of the best in Northern California.
5. Indulging in some all-American roadside kitsch along Hwy 101 at **Trees of Mystery** (p264).
6. Discovering the life of early settlers via the excellent **Mendocino County Museum** (p243) in Willits.
7. Enjoying the wonderful retro experience of a drive-in movie at the classic **Lakeport Auto Movies** (p237) in Clearlake.

Getting Around

Although Hwy 1 is popular with cyclists and there are bus connections, you will almost certainly need a car to explore this region. Those headed to the far north and on a schedule should take Hwy 101, the faster, inland route, and then cut over to the coast. Windy Hwy 1 hugs the coast, then cuts inland and ends at Leggett, where it joins Hwy 101. Neither Amtrak nor Greyhound serve cities on coastal Hwy 1.

AIR

Arcata-Eureka Airport (p254) is located north of McKinleyville on the North Coast, signposted west of Hwy 101. **Alaska Airlines** (☎1-800-252-722; www.alaskaair.com), **Penair** (www.penair.com), Delta, American Airlines and United Airlines are the main carriers to operate national flights to/from here but fares tend to be high. Flights come and go from several major Californian cities, including Los Angeles, San Francisco, Sacramento and San Diego. There are also regular flights from other US cities, including New York, Denver, Phoenix and Portland (Oregon).

In the far north of the region, Crescent City is home to the tiny Del Norte County Regional Airport (p266). Alaska Airlines and Penair are the main carriers to serve this airport. Most flights contact with the nearby hubs of Arcata-Eureka Airport and Portland Airport in Oregon, from where there are connecting flights to US cities further afield.

BUS

Brave souls willing to piece together bus travel through the region will face a time-consuming headache, but connections are possible to most (but certainly not all!) towns in the region. **Greyhound** (☎800-231-2222; www.greyhound.com; 📶) runs buses between San Francisco and Ukiah ($44, three hours, daily), Willits ($44, 3½ hours, daily), Rio Dell (near Fortuna; $57, six hours, daily), Eureka ($57, 6¾ hours, daily) and Arcata ($57, seven hours, daily).

The **Mendocino Transit Authority** (MTA; ☎800-696-4682, 707-462-1422; www.mendocinotransit.org; 241 Plant Rd, Ukiah; most 1-way fares $1.50-6) operates bus 65, which travels between Fort Bragg, Willits, Ukiah and Santa Rosa daily, with an afternoon return ($26.25, three hours, four daily). Bus 95 runs between Point Arena and Santa Rosa via Jenner, Bodega Bay and Sebastopol ($8.25, 3¼ hours, daily). Bus 75 heads north every weekday from Gualala to the Navarro River junction at Hwy 128, then runs inland through the Anderson Valley to Ukiah, returning in the afternoon ($6.75, 2½ hours, daily). The North Coast route 60 goes north between Navarro River junction and Albion, Little River, Mendocino and Fort Bragg, Monday to Friday ($2.25, 1½ hours, two daily).

North of Mendocino County, the **Redwood Transit System** (☎707-443-0826; www.redwoodtransit.org) operates buses ($3) Monday through Saturday between Scotia and Trinidad (2½ hours), stopping en route at Eureka (1¼ hours) and Arcata (1½ hours). **Redwood Coast Transit** (☎707-464-9314; www.redwoodcoast-transit.org) runs buses Monday to Saturday between Crescent City, Klamath ($1.50, one hour, three daily) and Arcata ($30, two hours, three daily), with numerous stops along the way.

TRAIN

Amtrak (☎800-872-7245; www.amtrakcalifornia.com) operates the Coast Starlight between Los Angeles and Seattle. From LA, Amtrak buses connect to several North Coast towns, including Leggett ($87, 11 hours, two daily) and Garberville ($87, 11½ hours, two daily).

COASTAL HIGHWAY 1

Down south it's called the 'PCH,' or Pacific Coast Hwy, but North Coast locals simply call it 'Hwy 1.' However you label it, get ready for a fabulous coastal drive, which cuts a winding course on isolated cliffs high above the crashing surf. Compared to the famous Big Sur coast, the serpentine stretch of Hwy 1 up the North Coast is more challenging, more remote and more *real,* passing farms, fishing towns and hidden beaches. Drivers use roadside pullouts to scan the hazy Pacific horizon for migrating whales and explore a coastline dotted with rock formations that are relentlessly pounded by the surf. The drive between Bodega Bay and Fort Bragg takes four hours of daylight driving without stops. At night in the fog, it takes steely nerves and much, much longer. The most popular destination is the cliffside charmer of Mendocino.

Considering their proximity to the Bay Area, Sonoma and Mendocino Counties remain unspoiled, and the austere coastal bluffs are some of the most spectacular in the country. But the trip north gets more rewarding and remote with every mile. By the time Hwy 1 cuts inland to join Hwy 101, the land along the Pacific – called the Lost Coast – offers the state's best-preserved natural gifts.

Coastal accommodations (including campgrounds) can fill from Memorial Day to Labor Day (late May to early September) and on fall weekends, and often require two-night stays, so reserve ahead. There is a good choice of places to lay your head along the highway, although the budget conscious may find a definite lack of chain motels in these parts.

Bodega Bay

Bodega Bay is the first pearl in a string of sleepy fishing towns that line the North Coast and was the setting of Hitchcock's terrifying 1963 avian psycho-horror flick *The Birds*. The skies are free from bloodthirsty gulls today (though you'd best keep an eye on the picnic); it's Bay Area weekenders who descend en masse for extraordinary beaches, tide pools, whale-watching, fishing, surfing and seafood. Mostly a few restaurants, hotels and shops on both sides of Hwy 1, the downtown is not made for strolling, but it is a great base for exploring the endless nearby coves of the Sonoma Coast State Beach. Hwy 1 runs through town and along the east side of Bodega Bay. On the west side, a peninsula resembling a crooked finger juts out to sea, forming the entrance to Bodega Harbor.

Sights & Activities

Surfing, beachcombing and sportfishing are the main activities here – the latter requires advance booking. From December to April, the fishing boats host whale-watching trips, which are also good to book ahead. Just about everyone in town sells kites, which are great for flying at Bodega Head. The excellent **Farm Trails** (www.farmtrails.org) guide at the Sonoma Coast Visitor Center has suggestions for tours of local ranches, orchards, farms and apiaries.

Bodega Head VIEWPOINT
(Bay Flat Rd) At the peninsula's tip, Bodega Head rises 265ft above sea level. It's great for whale-watching. Landlubbers enjoy hiking above the surf, where several good trails include a 3.75-mile trek to Bodega Dunes Campground and a 2.2-mile walk to Salmon Creek Ranch. Head west from Hwy 1 onto Eastshore Rd, then turn right at the stop sign onto Bay Flat Rd.

Ren Brown Collection Gallery GALLERY
(707-875-2922; www.renbrown.com; 1781 Hwy 1; 10am-5pm Wed-Sun) The renowned collection of modern Japanese prints and California works at this small gallery is a tranquil escape from the elements. Check out the Japanese garden at the back.

Bodega Marine Laboratory & Reserve SCIENCE CENTER
(707-875-2211; www.bml.ucdavis.edu; 2099 Westshore Rd; 2-4pm Fri; P) FREE Run by University of California (UC) Davis, this spectacularly diverse teaching and research reserve surrounds the research lab, which has studied Bodega Bay since the 1920s. The 263-acre reserve hosts many marine environments, including rocky intertidal coastal areas, mudflats and sand flats, salt marsh, sand dunes and freshwater wetlands. On most Friday afternoons docents give tours of the lab and surrounds.

Chanslor Ranch HORSEBACK RIDING
(707-875-3333,707-875-2721; www.horsenaroundtrailrides.com; 2660 N Hwy 1; rides from $125; 10am-5pm) Just north of town, this friendly outfit leads horseback expeditions along the coastline and the rolling inland hills. Ron, the trip leader, is an amiable, sun-weathered cowboy straight from central casting; he recommends taking the Salmon Creek ride or calling ahead for weather-permitting moonlight rides. The 90-minute beach rides are justifiably popular.

BLOODTHIRSTY BIRDS OF BODEGA BAY

Bodega Bay has the enduring claim to fame as the setting for Alfred Hitchcock's *The Birds*. Although special effects radically altered the actual layout of the town, you still get a good feel for the supposed site of the farm owned by Mitch Brenner (played by Rod Taylor). The once-cozy Tides Wharf & Restaurant (p217), where much avian-caused havoc occurs in the movie, is still there but since 1962 it has been transformed into a vast restaurant complex. Venture 5 miles inland to the tiny town of Bodega and you'll find two icons from the film: the schoolhouse and the church. Both stand just as they did in the movie – a crow overhead may make the hair rise on your neck.

Coincidentally, right after production of *The Birds* began, a real-life bird attack occurred in Capitola, the sleepy seaside town south of Santa Cruz. Thousands of seagulls ran amok, destroying property and attacking people.

Bodega Bay Sportfishing Center FISHING, WHALE-WATCHING
(☎707-875-3495; www.bodegacharters.com; 1410b Bay Flat Rd; fishing trips $135, whale-watching adult/child $50/35;) Beside the Sandpiper Cafe, this outfit organizes full-day fishing trips and three-hour whale-watching excursions. It also sells bait, tackle and fishing licenses. Call ahead to ask about recent sightings.

Bodega Bay Surf Shack SURFING
(☎707-875-3944; www.bodegabaysurf.com; 1400 N Hwy 1, Pelican Plaza; surfboard/SUP/kayak/bike rental from $17/40/45/16) If you want to get on the water, this easygoing one-stop shop has all kinds of rentals, lessons and good local information. It also rents bikes for landlubbers.

Festivals & Events

Bodega Bay Fishermen's Festival CULTURAL
(www.bbfishfest.org; Apr) At the end of April, this festival culminates in a blessing of the fleet, a flamboyant parade of vessels, an arts-and-crafts fair, kite-flying and feasting.

Bodega Seafood, Art & Wine Festival FOOD & DRINK
(www.winecountryfestivals.com; 16855 Bodega Hwy, Watt's Ranch; 10am-6pm Sat, to 5pm Sun late Aug;) Held over a weekend in late August, this festival of food and drink brings together the best beer- and wine-makers of the area, tons of seafood and activities for kids. It takes place in the town of Bodega.

Sleeping

There's a wide spread of options – RV and tent camping, quaint motels, B&Bs and fancy hotels. Several have lovely views of the bay and all fill up early during peak seasons and at weekends. Campers should consider heading just north of town to the state-operated sites.

Doran Regional Park CAMPGROUND $
(www.parks.sonomacounty.ca.gov; 201 Doran Park Rd; tent sites $7, RV sites without hookups $32; 7am-sunset;) Watch for the sign if you are approaching town from the south. There are a few campsites here and easy access to the protected 2-mile Doran Beach, which has a boat launch and picnic areas.

Westside Regional Park CAMPGROUND $
(www.parks.sonomacounty.ca.gov; 2400 Westshore Rd; tent sites $7, RV sites without hookups $32; 7am-sunset) This park caters mainly for RVs and boaters. It has windy exposures, beaches, hot showers, fishing and boat ramps.

Chanslor Guest Ranch RANCH $$
(☎707-875-2721; www.chanslorranch.com; 2660 Hwy 1; campsites $50, r from $144) A mile north of town, this working horse ranch has rooms and options for upscale camping. Wildlife programs and guided horse tours make this one sweet place, with sweeping vistas across open grasslands to the sea.

★ **Bay Hill Mansion** B&B $$$
(☎877-468-1588; www.bayhillmansion.com; 3919 Bay Hill Rd; d $279-299;) A luxe B&B in a spacious, modern mansion. The decor is tasteful and the cleanliness and comfort standards are some of the best we've ever seen. Get a private yoga class or massage, then the helpful hosts, Kirtis and Kristopher, can direct you to the area's best spots. Views overlook trees with just a peek at the bay.

The daily breakfast is more like a brunch, with a vast selection of delicious fare on offer. Other perks include a complimentary bottle of wine on arrival, cocktails at dusk and Nespresso machines in all rooms.

Bodega Bay Lodge & Spa LODGE $$$
(☎707-875-3525; www.bodegabaylodge.com; Doran Beach Rd; r $190-470;) Bodega's plushest option, this small oceanfront resort has an ocean-view swimming pool, a golf course, a Jacuzzi and a state-of-the-art fitness club. In the evenings it hosts wine tastings. The more expensive rooms have commanding views, but all have balconies. The other pluses on-site include Bodega Bay's best spa and Drakes restaurant, which is the fanciest dining in town.

Eating & Drinking

For the old-fashioned thrill of seafood by the docks, there are several options where you can enjoy sea views, along with a simple menu of clam chowder, fried fish and coleslaw. There are also fish and produce markets in town where self-caterers can pick up supplies, and a fair range of other eateries specializing in everything from fast-food hotdogs to Tex-Mex and super-sophisticated offerings.

★ **Fishetarian Fish Market** CALIFORNIAN $
(☎707-480-9037; www.fishetarianfishmarket.com; 599 Hwy 1; mains from $12; 11am-6pm Mon-Thu & Sun, to 7pm Fri & Sat;) A fish market,

deli and great place to eat with reggae as the soundtrack, an outdoor deck near the water and an expansive menu that includes colorful and imaginative organic salads, fried tofu (or calamari) with homemade fries, oysters, fish tacos, crab cakes and a fine clam chowder. Also serves craft beers on tap and decadent desserts.

Spud Point Crab Company SEAFOOD **$**
(707-875-9472; www.spudpointcrab.com; 1860 Westshore Rd; mains $6.75-12; 9am-5pm; P) In the classic tradition of dockside crab shacks, Spud Point serves salty-sweet crab sandwiches and *real* clam chowder (that consistently wins local culinary prizes). You can also buy a crab to take home if you fancy. Eat at picnic tables overlooking the marina. Take Bay Flat Rd to get here.

Lucas Wharf Restaurant & Bar SEAFOOD **$$**
(707-875-3522; www.lucaswharfrestaurant.com; 595 Hwy 1; mains $9-28; 11:30am-9pm Mon-Fri, 11am-9:30pm Sat & Sun; P) Located right on the water, this place specializes in sophisticated seafood options, with ingredients such as roasted cherry tomatoes accompanying dishes like Dungeness crab cakes and popcorn shrimp. Founded by a family of commercial fishers, the restaurant originated as a fish market, which is now next door, together with an upmarket deli. In other words, these folks know their seafood and you can guarantee it is flapping fresh.

Tides Wharf & Restaurant SEAFOOD **$$**
(707-875-3652; www.innatthetides.com; 835 Hwy 1; breakfast $9-24, lunch $17-30, dinner $25-38; 7:30am-9:30pm Mon-Thu, 7:30am-10pm Fri, 7am-10pm Sat, 7am-9:30pm Sun; P) Enjoy a stunning view of the bay and an upscale atmosphere. Seafood is the emphasis here, but pasta and meat dishes are also available. The black-and-white pics of the Hitchcock days add to the atmosphere and, if you're lucky, you may spy seals and dolphins from the vast picture window. The desserts are outstanding.

Terrapin Creek Cafe & Restaurant CALIFORNIAN **$$**
(707-875-2700; www.terrapincreekcafe.com; 1580 Eastshore Dr; lunch mains $12-19, dinner mains $23-30; 11am-2:30pm & 4:30-9pm Thu-Sun; P) This upscale restaurant is run by a husband-wife team who espouse the slow-food movement and serve local dishes sourced from the surrounding area. Comfort-food offerings such as black cod roasted in lemongrass and coconut broth are artfully executed, while the Dungeness crab salad is fresh, briny and perfect. Jazz and warm light complete the atmosphere.

Drakes CALIFORNIAN **$$$**
(888-875-2250; www.drakesbodegabay.com; 103 Hwy 1, Bodega Bay Lodge & Spa; mains $25-28, appetizers $8-17; 7am-10pm; P) This fancy spot offers a choice of dining experiences. The Drakes Sonoma Coast Kitchen offers breakfast and dinner, the latter concentrating on such classics as pan-seared duck breast and Black Angus rib-eye steak with accompaniments like orange and almond relish and Parmesan mash. The Fireside Lounge offers a relaxed setting for lighter bites, including Pacific oysters and garlic fries.

Gourmet Au Bay WINE BAR
(707-875-9875; www.gourmetaubay.com; 1412 Bay Flat Rd; 11am-6pm Thu-Tue;) This sophisticated wine bar moved to larger premises in 2017 and now offers sophisticated snacks to accompany your tipple. Head to the spacious deck where you can enjoy a salty breeze along with your wine tasting.

Information

Sonoma Coast Visitor Center (707-875-3866; www.bodegabay.com; 850 Hwy 1; 9am-5pm Mon-Thu & Sat, to 6pm Fri, 10am-5pm Sun) Opposite the Tides Wharf. Stop by for the best help on the coast and for a copy of the *North Coaster,* a small-press indie newspaper of essays and brilliant insights on local culture.

Sonoma Coast State Beach

Stretching 17 miles north from Bodega Head to Vista Trail, 4 miles north of Jenner, the glorious Sonoma Coast State Beach is actually a series of beaches separated by several beautiful rocky headlands. Some beaches are tiny, hidden in little coves, while others stretch far and wide. Most of the beaches are connected by vista-studded coastal hiking trails that wind along the bluffs. Bring binoculars and your camera – the views are stunning, with rock outcrops, mini islands, inlets and shifting tides. During summer there can be morning fog, which generally burns off by midday. Exploring this area makes an excellent day-long adventure, but facilities are zero, so bring water and food, as well as a fully charged cell phone, in case of emergency. Also note that the surf is often too treacherous to wade, so keep a close eye on children.

Sights & Activities

Schoolhouse Beach BEACH
(btwn Bodega Bay & Jenner; P) A very pleasant beach with parking (but no other facilities); can be prone to riptides so swimmers should take care.

Goat Rock BEACH
(5400-5900 N Hwy 1, Jenner; P) Famous for its colony of harbor seals, lazing in the sun at the mouth of the Russian River. Noted for its mystical-looking rock archway, as well.

Duncan's Landing BEACH
(6947 Cliff Ave, Bodega Bay; P) Small boats unload near this rocky headland in the morning. A good place to spot wildflowers in the spring.

Shell Beach BEACH
(Shell Beach Rd, Jenner; P) Just south of the small town of Jenner, a boardwalk and trail leads out to a stretch perfect for tide-pooling and beachcombing.

Salmon Creek Beach BEACH
(3095 Hwy 1, Bodega Bay; P) Situated around a lagoon, with 2 miles of hiking and good waves for surfing.

Portuguese Beach BEACH
(btwn Bodega Bay & Jenner; P) Very easy to access; sheltered coves between rocky outcroppings.

Sleeping

Unless you are willing to hammer down tent pegs (and even that is increasingly restricted; most camping is for day-use only), you will need to base yourself in Bodega Bay or Jenner. This is no real hardship, however, as both are just a few miles away either to the south or the north.

Wright's Beach Campground CAMPGROUND $
(☎800-444-7275; www.reserveamerica.com; 7095 Hwy 1; tent & RV sites $35, day use $8; P) Of the precious few parks that allow camping along Sonoma Coast State Beach, this is the best, even though sites lack privacy and there are no hot showers. There are just 27 sites but they can be booked six months in advance, and numbers one to 12 are right on the beach. There are BBQ pits for day use and it's a perfect launch for sea kayakers.

Bodega Dunes CAMPGROUND $
(☎800-444-7275; www.reserveamerica.com; 3095 Hwy 1, Ranch Rd, Bodega Bay; tent & RV sites $35, day use $8; P) The largest campground in the Sonoma Coast State Beach system of parks with close to 100 sites; it is also closest to Bodega Bay, so it gets a lot of use. Sites are in high dunes and have hot showers, but be warned – the foghorn sounds all night.

Jenner

Perched on the hills looking out to the Pacific and above the mouth of the Russian River, tiny Jenner offers access to the coast and the Russian River wine region. A **harbor-seal colony** sits at the river's mouth and pups are born here from March to August. There are restrictions about getting too close to the chubby, adorable pups – handling them can be dangerous and cause the pups to be abandoned by their mothers. Volunteers answer questions along the roped-off area where day-trippers can look on at a distance. The best way to see them is by kayak, and most of the year you will find **Water Treks Ecotours** (☎707-865-2249; www.watertreks.com; kayak rental from $30; ⌚hours vary) renting kayaks on the highway. Heading north on Hwy 1 you will begin driving on one of the most beautiful, windy stretches of California highway. You'll also probably lose cell-phone service – possibly a blessing.

Sleeping & Eating

River's End Inn COTTAGE $$
(☎707-865-2484; www.ilovesunsets.com; 11048 Hwy 1; cottages $169-279; P) Run by the same folk who own the superb River's End Restaurant, these ocean-view cottages are wood-paneled and have no TVs, wi-fi or phones, but many do come with fireplaces, breezy decks and breathtaking ocean views, complete with harbor seals. Children under 12 years old not recommended.

★ **Café Aquatica** CAFE $
(☎707-865-2251; 10439 Hwy 1; pastries & sandwiches $4-10; ⌚8am-5pm;) This is the kind of North Coast coffee shop you've been dreaming of: fresh pastries, fog-lifting organic coffee and chatty locals. The expansive view of the Russian River from the patio and gypsy sea-hut decor make it hard to leave, especially at weekends when a strumming

guitarist adds to the California dreamin' ambience.

River's End Restaurant CALIFORNIAN **$$$**
(☎707-865-2484; www.ilovesunsets.com; 11048 Hwy 1; lunch mains $15-26, dinner mains $26-42; ⊙noon-3:30pm & 5-9pm Fri-Mon; P📶) Unwind in style at this picture-perfect restaurant, perched on a cliff overlooking the river's mouth and a grand sweep of the Pacific Ocean. It serves world-class meals at world-class prices, but the real reward is the view.

Fort Ross State Historic Park

A curious glimpse into Tsarist Russia's exploration of the California coast, the salt-washed buildings of **Fort Ross State Historic Park** (☎707-847-3437; www.fortross.org; 19005 Hwy 1; per car $8; ⊙10am-4:30pm) offer a fascinating insight into the pre-American Wild West. It's a quiet, picturesque place with a riveting past. If you pass by on a weekday when the fort is closed (due to budget cuts), you still may be able to walk down and have a peek inside if a school group is there.

In March 1812, a group of 25 Russians and 80 Alaskans (including members of the Kodiak and Aleutian tribes) built a wooden fort here, near a Kashaya Pomo village. The southernmost outpost of the 19th-century Russian fur trade on America's Pacific Coast, Fort Ross was established as a base for sea-otter hunting operations and trade with Alta California, and for growing crops for Russian settlements in Alaska. The Russians dedicated the fort in August 1812 and occupied it until 1842, when it was abandoned because the sea-otter population had been decimated and agricultural production had never taken off.

Fort Ross State Historic Park, an accurate reconstruction of the fort, is 11 miles north of Jenner on a beautiful point. The original buildings were sold, dismantled and carried off to Sutter's Fort during the gold rush. The visitor center has a great museum with historical displays and an excellent bookshop on Californian and Russian history. Ask about hikes to the Russian cemetery.

On Fort Ross Heritage Day, the last Saturday in July, costumed volunteers bring the fort's history to life; check www.parks.ca.gov or call the visitor center for other special events.

Sleeping

Stillwater Cove Regional Park CAMPGROUND **$**
(☎reservations 707-565-2267; www.sonoma-county.org/parks; 22455 N Hwy 1; tent & RV sites $28; P) Two miles north of Timber Cove, this park has hot showers and hiking under Monterey pines. Sites 1, 2, 4, 6, 9 and 10 have ocean views.

Timber Cove Inn INN **$$$**
(☎707-847-3231; www.timbercoveinn.com; 21780 N Hwy 1; r $230-350; P🐕📶) A dramatic and quirky '60s-modern seaside inn that has been refurbished into a luxury lodge. The rustic architectural shell is stunning, and a duet of tinkling piano and crackling fire fills the vast open-plan lobby. Rooms have fireplaces and balconies or terraces. Prices vary according to the views. The Coast Kitchen restaurant offers a menu of well-prepared Californian cuisine.

Even those who don't bunk here should wander agape in the shadow of Benny Bufano's 93ft peace statue, a spectacular totem on the edge of the sea.

Salt Point State Park

Stunning 6000-acre **Salt Point State Park** (☎707-847-3221; www.parks.ca.gov; 25050 Hwy 1; per car $8; ⊙park sunrise-sunset, visitor center 10am-3pm Sat & Sun Apr-Oct; P) has sandstone cliffs that drop dramatically into the kelp-strewn sea and hiking trails that crisscross windswept prairies and wooded hills, connecting pygmy forests and coastal coves rich with tidepools. The 6-mile-wide park is bisected by the **San Andreas Fault** – the rock on the east side is vastly different from that on the west. Check out the eerily beautiful tafonis (honeycombed-sandstone formations) near Gerstle Cove. For a good roadside photo op, there's a pullout at mile marker 45.

Though many of the day-use areas have been closed off due to budget cuts, trails lead off Hwy 1 pullouts to views of the pristine coastline. The platform overlooking Sentinel Rock is just a short stroll from the Fisk Mill Cove parking lot at the park's north end. Further south, seals laze at **Gerstle Cove Marine Reserve**, one of California's first underwater parks. Tread lightly around tidepools and don't lift the rocks: even a glimpse of sunlight can kill some critters. If you're here between April and June, you must see **Kruse Rhododen-**

dron State Reserve. Growing abundantly in the forest's filtered light, magnificent, pink rhododendrons reach heights of over 30ft, making them the tallest species in the world; turn east from Hwy 1 onto Kruse Ranch Rd and follow the signs. Be sure to walk the short Rhododendron Loop Trail.

Sleeping

★Ocean Cove Lodge Bar & Grill MOTEL $
(707-847-3158; www.oceancovelodge.com; 23255 Hwy 1; r from $89;) Just a few minutes south of Salt Point State Park is Ocean Cove Lodge Bar & Grill, a godsend for those on a budget. It's just a basic motel but the location is fabulous, with uninterrupted ocean views (and whale-watching) beyond the sweeping lawns and hot tub. There's a surprisingly good American-style restaurant on the premises. The owner prides himself on the homemade cinnamon rolls made daily with an added hit of chili.

Salt Point State Park Campgrounds CAMPGROUND $
(800-444-7275; www.reserveamerica.com; Salt Point State Park; tent/RV sites $25/35; P) Two campgrounds, Woodside and Gerstle Cove, both signposted off Hwy 1, have sites with cold water. Inland Woodside (closed December to March) is well protected by Monterey pines. Gerstle Cove's trees burned over a decade ago and have only grown halfway back, giving the gnarled, blackened trunks a ghostly look when the fog twirls between the branches.

Sea Ranch

Though not without its fans, the exclusive community of Sea Ranch is a sort of weather-beaten Stepford-by-the-Sea. The ritzy subdivision that sprawls 10 miles along the coast is connected with a well-watched network of private roads, with hiking trails leading to the sea and along the bluffs. Approved for construction prior to the existence of the watchdog Coastal Commission, the community was a precursor to the concept of 'slow growth,' with strict zoning laws requiring that houses be constructed of only weathered wood. Though there are some pleasant short-term rentals here, don't break any community rules – like throwing wild parties – or security will come knockin'. For supplies and gasoline, go to Gualala. North of the Sea Ranch Lodge, you'll find the iconic nondenominational chapel; an extraordinary contemporary building surrounded by meadows of grazing cattle.

Sights

Stengel Beach BEACH
(Hwy 1, Mile 53.96; 6am-sunset May-Sep, from 8am Oct-Apr; P) One of a handful of idyllic beaches on this stretch of coastline, Stengel has a large, free car park and a short access trail lined by cypress trees that takes you to a wooden staircase leading to the beach.

Walk-On Beach BEACH
(Hwy 1, Mile 56.53; parking per day $7; 6am-sunset May-Sep, from 8am Oct-Apr; P) A short trail passes through a large grove of cypress trees leading to a staircase down to the pristine quarter-mile beach; note that there is also wheelchair access. Walkers can follow the stunning Bluff Top Trail from here, which leads north to Gualala Point Regional Park.

Shell Beach BEACH
(Hwy 1, Mile 55.24; parking per day $7; 6am-sunset May-Sep, from 8am Oct-Apr; P) A lovely beach comprising two sandy coves divided by a rocky headland. You can park just south of Whale Bone Reach Rd from where there is an approximately 2-mile access trail to the beach via pine trees and meadows. Note that there are no facilities, aside from toilets at the car park.

Sleeping

Depending on the season, it can be surprisingly affordable to rent a house in Sea Ranch. There are several agencies that can assist you in finding a place, including **Rams Head Realty & Rentals** (707-884-1427; www.ramshead.com; 309000 Hwy 1; 9am-6pm) and **Sea Ranch Rentals** (707-884-4235; www.searanchrentals.com; 39200 Hwy 1; 9am-6pm), both located in the center of nearby Gualala.

Sea Ranch Lodge HOTEL $$$
(707-785-2371; www.searanchlodge.com; 60 Sea Walk Dr; r $199-369; P) A marvel of '60s-modern California architecture, timber clad Sea Ranch has spacious, minimalist rooms, many with dramatic views of the ocean; some have hot tubs and fireplaces. On the downside, Sea Ranch lodge is starting to look just a little bit dated and readers have complained about a lack of insulation which can be a problem with noisy neighbors.

Gualala & Anchor Bay

Located at the mouth of the Gualala River on the Pacific Coast, Gualala (pronounced by most locals as 'Wah-la-la') is a Native American Pomo name meaning 'where the waters flow down'. It is northern Sonoma coast's hub for a weekend getaway as it sits squarely in the middle of the 'Banana Belt,' an area known for unusually sunny weather. Founded as a prosperous lumber town in the 1860s, the downtown stretches along Hwy 1 with a bustling commercial district that has a great grocery store and some cute, slightly upscale shops.

Just north, quiet Anchor Bay is the destination of choice for many visitors seeking a tranquil stay, as it is home to some exceptional accommodation choices with a string of secluded, hard-to-find beaches situated just to the north. Both Gualala and Anchor Bay are excellent jumping-off points for exploring the surrounding area.

Sights & Activities

Seven miles north of Anchor Bay, pull off at mile marker 11.41 for **Schooner Gulch**. A trail into the forest leads down cliffs to a sandy beach with tide pools. Bear right at the fork in the trail to reach iconic **Bowling Ball Beach**, where low tide reveals rows of big, round rocks resembling bowling balls. Consult tide tables for Arena Cove. The forecast low tide must be lower than +1.5ft on the tide chart for the rocks to be visible.

Gualala Arts Center ARTS CENTER
(707-884-1138; www.gualalaarts.org; 46501 Old State Hwy, Gualala; 9am-4pm Mon-Fri, noon-4pm Sat & Sun; P) Inland along Old State Hwy, at the south end of town, and beautifully built entirely by volunteers, this center hosts changing exhibitions, organizes the **Art in the Redwoods Festival** in late August, holds a range of art classes and has loads of info on local art.

Sleeping & Eating

Of the two towns, Gualala has more services than Anchor Bay, including places to stay, and is a more practical hub for exploring – there is a bunch of good motels, plus campgrounds and a handful of inns and B&Bs.

Gualala Point Regional Park CAMPGROUND $
(707-567-2267; http://parks.sonomacounty.ca.gov; 42401 Hwy 1, Gualala; tent & RV sites $35; P) Shaded by a stand of redwoods and fragrant California bay laurel trees, a short trail connects this creek-side campground to the windswept beach. The quality of sites, including several secluded hike-in spots, makes it the best drive-in camping on this part of the coast.

Gualala River Redwood Park CAMPGROUND $
(707-884-3533; www.gualalapark.com; Gualala Rd, Gualala; day use $6, tent/RV sites $42/49; P) Another excellent Sonoma County Park. Located inland from the Old State Hwy, you can camp and do short hikes along the Gualala River.

★**St Orres Inn** INN $$
(707-884-3303; www.saintorres.com; 36601 Hwy 1, Gualala; B&B $95-135, cottages $140-445; P) Famous for its striking Russian-inspired architecture: dramatic rough-hewn timbers, stained glass and burnished-copper domes, there's no place quite like St Orres. On the property's fairy-tale-like, wild mushroom-strewn 90 acres, hand-built cottages range from rustic to luxurious. The inn's fine restaurant is worth the splurge, with inspired California cuisine in one of the coast's most romantic rooms.

North Coast Country Inn B&B $$
(707-884-4537; www.northcoastcountryinn.com; 34591 S Hwy 1, Anchor Bay; r $185-235; P) Perched on an inland hillside beneath towering trees and surrounded by lovely gardens, the perks of this adorable place begin with the gregarious owner and a hot tub. The six spacious, country-style rooms are decorated with lovely prints and boast exposed beams, fireplaces, board games and private entrances.

★**Mar Vista Cottages** CABIN $$$
(707-884-3522; www.marvistamendocino.com; 35101 Hwy 1, Anchor Bay; cottages $190-310; P) These elegantly renovated 1930s fishing cabins offer a simple, stylish seaside escape with a vanguard commitment to sustainability. The harmonious environment is the result of pitch-perfect details: linens are line-dried over lavender, guests browse the organic vegetable garden to harvest their own dinner and chickens cluck around the grounds laying the next morning's breakfast. It often requires two-night stays.

Trinks CAFE $
(☎707-884-1713; www.trinkscafe.com; 39140 Hwy 1, Gualala; snacks & sandwiches $10-15; ⏰7am-4pm Mon-Tue, Fri & Sat, to 8pm Wed & Thu, 8am-4pm Sun; P📶) Tucked into the corner of a strip of shops with a seaview terrace, the overstuffed sandwiches are great value here. Be sure to leave room for a slice of fresh fruit pie; there are generally at least four to select from. Lightweights can opt for quiche and salad, while vegetarians will rejoice over the hearty veg-filled lentil bowl.

Anchor Bay Village Market MARKET $
(☎707-884-4245; 35513 S Hwy 1, Anchor Bay; ⏰8am-7pm Mon-Sat, to 6pm Sun; P) This grocery store specializes in organic produce and products, with a superb range including baked goods and deli items.

Information

Redwood Coast Visitors Center (☎707-884-1080; www.redwoodcoastchamber.com; 39150 Hwy 1, Shoreline Hwy, Gualala; ⏰noon-5pm Thu, Fri & Sun, from 11am Sat) A well-stocked tourist office with plenty of information on the area, including a free local map.

Point Arena

This laid-back little town of less than 450 residents combines creature comforts with relaxed, eclectic California living and is the first town up the coast where the majority of residents don't seem to be retired Bay Area refugees, but are rather a young, creative bunch who tout organic food, support their local theater and sell their fair share of dream catchers. The main street is part of scenic Hwy 1, with a small harbor at one end and a clutch of small arty shops, cafes and restaurants housed in pretty Victorian-era buildings running through the center of town. Peruse the shops and restaurants then follow the sign leading to the lighthouse at the north end of Main St, or head to the docks a mile west of town at Arena Cove and watch surfers mingle with fisherfolk and locals.

Sights

★**Point Arena Lighthouse** LIGHTHOUSE
(☎707-882-2809; www.pointarenalighthouse.com; 45500 Lighthouse Rd; adult/child $7.50/1; ⏰10am-3:30pm mid-Sep–mid-May, to 4:30pm mid-May–mid-Sep; P) This 1908 lighthouse (the tallest on the US West Coast) stands 10 stories high and is the only lighthouse in California you can ascend. Check in at the museum, then climb 145 steps to the top and see the Fresnel lens and the jaw-dropping view. You can stay on-site. The turnoff is 2 miles northwest of town off Hwy 1.

Stornetta Public Lands NATURE RESERVE
(Lighthouse Rd; P) For fabulous bird-watching, hiking on terraced rock past sea caves and access to hidden coves, head 1 mile down Lighthouse Rd from Hwy 1 and look for the Bureau of Land Management (BLM) signs on the left indicating these 1132-acre public lands. The best, most dramatic walking trail leads along the coast and also begins on Lighthouse Rd from a small parking area about a quarter-mile before the lighthouse parking area.

Sleeping

Point Arena Lighthouse Lodging RENTAL HOUSE $$
(☎707-882-2809; www.pointarenalighthouse.com; 45500 Lighthouse Rd; houses $150-250; P🚭📶) True lighthouse buffs should look into staying at the plain, three-bedroom, kitchen-equipped former coast-guard homes at the lighthouse. They're quiet, windswept retreats.

Wharf Master's Inn HOTEL $$
(☎707-882-3171; www.wharfmasters.com; 785 Iversen Ave; r $129-259; P🚭📶🐾) This is a cluster of comfortable, spacious rooms on a cliff overlooking fishing boats and a stilt pier. Recently reformed, they are eminently comfortable; several sporting four-poster beds. Most of the rooms have private balconies with uninterrupted sea views.

Eating & Drinking

Franny's Cup & Saucer BAKERY $
(☎707-882-2500; www.frannyscupandsaucer.com; 213 Main St; cakes from $2; ⏰8am-4pm Wed-Sat) The cutest patisserie on this stretch of coast is run by Franny and her mother, Barbara (a veteran of Chez Panisse in Berkeley). The fresh berry tarts and creative housemade chocolates seem too beautiful to eat, until you take the first bite and immediately want to order another. Once a month they pull out all the stops for a farmhouse dinner ($28).

Arena Market ORGANIC, DELI $
(☎707-882-3663; www.arenaorganics.org; 185 Main St; soup $6.50, sandwiches $8; ⏰7am-7pm Mon-Sat, 8am-6pm Sun; P📶) 🌿 The deli at

this fully stocked organic co-op makes excellent to-go veg and gluten-free options, including sandwiches, with ingredients generally sourced from local farms. The serve-yourself soup is delicious; you can enjoy it at one of the tables out front.

Uneda CALIFORNIAN $$
(707-882-3800; www.unedaeat.com; 206 Main St; mains $16-25; 5:30-8:30pm Wed-Sat) The owners are serious about food, they travel the world sourcing recipes and have a catering business as well as a food truck. The menu changes nightly depending on what is fresh in the market that day, but is always healthy and imaginative. There are just nine tables so reserve ahead of time. Cash only.

215 Main BAR
(www.facebook.com/215Main; 215 Main St; 2pm-2am Tue-Sun) Head to this open, renovated historic building to drink local beer and wine. There's jazz on the weekends.

☆ Entertainment

Arena Theater CINEMA
(707-882-3020; www.arenatheater.org; 214 Main St) Shows mainstream, foreign and art films in a beautifully restored movie house. Sue, the ticket seller, has been in that booth for 40 years. Got a question about Point Arena? Ask Sue.

Manchester

Follow Hwy 1 north beyond Point Arena, through gorgeous rolling fields dropping down from the hills to the blue ocean, and a turnoff leads to **Manchester State Beach**, a long, wild stretch of sand. If you visit from October to April, you may spy gray and humpback whales during their annual migration. Part of the protected **Manchester State Park** (707-882-2463; www.parks.gov.ca; Kinney Rd; tent sites $25-35; P), a 111-acre camping park, the area around here is remote and beautiful, with grazing land for sheep and cattle further inland and two freshwater streams noted for their salmon and steelhead (anglers take note). The population hovers around the 200 mark so there is not much here in terms of shops and facilities (only one grocery store), but it's a quick 7-mile drive east to Point Arena with its shops, restaurants and appealing places to stay.

Based inland around 8 miles to the north and actually closer to Elk, **Ross Ranch** (707-877-1834; www.rossranch.biz; 28300 Philo Greenwood Rd; rides $50-60;) organizes two-hour rides along Manchester Beach or in nearby woodlands and forest for groups of up to 10.

Toward the ocean, **Mendocino Coast KOA** (707-882-2375; www.manchesterbeachkoa.com; 44300 Kinney Rd; tent/RV sites from $32/65, cabins $75-85; P) is an impressive private campground with tightly packed campsites beneath enormous Monterey pines, a cooking pavilion, hot showers, a hot tub, bicycles and a community campfire area. The cabins are a great option for families who want to get the camping experience without roughing it.

TOP WHALE-WATCHING SPOTS

Watch for spouts, sounding and breaching whales and pods. Anywhere coastal will do, but the following are some of the North Coast's best:

- Bodega Head (p215)
- Mendocino Headlands State Park (p226)
- Jug Handle State Natural Reserve (p229)
- MacKerricher State Park (p232)
- Shelter Cove (p248) & Lost Coast (p246)
- Trinidad Head Trail (p259)
- Klamath River Overlook (p264)

Elk

Itty-bitty Elk is famous for its stunning clifftop views of 'sea stacks,' towering rock formations jutting out of the water. Otherwise, it's one of the cutest yet gentrified-looking villages before Mendocino. There is *nothing* to do after dinner, so bring a book if you're a night owl. And you can forget about the cell phone, too; reception here is nonexistent. Elk's visitor center (p224) has exhibits on the town's logging past. At the southern end of town, **Greenwood State Beach** sits where Greenwood Creek meets the sea and marks the spot where ships used to stop when carrying timber to San Francisco and China. There are some excellent walks along the cliffs offering dramatic ocean views combined with dense woods.

Sleeping & Eating

★Elk Cove Inn & Spa INN $$$

(☎800-725-2967; www.elkcoveinn.com; 6300 S Hwy 1; r $100-375, cottages $275-355; P ⊖ ☜ 🐾) Several upmarket B&Bs take advantage of the views but you simply can't beat those from Elk Cove Inn & Spa, located on a bluff with steps leading down to the driftwood-strewn beach below. Prices in the wide selection of rooms and cottages include breakfast, wine, champagne and cocktails, plus you can relax even further at the deluxe spa.

Elk Store DELI $

(☎707-877-3544; 6101 Hwy 1, Shoreline Hwy; sandwiches from $9; ⊙9am-6pm) Make a stop here for gourmet foods, gifts, Mendocino County wines and a great deli menu with build-your-own sandwiches, burritos, bagels and wraps, and an awesomely good clam chowder.

Queenie's Roadhouse Cafe CAFE $

(☎707-877-3285; 6061 S Hwy 1, Shoreline Hwy; mains $6-10; ⊙8am-3pm Thu-Mon; ☑) Everyone swears by this excellent, retro-chic classic diner for a creative range of breakfast (try the wild-rice waffles) and lunch treats, including a great burger and Reuben sandwich.

Information

Elk Visitor Center (☎707-937-5804; www.mendoparks.org/greenwood-state-beach-elk-ca/; Greenwood State Beach; ⊙11am-1pm Sat & Sun mid-Mar–Oct; ☜) This small visitor center-cum-museum provides information about the region and also has a photographic display about the history of Elk (formerly known as Greenwood) as a lumber town in the late 1800s.

Van Damme State Park

Three miles south of Mendocino, this sprawling 1831-acre **park** (☎707-937-5804; www.parks.ca.gov; 8001 N Hwy 1, Little River; per car $8; ⊙8am-9pm; P) draws beachcombers, divers and kayakers to its easy-access beach, and hikers to its pygmy forest. The latter is a unique and precious place, where acidic soil and an impenetrable layer of hardpan have created a miniature forest of decades-old trees. The visitor center has nature exhibits and programs.

You can reach the forest on the moderate 3.5-mile **Fern Canyon Scenic Trail**, which crosses back and forth over Little River and past the Cabbage Patch, a bog of skunk cabbage that's rich with wildlife.

Two pretty **campgrounds** (☎800-444-7275; www.reserveamerica.com; 8001 Hwy 1, Little River; tent/RV sites $25/35; P 🐾) are excellent for family car camping. They both have hot showers: one is just off Hwy 1, the other is in a highland meadow, which has lots of space for kids to run around. Nine environmental campsites (tent sites $25) lie just a 1¼-mile hike up Fern Canyon; there's untreated creek water.

For sea-cave kayaking tours contact **Kayak Mendocino** (☎707-937-0700; www.kayakmendocino.com, 8001 N Hwy 1, Little River; adult/child $60/40; ⊙tours 9am, 11:30am & 2pm).

Mendocino

Leading out to a gorgeous headland, Mendocino is the North Coast's salt-washed perfect village, with B&Bs surrounded by rose gardens, white-picket fences and New England–style redwood water towers. Bay Area weekenders walk along the headland among berry bramble and wildflowers, where cypress trees stand over dizzying cliffs. The town itself is full of cute shops – no chains – and has earned the nickname 'Spendocino,' for its upscale goods.

Built by transplanted New Englanders in the 1850s, Mendocino thrived late into the 19th century, with ships transporting redwood timber from here to San Francisco. The mills shut down in the 1930s, and the town was rediscovered in the 1950s by artists and bohemians. Today the culturally savvy, politically aware, well-traveled citizens welcome visitors, but eschew corporate interlopers – don't look for a Big Mac or Starbucks. To avoid crowds, come midweek or in the low season, when the vibe is mellower – and prices more reasonable.

Sights

Mendocino is lined with all kinds of interesting galleries, which hold openings on the second Saturday of each month from 5pm to 8pm.

Kwan Tai Temple TEMPLE

(Map p225; ☎707-937-5123; www.kwantaitemple.org; 45160 Albion St; ⊙by appointment) Peering in the window of this 1852 temple reveals an old altar dedicated to the Chinese god of war. Tours are available by appointment and provide a fascinating insight into the

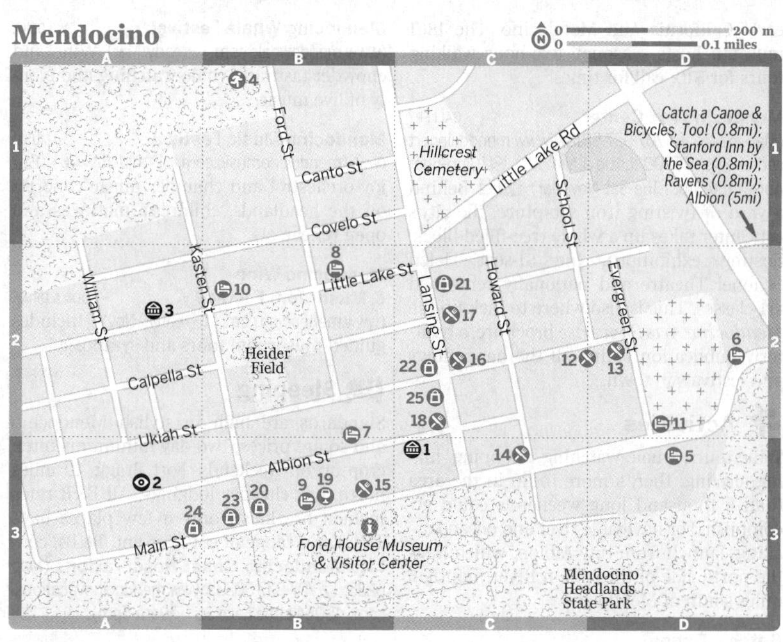

Mendocino

Sights

1 Kelley House Museum ... C3
2 Kwan Tai Temple ... A3
3 Mendocino Art Center ... A2

Activities, Courses & Tours

4 Mendocino Headlands State Park ... B1

Sleeping

5 Alegria ... D3
6 Didjeridoo Dreamtime Inn ... D2
7 MacCallum House Inn ... B2
8 Mendocino Coast Reservations ... B2
9 Mendocino Hotel ... B3
10 Packard House ... B2
11 Raku House ... D2

Eating

12 955 Ukiah Street ... C2
13 Café Beaujolais ... D2
14 Farmers Market ... C3
15 Flow ... B3
16 Frankie's ... C2
MacCallum House Restaurant ... (see 7)
17 Patterson's Pub ... C2
18 Tote Fête Deli & Burger Grill ... C2

Drinking & Nightlife

19 Dick's Place ... B3

Shopping

20 Gallery Bookshop ... B3
21 Harvest Market ... C2
22 Mendocino Chocolate Company ... C2
23 Out Of This World ... B3
24 Twist ... A3
25 Village Toy Store ... C2

history of the area's Chinese American immigrants, dating from the mid-19th century when they worked in the lumber industry.

Point Cabrillo Light Station LIGHTHOUSE
(☎707-937-6123; www.pointcabrillo.org; 45300 Lighthouse Rd; ⏰park sunrise-sunset, lighthouse 11am-4pm) FREE Restored in 1909, this stout lighthouse stands on a 300-acre wildlife preserve north of town, between Russian Gulch and Caspar Beach. Guided walks of the preserve leave at 11am on Sundays from May to September. You can also stay in the lighthouse keeper's house and cottages.

Kelley House Museum MUSEUM
(Map p225; ☎707-937-5791; www.mendocinohistory.org; 45007 Albion St; $2; ⏰11am-3pm Thu-Tue Jun-Sep, Fri-Mon Oct-May) Check out the research library and changing exhibits on

early California and Mendocino. The 1861 museum hosts seasonal, two-hour walking tours for $10; call for times.

Mendocino Art Center GALLERY
(Map p225; 707-937-5818; www.mendocinoartcenter.org; 45200 Little Lake St; 10am-5pm Apr-Oct, to 4pm Tue-Sat Nov-Mar) FREE Behind a yard of twisting iron sculpture, the city's art center takes up a whole tree-filled block, hosting exhibitions, the 81-seat Helen Schonei Theatre and nationally renowned art classes. This is also where to pick up the *Mendocino Arts Showcase* brochure, a quarterly publication listing all the happenings and festivals in town.

Activities

Wine tours, whale-watching, shopping, hiking, cycling: there's more to do in the area than a thousand long weekends could accomplish. For navigable river and ocean kayaking, launch from tiny Albion, which hugs the north side of the Albion River mouth, 5 miles south of Mendocino.

Catch a Canoe & Bicycles, Too! CANOEING, CYCLING
(707-937-0273; www.catchacanoe.com; 44850 Comptche-Ukiah Rd, Stanford Inn by the Sea; 3hr kayak, canoe or bicycle rental adult/child $28/14; 9am-5pm;) This friendly outfit rents bikes, kayaks and canoes (including redwood outriggers) for trips up the 8-mile Big River tidal estuary. Northern California's longest undeveloped estuary has no highways or buildings, only beaches, forests, marshes, streams, abundant wildlife and historic logging sites. Bring a picnic and a camera to enjoy the ramshackle remnants of century-old train trestles and majestic blue herons.

Mendocino Headlands State Park HIKING
(Map p225; 707-937-5804; www.parks.ca.gov; Ford St) FREE Mendocino Headlands State Park surrounds the village, where trails crisscross bluffs and rocky coves. Ask at the visitor center (p229) about guided weekend walks, including spring wildflower explorations and whale-watching jaunts.

Festivals & Events

For a complete list of Mendocino's many festivals, check with the visitor center or www.gomendo.com.

Mendocino Whale Festival WILDLIFE
(www.mendowhale.com; early Mar) Wine and chowder tastings, whale-watching and plenty of live music.

Mendocino Music Festival MUSIC
(www.mendocinomusic.com; mid-Jul;) Enjoy orchestral and chamber music concerts on the headlands, children's matinees and open rehearsals.

Mendocino Wine & Mushroom Festival FOOD & DRINK
(www.mendocino.com; early Nov) Includes guided mushroom tours and symposia.

Sleeping

Standards are high in stylish Mendocino and so are prices; two-day minimums often crop up on weekends. Fort Bragg, 10 miles north, has cheaper lodgings. All B&B rates include breakfast; only a few places have TVs. For a range of cottages and B&Bs, contact **Mendocino Coast Reservations** (Map p225; 707-937-5033; www.mendocinovacations.com; 45084 Little Lake St; 9am-5pm).

Russian Gulch State Park CAMPGROUND $
(reservations 800-444-7275; www.reserveamerica.com; tent & RV sites $35; P) In a wooded canyon 2 miles north of town, with secluded drive-in sites, hot showers, a small waterfall and the Devil's Punch Bowl (a collapsed sea arch).

★ **Didjeridoo Dreamtime Inn** B&B $$
(Map p225; 707-937-6200; www.didjeridooinn.com; 44860 Main St; r $112-160;) One of the town's more economical choices, rooms here are all different yet share the same homey, unpretentious atmosphere with tasteful artwork, antiques and parquet flooring. Several rooms have en suites, and a couple have mini hot tubs. The breakfast spread is excellent and on Sunday you are treated to some soothing live music. The front garden is a lovely place to sit.

MacCallum House Inn B&B $$
(Map p225; 707-937-0289; www.maccallumhouse.com; 45020 Albion St; r & cottages from $149, water-tower ste $259-359; P@) One of the finest B&B options in town with gardens in a riot of color. There are cheerful cottages, and a modern luxury home, but the most memorable space is within one of Mendocino's iconic, historic water towers – living quarters fill the ground floor, a sauna

is on the 2nd and there's a view of the coast from the top.

Andiron Seaside Inn & Cabins CABIN $$
(☎707-937-1543; http://theandiron.com; 6051 N Hwy 1, Little River; d $109-299;) Styled with hip vintage decor, this cluster of 1950s roadside cottages is a refreshingly playful option amid the cabbage-rose and lace aesthetic of Mendocino. Each cabin houses two rooms with complementing themes: 'Read' has old books, comfy vintage chairs and retro eyeglasses, while the adjoining 'Write' features a huge chalkboard and a ribbon typewriter.

Lighthouse Inn at Point Cabrillo B&B $$
(☎707-937-6124; www.pointcabrillo.org; Point Cabrillo Dr; cottages from $132, houses from $450;) On 300 acres, in the shadow of Point Cabrillo lighthouse, the stately lightkeeper's and assistant lightkeeper's houses, together with the staff's two turn-of-the-century cottages have been revamped into vacation rentals. All options have verandas and lush period decor but are not very private.

Packard House B&B $$
(Map p225; ☎707-937-2677; www.packardhouse.com; 45170 Little Lake St; r $175-225;) Decked out in contemporary style, this place is Mendocino's most chic and sleek B&B choice, with beautiful fabrics, colorful minimalist paintings and limestone bathrooms.

★**Alegria** B&B $$$
(Map p225; ☎707-937-5150; www.oceanfrontmagic.com; 44781 Main St; r $239-299;) A perfect romantic hideaway, beds have views over the coast, decks have ocean views and all rooms have wood-burning fireplaces; outside, a gorgeous path leads to a big, amber-gray beach. Ever-so-friendly innkeepers whip up amazing breakfasts served in the sea-view dining area. Less-expensive rooms are available across the street at bright and simple **Raku House** (Map p225; ☎800-780-7905; 998 Main St; r $109-139;).

★**Stanford Inn by the Sea** INN $$$
(☎707-937-5615; www.stanfordinn.com; 44850 Comptche-Ukiah Rd; r $211-299;) This masterpiece of a lodge standing on 10 lush acres has wood-burning fireplaces, knotty-pine walls, original art, stereos and top-quality mattresses in every room. Take a stroll in the organic gardens, where they harvest food for the excellent on-site restaurant, and a dip in the solarium-enclosed pool and hot tub, and it's a sublime getaway.

Brewery Gulch Inn B&B $$$
(☎707-937-4752; www.brewerygulchinn.com; 9401 N Hwy 1; d $245-495;) Just south of Mendocino, this bright, woodsy place has 10 modern rooms (all with flat-screen televisions, gas fireplaces and spa bathtubs), and guests enjoy touches like feather beds and leather reading chairs. The hosts pour heavily at the complimentary wine hour and leave out sweets for midnight snacking. Made-to-order breakfast is served in a small dining room overlooking the distant water.

Glendeven B&B $$$
(☎707-937-0083; www.glendeven.com; 8205 Hwy 1, Shoreline Hwy; r $216-280;) This historic 1860s estate 2 miles south of town has organic gardens, grazing llamas (with daily feedings at dusk), chickens for those breakfast eggs, forest and oceanside trails and a wine bar serving only Mendocino wines – and that's just the start. Romantic rooms have neutral tones, soothing decor, fireplaces and top-notch linens. Farm-to-table dinners are available at the bistro.

Eating

With quality to rival Napa Valley, the influx of Bay Area weekenders has fostered an excellent dining scene that enthusiastically espouses organic, sustainable principles. Make reservations. Gathering picnic supplies is easy at Harvest Market (p229) organic grocery store (with deli) and the **farmers market** (Map p225; cnr Howard & Main St; noon-2pm Fri May-Oct).

Tote Fête Deli & Burger Grill BURGERS $
(Map p225; ☎707-937-3383; 10450 Lansing St; burgers $9-15, mains $12-15; 11:30am-7:30pm Mon, Tue & Thu-Sat, to 5pm Sun) Dine in or take away at this serious burger place with its all-natural, grass-fed beef and 11 choices, including veggie and portobello-mushroom options. Also on the menu are seafood dishes, such as fish tacos, calamari and coconut shrimp, plus steaks, gourmet salads and sandwiches. The atmosphere is laid back; this is not the place for a romantic dinner.

Frankie's PIZZA $
(Map p225; ☎707-937-2436; www.frankiesmendocino.com; cnr Ukiah & Lansing Sts; pizza $13-16; 11am-9pm;) There is no Sicilian-style simplicity to these pizzas, they are

pure Californian with piled-high organic ingredients such as cremini mushrooms, Canadian bacon, roasted red peppers and pineapple (not combined, fortunately). It also serves healthy fare such as quinoa kale cakes and gluten-free falafel, plus soups, salads and Fort Bragg's famous Cowlick's ice cream.

Flow CALIFORNIAN $$
(Map p225; ☎707-937-3569; www.mendocinoflow.com; 45040 Main St; mains $14-20; ⏲8am-10pm; 📶🌱) Run by the Mendocino Cafe, this very busy place has the best views of the ocean in town from its 2nd-story perch. Brunch is a specialty as are Mexican-inspired small plates, artisan pizzas and a sublime local Dungeness crab chowder. Gluten-free and vegan options are available.

Ledford House MEDITERRANEAN $$
(☎707-937-0282; www.ledfordhouse.com; 3000 N Hwy 1, Albion; mains $14-30; ⏲5-8pm Wed-Sun; P) Watch the water pound the rocks and the sun set out of the Mendocino hubbub (8 miles south) at this friendly Cal-Med bistro. Try the cassoulet or the gnocchi. It's a local hangout and gets hoppin' with live jazz most nights.

Patterson's Pub PUB FOOD $$
(Map p225; www.pattersonspub.com; 10485 Lansing St; mains $13-16; ⏲10am-midnight, food to 11pm) If you pull into town late and hungry, you'll thank your lucky stars for this place; it serves quality pub grub – fish and chips, burgers and dinner salads – with cold beer. The only traditional Irish pub ambience spoiler is the plethora of flat-screen TVs. A busy brunch is served on Saturday and Sunday mornings from 10am to 2pm.

★**Café Beaujolais** CALIFORNIAN $$$
(Map p225; ☎707-937-5614; www.cafebeaujolais.com; 961 Ukiah St; lunch mains $10-18, dinner mains $23-38; ⏲11:30am-2:30pm Wed-Sun, dinner from 5:30pm daily; P) 🌿 Mendocino's iconic, beloved country-Cal-French restaurant occupies an 1893 farmhouse restyled into a monochromatic urban-chic dining room, perfect for holding hands by candlelight. The refined, inspired cooking draws diners from San Francisco, who make this the centerpiece of their trip. The locally sourced menu changes with the seasons, but the Petaluma duck confit is a gourmand's delight.

955 Ukiah Street CALIFORNIAN $$$
(Map p225; ☎707-937-1955; www.955restaurant.com; 955 Ukiah St; mains $18-37; ⏲from 6pm Thu-Sun) One of those semi-secret institutions, the menu here changes with what's available locally. When we visited, that meant wondrous things such as a roasted cauliflower, feta and caramelized-onion appetizer. The dimly lit, bohemian setting overlooks rambling gardens. Check the website for the excellent-value, three-course meal with wine for $25 every Thursday, and other events.

Don't miss the paintings by Emmy Lou Packard, who lived round the corner during the '60s and was famously both a communist and an assistant to Mexican painter and muralist, Diego Rivera.

MacCallum House Restaurant CALIFORNIAN $$$
(Map p225; ☎707-937-0289; www.maccallumhouse.com; 45020 Albion St; cafe dishes $12-18, mains $25-42; ⏲8:15-10am Mon-Fri, to 11am Sat & Sun, plus 5:30-9pm daily; P) 🌿 Sit on the veranda or fireside for a romantic dinner of all-organic game, fish or risotto primavera. Chef Alan Kantor makes *everything* from scratch and his commitment to sustainability and organic ingredients is nearly as visionary as his menu. The cafe menu, served at the Grey Whale Bar, is one of Mendocino's few four-star bargains.

Ravens CALIFORNIAN $$$
(☎707-937-5615; www.ravensrestaurant.com; Stanford Inn by the Sea, Comptche-Ukiah Rd; breakfast $11-15, mains $24-30; ⏲8am-10pm; P🌱) 🌿 Ravens brings haute-contemporary concepts to a completely vegetarian and vegan menu. Produce comes from the idyllic organic gardens of the Stanford Inn by the Sea (p227) and the bold menu takes on everything from sea-palm strudel and portabella sliders to decadent (guilt-free) desserts.

🍷 Drinking & Nightlife

Have cocktails at the **Mendocino Hotel** (Map p225; ☎707-937-0511; www.mendocinohotel.com; 45080 Main St; P🐾📶) or the Grey Whale Bar at the MacCallum House Inn (p226). For boisterousness and beer head straight to Patterson's Pub.

Dick's Place BAR
(Map p225; ☎707-937-6010; 45080 Main St; ⏲11:30am-2am) A bit out of place among the fancy-pants shops downtown, but an

excellent spot to check out the *other* Mendocino and do shots with rowdy locals. And don't miss the retro experience of dropping 50¢ in the jukebox to hear that favorite tune.

Shopping

Mendocino's walkable streets are great for shopping, and the ban on chain stores ensures unique, often upscale gifts. There are many small galleries in town where one-of-a-kind artwork is for sale.

Twist CLOTHING
(Map p225; 707-937-1717; www.mendocinotwist.com; 45140 Main St; 11am-5pm Mon-Fri, 10:30am-5:30pm Sat & Sun) Twist stocks eco-friendly, natural-fiber clothing and lots of locally made clothing and toys.

Mendocino Chocolate Company CHOCOLATE
(Map p225; 800-722-1107; www.mendocino-chocolate.com; 10466 Lansing St; 10am-5:30pm) This company has been around for 30 years in Fort Bragg, so it know its cocoa beans. This newer second outlet adds a sweet touch to Mendocino's shopping scene. Check out the exquisite handmade seashells in marbled white, milk and dark chocolate.

Harvest Market FOOD & DRINK
(Map p225; 707-937-5879; www.harvestmarket.com; 10501 Lansing St; 7:30am-10pm) The town's biggest grocery store has legit organic credentials, an excellent cold-food bar and great cheese and meat.

Village Toy Store TOYS
(Map p225; 707-937-4633; www.mendotoystore.com; 10450 Lansing St; 10am-6pm) Get a kite or browse the old-world selection of wooden toys and games that you won't find in the chains – hardly anything requires batteries.

Gallery Bookshop BOOKS
(Map p225; 707-937-2665; www.gallerybookshop.com; 319 Kasten St; 9:30am-6pm) Stocks a great selection of books on local topics, titles from California's small presses and specialized outdoor guides.

Out of This World SPORTS & OUTDOORS
(Map p225; 707-937-3335; www.outofthisworldshop.com; 45100 Main St; 10am-5:30pm) Birders, astronomy buffs and science geeks head directly to this telescope, binocular and science-toy shop.

Information

Ford House Museum & Visitor Center (Map p225; 707-537-5397; www.mendoparks.org; 45035 Main St; 11am-4pm) Enjoy maps, books, information and exhibits, including a scale model of 1890 Mendocino, plus a historical setting with original Victorian-period furniture and decor.

Jug Handle State Reserve

Between Mendocino and Fort Bragg, **Jug Handle** (707-937-5804; www.parks.ca.gov; Hwy 1, Caspar; sunrise-sunset;) FREE preserves an **ecological staircase** that you can view on a 5-mile (round-trip) self-guided nature trail. The reserve is also a good spot to stroll the headlands, whale-watch or lounge on the beach; you can pick up a printed guide detailing the area's geology, flora and fauna from the parking lot. Note that it's easy to miss the entrance; watch for the turnoff, just north of Caspar.

Five wave-cut terraces ascend in steps from the seashore, each 100ft and 100,000 years removed from the previous one, and each with its own distinct geology and vegetation. One of the terraces has a **pygmy forest**, similar to the better known example at Van Damme State Park, 9 miles south.

Jug Handle Creek Farm & Nature Center (707-964-4630; www.jughandlecreekfarm.com; 15501 N Hwy 1; tent sites $14, r & cabins adult/student $45/38; 9am-8pm;) is a nonprofit 39-acre farm with rustic cabins and hostel rooms in a 19th-century farmhouse. Call ahead about work-stay discounts. Drive 5 miles north of Mendocino to Caspar; the farm is on the east side of Hwy 1. Take the second driveway after Fern Creek Rd.

Fort Bragg

In the past, Fort Bragg was Mendocino's ugly stepsister, home to a lumber mill, a scrappy downtown and blue-collar locals who gave a cold welcome to outsiders. Since the mill closure in 2002, the town has started to reinvent itself, slowly warming to a tourism-based economy, with the downtown continuing to develop as a wonderfully unpretentious alternative to Mendocino (even if the southern end of town is hideous). Unlike the *entire* franchise-free 180-mile stretch of Coastal Hwy 1 between here and the Golden Gate, in Fort Bragg you can get a

Big Mac, grande latte or any of a number of chain-store products whose buildings blight the landscape. Don't fret. In downtown you'll find better hamburgers and coffee, old-school architecture and residents eager to show off their little town.

By car, twisting Hwy 20 provides the main access to Fort Bragg from the east, and most facilities are near Main St, a 2-mile stretch of Hwy 1. The Mendocino Transit Authority (p214) operates bus 65, which travels between Fort Bragg, Willits, Ukiah and Santa Rosa daily, with an afternoon return ($23, three hours, four daily). Monday to Friday, the North Coast route 60 goes north between Navarro River junction and Albion, Little River, Mendocino and Fort Bragg ($2.25, 1½ hours, two daily).

Sights & Activities

Fort Bragg has the same banner North Coast activities as Mendocino – beachcombing, surfing, hiking – but basing yourself here is much cheaper and arguably less quaint and pretentious. The wharf lies at Noyo Harbor – the mouth of the Noyo River – south of downtown. Here you can find whale-watching cruises and deep-sea fishing trips.

★Mendocino Coast Botanical Gardens GARDENS
(707-964-4352; www.gardenbythesea.org; 18220 N Hwy 1; adult/child/senior $14/5/10; 9am-5pm Mar-Oct, to 4pm Nov-Feb; P) This gem of Northern California displays native flora, rhododendrons and heritage roses. The succulent display alone is amazing and the organic garden is harvested by volunteers to feed area residents in need. The serpentine paths wander along 47 seafront acres south of town. Primary trails are wheelchair accessible.

Northcoast Artists Gallery GALLERY
(www.northcoastartists.org; 362 N Main St; 10am-6pm) An excellent local arts cooperative where 20 full-time members work in photography, glass, woodworking, jewelry, painting, sculpture, textiles and printmaking. Openings are on the first Friday of the month. Visit www.mendocino.com for a comprehensive list of galleries throughout Mendocino County.

Glass Beach BEACH
(Elm St) Named for (what's left of) the sea-polished glass in the sand, remnants of its days as a city dump, this beach is now part of MacKerricher State Park (p232). Take the headlands trail from Elm St, off Main St, but leave the glass – visitors are not supposed to pocket souvenirs.

Triangle Tattoo & Museum MUSEUM
(707-964-8814; www.triangletattoo.com; 356b N Main St; noon-7pm) FREE This one-off museum has an excellent exhibition of international tattoo art and explains the history in various cultures. You can also get a tattoo done here if you fancy.

★Skunk Train HISTORIC TRAIN
(707-964-6371; www.skunktrain.com; 100 W Laurel St; adult/child $84/42; 9am-3pm;) Fort Bragg's pride and joy, the vintage train got its nickname in 1925 for its stinky gas-powered steam engines, but today the historic steam and diesel locomotives are odorless. Passing through redwood-forested mountains, along rivers, over bridges and through deep mountain tunnels, the trains run from both Fort Bragg and Willits (p243) to the midway point of Northspur, where they turn around.

If you want to go to Willits, plan to spend the night. The depot is downtown at the foot of Laurel St, one block west of Main St.

All-Aboard Adventures FISHING, WHALE-WATCHING
(707-964-1881; www.allaboardadventures.com; 32400 N Harbor Dr; fishing trips $80, whale-watching $40) Captain Tim leads five-hour crabbing and salmon-fishing trips and two-hour whale-watching explorations during the whale migration.

Festivals & Events

Fort Bragg Whale Festival WILDLIFE
(www.mendowhale.com; Mar) Held on the third weekend in March, with microbrew tastings, crafts fairs and whale-watching trips.

Paul Bunyan Days CARNIVAL
(www.paulbunyandays.com; Sep) Held on Labor Day weekend in September, celebrate California's logging history with a logging show, square dancing, parade and fair.

Sleeping

Fort Bragg's lodging is cheaper than Mendocino's, but most of the motels along noisy Hwy 1 don't have air-conditioning, so you'll hear traffic through your windows. The best of the motel bunch is **Colombi Motel** (707-

964-5773; www.colombimotel.com; 647 E Oak St; 1-/2-bedroom units with kitchenette from $80/85;), which is in town. Most B&Bs do not have TVs and they all include breakfast.

Country Inn B&B $$
(707-964-3737; www.beourguests.com; 632 N Main St; r $125-170;) This gingerbread-trimmed B&B in the middle of town is an excellent way to dodge the chain motels for a good-value stay. The lovely family hosts are welcoming and easygoing and can offer good local tips. Breakfast can be delivered to your room and at night you can soak in a hot tub out back. There is a minimum two-night stay at weekends.

Grey Whale Inn B&B $$
(707-964-0640; www.greywhaleinn.com; 615 N Main St; r $110-172;) Situated in a historic (some say haunted!) building and former hospital on the north side of town (walking distance from downtown and glass beach), this comfortable, family-run inn has simple, straightforward rooms that are good value for families. Expect a warm welcome, especially from Sweetpea, the resident cat.

Shoreline Cottages MOTEL, COTTAGE $$
(707-964-2977; www.shoreline-cottage.com; 18725 Hwy 1; d $129-149;) Low-key, four-person rooms and cottages with kitchens surround a central, tree-filled lawn. The family rooms are a good bargain, and suites feature modern artwork and clean sight lines. All rooms have microwaves, cable TV, snacks and access to a library of DVDs, plus there's a communal hot tub.

Weller House Inn B&B $$$
(707-964-4415; www.wellerhouse.com; 524 Stewart St; r $200-310;) Rooms in this beautifully restored 1886 mansion have down comforters, underfloor heating, good mattresses and fine linens. The water tower is the tallest structure in town – and it has a hot tub at the top! Breakfast is in the massive redwood ballroom.

Eating

Similar to the lodging scene, the food in Fort Bragg is less spendy than Mendocino, but there are a number of truly excellent options, mainly located on or around Main St. Self-caterers should try the farmers market (p232) downtown or the **Harvest Market** (707-964-7000; cnr Hwys 1 & 20; 5am-11pm) for the best groceries.

★**Taka's Japanese Grill** JAPANESE $
(707-964-5204; 250 N Main St; mains $10.50-17; 11:30am-3pm & 4:30-9pm;) Although it may look fairly run of the mill, this is an exceptional Japanese restaurant. The owner is a former grader at the Tokyo fish market so the quality is tops and he makes a weekly run to San Francisco to source freshly imported seafood. Sushi, teriyaki dishes, noodle soups and pan-fried noodles with salmon, beef or chicken are just a few of the options.

Los Gallitos MEXICAN $
(707-964-4519; 130 S Main St; burritos $5.50-6.50; 11am-8pm Mon-Sat, from 10am Sun) A packed hole-in-the-wall that serves the best Mexican on the coast. Chips are homemade, the guacamole is chunky and the dishes, from the fresh fish tacos to homemade pork tamales and generous soups, are consistently flavorful and well beyond the standard glob of refried beans. It's located across the parking lot from the CVS.

Cowlick's Handmade Ice Cream ICE CREAM $
(707-962-9271; www.cowlicksicecream.com; 250b N Main St; scoops from $1.85; 11am-9pm) Just great ice cream in fun flavors, from classics such as mocha almond fudge to the very unusual, such as candy cap mushroom (tastes like maple syrup but better), ginger or blackberry chocolate chunk. The sorbets (try the grapefruit Campari) are also delish.

Headlands Coffeehouse CAFE $
(707-964-1987; www.headlandscoffeehouse.com; 120 E Laurel St; mains $4-8; 7am-10pm Mon-Sat, to 7pm Sun;) The town's best cafe is in the middle of the historic downtown, with high ceilings and lots of atmosphere. The menu gets raves for the Belgian waffles, homemade soups, veggie-friendly salads, panini and lasagna.

Silver's at the Wharf CALIFORNIAN $
(707-964-4283; www.silversatthewharf.com; 32260 N Harbor Dr; mains $10-15; 11am-9:30pm;) Given its position, overlooking the docks, you would expect this to be a swanky oysters-and-champagne sort of place. Far from it. The decor is stuck in the '60s and the cuisine is well prepared but solidly traditional, with a vast selection that includes pasta, rib-eye steak, Mexican fare and seafood, such as Pacific

NORTH COAST BEER TOUR

The craft breweries of the North Coast don't mess around – bold hop profiles, Belgian-style ales and smooth lagers are regional specialties, and they're produced with style. Some breweries are better than others, but the following tour makes for an excellent long weekend of beer tasting in the region.

Anderson Valley Brewing Company (p237), Boonville

North Coast Brewing Company (p232), Fort Bragg

Six Rivers Brewery (p257), near Arcata

Eel River Brewing (p250), Fortuna

Bay shrimp and calamari steak. Ideal for families.

Farmers Market MARKET **$**
(cnr E Laurel & N Franklin Sts; 3:30-6pm Wed May-Oct) This is an above-average farmers market with an excellent array of fresh produce, plus breads, preserves and locally produced cheese.

★**Piaci Pub & Pizzeria** ITALIAN **$$**
(707-961-1133; www.piacipizza.com; 120 W Redwood Ave; mains $8-20; 11am-9:30pm Mon-Thu, to 10pm Fri & Sat, 4-9:30pm Sun) Fort Bragg's must-visit pizzeria is known for its sophisticated wood-fired, brick-oven pizzas as much as for its long list of microbrews. Try the 'Gustoso' – with chèvre, pesto and seasonal pears, all carefully orchestrated on a thin crust. It's tiny, loud and fun, with much more of a bar atmosphere than a restaurant. Expect to wait at peak times.

North Coast Brewing Company AMERICAN **$$**
(707-964-2739; www.northcoastbrewing.com; 455 N Main St; mains $17-25; restaurant 4-10pm Sun-Thu, to 11pm Fri & Sat, bar from 2pm daily;) Though thick, rare slabs of steak and a list of specials demonstrate that they take the food as seriously as the bevvies, it's the burgers and garlic fries that soak up the fantastic selection of handcrafted brews. A great stop for serious beer lovers.

★**Cucina Verona** ITALIAN **$$$**
(707-964-6844; www.cucinaverona.com; 124 E Laurel St; mains $26-30; 9am-9pm) A real-deal Italian restaurant with no-fail traditional dishes, plus a few with a Californian tweak, such as butternut-squash lasagne and artichoke bruschetta. The atmosphere is as comforting as the cuisine, with dim lighting, a warm color scheme and unobtrusive live music most evenings. There is an extensive microbrewery selection on offer, as well as local and imported wines.

☆ Entertainment

Gloriana Musical Theater THEATER
(Eagles Hall Theater; 707-964-7469; www.gloriana.org; 210 N Corry St; tickets from $12; hours vary) Since 1976 this company has been staging high-standard musical theater and operettas.

Shopping

There's plenty of window-shopping in Fort Bragg's compact downtown, including a string of antique shops along Franklin St.

Fractalize Eco Boutique FASHION & ACCESSORIES
(707-672-2208; www.fractalizeecoboutique.com; 107 E Laurel St; 11am-5pm Wed-Sun) Sells a fabulous array of women's fashions in rich earth colors made with all-natural fabrics, including hemp and bamboo.

Outdoor Store SPORTS & OUTDOORS
(707-964-1407; www.mendooutdoors.com; 247 N Main St; 10am-5:30pm Mon-Sat, to 5pm Sun) If you're planning on camping on the coast or exploring the Lost Coast, this is the best outfitter in the region, stocking detailed maps of the region's wilderness areas, fuel for stoves and high-quality gear.

Information

Fort Bragg-Mendocino Coast Chamber of Commerce (707-961-6300; www.mendocinocoast.com; 332 S Main St; 10am-5pm Mon-Fri, to 3pm Sat;) The chamber of commerce has lots of helpful information about this stretch of coast and what's on. Its online guide is also worth checking out.

MacKerricher State Park

Three miles north of Fort Bragg, the **MacKerricher State Park** (707-964-9112; www.parks.ca.gov) preserves 9 miles of pristine rocky headlands, sandy beaches, dunes and tidepools.

The visitor center sits next to the whale skeleton at the park entrance. Hike the

Coastal Trail along dark-sand beaches and see rare and endangered plant species. **Lake Cleone** is a 30-acre freshwater lake stocked with trout and visited by over 90 species of birds. At nearby **Laguna Point** an interpretive boardwalk (accessible to visitors with disabilities) overlooks harbor seals and, from December to April, migrating whales. **Ricochet Ridge Ranch** (707-964-7669; www.horse-vacation.com; 24201 N Hwy 1; per hr/day $60/330; 9am-6:30pm) offers horseback-riding trips through redwoods or along the beach.

Just north of the park is **Pacific Star Winery** (707-964-1155; www.pacificstarwinery.com; 33000 Hwy 1; tastings $5; noon-5pm Thu-Mon), in a dramatic, rub-your-eyes-in-disbelief-beautiful location on a bluff over the sea. The wines don't get pros excited but they are very drinkable, the owners are friendly and you're encouraged to picnic at one of the many coast-side tables, stroll some of the short coastal trails along the cliffs and generally enjoy yourself (which isn't hard).

Popular **campgrounds** (800-444-2725; www.reserveamerica.com; tent & RV sites $35), nestled in pine forest, have hot showers and water; the first-choice reservable tent sites are numbers 21 to 59. Ten superb, secluded walk-in tent sites (numbers 1 to 10) are first-come, first-served.

Westport

If sleepy Westport feels like the peaceful edge of nowhere, that's because it is. The last hamlet before the Lost Coast, on a twisting 15-mile drive north of Fort Bragg, it is the last town before Hwy 1 veers inland on the 22-mile ascent to meet Hwy 101 in Leggett. The population here is around 60 and the town today consists of little more than a couple of choice places to stay, a fine pub, a small grocer and deli, and a couple of gas pumps. Westport dates from 1877 when it was called Beall's Landing after a (long-gone) timber loading facility built by Samuel Beall, the town's first white settler.

Head 1.5 miles north of town for the ruggedly beautiful **Westport-Union Landing State Beach** (707-937-5804; 40501 Hwy 1; tent sites $25;), which extends for 3 miles on coastal bluffs. A rough hiking trail leaves the primitive campground and passes by tidepools and streams, accessible at low tide.

Sleeping & Eating

Westport Inn INN $

(707-964-5135; www.westportinnca.com; 37040 Hwy 1, Shoreline Hwy; r from $80;) Dating from the 1970s, this simple place to stay has beach access and recently refurbished, pleasant rooms with fresh flowers and nice art work. The owner is charming and can provide meals on request.

★Westport Hotel & Old Abalone Pub INN $$

(877-964-3688; www.westporthotel.us; 38921 Hwy 1, Shoreline Hwy; r $150-245;) Westport Hotel & Old Abalone Pub is quiet enough to have a motto that brags 'You've finally found nowhere.' The rooms are sumptuous – feather duvets, hardwood furniture, plush carpeting – with excellent views. The classy historic pub downstairs is the only option for dinner, so be thankful it's a delicious sampling of whimsical California fusions and hearty, expertly presented pub food.

Howard Creek Ranch CABIN $$

(707-964-6725; www.howardcreekranch.com; 40501 N Hwy 1, Shoreline Hwy; r $90-198, cabins $105-198;) Howard Creek Ranch, sitting on 60 stunning acres of forest and farmland abutting the wilderness, has accommodations in an 1880s farmhouse or a few cabins including a carriage barn, whose way-cool redwood rooms have been expertly handcrafted by the owner. Rates include full breakfast. Bring hiking boots, not high heels.

ALONG HIGHWAY 101

To get into the most remote and wild parts of the North Coast on the quick, eschew winding Hwy 1 for inland Hwy 101, which runs north from San Francisco as a freeway, then as a two- or four-lane highway north of Sonoma County, occasionally pausing under the traffic lights of small towns.

Know that escaping the Bay Area at rush hour (weekdays between 4pm and 7pm) ain't easy. You might sit bumper-to-bumper through Santa Rosa or Willits, where trucks bound for the coast turn onto Hwy 20.

Although Hwy 101 may not look as enticing as the coastal route, it's faster and less winding, leaving you time along the way to detour into Sonoma and Mendocino Counties' wine regions (Mendocino claims to be the greenest wine region in the country), explore pastoral Anderson Valley, splash about Clear Lake or soak at hot-springs resorts outside Ukiah – time well spent indeed!

Hopland

Apparently using the most solar power per capita in the world, Hopland flaunts its eco-geek, green-living ways at every turn with more organic produce available than you can shake a carrot stick at, plus a sustainable-living demonstration site, complete with a bio-fuel pump that recycles vegetable oil from local restaurants! Hops were first grown here in 1866, but Prohibition brought the industry temporarily to a halt. Today, with its location as a gateway to Mendocino County's wine country, booze drives Hopland's economy again, with wine tasting the primary draw. Most of the tasting rooms are conveniently located right on Hwy 101, which runs through the center of town, and are generally small, boutique-style operations offering an enjoyable personalized experience.

Sights

For an excellent weekend trip, use Hopland as a base for exploring the regional wineries. More information about the constantly growing roster of wineries is available at www.destinationhopland.com. Find a map to the wine region at www.visitmendocino.com.

Brutocao Cellars TASTING ROOM
(☎800-433-3689; www.brutocaocellars.com; 13500 S Hwy 101; ⏰10am-5pm; P) FREE Located in a former 1920s schoolhouse in central Hopland, this fourth-generation family-owned winery has bocce courts, bold red wines and chocolate – a perfect combo. There is also, refreshingly, no charge for wine tasting here (although there is generally a limit to how much tippling you can do!). The gift shop specializes in gourmet goodies, great for gifts.

Real Goods Solar Living Center MUSEUM
(☎707-742-2460; www.solarliving.org; 13771 S Hwy 101; self-guided tour free, guided tour per person/family $3/5, wine tasting $5; ⏰center 9am-6pm daily, tours 11am & 3pm Sat & Sun Apr-Oct; P) This progressive, futuristic 12-acre campus is largely responsible for the area's bold green initiatives. The Real Goods Store, run by the same company that sold the first solar panel in the US in 1978, is an impressive straw-bale-house showroom. You can also enjoy an exhibition on permaculture and a demonstration of solar-powered water systems. Plus, on the off chance your car runs on bio-diesel, you can fill up your tank here.

Graziano Family of Wines WINERY
(☎707-744-8466; www.grazianofamilyofwines.com; 13251 S Hwy 101; ⏰10am-5pm; P) FREE The Italian Graziano family is one of the oldest grape-growing families in Mendocino County and specializies in 'Cal-Ital' wines – including Primitivo, Dolcetto, Barbera and Sangiovese – at some great prices. Wine tasting is complimentary.

Saracina Vineyards WINERY
(☎707-670-0199; www.saracina.com; 11684 S Hwy 101; tasting & tour $15; ⏰11am-5pm; P) The highlight of a tour here is the descent into the cool caves. Sensuous whites are all biodynamically and sustainably farmed.

Sleeping & Eating

Piazza de Campovida INN $$
(☎707-744-1977; www.piazzadecampovida.com; 13441 S Hwy 101; ste $185-220; P) Modern Californian meets Italian at this very comfortable inn where all of the spacious suites have Jacuzzis, fireplaces and private balconies. The homey taverna and pizzeria in front have big tables for communal dining and fantastic artisanal pizzas, craft beer and wine.

Burger My Way BURGERS $
(☎707-744-8762; 13600 Mountain House Rd, 76 Gas Station; burgers $6-8; ⏰8am-9pm; P) Look beyond the surroundings (this place is attached to a gas station) and instead concentrate on the quality of burgers, with some 17 varieties, including vegetarian, turkey and salmon. The fries are hand cut and crispy and there are non-burger options too, including a selection of Mexican dishes, sandwiches and salads. But it's the burgers that will have you salivating...

Bluebird Cafe DINER $
(☎707-744-1633; 13340 S Hwy 101; breakfast $11-13, lunch mains $10-15; ⏰7am-2pm Mon-Thu, to 7pm Fri-Sun;) This classic American diner serves hearty breakfasts and homemade pie (the summer selection of peach-blueberry pie is dreamy). For a more

exciting culinary adventure, try the wild-game burgers, such as elk, with a bite of horseradish.

Clear Lake

With over 100 miles of shoreline and 68 square miles of surface area, Clear Lake is the largest naturally occurring freshwater lake in California (Tahoe is bigger, but crosses the Nevada state line). In summer the warm water thrives with algae, giving it a murky green appearance and creating a fabulous habitat for fish, especially bass and catfish, so you can expect plenty of anglers here, particularly on weekends. Mt Konocti, a 4200ft-tall dormant volcano, lords over the scene. The lake is ringed by small, tasteful resorts with places to stay, dine and kick back enjoying the lake views. You can also rent boats, kayaks, paddleboards and just about anything else that floats on the water at one of several marinas. On a more somber note, the area was devastated by fire in the summer of 2015 with Middletown, in particular, being badly affected; a vigorous rebuilding program continues.

Locals refer to the northwest portion as 'upper lake' and the southeast portion as 'lower lake.' Likeable and well-serviced **Lakeport** (population 4695) sits on the northwest shore, a 45-minute drive east of Hopland along Hwy 175 (off Hwy 101); tiny, Old West style **Kelseyville** (population 3353) is 7 miles south. **Clearlake**, off the southeastern shore, is the biggest town.

Hwy 20 links the relatively bland north-shore hamlets of **Nice** (the northernmost town) and **Lucerne**, 4 miles southeast. **Middletown**, a cute village, lies 20 miles south of Clearlake at the junction of Hwys 175 and 29, 40 minutes north of Calistoga.

Sights

Clear Lake State Park STATE PARK
(707-279-2267, 707-279-4293; www.clearlakestatepark.org; 5300 Soda Bay Rd, Kelseyville; per car $8; sunrise-sunset; P) Four miles from Kelseyville, on the lake's southern shore, this park is idyllic and gorgeous, with hiking trails, fishing, boating and camping. The bird-watching is extraordinary. The visitor center has natural history and cultural diorama exhibits.

Sleeping & Eating

For the greatest range of places to stay, head to Lakeport, where most accommodations are conveniently located on and around Main St. Be sure to make reservations ahead on weekends and during summer, when people flock to the cool water. There

TOP CLEAR LAKE WINERIES

These four wineries are the best; some offer tours by appointment.

Kaz Winery (707-833-2536; www.kazwinery.com; 1435 Big Valley Rd, Lakeport; tasting $5-10; 11am-5pm Sat or by appointment; P) A cult favorite, supercool Kaz is about blends: whatever is in the organic vineyards goes into the wine – and they're blended at crush, not during fermentation. Expect lesser-known varietals like Tannat and Lenoir, and worthwhile cabernet-merlot blends. Bottles cost $26 to $45.

Brassfield Estate (707-998-1895; www.brassfieldestate.com; 10915 High Valley Rd, Clearlake Oaks; tasting $5; 11am-5pm May-Nov, from noon Dec-Apr; P) Remote, stunning Tuscan villa in the unique High Valley appellation surrounded by magnificent landscaped gardens.

Wildhurst (707-279-4302; www.wildhurst.com; 3855 Main St, Kelseyville; 10am-5pm; P) Looking like a Western movie set, downtown Kelseyville is where family-owned winery tasting rooms such as Wildhurst (tasting free) rustle beside hardware stores, soda fountains and cafes.

Langtry Estate Vineyards (707-995-7521; www.langtryestate.com; 21000 Butts Canyon Rd, Middletown; tasting $5, tours from $60; 11am-5pm; P) This winery has a stunning location on a hilltop overlooking the lake with picnic tables available for anyone who wants to pack a lunch. Visitors can opt for a wine tasting of six wines, a tasting plus tour, a vineyard tour or a historical tour that includes a wine tasting with appetizers at the nearby Lillie Langry mansion; the famous late actress owned the vineyard and house from 1888 until 1906.

are several campsites close to the lake, although be aware that they can flood if there are heavy rains, so always check in advance. For the budget conscious, Lakeport also has the most affordable options.

Clearlake

Visto del Lago Lakehouse CABIN $$
(707-356-9721; www.vdlresort.com; 14103 Lakeshore Dr, Clearlake; cottages $75-179;) Located right on the main road, so handy for shops and restaurants, these clean-as-a-whistle cottages are a delight. Sizes and facilities vary greatly, but all have well-equipped kitchenettes and are comfortably furnished. Other options may include hot tubs, fireplaces and Netflix; one cabin even has its own pool table. There is an outside Jacuzzi, swing chair and barbecue right on the lake.

Lakeport & Kelseyville

There are a number of motels along the main drags in Kelseyville and Lakeport, but if you want fresh air, Clear Lake State Park has four **campgrounds** (800-444-7275; www.reserveamerica.com; State Park Rd; tent & RV sites $35; year round;) with showers. The weekly **farmers market** (www.clearlakefarmersmarket.com/; Hwy 29 & Thomas Dr; 8:30am-noon Sat Jun-Oct) is in Kelseyville.

★**Lakeport English Inn** B&B $$
(707-263-4317; www.lakeportenglishinn.com; 675 N Main St, Lakeport; r $185-210, cottages $210;) The finest B&B at Clear Lake is an 1875 Carpenter Gothic with 10 impeccably furnished rooms, styled with a nod to the English countryside and with such quaint names as the Prince of Wales or (wait for it) Roll in the Hay. Weekends take high tea (nonguests welcome by reservation), with scones and real Devonshire cream.

★**Angelina's Bakery & Espresso** CAFE $
(707-263-0391; www.angelinas365.com; 365 N Main St, Lakeport; sandwiches from $5; 7am-5pm Mon-Fri, 8am-2pm Sat;) The best baked goodies in Clear Lake, especially the giant decadent muffins and gooey cinnamon rolls. Also makes sandwiches to order and serves savory pastries. The coffee is the real McCoy, with a caffeine kick that should set you up for the day.

Park Place AMERICAN $
(707-263-0444; www.parkplacelakeport.com; 50 3rd St, Lakeport; mains $7-11; 11am-9pm Tue-Sun, to 3pm Mon;) Simple but right on the waterfront, come to this bright and completely unpretentious eatery for basics like pasta, burgers and pizza made from sustainable, local produce at great prices. A local favorite.

Studebaker's Coffee House DELI $
(707-279-8871; 3990 Main St, Kelseyville; sandwiches from $6; 6am-4pm Mon-Fri, 7am-4pm Sat, 7am-2pm Sun) A friendly, old-style diner with plenty of character, from black-and-white checker linoleum floors to old photos on the wall. Great sandwiches, including vegetarian options, plus Mexican fare such as quesadillas and burritos; the coffee's good too.

★**Saw Shop Bistro** CALIFORNIAN $$
(707-278-0129; www.sawshopbistro.com; 3825 Main St, Kelseyville; small plates $10-16, mains $15-26; 11:30am-10pm Tue-Sat;) The best restaurant in Lake County serves a California-cuisine menu of wild salmon and rack of lamb, as well as a small-plates menu of sushi, lobster tacos, Kobe-beef burgers and flatbread pizzas. Laid-back atmosphere, too. Reservations recommended.

Northshore

Tallman Hotel HISTORIC HOTEL $$
(information 707-275-2244, reservations 707-275-2245; www.tallmanhotel.com; 9550 Main St, Upper Lake; r $185-265;) The centerpiece may be the smartly renovated historic hotel – tile bathrooms, warm lighting, thick linens – but the rest of the property's lodging, including the shady garden, walled-in swimming pool, brick patios and porches, exudes timeless elegance. Some garden rooms come with outdoor Japanese soaking tubs heated by an energy-efficient geothermal-solar system.

Featherbed Railroad Co HOTEL $$
(707-274-8378; www.featherbedrailroad.com; 2870 Lakeshore Blvd, Nice; cabooses $175-220;) A treat for train buffs and kids, Featherbed has 10 comfy, real cabooses on a grassy lawn. Some of the cabooses straddle the border between kitschy and tacky (the 'Easy Rider' has a Harley-Davidson headboard and a mirrored ceiling), but they're great fun if you keep a sense of humor. There's a tiny beach across the road.

Sea Breeze Resort COTTAGE $$

(☎707-998-3327; www.seabreezeresort.net; 9595 Harbor Dr, Glenhaven; cottages $125-180; ⏲Apr-Oct; P ⊜ ❄ 🛜) Just south of Lucerne on a small peninsula, lush green gardens surround seven spotless lakeside cottages. All but one have full kitchens.

Drinking & Nightlife

Library Park, in Lakeport, has free lakeside Friday-evening summer concerts, with blues and rockabilly tunes to appeal to road-trippers.

Kelsey Creek Brewing BREWERY

(☎707-279-2311; www.kelseycreekbrewing.com; 3945 Main St, Kelseyville; ⏲2-8pm Mon-Fri, noon-8pm Sat, noon-6pm Sun) A 'hop'-ping fun local's scene with excellent craft beer, peanut shells on the floor and a bring-your-own-food, bring-your-dog kind of laid-back vibe.

☆ Entertainment

Lakeport Auto Movies CINEMA

(www.lakeportautomovies.com; 52 Soda Bay Rd, Lakeport; 1/2/3 people per car $10/18/25; ⏲Fri & Sat Apr-Sep; 👪) Lakeport is home to one of the few surviving and wonderfully nostalgic drive-in movie theaters, with showings on Friday and Saturday nights.

Information

Lake County Visitor Information Center (☎800-525-3743; www.lakecounty.com; 255 N Forbes St, Lakeport; ⏲9am-5pm Mon-Sat, noon-4pm Sun) Has complete information and an excellent website, which allows potential visitors to narrow their focus by interests.

Getting Around

Lake Transit (☎707-994-3334, 707-263-3334; www.laketransit.org; 9240 Highway 53, Lower Lake) Operates weekday routes between Middletown, Calistoga and St Helena ($5, 35 minutes, three daily). Buses serve Ukiah ($8, two hours, four daily), from Clearlake via Lakeport ($5, 1¼ hours, seven daily). Since piecing together routes and times can be difficult, it's best to phone ahead.

Anderson Valley

A one-time redwood-logging community, rolling hills surround pocket-size Anderson Valley, more famous today for the apple orchards, vineyards, pastures and its general air of tranquility. Visitors come primarily to winery-hop; the winery scene here has been compared to the Napa Valley some 30 years ago. Most of the wineries are clustered between Boonville and Navarro, but you'll also find good hiking and cycling in the hills and the chance to escape civilization (although weekends can get busy with San Franciscans escaping the clamor of the city). Other things to check out include the craft breweries and the farmstead cheeses; look for signs on the roadside. Cheese is also sold at several of the vineyards and agreeably available for tasting along with the wine. Traveling through the valley is the most common route to Mendocino and Fort Bragg from San Francisco.

Boonville (population 1488) and **Philo** (population 349) are the valley's principal towns. From Ukiah, winding Hwy 253 heads 20 miles south to Boonville. Equally scenic Hwy 128 twists and turns 60 miles between Cloverdale on Hwy 101, south of Hopland, and Albion on coastal Hwy 1.

Sights & Activities

Philo Apple Farm FARM

(☎707-895-2333; www.philoapplefarm.com; 18501 Greenwood Rd, Philo; ⏲10am-5pm; P 👪) For the best fruit, skip the obvious roadside stands and head to this gorgeous farm for organic preserves, chutneys, heirloom apples and pears, as well as a tasteful array of homeware and furniture. For overnight guests, the farm also hosts **cooking classes**. You can make a weekend out of it by staying in one of the Philo Apple Farm Guest Cottages (p239).

Anderson Valley Brewing Company BREWERY

(☎707-895-2337; www.avbc.com; 17700 Hwy 253, Boonville; tasting from $2, tours & disc-golf course free; ⏲11am-6pm Sat-Thu, to 7pm Fri; P 👪) East of the Hwy 128 crossroads, this solar-powered brewery crafts award-winning beers in a Bavarian-style brewhouse. You can also toss around a Frisbee on the **disc-golf course** while enjoying the brews, but, be warned, the sun can take its toll. Tours leave at 1:30pm daily (no reservations).

Anderson Valley Historical Society Museum MUSEUM

(☎707-895-3207; www.andersonvalleymuseum.org; 12340 Hwy 128, Boonville; ⏲1-4pm Sat & Sun Feb-Nov; P) FREE Situated in a tastefully renovated red schoolhouse west of Boonville, this museum displays historical artifacts, including an interesting display centered on the Pomos (an indigenous Native American tribe who once populated this region and were famed for their beautiful woven baskets). You can examine the works here, ranging from 4ft-to-5ft storage baskets to tiny intricate examples barely the size of a finger tip.

Festivals & Events

Pinot Noir Festival WINE
(707-895-9463; www.avwines.com; Goldeneye Winery, Philo; May) One of Anderson Valley's many wine celebrations; held over four days toward the end of May.

Sierra Nevada World Music Festival MUSIC
(www.snwmf.com; Mendocino County Fairgrounds, 14400 Hwy 128, Boonville; mid-Jun) In the middle of June, over three days, the sounds of reggae and roots fill the air, co-mingling with the scent of Mendocino County's *other* cash crop.

Mendocino County Fair & Apple Show FAIR
(www.mendocountyfair.com; Mendocino County Fairgrounds, 14400 Hwy 128, Boonville; adult/child $9/6; mid-Sep;) A county classic autumnal fair with wine tasting, a rodeo and lively parades.

Sleeping

Overall the accommodation options are in the midrange to high-end categories, catering to San Franciscan weekenders seeking a self-pampering break with wine tasting, vineyard views and Egyptian-cotton sheets thrown in. If you are looking for somewhere more family and budget friendly, there are some excellent campsites in the valley, some with cabin accommodation available. The Anderson Valley Chamber of Commerce can advise on places to stay throughout the region.

Hendy Woods State Park CAMPGROUND $
(707-937-5804, reservations 800-444-7275; www.reserveamerica.com; Hwy 128; tent & RV sites $40, cabins $60; P) Bordered by the Navarro River on Hwy 128, west of Philo, this lovely park has hiking, picnicking and a forested campground with hot showers.

Other Place COTTAGE $$
(Sheep Dung Properties; 707-895-3979; www.sheepdung.com; 14655 CA-128, Boonville; cottages $190-350; P) Located outside of town on a ridge with blissful panoramic and vineyard views, the 500 acres of ranch land here surround private, fully equipped hilltop cottages. The owners also hire out a cottage in downtown Boonville that shares access to the ranch with its picturesque views and walking trails.

★ **Boonville Hotel** BOUTIQUE HOTEL $$$
(707-895-2210; www.boonvillehotel.com; 14050 Hwy 128, Boonville; d $295-365; P) Decked out in a contemporary American country feel with sea-grass flooring, pastel colors and fine linens, this historic hotel's rooms and suites are safe for urbanites who refuse to abandon style just because they've gone to the country. The rooms are all different and there are agreeable extras, including hammocks and fireplaces.

TOP ANDERSON VALLEY WINERIES

The valley's cool nights yield high-acid, fruit-forward, food-friendly wines. Pinot Noir, Chardonnay and dry Gewürztraminer flourish. Most wineries (www.avwines.com) sit outside Philo. Many are family-owned and offer free tastings; some give tours. The following are particularly noteworthy:

Navarro Vineyards (707-895-3686; www.navarrowine.com; 5601 Hwy 128, Philo; 8am-6pm Mon-Fri, to 5pm Sat & Sun; P) The best option around with award-winning Pinot Noir and dry Gewürztraminer; has twice-daily free tours (reservations accepted) and picnicking facilities.

Husch Vineyards (707-462-5370; www.huschvineyards.com; 4400 Hwy 128, Philo; 10am-6pm, to 5pm Nov-Mar; P) The oldest vineyard in the valley serves exquisite tastings inside a rose-covered cottage.

Bink Wines (707-895-2940; www.binkwines.com; 9000 Hwy 128, Philo; 11am-5pm Wed-Mon; P) This winery produces small-batch artisanal wines that get rave reviews. Bink is located within the Med-style Madrones complex, which houses a total of four local vintners, as well as a hotel, restaurant and gift shop.

★**Philo Apple Farm Guest Cottages** COTTAGE $$$
(☎707-895-2333; www.philoapplefarm.com; 18501 Greenwood Rd, Philo; d $250-300; P) Set within the orchard, guests of bucolic Philo Apple Farm (p237) choose from four exquisite cottages, each built with reclaimed materials. With bright, airy spaces, polished plank floors, simple furnishings and views of the surrounding trees, each one is an absolute dream.

Red Door cottage is a favorite because of the bathroom – you can soak in the slipper tub, or shower on the private deck under the open sky. The cottages often get booked with participants of the farm's cooking classes, so book well in advance. For a swim, the Navarro River is within walking distance.

Madrones HOTEL $$$
(☎707-895-2955; www.themadrones.com; 9000 Hwy 128, Philo; r $175-350; P) Tucked off the back of the Madrones Mediterranean-inspired complex that includes a restaurant and the wonderful Bink Wines tasting room, the spacious 'guest quarters' here are modern-country-luxe, with a tinge of Tuscany. Above all, they are eminently comfortable with plush furnishings, marshmallow-soft pillows, soft carpeting and a soothing color scheme.

Eating

Boonville restaurants seem to open and close as they please, so expect hours to vary based on season and whims. There are several places along Hwy 128 which can supply a picnic with fancy local cheese and fresh bread. Locally grown produce is the norm in these parts, so you can expect organic seasonal veg and a pleasing lack of fast-food options. Nope, gourmet burgers don't count.

Paysanne ICE CREAM $
(☎707-895-2210; www.sweetpaysanne.com; 14111 Hwy 128, Boonville; ice cream from $2.50; ⏰10am-6pm Sun-Thu;) Boonville's fantastic sweets shop serves the innovative flavors of Three Twins Ice Cream, whose delightful choices include Lemon Cookie and Strawberry Je Ne Sais Quoi (which has a hint of balsamic vinegar); it's the best ice cream to be found in the Anderson Valley according to the locals – and they know best.

Boonville General Store DELI $
(☎707-895-9477; 17810 Farrer Lane, Boonville; dishes $7-14; ⏰7:30am-3pm Mon-Thu, 7:30am-3pm & 5:30-8pm Fri, 8:30am-3pm Sat & Sun; P) Opposite the Boonville Hotel, this superb deli is good to stock up for picnics, offering gourmet sandwiches on homemade bread, thin-crust pizzas and organic cheeses. It also serves hearty homemade soups if you feel like grabbing a pew, as well as scrumptious breakfasts. Organic produce is used as far as possible and there are plenty of vegetarian options.

★**Table 128** CALIFORNIAN $$
(☎707-895-2210; www.boonvillehotel.com; 14050 Hwy 128, Boonville; lunch mains $10-14, dinner mains $19-31; ⏰6-8pm Thu-Mon Apr–mid-Jun, from 4:30pm mid-Jun–mid-Oct; P) Food-savvy travelers love the constantly changing New American menu here, featuring simple dishes done well, like Alaskan turbot, grilled local lamb, and cheesecake. The family-style service makes dinner a free-wheeling, elegant social affair, with big farm tables and soft lighting. It's got great wines, craft beers, scotch and cocktails.

Information

Anderson Valley Chamber of Commerce
(☎707-895-2379; www.andersonvalleychamber.com; 9800 Hwy 128, Boonville; ⏰9am-5pm Mon-Fri) Has tourist information and a complete schedule of annual events, plus can also advise on places to stay, including campsites.

Ukiah

As the county seat and Mendocino's largest city, Ukiah is mostly a utilitarian stop for travelers to refuel the car and get a bite. But, if you have to stop here for the night, you could do much worse: the town is a friendly place that's gentrifying. There is a plethora of cookie-cutter hotel chains, some cheaper mid-century motels and a handful of very good dining options. The coolest attractions, a pair of thermal springs and a sprawling campus for Buddhist studies complete with 10,000 golden Buddha statues, lie outside the city limits. There are also some excellent wineries and tasting rooms within easy access from the center; the helpful **Chamber of Commerce** (☎707-462-4705; www.gomendo.com; 200 S School St; ⏰9am-5pm Mon-Fri) can point you in the right direction. Ukiah has a pleasant, walkable shopping district along School St near the courthouse, where you can find some idiosyncratic small shops and larger chains.

Sights

Grace Hudson Museum & Sun House MUSEUM
(707-467-2836; www.gracehudsonmuseum.org; 431 S Main St; $4; 10am-4:30pm Wed-Sat, from noon Sun) One block east of State St, the collection's mainstays are paintings by Grace Hudson (1865–1937). Her sensitive depictions of Pomo people and other indigenous groups complement the ethnological work and Native American baskets collected by her husband, John Hudson. The lovely 1911 Sun House, adjacent to the museum, was the former Hudson home and is typical of the arts-and-crafts style of that era; docent-guided tours are available.

Festivals & Events

Redwood Empire Fair FAIR
(707-462-3884; www.redwoodempirefair.com; 1055 N State St; Jun & Aug;) There are two major fairs held here: the Redwood Empire Spring Fair, held over a weekend in early June, and the Redwood Empire Fair, held over a weekend in early August. Both have loads of events, ranging from quilt exhibitions to garden expos.

Ukiah Country PumpkinFest CULTURAL
(www.cityofukiah.com; late Oct;) In late October, with an arts-and-crafts fair, children's carnival and a fiddle contest.

Sleeping

Hampton Inn MOTEL $$
(707-462-6555; www.hamptoninn3.hilton.com; 1160 Airport Park Blvd; r $125-175;) The best of the chain gang in Ukiah, with a whiff of a Hilton about it (Hampton is now part of the Hilton portfolio). Expect excellent amenities, including a fitness center and comprehensive offerings for the business bunch. The recently updated rooms may still be hotel-chain bland but are comfortable, carpeted and spacious.

Eating

It'd be a crime to eat the fast-food junk located off the highway; Ukiah has a burgeoning food scene that pairs nicely with the surrounding wine country.

★ **Schat's Bakery & Cafe** CAFE $
(707-462-1670; www.schats.com; 113 W Perkins St; lunch mains $5-8, dinner mains $8-14; 5:30am-6pm Mon-Fri, to 5pm Sat) Founded by Dutch bakers, Schat's makes a dazzling array of chewy, dense breads, sandwiches, wraps, big salads, dee-lish hot mains, full breakfasts and homemade pastries.

Kilkenny Kitchen CAFE $
(707-462-2814; www.kilkennykitchen.com; 1093 S Dora St; sandwiches $8; 10am-3pm Mon-Fri;) Tucked into a neighborhood south of downtown, county workers love this chipper yellow place for the fresh rotation of daily soups and sandwich specials (a recent visit on a blazing-hot day found a heavenly, cold spinach and dill soup). The salads – like the cranberry, spinach with pecans and feta cheese – are also fantastic, and there's a kid's menu.

★ **Saucy Ukiah** PIZZA $$
(707-462-7007; www.saucyukiah.com; 108 W Standley St; pizzas $14-19, mains $13-19; 11:30am-9pm Mon-Thu, to 10pm Fri, noon-10pm Sat) Yes there are arty pizzas with toppings like organic fennel pollen and almond basil pesto but there are also amazing soups, salads, pastas and starters – Nana's meatballs are to die for and the 'kicking' minestrone lives up to its name. The small-town ambience is mildly chic but fun and informal at the same time.

Oco Time JAPANESE $$
(707-462-2422; www.ocotime.com; 111 W Church St; lunch mains $7-10, dinner mains $8-19; 11:15am-2:30pm Tue-Fri, 5:30-8:30pm Mon-Sat;) Shoulder your way through the locals to get Ukiah's best sushi, noodle bowls and *oco* (a delicious combo of seaweed, grilled cabbage, egg and noodles). The 'Peace Café' has a great vibe, friendly staff and interesting special rolls. Downside? The place gets mobbed, so reservations are a good idea.

Patrona MODERN AMERICAN $$
(707-462-9181; www.patronarestaurant.com; 130 W Standley St; lunch mains $10-16, dinner mains $15-34; 11am-9pm Sun-Thu, to 10pm Fri & Sat) Foodies flock to excellent Patrona for earthy, flavor-packed, seasonal and regional organic cooking in super stylish surrounds. The unfussy menu includes dishes such as roasted chicken, brined-and-roasted pork chops and housemade pasta, as well as local wines. Reservations recommended at weekends.

Ukiah Garden Cafe CALIFORNIAN **$$**
(☎707-462-1221; 1090 S State St; mains $17-24; ⏰11am-9pm Tue-Fri, from 4pm Mon & Sat; P) Meat lovers will be swooning at the top-quality steaks, roast prime rib and lamb and pork chops here. The chicken dishes are also winners but vegetarians will have to stick to the appetizers: think homemade fried mozzarella sticks or crispy zucchini with a creamy dip.

Himalayan Cafe NEPALI **$$**
(☎707-467-9900; www.thehimalayancafe.com; 1639 S State St; mains $15-18; ⏰5-9pm Mon,11am-3pm Tue-Sat) South of downtown, find delicately spiced Nepalese cooking – think tandoori breads and curries, including plenty of vegetarian options. Some Sundays there's a Nepalese buffet at 4pm.

Drinking & Nightlife

Dive bars and scruffy cocktail lounges line State St, especially to the north of town. For a wider and marginally classier selection, head to S State St and the surrounding streets.

Black Oak Coffee Roasters CAFE
(☎866-390-1427; www.blackoakcoffee.com; 476 N State St; ⏰6:30am-6pm Mon-Fri, 7am-5pm Sat & Sun; 📶) A big modern coffee house that roasts its own beans with some interesting and delicious choices such as a *café borgia latté* with artisan chocolate and orange essence or, for tea lovers, a *matcha chia* milkshake. Light breakfasts and lunches are also on offer.

Information

Army Corps of Engineers (☎707-462-7581; www.spn.usace.army.mil/mendocino; 1160 Lake Mendocino Dr; ⏰8am-4pm Mon-Fri May-Sep) The visitor center here can provide information about Lake Mendocino, including hiking and biking trails, as well as boating and campsites.

Bureau of Land Management (☎707-468-4000; www.blm.gov; 2550 N State St; ⏰10am-5pm Mon-Fri) Maps and information on backcountry camping, hiking and biking in wilderness areas.

Getting Around

Mendocino Transit Authority (☎707-462-1422; www.mendocinotransit.org; 241 Plant Rd) The Mendocino Transit Authority runs a sparse bus service covering major towns in the Mendocino region.

Around Ukiah

Vichy Springs Resort

This **spa resort** (☎707-462-9515; www.vichysprings.com; 2605 Vichy Springs Rd; s $175-235, d $235-285, ste s/d $255/315, cottages from $325; P) offers a tranquil retreat with a choice of rooms and suites in a historic 1870s inn with a shared terrace overlooking sweeping lawns. The cottages are airy and light with floral fabrics and light pine decor and a fully equipped kitchen. Guests can enjoy the spa facilities as well as hiking trails on the 700-acre property.

Vichy is the oldest continuously operating mineral-springs spa in California. The water's composition perfectly matches that of its famous namesake in Vichy, France. A century ago, Mark Twain, Jack London and Robert Louis Stevenson traveled here for the water's restorative properties, which ameliorate everything from arthritis to poison oak.

Today, the historic resort has the only warm-water, naturally carbonated mineral baths in North America. Unlike others, Vichy requires swimsuits (rentals $3). Day use (for guests and non-guests) costs $35 for two hours, $65 for a full day.

Facilities include a swimming pool, outdoor mineral hot tub, 14 indoor and outdoor tubs with natural 100°F (38°C) waters, and a grotto for sipping the effervescent waters. Massages and facials are available. The resort's hiking trails lead to a 40ft waterfall, an old cinnabar mine and 1100ft peaks – great for sunset views.

Orr Hot Springs

A soak in the thermal waters of the rustic **Orr Hot Springs resort** (☎707-462-6277; www.orrhotsprings.org; 13201 Orr Springs Rd; day-use adult/child $30/25; ⏰by appointment 10am-10pm) is heavenly. While it's not for the bashful, the clothing-optional resort is beloved by locals, back-to-the-land hipsters, backpackers and liberal-minded tourists. Still, you don't have to let it all hang out. Enjoy the private tubs, a sauna, a spring-fed, rock-bottomed swimming pool, steam room, massage and magical gardens. Soaking in the rooftop stargazing tubs on a clear night is magical. Make reservations.

You can stay here in one of the elegantly rustic **accommodations** (☎707-462-6277; www.orrhotsprings.org; 13201 Orr Springs Rd; tent site per adult/child $70/25, r & yurt $210, cottages $280; P). Accommodations include use of the spa and communal kitchen, while some share bathrooms; cottages have their own kitchens. There are also six yurts tucked into the woods here, offering total privacy.

Orr Hot Springs can be tricky to find. Drive south on Hwy 101 and take exit 551 for N State St. Turn left and head approximately a quarter mile north, turning left onto Orr Springs Rd. Follow the paved road over the hills for approximately 12 miles until you reach the signposted hot springs.

Ukiah Wineries

You'll notice the acres of grapes stretching out in every direction on your way into town. Winemakers around Ukiah enjoy many of the same climatic conditions that made Napa so famous. Pick up a wineries map from the Ukiah Chamber of Commerce (p239). Tasting fees are generally around $5.

Nelson Family Vineyards WINERY
(707-462-3755; www.nelsonfamilyvineyards.com; 550 Nelson Ranch Rd; 10am-5pm; P) Just north of Ukiah, this winery, vineyard and pear, olive and Christmas-tree farm with wondrous views over the valley is a great place to picnic (in a redwood grove), make friends and sip not-too-sweet Chardonnay and luscious red blends. Just one aside – it is a popular venue for weddings, which can affect visits by the public.

Parducci Wine Cellars WINERY
(707-463-5357; www.parducci.com; 501 Parducci Rd; wine tasting $5; 10am-5pm; P) Sustainably grown, harvested and produced, 'America's Greenest Winery' offers affordable, bold, earthy reds. The tasting room, lined in brick with low ceilings and soft lights, is a perfect little cave-like environment to get out of the summer heat, sip wine and chat about sustainability practices. Or head for the terrace overlooking the vineyards and organic gardens, complete with contented chickens.

Montgomery Woods State Natural Reserve

Two miles west of Orr Hot Springs, this 2743-acre **reserve** (707-937-5804; www.parks.ca.gov; 15825 Orr Springs Rd; P) FREE protects five old-growth virgin redwood groves, which are some of the best groves within a day's drive from San Francisco. A 2-mile loop **trail**, starting near the picnic tables and toilets, crosses the creek, winding through the serene groves. It's out of the way, so visitors are likely to have it mostly to themselves.

The trees here are impressive – some are up to 14ft in diameter – but remember to admire them from the trail, both to protect the root systems of the trees and to protect yourself from poison oak, which is all over the park.

City of Ten Thousand Buddhas

The showpiece at the **City of Ten Thousand Buddhas** (707-462-0939; www.cttbusa.org; 4951 Bodhi Way; 8am-6pm; P) is the beautiful temple with its 10,000 golden Buddha statues. Elsewhere enjoy pretty courtyards, lush landscaping and decorative peacocks. This Buddhist monastery and college is home to both nuns and monks and runs courses on Buddhism; check the website for more information. There is an interesting gift shop with souvenirs as well as literature on Buddhism.

The excellent **Jyun Kang Vegetarian Restaurant** (4951 Bodhi Way; mains $8-12; 11:30am-3pm Wed-Mon;) will have vegetarians (and vegas) swooning over the superb Asian-influenced dishes.

Willits

Twenty miles north of Ukiah, Willits mixes NorCal dropouts with loggers and ranchers (the high school has a bull-riding team). Lamp posts on the main drag are decorated with cowboys and similar, while the heart of the place has a small-town atmosphere with an appealing clutch of idiosyncratic small shops and some solid eating choices.

Though ranching, timber and manufacturing may be its mainstays, tie-dye and gray ponytails are de rigueur. For visitors, Willits has a couple of claims to fame: it is the eastern terminus of the Skunk Train and is also home to the oldest continuous rodeo in California. Willits Frontier Days & Rodeo, held annually here in July, attracts bucking bronco fans from all over the US. Fort Bragg is about 35 miles away on the coast; allow an hour to navigate twisty Hwy 20.

Sights & Activities

Ten miles north of Willits, Hwy 162/Covelo Rd makes for a superb drive following the route of the Northwestern Pacific Railroad along the Eel River and through the **Mendocino National Forest**. The trip is only about 30 miles, but plan on taking at least an hour on the winding road, passing exquisite river canyons and rolling hills. Eventually, you'll reach **Covelo**, known for its unusual round valley.

★Mendocino County Museum MUSEUM
(☎707-459-2736; www.mendocinomuseum.org; 400 E Commercial St; adult/child $4/1; ⊙10am-4:30pm Wed-Sun; P) Among the best community museums in this half of the state, this puts the lives of early settlers in excellent historical context – much drawn from old letters – and there's an entire 1920s soda fountain and barber shop inside. You could spend an hour perusing Pomo and Yuki basketry and artifacts, or reading about local scandals and countercultural movements.

Outside, the **Roots of Motive Power** (www.rootsofmotivepower.com) exhibit occasionally demonstrates steam logging and machinery.

Ridgewood Ranch HISTORIC SITE
(☎reservations 707-459-7910; www.seabiscuit heritage.org; 16200 Hwy 101; group/private tours $25/40; ⊙9:30am 1st & 3rd Sat May-Oct) Willits' most famous resident was the horse Seabiscuit, who grew up here. Three-hour tours for eight or more people are available by reservation and there are other events listed on the website; private tours are also available. Docent-led nature tours of the surrounding natural area are free with advance reservations.

Skunk Train HISTORIC TRAIN
(☎707-964-6371; www.skunktrain.com; E Commercial St; adult/child $54/34) This heritage railroad has its depot on E Commercial St, three blocks east of Hwy 101. Trains run between Willits and Fort Bragg (p230), passing through some lush redwood country en route.

Jackson Demonstration State Forest HIKING
(www.stateparks.com; Fort Bragg-Willits Rd) Fifteen miles west of Willits on Hwy 20, the forest offers day-use recreational activities, including hiking trails and mountain-biking. You can also camp here. A demonstration forest is so named as it is used for forestry education, research and sustainable felling techniques. Seek out the Chamberlain Creek Waterfall on the Chamberlain Creek Trail and Camellia Trail if you can. These beautiful falls are situated in a lush canyon surrounded by redwoods and ferns.

Festivals & Events

Willits Frontier Days & Rodeo RODEO
(www.willitsfrontierdays.com; adult/child $15/5; ⊙early Jul) Dating from 1926, Willits has the oldest continuous rodeo in California, occurring in the first week in July.

Sleeping

Quality accommodations are pretty sparse here. Some of the in-town motels – and there seems to be about a hundred of them – are dumps, so absolutely check out the room before checking in. Ask about Skunk Train packages. For only the most desperate campers, there are a couple of crowded, loud RV parks on the edges of town.

★Old West Inn MOTEL $
(☎707-459-4201; www.theoldwestinn.com; 1221 S Main St; r $79; P ⊖ ❄ 📶) The facade looks like a mock up of an Old West main street and each room has a theme, from the 'Stable' to the 'Barber Shop.' The decor is simple and comfy with just enough imagination to make it interesting. Besides that this is the cleanest, friendliest and most highly recommended place in town.

Baechtel Creek Inn & Spa BOUTIQUE HOTEL $$
(☎707-459-9063; www.baechtelcreekinn.com; 101 Gregory Lane; d $125-165; P ⊖ ❄ 📶 ≋ 🐾) As Willits' only upscale option, this place draws an interesting mix: Japanese bus tours, business travelers and wine-trippers. The standard rooms are nothing too flashy, but they have top-notch linens, iPod docks and tasteful art. Custom rooms come with local wine and more space. The immaculate pool and lovely egg breakfast on the patio are perks.

Eating

La Siciliana ITALIAN $
(☎707-459-5626; www.lasicilianawillits.com; 1611 S Main St; mains $11-13; ⊙11am-9pm Tue-Sun; 👪) The *sugo* (sauce) is pure Sicilian, the pesto is rich with basil and pine nuts, the olive oil is extra virgin and the pizza crust is crisp and thin. There is no dreaded ping of the microwave and everything is freshly made

in-house. That said, the prices are low and the atmosphere no-fuss and family friendly.

Aztec Grill MEXICAN $
(781 S Main St; burritos $5-8; ⏰5am-9pm) Yes this is in the Chevron Gas Station, but the unanimous vote from locals is that this is, hands down, the best Mexican food in town. Cheap too.

Loose Caboose Cafe SANDWICHES $
(☎707-459-1434; www.loosecaboosewillits.com; 10 Wood St; sandwiches $7-11; ⏰7:30am-3pm) People tend to get a bit flushed when talking about the sandwiches at the Loose Caboose, which gets jammed at lunch. The Reuben and Sante Fe chicken sandwiches are two savory delights. Look for a ramshackle entrance complete with a historic rail crossing sign.

Adam's Restaurant CALIFORNIAN $$$
(☎707-409-4378; 50 N Main St; mains $22-27; ⏰5-9pm Tue-Sun; 📶) Willits' swankiest address is known for its crab cakes and special occasion-worthy mains like big New York steaks, lamb osso buco or cajun chicken pasta, perhaps finished off with a blueberry crème brûlée. The ambience is simple and the service stellar. Check out its Facebook page.

Drinking & Nightlife

The main street through town is home to a couple of cafes, as well as a pub with regular live music and a dimly-lit bar (or two).

Shanachie Pub PUB
(☎707-459-9194; 50 N Main St; ⏰3pm-1am Mon-Sat) This is a friendly little garden-side dive with tons on tap and regular live music.

☆ Entertainment

Willits Community Theatre THEATER
(☎707-459-0895; www.willitstheatre.org; 37 W Van Lane; ⏰hours vary) Stages award-winning plays, poetry readings and comedy.

Shopping

JD Redhouse & Co CLOTHING, HOMEWARES
(☎707-459-1214; www.jdredhouse.com; 212 S Main St; ⏰9am-6pm Mon-Fri, from 10am Sat & Sun) Family-owned and operated, this central mercantile is a good reflection of Willits itself, balancing cowboy essentials – boots and grain, tools and denim – with treats for the weekend tourist. The Cowlick's counter (with excellent Mendocino-made ice cream) is a good place to cool off when the heat on the sidewalk gets intense.

Mariposa Market FOOD & DRINK
(☎707-459-9630; www.mariposamarket.com; 600 S Main St; ⏰8am-7pm Mon-Fri, from 9am Sat & Sun) Willits' natural-food grocery market has plenty of organic fresh fruit and veg, plus a juice bar and baked-goods section.

SOUTHERN REDWOOD COAST

There's some real magic in the loamy soil and misty air 'beyond the redwood curtain'; it yields the tallest trees and most potent herb on the planet. North of Fort Bragg, Bay Area weekenders and antique-stuffed B&Bs give way to lumber wars, pot farmers and an army of carved bears. The 'growing' culture here is palpable and the huge profit it brings to the region has evident cultural side effects – an omnipresent population of transients who work the harvests, a chilling respect for 'No Trespassing' signs and a political culture that is an uneasy balance between gun-toting libertarians, ultra-left progressives and typical college-town chaos. Nevertheless, the reason to visit is to soak in the magnificent landscape, which runs through a number of pristine, ancient redwood forests.

Information

Redwood Coast Heritage Trails (www.redwoods.info) gives a nuanced slant on the region, with itineraries based around lighthouses, Native American culture, the timber and rail industries, and maritime life.

Leggett

Leggett marks the redwood country's beginning and Hwy 1's end. There's not much going on here, aside from a single gas station, a grocery store, a small restaurant and a post office, however, fear not, there is plenty to do and see close by.

Visit 1000-acre **Standish-Hickey State Recreation Area** (☎707-925-6482; www.parks.ca.gov; 69350 Hwy 101; per car $8; 👪), 1.5 miles to the north, for picnicking, swimming and fishing in the Eel River and hiking trails among virgin and second-growth redwoods.

Chandelier Drive-Thru Tree Park (☎707-925-6464; www.drivethrutree.com; 67402 Drive Thru Tree Rd; per car $5; ⏲8:30am-9pm Jun-Aug, closes earlier Sep-May; P 🚸) has 200 private acres of virgin redwoods with picnicking and nature walks. And yes, there's a redwood with a square hole carved out, which cars can drive through. Only in America.

The 1949 tourist trap of **Confusion Hill** (☎707-925-6456; www.confusionhill.com; 75001 N Hwy 101; Gravity House adult/child $5/4; ⏲9am-6pm May-Sep, 10am-5pm Oct-Apr; 🚸) is an enduring curiosity and the most elaborate of the old-fashioned stops that line the route north.

Richardson Grove State Park

Fifteen miles to the north of Leggett, and bisected by the Eel River, serene **Richardson Grove** (☎707-247-3318; www.parks.ca.gov; 1600 Hwy 101, Garberville; per car $8) occupies 1400 acres of virgin forest. Many trees are over 1000 years old and 300ft tall, but there aren't many hiking trails. In winter, there's good fishing for silver and king salmon. For the last few years, CalTrans has been considering widening the road through Richardson Grove, which has sparked an intense protest.

The **visitor center** (⏲9am-2pm May-Sep) sells books inside a 1930s lodge, which often has a fire going during cool weather. The park is primarily a **campground** (☎reservations 800-444-7275; www.reserveamerica.com; 1600 Hwy 101; tent & RV sites $35; P), with three separate areas and hot showers; some remain open year-round. Summer-only Oak Flat on the east side of the river is shady and has a sandy beach.

Garberville

The main supply center for southern Humboldt County is the primary jumping-off point for both the Lost Coast, to the west, and the Avenue of the Giants, to the north. There's an uneasy relationship between the old-guard loggers and the hippies, many of whom came in the 1970s to grow sinsemilla (potent, seedless marijuana) after the feds chased them out of Santa Cruz. More recently there has also been a troubling number of homeless on the streets, especially during the warm summer months. Reggae

Southern Redwood Coast

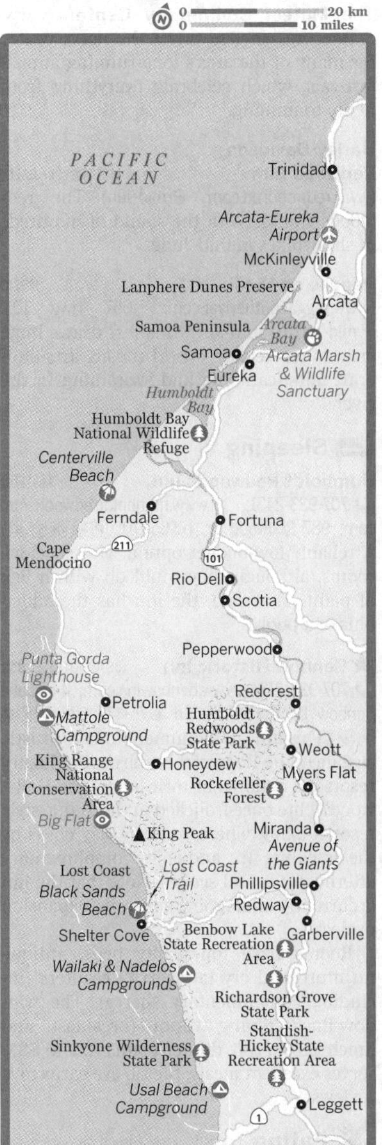

fans note that there is a popular music festival here in July attracting some top names in the genre. Two miles west, Garberville's ragtag sister, Redway, has fewer services. Garberville is about four hours north of San Francisco, one hour south of Eureka.

Festivals & Events

The **Mateel Community Center** (www.mateel.org), in Redway, is the nerve center for many of the area's long-running annual festivals, which celebrate everything from hemp to miming.

Harley-Davidson Redwood Run MOTORCYCLE RALLY
(www.redwoodrun.com; mid-Jun) The redwoods rumble with the sound of hundreds of shiny bikes in mid-June.

Reggae on the River MUSIC
(www.reggaeontheriver.com; 657 Hwy 101; mid-Jul) In mid-July, this fest draws huge crowds for reggae, world music, arts-and-craft fairs, camping and swimming in the river.

Sleeping

Humboldt Redwoods Inn MOTEL $
(707-923-2451; www.humboldtredwoodsinn.com; 987 Redwood Dr; r $65-110;) A reliable low-budget option with spacious rooms, although they could do with a lick of paint. That said, the inn has the added plus of a pool.

★**Benbow Historic Inn** HISTORIC HOTEL $$$
(707-923-2124; www.benbowinn.com; 445 Lake Benbow Dr, Garberville; d $175-475;) This inn is a monument to 1920s rustic elegance; the Redwood Empire's first luxury resort is a national historic landmark. Hollywood's elite once frolicked in the Tudor-style resort's lobby, where you can play chess by the crackling fire, and enjoy complimentary afternoon tea and scones. Note that the inn is currently undergoing a massive expansion project.

Rooms have top-quality beds, antique furniture and crystal sherry decanters (including complimentary sherry). The window-lined **dining room** (breakfast and lunch $10 to $15, dinner mains $22 to $32) serves excellent meals; the rib eye earns rave reviews.

Eating

Expect a small but varied choice of eateries, including some healthy options, as well as Mexican and down-home USA. Just about all the restaurants and cafes are located on Redwood Dr running through the center of town and essentially part of Hwy 101.

Woodrose Café BREAKFAST, AMERICAN $
(707-923-3191; www.woodrosecafe.com; 911 Redwood Dr; mains $9-18; 8am-2pm;) Garberville's beloved cafe serves organic omelets, veggie scrambles and buckwheat pancakes with *real* maple syrup in a cozy room. Lunch brings crunchy salads, sandwiches with all-natural meats and good burritos. Plenty of gluten-free options.

Bon Bistro & Bakery BAKERY $
(707-923-2509; 867 Redwood Dr; sandwiches from $5; 7am-3pm Mon-Fri, 8am-2pm Sat & Sun) At the southern, quieter end of town backed by lofty trees, this cozy spot has a cottage feel with its warm wood paneling and lacy curtains. Enjoy freshly baked breads, bagels and sandwiches with such tasty, unusual fillings as cashew chicken.

Cecil's New Orleans Bistro CAJUN $$
(707-923-7007; www.garbervillebistro.com; 733 Redwood Dr; mains $18-28; 5-9pm Thu-Mon) This 2nd-story eatery overlooks Main St and serves ambitious dishes that may have minted the California-Cajun style. Start with fried green tomatoes before launching into the smoked-boar gumbo. Check the website for music events.

Information

Find out what's really happening by tuning in to amazing community radio KMUD FM91 (www.kmud.org).

Garberville-Redway Area Chamber of Commerce (707-923-2613; www.garberville.org; 784 Redwood Dr; 10am-4pm daily May-Aug, 10am-4pm Mon-Fri Sep-Apr) Located inside the Redwood Drive Center, with plenty of information about the town including where to stay and what is on.

Lost Coast

The North Coast's superlative backpacking destination is a mystifying coastal stretch where narrow dirt trails ascend rugged coastal peaks. Here you'll find volcanic beaches of black sand and ethereal mist hovering above the roaring surf as majestic Roosevelt elk graze the forests. The King Range boldly rises 4000ft within 3 miles of the coast between where Hwy 1 cuts inland north of Westport to just south of Ferndale. The coast became 'lost' when the state's highway system deemed the region impassable in the early 20th century. The area north of the King Range is more accessible, if less dramatic.

In autumn, the weather is clear and cool. Wildflowers bloom from April through May and gray whales migrate from December through April. The warmest, driest months are June to August, but days are foggy. Note the weather can quickly change.

Aside from a few one-horse villages, Shelter Cove is the only option for services.

Information

The area is a patchwork of government-owned land and private property; visit the **Bureau of Land Management** (BLM; 707-825-2300, 707-986-5400; www.blm.gov; 768 Shelter Cove Rd; 8am-4:30pm Mon-Sat Sep-May, 8am-4:30pm Mon-Fri Jun-Aug) office for information, permits and maps. There are few circuitous routes for hikers, and rangers can advise on reliable (if expensive) shuttle services in the area.

For information about the flora and fauna stop by the **Needle Rock Visitor Center** (707-986-7711; www.parks.ca.gov; Bear Harbor Rd; per car $6; hours vary).

A few words of caution: lots of weed is grown around here and it's wise to stay on trail and to respect 'no trespassing' signs, lest you find yourself at the business end of someone's right to bear arms. And pot farmers don't pose the only threat: you'll want to check for ticks (Lyme disease is common) and keep food in bear-proof containers, which are required for camping.

Sinkyone Wilderness State Park

Named for the Sinkyone people who once lived here, this 7367-acre wilderness extends south of Shelter Cove along pristine coastline. The **Lost Coast Trail** passes through here for 22 miles, from Whale Gulch south to Usal Beach Campground. It takes at least three days to walk as it meanders along high ridges, providing bird's-eye views down to deserted beaches and the crashing surf (side trails descend to water level).

To get to Sinkyone, drive west from Garberville and Redway on Briceland-Thorn Rd, 21 miles through Whitethorn to Four Corners. Turn left (south) and continue for 3.5 miles down a very rugged road to the ranch house; it takes 1½ hours.

North of the **Usal Beach Campground** (707-247-3318; www.parks.ca.gov; tent sites $25; P), Usal Rd (County Rd 431) is much rougher and recommended only if you have a high-clearance 4WD and a chainsaw. Seriously.

King Range National Conservation Area

Stretching over 35 miles of virgin coastline, with ridge after ridge of mountainous terrain plunging to the surf, the 60,000-acre area tops out at namesake King's Peak (4087ft). The wettest spot in California, the range receives over 120in – and sometimes as much as 240in – of annual rainfall, causing frequent landslides; in winter, snow falls on the ridges. (By contrast, nearby sea-level Shelter Cove gets only 69in of rain and no snow.) Two-thirds of the area is awaiting wilderness designation. Note that for overnight hikes, you will need a backcountry-use permit, which can be obtained from the Bureau of Land Management.

Fire restrictions begin July 1 and last until the first soaking rain, usually in November. During this time, there are no campfires allowed outside developed campgrounds.

North of the King Range

Though it's less of an adventure, you can reach the Lost Coast's northern section year-round via paved, narrow Mattole Rd.

HIKING THE LOST COAST

The best way to see the Lost Coast is to hike, and the best hiking is through the southern regions within the Sinkyone and Kings Range wilderness areas. Some of the best trails start from Mattole Campground, just south of Petrolia, which is on the northern border of the Kings Range. It's at the ocean end of Lighthouse Rd, 4 miles from Mattole Rd (sometimes marked as Hwy 211), southeast of Petrolia.

Both Wailaki and Nadelos have developed **campgrounds** (tent sites $8) with toilets and water. There are another four developed campgrounds around the range, with toilets but no water (except Honeydew, which has purifiable creek water). There are multiple primitive walk-in sites. You'll need a bear canister and backcountry permit, both available from the Bureau of Land Management (p247).

Plan on three hours to navigate the sinuous 68 miles from Ferndale in the north to the coast at Cape Mendocino, then inland to Humboldt Redwoods State Park and Hwy 101. Don't expect redwoods: the vegetation is grassland and pasture. It's beautiful in spots – lined with sweeping vistas and wildflowers that are prettiest in spring.

You'll pass two tiny settlements, both 19th-century stage-coach stops. **Petrolia** has an all-in-one store that rents bear canisters, and sells supplies for the trail, good beer and gasoline. **Honeydew** also has a general store. The drive is enjoyable, but the Lost Coast's wild, spectacular scenery lies further south in the more remote regions.

Shelter Cove

The only sizable community on the Lost Coast, Shelter Cove is surrounded by the King Range National Conservation Area and abuts a large south-facing cove. It's a tiny seaside subdivision with an airstrip in the middle – indeed, many visitors are private pilots. Fifty years ago, Southern California swindlers subdivided the land, built the airstrip and flew in potential investors, fast-talking them into buying seaside land for retirement. But they didn't tell buyers that a steep, winding, one-lane dirt road provided the *only* access and that the seaside plots were eroding into the sea. Today, the large number of 'For Sale' plaques are a sobering sign of the times.

Today, there's still only one route, but now it's paved. Cell phones barely work here: this is a good place to disappear. A short drive brings you to the stunning Black Sands Beach stretching for miles northward.

Sleeping

Oceanfront Inn INN $$
(707-986-7002; www.sheltercoveoceanfrontinn.com; 10 Seal Ct; r $180-235, ste $250;) The recently renovated big, bright rooms here all have private balconies, fridges, microwaves, coffeemakers and phenomenal sea views, and the owners provide a basket of goodies; provisions are pretty scarce in this town. There is one suite complete with a full kitchen (minimum two-night stay). The nine-hole golf course across the street is within putting distance of the sea. The on-site Cove Restaurant is one of the top dining options in town.

Inn of the Lost Coast INN $$
(707-986-7521; www.innofthelostcoast.com; 205 Wave Dr, Shelter Cove; r from $225, ste from $240;) Shelter Cove's most family-friendly hotel has a choice of rooms and suites; the latter including options with a full kitchen, private hot tub and sauna and/or fireplace. The double rooms are spacious, with picture windows to maximize the breathtaking ocean views; most have private balconies.

Downstairs the Delgada Pizzeria & Bakery serves decent pizza, while the Fish Tank Cafe is a good stop for coffee, pastries and sandwiches.

Tides Inn HOTEL $$
(707-986-7900; www.sheltercovetidesinn.com; 59 Surf Pt; r $170, ste $195-390;) Perched above tide pools teeming with starfish and sea urchins, the squeaky-clean rooms here offer excellent views (go for the mini suites on the 3rd floor with their fireplaces and full kitchens). The suite options are good for families, and kids are greeted warmly with an activity kit by the innkeeper.

Spy Glass Inn INN $$$
(707-986-4030; www.spyglassinnsheltercove.com; 118 Dolphin Dr; ste $345-375;) Up on a hill a short walk from town, the four luxurious suites here all have sea-view Jacuzzi tubs, full kitchens, private decks and windows lit up by the expansive shoreline beyond. Note that there is a minimum two-night stay at weekends.

Eating

Shelter Cove General Store SUPERMARKET $
(707-986-7733; 7272 Shelter Cove Rd) For those who are self-catering, Shelter Cove General Store is 2 miles beyond town. Get groceries and gasoline here.

Cove Restaurant AMERICAN $$
(707-986-1197; www.sheltercoveoceanfrontinn.com; 10 Seal Ct; mains $10-44; 5-9pm Thu-Sun;) The first-choice place to eat, located at the Oceanfront Inn, this restaurant has everything from artichoke-mushroom lasagna to New York steaks.

Humboldt Redwoods State Park & Avenue of the Giants

Don't miss this magical drive through California's largest redwood park, **Humboldt**

Redwoods State Park (☎707-946-2409; www.parks.ca.gov; Hwy 101; P ♿) FREE, which covers 53,000 acres – 17,000 of which are old-growth – and contains some of the world's most magnificent trees. It also boasts three-quarters of the world's tallest 100 trees. Tree huggers take note: these groves rival (and some say surpass) those in Redwood National Park, which is a long drive further north, although the landscapes here are less diverse.

Exit Hwy 101 when you see the 'Avenue of the Giants' sign, take this smaller alternative to the interstate; it's an incredible, 32-mile, two-lane stretch. You'll find free driving guides at roadside signboards at both the avenue's southern entrance, 6 miles north of Garberville, near Phillipsville, and at the northern entrance, south of Scotia, at Pepperwood; there are access points off Hwy 101.

Three miles north, the **California Federation of Women's Clubs Grove** is home to an interesting four-sided hearth designed by renowned San Franciscan architect Julia Morgan in 1931 to commemorate 'the untouched nature of the forest.'

Primeval **Rockefeller Forest**, 4.5 miles west of the avenue via Mattole Rd, appears as it did a century ago. It's the world's largest contiguous old-growth redwood forest, and contains about 20% of all such remaining trees. Walk the 2.5-mile Big Trees Loop (note that at the time of research a footbridge had been taken out and you'll have to walk across a fallen tree to cross the river where the trail starts). You quickly walk out of sight of cars and feel like you have fallen into the time of dinosaurs.

In **Founders Grove**, north of the visitor center, the Dyerville Giant was knocked over in 1991 by another falling tree. A walk along its gargantuan 370ft length, with its wide trunk towering above, helps you appreciate how huge these ancient trees are.

The park has over 100 miles of trails for hiking, mountain biking and horseback riding. Easy walks include short nature trails in Founders Grove, Rockefeller Forest and **Drury-Chaney Loop Trail** (with berry picking in summer). Challenging treks include the popular **Grasshopper Peak Trail**, south of the visitor center, which climbs to the 3379ft fire lookout.

Humboldt Redwoods State Park Campgrounds CAMPGROUND $
(☎information 707-946-2263, reservations 800-444-7275; www.reserveamerica.com; tent & RV sites $20-35; P 🐾) The park runs three seasonal campgrounds with hot showers, one environmental camp, a hike/bike camp and primitive trail camps. Of the developed spots, Burlington Campground is beside the visitor center and near a number of trailheads; Hidden Springs Campground is 5 miles south along Avenue of the Giants; and Albee Creek Campground is on Mattole Rd past Rockefeller Forest.

Miranda Gardens Resort RESORT $$
(☎707-943-3011; www.mirandagardens.com; 6766 Avenue of the Giants, Miranda; cottages $125-300; P 🚭 🏊 🐾) The best indoor stay along the avenue. The cozy, dark, slightly rustic cottages have redwood paneling, some with fireplaces and kitchens, and are spotlessly clean. The grounds – replete with outdoor Ping Pong, a seasonal swimming pool and a play area for kids amid swaying redwoods – have wholesome appeal for families.

Riverbend Cellars WINERY $$
(☎707-943-9907; www.riverbendcellars.com; 12990 Avenue of the Giants, Myers Flat; ⏰noon-6pm) For something a bit posh, pull over here. The El Centauro red – named for Pancho Villa – is an excellent estate-grown blend.

ℹ Information

Humboldt Redwoods Visitor Center (☎707-946-2263; www.humboldtredwoods.org; Avenue of the Giants; ⏰9am-5pm Apr-Oct, 10am-4pm Nov-Mar) Located 2 miles south of Weott, a volunteer-staffed visitor center shows videos (three in total), sells maps and also has a small exhibition center about the local flora and fauna.

Scotia

For years, Scotia was California's last 'company town,' entirely owned and operated by the Pacific Lumber Company, which built cookie-cut houses and had an open contempt for long-haired outsiders who liked to get between their saws and the big trees. The company went belly up in 2006, sold the mill to another redwood company and, though the town still has a creepy *Twilight Zone* vibe, you no longer have to operate by the company's posted 'Code of Conduct.'

As you drive along Hwy 101 and see what appears to be a never-ending redwood forest, understand that this 'forest' sometimes consists of trees only a few rows deep –

called a 'beauty strip' – a carefully crafted illusion for tourists. Most old-growth trees have been cut.

There are dingy diners and a couple of bars in Rio Dell, across the river. Back in the day, this is where the debauchery happened: because it wasn't a company town, Rio Dell had bars and hookers. In 1969 the freeway bypassed the town and it withered. Upon entering the town from the north, there is a Hoby's Market and Deli located in the Scotia Center (a small shopping center).

The best reason to pull off here is the **Eel River Brewing Company Taproom & Grill** (☎702-725-2739; http://eelriverbrewing.com; 1777 Alamar Way, Fortuna; ⊙11am-11pm), where a breezy beer garden and excellent burgers ($11 to $15) accompany all-organic brews.

Ferndale

The North Coast's most charming town is stuffed with impeccable Victorians – known locally as 'butterfat palaces' because of the dairy wealth that built them. There are so many, in fact, that the entire place is a state and federal historical landmark. Dairy farmers built the town in the 19th century and it's still run by the 'milk mafia': you're not a local till you've lived here 40 years. A stroll down Main St offers a taste of super wholesome, small-town America, from galleries to old-world emporiums and soda fountains. Although Ferndale relies on tourism, it has avoided becoming a tourist trap and has no chain stores. Though a lovely place to spend a summer night, folk close the shutters early in winter and it may be hard to find a bite to eat late evening time, let alone a pint of something frothy.

Sights

Fern Cottage HISTORIC BUILDING
(☎707-786-4835; www.ferncottage.org; 2121 Centerville Rd; group tours per person $10; ⊙11am-3pm Thu-Sat) This 1866 Carpenter Gothic grew to a 32-room mansion. Only one family ever lived here, so the interior is completely, and charmingly, preserved. Tours are held at 11am, noon and 2pm.

Festivals & Events

This wee town has a packed social calendar, especially in the summer. If you're planning a visit, check the events page at www.victorianferndale.com.

Tour of the Unknown Coast SPORTS
(www.tuccycle.org; ⊙May) A challenging one-day event in late May, in which participants in the 100-mile bicycle race climb nearly 10,000ft. Widely recognized as being California's toughest cycle race.

Humboldt County Fair FAIR
(www.humboldtcountyfair.org; Humboldt County Fairgrounds; ⊙mid-Aug) Held in mid-August, the longest-running county fair in California.

Sleeping & Eating

Victorian Inn HISTORIC HOTEL $$
(☎707-786-4949; www.victorianvillageinn.com; 400 Ocean Ave; r $125-250;) The bright, sunny rooms inside this venerable, two-story former bank building (1890) are comfortably furnished with thick carpeting, period-style wallpaper, good linens and antiques.

Shaw House B&B $$
(☎707-786-9958; www.shawhouse.com; 703 Main St; r $129-175, ste $225-275;) Shaw House, an emblematic 'butterfat palace,' was the first permanent structure in Ferndale, completed by founding father Seth Shaw in 1866. Today, it's California's oldest B&B, set back on extensive grounds. Original details remain, including painted wooden ceilings. Most of the rooms have private entrances, and three have private balconies overlooking the large garden with its magnificent shady trees and suitably situated benches.

Hotel Ivanhoe HISTORIC HOTEL $$
(☎707-786-9000; www.ivanhoe-hotel.com; 315 Main St; r $95-145;) Ferndale's oldest hostelry opened in 1875. It has four antique-laden rooms and an Old West–style, 2nd-floor gallery, perfect for morning coffee. The adjoining saloon with dark wood and lots of brass is an atmospheric place for a nightcap, while the adjacent restaurant is a reliable choice for a meal.

★**Gingerbread Mansion** B&B $$$
(☎707-786-4000; www.gingerbread-mansion.com; 400 Berding St; r $175-495; P) This is the cream of dairyland elegance, an 1898 Queen Anne–Eastlake that's unsurprisingly the town's most photographed building. And the inside is no less extravagant, with each room having its own unique (and complex) mix of floral wallpaper, patterned carpeting, grand antique furniture and perhaps a fireplace, wall fresco, stained-glass window or Greek statue thrown in for kicks.

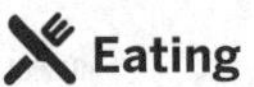

Eating

★Lost Coast Cafe VEGETARIAN $
(☎707-786-5330; 468 Main St; mains $7-10; ⏲10:30am-4pm Thu-Mon; ✎) Step into a homey kitchen, where the soups, sandwiches, salads and baked goods are easily the best vegetarian choices north of Fort Bragg. The owner, Mario, is a wonderful, friendly character and passionate about his cooking and Ferndale. Organic coffee is on the house. Cash only.

Humboldt Sweets BAKERY $
(☎707-786-4683; 614 Main St; scones $5; ⏲8am-5pm Fri-Sun) This cute-as-a-button small place is recommended for coffee and cake; favorites include coconut cream and carrot. Or opt for one of the giant buttery scones, including jalapeño, and cheddar cheese with spring onions. It also makes its own truffles and toffees for the ultimate sugar rush.

No Brand Burger Stand BURGERS $
(☎707-786-9474; 989 Milton Ave; burgers $7; ⏲11am-4pm; P) Hiding near the entrance to town by an industrial building, this hole-in-the-wall turns out a juicy jalapeño double cheeseburger that ranks easily as the North Coast's best burger. The shakes – so thick your cheeks hurt from pulling on the straw – are about the only other thing on the menu.

Farmhouse on Main Restaurant CALIFORNIAN $$
(☎707-786-9222; 460 Main St; mains $18-23; ⏲11am-2pm & 5-9pm Thu-Sun; ☎) This light-filled dining space is one of Ferndale's latest culinary hits with a menu of no-fuss favorites like rib-eye steak, pork cutlets, lamb shanks and braised beef served with appetizing sides such as a creamy polenta. Lightweights can opt for the salads and homemade soups, plus housemade artisan breads, quiches and similar.

☆ Entertainment

Ferndale Repertory Theatre THEATER
(☎707-786-5483; www.ferndale-rep.org; 447 Main St) This top-shelf community company produces excellent contemporary theater in the historic Hart Theatre Building.

Shopping

Main St is a great place to shop. Look for the handful of secondhand stores selling vintage cowboy boots and used designer jeans at reasonable prices.

Blacksmith Shop & Gallery METAL GOODS
(☎707-786-4216; www.ferndaleblacksmith.com; 455 & 491 Main St; ⏲9:30am-5pm) From wrought-iron art to sculpture and jewelry, this is the largest collection of contemporary blacksmithing in the US. Note that there are two venues here: the shop and the gallery, two doors apart, and it is well worth checking them both out.

Ferndale Arts Gallery ARTS & CRAFTS
(☎707-786-9634; www.ferndaleartgallery.com; 580 Main St; ⏲10am-5pm) This artists' co-operative runs a large gallery space selling prints, paintings, pottery, photography and greeting cards that showcase local artists from Humboldt County.

Humboldt Bay National Wildlife Refuge

This pristine **wildlife refuge** (☎707-733-5406; www.fws.gov/refuge/humboldt_bay; 1020 Ranch Rd, Loleta; ⏲8am-5pm; P 🚻) FREE protects wetland habitats for more than 200 species of birds migrating annually along the Pacific Flyway. Between the fall and early spring, when Aleutian geese descend en masse to the area, more than 25,000 geese might be seen in a cackling gaggle outside the visitor center.

The peak season for waterbirds and raptors runs September to March; for black brant geese and migratory shorebirds it's mid-March to late April. Gulls, terns, cormorants, pelicans, egrets and herons come year-round. Look for harbor seals offshore; bring binoculars. If it's open, drive out South Jetty Rd to the mouth of Humboldt Bay for a stunning perspective.

Pick up a map from the **Richard J Guadagno Headquarters & Visitor Center**. Exit Hwy 101 at Hookton Rd, 11 miles south of Eureka, turn north along the frontage road, on the freeway's west side. In April, look for the Godwit Days festival, a celebration of the spring bird migration.

Eureka

One hour north of Garberville, on the edge of the giant Humboldt Bay, lies Eureka, the largest bay north of San Francisco. With a strip-mall sprawl surrounding a lovely historic downtown, it wears its role as the county seat a bit clumsily. Despite a diverse and interesting community of artists, writers, pagans and other free-thinkers, Eureka's wild side slips out only occasionally – the Redwood Coast Jazz Festival has events all over town, and summer concerts rock out the F Street Pier – but mostly, Eureka goes to bed early. Make for Old Town, a small historic district with good shopping and a revitalized waterfront. For nightlife, head to Eureka's livelier sister up the road, Arcata.

Eureka was a major logging town in the late 19th century, and Victorian lumber-baron mansions dot the town; an impressive 16% or so of the city's Old Town buildings have been catalogued as important historical structures.

Sights

The free *Eureka Visitors Map*, available at tourist offices, details walking tours and scenic drives, focusing on architecture and history. **Old Town**, along 2nd and 3rd Sts from C St to M St, was once down-and-out, but has been refurbished into a buzzing pedestrian district. The F Street Plaza and Boardwalk runs along the waterfront at the foot of F St. Gallery openings fall on the first Saturday of every month.

Romano Gabriel Wooden Sculpture Garden GARDENS

(315 2nd St) The coolest thing to gawk at downtown is this collection of whimsical outsider art that's enclosed by aging glass. For 30 years, wooden characters in Gabriel's front yard delighted locals. After he died in 1977, the city moved the collection here.

Morris Graves Museum of Art MUSEUM

(707-442-0278; www.humboldtarts.org; 636 F St; $5; noon-5pm Wed-Sun;) Across Hwy 101, this excellent museum shows rotating Californian artists and hosts performances inside the 1904 **Carnegie library**, the state's first public library. If you are around for a while it also hosts art workshops and classes for adults and kids.

Sequoia Park PARK

(707-441-4263; www.sequoiaparkzoo.net; 3414 W St; park free, zoo adult/child $5/3; zoo 10am-5pm May-Sep, 10am-5pm Tue-Sun Oct-Apr; P) A 77-acre old-growth redwood grove is a surprising green gem in the middle of a residential neighborhood. It has biking and hiking trails, a children's playground and picnic areas, and a small **zoo**, the oldest in California.

Kinetic Museum Eureka MUSEUM

(707-786-3443; http://kineticgrandchampionship.com/kinetic-museum-eureka; 518 A St; admission by donation; 2:15-6:30pm Fri-Sun, also 6-9pm 1st Sat of month;) Come see the fanciful, astounding, human-powered contraptions used in the annual Kinetic Grand Championship (p256) race from Arcata to Ferndale. Shaped like giant fish and UFOs, these colorful piles of junk propel racers over roads, water and marsh during the May event.

Activities

Harbor Cruise CRUISE

(Madaket Cruises; 707-445-1910; www.humboldtbaymaritimemuseum.com; 1st St; narrated cruises adult/child $22/18; 1pm, 2:30pm & 4pm Wed-Sat, 1pm & 2:30pm Sun-Tue mid-May–mid-Oct;) Board the 1910 *Madaket*, the USA's oldest continuously operating passenger vessel, and learn the history of Humboldt Bay. Docked at the foot of C St, it originally ferried mill workers and passengers until the Samoa Bridge opened in 1971. The $10 sunset cocktail cruise serves from the smallest licensed bar in the state, and there's also a 75-minute wildlife cruise.

Hum-Boats Sail, Canoe & Kayak Center BOATING

(707-443-5157; www.humboats.com; 601 Startare Dr; kayak tours from $55; 9am-5pm Mon-Fri, to 6pm Sat & Sun Apr-Oct, to 2:30pm Nov-Mar) At Woodley Island Marina, this outfit rents kayaks and sailboats, offering lessons, tours, charters, sunset sails and full-moon paddles.

Tours

Blue Ox Millworks & Historic Park HISTORIC BUILDING

(707-444-3437; www.blueoxmill.com; 1 X St; adult/child 6-12yr $10/5; 9am-5pm Mon-Fri year-round, plus 9am-4pm Sat Apr-Nov;) One of only a few of its kind in the US, here antique tools and mills are used to produce authentic gingerbread trim for Victorian buildings. One-hour self-guided tours take you through the mill and historical buildings, including a blacksmith shop and 19th-century skid camp. Kids love the oxen. Be sure to leave time to peruse the gift shop.

Sleeping

Every brand of chain hotel is along Hwy 101. Room rates run high midsummer; you can sometimes find cheaper options in Arcata, to the north, or Fortuna, to the south. There is also a handful of motels that cost from $55 to $100 and have no air-conditioning; choose places set back from the road. The cheapest options are south of downtown on the suburban strip.

Inn at 2nd & C HISTORIC HOTEL **$$**
(☎707-444-3344; www.theinnat2ndandc.com; 139 2nd St; r from $129, ste from $209;) Formerly the Eagle House Inn, but reopened under new ownership in May 2017, this glorious Victorian hotel has been tastefully restored to combine Victorian-era decor with every possible modern amenity. The magnificent turn-of-the-century ballroom is used for everything from theater performances to special events. There is also a yoga studio and spa room. Breakfast, tea and complimentary cocktails are additional perks.

Although the hotel is non-smoking, the owners have thoughtfully designated an outside secluded area for smokers (with a bay view, no less!).

Cornelius Daly Inn B&B **$$**
(☎707-445-3638; www.dalyinn.com; 1125 H St; r with/without bathroom $185/130;) This impeccably maintained 1905 Colonial Revival mansion has individually decorated rooms with turn-of-the-20th-century European and American antiques. Guest parlors are trimmed with rare woods; outside are century-old flowering trees. The breakfasts reflect co-owner Donna's culinary skills with such gourmet offerings as apple-stuffed French toast.

Eureka Inn HISTORIC HOTEL **$$**
(☎707-497-6903; www.eurekainn.com; cnr 7th & F Sts; r from $119;) This majestic and enormous historic hotel with its mock Tudor frontage has been renovated. The style is cozy, in an early-20th-century-lodge, vaguely Wild West sort of way, the staff are extremely friendly and there's a decent bar and restaurant on the premises.

Carter House Inns B&B **$$$**
(☎707-444-8062; www.carterhouse.com; 301 L St; r $184-384;) Constructed in period style, this aesthetically remodeled hotel is a Victorian lookalike. Rooms have all modern amenities and top-quality linens; suites have in-room Jacuzzis and marble fireplaces. The same owners operate four other sumptuously decorated lodgings: a single-level house, two honeymoon hideaway cottages and a replica of an 1880s San Francisco mansion, which the owner built himself, entirely by hand.

Eating

You won't go hungry in this town, and health-conscious folk are particularly well catered to with two excellent natural-food grocery stores – **North Coast Co-op** (☎707-443-6027; www.northcoast.coop; cnr 4th & B Sts; 6am-9pm) and **Eureka Natural Foods** (☎707-442-6325; www.eurekanaturalfoods.com; 1626 Broadway St; 7am-9pm Mon-Sat, 8am-8pm Sun) – and two weekly farmers markets – one **street market** (cnr 2nd & F Sts; 10am-1pm Tue Jun-Oct) and one at the **Henderson Center** (☎707-445-3101; 2800 F St; 10am-1pm Thu Jun-Oct). The vibrant dining scene is focused in the Old Town district and has an excellent array of foodie options and price categories.

★**Cafe Nooner** MEDITERRANEAN **$**
(☎707-443-4663; www.cafenooner.com; 409 Opera Alley; mains $10-14; 11am-4pm Sun-Wed, to 8pm Thu-Sat;) Exuding a cozy bistro-style ambience with red-and-white checkered tablecloths and jaunty murals, this perennially popular restaurant serves natural, organic and Med-inspired cuisine with choices that include a Greek-style *meze* platter, plus kebabs, salads and soups. There's a healthy kid's menu, as well.

Ramone's Bakery & Cafe BAKERY, DELI **$**
(☎707-443-6027; www.ramonesbakery.com; 2297 Harrison Ave; mains $6-10; 7am-6pm Mon-Sat, 8am-4pm Sun;) Come here for delicious cakes, tarts, pies and pastries, as well as baguette sandwiches and salads; there are four other branches in town.

★**Brick & Fire** CALIFORNIAN **$$**
(☎707-268-8959; www.brickandfirebistro.com; 1630 F St, Eureka; dinner mains $14-23; 11:30am-9pm Mon & Wed-Fri, 5-9pm Sat & Sun;) Eureka's best restaurant is in an intimate, warm-hued, bohemian-tinged setting that is almost always busy. Choose from thin-crust pizzas, delicious salads (try the pear and blue cheese) and an ever-changing selection of appetizers and mains that highlight local produce and wild mushrooms. There's a weighty wine list and servers are well-versed in pairings.

Kyoto JAPANESE **$$**
(☎707-443-7777; 320 F St; sushi $4-6, mains $15-27; 11:30am-3pm & 5:30-9:30pm Wed-Sat) Renowned as the best sushi in Humboldt

County, dine in a tiny, packed room, where conversation with the neighboring table is inevitable. A menu of sushi and sashimi is rounded out by grilled scallops and fern-tip salad. North Coast travelers who absolutely need sushi should phone ahead for a reservation.

Jack's SEAFOOD $$
(707-273-5273; www.jacksseafoodeureka.com; 4 C St; mains $16-24; 11am-9pm;) Grab a pew by the large picture window overlooking the birds, the boats and Humboldt Bay. The seafood menu here includes all the classics, like steamer clams in a white wine broth and Dungeness crab cakes. Oysters are served three ways: smokey, traditional and raw. There are several pasta dishes, as well, and the salads are huge.

★Restaurant 301 CALIFORNIAN $$$
(707-444-8062; www.carterhouse.com; 301 L St; mains $24-40; 5-8:30pm) Part of the excellent Carter House Inn, Eureka's top table, romantic, sophisticated 301 serves a contemporary Californian menu, using produce from its organic gardens (tours available). The five-course tasting menu ($62, with wine pairings $107) is a good way to taste local seasonal food in its finest presentation.

Drinking & Nightlife

Eureka has some fine old bars and pubs, including live music venues, mainly located in and around the historic center. The annual jazz festival attracts some top musicians and also includes blues concerts (unfortunately the Blues on the Bay annual festival has been suspended in recent years).

Old Town Coffee & Chocolates CAFE
(707-445-8600; www.oldtowncoffeeeureka.com; 211 F St; 7am-9pm;) You'll smell roasting coffee blocks before you see this place. It's a local hangout in a historic building and has board games, local art on the wall and baked goods that include savory choices like bagels with hummus, and wraps.

Speakeasy BAR
(707-444-2244; 411 Opera Alley; 4-11pm Sun-Thu, to 2am Fri & Sat) Squeeze in with the locals at this New Orleans–inspired bar with regular live blues and an infectious convivial atmosphere.

2 Doors Down WINE BAR
(707-268-8959; www.2doorsdownwinebar.com; 1626 F St; 4:40-9:30pm Wed-Mon) Wonderfully cozy and inviting, this Victorian-feeling wine bar lets you create your own flights and will open any bottle on their list of 80-plus wines if you're getting two or more glasses from it. Plenty of snacks are available for order from Brick & Fire (p253) a couple of doors down.

Shanty BAR
(707-444-2053; 213 3rd St; noon-2am;) The coolest spot in town is grungy and fun. Play pool, Donkey Kong, Ms Pac-Man or Ping-Pong, or kick it on the back patio with local 20- and 30-something hipsters.

Entertainment

Morris Graves Museum of Art PERFORMING ARTS
(707-442-0278; www.humboldtarts.org; 636 F St; suggested donation $5) Hosts performing-arts events between September and May, usually on Saturday evenings and Sunday afternoons, but sometimes on other days as well.

Shopping

Eureka's streets lie on a grid: numbered streets cross lettered streets. For the best window-shopping, head to the 300, 400 and 500 blocks of 2nd St, between D and G Sts. The town's low rents and cool old spaces harbor lots of indie boutiques.

Information

Eureka Chamber of Commerce (707-442-3738; www.eurekachamber.com; 2112 Broadway; 8:30am-5pm Mon-Fri;) The main visitor information center is on Hwy 101.

Getting There & Around

Arcata-Eureka Airport (Humboldt County Airport; 707-839-5401; www.humboldtgov.org/1396/Aviation; 3561 Boeing Ave) The Arcata-Eureka Airport (ACV) is located north of McKinleyville on the North Coast, signposted west of Hwy 101 and with regular services to major cities in California and Oregon, as well as further afield. Several carriers operate from this airport including Penair (p214), United Airlines, Delta, American Airlines, United Airlines and Alaska Airlines (p214), though prices tend to be high.

Eureka Transit Service (707-443-0826; www.eurekatransit.org; Humboldt Transit Authority, 133 V St; single fare $1.70) Runs four routes throughout Eureka: the red, gold, green and purple routes. Fares may be paid on the bus and day or monthly passes are also available.

Samoa Peninsula

Grassy dunes and windswept beaches extend along the half-mile-wide, 7-mile long Samoa Peninsula. Stretches of it are spectacular, particularly the dunes, which are part of a 34-mile-long dune system – the largest in Northern California – and the wildlife viewing is excellent.

At the peninsula's south end, **Samoa Dunes Recreation Area** (707-825-2300; www.blm.gov; sunrise-sunset; P) FREE is good for picnicking and fishing. For wildlife, head to **Mad River Slough & Dunes**; from Arcata, take Samoa Blvd west for 3 miles, then turn right at Young St, the Manila turnoff. Park at the community center lot, from where a trail passes mudflats, salt marsh and tidal channels. There are over 200 species of birds: migrating waterfowl in spring and fall, songbirds in spring and summer, shorebirds in fall and winter, and waders year-round.

These undisturbed dunes reach heights of over 80ft. Because of the environment's fragility, access is by guided tour only. **Friends of the Dunes** (www.friendsofthedunes.org) leads free guided walks.

The **Samoa Cookhouse** (707-442-1659; www.samoacookhouse.net; 908 Vance Ave; all-you-can-eat meals per adult $13-17, child $5-9; 7am-3pm & 5-8pm; P) is the dining hall of an 1893 lumber camp. Hikers, hippies and lumberjacks get stuffed while sharing long, red-checked oilcloth-covered tables. There is no menu but you can guarantee that anything you order will be freshly made that day. Think fried chicken, pork ribs and bumper breakfasts. Vegetarians should call ahead.

Arcata

The North Coast's most progressive town, Arcata surrounds a tidy central square that fills with college students, campers, transients and tourists. Sure, it occasionally reeks of patchouli and its politics lean far left, but its earnest embrace of sustainability has fostered some of the most progressive civic action in America. Here, garbage trucks run on biodiesel, recycling gets picked up by tandem bicycle, wastewater gets filtered clean in marshlands and almost every street has a bike lane. Predictably enough, organic products and produce are the norm, art-and-craft markets are rampant and vegans are well catered to.

Founded in 1850 as a base for lumber camps, today Arcata is defined as a magnet for 20-somethings looking to expand their minds: either at Humboldt State University (HSU), and/or on the local highly potent marijuana. Since a 1996 state proposition legalized marijuana for medical purposes, the economy of the region has become inexorably tied to the crop.

Sights

Around Arcata Plaza are two National Historic Landmarks: the 1857 **Jacoby's Storehouse** (707-826-2426; www.facebook.com/pages/Jacoby-Storehouse; Arcata Plaza; hours vary) and the 1915 **Hotel Arcata** (707-826-0217; www.hotelarcata.com; 708 9th St). Another great historic building is the 1914 **Minor Theatre** (707-822-3456; www.minortheatre.com; 1013 10th St; hours vary), which some local historians claim is the oldest theater in the US built specifically for showing films.

Arcata Marsh & Wildlife Sanctuary WILDLIFE RESERVE
(www.cityofarcata.org; Klopp Lake) On the shores of Humboldt Bay, this sanctuary has 5 miles of walking trails and outstanding birding. The **Redwood Region Audubon Society** (707-826-7031; www.rras.org; donation welcome) offers guided walks on Saturdays at 8:30am, rain or shine, from the parking lot at I St's south end. Friends of Arcata Marsh offer guided tours Saturdays at 2pm from the Arcata Marsh Interpretive Center (p258).

Humboldt State University UNIVERSITY
(HSU; 707-826-3011; www.humboldt.edu; 1 Harpst Dr; P) The university on the northeastern side of town holds the Campus Center for Appropriate Technology (CCAT; www.ccathsu.com), a world leader in developing sustainable technologies. On Tuesday at 10am and Friday at 3pm you can take a tour of CCAT's house, a converted residence that uses only 4% of the energy of a comparably sized dwelling.

Activities

Finnish Country Sauna and Tubs SPA
(707-822-2228; http://cafemokkaarcata.com; 495 J St; per 30min adult/child $9.75/2; noon-11pm Sun-Thu, to 1am Fri & Sat;) Like some kind of Euro-crunchy bohemian dream, these private, open-air redwood hot tubs and sauna are situated around a small frog pond. The staff is easygoing, and the facility

is relaxing, simple and clean. Reserve ahead, especially on weekends.

HSU Center Activities OUTDOORS
(707-826-3357; www.humboldt.edu/centeractivities; Humboldt State University, 1 Harpst Dr; 10am-4pm Mon-Fri) An office on the 2nd floor of the University Center, beside the campus clock tower, sponsors myriad workshops, outings and sporting-gear rentals; non-students welcome.

Festivals & Events

Kinetic Grand Championship ART, SPORTS
(707-786-3443; www.kineticgrandchampionship.com; late May;) Arcata's most famous event is held Memorial Day weekend: people on amazing self-propelled contraptions travel 42 miles from Arcata to Ferndale over a period of three days.

Arcata Bay Oyster Festival FOOD & DRINK
(www.oysterfestival.net; 8th St; mid-Jun) A magical celebration of oysters and beer held on a Saturday in mid-June.

North Country Fair FAIR
(www.sameoldpeople.org; Arcata Plaza; Sep) A fun September street fair, where bands with names like the Fickle Hillbillies jam.

Sleeping

Arcata has affordable but limited lodgings. A cluster of hotels – Comfort Inn, Hampton Inn etc – is just north of town, off Hwy 101's Giuntoli Lane. There's cheap camping further north at Clam Beach. One of the best situated hotels is the old fashioned **Hotel Arcata** (707-826-0217; www.hotelarcata.com; 708 9th St; r $97-167;), right on the city's main square.

Fairwinds Motel MOTEL $
(707-822-4824; www.fairwindsmotelarcata.com; 1674 G St; s $70-75, d $80-90;) Serviceable rooms in a standard-issue motel, with some noise from Hwy 101. It's more expensive than the chain motels but has the advantage of being in town and also having an adjacent, reasonable (in price and quality) restaurant.

Lady Anne Inn INN $$
(707-822-2797; www.ladyanneinn.com; 902 14th St; r $115-220;) Dating from 1983, this eco inn is owned by the former mayor of Arcata, so he knows a fair bit about the town. The front garden is a dazzle of roses and native flowers and, while the rooms all differ, they continue the floral theme with decorative wallpaper and pastel paintwork. Dark wood antiques complete the look.

A couple of rooms have a claw-foot tub in the bedroom.

Arcata Stay ACCOMMODATION SERVICES $$
(707-822-0935; www.arcatastay.com; 814 13th St; apt from $169; 11am-5pm) A network of excellent and centrally situated apartments, B&Bs and cottage rentals. There is a two-night minimum and prices go down the longer you stay.

Eating

Great food abounds in restaurants throughout Arcata, almost all casual and most promoting organic produce and ingredients; vegetarians and vegans will have no problem in this town.

There are fantastic farmers markets, at the **Arcata Plaza** (www.humfarm.org; btwn 8th & 9th Sts; 9am-2pm Sat Apr-Nov, from 10am Dec-Mar) and in the parking lot of Wildberries Market. Just a few blocks north of downtown, there is a cluster of the town's best restaurants on G St, near Hwy 101.

Slice of Humboldt Pie CALIFORNIAN $
(707-630-5100; 828 I St; pies $4.50-7.50; 11am-10pm Mon-Thu, to 11pm Fri & Sat) Pies and cider are the mainstays here, ranging from chicken pot pie to cottage, steak and mushroom and savory *empanadas*, including chicken coconut curry and Thai chicken with satay sauce. Sweet pastry treats include peanut-butter fudge and traditional apple, while the ciders cover imports and local varieties. The decor is pure industrial chic with exposed pipes and soft gray paintwork.

T's Cafe CAFE $
(707-826-2133; 860 10th St; breakfast $8-13; 7am-2pm;) Housed in a wonderful early-20th-century mansion, try and grab the table on the front porch if you can. Inside, two cavernous rooms with mismatched furniture, local art, books, toys and magazines provide an informal kickback space for enjoying delicious breakfast classics such as eggs with corned beef hash, stuffed French toast and the specialty: seven choices of eggs Benedict.

Cafe Brio CAFE $
(707-822-5922; www.cafebrioarcata.com; 791 G St; mains $12-15; 7am-5pm Mon, Tue & Thu, to 6pm Wed, to 9pm Fri & Sat) Occupying an ace

THE ECONOMICS OF THE HUMBOLDT HERB

With an estimated one-fifth of Humboldt County's population farming its world-famous weed, a good chunk of the economy here has run, for decades, as bank-less, tax-evading and cash only – but it's also been prosperous enough to strongly support many local businesses. Back in the 1990s farmers could expect to get around $6000 a pound for their crops but since medical marijuana has become legal the price has dropped radically, to just above $1000 per pound. In November 2016 a further law was passed legalizing recreational cannabis use in the state, which some feel may lead to prices plummeting still further and the possibility of large farms and corporations putting the small farmers out of business.

position on the corner of this central square, the patisserie here serves sumptuous cakes, breakfasts are delish and the lunch salads, sandwiches and pies are a notch above the norm. There is also a coffee-cum-wine-bar for suppin'.

Japhy's Soup & Noodles NOODLES $
(☎707-826-2594; www.japhys.com; 1563 G St; mains $7.50-9; ⏰11:30am-8pm Mon-Fri) Big salads, tasty coconut curry, cold noodle salads with a vast choice of sauces and homemade soups – and cheap!

★ **Folie Douce** MODERN AMERICAN $$$
(☎707-822-1042; www.foliedoucearcata.com; 1551 G St; dinner mains $28-37, pizzas $17-24; ⏰11am-2pm Mon, 11am-2pm & 5:30-9pm Tue-Thu, 11am-2pm & 5:30-10pm Fri & Sat) Just a slip of a place, but with an enormous reputation. The short but inventive menu features seasonally inspired bistro cooking, from Asian to Mediterranean, with an emphasis on local organics. Wood-fired pizzas are renowned and desserts are pretty special, as well. A slice of artichoke-heart cheesecake perhaps? Dinner reservations essential.

Drinking & Nightlife

Dive bars and cocktail lounges line the plaza's northern side. Arcata is awash with coffeehouses and brewpubs.

★ **Six Rivers Brewery** MICROBREWERY
(☎707-839-7580; www.sixriversbrewery.com; 1300 Central Ave, McKinleyville; ⏰11:30am-11:30pm Sun & Tue-Thu, to 12:30am Fri & Sat, from 4pm Mon) One of the first female-owned breweries in California, the 'brew with a view' kills it in every category: great beer, amazing community vibe, occasional live music and delicious hot wings. The spicy chili-pepper ale is amazing. At first glance the menu might seem like ho-hum pub grub, but portions are fresh and huge. They also make a helluva pizza.

Redwood Curtain Brewing Company MICROBREWERY
(☎707-826-7222; www.redwoodcurtainbrewing.com; 550 S G St; ⏰noon-11pm Sun-Tue, to midnight Wed-Sat) This tiny gem of a brewery has a varied collection of rave-worthy craft ales and live music or DJs some nights. Plus it offers free wheat thins and goldfish crackers to munch on.

Cafe Mokka CAFE
(☎707-822-2228; www.cafemokkaarcata.com; cnr 5th & J Sts; ⏰noon-11pm Sun-Thu, to 1am Fri & Sat) Bohos head to this cafe at Finnish Country Sauna & Tubs (p255) for a mellow, old-world vibe, good coffee drinks and homemade cookies.

Humboldt Brews BAR
(☎707-826-2739; www.humbrews.com; 856 10th St; ⏰11:30am-midnight Sat-Thu, to 2am Fri) This popular dimly-lit beer house has a huge range of carefully selected beer taps, fish tacos, buffalo wings and for veggies, smoked tofu (pub grub $11 to $13). Regular live music and a pool table add to the entertainment.

Entertainment

Center Arts PERFORMING ARTS
(☎tickets 707-826-3928; www.humboldt.edu/centerarts; Humboldt State University, 1 Harpst Dr; ⏰hours vary) Hosts events on campus and you'd be amazed at who shows up. The place to buy tickets is at the University Ticket Office in the HSY Bookstore on the 3rd floor of the University Center.

Arcata Theatre CINEMA
(☎707-822-1220; www.arcatatheater.com; 1036 G St) An exquisite remodeling has revived this classic movie house, which shows art films,

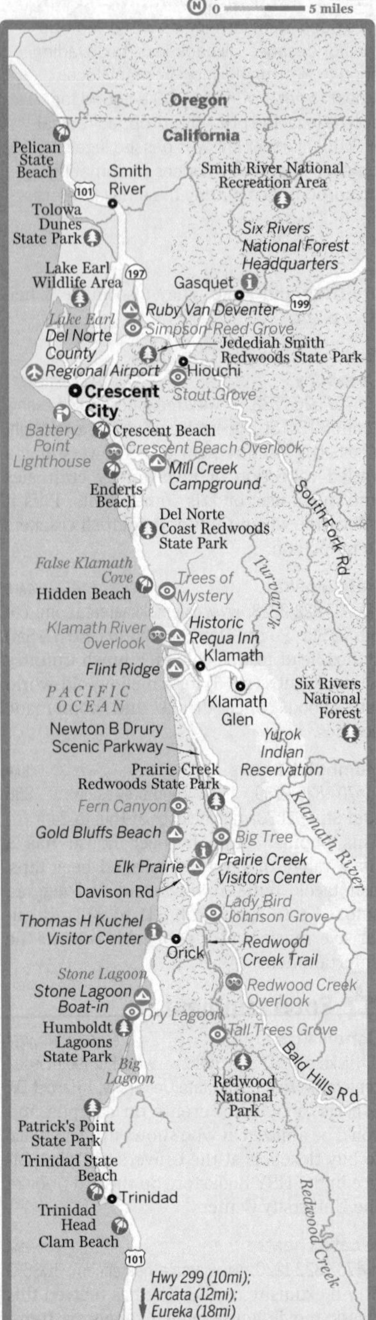

rock documentaries, silent films and more. Plus, it serves beer.

Information

Arcata Marsh Interpretive Center (707-826-2359; www.humboldt.edu/arcatamarsh; 569 South G St; 9am-5pm Tue-Sun, from 1pm Mon;) Staffed by the Friends of Arcata Marsh (FOAM), who give free guided tours on Saturday afternoons.

California Welcome Center (707-822-3619; www.arcatachamber.com; 9am-5pm) At the junction of Hwys 299 and 101; has area info.

Getting There & Around

Alaska Airlines, Penair, Delta, American Airlines and United Airlines are the main carriers to operate national flights to/from the Arcata-Eureka Airport (p254) but fares tend to be high. Flights come and go from several major Californian cities, including Los Angeles, San Francisco, Sacramento and San Diego. There are also regular flights from other US cities, including New York, Denver, Phoenix and Portland (Oregon).

Greyhound (p214) serves Arcata from San Francisco ($57, seven hours, daily). Redwood Transit System (p214) serves Arcata and Eureka on the Trinidad–Scotia routes Monday to Saturday ($3, 2½ hours).

Arcata city buses stop at the **Arcata & Mad River Transit Center** (707-825-8934; www.arcatatransit.org; 925 E St at 9th St). For shared rides, read the bulletin board at the North Coast Co-op.

Life Cycle Bike Shop (707-822-7755; www.lifecyclearcata.com; 1593 G St; per day $25; 9am-6pm Mon-Sat) rents, services and sells bicycles.

Only in Arcata: borrow a bike from **Library Bike** (www.arcata.com/greenbikes; 865 8th St; deposit $20; hours vary). They're beaters, but they ride.

NORTHERN REDWOOD COAST

Congratulations, traveler, you've reached the middle of nowhere, or at least the top of the middle of nowhere. Here, the trees are so large that the tiny towns along the road seem even smaller. The scenery is pure drama: cliffs and rocks, native lore, legendary salmon runs, mammoth trees, wild elk and RVing retirees. Leave time to dawdle and bask in the haunting natural grandeur of it all and, even though there are scores of mid-century motels, try and make an effort to sleep outdoors if possible. Then, as you gaze skywards, ponder the fact that giant redwoods once covered some 5000 square miles of coast here, before the brutal mass logging that took place around the turn of the 20th century (apparently some 95% of the trees were felled). Fortunately, conservation measures are now firmly in place to protect these magnificent trees that can live for thousands of years.

Trinidad

Cheery, tiny Trinidad perches prettily on the side of the ocean, combining upscale mid-century homes with a mellow surfer vibe. Somehow it feels a bit off-the-beaten-path even though tourism augments fishing to keep the economy going. Trinidad is also a big hit with ornithologists; it's home to one of the most diverse seabird colonies in California. The town gained its name when Spanish sea captains arrived on Trinity Sunday in 1775 and named the area La Santisima Trinidad (the Holy Trinity); later it was the site of bloody battles and raids against the local Native Americans during the Civil War. Around this period, it also experienced a boom, becoming an important port for miners. If you can, check out the superb beaches and rocky coves and stop for a seafood meal overlooking the water.

Sights & Activities

Trinidad is small: approach via Hwy 101 or from the north via Patrick's Point Dr (which becomes Scenic Dr further south). To reach town, take Main St.

The free town map at the information kiosk (p260) shows several fantastic hiking trails, most notably the **Trinidad Head Trail** with superb coastal views and excellent for **whale-watching** (December to April). Stroll along an exceptionally beautiful cove at **Trinidad State Beach**; take Main St and bear right at Stagecoach, then take the second turn left (the first is a picnic area) into the small lot.

Scenic Dr twists south along coastal bluffs, passing tiny coves with views back toward the bay. It peters out before reaching the broad expanses of **Luffenholtz Beach** (accessible via the staircase) and serene white-sand **Moonstone Beach**. Exit Hwy 101 at 6th Ave/Westhaven to get there. Further south Moonstone becomes **Clam Beach County Park**.

Surfing is good year-round, but potentially dangerous: unless you know how to judge conditions and get yourself out of trouble – there are no lifeguards here – surf in better-protected Crescent City.

HSU Telonicher Marine Laboratory AQUARIUM
(707-826-3671; www.humboldt.edu/marinelab; 570 Ewing St; $1; 9am-4:30pm Mon-Fri year-round, plus 10am-5pm Sat & Sun mid-Sep–mid-May; P) Near Edwards St, this marine lab has a touch tank, several aquariums (look for the giant Pacific octopus), an enormous whale jaw and a cool 3D map of the ocean floor. You can join a naturalist on **tide-pooling expeditions** (per person $3, minimum $20). All tours are by appointment only so call ahead and be sure to ask about conditions.

Sleeping

Most of the inns and motels line Patrick's Point Dr, north of town, and are family owned and welcoming, with fabulous ocean views. In the center, choices are limited to a cute B&B which gets booked up fast at weekends. **Trinidad Retreats** (www.trinidadretreats.com) and **Redwood Coast Vacation Rentals** (www.redwoodcoastvacationrentals.com) can also help you find a bed for the night.

View Crest Lodge LODGE $$
(707-677-3393; www.viewcrestlodge.com; 3415 Patrick's Point Dr; 1- & 2-bedroom cottages $95-240; P) On a hill above the ocean on the inland side, these well-maintained, modern and terrific-value cottages all have ocean views and added extras like fireplaces and hot tubs. They range from one to two bedroom and breakfast is included in the price.

Trinidad Inn INN $$
(707-677-3349; www.trinidadinn.com; 1170 Patrick's Point Dr; r $100-245; P) Sparklingly clean and attractively decorated rooms fill this upmarket, gray-shingled motel under tall trees. The accommodations vary considerably; some rooms have sitting rooms, fireplaces and fully equipped kitchens, others are straightforward double rooms with a TV and desk.

★ **Lost Whale Inn** B&B $$$
(707-677-3425; www.lostwhaleinn.com; 3452 Patrick's Point Dr; r $199-325, ste $408-750;

) Perched atop a grassy cliff, high above crashing waves and braying sea lions, this spacious, modern, light-filled B&B has stunning views out to the sea. The lovely gardens have a 24-hour hot tub and other perks include the superb breakfast and complimentary tea that is served at 4pm. The owner is Portuguese and family antiques feature in every room.

Turtle Rocks Oceanfront Inn B&B $$$
(707-677-3707; www.turtlerocksinn.com; 3392 Patrick's Point Dr; r $295-335;) Enjoy truly stunning sea vistas from every room at this plush, modern place on three peaceful, windswept acres. Rooms are spacious with terraces; number 3 comes particularly recommended with its warm blue decor. A complimentary buffet is served from 3pm to 6pm.

Trinidad Bay B&B B&B $$$
(707-677-0840; www.trinidadbaybnb.com; 560 Edwards St; r $200-350;) Opposite the lighthouse, this light-filled Cape Cod–style home overlooks the harbor and Trinidad Head. Breakfast may be delivered to your uniquely styled room and in the afternoon the house fills with the scent of freshly baked cookies. The Trinity Alps room has a kitchenette and is well set up for families.

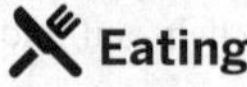

Eating

Trinidad is home to superb beaches and hideaway coves where packing a picnic is always a tempting option (thankfully the town has a solid choice of delis and supermarkets). Trinidad State Beach also has excellent picnicking facilities. The restaurants here are, unsurprisingly, centered on seafood and fish; several have coastal views to enhance that ocean-inspired dining experience.

Katy's Smokehouse & Fishmarket SEAFOOD $
(www.katyssmokehouse.com; 740 Edwards St; 9am-6pm) Makes its own chemical-free and amazingly delicious smoked and canned fish, using line-caught, sushi-grade seafood; the tuna has been voted number one in the US, no less. There's no restaurant, just grab some for a picnic.

Beachcomber Café CAFE $
(707-677-0106; 363 Trinity St; breakfast from $4; 7am-4pm Mon-Fri, 8am-4pm Sat & Sun;) Head here for the best breakfast in these parts, ranging from a hearty bowl of organic black beans with avocado and poached egg to moist and delicious homemade muffins. Also has plenty of newspapers and mags to peruse. Bring your own cup if you want a drink to go.

Lighthouse Café CALIFORNIAN $
(707-677-0390; 355 Main St; mains $6-9; 11am-7pm Tue-Sun;) Across from the Chevron, this fun little arty joint makes good food fast, using mostly organic ingredients – try the creative soups, fish and chips with hand-cut fries, local grass-fed beef burgers and homemade ice cream. Order at the counter and then sit inside or out.

Larrupin Cafe CALIFORNIAN $$$
(707-677-0230; www.thelarrupin.com; 1658 Patrick's Point Dr; mains $22-42; 5-9pm Tue-Sun;) Everybody loves Larrupin, where Moroccan rugs, chocolate-brown walls, gravity-defying floral arrangements and deep-burgundy Oriental carpets create a moody atmosphere perfect for a lovers' tryst. On the menu, expect consistently good mesquite-grilled seafood and meats – the smoked beef brisket is amazing. In the summer, book a table on the garden patio for live music some nights.

Information

Information Kiosk (www.trinidadcalif.com; cnr Patrick's Point Dr & Main St; 11am-5pm Jun-Sep, shorter hours Oct-May) Just west of the freeway. Pick up the pamphlet *Discover Trinidad* from here – it has an excellent map.

Trinidad Chamber of Commerce (707-667-1610; www.trinidadcalif.com) Information on the web, but no visitor center.

Patrick's Point State Park

Coastal bluffs jut out to sea at this 640-acre state park, where sandy beaches abut rocky headlands. Easy access to dramatic coastline makes this is a great bet for families, but any age will find a feast for the senses as they climb rock formations, search for breaching whales, carefully navigate tide pools and listen to barking sea lions and singing birds.

Sumêg is an authentic reproduction of a Yurok village, with hand-hewn redwood buildings where Native Americans gather for traditional ceremonies. In the native plant garden you'll find species for making traditional baskets and medicines.

On Agate Beach look for stray bits of jade and sea-polished agate. Follow the signs to tide pools. The 2-mile Rim Trail, an old

Yurok trail around the bluffs, circles the point with access to huge rocky outcrops. Don't miss Wedding Rock, one of the park's most romantic spots. Other trails lead around unusual formations like Ceremonial Rock and Lookout Rock.

The park's three well-tended **camp-grounds** (information 707-677-3570, reservations 800-444-7275; www.reserveamerica.com; 4150 Patrick's Point Dr; tent/RV sites $35/45; P) have coin-operated showers and clean bathrooms. Penn Creek and Abalone campgrounds are more sheltered than Agate Beach.

Humboldt Lagoons State Park

Stretching out for miles along the coast, Humboldt Lagoons has long, sandy beaches and a string of coastal lagoons. **Big Lagoon** and the even prettier **Stone Lagoon** are both excellent for kayaking and bird-watching. Sunsets are spectacular, with no artificial structures in sight. Picnic at Stone Lagoon's north end. The Stone Lagoon Visitor Center, on Hwy 101, has closed due to staffing shortages, but there's a toilet and a bulletin board displaying information.

A mile north, **Freshwater Lagoon** is also great for birding. South of Stone Lagoon, tiny **Dry Lagoon** (a freshwater marsh) has a fantastic day hike and good agate hunting. Park at Dry Lagoon's picnic area and hike north on the unmarked trail to Stone Lagoon; the trail skirts the southwestern shore and ends up at the ocean, passing through woods and marshland rich with wildlife. Mostly flat, it's about 2.5 miles one way – and nobody takes it because it's unmarked.

You will have to sleep under canvas in these parts. All campsites are first-come, first-served. The park runs two **environmental campgrounds** (tent sites $20; Apr-Oct; P); bring water. Stone Lagoon has six boat-in environmental campsites.

Humboldt County Parks also operates a lovely cypress-grove picnic area and campground: the **Big Lagoon County Park Campground** (707-445-7651; http://co.humboldt.ca.us; off Hwy 101; tent sites $20; P) beside Big Lagoon, a mile off Hwy 101, with flush toilets and cold water, but no showers.

Redwood National & State Parks

This richly forested region can be a little confusing regarding which park is where and what they all offer. The main parks in this jigsaw of mighty redwoods are: the Redwood National Park; Prairie Creek Redwoods State Park; Del Norte Coast Redwoods State Park and Jedediah Smith Redwoods State Park (famed for being a backdrop in the original *Star Wars* movie). Interspersed among the parks are a number of small towns, while to the south lies Orick (population 650), which offers a few storefronts, a gas station and an excellent visitor center. All the parks are an International Biosphere Reserve and World Heritage Site, yet they remain little visited when compared to their southern brethren, like the Sequoia National Park. It is worth contemplating that some of these trees have been standing here for time immemorial, predating the Roman Empire by over 500 years. Prepare to be impressed.

Redwood National Park

This park is the southernmost of a patchwork of state and federally administered lands under the umbrella of **Redwood National & State Parks** (707-465-7335; www.nps.gov/redw; Hwy 101, Orick; P) FREE. After picking up a map at the **visitor center**, you'll have a suite of choices for hiking. A few miles north along Hwy 101, a

THE ENDANGERED MARBLED MURRELET

Notice how undeveloped the Redwood National and State Parks have remained? Thank the marbled murrelet, a small white and brown-black auk that nests in old-growth conifers. Loss of nesting territory due to logging has severely depleted the bird's numbers but Redwood National Park scientists have discovered that corvid predators (ravens, jays etc) are also to blame. Because corvids are attracted to food scraps left by visitors, the number of snacking, picnicking or camping humans in the park greatly affects predation on the marbled murrelet. Restrictions on development to prevent food scraps and thus protect the birds are so strict that it's nearly impossible to build anything new.

trip inland on Bald Hills Rd will take you to Lady Bird Johnson Grove, with its 1-mile, kid-friendly loop trail, or get you lost in the secluded serenity of Tall Trees Grove.

To protect the Tall Trees Grove, a limited number of cars per day are allowed access; get permits at the visitor center. This can be a half-day trip itself, but you're well rewarded after the challenging approach (a 6-mile rumble on an old logging road behind a locked gate, then a moderately strenuous 4-mile round-trip hike). Another recommended hike is to Trillium Falls – a 2½-mile trail leading to a small waterfall, accessed from Davidson Rd at Elk Meadow.

Note that during the winter, several foot bridges crossing the Redwood Creek are removed due to the high waters. If you are hiking at this time of year, be sure to check with a ranger regarding the current situation before striding out.

Elk Meadow Cabins CABIN **$$$**

(☎866-733-9637; www.redwoodadventures.com; 7 Valley Green Camp Rd, Orick; cabins $239-289; P 📶 🐾) These spotless and bright cabins with equipped kitchens and all the mod-cons are in a perfect mid-parks location – they're great if you're traveling in a group and the most comfy choice even if you're not. Expect to see elk on the lawn in the mornings. Cabins sleep six to eight people and there's an additional $65 cleaning fee.

ℹ Information

Unlike most national parks, there are no fees and no highway entrance stations at Redwood National Park, so it's imperative to pick up the free map at the park headquarters in Crescent City (p266) or at the information center in Orick. Rangers here issue permits to visit Tall Trees Grove and loan bear-proof containers for backpackers.

For in-depth redwood ecology, buy the excellent official park handbook. The **Redwood Parks Association** (www.redwoodparksassociation.org) provides good information on its website, including detailed descriptions of all the park hikes.

Prairie Creek Redwoods State Park

Famous for some of the world's best virgin redwood groves and unspoiled coastline, this 14,000-acre **section** (www.parks.ca.gov; Newton B Drury Scenic Pkwy; per car $8; P 👪) 🌿 of Redwood National & State Parks has spectacular scenic drives and 70 miles of mainly shady hiking trails, many of which are excellent for children. Kids of all ages will enjoy the magnificent herd of elk here, which can generally be spied grazing at the Elk Prairie, signposted from the highway; the best times to be sure of seeing the elk are early morning and around sunset.

There are 28 **mountain-biking** and **hiking trails** through the park, from simple to strenuous. Only a few of these will appeal to hard-core hikers, who should take on the Del Norte Coast Redwoods. A few easy nature trails start near the visitor center, including Revelation Trail and Elk Prairie Trail. Stroll the recently reforested logging road on the Ah-Pah Interpretive Trail at the park's north end. The most challenging hike in this corner of the park is the spectacular 11.5-mile Coastal Trail which goes through primordial redwoods and is part of the California Coastal Trail (www.californiacoastaltrail.info).

Just past the Gold Bluffs Beach Campground the road deadends at Fern Canyon, the second busiest spot in the park, where 60ft fern-covered sheer-rock walls are so unusual that they were used in scenes from Steven Spielberg's *Jurassic Park 2: The Lost World*, as well as *Return of the Jedi*. This is one of the most photographed spots on the North Coast – damp and lush, all emerald green – and totally worth getting your toes wet to see.

Newton B Drury Scenic Parkway DRIVING

(Hwy 101, Orick; 👪) Just north of Orick is the turnoff for the 8-mile parkway, which runs parallel to Hwy 101 through untouched ancient redwood forests. This is a not-to-miss short detour off the freeway where you can view the magnificence of these trees. Numerous trails branch off from roadside pullouts, including family-friendly options and trails that fit ADA (American Disabilities Act) requirements, such as Big Tree Wayside and Revelation Trail.

★**Gold Bluffs Beach** CAMPGROUND **$**

(tent sites $35) This gorgeous campground sits between 100ft cliffs and wide-open ocean, but there are some windbreaks and solar-heated showers. Look for sites up the cliff under the trees. No reservations.

Elk Prairie Campground CAMPGROUND **$**

(☎reservations 800-444-7275; www.reserveamerica.com; Prairie Creek Rd; tent & RV sites $35; P 🐾) Elk roam this popular campground,

WORTH A TRIP

SMITH RIVER NATIONAL RECREATION AREA

West of Jedediah Smith Redwoods State Park, the Smith River, the state's last remaining undammed waterway, runs right beside Hwy 199. Originating high in the Siskiyou Mountains, its serpentine course cuts through deep canyons beneath thick forests. Chinook salmon (October to December) and steelhead trout (December to April) annually migrate up its clear waters. Camp (there are four developed campgrounds), hike (75 miles of trails), raft (145 miles of navigable white water) and kayak here, but check regulations if you want to fish. Stop by the **Six Rivers National Forest Headquarters** (707-457-3131; www.fs.fed.us/r5/sixrivers; 10600 Hwy 199, Gasquet; 8am-4:30pm daily May-Sep, 8am-4:30pm Mon-Fri Oct-Apr) to get your bearings. Pick up pamphlets for the **Darlingtonia Trail** and **Myrtle Creek Botanical Area**, both easy jaunts into the woods, where you can see rare plants and learn about the area's geology.

where you can sleep under redwoods or at the prairie's edge. There are hot showers, some hike-in sites and a shallow creek to splash in. Sites one to seven and 69 to 76 are on grassy prairies and get full sun; sites eight to 68 are wooded. To camp in a mixed redwood forest, book sites 20 to 27.

Del Norte Coast Redwoods State Park

Marked by steep canyons and dense woods north of Klamath, half the 6400 acres of this **park** (707-465-7335; www.parks.ca.gov; Mill Creek Rd; per car $8; P) are virgin redwood forest, crisscrossed by 15 miles of hiking trails, some of which pass by branches of Mill Creek (bring your fishing rod). The park also fronts 8 miles of rugged coastline.

Hwy 1 winds in from the coast at dramatic Wilson Beach, and traverses the dense forest, with groves stretching as far as you can see. Picnic on the sand at False Klamath Cove. Heading north, tall trees cling precipitously to canyon walls that drop to the rocky, timber-strewn coastline. Unfortunately, it is impossible to hike to the water – as of April 2017, the trail bridge located 1.75 miles in from the parking lot on Damnation Creek Trail was closed until further notice.

Serious hikers will be most greatly rewarded by the Damnation Creek Trail. It's only 4 miles long, but the 1100-ft elevation change and cliff-side red- wood makes it the park's best hike. The unmarked trailhead starts from a parking area off Hwy 101 at Mile 16.

Crescent Beach Overlook and picnic area has superb wintertime whale-watching. At the park's north end, watch the surf pound at Crescent Beach, just south of Crescent City via Enderts Beach Rd.

Mill Creek Campground (reservations 800-444-7275; www.reserveamerica.com; Mill Creek Rd; tent & RV sites $35; mid-May–Oct; P) has hot showers and 145 sites in a redwood grove, 2 miles east of Hwy 101 and 7 miles south of Crescent City. Sites 1-74 are woodsier; sites 75-145 sunnier. Hike-in sites are prettiest.

Pick up maps and inquire about guided walks at the Crescent City Information Center (p266) or the **Thomas H Kuchel Visitor Center** (707-465-7765; www.nps.gov/redw; Hwy 101, Orick; 9am-5pm Apr-Oct, to 4pm Nov-Mar;) in Orick.

Jedediah Smith Redwoods State Park

The northernmost park, Jedediah Smith is 9 miles northeast of Crescent City (via Hwy 101 north to Hwy 199 east). The redwood stands are so thick that few trails penetrate the park, but the outstanding 11-mile **Howland Hill Rd scenic drive** cuts through otherwise inaccessible areas (take Hwy 199 to South Fork Rd; turn right after crossing two bridges). It's a rough road, impassable for RVs, but if you can't hike, it's the best way to see the forest.

Stop for a stroll under enormous trees in **Simpson-Reed Grove**. There's a swimming hole and picnic area near the park entrance. An easy half-mile trail, departing from the far side of the campground, crosses the Smith River via a summer-only footbridge, leading to Stout Grove, the park's most famous grove. The visitor center sells hiking maps and nature guides.

Klamath

Giant metal-cast golden bears stand sentry at the bridge across the Klamath River, announcing Klamath, one of the tiny settlements that break up Redwood National & State Parks between Prairie Creek Redwoods State Park and Del Norte Coast Redwoods State Park. With a gas station/market, diner and a casino, Klamath is basically a wide spot in the road with some seriously great roadside kitsch at its edges. The Yurok Tribal Headquarters is in the town center and the entire settlement and much of the surrounding area is the tribe's ancestral land. The Yuroks are the largest group of Native Americans in the state of California.

Klamath is roughly an hour north of Eureka and is popular with hikers, campers and anglers; the river is famed for its wild freshwater salmon and is one of California's last free-flowing rivers after a proposal to build a dam here was thwarted in 1994.

Sights & Activities

The mouth of the **Klamath River** is a dramatic sight. Marine, riparian, forest and meadow ecological zones all converge and the birding is exceptional. For the best views, head north of town to Requa Rd and the **Klamath River Overlook** and picnic on high bluffs above driftwood-strewn beaches. On a clear day, this is one of the most spectacular viewpoints on the North Coast, and one of the best whale-watching spots in California (this is one of the mammal's first feeding stops as they come south from Alaska). For a good hike, head north along the Coastal Trail. You'll have the sand to yourself at **Hidden Beach**; access the trail at the northern end of Motel Trees.

Just south of the river, on Hwy 101, the scenic **Coastal Drive**, a narrow, winding country road, traces extremely high cliffs over the ocean. Due to erosion a 3.3-mile section of the 9.5-mile loop (between Carruther's Cove trailhead and the intersection of the Coastal Drive with Alder Camp Rd) has been closed to motor traffic since 2011, but it's still walkable.

TREES OF MYSTERY

It's hard to miss the giant statues of Paul Bunyan and Babe the Blue Ox towering over the parking lot at **Trees of Mystery** (707-482-2251; www.treesofmystery.net; 15500 Hwy 101; museum free, gondola adult/child $16/8; 8:30am-6:30pm Jun-Aug, 9am-6pm Sep & Oct, 9:30am-4:30pm Nov-May; P), a shameless tourist trap with a gondola running through the redwood canopy and a fun 'Tall Tales Forest' where chainsaw sculptures tell the tale of Paul Bunyan. It's perfect for families. The surprisingly wonderful **End of the Trail Museum** located behind the gift shop has an outstanding collection of Native American arts and artifacts, and it's free.

Sleeping

Woodsy Klamath is cheaper than Crescent City, but there aren't as many places to eat or buy groceries, and there's nothing to do at night but play cards. There are ample private RV parks in the area.

Flint Ridge Campground CAMPGROUND
(707-464-6101) FREE Four miles from the Klamath River Bridge via Coastal Dr, this tent-only, hike-in campground sits among a wild, overgrown meadow of ferns and moss. It's a 10-minute walk (half a mile) east, uphill from the parking area. There's no water, plenty of bear sightings (bear boxes on-site) and you have to pack out trash. But, hey, it's free.

Ravenwood Motel MOTEL $
(707-482-5911; www.ravenwoodmotel.com; 131 Klamath Blvd; r/ste with kitchen $95/140; P) The spotlessly clean rooms are individually decorated with furnishings and flair you'd expect in a city hotel, not a small-town motel. The same could be said of the surrounding attractions – there is a casino virtually next door!

★ **Historic Requa Inn** HISTORIC HOTEL $$
(707-482-1425; www.requainn.com; 451 Requa Rd; r $119-199; P) A woodsy country lodge on bluffs overlooking the mouth of the Klamath, the creaky and bright 1914 Requa Inn is a North Coast favorite and – even better – it's a carbon-neutral facility. Many of the charming, old-timey Americana rooms have mesmerizing views over the misty river, as does the dining room, which serves locally sourced, organic New American cuisine.

Crescent City

Crescent City is California's last big town north of Arcata. Founded as a thriving seaport and supply center for inland gold mines in the mid-19th century, the town's history was quite literally washed away in 1964, when half the town was swallowed by a tsunami. Of course, it was rebuilt (though mostly with the utilitarian ugliness of ticky-tacky buildings), but its marina was devastated by effects of the 2011 Japan earthquake and tsunami, when the city was evacuated. The economy depends heavily on shrimp and crab fishing, hotel tax and on Pelican Bay maximum-security prison, just north of town, which adds tension to the air and lots of cops to the streets.

Hwy 101 splits into two parallel one-way streets, with the southbound traffic on L St, northbound on M St. To see the major sights, turn west on Front St toward the lighthouse. Downtown is along 3rd St.

Sights

If you're in town in August, the **Del Norte County Fair** features a rodeo, and lots of characters.

North Coast Marine Mammal Center SCIENCE CENTER
(707-465-6265; www.northcoastmmc.org; 424 Howe Dr; 10am-5pm;) Just east of Battery Point, this is the ecologically minded foil to the garish Ocean World. The clinic treats injured seals, sea lions and dolphins and releases them back into the wild. There is an interesting gift shop.

Battery Point Lighthouse LIGHTHOUSE
(707-467-3089; www.delnortehistory.org; South A St; adult/child $3/1; 10am-4pm Wed-Sun Apr-Sep) The 1856 lighthouse still operates on a tiny, rocky island that you can easily reach at low tide. You can also get a tour of the on-site museum for $3. Note that the listed hours are subject to change due to tides and weather.

Beachfront Park PARK
(Howe Dr; P) Between B and H Sts, this park has a harborside beach with no large waves, making it perfect for little ones. Further east on Howe Dr, near J St, you'll come to **Kidtown**, with slides and swings and a make-believe castle.

Sleeping

Most people stop here for one night while traveling; motels are overpriced, but you'll pass a slew of good midrange hotels on the main arteries leading into and out of town, and you will generally have no problem finding a room, whatever the season. The county operates two excellent first-come, first-served campgrounds just outside of town and a couple of B&Bs have more recently opened up in town.

Curly Redwood Lodge MOTEL $
(707-464-2137; www.curlyredwoodlodge.com; 701 Hwy 101 S; r $79-107; P) The motel is a marvel: it's entirely built and paneled from a single curly redwood tree that measured over 18ft thick in diameter. Progressively restored and polished into a gem of mid-20th-century kitsch, the inn is like stepping into a time capsule and a delight for retro junkies. Rooms are clean, large and comfortable (request one away from the road).

Florence Keller Park CAMPGROUND $
(707-464-7230; www.co.del-norte.ca.us; 3400 Cunningham Lane; tent sites $10; P) County-run Florence Keller Park has 50 sites in a beautiful grove of young redwoods (take Hwy 101 north to Elk Valley Cross Rd and follow the signs). There are limited facilities at this campground: toilets, but no showers.

Bay View Inn HOTEL $
(800-742-8439; www.ccbvi.com; 310 Hwy 101 S; s/d $55/99; P) Bright, modern, updated rooms with microwaves and refrigerators fill this centrally located, independent hotel. It may seem a bit like a better-than-average highway-exit chain, but colorful bedspreads and warm hosts add necessary homespun appeal. The rooms upstairs in the back have views of the lighthouse and the harbor.

Anna Wulf Bed & Breakfast B&B $$
(707-464-5340; www.annawulfhousebedandbreakfast.com; 622 J St; r/ste $100/150; P) Nice, Victorian-style B&B built in 1896. It's not as frilly inside as the lavender exterior would predict. The Honeymoon Suite has an inviting clawfoot tub. Check-out time is civilized (noon) – refreshing in these parts.

★ **Scopa at the Sea** B&B $$$
(541-944-4156; www.scopaproperties.com; 344 N Pebble Beach Dr; r from $250; P) The Cape Cod–style architecture twinned with deluxe contemporary decor make this a

good option for those weary of motel chains. Furnished in warm earth colors with a design eye for detail, the en suites have tubs, as well as showers, while the front terrace is ideally placed for whale-watching. The breakfast highlights are the homemade breads and pastries made by innkeeper Deborah.

Eating

Crescent City has plenty of restaurants, including a large number of fast-food options located on Hwy 101. For fresh seafood, there are a couple of aptly located restaurants near the water that specialize in fresh shrimp and crab. There is an excellent farmers market held every Saturday from June to October at the Del Norte County Fairgrounds.

Good Harvest Cafe AMERICAN $
(707-465-6028; 575 Hwy 101 S; mains $7-16; 7:30am-9pm Mon-Sat, from 8am Sun;) This popular family owned cafe is in a spacious location across from the harbor. It's got a bit of everything – all pretty good – from soups and sandwiches to full meals and smoothies. Fine beers, a crackling fire and loads of vegetarian options make this among the best dining spots in town.

North Coast Ocean Sports & Grill GRILL $
(707-465-1465; www.northcoastoceansportsandgrill.com; 110 Anchor Way; mains $11-15; 11am-8pm;) A young, informal vibe, a no-frills sound menu of seafood, burgers and salads and exceptional ice cream mean this place is always packed out, especially in summer when folk spill out onto the front deck across from the ocean. It also rents out surf boards, kayaks and bikes.

Enoteca ITALIAN, AMERICAN $
(960 3rd St; mains $7-12; 11am-7pm Mon-Wed & Sat, to 8pm Thu, to 10pm Fri;) Stop in for salads, pasta, sandwiches or jazz on Friday nights. Hands down the most happening place downtown.

Chart Room SEAFOOD $$
(707-464-5993; www.ccchartroom.com; 130 Anchor Way; dinner mains $10-28; 7am-7pm Wed-Thu & Sun, to 8pm Fri & Sat, 11am-4pm Tue;) At the tip of the South Harbor pier, this joint is renowned far and wide for its fish and chips: batter-caked golden beauties that deliver on their reputation. It's often a hive of families, retirees, Harley riders and fisherfolk, so grab a beer at the small bar and wait for a table. Other recommendations include the creamy clam chowder.

Information

Crescent City Information Center (707-465-7335; www.nps.gov/redw; 1111 2nd St; 9am-5pm Apr-Oct, to 4pm Nov-Mar) On the corner of K St; you'll find rangers here and information about all four parks under its jurisdiction.

Crescent City-Del Norte Chamber of Commerce (707-464-3174; www.exploredelnorte.com; 1001 Front St; 9am-5pm daily May-Aug, 9am-5pm Mon-Fri Sep-Apr) A helpful office that can provide local information, as well as a map.

Getting There & Around

Alaska Airlines (p214) and Penair (p214) fly into tiny **Del Norte County Regional Airport** (CEC; 707-464-7288; www.flycrescentcity.com; 250 Dale Rupert Rd, Crescent City; 5am-7:30pm), located 3 miles northwest of town. There are frequent flights to Eureka as well as Portland, Redding and North Bend in Oregon.

Redwood Coast Transit (p214) serves Crescent City with local buses ($1), and runs buses Monday to Saturday to Klamath ($1.50, one hour, three daily) and Arcata ($30, two hours, three daily), with stops in between. Have the exact fare, the driver carries no change.

Drivers may experience delays on Hwy 101 between Klamath and Crescent City as corrosion continues to affect the highway, particularly after heavy rains.

Tolowa Dunes State Park & Lake Earl Wildlife Area

Two miles north of Crescent City, this **state park and wildlife area** (707-464-6101, ext 5112; Kellogg Rd; sunrise-sunset) encompasses 10,000 acres of wetlands, dunes, meadows and two lakes – **Lake Earl** and **Lake Tolowa**. This major stopover on the Pacific Flyway route brings over 250 species of birds here. Listen for the whistling, warbling chorus. On land, look for coyotes and deer, angle for trout, or hike or ride 20 miles of trails; at sea, spot whales, seals and sea lions.

The park and wildlife area are a patchwork of lands administered by California State Parks and the Department of Fish and Game (DFG). The DFG focuses on single-species management, hunting and fishing; the State Parks' focus is on ecodiversity and recreation. You might be hiking a vast expanse of pristine dunes, then suddenly hear a shotgun or a whining 4WD. Strict regulations limit where and when you can hunt and drive; trails are clearly marked.

To get here from Crescent City, take Northcrest Dr north off of Hwy 101, which becomes Lake Earl Dr. Turn left on Lower Lake Rd to Kellogg Rd, which leads to the park.

Pelican State Beach

The northernmost beach in California and the most northern spot on the California Coastal Trail, never-crowded **Pelican State Beach** (☎707-464-6101, ext 5151; Gilbert Way, Hwy 101; P) occupies 5 coastal acres just south of the Oregon border. There are no facilities and due to its easy-to-miss access, this beach has been described as the loneliest beach in California, but it's great for walking, beachcombing and kite flying; pick one up at one of the kite specialty shops just over the border in Oregon.

The beach is around 2 miles east of Pelican Bay State Prison; the only so-called super maximum security facility in California and a world away, one imagines, from the tranquility of this beautiful unspoiled beach.

Clifford Kamph Memorial Park CAMPGROUND **$**
(☎707-464-7230; 15100 Hwy 101; tent sites $10) Pitch a tent by the ocean (no windbreaks) at Clifford Kamph Memorial Park; no RVs. It's a steal for the beachside location and, even though sites are exposed in a grassy area and there isn't much privacy, all have BBQs.

Casa Rubio BOUTIQUE HOTEL **$$**
(☎707-487-4313; www.casarubio.com; 17285 Crissey Rd; r $98-178; P) The best reason to visit Pelican State Beach is to stay at secluded, charming Casa Rubio, where three of the four ocean-view rooms have kitchens. Surrounded by tropical gardens, a short path leads directly to the beach.

Central Coast

Includes ➡

Best Places to Eat

➡ Assembly (p276)
➡ Ember (p326)
➡ Foremost Wine Co (p320)
➡ Thomas Hill Organics (p318)
➡ La Cosecha Bar & Restaurant (p315)

Best Places to Sleep

➡ Post Ranch Inn (p300)
➡ Jabberwock (p286)
➡ Cass House Inn (p307)
➡ Avila La Fonda (p323)
➡ Summerwood Inn (p315)

Why Go?

Too often forgotten or dismissed as 'flyover' country between San Francisco and LA, this fairy-tale stretch of California coast is packed with wild beaches, misty redwood forests where hot springs hide, and rolling golden hills of fertile vineyards and farm fields.

Coastal Hwy 1 pulls out all the stops, scenery-wise. Flower-power Santa Cruz and the historic port town of Monterey are gateways to the rugged wilderness of the bohemian Big Sur coast. It's an epic journey snaking down to vainglorious Hearst Castle, past lighthouses and edgy cliffs atop which endangered condors soar.

Get acquainted with California's agricultural heartland along inland Hwy 101, called El Camino Real (the King's Highway) by Spanish conquistadors and Franciscan friars. Colonial missions still line the route, which passes through Paso Robles' flourishing wine and craft-beer country. Then soothe your nature-loving soul in collegiate San Luis Obispo, ringed by sunny beach towns and volcanic peaks.

When to Go

Santa Cruz

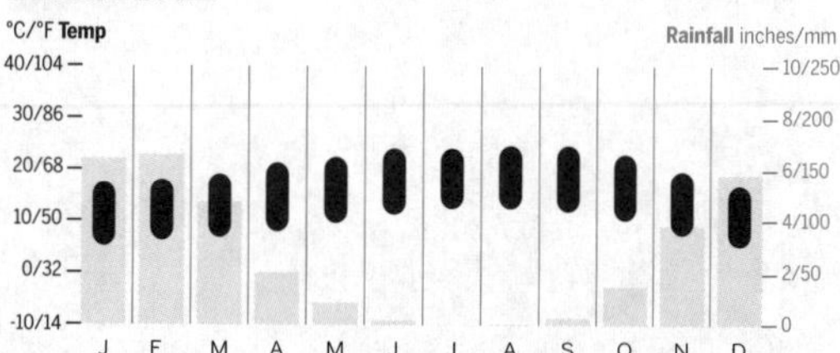

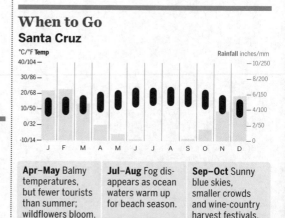

Apr–May Balmy temperatures, but fewer tourists than summer; wildflowers bloom.

Jul–Aug Fog disappears as ocean waters warm up for beach season.

Sep–Oct Sunny blue skies, smaller crowds and wine-country harvest festivals.

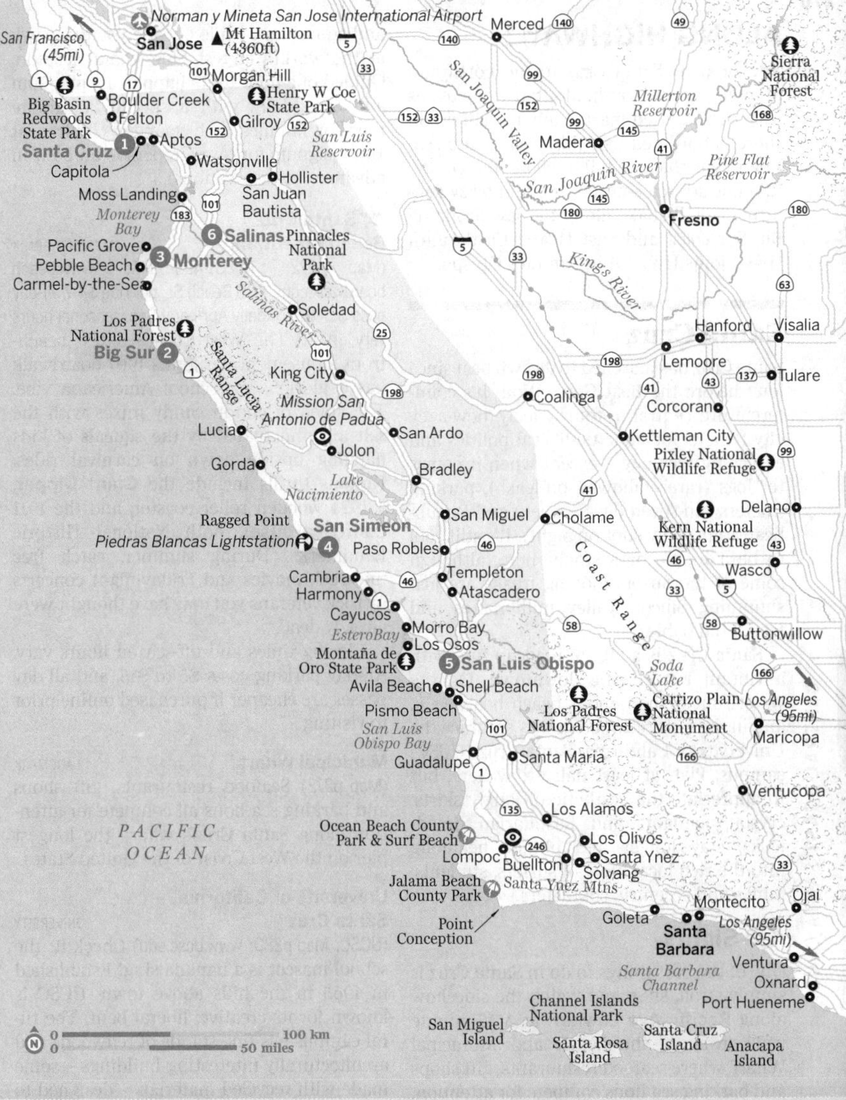

Central Coast Highlights

1. Learning to surf, and scaring yourself silly on the Giant Dipper along the famed beach boardwalk in **Santa Cruz** (p270).

2. Cruising Hwy 1, where the sky touches the sea along the rocky coastline of mystical **Big Sur** (p295).

3. Being mesmerized by aquatic denizens of the 'indoor ocean' at the superb aquarium in **Monterey** (p281).

4. Marveling at the jawdropping grandiosity of Hearst Castle in **San Simeon** (p303) after meeting the neighbors: ginormous elephant seals.

5. Chilling out in easygoing college town **San Luis Obispo** (p317), surrounded by beaches, vineyards and mountains.

6. Exploring **Salinas** (p311) and the blue-collar world of Nobel Prize–winning, down-to-earth novelist John Steinbeck.

ALONG HIGHWAY 1

Anchored by Santa Cruz to the north and Monterey to the south, Monterey Bay teems with richly varied marine life. Its half-moon shore is bordered by wild beaches and seaside towns that are full of character. On the 125-mile stretch south of the Monterey Peninsula, you'll snake along the jaw-dropping Big Sur coast and past Hearst Castle until Hwy 1 joins Hwy 101 in San Luis Obispo.

Santa Cruz

Santa Cruz has marched to its own beat since long before the Beat Generation. It's counterculture central, a touchy-feely, new-agey city famous for its leftie-liberal politics and easygoing ideology – except when it comes to dogs (rarely allowed off-leash), parking (meters run seven days a week) and Republicans (allegedly shot on sight). It's still cool to be a hippie or a stoner here, although some of the far-out-looking freaks are just slumming Silicon Valley millionaires and trust-fund babies.

Santa Cruz is a city of madcap fun, with a vibrant but chaotic downtown. On the waterfront is the famous beach boardwalk, and in the hills redwood groves embrace the University of California, Santa Cruz (UCSC) campus. Plan at least half a day here, but to appreciate the aesthetic of jangly skirts, crystal pendants and Rastafarian dreadlocks, stay longer and plunge headlong into the rich local brew of surfers, students, punks and eccentric characters.

Sights

One of the best things to do in Santa Cruz is simply stroll, shop and watch the sideshow along **Pacific Ave** downtown. A 15-minute walk away is the beach and Municipal Wharf, where seafood restaurants, gift shops and barking sea lions compete for attention. Ocean-view **West Cliff Dr** follows the waterfront southwest of the wharf, paralleled by a paved recreational path.

★Seymour Marine Discovery Center MUSEUM

(Map p280; ☎831-459-3800; http://seymourcenter.ucsc.edu; 100 Shaffer Rd; adult/child 3-16yr $8/6; ⏰10am-5pm Tue-Sun; P 👪) By Natural Bridges State Beach, this kids' educational center is part of UCSC's Long Marine Laboratory. Interactive natural-science exhibits include tidal touch pools and aquariums, while outside you can gawk at the world's largest blue-whale skeleton. Guided one-hour tours happen at 1pm, 2pm and 3pm daily, with a special 30-minute tour for families with younger children at 11am; sign up for tours in person an hour in advance (no reservations).

★Santa Cruz Beach Boardwalk AMUSEMENT PARK

(Map p272; ☎831-423-5590; www.beachboardwalk.com; 400 Beach St; per ride $4-7, all-day pass $37-82; ⏰daily Apr-early Sep, seasonal hours vary; P 👪) The West Coast's oldest beachfront amusement park, this 1907 boardwalk has a glorious old-school Americana vibe. The smell of cotton candy mixes with the salt air, punctuated by the squeals of kids hanging upside down on carnival rides. Famous thrills include the **Giant Dipper**, a 1924 wooden roller coaster, and the 1911 **Looff carousel**, both National Historic Landmarks. During summer, catch free midweek movies and Friday-night concerts by rock veterans you may have thought were already dead.

Closing times and off-season hours vary. All-day parking costs $5 to $15, and all-day passes are cheaper if purchased online prior to visiting.

Municipal Wharf LANDMARK

(Map p272) Seafood restaurants, gift shops and barking sea lions all compete for attention along Santa Cruz's wharf, the longest pier on the West Coast of the United States.

University of California, Santa Cruz UNIVERSITY

(UCSC; Map p280; www.ucsc.edu) Check it: the school mascot is a banana slug! Established in 1965 in the hills above town, UCSC is known for its creative, liberal bent. The rural campus has fine stands of redwoods and architecturally interesting buildings – some made with recycled materials – designed to blend in with rolling pastureland. Amble around the peaceful **arboretum** (Map p280; ☎831-502-2998; www.arboretum.ucsc.edu; cnr High St & Arboretum Rd; adult/child 6-17yr $5/2, free 1st Tue of each month; ⏰9am-5pm) and picturesquely decaying 19th-century structures from Cowell Ranch, upon which the campus was built.

Museum of Art & History MUSEUM

(Map p272; ☎831-429-1964; www.santacruzmah.org; McPherson Center, 705 Front St; adult/child 12-17yr $10/8, free 1st Fri of each month; ⏰11am-5pm

DON'T MISS

TOP SANTA CRUZ BEACHES

Sun-kissed Santa Cruz has warmer beaches than San Francisco or Monterey. *Baywatch* it isn't, but 29 miles of coastline reveal a few Hawaii-worthy beaches, craggy coves, some primo surf spots and big sandy stretches where your kids will have a blast. Fog may ruin many a summer morning; it often burns off by the afternoon.

West Cliff Dr is lined with scramble-down-to coves and plentiful parking. If you don't want sand in your shoes, park yourself on a bench and watch enormous pelicans dive for fish. You'll find bathrooms and showers at the lighthouse parking lot.

Locals favor less-trampled East Cliff Dr beaches, which are bigger and more protected from the wind, meaning calmer waters. Except at a small metered lot at 26th Ave, parking is by permit only on weekends (buy a $8 per-day permit at 9th Ave).

Main Beach (Map p272) *The* scene in Santa Cruz, with a huge sandy stretch, volleyball courts and swarms of people. Park on E Cliff Dr and walk across the *Lost Boys* trestle to the beach boardwalk (p270).

Its Beach (Map p280; 🐾) The only official off-leash beach for dogs (before 10am and after 4pm) in Santa Cruz is just west of the lighthouse. The field across the street is another good romping ground.

Natural Bridges State Beach (Map p280; ☎831-423-4609; www.parks.ca.gov; 2531 W Cliff Dr; per car $10; ⏲8am-sunset; P 👪) Best for sunsets, this family favorite has lots of sand, tide pools and monarch butterflies from mid-October through mid-February. It's at the far western end of W Cliff Dr.

Seacliff State Beach (☎831-685-6442; www.parks.ca.gov; State Park Rd, Aptos; per car $10; ⏲8am-sunset) Seacliff State Beach harbors a 'cement boat,' a quixotic freighter built of concrete that floated OK, but ended up here as a coastal fishing pier. During huge storms in February 2017, the boat actually broke apart but remains *in situ*.

Manresa State Beach (☎831-724-3750; www.parks.ca.gov; San Andreas Rd, Watsonville; per car $10; ⏲8am-sunset) Near Watsonville, the La Selva Beach exit off Hwy 1 leads here to this sparsely populated beach.

Moran Lake County Park (Map p280; E Cliff Dr; ⏲8am-sunset) With a good surf break and bathrooms, this pretty all-around sandy spot is further east of 26th Ave off E Cliff Dr.

Cowell's Beach (Map p272) Popular Santa Cruz surfing beach off WCliff Dr.

Sunset State Beach (☎831-763-7062; www.parks.ca.gov; San Andreas Rd, Watsonville; per car $10; ⏲8am-sunset) The La Selva Beach exit off Hwy 1, near Watsonville, brings you here, where you can have miles of sand and surf almost all to yourself.

Tue-Thu & Sat & Sun, to 9pm Fri) In Santa Cruz's downtown, rotating displays by contemporary California artists and exhibits that dive into local history are worth a quick look. Recent renovations include an adjacent courtyard with cafes and restaurants.

Sanctuary Exploration Center MUSEUM
(Map p272; ☎831-421-9993; www.montereybay.noaa.gov; 35 Pacific Ave; ⏲10am-5pm Wed-Sun; 👪) FREE Operated by the Monterey Bay National Marine Sanctuary, this educational museum near the beach boardwalk is an interactive multimedia experience that teaches kids and adults about the bay's marine treasures, watershed conservation and high-tech underwater exploration for scientific research.

Santa Cruz Surfing Museum MUSEUM
(Map p280; ☎831-420-6289; www.santacruzsurfingmuseum.org; 701 W Cliff Dr; by donation; ⏲10am-5pm Wed-Mon Jul 4-early Sep, noon-4pm Thu-Mon early Sep-Jul 3; 👪) A mile southwest of the wharf along the coast, this tiny museum inside an old lighthouse is packed with memorabilia, including vintage redwood surfboards. Fittingly, Lighthouse Point overlooks two popular surf breaks.

Mystery Spot LANDMARK
(☎831-423-8897; www.mysteryspot.com; 465 Mystery Spot Rd; $8; ⏲10am-4pm Mon-Fri, to 5pm Sat & Sun Sep-May, 10am-6pm Mon-Fri, 9am-7pm Sat & Sun Jun-Aug; P 👪) A kitschy, old-fashioned tourist trap, Santa Cruz's Mystery Spot has scarcely changed since it opened

Santa Cruz

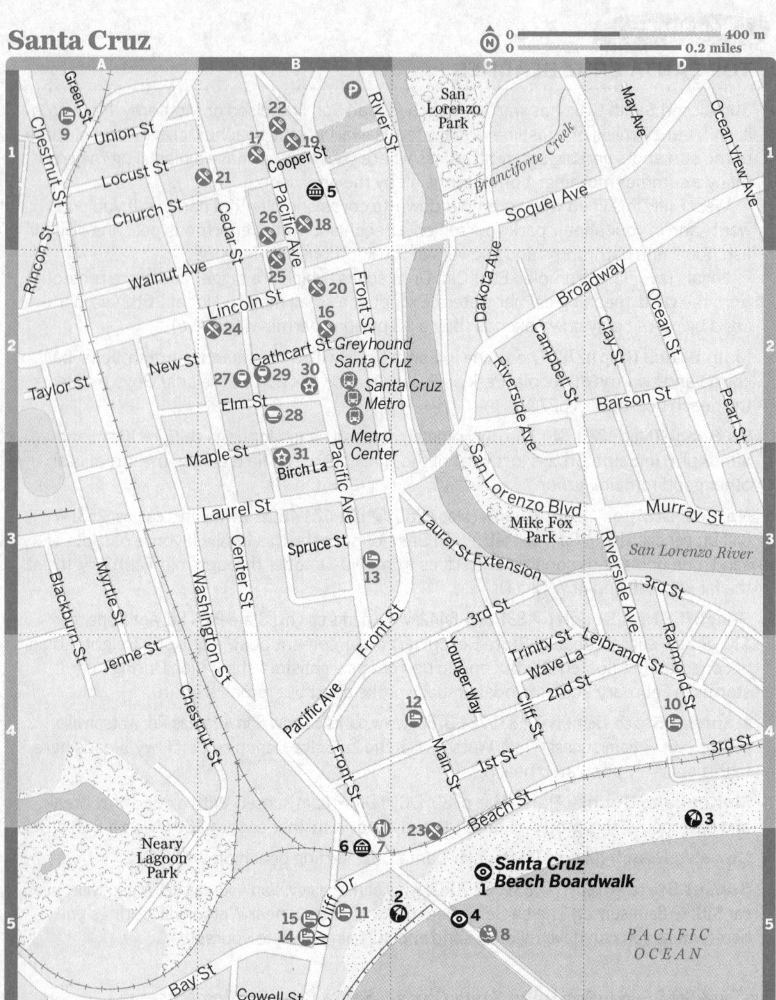

in 1940. On a steeply sloping hillside, compasses seem to point crazily, mysterious forces push you around and buildings lean at silly angles. Make reservations, or risk getting stuck waiting for a tour. It's about 4 miles northeast of downtown: take Water St to Market St north and continue on Branciforte Dr into the hills. Parking costs $5. Don't forget your bumper sticker!

Santa Cruz Museum of Natural History MUSEUM

(Map p280; ☎831-420-6115; www.santacruzmuseum.org; 1305 E Cliff Dr; adult/child under 18yr $4/free, free 1st Fri of each month; ⏰11am-4pm Tue-Fri & 10am-5pm Sat-Sun; 👪) The collections at this pint-sized museum include stuffed-animal mounts, Native Californian cultural artifacts and a touch-friendly tide pool that shows off sea critters living by the beach right across the street.

Activities

★Santa Cruz Food Tour FOOD

(☎866-736-6343; www.santacruzfoodtour.com; per person $59; ⏰2:30-6pm Fri & Sat) Combining Afghan flavors, a farm-to-table bistro, vegan cupcakes and artisan ice cream, these highly recommended walking tours

Santa Cruz

also come with a healthy serving of local knowledge and interesting insights into Santa Cruz history, culture and architecture. Sign up for a tour when you first arrive in town to get your bearings in the tastiest way possible.

Slow Adventure WALKING
(☎831-332-7923; www.slowadventure.us; per person $1495; ⊙Apr-Oct) Well-traveled Santa Cruz local Margaret Leonard arranges self-guided walking adventures around Monterey Bay. The full itinerary from Santa Cruz to Monterey takes six days and five nights, covering from 40 to 50 miles in total, and overnighting in very comfortable ocean-view accommodations along the way. Luggage is transferred independently, and highlights include birdlife, marine mammals and superb coastal views. Shorter four-day/three-night coastal adventures to the north and south of Santa Cruz are also available (per person $995 to $1095).

DeLaveaga Disc Golf Club GOLF
(Map p280; www.facebook.com/groups/DelaDDGC; Upper Park Rd;) FREE Touring pros and families with kids toss discs across this challenging hillside layout that peaks at Hole No 27, nicknamed 'Top of the World.' It's a couple of miles northeast of downtown Santa Cruz, off Branciforte Dr.

SUP Shack WATER SPORTS
(Map p280; ☎831-464-7467; www.supshacksantacruz.com; 2214 E Cliff Dr; rental/lessons from $20/59) Based in the calm waters of Santa Cruz Harbor, SUP Shack offers paddleboarding lessons and rentals. Kayaks and body boards are also available for rental.

Surfing

Year-round, water temperatures average under 60°F, meaning that without a wetsuit, body parts quickly turn blue. Surfing is incredibly popular, especially at experts-only **Steamer Lane** and beginners' Cowell's (p271), both off W Cliff Dr. Other favorite surf spots include **Pleasure Point Beach**, on E Cliff Dr toward Capitola, and Manresa State Beach (p271) off Hwy 1 southbound.

O'Neill Surf Shop SURFING
(Map p280; ☎831-475-4151; www.oneill.com; 1115 41st Ave; wetsuit/surfboard rental from $15/25; ⊙9am-8pm Mon-Fri, from 8am Sat & Sun) Head east toward Pleasure Point to worship at this internationally renowned surfboard-maker's flagship store, with branches on the beach boardwalk and downtown.

Richard Schmidt Surf School SURFING
(Map p280; ☎831-423-0928; www.richardschmidt.com; 849 Almar Ave; 2hr group/1hr private lesson $90/120;) Award-winning,

time-tested surf school can get you out there, all equipment included. Summer surf camps hook adults and kids alike.

Cowell's Beach Surf Shop SURFING
(Map p272; ☎831-427-2355; www.cowellssurfshop.com; 30 Front St; 2hr group lesson $90; ⊙8am-6pm, to 5pm Nov-Mar;) Rent surfboards, boogie boards, wetsuits and other beach gear near the wharf, where veteran staff offer local tips and lessons.

Kayaking

Kayaking lets you discover the craggy coastline and kelp beds where sea otters float.

Kayak Connection WATER SPORTS
(Map p280; ☎831-479-1121; www.kayakconnection.com; Santa Cruz Harbor, 413 Lake Ave; kayak rental/tour from $35/50; ⊙10am-5pm Mon, Wed & Fri, 9am-5pm Sat-Sun;) Rents kayaks and offers lessons and tours, including whale-watching, sunrise, sunset and full-moon trips. Also rents stand-up paddle boarding (SUP) sets (from $35), wetsuits ($10) and boogie boards ($10).

Venture Quest KAYAKING
(Map p272; ☎831-427-2267, 831-425-8445; www.kayaksantacruz.com; Municipal Wharf; kayak rental/tour from $35/56; ⊙10am-7pm Mon-Fri, from 9am Sat & Sun late May–late Sep, hours vary late Sep–mid-May) Convenient rentals on the wharf, plus whale-watching and coastal sea-cave tours, moonlight paddles and kayak-sailing trips. Book ahead for kayak-surfing lessons.

Whale-Watching & Fishing

Winter whale-watching trips run from December through April, though there's plenty of marine life to see on a summer bay cruise.

Many fishing trips depart from Santa Cruz's wharf, where a few shops rent fishing tackle and poles, if you're keen to join locals waiting patiently for a bite.

Stagnaro's BOATING
(Map p280; ☎info 831-427-0230, reservations 888-237-7084; www.stagnaros.com; 1718 Brommer St; adult/child under 14yr cruise from $22/15, whale-watching tour from $50/36) Longstanding tour operator offers scenic and sunset cruises around Monterey Bay during spring and summer, and whale-watching tours year-round.

Festivals & Events

Woodies on the Wharf CULTURAL
(www.santacruzwoodies.com; ⊙late June) Classic-car show features vintage surf-style station wagons on Santa Cruz's Municipal Wharf (p270).

Open Studio Art Tour ART
(www.firstfridaysantacruz.com) Step inside local artists' creative workshops over three weekends in October. The arts council also sponsors 'First Friday' art exhibitions on the first Friday of each month, including access to artists' ateliers at the heritage Tannery Arts Center located just north of downtown.

Sleeping

Santa Cruz does not have enough beds to satisfy demand: expect high prices at peak times for nothing-special rooms. Places near the beach boardwalk (p270) range from friendly to frightening. For a decent motel, cruise Ocean St inland or Mission St (Hwy 1). Several new hotels scheduled to open from late 2017 will improve the city's accommodations options. Contact the visitor center (p278) for details.

HI Santa Cruz Hostel HOSTEL $
(Map p272; ☎831-423-8304; www.hi-santacruz.org; 321 Main St; dm $28-31, r $85-140, all with shared bath; ⊙check in 5-10pm; @) Budget overnighters dig this cute hostel at the century-old Carmelita Cottages surrounded by flowering gardens, just two blocks from the beach. Cons: midnight curfew, daytime lockout (11am to 5pm) and three-night maximum stay. Reservations are essential. Street parking costs $2.

California State Park Campgrounds CAMPGROUND $
(☎reservations 800-444-7275; www.reserveamerica.com; tent & RV sites $35-65) Book well ahead to camp at state beaches off Hwy 1 south of Santa Cruz or up in the foggy Santa Cruz Mountains off Hwy 9. Family-friendly campgrounds include Henry Cowell Redwoods State Park in Felton and New Brighton State Beach in Capitola.

★ **Adobe on Green B&B** B&B $$
(Map p272; ☎831-469-9866; www.adobeongreen.com; 103 Green St; r $179; P) Peace and quiet are the mantras at this place, a short walk from Pacific Ave. The hosts are practically invisible, but their thoughtful touches are everywhere, from boutique-hotel amenities in spacious, stylish and solar-powered rooms to breakfast spreads from their organic gardens.

Carousel Beach Inn MOTEL $$
(Map p272; ☎831-425-7090; www.carousel-beach-inn.com; 110 Riverside Ave; r $159-229; P) Colorful decor and bright artwork feature

at this recently renovated motel that is the closest accommodations to the attractions of the Santa Cruz boardwalk. Prices surge in summer, but it's worth checking online for off-peak and seasonal discounts.

Seaway Inn MOTEL $$
(Map p272; 831-471-9004; www.seawayinn.com; 176 W Cliff Dr; r $139-150;) Good value and welcoming accommodations just a short walk uphill from the Santa Cruz Municipal Wharf. Try and stay on a weekday as prices surge on weekends.

Hotel Paradox HOTEL $$
(Map p280; 831-425-7100; www.thehotelparadox.com; 611 Ocean St; r from $229;) This downtown boutique hotel brings the great outdoors inside, with nature prints on the walls, textured wood panels and earth-toned furnishings. Relax in a cabana by the pool or next to an outdoor fire pit. Weekday rates can be reasonable, but summer weekends are ridiculously high-priced. Parking is $10.

Mission Inn MOTEL $$
(Map p280; 831-425-5455; www.mission-inn.com; 2250 Mission St; r $139-179;) Perfectly serviceable two-story motel with a garden courtyard, hot tub and complimentary continental breakfast. It's on busy Hwy 1 near the UCSC campus, away from the beach.

Pelican Point Inn INN $$
(Map p280; 831-475-3381; www.pelicanpointinnsantacruz.com; 21345 E Cliff Dr; ste $139-229;) Ideal for families, these roomy apartments near a kid-friendly beach come with everything you'll need for a lazy vacation, including kitchenettes. Weekly rates available. Pet fee $25.

Pacific Blue Inn B&B $$$
(Map p272; 831-600-8880; www.pacificblueinn.com; 636 Pacific Ave; r $189-289;) This downtown courtyard B&B is an eco-conscious gem, with water-saving fixtures and renewable and recycled building materials. Refreshingly elemental rooms have pillowtop beds, electric fireplaces and flat-screen TVs with DVD players. Free parking and loaner bikes. Pet fee $50.

Babbling Brook Inn B&B $$$
(Map p280; 831-427-2437; www.babblingbrookinn.com; 1025 Laurel St; r $229-329;) Built around a running stream with meandering gardens, the inn has cozy rooms decorated in French-provincial style. Most have gas fireplaces, some have Jacuzzis and all have featherbeds. There's afternoon wine and hors d'oeuvres, plus a full breakfast.

Dream Inn HOTEL $$$
(Map p272; 831-426-4330; www.dreaminnsantacruz.com; 175 W Cliff Dr; r $279-576;) Overlooking the wharf from a hillside perch, this chic hotel offers some of Santa Cruz's most stylish accommodations. Newly renovated rooms all have ocean views, while the beach and the revamped swimming pool area are just steps away. Don't miss having an end-of-day cocktail in the Jack O'Neill Lounge, named after Santa Cruz's iconic pioneer of surfing culture.

West Cliff Inn INN $$$
(Map p272; 831-457-2200; www.westcliffinn.com; 174 W Cliff Dr; r $210-425;) In a classy Victorian house west of the wharf, this boutique inn's quaint rooms mix seagrass wicker, dark wood and jaunty striped curtains. The most romantic suites have gas fireplaces and let you spy on the breaking surf. Rates include a breakfast buffet and afternoon wine, tea and snacks.

Eating

Downtown Santa Cruz is packed with casual cafes. If you're looking for seafood, wander the wharf's takeout counter joints. Mission St, near UCSC, and 41st Ave offer cheaper eats.

★ **Penny Ice Creamery** ICE CREAM $
(Map p272; 831-204-2523; www.thepennyicecreamery.com; 913 Cedar St; snacks $3-5; noon-11pm;) With a cult following, this artisan ice-cream shop crafts zany flavors such as bourbon-candied ginger, lemon-verbena–blueberry and ricotta apricot all from scratch using local, organic and wild-harvested ingredients. Even plain old vanilla is special: it's made using Thomas Jefferson's original recipe. Also at a **downtown kiosk** (Map p272; 1520 Pacific Ave; snacks $3-5; noon-6pm;) and near **Pleasure Point** (Map p280; 820 41st Ave; snacks $3-5; noon-9pm Sun-Thu, to 10pm Fri & Sat;).

★ **Santa Cruz Farmers Market** MARKET $
(Map p272; 831-454-0566; www.santacruzfarmersmarket.org; cnr Lincoln & Center Sts; 1:30-6:30pm Wed;) Organic produce, baked goods and arts-and-crafts and food booths all give you an authentic taste of the local vibe. Shorter fall and winter hours.

Akira JAPANESE $

(Map p280; ☎831-600-7093; www.akirasantacruz.com; 1222 Soquel Ave; sushi & sashimi $10-15; ⏲11am-11pm;) Head northeast of downtown Santa Cruz to Soquel Ave's restaurant strip for Akira's modern take on sushi, sashimi and other Japanese flavors. Combining sake, craft brews and a surf-town ambience, Akira's menu harnesses briny-fresh tuna, salmon, eel and shellfish for a huge variety of sushi. Bento boxes for lunch ($10 to $14) are good value, and there's a wide range of vegetarian options.

Buttercup Cakes CAFE $

(Map p272; ☎831-466-0373; www.facebook.com/scbuttercupcakes; 1141 Pacific Ave; snacks from $3; ⏲10am-9pm;) Vegan and organic ingredients all feature, but there's absolutely no trade-off in flavor with Buttercup's cupcakes and desserts. The downtown location is a handy coffee stop, too.

Walnut Ave Cafe BREAKFAST $

(Map p272; ☎831-457-2804; www.walnutavenuecafe.com; 106 Walnut Ave; mains $9-12; ⏲7am-3pm Mon-Fri, 8am-4pm Sat & Sun;) Line up at this clean, well-lit breakfast spot for fluffy Belgian waffles, blackened ahi tuna eggs benny, Mexican huevos rancheros with pulled pork and all kinds of veggie scrambles. Lunch brings less-exciting sandwiches, salads and soups. Dogs are welcome on the outdoor patio.

New Leaf Community Market SUPERMARKET $

(Map p272; ☎831-425-1793; www.newleaf.com; 1134 Pacific Ave; ⏲8am-9pm;) Organic and local produce, natural-foods groceries and deli take-out meals in the middle of downtown Santa Cruz.

Picnic Basket DELI $

(Map p272; ☎831-427-9946; www.facebook.com/pg/thepicnicbasketsc; 125 Beach St; snacks $6-11; ⏲7am-9pm;) Across the street from the beach boardwalk, this locavorian kitchen puts together creative sandwiches such as beet with lemony couscous or 'fancy pants' grilled cheese with fruit chutney, plus homemade soups, breakfast burritos and baked goods. Service can be standoffish, but ice-cream treats are sweet. It's open shorter hours in the off season.

★Assembly CALIFORNIAN $$

(Map p272; ☎831-824-6100; www.assembly.restaurant; 1108 Pacific Ave; brunch & lunch $12-16, dinner mains $22-28; ⏲11:30am-9pm Mon & Wed-Thu, to 10pm Fri, 10am-10pm Sat-Sun;) Farm-to-table and proudly regional flavors feature at this excellent bistro in downtown Santa Cruz. Assembly's Californian vibe belies real culinary nous in the kitchen, and the seasonal menu could include dishes such as chicken breast with crispy pancetta or a truffle-laced asparagus risotto. Don't miss trying the Scotch olives and meatballs with a tasting flight of local craft beers.

Soif BISTRO $$

(Map p272; ☎831-423-2020; www.soifwine.com; 105 Walnut Ave; small plates $5-17, mains $19-25; ⏲5-9pm Sun-Thu, to 10pm Fri & Sat;) Following a recent makeover, one of Santa Cruz's more established restaurants is now better than ever, and the chic and cosmopolitan decor showcases a stunning wine list – including tasting flights ($20.50) of local Santa Cruz varietals – and a well-curated menu with standouts like slow-roasted pork and scallops wrapped in bacon. Wine-matching suggestions are available for all dishes.

An on-site **wine shop** (noon-8pm Tue-Sun, 5-8pm Mon) also features many Californian wines.

Jaguar MEXICAN $$

(Map p280; ☎831-600-7428; www.jaguarrestaurantinc.com; 1116 Soquel Ave; mains $14-22; ⏲5-10pm Thu-Tue) Regional Mexican flavors feature at this bricks-and-mortar expansion of a popular long-standing Santa Cruz food stall. A strong adherence to organic ingredients shines in dishes like a delicious chicken mole (a Mexican dish with a rich spicy sauce), and a delicate ceviche packed with fresh seafood. Wines from local Santa Cruz vineyards partner well with the robust flavors.

Bantam CALIFORNIAN, ITALIAN $$

(Map p280; ☎831-420-0101; www.bantam1010.com; 1010 Fair Ave; shared plates $11-23, pizza $11-20; ⏲5-9pm Mon-Thu, to 9:30pm Fri-Sat;) Another opening in the up-and-coming dining scene in Santa Cruz's West End, Bantam's versatile space is often packed with SC locals enjoying wood-fired pizza, a savvy cocktail, the wine and craft-beer list, and moreish shared plates including squid, meatballs and pork belly. No reservations, but the informal and easygoing ambience means tables are turned over fairly promptly.

Laili AFGHANI $$

(Map p272; ☎831-423-4545; www.lailirestaurant.com; 101b Cooper St; mains $14-26; ⏲11:30am-2:30pm & 5-9pm Tue-Sun;) A chic downtown

LOCAL KNOWLEDGE

TOP SANTA CRUZ BREWERIES & BEER BARS

We asked Derek Wolfgram, home brewer and local beer columnist, to share a few of his favorite places for a pint:

Boulder Creek Brewery Outpost (☎831-338-7882; www.facebook.com/bouldercreekbrewery; 13101 Hwy 9, Boulder Creek; ⌚noon-9pm) High up in the mountains in the village of Boulder Creek, these guys brew amber 'Redwood Ale' and 'Dragon's Breath' American IPA. After a fire in 2016, they've relocated just across the road to this pop-up location while they rebuild.

Sante Adairius Rustic Ales (Map p280; ☎831-462-1227; www.rusticales.com; 103 Kennedy Dr; ⌚3-8pm Tue-Thu, from noon Fri-Sun) Off Hwy 1 east of Santa Cruz, Belgian-inspired and barrel-aged beers are a beer geek's dream.

Discretion Brewing (Map p280; ☎831-316-0662; www.discretionbrewing.com; 2703 41st Ave, Soquel; ⌚11:30am-9pm; 🐾) Rye IPA, English ales and traditional Belgian and German brews are always on tap, off Hwy 1. The raffish beer garden is dog-friendly, and ramen noodles and risotto both come with a proudly Californian farm-to-table accent.

Santa Cruz Mountain Brewing (Map p280; ☎831-425-4900; www.scmbrew.com; 402 Ingalls St, Ingalls St Courtyard; ⌚11:30am-10pm; 🐾) An essential part of the eating and drinking scene in the Ingalls St Courtyard on Santa Cruz's Westside, Santa Cruz Mountain Brewing is a rustic spot to combine brews and a burger. Crowd into the compact tasting room or share an outside table with friendly locals and their well-behaved canine pals. Our favorite beer is the robust Devout Scout.

From Friday to Sunday, adjacent urban wine-tasting rooms are also open, often offering live music.

Santa Cruz Ale Works (Map p280; ☎831-425-1182; www.santacruzaleworks.com; 150 Du Bois St; ⌚11am-6pm; 🐾) Hefeweizen and 'Dark Night' oatmeal stout are commendable at this dog-friendly brewpub with a deli. The beers are good, but the location in an office park lacks ambience.

dining oasis, family-owned Laili invites diners in with an elegant high-ceilinged dining room and garden patio. Share apricot-chicken flatbread, tart pomegranate eggplant, roasted cauliflower with saffron, succulent lamb kebabs and more. Reservations for dinner advised.

Engfer Pizza Works PIZZA **$$**

(Map p280; ☎831-429-1856; www.engferpizzaworks.com; 537 Seabright Ave; pizzas $11-27; ⌚4-9:30pm Tue-Sun; 🍷👪) Detour to find this old factory, where wood-fired oven pizzas are made from scratch with love – the no-name specialty is like a giant salad on roasted bread. Play Ping-Pong and down craft beers from local breweries while you wait. Try the Hot Hawaiian pizza with a Santa Cruz Ale Works Hefeweizen.

El Palomar MEXICAN **$$**

(Map p272; ☎831-425-7575; www.elpalomarsantacruz.com/; 1336 Pacific Ave; mains $10-22; ⌚11:30am-10pm Mon-Fri, 10am-10pm Sat-Sun; 👪) Always packed and consistently good (if not great), El Palomar serves tasty Mexican staples – try the ceviches – and fruity margaritas. Tortillas are made fresh by charming women in the covered courtyard.

Drinking & Nightlife

Santa Cruz's downtown overflows with bars, lounges and coffee shops. Heading west on Mission St (Hwy 1), craft breweries and wine-tasting rooms fill the raffish industrial ambience of the Smith St and Ingalls St courtyards.

Lupulo Craft Beer House CRAFT BEER

(Map p272; ☎831-454-8306; www.lupulosc.com; 233 Cathcart St; ⌚11:30am-10pm Sun-Thu, to 11:30pm Fri-Sat) Named after the Spanish word for hops, Lupulo Craft Beer House is an essential downtown destination for traveling beer fans. Modern decor combines with an ever-changing taplist – often including seasonal brews from local California breweries – and good bar snacks such as empanadas, tacos and charcuterie plates. Almost 400 bottled and canned beers create delicious panic for the indecisive drinker.

If you're a fan of hard-to-find Belgian beers, you'll be in hoppy heaven.

515 COCKTAIL BAR
(Map p272; 831-425-5051; www.515santacruz.com; 515 Cedar St; 5pm-late Mon-Fri, 10am-late Sat-Sun) Superior cocktails and eclectic food feature at this cosmopolitan spot near Santa Cruz's main drag. Settle into a huge armchair amid vintage-chic decor and enjoy cocktails based on the American classics – think Sazeracs, Negronis and Whisky Sours – or a cold craft brew from the well-curated tap list. 515 is open to 1:30am from Friday to Saturday.

Verve Coffee Roasters CAFE
(Map p272; 831-600-7784; www.vervecoffee.com; 1540 Pacific Ave; 6:30am-9pm;) To sip finely roasted artisan espresso or a cup of rich pour-over coffee, join the surfers and hipsters at this industrial-zen cafe. Single-origin brews and house blends rule. it's been so successful around their home patch that it's also opened satellite cafes in Los Angeles and Tokyo.

West End Tap & Kitchen CRAFT BEER
(Map p280; 831-471-8115; www.westendtap.com; 334d Ingalls St, Ingalls St Courtyard; 11:30am-9:30pm Sun-Thu, to 10pm Fri-Sat) Another recent opening amid the gathering of brewpubs, cafes and wine-tasting rooms in the Ingalls St Courtyard, West End Tap & Kitchen combines beers from Hermitage Brewing in San Jose – often including zingy sour beers – and a full menu including Mediterranean-style flatbreads and hearty steaks, pasta and burgers. Try Hermitage's Ale of the Imp 8% Imperial IPA.

Caffe Pergolesi CAFE
(Map p272; 831-426-1775; www.theperg.com; 418 Cedar St; 11am-9pm Mon-Sat, 11am-8pm Sun;) Discuss conspiracy theories over stalwart coffee, tea or beer at this landmark Victorian house with a big ol' tree-shaded veranda. There's live music some evenings.

Entertainment

Free tabloid *Good Times* (http://goodtimes.sc/) covers the music, arts and nightlife scenes in Santa Cruz.

Kuumbwa Jazz Center LIVE MUSIC
(Map p272; 831-427-2227; www.kuumbwajazz.org; 320 Cedar St; admission varies by gig) Hosting jazz luminaries since 1975, this nonprofit theater is for serious jazz cats snapping their fingers for famous-name performers in an electrically intimate room.

Moe's Alley LIVE MUSIC
(Map p280; 831-479-1854; www.moesalley.com; 1535 Commercial Way; admission varies by gig) In a way-out industrial wasteland, this joint puts on live sounds almost every night: jazz, blues, reggae, roots, salsa and acoustic world-music jams.

Catalyst LIVE MUSIC
(Map p272; 831-423-1338; www.catalystclub.com; 1011 Pacific Ave; admission varies by gig) Over the years, this stage for local bands has seen big-time national acts perform, from Queens of the Stone Age to Snoop Dogg. Expect loads of punk attitude and look forward to gigs ranging from classic reggae acts to the occasional Ned Flanders–inspired thrash-metal band (c'mon down Okilly Dokilly...).

Shopping

Stroll Pacific Ave and downtown side streets to find Santa Cruz's one-of-a-kind, locally owned boutiques. For vintage clothing and surf shops, amble 41st Ave around Portola Dr.

Bookshop Santa Cruz BOOKS
(Map p272; 831-423-0900; www.bookshopsantacruz.com; 1520 Pacific Ave; 9am-10pm Sun-Thu, to 11pm Fri & Sat) Vast selection of new books, a few used ones, popular and unusual magazines, and 'Keep Santa Cruz Weird' bumper stickers.

Donnelly Fine Chocolates FOOD
(Map p280; 831-458-4214; www.donnellychocolates.com; 1509 Mission St; 10:30am-6pm Tue-Fri, from noon Sat & Sun) The Willy Wonka of Santa Cruz makes stratospherically priced chocolates on par with the big city. Try the cardamom or chipotle truffles. Pricey, but worth it we reckon.

Information

Public Library (831-427-7707; www.santacruzpl.org; 224 Church St; 10am-7pm Mon-Thu, 10am-5pm Fri & Sat, 1-5pm Sun;) Free wi-fi and public internet terminals for California public-library cardholders (out-of-state visitors $10).

Santa Cruz Post Office (Map p280; 800-275-8777; www.usps.com; 850 Front St; 9am-5pm Mon-Fri)

Santa Cruz Visitor Center (Map p280; 831-425-1234; www.santacruzca.org; 303 Water St; 9am-noon & 1-4pm Mon-Fri, 11am-3pm Sat & Sun) Free public internet terminal, plus maps and brochures.

Getting There & Around

Greyhound Santa Cruz (Map p272; ☎800-231-2222; www.greyhound.com; Metro Center, 920 Pacific Ave) Greyhound has a few daily buses to San Francisco, Salinas, Santa Barbara and Los Angeles.

Santa Cruz Airport Shuttles (☎831-421-9883; www.santacruzshuttles.com) Santa Cruz Airport Shuttles runs shared shuttles to/from the airports at San Jose ($50), San Francisco ($80) and Oakland ($80), with a $5 cash discount; the second passenger pays $10.

Santa Cruz Metro (Map p272; ☎831-425-8600; www.scmtd.com; 920 Pacific Ave; single-ride/day pass $2/6) Local and regional buses converge on downtown's Metro Center. Destinations include San Jose, Capitola and Watsonville.

Santa Cruz Trolley (www.santacruztrolley.com; per ride 25¢) From late May through early September, the trolley shuttles between downtown and the beach from 11am until 9pm daily.

Around Santa Cruz

Santa Cruz Mountains

Winding between Santa Cruz and Silicon Valley, Hwy 9 is a 40-mile backwoods byway through the Santa Cruz Mountains, passing tiny towns, towering redwood forests and fog-kissed vineyards. The Santa Cruz Mountains Winegrowers Association (www.scmwa.com) publishes a free winery map, available at tasting rooms, including those that have opened more convenient tasting rooms in Santa Cruz.

Heading north from Santa Cruz, it's 7 miles to **Felton**, where there is forest ziplining adventures and also hiking in the **Henry Cowell Redwoods State Park** (☎info 831-335-4598, reservations 800-444-7275; www.parks.ca.gov; 101 N Big Trees Park Rd; entry per car $10, campsites $35; ⏰sunrise-sunset; P 👪) 🌿. Also in Felton is the pioneer-era fun and spectacle of **Roaring Camp Railroads** (☎831-335-4484; www.roaringcamp.com; 5401 Graham Hill Rd; adult/child 2-12yr from $29/22, parking $8; 👪). Seven miles further north on Hwy 9, stop in **Boulder Creek** for a bite and a cold beer at Boulder Creek Brewery Outpost (p277).

Follow Hwy 236 northwest for a further nine twisting miles from Boulder Creek to **Big Basin Redwoods State Park** (Map p38; ☎831-338-8860; www.parks.ca.gov; 21600 Big Basin Way; entry per car $10, campsites $35; ⏰sunrise-sunset; P 👪) 🌿 for excellent hiking. A 12.5-mile one-way section of the **Skyline to the Sea Trail** ends at Waddell Beach, almost 20 miles northwest of Santa Cruz on Hwy 1. On weekends between mid-March and mid-December, you can usually ride **Santa Cruz Metro** (☎831-425-8600; www.scmtd.com) bus 35A up to Big Basin in the morning and get picked up by bus 40 at the beach in the afternoon.

Capitola

Six miles east of Santa Cruz, the diminutive beach town of Capitola nestles quaintly between ocean bluffs. Show up for mid-September's **Capitola Art & Wine Festival**, or the famous **Begonia Festival** (www.begoniafestival.com), held over Labor Day weekend, with floral floats along Soquel Creek.

By the beach, downtown is laid out for strolling, where cute shops and touristy restaurants inhabit seaside houses. Drop by family-friendly **Capitola Beach Company** (Map p280; ☎831-462-5222; www.capitolabeachcompany.com; 131 Monterey Ave; surfboard/SUP rental from $12/20, surfing & SUP lessons from $85; ⏰10am-6pm) or **Capitola Surf & Paddle** (Map p280; ☎831-435-6503; www.capitolasurfandpaddle.com; 208 San Jose Ave; surfboard/SUP rental from $10/20, surfing & SUP lessons $65-75; ⏰10am-6pm) to rent water-sports gear or, if you book ahead, take surfing and stand-up paddleboarding lessons.

Catch an organic, fair-trade java buzz at **Mr Toots Coffeehouse** (Map p280; ☎831-475-3679; www.facebook.com/MrTootsCoffeehouse; 2nd fl, 231 Esplanade; ⏰7am-10pm; 📶) 🌿, which has an art gallery, live music and ocean-view deck. Head inland to **Gayle's Bakery & Rosticceria** (Map p280; ☎831-462-1200; www.gaylesbakery.com; 504 Bay Ave; dishes $4-11; ⏰6:30am-8:30pm; 👪), which has a deli to stock up for a beach picnic. A few miles east in Aptos, **Aptos St BBQ** (☎831-662-1721; www.aptosstbbq.com; 8059 Aptos St; mains $10-32; ⏰11am-9pm) pairs smoked tri-tip beef and pulled pork with California craft beers and live music.

The **Capitola Chamber of Commerce** (Map p280; ☎800-474-6522; www.capitolachamber.com; 716G Capitola Ave; ⏰10am-4pm) offers travel tips. Driving downtown can be a nightmare in summer and on weekends; use the parking lot behind City Hall, off Capitola Ave by Riverview Dr.

Moss Landing & Elkhorn Slough

Hwy 1 swings back toward the coast at Moss Landing, just south of the Santa Cruz County line, almost 20 miles north of Monterey.

Around Santa Cruz

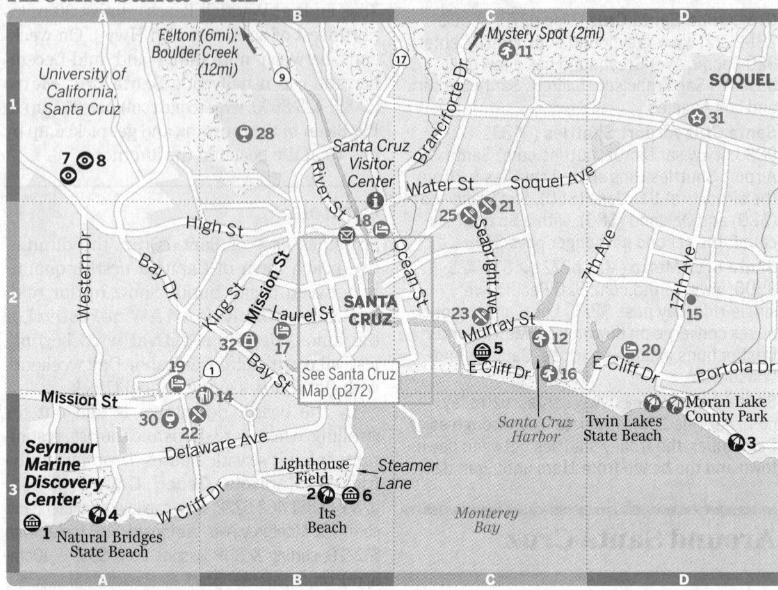

Around Santa Cruz

Top Sights

1 Seymour Marine Discovery Center A3

Sights

2 Its Beach B3
3 Moran Lake County Park D3
4 Natural Bridges State Beach A3
5 Santa Cruz Museum of Natural History C2
6 Santa Cruz Surfing Museum B3
7 UCSC Arboretum A1
8 University of California, Santa Cruz A1

Activities, Courses & Tours

9 Capitola Beach Company E2
10 Capitola Surf & Paddle E2
11 DeLaveaga Disc Golf Club C1
12 Kayak Connection C2
13 O'Neill Surf Shop E2
14 Richard Schmidt Surf School B3
15 Stagnaro's D2
16 SUP Shack C2

Sleeping

17 Babbling Brook Inn B2
18 Hotel Paradox B2
19 Mission Inn A2
20 Pelican Point Inn D2

Eating

21 Akira C2
22 Bantam A3
23 Engfer Pizza Works C2
24 Gayle's Bakery & Rosticceria E2
25 Jaguar C2
Penny Ice Creamery .... (see 13)

Drinking & Nightlife

26 Discretion Brewing E1
27 Mr Toots Coffeehouse E2
28 Santa Cruz Ale Works B1
Santa Cruz Mountain Brewing .... (see 22)
29 Sante Adairius Rustic Ales E1
30 West End Tap & Kitchen A3

Entertainment

31 Moe's Alley D1

Shopping

32 Donnelly Fine Chocolates B2

From the working fishing harbor, **Sanctuary Cruises** (☎info 831-917-1042, tickets 888-394-7810; www.sanctuarycruises.com; 7881 Sandholdt Rd; tours $45-55; 👪) 🌿 operates whale-watching and dolphin-spotting cruises year-round aboard biodiesel-fueled boats (reservations are essential). Devour dock-fresh seafood at warehouse-sized **Phil's Fish**

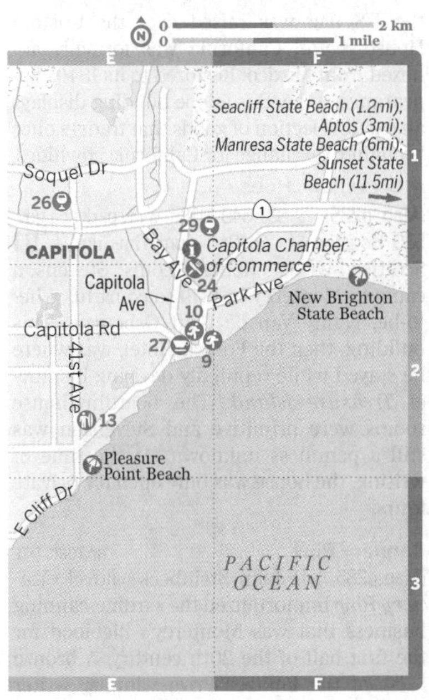

Market (☎831-633-2152; www.philsfishmarket.com; 7600 Sandholdt Rd; mains $10-26; ⏰10am-9pm; 👪) or, after browsing the antiques shops, lunch at **Haute Enchilada** (☎831-633-5483; www.hauteenchilada.com; 7902 Moss Landing Rd; mains $13-26; ⏰11am-9pm) 🌿, an inspired Mexican restaurant inside an art gallery.

On the eastern side of Hwy 1, **Elkhorn Slough National Estuarine Research Reserve** (☎831-728-2822; www.elkhornslough.org; 1700 Elkhorn Rd, Watsonville; adult/child under 16yr $4/free; ⏰9am-5pm Wed-Sun; P 👪) 🌿 is popular with bird-watchers and hikers, and can also be explored by cruising on an electric boat with **Whisper Charters** (☎800-979-3370; www.whispercharters.com; 2370 Hwy 1, Moss Landing; 2hr tour adult/child under 12yr $49/39; 👪) 🌿. Kayaking and SUP are also fantastic ways to see the slough, though not on a windy day or when the tides are against you. Reserve ahead for kayak or SUP rentals, guided tours and paddling instruction with **Kayak Connection** (☎831-724-5692; www.kayakconnection.com; 2370 Hwy 1, Moss Landing; kayak & SUP rental from $35, tours adult/child from $50/40; ⏰9am-5pm; 👪) 🌿 or **Monterey Bay Kayaks** (☎831-373-5357; www.montereybaykayaks.com; 2390 Hwy 1, Moss Landing; kayak & SUP rental/tour from $30/55; 👪) 🌿.

Around 10 miles north of Moss Landing on the edge of **Watsonville** are a couple of interesting shops to stop at en route north or south.

Monterey

Working-class Monterey is all about the sea. What draws many visitors is a world-class aquarium overlooking **Monterey Bay National Marine Sanctuary**, which protects dense kelp forests and a sublime variety of marine life, including seals and sea lions, dolphins and whales. The city itself possesses the best-preserved historical evidence of California's Spanish and Mexican periods, with many restored adobe buildings. An afternoon's wander through downtown's historic quarter promises to be more edifying than time spent in the tourist ghettos of Fisherman's Wharf and Cannery Row.

Sights

★**Monterey Bay Aquarium** AQUARIUM
(Map p285; ☎info 831-648-4800, tickets 866-963-9645; www.montereybayaquarium.org; 886 Cannery Row; adult/child 3-12yr/youth 13-17yr $50/30/40; ⏰10am-6pm; 👪) 🌿 Monterey's most mesmerizing experience is its enormous aquarium, built on the former site of the city's largest sardine cannery. All kinds of aquatic creatures are featured, from kid-tolerant sea stars and slimy sea slugs to animated sea otters and surprisingly nimble 800lb tuna. The aquarium is much more than an impressive collection of glass tanks – thoughtful placards underscore the bay's cultural and historical contexts.

Every minute, up to 2000 gallons of seawater are pumped into the three-story **kelp forest**, re-creating as closely as possible the natural conditions you see out the windows to the east. The large fish of prey are at their charismatic best during mealtimes; divers hand-feed at 11am. More entertaining are the sea otters, which may be seen basking in the **Great Tide Pool** outside the aquarium, where they are readied for reintroduction to the wild.

Even new-agey music and the occasional infinity-mirror illusion don't detract from the astounding beauty of jellyfish in the **Jellies Gallery**. To see marine creatures – including hammerhead sharks, ocean sunfish and green sea turtles – that outweigh kids many times over, ponder the awesome

Open Sea tank. Upstairs and downstairs you'll find **touch pools**, where you can get close to sea cucumbers, bat rays and tide-pool creatures. Younger kids love the **Splash Zone**, with interactive bilingual exhibits in English and Spanish, and penguin feedings at 10:30am and 3pm.

To avoid long lines in summer and on weekends and holidays, buy tickets in advance. A visit can easily become a full-day affair, so get your hand stamped and break for lunch. Metered on-street parking is limited. Parking lots offering daily rates are plentiful just uphill from Cannery Row.

★Monterey State Historic Park HISTORIC SITE

(Map p285; ☎info 831-649-7118; www.parks.ca.gov) FREE Old Monterey is home to an extraordinary assemblage of 19th-century brick and adobe buildings, administered as Monterey State Historic Park, and all found along a 2-mile self-guided walking tour portentously called the 'Path of History.' You can inspect dozens of buildings, many with charming gardens; expect some to be open while others aren't, according to a capricious schedule dictated by unfortunate state-park budget cutbacks.

➡ Pacific House

(Map p285; ☎831-649-7118; www.parks.ca.gov; 20 Custom House Plaza; walking tour adult/child $5/free; ⏰10am-4pm, closed Mon-Wed Nov-Mar; 👪) Find out what's currently open at Monterey State Historic Park, grab a free map and buy tickets for guided walking tours inside this 1847 adobe building, where fascinatingly in-depth exhibits cover the state's early Spanish, Mexican and American eras. Walking tours run at 10:30am, 12:30pm & 2pm Thursday to Sunday.

Nearby are some of the state park's historical highlights, including an **old whaling station** (Map p285; ⏰10am-2pm Tue-Fri) and **California's first theater** (Map p285). A 10-minute walk south is the **old Monterey jail** (Map p285; ☎831-646-5640; www.monterey.org; Dutra St; ⏰10am-4pm) FREE featured in John Steinbeck's novel *Tortilla Flat*.

➡ Custom House

(Map p285; ☎831-649-7111; www.parks.ca.gov; Custom House Plaza; ⏰10am-4pm; 👪) FREE In 1822, a newly independent Mexico ended the Spanish trade monopoly and stipulated that any traders bringing goods to Alta (Upper) California must first unload their cargoes here for duty to be assessed. In 1846, when the US flag was raised over the Custom House, *voilà*! California was formally annexed from Mexico. Restored to its 1840s appearance, today this adobe building displays an exotic selection of goods that traders once brought to exchange for California cowhides.

➡ Stevenson House

(Map p285; ☎831-649-7118; www.parks.ca.gov; 530 Houston St; ⏰10am-4pm Thu-Sun) FREE Scottish writer Robert Louis Stevenson came to Monterey in 1879 to court his wife-to-be, Fanny Van de Grift Osbourne. This building, then the French Hotel, was where he stayed while reputedly devising his novel *Treasure Island*. The boarding-house rooms were primitive and Stevenson was still a penniless unknown. At the time of writing, the house was only open for private tours.

Cannery Row HISTORIC SITE

(Map p285; 👪) John Steinbeck's novel *Cannery Row* immortalized the sardine-canning business that was Monterey's lifeblood for the first half of the 20th century. A bronze **bust** of the Pulitzer Prize–winning writer sits at the bottom of Prescott Ave, just steps from the unabashedly touristy experience that the famous row has devolved into. The historical **Cannery Workers Shacks** (Map p285) at the base of flowery Bruce Ariss Way provide a sobering reminder of the hard lives led by Filipino, Japanese, Spanish and other immigrant laborers.

Back in Steinbeck's day, Cannery Row was a hardscrabble, working-class melting pot, which the novelist described as 'a poem, a stink, a grating noise, a quality of light, a tone, a habit, a nostalgia, a dream.' Sadly, there's precious little evidence of that era now, as overfishing and climatic changes caused the sardine industry's collapse in the 1950s.

Dali17 GALLERY

(Map p285; ☎831-372-2608; www.dali17.com; 5 Custom House Plaza, Museum of Monterey; adult/child $20/10; ⏰10am-5pm Sun-Thu, 10am-7pm Fri-Sat) Escaping WWII in Europe, Spanish surrealist artist Salvador Dalí lived and worked in the Monterey and Carmel area in the 1940s. Comprising over 300 Dalí etchings, mixed media, lithographs and sculptures, this permanent exhibition in the Museum of Monterey is named after Carmel's 17-Mile Drive (p293), where the artist lived at Pebble Beach from 1943 to 1948.

Monterey Museum of Art MUSEUM
(MMA; www.montereyart.org; adult/child $10/free; 11am-5pm Thu-Mon) Downtown, **MMA Pacific Street** (Map p285; 831-372-5477; 559 Pacific St; adult/child $10/free; 11am-5pm Thu-Mon, to 8pm 1st Fri of month;) is particularly strong in California contemporary art and modern landscape painters and photographers, including Ansel Adams and Edward Weston. Southeast of downtown, **MMA La Mirada** (Map p285; 831-372-3689; 720 Via Mirada), a silent-film star's villa, has humble adobe origins that are exquisitely concealed. It is now only used for special museum events, and not generally open to the public. Check the website to see if anything is scheduled.

Royal Presidio Chapel & Heritage Center Museum CHURCH
(Map p285; 831-373-2628; www.sancarloscathedral.org; 500 Church St; donations accepted; 10am-noon Wed, to 3pm Fri, to 2pm Sat, 1-3pm Sun, also 10am-noon & 1:15-3:15pm 2nd & 4th Mon of month;) Built of sandstone in 1794, this graceful chapel is California's oldest continuously functioning parish and first stone building. The original 1770 mission church stood here before being moved to Carmel. As Monterey expanded under Mexican rule in the 1820s, older buildings were gradually destroyed, leaving behind this National Historic Landmark as the strongest reminder of the defeated Spanish colonial presence. On-site docents are happy to provide tours during opening hours.

Activities

Like its larger namesake in San Francisco, Monterey's **Fisherman's Wharf** is a tacky tourist trap, but also a jumping-off point for deep-sea fishing trips and whale-watching cruises. A short walk east at workaday **Municipal Wharf 2**, fishing boats bob and sway in the bay.

Dennis the Menace Park PLAYGROUND
(Map p285; www.monterey.org; 777 Pearl St; 10am-dusk, closed Tue Sep-May;) FREE The brainchild of Hank Ketcham, the creator of the classic *Dennis the Menace* comic strip, this ain't your standard dumbed-down playground suffocated by Big Brother's safety regulations. With lightning-fast slides, a hedge maze, a suspension bridge and towering climbing walls, even some adults can't resist playing here.

Whale-Watching

You can spot whales off the coast of Monterey Bay year-round. The season for blue and humpback whales runs from April to early December, while gray whales pass by from mid-December through March. Tour boats depart from Fisherman's Wharf and Moss Landing (p280). Reserve trips at least a day in advance; be prepared for a bumpy, cold ride.

Monterey Whale Watching BOATING
(Map p285; 831-372-2203; www.montereywhalewatching.com; 96 Fisherman's Wharf; 2½hr tour adult/child 5-11yr $45/35) Several daily departures; no children under age five or pregnant women allowed.

Monterey Bay Whale Watch BOATING
(Map p285; 831-375-4658; www.montereybaywhalewatch.com; 84 Fisherman's Wharf; 3hr tour adult/child 4-12yr from $44/29;) Morning and afternoon departures; young children and well-behaved dogs are welcome on board.

Diving & Snorkeling

Monterey Bay offers world-renowned diving and snorkeling, including off **Lovers Point** in Pacific Grove and at Point Lobos State Natural Reserve (p292) south of Carmel-by-the-Sea. You'll want a wetsuit year-round. In summer, upwelling currents carry cold water from the deep canyon below the bay, sending a rich supply of nutrients up toward the surface level to feed the bay's diverse marine life. These frigid currents also account for the bay's chilly water temperatures and the summer fog that blankets the peninsula.

Aquarius Dive Shop DIVING
(831-375-1933; www.aquariusdivers.com; 2040 Del Monte Ave; snorkel/scuba-gear rental $35/65, dive tours from $65; 9am-6pm Mon-Fri, 7am-6pm Sat-Sun) Talk to this five-star PADI operation for gear rentals, classes and guided dives into Monterey Bay.

Monterey Bay Dive Charters DIVING
(831-383-9276; www.mbdcscuba.com; scuba-gear rental $75, shore/boat dives from $65/85) Arrange shore or boat dives and rent a full scuba kit with wetsuit from this well-reviewed outfitter.

Kayaking & Surfing

Monterey Bay Kayaks KAYAKING
(Map p285; 831-373-5357; www.montereybaykayaks.com; 693 Del Monte Ave; kayak or SUP set rental per day from $35, tours from $45; 8:30am-5pm, extended hours in summer) Rents kayaks

Monterey

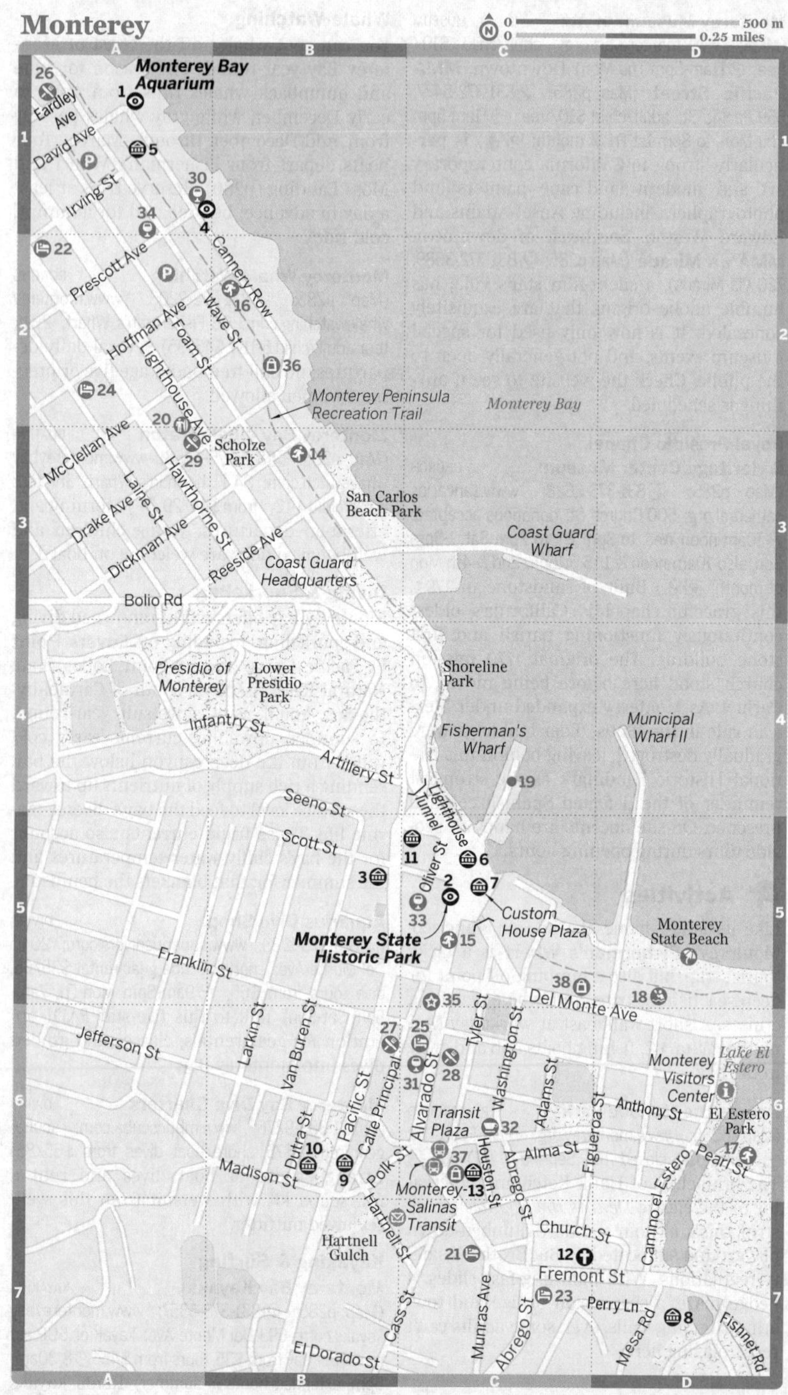

CENTRAL COAST MONTEREY

Monterey

Top Sights

1 Monterey Bay Aquarium A1
2 Monterey State Historic Park C5

Sights

3 California's First Theater B5
4 Cannery Row A1
5 Cannery Workers Shacks A1
6 Custom House C5
7 Dali17 C5
8 Monterey Museum of Art – La Mirada D7
9 Monterey Museum of Art – Pacific Street B6
10 Old Monterey Jail B6
11 Old Whaling Station C5
Pacific House (see 2)
12 Royal Presidio Chapel & Heritage Center Museum C7
13 Stevenson House C6

Activities, Courses & Tours

14 Adventures by the Sea B3
15 Adventures by the Sea C5
Bay Bikes (see 32)
16 Bay Bikes B2
17 Dennis the Menace Park D6
18 Monterey Bay Kayaks D5
Monterey Bay Whale Watch (see 19)
19 Monterey Whale Watching C4
20 Sunshine Freestyle Surf & Sport A2

Sleeping

21 Casa Munras C7
22 HI Monterey Hostel A2
23 Hotel Abrego C7
24 Jabberwock A2
25 Monterey Hotel C6

Eating

26 First Awakenings A1
27 Montrio Bistro B6
28 Old Monterey Marketplace C6
29 Zab Zab A3

Drinking & Nightlife

30 A Taste of Monterey A1
31 Alvarado Street Brewery C6
32 East Village Coffee Lounge C6
33 Peter B's Brewpub C5
34 Sardine Factory Lounge A1

Entertainment

35 Osio Cinema C5
Sly McFly's Fueling Station (see 30)

Shopping

36 Monterey Peninsula Art Foundation Gallery B2
37 Old Capitol Books C6
38 Wharf Marketplace C5

and SUP equipment, offers paddling lessons and leads guided tours of Monterey Bay, including full-moon and sunrise trips.

Sunshine Freestyle Surf & Sport SURFING
(Map p285; 831-375-5015; www.facebook.com/SunshineFreestyle; 443 Lighthouse Ave; surfboard/wetsuit/body board rental from $20/10/7; 10am-6pm Mon-Sat, 11am-5pm Sun) Monterey's oldest surf shop rents and sells all the surfing gear you'll need.

Cycling & Mountain Biking

Along an old railway line, the **Monterey Peninsula Recreational Trail** travels for 18 car-free miles along the waterfront, passing Cannery Row en route to Lovers Point in Pacific Grove. Road-cycling enthusiasts can make the round trip to Carmel along the 17-Mile Drive (p293). Mountain-bikers head to **Fort Ord National Monument** to pedal over 80 miles of single-track and fire roads; the **Sea Otter Classic** (www.seaotterclassic.com) races there in mid-April.

Adventures by the Sea CYCLING, KAYAKING
(Map p285; 831-372-1807; www.adventuresbythesea.com; 299 Cannery Row; rental per day kayak or bicycle $35, SUP set $50, kayak tours from $60; 9am-5pm, to 8pm in summer;) Beach cruisers, electric bikes and water-sports gear rentals and tours available at multiple locations on Cannery Row and **downtown** (Map p285; 210 Alvarado St; 9am-5pm, to 8pm in summer;).

Bay Bikes CYCLING
(Map p285; 831-655-2453; www.baybikes.com; 585 Cannery Row; bicycle rental per hour/day from $9/36, tours from $70; 9am-5pm Sun-Thu, to 6pm Fri, to 6:30pm Sat;) Cruiser, tandem, hybrid and road-bike rentals near the aquarium and also **downtown** (Map p285; 486 Washington St; 10am-5pm Sun-Mon, 10am-6pm Tue-Fri, 9am-6pm Sat;). Check out its handy free maps detailing local bike routes. Tours taking in Cannery Row, Pacific Grove or local wine-tasting are also available.

Festivals & Events

Castroville Artichoke Food & Wine Festival FOOD & DRINK
(831-633-2465; www.artichokefestival.org; late May/early Jun) Head 15 miles north of Monterey for 3D 'agro art' sculptures, cooking

demos, a farmers market and field tours. A recent addition is a wine-and-beer garden with tasty beverages from around the region.

Monterey County Fair CARNIVAL, FOOD
(www.montereycountyfair.com; late Aug & early Sep) Old-fashioned fun, carnival rides, horseback riding and livestock competitions, wine tasting and live music.

★**Monterey Jazz Festival** MUSIC
(www.montereyjazzfestival.org; mid-Sep) One of the world's longest-running jazz festivals (since 1958) showcases big-name headliners over a long spring weekend.

Sleeping

Book ahead for special events, on weekends and in summer. To avoid the tourist congestion and jacked-up prices of Cannery Row, look to Pacific Grove. Cheaper motels line Munras Ave, south of downtown, and N Fremont St, east of Hwy 1.

HI Monterey Hostel HOSTEL $
(Map p285; 831-649-0375; www.montereyhostel.org; 778 Hawthorne St; with shared bathdm $30-40; check in 4-10pm;) Four blocks from Cannery Row and the aquarium, this simple, clean hostel houses single-sex and mixed dorms, as well as private rooms accommodating up to five people (check online for rates). Budget backpackers stuff themselves silly with make-your-own-pancake breakfasts. Reservations strongly recommended. Take MST bus 1 from downtown's Transit Plaza (p288).

Veterans Memorial Park Campground CAMPGROUND $
(Map p290; 831-646-3865; www.monterey.org; Veterans Memorial Park; tent & RV sites $30) Tucked into the forest, this municipal campground has 40 grassy, non-reservable sites near a nature preserve's hiking trails. Amenities include coin-op hot showers, flush toilets, drinking water and barbecue fire pits. Three-night maximum stay.

Inn by the Bay MOTEL $$
(Map p290; 831-372-5409; www.innbythebaymonterey.com; 936 Munras Ave; d from $110;) An easy walk downhill to downtown Monterey, Inn on the Bay is the quiet achiever along the Munras Ave motel strip. Recent renovations have modernized the interiors, there are flat-screen TVs in the rooms, and a location set back from the street means it is uniformly quiet. A young, switched-on team at reception offer plenty of tips for enjoying Monterey and around.

Hotel Abrego BOUTIQUE HOTEL $$
(Map p285; 831-372-7551; www.hotelabrego.com; 755 Abrego St; r from $144;) At this downtown Monterey boutique hotel, most of the spacious, clean-lined contemporary rooms have gas fireplaces and chaise longues. Work out in the fitness studio, take a dip in the recently redeveloped outdoor pool or warm up in the hot tub. A new fire pit is a cozy addition for cooler Monterey evenings.

Casa Munras BOUTIQUE HOTEL $$
(Map p285; 831-375-2411; www.hotelcasamunras.com; 700 Munras Ave; r from $140;) Built around an adobe hacienda once owned by a 19th-century Spanish colonial don, chic modern rooms come with lofty beds and some have gas fireplaces, all inside two-story motel-esque buildings. Splash in a heated outdoor pool, unwind at the tapas bar or take a sea-salt scrub in the tiny spa. Pet fee $50.

Monterey Hotel HISTORIC HOTEL $$
(Map p285; 831-375-3184; www.montereyhotel.com; 406 Alvarado St; r $131-275;) In the heart of downtown and a short walk from Fisherman's Wharf, this 1904 edifice harbors five-dozen smallish but renovated rooms and suites with Victorian-styled furniture and plantation shutters. No elevator. A recently added boutique spa offers massage and beauty treatments.

★**Jabberwock** B&B $$$
(Map p285; 831-372-4777; www.jabberwockinn.com; 598 Laine St; r $249-339;) Barely visible through a shroud of foliage, this 1911 arts-and-crafts house hums a playful *Alice in Wonderland* tune through seven immaculate rooms, a few with fireplaces and Jacuzzis. Over afternoon tea and cookies or evening wine and hors d'oeuvres, ask the genial hosts about the house's many salvaged architectural elements. Weekends are more expensive and have a two-night minimum.

Also available is Tumtum Tree, a standalone cottage cradled by Monterey Cypress trees, and accommodating up to four guests.

Sanctuary Beach Resort HOTEL $$$
(831-883-9478; www.thesanctuarybeachresort.com; 3295 Dunes Dr, Marina; r from $260;) Be lulled to sleep by the surf at this low-lying retreat hidden in the sand dunes north of Monterey. Reached via golf carts, townhouses harbor petite rooms with gas

fireplaces and binoculars for whale-watching. Sunset bonfires bring out s'mores. The beach is an off-limits nature preserve, but there are public beaches and walking trails nearby. Pet fee $50.

Eating

Uphill from Monterey's Cannery Row, Lighthouse Ave features casual, budget-friendly eateries including Hawaiian barbecue and Thai flavors, through to sushi and Middle Eastern kebabs. Downtown around Alvarado St also features cafes and pub dining.

Zab Zab NORTHERN THAI $
(Map p285; 831-747-2225; www.zabzabmonterey.com; 401 Lighthouse Ave; mains $11-15; 11am-2:30pm & 5-9pm Tue-Fri, noon-9pm Sat-Sun;) Our pick of Lighthouse Ave's ethnic eateries, Zab Zab channels the robust flavors of northeast Thailand. The bijou cottage interior is perfect in cooler weather, but during summer the best spot is on the deck surrounded by a pleasantly overgrown garden. For fans of authentic Thai heat, go for the Kai Yang grilled chicken. Lunch boxes ($11 to $13) are good value.

Tricycle Pizza PIZZA $
(Map p290; www.tricyclepizza.com; 899 Lighthouse Ave; pizza $11-13; 3-9pm Wed-Fri, noon-9pm Sat) One of Monterey's favorite food trucks has graduated to a bricks-and-mortar location along Lighthouse Ave. Tricycle's crusty wood-fired pizza is still cooked in the original truck on-site, but there's now the option of takeout or dining in a hip, industrial space nearby. Try the sausage and mushroom with organic oregano, wood-fired mushrooms and fennel sausage.

Old Monterey Marketplace MARKET $
(Map p285; www.oldmonterey.org; Alvarado St, btwn Del Monte Ave & Pearl St; 4-7pm Tue Sep-May, to 8pm Jun-Aug;) Rain or shine, head downtown on Tuesdays for farm-fresh fruit and veggies, artisan cheeses, international food stalls and a scrumptious 'baker's alley.'

First Awakenings AMERICAN $
(Map p285; 831-372-1125; www.firstawakenings.net; American Tin Cannery, 125 Oceanview Blvd; mains $9-13; 7am-2pm Mon-Fri, to 2:30pm Sat & Sun;) Sweet and savory, all-American breakfasts and lunches and bottomless pitchers of coffee merrily weigh down outdoor tables at this cafe uphill from the aquarium. Try the unusual 'bluegerm' pancakes or a spicy Sonoran frittata.

Monterey's Fish House SEAFOOD $$
(831-373-4647; www.montereyfishhouse.com; 2114 Del Monte Ave; mains $11-25; 11:30am-2:30pm Mon-Fri & 5-9:30pm daily) Watched over by photos of Sicilian fishermen, dig into oak-grilled or blackened swordfish, barbecued oysters or, for those stout of heart, the Mexican squid steak. Reservations are essential (it's *so* crowded), but the vibe is island-casual: Hawaiian shirts seem to be de rigueur for men.

Montrio Bistro CALIFORNIAN $$$
(Map p285; 831-648-8880; www.montrio.com; 414 Calle Principal; shared plates $12-30, mains $25-44; 4:30-10pm Sun-Thu, to 11pm Fri & Sat) Inside a 1910 firehouse, Montrio combines leather walls and iron trellises, and the tables have butcher paper and crayons for kids. The eclectic seasonal menu mixes local, organic fare with Californian, Asian and European flair, including tapas-style shared plates and mini desserts. Well-priced bar snacks and happy-hour prices from 4:30pm daily are a fine end-of-the-day option.

Drinking & Nightlife

Prowl downtown Monterey's Alvarado St, touristy Cannery Row and locals-only Lighthouse Ave for watering holes.

★**Alvarado Street Brewery** CRAFT BEER
(Map p285; 831-655-2337; www.alvaradostreetbrewery.com; 426 Alvarado St; 11:30am-10pm Sun-Wed, to 11pm Thu-Sat) Vintage beer advertising punctuates Alvarado Street's brick walls, but that's the only concession to earlier days at this excellent craft-beer pub. Innovative brews harness new hop strains, sour and barrel-aged beers regularly fill the taps, and superior bar food includes Thai-curry mussels and truffle-crawfish mac 'n' cheese. In summer, adjourn to the alfresco beer garden out back.

Peter B's Brewpub BREWERY
(Map p285; 831-649-2699; www.facebook.com/PeterBsBrewpub; 2 Portola Plaza; 11am-11pm Sun-Thu, to midnight Fri-Sat) Often heaving with locals and tourists, Peter B's combines huge meals – the burgers are really good value – with a solid array of craft beers brewed on-site. Students crowd in to watch live sports on big-screen TVs, while visiting beer buffs work their way through beer sampling trays. Peter B's seasonal one-off brews are always worth trying.

A Taste of Monterey WINE BAR
(Map p285; www.atasteofmonterey.com; 700 Cannery Row; tasting flights $14-22; 11am-

6pm Sun-Thu, to 8pm Fri-Sat) Sample medal-winning Monterey County wines from as far away as the Santa Lucia Highlands while soaking up dreamy sea views, then peruse thoughtful exhibits on barrel-making and cork production. Shared plates, including crab cakes and smoked salmon, provide a tasty reason to linger.

Sardine Factory Lounge LOUNGE
(Map p285; ☎831-373-3775; www.sardinefactory.com; 701 Wave St; ⊙5pm-midnight) The legendary restaurant's fireplace lounge pours wines by the glass, delivers filling appetizers to your table and has a live piano player most nights.

East Village Coffee Lounge CAFE, LOUNGE
(Map p285; ☎831-373-5601; www.facebook.com/eastvillagemonterey; 498 Washington St; ⊙6am-10pm Mon-Fri, from 7am Sat & Sun;) Downtown Monterey coffee shop on a busy corner brews with fair-trade, organic beans. At night, it pulls off a big-city lounge vibe with film, open-mike and live-music nights and an all-important booze license. Check the Facebook page for event listings.

Entertainment

For comprehensive entertainment listings, browse the free tabloid *Monterey County Weekly* (www.montereycountyweekly.com).

Osio Cinema CINEMA
(Map p285; ☎831-644-8171; http://osiotheater.com; 350 Alvarado St; adult $10, before 6pm $7;) Downtown Monterey cinema screens indie dramas, cutting-edge documentaries and offbeat Hollywood films. Drop by its Cafe Lumiere for locally roasted coffee, loose-leaf tea, decadent cheesecake and wi-fi.

Sly McFly's Fueling Station LIVE MUSIC
(Map p285; ☎831-649-8050; www.slymcflysmonterey.com; 700 Cannery Row; ⊙11:30am-midnight Sun-Thu, to 2am Fri & Sat) Waterfront dive showcases live local blues, jazz and rock bands nightly after 8:30pm or 9pm. Skip the food, though.

Shopping

Cannery Row is jammed with claptrap shops, while downtown Monterey's side streets hide more one-of-a-kind finds.

Wharf Marketplace FOOD & DRINKS
(Map p285; ☎831-649-1116; www.thewharfmarketplace.com; 290 Figueroa St; ⊙7am-7pm) Inside an old railway station, this gourmet-food emporium carries bountiful farm goodness, artisanal products and wine from Monterey County and beyond. It's a good spot for a leisurely breakfast, too.

Monterey Peninsula Art Foundation Gallery ART
(Map p285; ☎831-655-1267; www.mpaf.org; 425 Cannery Row; ⊙11am-5pm) Taking over a cozy sea-view house, more than 30 local artists sell plein-air paintings and sketches alongside contemporary works in all media.

Old Capitol Books BOOKS
(Map p285; ☎831-333-0383; www.oldcapitolbooks.com; 559 Tyler St; ⊙10am-6pm Wed-Mon, to 7pm Tue) Tall shelves of new, used and antiquarian books, including rare first editions, California titles and John Steinbeck's works.

Information

Doctors on Duty (☎831-649-0770; www.doctorsonduty.com; 501 Lighthouse Ave; ⊙8am-8pm Mon-Sat, to 6pm Sun) Walk-in, non-emergency medical clinic.

Monterey Public Library (☎831-646-3933; www.monterey.org/library; 625 Pacific St; ⊙noon-8pm Mon-Wed, 10am-6pm Thu-Sat, 1-5pm Sun;) Free wi-fi and public internet terminals.

Monterey Visitors Center (Map p285; ☎831-657-6400; www.seemonterey.com; 401 Camino el Estero; ⊙9am-6pm Mon-Sat, to 5pm Sun, closes 1hr earlier Nov-Mar) Free tourist brochures and accommodations booking service; ask for a *Monterey County Literary & Film Map*.

Post Office (Map p285; ☎800-275-8777; www.usps.com; 565 Hartnell St; ⊙8:30am-5pm Mon-Fri, 10am-2pm Sat) Located just south of downtown Monterey.

Getting There & Away

Monterey is 43 miles south of Santa Cruz and 177 miles north of San Luis Obispo.

AIR

A few miles east of downtown off Hwy 68, **Monterey Regional Airport** (☎831-648-7000; www.montereyairport.com; 200 Fred Kane Dr) has flights with United (LA, San Francisco), American (Phoenix), Alaska (San Diego and LA) and Allegiant Air (Las Vegas). A taxi from downtown is around $20 (10 minutes), and to get here by public transport, catch buses 7, 56 or 93 ($2.50) from Monterey's **Transit Plaza** (Map p285; cnr Pearl & Alvarado Sts).

The **Monterey Airbus** (☎831-373-7777; www.montereyairbus.com;) shuttle service links Monterey with international airports in San Jose

($40, 1½ hours) and San Francisco ($50, 2½ hours) almost a dozen times daily; book online for discounts.

BUS

Monterey-Salinas Transit (MST; Map p285; ☎888-678-2871; www.mst.org; Jules Simmoneau Plaza; single-ride fares $1.50-3.50, day pass $10) operates local and regional buses; routes converge on downtown's Transit Plaza, including routes to Pacific Grove, Carmel and Big Sur. From late May until early September, MST's free trolley loops around downtown, Fisherman's Wharf and Cannery Row between 10am and 7pm or 8pm daily.

Pacific Grove

Founded as a tranquil Methodist summer retreat in 1875, Pacific Grove (or PG) maintained its quaint, holier-than-thou attitude well into the 20th century. The selling of liquor was illegal up until 1969, making it California's last 'dry' town. Today, leafy streets are lined by stately Victorian homes and a charming, compact downtown orbits Lighthouse Ave.

Sights & Activities

Pacific Grove's aptly named **Ocean View Blvd** affords views from Lovers Point Park west to Point Pinos, where it becomes **Sunset Dr**, offering tempting turnouts where you can stroll by pounding surf, rocky outcrops and teeming tide pools all the way to Asilomar State Beach. This seaside route is great for cycling, too – some say it rivals the famous 17-Mile Drive for beauty and, even better, it's free.

Asilomar State Beach BEACH

(Map p290; Sunset Dr) Negotiate a 1-mile trail boardwalk through rugged sand dunes. Note this beach is known for riptides and unpredictable surf, and care must be taken when swimming here.

Point Pinos Lighthouse LIGHTHOUSE

(Map p290; ☎831-648-3176; www.pointpinoslighthouse.org; 80 Asilomar Ave; suggested donation adult/child 6-12yr $4/2; ⏲1-4pm Thu-Mon) The West Coast's oldest continuously operating lighthouse has been warning ships off the hazardous tip of the Monterey Peninsula since 1855. Inside are modest exhibits on the lighthouse's history and, alas, its failures – local shipwrecks.

Monarch Grove Sanctuary PARK

(Map p290; www.cityofpacificgrove.org/visiting; 250 Ridge Rd; ⏲dawn-dusk; 👪) FREE Between November and February, over 25,000 migratory monarch butterflies cluster in this thicket of tall eucalyptus trees, secreted inland. During peak season, volunteer guides answer all of your questions between noon and 3pm, weather permitting.

Pacific Grove Golf Links GOLF

(Map p290; ☎831-648-5775; www.playpacificgrove.com; 77 Asilomar Blvd; green fees $43-64) Can't afford to play at famous Pebble Beach? This historic 18-hole municipal course, where deer freely range, has impressive sea views, and it's a lot easier (not to mention cheaper) to book a tee time here.

Sleeping

Antique-filled B&Bs have taken over many stately Victorian homes around downtown Pacific Grove and by the beach. Motels cluster at the peninsula's western end, off Lighthouse and Asilomar Aves.

Asilomar Conference Grounds LODGE $$

(Map p290; ☎831-372-8016; www.visitasilomar.com; 800 Asilomar Ave; r from $188; @🛜🐕) This state-park lodge sprawls by sand dunes in pine forest. Skip ho-hum motel rooms and opt for historic houses designed by early-20th-century architect Julia Morgan (of Hearst Castle fame) – the thin-walled, hardwood-floored rooms may be small, but they share a fireplace lounge. Head to the lodge lobby for Ping-Pong, pool tables and wi-fi. Bike rentals available.

Sunset Inn MOTEL $$

(Map p290; ☎831-375-3529; www.gosunsetinn.com; 133 Asilomar Blvd; r $99-235; 🛜) At this small motor lodge near the golf course and the beach, attentive staff hand out keys to crisply redesigned rooms that have hardwood floors, king-sized beds with cheery floral-print comforters and sometimes a hot tub and a fireplace.

Eating

Downtown PG teems with European-style bakeries, coffee shops and neighborhood cafes.

Jeninni Kitchen & Wine Bar MEDITERRANEAN $$

(Map p290; ☎831-920-2662; www.jeninni.com; 542 Lighthouse Ave; mains $18-32; ⏲4pm-late Thu-Tue, 9:30am-1:30pm Sun) Happy-hour

Monterey Peninsula

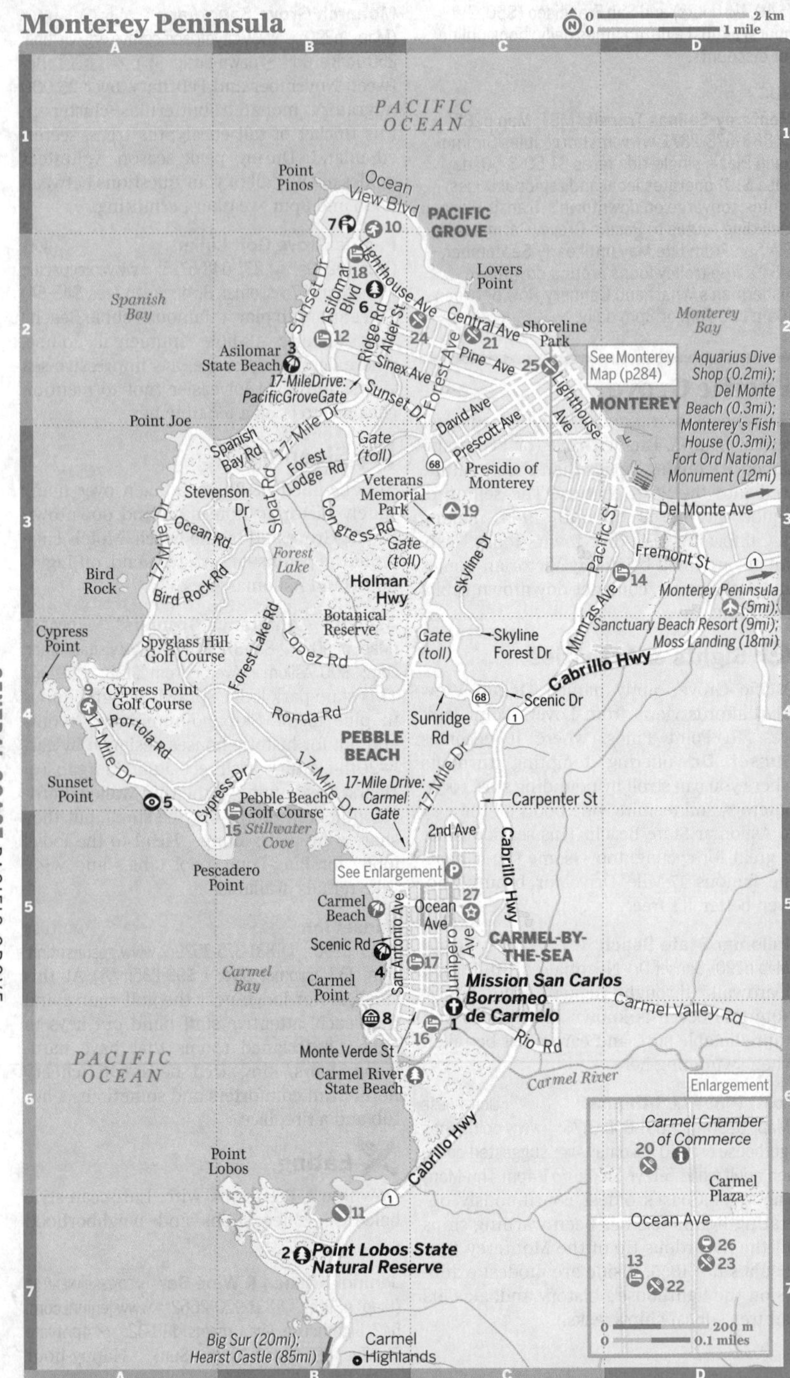

Monterey Peninsula

Top Sights
1 Mission San Carlos Borromeo de Carmelo C6
2 Point Lobos State Natural Reserve B7

Sights
3 Asilomar State Beach B2
4 Carmel Beach City Park B5
5 Lone Cypress A4
6 Monarch Grove Sanctuary B2
7 Point Pinos Lighthouse B1
8 Tor House B6

Activities, Courses & Tours
9 17-Mile Drive A4
10 Pacific Grove Golf Links B1
11 Whalers Cove B7

Sleeping
12 Asilomar Conference Grounds B2
13 Cypress Inn D7
14 Inn by the Bay D3
15 Lodge at Pebble Beach B5
16 Mission Ranch C6
17 Sea View Inn C5
18 Sunset Inn B2
19 Veterans Memorial Park Campground C3

Eating
20 Cultura Comida y Bebida D6
21 Jeninni Kitchen & Wine Bar C2
22 La Bicyclette D7
23 Mundaka D7
24 Passionfish C2
25 Tricycle Pizza C2

Drinking & Nightlife
26 Barmel D7
Scheid Vineyards .... (see 23)

Entertainment
27 Forest Theater C5

snacks from 4pm to 6pm segue to dinner at this bistro featuring the flavors of the Med. Housemade charcuterie and shared plates, such as crispy octopus, create a convivial ambience, while larger mains featuring venison, duck or lamb partner well with an informed wine list. On balmy summer nights, dine on the front patio watching Pacific Grove's passing parade.

Passionfish SEAFOOD $$$
(Map p290; ☎831-655-3311; www.passionfish.net; 701 Lighthouse Ave; mains $21-42; ⊙5-9pm Sun-Thu, to 10pm Fri & Sat; ☎) Fresh, sustainable seafood is artfully presented in any number of inventive ways, and a seasonally inspired menu also carries slow-cooked meats and vegetarian dishes spotlighting local farms. The earth-tone decor is spare, with tables squeezed conversationally close together. An ambitious world-ranging wine list is priced near retail, and there are as many Chinese teas as wines by the glass.

Reservations strongly recommended.

Drinking & Nightlife

Pacific Grove is largely a daytime destination, so make the short journey to Monterey for better after-dark action.

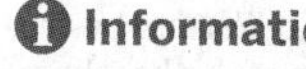

Information

Pacific Grove Chamber of Commerce (Map p290; ☎831-373-3304; www.pacificgrove.org; 584 Central Ave; ⊙9:30am-5pm Mon-Fri, 10am-3pm Sat)

Getting There & Around

MST (p289) bus 1 connects downtown Monterey and Cannery Row with Pacific Grove, continuing to Asilomar ($2.50, 15 minutes, every 30 to 60 minutes).

Carmel-by-the-Sea

With borderline fanatical devotion to its canine citizens, quaint Carmel has the well-manicured feel of a country club. Watch the parade of behatted ladies toting fancy-label shopping bags to lunch and dapper gents driving top-down convertibles along Ocean Ave, the village's slow-mo main drag.

Founded as a seaside resort in the 1880s – fairly odd, given that its beach is often blanketed in fog – Carmel quickly attracted famous artists and writers, such as Sinclair Lewis and Jack London, and their hangers-on. Artistic flavor survives in over 100 galleries that line downtown's immaculate streets, but sky-high property values have long obliterated any salt-of-the-earth bohemia.

Dating from the 1920s, Comstock cottages, with their characteristic stone chimneys and pitched gable roofs, still dot the town, making it look vaguely reminiscent of the English countryside. Even payphones, garbage cans and newspaper vending boxes are quaintly shingled.

Sights & Activities

Escape downtown Carmel's harried shopping streets and stroll tree-lined neighborhoods on the lookout for domiciles charming and peculiar. The Hansel and Gretel houses on Torres St, between 5th and 6th Avenues, are just how you'd imagine them. Another eye-catching house in the shape of a ship, made from local river rocks and salvaged ship parts, is on Guadalupe St near 6th Ave.

★Point Lobos State Natural Reserve — STATE PARK

(Map p290; ☎831-624-4909; www.pointlobos.org; Hwy 1; per car $10; ⏰8am-7pm, to 5pm early Nov–mid-Mar; P 👪) 🌿 They bark, they bathe and they're fun to watch – sea lions are the stars here at Punta de los Lobos Marinos (Point of the Sea Wolves), almost 4 miles south of Carmel, where a dramatically rocky coastline offers excellent tide-pooling. The full perimeter hike is 6 miles, but shorter walks take in wild scenery too, including **Bird Island**, shady cypress groves, the historical **Whaler's Cabin** and the **Devil's Cauldron**, a whirlpool that gets splashy at high tide.

The kelp forest at Whalers Cove is popular with snorkelers and scuba divers. Don't skip paying the entry fee by parking outside the park gates on the highway shoulder – California's state parks are chronically underfunded and need your help.

➡ Whalers Cove

(Map p290) Without donning a wetsuit, you can still get an idea of the underwater terrain with a 3D model located by the parking lot. Reserve snorkeling, scuba-diving, kayaking and SUP permits ($10 to $30) up to two months in advance online.

★Mission San Carlos Borromeo de Carmelo — CHURCH

(Map p290; ☎831-624-1271; www.carmelmission.org; 3080 Rio Rd; adult/child 7-17yr $6.50/2; ⏰9:30am-7pm; 👪) Monterey's original mission was established by Franciscan friar Junípero Serra in 1770, but poor soil and the corrupting influence of Spanish soldiers forced the move to Carmel two years later. Today this is one of California's most strikingly beautiful missions, an oasis of solemnity bathed in flowering gardens. The mission's adobe chapel was later replaced with an arched basilica made of stone quarried in the Santa Lucia Mountains. Museum exhibits are scattered throughout the meditative complex.

The spartan cell attributed to Serra looks like something out of *The Good, the Bad and the Ugly*, while a separate chapel houses his memorial tomb.

Don't overlook the gravestone of 'Old Gabriel,' a Native American convert whom Serra baptized, and whose dates put him at 151 years old when he died. People say he smoked like a chimney and outlived seven wives. There's a lesson in there somewhere.

Tor House — HISTORIC BUILDING

(Map p290; ☎844-285-0244; www.torhouse.org; 26304 Ocean View Ave; adult/child 12-17yr $12/7; ⏰tours hourly 10am-3pm Fri & Sat) Even if you've never heard of 20th-century poet Robinson Jeffers, a pilgrimage to this house built with his own hands offers fascinating insights into both the man and the bohemian ethos of Old Carmel. A porthole in the Celtic-inspired **Hawk Tower** reputedly came from the wrecked ship that carried Napoleon from Elba. The only way to visit the property is to reserve a tour (children under 12 years old not allowed), although the tower can be glimpsed from the street.

Carmel Beach City Park — BEACH

(Map p290; off Scenic Rd; 👪 🐾) Not always sunny, Carmel Beach is a gorgeous blanket of white sand, where pampered pups excitedly run off-leash. South of 10th Ave, bonfires crackle after sunset (until 10pm Monday through Thursday only).

Festivals & Events

Pebble Beach Food & Wine — FOOD & DRINK

(☎866-907-3663; www.pbfw.com) Excellent four-day gastronomy-focused festival sponsored by the prestigious *Food & Wine* magazine. Held in mid- to late-April.

Carmel International Film Festival — FILM

(www.carmelfilmfest.com; ⏰mid-Oct) Live music and over 100 independent film screenings. Animation, documentaries, features and short films are all covered.

Sleeping

Shockingly overpriced boutique hotels, inns and B&Bs fill up quickly in Carmel-by-the-Sea, especially in summer. Ask the chamber of commerce (p295) about last-minute deals. For better-value lodgings, head north to Monterey.

Mission Ranch INN $$
(Map p290; ☎831-624-6436; www.missionranchcarmel.com; 26270 Dolores St; r $140-340;) If woolly sheep grazing on green fields by the beach doesn't convince you to stay here, maybe knowing that Hollywood icon Clint Eastwood restored this historic ranch will. Accommodations are shabby-chic, even a tad rustic.

Sea View Inn B&B $$
(Map p290; ☎831-624-8778; www.seaviewinncarmel.com; El Camino Real, btwn 11th & 12th Aves; r $145-295;) Retreat from downtown Carmel's hustle to fireside nooks tailor-made for reading. The cheapest rooms with slanted ceilings are short on cat-swinging space. Rates include afternoon wine and noshes on the front porch.

Lodge at Pebble Beach RESORT $$$
(Map p290; ☎831-624-3811; www.pebblebeach.com; 1700 17-Mile Drive; r from $815;) The luxurious Lodge at Pebble Beach includes a spa and designer shops where the most demanding of tastes are catered to. Even if you're not a trust-fund baby, you can still soak up the rich atmosphere in the resort's art-filled public spaces and bay views from the cocktail lounge.

Cypress Inn BOUTIQUE HOTEL $$$
(Map p290; ☎831-624-3871; www.cypress-inn.com; cnr Lincoln St & 7th Ave; r/ste from $279/499;) Done up in Spanish Colonial style, this 1929 inn is co-owned by movie star Doris Day. Airy terracotta hallways with colorful tiles give it a Mediterranean feel, while sunny rooms face the courtyard. Pet fee $30.

Eating

Carmel's dining scene has traditionally been more about old-world atmosphere, but a few recent openings have added a more modern, cosmopolitan sheen.

Cultura Comida y Bebida MEXICAN $$
(Map p290; ☎831-250-7005; www.culturacarmel.com; Dolores St btwn 5th & 6th Aves; mains $19-32; 11:30am-midnight Thu-Sun, 5pm-midnight Mon-Tue) Located near art galleries in a brick-lined courtyard, Cultura Comida y Bebida is a relaxed bar and eatery inspired by the food of Oaxaca in Mexico. Pull up a seat at the elegant bar and sample a vertical tasting of mezcal, or partner Monterey squid tostadas

17-MILE DRIVE

What to See

Pacific Grove and Carmel are linked by the spectacularly scenic, if overhyped, **17-Mile Drive** (Map p290; www.pebblebeach.com; per car/bicycle $10/free), which meanders through Pebble Beach, a wealthy private resort. It's no chore staying within the 25mph limit – every curve in the road reveals another postcard vista, especially when wildflowers are in bloom. Cycling the drive is enormously popular: try to do it during the week, when traffic isn't as heavy, and ride with the flow of traffic from north to south.

Using the self-guided touring map you'll receive at the toll gate, you can pick out landmarks such as **Spanish Bay**, where explorer Gaspar de Portolá dropped anchor in 1769; treacherously rocky **Point Joe**, which was often mistaken for the entrance to Monterey Bay and thus became the site of shipwrecks; and **Bird Rock**, also a haven for harbor seals and sea lions. The pièce de résistance is the trademarked **Lone Cypress** (Map p290), which has perched on a seaward rock for possibly more than 250 years.

Besides the coastal scenery, star attractions at Pebble Beach include world-famous golf courses, where a celebrity and pro tournament happens every February. The luxurious **Lodge at Pebble Beach** (p293) has a spa and designer shops.

The Route

Operated as a toll road by the Pebble Beach Company, the 17-Mile Drive is open from sunrise to sunset. The toll can be refunded later as a discount on a $30 minimum food purchase at local restaurants.

Time & Mileage

There are five separate gates for the 17-Mile Drive; how far you drive and how long you take is up to you. To take advantage of the most scenery, enter on Sunset Dr in Pacific Grove and exit onto San Antonio Ave in Carmel-by-the-Sea.

WORTH A TRIP

CARMEL VALLEY

Where sun-kissed vineyards rustle beside farm fields, Carmel Valley is a peaceful side trip, just a 20-minute drive east of Hwy 1 along eastbound Carmel Valley Rd. At organic **Earthbound Farm Stand** (☎805-625-6219; www.ebfarm.com; 7250 Carmel Valley Rd; ⏰8am-6:30pm Mon-Sat, 9am-6pm Sun; 👪) 🌿, sample homemade soups and salads or harvest your own herbs from the garden. Several wineries further east offer tastings – don't miss the Pinot Noir bottled by **Boekenoogen** (Map p296; ☎831-659-4215; www.boekenoogen-wines.com; 24 W Carmel Valley Rd; tasting flights $10-15; ⏰11am-5pm; P). Afterwards, stretch your legs in the village of Carmel Valley, chock-a-block with genteel shops and bistros.

Corkscrew Cafe (Map p296; ☎831- 659-8888; www.corkscrewcafe.com; 55 W Carmel Valley Rd; mains $15-26; ⏰noon-9pm Wed-Mon) Just possibly Carmel Valley's coziest eatery, the Corkscrew Cafe combines a rustic wine-country vibe and a Mediterranean-influenced menu – think wood-fired salmon, pizza, and mushroom and lamb pasta – with a stellar local wine list. Relax into a Carmel Valley evening under the market umbrellas in the pleasant garden, and don't leave without checking out the quirky corkscrew museum.

Valley Greens Gallery (Map p296; ☎831-620-2985; www.valleygreensgallery.com; 16e E Carmel Valley Rd; 4-beer tasting flights $12; ⏰3-9pm Mon-Tue, 3-10pm Wed-Thu, 1-11pm Fri-Sat, 1-9pm Sun) One part funky art gallery and two parts craft-beer bar, Valley Greens is a stand-out destination amid Carmel Valley's laid-back main drag. Four rotating beer taps deliver some real surprises from smaller Californian breweries, old-school reggae and foosball tables create a fun ambience, and open-mike night from 6pm on Tuesdays is always worth catching.

and oak-roasted trout with cilantro, lime and garlic with Californian and French wines.

Mundaka TAPAS **$$**
(Map p290; ☎831-624-7400; www.mundakacarmel.com; San Carlos St, btwn Ocean & 7th Aves; small plates $8-15; ⏰5-9pm Sun-Thu, to 10pm Fri-Sat) This stone courtyard hideaway is a svelte escape from Carmel's stuffy 'newly wed and nearly dead' crowd. Taste Spanish tapas and housemade sangria while world beats spin. Partner the garlic prawns or grilled octopus with a chilled glass of local wine.

La Bicyclette FRENCH, ITALIAN **$$**
(Map p290; ☎831-622-9899; www.labicycletterestaurant.com; cnr Dolores St & 7th Ave; dinner mains $18-31; ⏰8am-10pm) 🌿 Rustic European comfort food using seasonal local ingredients packs canoodling couples into this bistro, with an open kitchen baking wood-fired-oven pizzas. Excellent local wines by the glass. It's also a top spot for a breakfast or lunch.

🍷 Drinking & Entertainment

Winery tasting rooms dot Carmel's compact and well-kept centre, and the best option for late-night drinks is the cool and energetic scene at Barmel.

Barmel WINE BAR
(Map p290; ☎831-626-2095; www.facebook.com/BarmelByTheSea; San Carlos St, btwn Ocean & 7th Aves; ⏰2pm-2am Mon-Fri, 1pm-2am Sat-Sun) Shaking up Carmel's conservative image and adding a dash of after-dark fun is this cool little Spanish-themed courtyard bar. There's live music from 7pm to 9pm from Thursday to Saturday, robust cocktails and an energetic, younger vibe.

Scheid Vineyards WINE BAR
(Map p290; ☎831-656-9463; www.scheidvineyards.com; San Carlos St, at 7th Ave; tasting flights $10-20; ⏰noon-7pm Sun-Thu, to 8pm Fri & Sat) Pop into Scheid Vineyards' wine-tasting room to sip a prodigious range of grape varietals, all grown in Monterey County. Red wine varietals including Merlot, Pinot Noir and Cabernet Sauvignon are local stars.

Forest Theater THEATER
(Map p290; ☎box office 831-622-0100; www.foresttheatercarmel.org; cnr Mountain View Ave & Santa Rita St) At this 1910 venue, community-theater musicals, dramas and comedies as well as film screenings take place under the stars by flickering fire pits.

Information

Carmel Chamber of Commerce (Map p290; 831-624-2522; www.carmelcalifornia.org; San Carlos St, btwn 5th & 6th Aves; 10am-5pm)

Getting There & Away

Carmel is about 5 miles south of Monterey via Hwy 1. There's free parking (no time limit) in a **municipal lot** (Map p290; cnr 3rd & Junípero Sts) behind the Vista Lobos building.

MST (888-678-2871; www.mst.org) 'Grapevine Express' bus 24 ($2.50, hourly) connects Monterey's Transit Plaza with downtown Carmel, the mission and Carmel Valley. Bus 22 ($3.50) stops in downtown Carmel and at the mission en route to/from Point Lobos and Big Sur three times daily between late May and early September, and twice daily on Saturday and Sunday only the rest of the year.

Big Sur

Big Sur is more a state of mind than a place to pinpoint on a map, and when the sun goes down, the moon and the stars are the area's natural streetlights. (That's if summer's fog hasn't extinguished them.) Raw beauty and an intense maritime energy characterize this land shoehorned between the Santa Lucia Range and the Pacific Ocean, and a first glimpse of the craggy, unspoiled coastline is a special moment.

In the 1950s and '60s, Big Sur – named by Spanish settlers living on the Monterey Peninsula, who referred to the wilderness as *el país grande del sur* ('the big country to the south') – became a retreat for artists and writers, including Henry Miller and Beat Generation visionaries such as Lawrence Ferlinghetti. Today Big Sur attracts self-proclaimed artists, new-age mystics, latter-day hippies and city slickers seeking to unplug and reflect more deeply on this emerald-green edge of the continent.

Sights

At Big Sur's state parks, your parking fee ($10) receipt is valid for same-day entry to all except Limekiln. Please don't skip paying the entry fee by parking illegally outside the parks along Hwy 1 – California's state parks have suffered severe budget cutbacks, and every dollar helps.

Garrapata State Park — PARK

(Map p296; 831-624-4909; www.parks.ca.gov; off Hwy 1;) FREE Over 4 miles south of Point Lobos on Hwy 1, pull over to hike coastal headlands, where you might spot whales cruising by offshore during winter, or into canyons of wildflowers and redwood trees. *Garrapata* is Spanish for 'tick,' of which there are many in the canyon and woods, so wearing long sleeves and pants is smart. Leashed dogs are allowed on the beach only.

Bixby Bridge — LANDMARK

(Map p296) Less than 15 miles south of Carmel, this landmark spanning Rainbow Canyon is one of the world's highest single-span bridges. Completed in 1932, it was built by prisoners eager to lop time off their sentences. There's a perfect photo-op pull-off on the bridge's north side. Before Bixby Bridge was constructed, travelers had to trek inland on what's now called the **Old Coast Rd**, a rough dirt route that reconnects after 11 miles with Hwy 1 near Andrew Molera State Park. When the weather is dry enough, the old road is usually navigable by 4WD or a mountain bike.

HIGHWAY 1 ROAD CLOSURES

At the time of writing, temporary road closures have shuttered a 23 mile stretch along Hwy 1 through Big Sur. To the north, the Pfeiffer Canyon Bridge has been condemned after the eroding hillside undermined the support columns. In the southern part of the region, mudslides have covered the road at Mud Creek, significantly changing the landscape and making the area inaccessible via car. The Pfeiffer Canyon Bridge is scheduled to reopen in September 2017. However, the California Department of Transportation has a larger challenge with the landslides. A plan was put forward in August 2017 to realign the highway across the landslide, but the enormous undertaking had no set date of completion at that time.

Until the road reopens, travelers can detour around Big Sur on Hwy 101 (p310). You'll miss out on some coastal views, but between stunning views of the California countryside, quaint towns and world-class wine tasting, it's a detour worth taking on its own merit.

Big Sur

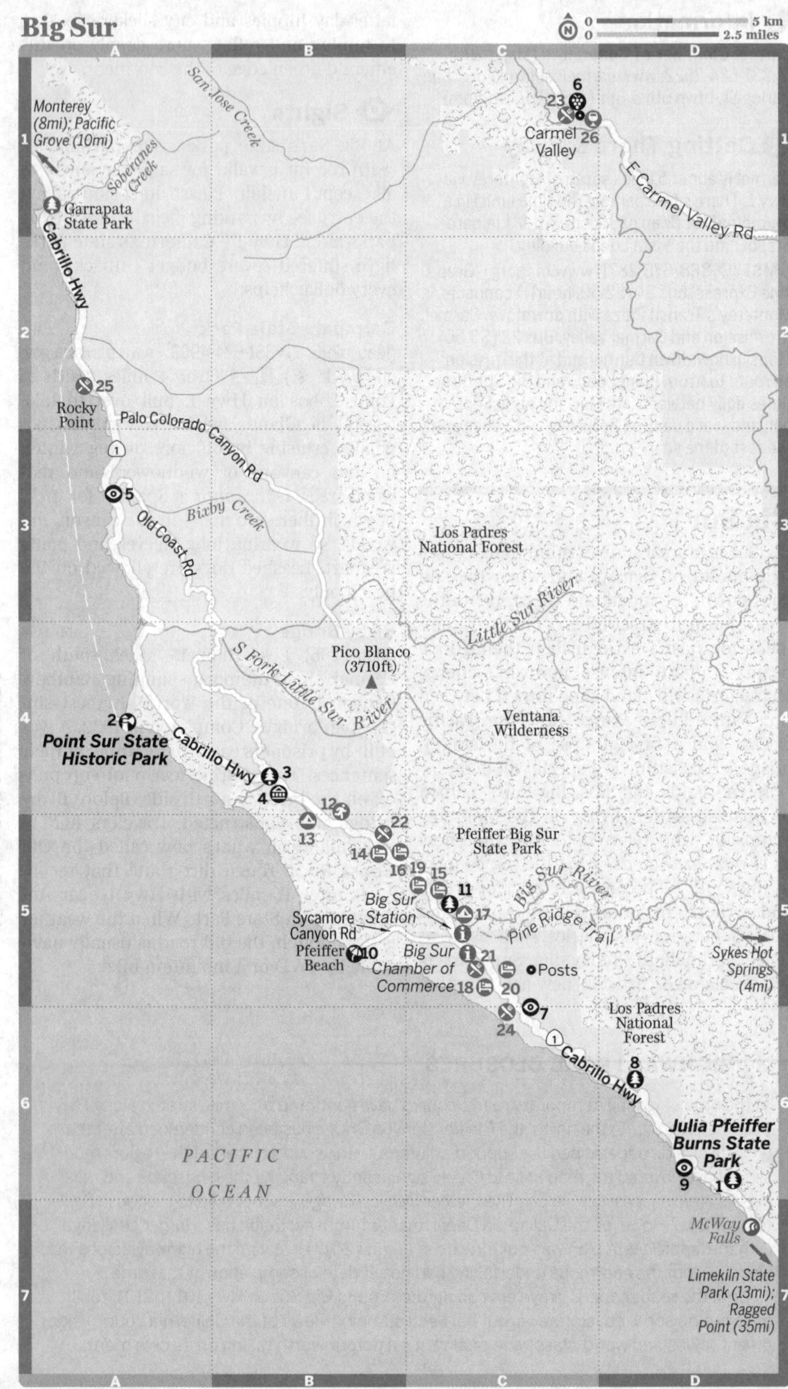

0 5 km
0 2.5 miles
Monterey (8mi); Pacific Grove (10mi)
San Jose Creek
Soberanes Creek
Carmel Valley
E Carmel Valley Rd
Garrapata State Park
Cabrillo Hwy
Rocky Point
Palo Colorado Canyon Rd
Bixby Creek
Old Coast Rd
Los Padres National Forest
Little Sur River
S Fork Little Sur River
Pico Blanco (3710ft)
Ventana Wilderness
Point Sur State Historic Park
Pfeiffer Big Sur State Park
Big Sur River
Big Sur Station
Pine Ridge Trail
Sycamore Canyon Rd
Pfeiffer Beach
Big Sur Chamber of Commerce
Posts
Sykes Hot Springs (4mi)
Los Padres National Forest
Julia Pfeiffer Burns State Park
McWay Falls
Limekiln State Park (13mi); Ragged Point (35mi)
PACIFIC OCEAN

★ Point Sur State Historic Park LIGHTHOUSE
(Map p296; ☎831-625-4419; www.pointsur.org; off Hwy 1; adult/child 6-17yr from $12/5; ⏲tours usually at 1pm Wed, 10am Sat & Sun Oct-Mar; 10am & 2pm Wed & Sat, 10am Sun Apr-Sep, also 10am Thu Jul & Aug) FREE A little over 6 miles south of Bixby Bridge (p295), Point Sur rises like a velvety green fortress out of the sea. It looks like an island, but is actually connected to land by a sandbar. Atop the volcanic rock sits an 1889 stone light station, which was staffed until 1974. During three-hour guided tours, ocean views and tales of the lighthouse keepers' family lives are engrossing. Meet your tour guide at the locked farm gate 0.25-miles north of Point Sur Naval Facility.

Special monthly moonlight tours are given between April and September. Call ahead to confirm all tour schedules. Show up early because space is limited (no reservations; some credit cards accepted).

Andrew Molera State Park STATE PARK
(Map p296; ☎831-667-2315; www.parks.ca.gov; Hwy 1; per car $10; ⏲30min before sunrise-30min after sunset; P ♿) Named after the farmer who first planted artichokes in California, this oft-overlooked park is a trail-laced pastiche of grassy meadows, ocean bluffs and rugged sandy beaches offering excellent wildlife watching. Look for the entrance just over 8 miles south of Bixby Bridge.

South of the parking lot, you can learn all about endangered California condors and long-term species recovery and monitoring programs inside the **Big Sur Discovery Center** (Map p296; ☎831-624-1202; www.ventanaws.org/discovery_center; ⏲10am-4pm Sat & Sun late May–early Sep; P ♿) FREE.

From the main parking lot, a short walk along the beach-bound trail passes through a first-come-first-serve campground, from where a gentle spur trail leads to the 1861 redwood **Cooper Cabin**, Big Sur's oldest building. Keep hiking on the main trail out toward a wild beach where the Big Sur River runs into the ocean; condors may be spotted circling overhead and migrating whales sometimes cruise by offshore.

Pfeiffer Big Sur State Park PARK
(Map p296; ☎831-667-2315; www.parks.ca.gov; 47225 Hwy 1; per car $10; ⏲30min before sunrise-30min after sunset; P ♿) Named after Big Sur's first European settlers who arrived in 1869, this is Big Sur's largest state park, where hiking trails loop through stately redwood groves. The most popular hike – to 60ft-high **Pfeiffer Falls**, a delicate cascade hidden in the forest, which usually runs from December to May – is a 2-mile round-trip. Built in the 1930s by the Civilian Conservation Corps (CCC), rustic **Big Sur Lodge** (Map p296; ☎831-667-3100; www.bigsurlodge.com; 47225 Hwy 1; d $309-439; P)

Big Sur

Top Sights
1 Julia Pfeiffer Burns State Park D6
2 Point Sur State Historic Park A4

Sights
3 Andrew Molera State Park B4
4 Big Sur Discovery Center B4
5 Bixby Bridge A3
6 Boekenoogen C1
7 Henry Miller Memorial Library C6
8 Los Padres National Forest D6
9 Partington Cove D6
10 Pfeiffer Beach B5
11 Pfeiffer Big Sur State Park C5

Activities, Courses & Tours
12 Molera Horseback Tours B4

Sleeping
13 Andrew Molera State Park Campground B5
14 Big Sur Campground & Cabins B5
15 Big Sur Lodge C5
16 Glen Oaks Motel B5
17 Pfeiffer Big Sur State Park Campground C5
18 Post Ranch Inn C5
19 Ripplewood Resort C5
20 Ventana Inn & Spa C5

Eating
21 Big Sur Bakery & Restaurant C5
Big Sur Deli & General Store .... (see 21)
22 Big Sur River Inn B5
Big Sur Roadhouse .... (see 16)
23 Corkscrew Cafe C1
24 Nepenthe C6
25 Rocky Point A2

Drinking & Nightlife
Big Sur Taphouse .... (see 21)
Maiden Publick House .... (see 22)
26 Valley Greens Gallery C1

Entertainment
Henry Miller Memorial Library .... (see 7)

stands near the park entrance, about 13 miles south of Bixby Bridge (p295).

★ Julia Pfeiffer Burns State Park PARK
(☎831-667-2315; www.parks.ca.gov; Hwy 1; per car $10; ⊙30min before sunrise-30min after sunset; P 🚻) 🍃 If you're chasing waterfalls, swing into this state park named for a Big Sur pioneer. From the parking lot, the 1.3-mile round-trip **Overlook Trail** rushes downhill toward the ocean, passing through a tunnel underneath Hwy 1. Everyone comes to photograph 80ft-high **McWay Falls**, which tumbles year-round over granite cliffs and freefalls into the sea – or the beach, depending on the tide. The park entrance is on the east side of Hwy 1, about 8 miles south of Nepenthe restaurant (p301). McWay Falls is the classic Big Sur postcard shot, with tree-topped rocks jutting above a golden beach next to swirling blue pools and crashing white surf. From trailside benches, you might spot migrating whales during winter.

Pfeiffer Beach BEACH
(Map p38; ☎831-667-2315; www.fs.usda.gov/lpnf; end of Sycamore Canyon Rd; per car $10; ⊙9am-8pm; P 🚻 🐾) This phenomenal, crescent-shaped and dog-friendly beach is known for its huge double-rock formation, through which waves crash with life-affirming power. It's often windy, and the surf is too dangerous for swimming. But dig down into the wet sand – it's purple! That's because manganese garnet washes down from the craggy hillsides above. To get here from Hwy 1, make a sharp right onto Sycamore Canyon Rd, marked by a small yellow sign that says 'narrow road' at the top. From the turnoff, which is a half-mile south of Big Sur Station on the ocean side of Hwy 1, it's two narrow, twisting miles down to the beach (RVs and trailers prohibited).

Henry Miller Memorial Library ARTS CENTER
(Map p296; ☎831-667-2574; www.henrymiller.org; 48603 Hwy 1; donations accepted; ⊙10am-5pm) FREE Novelist Henry Miller was a Big Sur denizen from 1944 to 1962. More of a beatnik memorial, alt-cultural venue and bookshop, this community gathering spot was never Miller's home. The house belonged to Miller's friend, painter Emil White, until his death and is now run by a nonprofit group. Stop by to browse and hang out on the front deck. It's 0.4 miles south of Nepenthe restaurant (p301).

Inside are copies of all of Miller's written works, many of his paintings and a collection of Big Sur and Beat Generation material, including copies of the top 100 books Miller said most influenced him. Check the online calendar for upcoming events.

Partington Cove BEACH
(off Hwy 1) FREE This is a raw, breathtaking spot where crashing surf salts your skin. On the steep, half-mile dirt hike down to the cove, you'll cross a cool bridge and go through an even cooler tunnel. The cove's water is unbelievably aqua and within it grow tangled kelp forests. Look for the unmarked trailhead turnoff inside a hairpin turn on the ocean side of Hwy 1, about 6 miles south of Nepenthe restaurant (p301) and 2 miles north of Julia Pfeiffer Burns State Park.

The trail starts just beyond the locked vehicle gate. There's no real beach access and ocean swimming isn't safe, but some people scamper on the rocks and look for tide pools as waves splash ominously. Originally used for loading freight, Partington Cove allegedly became a landing spot for Prohibition-era bootleggers.

Limekiln State Park PARK
(☎831-434-1996; www.parks.ca.gov; 63025 Hwy 1; per car $10; ⊙8am-sunset) Two miles south of Lucia, this park gets its name from the four remaining wood-fired kilns originally built here in the 1880s to smelt quarried limestone into powder, a key ingredient in cement building construction from Monterey to San Francisco. Tragically, pioneers chopped down most of the steep canyon's old-growth redwoods to fuel the kilns' fires. A 1-mile round-trip trail leads through a redwood grove to the historic site, passing a creekside spur trail to a delightful 100ft-high waterfall.

Los Padres National Forest FOREST
(☎805-968-6640; www.fs.usda.gov/lpnf; Hwy 1, almost opp Plaskett Creek Campground; 🐾) The tortuously winding 40-mile stretch of Hwy 1 south of Lucia to Hearst Castle is sparsely populated, rugged and remote, mostly running through national forest lands. Around 5 miles south of Kirk Creek Campground (p301) and Nacimiento-Fergusson Rd, almost opposite Plaskett Creek Campground (p301), is **Sand Dollar Beach** (http://campone.com; Hwy 1; per car $10, free with local USFS campground fee; ⊙9am-8pm; 🐾). From the picnic area, it's a five-minute walk to southern Big Sur's longest sandy

WORTH A TRIP

VENTANA WILDERNESS

The 240,000-acre Ventana Wilderness is Big Sur's wild backcountry. It lies within the northern Los Padres National Forest, which straddles the Santa Lucia Range running parallel to the coast. Most of this wilderness is covered with oak and chaparral, though canyons cut by the Big Sur and Little Sur Rivers support virgin stands of coast redwoods and the rare endemic Santa Lucia fir, which grows on steep, rocky slopes too.

Now regenerating after devastating wildfires in 2008, Ventana Wilderness is popular with adventurous backpackers. A much-trammeled overnight destination is Sykes Hot Springs, natural 100°F (35°C) mineral pools framed by redwoods. It's a moderately strenuous 10-mile, one-way hike along the Pine Ridge Trail, starting from Big Sur Station (p302), where you can get free campfire permits and pay for overnight trailhead parking ($5). Don't expect solitude on weekends during peak season (April through September) and always follow Leave No Trace (www.lnt.org) principles.

beach, a crescent-shaped strip of sand protected from winds by high bluffs. Nearby is **Jade Cove** (http://campone.com; Hwy 1; ⏲sunrise-sunset; 🐾) FREE and it's a short drive south to Salmon Creek Falls.

Heading south before leaving Lucia, make sure you've got at least enough fuel in the tank to reach the expensive gas stations at Gorda, about 11 miles south of Limekiln State Park, or Ragged Point, another 12 miles further south.

Ragged Point LANDMARK
(19019 Hwy 1) Your last – or first – taste of Big Sur's rocky grandeur comes at this craggy cliff outcropping with fabulous views of the coastline in both directions, about 15 miles north of Hearst Castle (p304). Once part of the Hearst empire, it's now taken over by a sprawling, ho-hum lodge with a pricey gas station. Heading south, the land grows increasingly wind-swept as Hwy 1 rolls gently down to the water's edge.

Salmon Creek Falls WATERFALL
(www.fs.usda.gov/lpnf; Hwy 1; P 👪 🐾) FREE Take a short hike to splash around in the pools at the base of this double-drop waterfall, tucked uphill in a forested canyon. The falls usually run from December through May, and the trail is dog-friendly. In a hairpin turn of Hwy 1, the roadside turnoff is marked only by a small brown trailhead sign, about 8 miles south of Gorda.

Activities

Esalen Hot Springs HOT SPRINGS
(☎831-667-3047; www.esalen.org; 55000 Hwy 1; per person $30; ⏲by reservation) At the private **Esalen Institute** (☎831-667-3000), clothing-optional baths fed by a natural hot spring sit on a ledge above the ocean. We're confident you'll never take another dip that compares scenery-wise, especially on stormy winter nights. Only two small outdoor pools perch directly over the waves, so once you've stripped and taken a quick shower, head outside immediately. Credit cards only.

Advance reservations are required. The signposted entrance is on Hwy 1, about 3 miles south of Julia Pfeiffer Burns State Park (p298).

Molera Horseback Tours HORSEBACK RIDING
(Map p296; ☎831-625-5486; www.molerahorsebacktours.com; Hwy 1; per person $58-96; 👪) Across Hwy 1 from Andrew Molera State Park (p297), Molera offers guided trail rides on the beach and through redwood forest. Walk-ins and novices are welcome; children must be at least six years old, with most rides recommended for ages 12 and up.

Sleeping

With few exceptions, Big Sur's lodgings do not have TVs and rarely have telephones. This is where you come to escape the world. There aren't a lot of rooms overall, so demand often exceeds supply and prices can be steep. Bigger price tags don't necessarily buy you more amenities either. In summer and on weekends, reservations are essential everywhere, from campgrounds to deluxe resorts.

Ripplewood Resort CABIN $$
(Map p296; ☎831-667-2242; www.ripplewoodresort.com; 47047 Hwy 1; cabins $140-250; 🐾 📶) North of Pfeiffer Big Sur State Park (p297), Ripplewood has gotten behind fiscal equality by charging the same rates year-round.

Throwback Americana cabins mostly have kitchens and sometimes even wood-burning fireplaces. Quiet riverside cabins are surrounded by redwoods, but roadside cabins can be noisy. Wi-fi in restaurant only.

★ **Post Ranch Inn** RESORT **$$$**

(Map p296; ☎831-667-2200; www.postranchinn.com; 47900 Hwy 1; d from $925; P ⊜ ❄ @ ⓦ ≋) The last word in luxurious coastal getaways, the exclusive Post Ranch pampers demanding guests with slate spa tubs, wood-burning fireplaces, private decks and walking sticks for coastal hikes. Ocean-view rooms celebrate the sea, while treehouses lack views and have a bit of sway. Paddle around the clifftop infinity pool after a shamanic-healing session or yoga class in the spa. No children allowed.

Panoramic sea-view Sierra Mar restaurant requires reservations for lunch and dinner; the gourmet breakfast buffet is served to guests only.

Ventana Inn & Spa RESORT **$$$**

(Map p296; ☎831-667-2331; www.ventanainn.com; 48123 Hwy 1; d from $596; ⓦ ≋) Almost at odds with Big Sur's hippie-alternative vibe, Ventana injects a little soul into its deluxe digs. Honeymooning couples and paparazzi-fleeing celebs pad from tai chi class to the Japanese baths and outdoor pools (one is famously clothing-optional), or hole up all day next to the wood-burning fireplace in their own private villa, hot-tub suite or ocean-view cottage.

Treebones Resort CABIN **$$$**

(☎877-424-4787; www.treebonesresort.com; 71895 Hwy 1; campsites $95, d with shared bath from $320; ⊜ ⓦ ≋) Don't let the word 'resort' throw you. Yes, it has an ocean-view hot tub, heated pool and massage treatments. But a unique woven 'human nest' and canvas-sided yurts with polished pine floors, quilt-covered beds, sink vanities and redwood decks are more like glamping, with little privacy. Communal bathrooms and showers are a short stroll away. Wi-fi in main lodge only.

Basic walk-in campsites (no vehicle access) are also available. Children must be at least six years old. Look for the signposted turnoff a mile north of Gorda, at the southern end of Big Sur.

Glen Oaks Motel MOTEL, CABIN **$$$**

(Map p296; ☎831-667-2105; www.glenoaksbigsur.com; 47080 Hwy 1; d $300-475; P ⊜ ⓦ) At this 1950s redwood-and-adobe motor lodge, rustic rooms and cabins seem effortlessly chic. Dramatically transformed by eco-conscious design, snug romantic hideaway rooms all have gas fireplaces. Woodsy cabins in a redwood grove have kitchenettes and share outdoor fire pits, or retreat to the one-bedroom house with a full kitchen.

Public Campgrounds

Camping is currently available at four of Big Sur's state parks and two United States Forest Service (USFS) campgrounds along Hwy 1.

CALIFORNIA'S COMEBACK CONDORS

When it comes to endangered species, one of the state's biggest success stories is the California condor (*Gymnogyps californianus*). These gigantic, prehistoric birds weigh over 20lb with a wingspan of up to 10ft, letting them fly great distances in search of carrion. They're easily recognized by their naked pink head and large white patches on the underside of each wing.

This big bird became so rare that in 1987 there were only 27 left in the world, and all were removed from the wild to special captive-breeding facilities. Read the whole gripping story in journalist John Moir's book *Return of the Condor: The Race to Save Our Largest Bird from Extinction*.

There are over 400 California condors alive today, with increasing numbers of captive birds being released back into the wild. It's hoped they will begin breeding naturally, although it's an uphill battle. Wild condors are still dying of lead poisoning caused by hunters' bullets in the game carcasses that the birds feed on.

The Big Sur coast and Pinnacles National Park (p313) offer excellent opportunities to view this majestic bird. In Big Sur, the Ventana Wildlife Society (www.ventanaws.org) occasionally leads two-hour guided condor-watching tours ($50) using radio telemetry to track the birds; for sign-up details, check the website or ask at the Big Sur Discovery Center (p297).

Big Sur Campground & Cabins CABIN, CAMPGROUND $$
(Map p296; ☎831-667-2322; www.bigsurcamp.com; 47000 Hwy 1; tent/RV sites from $63/73, cabins $175-430; P) On the Big Sur River and shaded by redwoods, cozy cabins sport full kitchens and fireplaces, while canvas-sided tent cabins share bathroom facilities. The riverside campground, where neighboring sites have little privacy, is popular with RVs. There are hot showers and a coin-op laundry, playground and general store.

Pfeiffer Big Sur State Park Campground CAMPGROUND $
(Map p296; ☎reservations 800-444-7275; www.reserveamerica.com; 47225 Hwy 1; tent & RV sites $35-50; P) Best for novice campers and families with young kids, here over 200 campsites nestle in a redwood-shaded valley. Facilities include drinking water, fire pits and coin-op hot showers and laundry.

Julia Pfeiffer Burns State Park Campground CAMPGROUND $
(Map p38; ☎831-667-2315; www.parks.ca.gov; Hwy 1; tent sites $30) Two small walk-in campsites sit up on a semi-shaded ocean bluff, with fire pits and vault toilets but no water. All campers must check in first at Pfeiffer Big Sur State Park (p297), 11 miles north.

Andrew Molera State Park Campground CAMPGROUND $
(Map p38; www.parks.ca.gov; Hwy 1; tent sites $25) Two-dozen primitive tent sites (no reservations) in a grassy meadow come with fire pits and drinking water, but no ocean views. The campground is a 0.3-mile walk from the parking lot.

Limekiln State Park Campground CAMPGROUND $
(Map p38; ☎805-434-1996; www.parks.ca.gov; 63025 Hwy 1; tent & RV sites $35;) In southern Big Sur, this quiet state park has two-dozen campsites huddled under a bridge next to the ocean. Drinking water, fire pits and coin-op hot showers are available.

USFS Kirk Creek Campground CAMPGROUND $
(☎reservations 877-444-6777; www.recreation.gov; Hwy 1; tent & RV sites $35) Over 30 exposed ocean-view blufftop campsites with drinking water and fire pits cluster close together, nearly 2 miles south of Limekiln State Park (p298).

USFS Plaskett Creek Campground CAMPGROUND $
(Map p38; ☎reservations 877-477-6777; www.recreation.gov; Hwy 1; tent & RV sites $35) Nearly 40 spacious, shady campsites with drinking water and vault toilets circle a forested meadow near Sand Dollar Beach (p299) in southern Big Sur.

Eating

Like Big Sur's lodgings, some restaurants and cafes alongside Hwy 1 can be overpriced and underwhelming, but stellar views at some locations do offset any mediocrity.

Big Sur Roadhouse CALIFORNIAN $
(Map p296; ☎831-667-2370; www.bigsurroadhouse.com; 47080 Hwy 1; snacks & mains $7-15; ⊙8am-2:30pm;) This modern roadhouse glows with color-splashed artwork and an outdoor fire pit. At riverside tables, fork into upscale California-inspired pub grub like spicy wings, pork sliders and gourmet burgers, with craft beer on tap. It's also a top spot for coffee and cake.

Big Sur Deli & General Store DELI $
(Map p296; ☎831-667-2225; www.bigsurdeli.com; 47520 Hwy 1; snacks $2-12; ⊙7am-8pm) With the most reasonable prices in Big Sur, this family-owned deli slices custom-made sandwiches and piles up tortillas with carne asada, pork *carnitas,* veggies or beans and cheese. The small market carries camping food, snacks, beer and wine.

Rocky Point CALIFORNIAN, SEAFOOD $$
(Map p296; ☎831-624-2933; www.rockypointrestaurant.com; 36700 Hwy 1; mains $18-36; ⊙11:30am-8pm Thu-Tue) Come for the hillside ocean-view terrace, where cocktails and Californian wines are served all day long, and the steak and seafood menu includes on-the-road treats like scallops, paella and crab cakes. The spectacularly located restaurant is 2.5 miles north of Bixby Bridge (p295).

Nepenthe CALIFORNIAN $$$
(Map p296; ☎831-667-2345; www.nepenthebigsur.com; 48510 Hwy 1; mains $18-50; ⊙11:30am-4:30pm & 5-10pm;) Nepenthe comes from a Greek word meaning 'isle of no sorrow,' and indeed, it's hard to feel blue while sitting by the fire pit on this aerial terrace. Just-okay California cuisine (try the renowned Ambrosia burger) takes a backseat to the views and Nepenthe's history – Orson Welles and Rita Hayworth briefly owned a cabin here in the 1940s. Reservations essential.

DRIVING HIGHWAY 1

Driving this narrow two-lane highway through Big Sur and beyond is very slow going. Allow about three hours to cover the distance between the Monterey Peninsula and San Luis Obispo, much more if you want to explore the coast. Traveling after dark can be risky and more to the point, it's futile, because you'll miss out on the seascapes. Watch out for cyclists and make use of signposted roadside pullouts to let faster-moving traffic pass.

Downstairs, cheaper but still expensive Café Kevah delivers coffee, baked goods, light brunches and head-spinning ocean views on its outdoor deck (closed during winter and bad weather).

Big Sur Bakery & Restaurant CALIFORNIAN **$$$**
(Map p296; ☎831-667-0520; www.bigsurbakery.com; 47540 Hwy 1; bakery items $3-14, mains $20-36; ⌚bakery from 8am daily, restaurant 9:30am-2pm Mon-Fri, 10am-2:30pm Sat & Sun, 5:30pm-late Wed-Sat) Behind the Shell station, this warmly lit, funky house has seasonally changing menus, on which wood-fired pizzas share space with rustic dishes like grilled swordfish or wood-roasted chicken. Fronted by a pretty patio, the bakery makes addictive cinnamon buns and super-stuffed sandwiches. Expect longish waits and standoffish service. Dinner reservations are essential.

Big Sur River Inn AMERICAN **$$$**
(Map p296; ☎831-667-2700; www.bigsurriverinn.com; 46840 Hwy 1; breakfast & lunch $15-20, dinner $15-40; ⌚8am-9pm;) Woodsy restaurant with a deck, overlooking a creek teeming with throaty frogs. The food is standard American (seafood, grilled meats and pastas, plus vegetarian options), but diner-style breakfasts and lunches such as berry pancakes and BLT sandwiches satisfy. Rooms (starting at $150), a general store, and gas are also available.

Drinking & Entertainment

Californian craft beers are a Big Sur highlight at the Big Sur Taphouse and the Maiden Publick House, while there are excellent wine lists at clifftop restaurants with rugged Pacific Ocean vistas.

Big Sur Taphouse BAR
(Map p296; ☎831-667-2225; www.bigsurtaphouse.com; 47520 Hwy 1; ⌚noon-10pm Mon-Fri, 10am-midnight Sat, to 10pm Sun;) Down California craft beers and regional wines on the back deck or by the fireplace inside this high-ceilinged wooden bar with board games, sports on the TVs and pub grub from the next-door deli.

Maiden Publick House PUB
(Map p296; ☎831-667-2355; Village Center Shops, Hwy 1; ⌚3pm-2am Mon-Thu, from 1pm Fri & from 11am Sat-Sun) Just south of the Big Sur River Inn, this dive has an encyclopedic beer bible and motley local musicians jamming, mostly on weekends. Sixteen rotating taps and three pages of bottled brews create havoc for the indecisive drinker.

Henry Miller Memorial Library PERFORMING ARTS
(Map p296; ☎831-667-2574; www.henrymiller.org; 48603 Hwy 1; ⌚10am-5pm & longer hours for specific events;) Just south of Nepenthe (p301), this nonprofit alternative space hosts a bohemian carnival of live-music concerts, author readings, open-mike nights and indie-film screenings outdoors, especially during summer.

Information

Visitors often wander into businesses along Hwy 1 and ask, 'How much further to Big Sur?' In fact, there is no town of Big Sur as such, though you may see the name on maps. Commercial activity is concentrated along the stretch north of Pfeiffer Big Sur State Park. Sometimes called 'the Village,' this is where you'll find most of the lodgings, restaurants and shops.

Big Sur Chamber of Commerce (Map p296; ☎831-667-2100; www.bigsurcalifornia.org; Hwy 1; ⌚9am-1pm Mon, Wed & Fri)

Big Sur Station (Map p296; ☎831-667-2315; www.bigsurcalifornia.org/contact.html; 47555 Hwy 1; ⌚9am-4pm) About 1.5 miles south of Pfeiffer Big Sur State Park, this multiagency ranger station has information and maps for state parks, the Los Padres National Forest and Ventana Wilderness. The location is also one of the spots along Big Sur where there is more reliable cellphone coverage.

Getting There & Around

Big Sur is best explored by car, since you'll be itching to stop frequently and take in the rugged beauty and vistas that reveal themselves after every hairpin turn. Even if your driving skills are up to these narrow switchbacks, others' aren't:

expect to average 35mph or less along the route. Parts of Hwy 1 are battle-scarred, evidence of a continual struggle to keep them open after landslides and washouts. Check current highway conditions with CalTrans (☎800-427-7623; www.dot.ca.gov) and fill up your gas tank beforehand.

MST (☎888-678-2871; www.mst.org) bus 22 ($3.50, 1¼ hours) travels from Monterey via Carmel and Point Lobos as far south as Nepenthe restaurant (p301), stopping en route at Andrew Molera State Park (p297) and the Big Sur River Inn. Buses run three times daily between late May and early September, and twice daily on Saturdays and Sundays only the rest of the year.

Point Piedras Blancas

Many lighthouses still stand along California's coast, but few offer such a historically evocative seascape. Federally designated an outstanding natural area, the jutting, windblown grounds of this 1875 **light station** (☎805-927-7361; www.piedrasblancas.gov; off Hwy 1; tours adult/child 6-17yr $10/5; ⊙tours 9:45am Mon-Tue & Thu-Sat mid-Jun–Aug, 9:45am Tue, Thu & Sat Sep–mid-Jun) have been replanted with native flora. Everything looks much the way it did when the first lighthouse keepers helped ships find safe harbor at San Simeon Bay. Guided tours meet at the old Piedras Blancas Motel, 1.5 miles north of the lighthouse gate on Hwy 1. No reservations are taken; call ahead to check tour schedules.

At a signposted vista point, around 4.5 miles north of Hearst Castle, you can observe a colony of northern elephant seals bigger than the one at Año Nuevo State Reserve near Santa Cruz. During peak winter season, about 18,000 seals seek shelter in the coves and beaches along this stretch of coast. On sunny days the seals usually 'lie around like banana slugs,' in the words of one volunteer. Interpretative panels along a beach boardwalk and blue-jacketed Friends of the Elephant Seal (www.elephantseal.org) guides demystify the behavior of these giant beasts.

Mission San Antonio De Padua

Remote and evocative, this historical mission sits in the Valley of the Oaks, once part of the sprawling Hearst Ranch landholdings and now inside the boundaries of the US Army's Fort Hunter Liggett. Around the grounds, you can inspect the remains of a grist mill and irrigation system with aqueducts. It's seldom crowded, and you may have this vast site all to yourself, except during Mission Days in late April and La Fiesta on the second Sunday of June.

The mission was founded in 1771 by Franciscan priest Junípero Serra. Built with Native Californian labor, the church has been restored to its early-19th-century appearance, with a wooden pulpit, canopied altar and decorative flourishes on whitewashed walls. A creaky door leads to a cloistered garden anchored by a fountain. The museum has a small collection of utilitarian items such as an olive press and a weaving loom once used in the mission's workshops.

You may be asked for photo ID and proof of your vehicle's registration at a nearby military checkpoint. From the north, take the Jolon Rd exit off Hwy 101 before King City and follow Jolon Rd (County Rte G14) about 18 miles south to Mission Rd. From the south, take the Jolon Rd (County Rte G18) exit off Hwy 101 and drive 22 miles northwest to Mission Rd.

San Simeon

Little San Simeon Bay sprang to life as a whaling station in 1852, by which time California sea otters had been hunted almost to extinction by Russian fur traders. Shoreline whaling was practiced to catch gray whales migrating between Alaskan feeding grounds and birthing waters in Baja California. In 1865 Senator George Hearst purchased 45,000 acres of ranch land and established a small settlement beside the sea. Designed by architect Julia Morgan, the historic 19th-century houses today are rented to employees of the Hearst Corporation's 82,000-acre free-range cattle ranch.

Sights & Activities

William Randolph Hearst Memorial State Beach BEACH
(www.parks.ca.gov; Hwy 1; ⊙dawn-dusk) FREE Across from Hearst Castle (p304), this bayfront beach is a pleasantly sandy stretch punctuated by rock outcroppings, kelp forests, a wooden pier (fishing permitted) and picnic areas with barbecue grills.

Kayak Outfitters KAYAKING
(☎805-927-1787; www.kayakcambria.com; Hwy 1; single/double kayak rentals from $20/40, tours

$50-110; ⏲10am-4pm or later mid-Jun–early Sep, call for off-season hours) Right on San Simeon's beach, you can rent sea kayaks, wetsuits, stand-up paddle boarding (SUP) sets, bodyboards and surfboards, or take a kayak-fishing trip or a guided paddle around San Simeon Cove. Sea kayaking along the famed Moonstone Beach south at Cambria is another excellent option.

Sleeping & Eating

Modern San Simeon is nothing more than a strip of unexciting motels and lackluster restaurants. There are better-value places to stay and eat in Cambria and beach towns further south, such as Cayucos and Morro Bay.

Hearst San Simeon State Park Campground CAMPGROUND $
(☎reservations 800-444-7275; www.reserveamerica.com; Hwy 1; tent & RV sites $25) About 5 miles south of Hearst Castle are two state-park campgrounds: **San Simeon Creek**, with coin-op hot showers and flush toilets; and undeveloped **Washburn**, located along a dirt road. Drinking water is available at both.

Morgan MOTEL $$
(☎805-927-3828; www.hotel-morgan.com; 9135 Hearst Dr; r from $179;) Although rates are high for these revamped motel-style accommodations, the oceanfront setting makes up for a lot, as do gas fireplaces in deluxe rooms. Complimentary continental breakfast and board games to borrow. Pet fee $25.

Sebastian's AMERICAN $
(☎805-927-3307; www.facebook.com/SebastiansSanSimeon; 442 SLO–San Simeon Rd; mains $9-14; ⏲11am-4pm Tue-Sun) Down a side road across Hwy 1 from Hearst Castle, this tiny historic market sells cold drinks, Hearst Ranch beef burgers, giant deli sandwiches and salads for beach picnics at San Simeon Cove. Hearst Ranch Winery tastings are available at the copper-top bar.

Hearst Castle

Pearched high on a hill, **Hearst Castle** (☎info 805-927-2020, reservations 800-444-4445; www.hearstcastle.org; 750 Hearst Castle Rd; tours) is a wondrous, historic, over-the-top homage to material excess. The estate sprawls across acres of lushly landscaped gardens, accentuated by shimmering pools and fountains, statues from ancient Greece and Moorish Spain and the ruins of what was in Hearst's day the world's largest private zoo (look for zebras grazing on the hillsides of neighboring Hearst Ranch). To see anything of this historic monument, you have to take a tour (try to book ahead).

The most important thing to know about William Randolph Hearst (1863–1951) is that he did not live like Citizen Kane. Not that Hearst wasn't bombastic, conniving and larger than life, but the moody recluse of Orson Welles' movie? Definitely not. Hearst also didn't call his 165-room estate a castle, preferring its official name, La Cuesta Encantada ('The Enchanted Hill'), or more often calling it simply 'the ranch.'

EYEING ELEPHANT SEALS

The elephant seals that visit coastal California each year follow a precise calendar. In November and December, bulls (adult males) return to their colony's favorite California beaches and start the ritual struggles to assert superiority. Only the largest, strongest and most aggressive 'alpha' males gather a harem of females. In January and February, adult females, already pregnant from last year's beach antics, give birth to pups and soon mate with the dominant males, who promptly depart on their next feeding migration. The bulls' motto is 'love 'em and leave 'em.'

At birth an elephant seal pup weighs about 75lb; while being fed by its mother, it puts on about 10lb a day. Female seals leave the beach in March, abandoning their offspring. For up to two months the young seals, now known as 'weaners,' lounge around in groups, gradually learning to swim, first in tidal pools, then in the ocean. The weaners depart by May, having lost 20% to 30% of their weight during a prolonged fast.

Between June and October, elephant seals of all ages and both sexes return in smaller numbers to the beaches to molt. Always observe elephant seals from a safe distance (minimum 25ft) and do not approach or otherwise harass these unpredictable wild animals, who surprisingly can move faster on the sand than you can!

From the 1920s into the '40s, Hearst and Marion Davies, his longtime mistress (Hearst's wife refused to grant him a divorce), entertained a steady stream of the era's biggest movers and shakers. Invitations were highly coveted, but Hearst had his quirks – he despised drunkenness, and guests were forbidden to speak of death.

California's first licensed woman architect Julia Morgan based the main building, Casa Grande, on the design of a Spanish cathedral, and over the decades she catered to Hearst's every design whim, deftly integrating the spoils of his fabled European shopping sprees, including artifacts from antiquity and pieces of medieval monasteries.

Much like Hearst's construction budget, the castle will devour as much of your time and money as you let it. In peak summer months, show up early enough and you might be able to get a same-day tour ticket, but it's always better to make reservations in advance.

Tours (adult/child 5-12yr from $25/12; daily except Thanksgiving, Christmas & New Year's Day, closing time varies) usually depart starting at 9am daily, with the last leaving the visitor center for the 10-minute ride to the hilltop by 4pm (later in summer). There are three main tours: the guided portion of each lasts about an hour, after which you're free to wander the gardens and terraces and soak up the views. Best of all are Christmas holiday and springtime evening tours, featuring living-history re-enactors who escort you back in time to the castle's 1930s heyday. For holiday and evening tours, book at least two weeks to a month beforehand.

Dress in plenty of layers: gloomy fog at the sea-level visitor center can turn into sunny skies at the castle's hilltop location, and vice versa. At the visitor center, a five-story-high theater shows a 40-minute historical film (free admission included with daytime tour tickets) about the castle and the Hearst family. Other facilities are geared for industrial-sized mobs of visitors. Before you leave, take a moment to visit the often-overlooked museum area at the back of the center.

RTA (☎805-541-2228; www.slorta.org) bus 15 makes a few daily round-trips to Hearst Castle via Cambria and Cayucos from Morro Bay ($23, 55 minutes), where you can transfer to bus 12 to San Luis Obispo.

Note that at the time of writing the famed Neptune Pool had been emptied for repairs, and restoration was expected to be completed by early- to mid-2018.

Cambria

With a whopping dose of natural beauty, the coastal idyll of Cambria is a lone pearl cast along the coast. Built on lands that once belonged to Mission San Miguel, one of the village's first nicknames was Slabtown, after the rough pieces of wood that pioneer buildings were constructed from. Today, just like at neighboring Hearst Castle, money is no object in this wealthy community, whose motto 'Pines by the Sea' is affixed to the back of BMWs that toodle around town.

Sights & Activites

Although its milky-white moonstones are long gone, Moonstone Beach still attracts romantics to its oceanfront boardwalk and truly picturesque rocky shoreline. For more solitude, take the Windsor Blvd exit off Hwy 1 and drive down to where the road dead-ends, then follow a 2-mile round-trip blufftop hiking trail across Fiscalini Ranch Preserve.

A 10-minute drive south of Cambria, past the Hwy 46 turnoff to Pasa Robles' wine country, tiny Harmony (population 18) is an easygoing slice of Americana where an 1865 creamery houses artists' workshops, and a charming winery sits on a nearby hillside. A few miles further south there's good hiking at **Harmony Headlands State Park** (www.parks.ca.gov; Hwy 1; ⏲6am-sunset) FREE.

Sleeping

Cambria's choicest motels and hotels line Moonstone Beach Dr, while quaint B&Bs cluster around the village.

Bridge Street Inn GUESTHOUSE $
(☎805-215-0724; www.bsicambria.com; 4314 Bridge St; r $50-90, vans $30; 📶) Inside a 19th-century parsonage and surrounded by a pleasant garden, this European-style guesthouse has a quaint, raffish charm. There's a communal kitchen and five rooms with shared bathroom facilities, and the BBQ area is well-used by international guests. One additional room has a separate toilet and washbasin. There's parking outside for one smaller campervan, but you'll need to book ahead.

Van guests can use the kitchen, bathroom and lounge facilities, and also jump on Bridge Street's wi-fi network.

Blue Dolphin Inn MOTEL **$$**
(☎805-927-3300; www.cambriainns.com; 6470 Moonstone Beach Dr; r from $188;) This sand-colored, two-story, slat-sided building may not look as upscale as other oceanfront motels, but rooms have romantic fireplaces, pillowtop mattresses and to-go breakfast picnics to take to the beach. Pet fee $25.

Fogcatcher Inn HOTEL **$$$**
(☎805-927-1400; www.fogcatcherinn.com; 6400 Moonstone Beach Dr; r from $204;) Moonstone Beach Dr hotels are nearly identical, but this one stands out with its pool and hot tub. Faux English Tudor–style cottages harboring quietly luxurious modern rooms, some with fireplaces and ocean views. Pet fee $75.

Eating & Drinking

It's a short walk between cutesy cafes and interesting restaurants in Cambria's East Village.

Linn's Easy as Pie Cafe AMERICAN **$**
(☎805-927-0371; www.linnsfruitbin.com; 4251 Bridge St; dishes $6-12; 10am-7pm Mon-Thu, to 8m Fri-Sat;) If you don't have time to visit Linn's original farm stand on Santa Rosa Creek Rd (a 20-minute drive east via Main St), you can fork into its famous olallieberry pie at this take-out counter that delivers soups, salads, sandwiches and comfort fare such as chicken pot pie to a sunny deck.

Robin's INTERNATIONAL **$$**
(☎805-927-5007; www.robinsrestaurant.com; 4095 Burton Dr; lunch $13-19, dinner $24-33; 11am-9pm Sun-Thu, to 9:30pm Fri-Sat;) Global flavors from Asia and India feature on the wide-ranging menu at Robin's. Relax under the shaded arbor canopy in the rustic courtyard and graze on Indian flatbreads or Vietnamese spring rolls, or tuck into surprising lamb-curry burritos. A stellar wine list is equally cosmopolitan, with labels from Australia, New Zealand, Spain and France complementing Californian favorites.

Harmony Cellars BAR
(☎805-927-1625; www.harmonycellars.com; 3255 Harmony Valley Rd, Harmony; tasting fee $7; 10am-5pm, to 5:30pm Jul & Aug) This popular hillside winery is strong on robust reds including Syrah, Cabernet Sauvignon and Zinfandel, and cheese and charcuterie platters ($30 to $48, must be ordered 24 hours in advance) are also available.

927 Beer Company CRAFT BEER
(☎805-203-5265.; www.927beer.com; 821 Cornwall St; noon-7pm Mon-Sat, to 6pm Sun) Enlivened by colorful music posters – 927's friendly owner is a big fan of Pearl Jam – this nano-brewery tucked away behind Main St in the West Village features a relaxed neighborhood tasting room that's a real hit with locals and their canine companions. Our favorite brews are the Mudhoney Oatmeal Stout and the zesty Belgian-style Saison.

Information

Cambria Chamber of Commerce (☎805-927-3624; www.cambriachamber.org; 767 Main St; 9am-5pm Mon-Fri, noon-4pm Sat & Sun) Staffed by a friendly crew ready to dispense maps and information.

Getting There & Away

Cambria is 140 miles south of Monterey and 39 miles north of San Luis Obispo. From San Luis Obispo, RTA (p321) bus 15 makes a few daily trips from Morro Bay via Cayucos to Cambria ($3, 35 minutes), stopping along Main St and Moonstone Beach Dr. Most buses continue north to Hearst Castle (p304).

Cayucos

With its historic storefronts housing antiques shops and eateries, the main drag of amiable, slow-paced Cayucos recalls an Old West frontier town. Just one block west of Ocean Ave, surf's up by the recently renovated pier.

Sights & Activities

Fronting a broad white-sand beach, Cayucos' long wooden pier is popular with fishers. It's also a sheltered spot for beginner surfers.

Estero Bluffs State Park PARK
(☎805-772-7434; www.parks.ca.gov; Hwy 1; sunrise-sunset) FREE Ramble along coastal grasslands and pocket beaches at this small state park, accessed from unmarked roadside pulloffs north of Cayucos. Look among the scenic sea stacks to spot harbor seals hauled out on tide-splashed rocks.

Good Clean Fun WATER SPORTS
(☎805-995-1993; www.goodcleanfuncalifornia.com; 136 Ocean Front Ln; group surfing lesson or kayak

tour from $75) By the beach, this friendly surf shop has all kinds of rental gear – wetsuits, body boards, surfboards, SUP sets and kayaks. Book in advance for surfing lessons and kayak (or kayak-fishing) tours.

Cayucos Surf Company SURFING
(805-995-1000; www.facebook.com/CayucosSurf; 95 Cayucos Dr; 1hr private/2hr group lesson $90/100; 10am-5pm Sun-Thu, to 6pm Fri & Sat) Near the pier, this landmark local surf shop rents surfboards, body boards and wetsuits. Call ahead for learn-to-surf lessons.

Sleeping

Cayucos doesn't lack for motels or beachfront inns. If there's no vacancy or prices look too high, head 6 miles south to Morro Bay (p308).

Shoreline Inn on the Beach HOTEL $$
(805-995-3681; www.cayucosshorelineinn.com; 1 N Ocean Ave; r $159-249;) There are few beachside lodgings on Hwy 1 where you can listen to the surf from your balcony for such a reasonable price tag. Standard-issue rooms are spacious and perked up by sea-foam painted walls. It's also dog-friendly (pet fee $35).

Seaside Motel MOTEL $$
(805-995-3809; www.seasidemotel.com; 42 S Ocean Ave; d $80-170;) Expect a superwarm welcome from the hands-on owners of this vintage motel with a pretty garden featuring Cape Cod chairs and ocean views. Country-kitsch rooms may be on the small side, though some have kitchenettes. Cross your fingers for quiet neighbors.

★ **Cass House Inn** INN $$$
(805-995-3669; www.casshousecayucos.com; 222 N Ocean Ave; d $265-345;) Inside a charmingly renovated 1867 Victorian inn, five boutique rooms beckon, some with ocean views, deep-soaking tubs and antique fireplaces to ward off chilly coastal fog. All rooms have plush beds, flat-screen TVs with DVD players and tasteful, romantic accents. The best eating and drinking in town is most pleasantly on-site.

Eating & Drinking

The versatile dining scene at Cacuyos stretches from excellent barbecue and fish tacos to fine dining in a heritage inn.

Brown Butter Cookie Co BAKERY $
(805-995-2076; www.brownbuttercookies.com; 98 N Ocean Ave; snacks from $2.50; 9am-6pm;) Seriously addictive cookies are baked in all sorts of flavors including almond, citrus, cocoa, coconut-lime and original butter. Buy a bagful to provide tasty sustenance as you negotiate a stroll along Cayucos' recently restored 1872 pier.

Ruddell's Smokehouse SEAFOOD $
(805-995-5028; www.smokerjim.com; 101 D St; dishes $4-13; 11am-6pm;) 'Smoker Jim' transforms fresh-off-the-boat seafood into succulently smoked slabs, sandwiches topped with spicy mustard and fish tacos slathered in a unique apple-celery relish. Squeeze yourself in the door to order. Dogs are allowed at the sidewalk tables. If you're lucky, you might chance upon the Ruddell's food truck on summer weekends at craft breweries around the region.

Cass House Grill CALIFORNIAN, FRENCH $$
(805-995-1014; www.casshousecayucos.com; Cass House Inn, 222 N Ocean Ave; mains $13-32; 11am-3pm & 4-8:30pm Thu-Sun mid-Sep–late May, plus Wed during summer) The Grill's wood-fired oven is harnessed for pizza, empanadas and grilled prawn and lamb, and a lighter touch is evident in roast salmon and a delicate fettucine crammed with seasonal produce. Many of the ingredients are sourced locally and from Cass House's own gardens, and the wine and beer list both offer Californian provenance. See www.casshousecayucosevents.com for special winemaker dinners.

The adjacent Cass House Bakery is open from 7am Thursday to Sunday for coffee, scones and muffins.

Schooners Wharf BAR
(www.schoonerswharf.com; 171 N Ocean Ave; 11am-midnight) Come for drinks on the ocean-view deck, rather than the fried seafood. The cocktails are punchy and there's an OK selection of draft beers from central Californian breweries. Vistas of Cayucos' heritage pier come free of charge.

Getting There & Away

Cayucos is 15 miles south of Cambria and 19 miles north of San Luis Obispo. **RTA** (805-541-2228; www.slorta.org) bus 15 travels three to five times daily from Morro Bay ($2, 15 minutes) to Cayucos, continuing north to Cambria ($2, 20 minutes) and Hearst Castle ($2, 35 minutes).

Morro Bay

Home to a commercial fishing fleet, Morro Bay's biggest claim to fame is Morro Rock, a volcanic peak jutting dramatically from the ocean floor. It's one of the Nine Sisters, a 21-million-year-old chain of rocks stretching all the way south to San Luis Obispo. The town's less boast-worthy landmark comes courtesy of the power plant, whose three cigarette-shaped smokestacks mar the bay views. Along this humble, working-class stretch of coast you'll find fantastic opportunities for kayaking, hiking and camping.

Sights & Activities

This town harbors natural riches that are easily worth a half-day's exploration. The bay itself is a deep inlet separated from the ocean by a 5-mile-long sand spit. South of Morro Rock is the **Embarcadero**, a small waterfront boulevard jam-packed with souvenir shops and eateries.

Morro Rock LANDMARK

Chumash tribespeople are the only people legally allowed to climb this volcanic rock, now the protected nesting ground of peregrine falcons. You can laze at the small beach on the rock's north side, but you can't drive all the way around it. Instead, rent a kayak to paddle the giant estuary, inhabited by two-dozen threatened and endangered species, including brown pelicans, snowy plovers and sea otters.

Morro Bay Skateboard Museum MUSEUM

(805-610-3565; www.mbskate.com; Embarcadero, Marina Sq; donations appreciated; noon-5pm Mon-Wed & Fri, from 10am Sat-Sun;) With exhibits, posters and more than 200 skateboards from the 1930s to the 21st century, this excellent privately operated museum is essential for anyone who's ever fallen under the spell of zipping along on four urethane wheels. Look forward to damn fine souvenir T-shirts and merchandise, too.

Morro Bay Whale Watching WHALE WATCHING

(805-772-9463; www.morrobaywhalewatching.com; 699 Embarcadero; adult/child/student $45/35/40; tours 9am & 12:30pm;) Humpback whales visit the Morro Bay area from May to October, and then from December to May more than 20,000 gray whales pass by on their annual migration. Other species often seen include minke whales, dolphins, porpoises, sea lions and sea otters. Bring along binoculars for coastal and pelagic birdlife. Excursions take place on an open catamaran, so dress warmly. Tours only depart with a minimum of six passengers.

Kayak Shack WATER SPORTS

(805-772-8796; www.morrobaykayakshack.com; 10 State Park Rd; kayak/SUP rental from $14/16; usually 9am-4pm late May-Jun, to 5pm Jul-early Sep, 9am-4pm Fri-Sun mid-Sep–late May) No one gets you out on the water faster than this laid-back kayak, canoe and SUP rental spot by the marina in Morro Bay State Park. A no-frills DIY operation, this is a calmer place to start paddling than the Embarcadero. Guided kayak tours are also offered in conjunction with Central Coast Outdoors.

Tours

Sub-Sea Tours BOATING

(805-772-9463; www.subseatours.com; 699 Embarcadero; 45min tour adult/child 3-12yr $18/10; hourly departures usually 11am-5pm;) For pint-sized views of kelp forests and schools of fish, take the kids on a spin around the bay in a yellow semi-submersible with underwater viewing windows. Departures may be limited to twice daily outside of the peak season.

Central Coast Outdoors TOURS

(805-528-1080; www.centralcoastoutdoors.com; tours $65-150) Leads kayaking tours (including sunset and full-moon paddles), guided hikes and cycling trips along the coast and to Paso Robles and Edna Valley vineyards.

Festivals & Events

Morro Bay Winter Bird Festival OUTDOORS

(805-234-1170; www.morrobaybirdfestival.org; Jan) Bird-watchers flock here for guided hikes, kayaking tours and naturalist-led field trips, during which over 200 species can be spotted along the Pacific Flyway.

Sleeping

Dozens of motels cluster along Hwy 1 and around Harbor and Main Sts, between downtown Morro Bay and the Embarcadero.

California State Park Campgrounds CAMPGROUND $

(reservations 800-444-7275; www.reserveamerica.com; tent & RV sites $25-50;) In **Morro Bay State Park**, over 240 campsites are fringed by eucalyptus and cypress trees; amenities include coin-op hot showers and an RV dump station.

At the north end of town off Hwy 1, **Morro Strand State Beach** (reservations 800-444-7275; www.reserveamerica.com; tent & RV sites $25-50) has 75 simpler oceanfront campsites.

456 Embarcadero Inn & Suites HOTEL $$
(805-772-2700; www.embarcaderoinn.com; 456 Embarcadero; r from $200;) Located at the quieter southern end of the Embarcadero, this recently renovated property features 33 chic and spacious rooms, some with excellent views of the estuary and Morro Rock. Decor is more modern than at a few other local accommodation spots, and online midweek discounts are good value. Ease into the Jacuzzi after an afternoon's kayaking.

Pleasant Inn Motel MOTEL $$
(805-772-8521; www.pleasantinnmotel.com; 235 Harbor St; r $169-229;) Two blocks uphill from the Embarcadero, this spiffy motel has nautical-esque rooms (some with compact kitchens) sporting sailboat photos on the walls, open-beam wooden ceilings and blue-and-white rugs underfoot. A recent renovation makes it one of the most welcoming places in town, and the team at reception have plenty of good restaurant advice. Pet fee $25.

Beach Bungalow Inn & Suites MOTEL $$
(805-772-9700; www.morrobaybeachbungalow.com; 1050 Morro Ave; d $180-230;) This butter-yellow motor court's chic, contemporary rooms are dressed up with hardwood floors, plush rugs, pillowtop mattresses and down comforters for foggy nights. Cape Cod chairs circle a compact fire pit in the middle of the complex. Complimentary breakfasts are delivered to guests' rooms and the pet fee is $30.

★**Anderson Inn** INN $$$
(805-772-3434; www.andersoninnmorrobay.com; 897 Embarcadero; d $269-349;) Like a small boutique hotel, this waterfront inn has just a handful of spacious, soothingly earth-toned rooms. If you're lucky, you'll get a gas fireplace, spa tub and harbor views. The friendly owners infuse the whole property with an easygoing Californian cool. Weekday rates offer the best value.

Eating

Predictably touristy seafood shacks line the Embarcadero, and a few other worthwhile eateries are scattered around Morro Bay.

Flavor Factory BURGERS $
(805-772-4040; www.facebook.com/FlavorFactoryMB; 420 Quintana Rd; soup & burgers $9-13; 11am-8pm Fri-Tue) Superlative gourmet burgers make this place located in a compact shopping mall worth seeking out. Classics like beef and bacon share the menu with ritzy combos with blue cheese or stuffed green chillies, and the concise list of six rotating craft beers is equally surprising. Even the seasonal soups and salad bar crammed with local produce prepared on-site are winners.

Giovanni's Fish Market & Galley SEAFOOD $
(877-521-4467; www.giovannisfishmarket.com; 1001 Front St; mains $5-15; market 9am-6pm, restaurant from 11am;) At this family-run joint on the Embarcadero, folks line up for batter-fried fish and chips and killer garlic fries. You'll have to dodge beggar birds on the outdoor deck. Inside there's a market with all the fixin's for a beach campground fish-fry.

The Galley Seafood Grill & Bar SEAFOOD $$$
(805-772-7777; www.galleymorrobay.com; 899 Embarcadero; mains $24-48; 11:30-10pm) Our pick of Morro Bay's Embarcadero restaurants, The Galley combines an absolute waterfront location and expert renditions of classic American dishes with a briny touch of the ocean. There's definitely nothing groundbreaking about the menu, but when you're hankering for crab cakes and fresh oysters, or perfectly grilled fish and a glass of white wine, this is where to come.

Drinking & Nightlife

Explore the Embarcadero for good wine and craft beer, or head up the hill to Morro Bay's Main St for live music and the occasional DJ.

★**Libertine Pub** PUB
(805-772-0700; www.libertinebrewing.com; 801 Embarcadero; noon-11pm Mon-Thu, 11am-11pm Fri-Sat, 10am-10pm Sun) Stroll down to the Embarcadero for barrel-aged and sour beers from one of California's most interesting breweries. Lots more excellent American craft beers are on the 48 taps, and entertainment comes from the bartenders spinning vintage vinyl, or occasional live gigs. Taster glasses make it easy for the traveling beer geek to dive in and explore some very special brews.

The Siren LOUNGE
(☎805-772-8478; www.thesirenmorrobay.com; 900 Main St; ⊙11am-2am Tue-Sat, from 9am Sun) A laidback spot for a quiet drink or game of pool during the week, The Siren is transformed into a rockin' live-music venue on Friday and Saturday nights. Beats range from blues and Americana through to indie rock and reggae, and crowding onto the dance floor is definitely encouraged after a few nine-buck cocktails or tasty craft brews.

Information

Morro Bay Visitor Center (☎805-225-1633; www.morrobay.org; 695 Harbor St; ⊙10am-5pm) Located a few blocks uphill from the Embarcadero, in the less touristy downtown area.

Getting There & Away

Morro Bay is 142 miles south of Monterey and 13 miles northwest of San Luis Obispo. From San Luis Obispo, **RTA** (☎805-541-2228; www.slorta.org) bus 12 travels hourly on weekdays and a few times daily on weekends along Hwy 1 to Morro Bay ($2.50, 25 minutes). Three to five times daily, bus 15 heads north to Cayucos ($2, 15 minutes), Cambria ($2, 35 minutes) and Hearst Castle ($2, 55 minutes).

From late May through early October, a **trolley** (single ride $1, day pass $3) loops around the waterfront, downtown and north Morro Bay, operating varying hours (no service Tuesday to Thursday).

Montaña de Oro State Park

In spring the hillsides are blanketed by bright California native poppies, wild mustard and other wildflowers, giving this **park** (Map p38; ☎805-528-0513; www.parks.ca.gov; 3550 Pecho Valley Rd, Los Osos; ⊙6am-10pm; P ♿) FREE its Spanish name, meaning 'mountain of gold.'

Wind-tossed coastal bluffs with wild, wide-open sea views make it a favorite spot with hikers, mountain bikers and horseback riders. The northern half of the park features sand dunes and an ancient marine terrace visible due to seismic uplifting.

Once used by smugglers, **Spooner's Cove** is now a postcard-perfect sandy beach and picnic area. If you go tidepooling, avoid disturbing the marine creatures and never remove them from their aquatic homes. You can hike along the grassy ocean bluffs, or drive uphill past the visitor center inside a historic ranch house to the start of the exhilarating 7-mile loop trail tackling **Valencia Peak** (1346ft) and **Oats Peak** (1347ft).

Sleeping

Montaña de Oro State Park Campground CAMPGROUND $
(☎reservations 800-444-7275; www.reserveamerica.com; Montaña de Oro State Park; tent & RV sites $25) Tucked into a small canyon, this minimally developed campground has pleasantly cool drive-up and environmental walk-in sites. Limited amenities include vault toilets, drinking water and fire pits.

Getting There & Away

To reach Montaña de Oro State Park by private car from the north, exit Hwy 1 in Morro Bay at South Bay Blvd; after 4 miles, turn right onto Los Osos Valley Rd (which runs into Pecho Valley Rd) for 6 miles. From the south, exit Hwy 101 in San Luis Obispo at Los Osos Valley Rd, then drive northwest for around 16 miles.

ALONG HIGHWAY 101

Driving inland along Hwy 101 is a quicker way to travel between the Bay Area and Southern California. Although it lacks the striking scenery of coastal Hwy 1, the historic El Camino Real (King's Highway), established by Spanish conquistadors and missionaries, has a beauty of its own. Along the way are plenty of sights worth stopping for – from oak-dappled golden hills and ghostly missions to jaw-dropping sights in Pinnacles National Park and sprawling wineries.

San Juan Bautista

In atmospheric old San Juan Bautista, where you can practically hear the whispers of the past, California's 15th mission is fronted by the state's only remaining original Spanish plaza. In 1876 the railroad bypassed the town, which has been a sleepy backwater ever since. Along 3rd St, evocative historic buildings mostly shelter antiques shops and petite garden restaurants. Hark! That cock you hear crowing is one of the town's roosters, which are allowed by tradition to stroll the streets at will.

Sights

Mission San Juan Bautista CHURCH

(831-623-4528; www.oldmissionsjb.org; 406 2nd St; adult/child 5-17yr $4/2; 9:30am-4:30pm;) Founded in 1797, this mission claims the largest church among California's original 21 missions. Unknowingly built directly atop the San Andreas Fault, the mission has been rocked by earthquakes. Bells hanging in the tower today include chimes that were salvaged after the 1906 San Francisco earthquake toppled the original mission. Scenes from Alfred Hitchcock's thriller *Vertigo* were shot here, although the bell tower in the movie's climactic scene was just a special effect.

Below the mission cemetery, you can spy a section of El Camino Real, the Spanish colonial road built to link California's first missions.

San Juan Bautista State Historic Park PARK

(831-623-4881; www.parks.ca.gov; 2nd St, btwn Mariposa & Washington Sts; museum adult/child $3/free; 10am-4:30pm) Buildings around the old Spanish plaza opposite the mission anchor this small historical park. Cavernous **stables** hint at San Juan Bautista in its 1860s heyday as a stagecoach stop. The 1858 **Plaza Hotel**, which started life as a single-story adobe building, now houses a little historical **museum**. Next door to the hotel, the **Castro-Breen Adobe** once belonged to Mexican general and governor José Castro. In 1848 it was bought by the Breen family, survivors of the Donner Party disaster.

Sleeping & Eating

San Juan Bautista features a few B&Bs but is conveniently visited as a day trip from Santa Cruz or Monterey.

Fremont Peak State Park Campground CAMPGROUND $

(reservations 800-444-7275; www.reserveamerica.com; San Juan Canyon Rd; tent & RV sites $25) A pretty but primitive 25-site campground with vault toilets (no water) is shaded by oak trees on a hilltop with distant views of Monterey Bay.

Vertigo Coffee CAFE $

(831-623-9533; www.facebook.com/vertigocoffee; 81 4th St; dishes $4-12; 7am-7pm Tue-Fri, from 8am Sat & Sun) Rich espresso and pour-over brews, wood-fired pizzas and garden salads make this coffee-roaster's shop a real find. Rotating exhibitions from local artists often fill the whitewashed walls, and seven taps of craft beer feature surprising brews from around the central Californian coast. Ask if anything from Brewery Twenty Five based in nearby Hollister is available.

Getting There & Away

San Juan Bautista is on Hwy 156, a few miles east of Hwy 101, about a 20-minute drive south of Gilroy. Public transport is very limited, and the town is best visited with your own transport. Further south, Hwy 101 enters the sun-dappled eucalyptus grove that James Stewart and Kim Novak drove through in *Vertigo*.

Gilroy

About 30 miles south of San Jose, the self-proclaimed 'garlic capital of the world' hosts the jam-packed **Gilroy Garlic Festival** (www.gilroygarlicfestival.com) over the last full weekend in July. Show up for the chow – garlic fries, garlic ice cream and more – and cooking contests under the blazing-hot sun.

Unusual **Gilroy Gardens** (408-840-7100; www.gilroygardens.org; 3050 Hecker Pass Hwy; adult/child 3-10yr $50/40; 11am-5pm Mon-Fri early Jun–mid-Aug, plus 10am-6pm Sat & Sun early Apr-Nov;) is a nonprofit family-oriented theme park focused on food and plants. You've got to really love flowers, fruit and veggies to get your money's worth, though. Most rides such as the 'Mushroom Swing' are tame. Buy tickets online to save. From Hwy 101, follow Hwy 152 west; parking is $12.

Heading east on Hwy 152 toward I-5 **Casa de Fruta** (408-842-7282; www.casadefruta.com; 10021 Pacheco Pass Hwy, Hollister; per ride $2.50-4; seasonal hours vary;) FREE is a commercialized farm stand with an old-fashioned carousel and choo-choo train rides for youngsters.

Salinas

Best known as the birthplace of John Steinbeck and nicknamed the 'Salad Bowl of the World,' Salinas is a working-class agricultural center with down-and-out streets. It makes a thought-provoking contrast with the affluence of the Monterey Peninsula, a fact of life that helped shape Steinbeck's novel *East of Eden*. Historic downtown stretches along Main St, with the National Steinbeck Center capping off its northern end.

Sights

★National Steinbeck Center MUSEUM

(☎831-775-4721; www.steinbeck.org; 1 Main St; adult/child 6-17yr $13/7; ⏰10am-5pm; 👪) This museum will interest almost anyone, even if you don't know anything about Salinas' Nobel Prize–winning native son, John Steinbeck (1902–68), a Stanford University dropout. Tough, funny and brash, he portrayed the troubled spirit of rural, working-class Americans in novels like *The Grapes of Wrath*. Interactive exhibits and short video clips chronicle the writer's life and works in an engaging way. Gems include Rocinante, the camper in which Steinbeck traveled around the USA while researching *Travels with Charley*.

Take a moment and listen to Steinbeck's Nobel acceptance speech – it's grace and power combined.

Steinbeck House HISTORIC BUILDING

(☎831-424-2735; www.steinbeckhouse.com; 132 Central Ave; ⏰restaurant 11:30am-2pm Tue-Sat, gift shop to 3pm) Steinbeck was born and spent much of his boyhood in this house, four blocks west of the museum. It's now a twee lunch cafe, which we're not sure he'd approve of. Guided tours are given on select summer Sundays; check online for details.

Festivals & Events

Steinbeck Festival CULTURAL

(www.steinbeck.org; ⏰early May) This three-day festival features films, lectures, live music and guided bus and walking tours.

California Rodeo Salinas RODEO

(www.carodeo.com; ⏰late Jul) Bull riding, calf roping, cowboy poetry and carnival rides.

California International Airshow OUTDOORS

(www.salinasairshow.com; ⏰late Sep) Professional stunt flying and vintage and military aircraft take wing.

Sleeping

Salinas has plenty of motels off Hwy 101, including at the Market St exit.

Laurel Inn MOTEL $

(☎831-449-2474; www.laurelinnsalinas.com; 801 W Laurel Dr; r from $95; P❄️📶🏊) If chain motels don't do it for you, this sprawling, family-owned cheapie has cozy rooms that are nevertheless spacious.

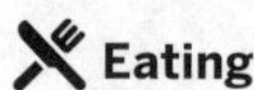

Eating

Cafes and restaurants feature in downtown Salinas, and at the time of research, spacious heritage buildings near the National Steinbeck Center were being repurposed to house new eating and drinking openings. Let us know what you discover.

First Awakenings AMERICAN $

(☎831-784-1125; www.firstawakenings.net; 171 Main St; mains $8-13; ⏰7am-2pm; 👪) Fork into diner-style breakfasts of fruity pancakes, crepes and egg skillets, or turn up later in the day for handcrafted sandwiches and market-fresh salads. Try the Sonoran frittata, an open-faced omelet crammed with spicy chorizo.

Giorgio's at 201 MEDITERRANEAN, PIZZA $$

(☎831-800-7573; www.201complex.com; 201 Main St; mains $15-37; ⏰4-9pm Mon-Thu, to 11pm Fri-Sat, 10am-3pm Sun) In a stately, high-ceilinged former bank, Giorgio's at 201 is the lead address in an expanding if compact enclave of restaurants and terrace cafes. Drop in for excellent pizza, pasta and Mediterranean cuisine – with occasional diversions into Asian flavors – and then check out what new eating, drinking or live-music destinations have been added since we last visited.

Drinking & Nightlife

Downtown Salinas has a compact selection of good pubs and bars, and the Alvarado Street Brewery & Tasting Room is definitely worth the short journey from central Salinas for craft-beer fans.

Farmers Union Pour House CRAFT BEER

(☎831-975-4890; www.facebook.com/FarmersUnionPourHouse; 217 Main St; ⏰2-10pm Tue-Thu & Sun, to midnight Fri-Sat) Brick-lined walls and wooden floors combine with a thoroughly modern big screen displaying the 24 different beers on tap. Food options include cheese and charcuterie boards, or you can order pizza and full meals from the separate restaurant next door. Up to 15 Californian wines are also available.

Alvarado Street Brewery & Tasting Room CRAFT BEER

(☎831-800-3332; www.alvaradostreetbrewery.com/salinas-brewery; 1315 Dayton St; ⏰3-8pm Tue-Fri, from 1pm Sat-Sun) This Salinas offshoot of the Monterey-based craft brewery is another excellent recent addition to the growing beer scene around Salinas. Location-wise, it's in an industrial park around 3 miles south of downtown. Ask if the stonking 10.5% Triple IPA is on tap.

Information

Salinas 411 (831-594-1799; www.salinas411.org; 222 Main St; 11am-8pm)

Getting There & Away

Salinas is 106 miles south of San Francisco and 126 miles north of San Luis Obispo.

Amtrak (800-872-7245; www.amtrak.com; 11 Station Pl) runs daily *Coast Starlight* trains north to Oakland ($18, three hours) and south to Paso Robles ($20, two hours), San Luis Obispo ($28, 3¼ hours), Santa Barbara ($41, 6¼ hours) and LA ($58, 9¼ hours).

Greyhound (800-231-2222; www.greyhound.com; Station Pl) has a few daily buses north to Santa Cruz ($16, 65 minutes) and San Francisco ($21, 3½ to five hours), and south to Santa Barbara ($40, 4¾ hours). Buses depart from the Salinas railway station.

From the nearby **Salinas Transit Center** (110 Salinas St), **MST** (888-678-2871; www.mst.org) bus 20 goes to Monterey ($3.50, one hour, every 30 to 60 minutes).

Pinnacles National Park

Named for the towering spires that rise abruptly out of the chaparral-covered hills east of Salinas Valley, this off-the-beaten-path park protects the remains of an ancient volcano. The best time to visit **Pinnacles National Park** (831-389-4486; www.nps.gov/pinn; per car $15;) is during spring or fall; summer heat is extreme.

Sights & Activites

Besides rock climbing (for route information, visit www.pinnacles.org), the park's biggest attractions are its two talus caves, formed by piles of boulders. **Balconies Cave** is almost always open for exploration. Scrambling through it is not an exercise recommended for claustrophobes, as it's pitch-black inside, making a flashlight essential. Be prepared to get lost a bit too. The cave is found along a 2.5-mile hiking loop from the west entrance. Nearer the east entrance, **Bear Gulch Cave** is closed seasonally, so as not to disturb a resident colony of Townsend's big-eared bats.

To really appreciate Pinnacles' stark beauty, you need to hike. Moderate loops of varying lengths and difficulty ascend into the **High Peaks** and include thrillingly narrow clifftop sections. In the early morning or late afternoon, you may spot endangered California condors soaring overhead. Get an early start to tackle the 9-mile round-trip trail to the top of **Chalone Peak**, granting panoramic views.

Rangers lead guided full-moon hikes and star-gazing programs on some weekend nights, usually in spring or fall. Reservations are required: call 831-389-4485 in advance or check for last-minute vacancies at the visitor center.

Sleeping & Eating

The **Pinnacles Campground Store** (831-389-4538; 3-4pm Mon-Thu, noon-6pm Fri, 9am-6pm Sat & Sun) sells water, drinks and basic snacks and supplies, but you're best to stock up for self-catering in supermarkets in King City or Salinas.

Pinnacles National Park Campground CAMPGROUND $
(877-444-6777; www.recreation.gov; tent/RV sites $23/36;) On the park's east side, this popular family-oriented campground has over 130 sites (some with shade), drinking water, coin-op hot showers, fire pits and an outdoor pool (usually closed from October to March).

Information

Pinnacles National Park Visitor Center (831-389-4485; 9:30am-5pm daily, to 8pm Fri late Mar-early Sep) Information, maps and books are available on the park's east side from the small NPS visitor center inside the campground store.

Getting There & Away

There is no road connecting the two sides of Pinnacles National Park. To reach the less-developed **west entrance** (7:30am-8pm), exit Hwy 101 at Soledad and follow Hwy 146 northeast for 14 miles. The **east entrance** (24hr), where you'll find the visitor center and campground, is accessed via lonely Hwy 25 in San Benito County, southeast of Hollister and northeast of King City.

San Miguel

Founded in 1797, **Mission San Miguel Arcángel** (805-467-3256; www.missionsanmiguel.org; 775 Mission St; adult/child 5-17yr $3/2; 10am-4:30pm) suffered heartbreaking damage during a 2003 earthquake.

Although repairs are still underway, the church, cemetery, museum and gardens are open. An enormous cactus out front was planted during the early days of the mission.

Hungry? Look for a couple of no-name Mexican delis, where the limited options include massive shrimp burritos.

Paso Robles

In northern San Luis Obispo County, Paso Robles is the heart of a historic agricultural region where grapes are now the biggest money-making crop. Scores of wineries along Hwy 46 produce a brave new world of more-than-respectable bottles. The Mediterranean climate and laidback lifestyle is yielding other bounties as well, and olive oil, craft beer and artisan distilleries are growing in popularity. Paso's historic downtown centers on Park and 12th Sts, where boutique shops and wine-tasting rooms await.

Sights & Activities

Around Paso Robles, you could spend days wandering country back roads off Hwy 46, running east and west of Hwy 101. Most wineries have tasting rooms and a few offer vineyard tours. For dozens more wineries and olive-oil farms to visit, browse www.pasowine.com.

Studios on the Park GALLERY
(805-238-9800; www.studiosonthepark.org; 1130 Pine St; noon-4pm Mon-Wed, to 6pm Thu & Sun, to 9pm Fri-Sat) Artists from around the Central Coast work and display their art at this collection of open studios on the eastern edge of Paso Robles' town square. Up to 15 different artists work from six studios, and other facilities include art galleries and an excellent fine art shop. Check the website for always-interesting special exhibitions and what interactive classes are scheduled.

Eastside

J Lohr Vineyards & Wines WINERY
(805-239-8900; www.jlohr.com; 6169 Airport Rd; tastings free-$10; 10am-5pm) A Central Coast wine pioneer, J Lohr owns vineyards in Napa Valley, Monterey's Santa Lucia Highlands and Paso's pastoral countryside. Knowledgeable staff guide you through a far-reaching wine list.

Tobin James Cellars WINERY
(805-239-2204; www.tobinjames.com; 8950 Union Rd; 10am-6pm) Anti-serious Old West saloon pours bold reds, including an outlaw 'Ballistic' Zinfandel and 'Liquid Love' dessert wine. No tasting fee.

Eberle Winery WINERY
(805-238-9607; www.eberlewinery.com; 3810 E Hwy 46; tastings free-$10; 10am-5pm) Offers lofty vineyard views and tours of its wine caves every half-hour from 10:30am to 5pm. Sociable tastings run the gamut of white and red varietals and Rhône blends.

Westside

Tablas Creek Vineyard WINERY
(805-237-1231; www.tablascreek.com; 9339 Adelaida Rd; tastings from $10; 10am-5pm) Breathe easy at this organic estate vineyard reached via a pretty winding drive up into the hills. Known for Rhône varietals, the signature blends also rate highly. Free tours at 10:30am and 2pm daily (reservations necessary).

Castoro Cellars WINERY
(805-238-0725; www.castorocellars.com; 1315 N Bethel Rd; tasting fee $5; 10am-5:30pm) Husband-and-wife team produces 'dam fine wine' (the mascot is a beaver, get it?), including from custom-crushed and organic grapes. Outdoor vineyard concerts happen during summer.

Thacher Winery WINERY
(805-237-0087; www.thacherwinery.com; 8355 Vineyard Rd; tastings $10; 11am-5pm Thu-Mon) Breathe deeply as you drive up the dirt road to this historic ranch that makes memorable Rhône blends – 'Controlled Chaos' is a perennial fave.

Festivals & Events

Wine Festival WINE, FOOD
(www.pasowine.com; mid-May) Oenophiles come for Paso's premier Wine Festival in mid-May, but the Vintage Paso weekend, focusing on Zinfandel wines, in mid-March and the Harvest Wine Weekend in mid-October are just as much fun.

California Mid-State Fair CARNIVAL, MUSIC
(www.midstatefair.com; mid-Jul) Twelve days of live rock and country-and-western concerts, farm exhibits, carnival rides and a rodeo draw huge crowds.

Sleeping

Adelaide Inn MOTEL $$
(805-238-2770; www.adelaideinn.com; 1215 Ysabel Ave; r $104-161;) Fresh-baked cookies, muffins for breakfast, mini golf and a fitness room keep families happy at this motel just off Hwy 101.

★ **Summerwood Inn** B&B $$$
(805-227-1111; www.summerwoodwine.com; 2175 Arbor Rd; d from $300;) Along Hwy 46 within an easy drive of dozens of wineries, this gorgeous inn renovated in cool neutral tones mixes vintage and modern elements. Each of the nine rooms is named after a wine varietal and has a gas fireplace and balcony overlooking the vineyards. Indulge with the chef's gourmet breakfast, afternoon hors d'oeuvres and evening desserts.

★ **Hotel Cheval** BOUTIQUE HOTEL $$$
(805-226-9995; www.hotelcheval.com; 1021 Pine St; d $330-475;) Near downtown Paso Robles, this European-style boutique hotel has 16 rooms arrayed around a sheltered inner courtyard. Spacious guest accommodation features flat-screen TVs and fireplaces, and rates include breakfast. Stylish shared spaces incorporate a library – decked out with sumptuous leather couches – and the Pony Bar, serving Californian wines, and featuring live music from 5pm on Friday and Saturday. Rates are around $60 cheaper on weekdays.

Inn Paradiso B&B $$$
(805-239-2800; www.innparadiso.com; 975 Mojave Ln; ste $395-425;) An intimate B&B pulls off no-fuss luxury with four suites decorated with art and antiques, and perhaps a fireplace, a deep soaking tub, a canopy king-sized bed or French balcony doors. Breakfast generously overflows with local and organic produce. Pet fee $50.

Eating

★ **La Cosecha Bar & Restaurant** LATIN AMERICAN, SPANISH $$
(805-237-0019; www.lacosechabr.com; 835 12th St; pizza $14-15, mains $21-30) The Honduran heritage of chef and owner Santos MacDonal shines through at this cosmopolitan bar and bistro translating from Spanish into 'the harvest.' That means a strong focus on local and seasonal produce crafted into dishes with a Latin American and Iberian flair. Combine one of Paso's best wine and beer lists with delicate Ecuadorian shrimp, paella or wood-fired pizza.

Check the website for regular dinner events partnering with local winemakers.

The Hatch Rotisserie & Bar AMERICAN $$
(805-221-5727; www.hatchpasorobles.com; 835 13th St; mains $15-23; 3-9pm Mon-Wed, to 10pm Thu, to 11pm Fri-Sat) Wood-fired treats in this heritage location combining shimmering chandeliers and rustic bricks include grilled octopus, rotisserie chicken and creamy bone marrow, and a sly sophistication is added to American comfort food including shrimp and grits and buttermilk fried chicken. Regular smoked-meat specials, craft beer and cocktails, and Paso Robles wine on tap all make The Hatch an essential destination.

Artisan CALIFORNIAN $$$
(805-237-8084; www.artisanpasorobles.com; 843 12th St; shared plates $14-16, mains $17-36; 4:30pm-9pm Mon-Thu, to 10pm Fri-Sat, 10am-2:30pm & 4:30-9pm Sun) Chef Chris Kobayashi often ducks out of the kitchen just to make sure you're loving his impeccable contemporary renditions of modern American cuisine, featuring sustainably farmed meats, wild-caught seafood and artisan California cheeses. Impressive wine, beer and cocktail menus. Reservations essential.

Drinking & Nightlife

Paso Robles is home to several excellent craft breweries, and the up-and-coming Tin City area south of the city also features cider bars, urban distilleries and wine-tasting rooms.

★ **Tin City Cider Co** CIDER
(805-293-6349; www.tincitycider.com; 3005a Limestone Way, Tin City; tastings $12; 1-7pm Tue-Thu, 1-8pm Fri, 11am-6pm Sat-Sun) Joining the tangle of breweries, distilleries and wine-tasting rooms in Paso Robles' Tin City neighborhood, Tin City Cider's thoroughly modern tasting room showcases tart and tangy tipples crafted from apples. Their standard range is crisp and refreshing, and more complex flavors underpin innovative variations fermented with Belgian brewers yeast, enlivened with passionfruit, or aged in bourbon barrels or French oak.

Silva Brewing CRAFT BEER
(805-369-2337; www.silvabrewing.com; 525 Pine St; 2-7pm Wed-Fri, noon-5pm Sat-Sun) Chuck Silva is US brewing aristocracy – he was

DON'T MISS

JAMES DEAN MEMORIAL

In Cholame, about 25 miles east of Paso Robles via Hwy 46, there's a memorial near the spot where *Rebel Without a Cause* star James Dean fatally crashed his Porsche on September 30, 1955, at the age of 24. Ironically, the actor had recently filmed a public-safety campaign TV spot, in which he said, 'The road is no place to race your car. It's real murder. Remember, drive safely. The life you save might be mine.'

Look for the shiny stainless-steel memorial wrapped around an oak tree outside the truck-stop Jack Ranch Cafe, which has old photographs and movie-star memorabilia inside.

previously with Green Flash Brewing in San Diego – and now he's crafting his own brews in a compact space in Paso Robles. Look forward to bold, hop-forward styles and also Belgian-influenced beers. Just through an adjoining door (literally!) is a separate craft-beer pub, so make a night of it.

Wine Shine DISTILLERY
(☎805-286-4453; www.wineshine.com; 3064 Limestone Way, Tin City; ⏲1-5pm Fri-Sun) Grape juice sourced from Paso Robles wineries is the versatile basis for the innovative spirits crafted by Wine Shine. Sample brandies tinged with mango, ginger or cinnamon and aged in oak barrels, or try Wine Shine's Manhattan Project whiskey that is a tribute to the classic days of American cocktails.

BarrelHouse Brewing Co BREWERY
(☎805-296-1128; www.barrelhousebrewing.com; 3055 Limestone Way, Tin City; ⏲2-8pm Wed-Thu, 11am-9pm Fri & Sat, to 8pm Sun) Detour south of downtown, where locals chill in the outdoor beer garden with ales, stouts, zingy sour beers and fruity Belgian-style brews. Live bands frequently play, and most evenings there's a local food truck in attendance. Make an afternoon of it.

Brewery tours run on a first-come, first-served basis at 3pm from Friday to Sunday. You'll need to wear closed-toe shoes for safety regulations.

Re:Find Distillery DISTILLERY
(☎805-239-9456; www.refinddistillery.com; 2725 Adelaida Rd; ⏲11am-5pm) Paso Robles' first micro-distillery makes crisp botanical brandy (gin) and also whiskey and flavored vodkas. Scores of lemons were being zested when we dropped by. Try all the spirits in the rustic and rural tasting room, and ask how the plans are going to open an urban tasting room in Paso Robles' iconic Fox Theater on the edge of downtown.

For more on the Paso Robles distillery scene see www.pasoroblesdistillerytrail.com, and download a touring map listing 10 different distilleries.

Shopping

Around Paso Robles' downtown square, side streets are full of wine-country boutiques.

Pasolivo FOOD & DRINKS
(☎805-227-0186; www.pasolivo.com; 8530 Vineyard Dr; ⏲11am-5pm) Located on a pleasantly winding back road in Paso Robles wine country, Pasolivo's olive-oil tasting room features bold and earthy oils flavored with basil, citrus and rosemary. The laid-back ranch-style surroundings make a pleasant break from wine-tasting, and the attached shop sells excellent artisan foods and olive oil–based soaps and beauty products.

Paso Robles General Store FOOD, GIFTS
(☎805-226-5757; www.generalstorepr.com; 841 12th St; ⏲10am-7pm) Stock up on picnic provisions such as California-made pistachio butter, fresh local baguettes, fruit jams and more, plus home goods like lavender soap. Many of the products are locally sourced, organic and sustainable. Also an excellent source of gifts and homewares.

Information

Paso Robles Chamber of Commerce (☎805-238-0506; www.travelpaso.com; 1225 Park St; ⏲8:30am-5pm Mon-Fri, 9am-5pm Sat, 10am-2pm Sun)

Geting There & Away

From an unstaffed **Amtrak station** (☎800-872-7245; www.amtrak.com; 800 Pine St), daily *Coast Starlight* trains head north to Salinas ($20, two hours) and Oakland ($32, 4¾ hours) and south to Santa Barbara ($29, 4¼ hours) and LA ($43, 7½ hours). Several daily Thruway buses link to more-frequent regional trains, including the *Pacific Surfliner*.

RTA (☎805-541-2228; www.slorta.org) bus 9 travels between San Luis Obispo and Paso Robles ($3, 70 minutes) hourly Monday to Friday, and a few times daily on weekends.

San Luis Obispo

Almost midway between LA and San Francisco, at the junction of Hwys 101 and 1, San Luis Obispo is a popular overnight stop for road-trippers. With no must-see attractions, SLO might not seem to warrant much of your time. Even so, this low-key town has an enviably high quality of life – in fact, it has been named America's happiest city. CalPoly university students inject a healthy dose of hubbub into the city's streets, bars and cafes throughout the school year. Nestled at the base of the Santa Lucia foothills, SLO is just a grape's throw from Edna Valley wineries, too.

Sights

San Luis Obispo Creek, once used to irrigate mission orchards, flows through downtown. Uphill from Higuera St, **Mission Plaza** is a shady oasis with restored adobe buildings and fountains overlooking the creek. Look for the **Moon Tree**, a coast redwood grown from a seed that journeyed on board *Apollo 14*'s lunar mission.

Mission San Luis Obispo de Tolosa CHURCH
(Map p319; ☎805-543-6850; www.missionsanluisobispo.org; 751 Palm St; suggested donation $5; ⏲9am-5pm late Mar-Oct, to 4pm Nov–mid-Mar; 👪) Those satisfyingly reverberatory bells heard around downtown emanate from this active parish dating from 1772. The fifth California mission founded by Padre Junípero Serra, it was named for a 13th-century French saint. The modest **church** has an unusual L-shape and whitewashed walls decorated with Stations of the Cross. An adjacent building contains an old-fashioned **museum** about daily life during the Chumash tribal and Spanish colonial periods. Interesting guided tours of the mission take place most days at 1:15pm.

San Luis Obispo Museum of Art MUSEUM
(Map p319; ☎805-543-8562; www.sloma.org; 1010 Broad St; ⏲11am-5pm, closed Tue early Sep-early Jul) FREE By the creek, this small gallery showcases the work of local painters, sculptors, printmakers and fine-art photographers, as well as traveling California art exhibitions.

Activities & Tours

For hiking with ocean views, head to Montaña de Oro State Park (p310), not far away from San Luis Obispo.

Margarita Adventures ZIPLINING, KAYAKING
(☎805-438-3120; www.margarita-adventures.com; 22719 El Camino Real, Santa Margarita; adult/child zip-line tour $119/89; ⏲8am-4:30pm Thu-Tue; 👪) Whoosh down five zip lines across the vineyards beneath the Santa Lucia Mountains at this historic ranch, about a 10-mile drive northeast of SLO via Hwy 101. Reservations are required and trips leave from Margarita Adventures' office in the main street of sleepy Margarita. Ziplining experiences are ten bucks cheaper from Monday to Friday.

Hop On Beer Tours FOOD & DRINK
(☎855-554-6766; www.hoponbeertours.com; per person $30) Jump aboard these sociable minibus tours to explore the San Luis Obispo and Paso Robles craft-beer scenes. Tours visit up to four different breweries. Check the website for timings of Social Tours open to the public – usually on Friday, Saturday or Sunday nights, two to four times per month – as Hop On also runs private tours.

Tours depart from downtown San Luis Obispo. Note that beer needs to be purchased separately.

Festivals & Events

SLO International Film Festival FILM
(www.slofilmfest.org; ⏲mid-Mar) This annual six-day celebration of film has been a mainstay of the SLO cultural calendar since 1993. Events and screenings are held around the greater San Luis Obispo County area, including in Paso Robles and Pismo Beach.

Concerts in the Plaza MUSIC, FOOD
(www.downtownslo.com; ⏲Fri nights, Jun-Sep) Downtown's Mission Plaza rocks out with local bands and food vendors.

Sleeping

Motels cluster off Hwy 101 in San Luis Obispo, especially off Monterey St northeast of downtown and around Santa Rosa St (Hwy 1). A slew of interesting new openings has increased the range of accommodation in town.

HI Hostel Obispo HOSTEL $
(Map p319; ☎805-544-4678; www.hostelobispo.com; 1617 Santa Rosa St; dm $32-39, r from $65, all with shared bath; ⏲check in 4:30-10pm; @📶) 🌿 On a tree-lined street near SLO's train station, this solar-empowered, avocado-colored hostel inhabits a converted Victorian, which gives it a bit of a B&B feel. Amenities include a kitchen, bike rentals (from $10 per day)

and complimentary sourdough pancakes and coffee for breakfast. BYOT (bring your own towel).

The Butler DESIGN HOTEL **$$**
(Map p319; ☎805-548-1884; www.thebutlerhotel.com; 1511 Monterey St; r $229-249;) Just six stylish rooms fill this unique property that used be an automotive workshop. There's definitely no grease and grime now evident in the rooms decked out with colorful artwork and featuring stellar bathrooms. Shared spaces include a lounge with design books, a record player (including plenty of vintage jazz vinyl), and a compact kitchen with drinks and snacks available.

Note that guest access is via a key code and there are no hotel staff resident at the property.

San Luis Creek Lodge HOTEL **$$**
(☎805-541-1122; www.sanluiscreeklodge.com; 1941 Monterey St; r $159-229;) Rubbing shoulders with neighboring motels, this boutique inn has fresh, spacious rooms with divine beds (and some have gas fireplaces and jetted tubs) inside three whimsically mismatched buildings built in Tudor, California arts-and-crafts, and Southern plantation styles. DVDs, chess sets and board games are free to borrow.

Madonna Inn HOTEL **$$**
(☎805-543 3000; www.madonnainn.com; 100 Madonna Rd; r $209-329;) The fantastically campy Madonna Inn is a garish confection visible from Hwy 101. Japanese tourists, vacationing Midwesterners and irony-loving hipsters adore the 110 themed rooms – including Yosemite Rock, Caveman and hot-pink Floral Fantasy (check out photos online). The urinal in the men's room is a bizarre waterfall. But the best reason to stop here? Old-fashioned cookies from the storybook bakery.

SLO Brew Lofts APARTMENT **$$$**
(Map p319; ☎805-543-1843; www.slobrew.com; 738 Higuera St; apts from $250;) Located above a brewpub and live-music venue, SLO Brew Lofts offer a unique urban stay in downtown. Apartments range from one to three bedrooms – the lofts are suitable for families or friends – and stylish decor is partnered by cool touches like a refrigerator stocked with SLO Brew's fine products, and record players with stacks of vintage vinyl. Expect some noise from downstairs, especially on weekends.

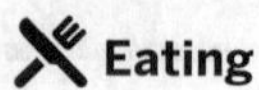

Eating

Downtown SLO has several excellent restaurants, befitting the area's farm-to-fork focus and wine-country heritage.

★ **San Luis Obispo Farmers Market** MARKET **$**
(Map p319; ☎805-541-0286; www.downtownslo.com; Higuera St; 6-9pm Thu;) The county's biggest and best weekly farmers market turns downtown SLO's Higuera St into a giant street party, with smokin' barbecues, overflowing fruit and veggie stands, live music and free sidewalk entertainment, from salvation peddlers to wackadoodle political activists. Rain cancels it.

★ **Thomas Hill Organics** BISTRO **$$**
(Map p319; ☎805-457-1616; www.thomashillorganics.com; 858 Monterey St; mains $22-40; 11am-late Mon-Sat, from 10am Sun;) More contemporary than its original namesake eatery in Paso Robles, Thomas Hill's San Luis Obispo opening presents seasonal menus amid a stylish combination of chandeliers and whitewashed walls. Secure a spot at the bar and combine Central Coast wines with a delicate salad of beets, burrata and pistachios, or devour a sausage-and-mushroom pizza with a zingy draft cider. For Sunday brunch and on warm summer evenings, the outside patio is the place to be.

Guiseppe's Cucina Rustica ITALIAN **$$**
(Map p319; ☎805-541-9922; www.giuseppesrestaurant.com; 849 Monterey St; pizza & sandwiches $13-16, mains $21-36; 11:30am-11pm) Visit Guiseppe's for a leisurely downtown lunch dining on excellent salads, pizza and antipasti, or to grab a take-out meatball or Caprese sandwich from the deli counter out the front. Out the back, the facade of the heritage Sensheimer Brothers building looks over a shaded courtyard that's equally suited to long dinners of slow-roasted chicken and SLO County wines.

Luna Red FUSION **$$**
(Map p319; ☎805-540-5243; www.lunaredslo.com; 1023 Chorro St; shared plates $6-20, mains $20-39; 11:30am-9:30pm Mon-Thu, to midnight Fri, 9am-11:30pm Sat, to 9pm Sun;) Local bounty from the land and sea, artisan cheeses and farmers-market produce pervade the chef's Californian, Asian and Mediterranean small-plates menu. Cocktails and glowing lanterns enhance a sophisticated ambience indoors, or

San Luis Obispo

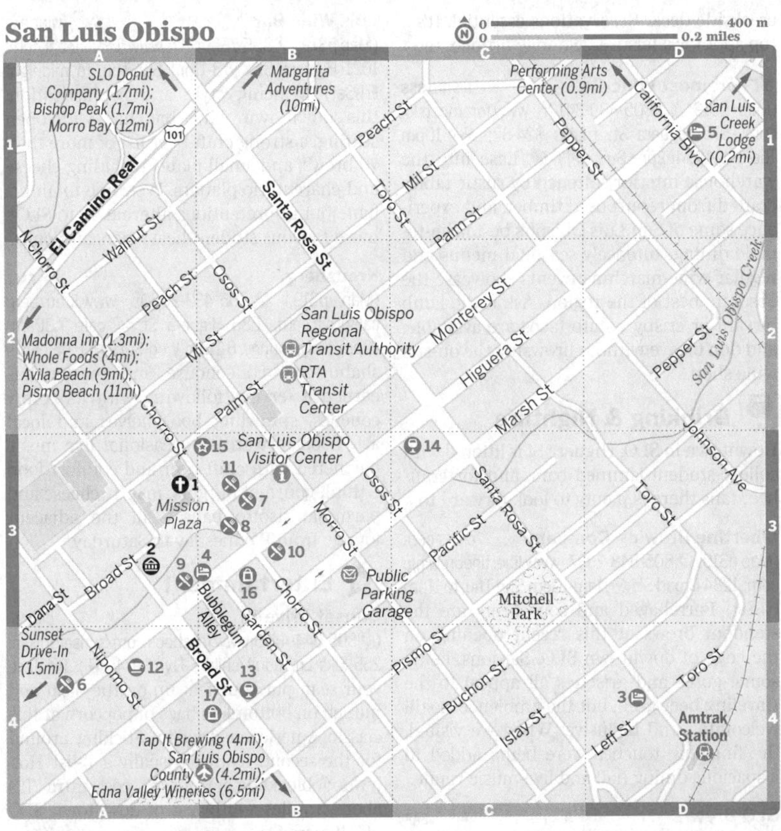

San Luis Obispo

Sights
1 Mission San Luis Obispo de Tolosa ... A3
2 San Luis Obispo Museum of Art ... A3

Sleeping
3 HI Hostel Obispo ... D4
4 SLO Brew Lofts ... B3
5 The Butler ... D1

Eating
6 Foremost Wine Co ... A4
7 Guiseppe's Cucina Rustica ... B3
8 Luna Red ... B3
9 Novo ... A3
10 San Luis Obispo Farmers Market ... B3
11 Thomas Hill Organics ... B3

Drinking & Nightlife
12 Kreuzberg ... A4
13 Libertine Brewing Company ... B4
14 Luis Wine Bar ... C3
SLO Brew ... (see 4)

Entertainment
15 Palm Theatre ... B3

Shopping
16 Hands Gallery ... B3
17 The Mountain Air ... B4

linger over brunch on the mission-view garden patio. Reservations recommended.

Novo FUSION $$
(Map p319; 805-543-3986; www.novorestaurant.com; 726 Higuera St; mains $18-36; 11am-9pm Mon-Thu, to 1am Fri & Sat, 10am-9pm Sun) Novo spins out moreish European, Latin and Asian-inspired tapas with an artistic eye towards classy presentation. Pick from dozens of international beers, wines or sakes, then savor the view from tables on the

creekside deck. Reservations essential. It's a top spot for a leisurely Sunday brunch, too.

★Foremost Wine Co BISTRO $$$
(Map p319; ☎805-439-3410; www.foremostslo.com; 570 Higuera St; mains $24-32; ⏱4-10pm Tue-Sat, 10am-2pm Sun;) Ease into the warehouse interior softened by rustic tables crafted from repurposed timber, and experience some of San Luis Obispo's best farm-to-table dining. Intensely seasonal menus and regular wine-matching events showcase the absolute best of the region. Ask if the lamb biryani or crispy potato tacos are available, and don't leave without browsing the on-site wine shop.

Drinking & Nightlife

Downtown in SLO, Higuera St is littered with college-student-jammed bars, and for craft-beer fans there is plenty to look forward to.

Libertine Brewing Company CRAFT BEER
(Map p319; ☎805-548-2337; www.libertinebrewing.com; 1234 Broad St; ⏱11am-10pm Sun-Thu, to 11pm Fri-Sat) Barrel-aged and sour beers are the standout brews at this recent opening on the edge of downtown SLO. Saisions, kettle sours, goses and grisettes all appeal to the traveling beer geek, but the ambience is still welcoming and inclusive. When we visited, the finishing touches were being added to a spacious dining hall and live-music venue.

SLO Brew BAR
(Map p319; ☎805-543-1843; www.slobrew.com; 736 Higuera St; ⏱11:30am-2am Tue-Sat, to midnight Sun-Mon) SLO Brew's versatile setup incorporates an on-site brewery with good pub meals – combine the Red Reggae wheat beer with the Yard Bird roast-chicken pizza – and it's also a rocking live-music venue with regular gigs. Past performers have included The Strokes and Lee 'Scratch' Perry, so it's definitely worth checking out who's playing.

Tap It Brewing BREWERY
(☎805-545-7702; www.tapitbrewing.com; 675 Clarion St; ⏱noon-6pm Sun, to 7pm Tue, to 8pm Wed, to 10pm Thu-Sat) Head out toward the airport to this upstart brewery's tap room, where cacti grow inside an old Jeep and live bands sometimes rock on the patio. Order up a beer-tasting rack, chill with the brewery's regular posse of visiting hounds, and look forward to being surprised by Tap It's always interesting seasonal brews.

Luis Wine Bar WINE BAR
(Map p319; ☎805-762-4747; www.luiswinebar.com; 1021 Higuera St; ⏱3-11pm Sun-Thu, to midnight Fri-Sat) Evincing style and sophistication, this downtown wine bar has wide-open seating, a strong craft-beer list of more than 70 brews, and small plates including cheese and charcuterie platters. Welcome to an urbane but unpretentious alternative to SLO's more raucous student-heavy bars and pubs.

Kreuzberg CAFE
(Map p319; ☎805-439-2060; www.kreuzbergcalifornia.com; 685 Higuera St; ⏱cafe 7:30am-10pm daily, lounge 6-11pm Wed-Sat;) This shabby-chic coffeehouse and roaster has earned a fervent following with its comfy couches, sprawling bookshelves and local art. Look forward to occasional live music partnered with craft beer and comfort food – think gourmet burgers, mac 'n' cheese and parmesan-risotto balls – in the adjacent lounge from Wednesday to Saturday.

☆ Entertainment

Sunset Drive-In CINEMA
(☎805-544-4475; www.facebook.com/sunsetdrivein; 255 Elks Ln; adult/child 5-11yr $9/4;) Recline your seat, put your feet up on the dash and munch on bottomless bags of popcorn at this classic Americana drive-in. Sticking around for the second feature (usually a B-list Hollywood blockbuster) doesn't cost extra. It's about 2 miles southwest of downtown SLO off Higuera St.

Palm Theatre CINEMA
(Map p319; ☎805-541-5161; www.thepalmtheatre.com; 817 Palm St; tickets $5-9) This small-scale movie house showing foreign and indie flicks just happens to be the USA's first solar-powered cinema. Seats are a bargain $5 on Mondays. Look for the SLO International Film Festival (p317) in March.

Shopping

For shopping fans to San Luis Obispo, downtown Higuera and Marsh Sts, along with all of the arcades and cross streets in between, are full of unique boutiques.

Hands Gallery ARTS & CRAFTS
(Map p319; ☎805-543-1921; www.handsgallery.com; 777 Higuera St; ⏱10am-6pm Mon-Wed, to 8pm Thu-Sat, 11am-5pm Sun) Brightly lit downtown shop sells vibrant contemporary pieces by California artisans, including jewelry,

fiber arts, sculptures, ceramics and blown glass.

The Mountain Air SPORTS & OUTDOORS
(Map p319; ☎805-543-1676; www.themountainair.com; 667 Marsh St; ⏲10am-6pm Mon-Sat, to 8pm Thu, 11am-4pm Sun) At this local outdoor outfitter, pick up anything from campstove fuel and tents to brand-name clothing and hiking boots.

Information

San Luis Obispo Visitor Center (Map p319; ☎805-781-2777; www.visitslo.com; 895 Monterey St; ⏲10am-5pm Sun-Wed, to 7pm Thu-Sat)

Mission San Luis Obispo Post Office (Map p319; ☎800-275-8777; www.usps.com; 893 Marsh St; ⏲10am-5pm Mon-Fri, to 2pm Sat) Centrally located in downtown SLO.

San Luis Obispo Library (☎805-781-5991; www.slolibrary.org; 995 Palm St; ⏲10am-5pm Wed-Sat, to 8pm Tue; 📶) Free wi-fi and public internet terminals.

French Hospital (☎805-543-5353; www.frenchmedicalcenter.org; 1911 Johnson Ave; ⏲24hr) Emergency-room services.

Getting There & Away

Amtrak (☎800-872-7245; www.amtrak.com; 1011 Railroad Ave) runs daily Seattle–LA *Coast Starlight* and twice-daily SLO–San Diego *Pacific Surfliner* trains. Both routes head south to Santa Barbara ($35, 2¾ hours) and Los Angeles ($57, 5½ hours). The *Coast Starlight* connects north via Paso Robles to Salinas ($28, 3 hours) and Oakland ($41, six hours). Several daily Thruway buses link to more regional trains.

Off Broad St, over 3 miles southeast of downtown, **San Luis Obispo County Regional Airport** (☎805-781-5205; www.sloairport.com; 903 Airport Dr) has scheduled flights with United (San Francisco and LA), American Airlines (Phoenix) and Alaska Airlines (Seattle). A new four-gate terminal opened at the airport in 2017.

There's no public bus transport to the airport and a taxi from downtown is around $18.

San Luis Obispo Regional Transit Authority (RTA; Map p319; ☎805-541-2228; www.slorta.org; single-ride fares $1.50-3, day pass $5) operates daily county-wide buses with limited weekend services. All buses are equipped with bicycle racks. Lines converge on downtown's **transit center** (Map p319; cnr Palm & Osos Sts).

Avila Beach

Quaint, sunny Avila Beach lures crowds with its strand of golden sand and a shiny seafront commercial district of restaurants, cafes and shops. Explore the arcades behind Front St for art galleries and winery tasting rooms. Two miles west of downtown, Port San Luis is a working fishing harbor with a rickety old pier.

Sights & Activities

For a lazy summer day at Avila Beach, you can rent beach chairs and umbrellas, surfboards, boogie boards and wetsuits underneath **Avila Pier**, off downtown's waterfront promenade. Over by the port, the beach has bonfire pits and the barking of sea lions accompanies your stroll atop **Harford Pier**, one of the Central Coast's most authentic fishing piers.

★ **Point San Luis Lighthouse** LIGHTHOUSE
(Map p322; ☎guided hike reservations 805-528-8758, trolley tour reservations 805-540-5771; www.pointsanluislighthouse.org; lighthouse $5, incl trolley tour adult/child 3-12yr $20/15; ⏲guided hikes 8:45am-1pm Wed & Sat, trolley tours noon & 1pm Wed & Sat) Just getting to this scenic 1890 lighthouse, overshadowed by Diablo Canyon nuclear power plant, is an adventure. The cheapest way to reach the lighthouse is via a rocky, crumbling, 3.75-mile round-trip hiking trail, for which guided-hike reservations are required. If you'd rather take it easy and ride out to the lighthouse, join an afternoon trolley tour (reservations also required). Inside the lighthouse you can inspect an original Fresnel lens and authentic Victorian-period furnishings.

The **Pecho Coast Trail** to the lighthouse is open only for guided hikes led by Pacific Gas & Electric (PG&E) docents, weather permitting. These guided hikes are free; children under nine years old are not allowed. Make reservations online at least two weeks in advance and bring plenty of water.

Avila Valley Barn FARM
(Map p322; ☎805-595-2816; www.avilavalleybarn.com; 560 Avila Beach Dr; ⏲9am-6pm mid-Mar–late Dec, to 5pm Thu-Mon Jan–mid-Mar; 👪) At this rural farmstand and pick-your-own berry farm, park alongside the sheep and goat pens, lick an ice-cream cone, then grab a basket and walk out into the fields to harvest jammy olallieberries in late spring and early summer, mid-summer peaches and nectarines, or autumn apples and pumpkins. During summer, the kids can jump aboard tractor rides or pony rides.

San Luis Obispo Bay

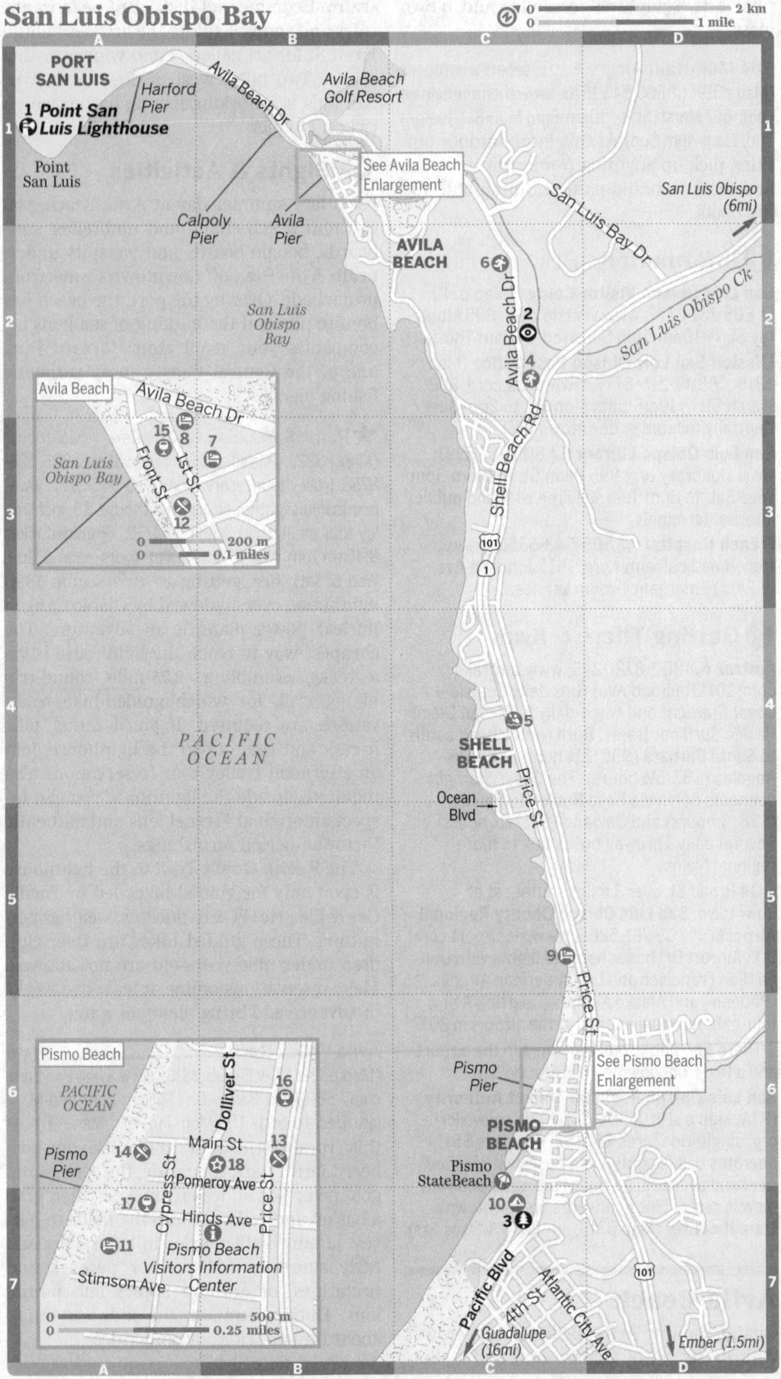

0 — 2 km
0 — 1 mile

PORT SAN LUIS
1 Point San Luis Lighthouse
Harford Pier
Avila Beach Dr
Avila Beach Golf Resort
Point San Luis
See Avila Beach Enlargement
Calpoly Pier
Avila Pier
AVILA BEACH
San Luis Bay Dr
San Luis Obispo (6mi)
San Luis Obispo Ck
San Luis Obispo Bay
Avila Beach Dr
Shell Beach Rd
PACIFIC OCEAN
SHELL BEACH
Ocean Blvd
Price St
See Pismo Beach Enlargement
Pismo Pier
PISMO BEACH
Pismo State Beach
Pacific Blvd
4th St
Atlantic City Ave
Guadalupe (16mi)
Ember (1.5mi)

Avila Beach
Avila Beach Dr
San Luis Obispo Bay
Front St
1st St
0 — 200 m
0 — 0.1 miles

Pismo Beach
PACIFIC OCEAN
Pismo Pier
Dolliver St
Main St
Cypress St
Pomeroy Ave
Price St
Hinds Ave
Pismo Beach Visitors Information Center
Stimson Ave
0 — 500 m
0 — 0.25 miles

San Luis Obispo Bay

Sycamore Mineral Springs SPA

(Map p322; ☎805-595-7302; www.sycamoresprings.com; 1215 Avila Beach Dr; 1hr per person $15-20; ⊗8am-midnight) Make time for a therapeutic soak in one of these private redwood hot tubs discreetly laddered up a woodsy hillside. Call in advance for reservations, especially during summer and after dark on weekends. Last reservation time is 10:30pm.

Avila Hot Springs HOT SPRINGS

(Map p322; ☎805-595-2359; www.avilahotsprings.com; 250 Avila Beach Dr; adult/child under 16yr $12/10; ⊗usually 8am-9pm Sun-Tue & Thu, to 10pm Wed, Fri & Sat;) Slightly sulfuric, lukewarm public swimming pool has kiddie waterslides that are usually open from noon to 5pm on Saturday and Sunday.

Sleeping

Accommodation in Avila Beach ranges from simple RV parking to a very comfortable boutique hotel.

★ **Avila La Fonda** INN $$$

(Map p322; ☎805-595-1700; www.avilalafonda.com; 101 San Miguel St; d from $269;) Downtown, this small boutique hotel is a harmonious mix of Mexican and Spanish colonial styles, with hand-painted tiles, stained-glass windows, wrought iron and rich wood. Gather around the fireplace for nightly wine and hors d'oeuvres. Complimentary beach gear to borrow for guests.

Avila Lighthouse Suites HOTEL $$$

(Map p322; ☎805-627-1900; www.avilalighthousesuites.com; 550 Front St; ste from $359;) Any closer to the ocean and your bed would actually be sitting on the sand. With families in mind, this apartment-style hotel offers suites and villas with kitchenettes. But it's the giant heated outdoor pool, Ping-Pong tables, putting green and life-sized checkers board that keep kids amused. Ask about steep off-season discounts. Reception is off First St.

Eating & Drinking

Avila's Front St promenade features cafes and upscale restaurants. At Port San Luis, Harford Pier is home to seafood shops that sell fresh catch right off the boats.

Avila Beach Farmers Market MARKET $

(Map p322; ☎805-801-1349; www.facebook.com/AvilaBeachFarmersMarket; Front St; ⊗4-8pm Fri early Apr-late Sep) With local farmers, food booths and rockin' live music, this outdoor street party takes over downtown's oceanfront promenade weekly from spring to fall.

PierFront Wine & Brew WINE BAR

(Map p322; ☎805-439-3400; www.pierfrontwineandbrew.com; 480 Front St; ⊗noon-7pm Sun-Thu, to 9pm Fri-Sat;) Californian craft beers and West Coast wines come with a side order of stellar sunset views of Avila's pier at this recent opening. Relax on a comfortable sofa in the eclectic interior or secure a sun-dappled spot under market umbrellas on the compact patio. Well-behaved dogs are welcomed as regulars, and PierFront's concise food menu includes flatbreads and cheese boards.

Getting There & Away

Avila is around 10 miles south of San Luis Obispo and 8 miles northwest of Pismo Beach.

Between 10am and 4pm on Saturdays and Sundays from late March until mid-October, a free **trolley** (SCT; ☎805-781-4472; www.slorta.org) loops from Pismo Beach around downtown Avila Beach to Port San Luis; from early June to early September, extended hours are 10am to 6pm Thursday through Sunday. There's no public transportation offered between mid-October and late March.

Pismo Beach

Backed by a wooden pier that stretches toward the setting sun, Pismo Beach is where James Dean once trysted with Pier Angeli. Fronted by an invitingly wide, sandy beach, this 1950s-retro town feels like somewhere straight out of *Rebel Without a Cause* or *American Graffiti*. If you're looking for a sand-and-surf respite from coastal road tripping, break your journey here.

Pismo likes to call itself the 'Clam Capital of the World,' but these days the beach is pretty much clammed out. You'll have better luck catching something fishy off the pier, where you can rent rods. To rent a wetsuit, body board or surfboard, cruise nearby surf shops.

Sights & Activities

Pismo Beach Monarch Butterfly Grove PARK

(Map p322; ☎805-773-5301; www.monarchbutterfly.org; Hwy 1; ⊙sunrise-sunset; 👪) FREE From November through February, over 25,000 black-and-orange monarchs make their winter home here. Forming dense clusters in the tops of eucalyptus trees, they might easily be mistaken for leaves. Between 10am and 4pm during the roosting season, volunteers can tell you all about the insects' incredible journey, which outlasts any single generation of butterflies. Look for a gravel parking pull-out on the ocean side of Pacific Blvd (Hwy 1), just south of Pismo State Beach's **North Beach Campground** (399 S Dolliver St; tent & RV sites $40; 🐾).

Central Coast Kayaks KAYAKING

(Map p322; ☎805-773-3500; www.centralcoastkayaks.com; 1879 Shell Beach Rd, Shell Beach; kayak or SUP set rental $20-25, classes $60-75, tours $60-120; ⊙9am-4:30pm Mon-Tue & Thu-Fri, to 5pm Sat-Sun) Paddle out among sea otters and seals and through mesmerizing sea caves, rock grottos, arches and kelp forests. Wetsuits, paddle jackets and booties available (small surcharge applies) with kayak rentals.

Festivals & Events

Wine, Waves & Beyond CULTURAL, FOOD

(www.winewavesandbeyond.com; ⊙early Jun) Surfing competitions, surf-themed movies, wine tasting and a big bash on the beach with live music and food.

Clam Festival FOOD & DRINK

(www.pismochamber.com; ⊙mid-Oct) Celebrate the formerly abundant and still tasty mollusc with a clam dig, chowder cookoff, food vendors and live music.

Sleeping

Pismo Beach has dozens of motels, but rooms fill up quickly and prices skyrocket in summer, especially on weekends. Resorts and hotels roost on cliffs north of town via Price St and Shell Beach Rd, while motels cluster near the beach and along Hwy 101.

Pismo Lighthouse Suites HOTEL $$

(Map p322; ☎805-773-2411; www.pismolighthousesuites.com; 2411 Price St; ste from $239; P ⊖ 📶 🏊 🐾) With everything a vacationing family needs – from kitchenettes to a life-sized outdoor chessboard, a putting green, table tennis and badminton courts – this contemporary all-suites hotel right on the beach is hard to tear yourself away from. Ask about off-season discounts and check out the on-site spa services. Pet fee $50.

Sandcastle Inn HOTEL $$$

(Map p322; ☎805-773-2422; www.sandcastleinn.com; 100 Stimson Ave; r $305; 📶) Many of these Eastern Seaboard–styled rooms are mere steps from the sand. The top-floor ocean-view patio is perfect for cracking open a bottle of wine at sunset or after dark by the fireplace.

Eating

Good restaurants – including cheaper seafood joints – feature in downtown Pismo Beach, especially along Price St, and the nearby adjoining town of Arroyo Grande also has good eating.

Doc Burnstein's Ice Cream Lab ICE CREAM $

(☎805-474-4068; www.docburnsteins.com; 114 W Branch St, Arroyo Grande; snacks $4-12; ⊙11am-9:30pm Sun-Thu, to 10:30pm Fri & Sat, reduced hours in winter; 👪) In Pismo's neighboring Arroyo Grande, Doc's scoops up fantastical flavors like Merlot raspberry truffle and the 'Elvis Special' (peanut butter with banana swirls). Live ice-cream lab shows start at

SCENIC DRIVE: HWY 1 SOUTH OF PISMO BEACH

What to See

Hwy 1 ends its fling with Hwy 101 at Pismo Beach, veering off toward the coast. Some truly wild, hidden beaches beckon along this back-door route to Santa Barbara.

Guadalupe Dunes

You almost expect to have to dodge tumbleweeds as you drive into the agricultural town of Guadalupe. Five miles further west at **Rancho Guadalupe Dunes Preserve** (www.countyofsb.org/parks/day-use/rancho-guadalupe-dunes.sbc; off Hwy 166; 7am-sunset; P) FREE, enormous Egyptian-esque film sets from Cecil B DeMille's 1923 Hollywood epic *The Ten Commandments* still lie buried in the sand. Learn more about the 'Lost City of DeMille,' the ecology of North America's largest coastal dunes, and the mystical Dunites who lived here during the 1930s back at downtown Guadalupe's small **Dunes Center** (805-343-2455; www.dunescenter.org; 1055 Guadalupe St; adult/child $5/free; 10am-4pm Wed-Sun) museum.

Surf & Ocean Beaches

These wind-whipped beaches, one surf beach with a lonely Amtrak train whistlestop platform station, cozy up to the Vandenberg Air Force Base. On the 10-mile drive west of Lompoc and Hwy 1 (take Hwy 246/W Ocean Ave), you'll pass odd-looking structures supporting spy and commercial satellite launches. Between March and September, both Surf Beach and **Ocean Beach** (www.countyofsb.org/parks/day-use/ocean-beach.sbc; Ocean Park Rd, off Hwy 246; 8am-sunset Oct-Feb) FREE may be closed to protect endangered Snowy Plovers during their nesting season.

Jalama Beach

Leaving Hwy 1 about 5 miles east of Lompoc, Jalama Rd follows 14 miles of twisting tarmac across ranch- and farmlands before arriving at utterly isolated **Jalama Beach County Park** (recorded info 805-736-3616; www.countyofsb.org/parks/jalama; Jalama Beach Rd, Lompoc; per car $10). To stay overnight, reserve a cabin in advance or arrive by 8am to get on the waiting list for a campsite in the crazily popular **campground** (805-568-2460; www.countyofsb.org/parks/jalama.sbc; 9999 Jalama Rd, Lompoc; tent/RV sites from $25/40, cabins $120-220; P) – look for the 'campground full' sign back near Hwy 1 to avoid a wasted trip. There is a local general store selling basics, but it's recommended to bring your food and drink supplies.

The Route

Heading south of Pismo Beach, Hwy 1 slowly winds along, passing through Guadalupe and Lompoc, where you can detour to **La Purísima Mission State Historic Park** (805-733-3713; www.lapurisimamission.org; 2295 Purísima Rd, Lompoc; per car $6; 9am-5pm, tours at 1pm Wed-Sun & public holidays Sep-Jun, daily Jul & Aug; P). Past Lompoc, Hwy 1 curves east to rejoin Hwy 101 south of Santa Barbara's wine country, near Gaviota.

Time & Mileage

With all of the detours described above, it's a 165-mile drive from Pismo Beach to Santa Barbara. The drive takes at least 3½ hours without any stops or traffic delays.

7pm sharp on Wednesday. From Hwy 101 southbound, exit at Grand Ave.

Frutiland La Casa Del Sabor MEXICAN $$

(805-541-3663; www.facebook.com/frutiland.frutiland; 803 E Grand Ave, Arroyo Grande; mains $8-14; 10am-6pm) Oversized, overstuffed Mexican *tortas* (sandwiches) will feed two, and there are two dozen varieties to choose from. Or order a platter of blue-corn-tortilla fish tacos with a mango or papaya *agua fresca* (fruit drink). To find this taco shack in Arroyo Grande, exit Hwy 101 southbound at Halcyon Rd.

Cracked Crab SEAFOOD $$

(Map p322; 805-773-2722; www.crackedcrab.com; 751 Price St; mains $16-59; 11am-9pm Sun-

Thu, to 10pm Fri & Sat;) Fresh seafood and regional wines are the staples at this super-casual, family-owned grill. When the famous bucket o'seafood, full of flying bits of fish, Cajun sausage, red potatoes and cob corn, gets dumped on your butcher-paper-covered table, make sure you're wearing one of those silly-looking plastic bibs. No reservations, but the wait is worth it.

★ Ember CALIFORNIAN $$$

(805-474-7700; www.emberwoodfire.com; 1200 E Grand Ave, Arroyo Grande; shared dishes $12-26, mains $26-36; 4-9pm Wed-Thu & Sun, to 10pm Fri & Sat) Chef Brian Collins, who once cooked at Alice Waters' revered Chez Panisse, has returned to his roots in SLO County. Out of this heart-warming restaurant's wood-burning oven come savory flatbreads, artfully charred squid and hearty red-wine-smoked short ribs. No reservations, so show up at 4pm or after 7:30pm, or be prepared for a very long wait for a table.

Sociable seating in the bar, where you can order off the full menu, is first-come, first-served. Look forward to being surprised with a different seasonal menu each month. The restaurant is west of Hwy 101 (southbound exit Halcyon Rd) in Arroyo Grande.

Oyster Loft CALIFORNIAN, SEAFOOD $$$

(Map p322; 805-295-5104; www.oysterloft.com; 101 Pomeroy Ave; mains $20-45; 5-9pm Sun-Thu & to 10pm Fri-Sat) Delve into the appetizers menu – including crab cakes or orange-glazed octopus – or kick off with tuna tataki or fresh oysters from the crudo raw bar. Mains including pan-fried halibut are still seafood-heavy, but do venture successfully into steaks and chicken. Look forward to excellent views of the surf and the Pismo Beach pier from the restaurant's elevated position. Reservations recommended although walk-in diners can sit at the bar.

Drinking & Nightlife

Pismo Beach has a standout craft-beer bar, and downtown Arroyo Grande along W Branch St has welcoming pubs, bistros and wine-tasting rooms.

The Boardroom BAR

(Map p322; 805-295-6222; www.theboardroompismobeach.com; 160 Hinds Ave; 2-10pm Mon-Wed, noon-10pm Sun & Thu, noon-1am Fri-Sat;) An exemplary range of craft beers – mainly from the West Coast of the US – combines with knowledgeable and friendly bartenders at this easygoing bar with a surfing ambience. Get to know the locals over a game of darts, maximize your travel budget during happy hour from 4pm to 6pm, and fill up on pizza, salads and panini.

Taste of the Valleys WINE BAR

(Map p322; 805-773-8466; www.pismowineshop.com; 911 Price St; noon-9pm Mon-Sat & to 8pm Sun) Inside a wine shop stacked floor to ceiling with hand-picked vintages from around California and beyond, ask for a taste of anything they've got open, or sample from a quite astounding list of more than 1000 wines poured by the glass.

Entertainment

Pismo Bowl BOWLING

(Map p322; 805-773 2482; www.pismobeachbowl.com; 277 Pomeroy Ave; game per person $4.25, shoe rental $3.25; noon-10pm Sun-Thu, to midnight Fri & Sat;) Epitomizing Pismo Beach's retro vibe, this old-fashioned bowling alley is just a short walk uphill from the pier. Blacklight 'cosmic' and karaoke bowling rule Friday and Saturday nights.

Information

Pismo Beach Visitors Information Center (Map p322; 805-773-4382; www.classiccalifornia.com; 581 Dolliver St; 9am-5pm Mon-Fri, 10am-2pm Sat) Free maps and brochures. A smaller kiosk on the pier is open from 11am to 4pm on Sunday.

Getting There & Around

Hourly from Monday to Friday, and a few times daily on weekends, **RTA** (805-541-2228; www.slorta.org) bus 10 links San Luis Obispo with Pismo's Premium Outlets mall ($2, 30 minutes), a mile from the beach, before continuing to downtown Arroyo Grande ($1.50, 15 minutes).

ADONIS VILLANUEVA/SHUTTERSTOCK ©

Pacific Coast Highways

Snaking more than 1000 miles along dizzying sea cliffs and over landmark bridges, passing ancient redwoods, historic lighthouses and quirky beach towns, California's two-lane coastal highways trace the edge of the continent as they connect the dots between perpetually sunny San Diego, star-powered Los Angeles and eclectic San Francisco.

Contents

Above Point Reyes National Seashore (p121)

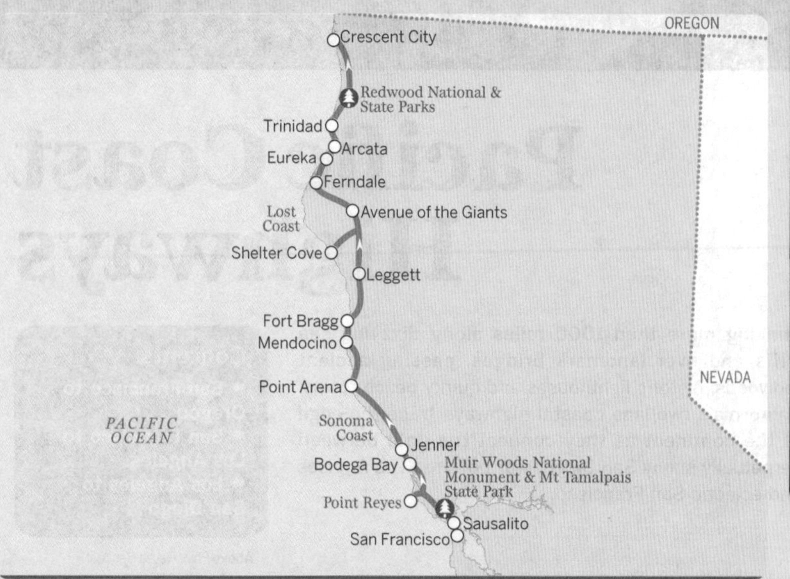
OREGON
Crescent City
Redwood National & State Parks
Trinidad
Arcata
Eureka
Ferndale
Lost Coast
Avenue of the Giants
Shelter Cove
Leggett
Fort Bragg
Mendocino
Point Arena
NEVADA
PACIFIC OCEAN
Sonoma Coast
Jenner
Bodega Bay
Muir Woods National Monument & Mt Tamalpais State Park
Point Reyes
Sausalito
San Francisco

San Francisco to Oregon

Northern California's redwood forests and fishing villages sprawl along the coast on Hwy 1 north of San Francisco and all the way up to Oregon on Hwy 101. Political radicals, artists, pot farmers and nature-loving hippies all gravitate here.

Get a primer on NorCal's left-leaning beatnik scene starting in **San Francisco**, a multicultural mosaic of neighborhoods. Explore top-notch museums and wide-open spaces in Golden Gate Park, then gather your friends around a sunset bonfire at Ocean Beach.

Jaunting north, outdoorsy Marin County has gorgeous beaches and miles of hiking and mountain-biking trails. Just across the Golden Gate Bridge discover the houseboat village of **Sausalito**, then go tramping around Marin County's **Muir Woods** and landmark **Mt Tamalpais**.

After more hiking and wildlife spotting at **Point Reyes**, devour fresh oysters at roadside stands along Hwy 1. Made infamous by Hitchcock's thriller *The Birds*, **Bodega Bay** is the gateway to the windswept Sonoma Coast. At **Jenner**, where the Russian River meets the sea, it's tempting to make a quick detour inland to wine country.

Keep going north, stopping to climb the **Point Arena** lighthouse, and pull over in the Victorian village of **Mendocino**. Beyond the windy fishing port of **Fort Bragg**, Hwy 1 snakes inland to join Hwy 101 at **Leggett**, where the Redwood Empire truly begins. Trundle north to the **Avenue of the Giants**, an unforgettably scenic drive.

To really get away from it all, detour west to **Shelter Cove** on the remote Lost Coast. When you crave civilization again, head to the farm town of **Ferndale**; the salty sea-dogs' lair of **Eureka**; the hippy-dippy university town of **Arcata**; and postcard-perfect **Trinidad**.

Onward to the reason you've driven all this way: California's redwoods, the tallest trees on earth. In **Redwood National & State Parks**, take time out for Tall Trees Grove, Fern Canyon, Gold Bluffs Beach and the winding Newton B Drury Scenic Parkway before rolling into **Crescent City**.

Top: View of San Francisco Bay from Mt Tamalpais (p115)
Bottom: Sausalito (p106)

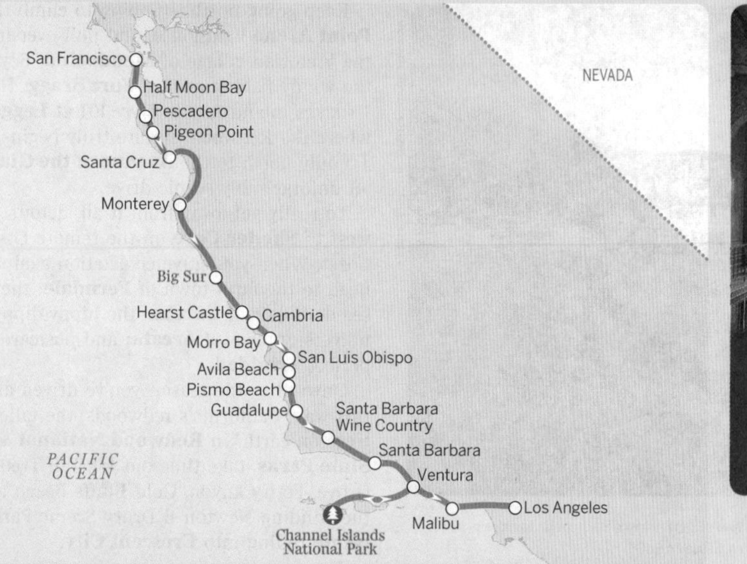
San Francisco
Half Moon Bay
Pescadero
Pigeon Point
Santa Cruz
Monterey
Big Sur
Hearst Castle
Cambria
Morro Bay
San Luis Obispo
Avila Beach
Pismo Beach
Guadalupe
Santa Barbara
Wine Country
Santa Barbara
Ventura
Malibu
Los Angeles
Channel Islands
National Park
PACIFIC
OCEAN
NEVADA

Top: Late afternoon on the Pacific Coast
Bottom: The Roman Pool, Hearst Castle (p304)

5 DAYS San Francisco to Los Angeles

Get away from the boring inland freeways that zip between San Francisco and LA and you'll discover that the Central Coast is a natural wonderland, from Monterey Bay's marine sanctuary and Big Sur's mystical redwood forests to the wildlife-rich Channel Islands.

Driving along Hwy 1 south of **San Francisco** via **Half Moon Bay** feels like you're dangling off the edge of the world. Pull over in the rural town of **Pescadero** for local farm bounty. Just further south at **Pigeon Point**, visit the first of many historic lighthouses you'll encounter.

If you love California's weird, wacky side, stop in **Santa Cruz**. Surfers hit the bodacious beaches, while kids go nuts on the carnival beach boardwalk. On the other side of the bay, **Monterey** has the rough-and-ready seafaring atmosphere of a John Steinbeck novel.

Heading south, Hwy 1 plunges into mysterious **Big Sur** (for temporary route changes, see p295), where modern-day hippies, beatniks and bohemians gather. Seek out hot springs and waterfalls, hike through misty redwood forests and keep looking skyward to spot endangered California condors soaring above ocean cliffs.

Beyond Big Sur, Hwy 1 tumbles downhill past **Hearst Castle**, a monumental hilltop mansion, before lazing in the seaside village of **Cambria**. Rent a kayak to paddle around **Morro Bay**, with its landmark volcanic rock. Slow down for the college town of **San Luis Obispo**, surrounded by vineyards and farms.

Soak up the sunshine at **Avila Beach** or go fishing off the pier at **Pismo Beach**. Follow Hwy 1 to detour out to the monumental sand dunes of **Guadalupe**, then head back inland and cross Hwy 101 onto bucolic back roads that wind through **Santa Barbara Wine Country**.

Let yourself fall under the spell of the Mediterranean climate, red-tiled roofs and golden beaches of **Santa Barbara**. From **Ventura**, sail out to **Channel Islands National Park** to get truly wet and wild. Hwy 1 keeps cruising south through star-studded **Malibu**, where celebrity sightings are as predictable as the tides, before hitting **LA**.

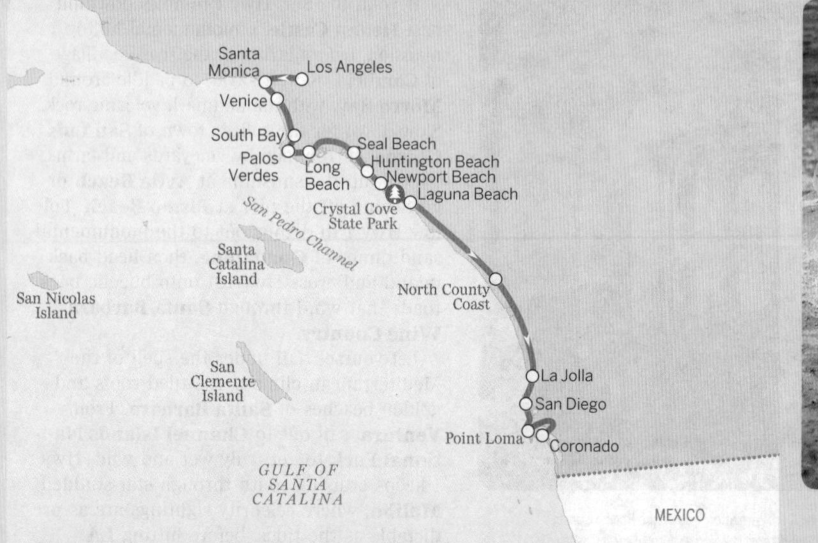
Santa
Monica
Los Angeles
Venice
South Bay
Palos
Verdes
Long
Beach
Seal Beach
Huntington Beach
Newport Beach
Laguna Beach
Crystal Cove
State Park
San Pedro Channel
Santa
Catalina
Island
San Nicolas
Island
North County
Coast
San
Clemente
Island
La Jolla
San Diego
Point Loma
Coronado
GULF OF
SANTA
CATALINA
MEXICO

Top: Sunset, Venice (p388)
Bottom: Sea lions, La Jolla (p473)

5 DAYS

Los Angeles to San Diego

It's time to drop the convertible top and cue up the California beach-life soundtrack. On this short stretch of Hwy 1, you can dive headfirst into a dreamscape of beautiful sand, epic waves and surf towns. Start in glam LA before cruising through Orange County's coast and laid-back San Diego.

Los Angeles is California's biggest, boldest and most diverse metropolis. At the city's western edge, take a spin on the solar-powered Ferris wheel atop the seaside pier at **Santa Monica** and Rollerblade along the beach boardwalk in oddball **Venice**. Dive into the arts and cultural scene Downtown, with its top-class museums, cutting-edge restaurants and bars.

Meanwhile fashionistas, surfers and bikini-clad beach-volleyball stars head to LA's **South Bay**, where you'll cruise by chic Manhattan Beach, funky Hermosa Beach and touristy Redondo Beach. Follow Hwy 1 around the **Palos Verdes** peninsula for mesmerizing sea views, then drop by the aquarium in family-friendly **Long Beach**.

Cross the Orange County line to old-fashioned **Seal Beach**, whose quaint main street leads out to a wooden pier. Next up is party-animal **Huntington Beach**, which legally owns the name 'Surf City USA.' Don strappy sandals and sunglasses for the white sands of the Balboa Peninsula in **Newport Beach**, where yachties mingle. Pause for a breath of fresh air and beachcombing at wild **Crystal Cove State Park**. Further south, the artists' colony of **Laguna Beach** is another movie-star beautiful hamlet you may never want to leave.

Along San Diego's **North County Coast** a colorful grab-bag of beach towns jostle between Hwy 1 and the ocean surf. Keep rolling south to fancy-pants **La Jolla**, a coastal village full of ritzy restaurants and boutiques, as well as gorgeous sea coves and nature reserves.

In **San Diego**, hang with regular folks at Pacific Beach, ride the roller coaster at Mission Beach or scarf down fish tacos and get a tattoo in bohemian Ocean Beach. Snap a panoramic photo from **Point Loma** before finishing up your journey with a cocktail at the swanky Hotel Del in **Coronado**.

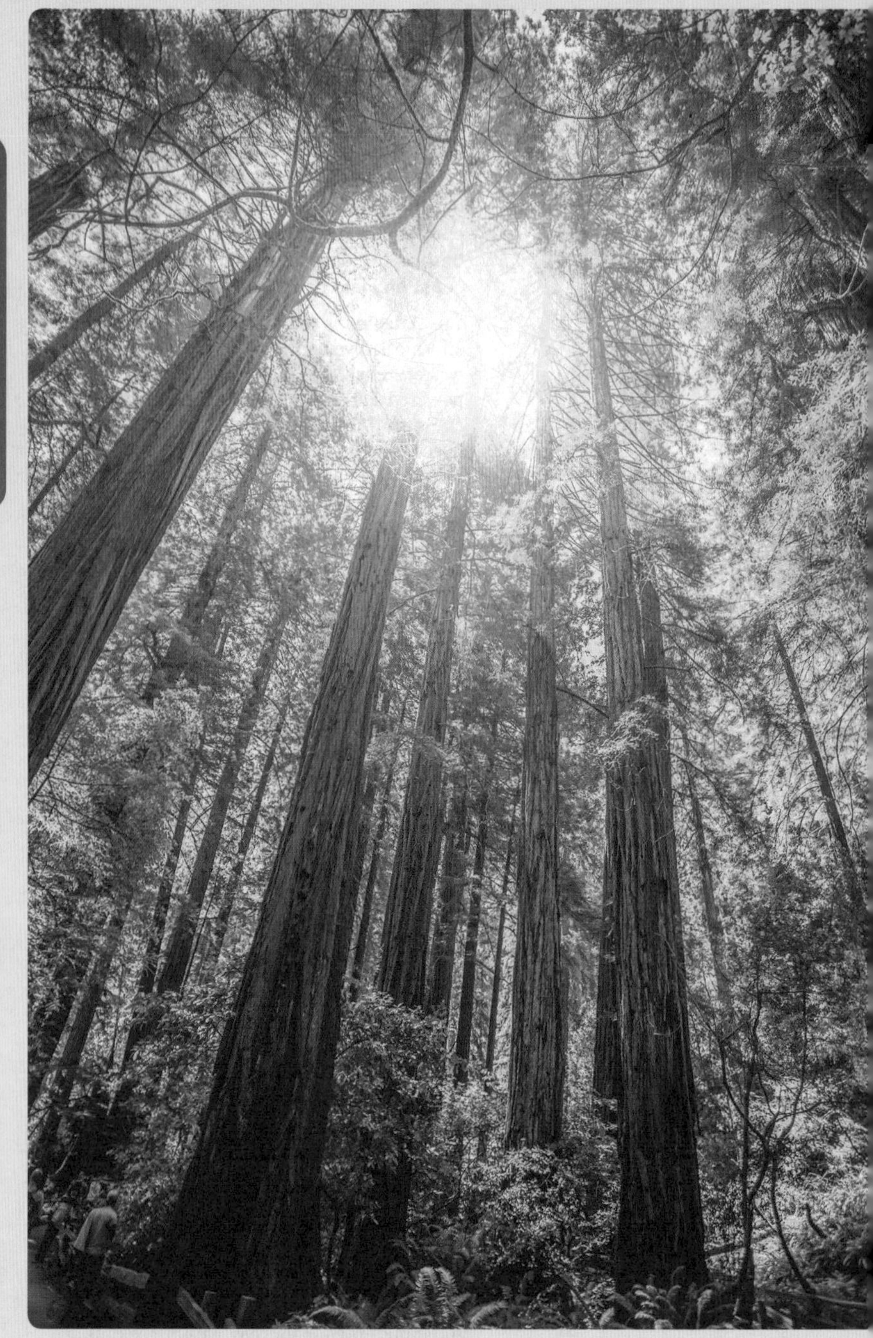

Muir Woods National Monument (p117)

Santa Barbara County

Includes ➡

Best Places to Eat

➡ Santa Barbara Shellfish Company (p351)
➡ Mesa Verde (p351)
➡ Bouchon (p352)
➡ Knead (p371)
➡ Yoichi's (p352)

Best Places to Sleep

➡ Belmondo El Encanto (p348)
➡ Pacific Crest Hotel (p347)
➡ Inn of the Spanish Garden (p349)
➡ Landsby (p364)
➡ Hotel Californian (p347)

Why Go?

Frankly put, this area is damn pleasant to putter around. Low-slung between lofty mountains and the shimmering Pacific, chic Santa Barbara's red-tiled roofs, white stucco buildings and Mediterranean vibe give credence to its claim of being the 'American Riviera.' It's an enticing place to loll on the beach, eat and drink extraordinarily well, shop a bit and push all your cares off to another day. The city's car-free campaign has brought electric shuttle buses, urban bike trails and earth-friendly wine tours. Mother Nature returns the love with hiking, biking, surfing, kayaking, scuba-diving and camping opportunities galore, from offshore Channel Islands National Park to arty Ojai, in neighboring Ventura County. Meanwhile, winemaking is booming in the bucolic Santa Ynez Mountains, west of Santa Barbara, where over a hundred wineries vie for your attention.

When to Go

Santa Barbara

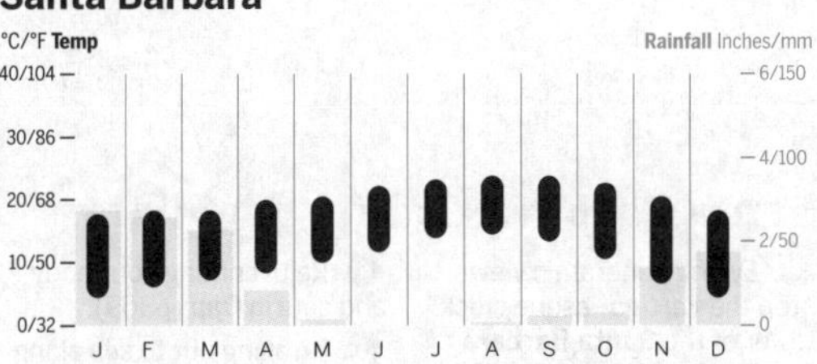

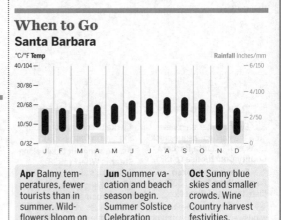

Apr Balmy temperatures, fewer tourists than in summer. Wildflowers bloom on Channel Islands.

Jun Summer vacation and beach season begin. Summer Solstice Celebration parade.

Oct Sunny blue skies and smaller crowds. Wine Country harvest festivities.

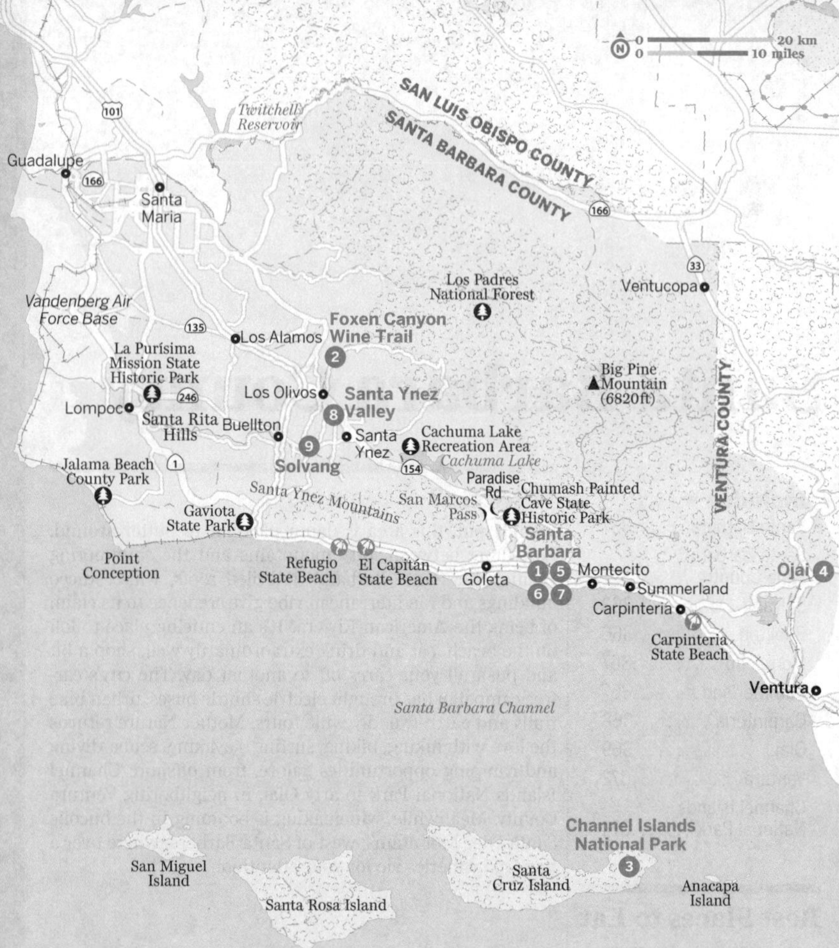

Santa Barbara County Highlights

1. Eyeing panoramic views atop the *Vertigo*–esque clock tower of the **Santa Barbara County Courthouse** (p337).
2. Following the **Foxen Canyon Wine Trail** (p357) to taste top-rated Pinot Noir.
3. Kayaking sea caves, hiking windswept cliffs and watching for whales in **Channel Islands National Park** (p374).
4. Rejuvenating your body and soul in **Ojai** (p369).
5. Strolling out to sea along **Stearns Wharf** (p338), California's oldest pier.
6. Ambling between wine-tasting rooms, hip bars and eateries, art galleries and unique shops in Santa Barbara's **Funk Zone** (p345).
7. Exploring Spanish-colonial history at **Mission Santa Barbara** (p337).
8. Pedaling past vineyards and organic farms through the **Santa Ynez Valley** (p361).
9. Eating *aebleskivers* (pancake popovers) by a kitschy windmill in the Danish village of **Solvang** (p363).

SANTA BARBARA

Perfect weather, beautiful buildings, excellent bars and restaurants, and activities for all tastes and budgets make Santa Barbara a great place to live (as the locals will proudly tell you) and a must-see place for visitors to Southern California. Check out the Spanish mission church first, then just see where the day takes you.

History

For hundreds of years before the arrival of the Spanish, Chumash tribespeople thrived in this region, setting up trade routes between the mainland and the Channel Islands and constructing redwood canoes known as *tomols*. In 1542 explorer Juan Rodríguez Cabrillo sailed into the channel and claimed it for Spain – then quickly met his doom (from a gangrenous leg injury) on a nearby island.

The Chumash had little reason for concern until the permanent return of the Spanish in the late 18th century. Catholic priests established missions up and down the coast, ostensibly to convert Native Americans to Christianity. Spanish soldiers often forced the Chumash to construct the missions and presidios (military forts) and provide farm labor; they also rounded up the tribespeople on the Channel Islands and forced them to leave. Back on the mainland, the indigenous population shrank dramatically, as many Chumash died of European diseases and ill treatment.

Mexican ranchers arrived after their country won independence in 1821. Easterners began migrating en masse after California's gold rush kicked off in 1849. By the late 1890s, Santa Barbara was an established SoCal vacation spot for the wealthy. After a massive earthquake in 1925, laws were passed requiring much of the city to be rebuilt in a faux-but-attractive Spanish Colonial–style,with white-stucco buildings and red-tiled roofs.

Sights

★MOXI MUSEUM

(Wolf Museum of Exploration + Innovation; Map p346; ☎805-770-5000; www.moxi.org; 125 State St; adult/child $14/10; ⊙10am-5pm; 👪) Part of the regeneration of this neglected strip of State St, Moxi's three floors filled with hands-on displays covering science, arts and technology themes will tempt families in, even when it's not raining outside. If all that interactivity gets too much, head to the roof terrace for views across Santa Barbara and a nerve-challenging walk across a glass ceiling.

Highlights include booths where you re-create sound effects from famous movie scenes, the 'mind ball' game where you use just your calm thoughts to move a metal ball against an opponent, and workshops that feature different make-and-learn activities.

Weekends get very busy with waits for many of the exhibits, so try to come during the week when it's quieter.

DON'T MISS

MEETING MONARCHS

If you're here in late fall or winter, ask at the Outdoors Santa Barbara Visitors Center (p356) about the best places to see migratory monarch butterflies roosting in the trees – an extraordinary sight.

★Santa Barbara County Courthouse HISTORIC BUILDING

(Map p346; ☎805-962-6464; http://sbcourthouse.org; 1100 Anacapa St; ⊙8am-5pm Mon-Fri, 10am-5pm Sat & Sun) FREE Built in Spanish-Moorish Revival style in 1929, the courthouse features hand-painted ceilings, wrought-iron chandeliers, and tiles from Tunisia and Spain. On the 2nd floor, step inside the hushed mural room depicting Spanish-colonial history, then head up to El Mirador, the 85ft clock tower, for arch-framed panoramas of the city, ocean and mountains.

You can explore on your own, but you'll get a lot more out of a free, one-hour docent-guided tour: 2pm daily, plus 10:30am Monday to Friday.

★Mission Santa Barbara CHURCH

(☎805-682-4713; www.santabarbaramission.org; 2201 Laguna St; adult $9, child 5-17yr $4; ⊙9am-5pm, last entry 4:15pm; P👪) California's 'Queen of the Missions' reigns above the city on a hilltop perch over a mile north of downtown. Its imposing Ionic facade, an architectural homage to an ancient Roman chapel, is topped by an unusual twin bell tower. Inside the mission's 1820 stone church, notice the striking Chumash artwork. In the cemetery the elaborate mausoleums of early California settlers stand out, while the graves of thousands of Chumash lie largely forgotten.

The self-guided tour starts in the pretty garden before heading to the cemetery (where Juana María, the Chumash girl made famous in *Island of the Blue Dolphins*, was buried). Next up is the church itself, followed by a series of rooms turned into a museum and exhibiting Chumash baskets, a missionary's bedroom and time-capsule black-and-white photos showing the last Chumash residents of the Mission and the damage done to the buildings after the 1925 earthquake. Docent-guided tours are usually given at 11am on Tuesday, Thursday and Friday, 10:30am on Saturday, and 12:30pm on Sunday; no reservations are taken.

The mission was established on December 4 (the feast day of St Barbara), 1786, as the 10th California mission. Of California's original 21 Spanish-colonial missions, it's the only one that escaped secularization under Mexican rule. Continuously occupied by Catholic priests since its founding, the mission is still an active parish church.

From downtown, take MTD bus 6 or 11, then walk five blocks uphill.

Santa Barbara Zoo ZOO

(805-962-6310; www.sbzoo.org; 500 Ninos Dr; adult $17, child under 13 $10; 10am-5pm; P) Small (so it's perfect for young kids) Santa Barbara Zoo has 146 species covering all creatures great and small, including several not found in many other zoos. Asian elephants Little Mac and Sujatha have been together here since 1972 and are hugely popular, as are the adorable meerkats. Don't miss the chance to see endangered California condors – probably your best bet for seeing them in the whole state – and giant anteaters. The antics of the Humboldt penguins always raise a smile.

Information panels give details on the animals and their habitats, plus tips for visitors on how to help preserve the creatures' natural environments (don't buy unsustainable palm oil, for example).

Parking is available (weekdays $7, weekends $10) or take the Waterfront shuttle for just 50¢.

Shoreline Park PARK

(Shoreline Dr; 8am-sunset; P) FREE For great views across the city, mountains and ocean (with the chance to spot whales in season and dolphins year-round), come to Shoreline Park, southwest of Santa Barbara. There are restrooms, picnic tables and a children's playground, and dogs are welcome.

Santa Barbara Museum of Natural History MUSEUM

(805-682-4711; www.sbnature.org; 2559 Puesta del Sol; adult $12, child 2-12yr $7, youth 13-17yr $8, incl planetarium show $16/12/12; 10am-5pm; P) The huge whale skeleton by the entrance whets the appetite for the city's natural history museum. The usual dioramas of stuffed animals are on display in dimly lit rooms (the bird collection is especially good on local species), but the joy of this place is that once you've learned about nature inside, you can head outside to the 'Museum's Backyard', a trail through woods by a creek, and engage with the real thing.

Santa Barbara Historical Museum MUSEUM

(Map p346; 805-966-1601; www.santabarbaramuseum.com; 136 E De La Guerra St; 10am-5pm Tue-Sat, from noon Sun) FREE Embracing a romantic cloistered adobe courtyard, this peaceful little museum tells the story of Santa Barbara. Its endlessly fascinating collection of local memorabilia ranges from the simply beautiful, such as Chumash woven baskets and Spanish-colonial-era textiles, to the intriguing, such as an intricately carved coffer that once belonged to Junípero Serra. Learn about the city's involvement in toppling the last Chinese monarchy, among other interesting lessons in local history.

Stearns Wharf WATERFRONT

(Map p346; www.stearnswharf.org; open daily, hours vary; P) FREE The southern end of State St gives way to Stearns Wharf, a rough wooden pier lined with souvenir shops, snack stands and seafood shacks. Built in 1872, it's the oldest continuously operating wharf on the West Coast, although the actual structure has been rebuilt more than once. During the 1940s it was co-owned by tough-guy actor Jimmy Cagney and his brothers. If you have kids, take them inside the **Sea Center** (Map p346; 805-962-2526; www.sbnature.org; 211 Stearns Wharf; adult $8.50, child 2-12yr $6, youth 13-17yr $7.50; 10am-5pm; P).

Santa Barbara Botanic Garden GARDENS

(805-682-4726; www.sbbg.org; 1212 Mission Canyon Rd; adult $12, child 2-12yr $6, youth 13-17yr $8; 9am-6pm Mar-Oct, to 5pm Nov-Feb; P) Take a soul-satisfying jaunt around this 40-acre botanic garden, devoted to California's native flora. Miles of partly wheelchair-accessible trails meander past cacti, redwoods and wildflowers and by the old mission dam, originally built by Chumash tribespeople to irrigate the mission's fields.

TOP 10 BEACHES IN SANTA BARBARA

Although Santa Barbara's beaches are beauty-pageant prize winners, don't expect sunsets over the ocean because most of this coast faces south.

East Beach (Map p346; www.santabarbaraca.gov/gov/depts/parksrec; E Cabrillo Blvd;) Santa Barbara's largest and most popular beach is a long, sandy stretch sprawling east of Stearns Wharf, with volleyball nets for pick-up games, a children's play area and a snack bar. On Sunday afternoons, artists set up booths along the sidewalk, near the bike path.

Butterfly Beach (Channel Dr) No facilities but quite a high chance of celebrity spotting (the nearby Four Seasons Biltmore hotel is a popular destination for the rich and famous) at this small beach.

West Beach (Map p346; W Cabrillo Blvd;) Central, palm-tree-backed stretch of sand, right next to Stearns Wharf and the harbor (swimming isn't advisable). It's also the setting for large outdoor city events such as Fourth of July celebrations.

Leadbetter Beach (805-564-5418; Shoreline Dr, at Loma Alta Dr; per vehicle $2; P) One of Santa Barbara's most popular beaches, always busy with surfers, wind- and kitesurfers, joggers and sunbathers. Facilities include reservable picnic areas and showers.

Goleta Beach County Park (www.countyofsb.org/parks/day-use/goleta-beach.sbc; Sandspit Rd, Goleta; 8am-sunset; P) Good beach for sunbathing, swimming and picnicking (nab a prized shaded spot if you can), or strolling the 1500ft-long pier for views out to the Channel Islands.

Arroyo Burro Beach County Park (Hendry's; 805-568-2460; www.countyofsb.org/parks; Cliff Dr, at Las Positas Rd; 8am-sunset; P) Swim (lifeguards on duty), stroll or just picnic on this gem of a stretch of sand, also known as Hendry's Beach, 5 miles southwest of Santa Barbara. It's flat, wide, away from tourists and great for kids, who can go tide-pooling. It's also a popular local surf spot and the eastern section is dog-friendly (there's even a dog wash in the parking lot).

El Capitán State Beach (Map p38; 805-968-1033; www.parks.ca.gov; El Capitan State Beach Rd, Goleta; $10 per vehicle; 8am-sunset; P) Head down from the low cliffs to enjoy swimming (confident bathers only), surfing and fishing from this pebbly beach, overlooked by native sycamore and oak trees. The seasonal beach store opens April to mid-September and sells basic groceries and camping supplies.

Thousand Steps Beach (Shoreline Dr, southern end of Santa Cruz Blvd; sunrise-10pm) Descend the cliffs on a historic staircase (don't worry, there aren't actually a thousand steps) for some windy beachcombing and tide-pooling (only at low tide), but no swimming. The beach is also accessible from Shoreline Park (p338) – head west along Shoreline Dr from the park and take a left on Santa Cruz Blvd.

Carpinteria State Beach (p368) Calm waters and tide pools make this idyllyic stretch of beach an ideal spot for families. Also a good location to see harbor seals and sea lions during winter.

Guided tours (included with admission) depart at 11am and 2pm on Saturday and Sunday, and 2pm on Monday. Leashed, well-behaved dogs are welcome.

If you're driving, head north from the mission to Foothill Blvd/Hwy 192, turn right and then left to continue on Mission Canyon Rd.

Santa Barbara Maritime Museum MUSEUM
(Map p346; 805-962-8404; www.sbmm.org; 113 Harbor Way; adult $8, child 6-17yr $5; 10am-5pm Thu-Tue; P) On the harborfront, this jam-packed, two-story exhibition hall celebrates the town's briny history with nautical artifacts, memorabilia and hands-on exhibits, including a big-game fishing chair from which you can 'reel in' a trophy marlin. Take a virtual trip through the Santa Barbara Channel, stand on a surfboard or watch deep-sea-diving documentaries in the theater. There's 90 minutes of free parking in the public lot or take the Lil' Toot water taxi (p357) from Stearns Wharf.

Southern California's Best Beaches

Hundreds of miles of Pacific beaches edge SoCal's golden coast – which makes choosing just one to visit almost impossible. Take your pick depending on what you prefer doing: launching your surfboard onto a world-famous break; snapping on a snorkel mask and peeking at colorful marine life; or just lazing on the sand.

1. Santa Monica (p387)
A carnival pier with a solar-powered Ferris wheel and a tiny aquarium for the kiddos sits atop this idyllic, 3-mile long strand, where LA comes to play.

2. Malibu (p387)
Celebrity residents aren't keen to share their paradisiacal pocket beaches, but with persistence and some insider tips, you too can share these million-dollar views.

3. Huntington Beach (p431)
Officially 'Surf City, USA,' Huntington Beach is everything you imagined SoCal beach life to be, from surfing by the pier to sunset bonfires on the sand.

4. Mission Beach (p454)
A day trip to San Diego's most fun-crazed beach should begin with a ride on the Giant Dipper wooden roller coaster and end with sunset along Ocean Front Walk.

5. Crystal Cove State Park (p439)
Tired of manicured beaches crowded with beach towels? Escape instead to this wilder, undeveloped Orange County gem for beachcombing and scuba diving.

6. Coronado (p454)
Pedal a beach cruiser along the Silver Strand, or frolic like Marilyn Monroe did on the golden sand fronting San Diego's landmark Hotel del Coronado.

7. East Beach (p339)
Next to historic Stearns Wharf, where Santa Barbara meets the sea, this easy-access beach fills with swimmers, volleyball players and even sea kayakers in summer.

8. Carpinteria State Beach (p368)
Even tots can get their feet wet or poke around the tide pools at this Santa Barbara County classic, where palm trees wave above soft sands.

1

3

4

MAREMAGNUM/GETTY IMAGES ©

LAGUNATICPHOTO/SHUTTERSTOCK ©

GAGLIARDIIMAGES/SHUTTERSTOCK ©

GERI LAVROV/GETTY IMAGES ©

VENTURE MEDIA GROUP/GETTY IMAGES ©

Santa Barbara Museum of Art MUSEUM
(Map p346; ☎805-963-4364; www.sbmuseart.org; 1130 State St; adult $10, child 6-17yr $6, all free 5-8pm Thu; ⊙11am-5pm Tue-Wed & Fri-Sun, to 8pm Thu; ♿) This thoughtfully curated, bite-sized art museum displays European and American masters – including Monet, Van Gogh and Degas – along with photography, classical antiquities and Asian artifacts and thought-provoking temporary exhibits. At the time of writing, some galleries were closed while the museum is retrofitted for earthquake protection.

Highlight tours of current exhibitions start at 1pm daily and are included in admission. It also has an interactive children's space, a museum shop and a cafe.

El Presidio de Santa Barbara State Historic Park HISTORIC SITE
(Map p346; ☎805-965-0093; www.sbthp.org; 123 E Canon Perdido St; adult $5, child under 17yr free; ⊙10:30am-4:30pm) Founded in 1782 to defend the mission, this adobe-walled fort built by Chumash laborers was Spain's last military stronghold in Alta California. But its purpose wasn't solely to protect – the presidio also served as a social and political hub, and as a stopping point for traveling Spanish military. Today this small urban park harbors some of the city's oldest structures. On a self-guided walking tour, be sure to stop at the chapel, its interior radiant with rich hues.

Activities

Cycling

A paved **recreational path** stretches 3 miles along the waterfront in both directions from Stearns Wharf, west to Leadbetter Beach beyond the harbor and east just past East Beach. For more pedaling routes, Santa Barbara Bikes to Go offers free downloadable DIY cycling tours of the city, mountains and Wine Country, along with links to bicycle rentals and specialty shops.

Wheel Fun Rentals CYCLING
(Map p346; ☎805-966-2282; http://wheelfunrentalssb.com; 23 E Cabrillo Blvd; ⊙8am-8pm; ♿) Hourly rentals of beach cruisers ($9.95), mountain bikes ($10.95) and two-/four-person surreys ($28.95/38.95), with discounted half-day and full-day rates. A second, seasonal branch is in the Fess Parker Double Tree Hotel at 633 E Cabrillo Blvd.

Santa Barbara Bikes To-Go CYCLING
(Map p346; ☎805-628-2444; www.sbbikestogo.com; 1 N Calle Cesar Chavez; bike rental per day $35-105; ⊙9am-5pm) Delivers top-quality road and hybrid mountain bikes to wherever you're staying in Santa Barbara. Rentals include helmets and emergency-kit saddle bags. Discounts for multiday, weekly and monthly rentals; reservations essential.

Kayaking & Boating

Paddle the calm waters of Santa Barbara's harbor or the coves of the Gaviota coast, or hitch a ride to the Channel Islands for awesome sea caves.

Some tour companies offer year-round whale-watching boat trips, mostly to see grays in winter and spring, and humpbacks and blues in summer.

Santa Barbara Adventure Company KAYAKING
(Map p346; ☎805-884-9283; www.sbadventureco.com; 32 E Haley St; ⊙office 8am-5pm Mon-Sat; ♿) The name says it all: if you want a company that provides a whole host of well-organized adventures then you've come to the right place. It offers everything from Channel Island kayaking ($179) to surf lessons ($89), and bike tours (from $119) to horseback riding ($150).

Paddle Sports Center KAYAKING
(Map p346; ☎805-617-3425; http://paddlesportsca.com; 117b Harbor Way; SUP/kayak rental from $20/12; ⊙usually 8am-6pm) Long-established, friendly outfitter offering year-round kayak and SUP rentals from Santa Barbara harbor and Goleta Beach. Walk-ins are welcome but reduced rates are available if you book online in advance.

Santa Barbara Sailing Center CRUISE, SAILING
(Map p346; ☎805-962-2826; www.sbsail.com; Marina 4, off Harbor Way; ⊙9am-6pm, to 5pm winter;

DIY WALKING TOURS

Santa Barbara's self-guided, 12-block **Red Tile walking tour** is a convenient introduction to downtown's historical highlights. The tour's name comes from the half-moon-shaped red clay tiles covering the roofs of many Spanish Revival–style buildings. You can download a free map of this walking tour, as well as other paths including along the waterfront, from Santa Barbara Car Free (www.santabarbaracarfree.org). For a lazy stroll between wine-tasting rooms, follow the city's Urban Wine Trail (p353).

SANTA BARBARA COUNTY IN...

One Day

Spend your first morning exploring Santa Barbara's historic mission (p337) before visiting downtown's museums, landmarks and shops along **State St**, stopping at the county courthouse (p337) for 360-degree views from its clock tower. Grab lunch on State St and then soak up some rays at the city's East Beach (p339), walking out on to Stearns Wharf (p338) and down by the harbor for sunset. After dark, head to the **Funk Zone** for dinner and drinks in Santa Barbara's coolest neighborhood.

Two Days

Head up to Santa Barbara's Wine Country. Enjoy a do-it-yourself vineyards tour by car, motorcycle or bicycle along a scenic wine trail – Foxen Canyon (p357) and the Santa Rita Hills (p360) are exceptionally beautiful. Pack a picnic lunch or grab a bite in charming Los Olivos (p362) or Danish-esque Solvang (p363).

Three Days

Spend the morning cycling along the coast, surfing or sea-kayaking on the Pacific, or hiking in the Santa Ynez foothills. In the afternoon, drive to posh Montecito (p367) for shopping and people-watching, or hang loose in Carpinteria (p368), a retro beach town.

Four Days

Head east for a stop in arty Ojai (p369), up in the mountains and known for its hot springs and spas, or book a day trip from Ventura (p372) by boat to explore one of the rugged Channel Islands (p374).

) Climb aboard the *Double Dolphin,* a 50ft sailing catamaran, for a two-hour coastal or sunset cruise ($35). Seasonal whale-watching trips ($40) and quick half-hour spins around the harbor to view marine life ($18) are more kid-friendly. It also offers kayak and SUP rentals and tours.

Condor Express CRUISE
(Map p346; 805-882-0088; www.condorcruises.com; 301 W Cabrillo Blvd; 2½/4½hr cruises adult from $50/99, child 5-12yr from $30/50;) Take a whale-watching excursion aboard the high-speed catamaran *Condor Express.* Whale sightings are guaranteed, so if you miss out the first time, you'll get a free voucher for another cruise.

Sunset Kidd's Sailing Cruises CRUISE
(Map p346; 805-962-8222; www.sunsetkidd.com; 125 Harbor Way; cruises $40) Float in an 18-passenger sailboat on a 2½-hour whale-watching trip or a two-hour morning, afternoon, sunset-cocktail or full-moon cruise. Reservations recommended.

Surfing

Unless you're a novice, conditions are too mellow in summer – come back in winter when ocean swells kick back up. Santa Barbara's **Leadbetter Point** is best for beginners. Experts-only **Rincon Point** awaits just outside Carpinteria.

Surf-n-Wear's Beach House SURFING
(Map p346; 805-963-1281; www.surfnwear.com; 10 State St; rental per hour/day wetsuit $4/16, bodyboard $4/16, surfboard $10/35, SUP set per day $50; 9am-6pm Sun-Thu, to 7pm Fri & Sat) Not far from Stearns Wharf, you can rent soft (foam) boards, bodyboards, wetsuits and SUP sets from this 1960s surf shop. It also sells modern and vintage surfboards, unique T-shirts and hoodies, colorful bikinis, shades, beach bags and flip-flops.

Hiking

Gorgeous day hikes await in the foothills of the Santa Ynez Mountains and elsewhere in the Los Padres National Forest. Most trails cut through rugged chaparral and steep canyons – sweat it out and savor jaw-dropping coastal views. Spring and fall are the best seasons for hiking, when temperatures are moderate. Always carry plenty of extra water and watch out for poison oak.

To find even more local trails to explore, browse Santa Barbara Hikes online (www.santabarbarahikes.com) or visit the Los Padres National Forest Headquarters (p355), west of the airport.

SANTA BARBARA FOR CHILDREN

Santa Barbara abounds with family-friendly fun for kids of all ages, from tots to tweens.

MOXI (p337) Santa Barbara's newest hands-on, kid-friendly attraction.

Santa Barbara Museum of Natural History (p338) Giant skeletons, an insect wall and a pitch-dark planetarium captivate kids' imaginations. It's a 0.5-mile drive uphill from the mission.

Santa Barbara Maritime Museum (p339) Peer through a periscope, reel in a virtual fish, watch underwater films or check out the model ships.

Santa Barbara Sailing Center (p342) Short sails around the harbor let young 'uns see sea lions up close.

Sea Center (p338) From touch tanks full of tide-pool critters and crawl-through aquariums to whale sing-alongs, it's interactive and educational. Hourly parking on the wharf costs $2.50.

Lil' Toot water taxi (p357) Take a joyride along the waterfront on this tiny yellow boat.

Chase Palm Park (Map p346; www.santabarbaraca.gov/gov/depts/parksrec; 323 E Cabrillo Blvd; ⌚sunrise-10pm; 👪) FREE Antique-carousel rides ($2, cash only) plus a shipwreck-themed playground decked out with seashells and a miniature lighthouse.

Arroyo Burro Beach County Park (p339) A wide, sandy beach, away from the tourists but not too far from downtown.

Tours

★Architectural Foundation of Santa Barbara — WALKING

(☎805-965-6307; www.afsb.org; adult $10, child under 12yr free; ⌚10am Sat & Sun weather permitting) Take time out of your weekend for a fascinating 90-minute guided walking tour of downtown's art, history and architecture. No reservations required; call or check the website for meet-up times and places.

Santa Barbara Trolley — BUS

(Map p346; ☎805-965-0353; www.sbtrolley.com; adult $22, child 3-12yr $8; ⌚10am-3pm; 👪) Biodiesel-fueled trolleys make a narrated 90-minute one-way loop stopping at 14 major tourist attractions around the city, including the mission and the zoo. They start from the visitor center (hourly departures 10am to 3pm) and the hop-on, hop-off tickets are valid all day (and one consecutive day) – pay the driver directly, or buy discounted tickets online in advance.

Land & Sea Tours — TOURS

(Map p346; ☎805-683-7600; www.out2seesb.com; 99 W Cabrillo Blvd; adult $30, child 2-9yr $15; ⌚noon & 2pm, also 4pm daily May-Oct; 👪) If you dig James Bond–style vehicles, take a narrated tour of the city on the *Land Shark,* an amphibious vehicle that drives right into the water. Trips depart from Stearns Wharf; buy tickets onboard (no reservations).

Festivals & Events

To find out what's happening now, check the events calendars at www.santabarbaraca.com and www.independent.com.

Santa Barbara International Film Festival — FILM

(☎805-963-0023; http://sbiff.org; 1528 Chapala St, Suite 203; from $60; ⌚late Jan-early Feb) Film buffs and Hollywood A-list stars show up for screenings of more than 200 independent US and foreign films.

I Madonnari Italian Street Painting Festival — ART, FOOD

(www.imadonnarifestival.com; ⌚Memorial Day weekend, generally last weekend in May; 👪; 🚌6, 11) FREE Colorful chalk drawings adorn Mission Santa Barbara's sidewalks over Memorial Day weekend, with Italian-food vendors and arts-and-crafts booths too.

★Summer Solstice Celebration — FESTIVAL

(☎805-965-3396; www.solsticeparade.com; ⌚late Jun) FREE Kicking off summer, this wildly popular and wacky float parade down State St feels like something out of Burning Man. Live music, kids' activities, food stands, a wine-and-beer garden and an arts-and-craft show happen all weekend long.

Santa Barbara County Fair FAIR
(805-925-8824; www.santamariafairpark.com; Santa Maria Fairpark, 937 S Thornburg St, Santa Maria; adult/child $10/8, child under 5yr free; mid-Jul;) This old-fashioned county fair combines agriculture exhibits, carnival rides and lots of food and wine. The fairgrounds are in Santa Maria, over an hour's drive northwest of Santa Barbara via Hwy 101.

French Festival CULTURE, ART
(805-963-8198; www.frenchfestival.com; Oak Park; mid-Jul; ; 3) FREE California's biggest Francophile celebration has lots of food and wine, world music and dancing, a mock Eiffel Tower and Moulin Rouge and even a poodle parade.

★**Old Spanish Days Fiesta** CULTURE, ART
(www.oldspanishdays-fiesta.org; late Jul-early Aug) FREE The entire city fills up for this long-running – if slightly overblown – festival celebrating Santa Barbara's Spanish and Mexican colonial heritage. Festivities include outdoor bazaars and food markets, live music, flamenco dancing, horseback and rodeo events and a big ole parade.

Sleeping

Prepare for sticker shock: even basic motel rooms by the beach command over $200 in summer. Don't arrive without reservations and expect to find anything reasonably priced, especially not on weekends. A good selection of renovated motels are tucked between the harbor and the 101 freeway, just about walking distance to everything. Cheaper motels cluster along upper State St and Hwy 101 northbound to Goleta and southbound to Carpinteria, Ventura and Camarillo.

★**Santa Barbara Auto Camp** CAMPGROUND $$
(888-405-7553; http://autocamp.com/sb; 2717 De La Vina St; d $175-215; P) Ramp up the retro chic and bed down with vintage style in one of five shiny metal Airstream trailers parked near upper State St, north of downtown. All five architect-designed trailers have unique perks, such as a clawfoot tub or extra twin-size beds for kiddos, as well as full kitchen and complimentary cruiser bikes to borrow.

Book ahead; two-night minimum may apply. Pet fee $25.

Agave Inn MOTEL $$
(805-687-6009; www.agaveinnsb.com; 3222 State St; r from $119; P) While it's still just a motel at heart, this boutique-on-a-budget property's 'Mexican pop meets modern' motif livens things up with a color palette from a Frida Kahlo painting. Flatscreen TVs, microwaves, minifridges and aircon make it a standout option. Family-sized rooms have a kitchenette and pull-out sofa beds. It's a little north of town so a car is a necessity, or good walking shoes.

Castillo Inn MOTEL $$
(Map p346; 800-965-8570; www.sbcastilloinn.com; 22 Castillo St; r from $175; P@) Minutes from West Beach, the harbor and Stearns Wharf, you can't get better priced accommodations in central Santa Barbara than at the Castillo Inn. The simply decorated rooms at this spruced-up motel are large and bright and a continental breakfast (just fruit and muffins) is included in the rate. Some rooms have terraces.

Harbor House Inn MOTEL $$
(Map p346; 805-962-9745; www.harborhouseinn.com; 104 Bath St; r from $180; P) Down by the harbor, this friendly, converted motel offers brightly lit studios with hardwood floors and a beachy design scheme. Most have full kitchen and one has a fireplace. Rates include a welcome basket of breakfast goodies (with a two-night minimum stay) and beach towels, chairs, umbrellas and three-speed bicycles to borrow.

Hotel Indigo BOUTIQUE HOTEL $$
(Map p346; 805-966-6586; www.indigosantabarbara.com; 121 State St; r from $180; P@) Poised between downtown and the beach, this petite Euro-chic boutique hotel has all the right touches: curated contemporary-art displays, outdoor terraces

SANTA BARBARA ART WALKS

Prime time for downtown gallery hopping is **First Thursday** (www.santabarbaradowntown.com), from 5pm to 8pm on the first Thursday of every month, when art galleries on and off State St throw open their doors for new exhibitions, artists' receptions, wine tastings and live music, all free. Closer to the beach but similar in aim is the **Funk Zone Art Walk** (http://funkzone.net), happening on a bimonthly basis from 5pm to 8pm and featuring free events and entertainment at offbeat art galleries, bars and restaurants.

Downtown Santa Barbara

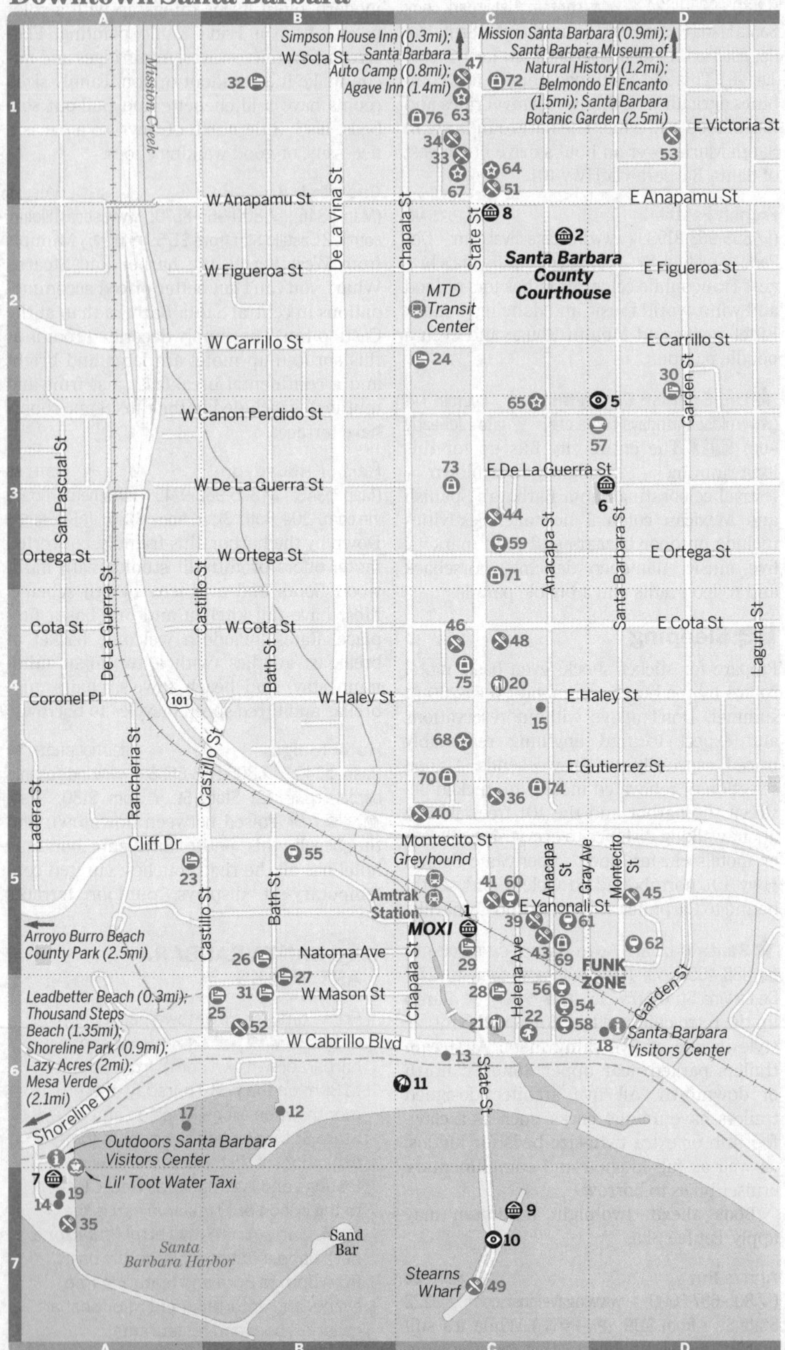
Simpson House Inn (0.3mi); Santa Barbara Auto Camp (0.8mi); Agave Inn (1.4mi)
Mission Santa Barbara (0.9mi); Santa Barbara Museum of Natural History (1.2mi); Belmondo El Encanto (1.5mi); Santa Barbara Botanic Garden (2.5mi)
W Sola St
Mission Creek
E Victoria St
W Anapamu St
E Anapamu St
De La Vina St
Chapala St
State St
Santa Barbara County Courthouse
W Figueroa St
E Figueroa St
MTD Transit Center
W Carrillo St
E Carrillo St
Garden St
W Canon Perdido St
E De La Guerra St
W De La Guerra St
San Pascual St
Ortega St
W Ortega St
E Ortega St
Anacapa St
Santa Barbara St
Castillo St
Cota St
W Cota St
E Cota St
Laguna St
De La Guerra St
Bath St
Coronel Pl
W Haley St
E Haley St
Rancheria St
E Gutierrez St
Ladera St
Cliff Dr
Montecito St
Greyhound
Amtrak Station
MOXI
E Yanonali St
Gray Ave
Helena Ave
FUNK ZONE
Arroyo Burro Beach County Park (2.5mi)
Natoma Ave
W Mason St
Leadbetter Beach (0.3mi); Thousand Steps Beach (1.35mi); Shoreline Park (0.9mi); Lazy Acres (2mi); Mesa Verde (2.1mi)
W Cabrillo Blvd
Santa Barbara Visitors Center
Shoreline Dr
Outdoors Santa Barbara Visitors Center
Lil' Toot Water Taxi
Santa Barbara Harbor
Sand Bar
Stearns Wharf

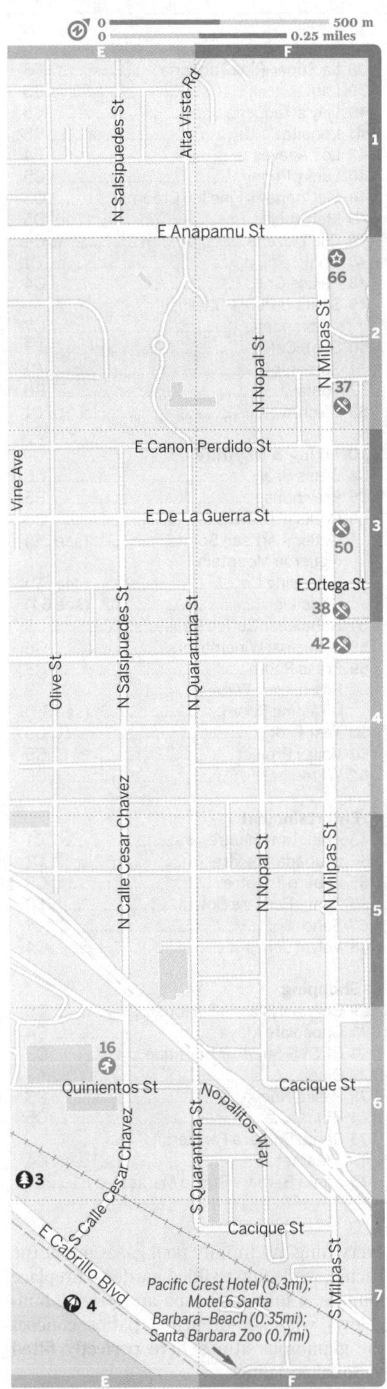

and ecofriendly green-design elements. Peruse local-interest and art-history books in the library nook, or retreat to your room and wrap yourself up in a plush bathrobe. Parking $30. Pet fee $40.

Marina Beach Motel MOTEL **$$**

(Map p346; ☎805-963-9311; www.marinabeachmotel.com; 21 Bath St; r from $155; P❄📶🐾) Family-owned since 1942, this whitewashed, one-story motor lodge that wraps around a grassy courtyard is worth a stay just for the location. Right by the beach, tidy remodeled rooms are comfy enough and some have kitchenette. Complimentary beach-cruiser bikes to borrow. Small pets OK (fee $15).

Franciscan Inn MOTEL **$$**

(Map p346; ☎805-963-8845; www.franciscaninn.com; 109 Bath St; r $155-215; P❄📶🏊) Settle into the relaxing charms of this Spanish Colonial two-story motel just over a block from the beach. Rooms differ in shape and decor, but some have kitchenette and all evince French-country charm. Embrace the friendly vibe, afternoon cookies and outdoor pool.

Motel 6 Santa Barbara-Beach MOTEL **$$**

(☎805-564-1392; www.motel6.com; 443 Corona del Mar; r $100-210; P❄📶🏊🐾) The very first Motel 6 to 'leave the light on for you' has been remodeled with IKEA-esque contemporary design, flat-screen TVs and multimedia stations. It fills nightly; book ahead. Wi-fi costs $3 extra every 24 hours. Pet fee $10.

★ **Hotel Californian** BOUTIQUE HOTEL **$$$**

(Map p346; www.thehotelcalifornian.com; 36 State St; r from $400; P❄📶🏊) Hotel Californian is the new kid on the once-rundown block that is the lower end of State St. Spearheading the area's rehabilitation, it would be worth staying just for the prime location (next to the beach, Stearns Wharf and the Funk Zone) but its appeal goes way beyond geography. A winning architectural mix of Spanish Colonial and North African Moorish styles set a glamorous tone.

★ **Pacific Crest Hotel** BOUTIQUE HOTEL **$$$**

(☎805-966-3103; www.pacificcrestsantabarbara.com; 433 Corona del Mar Dr; r from $235; P📶🏊) 🍃 Wonderfully friendly Greg and Jennifer make sure all guests feel at home at their boutique motel, close to East Beach and the zoo. Landscaped grounds welcome you, rooms are spacious (bathrooms are small but plans are afoot to enlarge them) and come in cool, neutral tones that provide a soothing experience.

Downtown Santa Barbara

★ **Belmondo El Encanto** LUXURY HOTEL $$$
(☎805-845-5800; www.elencanto.com; 800 Alvarado Pl; r from $475; P ❄ @ ☜ ≋ 🐾) Triumphantly reborn in 2013, this 1908 icon of Santa Barbara style is a hilltop hideaway for travelers who demand the very best of everything. An infinity pool gazes out at the Pacific, while flower-filled gardens, fireplace lounges, a full-service spa and private bungalows with sun-drenched patios concoct the glamorous atmosphere perfectly fitted to SoCal socialites.

CAMPING & CABINS AROUND SANTA BARBARA

You won't find a campground anywhere near downtown Santa Barbara, but less than a half-hour drive west via Hwy 101, right on the ocean, are **El Capitán & Refugio State Beaches** (reservations 800-444-7275; www.reserveamerica.com; off Hwy 101; tent & RV drive-up sites $35, hike-&-bike tent sites $10; P). You'll also find family-friendly campgrounds with varying amenities in the mountainous **Los Padres National Forest** (877-444-6777; www.recreation.gov; Paradise Rd, off Hwy 154; campsites $30) and at **Cachuma Lake Recreation Area** (Map p38; info 805-686-5055, reservations 805-568-2460; http://reservations.sbparks.org; 2225 Hwy 154; campsites $25-45, yurts $65-90, cabins $110-140; P), closer to Santa Barbara's Wine Country.

★Inn of the Spanish Garden BOUTIQUE HOTEL $$$
(Map p346; 805-564-4700; www.spanishgardeninn.com; 915 Garden St; r from $309; P) At this Spanish Colonial–style inn, casual elegance, first-rate service and a romantic central courtyard will have you lording about like the don of your own private villa. Rooms have a balcony or patio, beds have luxurious linens and bathrooms have oversized tubs. The concierge service is top-notch. Palms surround a small outdoor pool, or unwind with a massage in your room.

Simpson House Inn B&B $$$
(805-963-7067; www.simpsonhouseinn.com; 121 E Arrellaga St; r $325-610; P) Whether you book an elegant room with a claw-foot bathtub or a sweet cottage with a fireplace, you'll be pampered at this Victorian-era estate ensconced by English-style gardens. From gourmet vegetarian breakfasts through to evening wine, hors d'oeuvres and sweets receptions, you'll be well fed too. In-room mod cons include Netflix. Complimentary bicycles and beach gear to borrow.

The hotel is perfect for a romantic break and is for adults only.

Canary Hotel BOUTIQUE HOTEL $$$
(Map p346; 805-884-0300; www.canarysantabarbara.com; 31 W Carrillo St; r $325-575; P@) On a busy block downtown, this grand multistory hotel has a rooftop pool and sunset-watching perch for cocktails. Stylish accommodations show off four-poster beds and all mod cons. In-room spa services, Saturday yoga classes and bathroom goodies will soothe away stress, but ambient street noise may leave you sleepless (ask for an upper floor). Complimentary fitness-center access and cruiser bicycles.

Hungry? Taste local farm goodness at the hotel's downstairs restaurant, Finch & Fork.

Parking is $35; pets are welcome and stay for free.

White Jasmine Inn B&B $$$
(Map p346; 805-966-0589; www.whitejasmineinnsantabarbara.com; 1327 Bath St; r $170-350; P) Tucked behind a jasmine-entwined wooden fence, this cheery inn stitches together an arts-and-crafts bungalow and two quaint cottages. Rooms all have private bath and fireplace, most are air-conditioned and come with Jacuzzi. Full breakfast basket delivered daily to your door. No children under 12 years old allowed.

Brisas del Mar HOTEL $$$
(Map p346; 805-966-2219; http://brisasdelmarinn.com; 223 Castillo St; r from $210; P@) Kudos for all the freebies (DVDs, continental breakfast, afternoon wine and cheese, evening milk and cookies), the newer Mediterranean-style front section and the helpful staff. The outdoor pool and mountain-view sun decks are great for winding down after a day of sightseeing. It's on a noisy street three blocks north of the beach, so ask for a room in the back.

Eating

Restaurants abound along downtown's State St and by the waterfront, where you'll find a few gems among the touristy claptrap. More creative kitchens are found in the Funk Zone, while east of downtown, Milpas St has great taco shops. It's wise to book well in advance (a couple of weeks) for popular places or somewhere you're particularly keen to eat.

★Corazon Cocina MEXICAN $
(Map p346; 805-845-0282; www.facebook.com/sbcorazoncocina; 38 W Victoria St; 11am-9pm Tue-Sat, to 8pm Sun & Mon) The usual Mexican crowd-pleasers are all here (tacos *al pastor,* quesadillas, agua fresca) but made to such

perfection that previous versions pale in comparison. Head into the Santa Barbara Public Market and prepare to get food drunk (and to wait a while – it's popular).

★La Super-Rica Taqueria MEXICAN $

(Map p346; ☎805-963-4940; 622 N Milpas St; ⏰11am-9pm Thu-Mon) It's small, there's usually a line and the decor is basic, but all that's forgotten once you've tried the most authentic Mexican food in Santa Barbara. The fish tacos, tamales and other Mexican staples have been drawing locals and visitors here for decades, and were loved by TV chef and author Julia Childs.

★Lucky Penny PIZZA $

(Map p346; ☎805-284-0358; www.luckypennysb.com; 127 Anacapa St; pizzas $10-16; ⏰11am-9pm Sun-Thu, to 10pm Fri & Sat; 🌶) Shiny exterior walls covered in copper pennies herald a brilliant pizza experience inside this Funk Zone favorite, right beside the Lark (p352). Always jam-packed, it's worth the wait for a crispy pizza topped with a variety of fresh ingredients, many vegetarian-friendly, or a wood-oven-fired lamb-and-pork-meatball sandwich. The coffee is taken seriously too.

★McConnell's Fine Ice Creams DESSERTS $

(Map p346; ☎805-324-4402; www.mcconnells.com; 728 State St; pints from $10; ⏰11am-10pm Sun-Thu, to 11pm Fri & Sat; 👪) Just try walking past this place on State St if you have a sweet tooth. A Santa Barbara institution since 1949, McConnell's uses local milk and other ingredients to produce an array of flavors, from the classics such as chocolate and vanilla to the adventurous like Turkish coffee and cardamom and gingersnaps.

★Arigato Sushi JAPANESE $

(Map p346; ☎805-965-6074; www.arigatosb.com; 1225 State St; rolls from $7; ⏰5:30-10pm Sun-Thu, to 10:30pm Fri & Sat; ❄🌶) Phenomenally popular Arigato Sushi always has people milling around waiting for a table (no reservations taken) but it's worth the wait. Traditional and more unusual sushi, including lots of vegetarian options, plus salads and a dizzying array of hot and cold starters will make you order a sake pronto just to help you get through the menu.

It's noisy and bustling so not the place for a romantic dinner, unless you nab a table on the small patio on State St. Diners at the bar get to see the chefs in action right in front of them.

Dawn Patrol BREAKFAST $

(Map p346; ☎805-962-2889; www.dawnpatrolsb.com; 324 State St; breakfast $6-13; ⏰7:30am-2pm; 🌶) Bright and colorful decor helps wake you up, and the option to build your own hash breakfast ($12.50) sets you up for exploring Santa Barbara. Bread is housemade and other ingredients are locally sourced. Add a coffee, smoothie or a mimosa (go on, you're on vacation) and you have a great start to the day.

Shop Cafe BREAKFAST $

(Map p346; ☎805-845-1696; 730 N Milpas St; breakfast $6.50-15; ⏰8am-3pm; 🐾) Away from the hustle of State St, the Shop still gets crowded thanks to its top-quality breakfast offerings. The poached eggs on toast are on the healthier end of the menu spectrum. In the opposite direction are the Yolo (fried chicken, biscuit and gravy) and the Tugboat (eggs Benedict with your choice of protein).

Los Agaves MEXICAN $

(Map p346; ☎805-564-2626; www.los-agaves.com; 600 N Milpas St; mains $9.25-16.95; ⏰11am-9pm Mon-Fri, 9am-9pm Sat & Sun) In the heart of east Santa Barbara's Mexican culinary scene, Los Agaves stands out for its well-cooked food and hacienda-style decor. Start with the zucchini-blossom quesadillas if they're in season and then take your pick from the mostly seafood and meat dishes. There's always a wait but that allows you time to peruse the menu carefully.

El Buen Gusto MEXICAN $

(Map p346; ☎805-962-2200; 836 N Milpas St; dishes $2-8; ⏰8am-9pm; Ⓟ) At this red-brick strip-mall joint, order authentic south-of-the-border tacos, tortas, quesadillas and burritos with an agua fresca (fruit drink) or cold Pacifico beer. Mexican music videos and soccer games blare from the TVs. *Menudo* (tripe soup) and *birria* (spicy meat stew) are weekend specials.

Metropulos DELI $

(Map p346; ☎805-899-2300; www.metrofinefoods.com; 216 E Yanonali St; dishes $2-10; ⏰8:30am-5pm Mon-Fri, 10am-5pm Sat) Before a day at the beach, pick up custom-made sandwiches and fresh salads at this gourmet deli in the Funk Zone. Artisan breads, imported cheeses, cured meats, and California olives and wines will be bursting out of your picnic basket.

Lilly's Taquería MEXICAN $

(Map p346; ☎805-966-9180; http://lillystacos.com; 310 Chapala St; items from $1.60; ⏰10:30am-9pm Sun, Mon, Wed & Thu, to 10pm Fri & Sat) There's almost always a line roping around this downtown taco shack at lunchtime. But it goes fast, so you'd best be snappy with your order – the *adobada* (marinated pork) and *lengua* (beef tongue) are standout choices. Second location in Goleta, west of the airport, off Hwy 101.

Loquita TAPAS $

(Map p346; ☎805-880-3380; http://loquitasb.com; 202 State St; mains from $11; ⏰5-10pm Sun-Wed, to midnight Thu-Sat, 10am-2pm Sun brunch; 🍷) Spanish tapas done the Spanish way – simply and with top-quality ingredients. The wine list is a curated best-of-Spain selection, too, so pair your *pulpo* (octopus) with a crisp Albariño and eat with a smile on your face. Or loosen your belt for one of the best paellas this side of the Atlantic. Sunday's popular flamenco brunch is great fun.

★ **Mesa Verde** VEGAN $$

(☎805-963-4474; http://mesaverderestaurant.com; 1919 Cliff Dr; mains $15-21; ⏰11am-9pm; 🍷) 🌿 Perusing the menu is usually a quick job for vegetarians – but not at Mesa Verde. There are so many delicious, innovative all-vegan dishes on offer here (the tacos with jackfruit are a highlight) that meat-avoiding procrastinators will be in torment. If in doubt, pick a selection and brace yourself for flavor-packed delights. Meat-eaters welcome (and possibly converted).

Desserts are equally inspired – don't hesitate to try the chocolate ganache if it's available.

The location is in a residential neighborhood west of the action, but it's a quick drive to get here and most definitely worth the effort.

★ **Santa Barbara Shellfish Company** SEAFOOD $$

(Map p346; ☎805-966-6676; http://shellfishco.com; 230 Stearns Wharf; dishes $4-19; ⏰11am-9pm; 👪🐾) 'From sea to skillet to plate' sums up this end-of-the-wharf seafood shack that's more of a buzzing counter joint than a sit-down restaurant. Chase away the seagulls as you chow down on garlic-baked clams, crab cakes and coconut-fried shrimp at wooden picnic tables outside. Awesome lobster bisque, ocean views and the same location for almost 40 years.

Boathouse CALIFORNIAN $$

(☎805-898-2628; http://boathousesb.com; 2981 Cliff Dr; mains from $14; ⏰7:30am-close; 🍷👪) Water views and ocean air accompany your healthy dining at the Boathouse, right on Arroyo Burro Beach (p339). The outdoor patio is great for enjoying a cocktail and fancy salad with other beachgoers, while the walls inside display photos paying homage to the area's surfing and rowing heritage.

Opal CALIFORNIAN $$

(Map p346; ☎805-966-9676; http://opalrestaurantandbar.com; mains $16-30; ⏰11:30am-2:30pm Mon-Sat, 5-10pm Sun-Thu, 5-11pm Fri & Sat; 🍷) Start with a cocktail (martinis are a specialty) and take your time choosing from the inventive dishes on this Californian-cuisine-meets-French-bistro-style restaurant at the top end of State St. Strong flavors are brought together and work well in things like the homemade basil fettuccine with tiger shrimp or lemongrass salmon with Thai curry. Wine pairings are suggested for each dish.

Depending on how you're feeling, you'll either find the large open-plan dining space buzzing or noisy.

Toma MEDITERRANEAN $$

(Map p346; ☎805-962-0777; www.tomarestaurant.com; 324 W Cabrillo Blvd; ⏰5pm-close) Enjoy a glass of wine or a cocktail before tucking into some tasty pasta, flat breads or meat and seafood dishes at one of Santa Barbara's most popular restaurants. The decor's not the most exciting but the food more than compensates. Book well in advance.

Olio Pizzeria ITALIAN $$

(Map p346; ☎805-899-2699; www.oliopizzeria.com; 11 W Victoria St; shared plates $5-24, pizzas $15-21; ⏰11:30am-10pm; 🍷) Just around the corner from State St, this high-ceilinged pizzeria with a happening wine bar proffers crispy, wood-oven-baked pizzas, platters of imported cheeses and meats, garden-fresh *insalate* (salads), savory traditional Italian antipasti and sweet *dolci* (desserts). The entrance is off the parking-lot alleyway.

Palace Grill CAJUN, CREOLE $$

(Map p346; ☎805-963-5000; http://palacegrill.com; 8 E Cota St; mains lunch $10-22, dinner $17-32; ⏰11:30am-3pm daily, 5:30-10pm Sun-Thu, 5:30-11pm Fri & Sat; 👪) With all the exuberance of Mardi Gras, this N'awlins-style grill makes totally addictive baskets of housemade muffins and breads, and ginormous (if so-so) plates of jambalaya, gumbo ya-ya, blackened catfish and pecan chicken. Stiff cocktails and indulgent desserts make the grade. Act unsurprised when the staff lead the crowd in a rousing sing-along.

Brophy Brothers SEAFOOD $$

(Map p346; ☎805-966-4418; www.brophybros.com; 119 Harbor Way; mains $19-26; ⏰11am-10pm; P) A longtime favorite for its fresh-off-the-dock fish and seafood, rowdy atmosphere and salty harborside setting. Slightly less claustrophobic tables on the upstairs deck are worth the long wait – they're quieter and have the best ocean views. Or skip the long lines and start knocking back oyster shooters and Bloody Marys with convivial locals at the bar.

★**Yoichi's** JAPANESE $$$

(Map p346; ☎805-962-6627; www.yoichis.com; 230 E Victoria St; set 7-course menu $100; ⏰5-10pm Tue-Sun) Headline: *kaiseki* (traditional Japanese multicourse dining) comes to Santa Barbara and wows locals. It might have limited hours, take a chunk out of your wallet and need to be booked way in advance, but none of that has stopped Yoichi's being hailed as one of Santa Barbara's best (and slightly hidden away) eating experiences.

The set menu consists of seven courses, divided into different types of dishes (soup, sashimi, grilled and so on), each of which delivers on both flavor and presentation thanks to chef Yoichi's culinary skills and the beautiful, handmade, ceramic plates on which he serves his creations. And of course there's top quality and some unusual sakes to try too. It's tucked away on a quiet residential road a few blocks northeast of State St.

★**Lark** CALIFORNIAN $$$

(Map p346; ☎805-284-0370; www.thelarksb.com; 131 Anacapa St; shared plates $7-17, mains $19-48; ⏰5-10pm Tue-Sun, bar to midnight) There's no better place in Santa Barbara County to taste the bountiful farm and fishing goodness of this stretch of SoCal coast. Named after an antique Pullman railway car, this chef-run restaurant in the Funk Zone morphs its menu with the seasons, presenting unique flavor combinations such as crispy Brussels sprouts with dates or harissa and honey chicken. Make reservations. The cocktails and beer deserve serious consideration too.

★**Bouchon** CALIFORNIAN $$$

(Map p346; ☎805-730-1160; www.bouchonsantabarbara.com; 9 W Victoria St; mains $26-36; ⏰5-9pm Sun-Thu, to 10pm Fri & Sat) The perfect, unhurried, follow up to a day in the Wine Country is to feast on the bright, flavorful California cooking at pretty Bouchon (meaning 'wine cork'). A seasonally changing menu spotlights locally grown farm produce and ranched meats that marry beautifully with almost three-dozen regional wines available by the glass. Lovebirds, book a table on the candlelit patio.

Somerset CALIFORNIAN $$$

(Map p346; ☎805-845-7112; http://somersetsb.com; 7 E Anapamu St; mains from $28; ⏰5:30pm-close Mon-Fri, from 5pm Sat & Sun) The decor has an art-deco-meets-the-'70s wow factor and the olive-tree patio is as romantic as it gets at this relative newcomer to Santa Barbara's upscale dining scene. Chef Lauren Hermann is cooking up innovative dishes similar to those that earned her James Beard awards at two LA restaurants, using only local ingredients in creative ways. Book in advance – it's one of the hottest places in town despite some mixed reviews for the food.

Lazy Acres SUPERMARKET

(☎805-564-4410; www.lazyacres.com; 302 Meigs Rd; ⏰7am-11pm Mon-Sat, to 10pm Sun; P) High-quality supermarket standards, plus a salad and soup bar. It's a short drive southwest of town, follow W Carrillo St which turns into Meigs Rd.

Drinking & Nightlife

On lower State St, most of the boisterous watering holes have happy hours, tiny dance floors and rowdy college nights. The Funk Zone's eclectic mix of bars and wine-tasting rooms provides a trendier, more sophisticated alternative.

★**Brass Bear** CRAFT BEER

(Map p346; ☎805-770-7651; www.brassbearbrewing.com; 28 Anacapa St; ⏰noon-9pm Wed & Sun-Mon, to 10pm Thu, to 11pm Fri & Sat) Large glasses of wine and beer and a great grilled cheese make this cozy place, located up an alley off Anacapa (follow the murals), a worthy detour. Friendly staff add to the convivial atmosphere. Just be careful not to drink too much and end up taking some of the for-sale art on the walls home with you.

★**Good Lion** COCKTAIL BAR

(Map p346; ☎805-845-8754; www.goodlioncocktails.com; 1212 State St; ⏰4pm-1am) Grab a cocktail at the beautiful, blue-tiled bar, then grab a book from the shelves and settle into

DON'T MISS

URBAN WINE TRAIL

No wheels to head up to Santa Barbara's Wine Country? No problem. Ramble between over a dozen wine-tasting rooms (and microbreweries, too) downtown and in the Funk Zone near the beach. Pick up the Urban Wine Trail (www.urbanwinetrailsb.com) anywhere along its route. Most tasting rooms are open every afternoon or sometimes into the early evening. On weekends, join the beautiful people rubbing shoulders as they sip outstanding glasses of regional wines and listen to free live music.

For a sociable scene, start at Municipal Winemakers or Corks n' Crowns, both on Anacapa St. Then head up to Yanonali St, turning left for Riverbench Winery Tasting Room; Cutler's Artisan Spirits distillery, a storefront where you can sample bourbon whiskey, vodka and apple liqueur; and Figueroa Mountain Brewing Co. Walk further west to find more wine-tippling spots.

Or turn right on Yanonali St and stop at the Valley Project (p354) for a liquid education about Santa Barbara's five distinct wine-growing regions. A couple of blocks east on Santa Barbara St, Waterline has the Fox Wine tasting room, housed in a cool, multipurpose complex that offers beer and food too.

a leather banquette in this petite place that has a cool Montmartre-turn-of-the-20th-century feel (candles on the tables and absinthe in many of the cocktails helps with the Parisian atmosphere).

★ Municipal Winemakers BAR

(Map p346; ☎805-931-6864; www.municipalwinemakers.com; 22 Anacapa St; tastings $12; ⏰11am-8pm Sun-Wed, to 11pm Thu-Sat; 🐾) Dave, the owner of Municipal Winemakers, studied the vine arts in Australia and France before applying his knowledge in this industrially decorated tasting room and bar. Pale Pink rosé is a staple and hugely popular – enjoy a bottle on the large patio. For food, you can't beat the cheese plate, or at weekends a burger van parks outside.

★ Figueroa Mountain Brewing Co BAR

(Map p346; ☎805-694-2252; www.figmtnbrew.com; 137 Anacapa St; ⏰11am-11pm Sun-Thu, to midnight Fri & Sat) Father and son brewers have brought their gold-medal-winning hoppy IPA, Danish red lager and double IPA from Santa Barbara's Wine Country to the Funk Zone. Knowledgeable staff will help you choose before you clink glasses on the taproom's open-air patio while acoustic acts play. Enter on Yanonali St.

Test Pilot COCKTAIL BAR

(Map p346; ☎805-845-2518; www.testpilotcocktails.com; 211 Helena Ave; ⏰4pm-1am Mon-Thu, 4pm-2am Fri, 2pm-2am Sat, 2pm-1am Sun) Any actual test pilot would be grounded after one of the strong but delicious cocktails at this tiki bar in the Funk Zone. The decor follows a nautical theme; the drinks ($9 to $12) keep it simple with interesting twists on traditional concoctions. Expect foliage in your piña colada.

Waterline BREWERY

(Map p346; ☎805-845-1482; www.waterlinesb.com; 116-120 Santa Barbara St; ⏰varies; 🐾) Extending the Funk Zone a little further east is no bad thing, and Waterline's combination of two taprooms (Topa Topa and Lama Dog), a restaurant (the Nook) serving elevated bar food, a wine-tasting room (Fox Wine) and a clothing, art and accessories section (Guild-ed Table), means you might happily spend longer here than planned.

Riverbench Winery Tasting Room WINE BAR

(Map p346; ☎805-324-4100; www.riverbench.com; 137 Anacapa St; tastings $10; ⏰11am-6pm) Tasting room in the Funk Zone for the Santa Maria Valley vineyard of the same name. Amiable staff can guide you through a selection of Chardonnay and Pinot Noir, or a newer sparkling wine.

Corks n' Crowns BAR

(Map p346; ☎805-845-8600; www.corksandcrowns.com; 32 Anacapa St; tastings $7-20; ⏰11am-7pm, last call for tastings 6pm; 🐾) Sit on the sunny porch or inside the rustic-feel hut by the fire and try out the wines and beers from Santa Barbara in general and a few international destinations too. Tastings come in a flight of three for wine and four for beer – pours are generous. Board games are available – try Jenga after a tasting for added fun.

Cutler's Artisan Spirits DISTILLERY

(Map p346; ☎805-845-4040; http://cutlersartisan.com; 137 Anacapa St; tastings $10; ⏰1-6pm Thu-Sun) Family-run craft distillers producing whiskey, vodka, gin and apple pie (liqueur) since before (and during) Prohibition. The spirits are hard to find in stores so this is your chance to taste and then purchase up to three bottles (the maximum under local law) of their specialty liquors. The gin in particular is highly prized.

Valley Project BAR

(Map p346; ☎805-453-6768; www.thevalleyprojectwines.com; 116 E Yanonali St; tastings $12; ⏰noon-7pm Mon-Thu, to 8pm Fri-Sun) From the sidewalk, passersby stop just to peek through the floor-to-ceiling glass windows at a wall-sized map of Santa Barbara's Wine Country, all hand-drawn in chalk. Inside, wine lovers lean on the tasting bar while sipping flights of locally grown reds and whites.

Press Room PUB

(Map p346; ☎805-963-8121; 15 E Ortega St; ⏰11am-2am) This tiny pub can barely contain the college students and European travelers who cram the place to its seams. Pop in to catch soccer games, stuff the jukebox with quarters and enjoy jovial banter with the bartender.

Hollister Brewing Company BREWERY

(☎805-968-2810; www.hollisterbrewco.com; Camino Real Marketplace, 6980 Marketplace Dr, Goleta; ⏰11am-10pm) With over a dozen microbrews on tap, this place draws serious beer geeks out to Goleta, near the UCSB campus, off Hwy 101. IPAs are the permanent attractions, along with nitrogenated stout. Skip the food, though.

Handlebar Coffee Roasters CAFE

(Map p346; www.handlebarcoffee.com; 128 E Canon Perdido St; ⏰7am-5pm; 🐾) Bicycle-themed coffee shop brewing rich coffee and espresso drinks from small-batch roasted beans. Sit and sip yours on the sunny patio.

Brewhouse BREWERY

(Map p346; ☎805-884-4664; www.sbbrewhouse.com; 229 W Montecito St; ⏰11am-midnight; 📶🐾) Down by the railroad tracks, the boisterous Brewhouse crafts its own unique small-batch beer (Saint Barb's Belgian-style ales rule), serves wines by the glass, dishes up surprisingly good bar food and has cool art and rockin' live music Wednesday to Saturday nights.

☆ Entertainment

Santa Barbara's appreciation of the arts is evidenced not only by the variety of performances available on any given night, but also its gorgeous, often historic venues. For a current calendar of live music and special events, check www.independent.com or www.newspress.com/top/section/scene.

Santa Barbara Bowl LIVE MUSIC

(Map p346; ☎805-962-7411; http://sbbowl.com; 1122 N Milpas St; most tickets $35-125) Built by Works Progress Administration (WPA) artisans during the 1930s Great Depression, this naturally beautiful outdoor stone amphitheater has ocean views from the highest cheap seats. Kick back in the sunshine or under the stars for live rock, jazz and folk concerts in summer. Big-name acts like Brian Wilson, Radiohead and local graduate Jack Johnson have all taken the stage here.

Zodo's Bowling & Beyond BOWLING

(☎805-967-0128; www.zodos.com; 5925 Calle Real, Goleta; bowling lane per hour $22-55, shoe rental $4.50; ⏰8:30am-1:30am Wed-Sat, to midnight Sun-Tue; 👪) With over 40 beers on tap, pool tables and a video arcade (Skee-Ball!), this bowling alley near UCSB is good ol' family fun. Call ahead to get on the wait list and for schedules of open-play lanes and 'Glow Bowling' black-light nights with DJs. From Hwy 101 west of downtown, exit Fairview Ave north.

Arlington Theatre THEATRE

(Map p346; ☎805-963-4408; www.thearlingtontheatre.com; 1317 State St; ⏰box office 10am-6pm Mon-Sat, to 4pm Sun) Harking back to 1931, this Mission Revival–style movie palace has a Spanish courtyard and a star-spangled ceiling. It's a drop-dead gorgeous place to attend a film-festival screening, and has a series of high-profile performers throughout the year.

Velvet Jones MUSIC, COMEDY

(Map p346; ☎805-965-8676; http://velvet-jones.com; 423 State St; most tickets $10-25) Long-running downtown punk and indie dive for rock, hip-hop, comedy and 18-plus DJ nights for the city's college crowd. Many bands stop here between gigs in LA and San Francisco.

Granada Theatre THEATER, MUSIC

(Map p346; ☎805-899-2222; www.granadasb.org; 1214 State St; ⏰box office 10am-5:30pm Mon-Sat, noon-5pm Sun) This beautifully restored 1930s Spanish Moorish–style theater is home to the city's symphony, ballet and opera, as well as touring Broadway shows and big-name musicians.

Lobero Theatre THEATER, MUSIC
(Map p346; ☎805-963-0761; www.lobero.org; 33 E Canon Perdido St) One of California's oldest theaters (founded in 1873) presents modern dance, chamber music, jazz and world-music touring acts and stand-up comedy nights.

Soho LIVE MUSIC
(Map p346; ☎805-962-7776; www.sohosb.com; suite 205, 1221 State St; most tickets $8-50) One unpretentious brick room plus live music almost nightly equals Soho, upstairs inside a downtown office complex behind McDonald's. Lineups range from indie rock, jazz, folk and funk to world beats. Some all-ages shows.

Shopping

Downtown's **State St** is packed with shops of all kinds, and even chain stores conform to the red-roofed architectural style. The lower (beach) end has budget options, with quality and prices going up as the street does. For more local art galleries and indie shops, dive into the **Funk Zone**, east of State St, tucked in south of Hwy 101.

REI SPORTS & OUTDOORS
(Map p346; ☎805-560-1938; www.rei.com; 321 Anacapa St; ⏰10am-9pm Mon-Fri, to 7pm Sat, to 6pm Sun) If you forgot your tent or rock-climbing carabiners at home, the West Coast's most popular independent co-op outdoor retailer is the place to pick up outdoor recreation gear, active clothing, sport shoes and topographic maps.

Santa Barbara Public Market MARKET
(Map p346; ☎805-770-7702; http://sbpublicmarket.com; 38 W Victoria St; ⏰7:30am-10pm Mon-Wed, 7:30am-11pm Thu & Fri, 8am-11pm Sat, 8am-10pm Sun) Noodles, cupcakes, ice cream and Mexican magic from Corazon Cocina (p349) are just some of the tempting food options available at this central market, handy for a break from sightseeing or for takeout picnic provisions. Stop by too for coffee and wine, and have a break in the Garden, where dozens of beers come on tap.

Chocolate Maya CHOCOLATE
(Map p346; ☎805-965-5956; www.chocolatemaya.com; 15 W Gutierrez St; ⏰10am-6pm Mon-Fri, to 5pm Sat, to 4pm Sun) Personally sourced, fair-trade cacao from around the world means the chocolates on offer here not only taste good but make you feel good about yourself for buying them. Truffles are a specialty and ingredients are sometimes unusual (tarragon and pineapple, anyone?). Be adventurous or ask for recommendations.

Santa Barbara Farmers Market MARKET
(Map p346; ☎805-962-5354; www.sbfarmersmarket.org; 500 & 600 blocks of State St; ⏰4-7:30pm Tue mid-Mar–early Nov, 3-6:30pm Tue mid-Nov–mid-Mar, 8:30am-1pm Sat year-round; 👪) Stock up on fresh fruits and veggies, cheese, nuts and honey at the Tuesday Santa Barbara Farmers Market, which also happens again on Saturday morning at the corner of Santa Barbara and Cota Sts.

Diani CLOTHING
(Map p346; ☎805-966-7175; www.dianiboutique.com; 1324 State St, Arlington Plaza; ⏰10am-6pm Mon, 10am-7pm Tue-Sat, 11am-6pm Sun) Carries high-fashion, Euro-inspired designs, with a touch of funky California soul thrown in for good measure. Think Humanoid dresses, Rag & Bone skinny jeans and Stella McCartney sunglasses. A few doors down, Diani has expanded into shoes and homewares.

Channel Islands Surfboards SPORTS & OUTDOORS
(Map p346; ☎805-966-7213; www.cisurfboards.com; 36 Anacapa St; ⏰10am-7pm Mon-Sat, 11am-5pm Sun) Are you ready to take home a handcrafted, Southern California–born surfboard? Down in the Funk Zone, this surf shack is the place for innovative pro-worthy board designs, as well as surfer threads and beanie hats.

CRSVR Sneaker Boutique SHOES, CLOTHING
(Map p346; ☎805-962-2400; www.crsvr.com; 632 State St; ⏰11am-7pm) Check out this sneaker boutique run by DJs, not just for limited-edition Nikes and other athletic-shoe brands, but also T-shirts, jackets, hats and more urban styles for men.

Paseo Nuevo MALL
(Map p346; ☎805-963-7147; www.paseonuevoshopping.com; 651 Paseo Nuevo; ⏰10am-9pm Mon-Fri, 10am-8pm Sat, 11am-7pm Sun) This busy open-air mall is anchored by Macy's and Nordstrom department stores and offers all the usual clothing, accessories and beauty chains you could want, plus a few dining options.

Information

Los Padres National Forest Headquarters
(☎805-968-6640; www.fs.usda.gov/lpnf; 6750 Navigator Way, Goleta; ⏰8am-12pm & 1-4:30pm Mon-Fri) HQ for the whole Los Padres National Forest. Pick up maps, recreation passes etc.

Outdoors Santa Barbara Visitors Center
(Map p346; ☎805-456-8752; http://outdoorsb.sbmm.org; 4th fl, 113 Harbor Way; ⏰11am-5pm) Inside the same building as the maritime

museum, this volunteer-staffed visitor center offers info on Channel Islands National Park and a harbor-view deck.

Santa Barbara Central Library (☎805-564-5608; www.sbplibrary.org; 40 E Anapamu St; ⏰10am-7pm Mon-Thu, 10am-5:30pm Fri & Sat, 1-5pm Sun; 📶) Free internet access for up to two hours (photo ID required). Reserve in advance or try a walk-in.

Santa Barbara Visitors Center (Map p346; ☎805-568-1811, 805-965-3021; www.santabarbaraca.com; 1 Garden St; ⏰9am-5pm Mon-Sat, 10am-5pm Sun, closes 1hr earlier Nov-Jan) Pick up maps and brochures while consulting with the helpful but busy staff. The website offers free downloadable DIY touring maps and itineraries, from famous movie locations to wine trails, art galleries and outdoors fun. Self-pay metered parking lot nearby.

ℹ Getting There & Away

Small **Santa Barbara Airport** (www.flysba.com; 500 Fowler Rd, Goleta; 📶), 9 miles west of downtown via Hwy 101, has scheduled flights to/from LA, San Francisco and other western US cities.

Amtrak (☎800-872-7245; www.amtrak.com; 209 State St) trains run south to LA ($31, 2½ hours) via Carpinteria, Ventura and Burbank's airport, and north to San Luis Obispo ($22, 2¾ hours) and Oakland ($43, 8¾ hours), with stops in Paso Robles, Salinas and San Jose.

Greyhound (Map p346; ☎805-965-7551; www.greyhound.com; 224 Chapala St) operates a few direct buses daily to LA ($15, three hours), Santa Cruz ($42, six hours) and San Francisco ($40, nine hours).

Vista (☎800-438-1112; www.goventura.org) runs frequent daily 'Coastal Express' buses between Santa Barbara and Carpinteria ($3, 25 to 30 minutes) and Ventura ($3, 40 to 70 minutes); check online or call for schedules.

If you're driving on Hwy 101, take the Garden St or Carrillo St exits for downtown.

ℹ Getting Around

TO/FROM THE AIRPORT

A taxi to downtown or the waterfront costs about $30 to $35 plus tip. Car-rental agencies with airport lots include Alamo, Avis, Budget, Enterprise, Hertz and National; reserve in advance.

Santa Barbara Airbus (☎805-964-7759; www.sbairbus.com) shuttles between Los Angeles International Airport (LAX) and Santa Barbara ($49/94 one-way/round-trip, 2½ hours, eight departures daily). The more people in your party, the cheaper the fare. For more discounts, prepay online.

BICYCLE

For bicycle rentals, Wheel Fun Rentals (p342) has two locations close to Stearns Wharf.

GO GREEN IN SANTA BARBARA

Santa Barbara's biggest eco-travel initiative is **Santa Barbara Car Free** (www.santabarbaracarfree.org). Browse the website for tips on seeing the city without your car, plus valuable discounts on accommodations, vacation packages, rail travel and more. Still don't believe it's possible to tour Santa Barbara without a car? Let us show you how to do it.

From LA, hop aboard the *Pacific Surfliner* or *Coast Starlight* for a memorably scenic, partly coastal ride to Santa Barbara's Amtrak station (around 2½ hours), a few blocks from the beach and downtown. Then hoof it or catch one of the electric shuttles that zips north–south along State St and east–west along the waterfront. MTD buses 6 and 11 connect with the shuttle halfway up State St and will get you within walking distance of the famous mission (get off at Los Olivos St and walk uphill). For a DIY cycling tour, **Wheel Fun Rentals** (p342) is a short walk from the train station.

Even Santa Barbara's Wine Country is getting into the sustainable swing of things. More and more vineyards are implementing biodynamic farming techniques and following organic guidelines. Many vintners and oenophiles are starting to think that the more natural the growing process, the better the wine, too. **Sustainable Vine Wine Tours** (p362) whisks you around family-owned sustainable vineyards. Minimize your carbon footprint even further by following Santa Barbara's Urban Wine Trail (www.urbanwinetrailsb.com) on foot. If you love both wine and food, *Edible Santa Barbara* magazine (http://ediblecommunities.com/santabarbara) publishes insightful articles about vineyards and restaurants that are going green. It's available free at many local markets, restaurants and wineries.

Santa Barbara County abounds with ecofriendly outdoor activities, too. Take your pick of hiking trails, cycling routes, ocean kayaking, swimming, surfing or stand up paddle boarding (SUP). If you're going whale-watching, ask around to see if there are any alternative-fueled tour boats with trained onboard naturalists.

CAR

Downtown street parking or parking in any of a dozen municipal lots is free for the first 75 minutes; each additional hour costs $1.50.

LOCAL BUS

Local buses operated by the **Metropolitan Transit District** (MTD; ☎805-963-3366; www.sbmtd.gov) cost $1.75 per ride (exact change, cash only). Equipped with front-loading bike racks, these buses travel all over town and to adjacent communities; ask for a free transfer upon boarding. **MTD Transit Center** (Map p346; ☎805-963-3366; www.sbmtd.gov/passenger-information/transit-center.html; 1020 Chapala St; ⊙6am-7pm Mon-Fri, 9am-5pm Sat & Sun) has details about routes and schedules.

BUS	DESTINATION	FREQUENCY
5	Arroyo Burro Beach	hourly
11	State St, UCSB campus	every 30min
20	Montecito, Summerland, Carpinteria	hourly

SHUTTLE

MTD's electric **Downtown Shuttle** buses run along State St down to Stearns Wharf at 9am and 9:30am, and then every 15 minutes from 10am to 6pm daily. A second **Waterfront Shuttle** travels from Stearns Wharf west to the harbor and east to the zoo every 30 minutes from 10am to 6pm daily. Between Memorial Day (late May) and Labor Day (early September), both routes run every 10 to 15 minutes, including from 6pm to 9pm on Fridays and Saturdays. The fare is 50¢ per ride; transfers between routes are free.

TAXI

Taxis are metered around $3 at flagfall, with an additional $3 to $4 for each mile.

WATER TAXI

Lil' Toot water taxi (Map p346; ☎805-465-6676; www.celebrationsantabarbara.com; 113 Harbor Way; 1-way fare adult/child $5/1; ⊙usually noon-6pm Apr-Oct, hours vary Nov-Mar; 👪) provides an ecofriendly, biodiesel-fueled ride between Stearns Wharf and the harbor, docking in front of the maritime museum. Look for ticket booths on the waterfront. Trips run every half-hour, weather permitting.

SANTA BARBARA WINE COUNTRY

Oak-dotted hillsides, winding country lanes, rows of grapevines stretching as far as the eye can see – it's hard not to gush about the Santa Ynez and Santa Maria Valleys and the Santa Rita Hills wine regions.

This is an area made for do-it-yourself exploring. Locals here are friendly, from longtime landowners and farmers displaying small-town graciousness to vineyard owners who've fled big cities to follow their passion and who will happily share their knowledge and intriguing personal histories in intimate vineyard tasting rooms.

With around 100 local wineries, visiting can seem daunting, but the Santa Ynez Valley's five small towns – Los Olivos, Solvang, Buellton, Santa Ynez and Ballard – are all clustered within 10 miles of one another, so it's easy to stop, shop and eat whenever and wherever you like. Don't worry about sticking to a plan – instead, be captivated by the scenery and pull over wherever looks welcoming.

Wineries

The big-name appellations for Santa Barbara's Wine Country are the Santa Ynez Valley, Santa Maria Valley and Santa Rita Hills, plus smaller Happy Canyon and upstart Ballard Canyon. Wine-tasting rooms abound in Los Olivos and Solvang, handy for anyone with limited time.

The Santa Ynez Valley, where you'll find most of the wineries, lies south of the Santa Maria Valley. Hwy 246 runs east–west, via Solvang, across the bottom of the Santa Ynez Valley, connecting Hwy 101 with Hwy 154. North–south secondary roads bordered by vineyards include Alamo Pintado Rd from Hwy 246 to Los Olivos, and Refugio Rd between Santa Ynez and Ballard.

If you can't stay a night or two, then a half-day trip will allow you to see one winery or tasting room, have lunch and return to Santa Barbara. Otherwise make it a full day and plan to have lunch and possibly dinner before returning to the city.

Foxen Canyon Wine Trail

The scenic Foxen Canyon Wine Trail runs north from Hwy 154, just west of Los Olivos, deep into the heart of the rural Santa Maria Valley. It's a must-see for oenophiles or anyone wanting to get off the beaten path. For the most part, it follows Foxen Canyon Rd, though a couple of top spots lie close to Santa Maria town.

★Foxen WINERY

(Map p358; ☎805-937-4251; www.foxenvineyard.com; 7200 & 7600 Foxen Canyon Rd, Santa Maria; tastings $15-20; ⊙11am-4pm; P) On what was once a working cattle ranch, Foxen crafts

Santa Barbara Wine Country

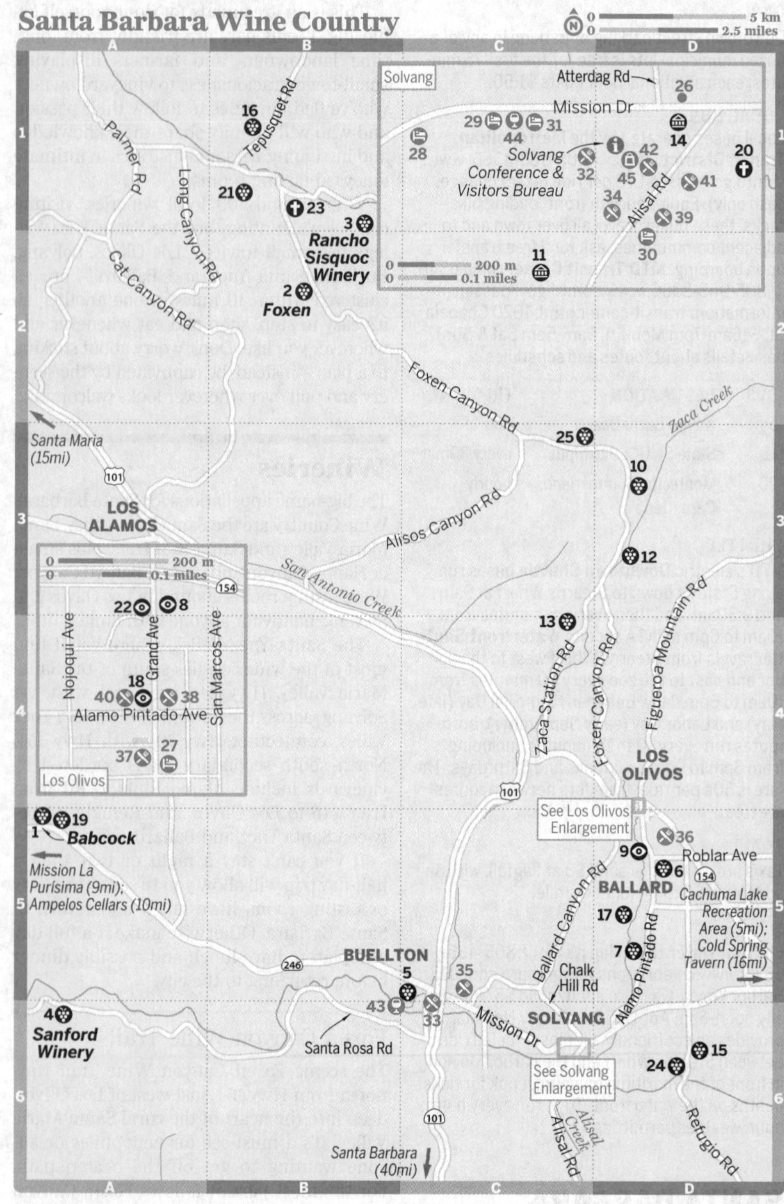

full-fruited Pinot Noir, warm Syrah, steel-cut Chardonnay and rich Rhône-style wines, all sourced from standout vineyards. The newer tasting room (for the Rhône-style tasting) is solar-powered, while the old 'shack' – a former blacksmith's with a corrugated-metal roof, funky-cool decor and leafy patio – pours Bordeaux-style and Cal-Ital varietals.

★ **Rancho Sisquoc Winery** WINERY
(Map p358; ☎805-934-4332; www.ranchosisquoc.com; 6600 Foxen Canyon Rd; tastings $10; ⏰10am-

Santa Barbara Wine Country

Top Sights
1 Babcock ... A5
2 Foxen ... B2
3 Rancho Sisquoc Winery ... B1
4 Sanford Winery ... A6

Sights
5 Alma Rosa Winery & Vineyards ... C5
6 Beckmen Vineyards ... D5
7 Buttonwood Farm Winery & Vineyard ... D5
8 Carhartt Vineyard Tasting Room ... A3
9 Clairmont Farms ... D5
10 Demetria Estate ... D3
11 Elverhøj Museum of History & Art ... C2
12 Fess Parker Winery & Vineyard ... D3
13 Firestone Vineyards ... C4
14 Hans Christian Andersen Museum ... D1
15 Kalyra Winery ... D6
16 Kenneth Volk Vineyards ... B1
17 Lincourt Vineyard ... D5
18 Los Olivos Tasting Room ... A4
19 Melville ... A5
20 Old Mission Santa Ines ... D1
21 Riverbench Vineyard & Winery ... B1
22 Saarloos + Sons ... A3
23 San Ramon Chapel ... B1
24 Sunstone Vineyards & Winery ... D6
25 Zaca Mesa Winery ... C3

Activities, Courses & Tours
Dr J's Bicycle Shop ... (see 26)
26 Santa Barbara Wine Country Cycling Tours ... D1

Sleeping
27 Fess Parker Wine Country Inn & Spa ... A4
28 Hadsten House ... C1
29 Hamlet Inn ... C1
30 Hotel Corque ... D2
31 Landsby ... C1

Eating
32 Aly's ... C1
33 Ellen's Danish Pancake House ... C6
34 First & Oak ... D1
35 Hitching Post II ... C5
Industrial Eats ... (see 5)
36 Los Olivos Grocery ... D5
37 Los Olivos Wine Merchant & Café ... A4
38 Panino ... A4
Paula's Pancake House ... (see 29)
39 Root 246 ... D1
40 Sides Hardware & Shoes ... A4
41 Solvang Bakery ... D1
42 Solvang Restaurant ... D1
Succulent Café ... (see 44)

Drinking & Nightlife
Bottlest Winery, Bar & Bistro ... (see 43)
Copenhagen Sausage Garden ... (see 45)
43 Figueroa Mountain Brewing Co ... B6
44 Solvang Brewing Company ... C1

Shopping
Book Loft ... (see 14)
45 Copenhagen House ... D1

4pm Mon-Thu, to 5pm Fri-Sun) This tranquil gem is worth the extra mileage, not just for the award-winning small-batch reds and whites, but for the delightfully rustic tasting room surrounded by pastoral views. The grounds are perfect for a picnic (fittingly, 'sisquoc' is Chumash for 'gathering place') so bring your own supplies or grab some of the on-site snacks, cheese and salami.

Turn right off Foxen Canyon Rd when you spot **San Ramon Chapel** (Map p358; ☎805-937-1334; www.sanramonchapel.org; Foxen Canyon Rd; ⊙grounds 6:30am-6:30pm; P) FREE, look out for the 'Winery' sign and follow the narrow, partly olive-tree-lined road for a mile or two.

Demetria Estate WINERY
(Map p358; ☎805-686-2345; www.demetriaestate.com; 6701 Foxen Canyon Rd, Los Olivos; tastings $25; ⊙by appointment; P) This hilltop retreat has the curving arches and thick wooden doors of your hospitable Greek uncle's country house, with epic views of vineyards and rolling hillsides. Tastings are by appointment only, but are worth it just to sample the biodynamically farmed Chardonnay, Syrah and Viognier, plus rave-worthy Rhône-style red blends.

Zaca Mesa Winery WINERY
(Map p358; ☎805-688-9339; www.zacamesa.com; 6905 Foxen Canyon Rd, Los Olivos; tastings $15-25, tours $30; ⊙10am-4pm daily year-round, to 5pm Fri & Sat late May-early Sep; 🐾) Stop by this barn-style tasting room for a rustic, sipping-on-the-farm ambience. Santa Barbara's highest-elevation winery, Zaca Mesa specializes in Syrah, but is also known for its estate-grown Rhône varietals and signature Z Cuvée red blend and Z Blanc white blend. An outsized outdoor chessboard and a tree-shaded picnic area that's dog-friendly add to the laid-back atmosphere.

Firestone Vineyards WINERY
(Map p358; ☎805-688-3940; www.firestonewine.com; 5017 Zaca Station Rd; tastings $10-15, incl tour $20; ⊙10am-5pm; P) Founded in the 1970s,

Firestone is Santa Barbara's oldest estate winery. Sweeping views of the vineyard from the sleek, wood-paneled tasting room are nearly as satisfying as the value-priced Cabernet Sauvignon and Bordeaux-style blends for which it's best known. Arrive in time for a winery tour, daily at 11:15am and 1:15pm, plus 3:15pm weekends (no reservations).

Kenneth Volk Vineyards WINERY

(Map p358; ☎805-938-7896; www.volkwines.com; 5230 Tepusquet Rd, Santa Maria; tastings $10; ⏲10:30am-4:30pm Thu-Mon, by appointment Tue & Wed) Only an established cult winemaker could convince oenophiles to drive so far out of their way to taste rare heritage varietals such as floral-scented Malvasia and inky Negrette, as well as standard-bearing Pinot Noir, Chardonnay, Cabernet Sauvignon and Merlot.

Riverbench Vineyard & Winery WINERY

(Map p358; ☎805-937-8340; www.riverbench.com; 6020 Foxen Canyon Rd, Santa Maria; tastings $15; ⏲10am-4pm) Riverbench has been creating prized Pinot Noir and Chardonnay since the early 1970s, and sparkling wines more recently. The rural tasting room is inside a butter-yellow arts-and-crafts farmhouse with panoramic views across the Santa Maria Valley. Out back is a picnic ground and bocce-ball court. Tours, cheese and chocolate pairings and other events available.

You can also sample its wines on Santa Barbara's Urban Wine Trail (p353).

Fess Parker Winery & Vineyard WINERY

(Map p358; ☎800-841-1104; www.fessparkerwines.com; 6200 Foxen Canyon Rd; tastings $14; ⏲10am-5pm) Besides its on-screen appearance as Frass Canyon in the movie *Sideways,* the winery's other claim to fame is its late founder Fess Parker, best known for playing Davy Crockett on TV. Fess has now passed on, but you can still enjoy his winery's award-winning Chardonnay and Pinot Noir on the newly extended patio, and buy a souvenir coonskin-cap-etched glass.

Santa Rita Hills Wine Trail

When it comes to country-road scenery, eco-conscious farming practices and top-notch Pinot Noir, the less-traveled Santa Rita Hills (www.staritahills.com) region holds its own. Almost a dozen tasting rooms line an easy driving loop west of Hwy 101 via Santa Rosa Rd and Hwy 246. Be prepared to share the roads with cyclists and an occasional John Deere tractor. More artisan winemakers hide out in the industrial warehouses of Buellton near Hwy 101 and further afield in Lompoc, where you can combine a visit to La Purísima (p364) mission with an exploration of the town's 'Wine Ghetto,' a concentration of tasting rooms centered on Industrial Way, located on the eastern edge of the town, generally open only at weekends. See www.lompoctrail.com for more information.

★**Babcock** WINERY

(Map p358; ☎805-736-1455; www.babcockwinery.com; 5175 E Hwy 246; tastings $15-18; ⏲11am-5:30pm; P) Hillside, family-owned vineyards overflowing with different grape varietals – Chardonnay, Sauvignon Blanc, Pinot Gris, Pinot Noir, Syrah, Cabernet Sauvignon and more – that let innovative small-lot winemaker Bryan Babcock be the star: 'Slice of Heaven' and 'Ocean's Ghost' Pinot Noirs alone are worthy of a pilgrimage. The eccentrically furnished tasting room offers vintage vinyl for sale and elevated views alongside the wine.

★**Sanford Winery** WINERY

(Map p358; ☎800-426-9463; www.sanfordwinery.com; 5010 Santa Rosa Rd; tastings $20-25; ⏲10am-4pm) Be enchanted by this romantic tasting room built of stone and handmade bricks, embraced by estate vineyards on historic Rancho La Rinconada. Watch the sun sink over the vineyards from the patio with a silky Pinot Noir or citrusy Chardonnay in hand. Hour-long winery tours are given at 11am daily ($50, book at least 48 hours in advance).

Alma Rosa Winery & Vineyards WINERY

(Map p358; ☎805-688-9090; www.almarosawinery.com; 181 Industrial Way; tastings $15; ⏲noon-6:30pm Mon-Fri, from 11am Sat & Sun; P) Richard Sanford left the powerhouse winery bearing his name to start this new winery with his wife, Thekla, using sustainable, organic farming techniques. The vineyard is closed to visitors at the moment, but tastings are held in the stylish, wood-heavy tasting room in Buellton; Pinot Noir, Chardonnay, Pinot Blanc and Pinot Gris are poured.

Ampelos Cellars TASTING ROOM

(☎805-736-9957; www.ampeloscellars.com; 312 N 9th Ave, Lompoc; tastings $10; ⏲11am-5pm Thu-Sun, to 4pm Mon) Danish grower Peter Work and wife Rebecca display their passion for the vine through biodynamic farming techniques and encyclopedic knowledge of their lots. Their Pinot Noir, Syrah and Grenache shine – you can sample them in Lompoc's 'Wine Ghetto,' an industrial area on the eastern edge of the town.

Melville WINERY

(Map p358; ☎805-735-7030; www.melvillewinery.com; 5185 E Hwy 246, Lompoc; tastings $10-20; ⏲11am-4pm Sun-Thu, to 5pm Fri & Sat; P) This beautiful Mediterranean hillside villa gives tastes of estate-grown, small-lot bottled Pinot Noir, Syrah and Chardonnay made by folks who believe in talking about pounds per plant, not tons per acre. Don't think there isn't variety though, with seven different clones of Pinot Noir alone grown. 'Vineyard to Bottle' tours are available noon and 2pm weekends ($25, 75 minutes).

Santa Ynez Valley

One of California's top viticulture regions, the Santa Ynez Valley is a compact area comprising a handful of small towns and dozens of vineyards. Put on the map back in 2004 by the movie *Sideways*, the area still draws the crowds and it's a hugely pleasant place to stay in upmarket lodgings, eat at high-quality restaurants and, of course, enjoy the many fine wines produced here. Los Olivos is the cutest town, Buellton the most down-to-earth, with incongruous Danish Solvang and tiny Santa Ynez and Ballard in between. Popular wineries cluster between Los Olivos and Solvang along Alamo Pintado Rd and Refugio Rd, south of Roblar Ave and west of Hwy 154.

Beckmen Vineyards WINERY

(Map p358; ☎805-688-8664; www.beckmenvineyards.com; 2670 Ontiveros Rd, Solvang; tastings $20; ⏲11am-5pm; P) Bring a picnic to one of the pond-side gazebos at this tranquil winery, where estate-grown Rhône varieties flourish on the unique terroir of Purisima Mountain. Biodynamic farming principles mean natural methods are used to prevent pests. To sample superb Syrah and a cuvée blend with Grenache, Syrah, Mourvèdre and Counoise, follow Roblar Ave west of Hwy 154 to Ontiveros Rd. Vineyard tours are offered at 11am daily ($25 including tasting; reservations required).

Lincourt Vineyard WINERY

(Map p358; ☎805-688-8554; www.lincourtwines.com; 1711 Alamo Pintado Rd, Solvang; tastings from $10; ⏲10am-5pm) Respected winemaker Bill Foley, who also owns Firestone Vineyards (p359) in Foxen Canyon, founded this vineyard in the 1990s on a former dairy farm. Today, the attractive, original 1926 farmhouse (built from a Sears catalog kit) is home to the tasting room: sip finely crafted Chardonnay and Pinot Noir and a dry French-style rosé, all made from locally grown grapes.

BEST SANTA BARBARA WINERIES FOR PICNICS

You won't have any problem finding picnic fare in Santa Barbara's Wine Country. The region is chock-full of local markets, delis and bakeries serving up portable sandwiches and salads. When picnicking at a winery, remember it's polite to buy a bottle of wine before spreading out your feast.

Beckmen Vineyards (p361)

Sunstone Vineyards & Winery (p361)

Zaca Mesa Winery (p359)

Lincourt Vineyard (p361)

Rancho Sisquoc Winery (p358)

Sunstone Vineyards & Winery WINERY

(Map p358; ☎805-688-9463; www.sunstonewinery.com; 125 N Refugio Rd, Santa Ynez; tastings $18; ⏲11am-5pm) Wander inside what looks like an 18th-century stone farmhouse from Provence and into a cool hillside cave housing wine barrels. Sunstone crafts Bordeaux-style wines made from 100% organically grown grapes. Bring a picnic to eat in the courtyard beneath gnarled oaks. Groups (eight or more) can order a wine-paired gourmet lunch to accompany their tasting ($30).

Kalyra Winery WINERY

(Map p358; ☎805-693-8864; www.kalyrawinery.com; 343 N Refugio Rd, Santa Ynez; tastings $12-14; ⏲11am-5pm Mon-Fri, from 10am Sat & Sun; P) Australian Mike Brown traveled halfway around the world to combine his two loves: surfing and winemaking. Try his full-bodied red blends, unusual white varietals or sweet dessert wines (the orange muscat is a crowd-pleaser), all in bottles with Aboriginal-art-inspired labels. Kalyra also pours at Helix, a smaller venue on Buellton's Industrial Way (noon to 5pm Friday to Sunday; $15), close to several other tasting rooms.

Buttonwood Farm Winery & Vineyard WINERY

(Map p358; ☎805-688-3032; www.buttonwoodwinery.com; 1500 Alamo Pintado Rd, Solvang; tastings $10-15; ⏲11am-5pm) Bordeaux

SANTA BARBARA WINE COUNTRY 101

Although large-scale winemaking has only been happening here since the 1980s, the climate of Santa Barbara's Wine Country has always been perfect for growing grapes. Two parallel, transverse mountain ranges – Santa Ynez and San Rafael – cradle the region and funnel coastal fog eastward off the Pacific into the valleys between. The further inland you go, the warmer it gets.

To the west, fog and low clouds may hover all day, keeping the weather crisp even in summer, while only a few miles inland, temperatures approach 100°F in July. These delicately balanced microclimates support two major types of grapes. Nearer the coast in the cooler Santa Maria Valley, Pinot Noir – a particularly fragile grape – and other Burgundian varietals such as Chardonnay thrive. Inland in the hotter Santa Ynez Valley, Rhône-style grapes do best, including Syrah and Viognier.

and Rhône varieties do well in the sun-dappled limestone soil at this friendly winery best for wine-tasting neophytes and dog owners. The trellised back patio, bordering a fruit-tree orchard, is a pleasant spot to relax with a bottle of zingy Sauvignon Blanc.

Tours

Full-day wine-tasting tours average $120 to $160 per person; most leave from Santa Barbara, and some require a minimum number of participants. The website www.sbcountywines.com has a detailed list.

★Sustainable Vine Wine Tours TOURS
(805-698-3911; www.sustainablevinewinetours.com; tours from $150) Biodiesel-van tours of wineries implementing organic and sustainable agricultural practices. Tours include stops at three tasting rooms, behind-the-scenes visits and organic picnic lunches. Pick-ups from any location in the Santa Barbara/Wine Country region.

Wine Edventures TOURS
(805-965-9463; www.welovewines.com; tours $120) Serves up a fun-lovin' side dish of local history and behind-the-scenes wine education on its shuttle-driven tasting tours, one of which visits a microbrewery, too. Price includes a picnic lunch and a bottle of local wine. Pick-ups from just about anywhere in the local area, including many Santa Barbara and Solvang hotels, are free.

Santa Barbara Wine Country Cycling Tours CYCLING
(Map p358; 805-686-9490; www.winecountrycycling.com; 1693 Mission Dr; tours from $170 per person; 9am-6pm Mon-Fri, to 5pm Sat, to 4pm Sun) Guided and DIY bike rides start from the same building as Dr J's (p364) and come in easy to moderate versions – except the Epic Cycling Tours which cover up to 65 miles around the Santa Ynez Valley and out to Jalama Beach (p325). Multiday trips also available.

Los Olivos

The posh ranching town of Los Olivos is many visitors' first stop when exploring Santa Barbara's Wine Country. Its four-block-long main street has rustic wine-tasting rooms, bistros and boutiques seemingly air-lifted straight out of Napa.

Sights

Clairmont Farms FARM
(Map p358; 805-688-7505; www.clairmontfarms.com; 2480 Roblar Ave; 11am-5pm Wed-Mon Apr-Oct, to 4pm Thu-Mon Nov-Mar; P) Natural beauty awaits just outside Los Olivos at this friendly, organic, family-owned farm, where purple lavender fields bloom like a Monet masterpiece, usually peaking mid-June to late July. Cruise the olive-tree-lined drive to the tiny shop selling bath and body products, and enjoy a lavender-scented picnic outside.

Sleeping & Eating

Options are limited and choices aren't cheap around these parts, but the quality is high.

Fess Parker Wine Country Inn & Spa SPA HOTEL $$$
(Map p358; 805-688-7788; www.fessparkerinn.com; 2860 Grand Ave; r from $395; @) Spacious rooms and suites, done out in calming, contemporary design, set the scene at this luxurious spa hotel in the center of Los Olivos. Fireplaces are standard, there's a heated pool and a decent-size gym, and breakfast and a wine tasting are included in the price.

Los Olivos Grocery DELI $

(Map p358; ☎805-688-5115; www.losolivosgrocery.com; 2621 W Hwy 154; ⊙7am-9pm; ✎) Eat in for breakfast or lunch (grab a table on the covered porch) or get sandwiches, artisan breads, salads, specialty cheeses, pickles and everything else you'll need for a vineyard picnic to go. Everything's produced inhouse or locally. It's a couple of minutes southeast of central Los Olivos, just off Hwy 154.

Panino SANDWICHES $

(Map p358; ☎805-688-9304; http://paninorestaurants.com; 2900 Grand Ave; sandwiches $10-12.50; ⊙10am-4pm; ✎) Take your pick from a huge range of gourmet deli sandwiches and salads: curry chicken is a perennial fave, but there are robust vegetarian options too. Order at the counter, then eat outside at an umbrella-covered table. There are other branches around Santa Barbara County, including in nearby Solvang and Santa Ynez.

Los Olivos Wine Merchant & Café CALIFORNIAN, MEDITERRANEAN $$

(Map p358; ☎805-688-7265; www.winemerchantcafe.com; 2879 Grand Ave; mains breakfast $9-12, lunch & dinner $13-29; ⊙11:30am-8:30pm daily, also 8-10:30am Sat & Sun) This wine-country landmark (as seen in *Sideways*) swirls up a casual-chic SoCal ambience with its wisteria-covered trellis entrance. It stays open between lunch and dinner for antipasto platters, hearty salads and crispy pizzas, and wine flights at the bar. Sit inside in the elegant dining room or outside on the covered patio.

★ **Sides Hardware & Shoes** AMERICAN $$$

(Map p358; ☎805-688-4820; http://sidesrestaurant.com; 2375 Alamo Pintado Ave; mains lunch $14-18, dinner $26-35; ⊙11am-2:30pm daily, 5-8:30pm Sun-Thu, to 9pm Fri & Sat; 👪) Behind its historic storefront, this bistro delivers haute country cooking. For lunch you can't beat the burgers, though there are lighter salads and tacos too. In the evenings (book ahead) start with the bacon steak (exactly what it says), followed by the fried chicken with garlicky kale or house-made vegetarian pasta. Sit out on the porch or in the open-plan dining room.

Drinking

Bring a book and buy a bottle of wine during your day-time vineyard visits if you want something to while away your Los Olivos evenings.

Los Olivos Tasting Room TASTING ROOM

(Map p358; ☎805-688-7406; http://site.thelosolivostastingroom.com; 2905 Grand Ave; tastings $10; ⊙11am-5pm) Inside a rickety 19th-century general store, this tasting room stocks rare vintages you won't find anywhere else. Well-oiled servers are by turns loquacious and gruff, but refreshingly blunt in their opinions about local wines, and pours are generous.

Saarloos + Sons TASTING ROOM

(Map p358; ☎805-688-1200; http://saarloosandsons.com; 2971 Grand Ave; tasting fee $10-15; ⊙11am-5pm, last pour 4:30pm) Wine snobs are given the boot at this shabby-chic tasting room pouring estate-grown, small-lot Syrah, Grenache Noir, Cabernet Sauvignon and Sauvignon Blanc. Pair your wine flight with a mini-cupcake and watch Los Olivos go by from the large outdoor deckchairs.

Carhartt Vineyard Tasting Room TASTING ROOM

(Map p358; ☎805-693-5100; www.carharttvineyard.com; 2990a Grand Ave; tasting fee $15; ⊙11am-6pm) An unpretentious tasting room inside a red-trimmed wooden shack that leads on to a shady garden patio out back, where a fun-loving younger crowd sips unfussy Zinfandel, Merlot and 'Not-So Petite' Syrah.

Solvang

Statues of the Little Mermaid and Hans Christian Andersen in the middle of Wine Country can only mean one thing: Solvang. A Danish village founded in 1911 on what was once a 19th-century Spanish-colonial mission, this Santa Ynez Valley town holds tight to its Danish heritage. With its knick-knack stores and cutesy motels, the town is almost as sickly sweet as the Scandinavian pastries sold to the crowds of day-trippers. But a few new businesses are toning down the kitsch and upping the modern-Scandi cool, plus the town has the best sleeping and eating options in the valley, making it a great base for exploration.

Sights

Hans Christian Andersen Museum MUSEUM

(Map p358; ☎805-688-2052; www.solvangca.com/museum; 2nd fl, 1680 Mission Dr; ⊙10am-5pm; 👪) FREE If you remember childhood fairy tales with fondness, stop by this tiny two-room museum. A larger-than-life bust of Denmark's favorite storyteller welcomes you to a mix of original letters, 1st-edition

WORTH A TRIP

MISSION LA PURÍSIMA

One of the most evocative of Southern California's missions, La Purísima was founded in 1787 and completely restored in the 1930s by the Civilian Conservation Corps (CCC). Today it's a **state historic park** (805-733-3713; www.lapurisimamission.org; 2295 Purísima Rd, Lompoc; per car $6; 9am-5pm, tours at 1pm Wed-Sun & public holidays Sep-Jun, daily Jul & Aug; P) with buildings furnished just as they were during Spanish-colonial times. The mission's fields still support livestock, while outdoor gardens are planted with medicinal plants and trees once used by Chumash tribespeople.

Start in the excellent visitor center, where exhibits tell stories of the Chumash, the Spanish missionaries and the work of the CCC. Self-guided visits are the usual way to explore the buildings themselves, though guided tours, lasting 1½ to 2 hours, are available too. The mission is just outside Lompoc, about 16 miles west of Hwy 101 (take Hwy 246 west from Buellton).

copies of his illustrated books, and a model of Andersen's childhood home. It's upstairs in the Book Loft (p366) building.

Elverhøj Museum of History & Art MUSEUM
(Map p358; 805-686-1211; www.elverhoj.org; 1624 Elverhoy Way; suggested donation adult $5, child under 13yr free; 11am-4pm Wed-Sun;) South of downtown, tucked away on a residential side street, this delightful little museum has modest but thoughtful exhibits on Solvang's Danish heritage, as well as Danish culture, art and history.

Old Mission Santa Ínes CHURCH
(Map p358; 805-688-4815; www.missionsantaines.org; 1760 Mission Dr; adult $5, child under 12yr free; 9am-4:30pm; P) Off Hwy 246 just east of Solvang's Alisal Rd, this historic Catholic mission (founded in 1804) was one of the settings for the Chumash revolt in 1824 against Spanish-colonial cruelty. A self-guided tour takes you through a small, dated museum, into the restored church, and through the pretty gardens to the cemetery. It's still an active parish today.

Activities

Solvang is best known by cyclists for the **Solvang Century races** (www.bikescor.com) in March. For self-guided cycling tours, visit www.solvangusa.com and www.bike-santabarbara.org and rent a bike from **Dr J's Bicycle Shop** (Map p358; 805-688-6263; www.drjsbikeshop.com; 1693 Mission Dr; day rates $45-85; 9am-6pm Mon-Fri, 9am-5pm Sat, 10am-4pm Sun).

Sleeping

Choices are the best in the region but sleeping in Solvang isn't cheap, not even at older motels with faux-Danish exteriors. On weekends, rates skyrocket and rooms fill fast, so book ahead.

★**Landsby** BOUTIQUE HOTEL $$
(Map p358; 805-688-3121; www.thelandsby.com; 1576 Mission Dr; r from $149;) Forget Solvang's cheesy Danish side, the Landsby is all about slick contemporary Scandinavian style. The principal decorative themes in this new arrival on the town's sleeping scene are white and wood, but cool design doesn't mean there's not a warm atmosphere. Start your day with the complimentary breakfast and finish it with a drink at the popular lobby bar.

The in-house Mad & Vin restaurant (meaning 'food and wine' in Danish) has similarly chic surroundings and a good menu of classic American dishes (mains $16 to $34).

Hamlet Inn MOTEL $$
(Map p358; 805-688-4413; www.thehamletinn.com; 1532 Mission Dr; r $99-229; P) This remodeled motel is to wine-country lodging what IKEA is to interior design: a budget-friendly, trendy alternative. Crisp, modern rooms have bright Danish-flag bedspreads and iPod docking stations. Free loaner bicycles and a bocce-ball court for guests add to the appeal.

Hadsten House BOUTIQUE HOTEL $$
(Map p358; 805-688-3210; www.hadstenhouse.com; 1450 Mission Dr; r $140-270; P) This revamped motel has luxuriously updated just about everything, except for its routine exterior. Inside, rooms are surprisingly plush, with flat-screen TVs, comfy duvets and high-end bath products. Spa suites come with jet tubs. There's a good in-house restaurant (Tuesday to Saturday).

Hotel Corque BOUTIQUE HOTEL **$$$**
(Map p358; 805-688-8000; www.hotelcorque.com; 400 Alisal Rd; r $179-409;) This clean-lined hotel is a relief from all things Danish. Overpriced rooms may look anonymous, but they're quite spacious. Amenities include an outdoor swimming pool and hot tub, plus access to the next-door fitness center, where you can work off all those Danish butter rings.

Eating

When it comes to eating, the emphasis is most definitely on Danish dishes, with pastry-producing bakeries abounding. A couple of non-Danish standouts provide a break from the sweet stuff though, with innovative menus showing off the rich local produce.

Paula's Pancake House DANISH **$**
(Map p358; 805-688-2867; www.paulaspancakehouse.com; 1531 Mission Dr; pancakes from $6.50; 6am-3pm;) *God Morgen!* Start the day Danish-style with a warm welcome and a hearty breakfast in which, clue in the name, pancakes feature heavily – over 30 years beating batter means Paula knows her stuff. The lunch menu ventures into burgers and sandwiches territory, but with breakfast served all day, there's no wrong time to put away some pancakes.

It's hugely popular and lines are long so prepare to either get here as soon as it opens or to wait a while.

Solvang Restaurant BAKERY **$**
(Map p358; 805-688-4645; www.solvangrestaurant.com; 1672 Copenhagen Dr; items from $4; 6am-3pm or 4pm Mon-Fri, to 5pm Sat & Sun;) Duck around the Danish-inscribed beams with decorative borders to order *aebleskivers* – round pancake popovers covered in powdered sugar and raspberry jam. They're so popular there's even a special takeout window, and if you develop a fondness for them you can buy all the ingredients (and the special pan) to make your own.

Solvang Bakery BAKERY **$**
(Map p358; www.solvangbakery.com; 438 Alisal Rd; items from $3.50; 7am-6:30pm Sun-Thu, to 8pm Fri & Sat;) Gingerbread is a specialty here (have a personalized holiday creation made for you) but that doesn't mean other bestsellers like the almond-butter ring and the jalapeño-cheese bread sit on the shelves for long either. The decor is exactly how you'd want this kind of place's decor to be.

★**First & Oak** CALIFORNIAN **$$**
(Map p358; 805-688-1703; www.firstandoak.com; 409 First St, Mirabelle Inn; mains $12-23; 5:30-8:45pm) Rich, innovative small plates in an elegant but cozy setting make First & Oak Solvang's best dining experience. The menu changes with the seasons but you can expect unusual takes on California cuisine, such as baked beets with bee pollen and whipped goat's cheese or linguini with soft-shell crab and yuzu emulsion. Inventive desserts round off a memorable meal.

★**Succulent Café** CALIFORNIAN **$$**
(Map p358; 805-691-9444; www.succulentcafe.com; 1555 Mission Dr; mains breakfast & lunch $5-15, dinner $16-36; 10am-3pm & 5-9pm Mon & Wed-Sun, from 8:30am Sat & Sun;) An inspired menu allows farm-fresh ingredients to speak for themselves at this family-owned gourmet cafe and market. Fuel up on breakfast biscuits with fried chicken, pulled pork and artisan grilled-cheese sandwiches for lunch, or pumpkin-seed-crusted lamb for dinner. On sunny days, eat outside on the patio, where dogs are welcome (they even have their own menu).

Aly's MODERN AMERICAN **$$$**
(Map p358; 805-697-7082; http://alysbyalebru.com; 451 2nd St; 5-8:45pm Thu-Mon) Fine cuisine isn't usually associated with Solvang, but Aly's meat- and fish-focused dishes hit the mark. The low-lit, simply furnished dining room complements the rich, flavorful food that is sourced locally and prepared with skill. If you're struggling to choose, go with the chef's tasting menu and pair it with carefully selected wines.

Root 246 AMERICAN **$$$**
(Map p358; 805-686-8681; www.root-246.com; 420 Alisal Rd; mains $26-39, brunch buffet adult $27, child 6-12yr $11; 5-9pm Tue-Thu, 5-10pm Fri & Sat, 10am-2pm & 5-9pm Sun) Next to Hotel Corque, chef Bradley Ogden's creative farm-to-table cuisine shows an artful touch. It's hard to beat the chicken and steaks, or come for the Sunday brunch buffet. Make reservations or seat yourself in the sleek fireplace lounge to sip California wines by the glass after 4pm. Service can be hit and miss.

Drinking & Nightlife

After dinner this town is deader than an ancient Viking, with a couple of notable exceptions, listed below.

Copenhagen Sausage Garden BEER GARDEN
(Map p358; ☎805-697-7354; www.csg-solvang.com; 1660 Copenhagen Dr; ⏰10am-midnight) Another sign of Solvang's attempts to stay up late, CSG keeps the beers (and wine) flowing well into the evening on its outdoor patio. Sausages from around the world (little flags on the menu help you choose the country you want, from Spain and Italy to Denmark and the US) provide the snacks, and occasional live music provides the entertainment.

Solvang Brewing Company BREWERY
(Map p358; ☎805-688-2337; http://solvangbrewing.com; 1547 Mission St; ⏰11am-midnight or later, from 4pm Wed) If you're done with wine but not with alcohol then the Brewing Company is the place to head. A decent selection of beers (including a stout and a couple of wheat ales) is complemented by filling pub grub and live music (usually Wednesday to Sunday). Plus it's one of the few places in town that stays open past sundown.

Shopping

Downtown Solvang's notoriously kitschy shops cover a half-dozen blocks south of Mission Dr/Hwy 246 between Atterdag Rd and Alisal Rd. For Danish cookbooks, handcrafted quilts and other homespun items, visit the Elverhøj Museum (p364).

★**Copenhagen House** DESIGN
(Map p358; ☎805-693-5000; http://thecopenhagenhouse.com; 1660 Copenhagen Dr; ⏰10am-5.30pm Mon-Fri, to 6pm Sat & Sun) The name stays true to Solvang's Danish roots but the eclectic mix of top-quality design goods, all from the motherland, couldn't be further from the town's usual tourist tat. Keep kids happy with some Lego, treat yourself to exquisite Pandora jewelry or a Bering watch, or buy some stylish home- and kitchenwares that make you feel cooler just looking at them.

Book Loft BOOKS
(Map p358; ☎805-688-6010; www.bookloftsolvang.com; 1680 Mission Dr; ⏰9am-8pm Tue-Thu, to 9pm Fri & Sat, to 6pm Sun & Mon) Long-running, independent bookshop carrying antiquarian and Scandinavian titles and children's storybooks. The Hans Christian Andersen Museum (p363) is upstairs.

Information

Solvang Conference & Visitors Bureau (Map p358; ☎805-688-6144; www.solvangusa.com; 1639 Copenhagen Dr; ⏰9am-5pm) Pick up free tourist brochures and winery maps at this kiosk in the town center, by the municipal parking lot and public restrooms.

Getting There & Away

Santa Ynez Valley Transit (☎805-688-5452; www.syvt.com; $1.50 each way; ⏰7am-7pm) runs local buses equipped with bike racks on a loop around Buellton, Solvang, Santa Ynez, Ballard and Los Olivos. Buses operate roughly between 7am and 7pm Monday through Saturday; one-way rides cost $1.50 (exact change only).

Buellton

Tiny Buellton was once best known for Andersen's Pea Soup Restaurant, and you can still get heaping bowls of the green stuff, a tradition going back almost 100 years. If split-pea soup doesn't appeal, then the growing drinking (beer as well as wine) and eating scene on Industrial Way, just south of Hwy 246, should do the trick instead.

Eating

★**Industrial Eats** AMERICAN $
(Map p358; ☎805-688-8807; http://industrialeats.com; 181 Industrial Way; mains $9-15; ⏰10am-9pm) Hugely and justifiably popular locals' hangout, housed in an eclectically decorated warehouse on Buellton's coolest street. Pizzas have traditional to what-the? toppings (eg duck and pistachio); the small plates are huge, innovative and eminently shareable; and the wine and beer are top-notch. On a changing menu perennial favorites include the shrimp and pancetta on toast combo and the beef-tongue Reuben.

Ellen's Danish Pancake House BREAKFAST $
(Map p358; ☎805-688-5312; www.ellensdanishpancakehouse.com; 272 Ave of Flags; mains $10-15; ⏰6am-8pm, to 2pm Mon; P) West of Hwy 101, just off Hwy 246, this old-fashioned, always-busy diner is where locals congregate for friendly service and the Wine Country's best Danish pancakes and sausages. Breakfast served all day.

Hitching Post II STEAK $$$
(Map p358; ☎805-688-0676; www.hitchingpost2.com; 406 E Hwy 246; mains $26-55; ⏰5-9:30pm Mon-Fri, from 4pm Sat & Sun; 👪) As seen in the movie *Sideways,* this dark-paneled chophouse offers oak-grilled steaks, pork ribs, smoked duck breast and rack of lamb. Every old-school meal comes with a veggie tray,

garlic bread, shrimp cocktail or soup, salad and potatoes. The Hitching Post makes its own Pinot Noir, and it's damn good (wine tastings at the bar start at 4pm).

 Drinking & Nightlife

Bottlest Winery, Bar & Bistro WINE BAR
(Map p358; ☎805-686-4742; http://avantwines.com; 35 Industrial Way; ⊙11am-9pm, dinner from 5pm) Small plates ($13–24) and dozens of wines come together in this 'winery restaurant,' formerly called Terravant. Step up to the Wine Wall to take your pick from 52 options and then add some crab cakes, pork belly or garden greens with burrata to the mix. Larger, meat and fish meals ($21–39) are also available. Happy hour (3pm to 5pm daily) brings prices down.

Figueroa Mountain Brewing Co BREWERY
(Map p358; ☎805-694-2252; www.figmtnbrew.com; 45 Industrial Way; ⊙11am-9pm; 🐾) Fig Mountain's original brewpub gives you a break from the wine with its award-winning, inhouse-brewed beers: Hoppy Poppy, Danish red lager and Davy Brown ale are three favorites. Soak them up with some great pub grub and enjoy the frequent live music and comedy nights. Or sit outside in the pet-friendly beer garden.

ℹ Getting There & Around

Central Coast Shuttle (☎805-928-1977; www.cclax.com; 1-way/round-trip LA–Buellton $70/128; ⊙info line 8am-7:30pm Mon-Fri, 9:30am-5:30pm Sat & Sun) will bus you from LAX to Buellton (book in advance online to avoid a non-prepaid small additional cost). Amtrak provides a couple of daily connecting Thruway buses to and from Solvang, but only if you're catching a train (or arriving on one) in Santa Barbara.

Santa Ynez Valley Transit runs local buses equipped with bike racks on a loop around Buellton, Solvang, Santa Ynez, Ballard and Los Olivos. You'll need exact change for the fare.

AROUND SANTA BARBARA

Can't quit your day job to follow your bliss? Don't despair: a long weekend in the mountains, valleys and beaches between Santa Barbara and LA will keep you inspired until you can. In this land of daydreams, perfect waves beckon off Ventura's coast, shady trails wind skyward in the Los Padres National Forest and spiritual Zen awaits you in Ojai Valley. Surf, stroll, seek – if outdoor rejuvenation is your goal, this is the place.

And then there's Channel Islands National Park, a biodiverse chain of islands shimmering just off the coast where you can kayak majestic sea caves, scuba dive in wavy kelp forests, wander fields of wildflower blooms or simply disappear from civilization at a remote wilderness campsite.

Montecito

Well-heeled, leafy Montecito, just east of Santa Barbara in the Santa Ynez foothills, is not just home to the rich and famous but to the obscenely rich and the uber-famous.

Though many homes hide behind manicured hedges these days, a taste of the Montecito lifestyle of yesteryear can be experienced by taking a tour of **Casa del Herrero** (☎805-565-5653; http://casadelherrero.com; 1387 E Valley Rd; 90min tour $25; ⊙10am & 2pm Wed & Sat, reservations 9am-5pm Mon-Sat; 🅿). The town's cafe- and boutique-filled main drag is Coast Village Rd (exit Hwy 101 at Olive Mill Rd).

Most visitors base themselves in Santa Barbara and visit Montecito (a 15-minute drive away) as a day trip. Upmarket, beachside Four Seasons Biltmore is an option if money is no object.

From Santa Barbara, MTD (p357) buses 14 and 20 run to and from Montecito ($1.75, 20 minutes, every 40 to 60 minutes); bus 20 also connects Montecito with Summerland and Carpinteria.

Summerland

This drowsy seaside community was founded in the 1880s by HL Williams, a real-estate speculator. Williams was also a spiritualist, whose followers believed in the power of mediums to connect the living with the dead. Spiritualists were rumored to keep hidden rooms for séances – a practice that earned the town the indelicate nickname of 'Spookville.'

Today, those wanting to connect to the past wander the town's antique shops, where you won't find any bargains, but you can ooh and aah over beautiful furniture, jewelry and art from decades or even centuries gone by.

To find the beach, turn south off exit 91 and cross the railroad tracks to cliffside **Lookout Park** (www.countyofsb.org/parks; Lookout Park Rd; 8am-sunset;) FREE which has a kids' playground, picnic tables, barbecue grills and access to a wide, relatively quiet stretch of sand (leashed dogs OK).

Grab breakfast or brunch at the Victorian seaside-style **Summerland Beach Café** (805-969-1019; www.summerlandbeachcafe.com; 2294 Lillie Ave; mains $7-14; 7am-3pm Mon-Fri, to 4pm Sat & Sun;), known for its fluffy omelets, and enjoy the ocean breezes on the patio. Or walk over to **Tinker's** (805-969-1970; 2275 Ortega Hill Rd; items $5-10; 11am-8pm;), an eat-out-of-a-basket burger shack that delivers seasoned curly fries and old-fashioned milkshakes.

From Santa Barbara, MTD bus 20 runs to Summerland ($1.75, 25 minutes, hourly) via Montecito, continuing to Carpinteria.

Carpinteria

Lying 11 miles east of Santa Barbara, the time-warped beach town of Carpinteria – so named because Chumash carpenters once built seafaring canoes here – is a laid-back place. You could easily spend an hour or two wandering in and out of antiques shops and beachy boutiques along Linden Ave, downtown's main street. To gawk at the world's largest vat of guacamole, show up for the California Avocado Festival in early October.

Sights & Activities

If you're an expert surfer, **Rincon Point** has long, glassy, right point-break waves. It's about 3 miles southeast of downtown, off Hwy 101 (exit Bates Rd).

Carpinteria State Beach BEACH
(805-968-1033; www.parks.ca.gov; end of Linden Ave; per car $10; 7am-sunset;) An idyllic, mile-long strand where kids can splash around in calm waters and go tide-pooling along the shoreline. In winter, you may spot harbor seals and sea lions hauled out on the sand, especially if you hike over a mile south along the coast to a bluff-top overlook.

Surf Happens SURFING
(Map p346; 805-966-3613; http://surfhappens.com; 13 E Haley St; 2hr private lesson from $160;) Welcoming families, beginners and 'Surf Happens Sisters,' these highly reviewed classes and camps led by expert staff incorporate the Zen of surfing. In summer, you'll begin your spiritual wave-riding journey. Make reservations in advance. The office is based in downtown Santa Barbara.

Festivals & Events

California Avocado Festival FOOD & DRINK
(www.avofest.com; 800 Linden Ave; early Oct) FREE Still going strong after 30 years, the annual California Avocado Festival is one of the state's largest free events, held in downtown Carpinteria. Bands play, avocado recipes are judged and the world's largest vat of guacamole makes a guest appearance.

Sleeping

Carpinteria's cookie-cutter chain motels and hotels are unexciting, but usually less expensive than those in nearby Santa Barbara.

Carpinteria State Beach Campground CAMPGROUND $
(800-444-7275; www.reserveamerica.com; 205 Palm Ave; tent & RV drive-up sites $45-70, hike-&-bike tent sites $10) Often crowded, this oceanfront campground offers lots of family-friendly amenities including flush toilets, hot showers, picnic tables and barbecue grills. Book ahead (reservations are taken up to seven months in advance).

Eating & Drinking

Tacos Don Roge MEXICAN $
(805-566-6546; www.facebook.com/tacosdonroge; 751 Linden Ave; items from $1.50; 10am-9pm) This Mexican taqueria stakes its reputation on a rainbow-colored salsa bar with up to a dozen different sauces to drizzle on piquant meat-stuffed, double-rolled corn tortillas – try the jalapeño or pineapple versions. If the spiciness gets you, grab an ice cream from Rainbows next door.

Padaro Beach Grill AMERICAN $
(805-566-9800; http://padarobeachgrill.com; 3765 Santa Claus Lane; mains $7-11; usually 10:30am-8pm Mon-Fri, from 11am Sat & Sun;) Off Hwy 101 west of downtown, this oceanfront grill makes darn good burgers (including vegan versions), grilled-fish tacos, sweet-potato fries and thick, hand-mixed milkshakes. The palm-tree-shaded garden is a relaxing place to devour them.

Corktree Cellars CALIFORNIAN $$
(805-684-1400; www.corktreecellars.com; 910 Linden Ave; small plates $7.50-14; usually 11:30am-9pm Tue-Thu & Sun, to 9:30pm Fri & Sat) Downtown's contemporary wine bar and

DON'T MISS

LOTUSLAND

In 1941 the eccentric opera singer and socialite Madame Ganna Walska bought the 37 acres that make up **Lotusland** (☎info 805-969-3767, reservations 805-969-9990; www.lotusland.org; 695 Ashley Rd; adult $45, child 3-18yr $20; ⏰tours by appt 10am & 1:30pm Wed-Sat mid-Feb–mid-Nov; P) with her lover and yoga-guru Theos Bernard. After marrying and then divorcing Bernard, she retained control of the gardens and spent the next four decades tending and expanding this incredible collection of rare and exotic plants from around the world; there are over 140 varieties of aloe alone. Come in summer when the lotuses bloom, typically during July and August.

Reservations are required for tours, but the phone is only attended from 9am to 5pm weekdays, to 1pm Saturday.

bistro offers tasty California-style tapas, charcuterie and cheese plates, and a good number of wine flights ($14).

Rincon Brewery CRAFT BEER
(☎805-684-6044; http://rinconbrewery.com; 5065 Carpinteria Ave; ⏰11am-9:30pm Sun-Thu, to 11pm Fri & Sat) Swap ocean waves for 'waves of grain' (their words) and knock back Belgian-style craft beers (among others) and a long menu of standard but tasty pub grub that keeps this place busy most nights of the week.

Island Brewing Co BREWERY
(☎805-745-8272; www.islandbrewingcompany.com; 5049 6th St, off Linden Ave; ⏰noon-9pm Mon-Thu, noon-10pm Fri, 11am-10pm Sat, 11am-9pm Sun; 🐾) Wanna hang loose with friendly beach bums and drink bourbon-barrel-aged brews? Find this locals-only, industrial space with an outdoor, dog-friendly patio by the railroad tracks – look for the Island sign.

Getting There & Away

Carpinteria is 11 miles east of Santa Barbara via Hwy 101 (southbound exit Linden Ave, northbound Casitas Pass Rd). From Santa Barbara, take MTD (p357) bus 20 ($1.75, 40 minutes, at least hourly) via Montecito and Summerland. **Amtrak** (☎800-872-7245; www.amtrak.com; 475 Linden Ave) has an unstaffed platform downtown; buy tickets online or by phone before catching one of five daily *Pacific Surfliner* trains west to Santa Barbara ($8.50, 15 to 20 minutes) and south to Ventura ($11, 25 minutes) or LA ($29, 2½ hours).

Ojai

Hollywood director Frank Capra chose the Ojai Valley to represent a mythical Shangri-la in his 1937 movie *Lost Horizon*. Today Ojai ('*OH*-hi', from the Chumash word for 'moon') attracts artists, organic farmers, spiritual seekers and anyone ready to indulge in day-spa pampering. Bring shorts and flip-flops: Shangri-la sure gets hot in summer.

Sights & Activities

Ojai Olive Oil Company FARM
(☎805-646-5964; www.ojaioliveoil.com; 1811 Ladera Rd; ⏰9am-4pm Mon-Fri, 10am-4pm Sat) FREE Outside town, family-owned Ojai Olive Oil Company has a tasting room open six days a week, and offers free talks and tours on Wednesdays (1pm to 4pm) and Saturdays (10am to 4pm). It also sells at the Ojai Farmers Market (p372) on Sundays. Dip bread into the various oils (and balsamic vinegars from Modena, its home) – the milder Provençale variety is the most popular.

Meditation Mount VIEWPOINT
(☎805-646-5508; https://meditationmount.org; 10340 Reeves Rd; ⏰8:30am-sunset Wed-Sun) FREE Ojai is famous for the rosy glow that emanates from its mountains at sunset (some days) – the so-called 'Pink Moment.' The ideal vantage point for catching the show is the peaceful lookout atop Meditation Mount. Head east of downtown on Ojai Ave/Hwy 150 for about 2 miles, turn left at Boccali's farm-stand restaurant and drive another 2.5 miles on Reeves Rd (there's some signage) until it heads uphill and dead-ends at a parking lot and meditation center.

As well as the view, the gardens are a scented delight and, in keeping with the name, meditation is available (8:30am guided classes, from 9am until close for private meditation).

Ojai Vineyard Tasting Room WINERY
(☎805-798-3947; www.ojaivineyard.com; 109 S Montgomery St; tastings $15; ⏰noon-6pm) Inside downtown's historic firehouse, Ojai Vineyard pours tastes of its delicate, small-batch

wines. It's best known for standard-bearing Chardonnay, Pinot Noir and Syrah, but the crisp Sauvignon Blanc, dry Riesling and zippy rosé are also worth sampling.

Ojai Valley Trail HIKING
(www.traillink.com/trail/ojai-valley-trail.aspx) FREE Running beside the highway, the 9-mile Ojai Valley Trail, converted from defunct railway tracks, is popular with walkers, runners, cyclists and equestrians. Pick it up downtown two blocks south of Ojai Ave, off Bryant St, then head west through the valley.

Mob Shop CYCLING
(805-272-8102; www.themobshop.com; 110 W Ojai Ave; bicycle rental per hour $12, day $25-50; 10am-5pm Mon & Wed-Fri, 9am-5pm Sat, 9am-4pm Sun) Bike rental (including electric and kid versions) for DIY, two-wheel exploration of Ojai, plus organized tours of the city and surrounding area. Mountain bikers can sign up for a descent of nearby Sulphur Mountain.

Spa Ojai SPA
(855-697-8780; www.ojairesort.com/spa-ojai; Ojai Valley Inn & Spa, 905 Country Club Rd) For the ultimate in relaxation, book a day at top-tier Spa Ojai in the Ojai Valley Inn, where nonresort guests pay an extra $20 to access swimming pools, a workout gym and mind/body fitness classes.

Day Spa of Ojai SPA
(805-640-1100; www.thedayspa.com; 209 N Montgomery St; treatments $21-190; 10:30am-5:30pm) Soothing everyday cares away for two decades now, this family-run operation is the place to come for facials, body wraps and hot-rock treatments for men and women. It specializes in Swedish massages, starting from $88.

Sleeping

Pricey but excellent quality would best describe the local accommodations scene. Book well in advance, especially for weekends.

★ Lavender Inn B&B $$
(805-646-6635; http://lavenderinn.com; 210 E Matilija St; r from $145;) For a central location in a historic 1874 schoolhouse building, you can't beat the Lavender Inn. Room decor ranges from quaint to modern; a hearty, healthy breakfast can be enjoyed on the porch overlooking the pretty garden; and the evening tapas and wine are nice touches.

An on-site spa sees to your relaxation needs, while the in-house cookery courses can satisfy any culinary aspirations. Just remember you *are* allowed to leave to explore Ojai itself, a short walk away.

Ojai Retreat B&B $$
(805-646-2536; www.ojairetreat.com; 160 Besant Rd; r $90-295;) On a hilltop on the outskirts of town, this peaceful place has a back-to-nature collection of 12 country arts-and-crafts-style guest rooms and cottage suites, all perfect for unplugging. Find a quiet nook for reading or writing (no TVs), ramble through the wonderful grounds, or practice your downward dog in a yoga class.

Emerald Iguana Inn BOUTIQUE HOTEL $$
(805-646-5277; www.emeraldiguana.com; 108 Pauline St; r/ste from $179/249;) Sister property of the Blue Iguana Inn, the Emerald Iguana is oriented more toward adults looking for a getaway but within walking distance of downtown Ojai. Local art hangs on the walls, in-room spa treatments can be arranged, and packages include romantic touches (wine, roses and chocolate). Two-bed cottages, complete with full kitchen, are available alongside comfortable standard rooms.

A two-night minimum is usually required. Book well in advance for weekends.

Ojai Rancho Inn MOTEL $$
(805-646-1434; http://ojairanchoinn.com; 615 W Ojai Ave; r $120-200;) At this low-slung motel next to the highway, pine-paneled rooms each have a king bed. Cottage rooms come with fireplaces, and some have Jacuzzis and kitchenettes. Besides competitive rates, the biggest bonuses of staying here are a small pool and sauna, shuffleboard, fire pit, and bicycles to borrow for the half-mile ride to downtown. Pet fee $20.

Blue Iguana Inn INN $$
(805-646-5277; www.blueiguanainn.com; 11794 N Ventura Ave; r/ste from $139/169;) Artsy iguanas lurk everywhere at this funky architect-designed inn – on adobe walls around Mediterranean-tiled fountains and anywhere else that reptilian style could bring out a smile. Roomy bungalow and cottage suites are unique, and the pool is a social scene for LA denizens. Rates include continental breakfast; two-night minimum stay on weekends. Some pets allowed with prior approval only.

For a more central location and romantic atmosphere, try the sister Emerald Iguana Inn, just north of downtown.

Ojai Valley Inn & Spa RESORT $$$

(☎805-646-1111, 855-697-8780; www.ojairesort.com; 905 Country Club Rd; r from $349; P ✻ @ 🛜 ≋ 🐾) At the west end of town, this pampering resort has landscaped gardens, tennis courts, swimming pools, a championship golf course and a fabulous spa. Luxurious rooms are outfitted with all mod cons, and some sport a fireplace and balcony. Recreational activities run the gamut from kids' camps and complimentary bikes to full-moon yoga and astrological readings. Nightly 'service' surcharge is $35.

If the resort's size puts you off, don't worry – a free golf-cart shuttle will whisk you to wherever you want to be.

On-site restaurant Olivella (p372) is one of the best in town.

Eating

You can guarantee top-quality ingredients in Ojai. Organic, sustainable and local are part of everyday culinary life here, and in keeping with the city's bohemian, hippie vibe, vegetarians and vegans will revel in the options available. The main drag, Ojai Ave, has plenty of places serving excellent food, but equally good choices are in out-of the-way but worth-seeking-out locations around town.

★Knead BAKERY, CAFE $

(☎310-770-3282; http://kneadbakingcompany.com; 469 E Ojai Ave; items $3.50-16; ⏲8am-2pm Wed-Sun) Family-run artisan bakery mixing batters with the best of Ojai's fresh fruit, herbs, honey and nuts. Get a slice of sweet tart (the lemon ricotta is sensational), a savory quiche or a made-to-order breakfast sandwich. Saturday's sticky buns fly off the shelves. Enjoy a mimosa, wine or beer too. No credit cards.

HiHo! BURGERS $

(☎805-640-4446; http://hihoburger.com; 401 E Ojai Ave; burgers from $10.95; ⏲11:30am-8pm Wed-Sun) Sometimes even health-conscious Ojai residents just want a burger, fries and a cola. HiHo! in the heart of downtown scratches that itch. It's a simple menu: wagyu-beef patties (vegetarian burgers available) served 'classic' (lettuce, cheese, ketchup) or 'HIHO' (same but with pickles and onion jam). Sit under the umbrellas and forget kale salads exist.

Bonnie Lu's Country Cafe BREAKFAST $

(☎805-646-0207; www.facebook.com/bonnielus; 328 E Ojai Ave; mains from $8; ⏲7am-2:30pm Thu-Tue) Central, and therefore busy (expect to wait at weekends), diner where all your breakfast favorites are available, including a variety of eggs Benedict, pancakes and biscuits with gravy. Not the place for a light start to the day.

Hip Vegan VEGAN $

(☎805-646-1750; www.hipvegancafe.com; 928 E Ojai Ave; mains $9.50-15; ⏲11am-5pm Mon & Thu, to 7pm Fri-Sun; 🖉 👪) 🌿 Tucked back from the street in a tiny garden (look for the arrow on the wall), this locals' kitchen stays true to Ojai's granola-crunching hippie roots with Mexican-leaning salads and sides, Asian-influenced sandwiches and classic SoCal date shakes and teas. The interior is spartan so grab a shaded picnic table outside.

Farmer & the Cook MEXICAN, VEGETARIAN $$

(☎805-640-9608; www.farmerandcook.com; 339 W Roblar Ave; mains $8.50-14.50; ⏲8:30am-8:30pm; 🖉 👪) 🌿 Flavorful, organic, vegetarian (some vegan) homemade Mexican cooking bursts out of this roadside market, which has its own farm nearby. Come for the squash and goat's-cheese tacos or the highly rated *huarache* (tortilla, potatoes, onions, pepper, feta and more), or, at dinner Thursday to Sunday, creative pizzas and a salad bar. Smoothies are available throughout the day.

Boccali's ITALIAN $$

(☎805-646-6116; http://boccalis.com; 3277 Ojai-Santa Paula Rd; mains $10-19; ⏲4-9pm Mon & Tue, from noon Wed-Sun; 🖉 👪) This roadside farm stand with red-and-white-checkered tablecloths does simple, big-portion Italian cooking. Much of the produce is grown behind the restaurant and the fresh tomato salad is often still warm from the garden. The real draws are the wood-oven pizzas and the seasonal strawberry shortcake. It's over 2 miles east of downtown via Ojai Ave.

★Suzanne's Cuisine INTERNATIONAL $$$

(☎805-640-1961; www.suzannescuisine.com; mains $18-36; ⏲11:30am-2:30pm & 5:30pm-close Mon & Wed-Sun) The eclectic menu in this Ojai locals' favorite ranges from French-inspired snails and hearty pasta dishes to healthy salads and excellent meat, fish and seafood options. It's a family-run affair with an attention to detail that reflects the dedication of the eponymous Suzanne. In summer ask for a table on the outside patio overlooking the charming garden.

Olivella CALIFORNIAN $$$

(☎855-697-8780; www.ojairesort.com/dining/olivella-restaurant; 905 Country Club Rd; mains $35-55; ⊙5:30-9pm Wed-Sun;) In the Ojai Valley Inn & Spa, this worth-getting-dressed-up-for (though you don't have to) restaurant is *the* place in Ojai for a special meal. Meat and pasta are the stars of the menu (the Bolognese sauce is a 19th-century chef-family recipe) but salads and fish dishes are equally tasty. Or push the boat out (and loosen the belt) with the four-course experience.

Service is friendly but can be disorganized.

Shopping

★**Bart's Books** BOOKS

(☎805-646-3755; www.bartsbooksojai.com; 302 W Matilija St; ⊙9:30am-sunset) One block north of Ojai Ave, this charming, unique indoor-outdoor space sells new and well-loved tomes. It's been going for well over a half century so demands at least a half-hour browse and a purchase or two – just don't step on the lurking but surprisingly nimble cat.

Ojai Farmers Market MARKET

(☎805-698-5555; www.ojaicertifiedfarmersmarket.com; 300 E Matilija St; ⊙9am-1pm Sun) It's no surprise that in an agriculturally blessed region, Ojai's farmers market is a beauty. There are the usual high-quality fruit and vegetables on offer each Sunday, plus seafood, meat, breads, chocolate, flowers and plants.

Ojai Clothing CLOTHING

(☎805-640-1269; http://ojaiclothing.com; 325 E Ojai Ave; ⊙noon-5pm Mon & Wed-Thu, noon-5:30pm Fri, 10am-5:30pm Sat, 11am-5pm Sun) Equally comfy for doing an interpretive dance or just hanging out, these earth-toned and vibrantly patterned casual pieces for women and men are made from soft cotton knits and woven fabrics.

Human Arts Gallery ARTS & CRAFTS

(☎805-646-1525; www.humanartsgallery.com; 246 E Ojai Ave; ⊙11am-5pm Mon-Sat, noon-5pm Sun) Browse the colorful handmade jewelry, sculpture, woodcarvings, glassworks, folk-art furnishings and more from over 150 American artists. A custom-design service is also available if you want a unique souvenir of your Ojai visit.

Information

Ojai Library (☎805-646-1639; www.vencolibrary.org/locations/ojai-library; 111 E Ojai Ave; ⊙10am-8pm Mon-Thu, noon-5pm Fri-Sun;) Free online computer terminals and wi-fi for public use.

Ojai Ranger Station (☎805-646-4348; www.fs.usda.gov/detail/lpnf; 1190 E Ojai Ave; ⊙8am-4:30pm Mon-Fri) Camping tips and trail maps for hiking to hot springs, waterfalls and mountaintop viewpoints in the Los Padres National Forest.

Ojai Visitors Bureau (☎805-640-3606; www.ojaivisitors.com; 109 N Blanche St; ⊙8am-4pm Mon-Fri) Provides brochures and other material to visitors.

Getting There & Away

Ojai is around 33 miles east of Santa Barbara via scenic Hwy 150, or 15 miles inland (north) from Ventura via Hwy 33. **Gold Coast Transit** (☎805-487-4222; www.goldcoasttransit.org) bus 16 runs from Ventura (including a stop near the Amtrak station) to downtown Ojai ($1.50, 45 minutes, hourly).

Ventura

The primary pushing-off point for Channel Island boat trips, the beach town of San Buenaventura may not look to be the most enchanting coastal city, but it has seaside charms, especially on the historic pier and downtown along Main St, north of Hwy 101 via California St.

Sights

South of Hwy 101 via Harbor Blvd, **Ventura Harbor** is the main departure point for boats to Channel Islands National Park.

Museum of Ventura County MUSEUM

(☎805-653-0323; www.venturamuseum.org; 100 E Main St; adult $5, child 6-17yr $1; ⊙11am-5pm Tue-Sun;) This tiny downtown museum has an excellently eclectic collection that includes exhibits on the local Chumash people and rotating exhibitions of local artists. The highlight though is the George Stuart Historical Figures gallery. An Ojai resident, Stuart made models of famous people from the past to help bring to life historical lectures he gave around the country. Look out for emperor Nero, Vlad Tepes (aka Dracula), Henry VIII (with, sadly, just two of his wives), Hitler and Putin.

San Buenaventura State Beach BEACH
(805-968-1033; www.parks.ca.gov; enter off San Pedro St; per car $10; dawn-dusk;) Along the waterfront off Hwy 101, this long white-sand beach is ideal for swimming, surfing or just lazing on the sand. A recreational cycling path connects to nearby **Emma Wood State Beach**, another popular spot for swimming, surfing and fishing.

Mission San Buenaventura CHURCH
(805-643-4318; www.sanbuenaventuramission.org; 211 E Main St; adult/child $4/2; 10am-5pm, from 9am Sat) Ventura's Spanish-colonial roots go back to this last mission founded by Junípero Serra in California in 1782. A stroll around the mellow parish church leads you through a garden courtyard and a small museum, past statues of saints, centuries-old religious paintings and unusual, unique wooden bells.

Eating

In downtown Ventura, Main St is chockablock with Mexicali taco shops, casual cafes and globally flavored kitchens.

★ **Paradise Pantry** DELI $
(805-641-9440; www.paradisepantry.com; 222 E Main St; sandwiches $12-16; 11am-8:30pm Tue-Thu, to 9:30pm Fri & Sat, Sun hours vary;) On the cafe side of Paradise Pantry you can grab a sandwich, soup, cheese or meat plate in a quietly buzzing atmosphere. On the deli side, you can stock up on supplies for a beach or Channel Island picnic (sandwiches can be made to go) and even grab some wine or beer to wash it all down.

Jolly Oyster SEAFOOD $
(805-798-4944; www.thejollyoyster.com; 911 San Pedro St; items $5-16; 11am-5pm Sat & Sun;) At San Buenaventura State Beach, the Jolly Oyster sells its own farm-raised oysters and clams. The main option is shucking your own (seat yourself at the nearby picnic tables) though their licensed truck prepares oysters on the half shell, baked and fried oysters, clam steamers and a bay-scallop ceviche. One-hour parking free.

Ventura Certified Farmers Market MARKET $
(805-529-6266; http://vccfarmersmarkets.com; cnr Santa Clara & Palm Sts; 8:30am-noon Sat;) Over 45 farmers and food vendors show up each week, offering fresh fruits and vegetables, home-baked bread and ready-made meals – Mediterranean, Mexican and more. Another farmers market sets up at midtown's Pacific View Mall from 9am to 1pm on Wednesdays.

★ **Lure Fish House** SEAFOOD $$$
(805-567-4400; www.lurefishhouse.com; 60 S California St; mains $17-37; 11:30am-9pm Sun-Thu, to 10pm Fri & Sat;) For seafood any fresher, you'd have to catch it yourself off Ventura pier. Go nuts ordering off a stalwart menu of sustainably caught seafood, organic regional farm produce and California wines. Make reservations or turn up at the bar during happy hour (4pm to 6pm Monday to Friday, 11:30am to 6pm Sunday) for strong cocktails, fried calamari and charbroiled oysters.

Drinking & Nightlife

You'll find plenty of rowdy dives down by the harbor and a couple of excellent craft-beer places around town.

★ **Topa Topa Brewing Company** CRAFT BEER
(805-628-9255; http://topatopa.beer; 104 E Thompson Blvd; noon-9pm Mon-Thu, noon-10pm Fri & Sat, 11am-8pm Sun;) Between the freeway and downtown Ventura is not exactly the most salubrious location, but the beer here makes up for the surroundings. Chief Peak IPA takes the medal but all the quality brewed-on-site options are worth trying. Food trucks (a different one every night, see the website for details) feed the hungry.

Surf Brewery BREWERY
(805-644-2739; http://surfbrewery.com; suite A, 4561 Market St; 4-9pm Tue-Thu, from 1pm Fri, noon-9pm Sat, noon-7pm Sun) Operating since 2011, Surf Brewery makes big waves with its hoppy and black IPAs and rye American pale ale. Beer geeks and food trucks gather at the sociable taproom in an industrial area, about 5 miles from downtown (take Hwy 101 southbound, exit Donlon St).

Shopping

★ **Copperfield's** GIFTS & SOUVENIRS
(805-667-8198; www.facebook.com/copperfieldsvta; 242 E Main St; 10am-6pm Mon-Sat, from 11am Sun) Part standard gift shop, part what can only be described as emporium of ephemera, this is the kind of place where you can buy a birthday card one day and an infra-compunctive resonance perversion ray gun the next (your guess is as good as ours). Quirky souvenirs don't come better than this.

Rocket Fizz FOOD & DRINKS
(805-641-1222; www.rocketfizz.com; 315 E Main St; 10:30am-8pm Mon-Thu, to 9pm Fri & Sat, to 7pm Sun) Part of a national retro-style soda-pop and old-fashioned candy-store chain, this is the place for stocking your cooler with all types of so-bad-but-so-good sweets and drinks before a day at the beach.

B on Main GIFTS & SOUVENIRS
(805-643-9309; www.facebook.com/b-on-main; 446 E Main St; 10:30am-6pm Mon-Thu, 10am-7pm Fri & Sat, 11am-5pm Sun) For coastal living, B sells nifty reproductions of vintage surf posters, shabby-chic furnishings, SoCal landscape art, locally made jewelry and beachy clothing for women.

Ormachea JEWELRY
(805-652-0484; www.ormacheajewelry.com; 451 E Main St; 11am-5:30pm Mon-Fri, to 6pm Sat, to 5pm Sun) Run by a third-generation Peruvian jewelry craftsman, Ormachea skillfully hammers out one-of-a-kind, handmade rings, pendants and bangles in a downtown studio.

ARC Foundation Thrift Store VINTAGE
(805-650-861; www.arcvc.org; 265 E Main St; 9am-6pm Mon-Thu, 9am-7pm Fri & Sat, 10am-6pm Sun) Loads of thrift stores, antiques malls and secondhand and vintage shops cluster downtown. Most are on Main St, west of California St, where ARC is always jam-packed with bargain hunters.

Information

Ventura Visitors & Convention Bureau
(805-648-2075; www.ventura-usa.com; 101 S California St; 9am-5pm Mon-Sat, 10am-4pm Sun) Downtown visitor center handing out free maps and tourist brochures. It also contains a gift shop.

Getting There & Away

Ventura is about 30 miles southeast of Santa Barbara via Hwy 101. **Amtrak** (800-872-7245; www.amtrak.com; Harbor Blvd, at Figueroa St) operates five daily trains north to Santa Barbara ($15, 45 minutes) via Carpinteria and south to LA ($24, 2¼ hours). Amtrak's platform station is unstaffed; buy tickets in advance online or by phone. **VCTC** (Ventura County Transportation Commission; 800-438-1112; www.goventura.org) runs several daily 'Coastal Express' buses between downtown Ventura and Santa Barbara ($3, 40 to 70 minutes) via Carpinteria; check online or call for schedules.

Channel Islands National Park

Don't let this off-the-beaten-path **national park** (Map p38; 805-658-5730; www.nps.gov/chis) FREE loiter for too long on your lifetime to-do list. It's easier to access than you might think, and the payoff is immense. Imagine hiking, kayaking, scuba diving, camping and whale-watching, and doing it all amid a raw, end-of-the-world landscape. Rich in unique flora and fauna, tide pools and kelp forests, the islands are home to 145 plant and animal species found nowhere else in the world, earning them the nickname 'California's Galapagos.'

Geographically, the Channel Islands are an eight-island chain off the Southern California coast, stretching from Santa Barbara to San Diego. Five of them – San Miguel, Santa Rosa, Santa Cruz, Anacapa and tiny Santa Barbara – comprise Channel Islands National Park.

Originally the Channel Islands were inhabited by Chumash tribespeople, who were forced to move to mainland Catholic missions by Spanish military forces in the early 1800s. The islands were subsequently taken over by Mexican and American ranchers during the 19th century and the US military in the 20th, until conservation efforts began in the 1970s and '80s.

Sights & Activities

Anacapa and Santa Cruz, the park's most popular islands, are within an hour's boat ride of Ventura. Both are doable day trips, though much larger Santa Cruz is a good overnight camping option. Bring plenty of water, because none is available on either island except at Scorpion Campground on Santa Cruz.

Most visitors arrive during summer, when island conditions are hot, dusty and bone-dry. Better times to visit are during the spring wildflower bloom or in early fall, when the fog clears. Winter can be stormy, but it's also great for wildlife-watching, especially whales.

Before you shove off from the mainland, stop by Ventura Harbor's NPS Visitor Center (p377) for educational natural-history exhibits, a free 25-minute nature film and on weekends and holidays, family-friendly activities and ranger talks.

Santa Cruz Island ISLAND

(www.nps.gov/chis/planyourvisit/santa-cruz-island.htm) Santa Cruz, the Channel Islands' largest at 96 sq miles, claims two mountain ranges and the park's tallest peak, Mt Diablo (2450ft). The western three-quarters is mostly wilderness, managed by the Nature Conservancy and only accessible with a permit (www.nature.org/cruzpermit). The rest, managed by the National Park Service, is ideal for an action-packed day trip or laid-back overnight stay. Boats land at either Prisoners Harbor or Scorpion Anchorage, a short walk from historic Scorpion Ranch.

You can swim, snorkel, dive and kayak here, and there are plenty of hiking options too, starting from Scorpion Anchorage. It's a 1-mile climb to captivating Cavern Point. Views don't get much better than from this windy spot. For a longer jaunt, continue 1.5 miles west, along the North Bluff Trail, to Potato Harbor. The 4.5-mile Scorpion Canyon Loop heads uphill to an old oil well and fantastic views, then drops through Scorpion Canyon to the campground. Alternatively, follow Smugglers Rd all the way to the pebble beach at Smugglers Cove, a strenuous 7.5-mile round-trip. From Prisoners Harbor there are several more strenuous trails including the 18-mile round-trip China Pines hike – your efforts will be rewarded by the chance to see the rare Bishop pine.

There's little shade on the island (so avoid midday summer walks), bring plenty of water (available at Scorpion Anchorage only) and make sure you're at the harbor in plenty of time to catch your return boat, otherwise you'll be stuck overnight.

Anacapa Island ISLAND

(www.nps.gov/chis/planyourvisit/anacapa.htm) Actually three separate islets totaling just over 1 sq mile, Anacapa gives a memorable introduction to the Channel Islands' ecology. It's also the best option if you're short on time. Boats dock year-round on the East Island where, after a short climb, you'll find 2 miles of trails offering fantastic views of island flora, a historic lighthouse, and rocky Middle and West Islands. You're bound to see western gulls too – the world's largest breeding colony is here.

Kayaking, diving, tide-pooling and watching seals and sea lions are popular outdoor activities, while inside the museum at the small visitor center, divers with video cameras occasionally broadcast images to a TV monitor you can watch during spring and summer.

Santa Rosa ISLAND

(www.nps.gov/chis/planyourvisit/santa-rosa-island.htm) The indigenous Chumash people called Santa Rosa 'Wima' (driftwood) because of the redwood logs that often came ashore here, with which they built plank canoes called *tomols*. This 84-sq-mile island has rare Torrey pines, sandy beaches and hundreds of plant and bird species. Beach, canyon and grasslands hiking trails abound, but high winds can make swimming, diving and kayaking tough for anyone but experts.

San Miguel ISLAND

(www.nps.gov/chis/planyourvisit/san-miguel-island.htm) While 14-sq-mile San Miguel can guarantee solitude and a remote wilderness experience, its westernmost location in the Channel Islands chain means it's often windy and shrouded in fog. Some sections are off-limits to protect the island's fragile ecosystem, which includes a caliche forest (hardened calcium-carbonate castings of trees and vegetation) and seasonal colonies of seals and sea lions. Peregrine falcons have been reintroduced, and some of the archeological sites from when the Chumash lived here date back almost 12,000 years.

Santa Barbara ISLAND

(www.nps.gov/chis/planyourvisit/santa-barbara-island.htm) Currently closed because of storm damage to its landing pier, Santa Barbara, only 1 sq mile and the smallest of the islands, is normally a jewel-box for nature lovers. Big, blooming coreopsis, cream cups

ISLAND OF THE BLUE DOLPHINS

For bedtime reading around the campfire, pick up Scott O'Dell's Newbery Medal–winning *Island of the Blue Dolphins*. This young-adult novel was inspired by the true-life story of a girl from the Nicoleño tribe who was left behind on San Nicolas Island during the early 19th century, when her people were forced off the Channel Islands. Incredibly, the girl survived mostly alone on the island for 18 years, before being discovered and brought to the mainland by a hunter in 1853. However, fate was not on her side, and she died just seven weeks later.

and chicory are just a few of the island's memorable plant species. You'll also find the humongous northern elephant seal here as well as Scripps's murrelets, a bird that nests in cliff crevices.

Get more information from the island's small visitor center. For the latest information on when it might open, check the website.

Tours

Most trips require a minimum number of participants, and may be canceled due to high surf or weather conditions.

Aquasports KAYAKING
(☎805-968-7231; www.islandkayaking.com) Aquasports offers day and overnight kayaking trips to Santa Cruz, Anacapa and along the coast near Santa Barbara, led by professional naturalists. Prices vary from $89 to $495, depending on the length of trip and whether you bring your own camping gear and arrange the ferry to the islands yourself.

Raptor Dive Charters DIVING
(☎805-650-7700; www.raptordive.com; 1559 Spinnaker Dr, Ventura) Certified and experienced divers can head out for some underwater action, including night dives, off Anacapa and Santa Cruz Islands. Prices start at $120; equipment rentals are available for a surcharge; and plenty of snacks, sandwiches and drinks are available on board.

Truth Aquatics OUTDOORS
(Map p346; ☎805-962-1127; www.truthaquatics.com; 301 W Cabrillo Blvd, Santa Barbara) Based in Santa Barbara, this long-running outfitter organizes seasonal (usually April to October) diving, kayaking and hiking day trips and three-day, all-inclusive excursions to the Channel Islands aboard specially designed dive boats.

Island Packers CRUISE
(☎805-642-1393; http://islandpackers.com; 1691 Spinnaker Dr, Ventura; Channel Island day trips from $59, wildlife cruises from $68) Main provider of boats for Channel Islands visits, with day trips and overnight camping excursions available. Boats mostly set out from Ventura but a few go from nearby Oxnard. It also offers wildlife cruises year-round, including seasonal whale-watching from late December to mid-April (gray whales) and mid-May through mid-September (blue and humpback whales).

Channel Islands Kayak Center KAYAKING
(☎805-984-5995; www.cikayak.com; 1691 Spinnaker Dr, Ventura; ⊙by appointment only) Book ahead to rent kayaks (from $12.50) and SUPs (from $25) or arrange a private guided kayaking tour of Santa Cruz or Anacapa (from $180 per person, two-person minimum).

Sleeping

Each island has a primitive year-round **campground** (☎reservations 877-444-6777; www.recreation.gov; tent sites $15) with pit toilets and picnic tables. Water is only available on Santa Cruz Island. You must pack everything in and out, including trash. Due to fire danger, campfires aren't allowed, but enclosed, gas campstoves are OK. Advance reservations are required for all island campsites.

CHANNEL ISLANDS NATIONAL PARK CAMPGROUNDS

CAMPGROUND	NUMBER OF SITES	ACCESS FROM BOAT LANDING	DESCRIPTION
Anacapa	7	0.5-mile walk with over 150 stairs	High, rocky, sun-exposed and isolated
Santa Barbara	10	Steep 0.25-mile walk uphill	Large, grassy and surrounded by trails
Santa Cruz (Scorpion Ranch)	31	Flat 0.5-mile walk	Popular with groups, often crowded and partly shady
San Miguel	9	Steep 1-mile walk uphill	Windy, often foggy with volatile weather
Santa Rosa	15	Flat 1.5-mile walk	Eucalyptus grove in a windy canyon

CALIFORNIA'S CHANNEL ISLANDS: PARADISE LOST & FOUND

Human beings have left a heavy footprint on the Channel Islands. Erosion was caused by overgrazing livestock and rabbits fed on native plants. The US military even used San Miguel as a practice bombing range. In 1969 an offshore oil spill engulfed the northern islands in an 800-sq-mile slick, killing thousands of seabirds and mammals. Meanwhile, deep-sea fishing has caused the destruction of three-quarters of the islands' kelp forests, which are key to the marine ecosystem.

Despite past abuses, the future isn't all bleak. Brown pelicans – decimated by the effects of DDT and reduced to one surviving chick in 1970 – have rebounded and are now off the endangered list, with healthy populations on West Anacapa and Santa Barbara Islands. On San Miguel Island, native vegetation has returned a half century after overgrazing sheep were removed. On Santa Cruz Island, the National Park Service and the Nature Conservancy have implemented multiyear plans to eliminate invasive plants and feral pigs.

Information

Channel Islands National Park Visitor Center (Robert J Lagomarsino Visitor Center; 805-658-5730; www.nps.gov/chis; 1901 Spinnaker Dr, Ventura; 8:30am-5pm;) Trip-planning information, books and maps are available on the mainland at the far end of Ventura Harbor. A free video, *A Treasure in the Sea*, gives some background on the islands, and weekends and holidays see ranger-led free programs at 11am and 3pm.

Getting There & Away

You can access the national park by taking a boat from Ventura or Oxnard or a plane from Camarillo. Trips may be canceled anytime due to high surf or weather conditions. Reservations are essential for weekends, holidays and summer trips.

The open seas on the boat ride out to the Channel Islands may feel choppy to landlubbers. To avoid seasickness, sit outside on the lower deck, keep away from the diesel fumes in the back, and focus on the horizon. The outbound trip is typically against the wind and a bit bumpier than the return. Over-the-counter motion-sickness pills (eg Dramamine) can make you drowsy. Boats usually brake when dolphins or whales are spotted – always a welcome distraction from any nausea.

AIR

If you're prone to seasickness or just want a memorable way to get to the Channel Islands, you can take a scenic flight to Santa Rosa or San Miguel with **Channel Islands Aviation** (805-987-1301; www.flycia.com; 305 Durley Ave, Camarillo). Half-day packages include hiking or a guided 4WD tour, while overnight camping excursions are more DIY.

BOAT

Island Packers offers regularly scheduled boat services to all islands, mostly from Ventura, but with a few sailings from Oxnard too. Anacapa and Santa Cruz are closer to the mainland and so less expensive to visit than other islands. Day trips are possible; overnight campers pay an additional surcharge. Be forewarned: if you do camp and seas are rough the following day, you could get stuck for an extra night or more.

Los Angeles

POP 10.1 MILLION

Includes ➡

Best Places to Eat

- ➡ Cassia (p404)
- ➡ Bestia (p399)
- ➡ Otium (p399)
- ➡ Gjelina (p404)
- ➡ Joss Cuisine (p401)

Best Places to Sleep

- ➡ Palihouse (p396)
- ➡ Chateau Marmont (p394)
- ➡ Hotel Indigo (p393)
- ➡ Petit Ermitage (p394)

Why Go?

LA runs deeper than her blond beaches, bosomy hills and ubiquitous beemers would have you believe. She's a myth. A beacon for countless small-town dreamers, rockers and risk-takers, an open-minded angel who encourages her people to live and let live without judgment or shame. She has given us Quentin Tarantino, Jim Morrison and Serena and Venus Williams, spawned skateboarding and gangsta rap, popularized implants, electrolysis and spandex, and has nurtured not just great writers, performers and directors, but also the ground-breaking yogis who first brought Eastern wisdom to the Western world.

LA is best defined by those simple life-affirming moments. A cracked-ice, jazz-age cocktail on Beverly Blvd, a hike high into the Hollywood Hills sagebrush, a pink-washed sunset over a thundering Venice Beach drum circle, the perfect taco. And her night music. There is always night music.

When to Go

Los Angeles

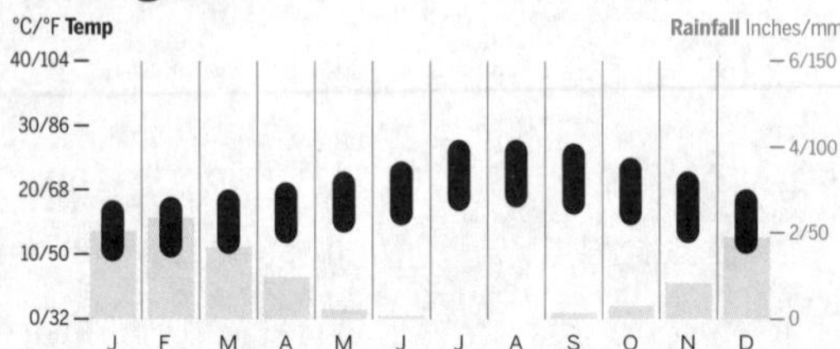

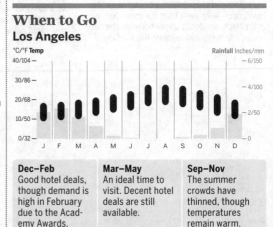

Dec–Feb Good hotel deals, though demand is high in February due to the Academy Awards.

Mar–May An ideal time to visit. Decent hotel deals are still available.

Sep–Nov The summer crowds have thinned, though temperatures remain warm.

Sights & Activities

Downtown Los Angeles & Boyle Heights

Downtown Los Angeles is historical, multi-layered and fascinating. It's a city within a city, alive with young professionals, designers and artists who have snapped up stylish lofts in rehabbed art-deco buildings. The growing gallery district along Main and Spring Sts draws thousands to its monthly art walks.

★ Broad MUSEUM

(Map p384; 213-232-6200; www.thebroad.org; 221 S Grand Ave; 11am-5pm Tue & Wed, to 8pm Thu & Fri, 10am-8pm Sat, to 6pm Sun; P; M Red/Purple Lines to Civic Center/Grand Park) The Broad (rhymes with 'road') is a must-visit for contemporary-art fans. It houses the world-class collection of local philanthropist and real-estate billionaire Eli Broad and his wife Edythe, with more than 2000 postwar pieces by the likes of Cindy Sherman, Jeff Koons, Andy Warhol, Roy Lichtenstein, Robert Rauschenberg, Keith Haring and Kara Walker.

★ Walt Disney Concert Hall NOTABLE BUILDING

(Map p384; 323-850-2000; www.laphil.org; 111 S Grand Ave; guided tours usually noon & 1:15pm Thu-Sat, 10am & 11am Sun; P; M Red/Purple Lines to Civic Center/Grand Park) FREE A molten blend of steel, music and psychedelic architecture, this iconic concert venue is the home base of the Los Angeles Philharmonic, but has also hosted contemporary bands such as Phoenix and classic jazz men such as Sonny Rollins. Frank Gehry pulled out all the stops: the building is a gravity-defying sculpture of heaving and billowing stainless steel.

★ MOCA Grand MUSEUM

(Museum of Contemporary Art; Map p384; 213-626-6222; www.moca.org; 250 S Grand Ave; adult/child $15/free, 5-8pm Thu free; 11am-6pm Mon, Wed & Fri, to 8pm Thu, to 5pm Sat & Sun) MOCA's superlative art collection focuses mainly on works created from the 1940s to the present. There's no shortage of luminaries, among them Mark Rothko, Dan Flavin, Willem de Kooning, and David Hockney, their creations housed in a postmodern building by award-winning architect Arata Isozaki. Galleries are below ground, yet sky-lit bright.

★ Grammy Museum MUSEUM

(Map p384; 213-765-6800; www.grammymuseum.org; 800 W Olympic Blvd; adult/child $13/11; 10:30am-6:30pm Mon-Fri, from 10am Sat & Sun; P) It's the highlight of LA Live (Map p384; 866-548-3452, 213-763-5483; www.lalive.com; 800 W Olympic Blvd; P). Music lovers will get lost in interactive exhibits, which define, differentiate and link musical genres. Spanning three levels, the museum's rotating exhibitions might include threads worn by the likes of Michael Jackson, Whitney Houston and Beyonce, scribbled words from the hands of Count Basie and Taylor Swift and instruments once used by world-renowned rock deities.

Union Station NOTABLE BUILDING

(Map p384; www.amtrak.com; 800 N Alameda St; P) Built on the site of LA's original Chinatown, Union Station opened in 1939 as America's last grand rail station. The marble-floored main hall, with cathedral ceilings, original leather chairs and 3000-pound chandeliers, is breathtaking. The station's Traxx Bar was once the telephone room, complete with operator to place customers' calls. The LA Conservancy runs 2½-hour walking tours of the station on Saturdays at 10am (book online).

Hollywood

No other corner of LA is steeped in as much mythology as Hollywood. It's here that you'll find the Hollywood Walk of Fame, the Capitol Records Tower and Grauman's Chinese Theatre, where the hand- and footprints of entertainment deities are immortalized in concrete. Look beyond the tourist-swamped landmarks of Hollywood Blvd and you'll discover a nuanced, multifaceted neighborhood where industrial streets are punctuated by edgy galleries and boutiques and where steep, sleepy streets harbor the homes of long-gone silver-screen stars.

★ Grauman's Chinese Theatre LANDMARK

(TCL Chinese Theatres; Map p390; 323-461-3331; www.tclchinesetheatres.com; 6925 Hollywood Blvd; guided tour adult/senior/child $16/13.50/8; M Red Line to Hollywood/Highland) Ever wondered what it's like to be in George Clooney's shoes? Just find his footprints in the forecourt of this world-famous movie palace. The exotic pagoda theater – complete with temple bells and stone heaven dogs from China – has shown movies since 1927.

★ Hollywood Museum MUSEUM

(Map p390; 323-464-7776; www.thehollywoodmuseum.com; 1660 N Highland Ave; adult/child $15/5; 10am-5pm Wed-Sun; M Red Line to Hollywood/Highland) For a taste of Old

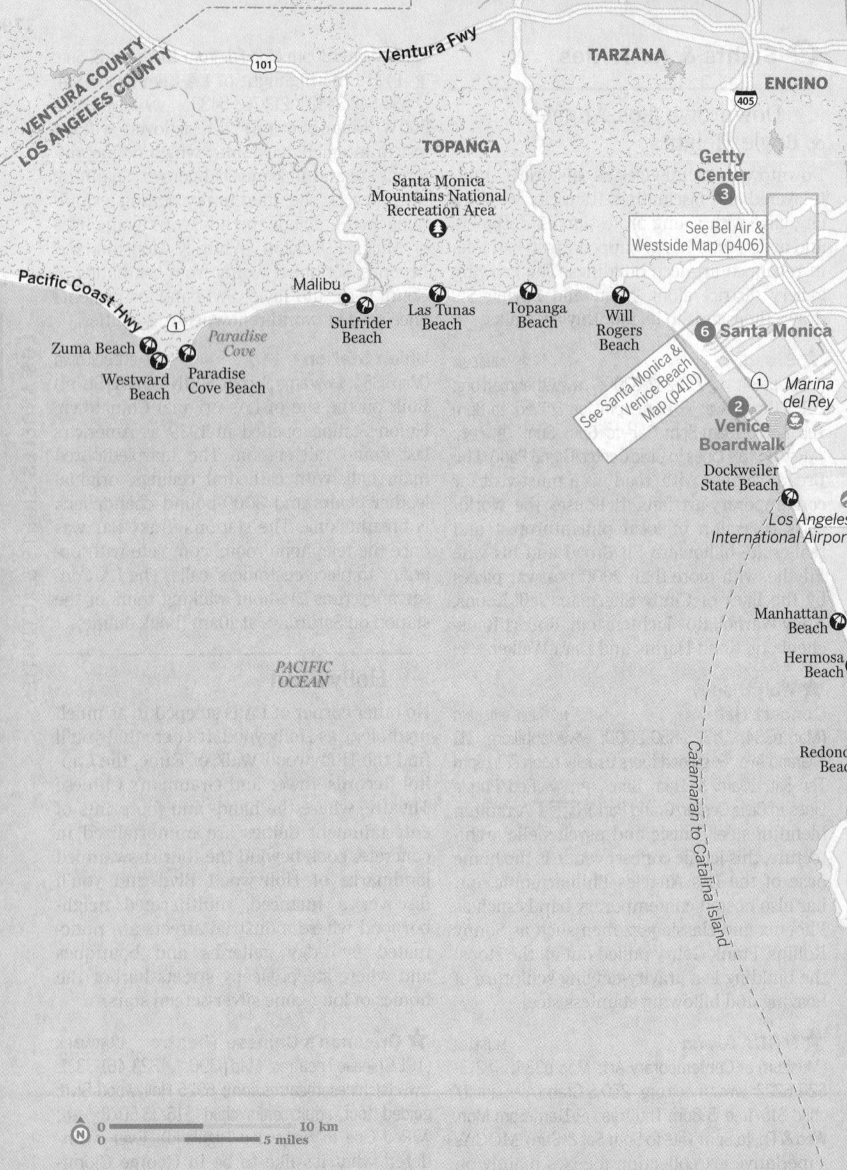

Los Angeles Highlights

1. Checking out LA's oldest buildings, its most glorious movie palaces and many of its hottest restaurants, bars and boutiques **downtown** (p399).

2. Strutting your stuff on **Venice Boardwalk** (p388) – one long, eclectic runway flanked by soaring palms, street artists and bulging Schwarzenegger wannabes.

3. Feeling your spirits soar surrounded by art, architecture, views and gardens at the **Getty Center** (p385).

4. Joining an obligatory stop for culture vultures at the **Los Angeles County Museum**

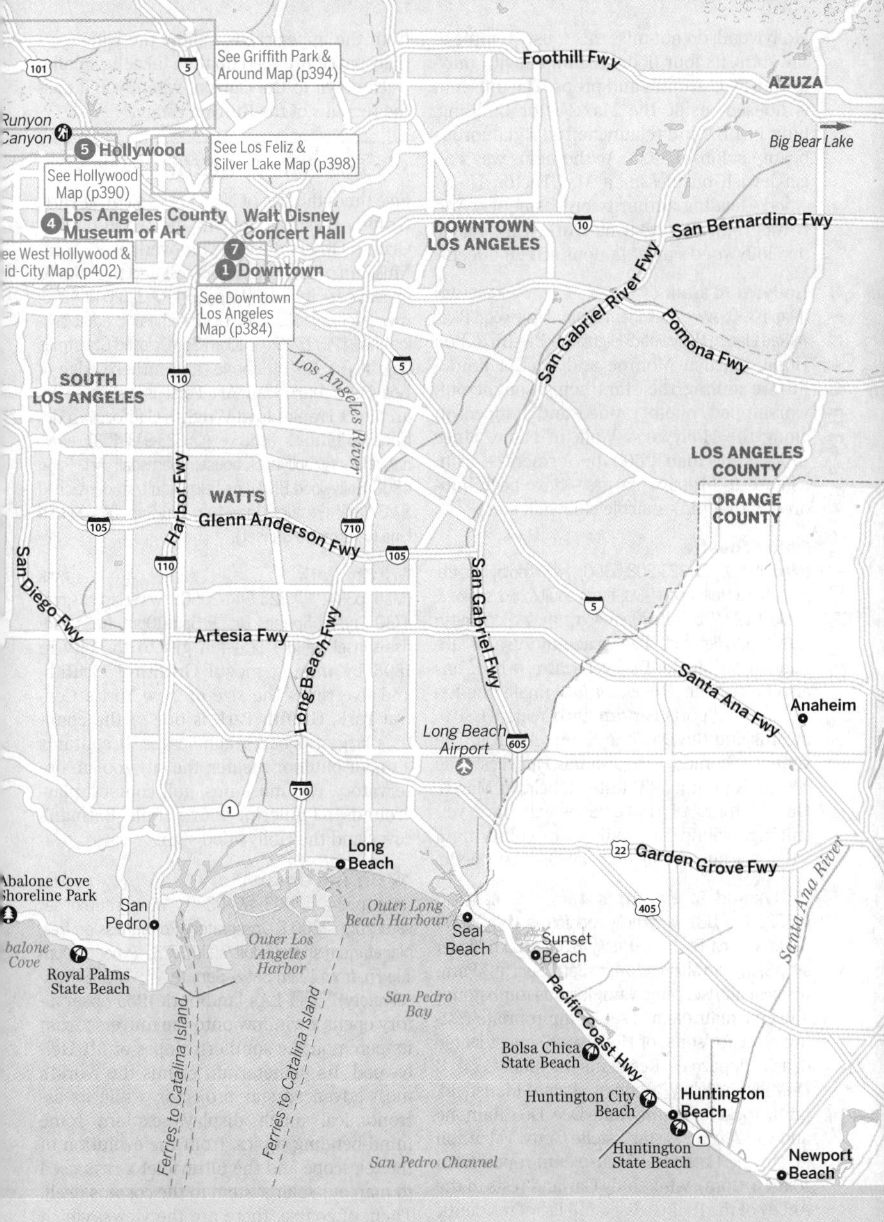

of Art (p383), the largest art museum in the western US and home to 100,000-plus works..

5 Hitting **Hollywood** (p405) bars and clubs for a night of tabloid-worthy decadence and debauchery.

6 Learning to surf, riding a solar-powered Ferris wheel or dipping your toes in the ocean in **Santa Monica** (p387).

7 Marveling at Pritzker Prize–winning architect Frank Gehry's **Walt Disney Concert Hall** (p379) with its undulating steel forms evoking the movement of music itself.

Hollywood, do not miss this musty temple to the stars, its four floors crammed with movie and TV costumes and props. The museum is housed inside the Max Factor Building, built in 1914 and relaunched as a glamorous beauty salon in 1935. At the helm was Polish-Jewish businessman Max Factor, Hollywood's leading authority on cosmetics. And it was right here that he worked his magic on Hollywood's most famous screen queens.

Hollywood Walk of Fame LANDMARK
(Map p390; www.walkoffame.com; Hollywood Blvd; Ⓜ Red Line to Hollywood/Highland) Big Bird, Bob Hope, Marilyn Monroe and Aretha Franklin are among the stars being sought out, worshipped, photographed and stepped on along the Hollywood Walk of Fame. Since 1960 more than 2600 performers – from legends to bit-part players – have been honored with a pink-marble sidewalk star.

Dolby Theatre THEATER
(Map p390; ☎323-308-6300; www.dolbytheatre.com; 6801 Hollywood Blvd; tours adult/child, senior & student $23/18; ⏲10:30am-4pm; P; Ⓜ Red Line to Hollywood/Highland) The Academy Awards are handed out at the Dolby Theatre, which has also hosted the *American Idol* finale, the Excellence in Sports Performance Yearly (ESPY) awards and the Daytime Emmy Awards. The venue is home to the annual PaleyFest, the country's premier TV festival, held in March. Guided tours of the theatre will have you sniffing around the auditorium, admiring a VIP room and nosing up to an Oscar statuette.

Hollywood Forever Cemetery CEMETERY
(☎323-469-1181; www.hollywoodforever.com; 6000 Santa Monica Blvd; ⏲usually 8:30am-5pm, flower shop 9am-5pm Mon-Fri, to 4pm Sat & Sun; P) Paradisiacal landscaping, vainglorious tombstones and epic mausoleums set an appropriate resting place for some of Hollywood's most iconic dearly departed. Residents include Cecil B DeMille, Mickey Rooney, Jayne Mansfield, punk rockers Johnny and Dee Dee Ramone and *Golden Girls* star Estelle Getty. Valentino lies in the Cathedral Mausoleum (open from 10am to 2pm), while Judy Garland rests in the Abbey of the Psalms. For a full list of residents, purchase a map ($5) at the flower shop.

★ **Runyon Canyon** HIKING
(www.runyoncanyonhike.com; 2000 N Fuller Ave; ⏲dawn-dusk) A chaparral-draped cut in the Hollywood Hills, this 130-acre public park is as famous for its buff runners and exercising celebrities as it is for the panoramic views from the upper ridge. Follow the wide, partially paved fire road up then take the smaller track down to the canyon, where you'll pass the remains of the Runyon estate.

Los Feliz & Griffith Park

Five times the size of New York's Central Park, Griffith Park is home to the world-famous Griffith Observatory, the oft-overlooked Autry Museum of the American West and the take-it-or-leave-it city **zoo** (Map p394; ☎323-644-4200; www.lazoo.org; 5333 Zoo Dr, Griffith Park; adult/senior/child $20/17/15; ⏲10am-5pm, closed Christmas Day; P 👪). Rising above the southern edge of Los Feliz, Barnsdall Art Park is crowned by architect Frank Lloyd Wright's Californian debut, **Hollyhock House** (☎323-913-4031; www.barnsdall.org/hollyhock-house; Barnsdall Art Park, 4800 Hollywood Blvd, Los Feliz; adult/student/child $7/3/free; ⏲tours 11am-4pm Thu-Sun; P; Ⓜ Red Line to Vermont/Sunset).

Griffith Park PARK
(Map p394; ☎323-644-2050; www.laparks.org; 4730 Crystal Springs Dr; ⏲5am-10pm, trails sunrise-sunset; P 👪) FREE A gift to the city in 1896 by mining mogul Griffith J Griffith, and five times the size of New York's Central Park, Griffith Park is one of the country's largest urban green spaces. It contains a major outdoor theater, the city zoo, an observatory, two museums, golf courses, playgrounds, 53 miles of hiking trails, Batman's caves and the Hollywood sign.

★ **Griffith Observatory** MUSEUM
(Map p394; ☎213-473-0890; www.griffithobservatory.org; 2800 E Observatory Rd; admission free, planetarium shows adult/child $7/3; ⏲noon-10pm Tue-Fri, from 10am Sat & Sun; P 👪; 🚌DASH Observatory) FREE LA's landmark 1935 observatory opens a window onto the universe from its perch on the southern slopes of Mt Hollywood. Its planetarium claims the world's most advanced star projector, while its astronomical touch displays explore some mind-bending topics, from the evolution of the telescope and the ultraviolet x-rays used to map our solar system to the cosmos itself. Then, of course, there are the views, which (on clear days) take in the entire LA basin, surrounding mountains and Pacific Ocean.

Silver Lake & Echo Park

Pimped with stencil art, inked skin and skinny jeans, Silver Lake and Echo Park are the epicenter of LA hipsterdom. Silver Lake is the

UNIVERSAL STUDIOS HOLLYWOOD

Although **Universal** (Map p394; ☎800-864-8377; www.universalstudioshollywood.com; 100 Universal City Plaza, Universal City; admission from $99, child under 3yr free; ⏰daily, hours vary; P 👪; M Red Line to Universal City) is one of the world's oldest continuously operating movie studios, the chances of seeing any filming action here, let alone a star, are slim to none. But never mind. This theme park on the studio's back lot presents an entertaining mix of thrill rides, live-action shows and a tram tour.

First-timers should head straight for the 45-minute narrated **Studio Tour** aboard a multi-car tram that drives around the sound stages in the front lot then heads to the back lot past the crash site from War of the Worlds, vehicles from Jurassic Park and the spooky Bates Motel from Psycho. Also prepare to brave a flash flood, survive a shark attack, a spitting dino and an 8.3-magnitude earthquake, before facing down King Kong in a new 3-D exhibit created by Peter Jackson. It's a bit hokey, but fun.

Newly opened, the phenomenally popular **Wizarding World of Harry Potter** is the park's biggest attraction. Climb aboard the Flight of the Hippogriff roller coaster and the 3-D ride Harry Potter and the Forbidden Journey.

more upwardly mobile of the pair, home to revitalized modernist homes, sharing-plate menus and obscure fashion labels on boutique racks. To the southeast lies grittier Echo Park, one of LA's oldest neighborhoods. Despite its own ongoing gentrification, it continues to offer a contrasting jumble of rickety homes, Mexican *panderias* (bakeries), indie rock bars, vintage stores, design-literate coffee shops and the serenity of its namesake lake, featured in Polanski's *Chinatown*.

Silver Lake and Echo Park are more about the vibe than ticking off sights. Consider starting your explorations at Silver Lake Junction (the intersection of Sunset and Santa Monica Blvds), grabbing coffee and exploring the well-curated stores that dot Sunset Blvd. The Echo Park stretch of Sunset Blvd is home to its own booty of small galleries and cool shops. When fatigue kicks in, retire to Echo Park Lake, where you can chill on the well-tended lawns or on the water itself in a pedal boat.

Neutra VDL House ARCHITECTURE

(www.neutra-vdl.org; 2300 Silver Lake Blvd, Silver Lake; adult/senior/child $15/10/free; ⏰guided tours 11am-3pm Sat, last tour commences 2:30pm) Built in 1932, burnt to a crisp in 1963 then subsequently rebuilt, the light-washed former home and laboratory of modernist architect Richard Neutra is a leading example of mid-century Californian design. Indeed, the site was declared a National Historic Landmark in 2017. Thirty-minute guided tours of the property run most Saturdays, shedding light on the Austrian-born architect's theories and stylistic evolution. Reservations not required. Always check the website as tours are not run some weeks.

West Hollywood & Mid-City

Welcome to West Hollywood (WeHo), an independent city with way more personality (some might say, frivolity) than its 1.9-sq-mile frame might suggest. Upscale and low-rent (but rising), gay fabulous and Russian-ghetto chic, this is a bastion of LA's fashionista best and home to some of the trashiest shops you'll ever see.

Mid-City, to the south and east, encompasses the Miracle Mile (home to some of the best museums in the west), the Orthodox-Jewish-meets-hipster Fairfax district and the legendary rock, punk and vintage shopping strip of Melrose Ave.

★Original Farmers Market MARKET

(Map p402; ☎323-933-9211; www.farmersmarketla.com; 6333 W 3rd St, Fairfax District; ⏰9am-9pm Mon-Fri, to 8pm Sat, 10am-7pm Sun; P 👪) Long before the city was flooded with farmers markets, there was *the* farmers market. Fresh produce, roasted nuts, doughnuts, cheeses, blini – you'll find them all at this 1934 landmark. Casual and kid friendly, it's a fun place for a browse, snack or for people-watching.

★Los Angeles County Museum of Art MUSEUM

(LACMA; Map p402; ☎323-857-6000; www.lacma.org; 5905 Wilshire Blvd, Mid-City; adult/child $15/free, 2nd Tue each month free; ⏰11am-5pm Mon, Tue & Thu, to 8pm Fri, 10am-7pm Sat & Sun; P; 🚌Metro lines 20, 217, 720, 780 to Wilshire & Fairfax) The depth and wealth of the collection at the largest museum in the western US is stunning. LACMA holds all the major players – Rembrandt, Cézanne, Magritte, Mary

Downtown Los Angeles

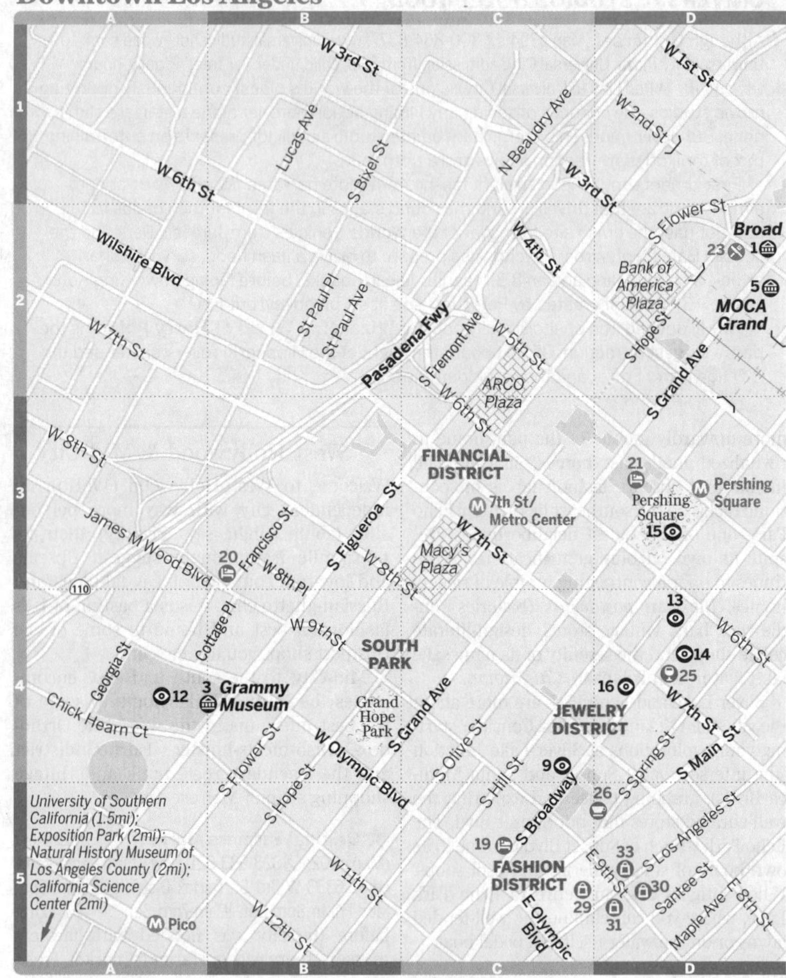

Cassat, Ansel Adams – plus millennia worth of Chinese, Japanese, pre-Columbian and ancient Greek, Roman and Egyptian sculpture. Recent acquisitions include massive outdoor installations such as Chris Burden's *Urban Light* (a surreal selfie backdrop of hundreds of vintage LA streetlamps) and Michael Heizer's *Levitated Mass,* a surprisingly inspirational 340-ton boulder perched over a walkway.

★ Petersen Automotive Museum MUSEUM
(Map p402; ☎323-930-2277; www.petersen.org; 6060 Wilshire Blvd, Mid-City; adult/senior & student/child $15/12/7; ⏰10am-6pm; P 👪; 🚌Metro lines 20, 217, 720, 780 to Wilshire & Fairfax) A four-story ode to the auto, the Petersen Automotive Museum is a treat even for those who can't tell a piston from a carburetor. A futuristic makeover (by Kohn Pederson Fox) in late 2015 left it fairly gleaming from the outside; the exterior is undulating bands of stainless steel on a hot-rod-red background. The once-dowdy inside is now equally gripping, with floors themed for the history, industry and artistry of motorized transportation.

La Brea Tar Pits & Museum MUSEUM
(Map p402; www.tarpits.org; 5801 Wilshire Blvd, Mid-City; adult/student & senior/child $12/9/5,

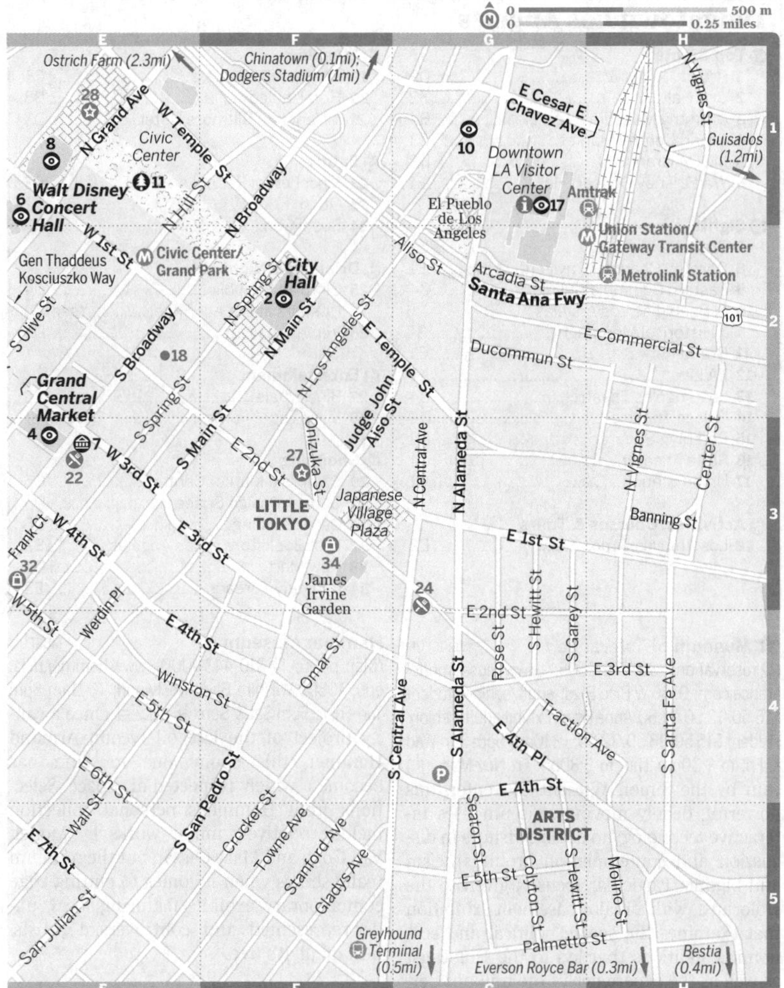

1st Tue of month Sep-Jun free; ⌚9:30am-5pm; P 👪) Mammoths, saber-toothed cats and dire wolves used to roam LA's savannah in prehistoric times. We know this because of an archaeological trove of skulls and bones unearthed at the La Brea Tar Pits, one of the world's most fecund and famous fossil sites.

Beverly Hills, Bel Air, Brentwood & Westwood

A triptych of megamansions, luxury wheels and tweaked cheekbones, Beverly Hills, Bel Air and Brentwood encapsulate the LA of international fantasies.

★Getty Center MUSEUM
(☎310-440-7300; www.getty.edu; 1200 Getty Center Dr, off I-405 Fwy; ⌚10am-5:30pm Tue-Fri & Sun, to 9pm Sat; P 👪; 🚌734, 234) FREE In its billion-dollar, in-the-clouds perch, high above the city grit and grime, the Getty Center presents triple delights: a stellar art collection (everything from medieval triptychs to baroque sculpture and impressionist brushstrokes), Richard Meier's cutting-edge architecture, and the visual splendor of seasonally changing gardens. Admission is free, but parking is $15 ($10 after 3pm).

Downtown Los Angeles

Top Sights
1 Broad ... D2
2 City Hall ... F2
3 Grammy Museum ... B4
4 Grand Central Market ... E3
5 MOCA Grand ... D2
6 Walt Disney Concert Hall ... E1

Sights
7 Bradbury Building ... E3
8 Dorothy Chandler Pavilion ... E1
9 Eastern Columbia Building ... C4
10 El Pueblo de Los Ángeles Historical Monument ... G1
11 Grand Park ... E1
12 LA Live ... A4
13 Los Angeles Theatre ... D4
14 Palace Theatre ... D4
15 Pershing Square ... D3
16 State Theatre ... D4
17 Union Station ... G1

Activities, Courses & Tours
18 Los Angeles Times ... E2

Sleeping
19 Ace Hotel ... C5
20 Hotel Indigo ... B3
21 Millennium Biltmore Hotel ... D3

Eating
22 Maccheroni Republic ... E3
23 Otium ... D2
24 Sushi Gen ... G3

Drinking & Nightlife
25 Clifton's Republic ... D4
Upstairs at the Ace Hotel ... (see 19)
26 Verve ... D5

Entertainment
27 Blue Whale ... F3
28 Mark Taper Forum ... E1

Shopping
29 California Market Center ... C5
30 Cooper Design Space ... D5
31 Gerry Building ... D5
32 Last Bookstore in Los Angeles ... E3
33 New Mart ... D5
34 Raggedy Threads ... F3

★ Museum of Tolerance — MUSEUM

(reservations 310-772-2505; www.museumoftolerance.com; 9786 W Pico Blvd; adult/senior/student $15.50/12.50/11.50, Anne Frank Exhibit adult/senior/student $15.50/13.50/12.50; 10am-5pm Sun-Wed & Fri, to 9:30pm Thu, to 3:30pm Fri Nov-Mar; P) Run by the Simon Wiesenthal Center, this powerful, deeply moving museum uses interactive technology to engage visitors in discussion and contemplation around racism and bigotry. Particular focus is given to the Holocaust, with a major basement exhibition that examines the social, political and economic conditions that led to the Holocaust as well as the experience of the millions persecuted. On the museum's 2nd floor, another major exhibition offers an intimate look into the life and effect of Anne Frank.

University of California, Los Angeles — UNIVERSITY

(UCLA; Map p406; www.ucla.edu; P) Founded in 1919, the alma mater of Jim Morrison, Kareem Abdul Jabbar and Jackie Robinson ranks among the nation's top universities. The campus is vast: walking briskly from one end to the other takes at least 30 minutes. You could easily spend a couple of hours exploring its manicured, sycamore-shaded lawns, profuse gardens, Romanesque Revival architecture and cultural assets.

Hammer Museum — MUSEUM

(Map p406; 310-443-7000; www.hammer.ucla.edu; 10899 Wilshire Blvd, Westwood; 11am-8pm Tue-Fri, to 5pm Sat & Sun; P) FREE Once a vanity project of the late oil tycoon Armand Hammer, this eponymous museum has become a widely respected art space. Selections from Hammer's personal collection include relatively minor works by Monet, Van Gogh and Mary Cassat, but the museum really shines when it comes to cutting-edge contemporary exhibits featuring local, under-represented and controversial artists. Best of all, it's free.

Westwood Village Memorial Park Cemetery — CEMETERY

(Map p406; 310-474-1579; 1218 Glendon Ave, Westwood; 8am-6pm; P) You'll be spending quiet time with entertainment heavyweights at this compact cemetery, hidden behind Wilshire Blvd's wall of high-rise towers. The northeast mausoleum houses Marilyn Monroe's simple crypt, while just south of it, the Sanctuary of Love harbors Dean Martin's crypt. Beneath the central lawn lie a number of iconic names, including actress Natalie Wood, pin-up Bettie Page and crooner Roy Orbison (the latter lies in an unmarked grave to the left of a marker labeled 'Grandma Martha Monroe').

Skirball Cultural Center MUSEUM
(☎310-440-4500; www.skirball.org; 2701 N Sepulveda Blvd; adult/student & senior/under 13yr $12/9/7, Thu free; ⊙noon-5pm Tue-Fri, 10am-5pm Sat & Sun; P) Although it is, technically speaking, the country's largest Jewish museum and cultural center, the Skirball has something for all. The preschool set can board a gigantic wooden **Noah's Ark**, while grown-ups gravitate to the permanent exhibit, an engagingly presented romp through 4000 years of history, traditions, trials and triumphs of the Jewish people.

Malibu & Pacific Palisades

Malibu enjoys near-mythical status thanks to its large celebrity population (it's been celebrity central since the 1930s) and the incredible beauty of its 27 miles of coastal mountains, pristine coves, wide sweeps of golden sand and epic waves. Despite its wealth and star quotient, the best way to appreciate Malibu is through its natural assets, so grab your sunscreen and a towel and head to the beach.

★**El Matador State Beach** BEACH
(☎818-880-0363; 32215 Pacific Coast Hwy, Malibu; P) Arguably Malibu's most stunning beach, where you park on the bluffs and stroll down a trail to sandstone rock towers that rise from emerald coves. Topless sunbathers stroll through the tides, and dolphins breech the surface beyond the waves. It's been impacted by coastal erosion, but you can still find a sliver of dry sand tucked against the bluffs.

★**Getty Villa** MUSEUM
(☎310-430-7300; www.getty.edu; 17985 Pacific Coast Hwy, Pacific Palisades; ⊙10am-5pm Wed-Mon; P; line 534 to Coastline Dr) FREE Stunningly perched on an ocean-view hillside, this museum in a replica 1st-century Roman villa is an exquisite, 64-acre showcase for Greek, Roman and Etruscan antiquities. Dating back 7000 years, they were amassed by oil tycoon J Paul Getty. Galleries, peristiles, courtyards and lushly landscaped gardens ensconce all manner of friezes, busts and mosaics, millennia-old cut, blown and colored glass and brain-bending geometric configurations in the Hall of Colored Marbles. Other highlights include the Pompeii fountain and Temple of Herakles.

Zuma Beach BEACH
(30000 Pacific Coast Hwy, Malibu; P; MTA 534) Zuma is easy to find, and thanks to the wide sweep of blonde sand that has been attracting valley kids to the shore since the 1970s, it gets busy on weekends and summer afternoons. Pass around Point Dume to **Westward Beach** (6800 Westward Rd, Malibu; P; MTA 534).

Will Rogers State Historic Park MONUMENT, PARK
(☎310-454-8212; www.parks.ca.gov; 1501 Will Rogers State Park Rd, Pacific Palisades; parking $12; ⊙8am-sunset, ranch house tours hourly 11am-3pm Thu & Fri, 10am-4pm Sat & Sun; P; MTA lines 2 & 302) This park sprawls across ranch land once owned by Will Rogers (1875–1935), an Oklahoma-born cowboy turned humorist, radio-show host and movie star (in the early 1930s he was the highest-paid actor in Hollywood). In the late '20s, he traded his Beverly Hills manse for a 31-room **ranch house** (☎tours 310-454-8212 x103; www.parks.ca.gov/?page_id=26257; 1501 Will Rogers State Park Rd, Pacific Palisades, Will Rogers State Historic Park; ⊙tours hourly 11am-3pm Thu & Fri, 10am-4pm Sat & Sun) and lived here until his tragic 1935 death in a plane crash.

Topanga Canyon SCENIC DRIVE
(Topanga Canyon Rd) Take this sinuous road from the sea and climb into a primordial canyon cut deep in the Santa Monica Mountains. The drive lays bare naked boulders and reveals jagged chaparral-covered peaks from every hairpin turn. The road is shadowed by lazy oaks and glimmering sycamores, and the whole thing smells of wind-blown black sage and 'cowboy cologne' (artemisia).

Santa Monica

Santa Monica is LA's cute, alluring, hippie-chic little sister, its karmic counterbalance and, to many, its salvation. Surrounded by LA on three sides and the Pacific on the fourth, SaMo is a place where real-life Lebowskis sip White Russians next to martini-swilling Hollywood producers, celebrity chefs dine at family-owned taquerias, and soccer moms and career bachelors shop at abundant farmers markets. All the while, kids, out-of-towners and those who love them flock to wide beaches and the pier, where the landmark Ferris wheel and roller coaster welcome one and all.

Once the very end of the mythical Route 66, and still a tourist love affair, the **Santa**

Monica Pier (Map p410; ☎310-458-8901; www.santamonicapier.org; 👪) dates back to 1908, is stocked with rides and arcade games and blessed with spectacular views, and is the city's most compelling landmark. After a stroll on the pier, hit the **beach** (Map p410; ☎310-458-8411; www.smgov.net/portals/beach; 🚌Big Blue Bus 1). We like the stretch just north of Ocean Park Blvd. Or rent a bike or some skates from **Perry's Café** (Map p410; ☎310-939-0000; www.perryscafe.com; Ocean Front Walk; bikes per hour/day from $10/30, boogie boards $7/20; ⏰9am-7:30pm Mon-Fri, from 8:30am Sat & Sun) and explore the 22-mile **South Bay Bicycle Trail** (Map p410; ⏰sunrise-sunset; 👪).

Venice

If you were born too late, and have always been a little jealous of the hippie heyday, come down to the Boardwalk and inhale a (not just) incense-scented whiff of Venice, a boho beach town and longtime haven for artists, new agers, road-weary tramps, freaks and free spirits. This is where Jim Morrison and the Doors lit their fire, where Arnold Schwarzenegger pumped himself to stardom, and the place the late Dennis Hopper once called home. These days, even as tech titans move in, the Old Venice spirit endures.

★Venice Boardwalk WATERFRONT

(Ocean Front Walk; Map p410; Venice Pier to Rose Ave) Life in Venice moves to a different rhythm and nowhere more so than on the famous Venice Boardwalk, officially known as Ocean Front Walk. It's a freak show, a human zoo and a wacky carnival alive with Hula-hoop magicians, old-timey jazz combos, solo distorted garage rockers and artists (good and bad) – as far as LA experiences go, it's a must.

★Abbot Kinney Boulevard AREA

(Map p410; 🚌Big Blue Bus line 18) Abbot Kinney, who founded Venice in the early 1900s, would probably be delighted to find that one of Venice's best-loved streets bears his name. Sort of a seaside Melrose with a Venetian flavor, the mile-long stretch of Abbot Kinney Blvd between Venice Blvd and Main St is full of upscale boutiques, galleries, lofts and sensational restaurants. A few years back, GQ named it America's coolest street, and that cachet has only grown since.

★Venice Skatepark SKATEBOARDING

(Map p410; www.veniceskatepark.com; 1500 Ocean Front Walk, Venice; ⏰dawn-dusk) Long the destination of local skate punks, the concrete at this skate park has now been molded and steel-fringed into 17,000 sq ft of vert, tranny and street terrain with unbroken ocean views. The old-school-style skate run and the world-class pool are most popular for high flyers and gawking spectators. Great photo opps, especially as the sun sets.

★Muscle Beach GYM

(Map p410; ☎310-399-2775; www.musclebeach.net; 1800 Ocean Front Walk, Venice; per day $10; ⏰8am-7pm Mon-Sat, 10am-4pm Sun Apr-Sep, shorter hours rest of year) Gym rats with an exhibitionist streak can get a tan and a workout at this famous outdoor gym right on the Venice Boardwalk, where Arnold Schwarzenegger and Franco Columbo once bulked up.

Venice Boardwalk Bike Rental CYCLING, SKATING

(Map p410; ☎310-396-2453; 517 Ocean Front Walk, Venice; 1hr/2hr/day bikes $7/12/20, surfboards $10/20/30, skates $7/12/20) Located in the Gingerbread Court complex, which was built by Charlie Chaplin, are a few shops, a cafe, some apartments above and this reliable Venice outfitter.

Long Beach & San Pedro

Along LA County's southern shore and adjacent to Orange County, the twin ports of Long Beach and San Pedro provide attractions from ship to hip. Ramble around the art deco ocean liner *Queen Mary*, scramble around the *Battleship Iowa*, or immerse yourself in the Aquarium of the Pacific. Then go for retro shopping and coastal cliff views.

★Aquarium of the Pacific AQUARIUM

(☎tickets 562-590-3100; www.aquariumofpacific.org; 100 Aquarium Way, Long Beach; adult/senior/child $30/27/19; ⏰9am-6pm; 🅿👪) Long Beach's most mesmerizing experience, the Aquarium of the Pacific is a vast, high-tech indoor ocean where sharks dart, jellyfish dance and sea lions frolic. More than 11,000 creatures inhabit four re-created habitats: the bays and lagoons of Baja California, the frigid northern Pacific, tropical coral reefs and local kelp forests.

★Museum of Latin American Art MUSEUM

(☎562-437-1689; www.molaa.org; 628 Alamitos Ave, Long Beach; adult/senior & student/child $10/7/free, Sun free; ⏰11am-5pm Wed, Thu, Sat & Sun, to 9pm Fri; 🅿) This gem of a museum is the only one in the US to present

DON'T MISS

SOUTH BAY BEACHES

When you've had all the Hollywood ambition, artsy pretension, velvet ropes and mind-numbing traffic you can take, head south of the airport, where this string of beach towns along Santa Monica Bay will soothe that mess from your psyche in one sunset. Buff volleyballers brush elbows with well-to-do University of Southern California (USC) alumni and an increasingly interesting restaurant scene.

It all starts with Manhattan Beach, just 15 minutes from LAX. A bastion of surf music and the birthplace of beach volleyball, Manhattan Beach has also gone chic. Its downtown area along Manhattan Beach Blvd has seen an explosion of trendy restaurants, boutiques and hotels. Yet, even with this Hollywood-ification, it remains a serene seaside enclave with prime surf on either side of the pier. To its south, Hermosa Beach is indeed *muy hermosa* (Spanish for 'very beautiful') – long, flat and dotted with permanent volleyball nets – and probably the funkiest of the three towns. Next up, Redondo Beach is a working-class beach town and the most ethnically diverse of the three.

As the coast winds to the south end of Santa Monica Bay you can follow it uphill to the Palos Verdes Peninsula. It's a revelation of sand-swept silver bays and the shadows of Catalina Island whispering through a fog rising from cold Pacific blue. Long, elegant and perfectly manicured lawns front sprawling mansions, and to the north, south and east there's nothing but layered jade hills forming the headland that cradles the bay's southernmost reach, before it turns a corner east toward Long Beach.

art created since 1945 in Latin America and in Latino communities in the US, in important temporary and traveling exhibits. Blockbuster shows have recently included Caribbean art and the works of LA's own Frank Romero.

★Battleship Iowa MUSEUM, MEMORIAL

(☎877-446-9261; www.pacificbattleship.com; Berth 87, 250 S Harbor Blvd, San Pedro; adult/senior/child $20/17/12; ⏱10am-5pm, last entry 4pm; P 👪; 🚌Metro Silver Line) This WWII to Cold War–era battleship is now permanently moored in San Pedro Bay and open to visitors as a museum. It's massive – 887ft long (that's 5ft longer than *Titanic*) and about as tall as an 18-story building. Step onto the gangway and download the app to take a self-guided audio tour of everything from the stateroom where FDR stayed to missile turrets and the enlisted men's galley, which churned out 8000 hot meals a day during WWII.

Retro Row AREA

(www.4thstreetlongbeach.com; 4th St btwn Junipero St & Cherry Ave, Long Beach) This blocks-long stretch of 4th St is a fab destination for retro fashion, fun cafes and restaurants and an awesome art-house theater.

Queen Mary SHIP

(☎877-342-0738; www.queenmary.com; 1126 Queens Hwy, Long Beach; tours adult/child from $27/17.50; ⏱tours 10am-6pm or later; P 👪; 🚌Passport, ⛴AquaBus, AquaLink) Long Beach's 'flagship' attraction is this grand – and supposedly haunted! – British luxury liner. Larger and more luxurious than even the *Titanic,* she transported royals, dignitaries, immigrants, WWII troops and vacationers between 1936 and 1966 and has been moored here since 1967. Sure it's a tourist trap, but spend time with the memorabilia and you may envision dapper gents escorting ladies in gowns to the art deco lounge for cocktails, or to the sumptuous Sir Winston's for dinner.

Point Fermin Park & Around PARK

(San Pedro) Locals come to this grassy community park on the bluffs to jog, picnic, watch wind- and kitesurfers, cool off in the shade of spreading magnolias, gaze at the silhouette of Catalina Island, wonder at never-ending waves pounding a rugged crescent coastline and enjoy live jazz on balmy summer Sundays.

Exposition Park & South LA

The world's oldest beings (dinosaur skeletons) and space-age technology (the Space Shuttle Endeavour) come together under one roof at the California Science Center, one of a trio of great museums in 'Expo Park,' a quick train ride from Downtown LA and a straight shot on the same train to Santa Monica. Several miles away, you may be equally inspired by Watts Towers, a masterpiece of folk art 33 years in the making, and

Hollywood

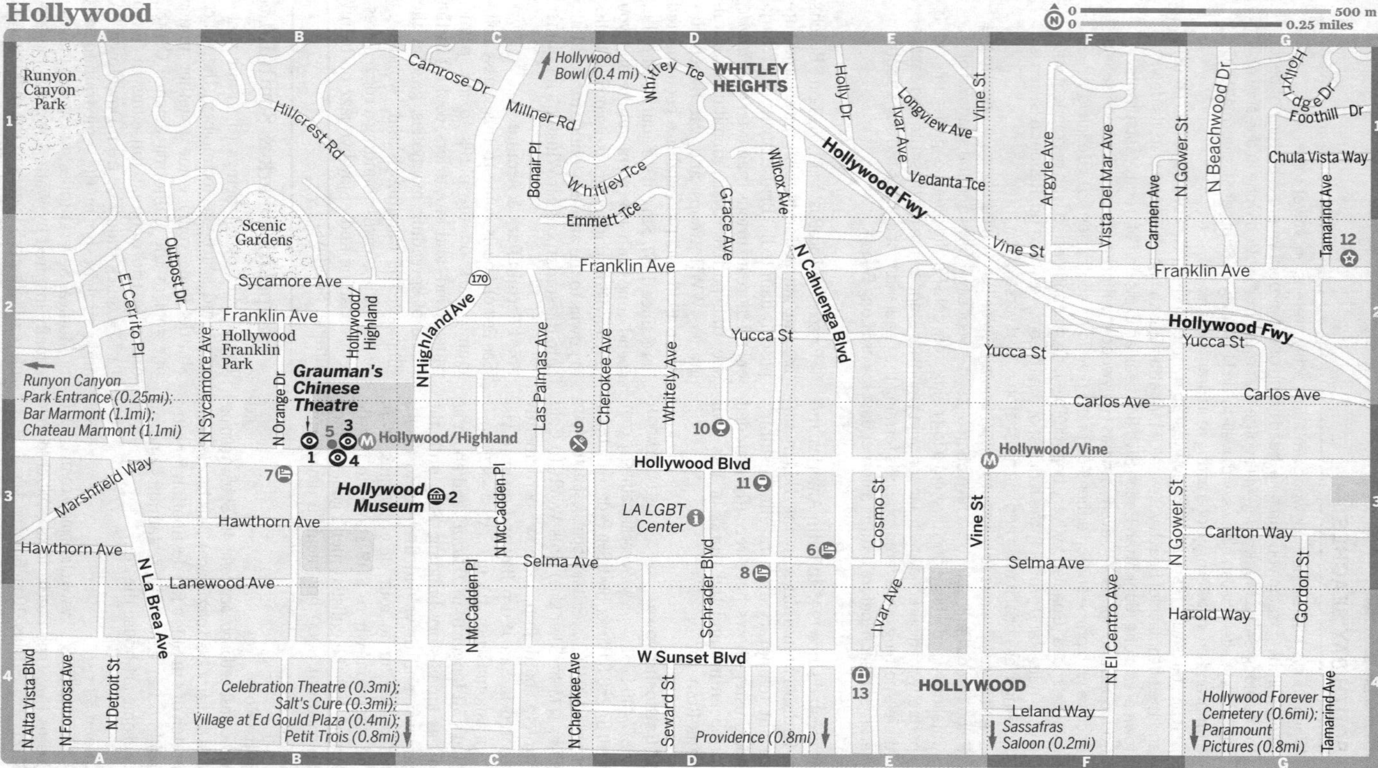
0 500 m
0 0.25 miles
Runyon Canyon Park
Hillcrest Rd
Camrose Dr
Millner Rd
Hollywood Bowl (0.4mi)
Whitley Tce
WHITLEY HEIGHTS
Holly Dr
Longview Ave
Ivar Ave
Vine St
Argyle Ave
Vista Del Mar Ave
Carmen Ave
N Gower St
N Beachwood Dr
Hollyridge Dr
Foothill Dr
Chula Vista Way
Tamarind Ave
12
Bonair Pl
Whitley Tce
Emmett Tce
Grace Ave
Wilcox Ave
Hollywood Fwy
Vedanta Tce
Scenic Gardens
Outpost Dr
El Cerrito Pl
Sycamore Ave
Franklin Ave
170
N Cahuenga Blvd
Hollywood/Highland
N Highland Ave
Hollywood Franklin Park
N Sycamore Ave
Las Palmas Ave
Cherokee Ave
Whitely Ave
Yucca St
Carlos Ave
Runyon Canyon Park Entrance (0.25mi); Bar Marmont (1.1mi); Chateau Marmont (1.1mi)
N Orange Dr
Grauman's Chinese Theatre
5
3
1
4
9
10
Hollywood/Vine
Hollywood Blvd
7
Marshfield Way
Hollywood Museum
2
N McCadden Pl
11
LA LGBT Center
Cosmo St
Vine St
N Gower St
Carlton Way
Hawthorn Ave
6
Selma Ave
8
Schrader Blvd
Lanewood Ave
N La Brea Ave
Ivar Ave
N El Centro Ave
Harold Way
Gordon St
W Sunset Blvd
N Alta Vista Blvd
N Formosa Ave
N Detroit St
Celebration Theatre (0.3mi); Salt's Cure (0.3mi); Village at Ed Gould Plaza (0.4mi); Petit Trois (0.8mi)
N Cherokee Ave
Seward St
Providence (0.8mi)
13
HOLLYWOOD
Leland Way
Sassafras Saloon (0.2mi)
Hollywood Forever Cemetery (0.6mi); Paramount Pictures (0.8mi)

Hollywood

Top Sights
1 Grauman's Chinese Theatre............ B3
2 Hollywood Museum C3

Sights
3 Dolby Theatre B3
4 Hollywood Walk of Fame.................. B3

Activities, Courses & Tours
5 TMZ Celebrity Tour.......................... B3

Sleeping
6 Dream E3
7 Hollywood Roosevelt Hotel.............. B3
8 Mama Shelter D3

Eating
9 Musso & Frank Grill......................... C3

Drinking & Nightlife
10 No Vacancy.................................... D3
11 Sayers Club.................................... D3

Entertainment
12 Upright Citizens Brigade Theatre G2

Shopping
13 Amoeba Music................................. E4

by the spirit of Leimert Park, the heart of LA's African-American community.

Natural History Museum of Los Angeles — MUSEUM

(213-763-3466; www.nhm.org; 900 Exposition Blvd, Exposition Park; adult/student & senior/child $12/9/5; 9:30am-5pm; P; M Expo Line to Expo/Vermont) Dinos to diamonds, bears to beetles, hissing roaches to African elephants – this museum will take you around the world and back, through millions of years in time. It's all housed in a beautiful 1913 Spanish Renaissance–style building that stood in for Columbia University in the first Toby McGuire *Spider-Man* movie – yup, this was where Peter Parker was bitten by the radioactive arachnid. There's enough to see here to fill several hours.

California Science Center — MUSEUM

(film schedule 213-744-2019, info 323-724-3623; www.californiasciencecenter.org; 700 Exposition Park Dr, Exposition Park; IMAX movie adult/child $8.50/5.25; 10am-5pm;) FREE Top billing at the Science Center goes to the Space Shuttle Endeavour, one of only four space shuttles nationwide, but there's plenty else to see at this large, multistory, multimedia museum filled with buttons to push, lights to switch on and knobs to pull. A simulated earthquake, baby chicks hatching and a giant techno-doll named Tess bring out the kid in everyone. Admission is free, but special exhibits, experiences and IMAX movies cost extra.

California African American Museum — MUSEUM

(213-744-7432; www.caamuseum.org; 600 State Dr, Exposition Park; 10am-5pm Tue-Sat, from 11am Sun; P) FREE CAAM does an excellent job of showcasing African-American artists and the African-American experience, with a special focus on California and LA. Exhibits change a few times each year in galleries around a sunlit atrium.

Los Angeles Memorial Coliseum — STADIUM

(213-741-0410; www.lacoliseum.com; 3911 S Figueroa St, Exposition Park; guided/self-guided tours $25/10; self-guided tours 10am-4pm Wed-Sun, guided tours 10:30am & 1:30pm Wed-Sun; M Expo Line to Exposition Park/USC) Built in 1923, this grand stadium hosted the 1932 and 1984 Summer Olympic Games, the 1959 baseball World Series and two Super Bowls, and is the temporary home stadium for the **Los Angeles Rams** (www.therams.com) and permanent home of University of Southern California Trojans (American) football teams. Informative guided tours dish the history and take you inside locker rooms, press box, the field and more (blackout dates apply).

★ Watts Towers — LANDMARK

(213-847-4646; www.wattstowers.us; 1761-1765 E 107th St, Watts; adult/child 13-17yr & senior/child under 13yr $7/3/free; tours 11am-3pm Thu & Fri, 10:30am-3pm Sat, noon-3pm Sun; P; M Blue Line to 103rd St) The three Gothic spires of the fabulous Watts Towers rank among the world's greatest monuments of folk art. In 1921 Italian immigrant Simon Rodia set out 'to make something big' and then spent 33 years cobbling together this whimsical free-form sculpture from concrete, steel and a motley assortment of found objects: green 7-Up bottles to sea shells, tiles, rocks and pottery.

Pasadena & the San Gabriel Valley

One could argue that there's more blueblood, meat-eating, robust Americana in Pasadena than in all other LA neighborhoods combined. Here you'll find a community with a preppy old soul, a historical perspective, an appreciation for art and jazz and a progressive undercurrent. The Rose Parade and Rose Bowl football game may have given Pasadena its long-lasting fame, but it's the spirit of this genteel city and its location beneath the lofty San Gabriel Mountains that make it a charming and attractive place to visit year-round.

★Huntington Library, Art Collections & Botanical Gardens MUSEUM, GARDEN
(☎626-405-2100; www.huntington.org; 1151 Oxford Rd, San Marino; adult weekday/weekend & holidays $23/25, child $10, 1st Thu each month free; ⊙10am-5pm Wed-Mon; P) One of the most delightful, inspirational spots in LA, the Huntington is rightly a highlight of any trip to California thanks to a world-class mix of art, literary history and over 120 acres of themed gardens (any one of which would be worth a visit on its own), all set amid stately grounds. There's so much to see and do that it's hard to know where to begin; allow three to four hours for even a basic visit.

Norton Simon Museum MUSEUM
(www.nortonsimon.org; 411 W Colorado Blvd, Pasadena; adult/child $12/free; ⊙noon-5pm Mon, Wed & Thu, 11am-8pm Fri & Sat, 11am-5pm Sun; P) Rodin's *Burghers of Calais* standing guard by the entrance is only a mind-teasing overture to the full symphony of art in store at this exquisite museum. Norton Simon (1907–93) was an entrepreneur with a Midas touch and a passion for art who parlayed his millions into an admirable collection of Western art and Asian sculpture. Meaty captions really help tell each piece's story.

Los Angeles County Arboretum & Botanic Garden GARDENS
(www.arboretum.org; 301 N Baldwin Ave, Arcadia; adult/student & senior/child 5-12yr $9/6/4, 3rd Tue of month free; ⊙9am-4:30pm) It's easy to spend hours amid the global vegetation, waterfalls, spring-fed lake and historic buildings of this fantastic, rambling, 127-acre park. Originally the private estate of real-estate tycoon Elias 'Lucky' Baldwin, it's so huge there's even a tram to haul those who are foot-weary.

San Gabriel Mission LANDMARK
(☎626-457-3035; www.sangabrielmission.org; 428 S Mission Dr, San Gabriel; adult/child 6-17yr $6/3; ⊙9am-4:30pm Mon-Sat, 10am-4pm Sun; P 👪) In 1781, settlers departed from this mission to found El Pueblo de Los Angeles in today's Downtown area. Set about 3 miles southeast of Pasadena in the city of San Gabriel, it's the fourth in the chain of 21 missions in California and is one of the prettiest.

☞ Tours

★Paramount Pictures TOURS
(☎323-956-1777; www.paramountstudiotour.com; 5555 Melrose Ave; tours from $55; ⊙tours 9:30am-5pm, last tour 3pm) *Star Trek*, *Indiana Jones* and *Shrek* are among the blockbusters that originated at Paramount, the country's second-oldest movie studio and the only one still in Hollywood proper. Two-hour tours of the studio complex are offered year-round, taking in the back lots and sound stages. Guides are usually passionate and knowledgeable, offering fascinating insight into the studio's history and the movie-making process in general.

★Esotouric BUS
(☎213-915-8687; www.esotouric.com; tours $58) Discover LA's lurid and fascinating underbelly on these offbeat, insightful and entertaining walking and bus tours themed around famous crime sites (Black Dahlia anyone?), literary lions (Chandler to Bukowski) and more.

★Los Angeles Conservancy WALKING
(☎213-623-2489; www.laconservancy.org; adult/child $15/10) Downtown LA's intriguing historical and architectural gems – from an art deco penthouse to a beaux-arts ballroom and a dazzling silent-movie theater – are revealed on this nonprofit group's 2½-hour walking tours. To see some of LA's grand historic movie theaters from the inside, the conservancy also offers the Last Remaining Seats film series, screening classic movies in gilded theaters.

TMZ Celebrity Tour BUS
(Map p390; ☎844-869-8687; www.tmz.com/tour; 6925 Hollywood Blvd; adult/child $54/44; ⊙tours departing Hard Rock Cafe Hollywood 12:15pm, 3pm & 5:30pm Thu-Tue, 12:15pm & 3pm Wed; M Red Line to Hollywood/Highland) Cut the shame; we know you want to spot celebrities, glimpse their homes and laugh at their dirt. Join this super-fun tour imagined by the paparazzi made famous. Tours run for two hours, and you'll likely meet some of the TMZ stars...and perhaps even celebrity guests on the bus.

Melting Pot Food Tours WALKING
(☎424-247-9666; www.meltingpottours.com; adult/child from $59/45) Duck into aromatic alleyways, stroll through fashionable shopping districts and explore LA landmarks

while tasting some of the city's best ethnic eats in Pasadena, Mid-City and East LA.

Festivals & Events

Tournament of Roses Parade PARADE
(www.tournamentofroses.com; viewing stands $50-95, sidewalk viewing free; Jan 1) Presented annually since 1890, this parade along Colorado Blvd through downtown Pasadena calls itself 'America's New Year Celebration.' The highlight: masterfully decorated floats covered entirely with flowers and plant material – seeds to fruit to fronds. Can't make it to the parade? Check out the Showcase of Floats nearby for the couple days afterwards. Standing and seated viewing available. Held on January 2 if January 1 is a Sunday.

Night on Broadway CULTURAL
(http://nightonbroadway.la; Broadway; Jan) A pumping, one-night-only arts and music festival on Broadway, with both emerging and established bands, DJs, performance art, food trucks and no shortage of DTLA cool.

Smorgasburg FOOD & DRINK
(http://la.smorgasburg.com/info; Alameda Produce Market, 746 Market Ct, Downtown; 10am-5pm Sun) This weekly, hipster-chic, open-air food fest originated in Brooklyn, but it's held there only half the year since Brooklyn's weather, well, kinda sucks the other half. Sunny DTLA to the rescue, with this year-round spin off. Dozens of food purveyors get ridonkulously creative (Filipino stews, berry kombucha, coconut bowls, raindrop cake etc), alongside stalls selling crafts, apparel, vintage goods and more.

Venice Art Walk ART
(www.theveniceartwalk.org; tickets $50; mid-May) Each May the Venice Family Clinic sponsors this art auction and studio tour to help raise funds for the clinic, which brings health care to 24,000 under-served men, women and children each year. With a ticket, you receive a map and pass that grants entry into more than 50 local studios featuring hundreds of original pieces, whether you plan on bidding or not.

Sleeping

From rock-and-roll Downtown digs to fabled Hollywood hideaways, LA serves up a dizzying array of slumber options. The key is to plan well ahead. Do your research and find out which neighborhood is most convenient for your plans and best appeals to your style and interests. Trawl the internet for deals, and consider visiting between January and April, when room rates and occupancy are usually at their lowest (Oscars week aside).

Downtown Los Angeles & Boyle Heights

★**Hotel Indigo** HOTEL $$$
(Map p384; 877-270-1392; www.ihg.com; 899 Francisco St, Downtown; d from $229; P ❄ ; M Red/Purple Lines to 7th St/Metro Center) This freshly minted, 350-room property celebrates Downtown's colorful backstory: wagon-shaped lobby lights pay tribute to the Fiesta de Las Flores, blown-up paparazzi shots around the elevators nod to vaudeville and early movie days, while the restaurant's tunnel-like booths allude to speakeasies. Rooms are plush and svelte, with city-themed splashbacks and deco-inspired bathrooms that pay tribute to early film star Anna May Wong.

Ace Hotel HOTEL $$$
(Map p384; 213-623-3233; www.acehotel.com/losangeles; 929 S Broadway; lofts from $400; P ❄) The ever-hip, buzzy, 182-room Ace is big on quirky details: Haas Brothers murals in the lobby and restaurant, whimsically themed cocktails at the rooftop bar and retro-inspired rooms with boxer-style robes, blank music sheets and, in many cases, record players or guitars. Small rooms can feel tight, so consider opting for a medium. Valet parking is $36 a night.

Hollywood

★**Mama Shelter** BOUTIQUE HOTEL $$
(Map p390; 323-785-6666; www.mamashelter.com; 6500 Selma Ave; r from $179; ❄ @ ; M Red Line to Hollywood/Vine) Hip, affordable Mama Shelter keeps things playful with its lobby gumball machines, foosball table and live streaming of guests' selfies and videos. Standard rooms are small but cool, with quality beds and linen and subway-tiled bathrooms with decent-sized showers. Quirky in-room touches include movie scripts, masks and Apple TVs with free Netflix. The rooftop bar is one of LA's best.

★**Dream** BOUTIQUE HOTEL $$$
(Map p390; 323-844-6417; www.dreamhotels.com; 6417 Selma Ave; r from $382; P ❄ ; M Red Line to Hollywood/Vine) This 179-room complex is inspired by mid-century style and designed by the acclaimed Rockwell Group.

Griffith Park & Around

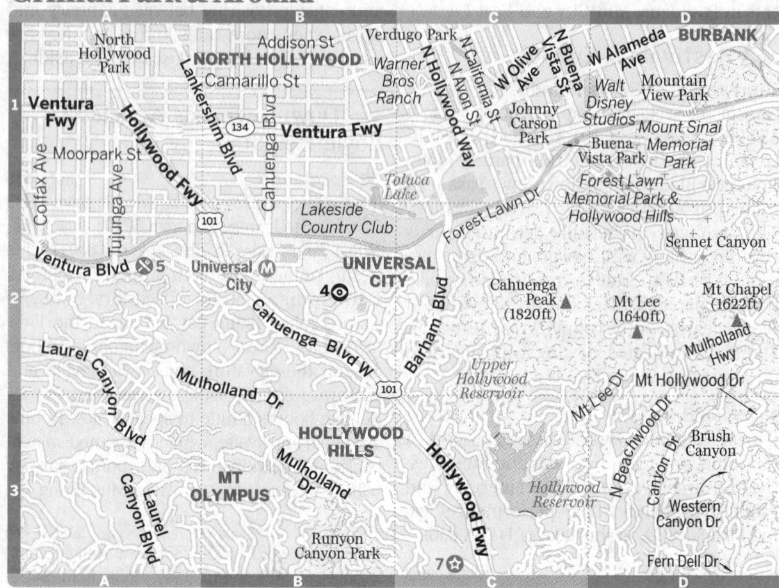

It's a hip, sceney spot, with a massive rooftop pool area and a branch of legendary New York bar Beauty & Essex. Entry-level rooms aren't especially strong on space, though all offer floor-to-ceiling windows and pared-back elegance in neutral, hangover-friendly hues.

★**Hollywood Roosevelt Hotel** HISTORIC HOTEL **$$$**
(Map p390; 323-856-1970; www.thehollywoodroosevelt.com; 7000 Hollywood Blvd; d from $282; P ❄ @ ᯤ ≋; M Red Line to Hollywood/Highland) Roosevelt heaves with Hollywood lore: Shirley Temple learned to tap dance on the stairs off the lobby, Marilyn Monroe shot her first print ad by the pool (later decorated by David Hockney) and the ghost of actor Montgomery Clift can still be heard playing the bugle. Poolside rooms channel a modernist, Palm Springs vibe, while those in the main building mix contemporary and 1920s accents.

West Hollywood & Mid-City

★**Petit Ermitage** BOUTIQUE HOTEL **$$$**
(Map p402; 310-854-1114; www.petitermitage.com; 8822 Cynthia St, West Hollywood; ste from $315; P ❄ @ ᯤ ≋) Bohemian-chic environs with Turkish rugs, old-world antiques, rooftop bars and fine booze set apart this intimate, one-of-a-kind hotel. No two of its 79 suites are the same, but all feature Venetian-style plaster walls, fireplaces, fun minibar snacks, and some have wet bar and kitchenette. Guests have exclusive access to an impressive art collection lining the halls, lots of chill spaces, and the rooftop bar/butterfly sanctuary.

★**Mondrian** HOTEL **$$$**
(Map p402; 323-650-8999, reservations 800-606-6090; www.mondrianhotel.com; 8440 Sunset Blvd, West Hollywood; r/ste from $329/369; P @ ᯤ ≋) This chic, sleek tower has been an LA showplace since the 1990s. Giant doors facing the Sunset Strip frame the entrance, opening to a lobby of minimalist elegance: white walls, blond woods, billowy curtains and model-good-looking staff. Upstairs, mood-lit hallways with tiny light boxes (by famed light artist James Turrell) lead to rooms with chandeliers, rain showers and down duvets.

★**Chateau Marmont** HOTEL **$$$**
(323-656-1010; www.chateaumarmont.com; 8221 W Sunset Blvd, Hollywood; r $450, ste from $820; P ⊖ ❄ ᯤ ≋) The French-flavored indulgence may look dated, but this faux castle has long lured A-listers with its hilltop perch, five-star mystique and legendary discretion. Howard Hughes used to spy on bikini beauties from the same balcony suite that became the favorite of U2's Bono. If nothing

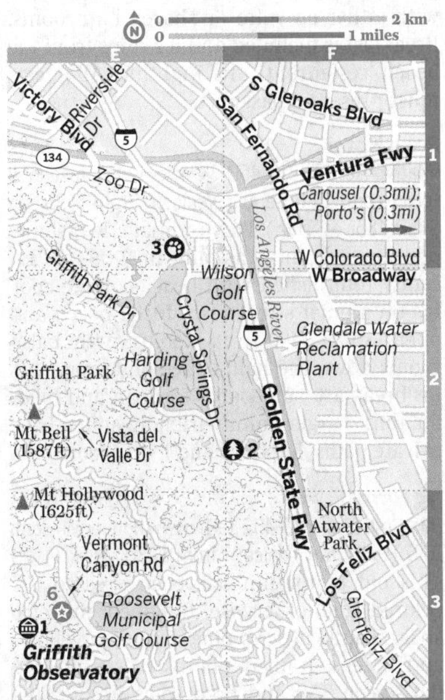

else, it's worth stopping by for a cocktail at Bar Marmont (p407).

Beverly Hills, Bel Air, Brentwood & Westwood

★ Montage HOTEL **$$$**

(☎888-860-0788; www.montagebeverlyhills.com; 225 N Canon Dr, Beverly Hills; r/ste from $695/1175; P@📶🏊) Drawing on-point eye candy and serious wealth, the 201-room Montage balances elegance with warmth and affability. Models and moguls lunch by the gorgeous rooftop pool, while the property's sprawling five-star spa is a marvel, with both single-sex and unisex plunge pools. Rooms are classically styled, with custom mattresses, dual marble basins, spacious showers and deep-soaking tubs.

Beverly Hills Hotel LUXURY HOTEL **$$$**

(☎310-276-2251; www.beverlyhillshotel.com; 9641 Sunset Blvd, Beverly Hills; r/bungalows from $525/715; P❄@📶🏊🐾) The revered 'Pink Palace' packs more Hollywood lore than any other hotel in town. Slumber in one of 208 elegantly appointed hotel rooms or live like the stars in one of 23 discreet, self-contained bungalows. Interiors in the latter are inspired by the stars who've stayed there, from Liz Taylor in number 5 to Frank Sinatra in 22.

Griffith Park & Around

Hotel Bel-Air HOTEL **$$$**

(Map p406; ☎310-472-1211; www.hotelbelair.com; 701 Stone Canyon Rd, Bel Air; r from $525; P❄📶🏊) This tranquil, 12-acre Spanish Colonial estate is a popular hideaway for royalty – Hollywood or otherwise. Leafy and low-key (we love the outdoor fireplaces), it exudes intimacy and restrained luxury, from the plush, living-room-style lobby with central fireplace to the dark, slinky bar and discreet alcoves of Wolfgang Puck's outstanding Californian restaurant. The pink-stucco rooms come with private entrances and French furnishings.

Malibu & Pacific Palisades

Point Mugu State Park Campground CAMPGROUND **$**

(☎800-444-7275; www.reserveamerica.com; 9000 Pacific Coast Hwy, Malibu; campsite $45, day use $12; P) You have two choices here: the creekside campsites shaded by gnarled, native sycamores and oaks, or the windswept beachside spots that are visible (and well within earshot) from the highway. All are within walking distance of flush toilets and coin-operated hot showers.

★ Malibu Beach Inn INN **$$$**

(☎310-651-7777; www.malibubeachinn.com; 22878 Pacific Coast Hwy, Malibu; r from $595; P❄📶) This intimate, adult-oriented hacienda was recently given a four-star upgrade by Waldo Hernandez, celebrity designer who has done work for the likes of the former Brangelina. The look is ocean-friendly grays and blues, and you might just find yourself face-to-face with well-curated art pieces by the likes of Jasper Johns and Andy Warhol.

Santa Monica

HI Los Angeles-Santa Monica HOSTEL $

(Map p410; 310-393-9913; www.hilosangeles.org; 1436 2nd St; dm low season $27-45, May-Oct $40-55, r with shared bath $109-140, with private bath $160-230; ; Expo Line to Downtown Santa Monica) Near the beach and Promenade, this hostel has an enviable location and recently modernized facilities that rival properties charging many times more. Its approximately 275 beds in single-sex dorms are clean and safe, private rooms are decorated with hipster chic, and public spaces (courtyard, library, TV room, dining room, communal kitchen) let you lounge and surf.

★ **Palihouse** BOUTIQUE HOTEL $$$

(Map p410; 310-394-1279; www.palihousesantamonica.com; 1001 3rd St; r/studios from $315/350;) LA's grooviest hotel brand (not named Ace) occupies the 38 rooms, studios and one-bedroom apartments of the 1927 Spanish-Colonial Embassy Hotel, with antique-meets-hipster-chic style. Each comfy room is slightly different, but look for picnic-table-style desks, and wallpaper with intricate sketches of animals. Most rooms have full kitchens.

Casa del Mar HOTEL $$$

(Map p410; 310-581-5533; www.hotelcasadelmar.com; 1910 Ocean Way; r from $525;) This mid-1920s beachfront building has alluring Spanish-Mediterranean style and 129 rooms and suites in whites and pale blues designed by Michael Smith, who did the Obama family's private residence. Room rates basically correlate with best views. 'Casa' is most definitely not a thumping pool-party scene, but there is a beach concierge for bikes, blades and umbrellas. It's across the street from **Shutters** (Map p410; 310-458-0030; www.shuttersonthebeach.com; 1 Pico Blvd; r $525;), its sister hotel. Parking is $45.

Venice

Samesun HOSTEL $

(Map p410; 310-399-7649, reservations 888-718-8287; www.samesun.com; 25 Windward Ave, Venice; dm $39-60, r with shared/private bath from $110/150;) This hostel in a refurbished 1904 building has spectacular rooftop views of Venice Beach, bright, beachy swatches of color and four- to eight-person dorms, as well as some private rooms with either en suite or shared bathrooms. Breakfast is included and it's steps from the beach, restaurants and nightlife. All guests must present a passport.

Rose Hotel INN $$

(Map p410; 310-450-3474; www.therosehotelvenice.com; 15 Rose Ave, Venice; r from $185, ste $450-485;) This intimate, low-slung, pension-style inn was built in 1908 and recently refurbished with beach-cottage cool. It's on a quiet street just off the beach and offers small (150-sq-ft) rooms with bathrooms down the hall, coffee and croissants for breakfast, surfboards for loan and bikes for rent. Larger, family-friendly suites have private baths, kitchens and living rooms.

★ **Hotel Erwin** BOUTIQUE HOTEL $$$

(Map p410; 310-452-1111; www.hotelerwin.com; 1697 Pacific Ave, Venice; r from $280;) This old motor inn has been dressed up, colored and otherwise funkified in retro style. Think eye-popping oranges, yellows and greens, framed photos of graffiti art, flat-screen TVs and ergo sofas in the spacious rooms. Book online for the best deals. Whether or not you stay here, the High (p407) rooftop lounge is a wonderful place for a sundowner.

Long Beach & San Pedro

★ **Hotel Maya** BOUTIQUE HOTEL $$

(562-435-7676; www.hotelmayalongbeach.com; 700 Queensway Dr, Long Beach; r from $179;) West of the *Queen Mary*, this boutique property hits you with hip immediately upon entering the rusted-steel, glass and magenta paneled lobby. The feel continues in the 199 rooms (coral tile, river-rock headboards, Mayan-icon accents), set in four 1970s-era hexagons with views of downtown Long Beach that are worth the upcharge.

Queen Mary Hotel SHIP $$

(877-342-0738; www.queenmary.com; 1126 Queens Hwy, Long Beach; r from $99; ; Passport) There's an irresistible romance to ocean liners, and this nostalgic retreat time warps you to a long-gone, slower-paced era. Yes, the rooms are small, but hallways are lined with bird's-eye maple veneer, period artwork and display cases of memorabilia from the Cunard days. First-class staterooms are atmospherically refurbished with original art-deco details.

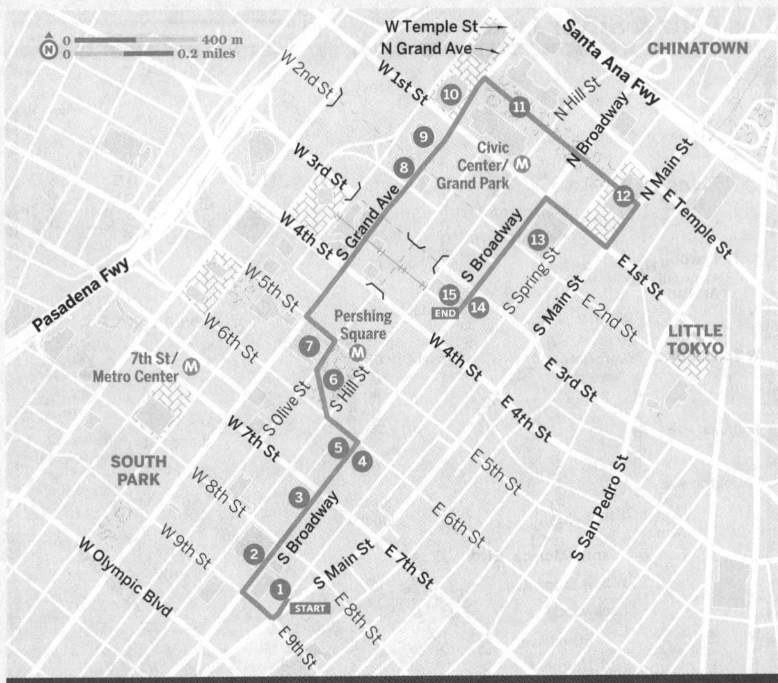

City Walk
Downtown Revealed

START VERVE
END GRAND CENTRAL MARKET
LENGTH 2.5 MILES; 2½ TO THREE HOURS

Grab a coffee at 1 **Verve** then head one block northwest along 9th St to Broadway. Dominating the intersection is the 2 **Eastern Columbia Building**, an art-deco beauty with a spectacular entrance. Head north on Broadway through the old theater district. Its heady soup of beaux-arts architecture and trendy new enterprises sums up the Downtown renaisance in just a few short blocks. Take note of the 3 **State Theatre**, 4 **Palace Theatre** and 5 **Los Angeles Theatre**. The Palace made a cameo in Michael Jackson's *Thriller* music video.

Turn left at 6th St and continue along for two blocks, passing 6 **Pershing Square** on your way to the historic 7 **Millennium Biltmore Hotel**; its cameos include *Fight Club* and *Mad Men*. Step inside for a look at its opulent interiors and to ask for directions to the Historical Corridor to scan the fascinating photograph of the 1937 Academy Awards, held on this very site.

Head right into Grand Ave, which will lead you to one of Downtown's most extraordinary contemporary buildings: modern-art museum 8 **Broad** (p379). The courtyard is home to hot-spot restaurant Otium, featuring a mural by artist Damian Hirst. On the other side of the Broad is Frank Gehry's showstopping 9 **Walt Disney Concert Hall** (p379), home to the LA Philharmonic. Beside it is the LA Phil's former home, 10 **Dorothy Chandler Pavilion**. Across the street is 11 **Grand Park**, a good spot to catch your breath.

Soaring at the end of the park is 12 **City Hall**. Head up its tower for stunning (and free) views and take in the building's breathtaking rotunda on level three. Done, head south along Main St, turning right into 1st St and passing the art-deco headquarters of the 13 **Los Angeles Times**. Turn left onto Broadway, eyeing up the beautiful atrium inside the 14 **Bradbury Building** before lunch at 15 **Grand Central Market**.

Los Feliz & Silver Lake

Los Feliz & Silver Lake

Eating

1 HomeState A2
2 Jeni's Splendid Ice Creams B1
3 Night + Market Song C4
4 Sqirl B4

Drinking & Nightlife

5 Virgil B3

Entertainment

6 Cavern Club Theater C2

Pasadena & the San Gabriel Valley

★Bissell House B&B B&B $$

(☎626-441-3535; www.bissellhouse.com; 201 S Orange Grove Ave, South Pasadena; r from $159; P Wi-Fi Pool) Antiques, hardwood floors and a crackling fireplace make this secluded Victorian (1887) B&B on 'Millionaire's Row' a bastion of warmth and romance. The hedge-framed garden feels like a sanctuary, and there's a pool for cooling off on hot summer days. The Prince Albert room has gorgeous wallpaper and a claw-foot tub. All seven rooms have private baths.

★Langham RESORT $$$

(☎626-568-3900; www.pasadena.langhamhotels.com; 1401 S Oak Knoll Ave, Pasadena; r from $289; P No smoking A/C @ Wi-Fi Pool) Opened as the Huntington Hotel in 1906, this place spent several decades as the Ritz-Carlton before recently donning the robes of Langham. But some things don't change, and this incredible 23-acre, palm-dappled, beaux-arts country estate – complete with rambling gardens, giant swimming pool and covered picture bridge – has still got it. Rooms would cost hundreds more elsewhere in town.

Eating

Downtown Los Angeles & Boyle Heights

★ Mariscos 4 Vientos MEXICAN $

(☎323-266-4045; www.facebook.com/Mariscos4Vientos; 3000 E Olympic Blvd; dishes $2.25-14; ⏲9am-5:30pm Mon-Thu, to 6pm Fri-Sun) You'll find the greatest shrimp taco of your life at no-frills Mariscos 4 Vientos. Order from the truck (if you're in a hurry) or grab a table inside the bustling dining room. Either way, surrender to corn tortillas folded and stuffed with fresh shrimp, then fried and smothered in *pico de gallo* (fresh salsa).

★ Guisados TACOS $

(☎323-264-7201; www.guisados.co; 2100 E Cesar Chavez Ave, Boyle Heights; tacos from $2.75; ⏲10:30am-8pm Mon-Thu, to 9pm Fri, 9am-9pm Sat, 9am-5pm Sun; Ⓜ Gold Line to Mariachi Plaza) Guisados' citywide fame is founded on its *tacos de guisados;* warm, thick, nixtamal tortillas made to order and topped with sultry, smoky, slow-cooked stews. Do yourself a favor and order the sampler plate ($7.25), a democratic mix of six mini tacos. The *chiles torreados* (blistered, charred chili) taco is a must for serious spice-lovers. The gourmet coffee isn't bad either.

★ Maccheroni Republic ITALIAN $$

(Map p384; ☎213-346-9725; www.maccheronirepublic.com; 332 S Broadway; mains $11-18; ⏲11:30am-2:30pm & 5:30-10pm Mon-Thu, 11:30am-2:30pm & 5:30-10:30pm Fri, 11:30am-10:30pm Sat, 11:30am-9pm Sun) Tucked away on a still-ungentrified corner is this gem with a leafy heated patio and tremendous Italian slow-cooked food. Don't miss the *polpettine di gamberi* (flattened ground shrimp cakes fried in olive oil), and its range of delicious housemade pastas. Perfectly al dente, the pasta is made using organic semolina flour and served with gorgeous crusty bread to mop up the sauce.

★ Bestia ITALIAN $$$

(☎213-514-5724; www.bestiala.com; 2121 7th Pl; pizzas $16-19, pasta $19-29, mains $28-120; ⏲5-11pm Sun-Thu, to midnight Fri & Sat; Ⓟ) Years on, this loud, buzzing, industrial dining space remains the most sought-after reservation in town (book at least a week ahead). The draw remains its clever, produce-driven takes on Italian flavors, from pizzas topped with housemade *'nduja* (a spicy Calabrian paste), to a sultry stinging-nettle raviolo with egg, mixed mushrooms, hazelnut and ricotta. The wine list celebrates the boutique and obscure.

★ Otium MODERN AMERICAN $$$

(Map p384; ☎213-935-8500; http://otiumla.com; 222 S Hope St, Downtown; dishes $15-45; ⏲11:30am-2:30pm & 5:30-10pm Tue-Thu, 11:30am-2:30pm & 5:30-11pm Fri, 11am-2:30pm & 5:30-11pm Sat, 11am-2:30pm & 5:30-10pm Sun; 📶) In a modernist pavilion beside the Broad is this fun, of-the-moment hot spot helmed by chef Timothy Hollingsworth. Prime ingredients conspire in unexpected ways, from the crunch of wild rice and amaranth in an eye-candy salad of avocado, beets and pomegranate, to a twist of lime and sake in flawlessly al dente whole-wheat bucatini with Dungeness crab.

★ Sushi Gen JAPANESE $$$

(Map p384; ☎213-617-0552; www.sushigen.org; 422 E 2nd St; sushi $11-23; ⏲11:15am-2pm & 5:30-9:45pm Tue-Fri, 5-9:45pm Sat; Ⓟ; Ⓜ Gold Line to Little Tokyo/Arts District) Come early to grab a table at this classic sushi spot, where bantering Japanese chefs carve thick slabs of melt-in-your-mouth salmon, buttery *toro* (tuna belly), Japanese snapper and more. At lunch, perch yourself at the sushi counter for à la carte options, or queue for a table in the dining room, where the sashimi lunch special ($17) is a steal. You'll find the place in Honda Plaza.

Hollywood

★ Petit Trois FRENCH $$

(☎323-468-8916; http://petittrois.com; mains $14-36; ⏲noon-10pm Sun-Thu, to 11pm Fri & Sat; Ⓟ) Good things come in small packages…like tiny, no-reservations Petit Trois! Owned by acclaimed TV chef Ludovic Lefebvre, its two long counters are where food-lovers squeeze in for smashing, honest, Gallic-inspired grub, from a ridiculously light Boursin-stuffed omelette to a showstopping double cheeseburger served with a standout foie gras–infused red-wine bordelaise.

★ Salt's Cure MODERN AMERICAN $$

(☎323-465-7258; http://saltscure.com; 1155 N Highland Ave; mains $17-34; ⏲11am-11pm Mon-Thu, to midnight Fri, 10am-midnight Sat, 10am-11pm Sun) Wood-paneled, concrete-floored Salt's Cure is an out, proud locavore. From the in-season vegetables to the house-butchered and cured meats, the menu celebrates all things Californian. Expect sophisticated takes on rustic comfort grub, whether it's capicollo with chili paste or tender duck breast paired with impressively light oatmeal griddle cakes and blackberry compote.

★ **Musso & Frank Grill** STEAK $$
(Map p390; ☎323-467-7788; www.mussoandfrank.com; 6667 Hollywood Blvd; mains $15-52; ⏱11am-11pm Tue-Sat, 4-9pm Sun; Ⓟ; Ⓜ Red Line to Hollywood/Highland) Hollywood history hangs in the thick air at Musso & Frank Grill, Tinseltown's oldest eatery (since 1919). Charlie Chaplin used to knock back vodka gimlets, Raymond Chandler penned scripts in the high-backed booths, and movie deals were made on the old phone at the back (the booth closest to the phone is favored by Jack Nicholson and Johnny Depp).

★ **Providence** MODERN AMERICAN $$$
(☎323-460-4170; www.providencela.com; 5955 Melrose Ave; lunch mains $40-45, tasting menus $120-250; ⏱noon-2pm & 6-10pm Mon-Fri, 5:30-10pm Sat, 5:30-9pm Sun; Ⓟ) The top restaurant pick by preeminent LA food critic Jonathan Gold for four years running, this two-starred Michelin darling turns superlative seafood into arresting, nuanced dishes that might see abalone paired with eggplant, turnip and nori, or spiny lobster conspire decadently with macadamia nut and earthy black truffle. À la carte options are available at lunch only.

Los Feliz & Griffith Park

★ **HomeState** TEX-MEX $
(Map p398; ☎323-906-1122; www.myhomestate.com; 4624 Hollywood Blvd, Los Feliz; tacos $3.50, dishes $7-10; ⏱8am-3pm; Ⓜ Red Line to Vermont/Sunset) Texan expat Briana Valdez is behind this rustic ode to the Lone Star State. Locals queue patiently for authentic breakfast tacos such as the Trinity, a handmade flour tortilla topped with egg, bacon, potato and cheddar. Then there's the *queso* (melted cheese) and our lunchtime favorite, the brisket sandwich, a coaxing combo of tender meat, cabbage slaw, guacamole and pickled jalapeños in pillow-soft white bread.

★ **Jeni's Splendid Ice Creams** ICE CREAM $
(Map p398; ☎323-928-2668; https://jenis.com; 1954 Hillhurst Ave, Los Feliz; 2/3/4 flavors $5.50/6.50/7.50; ⏱11am-11pm) Rarely short of a queue, this Ohio import scoops some of the city's creamiest, most inventive ice cream. Forget plain vanilla. Here, signature flavors include brown butter almond brittle and a riesling poached-pear sorbet.

Silver Lake & Echo Park

★ **Sqirl** CAFE $
(Map p398; ☎323-284-8147; http://sqirlla.com; 720 N Virgil Ave; dishes $5-15; ⏱6:30am-4pm Mon-Fri, from 8am Sat & Sun; 📶✎; Ⓜ Red Line to Vermont/Santa Monica) Despite its somewhat-obscure location, this tiny, subway-tiled cafe is forever pumping thanks to its top-notch, out-of-the-box breakfast and lunch offerings. Join the queue to order made-from-scratch wonders such as long-cooked chicken and rice porridge served with dried lime, ginger, turmeric, cardamon ghee and tomato, or the cult-status ricotta toast, a symphony of velvety house-made ricotta, thick-cut 'burnt' brioche and Sqirl's artisanal jams.

★ **Night + Market Song** THAI $
(Map p398; ☎323-665-5899; www.nightmarketla.com; 3322 Sunset Blvd; dishes $7-15; ⏱noon-3pm Mon-Fri, 5-11pm Mon-Sat; ✎) After cultivating a cult following in WeHo, this gleefully garish temple to real-deal Thai and Cambodian street food is killing it in the hipster heartlands. Invigorate the taste buds with spicy larb (minced-meat salad), proper pad Thai and harder-to-find specialties such as Isaan-style fermented pork sausage.

★ **Ostrich Farm** MODERN AMERICAN $$
(☎213-537-0657; http://ostrichfarmla.com; 1525 Sunset Blvd; dinner mains $19-29; ⏱10am-2pm Tue-Fri, to 3pm Sat & Sun, also 5:30-10pm Mon-Thu, 5:30-11pm Fri & Sat) Flickering tea lights and charming, competent barkeeps crank up the charm at this intimate, convivial space, owned and run by a husband-and-wife team. You won't find ostrich on the menu (the name refers to a former railway that reached Griffith Park), just honest takes on American classics, many of them cooked over the kitchen's wood-fired grill.

West Hollywood & Mid-City

★ **Night + Market** THAI $
(Map p402; ☎310-275-9724; www.nightmarketla.com; 9043 W Sunset Blvd, West Hollywood; dishes $8-15; ⏱11:30am-2:30pm Tue-Thu, 5-10:30pm Tue-Sun) Set behind Talésai, a long-running Thai joint, this related kitchen pumps out outstanding Thai street food and Thai-inspired hybrids such as catfish tamales. Pique the appetite with *larb lanna* (chopped pork salad), push the envelope with rich *pork toro* (grilled pork collar).

LA'S FASHION DISTRICT DEMYSTIFIED

Bargain hunters love the 100-block warren of fashion in southwestern Downtown that is the Fashion District. Deals can be amazing, but first-timers are often bewildered by the district's size and immense selection. For orientation, check out www.fashiondistrict.org.

Basically, the area is subdivided into several distinct retail areas, with womens wear and accessories constituting the bulk of the offerings:

➡ Women – Santee St between 9th St and Pico Blvd; Pico Blvd between Main and Santee Sts; Wall and Maple Sts between Olympic Blvd and 12th St.

➡ Children – 12th St and Pico Blvd between Maple Ave and San Julian St.

➡ Men – Main, Los Angeles and Santee Sts, between Pico Blvd and 16th St, plus Los Angeles St between 7th and 9th Sts.

➡ Textiles – The blocks bordered by 8th St, Olympic Blvd, Maple Ave and San Julian St.

➡ Jewelry and accessories – Santee Alley, Olympic Blvd between Main St and Wall St, plus Main and Santee Sts between Olympic and Pico Blvds.

Shops are generally open from 10am to 5pm daily, with Saturday being the busiest day because that's when many wholesalers open up to the public. Around a third of the shops are closed on Sunday. Cash is king and haggling may get you 10% or 20% off, especially when buying multiple items. Refunds or exchanges are a no-no, so choose carefully and make sure items are in good condition. Most stores don't have dressing rooms. Sample sales are usually held on the last Friday of every month, with popular showrooms including the **California Market Center** (Map p384; ☎213-630-3600; www.californiamarketcenter.com; 110 E 9th St), **Cooper Design Space** (Map p384; ☎213-627-3754; www.cooperdesignspace.com; 860 S Los Angeles St), **New Mart** (Map p384; ☎213-627-0671; www.newmart.net; 127 E 9th St) and the **Gerry Building** (Map p384; www.gerrybuilding.com; 910 S Los Angeles St). Upcoming sales are posted on the LA Fashion District Facebook page (www.facebook.com/LAFashionDist).

★ **Gracias Madre** VEGAN, MEXICAN $$
(Map p402; ☎323-978-2170; www.graciasmadreweho.com; 8905 Melrose Ave, West Hollywood; mains lunch $10-13, dinner $12-18; ⏲11am-11pm Mon-Fri, from 10am Sat & Sun; ✎) Gracias Madre shows just how tasty organic, plant-based Mexican cooking can be. Sit on the gracious patio or in the cozy interior and feel good as you eat healthy: sweet-potato flautas, coconut 'bacon,' plantain 'quesadillas,' plus salads and bowls.

Canter's DELI $$
(Map p402; ☎323-651-2030; www.cantersdeli.com; 419 N Fairfax Ave, Mid-City; ⏲24hr; P) As old-school delis go, Canter's is hard to beat. A fixture in the traditionally Jewish Fairfax district since 1931, it serves up the requisite pastrami, corned beef and matzo-ball soup with a side of sass by seen-it-all waitresses, in a rangy room with deli and bakery counters up front.

★ **Ray's** MODERN AMERICAN $$$
(Map p402; ☎323-857-6180; www.raysandstarkbar.com; 5905 Wilshire Blvd, Los Angeles County Museum of Art; mains $17-36; ⏲11:30am-8pm Mon-Tue & Thu, to 10pm Fri, 10am-8pm Sat & Sun; P; 🚌MTA 20) Seldom does a restaurant blessed with as golden a location as this one – on the plaza of LACMA (p383) – live up to the address. Ray's does. Menus change seasonally and often daily with farm-to-table fresh ingredients – some grown in the restaurant's own garden. You can expect some form of burrata, kale salad and pizzas to be on the menu.

Beverly Hills, Bel Air, Brentwood & Westwood

★ **Joss Cuisine** CHINESE $$
(☎310-277-3888; www.josscuisine.com; 9919 S Santa Monica Blvd, Beverly Hills; dishes $15-30; ⏲noon-3pm Mon-Fri, 5:30-10pm daily) With fans including Barbra Streisand, Gwenyth Paltrow and Jackie Chan, this warm, intimate nosh spot serves up superlative, MSG-free Chinese cuisine at noncelebrity prices. Premium produce drives a menu of exceptional dishes, from flawless dim sum and ginger fish broth, to crispy mustard prawns and one of the finest Peking ducks you'll encounter this side of East Asia. Reservations recommended.

West Hollywood & Mid-City

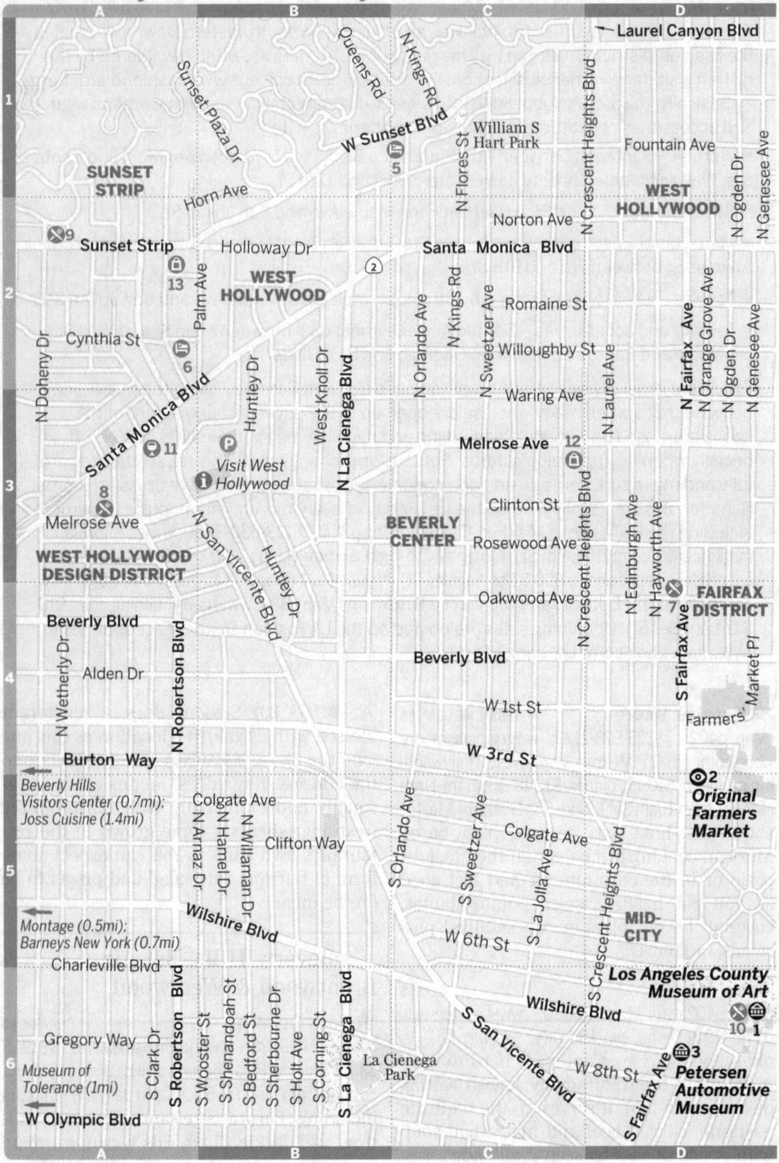

Malibu & Pacific Palisades

★ **Saddle Peak Lodge** AMERICAN $$$

(☎818-222-3888; www.saddlepeaklodge.com; 419 Cold Canyon Rd, Calabasas; appetizers $14-23, mains $34-62; ⏰5-9pm Mon-Fri, to 10pm Sat, 10:30am-2pm & 7-9pm Sun; 🅿) Rustic as a Colorado mountain lodge, and tucked into the Santa Monica Mountains with a creek running beneath, Saddle Peak Lodge serves up elk, venison, buffalo and other game in a setting watched over by mounted versions of the same. Though the furnishings are rustic timber, this is fine dining, so don't come

West Hollywood & Mid-City

Top Sights

1 Los Angeles County Museum of Art ... D6
2 Original Farmers Market ... D5
3 Petersen Automotive Museum ... D6

Sights

4 La Brea Tar Pits & Museum ... E6

Sleeping

5 Mondrian ... C1
6 Petit Ermitage ... A2

Eating

7 Canter's ... D4
8 Gracias Madre ... A3
9 Night + Market ... A2
10 Ray's ... D6

Drinking & Nightlife

11 The Abbey ... A3

Shopping

12 Fred Segal ... C3
13 Mystery Pier Books ... A2

here after a day on the trail. The 6-mile drive up Malibu Canyon is nothing short of inspirational – and occasionally hair-raising.

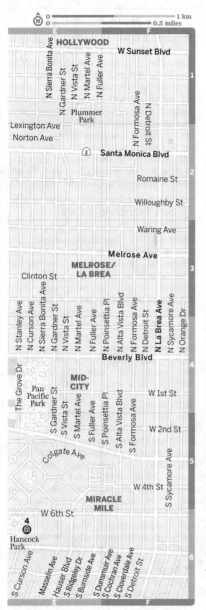

★Inn of the Seventh Ray ORGANIC $$$
(☎310-455-1311; www.innoftheseventhray.com; 128 Old Topanga Canyon Rd, Topanga; mains lunch $12-19, dinner $23-44; ⏱10am-3pm & 5:30-10pm; P ✎) If you lived through the 1960s, you might experience flashbacks at this new-agey hideaway in an impossibly idyllic creekside setting in Topanga Canyon. It grills hanger steaks and roast lamb belly, but it also bubbles soba noodles and makes a nice squid-ink pasta, all served on elegant white tablecloths.

★Nobu Malibu JAPANESE $$$
(☎310-317-9140; www.noburestaurants.com; 22706 Pacific Coast Hwy, Malibu; dishes $8-46; ⏱noon-10pm Mon-Thu, 9am-11pm Fri & Sat, to 10pm Sun; P) Chef Nobu Matsuhisa's empire of luxe Japanese restaurants began in LA, and the Malibu outpost is consistently one of LA's hot spots. East of the pier, it's a cavernous, modern wood chalet with long sushi bar and a dining room that spills onto a patio overlooking the swirling sea. Remember, it's the cooked food that built the brand.

Santa Monica

★Santa Monica Farmers Markets MARKET $
(Map p410; www.smgov.net/portals/farmersmarket; Arizona Ave, btwn 2nd & 3rd Sts; ⏱Arizona Ave 8:30am-1:30pm Wed, 8am-1pm Sat, Main St 8:30am-1:30pm Sun; 👪) You haven't really experienced Santa Monica until you've explored one of its weekly outdoor farmers markets stocked with organic fruits, vegetables, flowers, baked goods and freshly

shucked oysters. The mack daddy is the Wednesday market, around the intersection of 3rd and Arizona – it's the biggest and arguably the best for fresh produce, and often patrolled by local chefs.

★**Milo & Olive** ITALIAN $$
(☎310-453-6776; www.miloandolive.com; 2723 Wilshire Blvd; dishes $7-20; ⏲7am-11pm) We love this place for its small-batch wines, incredible pizzas, terrific breakfasts (creamy polenta and poached eggs anyone?), breads and pastries, all of which you may enjoy at the marble bar or shoulder to shoulder with new friends at one of two common tables. It's a cozy neighborhood joint so it doesn't take reservations.

★**Cassia** SOUTHEAST ASIAN $$$
(Map p410; ☎310-393-6699; 1314 7th St; appetizers $12-24, mains $18-77; ⏲5-10pm Sun-Thu, to 11pm Fri & Sat; P) Ever since it opened in 2015, open, airy Cassia has made about every local and national 'best' list of LA restaurants. Chef Bryant Ng draws on his Chinese-Singaporean heritage in dishes such as *kaya* toast (with coconut jam, butter and a slow-cooked egg), 'sunbathing' prawns, and the encompassing Vietnamese *pot au feu:* short-rib stew, veggies, bone marrow and delectable accompaniments.

Venice

★**Butcher's Daughter** VEGETARIAN, CAFE $$
(Map p410; ☎310-981-3004; www.thebutchersdaughter.com; 1205 Abbot Kinney Blvd, Venice; dishes $10-22; ⏲8am-10pm) Find yourself a seat around the central counter or facing busy Abbot Kinney to tuck in to stone-oven pizzas, handmade pastas and veggie faves such as whole roasted cauliflower and butternut-squash risotto. It's Aussie-owned, meaning great coffee. Light, airy and fun. Welcome to California!

★**Gjelina** AMERICAN $$$
(Map p410; ☎310-450-1429; www.gjelina.com; 1429 Abbot Kinney Blvd, Venice; veggies, salads & pizzas $10-18, large plates $15-45; ⏲8am-midnight; 👪; 🚌Big Blue Bus line 18) If one restaurant defines the new Venice, it's this. Carve out a slip on the communal table between the hipsters and yuppies, or get your own slab of wood on the elegant stone terrace, and dine on imaginative small plates (raw yellowtail spiced with chili and mint and drenched in olive oil and blood orange) and sensational thin-crust, wood-fired pizza.

Long Beach & San Pedro

★**Fourth & Olive** ALSATIAN $$
(☎562-269-0731; www.4thandolive.com; 743 E 4th St, East Village, Long Beach; mains $15-29; ⏲4:30-10pm Mon & Tue, 11am-10pm Wed, Thu & Sun, 11am-11pm Fri & Sat) There's much to love about this new Cal-French bistro: farmers-market produce, small-farm-raised beef and pork, housemade sausages, classic dishes such as *steak frites* and *choucroute garnie,* and low-key service, all under a high-raftered roof with generous windows to watch the world go by. *And* many of its staff are disabled veterans, so you're doing good while eating well.

San Fernando Valley

Porto's CUBAN, BAKERY $
(☎818-956-5996; www.portosbakery.com; 315 N Brand Blvd, Glendale; ⏲6:30am-8pm Mon-Sat, 7am-6pm Sun; 👪) Locals obsess over Porto's. There always seems to be a queue somewhere in this sprawling bakery-cafe, where different stations dispense hearty sandwiches, luscious cakes and obsession-worthy *pasteles* (small pastries). Deep-fried potato balls filled with meat or cheese and jalapeño define comfort food, as do flaky guava-cheese pastries and meaty sandwiches such as *medianoche* and Cuban. There's simple cafeteria-style seating. Olé, y'all!

★**Daichan** JAPANESE $$
(Map p394; ☎818-980-8450; 11288 Ventura Blvd, Studio City; mains $8-20; ⏲11:30am-3pm & 5:30-9pm Mon-Fri, noon-3pm & 5-9pm Sat; P) Tucked away in an unassuming mini-mall, and stuffed with knickknacks, pasted with posters and staffed by a sunny, sweet owner-operator, this offbeat, home-style Japanese diner offers some of the best (and tastiest) deals on Sushi Row. Fried seaweed tofu *gyōza* (dumplings) are divine and so are the bowls – especially the *negitoro* bowl, which puts fatty tuna over rice, lettuce and seaweed.

★**Carousel** MIDDLE EASTERN $$
(☎818-246-7775; www.carouselrestaurant.com; 304 N Brand Blvd, Glendale; mezes $6.75-11, mains lunch $12-18.50, dinner $15.50-28; ⏲11am-9:30pm Tue-Thu, to 10:30pm Fri & Sat, to 8:30pm Sun; P) Carousel may call itself a Lebanese restaurant, but this huge place has a commensurately huge following among Glendale's Armenian community. We can see why: succulent shawarma and kebabs, mounds of *mezzas* (small plates, hummus to steak

tartare) and desserts made with *ashta* (condensed milk) and honey are knockouts.

Pasadena & the San Gabriel Valley

★Din Tai Fung CHINESE $
(☎626-574-7068; www.dintaifungusa.com; 1108 S Baldwin Ave, Arcadia; dumplings $10-14, dishes $4.50-11.50; ⏰11am-9:30pm Mon-Fri, 10am-9:30pm Sat, 10am-9pm Sun; P) It's a testament to the SGV's ethnic Chinese community that Taiwan's most esteemed dumpling house opened its first US outpost here. The menu of dumplings, greens, noodles, desserts, teas and smoothies is as long as the phone directory at a medium-size corporation, but everyone orders pork *xiaolongbao* – steamed dumplings juicy with rich broth. Expect long waits – it's worth it.

NBC Seafood DIM SUM $
(☎626-282-2323; www.nbcrestaurant.com; 404-A Atlantic Blvd, Monterey Park; dim sum $3-7, mains $10-17; ⏰8am-10pm, dim sum until 3pm; P) Behind the rotunda facade, this SGV dim-sum institution seats 388 at a time. At peak hours (roughly 10am to 1pm on weekends) all seats are full, with a line out the door. Shrimp *har gao*, pan-fried leek dumplings and addictive shrimp on sugarcane are worth the wait.

★Union ITALIAN $$
(☎626-795-5841; www.unionpasadena.com; 37 E Union St, Pasadena; dishes $14-38; ⏰5-11pm Mon-Fri, from 4pm Sat & Sun) A cheerful, sophisticated energy animates James Beard–nominated chef Bruce Kalman's restaurant, offering California interpretations of northern Italian cuisine. The menu changes daily, but standards include pork meatballs, squid-ink pasta, fish caught from the waters of nearby Santa Barbara and a subtle and delicious olive-oil cake for dessert. Everything's made in-house, from breads to pastas to cheeses.

Drinking & Nightlife

Downtown Los Angeles & Boyle Heights

★Everson Royce Bar COCKTAIL BAR
(☎213-335-6166; www.erbla.com; 1936 E 7th St; ⏰5pm-2am) Don't be fooled by the unceremonious grey exterior. Behind that wall lies a hopping Arts District hangout, with a buzzy, bulb-strung outdoor patio. The barkeeps here are some of the city's best, using craft liquor to concoct drinks such as the prickly-pear Mateo Street Margarita.

★Clifton's Republic COCKTAIL BAR
(Map p384; ☎213-627-1673; www.cliftonsla.com; 648 S Broadway; ⏰11am-midnight Tue-Thu, to 2am Fri, 10am-2:30am Sat, 10am-midnight Sun; 📶; Ⓜ Red/Purple Lines to Pershing Sq) Opened in 1935 and back after a $10-million renovation, multilevel, mixed-crowd Clifton's defies description. You can chow retro-cafeteria classics (meals around $14.75) by a forest waterfall, order drinks from a Gothic church altar, watch burlesque performers shimmy in the shadow of a 40ft faux redwood, or slip through a glass-paneled door to a luxe tiki paradise.

★Upstairs at the Ace Hotel BAR
(Map p384; www.acehotel.com/losangeles; 929 S Broadway, Downtown; ⏰11am-2am) What's not to love about a rooftop bar with knockout Downtown views, powerful cocktails and a luxe, safari-inspired fit out? Perched on the 14th floor of the Ace Hotel, this chilled, sophisticated space has on-point DJs and specially commissioned artworks that include an installation made using Skid Row blankets.

Hollywood

★Sassafras Saloon BAR
(☎323-467-2800; www.sassafrashollywood.com; 1233 N Vine St; ⏰5pm-2am) You'll be pining for the bayou at the hospitable Sassafras Saloon, where hanging moss evokes sultry Savannah. Cocktails include a barrel-aged Sazerac, while themed nights include live jazz on Sunday and Monday, brass bands and acrobatics on Tuesday, burlesque and blues on Wednesday, karaoke on Thursday, and DJ-spun tunes on Friday and Saturday.

★Sayers Club CLUB
(Map p390; ☎323-871-8233; www.facebook.com/TheSayersClub; 1645 Wilcox Ave; cover varies; ⏰9pm-2am Tue & Thu-Sat; Ⓜ Red Line to Hollywood/Vine) When established stars such as the Black Keys, and even movie stars such as Joseph Gordon-Levitt, decide to play secret shows in intimate environs, they come to the back room at this brick-house Hollywood nightspot, where the booths are leather, the lighting moody and the music satisfying.

★No Vacancy BAR
(Map p390; ☎323-465-1902; www.novacancyla.com; 1727 N Hudson Ave; ⏰8pm-2am; Ⓜ Red Line to Hollywood/Vine) If you prefer your cocktail sessions with plenty of wow factor, make a reservation

Bel Air & Westside

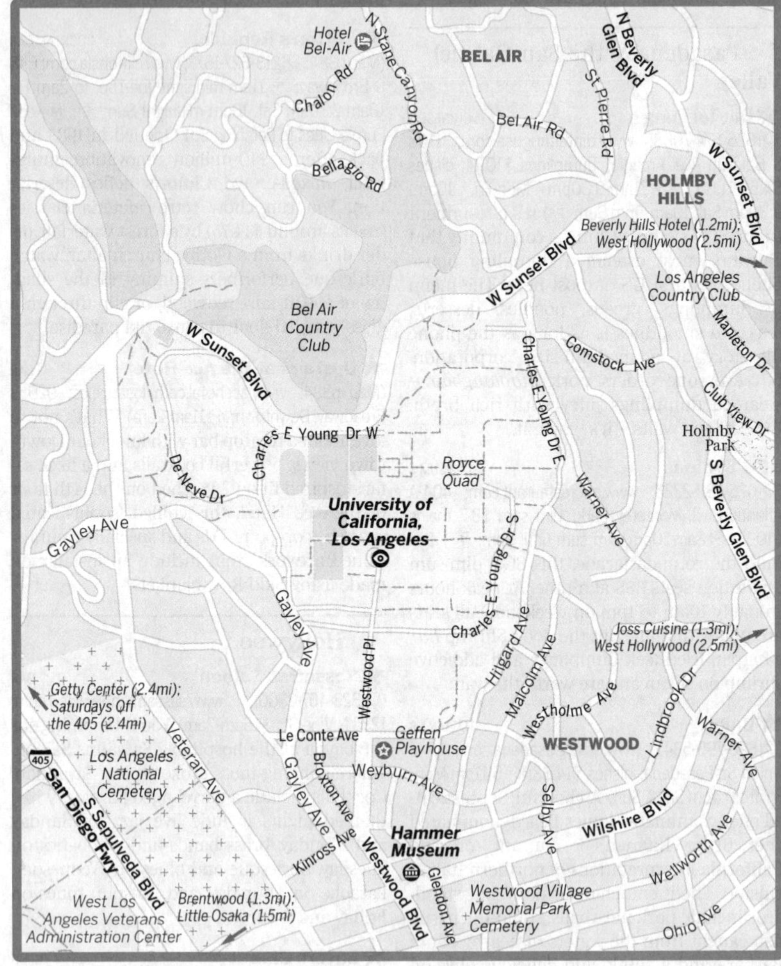

online, style up (no sportswear, shorts or logos) and head to this old shingled Victorian. A vintage scene of dark timber panels and elegant banquettes, it has bars in nearly every corner, tended by clever barkeeps while burlesque dancers and a tightrope walker entertain the droves of party people.

Silver Lake & Echo Park

★Virgil BAR

(Map p398; ☎323-660-4540; www.thevirgil.com; 4519 Santa Monica Blvd, Silver Lake; ⏰7pm-2am) An atmospheric, vintage-styled neighborhood hangout serving quality cocktails to local hipsters and arty types. A stocked calendar of entertainment includes top-notch live-comedy nights, with hilarious, subversive erotic fan-fiction improv on the third Sunday of the month. Other rotating events include booze-fueled spelling bees, storytelling events, bands and themed club nights, including '80s-themed Funkmosphere on Thursdays. Did we mention the jukebox?

Red Lion Tavern BEER HALL

(☎323-662-5337; http://redliontavern.net; 2366 Glendale Blvd, Silver Lake; ⏰11am-2am, beer garden to 11pm Sun-Thu & 1am Fri & Sat; 📶) Chipped, worn and armed with retro cigarette vending machine, this old-school beer dive has been pouring German suds since 1959. The snug, woody downstairs bar feels like a Teutonic version of *Cheers,* while upstairs is an even cozier bar and a super-popular beer garden. Beer flights are $10 and edibles include fantastic pretzels and a sausage platter large enough for two.

West Hollywood & Mid-City

★Abbey GAY & LESBIAN

(Map p402; ☎310-289-8410; www.theabbeyweho.com; 692 N Robertson Blvd, West Hollywood; ⏲11am-2am Mon-Thu, from 10am Fri, from 9am Sat & Sun) It's been called the best gay bar in the world, and who are we to argue? Once a humble coffee house, the Abbey has expanded into WeHo's bar/club/restaurant of record. Always a party, it has so many different flavored martinis and mojitos that you'd think they were invented here, plus a full menu of upscale pub food (mains $14 to $21).

★Bar Marmont BAR

(☎323-650-0575; www.chateaumarmont.com; 8171 Sunset Blvd, Hollywood; ⏲6pm-2am) Elegant, but not stuck up; been around, yet still cherished. With high ceilings, molded walls and terrific martinis, the famous and the wish-they-weres still flock here. If you time it right you might see celebs – the Marmont doesn't share who (or else they'd stop coming – get it?). Come midweek. Weekends are for amateurs.

Santa Monica

★Bungalow LOUNGE

(Map p410; www.thebungalowsm.com; 101 Wilshire Blvd, Fairmont Miramar Hotel; ⏲5pm-2am Mon-Fri, noon-2am Sat, noon-10pm Sun) A Brent Bolthouse nightspot, the indoor-outdoor lounge at the Fairmont Miramar was one of the hottest nights out in LA when it burst onto the scene a couple of years ago. It's since settled down, and like most Westside spots can be too dude-centric late in the evening, but the setting is elegant, and there's still beautiful mischief to be found here.

★Basement Tavern BAR

(Map p410; www.basementtavern.com; 2640 Main St; ⏲5pm-2am) A creative speakeasy, housed in the basement of the Victorian, and our favorite well in Santa Monica. We love it for its craftsman cocktails, cozy booths, island bar and nightly live-music calendar that features blues, jazz, bluegrass and rock bands. It gets way too busy on weekends for our taste, but weeknights can be special.

Venice

★High ROOFTOP BAR

(Map p410; ☎424-214-1062; www.highvenice.com; 1697 Pacific Ave, Hotel Erwin, Venice; ⏲3-10pm Mon-Thu, to midnight Fri, noon-midnight Sat, noon-10pm Sun) Venice's only rooftop bar is quite an experience, with 360-degree views from the shore to the Santa Monica Mountains – if you can take your eyes off the beautiful people. High serves creative seasonal cocktails (blood-orange julep, lemon apple hot toddy, Mexican hot chocolate with tequila) and dishes like beef or lamb sliders, meze plates and crab dip. Reservations recommended.

Intelligentsia Coffeebar CAFE

(Map p410; ☎310-399-1233; www.intelligentsiacoffee.com; 1331 Abbot Kinney Blvd, Venice; ⏲6am-8pm Mon-Thu, to 10pm Fri, 7am-10pm Sat, 7am-8pm Sun; 📶; 🚌Big Blue Bus line 18) In this hip, industrial, minimalist monument to the coffee gods, perfectionist baristas – who roam the central bar and command more steaming machines than seems reasonable – never short you on foam or caffeine, and the Cake Monkey scones and muffins are addictive.

☆ Entertainment

★Hollywood Bowl CONCERT VENUE

(Map p394; ☎323-850-2000; www.hollywoodbowl.com; 2301 N Highland Ave; rehearsals free, performance costs vary; ⏲Jun-Sep) Summers in LA just wouldn't be the same without alfresco melodies under the stars at the Bowl, a huge natural amphitheater in the Hollywood Hills. Its annual season – which usually runs from June to September – includes symphonies, jazz bands and iconic acts such as Blondie, Bryan Ferry and Angélique Kidjo. Bring a sweater or blanket as it gets cool at night.

★Blue Whale JAZZ

(Map p384; ☎213-620-0908; www.bluewhalemusic.com; 123 Onizuka St, Suite 301; cover $5-20; ⏲8pm-2am, closed 1st Sun of month; Ⓜ Gold Line to Little Tokyo/Arts District) An intimate, concrete-floored space on the top floor of Weller Court in Little Tokyo, Blue Whale serves top-notch jazz nightly from 9pm. The crowd is eclectic, the beers craft and the bar bites decent. Acts span emerging and edgy to established, and the acoustics are excellent. Note: bring cash for the cover charge.

★**Greek Theatre** LIVE MUSIC
(Map p394; ☎844-524-7335; www.lagreektheatre.com; 2700 N Vermont Ave; ⊙Apr-Oct) The 'Greek' in the 2010 film *Get Him to the Greek* is this 5900-capacity outdoor amphitheater, tucked into a woodsy Griffith Park hillside. A more intimate version of the Hollywood Bowl, it's much loved for its vibe and variety – recent acts include PJ Harvey, John Legend and Pepe Aguilar. Parking (cash only) is stacked, so plan on a postshow wait.

★**Saturdays Off the 405** LIVE MUSIC
(www.getty.edu; Getty Center; ⊙6-9pm Sat May-Sep) From May to September, the Getty Center courtyard fills with evening crowds for a delicious collision of art, brilliant live acts and beat-pumping DJ sets.

★**Geffen Playhouse** THEATER
(Map p406; ☎310-208-5454; www.geffenplayhouse.com; 10886 Le Conte Ave, Westwood) American magnate and producer David Geffen forked over $17 million to get his Mediterranean-style playhouse back into shape. The center's season includes both American classics and freshly minted works, and it's not unusual to see well-known film and TV actors treading the boards.

★**Mark Taper Forum** THEATER
(Map p384; ☎213-628-2772; www.centertheatregroup.org; 135 N Grand Ave) Part of the Music Center, the Mark Taper is one of the three venues used by the Center Theatre Group, SoCal's leading resident ensemble and producer of Tony-, Pulitzer- and Emmy-winning plays. It's an intimate space with only 15 rows of seats arranged around a thrust stage, so you can see every sweat pearl on the actors' faces.

★**Comedy & Magic Club** LOUNGE
(www.comedyandmagicclub.com; 1018 Hermosa Ave; ⊙Tue-Sun) Live music and comedy right on the Hermosa strip. It has something going almost every night, including some big names: David Spade, Arsenio Hall, Alonzo Bodden, Jon Lovitz, and 10 – count 'em, 10! – comedians most Fridays and Saturdays. Sunday means Jay Leno live and up close; he's the place's big draw.

★**Upright Citizens Brigade Theatre** COMEDY
(Map p390; ☎323-908-8702; http://franklin.ucbtheatre.com; 5919 Franklin Ave; tickets $5-12) Founded in New York by *Saturday Night Live* alums Amy Poehler and Ian Roberts along with Matt Besser and Matt Walsh, this sketch-comedy group cloned itself in Hollywood in 2005. With numerous nightly shows spanning anything from stand-up comedy to improv and sketch, it's arguably the best comedy hub in town. Valet parking costs $7.

Shopping

Downtown Los Angeles

★**Last Bookstore in Los Angeles** BOOKS
(Map p384; ☎213-488-0599; www.lastbookstorela.com; 453 S Spring St; ⊙10am-10pm Mon-Thu, to 11pm Fri & Sat, to 9pm Sun) What started as a one-man operation out of a Main St storefront is now California's largest new-and-used bookstore, spanning two levels of an old bank building. Eye up the cabinets of rare books before heading upstairs, home to a horror-and-crime book den, a book tunnel and a few art galleries to boot.

★**Raggedy Threads** VINTAGE
(Map p384; ☎213-620-1188; www.raggedythreads.com; 330 E 2nd St; ⊙noon-8pm Mon-Sat, to 6pm Sun; Ⓜ Gold Line to Little Tokyo/Arts District) A tremendous vintage Americana store just off the main Little Tokyo strip. There's plenty of beautifully ragged denim, with a notable collection of pre-1950s workwear from the US, Japan and France. You'll also find a good number of Victorian dresses, soft T-shirts and a wonderful turquoise collection at decent prices.

Hollywood

Amoeba Music MUSIC
(Map p390; ☎323-245-6400; www.amoeba.com; 6400 W Sunset Blvd; ⊙10:30am-11pm Mon-Sat, 11am-10pm Sun) When a record store not only survives but thrives in this techno age, you know it's doing something right. Flip through 500,000 new and used CDs, DVDs, videos and vinyl at this granddaddy of music stores, which also stocks band-themed T-shirts, music memorabilia, books and comics. Handy listening stations and the store's outstanding *Music We Like* booklet keep you from buying lemons.

West Hollywood & Mid-City

WeHo and Mid-City are by far the best and most diverse shopping territory in a city that often feels like it's built by and for shopaholics. Melrose Ave, between La Brea and Fairfax Aves, gets most of the buzz, thanks to the boutiques stuck together like block-long hedgerows. Most of their gear is rather low-brow and low-end, with some unique gems and fab vintage stores. If you want the high-end stuff, make your way west of Fairfax on Melrose or 3rd St. Both Beverly Blvd and La Brea Ave are stocked with gorgeous interiors showrooms and galleries, with the occasional fashion boutique mixed in. Fairfax Ave, between Beverly and Melrose, is where hip-hop and skate culture collide.

Then there are the megamalls: the Beverly Center and its smaller sister, Beverly Connection, across the street, and the Grove, each with dozens of high-to-middle-end shops and department stores, and often big hangout spots in their own right.

★Fred Segal FASHION & ACCESSORIES
(Map p402; ☎323-651-4129; www.fredsegal.com; 8100 Melrose Ave, Mid-City; ⏰10am-7pm Mon-Sat, noon-6pm Sun) Celebs and beautiful people circle for the very latest from Babakul, Aviator Nation and Robbi & Nikki at this warren of high-end boutiques under one impossibly chic but slightly snooty roof. The only time you'll see bargains (sort of) is during the two-week blowout sale in September.

★Mystery Pier Books BOOKS
(Map p402; www.mysterypierbooks.com; 8826 W Sunset Blvd, West Hollywood; ⏰11am-7pm Mon-Sat, noon-5pm Sun) An intimate, hidden-away courtyard shop that specializes in selling signed shooting scripts from past blockbusters, and 1st editions from Shakespeare ($2500 to $4000), Salinger ($21,000) and JK Rowling ($30,000 and up).

Beverly Hills & the Westside

Downtown Beverly Hills is the area's retail heartland, heaving with both well-known and more obscure luxury fashion and jewelry brands from mainly Europe and the US. The most famous (and most expensive) strip is Rodeo Dr, with boutiques also on the surrounding streets. Among these is N Beverly Dr, dotted with higher-end midrange fashion and lifestyle brands. To the south, Wilshire Blvd offers high-end department stores, including fashion-forward Barneys.

Barneys New York DEPARTMENT STORE
(☎310-276-4400; www.barneys.com; 9570 Wilshire Blvd; ⏰10am-7pm Mon-Wed, Fri & Sat, to 8pm Thu, 11am-6pm Sun; 📶) The Beverly Hills branch of New York's most fashion-forward department store delivers four floors of sharply curated collections for women and men. Expect interesting pieces from luxe Euro brands as well as unique pieces from homegrown labels like 3.1 Philip Lim and Warm.

Venice

Abbot Kinney Blvd has become one of LA's top shopping destinations. Bargains are few and far between here, but there's a lot of tantalizing stuff – clothing, gifts, accessories and more. As rents have risen, there has been spillover to surrounding streets.Along the Venice Boardwalk, shops and stalls sell everything from cheap sunglasses and microbikinis to incense and the inevitable tacky T-shirts.

Linus SPORTS & OUTDOORS
(Map p410; ☎310-301-1866; www.linusbike.com; 1817 Lincoln Blvd, Venice; ⏰11am-7pm; 🚌Big Blue Bus line 3) You've learned to eat, talk and appreciate art like a Venetian; now get around like one. The ultimate Venice bike shop assembles sturdy, steel-frame bikes such as the Dutchi and the Roadster. You can't carry a bike home with you, you say? It also sells enviable accessories such as bike bags, baskets, cup holders and even beer holsters.

Alexis Bittar JEWELRY
(Map p410; ☎310-452-6901; www.alexisbittar.com; 1612 Abbot Kinney Blvd, Venice; ⏰11am-7pm Mon-Sat, noon-6pm Sun) High-end women's jewelry known for Bittar's use of lucite, which is hand carved and painted in his Brooklyn studio. Some of it looks like stone. He started by selling it on the streets in Manhattan, where he was picked up by the MoMA store.

ℹ Information

INTERNET ACCESS

Cybercafes are a dying breed in LA, though free public wi-fi is proliferating, with hot spots including LAX, Pershing Sq and Grand Central Market in Downtown, Echo Park Lake, the Griffith Observatory, the Hollywood & Highland mall, Beverly Canon Gardens in Beverly Hills, Venice Beach and Santa Monica Pier.

POST

Call the **toll-free line** (☎310-247-3470; www.usps.com; 325 N Maple Dr; ⏰9am-5pm Mon-Fri, 9:30am-1pm Sat) for the nearest post-office branch.

TOURIST INFORMATION

Beverly Hills Visitors Center (☎310-248-1015; www.lovebeverlyhills.com; 9400 S Santa Monica Blvd, Beverly Hills; ⏰9am-5pm Mon-Fri, from 10am Sat & Sun; 📶) Sightseeing, activities, dining and accommodations information focused on the Beverly Hills area.

Downtown LA Visitor Center (Map p384; www.discoverlosangeles.com; Union Station, 800 N Alameda St; ⏲9am-5pm; Ⓜ Red/Purple/Gold Lines to Union Station) Maps and general tourist information in the lobby of Union Station.

Long Beach Area Convention & Tourism Bureau (☎562-628-8850; www.visitlongbeach.com; 3rd fl, One World Trade Center, 301 E Ocean Blvd, Long Beach; ⏲11am-7pm Sun-Thu, 11:30am-7:30pm Fri & Sat Jun-Sep, 10am-4pm Fri-Sun Oct-May) Tourist office located in downtown Long Beach.

Marina del Rey (☎310-305-9545; www.visitmarinadelrey.com; 4701 Admiralty Way, Marina del Rey; ⏲9am-5pm Mon-Fri, 10am-4pm Sat & Sun) Maps and information on sights, activities, events and accommodations in the Marina del Rey area.

Visit Pasadena (☎626-795-9311; www.visitpasadena.com; 300 E Green St, Pasadena; ⏲8am-5pm Mon-Fri, 10am-4pm Sat) Visitor information with a focus on Pasadena attractions and events.

Santa Monica Visitor Information Center (Map p410; ☎800-544-5319; www.santamonica.com; 2427 Main St) The main tourist information center in Santa Monica, with free guides, maps and helpful staff.

Visit West Hollywood (Map p402; www.visitwesthollywood.com; Pacific Design Center Blue Bldg, 8687 Melrose Ave, Suite M60, West Hollywood; ⏲9am-5pm Mon-Fri; 📶) Information on attractions, accommodations, tours and more in the West Hollywood area.

Getting There & Away

AIR

The main LA gateway is Los Angeles International Airport (p527). Its nine terminals are linked by the free LAX Shuttle A, leaving from the lower (arrival) level of each terminal. Cabs and hotel and car-rental shuttles stop here as well. A free minibus for travelers with disabilities can be ordered by calling ☎310-646-6402. Ticketing and check-in are on the upper (departure) level.

The hub for most international airlines is the Tom Bradley International Terminal.

Some domestic flights operated by Alaska, American Eagle, Delta Connection, JetBlue, Southwest and United also arrive at **Burbank Hollywood Airport** (BUR, Bob Hope Airport; www.burbankairport.com; 2627 N Hollywood Way, Burbank), which is handy if you're headed for Hollywood, Downtown or Pasadena.

To the south, on the border with Orange County, the small **Long Beach Airport** (www.lgb.org; 4100 Donald Douglas Dr, Long Beach) is convenient for

Santa Monica & Venice Beach

Top Sights
1 Abbot Kinney Boulevard B6
2 Santa Monica Pier A3
3 Venice Boardwalk A6

Sights
4 Santa Monica State Beach A2

Activities, Courses & Tours
5 Muscle Beach A6
6 Perry's Café & Rentals A2
7 South Bay Bicycle Trail A3
8 Venice Boardwalk Bike Rental A5
9 Venice Skatepark A6

Sleeping
10 Casa del Mar A3
11 HI Los Angeles-Santa Monica A2
12 Hotel Erwin A6
13 Palihouse B1
14 Rose Hotel A5
15 Samesun A6
16 Shutters on the Beach A3

Eating
17 Butcher's Daughter B6
18 Cassia B2
19 Gjelina B7
20 Santa Monica Farmers Markets B2

Drinking & Nightlife
21 Basement Tavern B4
22 Bungalow A2
High .... (see 12)
23 Intelligentsia Coffeebar B6

Shopping
24 Alexis Bittar B7
25 Linus B6

Disneyland and is served by Alaska, JetBlue and Southwest.

BUS

The main bus terminal for **Greyhound** (☎213-629-8401; www.greyhound.com; 1716 E 7th St) is in an industrial part of Downtown, so try not to arrive after dark. Take bus 18, 60, 62 or 760 to the 7th St/Metro Center metro station, from where metro trains head to Hollywood (Red Line), Koreatown (Purple Line), Culver City and Santa Monica (Expo Line) and Long Beach (Blue Line). Both the Red and Purple Lines reach Union Station, from where you can catch the Metro Gold Line (for Highland Park and Pasadena).

CAR & MOTORCYCLE

If you're driving into LA, there are several routes by which you might enter the metropolitan area.

From San Francisco and Northern California, the fastest route to LA is on I-5 through the San Joaquin Valley. Hwy 101 is slower but more picturesque, while the most scenic – and slowest – route is via Hwy 1 (Pacific Coast Hwy, or PCH).

From San Diego and other points south, I-5 is the obvious route. Near Irvine, I-405 branches off I-5 and takes a westerly route to Long Beach and Santa Monica, bypassing Downtown LA entirely and rejoining I-5 near San Fernando.

From Las Vegas or the Grand Canyon, take I-15 south to I-10 then head west into LA. I-10 is the main east–west artery through LA and continues on to Santa Monica.

TRAIN

Amtrak (www.amtrak.com) trains roll into Downtown's historic **Union Station** (☎800-872-7245; www.amtrak.com; 800 N Alameda St). Interstate trains stopping in LA are the daily *Coast Starlight* to Seattle, the daily *Southwest Chief* to Chicago and the thrice-weekly *Sunset Limited* to New Orleans. The *Pacific Surfliner* travels numerous times daily between San Diego, Santa Barbara and San Luis Obispo via LA.

Getting Around

TO/FROM THE AIRPORT

LAX FlyAway (☎866-435-9529; www.lawa.org/FlyAway) runs to Union Station (Downtown), Hollywood, Van Nuys, Westwood Village near UCLA, and Long Beach. A one-way ticket costs $9.75.

For scheduled bus services, catch the free shuttle bus from the airport toward parking lot C. It stops by the LAX City Bus Center hub for buses serving all of LA County. For Santa Monica or Venice, change to the Santa Monica Big Blue Bus lines 3 or Rapid 3 ($1.25). If you're headed for Culver City, catch Culver City bus 6 ($1). For Manhattan, Hermosa or Redondo Beaches, hop aboard Beach Cities Transit 109 ($1). Taxis are readily available.

BICYCLE

Most buses have bike racks, and bikes ride for free, although you must securely load and unload them yourself. Bicycles are also allowed on Metro Rail trains at all times.

LA has a number of bike-sharing programs. The following are especially useful for visitors:

Metro Bike Share (https://bikeshare.metro.net) Has more than 60 self-serve bike kiosks in the Downtown area, including Chinatown, Little Tokyo and the Arts District. Pay using your debit or credit card ($3.50 per 30 minutes) or TAP card, though you will first need to register it on the Metro Bike Share website. The

LGBTQ LOS ANGELES

LA is one of the country's gayest cities, and has made a number of contributions to gay culture. Your gaydar may well be pinging throughout the county, but the rainbow flag flies especially proudly in Boystown, along Santa Monica Blvd in West Hollywood, which is flanked by dozens of high-energy bars, cafes, restaurants, gyms and clubs. Most cater to gay men, although there's plenty for lesbians and mixed audiences. Thursday through Sunday nights are prime time.

Beauty reigns supreme among the buff, bronzed and styled of Boystown. Elsewhere the scene is considerably more laid-back and less body conscious. The crowd in Silver Lake is more mixed-age and runs from cute hipsters to leather-and-Levi's, while Downtown's burgeoning scene is an equally eclectic mix of hipsters, East LA Latinos, general counterculture types and business folk. Venice and Long Beach have the most relaxed, neighborly scenes.

If nightlife isn't your scene, there are plenty of other ways to meet, greet and engage. Outdoor options include the **Frontrunners** (www.lafrontrunners.com) running club and the **Great Outdoors** (www.greatoutdoorsla.org) hiking club. The latter runs day and night hikes, as well as neighborhood walks. For insight into LA's fascinating queer history, book a walking tour with **Out & About Tours** (www.thelavendereffect.org/tours; tours from $30).

There's gay theater all over town, but the **Celebration Theatre** (☎323-957-1884; www.celebrationtheatre.com; 6760 Lexington Ave, Hollywood) ranks among the nation's leading stages for LGBTQ plays. The **Cavern Club Theater** (Map p398; www.cavernclubtheater.com; 1920 Hyperion Ave, Silver Lake) pushes the envelope, particularly with uproarious drag performers; it's downstairs from Casita del Campo restaurant. If you're lucky enough to be in town when the **Gay Men's Chorus of Los Angeles** (www.gmcla.org) is performing, don't miss out: this amazing group has been doing it since 1979.

The **LA LGBT Center** (Map p390; ☎323-993-7400; www.lalgbtcenter.org; 1625 Schrader Blvd; ⏱9am-9pm Mon-Fri, to 1pm Sat) is a one-stop service and health agency, and its affiliated **Village at Ed Gould Plaza** (☎323-993-7400; https://lalgbtcenter.org; 1125 N McCadden Pl, Hollywood; ⏱6-10pm Mon-Fri, 9am-5pm Sat; P) offers art exhibits, theater and film screenings throughout the year.

The festival season kicks off in mid- to late May with the **Long Beach Pride Celebration** (☎562-987-9191; www.longbeachpride.com; 450 E Shoreline Dr, Long Beach; parade free, festival admission adult/child & senior $25/free; ⏱mid-May) and continues with the three-day **LA Pride** (www.lapride.org) in mid-June with a parade down Santa Monica Blvd. On Halloween (October 31), the same street brings out 500,000 outrageously costumed revelers of all persuasions.

smartphone app offers real-time bike and rack availability.

Breeze Bike Share (www.santamonicabikeshare.com; per hour $7, monthly/annually $25/99) Runs self-serve kiosks all over Santa Monica, Venice and Marina del Rey.

CAR & MOTORCYCLE

Unless time is no factor – or money is extremely tight – you're going to want to spend some time behind the wheel, although this means contending with some of the worst traffic in the country.

Parking at motels and cheaper hotels is usually free, while fancier ones charge anywhere from $8 to around $45 for the privilege.

The usual international car-rental agencies have branches at LAX and throughout LA. For Harley rentals, go to Route 66. Rates start from $149 per six hours, or $185 for one day. Discounts are available for longer rentals.

PUBLIC TRANSPORTATION

Most public transportation is handled by **Metro** (☎323-466-3876; www.metro.net), which offers maps, schedules and trip-planning help through its website.

To ride Metro trains and buses, buy a reusable TAP card. Available from TAP vending machines at Metro stations with a $1 surcharge, the cards allow you to add a preset cash value or day passes. The regular base fare is $1.75 per boarding, or $7 for a day pass with unlimited rides. Both single-trip tickets and TAP cards loaded with a day pass are available on Metro buses (ensure you have the exact change). When using a TAP card, tap the card against the sensor at station entrances and aboard buses.

TAP cards are accepted on DASH and municipal bus services and can be reloaded at vending machines or online on the TAP website (www.taptogo.net).

Metro Buses

Metro operates about 200 bus lines across the city and offers three types of bus services:

- Metro Local buses (painted orange) make frequent stops along major thoroughfares throughout the city.
- Metro Rapid buses (painted red) stop less frequently and have special sensors that keep traffic lights green when a bus approaches.
- Commuter-oriented Metro Express buses (painted blue) connect communities with Downtown LA and other business districts and usually travel via the city's freeways.

Metro Rail

The Metro Rail network consists of two subway lines, four light-rail lines and two express bus lines. Six lines converge in Downtown.

Red Line The most useful for visitors. A subway linking Downtown's Union Station to North Hollywood (San Fernando Valley) via central Hollywood and Universal City; connects with the Blue and Expo Lines at the 7th St/Metro Center station in Downtown and the Metro Orange Line express bus at North Hollywood.

Blue Line Light-rail line running from Downtown to Long Beach; connects with the Red and Expo Lines at 7th St/Metro Center station and the Green Line at Willowbrook/Rosa Parks station.

Expo Line Light-rail line linking USC and Exposition Park with Culver City and Santa Monica to the west and Downtown LA to the northeast, where it connects with the Red Line at 7th St/Metro Center station.

Gold Line Light-rail line running from East LA to Little Tokyo/Arts District, Chinatown and Pasadena via Union Station, Mt Washington and Highland Park; connects with the Red Line at Union Station.

Green Line Light-rail service between Norwalk and Redondo Beach; connects with the Blue Line at Willowbrook/Rosa Parks.

Orange Line Express bus linking the west San Fernando Valley to North Hollywood, from where the Red Line subway shoots south to Hollywood and Downtown LA.

Purple Line Subway line between Downtown LA, Westlake and Koreatown; shares six stations with the Red Line.

Silver Line Express bus linking the El Monte regional bus station to the Harbor Gateway Transit Center in Gardena via Downtown LA. Some services continue to San Pedro.

Most lines run from around 4:30am to 1am Sunday to Thursday, and until around 2:30am on Friday and Saturday nights. Frequency ranges from up to every five minutes in rush hour to every 10 to 20 minutes at other times. Schedules for all lines are available at www.metro.net.

Municipal Buses

Santa Monica–based **Big Blue Bus** (☎310-451-5444; www.bigbluebus.com) serves much of western LA, including Santa Monica, Venice, Westwood and LAX ($1.25). Its express bus 10 runs from Santa Monica to Downtown ($2.50, one hour).

The **Culver City Bus** (www.culvercity.org/enjoy/culver-city-bus) runs services throughout Culver City and the Westside. This includes a service to Aviation/LAX station on the metro Green Line ($1), from where a free shuttle connects to LAX.

Long Beach Transit (www.lbtransit.com; $1.25 per ride) serves Long Beach and surrounding communities. All three municipal bus companies accept payment by TAP card.

AROUND LOS ANGELES

Ditch the congestion, crowds and smog, and use LA as a hub to all the natural glory of California. Get an early start to beat the traffic, point the compass across the ocean or up into the mountains.

Catalina Island

Mediterranean-flavored Santa Catalina Island is a popular getaway for harried Angelenos drawn by fresh air, seemingly endless sunshine, seaside fun and excellent hiking in a unique microclimate.

Originally the home of Tongva native people, Catalina has gone through stints as a hangout for Spanish explorers, Franciscan friars, sea-otter poachers, smugglers and Union soldiers. In 1919 it was snapped up by chewing-gum magnate William Wrigley Jr (1861–1932), who had buildings constructed in the Spanish Mission style and for years sent his Chicago Cubs baseball team here for spring training. Apart from its human population (about 4100), Catalina's highest-profile residents are a herd of bison, brought here for a movie shoot and who ended up breeding.

Today most of the island is owned by the **Catalina Island Conservancy** (☎310-510-2595; www.catalinaconservancy.org; 125 Clarissa Ave, Avalon; biking/hiking permits $35/free), and 88% of the island's 75 square miles is a nature preserve requiring (easily available) permits for access to hiking and cycling.

Even if Catalina sinks under the weight of day-trippers in summer and whenever cruise ships anchor offshore, if you stay overnight you may well feel the ambience go from frantic to, as the song says, 'romance, romance, romance, romance.'

Commercial activity is concentrated in the town of Avalon (population about 3775), which is small enough to be explored in an hour or two, so there's plenty of time for hiking, swimming and touring.

The only other settlement is Two Harbors (population about 300) on the remote west coast, which has a general store, a dive and kayak center, a snack bar and a lodge.

Avalon lodging has long been pretty dowdy, but recent renovations are upgrading rooms while preserving the island's traditional charm. Rates soar on weekends and between May and September; they're about 30% to 60% lower at other times. For camping information, see www.visitcatalinaisland.com/avalon/camping.php.

Activities

There are plenty of activities right in Avalon and on the harbor, as well as hiking, mountain biking and ziplining inland with the chance to spot eagles and bison. If you're going into the backcountry, there's very little shade, so take a hat, sunscreen and plenty of water.

In Avalon you can hang out on the privately owned **Descanso Beach** (310-510-7410; www.visitcatalinaisland.com/activities-adventures/descanso-beach-club; 1 St Catherine Way, Avalon). There's good snorkeling at **Lovers' Cove** and at **Casino Point (Avalon Underwater Park)**, a marine reserve that's also the best shore dive. Another way to escape the throngs is by kayaking to the quiet coves along Catalina's rocky coastline. **Catalina Island Expeditions** (Descanso Beach Ocean Sports; 310-510-1226; www.kayakcatalinaisland.com; Descanso Beach Club; single/double kayak rental per hour $22/30, per day $52/72, SUP per hour/day from $24/60, 2hr tours per person $48) rents snorkeling gear, SUP kits and kayaks, and also runs guided kayaking tours and kayak camping trips.

To get into the protected backcountry, hop on the **Safari Bus** (310-510-4205; www.visitcatalinaisland.com/activities-adventures/two-harbors/safari-bus; mid-Jun–early Sep), which goes all the way to Two Harbors. You must book in advance and get a permit (and maps) from the Catalina Island Conservancy if you're going to be hiking or mountain biking.

Alternatively, you could just hop on an air-conditioned tour bus and let someone else show you around. Both **Catalina Adventure Tours** (877-510-2888; www.catalinaadventuretours.com; Green Pier, Avalon; tours adult/child & senior from $45/42) and **Discovery Tour Plaza** (800-626-1496; www.visitcatalinaisland.com/island-info/tour-plaza; 10 Island Plaza, Avalon; tours $19-124) operate historical Avalon itineraries and jaunts further out with memorable views of the rugged coast, deep canyons and sandy coves, and possible encounters with eagles and a herd of bison.

Snorkelers and certified scuba divers can rent equipment at Descanso Beach to glimpse local shipwrecks and kelp forests. **Two Harbors Dive and Recreation Center** (310-510-4272; www.visitcatalinaisland.com/activities-adventures/two-harbors/dive-recreation-center; 1 Banning House Rd, Two Harbors; guided trips from $99; 9am-5pm) accesses pristine dive sites off the island's less developed coast.

Getting There & Away

A few companies operate ferries to Avalon and Two Harbors. Reservations are recommended at any time and especially during summer. The use of cars on Catalina is restricted, so there are no vehicle ferry services.

Catalina Express (800-613-1212; www.catalinaexpress.com) Ferries to Avalon from San Pedro, Long Beach and Dana Point in Orange County, and to Two Harbors from San Pedro. It takes one to 1½ hours, with up to three ferries daily. You'll ride free on your birthday...true story.

Catalina Flyer (800-830-7744; www.catalinaferries.com) Catamaran to Avalon and Two Harbors from Balboa Harbor in Newport Beach (one to 1½ hours).

Big Bear Lake

Big Bear Lake is a low-key, family-friendly mountain resort (elevation 6750ft) about 110 miles northeast of LA. Snowy winters lure scores of ski bunnies and boarders to its two mountains, while summer brings hikers, mountain bikers and watersports enthusiasts wishing to escape the stifling heat down in the basin. Even getting here via the spectacular, curvy, panorama-filled **Rim of the World Scenic Byway** (Hwy 18) is a treat.

The purchase of Big Bear's two mountains – Snow Summit and Bear Mountain – by the owners of Mammoth Mountain ski resort in the Eastern Sierra has injected the town not only with money but also with new energy. The vibe has especially picked up in the downtown area, the Village, where upscale bars, restaurants and shops have opened.

Around Los Angeles

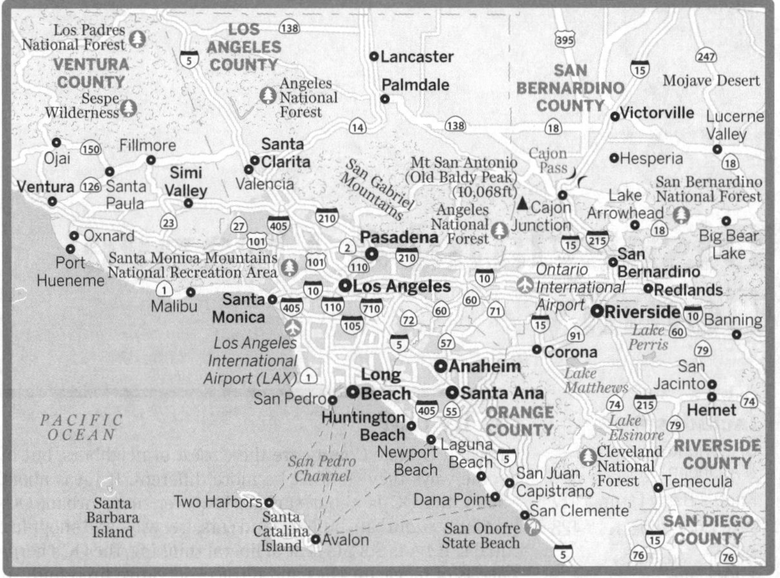

Activities

Big Bear's two ski mountains are jointly managed by **Big Bear Mountain Resorts** (☎844-462-2327; www.bigbearmountainresorts.com; 2-park lift ticket adult/child $56/46; ⊙usually Dec-Apr; 👪). The higher of the two, **Bear Mountain** (8805ft) is nirvana for freestyle freaks with more than 150 jumps, 80 jibs, and two pipes including a 580ft in-ground superpipe. **Snow Summit** (8200ft) is more about traditional downhill and has trails for everyone. Altogether the mountains are served by 26 lifts and crisscrossed by more than 55 runs.

Sleeping & Eating

On snowy winter weekends, demand often exceeds capacity, so plan ahead. The two hostels offer the cheapest digs, private villas the priciest and in between you'll find plenty of aging motels along the main highway and 2000 private cabins tucked into the woods.

For cheap sleeps tuck into the clean and friendly **Big Bear Hostel** (☎909-866-8900; www.bigbearhostel.com; 527 Knickerbocker Rd; dm $20-40, d $45-68; P@📶). **Switzerland Haus** (☎909-866-3729, 800-335-3729; www.switzerlandhaus.com; 41829 Switzerland Dr; r $125-249; @📶) offers comfy rooms with mountain-view patios and a Nordic sauna. **Himalayan** (☎909-866-2907; www.himalayanbigbear.com; 672 Pine Knot Ave; mains $10-19; ⊙11am-9pm Sun-Tue, to 10pm Fri & Sat; 🌿👪) is a popular Nepali and Indian kitchen with speedy service.

Information

Big Bear Discovery Center (☎909-382-2790; http://mountainsfoundation.org; 40971 N Shore Dr/Hwy 38, Fawnskin; ⊙8am-4:30pm, closed Wed & Thu mid-Sep–mid-May) Nonprofit visitor center dispenses information and maps on all outdoor-related activities around Big Bear, including camping. Also sells the National Forest Adventure Pass.

Big Bear Visitors Center (☎909-866-7000; www.bigbear.com; 630 Bartlett Rd; ⊙9am-5pm; 📶) Has lots of free flyers, maps and wi-fi, and sells trail maps and the National Forest Adventure Pass.

Getting There & Away

Big Bear is on Hwy 18, an offshoot of Hwy 30 in San Bernardino. A quicker approach is via Hwy 330, which starts in Highland and intersects with Hwy 18 in Running Springs. If you don't like serpentine mountain roads, pick up Hwy 38 near Redlands, which is longer, but easier on the queasy. Less traffic too, handy on peak weekends.

Mountain Transit (☎909-878-5200; http://mountaintransit.org) buses connect Big Bear with the Greyhound and Metrolink stations in San Bernardino at least twice daily ($10, 1¼ hours).

Disneyland & Orange County

Includes ➜

Best Places to Eat

- ➜ Walt's Wharf (p430)
- ➜ Napa Rose (p424)
- ➜ Driftwood Kitchen (p443)
- ➜ Ramos House Café (p445)

Best Places to Sleep

- ➜ Paséa (p433)
- ➜ Disney's Grand Californian Hotel & Spa (p422)
- ➜ Montage (p443)
- ➜ Crystal Cove Beach Cottages (p440)

Why Go?

LA and Orange County are the closest of neighbors, but in some ways they couldn't be more different. If LA is about stars, the OC is about surfers. LA: ever more urban, OC: proudly *sub*urban, built around cars, freeways and shopping malls. If LA is SoCal's seat of liberal thinking, the OC's heritage is of megachurches and ultraconservative firebrands. If LA is Hollywood glam, the OC is *Real Housewives.*

Tourism is dominated by Disneyland in Anaheim in northern OC, and beach communities promising endless summer – and very different lifestyles as you progress down the coast from Seal Beach to Huntington Beach, Newport Beach to Laguna Beach.

While there's some truth to those stereotypes of life behind the 'Orange Curtain,' this diverse county's 789 sq miles, 34 cities and 3.15 million people create deep pockets of individuality and beauty, while cool, urbanesque spots keep the OC 'real,' no matter one's reality.

When to Go

Anaheim

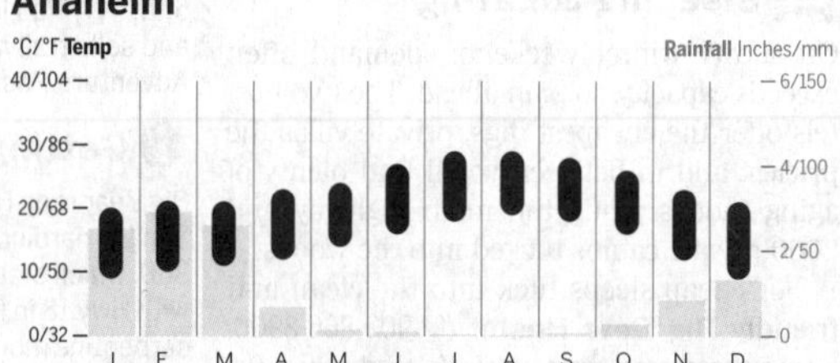

May Visitation dips from spring break to Memorial Day. Mostly sunny, balmy temperatures.

Jul & Aug Summer vacation and beach season peak. Surfing and art festivals by the coast.

Sep Blue skies, cooler temperatures inland, fewer crowds. Tall Ships Festival at Dana Point.

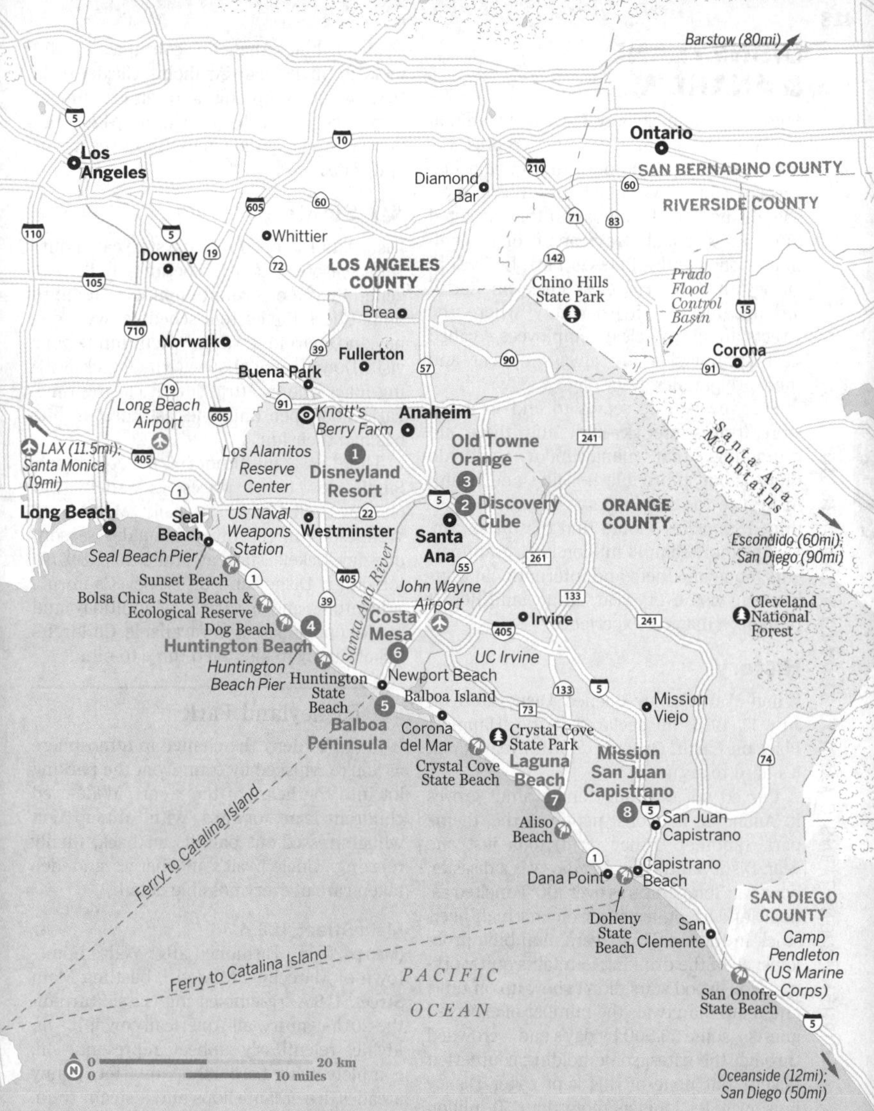

Disneyland & Orange County Highlights

1 Screaming your head off on Space Mountain before catching the fireworks show at **Disneyland Resort** (p418).

2 Fighting outrageous bed hair inside the eye of a hurricane in Santa Ana's **Discovery Cube** (p428).

3 Shopping for vintage treasures and slurping milkshakes in **Old Towne Orange** (p428).

4 Building a beach bonfire after a day of surfing waves at **Huntington Beach** (p431).

5 Cycling past Newport Beach's as-seen-on-TV sands on **Balboa Peninsula** (p434).

6 Discovering Orange County's alternative side at the Lab and the Camp 'antimalls'. in **Costa Mesa** (p438).

7 Watching the sun dip below the horizon at **Laguna Beach** (p440).

8 Being awed by the Spanish colonial history and beauty of **Mission San Juan Capistrano** (p444).

DISNEYLAND & ANAHEIM

Mickey is one lucky guy. Created by animator Walt Disney in 1928, this irrepressible mouse caught a ride on a multimedia juggernaut (film, TV, publishing, music, merchandising and theme parks) that rocketed him into a global stratosphere of recognition, money and influence. Plus, he lives in Disneyland, the 'Happiest Place on Earth,' an 'imagineered' hyper-reality where the streets are always clean, employees – called 'cast members' – are always upbeat and there are parades every day.

Sure, every ride seems to end in a gift store, prices are sky-high and there are grumblings that management could do more about affordable housing and health insurance for employees – but even determined grouches should find reason to grin. For the more than 14 million kids, grandparents, honeymooners and international tourists who visit every year, Disneyland Resort remains a magical experience.

History

When Walt Disney opened Disneyland on July 17, 1955, he declared it the 'Happiest Place on Earth.' Over six decades years later, it's hard to argue.

Carved out of orange and walnut groves in Anaheim, the construction of the 'theme park' (another Disney term) took just one year. Disneyland's opening day was a disaster, however. Temperatures over 100°F melted asphalt underfoot, leaving women's high heels stuck in the tar. There were plumbing problems: all of the drinking fountains quit working. Hollywood stars didn't show up on time, and more than twice the number of expected guests – some 28,000 by day's end – crowded through the gates, some holding counterfeit tickets. But none of this kept eager Disney fans away for long, as more than 50 million tourists visited in its first decade alone.

During the 1990s, Anaheim undertook a staggering $4.2 billion revamp and expansion, cleaning up rundown stretches and establishing the first tourist police force in the US. In 2001 a second theme park, Disney's California Adventure (DCA), was added, designed to salute the state's most famous natural landmarks and cultural history. More recently added was Downtown Disney, an outdoor pedestrian mall. The ensemble is called Disneyland Resort.

Meanwhile, Anaheim continues to fill in with malls like Anaheim GardenWalk (p425) and shopping and entertainment areas like the Packing District (p426) and Center Street (p426), plus improved roads and transit.

Sights

Disneyland is open 365 days a year; hours vary seasonally and sometimes daily, but generally you can count on at least 10am to 8pm. Check the current schedule (www.disneyland.com) in advance when timing your visit. Don't worry about getting stuck waiting for a ride or attraction at closing time. Parks stay open until the last guest in line has had their fun.

There is a multitude of ticket options. Single day ticket prices vary daily but on low-traffic days (typically Monday to Wednesday in the off or shoulder season) one-day tickets start at adult/child $97/91 for either Disneyland or Disney California Adventure, and a variety of multiday and 'park-hopper' passes are available. Children's tickets apply to kids aged three to nine.

Disneyland Park

It's hard to deny the change in atmosphere as you're whisked by tram from the parking lot into the heart of the resort. Wide-eyed children lean forward with anticipation while stressed-out parents sit back, finally relaxing. Uncle Walt's in charge, and he's taken care of every possible detail.

Main Street, U.S.A. AREA
(Map p420; 👪) Fashioned after Walt's hometown of Marceline, Missouri, bustling Main Street, U.S.A. resembles the classic turn-of-the-20th-century, all-American town. It's an idyllic, relentlessly upbeat representation, complete with barbershop quartet, penny arcades, ice-cream shops and a steam train. The music playing in the background is from American musicals, and there's a flag-retreat ceremony every afternoon.

Great Moments with Mr. Lincoln (Map p420; https://disneyland.disney.go.com/attractions/disneyland/disneyland-story; 👪), a 15-minute Audio-Animatronics presentation on Honest Abe, sits inside the fascinating **Disneyland Story** exhibit. Nearby, kids love seeing old-school Disney cartoons like *Steamboat Willie* inside **Main Street Cinema**.

Main Street ends in the **Central Plaza** (Map p420;). Lording over the plaza is **Sleeping Beauty Castle** (Map p420; https://disneyland.disney.go.com/attractions/disneyland/sleeping-beauty-castle-walkthrough;), the castle featured on the Disney logo. Inside the iconic structure (fashioned after a real 19th-century Bavarian castle), dolls and big books tell the story of Sleeping Beauty.

Tomorrowland AREA

(Map p420;) How did 1950s imagineers envision the future? As a galaxy-minded community filled with monorails, rockets and Googie-style architecture, apparently. In 1998 this 'land' was revamped to honor three timeless futurists: Jules Verne, HG Wells and Leonardo da Vinci. These days, though, the *Star Wars* franchise gets top billing. **Hyperspace Mountain** (Map p420; https://disneyland.disney.go.com/attractions/disneyland/hyperspace-mountain;), Tomorrowland's signature attraction and one of the USA's best roller coasters, hurtles you into complete darkness at frightening speed, and **Star Wars Launch Bay** (Map p420; https://disneyland.disney.go.com/attractions/disneyland/star-wars-launch-bay;) shows movie props and memorabilia.

Meanwhile, **Star Tours** (Map p420; https://disneyland.disney.go.com/attractions/disneyland/star-tours;) clamps you into a Starspeeder shuttle for a wild 3D ride through the desert canyons of Tatooine on a space mission.

If it's retro high-tech you're after, the **monorail** glides to a stop in Tomorrowland, its rubber tires traveling a 13-minute, 2.5-mile round-trip route to Downtown Disney. Just outside Tomorrowland station, kiddies will want to shoot laser beams on **Buzz Lightyear Astro Blaster** (Map p420; https://disneyland.disney.go.com/attractions/disneyland/buzz-lightyear-astro-blasters;) and drive their own miniature cars in the classic **Autopia** (Map p420; https://disneyland.disney.go.com/attractions/disneyland/autopia;) ride. Then jump aboard the **Finding Nemo Submarine Voyage** (Map p420;) to look for the world's most famous clownfish from within a refurbished submarine and rumble through an underwater volcanic eruption.

Fantasyland AREA

(Map p420;) Fantasyland is filled with the characters of classic children's stories. If you only see one attraction here, visit **"it's a small world,"** (Map p420;) a boat ride past hundreds of Audio-Animatronics dolls of children from different cultures all singing an earworm of a theme song.

Another classic, the **Matterhorn Bobsleds** (Map p420; https://disneyland.disney.go.com/attractions/disneyland/matterhorn-bobsleds;) is a steel-frame roller coaster that mimics a bobsled ride down a mountain. Fans of old-school attractions will also get a kick out of *The Wind in the Willows*–inspired **Mr. Toad's Wild Ride** (Map p420;), a loopy jaunt through London.

Younger kids love whirling around the **Mad Tea Party** (Map p420;) teacup ride and **King Arthur Carrousel** (Map p420; https://disneyland.disney.go.com/attractions/disneyland/king-arthur-carrousel;), then cavorting with characters in nearby **Mickey's Toontown** (Map p420;), a topsy-turvy mini-metropolis where kiddos can traipse through Mickey and Minnie's houses and dozens of storefronts.

DISNEYLAND IN...

One Day

Get to **Disneyland Park** early. Stroll Main Street, U.S.A. toward Sleeping Beauty Castle. Enter Tomorrowland to ride Hyperspace Mountain. In Fantasyland don't miss the classic "it's a small world" ride or race down the Matterhorn Bobsleds. Grab a FASTPASS for the Indiana Jones Adventure or the Pirates of the Caribbean before lunching in New Orleans Square. Plummet down Splash Mountain, then visit the Haunted Mansion before the fireworks begin.

Two Days

On the second day, at **Disney California Adventure**, take a virtual hang-gliding ride on Soarin' Around the World and let kids tackle the Redwood Creek Challenge Trail before having fun at Paradise Pier with its roller coaster, Ferris wheel and carnival games. Watch the Pixar•Play Parade, then ride the Radiator Springs Racers in Cars Land or cool off – fast! – on the Grizzly River Run. After dark, drop by World of Color show.

Disneyland Resort

Frontierland AREA

(Map p420; 👪) This Disney 'land' is a salute to old Americana: the Mississippi-style paddle-wheel **Mark Twain Riverboat** (Map p420; https://disneyland.disney.go.com/attractions/disneyland/mark-twain-riverboat; 👪), the 18th-century replica **Sailing Ship Columbia** (Map p420; https://disneyland.disney.go.com/attractions/disneyland/sailing-ship-columbia; 👪), a rip-roarin' Old West town with a shooting gallery and the **Big Thunder Mountain Railroad** (Map p420; https://disneyland.disney.go.com/attractions/disneyland/big-thunder-mountain-railroad; 👪), a mining-themed roller coaster. The former Tom Sawyer Island – the only attraction in the park personally designed by Uncle Walt – has been reimagined in the wake of the *Pirates of the Caribbean* movies and renamed the **Pirate's Lair on Tom Sawyer Island** (Map p420; https://disneyland.disney.go.com/attractions/disneyland/pirates-lair-on-tom-sawyer-island; 👪).

Adventureland AREA

(Map p420; 👪) Loosely deriving its jungle theme from Southeast Asia and Africa, Adventureland has a number of attractions, but the hands-down highlight is the safari-style **Indiana Jones™ Adventure** (Map p420; https://disneyland.disney.go.com/attractions/

Disneyland Resort

disneyland/indiana-jones-adventure;). Nearby, little ones love climbing the stairways of **Tarzan's Treehouse** (Map p420; https://disneyland.disney.go.com/attractions/disneyland/tarzans-treehouse;). Cool down on the **Jungle Cruise** (Map p420; https://disneyland.disney.go.com/attractions/disneyland/jungle-cruise;), viewing exotic Audio-Animatronics animals from rivers of South America, India, Africa and Southeast Asia. And the classic **Enchanted Tiki Room** (Map p420; https://disneyland.disney.go.com/attractions/disneyland/enchanted-tiki-room;) features carvings of Hawaiian gods and goddesses and a show of singing, dancing Audio-Animatronics birds and flowers.

Pirates of the Caribbean RIDE

(Map p420; https://disneyland.disney.go.com/attractions/disneyland/pirates-of-the-caribbean; New Orleans Sq;) Pirates of the Caribbean is the longest ride in Disneyland (17 minutes) and one of the longest running, opened in 1967. That's half a century of Audio-Animatronics pirates singing 'Yo-ho, yo-ho, a pirate's life for me' as they cruise by on a boat. You'll float through the subterranean haunts of tawdry pirates, where dead buccaneers perch atop their mounds of booty and Captain Jack Sparrow pops up occasionally.

Critter Country AREA

(Map p420;) Critter Country's main attraction is **Splash Mountain** (Map p420; https://

disneyland.disney.go.com/attractions/disneyland/splash-mountain;), a flume ride through the story of Brer Rabbit and Brer Bear, based on the controversial 1946 film *Song of the South*. Just past Splash Mountain, hop in a mobile beehive on **The Many Adventures of Winnie the Pooh** (https://disneyland.disney.go.com/attractions/disneyland/many-adventures-of-winnie-the-pooh;). Nearby on the Rivers of America, you can paddle **Davy Crockett's Explorer Canoes** (https://disneyland.disney.go.com/attractions/disneyland/davy-crocketts-explorer-canoes;) on summer weekends.

Disney California Adventure

Across the plaza from Disneyland's monument to fantasy is Disney California Adventure (DCA), an ode to California's geography, history and culture – or at least a sanitized G-rated version. DCA, which opened in 2001, covers more acres than Disneyland and feels less crowded, and it has more modern rides and attractions inspired by coastal amusement parks, the inland mountains and redwood forests, the magic of Hollywood, and car culture by way of the movie *Cars*.

Cars Land AREA

(Map p420;) This land gets kudos for its incredibly detailed design based on the popular Disney•Pixar *Cars* movies. Top billing goes to the wacky **Radiator Springs Racers** (Map p420; https://disneyland.disney.go.com/attractions/disney-california-adventure/radiator-springs-racers), a race-car ride that bumps around a track painstakingly decked out like the Great American West.

Grizzly Peak AREA

() Grizzly Peak is broken into sections highlighting California's natural and human achievements. Its main attraction, **Soarin' Around the World** (Map p420; https://disneyland.disney.go.com/attractions/disney-california-adventure/soarin), is a virtual hang-gliding ride using Omnimax technology that 'flies' you over famous landmarks. Enjoy the light breeze as you soar, keeping your nostrils open for aromas blowing in the wind.

Grizzly River Run (Map p420;) takes you 'rafting' down a faux Sierra Nevada river – you will get wet, so come when it's warm. While fake flat-hatted park rangers look on, kids can tackle the Redwood Creek Challenge Trail, with its 'Big Sir' redwoods, wooden towers and lookouts, and rock slide and climbing traverses.

Paradise Pier AREA

(Map p420;) If you like carnival rides, you'll love Paradise Pier, designed to look like a combination of all the beachside amusement piers in California. The state-of-the-art **California Screamin'** (Map p420; https://disneyland.disney.go.com/attractions/disney-california-adventure/california-screamin;) roller coaster resembles an old wooden coaster, but it's got a smooth-as-silk steel track: it feels like you're being shot out of a cannon. Just as popular is **Toy Story Midway Mania!** (Map p420; https://disneyland.disney.go.com/attractions/disney-california-adventure/toy-story-mania) – a 4-D ride where you earn points by shooting at targets while your carnival car swivels and careens through an oversize, old-fashioned game arcade.

Hollywood Land AREA

(Map p420;) California's biggest factory of dreams is presented here in miniature, with soundstages, movable props, and – of course – a studio store. A new *Guardians of the Galaxy*–themed ride is a top attraction; another is a one-hour live stage version of *Frozen*, at the Hyperion Theater (p426).

Activities

Redwood Creek Challenge Trail CLIMBING

(Map p420; Grizzly Peak) At this attraction in Disney California Adventure, more-active kids of all ages can tackle the Redwood Creek Challenge Trail, climbing rock faces, sliding down a rock slide and walking through the 35ft 'Big Sir' redwood stump. Flat-hatted faux park rangers look on.

Sleeping

Disneyland Resort

For the full-on Disney experience, there are three different hotels within Disneyland Resort, though there are less-expensive options just beyond the Disney gates in Anaheim. If you want a theme-park hotel for less money, try Knott's Berry Farm (p428).

★Disney's Grand Californian Hotel & Spa RESORT $$$

(Map p420; info 714-635-2300, reservations 714-956-6425; https://disneyland.disney.go.com/grand-californian-hotel; 1600 S Disneyland Dr; d from $360;) Soaring timber beams rise above the cathedral-like lobby of the six-story Grand Californian, Disney's homage to the

DISNEYLAND TO-DO LIST

- Make area hotel reservations or book a Disneyland vacation package.
- Sign up for online resources including blogs, e-newsletters and resort updates, such as Disney Fans Insider.
- Check the parks' opening hours, live show and entertainment schedules online.
- Make dining reservations for sit-down restaurants or special meals with Disney characters.
- Buy print-at-home tickets and passes online.
- Recheck the next day's opening hours and Anaheim Resort Transportation (p427) or hotel shuttle schedules.
- Pack a small day pack with sunscreen, hat, sunglasses, swimwear, change of clothes, jacket or hoodie, lightweight plastic rain poncho, and extra batteries and memory cards for digital and video cameras.
- Fully charge your electronic devices, including cameras and phones.
- Download the Disneyland app to your smartphone.

arts-and-crafts movement. Rooms have triple-sheeted beds, down pillows, bathrobes and all-custom furnishings. Outside there's a faux-redwood waterslide into the pool. At night, kids wind down with bedtime stories by the lobby's giant stone hearth.

Disneyland Hotel HOTEL **$$$**
(Map p420; 714-778-6600; www.disneyland.com; 1150 Magic Way, Anaheim; r $210-395; P @) Built in 1955, the year Disneyland opened, the park's original hotel has been rejuvenated with a dash of bibbidi-bobbidi-boo. There are three towers with themed lobbies (adventure, fantasy and frontier), and the 972 good-sized rooms now boast Mickey-hand wall sconces in bathrooms and headboards lit like the fireworks over Sleeping Beauty Castle (p419).

Disney's Paradise Pier Hotel HOTEL **$$$**
(Map p420; info 714-999-0990, reservations 714-956-6425; http://disneyland.disney.go.com/paradise-pier-hotel; 1717 S Disneyland Dr, Anaheim; d from $240; P @) Sunbursts, surfboards and a giant superslide are all on deck at the Paradise Pier Hotel, the smallest (472 rooms), cheapest and maybe the most fun of the Disney hotel trio. Kids will love the beachy decor and game arcade, not to mention the pool and the tiny-tot video room filled with mini Adirondack chairs.

Anaheim

While the Disney resorts have their own hotels, there are a number of worthwhile hotels just off-site or a few miles away, and every stripe of chain hotel you can imagine. Generally Anaheim's hotels are good value relative to those in the OC beach towns.

Ayres Hotel Anaheim HOTEL **$$**
(714-634-2106; www.ayreshotels.com/anaheim; 2550 E Katella Ave; r incl breakfast $139-219; P @) This well-run minichain of business hotels delivers solid-gold value. The 133 recently renovated rooms have microwaves, minifridges, safes, wet bar, pillow-top mattresses and design inspired by the Californian arts-and-crafts movement. Fourth-floor rooms have extra-high ceilings. Rates include a full breakfast and evening social hours Monday to Thursday with beer, wine and snacks.

Residence Inn Anaheim Resort/ Convention Center HOTEL **$$**
(Map p420; 714-782-7500; www.marriott.com; 640 W Katella Ave; r from $179; P @) This new hotel near the convention center, yet only about 10 minutes on foot to Disneyland, shines with sleek linens, marble tables and glass walls within in-room kitchens, big windows and a sweet rooftop pool deck with Jacuzzi and a splash zone for kids. Rates include full breakfast, and there's also a gym and laundry machines.

Hotel Indigo Anaheim BOUTIQUE HOTEL **$$**
(Map p420; 714-772-7755; www.ihg.com; 435 W Katella Ave; r from $170; P @) This friendly, professional 104-room hotel has a clean, mid-century modernist look with hardwood floor and pops of color, fitness center, pool and guest laundry. Mosaic murals are modeled after the walnut trees that

FASTPASS

Disneyland and Disney California Adventure's FASTPASS system can significantly cut your wait times.

➡ Walk up to a FASTPASS ticket machine – located near the entrance to select theme-park rides – and insert your park entrance ticket or annual passport. You'll receive a slip of paper showing the 'return time' for boarding (it's always at least 40 minutes later).

➡ Show up within the window of time on the ticket and join the ride's FASTPASS line. There'll still be a wait, but it's shorter (typically 15 minutes or less). Hang on to your FASTPASS ticket until you board the ride.

➡ If you're running late and miss the time window printed on your FASTPASS ticket, you can still try joining the FASTPASS line, although showing up before your FASTPASS time window is a no-no.

You're thinking, what's the catch, right? When you get a FASTPASS, you will have to wait at least two hours before getting another one (check the 'next available' time printed at the bottom of your ticket).

So, make it count. Before getting a FASTPASS, check the display above the machine, which will tell you what the 'return time' for boarding is. If it's much later in the day, or doesn't fit your schedule, a FASTPASS may not be worth it. Ditto if the ride's current wait time is just 15 to 30 minutes.

once bloomed here. It's about 15 minutes' walk or a quick drive to Disneyland and steps from shops and restaurants at Anaheim GardenWalk.

Eating

From stroll-and-eat Mickey-shaped pretzels ($4) and jumbo turkey legs ($10) to deluxe, gourmet dinners (sky's the limit), there's no shortage of eating options, though mostly pretty expensive and targeted to mainstream tastes. Phone **Disney Dining** (☎714-781-3463; http://disneyland.disney.go.com/dining) to make reservations up to 60 days in advance. Restaurant hours vary seasonally, sometimes daily. Check the Disneyland app or Disney Dining website for same-day hours. Driving just a couple miles into Anaheim will expand the offerings and price points considerably.

Disneyland Park

Blue Bayou SOUTHERN US **$$$**
(Map p420; ☎714-781-3463; https://disneyland.disney.go.com/dining/disneyland/blue-bayou-restaurant; New Orleans Sq; mains lunch $28-41, dinner $30-48; ⏰lunch & dinner; 👪) Surrounded by the 'bayou' inside the Pirates of the Caribbean (p421) attraction, this is the top choice for sit-down dining in Disneyland Park and is famous for its Creole and Cajun specialties at dinner. Order fresh-baked pecan pie topped by a piratey souvenir for dessert (*ahh*, then *argh*!).

Jolly Holiday Bakery Cafe RESTAURANT, BAKERY **$**
(Map p420; https://disneyland.disney.go.com/dining/disneyland/jolly-holiday-bakery-cafe; Main Street, U.S.A.; mains $8.50-11; ⏰breakfast, lunch & dinner; 👪) At this Mary Poppins–themed restaurant, the Jolly Holiday combo (grilled cheese and tomato basil soup for $9) is a decent deal and very satisfying. The cafe does other sandwiches on the sophisticated side, like the mozzarella caprese or turkey on ciabatta. Great people-watching from outdoor seating.

Downtown Disney & Hotels

★ **Napa Rose** CALIFORNIAN **$$$**
(Map p420; ☎714-300-7170; https://disneyland.disney.go.com/dining; Grand Californian Hotel & Spa; mains $38-48, 4-course prix-fixe dinner from $100; ⏰5:30-10pm; 👪) High-back arts-and-crafts style chairs, leaded-glass windows and towering ceilings befit Disneyland Resort's top-drawer restaurant. On the plate, seasonal 'California Wine Country' (read: NorCal) cuisine is as impeccably crafted as Sleeping Beauty Castle. Kids' menu available. Reservations essential. Enter the hotel from Disney California Adventure or Downtown Disney.

Steakhouse 55 AMERICAN **$$$**
(Map p420; ☎714-781-3463; 1150 Magic Way, Disneyland Hotel; mains breakfast $14-25, dinner $31-57; ⏰7am-11pm & 5-10:30pm) Nothing at Disneyland is exactly a secret, but this clubby, grown-up hideaway comes pretty darn close. Dry-rubbed, bone-in rib eye, Australian lob-

ster tail, heirloom potatoes and green beans with applewood-smoked bacon uphold a respectable chophouse menu. There's also a full bar, good wine list and (we hope well-behaved) kids' menu.

Disney California Adventure

Pacific Wharf Cafe FOOD HALL $

(Map p420; https://disneyland.disney.go.com/dining/disney-california-adventure/pacific-wharf-cafe; mains $10-11.50; breakfast, lunch & dinner;) This counter-service collection of restaurants shows off some of California's ethnic cuisines (Chinese, Mexican etc) as well as hearty soups in sourdough bread bowls, farmers-market salads and deli sandwiches. We like to eat at umbrella-covered tables by the water.

Wine Country Trattoria ITALIAN $$

(Map p420; https://disneyland.disney.go.com/dining/disney-california-adventure/wine-country-trattoria; Pacific Wharf; mains lunch $15-21, dinner $17-23; lunch & dinner;) If you can't quite swing the Napa Rose or Carthay Circle, this sunny Cal-Italian terrace restaurant is a fine backup. Fork into Italian pastas, salads or veggie paninis, washed down with Napa Valley wines.

★ **Carthay Circle** AMERICAN $$$

(Map p420; https://disneyland.disney.go.com/dining/disney-california-adventure/carthay-circle-restaurant; Buena Vista St; mains lunch $24-34, dinner $32-45; lunch & dinner;) Decked out like a Hollywood country club, new Carthay Circle is the best dining in either park, with seasonal steaks, seafood, pasta, smart service and a good wine list. Your table needs at least one order of fried biscuits, stuffed with white cheddar, bacon, and jalapeño and served with apricot honey butter.

Anaheim

Most restaurants on the streets surrounding Disneyland are chains, though **Anaheim GardenWalk** (www.anaheimgardenwalk.com; 400 W Disney Way; 11am-9pm;) has some upscale ones. It's about a 10-minute walk from Disneyland's main gate.

★ **Olive Tree** MIDDLE EASTERN $$

(714-535-2878; 512 S Brookhurst St; mains $8-16; 10am-9pm Mon-Sat, to 8pm Sun) In Little Arabia, this simple restaurant in a nondescript strip mall ringed by flags of Arab nations has earned accolades from local papers to *Saveur* magazine. You *could* get standards like falafel and kebabs, but daily specials are where it's at; Saturday's *kabseh* is righteous, fall-off-the-bone lamb shank over spiced rice with currants and onions.

Umami Burger BURGERS $$

(714-991-8626; www.umamiburger.com; 338 S Anaheim Blvd; mains $11-15; 11am-11pm Sun-Thu, to midnight Fri & Sat) The Anaheim outpost of this LA-based mini-chain sets the right tone for the Packing District (p426). Burgers span classic to truffled. Try the Hatch burger with roasted green chilies or the Manly with beer cheddar and bacon lardons. Get 'em with deep-fried 'smushed' potatoes with house-made ketchup, and top it off with a salted chocolate ice-cream sandwich. Full bar.

Drinking

You can't buy alcohol in Disneyland, but you can at Disney California Adventure, Downtown Disney and Disney's trio of resort hotels (p422). Downtown Disney offers bars, live music, a 12-screen cinema and more. Some restaurants and bars stay open as late as midnight on Fridays and Saturdays.

Golden Vine Winery BAR

(Map p420; Pacific Wharf, Disney California Adventure) This centrally located terrace is a great place for relaxing and regrouping in Disney California Adventure. Nearby at Pacific Wharf, walk-up window **Rita's Baja Blenders** whips up frozen cocktails like marga – you know – ritas, and nonalcoholic blended strawberry and lemon drinks.

Entertainment

It's tiki to the max and good, clean fun at **Trader Sam's Enchanted Tiki Lounge** (Map p420; https://disneyland.disney.go.com/dining/disneyland-hotel/trader-sams; 1150 Magic Way, Disneyland Hotel; 11:30am-1:30am). You can also hear big-name acts at **House of Blues** (714-778-2583; www.houseofblues.com/anaheim; 400 W Disney Way, Anaheim Garden Walk; hours vary) or jazz at **Ralph Brennan's New Orleans Jazz Kitchen** (Map p420; 714-776-5200; http://rbjazzkitchen.com; Downtown Disney; mains lunch/dinner $14-19/$24.50-38.50; 8am-10pm Sun-Thu, to 11pm Fri & Sat;).

★ **World of Color** LIVE PERFORMANCE

(Map p420; https://disneyland.disney.go.com/entertainment/disney-california-adventure/world-of-color; Paradise Pier) Disney California Adventure's premier show is the 22-minute *World of Color*, a dazzling nighttime display of lasers,

WORTH A TRIP

ANAHEIM PACKING DISTRICT & CENTER STREET

The **Anaheim Packing District** (www.anaheimpackingdistrict.com; S Anaheim Bl) launched in 2013 around a long-shuttered 1925 Packard dealership and the 1919 orange packing house a couple miles from Disneyland, near the city's actual downtown.

It relaunched in 2013–14 with chic new restaurants like **Umami Burger** (p425), the **Anaheim Brewery** (www.anaheimbrew.com; 336 S Anaheim Blvd; 5-9pm Tue-Thu, 5-11pm Fri, noon-11pm Sat, 1-7pm Sun), an evolving collection of shops and a park for events.

About a quarter-mile from here is **Center Street** (www.centerstreetanaheim.com; W Center St), a quietly splashy redeveloped neighborhood with an ice rink designed by starchitect Frank Gehry, and a couple of blocks of hip shops. Dining offerings include the fabulous food hall of the **Packing House** (714-533-7225; www.anaheimpackingdistrict.com; 440 S Anaheim St; opens 9am, closing hours vary), and the creative vegan dishes at **Healthy Junk** (714-772-5865; www.thehealthyjunk.com; 201 Center St Promenade; mains $4-10; 10am-9pm Mon-Fri, 11am-9pm Sat, 11am-5pm Sun;).

lights and animation projected over Paradise Bay. It's so popular, you'll need a FASTPASS ticket. Otherwise, several of the restaurants around DCA offer meal-and-ticket packages. Failing that, space is available without a ticket on a first-come, first-served basis.

Hyperion Theater THEATER
(Map p420; https://disneyland.disney.go.com/entertainment/disney-california-adventure/frozen-live-at-hyperion; Hollywood Land) A live stage version of the animated movie musical *Frozen* is presented here, with actors, the hit songs and Broadway-style costumes, sets and lighting.

Shopping

Each 'land' has its own shopping, appropriate to its particular theme, whether the Old West, Route 66 or a seaside amusement park. There's no shortage of ways to spend on souvenirs, clothing and Disneyana and plenty other non-Disney goods. For collectors, **Disney Gallery** (Map p420; https://disneyland.disney.go.com; Main Street, U.S.A.) and **Off the Page** (Map p420; Hollywood Land, Disney California Adventure) sell high-end art and collectibles like original sketches and vintage reproduction prints.

There are plenty of opportunities to drop cash in stores of **Downtown Disney** (not just Disney stuff either), restaurants and entertainment venues. Apart from the Disney merch, a lot of it is shops you can find elsewhere, but in the moment it's still hard to resist. Most shops here open and close with the parks.

Information

Before you arrive, visit **Disneyland Resort** (live assistance 714-781-7290, recorded info 714-781-4565; www.disneyland.com) for more information. You can also download the Disneyland Explorer app for your mobile device.

LOCKERS

Self-service lockers with in-and-out privileges cost $7 to $15 per day. You'll find them on Main Street, U.S.A. (p418; Disneyland), in **Sunshine Plaza** (Disney California Adventure) and at the **picnic area** just outside the theme park's main entrance, near Downtown Disney.

MEDICAL SERVICES

You'll find first-aid facilities at Disneyland (Main Street, U.S.A.), Disney California Adventure (Pacific Wharf) and Downtown Disney (next to Ralph Brennan's Jazz Kitchen).

Anaheim Urgent Care (714-533-2273; 831 S State College Blvd, Anaheim; 8am-8pm Mon-Fri, 9am-5pm Sat & Sun) Walk-in nonemergency medical clinic.

Anaheim Global Medical Center (657-230-0265; www.anaheim-gmc.com; 1025 S Anaheim Blvd, Anaheim; 24hr) Hospital emergency room.

MONEY

Disneyland's City Hall offers foreign-currency exchange. In Disney California Adventure, head to the guest relations lobby. Multiple ATMs are found in both theme parks and at Downtown Disney.

Travelex (714-687-7977; 100 West Lincoln Ave, inside US Bank, Anaheim; 9am-5pm Mon-Fri, to 1pm Sat) Also exchanges foreign currency near Anaheim City Hall.

TOURIST INFORMATION

For information or help inside the parks, just ask any cast member or visit Disneyland's **City Hall** (Map p420; 714-781-4565; Main Street, U.S.A.) or Disney California Adventure's guest relations lobby.

Visit Anaheim (Map p420; 855-405-5020; http://visitanaheim.org; 800 W Katella Ave, Anaheim Convention Center) The city's official tourism bureau has information on lodging, dining and transportation, during events at the Convention Center.

Getting There & Away

Disneyland and Anaheim can be reached by car (off the I-5 Fwy) or Amtrak or Metrolink trains at Anaheim's **ARTIC** (Anaheim Regional Transportation Intermodal Center; 2150 E Katella Ave, Anaheim) transit center. From here it's a short taxi, ride share or Anaheim Resort Transportation shuttle to Disneyland proper. The closest airport is Orange County's **John Wayne Airport** (SNA; www.ocair.com; 18601 Airport Way, Santa Ana).

AIR

Most international travelers arrive at Los Angeles International Airport (LAX), but for easy-in, easy-out domestic travel, the manageable John Wayne Airport in Santa Ana is served by all major US airlines and Canada's WestJet. It's near the junction of Hwy 55 and I-405 (San Diego Fwy).

CAR & MOTORCYCLE

Disneyland Resort is just off I-5 (Santa Ana Fwy), about 30 miles southeast of Downtown LA. Take the Disneyland Dr exit if you're coming from the north, or the Katella Ave/Disney Way exit from the south.Arriving at Disneyland Resort is like arriving at an airport. Giant, easy-to-read overhead signs indicate which ramps you need to take for the theme parks, hotels or Anaheim's streets.

TRAIN

Amtrak (☎800-872-7245; www.amtrak.com; 2626 E Katella Ave, ARTIC) has almost a dozen daily trains to/from LA's Union Station ($15, 40 minutes) and San Diego ($28, 2¼ hours). Less frequent **Metrolink** (☎800-371-5465; www.metrolinktrains.com; 22150 E Katella Ave, Anaheim, ARTIC) commuter trains connect Anaheim to LA's Union Station ($8.75, 50 minutes), Orange ($2.50, six minutes), San Juan Capistrano ($8.50, 40 minutes) and San Clemente ($10, 50 minutes).

SHUTTLE

Anaheim Resort Transportation operates some 20 shuttle routes between Disneyland and area hotels, convention centers, malls, stadiums and the transit center, saving traffic jams and parking headaches. Shuttles typically start running an hour before Disneyland opens, operating from 7am to midnight daily during summer. Departures are typically two to three times per hour, depending on the route. Purchase single or multiday ART passes at kiosks near ART shuttle stops or online in advance.

Many hotels and motels offer their own free shuttles to Disneyland and other area attractions; ask when booking.

Getting Around

CAR & MOTORCYCLE

All-day parking at Disneyland Resort costs $20 ($25 for oversize vehicles). Enter the 'Mickey & Friends' parking structure from southbound Disneyland Dr, off Ball Rd. Walk outside and follow the signs to board the free tram to Downtown Disney and the theme parks. The parking garage opens one hour before the parks do.

SHUTTLE

Anaheim Resort Transportation (ART; ☎888-364-2787; www.rideart.org; adult/child fare $3/1, day pass $5.50/2, multiple-day passes available) ART connects the Disney resorts with hotels and other locations around Anaheim and nearby. Day passes can be purchased at hotels or via the ART Ticketing app (www.rideart.org/fares-and-passes).

TRAIN & MONORAIL

With an admission ticket to Disneyland, you can ride the monorail between Tomorrowland and the far end of Downtown Disney, near the Disneyland Hotel. It sure beats walking both ways along crowded Downtown Disney.

AROUND DISNEYLAND

Within 10 easy miles of the Mouse House you'll find a big scoopful of sights and attractions that are worth a visit in their own right.

Knott's Berry Farm

America's oldest theme park, **Knott's** (☎714-220-5200; www.knotts.com; 8039 Beach Blvd, Buena Park; adult/child 3-11yr $75/42; ⊙from 10am, closing hours vary 5-11pm; P 👪) is smaller and less frenetic than Disneyland, but it can be more fun, especially for thrill-seeking teens, roller-coaster fanatics and younger kids.

The park opened in 1932, when Walter Knott's boysenberries (a blackberry-raspberry hybrid) and his wife Cordelia's fried-chicken dinners attracted crowds of local farmhands. Mr Knott built an imitation ghost town to keep them entertained, and eventually hired local carnival rides and charged admission.

Today Knott's keeps the Old West theme alive and thriving with shows and demonstrations at **Ghost Town**, but it's the thrill rides that draw the big crowds. The **Sierra Sidewinder** roller coaster rips through banks and turns while rotating on its axis. The suspended, inverted **Silver Bullet** screams through a corkscrew, a double spiral and an outside loop. **Xcelerator** is a 1950s-themed roller coaster that blasts you from 0mph to 82mph in under 2½ seconds with a hair-raising twist at the top. **Perilous Plunge** whooshes at 75mph down a 75-degree angled water chute that's almost as tall as Niagara Falls.

Opening hours vary seasonally, and online savings can be substantial (eg $10 off adult admission for buying print-at-home tickets).

Next door to Knott's Berry Farm is the affiliated water park **Soak City** (☎714-220-5200; www.soakcityoc.com; 8039 Beach Blvd, Buena Park; adult/child 3-11yr $43/38; ⏲10am-5pm, 6pm or 7pm mid-May–mid-Sep; P 👪), boasting a 750,000-gallon wave pool and dozens of high-speed slides, tubes and flumes. You must have a bathing suit without rivets or metal pieces to go on some slides. Bring a beach towel and a change of dry clothes.

Sleeping & Eating

Knott's Berry Farm Hotel (☎714-995-1111, 866-752-2444; www.knottshotel.com; 7675 Crescent Ave, Buena Park; r $79-169; P @ 📶 🏊) is a high-rise with bland rooms, outdoor pool, fitness center and tennis and basketball courts. For young Charlie Brown fans, ask about Camp Snoopy rooms, where kids are treated to *Peanuts*-themed decor (doghouse headboards? Awesome!), telephone bedtime stories and a goodnight 'tuck-in' visit from Snoopy himself.

The park has plenty of carnival-quality fast food, but the classic meal is the button-busting fried chicken and mashed potato dinner at the nuthin'-fancy **Mrs Knott's Chicken Dinner Restaurant** (☎714-220-5055; 8039 Beach Blvd, Buena Park; chicken dinner lunch $17, dinner $22; ⏲11am-9pm Mon-Fri, 8am-10pm Sat, 7am-9pm Sun; 👪).

Discovery Cube

Follow the giant 10-story cube – balanced on one of its points – to the **Discovery Cube** (☎714-542-2823; www.discoverycube.org; 2500 N Main St, Santa Ana; adult/child 3-14yr & senior $16/13, 4-D movies $2 extra; ⏲10am-5pm; P 👪), the county's best educational kiddie attraction. About 100 hands-on displays await, covering everything from dinosaurs to robotics, rockets to the water supply, the environment to hockey. In the Grand Hall of Science, you might learn the science of tornadoes or the physics of pulleys, while the Discovery Theater screens 4-D movies.

Elsewhere, step into the eye of a hurricane or grab a seat in the Shake Shack to virtually experience a magnitude 6.4 quake. Special science-themed exhibits, like the annual Bubblefest, are fun too. There was a 44,000-sq-ft expansion of the facilities in 2015.

Best allow a good four hours here, more if your kids are budding scientists. It's about 5 miles southeast of Disneyland via the I-5.

Bowers Museum & Kidseum

From its stately, Spanish Colonial–style shell, the **Bowers Museum** (☎714-567-3600; www.bowers.org; 2002 N Main St, Santa Ana; Tue-Fri adult/child 12-17yr & senior $13/10, Sat & Sun $15/12, special exhibit surcharge varies; ⏲10am-4pm Tue-Sun; 🚌53, 83) explodes onto the scene every year or so with remarkable exhibits that remind LA-centric museum-goers that the Bowers, too, is a local and national power player. Permanent exhibits are equally impressive, a rich collection of pre-Columbian, African, Chinese and Native American art, plus California art from the missions to Laguna Beach–style plein air painting. Our favorite: the Spirits and Headhunters gallery, showing jewelry, armaments, masks and religious articles of the Pacific Islands.

Docent-guided gallery tours are given every afternoon, and the airy cafe Tangata serves great lunches and California wines by the glass.

Admission to the Bowers also covers the affiliated **Kidseum** (☎714-480-1520; 1802 N Main St, Santa Ana; $8, child 2yr & younger free; ⏲10am-4pm Sat & Sun, 10am-4pm Tue-Fri during school holidays; 👪; 🚌53, 83), a quick walk away; check in advance for its opening hours, which are more limited.

The museum is 6 miles southeast of Disneyland, off I-5 in Santa Ana. Admission is free on the first Sunday of each month. Public parking costs $6.

Old Towne Orange

The city of Orange, 7 miles southeast of Disneyland, retains its charming historical center, called Old Towne Orange. It's where locals go, and visitors will find it well worth the detour for antiques and vintage clothing shops, smart restaurants and pure SoCal nostalgia.

Orange was originally laid out by Alfred Chapman and Andrew Glassell, who in 1869 received the 1-sq-mile piece of real estate in lieu of legal fees. Orange became California's only city laid out around a central plaza, a traffic circle where present-day Glassell St and Chapman Ave meet, and it remains pleasantly walkable today.

Eating

★ Linx HOT DOGS $
(☎714-744-3647; www.linxdogs.com; 238 W Chapman Ave; mains $5.50-14; ⏰11am-10pm Mon-Wed, to 11pm Thu & Fri, 10am-11pm Sat, 10am-10pm Sun) First things first: they're not hot dogs, they're 'haute' dogs, homemade and topped with your choice of combinations (the BBQ, Bacon and Blues comes with barbecue sauce, bacon marmalade and blue cheese bacon aioli). Burgers come with fries. There's a daily-changing craft-beer selection, and bread pudding for dessert with chocolate ganache and strawberries.

Burger Parlor BURGERS $
(☎714-602-8220; www.burgerparlor.com; 149 N Glassell St; mains $8-11; ⏰11am-9pm Sun-Wed, to 11pm Thu-Sat; 👪) Chef Joseph Mahon has parlayed his work at a Michelin-starred restaurant into gourmet burgers that have been named the OC's best. The cheerily contemporary counter service Orange location dishes up the same award-winning Smokey and Parlor burgers, plus fries and onion rings. Bonus: you can get any burger on lettuce instead of a bun (because California).

★ Watson Soda Fountain Café DINER $$
(☎714-202-2899; www.watsonscafe.com; 116 E Chapman Ave; mains $8-18; ⏰7am-9pm Sun-Wed, to 10pm Thu, to midnight Fri & Sat) Established 1899, this former drugstore was recently refurbished to a period design (check out the old safe, apothecary cabinets and telephone switchboard). It offers old-fashioned soda-fountain treats such as malts, milkshakes and sundaes, as well as burgers, fries, fried pickle chips and breakfast all day.

Haven Gastropub GASTROPUB $$
(☎714-221-0680; www.havengastropub.com; 190 S Glassell St; items $8-27; ⏰11am-2am Mon-Fri, from 9am Sat & Sun) Come with your sweetie or a group to share plates like beef poutine with cheese curds and sous vide egg, Brussels sprouts with flash-fried prosciutto or mac and cheese with truffle béchamel, and the burger is so good you'll probably want to share that too. There's a great, ever-changing craft-beer list and lots of windows to watch the scene.

Shopping

Shops line up primarily north and south, and to a lesser extent east and west, of Old Towne's **plaza** (cnr Chapman Ave & Glassell St), where you can find the OC's most concentrated collection of antiques, collectibles and vintage and consignment shops. It's fun to browse and some are very well curated. That said, real bargains are rare and you'll want to make sure the pieces are authentic.

Joy Ride VINTAGE
(☎714-771-7118; www.joyridevintage.com; 109 W Chapman Ave; ⏰11am-7pm) The brother shop of Elsewhere Vintage, Joy Ride has a similar vibe only with men's clothing: 1950s bowling shirts to immaculately maintained wool blazers, plus vintage cameras, straight-edge razors and other manly pursuits. It even has a hat repair clinic.

Elsewhere Vintage VINTAGE
(☎714-771-2116; www.elsewherevintage.com; 105 W Chapman Ave; ⏰11am-7pm) A hipster's love affair, this ladies' vintage store hangs sundresses next to hats, leather handbags and fabulous costume jewelry, all with a special emphasis on the 1920s to the '60s.

Getting There & Away

The drive from Anaheim takes under 20 minutes: take I-5 south to Hwy 22 east, then drive north on Grand Ave, which becomes Glassell St, for just over a mile. Both **Amtrak** (☎800-872-7245; www.amtrak.com) and **Metrolink** (☎800-371-5465; www.metrolinktrains.com) commuter trains stop at Orange's **train station** (191 N Atchison St), a few blocks west of the plaza with connections to Anaheim and LA's Union Station. **OCTA** (p430) bus line 59 also runs from Anaheim.

ORANGE COUNTY BEACHES

Orange County's 42 miles of beaches are a land of gorgeous sunsets, prime surfing, just-off-the-boat seafood and serendipitous discoveries. Whether you're learning to surf the waves at Seal Beach, piloting a boat around Newport Harbor, or spotting whales on a cruise out of yacht-filled Dana Point harbor, you'll discover each town has a distinctive charm.

Seal Beach

The OC's first beach town driving south from LA County, 'Seal' is one of the last great California beach towns and a refreshing alternative to the more crowded coast further south. Its 1.5 miles of pristine beach sparkle like a crown, and that's without mentioning three-block Main St, a stoplight-free zone with mom-and-pop restaurants and indie shops that are low on 'tude and high on charm.

Although the town's east side is dominated by the sprawling retirement community Leisure World and the huge US Naval Weapons Station (look for grass-covered bunkers), all that fades away along the charming Main St and the oceanfront.

Sights & Activities

Amble Main St and check out the laid-back local scene – barefoot surfers, friendly shopkeepers and silver-haired foxes scoping the way-too-young beach bunnies. Where Main St ends, walk out onto **Seal Beach Pier**, extending 1865ft over the ocean.

M&M Surfing School SURFING

(☎714-846-7873; www.surfingschool.com; 802 Ocean Ave; 1hr/3hr group lesson $77/85; ⌚lessons 8am-noon early Sep–mid-Jun and Sat & Sun all year, to 2pm Mon-Fri mid-Jun–early Sep; 👪) Offers group and private lessons that include surfboard and wet-suit rental, for students age five and up. Look for its van in the parking lot just north of the pier, off Ocean Ave at 8th St.

Eating

★ **Walt's Wharf** SEAFOOD $$$

(☎562-598-4433; www.waltswharf.com; 201 Main St; mains lunch $13-29, dinner $17-40; ⌚11am-9pm) Everybody's favorite for fresh fish (some drive in from LA), Walt's packs them in on weekends. You can't make reservations for dinner (though they're accepted for lunch), but it's worth the wait for the oak-fire-grilled seafood and steaks in the many-windowed ground floor or upstairs in captain's chairs. Otherwise, eat at the bar.

★ **Mahé** SUSHI, FUSION $$$

(☎562-431-3022; www.eatatmahe.com; 1400 Pacific Coast Hwy; mains lunch $15-20, dinner $15-39; ⌚opens 4pm Mon-Thu, 3pm Fri, 11:30am Sat, 10am Sun, closing hours vary) Raw-fish fans gather barside at this beach-chic sushi bar with live bands some nights in the back room. Baked scallop parmesan, ahi *tataki* wraps, and filet mignon with Gorgonzola cream all hang out on the Cal-Japanese menu. It's about five blocks from Main St but worth the walk.

Drinking

On Main St you'll find a surprising number of Irish pubs, alongside coffee bars, though we're particularly fond of cozy Bogart's, right across from the ocean.

Bogart's Coffee House CAFE

(☎562-431-2226; www.bogartscoffee.com; 905 Ocean Ave; ⌚6am-9pm Mon-Thu, to 10pm Fri, 7am-10pm Sat, 7am-9pm Sun; 📶) Around the corner from Main St, sip organic espresso drinks on the leopard-print sofa and play Scrabble as you watch the surf roll in on the beach across the street. Bogart's hosts live music Friday and Saturday nights, plus a regular open mike on Tuesdays.

Entertainment

Jazz, folk and bluegrass bands play by the pier at the foot of Main St from 6pm to 8pm every Wednesday during July and August for the annual **Summer Concerts in the Park** (http://sealbeachchamber.org; Eisenhower Park; ⌚6pm Wed Jul & Aug). The rest of the time, Main St is the kind of place where you'll find sidewalk musicians.

Shopping

Harbour Surfboards SPORTS & OUTDOORS

(☎562-430-5614; www.harboursurfboards.com; 329 Main St; ⌚9am-7pm, to 6pm Sun) This place has been making surfboards since 1959, but it's also about the surf-and-skate lifestyle, man. Eavesdrop on local surfers talking about their wax as you pillage the racks of hoodies, wet suits, beach T-shirts and beanie hats.

Tankfarm & Co. FASHION & ACCESSORIES

(☎562-594-4800; www.tankfarmco.com; 212 Main St; ⌚10am-6pm Sun-Thu, to 8pm Fri & Sat) On a street dominated by women's clothing and beachwear, Seal Beach–based Tankfarm carries duds for dudes craving the outdoor lifestyle: board shorts, hoodies, flannels and blankets from brands like Herschel and Deus Ex Machina, plus its own cool tees, woven shirts and accessories from pomade to enamel mugs reading 'coffee, whiskey or beer.' Worthy goals all.

Getting There & Around

Orange County Transport Authority (OCTA; ☎714-560-6282; www.octa.net; ride/day pass

RICHARD NIXON LIBRARY & MUSEUM

The **Nixon Library** (☎714-993-5075; www.nixonfoundation.org; 18001 Yorba Linda Blvd, Yorba Linda; adult/child 5-11yr/student/senior $16/6/10/12; ⊙10am-5pm Mon-Sat, 11am-5pm Sun; P) offers a fascinating walk though America's modern history and that of this controversial native son of Orange County (1913–94), who served as president from 1969 to 74. Noteworthy exhibits include a full-size replica of the White House East Room, recordings of conversations with *Apollo 11* astronauts on the moon, access to the ex-presidential helicopter – complete with wet bar and ashtrays – and excerpts from landmark TV appearances including the Kennedy-Nixon debates and Nixon's famous self-parody on the *Laugh-In* comedy show. Exhibits about Watergate, the infamous scandal that ultimately brought down Nixon's administration, also figure prominently.

The library is in the residential community of Yorba Linda in northeastern Orange County, about 10 miles northeast of Anaheim. To get here, take Hwy 57 north and exit east on Yorba Linda Blvd, then continue straight and follow the signs.

$2/5) bus 1 connects Seal Beach with the OC's other beach towns and LA's Long Beach every hour; the one-way fare is $2 (exact change). Long Beach Transit lines 131 and 171 also stop in Seal Beach.

There's two-hour free parking along Main St between downtown Seal Beach and the pier, but it's difficult to find a spot in summer. Public parking lots by the pier cost $3 per two hours, $6 all day. Free parking along residential side streets is subject to posted restrictions.

Huntington Beach

'No worries' is the phrase you'll hear over and over in Huntington Beach, the town that goes by the trademarked nickname 'Surf City USA.' In 1910 real-estate developer and railroad magnate Henry Huntington hired Hawaiian-Irish surfing star George Freeth to give demonstrations. When legendary surfer Duke Kahanamoku moved here in 1925, that solidified its status as a surf destination. Buyers for major retailers come here to see what surfers are wearing, then market the look.

Long considered a low-key, not-quite-fashionable beach community with its share of sidewalk-surfing skate rats and hollering late-night barflies, its downtown has undergone a couple of makeovers, first along **Main Street** and then at the sparkling new **Pacific City** (www.gopacificcity.com; 21010 Pacific Coast Hwy; ⊙hours vary) shopping center.

Still, HB remains a quintessential spot to celebrate the hang-loose SoCal coastal lifestyle: consistently good waves, surf shops, a surf museum, bonfires on the sand, a canine-friendly beach, and hotels and restaurants with killer views.

Sights

Bolsa Chica State Beach BEACH

(www.parks.ca.gov; Pacific Coast Hwy, btwn Seapoint & Warner Aves; parking $15; ⊙6am-10pm; P) A 3-mile-long strip of sand favored by surfers, volleyball players and fishers, Bolsa Chica State Beach stretches alongside Pacific Coast Hwy between **Huntington Dog Beach** (www.dogbeach.org; 100 Goldenwest Street; ⊙5am-10pm; P) to the south and Sunset Beach to the north. Even though it faces a monstrous offshore oil rig, Bolsa Chica (meaning 'Little Pocket' in Spanish) gets mobbed on summer weekends. You'll find picnic tables, fire rings and beach showers, plus a bike path running north to Anderson Ave in Sunset Beach and south to Huntington State Beach.

Huntington City Beach BEACH

(www.huntingtonbeachca.gov; ⊙5am-10pm; P 🚻) One of SoCal's best beaches, the sand surrounding the pier at the foot of Main St gets packed on summer weekends with surfers, volleyball players, swimmers and families. Bathrooms and showers are located north of the pier at the back of the snack-bar complex. In the evening volleyball games give way to beach bonfires.

Huntington Beach Pier HISTORIC SITE

(cnr Main St & Pacific Coast Hwy; ⊙5am-midnight) The 1853ft Huntington Pier is one of the West Coast's longest. It has been here – in one form or another – since 1904, though the mighty Pacific has damaged giant sections or completely demolished it multiple times since then. The current concrete structure was built in 1983 to withstand 31ft waves or a 7.0-magnitude earthquake, whichever hits HB first. On the pier you can rent fishing gear from **Let's Go Fishing**

TOP BEACHES IN ORANGE COUNTY

- **Seal Beach** (p430)
- **Bolsa Chica State Beach** (p431)
- **Huntington City Beach** (p431)
- **Balboa Peninsula** (p434)
- **Crystal Cove State Beach** (p439)
- **Aliso Beach County Park** (p442)
- **Doheny State Beach** (p446)

(714-960-1392; 21 Main Street, Huntington Beach Pier; fishing sets per hour/day $6/15; hours vary) bait and tackle shop.

Huntington State Beach BEACH
(714-536-1454; www.parks.ca.gov; 6am-10pm; P) Want even more surf and sand? South of the pier, Huntington State Beach extends 2 miles from Beach Blvd (Hwy 39) to the Santa Ana River and Newport Beach boundary. All-day parking costs $15.

International Surfing Museum MUSEUM
(714-960-3483; www.surfingmuseum.org; 411 Olive Ave; adult/child $2/1; noon-5pm Tue-Sun) The world's biggest surfboard (in the *Guinness World Records*) fronts this small museum, an entertaining stop for surf-culture enthusiasts. Temporary exhibits chronicle the sport's history with photos, vintage surfboards, movie memorabilia and surf music. For the best historical tidbits, spend a minute chatting with the all-volunteer staff.

Activities

Huntington is a one-stop shop for outdoor pleasures by OC beaches. If you forgot to pack beach gear, you can rent umbrellas, beach chairs, volleyballs and other essentials from **Zack's** (714-536-0215; www.zackssurfcity.com; 405 Pacific Coast Hwy; group lessons $85, surfboard rentals per hour/day $12/35, wetsuits $5/15), just north of the pier. Just south of the pier on the Strand, friendly **Dwight's Beach Concession** (714-536-8083; www.dwightsbeachconcession.com; 201 Pacific Coast Hwy; surfboard rentals per hour/day $10/40, bicycle rentals from $10/30; 9am-5pm Mon-Fri, to 6pm Sat & Sun), around since 1932, rents bikes, boogie boards, umbrellas and chairs. **Huntington Surf & Sport** (www.hsssurf.com; 300 Pacific Coast Hwy; 8am-9pm Sun-Thu, to 10pm Fri & Sat) also rents boards and wetsuits.

Vans Off the Wall Skatepark OUTDOORS
(714-379-6666; 7471 Center Dr; helmet & pad set rentals $5; 9am-8pm daily) FREE This custom-built facility by the OC-based sneaker and skatewear company has plenty of ramps, bowls, dips, boxes and rails for boarders to catch air. BYOB (board). Helmets and pads required for visitors under 18. The biggest drawback is the location, about 6 miles from Huntington Beach Pier on the north side of town, so you'll need your own transport.

Festivals & Events

Every Tuesday brings **Surf City Nights** (www.surfcitynights.com; 1st 3 blocks Main St; 5-9pm Tue), a street fair with a petting zoo and bounce house for the kids, crafts, sidewalk sales for the grown-ups, and live music and farmers-market goodies for everyone.

Car buffs, get up early on Saturday mornings for the **Donut Derelicts Car Show** (www.donutderelicts.com; cnr Magnolia St & Adams Ave; Sat mornings), a weekly gathering of woodies, beach cruisers and pimped-out street rods at the corner of Magnolia St and Adams Ave, 2.5 miles inland from Pacific Coast Hwy.

Vans US Open of Surfing SURFING
(www.usopenofsurfing.com; Huntington Beach Pier; late Jul & early Aug) This six-star competition lasts more than a week and draws more than 600 world-class surfers. Other festivities include beach concerts, motocross shows and skateboard jams.

Huntington Harbor Cruise of Lights CHRISTMAS
(www.cruiseoflights.org; 16889 Algonquin St; adult/child $19/12; mid- to late Dec) If you're here for the Christmas holidays, don't miss the evening boat tour past harborside homes twinkling with holiday lights. Run by the Philharmonic Society, cruise proceeds go to support youth music education programs.

Sleeping

Huntington Surf Inn MOTEL $$
(714-536-2444; www.huntingtonsurfinn.com; 720 Pacific Coast Hwy; r $119-209; P) You're paying for location at this two-story 1960s era motel just north of Main St and across from the beach. Smallish rooms are individually decorated with surf and skateboard art – cool, brah – with firm mattresses and fridges, and microwaves on request. There's a small common deck area with a beach view.

★**Paséa** RESORT $$$
(☎888-674-3634; http://meritagecollection.com/paseahotel; 21080 Pacific Coast Hwy; r from $359; P ⊖ ❄ @ 📶 ≋) This hotel is slick and serene, with tons of light and air. Floors are themed for shades of blue from denim to sky, and each of its 250 shimmery, minimalist, high-ceilinged rooms has an ocean-view balcony. As if the stunning pool, gym and Balinese-inspired spa weren't enough, it connects to Pacific City. (p431)

★**Shorebreak Hotel** BOUTIQUE HOTEL $$$
(☎714-861-4470; www.shorebreakhotel.com; 500 Pacific Coast Hwy; r from $269; P ⊖ ❄ @ 📶 🐾) Stow your surfboard (lockers provided) as you head inside HB's hippest hotel, a stone's throw from the pier. The Shorebreak has 'surf ambassadors,' a wetsuit mural in the lobby, pseudo-steampunk fitness center with climbing wall, and hardwood furniture and surfboard headboards in geometric-patterned rooms. Minibars stock surfboard wax, in case you, you know, forgot yours.

Eating

★**Lot 579** FOOD HALL
(www.gopacificcity.com/lot-579; Pacific City, 21010 Pacific Coast Hwy; ⏲hours vary; P 📶 👪) The food court at HB's stunning new ocean-view mall offers some unique and fun restaurants for pressed sandwiches (Burnt Crumbs – the spaghetti grilled cheese is so Instagrammable), Aussie meat pies (Pie Not), coffee (Portola) and ice cream (Han's). For best views, take your takeout to the deck, or eat at American Dream (brewpub) or Bear Flag Fish Company.

★**Sancho's Tacos** MEXICAN $
(☎714-536-8226; www.sanchostacos.com; 602 Pacific Coast Hwy; mains $3-10; ⏲8am-9pm Mon-Sat, to 8pm Sun; P) There's no shortage of taco stands in HB, but locals are fiercely dedicated to Sancho's, across from the beach. This two-room shack with patio grills flounder, shrimp and tri-tip to order.

Cucina Alessá ITALIAN $$
(☎714-969-2148; http://cucinaalessarestaurants.com; 520 Main St; mains lunch $9-13, dinner $12-25; ⏲11am-10pm) Every beach town needs its favorite go-to Italian kitchen. Alessa wins hearts and stomachs with classics like Neapolitan lasagna, butternut-squash ravioli and chicken marsala. Lunch brings out panini, pizzas and pastas, plus breakfasts including frittata and 'famous' French toast. Get sidewalk seating, or sit behind big glass windows.

Drinking & Nightlife

★**Bungalow** CLUB
(☎714-374-0399; www.thebungalow.com/hb; Pacific City, 21058 Pacific Coast Hwy, Suite 240; ⏲5pm-2am Mon-Fri, noon-2am Sat, noon-10pm Sun) This Santa Monica landmark of cool has opened a second location here in Pacific City, and with its combination of lounge spaces, outdoor patio, cozy, rustic-vintage design, specialty cocktails, DJs who know how to get the crowd going and – let's not forget – ocean views, it's already setting new standards for the OC. The food menu's pretty great too.

Saint Marc BAR
(☎714-374-1101; www.saintmarcusa.com; Pacific City, 21058 Pacific Coast Hwy; ⏲11am-midnight Mon-Wed, to 2am Thu & Fri, 10am-2am Sat, to 10pm Sun) Indoor-outdoor Saint Marc is technically a restaurant, but it's just so darn much fun as a bar: giant beer-pong table, beer bombers, wine on draft, infused vodkas, red Solo Cup cocktails and, um, jello shots! Should you get hungry, food ranges from cheese boards to New Orleans–inflected meals, or just go for bacon by the slice from the bacon bar.

Information

Visit Huntington Beach Information Kiosk
(☎714-969-3492, 800-729-6232; www.surfcityusa.com; Pier Plaza, 325 Pacific Coast Hwy; ⏲10:30am-7pm Mon-Fri, from 10am Sat & Sun, shorter hrs in winter) Visitor information kiosk by the pier.

Getting There & Around

Pacific Coast Hwy (PCH) runs alongside the beach. Main St intersects PCH at the pier. Heading inland, Main St ends at Hwy 39 (Beach Blvd), which connects north to I-405.

Public parking lots by the pier and beach – when you can get a spot – are 'pay and display' for $1.50 per hour, $15 daily maximum. Self-service ticket booths scattered across the parking lot take dollars or coins. More municipal lots alongside PCH and around downtown cost at least $15 per day in summer, typically with an evening flat rate of $5 after 5pm. On-street parking meters cost $1 per 40 minutes.

OCTA (p430) bus 1 connects HB with the rest of OC's beach towns every hour; one-way/day pass $2/5, payable on board (exact change). When we passed through, a free **Surf City USA Shuttle** (www.surfcityusashuttle.com; ⏲10am-10pm Fri & Sat, 10am-8pm Sun, mid-Jun–early Sep) was making a loop around beach and inland areas.

Newport Beach

There are really three Newport Beaches: paradise for wealthy Bentley- and Porsche-driving yachtsmen and their trophy wives; perfect waves and beachside dives for surfers and stoners; and glorious sunsets and seafood for the rest of the folk, trying to live the day-to-day. Somehow, these diverse communities all seem to live – mostly – harmoniously.

For visitors, the pleasures are many: just-off-the-boat seafood, boogie-boarding the human-eating waves at the Wedge, and the ballet of yachts in the harbor. Just inland, more lifestyles of the rich and famous revolve around Fashion Island (p437), a posh outdoor mall and one of the OC's biggest shopping centers.

Sights

★Orange County Museum of Art MUSEUM

(Map p436; ☎949-759-1122; www.ocma.net; 850 San Clemente Dr; adult/student & senior/child under 12yr $10/7.50/free; ⏰11am-5pm Wed-Sun, to 8pm Fri; P 👪) This engaging museum highlights California art and cutting-edge contemporary artists, with exhibitions rotating through two large spaces. Recent exhibitions have included the California-Pacific Triennial and works by Robert Rauschenberg. There's also a sculpture garden, eclectic gift shop and a theater screening classic, foreign and art-related films.

Upper Newport Bay Ecological Preserve NATURE RESERVE

(☎949-640-1751; www.ocparks.com/parks/newport; 2301 University Dr; ⏰7am-sunset; P) FREE The brackish water of this 752-acre reserve, where runoff from the San Bernardino Mountains meets the sea, supports more than 200 species of birds. This is one of the few estuaries in Southern California that has been preserved, and it's an important stopover on the Pacific Flyway migration route. There are also trails for jogging and cycling.

Discovery Cube's Ocean Quest MUSEUM

(Map p436; ☎949-675-8915; www.oceanquestoc.org; 600 E Bay Ave; adult/child 2 & under $5/free; ⏰hours vary; P 👪) In the **Balboa Fun Zone** (Map p436; www.thebalboafunzone.com; 600 E Bay Ave; Ferris wheel $4; ⏰Ferris wheel 11am-6pm Sun-Thu, to 9pm Fri, to 10pm Sat; 👪), this newly refurbished museum was recently taken over by Santa Ana's Discovery Cube (p428) and runs educational programs for local schools and field trips. When not hosting school groups, it opens to the public and shows traveling exhibits. Check the website for opening hours, what's on and for occasional whale-watching trips.

Activities

Balboa Peninsula AREA

(Map p436) Four miles long but less than a half-mile wide, the Balboa Peninsula has a white-sand beach on its ocean side and countless stylish homes, including the 1926 **Lovell Beach House** (Map p436; 1242 W Ocean Front). It's just inland from the paved beachfront **recreational path**, across from a small **playground**. Hotels, restaurants and bars cluster around the peninsula's two famous piers: **Newport Pier** near the western end and **Balboa Pier** at the eastern end. The two-mile oceanfront strip between them teems with beachgoers; people-watching is great.

Near Newport Pier, several shops rent umbrellas, beach chairs, volleyballs and other necessities. For swimming, families will find a more relaxed atmosphere and calmer waves at 10th St and 18th St. The latter beach, also known as **Mothers Beach** (Map p436; Marina Park, 18th St; 👪), has a lifeguard, restrooms and a shower.

At the very tip of Balboa Peninsula, by the West Jetty, the **Wedge** (Map p436) is a bodysurfing, bodyboarding and knee-boarding spot for experts; newcomers should head a few blocks west. Park on Channel Rd or E Ocean Blvd and walk through tiny West Jetty View Park.

Spa Gregorie's SPA

(Map p436; ☎949-644-6672; www.spagregories.com; 200 Newport Center Dr, Suite 100; 1hr massage from $109, facial from $119) After power shopping at Fashion Island (p437), indulge yourself at Spa Gregorie's. After you've been rejuvenated by the quiet room, step in to your massage, facial or body treatment.

Surfing

Surfers flock to the breaks at the small jetties surrounding the Newport Pier between 18th and 56th streets. Word of warning: locals can be territorial. For lessons, try Huntington Beach or Laguna Beach instead.

Rent surf, bodysurfing and stand-up paddleboard equipment and gear at **15th Street Surf & Supply** (Map p436; ☎949-751-7867; https://15thstsurfsupply.com; 103 15th St; boogie boards per hour/day $7/15, surfboards $15/40; ⏰9am-7pm).

Boating

Take a boat tour or rent your own kayak, sailboat or outboard motorboat. Even better, rent a flat-bottomed electric boat that you pilot yourself and cruise with up to 12 friends. Find boats at Duffy Electric Boat Rentals or **Balboa Boat Rentals** (Map p436; ☎949-673-7200; http://boats4rent.com; 510 E Edgewater Pl; per hr kayaks from $18, pontoon boats $105, powerboats from $75, electric boats from $80; ⏰10am-7pm, extended hrs in summer).

Duffy Electric Boat Rentals BOATING
(Map p436; ☎949-645-6812; www.duffyofnewportbeach.com; 2001 W Coast Hwy; first 2hr $199; ⏰10am-8pm) These heated electric boats with canopies are a Newport tradition. Bring tunes, food and drinks for a fun evening toodling around the harbor like a local. No boating experience required; maps provided.

Cycling & Skating

To experience fabulous ocean views, ride a bike along the paved **recreational path** that encircles almost the entire Balboa Peninsula. Inland cyclists like the paved **scenic loop** around Upper Newport Bay Nature Preserve. There are many places to rent bikes near Newport and Balboa Piers.

Diving

There's terrific diving just south of Newport Beach at the underwater park at Crystal Cove State Park (p439), where divers can check out reefs, anchors and an old military plane-crash site.

Tours

Davey's Locker BOATING
(Map p436; ☎949-673-1434; www.daveyslocker.com; 400 Main St; per adult/child 3-12yr & senior 2½hr whale-watching cruise from $32/26, half-day sportfishing $41.50/34) At **Balboa Pavilion** (Map p436; www.balboapavilion.com; 400 Main St); offers whale-watching and sportfishing trips.

Fun Zone Boat Co BOATING
(Map p436; ☎949-673-0240; www.funzoneboats.com; 700 Edgewater Pl; 45min cruise per adult/child 5-11yr/senior from $14/7/11) Sea lion-watching and celebrity home tours depart from the Fun Zone.

Festivals & Events

Newport Beach Film Festival FILM
(www.newportbeachfilmfest.com; ⏰mid-Apr) Roll out the red carpet for screenings of over 350 mostly new independent and foreign films. Some films shown here, such as *Crash*, *Waitress*, *(500) Days of Summer* and *Chef* have gone on to become classics, while earlier classics like *Sunset Boulevard* get anniversary screenings.

Christmas Boat Parade CHRISTMAS
(www.christmasboatparade.com; ⏰Dec) The week before Christmas brings thousands of spectators to Newport Harbor to watch a century-old tradition. The 2½-hour parade of up to 150 boats, including some fancy multi-million-dollar yachts all decked out with Christmas lights and holiday cheer, begins at 6:30pm. Watch for free from the Fun Zone or **Balboa Island** (Map p436; http://explorebalboaisland.com; P), or book ahead for a harbor boat tour.

Sleeping

A Newport stay ain't cheap, but outside of the peak season rates often drop 40% or more. Otherwise, to save some dough, you'll find chain hotels and motels further inland, especially around John Wayne Airport, in Costa Mesa, and around the triangle junction of Hwy 55 (Costa Mesa Fwy), toll road Hwy 73 and I-405 (San Diego Fwy).

Newport Dunes Waterfront Resort CABIN, CAMPGROUND $
(Map p436; ☎949-729-3863; www.newportdunes.com; 1131 Back Bay Dr; campsite from $64, cottage/1-bedroom cottage from $90/165; P@) RVs and tents aren't required for a stay at this upscale campground: two dozen tiny, well-kept A-frames and picket-fenced one-bedroom cottages are available, all within view of Newport Bay. A fitness center and walking trails, kayak rentals, board games, family bingo, ice-cream socials, horseshoe and volleyball tournaments, an outdoor pool and playground, and summertime movies on the beach await. Wheelchair-accessible.

★**Newport Beach Hotel** BOUTIQUE HOTEL $$
(Map p436; ☎949-673-7030; www.thenewportbeachhotel.com; 2306 W Oceanfront Blvd; r/stes from $235/425; P) There's charm to spare in this intimate, 20-room beachfront inn, built in 1904 and updated with beach-chic style. Relax over tea, fruit and cookies in the ocean-view lobby with rattan chairs and white wainscoting, then head upstairs where rooms of different sizes are done up with clean whites and pastel blues, some with spa tubs and ocean views.

Newport Beach

Newport Beach

Top Sights

1 Orange County Museum of Art D1

Sights

2 Balboa Fun Zone A3
3 Balboa Island C2
4 Balboa Pavilion B3
5 Balboa Peninsula B2
6 Discovery Cube's Ocean Quest A3
7 Lovell Beach House A2
8 Main Beach D3
9 Mothers Beach A2
10 Pirate's Cove D3
11 The Wedge D3

Activities, Courses & Tours

12 15th Street Surf & Supply A2
13 Balboa Boat Rentals A3
Davey's Locker .... (see 4)
14 Duffy Electric Boat Rentals A1
15 Fun Zone Boat Co A3
16 Spa Gregorie's D2

Sleeping

17 Doryman's Oceanfront Inn A2
18 Newport Beach Hotel A2
19 Newport Dunes Waterfront Resort C1

Eating

20 Bear Flag Fish Company A1
Dory Deli .... (see 17)

Drinking & Nightlife

21 Alta Coffee Warehouse A1
Muldoon's .... (see 16)

Shopping

22 Fashion Island D1

Doryman's Oceanfront Inn B&B **$$$**

(Map p436; ☎949-675-7300; www.dorymansinn.com; 2102 W Oceanfront; r $299-399; P ⊜ ❄ ☜) This 2nd-floor oceanfront B&B was built in 1891 and retains that Victorian country style. Each of the 11 rooms is unique, and some boast ocean views and fireplaces. It has a great location by Newport Pier (view it from the roof deck), although it can get loud in summer with the 24-hour activities. Parking and breakfast (quiche, bagels, fruit and more) included.

Eating

Dozens of restaurants and pubs throughout Newport offer fish dinners (as you'd expect), plus nouveau Japanese and modern Mexican.

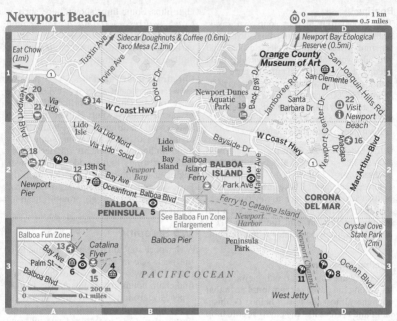

★**Bear Flag Fish Company** SEAFOOD $
(Map p436; ☎949-673-3474; www.bearflagfishco.com; 3421 Via Lido; mains $10-16; ⏰11am-9pm Tue-Sat, to 8pm Sun & Mon; 👪) This is *the* place for generously sized, grilled and *panko*-breaded fish tacos, ahi burritos, spankin' fresh ceviche and oysters. Pick out what you want from the ice-cold display cases, then grab a picnic-table seat. About the only way this seafood could be any fresher is if you caught and hauled it off the boat yourself!

Dory Deli DELI $
(Map p436; ☎949-220-7886; www.dorydeli.com; 2108 W Oceanfront; mains $7-12; ⏰6am-8pm Sun-Thu, to 9pm Fri & Sat) This hip new beachfront storefront does hot and cold sandwiches like the Rubinstein, Lifeguard Club and the steak-filled Rocky Balboa, plus fresh-caught fish-and-chips. For breakfast, you could be good and get the yoga pants burrito, or sin a little with chicken and waffles. Full bar too! Sure, we'll stop in after surfing...

Eat Chow CALIFORNIAN $$
(☎949-423-7080; www.eatchownow.com; 211 62nd St; mains $9-18; ⏰8am-9pm Mon-Thu, to 10pm Fri, 7am-10pm Sat, 7am-9pm Sun) Hidden a block behind W Coast Hwy, Eat Chow's crowd is equal parts tatted hipsters and ladies who lunch, which makes it very Newport indeed. They all queue happily for rib-eye Thai beef salads, grilled-salmon tacos with curry slaw, and bodacious burgers like the Chow BBQ burger with homemade barbecue sauce, smoked Gouda, crispy onions and more. Groovy indie-rock soundtrack.

Drinking

★**Alta Coffee Warehouse** COFFEE
(Map p436; www.altacoffeeshop.com; 506 31st St; ⏰6am-10pm Mon-Fri, from 7am Sat & Sun) Hidden on a side street, this cozy coffeehouse in a beach bungalow with a covered patio lures locals with live music and poetry readings, art on the brick walls and honest baristas who dish the lowdown on the day's soups, savories, popular comfort food and baked goods like carrot cake and cheesecake. It's the kind of place that keeps a shelf of mugs for frequent customers, of whom there are many. The kitchen closes at 9:30pm.

★**Muldoon's** BAR
(Map p436; ☎949-640-4110; www.muldoonspub.com; 202 Newport Center Dr; ⏰opens 11:30am Mon-Sat, 10am Sun, closing hours vary) At upscale, upbeat, much-admired Muldoon's, choose from indoor, outdoor (under a leafy tree) and bar seating and enjoy decent, if pricey, Irish pub grub, 10 beers on tap and live acoustic sounds Thursday through Saturday nights and many Sunday afternoons.Our only complaint: it's a drive from the beach, in an office park by Fashion Island.

Shopping

Fashion Island (Map p436; ☎949-721-2000, 855-658-8527; www.shopfashionisland.com; 401 Newport Center Dr; ⏰10am-9pm Mon-Fri, to 7pm Sat, 11am-6pm Sun), inland from the beach, is Newport's biggest, most established shopping center (over 200 shops), but the new **Lido Marina** district is gearing up to give it a run for its money on a smaller scale: about two dozen establishments including stylish boutiques and casual indoor-outdoor dining. On Balboa Island, **Marine Avenue** is lined with darling shops in an old-fashioned village atmosphere, a good place to pick up something for the kids, unique gifts and beachy souvenirs, or jewelry, art and antiques for yourself.

Information

Visit Newport Beach (Map p436; www.visitnewportbeach.com; 401 Newport Center Dr, Fashion Island, Atrium Court, 2nd fl; ⏰10am-9pm Mon-Fri, to 7pm Sat, to 6pm Sun) The city's official visitor center hands out free brochures and maps.

Balboa Branch Library (www.city.newport-beach.ca.us/nbpl; 100 E Balboa Blvd; ⏰9am-6pm Tue & Thu-Sat, to 9pm Mon & Wed; 📶) Near the beach; ask for a free internet-terminal guest pass.

Getting There & Around

BUS

OCTA (p430) bus 1 connects Newport Beach and Fashion Island mall with the OC's other beach towns, including Corona del Mar just east, every 30 minutes to one hour. From the intersection of Newport Blvd and Pacific Coast Hwy, bus 71 heads south along the Balboa Peninsula to Main Ave every hour or so. On all routes, the one-way fare is $2 (exact change).

BOAT

The West Coast's largest passenger catamaran, the **Catalina Flyer** (Map p436; ☎949-673-5245; www.catalinainfo.com; 400 Main St; round-trip adult/child 3-12yr/senior $70/53/65, per bicycle $7), makes a daily round-trip to Catalina Island, taking 75 minutes each way. It leaves Balboa Pavilion around 9am and returns before 6pm; check online for discounts.

Balboa Island Ferry (Map p436; www.balboaislandferry.com; 410 S Bay Front; adult/child $1/50¢, car incl driver $2; ⏲6:30am-midnight Sun-Thu, to 2am Fri & Sat)

CAR & MOTORCYCLE

Frequently jammed from dawn till dusk, Hwy 55 (Newport Blvd) is the main access road from I-405 (San Diego Fwy); it intersects with Pacific Coast Hwy near the shore. In town, Pacific Coast Hwy is called W Coast Hwy or E Coast Hwy, both in mailing addresses and conversationally by locals.

The municipal lot beside Balboa Pier costs 50¢ per 20 minutes, or $15 per day. Street parking meters on the Balboa Peninsula cost 50¢ to $1 per hour. Free parking on residential streets, just a block or two from the sand, is time-limited and subject to other restrictions. In summer expect to circle like a hawk for a space.

Around Newport Beach

Costa Mesa

So close to Newport Beach that they're often lumped together, Costa Mesa at first glance looks like just another landlocked suburb transected by the I-405, but top venues attract some 24 million visitors each year. South Coast Plaza is SoCal's largest mall – properly termed a 'shopping resort' – while Orange County's cultural heart is steps away in the performing-arts venues Segerstrom Center for the Arts and South Coast Repertory, lending the city's slogan, City of the Arts.

If that all sounds rather hoity-toity, a pair of 'anti-malls' called the Lab and the Camp brings hipster cool, while strip malls throughout town reveal cafes serving surprisingly tasty dishes, ethnic-food holes-in-the-wall, bars and clubs. A new food hall, the OC Mix, is shaking it up even more. There's some distance between all of these destinations, but combined they make Costa Mesa one of the OC's most interesting enclaves.

Eating

★Taco Mesa MEXICAN $

(☎949-642-0629; www.tacomesa.net; 647 W 19th St; mains $3-13; ⏲7am-11pm; 👪) Brightly painted in Mexican Day of the Dead art, this out-of-the-way stand is a local institution for fresh, healthy, sustainably farmed tacos of steak, beer-battered fish and more, with an awesome salsa bar. We like the tacos blackened, with cheese, chipotle sauce, cabbage relish and *crema fresca*. The *niños* (kids) menu offers quesadillas and such.

Sidecar Doughnuts & Coffee DESSERTS $

(☎949-873-5424; www.sidecardoughnuts.com; 270 E 17th St; doughnuts from $2.75; ⏲6:30am-4pm Sun-Thu, to 9pm Fri & Sat; 👪) It may be in the back corner of a nondescript strip mall, but Sidecar's a landmark nonetheless. Crowds line up out the door (especially on weekends) for what are billed as the 'world's freshest doughnuts.' Changing out daily and monthly, Sidecar bakes one-of-a-kind flavors like black velvet, Saigon cinnamon crunch, maple bacon, huckleberry, and butter and salt.

OC Mix FOOD HALL $

(www.socoandtheocmix.com; 3303 Hyland Ave; ⏲10am-9pm, individual shop hours vary) Costa Mesa's newest food destination brings together purveyors of coffees, cheeses, oysters and more. Also here is Taco Maria, whose Michelin-starred chef started with a food truck and was recently named *Food & Wine* magazine's best new chef. It's in the middle of the SOCO outdoor mall, where foodies will also want to flock to Surfas cooking store.

Memphis SOUTHERN US $$

(☎714-432-7685; www.memphiscafe.com; 2920 Bristol St; mains brunch $7-17, dinner $14-28; ⏲8am-9:30pm Sun-Wed, to 11pm Thu-Sat) Inside a vintage mid-century-modern building, this fashionable eatery is all about down-home flavor – think pulled-pork sandwiches, popcorn shrimp, gumbo and buttermilk-battered fried chicken. There's brunch daily, happy hour at the bar, and weeknight dinner specials cost a mere $10.

Drinking

Milk + Honey CAFE

(☎714-708-0092; www.milkandhoneycostamesa.com; the Camp, 2981 Bristol St; ⏲7am-10pm Mon-Thu, 8am-11pm Fri & Sat, 8am-10pm Sun; 📶) This minimalist cool cafe takes fair-trade, shade-grown and organic coffee a little further, with unusual flavor combinations that (mostly) work: Spanish latte, lavender latte, plus chai tea, fruit smoothies, seasonal fro-yo flavors and Japanese-style shave ice with flavors like strawberry, red bean and almond. There's a small menu of sandwiches and delectable snacks like macarons and peanut butter cookie sandwiches.

Ruin BAR

(☎714-884-3189; http://theruinbar.com; the Lab, 2930 Bristol St; ⊙4pm-1am Tue & Wed, noon-1am Thu-Sat) This intimate, eclectic bar is decorated kind of like grandma's attic...if grandma collected faux buffalo heads, piano fronts and a ski gondola, and crocheted her trees in yarn. There's a constantly changing selection of beers on tap and cocktails made from soju, the Korean distilled spirit. It's on the southern side of the Lab.

☆ Entertainment

Segerstrom Center for the Arts THEATER, CONCERT HALL

(☎714-556-2787; www.scfta.org; 600 Town Center Dr) The county's main performance venue is home to the Pacific Symphony, Philharmonic Society of Orange County and Pacific Chorale and draws international performing-arts luminaries and Broadway shows, in three main theaters. Check the website for the wide-ranging calendar.

South Coast Repertory THEATER

(☎714-708-5555; www.scr.org; 655 Town Center Dr) Next to Segerstrom Center, South Coast Rep was started by a band of plucky theater grads in the 1960s and has evolved into a multiple Tony Award–winning company. It's managed to hold true to its mission to 'explore the most urgent human and social issues of our time' with groundbreaking, original plays from fall through to spring.

Shopping

★**Camp** MALL

(☎714-966-6661; www.thecampsite.com; 2937 Bristol St; ⊙11am-8pm Mon-Sat, to 5pm Sun, individual shop hours vary) Vegans, treehuggers and rock climbers, lend me your ears. The Camp offers one-stop shopping for all your outdoor and natural-living needs. **Active Ride Shop** and **Seed People's Market** for outdoor gear and fair-trade home goods are among the stores clustered along a leafy outdoor walkway. Parking spaces are painted with inspirational quotes like 'Show Up for Life.' If the parking spaces are full, there's valet parking.

Among the several dining and drinking options here are **Native Foods** (www.nativefoods.com; the Camp, 2937 Bristol St; mains $8-10; ⊙11am-10pm;), Milk + Honey and **Wine Lab** (☎714-850-1780; www.winelabcamp.com; the Camp, 2937 Bristol St, Suite A101B; ⊙noon-10pm Tue-Thu, to 11pm Fri & Sat, to 9pm Sun, 4-9pm Mon).

★**Lab** MALL

(☎714-966-6661; www.thelab.com; 2930 Bristol St; ⊙10am-9pm Sun-Thu, to 10pm Fri & Sat, individual shop hours vary;) Sister property to the Camp cross the street, this outdoor, ivy-covered 'anti-mall' is the original in-your-face alternative to **South Coast Plaza** (☎800-782-8888; www.southcoastplaza.com; 3333 Bristol St; ⊙10am-9pm Mon-Fri, to 8pm Sat, 11am-6:30pm Sun), even if nowadays more (cool) national chains have moved in. Sift through vintage clothing, unique sneakers and trendy duds for teens, tweens and 20-somethings. For short attention spans, contemporary art exhibitions are displayed in shipping containers at ARTery.

Dining options here include **Habana** (☎714-556-0176; www.habanacostamesa.com; the Lab, 2930 Bristol St; mains lunch $13-20, dinner $20-30; ⊙11am-1am Sun-Thu, 11:30am-2am Fri & Sat), Ruin and more. Fun fact: the Lab is in a former goggle factory.

Corona del Mar

Just south of Balboa Peninsula is Corona del Mar, a ritzy bedroom community on the privileged eastern flanks of the Newport Channel with plenty of upscale stores and restaurants and some of SoCal's most celebrated ocean views from the bluffs, not to mention postcard-perfect beaches with rocky coves and child-friendly tide pools.

A half-mile long, **Main Beach** (Corona del Mar State Beach; Map p436; ☎949-644-3151; www.newportbeachca.gov; off E Shore Ave; ⊙6am-10pm;) lies at the foot of rocky cliffs. There are restrooms, fire rings (arrive early to snag one) and volleyball courts. All-day parking costs $15, but spaces fill by 9am on weekends. Scenes from the classic TV show *Gilligan's Island* were shot at waveless, family-friendly **Pirate's Cove** (Map p436;); take the nearby stairs off the north end of the Main Beach parking lot.

Crystal Cove State Park

A few miles of open beach and 2400 acres of undeveloped woodland at this **state park** (Map p38; ☎949-494-3539; www.parks.ca.gov; 8471 N Coast Hwy; per car $15; ⊙6am-sunset;) let you forget you're in a crowded metropolitan area, at least once you get past the parking lots and stake out a place on the sand. Overnight guests can stay in the dozens of vintage cottages (reserve well in advance), and anyone can stop for a meal or cocktails at the landmark Beachcomber restaurant.

Crystal Cove is also an underwater park. Scuba enthusiasts can check out two historic anchors dating from the 1800s as well as the crash site of a Navy plane that went down in the 1940s. Alternatively you can just go tide-pooling, fishing, kayaking and surfing along the undeveloped shoreline. On the park's inland side, miles of hiking and mountain-biking trails await.

Sleeping & Eating

Crystal Cove State Park Campground CAMPGROUND $
(800-444-7275; www.reserveamerica.com; 8471 N Coast Hwy, Laguna Beach; tent & RV sites $25-75; P) The Moro Campground of this beachside park accommodates both campers and/or tents and has toilets, showers and more. Heartier campers might opt for a variety of simpler, environmentally friendly and undeveloped 'primitive' campsites (no drinking water or showers) accessible only via a strenuous 3-mile hike.

★ **Crystal Cove Beach Cottages** CABIN $$
(reservations 800-444-7275; www.crystalcovealliance.org; 35 Crystal Cove, Crystal Cove State Park Historic District; r with shared bath $35-140, cottages $171-249; check-in 4-9pm; P) Right on the beach, these two dozen preserved cottages (circa 1930s to '50s) now host guests for a one-of-a-kind stay. Each cottage is different, sleeping between two and eight people in a variety of private or dorm-style accommodations. To snag one, book on the first day of the month seven months before your intended stay – or pray for cancellations.

Beachcomber Café AMERICAN $$
(949-376-6900; www.thebeachcombercafe.com; 15 Crystal Cove; mains breakfast $9-19, lunch $14-21, dinner $20-47; 7am-9:30pm) The atmospheric Beachcomber Café lets you soak up the vintage 1950s beach vibe as you tuck into macadamia-nut pancakes, roasted turkey club sandwiches or more serious surf-and-turf. Sunset is the magic hour for Polynesian tiki drinks by the sea.

Laguna Beach

It's easy to love Laguna: secluded coves, romantic cliffs, azure waves and waterfront parks imbue the city with a Riviera-like feel. But nature isn't the only draw. From public sculptures and art festivals to free summer shuttles, the city has taken thoughtful steps to promote tourism while discreetly maintaining its moneyed quality of life (MTV's reality show *Laguna Beach* being one drunken, shameless exception).

Sights

With 30 public beaches sprawling along 7 miles of coastline, Laguna Beach is perfect for do-it-yourself exploring. There's always another stunning view or hidden cove just around the bend. Although many of the coves are blocked from street view by multi-million-dollar homes, a good local map or sharp eye will take you to stairways leading from the Pacific Coast Hwy down to the beach. Just look for the 'beach access' signs, and be prepared to pass through people's backyards to reach the sand. Unlike its neighbors to the north, Laguna doesn't impose a beach curfew. You can rent beach chairs, umbrellas and boogie boards from **Main Beach Toys** (Map p441; 949-494-8808; 150 Laguna Ave; chairs/umbrellas/boards per day $10/10/15; 9am-9pm).

Pacific Marine Mammal Center NATURE CENTER
(949-494-3050; www.pacificmmc.org; 20612 Laguna Canyon Rd; donations welcome; 10am-4pm; P) FREE A nonprofit organization dedicated to rescuing and rehabilitating injured or ill marine mammals, this center northeast of town has a small staff and many volunteers who help nurse Orange County's rescued pinnipeds – mostly sea lions and seals – before releasing them back into the wild. Visitors can view outdoor pools and holding pens – but remember, this is a rescue center, not SeaWorld. Still, it's educational and heartwarming. Admission is free, but donations and gift-shop purchases (say, a stuffed animal) help.

Laguna Art Museum MUSEUM
(Map p441; 949-494-8971; www.lagunaartmuseum.org; 307 Cliff Dr; adult/student & senior/child under 13yr $7/5/free, 5-9pm 1st Thu of month free; 11am-5pm Fri-Tue, to 9pm Thu) This breezy museum has changing exhibitions featuring contemporary California artists, and a permanent collection heavy on California landscapes, vintage photographs and works by early Laguna bohemians. Free guided tours are usually given at 11am Tuesday, Thursday and Saturday, and there's a unique gift shop.Hours may be extended during some exhibitions.

Laguna Beach

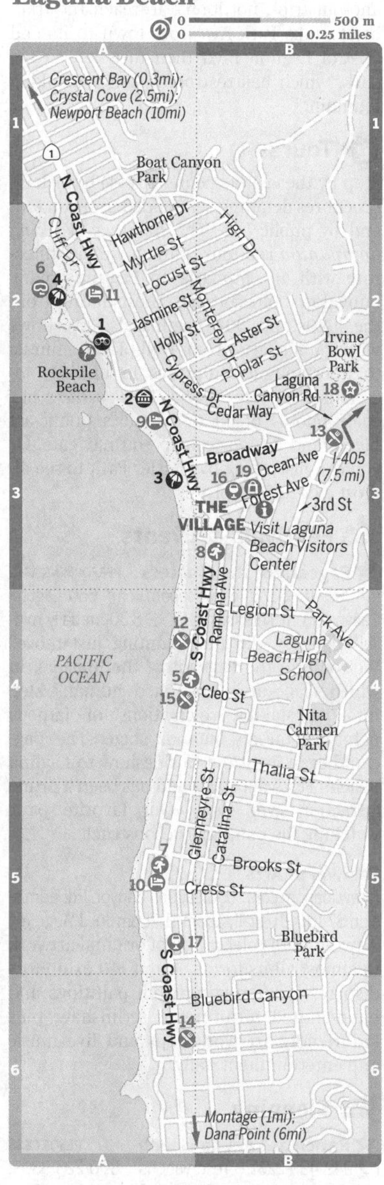

Laguna Beach

Sights

1 Heisler Park A2
2 Laguna Art Museum A3
3 Main Beach A3
4 Picnic Beach A2

Activities, Courses & Tours

5 CA Surf 'n' Paddle A4
6 Divers Cove A2
7 La Vida Laguna A5
8 Main Beach Toys B3

Sleeping

9 Inn at Laguna Beach A3
10 La Casa del Camino A5
11 Laguna Beach House A2

Eating

12 Driftwood Kitchen A4
13 Laguna Beach Farmers Market B3
14 Mozambique A6
15 Orange Inn A4

Drinking & Nightlife

16 Laguna Beach Brewery & Grille B3
17 Main Street A5
Rooftop Lounge .... (see 10)

Entertainment

18 Laguna Playhouse B2

Shopping

19 Hobie Surf Shop B3

Central Beaches

Near downtown's village, **Main Beach** (Map p441; 🚻) has volleyball and basketball courts, a playground and restrooms. It's Laguna's best beach for swimming. Just north at Picnic Beach, it's too rocky to surf; tide pooling is best. Pick up a tide table at the visitors bureau.

Above **Picnic Beach** (Map p441), the grassy, bluff-top **Heisler Park** (Map p441; 375 Cliff Dr) offers vistas of craggy coves and deep-blue sea. Bring your camera – with its palm trees and bougainvillea-dotted bluffs, the scene is definitely one for posterity. A scenic walkway also connects Heisler Park to Main Beach.

North of downtown, Crescent Bay has big hollow waves good for bodysurfing, but parking is difficult; try the bluffs atop the beach. The views here are reminiscent of the Amalfi Coast.

Southern Beaches

About 1 mile south of downtown, secluded **Victoria Beach** (Victoria Dr) has volleyball courts and La Tour, a Rapunzel's-tower-like structure from 1926. Skimboarding (at the south end) and scuba diving are popular here. Take the stairs down Victoria Dr; there's limited parking along Pacific Coast Hwy.

Further south, **Aliso Beach County Park** (949-923-2280; http://ocparks.com/beaches/aliso; 31131 S Pacific Coast Hwy; parking per hr $1; 6am-10pm;) is popular with surfers, boogie boarders and skimboarders. With picnic tables, fire pits and a play area, it's also good for families. Pay-and-display parking costs $1 per hour, or drive south and park on Pacific Coast Hwy for free.

Jealously guarded by locals, **Thousand Steps Beach** (off 9th Ave) is hidden about 1 mile south of Aliso Beach. Just past Mission Hospital, park along Pacific Coast Hwy or residential side streets. At the south end of 9th St, more than 200 steps (OK, so it's not 1000) lead down to the sand. Though rocky, the beach is great for sunbathing, surfing and bodysurfing.

Activities

With its coves, reefs and rocky outcroppings, Laguna is one of the best SoCal beaches for diving and snorkeling. Check weather and surf conditions with the city's **marine safety forecast line** (949-494-6573) beforehand, as drownings have happened. The visitors bureau has tide charts.

Divers Cove SNORKELING

(Map p441) Down below Heisler Park (p441) is Divers Cove, a deep, protected inlet popular with snorkelers and, of course, divers. It's part of the Glenn E Vedder Ecological Reserve, an underwater park stretching to the northern border of Main Beach (p441).

La Vida Laguna WATER SPORTS

(Map p441; 949-275-7544; www.lavidalaguna.com; 1257 S Coast Hwy; 2hr guided tour from $85) Take a guided kayaking tour of the craggy coves of Laguna's coast and you might just see a colony of sea lions. Make reservations online.

Hiking

Surrounded by a green belt – a rarity in SoCal – Laguna has great nature trails for hikes. If you love panoramic views, take the short, scenic drive to **Alta Laguna Park**, a locals-only park, up-canyon from town. There, the moderate **Park Avenue Nature Trail**, a 1.25-mile one-way hike, takes you through fields of spring wildflowers. Open to hikers and mountain bikers, the 2.5-mile **West Ridge Trail** follows the ridgeline of the hills above Laguna. Both trails are in-and-out trips, not loops. To reach the trailheads, take Park Ave from town to its end at Alta Laguna Blvd then turn left to the park, which has restrooms and a drinking fountain.

Tours

Stop by the visitors center (p444) to pick up brochures detailing self-guided tours on foot and by public bus. The *Heritage Walking Companion* is a tour of the town's architecture with an emphasis on Laguna's many bungalows and cottages, most dating from the 1920s and '30s. Laguna also overflows with public art, from well-placed murals to freestanding sculptures in unlikely locations. The free *Public Art Brochure* has color photos of all of Laguna's public-art pieces and a map to help you navigate. Or you can just swing by Heisler Park to see almost a dozen sculptures.

Festivals & Events

★**Pageant of the Masters** PERFORMING ARTS

(800-487-3378; www.foapom.com; 650 Laguna Canyon Rd; tickets from $15; 8:30pm daily mid-Jul–Aug) Hey, did that painting just move? Welcome to the Pageant of the Masters, in which elaborately costumed humans step into painstaking re-creations of famous paintings on an outdoor stage. The pageant began in 1933 as a sideshow to Laguna Beach's Festival of Arts and has been a prime attraction ever since. Our favorite part: watching the paintings deconstruct.

Festival of Arts ART

(www.foapom.com; 650 Laguna Canyon Rd; admission $7-10; usually 10am-11:30pm Jul & Aug;) A two-month celebration of original artwork in almost all its forms. About 140 exhibitors display works ranging from paintings and hand-crafted furniture to scrimshaw, plus kid-friendly art workshops and live music and entertainment daily.

Sleeping

★**Ranch at Laguna Beach** RESORT $$$

(949-499-2271, reservations 800-223-3309; www.theranchlb.com; 31106 S Coast Hwy; r from $399;) Laguna's newest resort is secluded away in Aliso Creek Canyon on the south side of town. Ninety-seven rooms, casitas and town homes are in multiple buildings spread across the 87-acre property, sporting a subtle, rustic refinement with board-and-batten construction and Mexican-tile bathrooms.

★Montage RESORT $$$

(☎949-715-6000; www.montagelagunabeach.com; 30801 S Coast Hwy; r from $595; P @ 🛜 ≋) You'll find nowhere more indulgent on the OC's coast than this over-the-top luxury waterside resort, especially if you hide away with your lover in a secluded bungalow. Even the most basic of its 248 rooms are plush and generous, offering California craftsman style, marble bathrooms, lemon verbena bath products and unobstructed ocean views.

★Laguna Beach House HOTEL $$$

(Map p441; ☎949-497-6645; www.thelagunabeachhouse.com; 475 N Coast Hwy; r $205-419; P ⊖ ❄ 🛜 ≋ 🐾) Be it good feng shui, friendly staff or proximity to the beach, this 36-room courtyard inn feels right. From the surfboards in the lobby to colorful throw pillows and clean white walls and linens, the decor is contemporary, comfy and clean. Settle into the outdoor heated Jacuzzi with a glass of wine as the sun drops over the ocean.

Inn at Laguna Beach HOTEL $$$

(Map p441; ☎949-497-9722; www.innatlagunabeach.com; 211 N Coast Hwy; r $250-500; P ❄ 🛜 ≋ 🐾) Pride of place goes to this three-story white, modern hotel, at the north end of Main Beach (p441). Its 70 keen rooms were recently renovated with rattan furniture, blond woods, marble, French blinds and pillow-top beds. Some have balconies overlooking the water. Extras include DVD and CD players, bathrobes, beach gear to borrow and nightly ocean-view wine reception.

You can step from the pool deck directly into Heisler Park (p441). Our favorite part is the terrace where you can bring your own lunch or dinner and enjoy 270-degree views. Staff are welcoming and professional. A $15 resort fee covers wi-fi, those wine hours, cookies and milk, and morning coffee. Parking $30.

✕ Eating

Laguna Beach Farmers Market MARKET $

(Map p441; ☎714-573-0374; www.facebook.com/lagunabeachfm; 505 Forest Ave; ⏲8am-noon Sat) Local farmers and merchants sell their wares each Saturday, an ever-changing seasonal selection of both produce and prepared foods.

ⓘ TIDE-POOL ETIQUETTE

Tread lightly on dry rocks only and don't pick anything up that you find living in the water or on the rocks.

Orange Inn DINER $

(Map p441; ☎949-494-6085; www.orangeinncafe.com; 703 S Coast Hwy; mains $7-13; ⏲5:30am-5:30pm) Birthplace of the smoothie (in the *Guinness World Records*), this little shop from 1931 continues to pack in surfers fueling up before hitting the waves. It also serves date shakes, big omelets and breakfast burritos, homemade muffins and deli sandwiches on whole-wheat or sourdough bread.

The namesake Orange Inn smoothie ($6) contains strawberries, blueberries, bananas, dates, juice and bee pollen. Orange you glad you heard about it?

★Driftwood Kitchen AMERICAN $$$

(Map p441; ☎949-715-7700; www.driftwoodkitchen.com; 619 Sleepy Hollow Lane; mains lunch $15-36, dinner $24-39; ⏲9-10:30am & 11am-2:30pm Mon-Fri, 5-9:30pm Sun-Thu, to 10:30pm Fri & Sat, 9am-2:30pm Sat & Sun) Ocean views and ridonkulous sunsets alone ought to be enough to bring folks in, but gourmet Driftwood steps up the food with seasonal menus centered around fresh, sustainable seafood, plus options for landlubbers. Inside it's all beachy casual, whitewashed and pale woods. And the cocktails are smart and creative.

Speaking of cocktails, there's a less-expensive sandwich- and salad-focused menu (mains $9–19) at the adjacent Stateroom bar.

Mozambique AFRICAN $$$

(Map p441; ☎949-715-7777; www.mozambiqueoc.com; 1740 S Coast Hwy; dinner mains $18-44; ⏲11am-10pm Mon-Thu, to midnight Fri & Sat, 10am-10pm Sun) Macaws and toucans welcome you to this trendy, sophisticated, three-level ode to exotically spiced dishes from southern Africa – peri-peri prawns, chicken pops, grilled pineapple to soaring steaks and seafood, in small plates to pricey surf and turf ($68). Who knows, you might see a *Real Housewives* cast member hiding out in the rooftop bar. There's live music nightly; Sunday reggage gets jammed.

DON'T MISS

FIRST THURSDAYS

Once a month, downtown Laguna Beach gets festive during the **First Thursdays Gallery Art Walk** (☎949-683-6871; www.firstthursdaysartwalk.com; ⌚6-9pm 1st Thu of month). You can make the rounds of 30 local galleries and the Laguna Art Museum (p440) via free shuttles circling Laguna's art gallery districts.

Drinking & Nightlife

There are almost as many watering holes in downtown's village as there are art galleries. Most cluster along S Coast Hwy and Ocean Ave, making for an easy pub crawl. If you drink, don't drive; local cops take driving under the influence (DUI) very seriously.

Although Laguna has one of SoCal's largest gay populations, the once-thriving gay nightlife has virtually vanished. The one remaining gay bar, **Main Street** (Map p441; ☎949-494-0056; www.mainstreet-bar.com; 1460 S Coast Hwy; ⌚4pm-2am Tue-Sat, to 10pm Sun; closing hours vary), is hit or miss.

Laguna Beach Brewery & Grille MICROBREWERY
(Map p441; ☎949-497-3381; www.lagunabeachbrewery.net; 237 Ocean Ave; ⌚11:30am-10:30pm Tue-Thu, to 11:30pm Fri & Sat, 10am-9pm Sun) For pub grub and microbrews after a day of surfing, this place lines up copper vats behind the bar, pouring its own Miel de Laguna blond and Solar amber ales to go with regional Mexican cooking: homemade tortillas, Rosarito-style lobster tacos and ceviche. Kick back on the outdoor patio for primo people-watching. Live music Wednesdays to Saturdays.

Rooftop Lounge BAR
(Map p441; www.rooftoplagunabeach.com; 1289 S Coast Hwy; ⌚11:30am-9pm Mon-Thu, to 10pm Fri & Sat, 10:30am-9pm Sun) Perched atop La Casa del Camino this bar, with 270-degree coastal views and a friendly vibe, has locals singing hallelujahs. Mango and wild berry mojitos add some spice to the cocktail menu, and you can snack on plates like meatballs in guava barbecue sauce. Enter through the hotel's lobby and take the elevator to the top.

☆ Entertainment

Laguna Playhouse THEATER
(Map p441; ☎949-497-2787; www.lagunaplayhouse.com; 606 Laguna Canyon Rd) Orange County's oldest continuously operating community theater stages lighter plays in summer, more serious works in winter.

Shopping

Downtown's village is a shopper's paradise, with hidden courtyards and eclectic little bungalows that beg further exploration. Forest Ave has the highest concentration of chic boutiques, but south of downtown, Pacific Coast Hwy has its fair share of fashionable and arty shops where you can balance your chakras or buy vintage rock albums and posters.

Hobie Surf Shop SPORTS & OUTDOORS
(Map p441; ☎949-497-3304; www.hobiesurfshop.com; 294 Forest Ave; ⌚9am-7pm) Hobart 'Hobie' Alter started his internationally known surf line in his parents' Laguna Beach garage in 1950. Today, this is one of only a handful of logo retail shops where you can stock up on surfboards and beachwear (love those flip-flops in rainbow colors!) for both babes and dudes.

ⓘ Information

Visit Laguna Beach Visitors Center (Map p441; ☎949-497-9229; www.lagunabeachinfo.com; 381 Forest Ave; ⌚10am-5pm;) Helpful staff, bus schedules, restaurant menus and free brochures on everything from hiking trails to self-guided walking tours.

ⓘ Getting There & Away

From I-405, take Hwy 133 (Laguna Canyon Rd) southwest. If you're coming from along the coast, Hwy 1 goes by several names in Laguna Beach: south of Broadway, downtown's main street, it's called South Coast Hwy; north of Broadway it's North Coast Hwy. Locals also call it Pacific Coast Hwy (PCH).

OCTA (p430) bus 1 heading along the coast connects Laguna Beach with Orange County's other beach towns, including Dana Point heading south, every 30 to 60 minutes. The one-way fare is $2 (exact change).

Around Laguna Beach

San Juan Capistrano

Famous for its swallows that fly back to town every year on March 19 (though sometimes they're just a bit early), San Juan Capistrano is home to the 'jewel of the California missions'. California missions were

Roman Catholic outposts established in the late 18th and early 19th centuries. Amid that photogenic mission streetscape of adobe, tile-roofed buildings, and historic wood-built cottages, there's enough history and charm here to make almost a day of it.

'San Juan Cap' is a little town, just east of Dana Point and just over 10 miles southeast of downtown Laguna Beach.

Sights

★Mission San Juan Capistrano CHURCH
(☎949-234-1300; www.missionsjc.com; 26801 Ortega Hwy; adult/child $9/6; ⏰9am-5pm; 👪) Plan on spending at least an hour poking around the sprawling mission's tiled roofs, covered arches, lush gardens, fountains and courtyards – including the padre's quarters, soldiers' barracks and the cemetery. Admission includes a worthwhile free audio tour with interesting stories narrated by locals. The mission is at the corner of Ortega Hwy and Camino Capistrano.

Particularly moving are the towering remains of the **Great Stone Church**, almost completely destroyed by a powerful earthquake on December 8, 1812. The **Serra Chapel** – whitewashed outside with restored frescoes inside – is believed to be the oldest existing building in California (1782). It's certainly the only one still standing in which Junípero Serra (the founder of the mission) gave Mass. Serra founded the mission on November 1, 1776, and tended it personally for many years.

There's a special audio tour for the elementary-school set, called Saved by the Mission Bell, included in children's admission.

Los Rios Historic District HISTORIC SITE
One block southwest of the mission, next to the Capistrano train depot, this peaceful assemblage of a few dozen historic cottages and adobes now mostly houses cafes and gift shops. To see 1880s-era furnishings and decor, as well as vintage photographs, stop by the tiny **O'Neill Museum** (31831 Los Rios St; adult/child $1/50¢; ⏰9am-noon & 1-4pm Tue-Fri, noon-3pm Sat & Sun).

Eating & Drinking

★El Campeon MEXICAN $
(31921 Camino Capistrano, El Adobe Plaza; items $2-9; ⏰6:30am-9pm; 👪) For real-deal Mexican food, in a strip mall south of the mission, try this multiroom restaurant, *panadería* (bakery) and *mercado* (grocery store). Look for tacos, tostadas and burritos in freshly made tortillas, *posole* (hominy stew) and pork carnitas served cafeteria-style, and *aguas frescas* (fruit drinks) in flavors like watermelon, strawberry and grapefruit.

★Ramos House Café CALIFORNIAN $$
(☎949-443-1342; www.ramoshouse.com; 31752 Los Rios St; weekday mains $17-21, weekend brunch $44; ⏰8:30am-3pm) The best spot for breakfast or lunch in the Los Rios Historic District, this Old West–flavored, wood-built house from 1881 (with brick patio) does organically raised comfort food flavored with herbs grown on-site: blueberry *pain perdu* (French toast) with lemon curd, apple-cinnamon beignets, basil-cured salmon lox or spicy crab-cake salad with smoked chili rémoulade. Breads are baked in-house daily.

El Adobe de Capistrano MEXICAN $$
(www.eladobedecapistrano.com; 31891 Camino Capistrano; mains lunch $11-24, dinner $16-38; ⏰11am-9pm Mon-Thu, to 10pm Fri & Sat, 10am-9pm Sun) In a building that traces its origins to 1797, this sprawling, beam-ceilinged 'Mexican steakhouse' and bar does a big business in the standards (enchiladas, fajitas) through to blackened fish or lobster tacos, garlic shrimp and grilled steaks. It was a favorite of President Nixon, who lived in nearby San Clemente, which might be good or bad depending on your outlook.

Coach House CLUB
(☎949-496-8930; www.thecoachhouse.com; 33157 Camino Capistrano; ⏰hours vary) Long-running live-music venue featuring a roster of local and national rock, indie, alternative and tribute bands; expect a cover charge of $15 to $40, depending on who's playing. Recent performers include classic rockers like Blue Öyster Cult, rockers Los Lonely Boys, plus comedy acts like Louie Anderson. Check the website for show times.

Getting There & Around

From Laguna Beach, ride OCTA (p430) bus 1 south to Dana Point. At the intersection of Pacific Coast Hwy and Del Obispo St, catch bus 91 northbound toward Mission Viejo, which drops you near the mission. Buses run every 30 to 60 minutes. The trips takes about an hour. You'll have to pay the one-way fare ($2, exact change) twice.

Drivers should take I-5 exit 82 (Ortega Hwy), then head west about 0.25 miles. There's free three-hour parking on streets and in municipal lots.

WORTH A TRIP

TRESTLES SURF BREAK

Surfers won't want to miss world-renowned **Trestles**, in protected **San Onofre State Beach** (☎949-492-4872; www.parks.ca.gov; parking per day $15; P), just southeast of San Clemente. This beach is famous for its natural surf break that consistently churns out perfect waves, even in summer. There are also rugged bluff-top walking trails, swimming beaches and a developed inland **campground** (☎949-361-2531, reservations 800-444-7275; www.reserveamerica.com; San Mateo Campground, 830 Cristianitos Rd, San Onofre State Beach; San Mateo sites $40-65, bluff sites $40; P).

Trestles is a great success story for environmentalists and surfers, who for over a decade fought the extension of a nearby toll road. Visit savetrestles.surfrider.org to learn more.

To reach the beach, exit I-5 at Basilone Rd, then hoof to Trestles along the nature trail.

The **Amtrak** (☎800-872-7245; www.amtrak.com; 26701 Verdugo St) depot is one block south and west of the mission. You could arrive by train from LA ($21, 75 minutes) or San Diego ($22, 90 minutes) in time for lunch, visit the mission and be back in the city for dinner. A few daily **Metrolink** (☎800-371-5465; www.metrolinktrains.com) commuter trains link San Juan Capistrano to Orange ($8, 45 minutes), with limited connections to Anaheim.

Dana Point

Dana Point was once called 'the only romantic spot on the coast.' Too bad that quote dates from seafarer Richard Dana's voyage here in the 1830s. Its built-up, parking-lotted harbor detracts from the charm its neighbors have, but it still gets a lot of visitors to its lovely beaches and port for whale-watching, sportfishing and the like.

Sights & Activities

Doheny State Beach BEACH
(Map p38; ☎949-496-6171; www.dohenystatebeach.org; 25300 Dana Point Harbor Dr; per car $15; ⊙park 6am-10pm, visitor center 10am-4pm Wed-Sun; P) Adjacent to the southern border of Dana Point Harbor, this mile-long beach is great for swimmers, surfers, surf fishers and tide-poolers. You'll also find picnic tables with grills, volleyball courts and a butterfly exhibit at the 62-acre coastal park. Stop by the park's **visitor center** to check out the five aquariums, mounted birds and 500-gallon simulated tide pool. Free wi-fi at the snack bar.

Salt Creek Beach BEACH
(☎949-923-2280; www.ocparks.com/beaches/salt; 33333 S Pacific Coast Hwy, off Ritz Carlton Dr; ⊙5am-midnight; P) Just south of the Laguna Beach boundary, this 18-acre county-run park is popular with surfers, sunbathers, bodysurfers and tide-poolers. Families make the most of the park's picnic tables, grills, restrooms and showers – all sprawling beneath the elegant bluff-top Ritz-Carlton resort. Open in summer, a beach concession stand rents boogie boards, beach chairs and umbrellas. Pay-and-display parking costs $1 per hour.

Wheel Fun Rentals CYCLING
(☎949-496-7433; www.wheelfunrentals.com; 25300 Dana Point Harbor Dr; cruiser rental per hour/day $10/28; ⊙9am-sunset daily late May-early Sep, Sat & Sun early Sep-late May) Wheel Fun covers the basic beach cruisers all the way up to choppers and four-seater surreys.

Capo Beach Watercraft Rentals BOATING
(☎949-661-1690; www.capobeachwatercraft.com; 34512 Embarcadero Pl; jet ski before/after 11:30am per hour Mon-Fri $85/105, Sat & Sun $100/120) This place rents kayaks and jet skis. Go through the gate and look for the small blue building.

Pure Watersports Dana Point BOATING
(Dana Point Jet Ski & Kayak Center; ☎949-661-4947; www.danapointjetski.com; 34671 Puerto Pl; rentals per hr kayak and SUP from $15, jet ski from $95; ⊙10am-6pm Mon-Fri, from 9am Sat & Sun) This friendly outfit rents jet skis and kayaks.

Beach Cities Scuba WATER SPORTS
(☎949-443-3858; www.beachcitiesscuba.com; 34283 Pacific Coast Hwy; rentals without/with snorkeling gear $65/95, dive boat trips $120; ⊙hours vary) Rents scuba equipment.

Tours

Capt Dave's Dolphin & Whale Safari BOATING
(949-488-2828; www.dolphinsafari.com; 34451 Ensenada Pl; adult/child 3-12yr from $65/45) This popular outfit runs year-round dolphin- and whale-watching trips on a catamaran equipped with underwater viewing pods and a listening system for you to hear what's going on below the surface.

Dana Wharf Sportfishing BOATING
(888-224-0603; www.danawharf.com; 34675 Golden Lantern St; sportfishing trips adult/child 3-12yr/senior from $46/29/41, whale-watching tours from $45/29/35) Half-day sportfishing trips are best for beginners. Whale-watching tours for families operate both winter and summer.

Festivals & Events

Festival of Whales STREET CARNIVAL, CULTURAL
(www.dpfestivalofwhales.com; early–mid-Mar) For two weekends, a parade, street fair, nature walks and talks, canoe races, surfing clinics, art exhibitions, live music, and surf 'woody' wagon and hot-rod show make up the merriment.

Doheny Blues Festival MUSIC
(www.omegaevents.com/dohenyblues; Doheny State Beach; mid-May) Blues, rock and soul legends perform alongside up-and-comers over a weekend of funky live-music performances and family fun at Doheny State Beach. Recent headliners have included Joe Walsh, Melissa Etheridge, Mavis Staples and Chris Isaak.

Sleeping & Eating

Mostly chain midrange motels and luxury resorts are what you'll find along Pacific Coast Hwy. Restaurants around Dana Point Harbor serve straight-off-the-boat seafood.

Doheny State Beach CAMPGROUND $
(800-444-7275; www.reserveamerica.com; 25300 Dana Point Harbor Dr; inland/beachfront campsites from $40/60; P) Regularly voted the county's best campground, Doheny State Beach offers picnic tables, fire rings, restrooms and showers, but little shade.

Ritz-Carlton Laguna Niguel RESORT $$$
(949-240-2000; www.ritzcarlton.com; 1 Ritz-Carlton Dr; r from $599; P) A longtime OC favorite, this five-star property is perched on a 150ft cliff above the ocean – lovely strolling paths take you there. Sea-blue carpets and crisp white linens in rooms seem to enhance the fabulous views of the coast and ocean. Six dining and drinking options, a spa and daily activities round out the experience for well-heeled travelers.

Turk's GRILL $$
(949-496-9028; 34683 Golden Lantern St; mains $5-16; 8am-2am, shorter hrs winter) At Dana Wharf, this trapped-in-amber dive bar is so dark it feels like you're drinking while jailed in the brig of a ship, but never mind. There's plenty of good pub grub (including burgers and fish-and-chips), Bloody Marys and beers, a mellow crowd and a groovy jukebox.

Information

Dana Point Chamber of Commerce & Visitor Center (949-248-3501; www.danapoint.org; cnr Golden Lantern & Dana Point Harbor Dr; 9am-4pm Fri-Sun late May-early Sep) Stop at this tiny booth for tourist brochures and maps. Gung-ho volunteers sure love their city.

Getting There & Around

From the harbor, **Catalina Express** (800-481-3470; www.catalinaexpress.com; 34675 Golden Lantern St; round-trip adult/child 2-11yr/senior $76.50/70/61) makes daily round-trips to Catalina Island, taking 90 minutes each way.

OCTA (p430) bus 1 connects Dana Point with the OC's other beach towns every 30 to 60 minutes. The one-way fare is $2 (exact change).

Four-hour public parking at the harbor is free, or pay $5 per day (overnight $10).

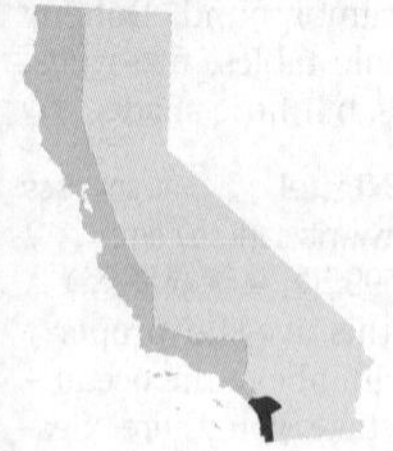

San Diego & Around

POP 1,394,928

Includes ➡

Best Places to Eat

- Clayton's Coffee Shop (p465)
- The Patio on Lamont (p466)
- Pacific Beach Fish Shop (p466)
- Big Kitchen (p461)

Best Places to Sleep

- Hotel del Coronado (p459)
- La Valencia (p474)
- USA Hostels San Diego (p458)
- US Grant Hotel (p458)

Why Go?

New York has its cabbie, Chicago its bluesman and Seattle its coffee-drinking boho. San Diego has its surfer dude, with his tousled hair, great tan and gentle enthusiasm; he looks like he's on a perennial vacation, and when he wishes you welcome, he really means it.

San Diego calls itself 'America's Finest City' and its breezy confidence and sunny countenance filter down even to folks you encounter every day on the street. It feels like a collection of villages each with their own personality, but it's the nation's eighth-largest city and we're hard-pressed to think of a place of any size that's more laid-back.

What's not to love? San Diego bursts with world-famous attractions for the entire family, including the zoo, Legoland and the museums of Balboa Park, plus a bubbling Downtown, beautiful hikes for all, more than 60 beaches and America's most perfect weather.

When to Go

San Diego

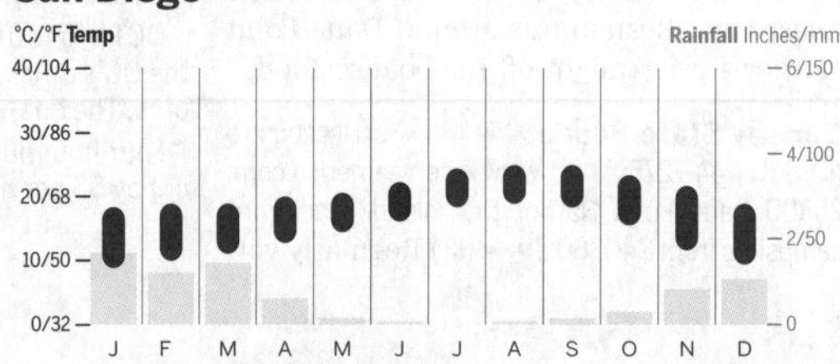

Jun–Aug High season; temperatures and hotel rates are highest, watch out for cloudy skies in June.

Sep–Oct, Mar–May Shoulder seasons; moderate rates, warm with blue skies.

Nov–Feb Low season but far from cold, and your chance to spot whales off the coastline.

CENTRAL & COASTAL SAN DIEGO

Whoosh – here comes a skateboarder. And there goes a wet-suited surfer toting his board to the break, while a Chanel-clad lady lifts a coffee cup off a porcelain saucer. Downtown San Diego and its nearby coastal communities offer all that and more.

San Diego's Downtown is the region's main business, financial and convention district. Whatever intense urban energy Downtown generally lacks, it makes up in spirited shopping, dining and nightlife in the historic Gaslamp Quarter, while the East Village and North Park are hipster havens. The waterfront Embarcadero is good for a stroll,

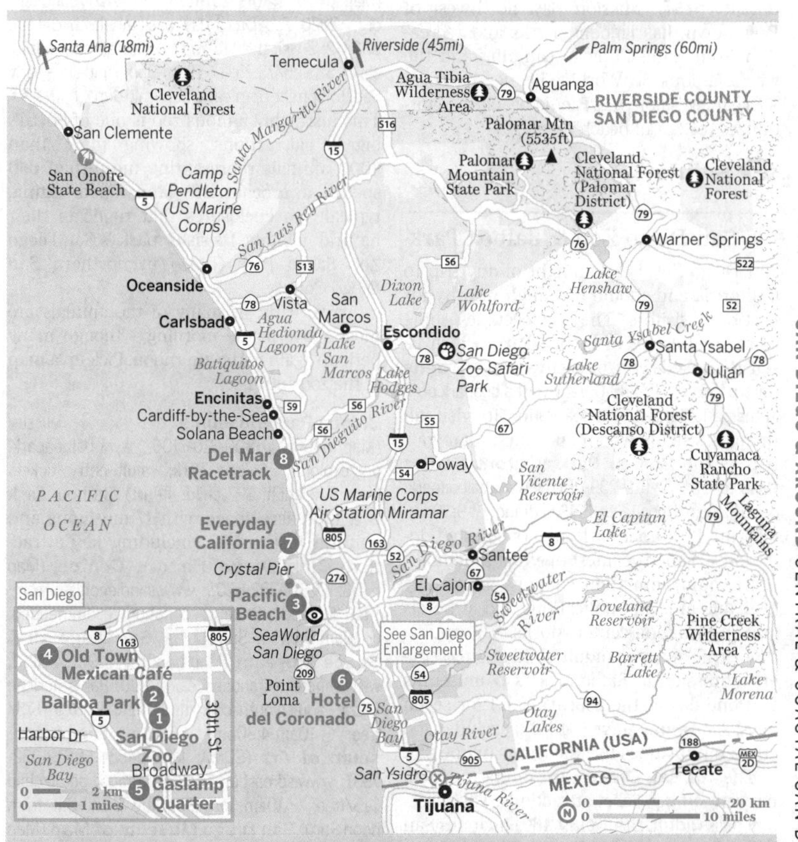

San Diego & Around Highlights

1. Cooing at koalas and pandering to pandas at **San Diego Zoo** (p450).
2. Museum hopping in **Balboa Park** (p450), then sampling fish tacos or the next great taste in Hillcrest and North Park.
3. Sunning and skating on the **Pacific Beach** (p454) boardwalk and catching an epic sunset on the pier.
4. Eating tortillas and swilling margaritas in a legendary the **Old Town Mexican Café** (p463).
5. Downtown pub-crawling and a dueling piano show at **Shout House** (p469) in the Gaslamp Quarter.
6. Marveling at the history and architecture at one of San Diego's prominent landmarks, **Hotel del Coronado** (p454).
7. Kayaking with **Everyday California** (p474) at La Jolla.
8. Mingling with Southern California's hoi polloi at **Del Mar Racetrack** (p477).

and in the northwestern corner of Downtown, vibrant Little Italy is full of good eats, and Old Town is the seat of local history.

The city of Coronado, with its landmark 1888 Hotel del Coronado (p454) and top-rated beach, sits across San Diego Bay from Downtown. At the entrance to the bay, Point Loma has sweeping views across sea and city from the Cabrillo National Monument (p454). Mission Bay, northwest of Downtown, has lagoons, parks and recreation from waterskiing to camping and the world-famous SeaWorld. The nearby coast – Ocean, Mission and Pacific beaches – epitomizes the SoCal beach scene.

Sights

San Diego Zoo & Balboa Park

San Diego Zoo is a highlight of any trip to California and should be a high priority for first-time visitors. The zoo occupies some prime real estate in Balboa Park, which itself is packed with museums and **gardens** (Map p456; ☎619-239-0512; www.balboapark.org/in-the-park/Gardens; Balboa Park). To visit all the park's sights would take days; plan your trip at the **Balboa Park Visitors Center** (Map p456; ☎619-239-0512; www.balboapark.org; House of Hospitality, 1549 El Prado; ⏲9:30am-4:30pm). Pick up a park map (suggested donation $1) and the latest opening schedule.

Discount admission coupons are widely available in local publications and at hotels and information-center kiosks. The **multi-day explorer pass** (adult/child $97/62) covers admission to Balboa Park's 17 museums and one day at the zoo; it's valid for seven days. A **one-day pass** ($46/27) excludes zoo entry, but includes five museums in one day.

The **Go San Diego** card offers up to 55 per cent off big-ticket attractions. The three-day pass (adult/child $189/169) includes San Diego Zoo, many of Balboa Park's museums, SeaWorld, Legoland, the USS *Midway* Museum and San Diego Zoo Safari Park.

Free tours depart Balboa Park's Visitors Center. To uncover the park's architectural heritage nature and history, led by volunteers and rangers, see www.balboapark.org/explore/tours for timings.

Balboa Park is easily reached from Downtown on bus 7 along Park Blvd. By car, Park Blvd provides easy access to free parking. El Prado is a pedestrian road running through the park and between museums; visitors can access it via Laurel St, then cross Cabrillo Bridge with the Cabrillo Fwy (CA 163) 120ft below; hanging greenery here makes it look like a rainforest gorge.

The free **Balboa Park Tram** bus makes a continuous loop around the park; however, it's easiest and most enjoyable to walk.

★San Diego Zoo ZOO

(Map p456; ☎619-231-1515; http://zoo.sandiego.org; 2920 Zoo Dr; 1-day pass adult/child from $52/42; 2-visit pass to zoo &/or safari park adult/child $83.25/73.25; ⏲9am-9pm mid-Jun–early Sep, to 5pm or 6pm early Sep–mid-Jun; P) This justifiably famous zoo is one of SoCal's biggest attractions, showing more than 3000 animals representing more than 650 species in a beautifully landscaped setting, typically in enclosures that replicate their natural habitats. Its sister park is San Diego Zoo Safari Park (p479) in northern San Diego County.

Arrive early, as many of the animals are most active in the morning – though many perk up again in the afternoon. Pick up a map at the zoo entrance.

Balboa Park Museums MUSEUM

(Map p456; ☎800-310-7106; www.balboapark.org/explorer; Balboa Park; multi-entry tickets from $46 adult, $27 child; P) Balboa Park is a 1200-acre space with 17 museums and cultural institutions, including key attractions **San Diego History Center** (Map p456; ☎619-232-6203; www.sandiegohistory.org; 1649 El Prado, Suite 3; donation recommended; ⏲10am-5pm Tue-Sun) FREE, **San Diego Air & Space Museum** (Map p456; ☎619-234-8291; www.sandiegoairandspace.org; 2001 Pan American Plaza; adult/youth/child under 2 $19.75/$10.75/free; ⏲10am-4:30pm), **San Diego Museum of Art** (SDMA; Map p456; ☎619-232-7931; www.sdmart.org; 1450 El Prado; adult/child $15/free; ⏲10am-5pm Mon, Tue & Thu-Sat, from noon Sun), **San Diego Museum of Man** (Map p456; ☎619-239-2001; www.museumofman.org; Plaza de California, 1350 El Prado; adult/child/teen $13/6/8; ⏲10am-5pm) and **San Diego Natural History Museum** (Map p456; ☎877-946-7797; www.sdnhm.org; 1788 El Prado; adult/youth 3-17/child under 2 $19/12/free; ⏲10am-5pm). All attractions are easily walkable, or jump aboard the park's tram to whizz around them all at speed.

★New Children's Museum MUSEUM

(Map p460; ☎619-233-8792; www.thinkplaycreate.org; 200 W Island Ave; $13; ⏲10am-4pm Mon, Wed,

FREE STUFF

Balboa Park Gardens A number of gardens, reflecting different horticultural styles and environments.

Hotel del Coronado (p454) Forever associated with Marilyn Monroe and *Some Like It Hot.*

Old Town San Diego State Historic Park (p453) Surrounded by trees and period buildings housing museums, shops and restaurants.

Spreckels Organ Pavilion Said to be the world's largest outdoor musical instrument.

Botanical Building Each season gives this stunning structure a different look.

Mission & Pacific Beaches (p454) Home to Ocean Front Walk and plenty of other distractions.

Coronado Municipal Beach (p454), consistently ranked in America's top 10.

Thu & Sat, 9.30am-4pm Fri, noon-4pm Sun;) This interactive children's museum offers interactive art meant for kids. Installations are designed by artists, so tykes can learn principles of movement and physics while simultaneously being exposed to art and working out the ants in their pants. Exhibits change every 18 months or so, so there's always something new.

Spreckels Organ Pavilion NOTABLE BUILDING
(Map p456; 619-702-8138; http://spreckelsorgan.org; Balboa Park) FREE Going south from Plaza de Panama, you can't miss the circle of seating and the curved colonnade in front of the band shell housing the organ said to be the world's largest outdoor pipe organ. Donated by the Spreckels family of sugar fortune and fame, the pipe organ came with the stipulation that San Diego must always have an official organist. Make a point of attending the free **concerts**, held throughout the year at 2pm Sundays and on Monday evenings in summer (7.30pm to 9.30pm).

Botanical Building GARDENS
(Map p456; www.balboapark.org/tours/botanical-bldg; 1549 El Prado; 10am-4pm) FREE The Botanical Building looks lovely from El Prado, where you can see it reflected in the large lily pond that was used for hydrotherapy in WWII when the navy took over the park. The building's central dome and two wings are covered with redwood lattice panels, which let filtered sunlight into the collection of tropical plants and ferns. The planting changes every season; in December there's a particularly beautiful poinsettia display.

Little Italy

Little Italy was settled in the mid-19th century by Italian immigrants, mostly fishermen and their families, who lived off a booming fish industry and whiskey trade.

Over the last few years, the Italian community has been joined by exciting contemporary architecture, galleries, gourmet restaurants, and design and architecture businesses. Fun bars and restaurants have made this one of San Diego's hippest neighborhoods.

Gaslamp Quarter

Gaslamp Museum & William Heath Davis House MUSEUM
(Map p460; 619-233-4692; www.gaslampquarter.org; 410 Island Ave; adult/senior & student $5/4, walking tour $10/8; 10am-5pm Tue-Sat, noon-4pm Sun) This house, a prefab affair brought from Maine in 1850, contains a small museum with 19th-century furnishings, plus historic newspaper clippings in the basement. From here, the Gaslamp Quarter Historical Foundation leads a weekly, 90-minute **walking tour** of the neighborhood on Thursdays at 1pm ($20 per person), which includes admission to the house.

Old Town

Under the Mexican government, which took power in San Diego in 1821, any settlement with a population of 500 or more was entitled to become a 'pueblo,' and the area below the Presidio became the first official civilian Mexican settlement in California – the Pueblo de San Diego.

Metropolitan San Diego

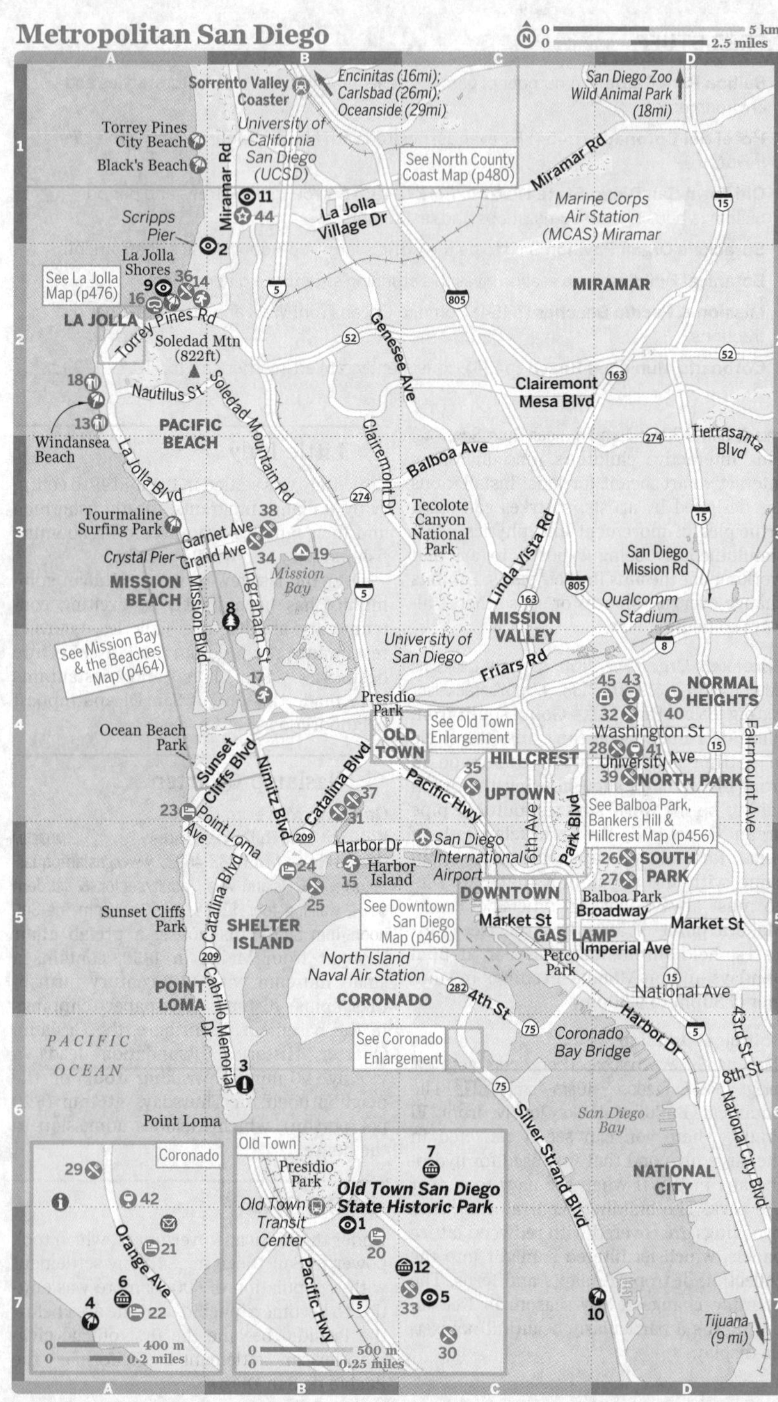

Metropolitan San Diego

Top Sights
1 Old Town San Diego State Historic Park B7

Sights
2 Birch Aquarium at Scripps B2
3 Cabrillo National Monument B6
4 Coronado Municipal Beach A7
5 El Campo Santo C7
6 Hotel del Coronado A7
7 Junípero Serra Museum C6
8 Mission Bay B3
9 San Diego-La Jolla Underwater Park Ecological Reserve A2
10 Silver Strand State Beach D7
11 University of California San Diego B1
12 Whaley House C7

Activities, Courses & Tours
13 Big Rock A2
14 Everyday California A2
15 Harbor Sailboats B5
Point Loma Sport Fishing .... (see 24)
16 San Diego-La Jolla Underwater Park A2
17 Seaforth Sportfishing B4
18 Windansea Beach A2

Sleeping
19 Campland on the Bay B3
20 Cosmopolitan Hotel B7
21 El Cordova Hotel A7
22 Hotel del Coronado A7
23 Inn at Sunset Cliffs A4
24 Pearl B5

Eating
1500 Ocean .... (see 22)
25 Bali Hai B5
26 Big Kitchen D5
27 Buona Forchetta D5
28 Carnitas' Snack Shack D4
29 Clayton's Coffee Shop A6
30 El Agave C7
31 Liberty Public Market B4
32 Nomad Donuts D4
33 Old Town Mexican Café C7
34 Pacific Beach Fish Shop B3
Point Loma Seafoods .... (see 24)
35 Saffron C4
Shakespeare Pub & Grille .... (see 35)
36 Shore Rider Cafe A2
37 Stone Brewing World Bistro & Gardens B4
38 The Patio on Lamont B3
39 Urban Solace D4

Drinking & Nightlife
40 Blind Lady Ale House D4
41 Coin-Op Game Room D4
42 Mc P's Irish Pub A6
43 Polite Provisions D4

Entertainment
44 La Jolla Playhouse B1

Shopping
45 Adams Avenue D4
Liberty Station .... (see 31)

In 1968 the area was named **Old Town San Diego State Historic Park** (Map p452; ☎619-220-5422; www.parks.ca.gov; 4002 Wallace St; ⏰visitor center & museums 10am-5pm daily; P 🚻) FREE, archaeological work began, and the few surviving original buildings were restored. Now it's a pedestrian district of trees, a large open plaza, and shops and restaurants.

There's the park visitor center and an excellent history museum in the Robinson-Rose House at the southern end of the plaza. The **Whaley House** (Map p452; ☎619-297-7511; www.whaleyhouse.org; 2476 San Diego Ave; adult/child before 5pm $8/6, after 5pm $13/8; ⏰10am-9:30pm daily summer, 10am-4:30pm Sun-Tue, to 9:30pm Thu-Sat rest of the year) is the city's oldest brick building and nearby is **El Campo Santo** (Map p452; San Diego Ave, btwn Arista & Conde Sts), a notable 1849 cemetery. The **Junípero Serra Museum** (Map p452; ☎619-232-6203; www.sandiegohistory.org/serra_museum; 2727 Presidio Dr; by donation; ⏰10am-4pm Fri-Sun early Jun-early Sep, 10am-5pm Sat & Sun early Sep-early Jun; P 🚻) is named for the Spanish padre who established the first Spanish settlement in California, in 1769, and has artifacts of the city's mission and rancho periods.

Embarcadero & the Waterfront

South and west of the Gaslamp Quarter, San Diego's well-manicured waterfront **promenades** stretch along Harbor Dr, and are perfect for strolling or jogging. Southwest of the ship museums is Seaport Village (p469), with restaurants and gift shops, and the convention center (1989), with its sail-inspired roof that stretches for a half mile. Another gathering place is the former police headquarters (p469), now a shopping center.

USS Midway Museum MUSEUM
(Map p460; ☎619-544-9600; www.midway.org; 910 N Harbor Dr; adult/child $20/$10; ⏰10am-

5pm, last admission 4pm; P 👪) The giant aircraft carrier USS *Midway* was one of the navy's flagships from 1945 to 1991, last playing a combat role in the first Gulf War. On the flight deck of the hulking vessel, walk right up to some 29 restored aircraft including an F-14 Tomcat and F-4 Phantom jet fighter. Admission includes an audio tour along the narrow confines of the upper decks to the bridge, admiral's war room, brig and 'pri-fly' (primary flight control; the carrier's equivalent of a control tower). Parking costs $10.

★Maritime Museum MUSEUM
(Map p460; ☎619-234-9153; www.sdmaritime.org; 1492 N Harbor Dr; adult/child $16/8; ⏲9am-9pm late May-early Sep, to 8pm early Sep-late May; 👪) This museum is easy to find: look for the 100ft-high masts of the iron-hulled square-rigger *Star of India*. Built on the Isle of Man and launched in 1863, the tall ship plied the England–India trade route, carried immigrants to New Zealand, became a trading ship based in Hawaii and, finally, ferried cargo in Alaska. It's a handsome vessel, but don't expect anything romantic or glamorous on board.

Coronado

Across the bay from downtown San Diego, Coronado is a civilized escape from the jumble of the city and the chaos of the beaches. After crossing the bay by ferry or via the elegantly curved 2.12-mile-long Coronado Bay Bridge, follow the tree-lined, manicured median strip of Orange Ave a mile or so toward the commercial center, Coronado Village. Then park your car; you won't need it again until you leave.

As an alternative to ferries, water taxis and bike rentals, bus 901 from downtown San Diego runs along Orange Ave to the Hotel del Coronado. The Old Town Trolley (p457) tour stops in front of **Mc P's Irish Pub** (Map p452; ☎619-435-5280; www.mcpspub.com; 1107 Orange Ave; ⏲11am-late Mon-Sat, 10am-late Sun; 🐾).

The story of Coronado is in many ways the story of the **Hotel del Coronado** (Map p452; ☎619-435-6611; www.hoteldel.com; 1500 Orange Ave, Coronado; P 👪), opened in 1888 by John D Spreckels, the millionaire who bankrolled the first rail line to San Diego, took over Coronado and turned the island into one of the West Coast's most fashionable getaways. The **beach** (Map p452; www.coronado.ca.us; P 👪) is consistently ranked in America's top 10.

Point Loma

On maps Point Loma looks like an elephant's trunk guarding the entrance to San Diego Bay. Highlights are the Cabrillo National Monument (at the end of the trunk), the shopping and dining of Liberty Station (at its base) and harborside seafood meals.

Cabrillo National Monument MONUMENT
(Map p452; ☎619-557-5450; www.nps.gov/cabr; 1800 Cabrillo Memorial Dr; per car $10; ⏲9am-5pm; P 👪) 🌿 Atop a steep hill at the tip of the peninsula, this is San Diego's finest locale for history, views and nature walks. It's also the best place in town to see the gray-whale migration (January to March) from land. You may forget you're in a major metropolitan area.

The **visitor center** has a comprehensive, old-school presentation on Portuguese explorer Juan Rodríguez Cabrillo's 1542 voyage up the California coast, plus exhibits on early Native Californian inhabitants and the area's natural history.

Ocean Beach

San Diego's most Bohemian seaside community is a place of seriously scruffy haircuts, facial hair and body art. You can get tattooed, shop for antiques and walk into a restaurant barefoot and shirtless without anyone batting an eyelid. **Newport Avenue**, the main drag, runs perpendicular to the beach through a compact business district of bars, surf shops, music stores, used-clothing stores and antiques consignment stores.

Mission Bay, Mission Beach & Pacific Beach

The big ticket attraction around Mission Bay is SeaWorld, while the nearby Mission, Ocean and Pacific Beaches are the SoCal of the movies.

Mission & Pacific Beaches BEACH
(Map p464) FREE Central San Diego's best beach scene is concentrated in a narrow strip of land between the ocean and Mission Bay. There's amazing people-watching is on the **Ocean Front Walk**, the boardwalk that connects the two beaches. From South Mission Jetty to Pacific Beach Point, it's crowded with joggers, in-line skaters and cyclists any time of the year. On warm summer weekends, oiled bodies, packed like sardines, cover the beach from end to end and cheer the setting sun.

While there's lots to do here, perhaps the best use of an afternoon is to walk along the boardwalk, then spread a blanket or kick back over cocktails and take in the scenery.

A block off Mission Beach, Mission Blvd (the main north–south road), is lined with surf, smoke and swimwear shops. **Cheap Rentals** (Map p464; ☎800-941-7761, 858-488-9070; 3689 Mission Blvd, Pacific Beach; foam surfboards from $7 per hour; ⏰10am-6pm) loans bikes, skates and surfboards.

In Pacific Beach, to the north, activity extends inland, particularly along Garnet (pronounced gar-*net*) Ave, lined with bars, restaurants and shops, mostly targeted at a 20-something crowd. At the ocean end of Garnet Ave, **Crystal Pier** is a mellow place to fish or gaze out to sea.

At peak times these beaches can get supercrowded: parking around noon is just not gonna happen.

Belmont Park AMUSEMENT PARK

(Map p464; ☎858-228-9283; www.belmontpark.com; 3146 Mission Blvd; per ride $3-6, all-day pass adult/child $30/20; ⏰from 11am daily, closing times varies; Ⓟ) This old-style family-amusement park at the southern end of Mission Beach has been here since 1925. There's a large indoor pool, known as the **Plunge**, and a classic wooden roller coaster named the **Giant Dipper**, plus adventure golf, a new escape-room game, a carousel and other classics. More modern attractions include wave machines like **Flowrider** (Map p464; WaveHouse Beach Club, 3125 Ocean Front Walk; wave-riding per hour $30) FREE, for simulated surfing. Even if it sits on dry land, Belmont is to San Diego what the Santa Monica Pier amusement park is to LA. During winter months check for closures due to ride maintenance.

Mission Bay PARK

(Map p452; www.sandiego.gov/park-and-recreation; Ⓟ👪) Just east of Mission and Pacific Beaches is this 7-sq-mile playground, with 27 miles of shoreline and 90 acres of parks on islands, coves and peninsulas. Sailing, windsurfing and kayaking dominate northwest Mission Bay, while waterskiers zip around **Fiesta Island**. Kite flying is popular in **Mission Bay Park**, beach volleyball is big on Fiesta Island, and there's delightful cycling and inline skating on the miles of bike paths.

Although hotels, boat yards and other businesses dot about one-quarter of the land, it feels wide open. Fun fact: Spanish explorers called this expanse at the mouth of the San Diego River 'False Bay' – it formed a shallow bay when the river flowed and a marshy swamp when it didn't. After WWII, a combination of civic vision and coastal engineering turned it into a recreational area.

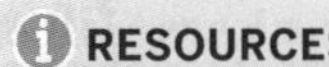

RESOURCES

Lonely Planet (www.lonelyplanet.com/usa/san-diego) Destination information, hotel bookings, traveler forum and more.

San Diego Tourism (www.sandiego.org) Search hotels, sights, dining, rental cars and more, and make reservations.

Activities

There are plenty of hikes in San Diego, but most outdoor activities involve the ocean. These waters are a dream for surfers, paddleboarders, kayakers and boaters.

Surfing

A good number of residents moved to San Diego just for the surfing, and boy, is it good. Even beginners will understand why.

Fall brings strong swells and offshore Santa Ana winds. In summer swells come from the south and southwest, and in winter from the west and northwest. Spring brings more frequent onshore winds, but the surfing can still be good. For the latest beach, weather and surf reports, call **San Diego County Lifeguard Services** (☎619-221-8824).

Beginners should head to Mission or Pacific Beach, for beach breaks (soft-sand bottomed). North of Crystal Pier, **Tourmaline Surfing Park** is a crowded, but good, improvers spot for those comfortable surfing reef.

Rental rates vary depending on the quality of the equipment, but figure on soft boards from around $15/45 per hour/full day; wet suits cost $7/28. Packages are available.

Diving & Snorkeling

Off the coast of San Diego County, divers will find kelp beds, shipwrecks (including the *Yukon,* a WWII destroyer sunk off Mission Beach in 2000) and canyons deep enough to host bat ray, octopus and squid. For current conditions, call San Diego County Lifeguard Services.

Fishing

The most popular public fishing piers are Imperial Beach Pier, Embarcadero Fishing Pier, Shelter Island Fishing Pier, Ocean Beach Pier

Balboa Park, Bankers Hill & Hillcrest

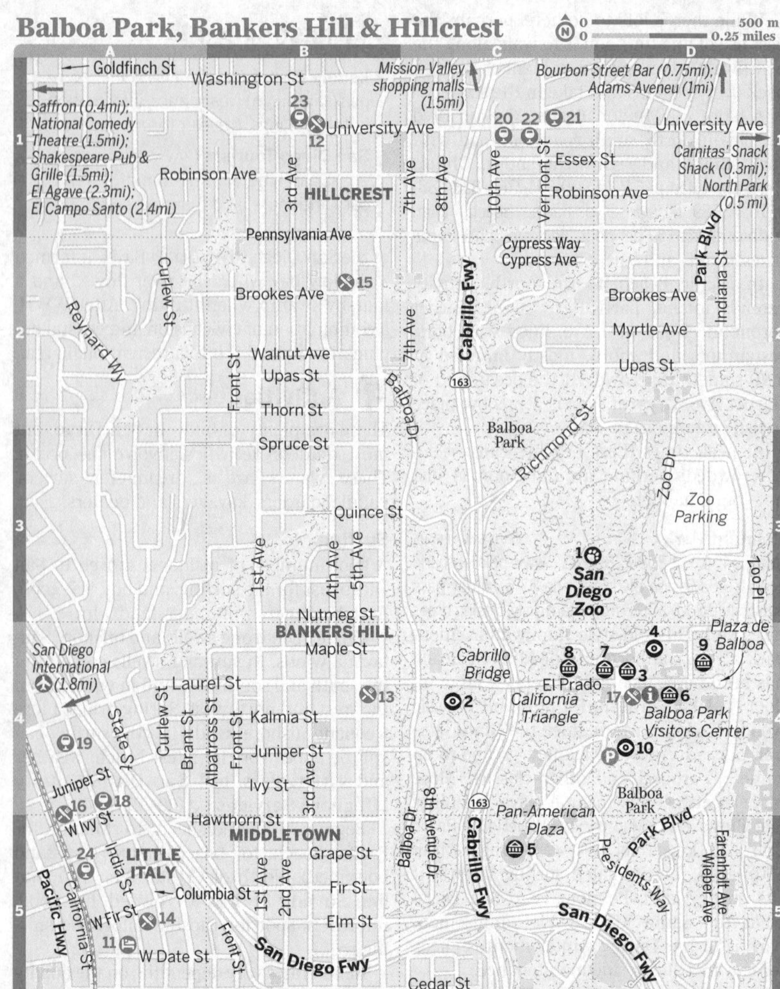

and Crystal Pier at Pacific Beach. Generally the best pier fishing is from April to October, and no license is required. For offshore fishing, catches can include barracuda, bass and yellowtail and, in summer, albacore tuna. A state fishing license is required for people over 16 for offshore fishing; visit www.wildlife.ca.gov for details or book a daily fishing trips with a tour company like **Point Loma Sport Fishing** (Map p452; ☎619-223-1627; www.pointlomasportfishing.com; 1403 Scott St, Point Loma; half-day trips from $45) including those around Coronado and Point Loma.

Boating

San Diego offers rental of powerboats (from $130 per hour), sailboats (from $30 per hour), and kayaks (from $18 per hour) and canoes on Mission Bay from **Mission Bay Sportcenter** (Map p464; ☎858-488-1004; www.missionbaysportcenter.com; 1010 Santa Clara Pl; rentals $3-230).

Kayaking

Ocean kayaking is a good way to observe sea life, and explore cliffs and caves inaccessible from land. Guided tours and lessons are available from **Family Kayak** (☎619-277-1169; www.familykayak.com; adult/child from $45/20; 👪).

Balboa Park, Bankers Hill & Hillcrest

Top Sights
1 San Diego Zoo C3

Sights
2 Balboa Park Gardens C4
3 Balboa Park Museums D4
4 Botanical Building D4
5 San Diego Air & Space Museum C5
6 San Diego History Center D4
7 San Diego Museum of Art D4
8 San Diego Museum of Man C4
9 San Diego Natural History Museum D4
10 Spreckels Organ Pavilion D4

Sleeping
11 La Pensione Hotel A5

Eating
12 Bread & Cie B1
13 Cucina Urbana B4
14 Filippi's Pizza Grotto A5
15 Hash House a Go Go B2
16 Juniper & Ivy A4
17 Prado D4

Drinking & Nightlife
18 Ballast Point Tasting Room & Kitchen A4
19 El Camino A4
20 Flicks C1
21 Gossip Grill C1
22 Rich's C1
23 Urban Mo's B1
24 Waterfront A5

Sailing

Experienced sailors are able to charter boats ranging from catamarans to yachts. Prices start at about $105 for four hours at **Harbor Sailboats** (Map p452; ☎800-854-6625, 619-291-9568; www.harborsailboats.com; 2040 Harbor Island Dr, Suite 104; lessons for nonmembers from $350, plus port fee) and rise steeply. Other charter operators can be found around **Shelter and Harbor Islands** (on the west side of San Diego Bay near the airport).

Whale-Watching

Gray whales pass San Diego from mid-December to late February on their way south to Baja California, and again in mid-March on their way back up to Alaskan waters. Their 12,000-mile round-trip journey is the longest migration of any mammal on earth.

Cabrillo National Monument (p454) is the best place to see the whales from land, where you'll also find exhibits, whale-related ranger programs and a shelter from which to watch the whales breach (bring binoculars).

Half-day whale-watching boat trips are offered by most of the companies that run daily fishing trips, like **Seaforth Sportfishing** (Map p452; ☎619-224-3383; www.seaforthlanding.com; 1717 Quivira Rd, Mission Bay; trips from $24-300). The trips generally cost $24 per adult excursion, sometimes with a guaranteed sighting or a free ticket. Look for coupons and special offers at tourist kiosks and online.

Tours

Brewery Tours of San Diego BREWERY
(☎619-961-7999; www.brewerytoursofsandiego.com; per person $75-95) San Diego has one of America's best craft-brew scenes, with dozens of small breweries. To leave the driving to someone else, this outfits offers a variety of bus tours each week to an assortment of breweries. Price varies by amount and type of drink and food provided.

San Diego Food Tours FOOD & DRINK
(☎619-233-8687; http://sodiegotours.com/san-diego-food-tours/; from $50) Walking tours showcase the city's gastronomic treasures from Gaslamp, Little Italy and the Old Town, with some enthusiastic native San Diegan guides. Come hungry.

Old Town Trolley Tours & Seal Tours TOURS
(☎855-396-7433; www.trolleytours.com; adult/child $40/25) Not to be confused with the municipal San Diego Trolley, this outfit operates hop-on-hop-off, open-air buses decorated like old-style streetcars, looping around the main attractions of Downtown and Coronado in about two hours, leaving every 30 minutes or so. The main trolley stand is in Old Town, but you can start or stop at any of the well-marked trolley-tour stops. It also operates 90-minute amphibious **Seal Tours** which depart from Seaport Village (p469) and tour the bay via Shelter Island.

Festivals & Events

San Diego Crew Classic SPORTS
(www.crewclassic.org; ⊙late Mar/early Apr) The national college rowing regatta takes place in Mission Bay.

San Diego Rock 'n' Roll Marathon SPORTS
(www.runrocknroll.competitor.com; ⊙early Jun) Live bands perform at each mile mark of this 26.2-mile race, with a big concert at the finish line.

San Diego County Fair FAIR
(www.sdfair.com; Del Mar Fairgrounds; early Jun-early Jul) More than a million people watch headline acts, enjoy hundreds of carnival rides and shows, and pig out on 'fair fare' (plus some healthier options).

San Diego LGBT Pride LGBT
(www.sdpride.org; mid-Jul) The city's gay community celebrates in Hillcrest and Balboa Park at the month's end, with parades, parties, performances, art shows and more.

Opening Day at Del Mar Racetrack SPORTS
(www.dmtc.com; mid- to late Jul) Outrageous hats, cocktails and general merriment kick off the horse-racing season, 'where the turf meets the surf.' Racing through early September.

Comic-Con International CONVENTION
(www.comic-con.org; San Diego Convention Center; late Jul) America's largest event for collectors of comic, pop-culture and movie memorabilia has gone from geek chic to trendmaker.

Fleet Week MILITARY
(www.fleetweeksandiego.org; early Oct) The US military shows its pride in events including a sea and air parade, special tours of ships, the Miramar Air Show and the Coronado Speed Festival (featuring vintage cars).

Little Italy Festa FOOD & DRINK, CULTURAL
(www.littleitalysd.com; early Oct) Come for the tastes and aromas of old Italia, and stay for Gesso Italiano, chalk-art drawn directly onto the streets.

San Diego Beer Week BEER, FOOD & DRINK
(http://sdbw.org; early Nov) Celebrating all things hoppy: take part in beer-tasting breakfast, dinners with beer pairing, and roam around the giant beer garden with dozens of San Diego's best breweries and chefs.

San Diego Bay Wine & Food Festival FOOD & DRINK
(www.sandiegowineclassic.com; mid-Nov) Cooking classes, wine-tasting parties, gourmet food stands and more.

Harbor Parade of Lights HOLIDAY FESTIVAL
(www.sdparadeoflights.org; Dec) Dozens of decorated, illuminated boats float in procession on San Diego's harbor on two Sunday evenings in December.

December Nights HOLIDAY FESTIVAL
(www.balboapark.org/decembernights; early Dec) This festival in Balboa Park includes crafts, carols and a candlelight parade.

Sleeping

We list high-season (summer) rates for single- or double-occupancy rooms. Prices drop significantly between September and June, but whatever time of year, ask about specials, suites and package deals. San Diego Tourism runs a **room-reservation line** (800-350-6205; www.sandiego.org).

For camping try **Campland on the Bay** (Map p452; 858-581-4260, 800-422-9386; www.campland.com; 2211 Pacific Beach Dr, Mission Bay; RV & tent sites $55-432, beachfront from $225;) or **KOA** (800-562-9877, 619-427-3601; www.sandiegokoa.com; 111 N 2nd Ave, Chula Vista; tent sites from $55, RV sites with hookups from $66, cabins from $95, deluxe cabins from $210;), about 8 miles south, with good camping facilities for families like a pool, bike rental, Jacuzzi and off-leash dog park; deluxe cabins include linens, private bathrooms and pots and pans.

Downtown San Diego

Downtown is San Diego's most convenient place to stay, for its wealth of restaurants and hotels and its easy access to transit.

★**USA Hostels San Diego** HOSTEL $
(Map p460; 619-232-3100, 800-438-8622; www.usahostels.com; 726 5th Ave; dm/r with shared bath from $32/80;) Lots of charm and color at this convivial hostel in a former Victorian-era hotel. Look for cheerful rooms, a full kitchen, and a communal lounge. Rates include linens, lockers and bagels for breakfast. Surrounded by bars, it's smack-bang in the middle of Gaslamp's nightlife scene, so bring earplugs if you're a light sleeper.

★**La Pensione Hotel** BOUTIQUE HOTEL $$
(Map p456; 619-236-8000, 800-232-4683; www.lapensionehotel.com; 606 W Date St; r from $145-200;) Despite the name, Little Italy's La Pensione isn't a pension but an intimate, friendly, recently renovated hotel of 67 rooms with queen-size beds and private bathrooms. It's set around a frescoed courtyard and is just steps to the neighborhood's dining, cafes and galleries, and walking distance to most Downtown attractions. There's an attractive cafe downstairs, and a recently introduced spa. Parking is $20.

★**US Grant Hotel** LUXURY HOTEL $$$
(Map p460; 800-237-5029, 619-232-3121; www.starwood.com; 326 Broadway; r from $211;) This 11-stories high 1910 hotel

was built as the fancy city counterpart to the Hotel del Coronado (p454) and hosted everyone from Albert Einstein to Harry Truman. Today's quietly flashy lobby combines chocolate-brown and ocean-blue accents, and rooms boast original artwork on the headboards. It's owned by members of the Sycuan tribe of Native Americans. Parking costs $48.

Old Town

Base yourself in San Diego's Old Town, and you may not need a car. Many lodgings offer free airport shuttles, and there are convenient transit links on the other side of the state park.

Cosmopolitan Hotel B&B $$
(Map p452; 619-297-1874; http://oldtowncosmopolitan.com; 2660 Calhoun St; r $139-195; front desk 9am-9pm;) Right in Old Town State Park, this creaky, 10-room hotel is restored to its 1870 glory and has oodles of charm, antique furnishings and is possibly haunted (!). There's a **restaurant** downstairs for lunch and dinner, with live music on Fridays and Saturday evenings. Breakfast is a simple affair centered on coffee and scones. Free wi-fi and free parking.

Coronado

A stay in Coronado Village – around the Hotel del Coronado – puts you close to the beach, shops and restaurants. The northern end is an easy walk to the ferry. Or get away from it all near the deserted **Silver Strand Beach**; a car is advisable here if you're looking to explore further afield.

El Cordova Hotel HISTORIC HOTEL $$
(Map p452; 800-229-2032, 619-435-4131; www.elcordovahotel.com; 1351 Orange Ave; r from $189;) This exceedingly cozy Spanish-style former mansion from 1902 has rooms and suites around an outdoor courtyard of shops, restaurants, pool, hot tub and barbecue grills. Rooms are charming in an antiquey sort of way, though nothing fancy; they include TVs with free HBO.

★**Hotel del Coronado** LUXURY HOTEL $$$
(Map p452; 800-468-3533, 619-435-6611; www.hoteldel.com; 1500 Orange Ave; r from $297;) San Diego's iconic hotel provides the essential Coronado experience: over a century of history (p454), a pool, full-service spa, shops, restaurants, manicured grounds, a white-sand beach and an ice-skating rink during Christmas season. Even the basic rooms have luxurious marbled bathrooms. Note: half the accommodations are not in the main Victorian-era hotel (368 rooms) but in an adjacent seven-story building constructed in the 1970s. For a sense of place, book a room in the original hotel. Self-parking is $39.

Point Loma Area

Although it's a bit out of the way, Point Loma boasts some fun accommodations. Head to **Shelter Island** for tiki-style hotels.

Pearl MOTEL $$
(Map p452; 619-226-6100, 877-732-7573; www.thepearlsd.com; 1410 Rosecrans St; r $125-199;) The mid-century-modern Pearl feels more Palm Springs than San Diego. The 23 rooms in its 1959 shell have soothing blue hues, trippy surf motifs and fishbowls. There's a lively pool scene (including **'dive-in' movies** on Wednesday nights), or play Jenga or Parcheesi in the groovy, shag-carpeted lobby. Light sleepers: request a room away from busy street traffic.

Ocean Beach

Ocean Beach (OB) is a happening hippy 'hood, but it is also under the outbound flight path of San Diego airport. Light sleepers might prefer to stay elsewhere or bring earplugs.

Ocean Beach International Hostel HOSTEL $
(Map p464; 619-223-7873, 800-339-7263; www.californiahostel.com; 4961 Newport Ave; dm $29-45, r from $110;) Central OB's cheapest option is easy to spot with its psychedelic colored exterior and peace sign on the top of the building. Only a couple of blocks from the ocean, it's a simple but friendly and fun place reserved for international travelers, with free wi-fi and breakfast. Entertainment comes in the form of music nights and board games.

Inn at Sunset Cliffs INN $$
(Map p452; 619-222-7901, 866-786-2453; www.innatsunsetcliffs.com; 1370 Sunset Cliffs Blvd; r/ste from $175/289;) At the south end of Ocean Beach, wake up to the sound of surf crashing onto the rocky shore. This low-key 1950s charmer wraps around a flower-bedecked courtyard with a small heated pool. Its 24 breezy rooms are compact, but most have attractive stone-and-tile bathrooms, and some suites have full kitchens.

Downtown San Diego

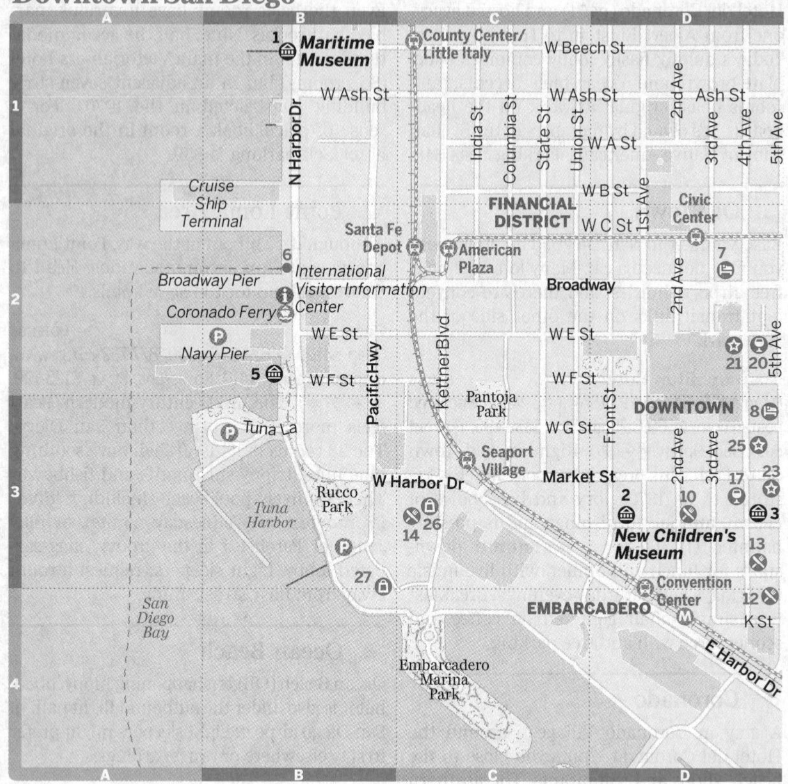

Downtown San Diego

Top Sights
1 Maritime Museum....B1
2 New Children's Museum....D3

Sights
3 Gaslamp Museum & William Heath Davis House....D3
4 Petco Park....E4
5 USS *Midway* Museum....B2

Activities, Courses & Tours
6 Flagship Cruises....B2

Sleeping
7 US Grant Hotel....D2
8 USA Hostels San Diego....D3

Eating
9 Basic....E3
10 Café 222....D3
11 Café Chloe....E3
12 Gaslamp Strip Club....D4
Neighborhood....(see 19)
13 Oceanaire....D3
14 Puesto at the Headquarters....C3
15 Valentine's....E1

Drinking & Nightlife
16 Bang Bang....E3
17 Dublin Square....D3
18 East Village Tavern & Bowl....E3
19 Noble Experiment....E3
20 Star Bar....D2

Entertainment
21 Arts Tix....D2
22 House of Blues....E2
23 Prohibition Lounge....D3
24 San Diego Symphony....E1
25 Shout House....D3

Shopping
26 Headquarters at Seaport District....C3
27 Seaport Village....B3

Mission Bay, Mission Beach & Pacific Beach

Just east of Mission Beach, Mission Bay has waterfront lodging at lower prices than accommodations on the ocean.

Catamaran Resort Hotel RESORT **$$**
(Map p464; 800-422-8386, 858-488-1081; www.catamaranresort.com; 3999 Mission Blvd; r from $139;) Tropical landscaping and tiki decor fill this resort backing onto Mission Bay (there's a luau on some summer evenings!). A plethora of activities make it a perfect place for families (sailing, kayaking, tennis, biking, skating, spa-ing, etc), or board the **Bahia Belle** (Map p464; www.sternwheelers.com; 998 W Mission Bay Dr; $10) here. Rooms are in low-rise buildings or in a 14-story tower; some have views and full kitchens.

Tower 23 BOUTIQUE HOTEL **$$$**
(Map p464; 858-270-2323, 866-869-3723; www.t23hotel.com; 723 Felspar St, Pacific Beach; r from $270;) If you like your oceanfront stay with contemporary cool style, this modernist place has an awesome location, minimalist decor, lots of teals and mint blues, water features and a sense of humor. There's no pool, but dude, you're right on the beach. Parking is $30.

Crystal Pier Hotel & Cottages COTTAGE **$$$**
(Map p464; 800-748-5894; www.crystalpier.com; 4500 Ocean Blvd, Pacific Beach; d $185-525;) Charming, wonderful and unlike any other place in San Diego, Crystal Pier has cottages built right on the pier above the water. Almost all 29 cottages have full ocean views and kitchens; most date from the 1930s. Newer, larger cottages sleep up to six. Book eight to 11 months in advance for summer reservations. Minimum-stay requirements vary by season. No air-conditioning. Rates include parking.

Eating

San Diego has a thriving dining culture, with an emphasis on Mexican, Californian and seafood. San Diegans eat dinner early, usually around 6pm or 7pm, and most restaurants are ready to close by 10pm. Breakfast is a big affair, and there's a growing locavore and gourmet scene, especially in North Park. Less-expensive options are fun and satisfying. Reservations are recommended.

Balboa Park & Around

Big Kitchen BREAKFAST **$**
(Map p452; 619-234-5789; www.bigkitchencafe.com; 3003 Grape St, South Park; mains $5-13.50; 7:30am-2:30pm;) Here since the '70s, this neighborhood joint is decorated with bric-a-brac, progressive bumper stickers, homages to The Beatles and pictures of Whoopi Goldberg – she once worked here as a dishwasher. The kitchen serves American classics like stacks of pancakes, 10 different types of burgers and big-bowl specialties; chili, soup and mac 'n' cheese.

★**Nomad Donuts** DESSERTS **$**
(Map p452; 619-431-5000; https://nomaddonuts.com; 4504 30th St; doughnuts from $4; 6am-2pm Mon-Fri, 8am-2pm Sat & Sun) If you think you know donuts, think again. This artisanal doughnut shop is headed up by pastry chef Kristianna Zabala, who hand

crafts every batch using cage-free, organic eggs and other ingredients from farmers markets. The menu changes daily, and when they're gone they're gone. Our faves include bacon flavor, charred blueberry–cream cheese, and the ube taro coconut doughnut.

★ Buona Forchetta ITALIAN **$$**
(Map p452; ☎ 619-381-4844; www.buonaforchettasd.com; 3001 Beech St; small plates $6-15, pizzas $8-25; ⏱ noon-3pm Tue-Fri, 5-10pm Mon-Thu, to 11pm Fri, noon-11pm Sat, noon-10pm Sun; 🐾) A gold-painted brick wood-fired oven imported from Italy delivers authentic Neapolitan pizzas straight to jammed-together family-sized tables at this South Park trattoria with a dog-friendly patio. No reservations.

★ Prado CALIFORNIAN **$$$**
(Map p456; ☎ 619-557-9441; www.pradobalboa.com; 1549 El Prado; lunch $8-19, dinner $8-37; ⏱ 11:30am-3pm Mon, 11am-10pm Tue-Thu, 11:30am-9:30pm Sat, 11am-9pm Sun; 👪) In one of San Diego's more beautiful dining rooms, feast on Cal-eclectic cooking by one of San Diego's most renowned chefs: bakery sandwiches, lobster bucatini, and thyme-roasted Jidori half-chicken. Go for a civilized lunch on the verandah or for afternoon cocktails and appetizers in the bar.

Little Italy

Little Italy is – surprise! – happy hunting ground for Italian cooking and cafes on India St and around Date St, and some non-Italian newcomers are rounding out the scene. Ballast Point Tasting Room & Kitchen (p467) also does some great dishes.

Valentine's MEXICAN **$**
(Map p460; ☎ 619-234-8256; 1157 6th Ave; tacos & mains $3-10; ⏱ 8am-midnight Sun-Thu, to 3am Fri & Sat) There's nothing urbane about this home-style Mexican joint, but it's a local institution. Apart from the usual tacos and burritos, the carne asada fries (french fries topped like nachos with grilled beef, sour cream, guacamole and such) are messy, coronary-inducing and oh so *bueno*. Late weekend hours mean it's great after a rager.

Filippi's Pizza Grotto PIZZA, DELI **$$**
(Map p456; ☎ 619-232-5094; www.realcheesepizza.com; 1747 India St; dishes $10-24; ⏱ 11am-10pm Sun & Mon, to 10:30pm Tue-Thu, to 11:30pm Fri & Sat; 👪) There are often lines out the door for Filippi's old-school Italian cooking (pizza, spaghetti and ravioli) served on red-and-white-checked tablecloths in the dining room festooned with murals of *la bella Italia*. The front of the restaurant is an excellent Italian **deli**.

★ Juniper & Ivy CALIFORNIAN **$$$**
(Map p456; ☎ 619-269-9036; www.juniperandivy.com; 2228 Kettner Blvd; small plates $10-23, mains $19-45; ⏱ 5-10pm Sun-Thu, to 11pm Fri & Sat) The menu changes daily at chef Richard Blais' highly rated San Diego restaurant, opened in 2014. The molecular gastronomy includes dishes in the vein of lobster congee, Hawaiian snapper with Valencia Pride mango, ahi (yellowfin tuna) with creamed black trumpets, and pig-trotter *totelloni*. It's in a rockin' refurbished warehouse.

Gaslamp Quarter

There are some 100 restaurants in the Gaslamp, many of them very good. Some have bar scenes too.

Café 222 BREAKFAST **$**
(Map p460; ☎ 619-236-9902; www.cafe222.com; 222 Island Ave; mains $7-11; ⏱ 7am-1:45pm) Downtown's favorite breakfast place serves renowned peanut-butter-and-banana French toast; buttermilk, orange-pecan or granola pancakes; and eggs in scrambles or Benedicts. It also sells lunchtime sandwiches and salads, but we always go for breakfast (available until closing).

Gaslamp Strip Club STEAK **$$**
(Map p460; ☎ 619-231-3140; www.gaslampsteak.com; 340 5th Ave; mains $17-27; ⏱ 5-10pm Sun-Thu, to midnight Fri & Sat) Pull your own bottle from the wine vault, then char your own favorite cut of steak, chicken or fish on the open grills in the retro-Vegas dining room at Downtown's most novel steak house. No steak costs more than $27. Fab, creative martinis and 'pin-up' art by Alberto Vargas. Tons of fun. No one under 21 allowed. Happy hour 5pm-7pm Sunday-Thursday.

Oceanaire SEAFOOD **$$$**
(Map p460; ☎ 619-858-2277; www.theoceanaire.com; 400 J St; mains $30-65; ⏱ 5-10pm Sun-Thu, to 11pm Fri & Sat) The look is art-deco ocean liner, and the service is just as elegant, with an oyster bar and creations like chicken-fried lobster with truffled honey, and California sole Florentine stuffed with crab meat. If you don't feel like a total splurge, look out for happy-hour deals with bargain-priced oysters and fish tacos in the bar (times vary).

East Village

Neighborhood PUB FOOD $$
(Map p460; 619-446-0002; www.neighborhoodsd.com; 777 G St; mains $7-14; noon-midnight) Lit with filament bulbs and decorated with exposed beams, pipework overhead and a big mural of Downtown San Diego, this place is often used as a hangout while people are waiting to get entry to the next-door speakeasy Noble Experiment (p468), but it's a great spot in its own right, serving dozens of craft ales and hipster pub eats.

Basic PIZZA $$
(Map p460; 619-531-8869; www.barbasic.com; 410 10th Ave; small/large pizzas from $14/32; 11:30am-2am) East Village hipsters feast on fragrant thin-crust, brick-oven-baked pizzas under Basic's high ceiling (it's in a former warehouse). Small pizzas have a large footprint but are pretty light. Toppings span the usual to the newfangled, like the mashed pie with mozzarella, mashed potatoes and bacon. Wash them down with beers (craft, naturally) or one of several cocktails.

Café Chloe FRENCH $$$
(Map p460; 619-232-3242; www.cafechloe.com; 721 9th Ave; dinner $9-31; 8am-10pm Mon-Sat, 8:30am-9:30pm Sun) This delightful corner French bistro has a simple style and gets the standards perfect, and everything else as well. Classics include onion tart, French toast, *moules* (mussels) or steak *frites* (steak and chips) served with herb butter and salad. There's also trout salad, and wonderful egg dishes for weekend brunch.

Bankers Hill & Old Town

The restaurant scene is booming here.

★**Old Town Mexican Café** MEXICAN $$
(Map p452; 619-297-4330; www.oldtownmexcafe.com; 2489 San Diego Ave; mains $5-17; 7-11pm weekdays, to midnight weekends;) Other restaurants come and go, but this place has been in this busy adobe with hardwood booths since the 1970s. While you wait to be seated, watch the staff turn out tortillas. Then enjoy *machacas* (shredded pork with onions and peppers), carnitas and Mexican ribs. For breakfast: *chilaquiles* (tortilla chips with salsa or mole, broiled or grilled with cheese).

★**Cucina Urbana** CALIFORNIAN, ITALIAN $$$
(Map p456; 619-239-2222; www.urbankitchengroup.com/cucina-urbana-bankers-hill/; 505 Laurel St, Bankers Hill; mains lunch $15-23, dinner $12-31; 11:30am-2pm Tue-Fri, 5-9pm Sun & Mon, 5-10pm Tue-Thu, 5pm-midnight Fri & Sat) In this corner place with modern rustic ambience, business gets done, celebrations get celebrated and friends hug and kiss over refined yet affordable Cal-Ital cooking. Look for short-rib pappardelle, pizzas like spicy coppa pork and pineapple or pear and Gorgonzola with caramelized onion, and smart cocktails and local 'brewskies.' Reservations recommended.

El Agave MEXICAN $$$
(Map p452; 619-220-0692; www.elagave.com; 2304 San Diego Ave; mains lunch $10-20, dinner $11-33; 11am-10pm; P) Candlelight flickers in this romantic 2nd-floor, white-tablecloth, high-end place catering to cognoscenti. The mole is superb (nine types to choose from), and there are a whopping 1500 different tequilas covering just about every bit of wall.

LGBTQ SAN DIEGO

San Diego's main LGBTQ-friendly area is Hillcrest, which has a large concentration of bars, restaurants, cafes and shops flying the rainbow flag. The scene is more casual, friendly and unpretentious than neighboring LA or San Francisco. The premier lesbian bar is **Gossip Grill** (Map p456; 619-260-8023; www.thegossipgrill.com; 1220 University Ave; noon-2am Mon-Fri, 10am-2am Sat & Sun), while **Flicks** (Map p456; 619-297-2056; www.sdflicks.com; 1017 University Ave; 9am-late Sun, 4pm-late Mon, Wed & Thu, 2pm-late Tue & Fri, noon-late Sat), **Rich's** (Map p456; 619-295-2195; www.richssandiego.com; 1051 University Ave; 10pm-2am Wed-Sun) and **Urban Mo's** (Map p456; 619-491-0400; www.urbanmos.com; 308 University Ave, Hillcrest; 9am-1:30am) are mixed, host various themed nights and are always lively spots to grab a drink. For current LGBTQ events and news visit the **Gay San Diego website** (http://gay-sd.com) or pick up a paper copy, distributed in newspaper racks around town.

North Park & Hillcrest

Hillcrest is well established and North Park is a hub of innovation.

★**Carnitas' Snack Shack** CALIFORNIAN, MEXICAN $

(Map p452; ☎619-294-7665; http://carnitassnackshack.com; 2632 University Ave; mains $8-13; ⏲11am-midnight; 👪) Eat honestly priced, pork-inspired slow food in a cute outdoor patio with natural wooden features. Wash dishes like the triple-threat pork sandwich (with schnitzel, bacon, pepperoncini, pickle relish, shack aioli and an Amish bun) down with local craft ales. Happy hour runs from 3pm–6pm Monday-Friday with $5 tacos, $5 drafts and $6 wines.

Bread & Cie BAKERY, CAFE $

(Map p456; ☎619-683-9322; www.breadandcie.com; 350 University Ave, Hillcrest; mains $6-11; ⏲7am-7pm Mon-Fri, to 6pm Sat, 7:30am-6pm Sun; 🅿) Aside from crafting some of San Diego's best artisan breads (including anise and fig, black olive, and walnut and raisin), this wide-open bakery-deli makes fabulous sandwiches with fillings such as curried-chicken salad and ham and Swiss cheese. Boxed lunches cost $11.50. Great pastries too.

★**Hash House a Go Go** AMERICAN $$

(Map p456; ☎619-298-4646; www.hashhouseagogo.com; 3628 5th Ave, Hillcrest; breakfast $10-22, dinner mains $15-29; ⏲7.30am-2.30pm Mon, 7:30am-2pm & 5:30-9pm Tue-Thu, to 2:30pm and 9:30pm Fri-Sun; 👪) This buzzing bungalow makes biscuits and gravy straight outta Indiana, towering Benedicts, large-as-your-head pancakes and – wait for it – hash seven different ways. Eat your whole breakfast, and you won't need to eat the rest of the day. It's worth coming back for the equally massive burgers, sage-fried chicken and award-winning meatloaf sandwich. No wonder it's called 'twisted farm food.'

★**Urban Solace** CALIFORNIAN $$

(Map p452; ☎619-295-6464; www.urbansolace.net; 3823 30th St, North Park; mains lunch $12-22, dinner $14-27; ⏲11am-9pm Mon-Tue, to 9:30pm Wed-Thu, to 10:30pm Fri, 10:30am-10:30pm Sat, 9:30am-2:30pm & 4-9pm Sun) North Park's young hip gourmets revel in creative comfort food here: quinoa-veg burger; 'duckaroni' (mac 'n' cheese with duck confit); and pulled chicken and dumplings. The setting's surprisingly chill for such great eats; maybe it's the creative cocktails.

Mission Bay & the Beaches

Sights
1 Belmont Park....B4
2 Mission & Pacific Beaches....B1
3 Mission Bay....B3

Activities, Courses & Tours
4 Bahia Belle....B4
5 Cheap Rentals....B3
6 Flowrider....A4
7 Mission Bay Sportcenter....B3

Sleeping
8 Catamaran Resort Hotel....B2
9 Crystal Pier Hotel & Cottages....B1
10 Ocean Beach International Hostel....A7
11 Tower 23....B1

Eating
12 Hodad's....A7
JRDN....(see 11)
13 Ocean Beach People's Market....B7
14 Sundara....A7

Drinking & Nightlife
15 Coaster Bar and Grill....B4
16 Jungle Java....A7
17 The Grass Skirt....B1

Entertainment
18 Winston's....A7

Shopping
19 Galactic....A7

Mission Hills

Mission Hills is the neighborhood north of Little Italy and west of Hillcrest. On India St, where it meets Washington St, there's a block of well-regarded eateries.

Saffron THAI $$
(Map p452; 619-574-7737; www.saffronsandiego.com; 3731 India St; mains $7-15; 10:30am-10pm Mon-Sat, 11am-10pm Sun) This multi-award-winning, hole-in-the-wall is actually two shops – **Saffron Thai Grilled Chicken** and **Noodles & Saté**, but you can get both at either shop and enjoy it in the noodle shop. Chicken is cooked over a charcoal grill and comes with a choice of sauces, salad, jasmine rice and a menu of finger foods.

Shakespeare Pub & Grille PUB FOOD $$
(Map p452; 619-299-0230; www.shakespearepub.com; 3701 India St; dishes $6-15; 10:30am-midnight Mon-Thu, to 1am Fri, 8am-1am Sat, 8am-midnight Sun) One of San Diego's most authentic English ale houses, Shakespeare is the place for darts, soccer by satellite, beer on tap and pub grub, including fish-and-chips, and bangers and mash. One thing they don't have in Britain: a great sundeck. On weekends, load up with a British breakfast: bacon, mushrooms, black and white pudding and more.

Embarcadero & the Waterfront

★**Puesto at the Headquarters** MEXICAN $$
(Map p460; 610-233-8880; www.eatpuesto.com; 789 W Harbor Dr, The Headquarters; mains $11-19; 11am-10pm) This eatery serves Mexican street food that knocked our *zapatos* off: innovative takes on traditional tacos like chicken (with hibiscus, chipotle, pineapple and avocado) and some out-there fillings like zucchini and cactus. Other highlights: crab guacamole, the lime-marinated shrimp ceviche, and the grilled Baja striped bass.

Coronado

★**Clayton's Coffee Shop** DINER $
(Map p452; 619-435-5425; www.facebook.com/claytonscoffeeshop; 979 Orange Ave; mains $7-13; 6am-10pm;) Some diners only look old-fashioned. This one is the real deal from the 1940s, with red leatherette swivel stools and booths with mini jukeboxes. It does famous all-American breakfasts and some Mexican specialties like *machaca* with eggs and cheese, and it's not above panini and croque monsieur sandwiches. For dessert: mile-high pie from the counter.

1500 Ocean CALIFORNIAN $$$
(Map p452; 619-435-6611; www.hoteldel.com/1500-ocean; Hotel del Coronado, 1500 Orange Ave; mains $38-52; 5:30-10pm Tue-Sat, plus Sun summer; P) It's hard to beat the romance of supping at the Hotel del Coronado (p454), especially at a table overlooking the sea from the verandah of its first-class dining room, where silver service and coastal cuisine with local ingredients set the perfect tone for popping the question or feting an important anniversary.

Point Loma Area

A hot spot for seafood restaurants, plus the recently opened Liberty Public Market (p466) with more than 30 local artisan vendors touting their flavors – you can easily spend a hour or so wandering around sampling them all.

★Point Loma Seafoods SEAFOOD $
(Map p452; ☎619-223-1109; www.pointlomaseafoods.com; 2805 Emerson St; mains $7-16; ⏰9am-7pm Mon-Sat, 10am-7pm Sun; P 👪) For off-the-boat-fresh seafood sandwiches, salads, sashimi, fried dishes and icy-cold beer, order at the counter at this fish-market-cum-deli and grab a seat at a picnic table on the upstairs, harbor-view deck. It also does great sushi and takeout dishes from ceviche to clam chowder.

★Liberty Public Market MARKET $
(Map p452; ☎619-487-9346; http://libertypublicmarket.com; 2820 Historic Decatur Rd; ⏰7am-10pm) What the Ferry Building Marketplace is to San Francisco, the newly opened Liberty Public Market is to San Diego. Inside this converted old Navy building are more than 30 hip artisan vendors such as Baker & Olive, Wicked Maine Lobster, Mastiff Sausage Company, Mama Made Thai, Le Parfait Paris, Cecilia's Taqueria and FishBone Kitchen.

Stone Brewing World Bistro & Gardens PUB FOOD $$
(Map p452; ☎619-269-2100; www.stonebrewing.com/visit/bistros/liberty-station; Liberty Station, 2816 Historic Decatur Rd; mains lunch $15-24, dinner $16-28; ⏰11:30am-9pm Mon-Fri, until 10pm Sat & Sun; P) Local brewer Stone has transformed the former mess hall of the naval training center at **Liberty Station** (Map p452; www.libertystation.com; 2640 Historic Decatur Rd) into a temple to local craft beer. Tuck into standard-setting, spin-the-globe dishes – beer-battered fish tacos, *yakisoba* (Japanese stir-fried noodles) bowls with Jidori chicken, and spicy lamb sausage rigatoni – at long tables or comfy booths under its tall beamed ceiling, or beneath twinkling lights in its courtyard.

Bali Hai POLYNESIAN $$$
(Map p452; ☎619-222-1181; www.balihairestaurant.com; 2230 Shelter Island Dr; dishes lunch $8-19, dinner $19-29, small plates from $10, Sun brunch adult/child $35/17; ⏰11:30am-9pm Mon-Thu, to 10pm Fri & Sat, 9:30am-9pm Sun; P) Near the tiki-themed hotels of Point Loma, this longtime, special-occasion restaurant serves Hawaiian-themed meals like tuna *poke* (cubed raw fish mixed with shōyu, sesame oil, salt, chili pepper and other condiments), *pupus* (small plates), chicken of the gods (with tangy orange-chili and a coconut–brown rice cake) and a massive Sunday champagne-brunch buffet. The best part: views clear across San Diego Bay through its circular wall of windows.

Ocean Beach

★Hodad's BURGERS $
(Map p464; ☎619-224-4623; www.hodadies.com; 5010 Newport Ave; dishes $4-15; ⏰11am-10pm) Since the flower-power days of 1969, OB's legendary burger joint has served great shakes, massive baskets of onion rings and succulent hamburgers wrapped in paper. The walls are covered in license plates, grunge/surf-rock plays (loud!) and your bearded, tattooed server might sidle into your booth to take your order. No shirt, no shoes, no problem, dude.

Ocean Beach People's Market VEGETARIAN $
(Map p464; ☎619-224-1387; www.obpeoplesfood.coop; 4765 Voltaire St; dishes $8, salads per pound from $7.89; ⏰8am-9pm; 🖉) 🌿 For strictly vegetarian groceries and fabulous prepared meals and salads north of central Ocean Beach, this organic cooperative does bulk foods, and excellent counter-service soups, sandwiches, salads and wraps.

Sundara INDIAN $$
(Map p464; ☎619-889-0639; www.sundaracuisine.com; 1774 Sunset Cliffs Blvd; mains $11-12; ⏰5-9.30pm Sun-Thu, to 10pm Fri & Sat; 🖉) This little, modern, neat-as-a-pin place has a tiny but well-chosen menu of curries and tandoori chicken, and a much longer menu of craft and bottled beers from as far away as India. It's adorned with simple black-and-white photos of Indian street scenes.

Pacific Beach

★Pacific Beach Fish Shop SEAFOOD $
(Map p452; ☎858-483-1008; www.thefishshop-pb.com; 1775 Garnet Ave; tacos/fish plates from $4.50/15.50; ⏰11am-10pm) You can't miss this fishy-themed joint with its enormous swordfish hanging outside. Inside, it's a casual, communal bench affair. Choose from more than 10 types of fresh fish at the counter, from ahi to red snapper, then pick your marinade (garlic butter to chipotle glaze), then select your style – fish plate with rice and salad, taco or sandwich perhaps?

★The Patio on Lamont AMERICAN $$
(Map p452; ☎858-412-4648; www.thepatioonlamont.com; 4445 Lamont St; dishes $7-26;

9am-midnight) Popular local hangout serving beautifully prepared New American small plates and cocktails. Try the crab and ahi tower or crispy artichoke with goat's cheese in a cozy fairy-lit patio area (with outside heaters in winter). Daily happy hours on selected beers and cocktails ($5/6) run from 3pm to 6pm and 10pm to midnight.

JRDN CALIFORNIAN **$$$**
(Map p464; 858-270-5736; www.t23hotel.com/dine; Tower 23 Hotel, 723 Felspar St; breakfast & lunch dishes $11-21, dinner mains $28-49; 9am to 4pm Mon-Fri, 5pm to 9:30pm Sun-Thu, to 10pm Fri & Sat;) A big heaping dose of chic amid PB's congenital laid-back feel. There's both an ocean view and a futuristic interior (and most excellent bar scene). Sustainably farmed meats and seafood join local veggies to create festivals on the plate. Try dishes like farmers-market apple salad, day-boat scallops, oysters on the half shell or local yellowtail.

Drinking & Nightlife

San Diego's bar scene is diverse, ranging from live-music pubs and classic American pool bars, to beach bars with tiki cocktails, gay clubs offering drag shows, and even a few hidden speakeasies. It's easy to find a local craft beer in town, or you can venture out to one of the 100 breweries or vineyards in the Temecula area.

Little Italy

El Camino LOUNGE
(Map p456; 619-685-3881; www.elcaminosd.com; 2400 India St; 5pm-late Mon-Sat, from 11am Sun) We're not sure what it means that this buzzy watering hole has a Día de los Muertos (Mexican Day of the Dead holiday) theme in the flight path of San Diego Airport – watch planes land from the outdoor patio – but whatever, dude. The clientele is cool, design mod, the cocktails strong and the Mexican victuals *fabuloso*.

Waterfront BAR
(Map p456; 619-232-9656; www.waterfrontbarandgrill.com; 2044 Kettner Blvd; 6am-2am) San Diego's first liquor license was granted to this place in the 1930s (it was on the waterfront until the harbor was filled and the airport built). A room full of historic bric-a-brac, big windows looking onto the street and the spirits of those who went before make this a wonderful place to spend the afternoon or evening.

Ballast Point Tasting Room & Kitchen PUB
(Map p456; 619-255-7213; www.ballastpoint.com; 2215 India St; 11am-11pm) This San Diego–based brewery does 4oz tasters of its beers for just $5, which could be the best deal in town. Enjoy them with a full menu including housemade pretzels, beer-steamed mussels, salads or a truffle burger.

Gaslamp Quarter

The Gaslamp has the city's highest concentration of nightlife venues. Many do double (even triple) duty as restaurants, bars and clubs.

★**Bang Bang** BAR
(Map p460; 619-677-2264; www.bangbangsd.com; 526 Market St; cocktails $14-26; 5-10:30pm Wed-Thu, to 2am Fri & Sat) Beneath lantern light, the Gaslamp's hottest new spot brings in local and world-renowned DJs and serves sushi and Asian small plates like dumplings and *panko*-crusted shrimp to accompany the imaginative cocktails (some in giant goblets meant for sharing with your posse). Plus, the bathrooms are shrines to Ryan Gosling and Hello Kitty: in a word, awesome. At the weekend and for special events, the place turns into a club: expect a cover charge later in the evening.

Dublin Square IRISH PUB
(Map p460; www.dublinsquareirishpub.com; 544 4th Ave; 11:30am-2am weekdays, from 9am Sat & Sun) Guinness? Check. Corned beef? Check. But what sets this rambling pub apart are its long happy hours (lasting five hours early in the week) and its live music, usually in the form of a lively covers band; check the website for the schedule. Brunch is served between 9am and 2pm on weekends, and lunch and dinner from 11:30am to 10.30pm daily.

Star Bar BAR
(Map p460; 619-234-5575; 423 E St; 6am-2am) When you've had it with gentrified style and you're looking for a historic dive, head to this old-school bar (decorated year-round with Christmas lights) for possibly the cheapest drinks in Gaslamp. It's open 20 hours a day, 365 days a year.

East Village

While out-of-towners frolic happily in the Gaslamp Quarter, San Diego locals and hipsters instead head east to these more insider-y bars.

Noble Experiment BAR
(Map p460; 619-888-4713; http://nobleexperimentsd.com; 777 G St; 7pm-2am Tue-Sun) This place is literally a find. Open a secret door and enter a contemporary speakeasy with miniature gold skulls on the walls, classical paintings on the ceilings and inventive cocktails on the list (from $12). The hard part: getting in. Text for a reservation, and they'll tell you if your requested time is available and how to find it; it's also possible to turn up to the bar upstairs (Neighborhood) (p463) and put your name on a waiting list.

East Village Tavern & Bowl SPORTS BAR
(Map p460; 619-677-2695; www.tavernbowl.com; 930 Market St; 11am-12am Sun-Thu, to 2am Sat & Sun) This large sports bar a few blocks from baseball stadium **Petco Park** (Map p460; 619-795-5011; www.padres.com; 100 Park Blvd; tours adult/child/senior $15/10/10; 10:30am & 12:30pm Sun-Fri, 3pm Sat;) has six bowling lanes (thankfully, behind a wall for effective soundproofing). Pub menu (dishes $5 to $14; bacon-jam sliders, mac 'n' cheese balls) is served all day.

North Park & Hillcrest

Hillcrest has the greatest concentration of bars, particularly gay spots, while North Park has a cool, hipster vibe.

★**Coin-Op Game Room** BAR, GAME ROOM
(Map p452; 619-255-8523; www.coinopsd.com; 3926 30th St, North Park; 4pm-1am Mon-Fri, noon-1am Sat & Sun) Dozens of classic arcade games – pinball to Mortal Kombat, Pac-Man and Big Buck Safari to Master Beer Bong – line the walls of this hipster bar in North Park. All the better to quaff craft beers and cocktails like The Dorothy Mantooth (gin, Giffard Violette, lime, cucumber, Champagne) and chow on truffle-parm tots, fried-chicken sandwiches or fried oreos.

★**Polite Provisions** COCKTAIL BAR
(Map p452; 619-677-3784; www.politeprovisions.com; 4696 30th St, North Park; 3pm-2am Mon-Thu, 11:30am-2am Fri-Sun) With a French-bistro feel and plenty of old-world charm, Polite Provisions' hip clientele sip cocktails at the marble bar, under a glass ceiling, and in a beautifully designed space, complete with vintage cash register, wood-paneled walls and tiled floors. Many cocktail ingredients, syrups, sodas and infusions are homemade and displayed in apothecary-esque bottles.

Blind Lady Ale House PUB
(Map p452; 619-225-2491; http://blindlady.blogspot.com; 3416 Adams Ave; 5pm-midnight Mon-Thu, from 11:30am Fri-Sun) A superb neighborhood pub, with creative decor like beer cans piled floor to ceiling and longboard skateboards attached to the walls. It sells craft ales on pump and prepares fresh pizza (from $7). Vegetarians should try the meat-free Mondays offering pies with inventive flavors.

Coronado to Pacific Beach

Pacific Beach (PB) is party central on the coast, with mostly 20-somethings on a beach bar bender (drivers: watch for tipsy pedestrians). If you've been there/done that, you might prefer one of the quieter coffeehouses or restaurant bars, or head to Ocean Beach or Coronado.

Jungle Java CAFE
(Map p464; 619-224-0249; http://daniellemariehargis.wixsite.com/jungle-java/home; 5047 Newport Ave, Ocean Beach; coffees from $2; 7am-6pm Mon-Sun;) Funky-dunky, canopy-covered cafe and plant shop, also crammed with crafts and art treasures. A chilled place to sip on a coffee, smoothie or chai latte, tuck into a pastry and surf the free wi-fi.

Coaster Bar and Grill BAR
(Map p464; 858-488-4438; http://thecoasterbarandgrill.com; 744 Ventura Pl, Mission Beach; 10am-2am Mon-Fri, 8am-2am Sat & Sun) Old-fashioned neighborhood dive bar with views of the Belmont Park roller coaster. It draws an unpretentious crowd and has more than 50 beers on tap; good margaritas too.

The Grass Skirt COCKTAIL BAR
(Map p464; 858-412-5237; http://thegrassskirt.com; 910 Grand Ave; 5pm-2am) Through a secret doorway, disguised as a refrigerator in the next-door **Good Time Poke** cafe, you'll step into a lost Hawaiian world with Polynesian wood carvings, thatched verandahs, fire features and tiki-girl figurines made into lamps. Sipping on your daiquiri or pina colada there are more surprises to come…listen out for immersive weather sounds and lighting effects.

☆ Entertainment

Check out the San Diego *City Beat* or *UT San Diego* for the latest movies, theater, galleries and music gigs around town. **Arts Tix** (Map p460; 858-437-9850; www.sdartstix.com; 28 Horton Plaza; 10am-4pm Tue-Thu, to 6pm Fri & Sat, to 2pm Sun), in a kiosk near Westfield

Horton Plaza (next to Balboa Theatre), has half-price tickets for same-day evening or next-day matinee performances and offers discounted tickets to other events. **Ticketmaster** (☎800-653-8000; www.ticketmaster.com) and House of Blues sell tickets to other gigs around the city.

Prohibition Lounge LIVE MUSIC
(Map p460; http://prohibitionsd.com; 548 5th Avenue; ⏰8:00pm-1:30am Wed-Sat) Find the unassuming doorway on 5th Ave with 'Eddie O'Hare's Law Office' on it, then flip the light switch on to alert the doorman, who'll guide you into a dimly lit basement serving craft cocktails, with patrons enjoying live jazz (music from 9:30pm). Come early as it gets busy fast; at weekends expect a waitlist.

Shout House LIVE MUSIC
(Map p460; ☎619-231-6700; www.theshouthouse.com; 655 4th Ave; cover free-$10) Good, clean fun at this cavernous Gaslamp bar with dueling pianos. Talented players have an amazing repertoire, including classics, rock and more. The lively crowd ranges from college age to conventioneers.

House of Blues BLUES
(Map p460; ☎619-299-2583; www.houseofblues.com/sandiego; 1055 5th Ave; ⏰4-11pm) Live blues music, DJs, rock bands, karaoke, trivia nights and more. Free shows on certain nights with dinner. Scheduled gigs are priced individually depending on the popularity of the artist.

San Diego Symphony CLASSICAL MUSIC
(Map p460; ☎619-235-0800; www.sandiegosymphony.com; 750 B St, Jacobs Music Center; from $20; ⏰show times vary) This accomplished orchestra presents classical and family concerts at **Jacobs Music Center**. Look for summer concerts at Embarcadero Marina Park South.

Winston's LIVE MUSIC
(Map p464; ☎619-222-6822; www.winstonsob.com; 1921 Bacon St, Ocean Beach; ⏰1pm until late) Bands play most nights, and each night has a different happening: open mike, karaoke, comedy, cover bands, local artists etc.

Shopping

San Diego is chock-full of shops selling everything from local-pride souvenirs to Mexican gifts, adventure goods, beachwear and antiques. Keep your eyes peeled in neighborhood streets for independent shops and boutiques trading in local wares. Farmers markets are also a big hit around town. Plus, there are plenty of slightly-out-of-town malls for everyday big brands and luxury fashion items.

SURF & SUDS

There are now more than 100 craft breweries operating in the San Diego area. The **San Diego Brewers Guild** (www.sandiegobrewersguild.org) counts some 40-plus member establishments. Go to the guild's website for a map or pick up one of its pamphlets around town, and start planning your brewery-hopping tour. To leave the driving to someone else, Brewery Tours of San Diego (p457) offers bus tours to different breweries for a variety of tastes. Tour price varies by timing and whether a meal is served.

Check our recommendations to get you started, and see also Stone Brewing (p466) and Ballast Point Tasting Room & Kitchen (p467)..

Headquarters at Seaport District MALL
(Map p460; ☎619-235-4013; www.theheadquarters.com; 789 W Harbor Dr; ⏰10am-9pm Mon-Sat, to 8pm Sun) San Diego's fairly new shopping center (opened 2013) is also one of its oldest buildings: the 1939 former police headquarters has turned into some 30 shopping, dining and entertainment options. There's a small exhibit of vintage handcuffs, badges and jail cells for you and up to 15 of your friends.

Seaport Village SHOPPING DISTRICT
(Map p460; ☎619-235-4014; www.seaportvillage.com; 849 West Harbor Dr; ⏰10am-10pm Jun-Aug, to 9pm Sep-May; 👪) Neither seaport nor village, this 14-acre collection of novelty shops and restaurants has a faux New England theme. It's touristy and twee but good for souvenir shopping and casual eats.

Galactic COMICS
(Map p464; ☎619-226-6543; 4981 Newport Ave; ⏰11am-8pm) Lose time perusing the shelves of this cubbyhole comic-book store. It also rents new DVDs and has a bunch of retro arcade games to play inside.

Adams Avenue ANTIQUES
(Map p452; www.adamsaveonline.com; Adams Ave) This is San Diego's main 'antique row,' featuring dozens of shops selling furniture, art and antiques from around the world. Take a rest from all the shopping at the Blind Lady Ale House, serving pizzas and craft beers.

TRAVELING TO TIJUANA

Just beyond the busiest land border in the western hemisphere, Tijuana, Mexico (population around 1.7 million) was for decades a cheap, convivial escape for hard-partying San Diegans, Angelenos, sailors and college kids. A decade ago, a double whammy of drug-related violence and global recession turned once-bustling tourist areas into ghost towns, but *tijuanenses* (as the locals call themselves) have been slowly but surely reclaiming their city. The difference from squeaky-clean San Diego is palpable from the moment you cross the border, but so are many signs of new life for those who knew TJ in the bad old days.

Avenida Revolución (aka La Revo) is the main tourist drag, though its charm is marred by cheap clothing and souvenir stores, strip joints, pharmacies selling bargain-priced medications to Americans, and touts best rebuffed with a firm 'no.' It's a lot more appealing just beyond La Revo, toward and around **Avenida Constitución**, where sightseeing highlights include **Catedral de Nuestra Señora de Guadalupe** (Cathedral of our Lady of Guadalupe; cnr Av Niños Héroes & Calle 2a), Tijuana's oldest church, **Mercado El Popo** (cnr Calle 2a & Av Constitución), an atmospheric market hall selling wares from tamarind pods to religious iconography and **Pasaje Rodríguez** (Av Revolución, btwn Calles 3a & 4a; noon- 10pm), an arcade filled with hipster coffee shops, local design shops and colorful street art.

A short ride away, **Museo de las Californias** (Museum of the Californias; from US 011-52-664-687-9600; www.cecut.gob.mx; Centro Cultural Tijuana, cnr Paseo de los Héroes & Av Independencia; adult/child under 12yr M$27/free; 10am-6pm Tue-Sun; P), inside the architecturally daring **Centro Cultural Tijuana** (CECUT; from US 011-52-664-687-9600; www.cecut.gob.mx; cnr Paseo de los Héroes & Av Independencia; 9am-7pm Mon-Fri, 10am-7pm Sat & Sun;), aka El Cubo (the Cube), offers an excellent history of the border region from prehistory to the present; there's signage in English. If you're in town on a Friday night, check

Information

INTERNET ACCESS

All public libraries and most coffeehouses and hotel lobbies in San Diego offer free wi-fi. Libraries also offer computer terminals for access.

San Diego Main Library (619-236-5800; www.sandiego.gov/public-library; 330 Park Blvd; 9:30am-7pm Mon-Thu, to 6pm Fri & Sat, noon-6pm Sun;) The city's new main library branch is a dazzler architecturally and has all the services you could want (including wi-fi).

MEDIA

Free listings magazines *Citybeat* (http://sdcitybeat.com) and *San Diego Reader* (www.sdreader.com) cover the active music, art and theater scenes. Find them in shops and cafes.

KPBS 89.5 FM (www.kpbs.org) National Public Radio station.

San Diego Magazine (www.sandiegomagazine.com) Glossy monthly.

UT San Diego (www.utsandiego.com) The city's major daily.

POST

For post-office locations, call 800-275-8777 or log on to www.usps.com.

Coronado Post Office (Map p452; 619-435-1142; www.usps.com; 1320 Ynez Pl; 8:30am-5pm Mon-Fri, 9am-noon Sat)

Downtown Post Office (Map p460; 800-275-8777; www.usps.com; 815 E St; 9am-5pm Mon-Fri)

TOURIST INFORMATION

Coronado Visitors Center (Map p452; 619-437-8788, 866-599-7242; www.coronadovisitorcenter.com; 1100 Orange Ave; 9am-5pm Mon-Fri, 10am-5pm Sat & Sun)

International Visitor Information Center (Map p460; 619-236-1242; www.sandiego.org; 1140 N Harbor Dr; 9am-5pm Jun-Sep, to 4pm Oct-May) Across from the B St Cruise Ship Terminal, helpful staff offer very detailed neighborhood maps, sell discounted tickets to attractions and maintain a hotel-reservation hotline.

Getting There & Away

AIR

Most flights to **San Diego International Airport-Lindbergh Field** (SAN; Map p452; 619-400-2404; www.san.org; 3325 N Harbor Dr;) are domestic. The airfield sits just 3 miles west of Downtown; plane-spotters will thrill watching jets come in over Balboa Park for landing. Coming from overseas, you'll likely change flights – and clear US customs – at one of the major US gateway airports, such as LA, San Francisco, Chicago, New York or Miami.

The standard one-way fare between LA and San Diego is about $115 and takes about 35 minutes;

out a **lucha libre** (Mexican wrestling; ☎from US 011-52-664-250-9015; Blvd Díaz Ordaz 12421, Auditorio Municipal Fausto Gutierrez Moreno; US$8-35) match at the Auditorio Municipal Fausto Gutiérrez Moreno, where oversized men in gaudy masks do Mexican wrestling.

Turista Libre (www.turistalibre.com) runs a variety of public and private tours in English, led by an American expat with endless enthusiasm for the city and its lesser-known nooks and crannies.

A passport is required to cross the border, and to reenter the US. By car, take I-5 south and look for either signs to Mexico or for the last US exit, where you can park at one of the many lots in the area (from $10 for five hours, from $20 for 24 hours). If traveling by taxi from the Mexican side of the border, be sure to take a taxi with a meter. Uber is also available for travelers with internet service on their phones. By public transport from San Diego, the **San Diego Trolley** (☎619-233-3004; www.sdmts.com) runs from Downtown to **San Ysidro border crossing** (☎619-690-8900; www.cbp.gov; 720 E San Ysidro Blvd; ⏲24hr). To cross the border on foot, follow the signs to Mexico, and a turnstile, which you walk through into Mexico. Follow signs reading 'Centro Downtown.' Be aware, there can be long waits to reenter the US by foot.

Driving into Mexico is easy for those with their own cars, but you will need to purchase extra road insurance for the time you are in Mexico, and international road-side assistance is advisable. Exercise caution when driving around northern Baja California. Nighttime smash-and-grab theft does happen, and there have been instances of carjackings in Mexico. It is sensible to avoid traveling at night and to use toll roads where possible. Visit government travel-advice websites for more information. Visit https://bwt.cbp.gov for updated border wait times.

unless you're connecting through LA, you're usually better off driving or taking the train.

To/from other US cities, San Diego flights are generally up to about $140 more expensive than those to LA. All major US airlines serve San Diego, plus Air Canada, British Airways, Mexico's Volaris and the Canadian carrier WestJet.

BUS

Greyhound (Map p460; ☎619-515-1100, 800-231-2222; www.greyhound.com; 1313 National Ave; ⏲ticket office 5am-11:59pm) serves San Diego from cities across North America from its Downtown location. Inquire about discounts and special fares, many available only online.

Buses depart frequently for LA; standard fares (one-way/round-trip) start at $14 and the trip takes 2½ to four hours. There are several daily departures to Anaheim (singles from $12, about 2¼ hours).

Buses to San Francisco (from $59, 12 hours, about seven daily) require a transfer in Los Angeles; round-trip airfares often cost about the same. Most buses to Las Vegas (one-way from $23, eight to nine hours, about eight daily) require a transfer in LA or San Bernardino.

CAR & MOTORCYCLE

Allow at least two hours to reach San Diego from LA in nonpeak traffic. If there are two or more passengers in your car you can use the high-occupancy vehicle lanes.

TRAIN

Amtrak (☎800-872-7245; www.amtrak.com; 1050 Kettner Blvd) runs the *Pacific Surfliner* several times daily to Anaheim (two hours), Los Angeles (2¾ hours) and Santa Barbara (6½ hours) from the historic **Union Station** (Santa Fe Depot; ☎800-872-7245; 1050 Kettner Blvd; ⏲3am-11:59pm). Trains run to stations in Oceanside, Carlsbad, Encinitas, Solana Beach, Sorrento Valley, Old Town and Downtown. Fares start from around $30, and the coastal views are enjoyable.

ℹ Getting Around

While most people get around San Diego by car, it's possible to have an entire vacation here using municipal buses and trolleys run by the Metropolitan Transit System and your own two feet. Most buses/trolleys cost $2.25/2.50 per ride. Transfers are not available, so purchase a day pass if you're going to be taking more than two rides in a day; a refillable **Compass Card** ($2 one-time purchase) will save hassles. The **MTS Transit Store** (Map p460; ☎619-234-1060; www.sdmts.com; 1255 Imperial Ave; ⏲8am-5pm Mon-Fri) is one-stop shopping for route maps, tickets and one-/two-/three-/four-day passes ($5/9/12/15). Same-day passes are also available from bus drivers. At trolley stations, purchase tickets from vending machines.

BICYCLE

While in San Diego, mostly flat Pacific Beach, Mission Beach, Mission Bay and Coronado are all great places to ride a bike. Visit **iCommute** (www.icommutesd.com) for maps and information about biking in the region. Public buses are equipped with bike racks.

A few outfits rent bicycles, from mountain and road bikes to kids' bikes and cruisers. In general, expect to pay about $8 per hour, $15–$22 per half-day (four hours) and $25–$30 per day.

BOAT

Flagship Cruises (Map p460; ☎619-234-4111; www.flagshipsd.com; 990 N Harbor Dr; tours adult/child from $24/12;) operates the hourly **Coronado Ferry** (Map p460; ☎800-442-7847; www.flagshipsd.com; 990 N Harbor Dr; 1 way $4.75; ⏲9am-10pm) shuttling between San Diego's **Broadway Pier** (1050 N Harbor Dr) on the Embarcadero and the ferry landing at the foot of B Ave in Coronado, two blocks south of Orange Ave. Bikes are permitted on board at no extra charge. Flagship also operates a water taxi, serving mostly Downtown and Coronado.

BUS

MTS (p471) covers most of San Diego's metropolitan area, North County, La Jolla and the beaches. It's most convenient if you're based Downtown and not staying out late.

Useful routes to/from Downtown:

BUS ROUTE NUMBER	STOPS IN SAN DIEGO
3	Balboa Park, Hillcrest, UCSD Medical Center
7	Gaslamp, Balboa Park, Zoo, Hillcrest, North Park
8/9	Old Town, Pacific Beach, SeaWorld
30	Gaslamp, Little Italy, Old Town, Pacific Beach, La Jolla, University Town Center
35	Old Town, Ocean Beach
901	Gaslamp, Coronado, Imperial Beach

CAR

All the big-name car-rental companies have desks at the San Diego airport (p470); lesser-known companies may be cheaper. Shop around – prices vary widely, even from day to day within the same company. The airport has free direct phones to a number of car-rental companies. Rental rates tend to be comparable to LA ($30 to $80 per day plus insurance fees). Smaller agencies include **West Coast Rent a Car** (☎619-544-0606; http://westcoastrentacar.net; 834 W Grape St; ⏲9am-6pm Mon-Sat, to 5pm Sun), in Little Italy.

METROPOLITAN TRANSIT SYSTEM (MTS)

The Metropolitan Transit System runs buses and trolleys throughout central San Diego and beyond. For route and fare information, call ☎619-233-3004 or ☎800-266-6883; operators are available 5:30am to 8:30pm Monday to Friday, and 8am to 5pm Saturday and Sunday (note that the 800 number works only within San Diego). For 24-hour automated information, call ☎619-685-4900. Visit www.sdmts.com/schedules-real-time to plan your route online.

One paying adult may travel with up to two children aged 5 and under for free on buses with a valid MTS ticket. On Saturdays and Sundays up to two children (age 12 and under) may ride for free with one fare-paying adult (age 18 or older) on all MTS routes.

TAXI & RIDESHARE

Taxi fares vary, but plan on about $12 for a 3-mile journey. Established companies include **Orange Cab** (☎619-223-5555; www.orangecabsandiego.net) and **Yellow Cab** (☎619-444-4444; www.driveu.com). Recently app-based ride-share companies such as **Uber** (www.uber.com) and **Lyft** (www.lyft.com) have entered the market with lower fares.

TROLLEY

Municipal trolleys, not to be confused with **Old Town Trolley tourist buses** (p457), operate on three main lines in San Diego. From the transit center across from the Santa Fe Depot, **Blue Line** trolleys go south to San Ysidro (on the Mexico border) and north to **Old Town Transit Center** (Map p452; www.amtrak.com; 4009 Taylor St). The **Green Line** runs from Gas Lamp to Old Town east through Mission Valley. The **Orange Line** connects the Convention Center and Seaport Village with Downtown, but otherwise it's less useful for visitors. Trolleys run between about 4:15am and 1am daily at 15-minute intervals during the day, and every 30 minutes in the evening. Fares are $2.50 per ride, valid for two hours from the time of purchase at vending machines on the station platforms.

LA JOLLA & NORTH COUNTY COAST

Immaculately landscaped parks, white-sand coves, upscale boutiques, top restaurants, and cliffs above deep, clear-blue waters make it easy to understand why 'La Jolla' translates from Spanish as 'The Jewel.' Pronounced la-*hoy*-yah, the name may actually date from Native Americans who inhabited the area from 10,000 years ago to the mid-19th century, and called the place 'mut la hoya, la hoya' – the place of many caves.

Northward from La Jolla, North County's coast evokes the San Diego of 40 years ago. Pretty Del Mar continues through low-key Solana Beach, Encinitas and Carlsbad (home of Legoland), before hitting Oceanside, home to Camp Pendleton Marine Base. All the beaches are terrific, and the small seaside towns are great for days of soaking up the laid-back SoCal scene and working on your tan. All that, and only about a half-hour's drive from Downtown San Diego.

La Jolla

Sights

★Children's Pool BEACH
(La Jolla seals; Map p474; 850 Coast Blvd) Built in the 1930s, La Jolla's Children's Pool was created as a family beach space, but since then it's been descended on by herds of seals and sea lions. Despite the pinnipeds' particularly pungent odor, tourists come in droves to see them larking around, swimming, fighting and mating. Visitors can get extremely close via a concrete platform surrounding the cove, and the seals don't seem to mind – but there's strictly no touching, feeding or selfies to be taken with the seals.

The future of the seals remains in debate, as divers and swimmers claim their presence increases bacteria levels in the water, yet animal-rights groups want to protect the cove and make it an official seal rookery. At the time of writing, courts ruled that the beach was to remain closed to swimmers, to protect the mums, pups and baby seals during pupping season (December 15 to May 15) when they are most vulnerable. But the future of the Children's Pool remains to be seen.

Birch Aquarium at Scripps AQUARIUM
(Map p452; 858-534-3474; www.aquarium.ucsd.edu; 2300 Expedition Way; adult/child $18.50/14; 9am-5pm; P) Marine scientists were working at the Birch Aquarium at Scripps Institution of Oceanography (SIO) as early as 1910 and, helped by donations from the Scripps family, the institute has grown to be one of the world's largest marine research institutions. It is now a part of University of California (UC) San Diego. Off N Torrey Pines Rd, the aquarium has brilliant displays. The **Hall of Fishes** has more than 60 fish tanks, simulating marine habitats from the Pacific Northwest to tropical seas.

★Cave Store CAVE
(Map p474; 858-459-0746; www.cavestore.com; 1325 Coast Blvd; adult/child $5/3; 10am-4:30pm Mon-Fri, to 5pm Sat & Sun) Waves have carved a series of caves into the sandstone cliffs east of La Jolla Cove. The largest is called **Sunny Jim Cave**, which you can access via this store. Taller visitors, watch your head as you descend the 145 steps.

Athenaeum LIBRARY
(Map p474; 858-454-5872; www.ljathenaeum.org; 1008 Wall St; 10am-5:30pm Tue-Sat, to 8:30pm Wed) Housed in a graceful Spanish renaissance structure, this space is devoted exclusively to art and music. Its reading room is a lovely place to relax and flick through a book, and it hosts a series of lectures plus live music, from classical to jazz.

San Diego-La Jolla Underwater Park Ecological Reserve DIVING, SNORKELING
(Map p452) Look for the white buoys offshore from Point La Jolla north to Scripps Pier that mark this protected zone with a variety of marine life, kelp forests, reefs and canyons. Waves have carved caves into the sandstone cliffs east of the cove.

University of California San Diego UNIVERSITY
(UCSD; Map p452; 858-534-2230; http://ucsd.edu; 9500 Gilman Dr) UCSD was established in 1960 and now has more than 30,000 students and a strong reputation, particularly for mathematics and science. It lies on rolling coastal hills in a parklike setting, surrounded by tall, fragrant eucalyptus. Its most distinctive structure is the **Geisel Library**, an upside-down pyramid named for children's author Theodor Geisel, aka Dr Seuss of *Cat in the Hat* fame; there's a collection of his drawings and books. Download a map of UCSD's excellent collection of public art at http://stuartcollection.ucsd.edu.

Activities

★Torrey Pines State Natural Reserve HIKING
(Map p480; 858-755-2063; https://torreypine.org/parks/trails.html; 12600 North Torrey Pines Rd; 7:15am-sunset, visitors center 9am-6pm) FREE Walkers and hikers explore 8 miles of **trails** in 2000 acres of well-trodden coastal state park. Choose from routes of varying difficulties, including the 0.7-mile Guy Fleming Trail, with panoramic sea views and paths through wildflowers, ferns and cacti, or the 1.4-mile

La Jolla

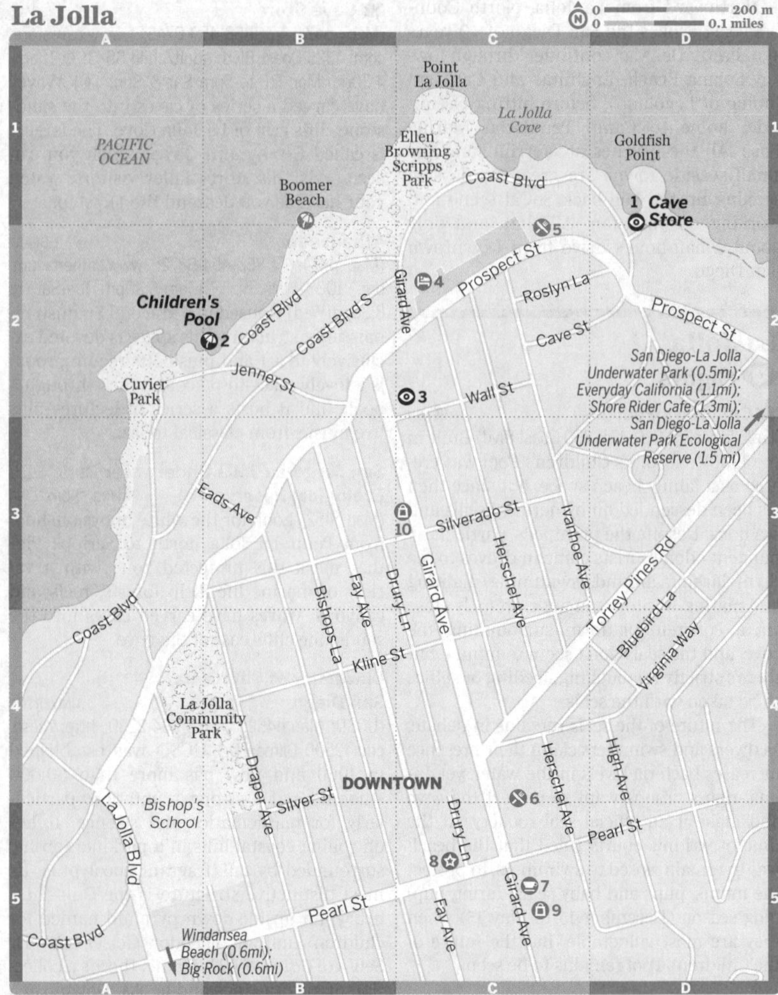

La Jolla

Top Sights
1 Cave Store D1
2 Children's Pool B2

Sights
3 Athenaeum C2

Sleeping
4 La Valencia C2

Eating
5 George's at the Cove C2
6 Harry's Coffee Shop C4

Drinking & Nightlife
7 Pannikin C5

Entertainment
8 Comedy Store C5

Shopping
9 DG Wills C5
10 Warwick's C3

Razor Point Trail with a good whale-spotting lookout during winter months.

Everyday California ADVENTURE SPORTS
(Map p452; ☎858-454-6195; www.everydaycalifornia.com; 2246 Avenida de la Playa; kayak tours from $50; ⏰9am-5pm) This adventure outfit offers paddleboard hire, kayak hire (during summer), snorkel sets and kayaking tours year-round along La Jolla's coastline and ecological reserve. On the 90-minute tours there's a good chance of spotting sea lions and seals in the water, and if you're lucky dolphins and whales (in winter). When sea conditions are safe, kayakers can venture into **Emerald Cave**.

La Jolla Beaches BEACH
Some of the county's best beaches are north of the Shores in Torrey Pines City Park, between the **Salk Institute** (Map p480; ☎858-453-4100; www.salk.edu; 10010 N Torrey Pines Rd; tours $15; ⏰tours by reservation 11:45am Mon-Fri; P) and **Torrey Pines State Natural Reserve** (Map p480; ☎858-755-2063; www.torreypine.org; 12600 N Torrey Pines Rd; ⏰7:15am-sunset, visitor center 10am-4pm Oct-Apr, 9am-6pm May-Sep; P) FREE. Hanggliders and paragliders launch into the sea breezes rising over the cliffs at **Torrey Pines Gliderport** (Map p480; ☎858-452-9858; www.flytorrey.com; 2800 Torrey Pines Scenic Dr; 20min paragliding $175, hang-gliding tandem flight per person $225), at the end of Torrey Pines Scenic Dr. It's a beautiful sight – tandem flights are available if you can't resist trying it. La Jolla Shores and Black's Beach are popular surfing spots.

San Diego-La Jolla Underwater Park SNORKELING, DIVING
(Map p452) Some of California's best and most accessible diving is in this reserve, accessible from La Jolla Cove. With an average depth of 20ft, the 6000 acres of look-but-don't-touch underwater real estate are great for snorkeling too. Ever-present are the spectacular, bright-orange Garibaldi fish – California's official state fish and a protected species (there's a hefty fine for poaching one).

Sleeping

★**Lodge at Torrey Pines** LUXURY HOTEL $$$
(Map p480; ☎858-453-4420; www.lodgetorreypines.com; 11480 N Torrey Pines Rd; r from $359; P@) Inspired by the architecture of Greene & Greene, the turn-of-the-20th-century arts-and-crafts masters who designed the Gamble House (www.gamblehouse.org) in Pasadena, the lodge's discreetly luxurious rooms have Mission oak-and-leather furniture à la Stickley, Tiffany-style lamps, plein air paintings and basket-weave bathroom-floor tiling in marble. There's a stellar full-service spa and a croquet lawn. Parking costs $25.

La Valencia HISTORIC HOTEL $$$
(Map p474; ☎858-454-0771, 800-451-0772; www.lavalencia.com; 1132 Prospect St; r from $314; P@) This 1926 pink-walled, Mediterranean-style landmark was designed by William Templeton Johnson. Among its 115 rooms, those in the main building are rather compact while the villas are spacious, but the property wins for its Old Hollywood romance. Even if you don't stay, consider lifting a toast – and a pinkie – to the sunset from its Spanish Revival lounge, La Sala. Parking is $30.

Eating

★**Shore Rider Cafe** CALIFORNIAN $
(Map p452; ☎858-412-5308; www.shoreridersd.com; 2168 Avenida de la Playa; dishes $9-15; ⏰11am-10pm Mon-Thu, to 11pm Fri, 9am-11pm Sat, to 10pm Sun) For tasty eats in a surf vibe right near the beach, head to Shore Rider's new mellow open-air patio, where they play California rock and serve beer on tap and lunch plates like mahimahi and shrimp ceviche, blue cheese and bacon fries and SoCal salads. For weekend brunch (9–1pm Saturday-Sunday): shrimp ranchero, French toast or 'dinosaur eggs.'

Harry's Coffee Shop DINER $
(Map p474; ☎858-454-7381; http://harryscoffeeshop.com/; 7545 Girard Ave; dishes $5-13; ⏰6am-3pm) This classic 1960 coffee shop has a posse of regulars from blue-haired socialites to sports celebs. The food is American at its best – pancakes, tuna melts, burgers (and a local concession, breakfast burritos). Wash it down with mimosas, Greyhound cocktails, Bloody Marys or beer, and soak up the special aura of the place.

★**George's at the Cove** CALIFORNIAN $$$
(Map p474; ☎858-454-4244; www.georgesatthecove.com; 1250 Prospect St; mains $16-46; ⏰11am-10pm Sun-Thu, to 11pm Fri & Sat) The Euro-Cal cooking is as dramatic as the oceanfront location, thanks to the bottomless imagination of chef Trey Foshee. George's has graced just about every list of top restaurants in California, and indeed the USA. Four venues allow you to enjoy it at different price points: Ocean Terrace, George's

California Modern and the no-reservations Level 2 and Modern Bar.

Drinking & Nightlife

Pannikin CAFE

(Map p474; 858-454-5453; https://pannikincoffeeandtea.com/; 7467 Girard Ave; drinks from $2; 6am-6pm;) A few blocks from the water, this clapboard shack of a cafe with a generous balcony is popular for its organic coffees, Italian espresso and Mexican chocolate. Like all the Pannikins, it's a North County institution. Also sells sandwiches, pastries and salads.

Entertainment

Comedy Store COMEDY

(Map p474; 858-454-9176; http://lajolla.thecomedystore.com; 916 Pearl St; show times vary) One of the area's most established comedy venues, the Comedy Store also serves popcorn, drinks and barrels of laughs. Expect a cover charge (from $10 on weekdays and $20 on weekends, with a two-drink minimum), and some of tomorrow's big names. Look out for free open-mike nights.

La Jolla Playhouse THEATER

(Map p452; 858-550-1010; www.lajollaplayhouse.org; 2910 La Jolla Village Dr; tickets $20-75) Inside the Mandell Weiss Center for the Performing Arts, this theater has sent dozens of productions to Broadway, including *Jersey Boys*, *Peter and the Starcatcher* and 2010 Tony winner *Memphis*.

Shopping

La Jolla's skirt-and-sweater crowd pays retail for cashmere sweaters and expensive tchotchkes downtown: paintings, sculpture and decorative items. Small boutiques fill the gaps between Talbot's, Banana Republic, Ralph Lauren and Jos. A. Bank.

DG Wills (Map p474; 858-456-1800; www.dgwillsbooks.com; 7461 Girard Ave; 10am-7pm Mon-Sat, 11am-5pm Sun) and **Warwick's** (Map p474; 858-454-0347; www.warwicks.com; 7812 Girard Ave; 9am-6pm Mon-Sat, 10am-5.30pm Sun) have good book selections and host readings and author events.

Getting There & Away

Bus number 30 connects La Jolla with Bird Rock, Pacific Beach, Mission Bay Park and the **Old Town Transit Center** (p472). There's a bus stop at Silverado St and Herschel St in La Jolla. The full journey takes around 45 minutes and costs $2.25 one way.

By car, via I-5 from Downtown San Diego, take the La Jolla Pkwy exit and head west toward Torrey Pines Rd, from where it's a right turn onto Prospect St.

Del Mar

The ritziest of North County's seaside suburbs, with a Tudor aesthetic that somehow doesn't feel out of place, Del Mar boasts good (if pricey) restaurants, unique galleries, high-end boutiques and, north of town, the West Coast's most renowned horse-racing track, also the site of the annual county fair. Downtown Del Mar (sometimes called 'the village') extends for about a mile along Camino del Mar. At its hub, where 15th St crosses Camino del Mar, the tastefully designed **Del Mar Plaza** (Map p480; 858-847-2284; http://delmarplaza.com; 1555 Camino Del Mar) shopping center has restaurants, boutiques and upper-level terraces that look out to sea.

Sights & Activities

Seagrove Park PARK

(Map p480; Coast Blvd) At the end of 15th St, this park abuts the beach and overlooks the ocean. This little stretch of well-groomed lawn is a community hub and perfect for a picnic.

★**Los Penasquitos Canyon Trail** HIKING

(Map p480; county ranger 858-538-8066; www.sandiego.gov/park-and-recreation/parks/osp/lospenasquitos; entry via Park Village Rd & Celome Way; sunrise-sunset) FREE A 20-minute drive inland is a series of wonderful, mostly flat, shady and sunny paths snaking through a lush valley and past a cascading waterfall surrounded by volcanic rock. The main 7-mile pathway is moderately trafficked with runners, walkers and mountain bikers. Lookout for butterflies, mule deer and bobcats. Stay alert when exploring – rattlesnakes also favor these arid pathways.

California Dreamin' BALLOONING

(800-373-3359; www.californiadreamin.com; per person from $298) Brightly colored hot-air balloons are a trademark of the skies above Del Mar, on the northern fringe of the San Diego metropolitan area. For flights, contact California Dreamin', which also serves Temecula.

Sleeping & Eating

Hotel Indigo San Diego Del Mar BOUTIQUE HOTEL $$
(Map p480; ☎858-755-1501, 877-846-3446; www.hotelindigosddelmar.com; 710 Camino Del Mar; r from $165;) This collection of whitewashed buildings with gray clay-tiled roofs has two outdoor heated pools, a spa, and new fitness and business centers. Rooms have hardwood floors, mosaic-tile accents and beach-inspired motifs. Some units have kitchenettes and distant ocean views. The hotel's **Ocean View Bar & Grill** serves breakfast and dinner. Free parking.

L'Auberge Del Mar Resort & Spa RESORT $$$
(Map p480; ☎858-259-1515, 800-245-9757; www.laubergedelmar.com; 1540 Camino Del Mar; r from $299;) Rebuilt in the 1990s on the grounds of the historic Hotel del Mar, where 1920s Hollywood celebrities once frolicked, L'Auberge continues a tradition of European-style elegance with luxurious linens, a spa and lovely grounds. It feels so intimate and the service is so individual, you'd never know there are 120 rooms. Parking is $25.

Americana MODERN AMERICAN $$
(Map p480; ☎858-794-6838; 1454 Camino del Mar; dishes breakfast & lunch $7-14, dinner $9-25; 7am-late) This quietly chichi and much-loved local landmark serves a diverse lineup of regional American cuisine: cheese grits to chicken Reubens, sesame salmon on succotash to seared duck breast with Israeli couscous, plus artisan cocktails, all amid checkerboard linoleum floors, giant windows and homey wainscoting. Breakfast served until 3pm.

Brigantine SEAFOOD $$$
(Map p480; ☎858-481-1166; www.brigantine.com; 3263 Camino del Mar; lunch $9-17, dinner $16-32; 11:30am-2:30pm Mon-Sat, 5pm-8:30pm Sun-Thur, 5pm-9pm Fri-Sat) Try San Diego–style surf 'n' turf at this posh seafood joint. Menu items include wok-charred ahi, classic filet mignon, Parmesan-crusted sautéed sand dabs, and macadamia-crusted fresh mahimahi. There's an oyster bar and happy hour (all night $1 off well drinks, and $2 off bar-menu items) on Mondays and between 4pm and 6pm Tues through Sun.

Entertainment

Del Mar Racetrack & Fairgrounds HORSE RACING
(Map p480; ☎858-792-4242; www.dmtc.com; 2260 Jimmy Durante Blvd; from $6; race season mid-Jul–early Sep) Del Mar's biggest draw during summer months was founded in 1937 by a prestigious group which included Bing Crosby. It's worth trying to brave the crowds on opening day (tickets from $10), if nothing else to see the amazing spectacle of ladies wearing over-the-top hats. The rest of the season, enjoy the visual perfection of the track's lush gardens and pink, Mediterranean-style architecture. On opening day, the racetrack runs free double-decker shuttle buses to and from the **Solana Beach train station** (Solana Beach Transit Center; 105 N Cedros Ave).

Getting There & Away

The 101 bus runs between La Jolla and Oceanside, stopping at Camino Del Mar and15th St. Route takes approximately one hour, one-way fares $1.75.

By car, N Torrey Pines Rd from La Jolla is the most scenic approach from the south. Heading north, the road (S21) changes its name from Camino del Mar to Coast Hwy 101 to Old Hwy 101. If you're in a hurry or headed out of town, the faster I-5 parallels it to the east. Traffic can snarl everywhere during rush hour and race or fair season.

Solana Beach

Solana Beach is the next town north from Del Mar – it's not as posh, but it has good beaches and lots of contemporary style. Don't miss the **Cedros Design District** (Map p480; www.shopcedros.com; Cedros Ave), four blocks on Cedros Ave where interior designers from all over the region come for inspiration and merchandise from buttons to bathrooms, paint to photographs and even garden supplies. Aside from a beautiful coastline, this kind of shopping is a Solana highlight.

Belly Up (Map p480; ☎858-481-8140; www.bellyup.com; 143 S Cedros Ave; tickets $10-45; show times vary) is a converted warehouse and bar that consistently books good bands from jazz to funk, and big names from Jimmy Buffett and Aimee Mann to Merle Haggard and tribute bands. There's also a new **microbrewery** (Map p480; ☎858-345-1144; https://culturebrewingco.com/; 111 S Cedros Ave, Suite 200; pints from $5; noon-9pm Mon-Sun) a few doors down.

Getting There & Away

The 101 bus route (running from La Jolla to Oceanside roughly every hour) stops at Hwy 101 and Lomas Santa Fe Dr. The route takes around one hour and costs $1.75 per single journey.

It takes roughly 25 minutes by car to reach Solana from Downtown San Diego, heading north on the I-5.

Coaster (www.gonctd.com) commuter trains run in the morning and evening between Oceanside and downtown San Diego via Solana Beach, with fares from $8 around three daily Amtrak *Surfliner* (www.amtrak.com). Trains run through Solana Beach, with fares starting from $10. Check the websites for timetables.

Cardiff-by-the-Sea

Beachy Cardiff is good for surfing and popular with a laid-back crowd. The town center has the perfunctory supermarkets and everyday shops along San Elijo Ave, about 0.25 miles from the ocean and across the railroad tracks, but the real action is the miles of restaurants, cafes and surf shops along Hwy 101.

Sleeping & Eating

The best option if you want to spend the night is the **San Elijo State Beach Campground** (Map p480; ☎760-753-5091, reservations 800-444-7275; www.parks.ca.gov; 2050 S Coast Hwy 101; summer tent/RV sites from $35/60; P 📶). Sitting right next to the beach, it has the best views in town. For dinner, head for **Las Olas** (Map p480; ☎760-942-1860; www.lasolasmex.com; 2655 S Coast Hwy 101; mains $9-19; ⏰11am-9pm Mon-Thu, to 9:30pm Fri, 10am-9:30pm Sat, to 9pm Sun; 👪), which serves fish tacos with a sea view. Lobster is served in the style of legendary Baja California lobster village Puerto Nuevo. House cocktails include pineapple and chili margaritas and drinks made with RIP (rum infused with pineapple). **Ki's Restaurant** (Map p480; ☎760-436-5236; www.kisrestaurant.com; 2591 S Coast Hwy 101; mains breakfast $6-15, lunch $9-15, dinner $6-24; ⏰8am-9pm Sun-Thu, to 8:30pm Fri & Sat; P ✎) 🍃 is also a solid option. Upstairs, there's a great ocean view from the sit-down restaurant and bar, where from 4:30pm daily fancier dishes like Jidori chicken or macadamia-coated mahimahi with Thai peanut sauce are served with ingredients from nearby family farms.

Getting There & Away

The easiest way to reach Cardiff is by car, as it's a short 20- to 30-minute drive from central San Diego. However, the **North County Transit District (NCTD)** (NCTD; ☎760-966-6500; www.gonctd.com) runs bus route 101, connecting UC San Diego with Torrey Pines, Del Mar, Cardiff and Encinitas. In Cardiff, it stops near **San Elijo State Beach** (Map p480; P) and the adjacent campground. There's another stop further south in Cardiff, outside Ki's Restaurant and **Cardiff State Beach** (Map p480; ☎760-753-5091; www.parks.ca.gov; ⏰7am-sunset; P). It runs roughly every hour and takes an hour from start to finish. Fares cost $1.75.

Encinitas

Peaceful Encinitas has a decidedly down-to-earth surf vibe and a laid-back, beach-town main street, perfect for a relaxing day trip or weekend escape. North of central Encinitas, yet still part of the city, is **Leucadia**, a leafy stretch of N Hwy 101 with a hippie vibe of used-clothing stores and taco shops.

Sights

Self-Realization Fellowship Retreat RELIGIOUS SITE

(Map p480; ☎760-436-7220; http://encinitastemple.org; 215 K St; ⏰meditation garden 9am-5pm Tue-Sat, from 11am Sun, hermitage 2-4pm Sun) FREE Yogi Paramahansa Yogananda founded his center here in 1937, and the town has been a magnet for holistic healers and natural-lifestyle seekers ever since. The gold lotus domes of the hermitage – conspicuous on South Coast Hwy 101 – mark the southern end of Encinitas and the turn-out for **Swami's Beach**, a powerful reef break surfed by territorial locals. The fellowship's compact but lovely **Meditation Garden** has wonderful ocean vistas, a stream and a koi pond.

San Diego Botanic Garden GARDENS

(Map p480; ☎760-436-3036; www.sdbgarden.org; 230 Quail Gardens Dr; adult/child/senior $14/8/10; ⏰9am-5pm; P 👪) This 37-acre garden has a large collection of California native plants as well as flora of different regions of the world, including Australia and Central America. There are special activities in the children's garden (10am Tuesday to Thursday); check the website for a schedule. Parking $2.

Entertainment

La Paloma Theatre CINEMA

(Map p480; ☎760-436-7469; www.lapalomatheatre.com; 471 S Coast Hwy 101) Built in 1928, this landmark – and central Encinitas' main venue – shows arthouse movies nightly and *The Rocky Horror Picture Show* on Fridays at midnight, and stages occasional concerts.

WORTH A TRIP

SAN DIEGO ZOO SAFARI PARK

Since the early 1960s, the San Diego Zoological Society has been developing this 1800-acre, open-range **zoo** (☎760-747-8702; www.sdzsafaripark.org; 15500 San Pasqual Valley Rd, Escondido; 1-day adult/child $52/42, 2-visit pass to zoo and/or safari park adult/child $83.25/73.25; ⏰8am-6pm, to 7pm late Jun–mid-Aug; P 👪) where herds of giraffes, zebras, rhinos and other animals roam the open valley floor. For an instant safari feel, board the Africa Tram ride, which tours you around the second-largest continent in under half an hour.

Elsewhere, animals are in enclosures so naturalistic it's as if the humans are guests, and there's a petting krall and animal shows; pick up a map and schedule. Additional 'safaris,' like ziplining, a chance to observe a cheetah whizz by while chasing a mechanical rabbit, and even sleepovers (yowza!) are available with reservations and additional payment.

The park's just north of Hwy 78, 5 miles east of I-15 from the Via Rancho Parkway exit. Plan on 45 minutes transit by car from San Diego, except in rush hour when that figure can double. For bus information contact **North County Transit District** (NCTD; ☎760-966-6500; www.gonctd.com)..

Sleeping

Leucadia Beach Inn MOTEL $
(Map p480; ☎760-943-7461; www.leucadiabeachinn.org; 1322 N Coast Hwy; r $85-145; P 📶 🐾) All the sparkling-clean rooms in this charming 1920s courtyard motel have tile floors and bright paint jobs, and many have kitchenettes. The beach is a few blocks' walk. It's across Hwy 101 from the train tracks, so light sleepers should pack earplugs.

Eating

★**Fish 101** SEAFOOD $
(Map p480; ☎760-634-6221; www.fish101restaurant.com; 1468 N Coast Hwy 101; mains $10-14) In this casual grown-up fish shack, order at the counter, sidle up to a butcher-block table, sip craft beer or Mexican coke from a mason jar and tuck into albacore-tuna *poke*, clam chowder, shrimp po'boy or fish-and-chips. Simple grilling techniques allow the catch's natural flavors to show through, and healthy rice-bran oil is used for frying.

Eve VEGAN $
(Map p480; ☎760-230-2560; www.eveencinitas.com; 575 S Coast Hwy 101; Buddha bowls $12; ⏰8am-9pm; ✎) 🌿 One part coffee shop, one part lounge and one part restaurant, this new vegan eatery serves hearty salad bowls heaped with goodness. Opt for a superfood smoothie, local kombucha or Buddha bowl. Our fave is the Legendary Hero flavor with braised kale, sprouts, beets, carrots, brown rice, hemp seed, walnuts, cranberries and tahini sauce.

★**Trattoria I Trulli** ITALIAN $$
(Map p480; ☎760-943-6800; www.trattoriaitrullisd.com; 830 S Coast Hwy 101; mains lunch $9-19, dinner $9-28; ⏰11am-2:30pm daily, 5-9.30pm Sun-Thu, to 10pm Fri & Sat) Country-style seating indoors and great peoople-watching on the sidewalk. Just one taste of the homemade ravioli or lasagna, salmon with arugula, capers and red onion, or *pollo uno zero uno* (101; chicken stuffed with cheese, spinach and artichokes in mushroom sauce) and you'll know why this mom-and-pop Italian trattoria is always packed. Reservations are recommended.

East Village Asian Diner FUSION $$
(Map p480; ☎760-753-8700; www.eateastvillage.com; 628 S Coast Hwy 101; mains $9-12; ⏰11:30am-2:30pm & 5-10pm Mon-Sat, to 9pm Sun; ✎) This cool diner-decorated eatery fuses mostly Korean cooking with Western and other Asian influences (witness the 'super awesome' beef-and-kimchi burrito). Try noodle dishes (Thai peanut, beef and broccoli etc), or build your own 'monk's stone pot,' a superheated rice bowl to which you can add ingredients from pulled pork to salmon. Sauces are made in-house.

Getting There & Away

The 101 bus, costing $1.75 for a single one-zone fare, travels between La Jolla and Oceanside, stopping at Encinitas Station roughly every 45 minutes. The entire bus route takes around one hour, depending on traffic. It takes half an hour to drive to Encinitas by car from Downtown San Diego. Roughly three Amtrak *Surfliner* trains stop at **Encinitas Station** (25 E D St) per day, with fares from around $10. The NCTD *Coaster*, with single fares from $8, also goes through here, running approximately every hour during rush-hour periods.

North County Coast

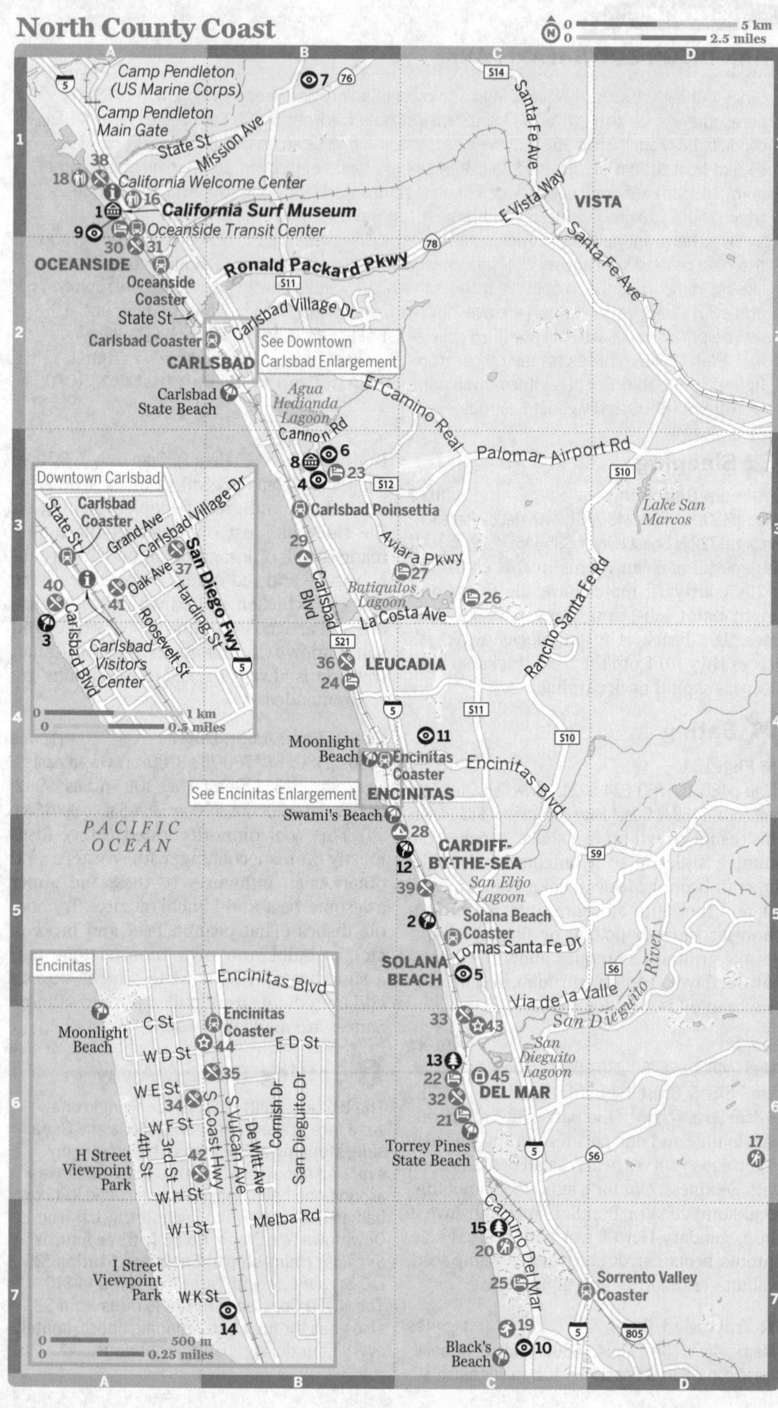

SAN DIEGO & AROUND ENCINITAS

North County Coast

Carlsbad

Most visitors come to Carlsbad for Legoland and head right back out, and that's too bad because they've missed the charming, intimate Carlsbad Village with shopping, dining and beaching nearby. It's bordered by I-5 and Carlsbad Blvd, which run north–south and are connected by Carlsbad Village Dr running east–west.

Carlsbad came into being with the railroad in the 1880s. John Frazier, an early homesteader, sank a well and found water that had a high mineral content, supposedly identical to that of spa water in Karlsbad, Bohemia (now in the Czech Republic). He built a grand Queen Anne–style spa hotel, which prospered until the 1930s and is now a local landmark.

If you've come looking for the Carlsbad Caverns, you're outta luck. Those are in New Mexico.

Sights

Legoland California Resort AMUSEMENT PARK

(Map p480; 760-918-5346; www.legoland.com/california; 1 Legoland Dr; adult/child 3-12yr from $95/89; hours vary, at least 10am-5pm year-round; P) A fantasy environment built largely of those little colored plastic blocks from Denmark. Many rides and attractions are targeted to elementary schoolers: a junior 'driving school' a jungle cruise lined with Lego animals, wacky 'sky cruiser' pedal cars on a track, and fairy-tale-, princess-, pirate-, adventurer- and dino-themed escapades. If you have budding scientists (age 10 and over) with you, sign them up on arrival at the park for an appointment for **Mindstorms**, where they can make computerized Lego robots. There are also lots of low-thrill activities like face-painting and princess-meeting.

Carlsbad Coast BEACH

(Map p480; P) Carlsbad's long, sandy beaches are great for walking and searching for seashells. Good access is from Carlsbad Blvd, two blocks south of Carlsbad Village Dr, where there's a boardwalk, restrooms and free parking.

Carlsbad Ranch Flower Fields GARDENS
(Map p480; ☎760-431-0352; www.theflowerfields.com; 5704 Paseo del Norte; adult/child 3-10yr $14/7; ⊙usually 9am-6pm Mar–mid-May; P ♿) The 50-acre flower fields of Carlsbad Ranch are ablaze in a sea of the carmine, saffron and snow-white blossoms of giant tecolote ranunculus. Take the Palomar Airport Rd exit off of I-5, head east and turn left on Paseo del Norte. It takes roughly 30 minutes from Downtown San Diego.

Museum of Making Music MUSEUM
(Map p480; www.museumofmakingmusic.org; 5790 Armada Dr; adult/child under 3 yr/student $10/free/7; ⊙10am-5pm Tue-Sun) Historical exhibits and listening stations of 450 instruments from the 1890s to the present, from manufacturing to the distribution of popular music.

Sleeping

If you're looking for a budget stay in Carlsbad, there's camping on the beach. Those in search of luxury have come to the right place: Carlsbad is home to fancy golf resorts and spa stays.

Legoland Hotel HOTEL **$$$**
(Map p480; ☎877-534-6526, 760-918-5346; www.legoland.com/california; 5885 The Crossings Dr; r from $328; P ❄ @ 🛜 ≋) Lego designers were let loose on this hotel, just outside Legoland's main gate. Thousands of Lego models (dragons to surfers) populate the property, and the elevator turns into a disco between floors. Each floor has its own theme (pirate, adventure, kingdom), down to the rooms' wallpaper, props, even the shower curtains.

South Carlsbad State Park Campground CAMPGROUND **$**
(Map p480; ☎760-438-3143, reservations 800-444-7275; www.reserveamerica.com; 7201 Carlsbad Blvd; ocean-/streetside tent & RV sites $50/35, ocean/inland tent & RV sites with hookups $75/60; P) Three miles south of town and sandwiched between Carlsbad Blvd and the beach, this campground has more than 200 tent and RV sites; all spaces accommodate both tents and RVs.

Eating & Drinking

State St (just north of Carlsbad Village Dr) is Carlsbad's most charming stretch, with a number of restaurants worth browsing.

For a luxury experience, also check out the restaurants at **Omni La Costa Resort & Spa** (Map p480; ☎800-854-5000, 760-438-9111; www.lacosta.com; 2100 Costa Del Mar Rd; r from $322; P @ 🛜 ≋ 🐾) and **Park Hyatt Aviara Resort** (Map p480; ☎760-603-6800; www.parkhyattaviara.com; 7100 Aviara Resort Dr; r from $349; P @ 🛜 ≋ 🐾). At the other end of the scale are the brewpub Pizza Port, and the local branch of Mexican **Las Olas** (Map p480; ☎760-434-5850; www.lasolasmex.com; 2939 Carlsbad Blvd; ⊙11am-9pm Mon-Thu, to 9:30pm Fri, 10am-9:30pm Sat, to 9pm Sun).

French Bakery Cafe BAKERY, CAFE **$**
(Map p480; ☎760-729-2241; www.carlsbadfrenchpastrycafe.com/; 1005 Carlsbad Village Dr; mains $6; ⊙7am-7pm Mon-Sat, 7.30am-5pm Sun; 🛜) Its location may be in a drab-looking shopping center just off I-5, but it's the real deal for croissants and brioches (baked daily) and kick-start espresso, plus omelets, salads and sandwiches.

Pizza Port PIZZA **$$**
(Map p480; ☎760-720-7007; www.pizzaport.com; 571 Carlsbad Village Dr; pizzas $7-24; ⊙11am-10pm Mon-Thu, to midnight Fri & Sat, 10am-11pm Sun; ♿) Rockin' and raucous local brewpub chain with surf art, rock music and 'anti-wimpy' pizzas to go with the signature Sharkbite Red Ale. Multiple locations.

Information

Carlsbad Visitors Center (Map p480; ☎760-434-6093; www.visitcarlsbad.com; 400 Carlsbad Village Dr; ⊙10am-5pm Mon-Fri, to 4pm Sat, to 3pm Sun.) Housed in the original 1887 Santa Fe train depot.

Getting There & Away

The 101 bus route runs between La Jolla's Westfield UTC shopping center and Oceanside, stopping at Carlsbad Village Station en route. Fares are $1.75 one way; the full bus journey takes roughly one hour.

Coaster and *Pacific Surfliner* trains run from Downtown's Santa Fe Depot (p471) along the breadth of the coastline, stopping at **Carlsbad Village Station** (☎800-872-7245; 2775 State St). *Coasters* (www.gonctd.com) run nearly every hour in the morning and evenings and start from $8 for a single one-zone journey; *Surfliner* (https://tickets.amtrak.com) trains run roughly three times a day, with fares from $10.

TEMECULA WINE REGION

Temecula has become a popular short-break destination for its Old West Americana main street, nearly two dozen wineries and California's largest casino, Pechanga.

Temecula means 'Place of the Sun' in the language of the native Luiseño people, who were present when Father Fermín Lasuén became the first Spanish missionary to visit in 1797. In the 1820s the area became a ranching outpost for the Mission San Luis Rey, in present-day Oceanside. Later, Temecula became a stop on the Butterfield stagecoach line (1858–61) and the California Southern railroad.

But it's Temecula's late 20th-century growth that's been most astonishing, from 2700 people in 1970 – the city didn't get its first traffic light until 1984 – to some 106,700 residents today. Between Old Town and the wineries is an off-putting, 3-mile buffer zone of suburban housing developments and shopping centers. Ignore that and you'll do fine.

Sample plenty of creative wines in the Temecula area, including the almond champagne at **Wilson Creek** (www.wilsoncreekwinery.com; 35960 Rancho California Rd; tasting $20; ⏲10am-5pm; 🅿). Get a designated driver to ferry you around the vineyards during the afternoon (many tasting rooms close at 5pm) or book on a tasting tour with **Grapeline Temecula** (☎888-894-6379; www.gogrape.com; shuttle service/tours from $69/89).

Of an evening, artisan restaurant and bar **Crush & Brew** (☎951-693-4567; www.crushnbrew.com; 28544 Old Town Front St, Suite 103; ⏲11:30am-10pm Sun-Thu, to midnight Fri & Sat) serves hand-crafted cocktails, or line-dancing dive the **Temecula Stampede** (☎951-695-1761; www.thetemeculastampede.com; 28721 Old Town Front Street; $5-10 cover Fri & Sat; ⏲Mon, Fri & Sat 6pm-2am, Thu 8pm-2am) is open for a late-night drink.

Many Temecula-area wineries offer entertainment, from guitar soloists to chamber concerts. Check at the **visitors center** (☎888-363-2852, 951-491-6085; www.visittemeculavalley.com; 28690 Mercedes St; ⏲9am-5pm Mon-Sat) or **Visit Temecula Valley** (www.visittemeculavalley.com) for upcoming events. If you fancy a bit of line dancing or mechanical bull-riding, try the **Temecula Stampede** (p483).

Temecula is just off the I-15 freeway, which begins in San Diego. Either of the Rancho California Rd or Rte 79 exits will take you to Old Town Front St. Allow 60 minutes from San Diego, 70 from Anaheim, 80 from Palm Springs or 90 from LA.

Greyhound (☎800-231-2222, 951-676-9768; www.greyhound.com; 28464 Old Town Front St) routes head to central San Diego twice daily (from $11 one way, when purchased in advance online). Journeys take roughly one hour and thirty minutes with no traffic.

Oceanside

The largest North County town, Oceanside is home to many who work at giant Camp Pendleton Marine Base just to the north. The huge military presence mixes with an attractive natural setting, surf shops, head (marijuana) shops and a downtown that's slowly revitalizing.

Little remains from the 1880s streetscape, when the new Santa Fe coastal railway came through Oceanside, but a few buildings designed by Irving Gill and Julia Morgan still stand. The Welcome Center (p484) has a pamphlet describing a self-guided history walk.

Sights & Activities

★California Surf Museum MUSEUM
(Map p480; ☎760-721-6876; www.surfmuseum.org; 312 Pier View Way; adult/child/student $5/free/3, first Tue of month free; ⏲10am-4pm Fri-Wed, to 8pm Thu; 👪) It's easy to spend an hour in this heartfelt museum of surf artifacts, from a timeline of surfing history to surf-themed art and a radical collection of boards, including the one chomped by a shark when it ate the arm of surfer Bethany Hamilton. Special exhibits change frequently along different themes (eg Women of Surfing and Surfers of the Vietnam War).

Mission San Luis Rey de Francia HISTORIC SITE
(Map p480; ☎760-757-3651; www.sanluisrey.org; 4050 Mission Ave; adult/child 5yr & under/youth 6-18yr/senior $7/free/3/5; ⏲9:30am-5pm) About 4.5 miles inland from central Oceanside, this was the largest California mission and the most successful in recruiting Native American converts. At one point some 3000 neophytes lived and worked here. After the Mexican government secularized the missions, San Luis

fell into ruin; the adobe walls of the church, from 1811, are the only original parts left. Inside are displays on work and life in the mission, with some original religious art and artifacts.

Oceanside Pier PIER

(Map p480) This wooden pier extends more than 1900ft out to sea. Bait-and-tackle shops rent poles to the many anglers who line its wooden fences (per hour/day $5/15). Two major surf competitions – the West Coast Pro-Am and the National Scholastic Surf Association (NSSA) – take place near the pier each June.

Surfcamps USA SURFING

(Map p480; 760-889-8984; www.surfcampsusa.com; 1202 N Pacific St; lessons per person from $55;) Newbies and not-so newbies can take two-hour private or group lessons from this popular operator. All equipment is included.

Asylum Surf SURFING

(Map p480; 760-722-7101; www.asylumboardshop.com; 310 Mission Ave; surfboards 3hr/day $15/25, wetsuits $10/15) Surfers can rent equipment here.

Sleeping & Eating

Good rates can be found on rooms in Oceanside, where accommodation mainly consists of chain hotels and motels. The Springhill Suites by Marriott is a favorite: right next to the beach, in the center of the action and with dreamy views of the Pacific Ocean.

★Springhill Suites Oceanside Downtown HOTEL $$

(Map p480; 760-722-1003; www.shsoceanside.com; 110 N Myers St; r $149-379;) This modern, six-story, ocean-view hotel is awash in summery yellows and sea blues in the lobby. Rooms have crisp lines and distressed-wood headboards, and ocean- and pier-view rooms have balconies or patios. Best views are from the pool and hot tub on the top floor, where there's also a fitness center. Hot breakfast buffet included. Parking is $26.

101 Café DINER $

(Map p480; 760-722-5220; http://101cafe.net; 631 S Coast Hwy; mains $6-10; 7am-7pm Mon-Thu, to 9pm Fri-Sun;) This tiny, streamlined modern diner (1928) serves all-American classics from omelets and burgers to chicken-fried steak with country gravy, or steak and eggs and hash browns. Check out the local historic photos on the wall. If you're lucky, you'll catch the owner and can quiz him about local history.

Harbor Fish & Chips SEAFOOD $

(Map p480; 760-722-4977; 276 Harbor Dr S; mains $8-16; 11am-7pm Mon-Thu, to 8pm Fri & Sat;) There's nothin' fancy about this harborside chippie from the '60s, but when the fish is fried to a deep crackle and you eat it at a picnic table on the dock while classic pop tunes play on the radio, you'll feel pretty good. There's a large local following and taxidermied catches on the walls.

That Boy Good BARBECUE $$

(TBG; Map p480; 760-433-4227; www.tbgbbq.com; 207 N Coast Hwy; mains $9-25; from 4pm Mon, from 11am Tue-Sun) This shrine to the Mississippi Delta serves belly-busting portions of fried chicken and waffles, dirty fries (piled with chili) and Cajun catfish. Wash it all down with a craft or canned beer or the BBQ Bloody Mary, topped with a rib.

Ruby's Diner DINER $$

(Map p480; 760-433-7829; www.rubys.com; 1 Oceanside Pier; mains $9-14; 7am-9pm Sun-Thu, to 10pm Fri & Sat;) This '50s-style diner has good burgers and milkshakes, big breakfasts and a full bar. Yes, it's a chain, but it's right at the end of the pier.

Information

California Welcome Center (Map p480; 760-721-1101, 800-350-7873; www.visitoceanside.org; 928 N Coast Hwy; 9am-5pm) Helpful, informative staff dispense coupons for local attractions, as well as maps and information for the San Diego area, plus help booking lodgings in Oceanside. It's just off the freeway exit.

Getting There & Away

Local buses and trains stop at the **Oceanside Transit Center** (Map p480; 235 S Tremont St).

Coaster (www.gonctd.com) trains run almost an hour apart in the morning and evenings and fares start from $8 for a single one-zone journey. There are around three *Surfliner* (https://tickets.amtrak.com) trains a day, with fares from $10.

The 101 bus route (running from La Jolla to Oceanside) runs approximately every hour. It costs $1.75 per single, and takes roughly an hour from the start of the route to the end.

Traveling by car via I-5 from Downtown San Diego, take the La Jolla Pkwy exit, and head west toward Torrey Pines Rd, from where it's a right turn to Oceanside's Prospect St.

Understand Coastal California

Coastal California Today

Coastal California is today the creative culmination of generations of big dreamers. The fantasies spun by Hollywood and the cutting-edge tech of Silicon Valley have come to dominate the digital transmissions and cultural trends of the entire planet. Meanwhile, the state's iconic images of tanned surfers and sunny sands endure, never mind thornier real-life questions about how to manage a burgeoning human population and its accompanying challenges of never-ending traffic gridlock, housing shortages and a sky-high cost of living.

Best in Print

The Tortilla Curtain (TC Boyle; 1995) Mexican-American culture clash and chasing the Californian dream.

My California: Journeys by Great Writers (Angel City Press; 2004) Insightful stories by talented chroniclers.

Where I Was From (Joan Didion; 2003) California-born essayist shatters palm-fringed fantasies.

The Joy Luck Club (Amy Tan; 1989) Tales of Chinese immigrants and their daughters in San Francisco.

Best Music

California Girls (Beach Boys; 1965) Early California surf sounds.

California Dreaming (The Mamas & the Papas; 1966) Counterculture folk rock hit.

California (Joni Mitchell; 1971) Haunting stream-of-consciousness ballad.

California Sun (Ramones; 1977) The definitive cover version.

California Love (2Pac; 1996) Comeback single featuring Dr Dre.

Californication (Red Hot Chili Peppers; 1999) Pop-punk portmanteau.

California (Phantom Planet; 2002) Theme song from *The OC*.

Beverly Hills (Weezer; 2005) Sarcastic rock anthem.

California Gurls (Katy Perry; 2010) Pop diva meets rapper Snoop Dogg.

People & Politics

Even if you've seen it in the movies or on TV, coastal California may be a shock to the system. Venice Beach skateboarders, Humboldt hippies, Marin County wild-mushroom hunters, 'Bezerkely' professors and Silicon Valley millionaires aren't on different channels. They all live here, a place where tolerance for other people's beliefs, be they conservative, liberal or wacky, is the social glue.

Still controversial elsewhere in the USA, medical marijuana is old news for Californians, who approved a state proposition allowing its use back in 1996 – although the proliferation of raids on MMJ dispensaries and rumors of Mexican cartel intervention have raised eyebrows. Two decades later, California followed Colorado's lead in legalizing marijuana for recreational use, with 56% of voters casting their ballots in favor of Proposition 64 in 2016.

Environmentalism

There's no denying that California's culture of conspicuous consumption is exported via Hollywood flicks and reality TV (hello, *Real Housewives of Orange County*). But since the 1960s, Californians have trailblazed another, 'greener' way by choosing more sustainable foods and low-impact lifestyles, preserving old-growth forests with tree-sitting activism, declaring urban nuclear-free zones, pushing for environmentally progressive legislation and establishing the biggest US market for hybrid vehicles. Over 60% of Californians admit that, yes, they've actually hugged a tree.

That shouldn't really come as a surprise. It was Californians who helped kick-start the world's conservation movement in the midst of the 19th-century industrial revolution, with laws curbing industrial dumping, swaths of prime real estate set aside as urban green space, and pristine wilderness protected by national and state parks. Today, even conservative California politicians may prioritize environmental issues on their agendas – at least as much as the state's economic recovery and several recent years of severe drought allow.

Fast Companies & Technology

You might not get a word in edgewise when it comes to discussing the environment with a local, but California's technological innovations need no introduction by anyone. Perhaps you've heard of PCs, iPods, Google and the internet? The home of Silicon Valley and a burgeoning biotech industry, Northern California gives Southern California's gargantuan entertainment industry a run for its money as the state's main economic powerhouse.

But even these industries weren't enough to salvage the state's ravaged economy, which spiraled out of control during the US recession beginning in 2008. California's budget crises brought deep cuts to environmental protections, education, social services and other public programs, including state parks. Governor Jerry Brown (Democrat) and state legislators have reversed many of these austerity measures as the economy bounces back.

Growing Pains

The biggest problem California faces is growth. Because of the Golden State's adaptability and charms, the human wave of domestic migration and international immigration continued to crest until the last decade. Still, many Americans who heed the mid-19th-century advice to 'Go West, young man!' wind up on California's shores, as do many of the USA's new foreign-born arrivals.

With this burgeoning humanity comes almost unbelievably high costs of living and real estate. Public transportation is often inadequate, so everyone hits the tortured freeways. Meanwhile, the gap between California's richest and poorest citizens dramatically keeps widening. Nowhere in the nation is income inequality greater than in San Francisco, where artists, working-class families and other long-time tenants are being evicted to build luxury condos for wealthy, young tech-company employees, whose private commuter buses infuriatingly clog city streets.

Sheer human impact is a palpable force almost everywhere in coastal California and begs the question that Rodney King asked back in 1992: 'Can we all get along?' Like California's future, the answer to that question is unknown.

POPULATION: **39.5 MILLION**

AREA: **155,780 SQ MILES**

MILES OF COASTLINE: **840**

GDP: **$2.46 TRILLION**

MEDIAN HOUSEHOLD INCOME: **$64,500**

if California were 100 people

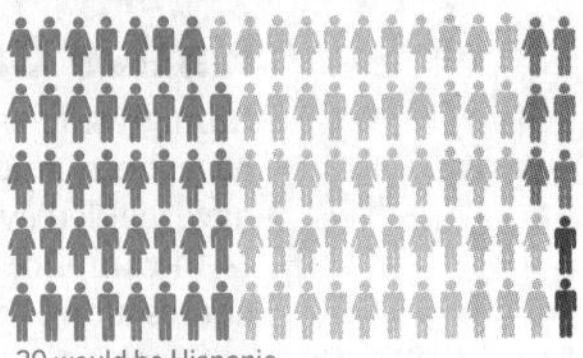

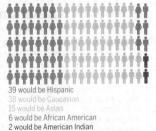

39 would be Hispanic
38 would be Caucasian
15 would be Asian
6 would be African American
2 would be American Indian

belief systems

(% of population)

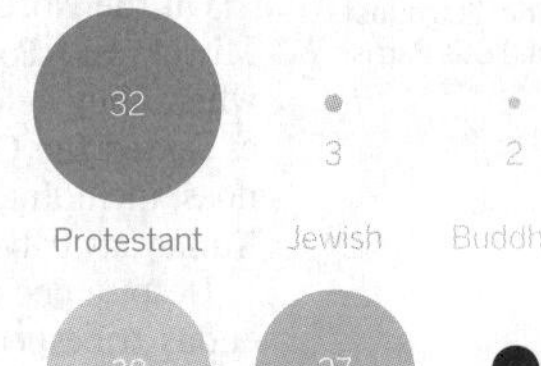

population per sq mile

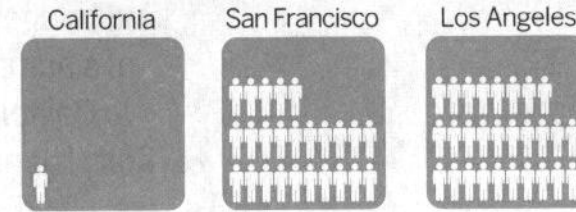

History

When European explorers first arrived in the 16th century, more than 100,000 Native Americans called this land home. Spanish conquistadors and priests marched through in search of a fabled 'city of gold' before establishing Catholic missions and presidios (military forts). After winning independence from Spain, Mexico briefly ruled California, but then got trounced by the fledgling USA just before gold was discovered here in 1848. Immigrant waves of star-struck California dreamers have washed up on these Pacific shores ever since.

Native Californians

Immigration is hardly a new phenomenon here, since human beings have been migrating to California for millennia. Archaeological sites have yielded evidence – from large middens of seashells along the beaches to campfire sites on the Channel Islands – of humans making their homes along this coast as early as 13,000 years ago.

Find out about the traditions and lifestyles of California's Native American tribes in the readable natural-history guide *California Indians and Their Environment* by Kent Lightfoot and Otis Parrish.

Speaking some 100 distinct languages, California's indigenous people mostly lived in small communities and a few migrated with the seasons. Their diet was largely dependent on acorn meal, supplemented by small game such as rabbits and deer, and fish and shellfish. They were skilled craftspeople, making earthenware pots, animal-skin and plant-fiber clothing, dugout canoes carved from redwood logs, fishing nets, bows, arrows and spears with chipped stone points. The most developed craft was basketry; baskets were often decorated with intricate geometric designs and some were so tightly woven they could hold water.

On the North Coast, fishing communities such as the Ohlone, Coast Miwok and Pomo built subterranean roundhouses and sweat lodges, where they held ceremonies, told stories and gambled. Chumash villages dotted the Central Coast, where tribespeople fished and paddled canoes, including out to the Channel Islands. Further south, the nomadic Kumeyaay tribe hunted, foraged and fished near present-day San Diego.

Despite pockets of armed resistance and violent revolts, many indigenous tribespeople were made to construct Spanish missions and presidios in the late 18th and early 19th centuries. Within 100 years of the

TIMELINE

20,000 BC

First people start crossing from Asia into North America via the Bering Strait land bridge. The bones of a human found on California's Santa Rosa Island date back 13,000 years.

AD 1542

Portuguese navigator Juan Rodríguez Cabrillo and his Spanish crew become the first Europeans to sight the mainland of New Spain's west coast, anchoring in today's San Diego Bay.

1769

Spain attempts to colonize California when Padre Junípero Serra and Captain Gaspar de Portolá lead an expedition to establish the first Catholic missions in Alta California, starting in San Diego.

Spanish colonists first arrival in 1769, California's indigenous population had plummeted by 80% to just 20,000 people due to foreign diseases, conscripted labor, violence, hunger and culture shock.

Native Californians were further dispossessed of tribal lands during the Mexican colonial and early American periods. It wasn't until the 20th century – when the US government began recognizing some tribes as sovereign nations, granting Native Americans citizenship and voting rights in 1924 – that California's indigenous population began to rebound.

Political activism, including the 'Red Power' protests of the American Indian Movement (AIM) starting in the late 1960s, led to a cultural renaissance and secured some tribes economic assistance from state and federal agencies. Deprived of their traditional land base and means of livelihood centuries ago, many California tribes have turned to casino gaming to relieve unemployment on their reservations.

A New World for Europeans

Following the conquest of Mexico in the early 16th century, Spain turned its attention toward exploring the edges of a new empire, fueled by curiosity, lust for power and, above all, greed. In 1542 the Spanish crown engaged Juan Rodríguez Cabrillo, a Portuguese explorer and retired conquistador, to lead an expedition up the West Coast to find the fabled golden land beyond Mexico.

When Cabrillo sailed into what is now San Diego Bay in 1542, he and his crew became the first Europeans to see mainland California. Staring back at them from shore were the Kumeyaay. Cabrillo's ships sat out a storm in the harbor, then sailed northward. They made a stop at the Channel Islands where Cabrillo broke a leg, fell ill, died and was buried on what is now San Miguel Island. The expedition continued as far as Oregon, but returned with no evidence of a city of gold.

Unimpressed Spanish colonial authorities ignored California for the next half century or so, until they decided they needed to secure some ports on the Pacific coast, and sent Sebastián Vizcaíno to find them. Vizcaíno's first expedition was a disaster that didn't get past Baja (Lower) California, but in his second attempt, in 1602, he rediscovered the harbor at San Diego and became the first European to set foot in what Spaniards called Alta (Upper) California.

Meanwhile, the English privateer Sir Francis Drake sailed up the California coast in 1579. He missed the entrance to San Francisco Bay, but pulled in near what is now called Point Reyes to repair his ship. Coastal Miwok tribespeople believed the English mariners to be the spirits of the dead returned from the afterworld. Drake quickly claimed their land for Queen Elizabeth, named it Nova Albion (New England) and sailed on to other adventures, journeying north up the Pacific coast to Alaska.

1781

Spanish governor Felipe de Neve and a tiny band of settlers set out from Mission San Gabriel and trek just 9 miles away to found Los Angeles.

1821

Mexican independence ends Spanish colonial dreams. Mexico inherits 21 Catholic missions in various states of disrepair, but quickly reorganizes Alta California into ranchos (land grants).

1826–32

Teenage Kit Carson helps blaze the Santa Fe Trail, which eventually leads to Los Angeles through 900 miles of rattlesnake-filled high desert and plains guarded by Native American tribes.

1848

After winning the Mexican-American War and signing the Treaty of Guadalupe Hidalgo, the US takes control of Alta California, just as gold is discovered in the Sierra Nevada foothills.

Spain's Mission Impossible

The distance between each of California's Spanish colonial missions equaled a day's journey by horseback. Learn more about the missions' historical significance and cultural influence at www.missionscalifornia.com.

In the 18th century, as Russian ships came to California's coast in search of sea-otter pelts, and British trappers and explorers spread throughout the West, Spain finally grew worried that its claim to the territory might be challenged. Conveniently, the Catholic Church was anxious to start missionary work among the native peoples, so the Church and Spanish crown combined forces. For the glory of God and the tax coffers of Spain it was decided that Catholic missions protected by presidios would be built across California.

On July 1, 1769, a sorry lot of about 100 missionaries and soldiers, led by the Franciscan priest Junípero Serra and the military commander Gaspar de Portolá, limped ashore at San Diego Bay. They had just spent several weeks at sea sailing from Baja California; about half of their cohort had died en route and many of the survivors were sick or near death. It was an inauspicious beginning for Mission San Diego de Alcalá, the first in a chain of 21 Spanish missions in Alta California.

Ostensibly, the Spanish presidios' purpose was to defend the Catholic missions and deter foreign intruders. The idea was to have Native American converts live inside the missions, learn trade and agricultural skills, and ultimately establish pueblos, which would be like little Spanish towns. Or so the plan went.

But the presidios created more threats than they deterred, as the soldiers aroused local hostility by raiding and looting tribal camps and kidnapping and raping indigenous women. Not only were Spanish presidios in Alta California militarily weak, their weaknesses were well known to Russia and Britain, and they didn't much strengthen Spain's claims to California.

Don't-Miss Missions

- *San Juan Capistrano*
- *Santa Barbara*
- *La Purísima (Santa Barbara County)*
- *San Carlos Borroméo de Carmelo (Carmel-by-the-Sea)*
- *San Juan Bautista*

Ultimately, the mission period was a failure. The Spanish population remained small, the missions achieved little more than mere survival, foreign intruders were not effectively deterred and more Native Americans died than were converted. Several of California's original Spanish missions still stand today, though a few are in ruins – some toppled by earthquakes, others broken by forced secularization under Mexican rule.

From Mexico to Manifest Destiny

When Mexico gained independence from Spain in 1821, many in that new nation looked to California to satisfy their thirst for private land. By the mid-1830s all but one Spanish mission had been secularized, so that Mexican governors could dole out hundreds of free land grants, or ranchos. By law, half of the land grants were supposed to go to Native Californians who worked at the missions, but few actually received their entitlements.

1850

After debate about whether it would be a slaveholding or free state (Congress chooses the latter), California enters the Union. Its first constitution is written in both Spanish and English.

1869

A golden spike is nailed in Utah, completing the first transcontinental railroad linking California with the East Coast. Gold is uncovered outside San Diego, unleashing a mini mining frenzy.

1882

The US Chinese Exclusion Act suspends new immigration from China, denies citizenship to those already in the country and sanctions racially targeted laws that stay on the books until 1943.

1892

Oil is discovered by Edward Doheny in Downtown LA, near where Dodger Stadium stands today, sparking a major oil boom. Within a decade, LA's population doubles to over 100,000 people.

The new landowners, called rancheros or Californios, prospered by raising livestock for the profitable hide and tallow trade. Rancheros became the social, cultural and political elite of Alta California under Mexican rule. Meanwhile, American explorers, trappers, traders, whalers, settlers and other opportunists showed increasing interest in the territory, seizing on economic prospects that the rancheros largely ignored. Some Americans who started businesses here converted to Catholicism, married locals and successfully assimilated into ranchero society.

Impressed by California's untapped riches and hoping to fulfill the promise of Manifest Destiny (the USA's imperialist doctrine of extending its borders from coast to coast), President Andrew Jackson sent an emissary to offer the financially strapped Mexican government $500,000 for California in 1835. Though American settlers were by then showing up in Alta California by the hundreds, Jackson's emissary was tersely rejected. Soon, a political storm was brewing.

In 1836 Texas seceded from Mexico and declared itself an independent republic. When the US annexed Texas in 1845, Mexico broke off diplomatic relations and ordered all foreigners without proper papers to be deported from California. In turn, the US declared war on Mexico and began an invasion. US naval units quickly occupied every port on California's coast, including Monterey, then the capital of Alta California.

Militarily speaking, California remained a sideshow while the war was mostly fought in Mexico. The capture of Mexico City by US troops in September 1847 put an end to hostilities. By signing the Treaty of Guadalupe Hidalgo on February 2, 1848, the Mexican government ceded much of its northern territory (including Alta California) to the USA, just in time for California's gold rush to begin.

In 1873 German immigrant and San Francisco store owner Levi Strauss received a patent for his hard-wearing, riveted denim pants, originally designed for California's gold prospectors and – voilà! – American blue jeans were born.

Eureka! California's Gold Rush

Gold was discovered at Sutter's Creek, in California's Sierra Nevada foothills, on January 24, 1848. By the next year, surging rivers of wagon trains were creaking into California filled with miners, pioneers, savvy entrepreneurs, outlaws and prostitutes, all seeking their fortunes. In 1850, when California was fast tracked for admission as the 31st US state, the foreign population had ballooned from 15,000 to 93,000.

With each wave of new arrivals, profits dropped and gold was harder to find. When surface gold became scarce, miners picked, shoveled and dynamited through mountains. Hills were stripped bare, erosion wiped out vegetation, streams silted up and mercury washed down rivers all the way into San Francisco Bay. The city of San Francisco became a hotbed of gambling, prostitution, drink and chicanery, earning it the moniker of 'Barbary Coast,' an allusion to Africa's north coast where pirates preyed.

1906

A massive earthquake levels entire blocks of San Francisco in less than a minute, setting off fires that rage for three days. Survivors start rebuilding immediately.

1913

The Los Angeles Aqueduct, built under the direction of chief engineer William Mulholland, starts supplying a thirsty metropolis with water controversially taken from the eastern Sierra Nevada.

1934

A longshoremen's strike in San Francisco ends with dozens of labor activists shot or beaten by police. After mass funeral processions and a citywide strike, shipping magnates meet union demands.

1942

During WWII, Executive Order 9066 sends nearly 120,000 Japanese Americans to internment camps. The Japanese American Citizens League files lawsuits, providing legal support for the 1964 Civil Rights Act.

In the 1860s California vicariously experienced a second mining boom after the discovery of the Comstock silver lode in present-day Nevada. Exploiting this mother lode required deep-mining techniques, which in turn necessitated California's big-shouldered industrial companies, stocks, trading and speculation. In fact, San Francisco made more money speculating on silver than Nevada did mining it: grandiose mansions sprouted on Nob Hill, and California's new business tycoons became renowned for their unscrupulous audacity.

Riches from Railroads, Real Estate & Oil

Opening the floodgates to massive migration into the West in 1869, the transcontinental railroad shortened the trip from New York to San Francisco from two months to less than four days. Nouveau riche San Francisco became California's metropolitan center. Meanwhile, Southern California's parched climate, its distance from water resources and relatively small population made it less attractive to profit-minded railroad moguls, though wheeling and dealing finally resulted in a spur line to LA during the mid-1870s.

By that time, rampant speculation had raised land prices in California to levels no farmer or new immigrant could afford. The railroad brought in products that undersold goods made in California, while some 15,000 Chinese laborers – no longer needed for railroad construction work or mining – flooded the labor market, especially in San Francisco. A period of antiforeign discrimination and unrest ensued, which culminated in federal legislation banning Chinese immigration outright in 1882.

Top California History Books

California: A History (Kevin Starr)

Journey to the Sun (Gregory Orfalea)

City of Quartz (Mike Davis)

During the same period, agriculture diversified, with new crops – especially oranges – being grown in Southern California for markets on the East Coast and abroad. As California-grown oranges found their way onto New York grocery shelves, a hard-sell advertising campaign for the Golden State began. Folks back East heeded the self-interested advice of crusading magazine and newspaper editor Horace Greeley to 'Go West, young man!'

Sneakily, much of the land granted to railroads was flipped and sold in big lots to speculators who also acquired, with the help of corrupt politicians and bureaucrats, a majority of the farmland intended for new settlers. A major share of agricultural land was consolidated in the hands of a few city-based landlords, establishing the still-existing pattern of industrial 'agribusiness' (rather than small family farms) dependent on large-scale irrigation projects and cheap migrant farm labor.

LA had other natural resources waiting to be exploited, albeit hidden underground. In 1892 a flat-broke mining prospector and real-estate speculator named Edward Doheny dug a well near Downtown LA that would change Southern California forever. Inside of a year, Doheny's well

1943
Tension between Americans and Mexicans reaches boiling point during the Zoot Suit Riots, which pit US military servicemen against zoot-suit-clad Mexican teens while LA police look on.

1955
In Anaheim, Disneyland opens to bad press, as crowds swarm the theme park, temperatures hit 101°F (38°C), ladies' high-heeled shoes sink into the still-soft asphalt and drinking fountains don't work.

1965
It takes 4000 National Guard troops to help quell the six-day Watts Riots in LA, which cause death, devastation and over $40 million in property damage. That same year, Rodney King is born.

1966
Ronald Reagan is elected governor of California, setting a career precedent for fading film stars. He served until 1975, then in 1981 became the 40th US President.

was producing 40 gallons of 'black gold' (oil) daily, and SoCal's oil industry was born.

Labor & Military Might

The Great Depression saw another wave of immigrants, this time of American farm families who were fleeing the Dust Bowl on the drought-stricken Great Plains. At the end of Route 66 in the promised land of California, they often found social discrimination and only scant pay and deplorable working conditions on company-owned farms, as fictionalized in John Steinbeck's harrowing Pulitzer Prize–winning novel *The Grapes of Wrath*. Outbreaks of social and labor protest led to the rapid growth of the Democratic Party in California, as well as growing trade unions for blue-collar workers.

Many of California's Depression-era public-works projects, which were sponsored by the federal government, have had lasting benefits for residents and tourists alike, including the restoration of historic Spanish missions and improvements to highways and public parks. But it was really California's cutting-edge aviation industry – pumped up by billions of dollars from federal military contracts – that helped boost the state out of the Great Depression.

California's workforce permanently changed during WWII, when women and African Americans were recruited for wartime industries and Mexican workers were brought in to fill agricultural labor shortages. After the Japanese bombed Pearl Harbor on December 7, 1941, San Diego became the headquarters of the entire US Pacific Fleet. Throughout WWII, as Southern California's aircraft manufacturing plants turned out planes by the thousands, San Francisco Bay Area workers (including women, nicknamed 'Rosie the Riveters') built hundreds of warships. Military contracts attracted top-notch engineers and scientists, who later launched California's high-tech industry.

After WWII many servicepeople decided to settle permanently on the West Coast. Within a decade after the war, California's population had grown by 40%, reaching 13 million. The state's military-industrial complex continued to prosper during the Cold War era, providing jobs in everything from avionics and missile manufacturing to nuclear-submarine maintenance. Military spending peaked in the 1980s under ex-California governor and then US president Ronald Reagan.

The classic film *Chinatown* (1974) is the fictionalized yet surprisingly realistic account of the brutal early 20th-century water wars that were waged to build Los Angeles.

Bohemians, Beats & Boomers

Unconstrained by the burden of traditions and promoted by film and TV, California has long been a leader in new attitudes and social movements. During the postwar boom of the 1950s, the Beat movement in San Francisco's North Beach railed against the banality and conformity

1968

Presidential candidate Robert Kennedy is assassinated at the Ambassador Hotel in LA by Palestinian immigrant and anti-Zionist Sirhan Sirhan, who remains in jail in San Diego County today.

1969

UCLA professor Len Kleinrock sends data from a computer in Los Angeles to another at Stanford University, typing just two characters before the system crashes. The internet is born.

1977

San Francisco Supervisor Harvey Milk becomes the first openly gay man elected to US public office. Milk sponsors a gay-rights bill before his 1978 murder by political opponent Dan White.

1992

Three of four white police officers charged with beating African American motorist Rodney King are acquitted by a predominantly white jury. Following the trial, Los Angeles endures six days of riots.

of suburban life, instead choosing bohemian coffeehouses for jazz, poetry and pot.

When the baby boomers came of age, many hippies took up where the Beat generation left off, heeding 1960s countercultural icon Timothy Leary's counsel to 'turn on, tune in, and drop out.' Sex, drugs and rock and roll ruled the day. With the foundations for social revolution already laid, protestors up and down California's coast marched against the Vietnam War and for civil rights in the late 1960s, then again for gay liberation starting in the '70s.

Since the 1980s, coastal California has become synonymous with a healthy lifestyle obsession, with more yoga classes and self-actualization workshops than you could shake a shaman's stick at. Remember that in-line skating, snowboarding and mountain biking started here first. Be careful what you scoff at: from pet rocks to soy burgers, California's flavor of the month is often next year's global trend.

High Tech Booms & Busts

In the 1950s Stanford University in Palo Alto needed to raise money to finance postwar growth, so it built an industrial park and leased space to high-tech companies like Hewlett-Packard, which formed the nucleus of Silicon Valley. When Hewlett-Packard introduced the first personal computer in 1968, advertisements breathlessly gushed that the 'light' (40lb) machine could 'take on roots of a fifth-degree polynomial, Bessel functions, elliptic integrals and regression analysis' – all for just $4900 (almost $35,000 today).

To read more about the garage-workshop culture of Silicon Valley go to www.folklore.org, which covers the crashes and personality clashes that made geek history.

Consumers didn't know quite what to do with computers, but in his 1969 Whole Earth Catalog, author (and former LSD tester for the CIA) Stewart Brand explained that the technology governments used to run countries could empower ordinary people. Hoping to bring computer power to the people, 21-year-old Steve Jobs and Steve Wozniak introduced the Apple II at the 1977 West Coast Computer Faire. Still, the question remained: what would ordinary people do with all that computing power?

By the mid-1990s an entire dot-com industry boomed in Silicon Valley with online start-ups, and suddenly people were getting everything – their mail, news, politics, pet food and, yes, sex – online. But when dot-com profits weren't forthcoming, venture-capital funding dried up and fortunes in stock options disappeared when the dot-com bubble burst and the Nasdaq Stock Market plummeted on March 10, 2000. Overnight, 26-year-old vice-presidents and Bay Area service-sector employees alike found themselves jobless. But as online users continued to look for useful information – and one another – in those billions of web pages, search engines and social media boomed.

1994

Orange County, one of the wealthiest municipalities in the US, declares bankruptcy after the county treasurer loses $1.7 billion investing in risky derivatives and pleads guilty to felony charges.

1994

The 6.7-magnitude Northridge earthquake strikes LA on January 17, killing 72 and causing $20 billion in property damage – one of the costliest natural disasters in US history.

2003

Republican Arnold Schwarzenegger (aka 'The Governator') is elected governor of California. Schwarzenegger breaks party ranks on environmental issues and wins re-election in 2007.

2004

Google's stock market launch raises a historic $1.9 billion at $85 per share. Since then share prices have increased over 1000% and the company's market value now exceeds $570 billion.

Meanwhile, California's biotech industry took off. In 1976 an upstart company called Genentech was founded in the San Francisco Bay Area, and quickly got to work cloning human insulin and introducing the Hepatitis B vaccine. In 2004 California voters approved a $3 billion bond measure for stem-cell research, and by 2008 California had become the USA's biggest funder of stem-cell research, as well as the focus of Nasdaq Stock Market's new Biotechnology Index.

Then came the unraveling of the US subprime mortgage-lending market, which triggered the stock-market crash of 2008 and mired the nation in a recession with massive unemployment. By 2010 California was so broke that Governor Jerry Brown (Democrat) was forced to make massive cuts to social services, education and state-parks funding. It took several years for the state's economy to start making a real recovery, complicated by other problems like long-term unemployment and a worrying number of years of severe drought.

But don't worry: California has always been a comeback kid. Just you wait and see.

2005

Antonio Villaraigosa elected mayor of LA, the first Latino to hold that office since 1872. Born poor in East LA, he says in his victory speech, 'I will never forget where I came from.'

2008

A slim majority of California voters pass Proposition 8, defining legal marriage as between a man and a woman. Courts eventually rule the law unconstitutional, and same-sex marriages resume in 2013.

2013

After years of construction delays and engineering controversies, the eastern span of the San Francisco–Oakland Bay Bridge opens. At $6.4 billion, it's the costliest public-works project in California history.

2016

A majority of California voters pass Proposition 64, legalizing the recreational use of marijuana statewide for ages 21 and up – and simultaneously impose a 15% tax on retail cannabis sales.

The Way of Life

In the coastal California dream world, you wake up, have a shot of wheatgrass juice, and roll down to the beach where the surf's up. Lifeguards wave as they go jogging by in bikinis and Speedos. You skateboard down the boardwalk to yoga class, where everyone admires your downward dog. Afterward, a food truck pulls up with your favorite: *kalbi* (Korean barbecue short-rib) tacos. But wait a sec, can anyone actually make those California dreams come true here?

Living the Dream

SoCal inventions include the space shuttle, Mickey Mouse, whitening toothpaste, the hula hoop (or at least its trademark), Barbie, skateboard and surfboard technology, the Cobb salad and the fortune cookie.

Let's keep dreaming. Napping on the beach afterward, you awake to find a casting agent hovering over you, blocking your sunlight, imploring you to star in a movie based on a best-selling comic book. You say you'll have your lawyer look over the papers, and by your lawyer you mean your roommate who plays one on TV. The conversation is cut short when you get a text to meet up with some friends at a bar.

That casting agent was a stress case – she wanted an answer in, like, a month – so you swing by your medical-marijuana dispensary and a tattoo parlor to get 'Peace' inscribed on your bicep as a reminder to yourself to stay chill. At the bar, you're called onstage to play a set with the band, and afterward you complain to the drummer about how the casting agent harshed your mellow. She recommends a Wine Country getaway, but you're already doing that Big Sur primal-scream chakra-cleansing retreat this weekend.

You head back to your beach house to update your status on your social-networking profile, simultaneously alerting your 10,000 Twitter followers to the major events of the day: 'Killer taco, solid downward dog, peace tattoo, movie offer.' Then you repeat your nightly self-affirmations: 'I am a child of the universe...I am blessed, or at least not a New Yorker...om.'

According to a 2008 Cambridge University study, creativity, imagination, intellectualism and mellowness are all defining personality characteristics of Californians compared with inhabitants of other states. (New Yorkers were found to be 'neurotic' and 'unfriendly.')

Stereotypes Versus Reality

Now for the reality check. Any Northern Californian hearing your California dream is bound to get huffy. What, political protests and open-source software inventions don't factor in your dreams? But Southern Californians will also roll their eyes at the silicone-and-spray-tan stereotypes: they didn't create CalTech's Jet Propulsion Lab and almost half the world's movies by slacking off.

Still, there is some truth to your California dreamscape. Nearly 70% of Californians live near the coast rather than inland, even though the beaches aren't always sunny or swimmable (the odds of that increase the further south you go, thus SoCal's inescapable associations with surf, sun and prime-time TV soaps and reality shows). And there's truth in at least one other outdoorsy stereotype: over 60% of Californians admit to having hugged a tree.

Regional Identity

Feel free to believe everything you've ever heard about Californians, just so long as you realize the stereotypes are exaggerated. Sure, tweens snap chewing gum in the shopping malls of the San Fernando Valley north of LA, blond surfers shout 'Dude!' across San Diego beaches, hippies gather for drum circles in San Francisco's Golden Gate Park, and tree huggers toke on joints in the North Coast woods but, all in all, it's hard to peg the coastal population.

California Babylon: A Guide to Sites of Scandal, Mayhem and Celluloid in the Golden State (2000), by Kristan Lawson and Anneli Rufus, is a guilty-pleasure guide to infamous and bizarre locations throughout the state.

San Francisco & the North Coast

In the San Francisco Bay Area, the politics tend to be liberal and the people open-minded, with a strong live-and-let-live ethic and devotion to the Great Outdoors. In overwhelmingly white and wealthy Marin County, civic pride sometimes borders on narcissism. San Francisco is more of a melting pot, but there aren't a lot of lower-income citizens since rents have risen sky-high with the invasion of high-salaried techies. The East Bay, especially Oakland and Berkeley, and San Jose to the south are more ethnically diverse.

Woodsy types live further up the North Coast – think beards and buffalo-plaid flannel. There aren't a lot of people way up there, and there's not a lot of money floating around either (apart from marijuana growers). Conservative radio stations shout on several frequencies, but at the other end of the political spectrum, some of the state's most progressive liberals and borderline eco-fanatics live way up north. If you spot a beat-up old Volvo chugging along the highway, chances are it's running on biodiesel, probably oil recycled from fast-food restaurants.

Central Coast

With smaller pockets of population, the hard-to-classify Central Coast starts south of San Francisco near wacky, left-of-center Santa Cruz and stretches all the way down to posh, progressively liberal Santa Barbara. Along the way, coastal Hwy 1 winds past working-class Monterey, made famous by John Steinbeck's novels; the bohemian Big Sur coast, where beatnik artists, hippies and back-to-landers stake their claims; the quaint 'villages' of Carmel-by-the-Sea and Cambria, where the 'newly wed and nearly dead' own multi-million-dollar homes; and the laid-back, liberal college town of San Luis Obispo, over halfway from San Francisco to LA.

Wherever you go along the Central Coast, you'll run into people who care passionately about environmental conservation and enthusiastically support local farmers, ranchers, winemakers and craft brewers.

Mike Davis' *City of Quartz* (1990) is an excoriating history of LA and a glimpse into its possible future. Davis and collaborators examine San Diego's underbelly in *Under the Perfect Sun: The San Diego Tourists Never See* (2003).

Los Angeles & Central California

Southern California is America at its extremes, with all the good and bad that this entails. Its people are among the nation's richest and poorest, most established and newest arrivals, most refined and roughest, most erudite and most airheaded. What binds them together isn't a shared ethnicity or language, but choosing to be Californian.

Composed of dozens of independent cities, LA is California's most cosmopolitan and racially diverse metro area. Although explosive race-related incidents have received high-profile exposure, as with the riots of 1965 and again in 1992, day-to-day civility between races is the norm. Tensions just as likely reflect the disparity between haves and have-nots, for example between Beverly Hills mansions and the impoverished inner city of South Central.

Orange County, where beautifully bronzed, buff bodies soak up rays, stretches between LA and San Diego. But make no mistake: it's no beach bums' paradise. Until recent waves of immigration tipped the scales toward liberal voters, the politics 'behind the Orange Curtain' were

THE WAY CALIFORNIANS TALK: IT'S COMPLICATED

Political correctness thrives along the coast. In fact, most people are so determined to get along that it can be hard to find out what somebody really thinks. This increases the further south you go, reaching its Zen-like zenith of 'niceness' in San Diego.

Self-help jargon has thoroughly infiltrated the daily language of coastal Californians. For example, the word 'issue' is constantly bandied about. Generally this is a way to refer to someone else's problems without implying that the person has...well, problems.

The mantra 'Can we all just get along?' flies out the window on busy freeways (almost always called by number, not name, and preceded by 'the' – as in, 'I'm taking the 101 to LA.') Expect to encounter unpredictable drivers with road rage who won't hesitate to cut you off, then flip you the 'bird.'

If someone you just met says, 'Let's get together sometime,' in most parts of the world that means, 'Call me.' Not in California, where it probably means, 'It's been nice talking to you, and now I have to go.' Often the other person never calls and, if you do, you may never hear back. Don't take it too personally.

overwhelmingly conservative. Republicans were welcomed with open arms at $2000-a-plate fundraising dinners, and many people still live in exclusive gated communities that have limited tolerance for outsiders. This conservative sociopolitical trend extends south to San Diego, which also has a sizable US military population.

Lifestyle

Few Californians can afford to spend their entire day tanning, sipping lattes and doing yoga, what with UVA/UVB rays, the rent and gas prices to consider. Most Californians effectively live in their car, commuting an average of nearly 30 minutes each way to work and spending almost $1 out of every $10 earned on car-related expenses. But they have zoomed ahead of the national energy-use curve in their smog-checked cars, buying more hybrid and fuel-efficient vehicles than any other state.

Few coastal Californians could afford a beach dream-home, and most rent rather than own on a median annual household income of $61,800. All of the top 10 most expensive US housing markets are in California, and in the two most expensive areas, Saratoga (near Silicon Valley) and Newport Beach, the average house costs over $2 million. Almost half of all Californians reside in cities, but most of the other half live in the suburbs, where the cost of living is just as high, if not higher.

Even so, coastal Californian cities (especially San Francisco and San Diego) consistently top national quality-of-life indexes. Self-help, fitness and body modification are major industries, successfully marketed since the 1970s as 'lite' versions of religious experience – all the agony and ecstasy of the major religious brands, without all those heavy commandments. Exercise and fresh food help keep Californians among the fittest in the nation. Yet over 750,000 Californians are apparently ill enough to merit prescriptions for medical marijuana. Dispensaries have proliferated up and down the coast, now outnumbering Starbucks coffee shops in some places. That trend will only grow bigger, now that California voters legalized recreational marijuana use in 2016.

Homelessness is not part of the California dream, but it's a reality for at least 114,000 Californians, representing 20% of the total US homeless population. The demographic of homeless people is varied, but the largest contingent of homeless Californians are US military veterans – estimated at more than 15,000 people. What's more, in the 1970s mental-health programs were cut, and state-funded drug-treatment programs were dropped in the 1980s, leaving many Californians with mental illnesses and substance-use problems no place to go.

Also standing in line at homeless shelters are the working poor, unable to afford to rent even a small apartment on minimum-wage salaries. Rather than addressing the underlying causes of homelessness, some California cities have criminalized loitering, panhandling, even sitting on sidewalks. More than three out of every 1000 Californians already sit in the state's notoriously overcrowded jails, the majority for drug-related crimes.

Population

If you are the average Californian, statistically you're likely to be Latina, aged about 35, living in densely populated LA, Orange or San Diego County, and speak more than one language. There's a one in four chance you were born outside the US, and if you were born in the US, the odds are almost 50/50 that you moved here recently from another state.

Immigration

With almost 39 million residents, California is the most populous US state: one in every nine Americans lives here. It's also one of the fastest-growing states, with three of America's 10 biggest cities (Los Angeles, San Diego and San Jose) and over 300,000 newcomers every year. You still don't believe it's crowded here? California's population density is 239 people per sq mile – almost triple the national average.

One of every four immigrants to the US lands in California, with the largest segment coming from Mexico. Most legal immigrants are sponsored by family members who already live here. In addition, an estimated two million or more undocumented immigrants currently live in California. But this is not a radical new development: before California became a US state in 1850 it was a territory of Mexico and Spain, and historically most of the state's growth has come from immigration.

Multiculturalism

Many coastal Californians idealize their state as an open-minded, easygoing multicultural society that gives everyone a chance to live the American (or Californian) dream. No one should be expected to give up their cultural or personal identity just to become Californian: Chicano pride, Black Power, and gay pride all built political bases here.

While equal opportunity may be a shared goal, in practice it's very much a work in progress. Historically, California's Chinatowns, Japantowns and other immigrant enclaves were often created by segregationist sentiment, not by choice. Even racially integrated metro areas of coastal California can be quite segregated in terms of income, language, education and, perhaps most surprisingly (given the state's position as a high-tech industry leader in Silicon Valley), internet access.

California's Latino and Asian populations are steadily increasing. More than 30% of the US's Asian American population lives in California, and Latino residents became the state's majority ethnic group in 2014. Latino identity is deeply enmeshed in everyday life in California, from Tejano tunes and taco trucks to JLo and Spanish-language TV. Despite being just over 7% of the population and relatively late arrivals to California with the WWII shipping boom, African Americans have also shaped California's culture, from jazz and hip-hop to fashion, sports and beyond.

New & Old Religions

Religious tolerance is usually the rule. Although Californians are less churchgoing than the American mainstream, and one in four Californians professes no religion at all, it's one of the most religiously diverse states. More than a quarter of residents are Catholic, partly due to a large Latino population, while another third are Protestant. There are also almost four million Muslims and over seven million Hindus statewide, LA has one of the 10 biggest Jewish communities in the country, and California has the largest number of Buddhists anywhere outside of Asia.

Despite their proportionately small numbers, California's alternative religions and utopian communities dominate the popular imagination, from modern pagans to new-age healers. California made national headlines in the 1960s with gurus from India, in the 1970s with Jim Jones' Peoples Temple and Erhard Seminars Training (EST), and in the 1990s with Heaven's Gate UFO-millennialist cult in San Diego. The controversial Church of Scientology is still seeking acceptance with celebrity proponents from movie-star Tom Cruise to musician Beck.

California is also a stronghold of fundamentalist and evangelical Christian churches, which have proliferated for the last century, notably in SoCal. In 1924 the world's first broadcast preacher, Aimee Semple McPherson, opened her own radio station to spread the word from LA's Angelus Temple, home of the Foursquare Church, a Pentecostal Christian sect. She pioneered the way for other 20th-century radio and televangelists such as Rick Warren of Orange County's Saddleback Church and the Schuller family of the *Hour of Power* show, formerly broadcast from the Crystal Cathedral (now called Christ Cathedral) near Anaheim.

Sports

California has more professional sports teams than any other state. If you doubt that Californians get excited about sports, go ahead and just try to find tickets before they sell out for an Oakland Raiders or San Diego Chargers football, San Francisco Giants or LA Dodgers baseball, LA Clippers basketball or LA Kings hockey game. You can score less-expensive tickets more easily for pro women's basketball in LA, pro hockey in Anaheim or San Jose, and pro soccer in LA or San Jose.

According to a recent study, Californians are less likely to be couch potatoes than other Americans. Nevertheless, when one of California's professional sports team plays another, the streets are deserted and all eyes glued to the tube. College sports rivalries, such as University of California (UC) Berkeley's Cal Bears versus Stanford University's Cardinals and the University of Southern California (USC) Trojans versus the UCLA Bruins, are equally fierce.

The roaring Grand Prix, a Formula 1 race, takes over the streets of Long Beach, just south of LA, every April. In San Diego County, Del Mar boasts the state's ritziest horse-racing track, while LA County's historic Santa Anita Park racetrack featured in the classic Marx Brothers movie *A Day at the Races* and the short-lived HBO series *Luck*.

Surfing first hit California in 1914, when Irish-Hawaiian surfer George Freeth gave demonstrations at Huntington Beach in Orange County. Today surfing is the coast's coolest spectator sport, with waves sometimes reaching 100ft at the annual Mavericks invitational competition near Half Moon Bay, south of San Francisco.

Extreme sports date back to the 1970s when skateboarders on LA's Santa Monica–Venice border honed their craft by breaking into dry swimming pools in the backyards of mansions, as chronicled in the 2005 film *Lords of Dogtown*. Extreme-sports deity Tony Hawk, a professional skateboarder and X Games champ, hails from San Diego County.

On Location: Film & TV

Try to imagine living in a world without Orson Welles whispering 'Rosebud,' Judy Garland clicking her heels three times or the Terminator threatening 'I'll be back.' Shakespeare claimed that 'all the world's a stage,' but in California it's actually more of a film or TV set. With dozens of TV shows and scores of movies shot here annually, every palm-lined boulevard or beach seems to come with its own IMDb resume.

It's a myth that most movie production took place in Hollywood, the social hub of 'the Industry.' Of the major motion-picture studios, only Paramount Pictures is in Hollywood proper, surrounded by block after block of production-related businesses, such as lighting and post-production. The high cost of filming has sent location scouts beyond LA's San Fernando Valley (where most movie and TV studios are found) and even north of the border to Canada. A few production companies are based in the San Francisco Bay Area, including Francis Ford Coppola's American Zoetrope, George Lucas' Industrial Light & Magic, and Pixar.

With increasing regularity, Hollywood films feature California as both a setting and a topic and, in some cases, almost as a character. LA especially loves to turn the camera on itself, often from a film-noir angle. Meanwhile, SoCal has become a versatile backdrop for edgy cable TV dramas and vapid reality-TV shows.

The Industry

You might know it as the TV and movie business, but to Southern Californians it's simply 'the Industry.' It all began in the humble orchards of Hollywoodland, a residential suburb of Los Angeles where entrepreneur-

CALIFORNIA ON CELLULOID

The Maltese Falcon (1941) John Huston directs Humphrey Bogart as Sam Spade, the classic San Francisco private eye.

Sunset Boulevard (1950) Billy Wilder's classic stars Gloria Swanson and William Holden in a bonfire of Hollywood vanities.

Vertigo (1958) The Golden Gate Bridge dazzles and dizzies in Alfred Hitchcock's noir thriller.

The Graduate (1967) Dustin Hoffman flees status-obsessed California suburbia to search for meaning, heading across the Bay Bridge to Berkeley (in the wrong direction).

Chinatown (1974) Roman Polanski's gripping version of the early-20th-century water wars that made and nearly broke LA.

Blade Runner (1982) Ridley Scott's sci-fi cyberpunk thriller projects a future LA of high-rise corporate fortresses and chaotic streets.

The Player (1992) Directed by Robert Altman and starring Tim Robbins, this satire on 'the Industry' features dozens of cameos by actors spoofing themselves.

The Big Lebowski (1998) Through myriad misadventures in the Coen brothers' zany LA farce, The Dude abides.

Milk (2008) Gus Van Sant directs Sean Penn in an Oscar-winning performance as Harvey Milk, the first openly gay man to hold a major US political office.

ial moviemakers established studios in the early 20th century. Within a few years, immigrants turned a humble orchard into Hollywood. In 1915 Polish immigrant Samuel Goldwyn joined with Cecil B DeMille to form Paramount Studios, while German-born Carl Laemmle opened nearby Universal Studios, selling lunch to curious guests to help underwrite his moving pictures. A few years later, a family of Polish immigrants arrived from Canada, and Jack Warner and his brothers soon set up a movie studio of their own.

With perpetually balmy weather and more than 315 days of sunshine a year, SoCal proved an ideal shooting location, and moviemaking flourished. In those early Wild West movie-making days, patent holders such as Thomas Edison sent agents to collect payments, or repossess movie equipment. Fledgling filmmakers saw them coming, and made runs for the Mexican border with their equipment. Palm Springs became a favorite weekend hideaway for Hollywood stars, partly because its distance from LA (just under 100 miles) was as far as they could travel under restrictive studio contracts.

Seemingly overnight, Hollywood studios made movie magic. Fans lined up for premieres in LA movie palaces for red-carpet glimpses of early silent-film stars such as Charlie Chaplin and Harold Lloyd. Moviegoers nationwide celebrated the first big Hollywood wedding in 1920, when swashbuckler Douglas Fairbanks married 'America's sweetheart' Mary Pickford. Years later, their divorce would be one of Hollywood's biggest scandals, but the United Artists studio they founded with Charlie Chaplin endures today. When the silent-movie era gave way to 'talkies' with the 1927 musical *The Jazz Singer*, the world hummed along.

Top California Film Festivals

AFI Fest (www.afi.com/afifest)

LA Film Fest (www.lafilmfest.com)

Frameline LGBT Film Fest (www.frameline.org)

Palm Springs International Film Festival (www.psfilmfest.org)

San Francisco International Film Festival (www.sffs.org)

Sonoma International Film Festival (www.sonomafilmfest.org)

Hollywood & Beyond

By the 1920s Hollywood became the industry's social and financial hub, but it's a myth that most movie production took place there. Most movies have long been shot elsewhere around LA, in Culver City (at MGM, now Sony Pictures), Studio City (at Universal Studios) and Burbank (at Warner Bros and later Disney).

Moviemaking hasn't been limited to LA, either. Founded in 1910, the American Film Manufacturing Company (aka Flying 'A' Studios) churned out box-office hits in San Diego and then Santa Barbara. Balboa Studios in Long Beach was another major silent-era dream factory. Both San Francisco and LA remain major hubs for independent filmmakers and documentarians.

But not every Californian you meet is in the Industry, even in Tinseltown. The Los Angeles Economic Development Council reports that only 1.6% of people living in LA County today are employed directly in film, TV

HOLLYWOOD'S GOLDEN YEARS

'The Industry,' as it's called, grew out of the humble orchards of Hollywoodland, a residential neighborhood of Los Angeles, where entrepreneurial moviemakers (including many European immigrants) established studios. Starting in 1913, Hollywood's first full-length feature, a silent Western drama called *The Squaw Man,* was shot by director Cecil B DeMille. The silent-movie era gave way to 'talkies' in 1927, the same year that Sid Grauman opened his landmark Chinese Theatre on Hollywood Blvd.

During the 1930s and '40s, American literary lions such as F Scott Fitzgerald, Dorothy Parker, Truman Capote, William Faulkner and Tennessee Williams did stints as Hollywood screenwriters. In the 1950s, during the anti-communist 'Red Scare' of the Cold War era, the federal government's House Un-American Activities Committee investigated and subsequently blacklisted many Hollywood actors, directors and screenwriters, some of whom left for self-imposed exile in Europe, never to return.

and radio production. The high cost of filming has sent location scouts far beyond LA's San Fernando Valley (where most of California's movie and TV studios are found) to Vancouver, Toronto and Montreal, where film production crews are welcomed with open arms (and sweet deals) to 'Hollywood North.' California recently passed a $330 tax credit to lure filmmakers back to Cali, and it seems to be working – more 2016 TV pilots were shot here than in any other location.

Still, for Hollywood dreamers and movie buffs, LA remains *the* place for a pilgrimage. You can tour major movie studios, be part of a live TV studio audience, line up alongside the red carpet for an awards ceremony, catch movie premieres at film festivals, wander the Hollywood Walk of Fame and discover what it's like to live, dine and party with the stars.

Director Alfred Hitchcock set some of his best thrillers in coastal California, including *Vertigo* (1958), with unforgettable shots of San Francisco's Golden Gate Bridge and Muir Woods, and *The Birds* (1963), set in Bodega Bay.

The Art of Animation

In 1923 a young cartoonist named Walt Disney arrived in LA, and within five years he had a hit called *Steamboat Willie* and a breakout star called Mickey Mouse. That film spawned the entire Disney empire, and dozens of other California animation studios have followed with films, TV programs and special effects. Among the most beloved are Warner Bros (Bugs Bunny et al in *Looney Tunes*), Hanna-Barbera (*The Flintstones, The Jetsons, Yogi Bear* and *Scooby-Doo*), DreamWorks *(Shrek, Madagascar, Kung-Fu Panda)* and Film Roman *(The Simpsons)*. Even if much of the hands-on work takes place overseas (in places such as South Korea), concept and supervision still takes place in LA and the San Francisco Bay Area.

In San Francisco, George Lucas' Industrial Light & Magic is made up of a team of high-tech wizards who produce computer-generated special effects for blockbuster series such as *Star Wars, Jurassic Park, Indiana Jones* and *Harry Potter*. Just across the San Francisco Bay, Pixar Animation Studios has produced an unbroken string of animated hits, including *Toy Story, Finding Dory, Inside Out, WALL-E, Cars* and *Brave*.

The Small Screen

After a year of tinkering, San Francisco inventor Philo Farnsworth transmitted the first television broadcast in 1927 of…a straight line. Giving viewers something actually interesting to watch would take a few more years. The first TV station began broadcasting in Los Angeles in 1931, beaming iconic images of California into living rooms across America and around the world with *Dragnet* (1950s), *The Beverly Hillbillies* (1960s), *The Brady Bunch* and *Charlie's Angels* (1970s), *LA Law* (1980s), and *Baywatch, Buffy the Vampire Slayer* and *The Fresh Prince of Bel-Air* (1990s). *Beverly Hills 90210* (1990s) made that LA zip code into a status symbol, while *The OC* (2000s) glamorized Orange County and *Silicon Valley* (2014–now) satirizes NorCal start-ups. Reality-TV fans will recognize Southern California locations from *Top Chef, Real Housewives of Orange County* and *Keeping Up with the Kardashians*.

A young cartoonist named Walt Disney arrived in LA in 1923, and five years later had his first breakout hit, *Steamboat Willie*, starring a mouse named Mickey, which eventually spawned the entire Disney empire.

A suburban San Francisco start-up changed the TV game in 2005, launching a streaming video on a platform called YouTube. With on-demand streaming services competing with cable channels to launch original series, we are entering a new golden age of television. Netflix Studios (in Silicon Valley and LA), Amazon Studios (Santa Monica) and Hulu Studios (Santa Monica) are churning out original series, feeding binge-watching cravings with futuristic dystopias such as *Stranger Things* and *The Handmaid's Tale*. Only time will tell if streaming services will also yield breakthrough Californian comedies to compare with Showtime's sharp-witted suburban pot-growing dramedy *Weeds* or HBO's *Curb Your Enthusiasm*, an insider satire of the industry featuring *Seinfeld* co-creator Larry David and Hollywood celebrities playing themselves.

Music & the Arts

Coastal California has long supported thriving music and arts scenes that aren't afraid to be completely independent, even outlandish at times. Californians themselves acknowledge that their music is eclectic, ranging from pitch-perfect opera to off-key punk. Meanwhile, critics have tried and failed to find any consistency in the styles and schools of art and architecture that have flourished here – but in the context of the most racially and ethnically diverse US state, that kind of infinite variety makes perfect sense.

Music

In your California dream, you're a DJ – so what kind of music do you play? Beach Boys covers, West Coast rap, bluegrass, original punk, classic soul, hard bop, heavy-metal riffs on opera? To please Californian crowds, try all of the above. To hear the world's most eclectic playlist, just walk down a city street in California.

Much of the traditional recording industry is based in LA, and SoCal's film and TV industries have produced many pop princesses and airbrushed boy bands. But NorCal DIY tech approach is launching YouTube artists daily, and encouraging Californians to make strange sounds in their garages with Moog machines and keytars. None of this would be possible without California's decades of innovation, musical oddities and wild dance parties.

An Eclectic Early Soundtrack

Wanna hear the next breakout indie band before they make it big? Tune into the *Morning Becomes Eclectic* show on Southern California's KCRW radio station (www.kcrw.com) for live in-studio performances and interviews with musicians.

Chronologically speaking, Mexican folk music arrived in California first, during the rancho era. The gold rush brought an influx of new arrivals, and rancheros had to belt to be heard over competing sounds of bluegrass, Chinese classical music and bawdy dancehall ragtime. But Italian opera arias became the breakout hits of early California, with divas paid fortunes in gold dust for encores.

By the turn of the 20th century, the city of San Francisco alone had 20 concert and opera halls before the 1906 earthquake literally brought down the houses. Performers converged on the shattered city for marathon free public performances that turned arias into anthems for the city's rebirth. San Francisco's War Memorial Opera House today is home to North America's second-largest opera company, after NYC's Metropolitan Opera.

Swing, Jazz, Blues & Soul

Swing was the next big thing to hit California. In the 1930s and '40s, big bands sparked a lindy-hopping craze in LA, and sailors on shore leave hit San Francisco's integrated underground jazz clubs.

California's African American community grew with the 'Great Migration' during the WWII shipping and manufacturing boom, and from this thriving scene emerged the West Coast blues sound. Texas-born bluesman T-Bone Walker worked in LA's Central Ave clubs before making hit records of his electric-guitar stylings for Capitol Records. Throughout the 1940s and '50s, West Coast blues was nurtured in San Francisco and

Oakland by guitarists such as Pee Wee Crayton and Oklahoma-born Lowell Fulson.

With Beat poets riffing over improvised bass lines and audiences finger-snapping their approval, the cool West Coast jazz of Chet Baker and Bay Area–born Dave Brubeck emerged from San Francisco's North Beach neighborhood in the 1950s. Meanwhile, in the African American cultural hub along LA's Central Ave, the hard bop of Charlie Parker and Charles Mingus kept SoCal's jazz scene alive and swinging.

In the 1950s and '60s, doo-wop, rhythm and blues, and soul music were all in steady rotation at nightclubs in South Central LA, considered the 'Harlem of the West.' Soulful singer Sam Cooke ran his own hit-making record label, attracting soul and gospel talent to LA.

Rockin' Out

The first homegrown rock-and-roll talent to make it big in the 1950s was Richie Valens, born in the San Fernando Valley, whose 'La Bamba' was a rockified version of a Mexican folk song. Dick Dale experimented with reverb effects in Orange County in the 1950s, becoming known as 'the King of the Surf Guitar.' He topped the charts with his band the Del-Tones in the early '60s, influencing everyone from the Beach Boys to Jimi Hendrix – you might recognize his recording of 'Miserlou' from the movie *Pulp Fiction*.

Guitar got psychedelic in 1960s California. When Joan Baez and Bob Dylan had their Northern California fling in the early 1960s, Dylan plugged in his guitar and pioneered folk rock. Janis Joplin and Big Brother & the Holding Company developed their own shambling musical stylings in San Francisco, splintering folk rock into psychedelia. Emerging from the same San Francisco Fillmore scene, Jefferson Airplane turned Lewis Carroll's children's classic *Alice's Adventures in Wonderland* into the psychedelic hit 'White Rabbit.' For many 1960s Fillmore headliners, the show ended too soon with drug overdoses – though for the original jam band, the Grateful Dead, the song remained the same until guitarist Jerry Garcia died in rehab in 1995.

On LA's famous Sunset Strip, LA bands were also blowing minds at the legendary Whisky a Go Go nightclub – especially the Byrds and the Doors, fronted by the legendary Jim Morrison. But the California sound also got down with iconic funk bands War from Long Beach, Tower of Power from Oakland, and San Francisco's Sly and the Family Stone.

The '70s music scene in LA was divided by zip codes and production values. High in the hills above the Sunset Strip was Laurel Canyon, where Joni Mitchell, David Crosby and Graham Nash held legendary jam sessions. Meanwhile down at Sunset Strip's seedy Tropicana Motel, local characters found their way into the bluesy storytelling of singer-songwriters Tom Waits and Rickie Lee Jones. Record labels produced arena bands to a high polish, creating the slick country-pop of the Eagles and Jackson Browne and finessing Mexican-American fusion with Linda Ronstadt and Santana. But in tiny clubs with battered guitars, a bunch of kids (Black Flag, The Germs, X) were making up songs and the LA punk scene as they went along.

In the 1950s, the hard-edged, honky-tonk Bakersfield Sound emerged inland in California's Central Valley, where Buck Owens and the Buckaroos and Merle Haggard performed their own twists on Nashville country hits for hard-drinkin' audiences of Dust Bowl migrants and cowboy ranchers.

Post-Punk to Pop

The 1980s saw the rise of such influential LA crossover bands as Bad Religion (punk) and Suicidal Tendencies (hardcore/thrash), while more mainstream all-female bands the Bangles and the Go-Gos, new wavers Oingo Boingo, and California rockers Jane's Addiction and Red Hot Chili Peppers took the world by storm. Hollywood's Guns N' Roses set the '80s standard for arena rock, while San Francisco's Metallica showed the world how to head bang with a vengeance. Avant-garde rocker Frank

Zappa earned a cult following and a rare hit with the 1982 single *Valley Girl*, in which his 14-year-old daughter Moon Unit taught the rest of America to say 'Omi*go*-o-od!' like an LA teenager.

By the 1990s California's alternative rock acts took the national stage, including songwriter Beck, political rockers Rage Against the Machine and Orange County's ska-rockers No Doubt, fronted by Gwen Stefani. Hailing from East LA, Los Lobos was king of the Chicano (Mexican American) bands, an honor that has since passed to Ozomatli.

Berkeley's 924 Gilman Street club revived punk in the '90s, launching the career of Grammy Award–winning Green Day. Riding the wave were Berkley ska-punk band Rancid, surf-punk Sublime from Long Beach, San Diego–based pop-punksters Blink 182, and Orange County's resident loudmouths, the Offspring.

Waiting for the Sun: A Rock & Roll History of Los Angeles, by Barney Hoskyns, follows the twists and turns of the SoCal music scene from the Beach Boys to Black Flag.

Rap & Hip-Hop

Since the 1980s, West Coast rap and hip-hop have spoken truth and hit the beat. When the NWA album *Straight Outta Compton* was released in 1989, it launched the careers of Eazy E, Ice Cube and Dr Dre, and established gangsta rap. Dre co-founded Death Row Records, which helped launched megawatt talents such as Long Beach bad boys Snoop Dogg, Warren G and the late Tupac Shakur. The son of a Black Panther leader who'd fallen on hard times, Tupac combined party songs and hard truths learned on Oakland streets until his untimely shooting in 1996 in a suspected East Coast/West Coast rap feud. Feuds also checkered the musical career of LA rapper Game, whose 2009 *R.E.D Album* brought together an all-star lineup of Diddy, Dr Dre, Snoop Dogg and more.

Throughout the 1980s and '90s, California maintained a grassroots hip-hop scene in Oakland and LA. Reacting against the increasing commercialization of hip-hop in the late 1990s, the Bay Area scene produced underground 'hyphy' (short for hyperactive) artists such as E-40. Political commentary and funk hooks have become signatures of East Bay groups Blackalicious, the Coup and Michael Franti & Spearhead.

Architecture

There's more to California than beach houses and boardwalks. Californians have adapted imported styles to the climate and available materials, building cool, adobe-inspired houses in San Diego and fog-resistant redwood-shingle houses in Mendocino. After a century and a half of Californians grafting on inspired influences and eccentric details as the mood strikes them, the element of the unexpected is everywhere: tiled Maya deco facades in Oakland, Shinto-inspired archways in LA, English thatched roofs in Carmel and chinoiserie streetlamps in San Francisco. California's architecture was postmodern before the word even existed.

Oddball Architecture

- *Hearst Castle, San Simeon*
- *Theme Building, LAX Airport*
- *Binoculars Building, Venice*
- *Tor House, Carmel-by-the-Sea*
- *Solvang, Santa Barbara Wine Country*
- *Winchester Mystery House, San Jose*

Spanish Missions & Victorian Queens

In the late 18th century, the first Spanish missions were built around courtyards, using materials that Native Californians and colonists found on hand: adobe, limestone and grass. Many missions crumbled into disrepair under Mexican rule in the early 19th century, but the style remained practical for the climate and many Californian settlers later adapted it into the rancho adobe style.

Once the Gold Rush got rolling, California's nouveau riche imported materials to construct grand mansions matching European fashions, and raised the stakes with ornamental excess. Many millionaires favored the gilded Queen Anne style. Outrageous examples of Victorian architecture, including 'painted ladies' and 'gingerbread' houses, are seen in San Francisco, Ferndale and Eureka.

Many turn-of-the-20th-century architects rejected frilly Victorian styles in favor of simpler, classical lines. Spanish Colonial Revival architecture, also known as Mission Revival style, hearkened back to early California missions with restrained and functional details: arched doors and windows, long covered porches, fountain courtyards, solid walls and red-tile roofs. Several SoCal train depots showcase this style, as do San Diego's Balboa Park and downtown Santa Barbara.

Arts & Crafts to Art Deco

Simplicity and harmony were hallmarks of California's early-20th-century arts-and-crafts style. Influenced by Japanese design principles and England's arts-and-crafts movement, its woodwork and handmade touches marked a deliberate departure from the Industrial Revolution's mechanization. Pasadena architects Charles and Henry Greene and the Bay Area's Bernard Maybeck and Julia Morgan popularized the versatile one-story bungalow, with overhanging eaves and sleeping porches.

Cosmopolitan California couldn't be limited to any one set of international influences. In the 1920s, the international art deco style took elements from the ancient world – Mayan glyphs, Egyptian pillars, Babylonian ziggurats – and flattened them into modern motifs to cap stark facades and outline skyscrapers, notably in LA and downtown Oakland. Later, streamline moderne kept decoration to a minimum and mimicked the aerodynamic look of ocean liners and airplanes.

In 1919 newspaper magnate William Randolph Hearst commissioned California's first licensed female architect, Julia Morgan, to build Hearst Castle. It would take her decades to finish.

Naked Modernism

Clothing-optional California has never been shy about showcasing its assets. Starting in the 1960s, California embraced the stripped-down, glass-wall aesthetics of the international style championed by Bauhaus architects Walter Gropius, Ludwig Mies van der Rohe and Le Corbusier.

In LA, Austrian-born Richard Schindler and Richard Neutra adapted this minimalist modern style to residential houses, with open floorplans and floor-to-ceiling windows perfectly suited to SoCal's see-and-be-seen culture. Neutra and Schindler were also influenced by Frank Lloyd Wright, who designed LA's not quite successful Hollyhock House in a style he dubbed 'California Romanza.'

Together with Charles and Ray Eames, Neutra contributed to the experimental Case Study Houses, several of which still jut out of the LA landscape and are used as filming locations for the likes of *LA Confidential*.

Postmodern Evolutions

True to its anti-establishment nature, California veered away from strict high modernism to add unlikely postmodern shapes to the local landscape. In 1997 Richard Meier made his mark on West LA with the Getty Center, a cresting white wave of a building on a sunburned hilltop. Canadian-born Frank Gehry relocated to Santa Monica, and his billowing, sculptural style for Downtown LA's Walt Disney Concert Hall winks cheekily at shipshape streamline moderne. Next door stands the Broad Museum, with its unusual honeycombed fiberglass facade, opened in 2015.

Into the 21st century, San Francisco has championed a brand of postmodernism by Pritzker Prize–winning architects that magnifies and mimics California's great outdoors, especially in Golden Gate Park. Swiss architects Herzog & de Meuron clad the de Young Museum in copper, which is slowly oxidizing green to match its park setting. Nearby, Renzo Piano literally raised the roof on sustainable design at the LEED platinum-certified California Academy of Sciences, capped by a living-roof garden.

Jim Heimann's *California Crazy and Beyond: Roadside Vernacular Architecture* is a romp through the zany, whimsical building-blocks world of California, where lemonade stands look like giant lemons and motels are shaped like tepees.

Visual Arts

The earliest European artists to capture California were trained cartographers accompanying Western explorers, although their images of California as an island show more imagination than scientific rigor. This mythologizing tendency continued throughout California's Gold Rush, as artists alternated between caricatures of Wild West debauchery and manifest-destiny propaganda urging pioneers to settle in the golden West. The completion of the transcontinental railroad in 1869 brought an influx of romantic painters, who created epic California wilderness landscapes. In the early 20th century, homegrown colonies of California impressionist plein air painters emerged at Laguna Beach and Carmel-by-the-Sea.

With the invention of photography, the improbable truth of California's landscape and its inhabitants was revealed. Pirkle Jones saw expressive potential in California landscape photography after WWII, while San Francisco–born Ansel Adams' sublime photographs had already started doing justice to Yosemite. Adams founded Group f/64 with Edward Weston from Carmel and Imogen Cunningham in San Francisco. Berkeley-based Dorothea Lange turned her unflinching lens on the plight of Californian migrant workers in the Great Depression and Japanese Americans forced to enter internment camps in WWII.

To find museums, art galleries, fine-art exhibition spaces and calendars of upcoming shows throughout SoCal, check out *ArtScene* (www.artscenecal.com) and *Artweek LA* (www.artweek.la) magazines.

As the postwar American West became crisscrossed with freeways and divided into planned communities, Californian painters captured the abstract forms of manufactured landscapes on canvas. In San Francisco, Richard Diebenkorn and David Park became leading proponents of Bay Area Figurative Art, while sculptor Richard Serra captured urban aesthetics in massive, rusting monoliths resembling ship prows and industrial Stonehenges. Pop artists captured SoCal's ethos of conspicuous consumerism through Wayne Thiebaud's still-life gumball machines, British émigré David Hockney's acrylic paintings and Ed Ruscha's canvas and film studies.

To see coastal California's contemporary art at its most experimental, browse the SoCal gallery scenes in Downtown LA and Culver City, then check out San Francisco's Mission District and SOMA neighborhood.

Latino Mural Movements in California

Beginning in the 1930s, when the federal Works Progress Administration sponsored schemes to uplift and beautify cities across the country, murals came to define California cityscapes. Mexican muralists Diego Rivera, David Alfaro Siqueiros and José Clemente Orozco sparked an outpouring of murals across LA that today number in the thousands. Rivera was also brought to San Francisco to paint murals at the San Francisco Art Institute, and his influence is reflected in the interior of San Francisco's Coit Tower and hundreds of murals across the Mission District. Murals gave voice to Chicano pride and protests over US Central American policies in the 1970s, notably in San Diego's Chicano Park, San Francisco's Balmy Alley and East LA murals by collectives such as East Los Streetscapers.

Theater

In your California dream you're discovered by a movie talent scout, but most Californian actors actually get their start in theater. Home to about 25% of the nation's professional actors, LA is the USA's second-most influential city for theater, after NYC. Meanwhile San Francisco has been a national hub for experimental theater since the 1960s.

Spaces to watch around LA include the Geffen Playhouse close to UCLA, the Ahmanson Theatre and Mark Taper Forum in Downtown

LA, and the Actors' Gang Theatre, co-founded by actor Tim Robbins. Small theaters flourish in West Hollywood (WeHo) and North Hollywood (NoHo), the West Coast's versions of off- and off-off-Broadway. Influential multicultural theaters include Little Tokyo's East West Players, while critically acclaimed outlying companies include the innovative Long Beach Opera and Orange County's South Coast Repertory in Costa Mesa.

San Francisco's priorities have been obvious since the great earthquake of 1906, when survivors were entertained in tents set up amid the smoldering ruins, and its famous theaters were rebuilt well before City Hall. Today SF is undergoing a performing-arts renaissance, against the long odds of rising rents and federal funding cuts. Tickets are affordable and programs sensational at historic theaters, and new venues are opening mid-Market, in the Tenderloin and in North Beach. Major productions destined for the lights of Broadway and London premiere at the American Conservatory Theater, and its new experimental venue, The Strand. The Magic Theatre gained a national reputation in the 1970s, when Sam Shepard was the theater's resident playwright, and it still premieres innovative California playwrights today. An audience-interactive troupe, We Players, stages classic plays, including Shakespearean dramas, at unusual locations such as Alcatraz. Across the Bay the Berkeley Repertory Theatre has launched acclaimed productions based on such unlikely subjects as the rise and fall of Jim Jones' Peoples Temple.

By the Book

Californians make up the largest market for books in the US, and read much more than the national average. Skewing the curve is bookish San Francisco, with more writers, playwrights and book purchases per capita than any other US city. The West Coast is a magnet for novelists, poets and storytellers, and California's multicultural literary community today is stronger than ever.

Early Voices of Social Realism

Feel the pulse of California's heartland in *Highway 99: A Literary Journey Through California's Central Valley*, edited by Oakland-based writer Stan Yogi. It's full of multicultural perspectives, from early European settlers to 20th-century Mexican and Asian immigrant farmers.

Arguably the most influential author to emerge from California was John Steinbeck, born in Salinas in 1902 in the heart of Central Valley farm country. He explored the lives and struggles of diverse California communities: Mexican American WWI vets adjusting to civilian life in *Tortilla Flat*, flat-broke wharf characters attempting to throw a party on *Cannery Row*, and migrant farm workers just trying to survive the Great Depression in his Pulitzer Prize–winning book *The Grapes of Wrath*. Acclaimed social realist Eugene O'Neill took his 1936 Nobel Prize money and transplanted himself near San Francisco, where he wrote the autobiographical play *Long Day's Journey into Night*.

Novelists took on the myth of California's self-made millionaires, exposing the tarnish on the Gold State. Classics in this vein include Upton Sinclair's *Oil!*, exposing the schemes of real-life LA oil-tycoon Edward Mahoney that resulted in the Teapot Dome bribery scandal. Aldous Huxley's *After Many a Summer* is based on the life of publisher William Randolph Hearst, the reclusive and vengeful media mogul who also inspired the Orson Welles' film *Citizen Kane*. When F Scott Fitzgerald moved to Hollywood to write scripts, he found the inspiration for his final novel, *The Last Tycoon*, the story of a 1930s movie producer slowly working himself to death.

California became synonymous with adventure through the talents of early chroniclers such as Mark Twain and Bret Harte. Professional hell-raiser Jack London was a wild child from the Oakland docks who traveled the world with little more than his wits and a canoe. He

READING CALIFORNIA

Central Coast *Selected Poetry of Robinson Jeffers* – In the looming, windswept pines surrounding his Tor House, Jeffers found inspiration for hauntingly beautiful poems.

Central Valley *Woman Warrior: Memoirs of a Girlhood Among Ghosts* (Maxine Hong Kingston) – A gripping tale of growing up Chinese American, and finding Californian identity.

Gold Country *Roughing It* (Mark Twain) – The master of sardonic wit tells of earthquakes, silver booms and busts, and getting by for a month on a dime in the Wild West.

Sierra Nevada *Riprap and Cold Mountain Poems* (Gary Snyder) – Influenced by Japanese and Chinese spirituality and classical literature, the Beat poet captures the meditative nature of open wilderness.

became the world's most successful adventurer and travel writer, sailing the seven seas, getting swept up in the Klondike gold rush, and dictating his adventures with an early recording device on his pioneering permaculture ranch in Sonoma.

Pulp Noir & Science Fiction

With mysterious fog and neon signs to set the mood, San Francisco and Los Angeles became crime-drama pulp-fiction capitals and the setting of choice for noir mystery movies. Dashiell Hammett *(The Maltese Falcon)* made a cynical San Francisco private eye into a modern antihero, while hard-boiled crime writer Raymond Chandler set the scene for murder and double-crossing dames in Santa Monica. The masterminds behind California's 1990s neo-noir crime fiction renaissance were James Ellroy *(LA Confidential)*, the late Elmore Leonard *(Get Shorty)* and Walter Mosley *(Devil in a Blue Dress)*, whose Easy Rawlins detective novels are set in South Central LA.

California technology has long inspired science fiction. Raised in Berkeley, Philip K Dick imagined dystopian futures, including a Los Angeles ruled by artificial intelligence in *Do Androids Dream of Electric Sheep?* It was adapted into the 1982 sci-fi movie classic *Blade Runner*. Dick's novel *The Man in the High Castle* presents the ultimate what-if scenario: imagine San Francisco circa 1962 if Japan, fascist Italy and Nazi Germany had won WWII. Berkeley-born Ursula K Le Guin *(The Left Hand of Darkness, A Wizard of Earthsea)* brings feminism to the genre of fantasy, imagining parallel realities where heroines confront forces of darkness.

Road-trip through California with local storytellers as your copilots in *My California: Journeys by Great Writers*. Proceeds from purchases via Angel City Press (www.angelcitypress.com) support the California Arts Council.

Social Movers & Shakers

After surviving WWII, the Beat Generation refused to fall in line with 1950s conformity, defying McCarthyism with poignant, poetic truths. San Francisco Beat scene luminaries included Jack Kerouac *(On the Road)*, Allen Ginsberg *(Howl)* and Lawrence Ferlinghetti, the Beats' patron publisher who co-founded City Lights Bookstore. Censors called *Howl* obscene, and Ferlinghetti was arrested for publishing it – but he won his trial in a landmark decision for free speech. Beat poets broke style rules and crossed genres, including poet-painter-playwright Kenneth Rexroth and Buddhist philosopher-poet Gary Snyder.

But no author has captured California culture with such unflinching clarity as Joan Didion, whose prose burns through the page like sun on a misty California morning. Her collection of literary nonfiction essays *Slouching Towards Bethlehem* captures 1960s flower power at the exact moment it blooms and wilts. Didion pioneered immersive first-person New Journalism with fellow '60s California chroniclers Hunter S Thompson *(Hells Angels: A Strange and Terrible Saga)* and Tom Wolfe *(The Electric Kool-Aid Acid Test)*.

In the 1970s, Charles Bukowski's semiautobiographical novel *Post Office* captured down-and-out Downtown LA, while Richard Vasquez' *Chicano* took a dramatic look at LA's Latino barrio. Armistead Maupin captured the rise of disco, cults, medical marijuana, feminism and gay pride in 1970s San Francisco as it happened in his serialized *Tales of the City*. Bret Easton Ellis followed the short lives and fast times of coked-up Beverly Hills teenagers in *Less Than Zero*, the definitive chronicle of '80s excess. Amy Tan's *The Joy Luck Club* weaves together the stories of four Chinese immigrants and their American-born daughters in a textured tale of aspiration and survival in San Francisco's Chinatown.

Each word Berkeley-based US Poet Laureate Robert Hass commits to the page in his Pulitzer Prize–winning *Time and Materials* is as essential and uplifting as a rivet in the Golden Gate Bridge.

Ever since the rise of California's underground comics in the '60s, no California bookshelf can be considered complete without graphic novels and 'zines. As you travel through California, you'll recognize characters straight out of local comics – arty, angsty teens from Daniel Clowes' *Ghostworld* and *Art School Confidential*, street-corner prophets from Wendy McNaughton's *Meanwhile in San Francisco*, and soul-searching techies from Paul Madonna's *Everything Is Its Own Reward*. To see what's on California's mind lately, pick up the latest copies of literary magazines *The Believer* and *McSweeney's*, founded by author Dave Eggers. You'll find them at his youth literary nonprofit 826 Valencia and its LA offshoot, the Time Travel Mart.

The Land & Wildlife

From misty redwood forests and rocky headlands to sunny beaches and arid canyons, coastal California is home to a bewildering variety of ecosystems. In fact, 30% of all plant and reptile species and almost half of all bird and mammal species that inhabit the USA are found in California, which boasts the highest biodiversity in North America. This is a land of record-breaking superlatives, including the planet's tallest trees.

Marine Mammals

Spend even one day along California's coast and you may spot pods of bottle-nosed dolphins and porpoises swimming and doing acrobatics in the ocean. Playful sea otters and harbor seals typically stick closer to shore, especially around public piers and protected bays. Since the 1989 earthquake, loudly barking sea lions have been piling up on San Francisco's Pier 39, much to the delight of ogling tourists. Other excellent places to see wild pinnipeds include Point Lobos State Natural Reserve south of Monterey, Point Reyes National Seashore in Marin County, and Channel Islands National Park, offshore from Ventura and Santa Barbara.

Once threatened by extinction, gray whales now migrate in growing numbers along California's coast between December and April. Adult whales live up to 60 years, are longer than a city bus and can weigh up to 40 tons, making quite a splash when they dive below or leap out of the water. Every year they travel from summertime feeding grounds in the arctic Bering Sea, down to southern breeding grounds off Baja California – and then all the way back up again, making a 10,000-mile round-trip.

If you can't tell a tufted sea lion from a whiskered harbor seal, pick up one of the excellent California Natural History Guides published by the University of California Press (www.californianaturalhistory.com).

Northern elephant seals have made a remarkable comeback along California's coast, after being hunted almost to extinction by the late 19th century for their oil-rich blubber. In winter the behemoth bulls engage in mock – and sometimes real – combat, all the while making odd guttural grunts, as their harems of female seals and young pups look on. Año Nuevo State Reserve, north of Santa Cruz, is a protected breeding ground, and there's a smaller rookery at Point Reyes, north of San Francisco. California's biggest colony of northern elephant seals hauls out by Point Piedras Blancas near Hearst Castle, south of Big Sur.

Land Mammals

California's most symbolic land animal – it graces the state flag – is the grizzly bear. Grizzlies once roamed California's beaches and grasslands in large numbers, eating everything from whale carcasses to acorns, but were extirpated in the 1920s after relentless hunting. All that remains now are the grizzlies' smaller cousins, black bears. Despite their name, their fur ranges in color from black to dark brown, cinnamon or even blond. These burly omnivores, who feed on berries, nuts, roots, grasses, insects, eggs, small mammals and fish, are rarely seen along the coast, preferring to live in mountainous forests further inland.

As foreign settlers moved into California in the 19th century, many other large mammals fared almost as poorly as grizzly bears. Immense herds of tule elk were hunted to near extinction by the 1860s. A small remnant herd of tule elk was moved to Point Reyes National Seashore in the 1970s, where the population has since rebounded. Much larger Roosevelt elk once ranged from San Francisco Bay all the way into Canada, but by the 1920s there were only 15 left. Today, species conservation efforts have increased the population to more than 1000 Roosevelt elk, protected by Redwood National and State Parks.

Peak mating season for northern elephant seals along the Pacific coast just happens to coincide with Valentine's Day (February 14).

Mountain lions (also called cougars) hunt throughout California, especially in woodsy areas teeming with deer. Solitary lions, which can grow 8ft in length and weigh 175lb, are formidable predators. A few attacks on humans have occurred, usually where human encroachment pushes hungry lions to their limits – for example, at the boundaries between wilderness and rapidly developing suburbs.

Birds & Butterflies

California lies on major migratory routes for over 350 species of bird, which either pass through the state or linger during winter. It's an essential stop on the migratory Pacific Flyway between Alaska and Mexico, and almost half of North America's bird species use the state's coastal and inland refuges for rest and refueling. Migration peaks during the wetter winter season, but you can spot an enormous variety of birds year-round at California's coastal beaches, estuaries, wetlands and bays.

Year-round avian residents along California's coast include gulls, grebes, terns, cormorants, sandpipers and little sanderlings that chase receding waves along the shore, looking for critters in the freshly turned sand. A few of California's beaches are closed between March and September to protect endangered western snowy plovers, who lay their eggs in exposed ground scrapes in the sand. Snowy plovers are easily frightened by humans, dogs and noisy off-highway vehicles (OHV), which can cause them to run off and abandon their eggs to burn in the sun.

As you drive along the Big Sur coast, look skyward to spot the largest flying bird in North America, the endangered California condor, which also soars over Pinnacles National Park and Los Padres National Forest. Keep an eye out for regal bald eagles, which have regained a foothold on the Channel Islands. The northern spotted owl, today a threatened species due to destructive logging practices, is protected inside Headwaters Forest Reserve near Eureka.

The Audubon Society's California chapter website (http://ca.audubon.org) offers helpful birding checklists, descriptions of key species statewide and a newsy blog (www.audublog.org).

Another iconic species that takes flight in coastal California, monarch butterflies are gorgeous orange creatures that follow amazing long-distance, multigenerational migration patterns in search of milkweed, their only source of food. Tens of thousands of monarchs hibernate in coastal California during winter, notably along the Central Coast at Santa Cruz, Pacific Grove, Pismo Beach and around Santa Barbara.

Trees & Flowers

Imagine how in centuries past almost all of California's coast, from the Oregon border south to Santa Cruz, was covered with stands of coast redwoods. Today less than 5% of these old-growth forests, whose complexity has been found by scientists to match that of tropical rainforests, remain. Officially the world's tallest trees, coast redwoods are those towering giants with spongy red bark, flat needles and olive-sized cones that rely on fog as their primary water source. On the damp forest floor beneath them, look for western sword ferns, redwood sorrel and velvety green mosses.

Other rare native tree species in coastal California include Monterey and Torrey pines, gnarled trees that have adapted to harsh coastal conditions such as high winds, sparse rainfall and sandy, stony soils. They too derive much of their water from the billowing coastal fog. Today, Torrey pines grow only at Torrey Pines State Natural Reserve near San Diego and in the Channel Islands, home to dozens more endemic plant species. On Catalina Island, you'll also find Catalina ironwood and mahogany trees.

California's myriad flowering plants are both flamboyant and subtle. Many species are so obscure or similar-looking that only a botanist could tell them apart. But in spring you end up with riotous carpets of wildflowers. Those famous 'golden hills' of California are actually the result of many plants drying up in preparation for the long, dry summer. Here plants have adapted to long periods of almost no rain by growing prolifically during California's mild wet winters, springing to life with the first rains in fall and blooming as early as February.

National & State Parks

Most Californians rank outdoor recreation as vital to their quality of life. Statewide, the amount of preserved land has steadily grown due to important pieces of legislation passed since the 1960s. The landmark 1976 California Coastal Act saved the coastline from further development, while the controversial 1994 California Desert Protection Act angered many ranchers, miners and off-roaders.

Today California State Parks (www.parks.ca.gov) protects nearly a third of the state's coastline, along with redwood forests, lakes, canyons, waterfalls, wildlife preserves and historical sites. In recent years federal and state budget shortfalls and politically motivated underfunding of California's parks have been responsible for park closures, reduced visitor services and

NATIVE WILDLIFE VS ALIEN INVADERS

Although the staggering numbers of land and sea animals, boundless virgin forests and wildflower fields that greeted California's early settlers are now mostly a thing of the past, it's still possible to see wildlife thriving along the coast in the right places and at the right times of year, from emerald hillsides blanketed by golden poppies to migratory gray whales. However, some of coastal California's endemic species of flora and fauna are but shadow populations today, hovering at the edge of survival, pushed up against the state's ever-burgeoning human population.

Once a biodiverse 'island' protected by the Pacific Ocean and the Sierra Nevada mountains, California has been overrun by alien species introduced by foreigners ever since the first Spanish colonists arrived in the late 18th century, right up through the gold rush era and post-WWII boom. Significantly altered and compromised habitats, both on land and water, have made this coast an easy target for invasive plants and animals, including highly aggressive species that damage both California's ecosystems and the economy.

In San Francisco Bay alone, one of the most important estuaries in the world, there are now over 230 alien species choking the aquatic ecosystem and in some areas they already comprise as much as 95% of the total biomass. Pushing out native flora all along the coast, ice plant – a ropy green ground cover with purple and white flowers that creeps over beach dunes and takes over headlands – originally came from South Africa. Volunteers all along the coast are kept busy pulling out invasive plants and restoring native flora.

During construction of California's 19th-century railways, fast-growing eucalyptus trees were imported from Australia to make railroad ties, but the wood proved poor and split when driven through with a stake. The trees now grow like weeds, fueling summertime wildfires with their flammable, explosive seed capsules. Even California's snails come from far away, brought here in the 1850s from France to produce escargot. Now they're everywhere, along with Atlantic crabs, which destroy native oyster beds.

Out of necessity but also by choice, California has become a leader in wildlife and ecosystem conservation. Monterey Bay National Marine Sanctuary (http://montereybay.noaa.gov) harbors one of the West Coast's deepest underwater canyons and protects hundreds of species of fish and over 30 species of marine mammal, including migratory whales. All along the coast, protecting and restoring native habitats, tagging and monitoring endangered wildlife, and captive-breeding-and-release programs are showing hopeful results.

increased park-entry and outdoor-recreation fees. This continually happens, even though it's in California's economic best interests to keep its parks in business, since revenues from recreational tourism consistently outpace competing 'natural resource extraction' industries such as mining.

Unfortunately, some of California's parks are being loved to death. Too many visitors stress the environment, and it's increasingly difficult to balance public access with conservation. At popular state beaches in Southern California during summer, it's almost impossible to find a parking space, let alone space on the sand. To avoid the biggest crowds and reduce your impact on parks, try to visit outside of peak season (usually summer) and take public transportation or cycle there.

In 2006 the world's tallest tree was discovered in a remote area of Redwood National Park (its location is kept secret to protect it). It's named Hyperion and stands a whopping 379ft tall.

Other natural areas of coastal California, including those managed by the National Park Service (www.nps.gov/state/CA), may go relatively untouched most of the year, which means you won't have to reserve permits, campsites or lodging many months in advance. Just inland from the coast, several national forests in California, managed by the US Forest Service (USFS; www.fs.usda.gov/r5), are less-trammeled areas worth exploring, including in Big Sur. National wildlife refuges (NWR), especially favored by bird-watchers, are run by the US Fish & Wildlife Service (USFWS; www.fws.gov/refuges). More remote wilderness tracts, including the Lost Coast, are overseen by the Bureau of Land Management (BLM; www.blm.gov/california).

Shake, Rattle & Roll

California is a complex geological landscape formed from fragments of rock and earth crust scraped together as the North American continent drifted westward over hundreds of millions of years. The crumpled Coast Ranges, the depressed Central Valley and the still-rising Sierra Nevada mountains all provide evidence of gigantic geological forces exerted as the continental and ocean plates crushed together.

Everything changed about 25 million years ago, when ocean plates stopped colliding and instead started sliding against each other. Today California sits on one of the world's major earthquake fault zones, at the dramatic meeting of two moving plates: the eastern edge of the Pacific Plate, made up of the Pacific Ocean floor and much of California's coastline, and the western edge of the continental North American Plate.

The primary boundary between these two plates is the massive San Andreas Fault, which runs for about 800 miles and has spawned numerous smaller faults that extend their treacherous fingers toward California's shoreline. Because this contact zone doesn't slide smoothly, but catches and slips irregularly, it rattles California with an ongoing succession of tremors and earthquakes.

California's Monster Quakes

In 1906 California's most famous earthquake measured 7.8 on the Richter scale and demolished San Francisco, leaving more than 3000 people dead. The Bay Area made headlines again in 1989 when the Loma Prieta earthquake (magnitude 7.1), which lasted just 15 seconds, caused a section of the Bay Bridge and I-880 in Oakland to collapse. Today, you can walk right up to the epicenter of the Loma Prieta quake in the Forest of Nisene Marks State Park, south of Santa Cruz.

Los Angeles' last 'big one' was in 1994, when the Northridge quake (magnitude 6.7) caused parts of the freeways and the scoreboard at Anaheim Stadium to fall down. With its epicenter in the San Fernando Valley, the Northridge quake's seismic waves were felt as far away as Las Vegas, NV. Dozens of deaths, thousands of injuries and estimated damages of up to $25 billion make it the most costly quake in California history.

Survival Guide

Directory A–Z

Accommodations

Coastal California has a wide range of accommodations, from campsites and hostels by the beach to motels, hotels and deluxe resorts. If you're planning on visiting during high season, the sooner you book the better – as far ahead as three to six months for a July visit.

➡ **B&Bs** Personable inns range from frilly Victorians to modern abodes.

➡ **Campgrounds** Budget-conscious travelers pitch tents along the coast.

➡ **Hostels** Cheap, but sparse outside of cities and bigger beach towns.

➡ **Hotels and resorts** Often offer amazing ocean views and extra amenities like swimming pools.

➡ **Motels** Handy for road-trippers and less expensive than hotels.

Amenities

➡ In Southern California, nearly all lodgings have air-conditioning, but in Northern California where it rarely gets hot, the opposite is true. In coastal areas as far south as Santa Barbara, only fans may be provided.

➡ Some accommodations offer online computer terminals for guests. A fee may apply (eg at full-service business centers inside hotels).

➡ There may be a fee for wireless internet, especially for in-room access. Look for free wi-fi hot spots in hotel public areas (eg lobby, poolside).

➡ Many lodgings are now exclusively nonsmoking. Where they still exist, smoking rooms are often left unrenovated and in undesirable locations. Expect a hefty 'cleaning fee' ($150 or more) if you light up in designated nonsmoking rooms.

Seasons & Reservations

➡ High season in coastal California runs from June to August.

➡ Demand and prices spike even higher around major holidays and for festivals, when some properties impose multiday minimum stays.

➡ Reservations are recommended for weekend and holiday travel year-round, and every day of the week during high season.

➡ Bargaining may be possible for walk-in guests without reservations at off-peak times.

Rates & Discounts

➡ Quoted rates typically do not include lodging taxes, which average more than 12%.

➡ Generally, midweek rates are lower except at city hotels geared toward business travelers, which lure leisure travelers with weekend deals.

➡ Discount membership cards (eg AAA, AARP) may get you 10% off standard rates at participating hotels and motels.

➡ Look for freebie ad magazines packed with hotel and motel discount coupons at gas stations, highway rest areas and tourist offices.

B&Bs

If you want an atmospheric alternative to impersonal motels and hotels, bed-and-breakfast inns might be for you. They often inhabit fine old Victorian houses or other heritage buildings, though some are more modern seaside inns. People who like privacy may find B&Bs too intimate.

Rates often include a cooked breakfast, but oc-

BOOK YOUR STAY ONLINE

For more accommodation reviews by Lonely Planet writers, check out http://lonelyplanet.com/hotels/. You'll find independent reviews, as well as recommendations on the best places to stay. Best of all, you can book online.

casionally breakfast is *not* provided (never mind what the name 'B&B' suggests). Amenities vary widely, but rooms with TV and telephone are the exception; the cheapest rooms share bathrooms.

Most B&Bs require advance reservations and don't accept drop-in guests; always call ahead. Smoking is generally prohibited and children are usually not welcome. Expect minimum-stay requirements, especially on weekends and in high season.

Standards are high at places certified by the California Association of Boutique & Breakfast Inns (www.cabbi.com).

Camping

In coastal California, camping is much more than just a cheap way to spend the night. The best campsites let you wake up on the beach or under a canopy of redwood trees. If you didn't bring your own tent, you can buy (and occasionally rent) camping gear at outdoor outfitters and sporting-goods shops in most cities and some towns.

Most public and private campgrounds in coastal areas are open year-round, including the following types:

Primitive campgrounds Usually campsites have fire pits, picnic tables and access to drinking water and vault toilets; most common in national forests (United States Forest Service) and on Bureau of Land Management (BLM) land.

Developed campgrounds Typically found in state and national parks, these offer more amenities, including flush toilets, BBQ grills and occasionally coin-operated hot showers.

Private campgrounds Catering mainly to RVers with full electricity and water hookups and dump stations; tent sites may be sparse and uninviting. Hot showers and coin-op laundry are usually available, and possibly wi-fi, a swimming pool and camping cabins too.

PRACTICALITIES

- **DVDs** Coded for region 1 (USA and Canada only).
- **Newspapers** *Los Angeles Times* (www.latimes.com), *San Francisco Chronicle* (www.sfchronicle.com), *Mercury News* (www.mercurynews.com), *San Diego Union-Tribune* (www.sandiegouniontribune.com).
- **Radio** National Public Radio (NPR), lower end of FM dial.
- **TV** PBS (public broadcasting); cable: CNN (news), ESPN (sports), HBO (movies), Weather Channel.

Walk-in (environmental) sites Providing more peace and privacy, and usually cheaper than drive-in campsites. A few state-park campgrounds reserve these sites for long-distance hikers and cyclists only.

CAMPGROUND RATES & RESERVATIONS

Many public and private campgrounds accept reservations for all or some of their sites, while a few are strictly first-come, first-served. Overnight fees range from $10 or less for the most primitive and remote campsites to $60 or more for developed oceanfront sites with recreational vehicle (RV) pull-throughs and full hookups.

Booking services can be used to search for campground locations and amenities, check current availability and make reservations (a fee of up to $10 may apply).

Recreation.gov To reserve a campsite or cabin on federal lands you must book through this service.

ReserveCalifornia.com Reservations for California state-park campgrounds and cabins that accept advance bookings, as well as East Bay regional parks and some private campgrounds.

Kampgrounds of America (KOA; ☎888-562-0000; www.koa.com) National chain of reliable but more expensive private campgrounds offering full facilities, including for RVs.

Hostels

Coastal California has 15 hostels affiliated with Hostelling International USA (www.hiusa.org). Dorms in HI hostels are typically gender-segregated and alcohol and smoking are prohibited. HI-USA membership cards ($28 per year) get you $3 off per night.

California also has dozens of independent hostels, particularly in coastal areas. They generally have more relaxed rules and often no curfew. Some hostels include a light breakfast in their rates, arrange local tours or offer pickups at transportation hubs. Facilities typically include mixed dorms, semiprivate rooms with shared bathrooms, communal kitchens, lockers, internet access and coin-operated laundry.

Some hostels say they accept only international travelers, basically to keep out homeless locals, but Americans who look like travelers (eg you're in possession of a plane ticket) may be admitted, especially during slow periods.

Dorm-bed rates average $25 to $60 per night, including tax. Reservations are always a good idea, especially in high season. Most hostels take reservations online or by phone. Online booking services may offer lower rates.

Hotels & Motels

- At midrange motels and hotels, expect clean, comfortable rooms with a private bathroom and such standard amenities as a cable TV, telephone, coffeemaker and perhaps a microwave and minifridge.

SLEEPING PRICE RANGES

The following price ranges refer to a private room with bathroom during high season, unless otherwise specified. Taxes and breakfast are not normally included in the price.

$ less than $100, $150 in San Francisco

$$ $100 to $250, $150 to $350 in San Francisco

$$$ more than $250, $350 in San Francisco

- Top-end hotels and resorts offer more amenities and perhaps a scenic location, high design or historical ambience. Pools, fitness rooms, business centers and full-service restaurants and bars are all standard.
- Rooms are often priced by the size and number of beds, rather than the number of occupants. A room with one double or queen-size bed usually costs the same for one or two people, while a room with a king-size bed or two double beds costs more.
- There is often a small surcharge for the third and fourth adult, but children under a certain age (this varies) may stay free. Cribs or rollaway cots usually incur an additional fee.
- Beware that suites or 'junior suites' may simply be oversized rooms; ask about the layout when booking.
- Recently renovated or larger rooms, or those with a view, are likely to cost more. Descriptors like 'oceanfront' and 'ocean view' are liberally used, and you may require a telescope to spot the surf.
- Rates may include breakfast, which could be just a stale doughnut and weak coffee, an all-you-can-eat hot and cold buffet, or anything in between.
- Some motels and hotels are now entirely smoke-free, meaning you're not allowed to smoke anywhere on the property, or even outdoors within a certain distance of entryways.

Customs Regulations

Currently, non-US citizens and permanent residents may import the following:

- 1L of alcohol (if you're over 21 years old)
- 200 cigarettes (one carton) or 100 cigars (if you're over 18 years old)
- $100 worth of gifts

Amounts higher than $10,000 cash, traveler's checks, money orders and other cash equivalents must be declared. Don't even think about bringing illegal drugs.

For more complete, up-to-date information, check with US Customs & Border Protection (www.cbp.gov).

Discount Cards

'America the Beautiful' Annual Pass (http://store.usgs.gov/pass; 12-month pass $80) Admits four adults and all children under 16 years for free to all national parks and federal recreational lands (eg USFS, BLM) for 12 months from the date of purchase. US citizens and permanent residents aged 62 years and older are eligible for a lifetime Senior Pass ($10), which grants free entry and 50% off some recreational-use fees such as camping.

American Association of Retired Persons (AARP; ☎888-687-2277; www.aarp.og) This advocacy group for Americans 50 years and older offers member discounts (usually 10%) on hotels, car rentals and more. Annual membership costs $16.

American Automobile Association (AAA; ☎800-922-8228; www.aaa.com) Members of AAA and its foreign affiliates (eg CAA, AA) enjoy small discounts (usually 10%) on Amtrak trains, car rentals, motels and hotels, chain restaurants and shopping, tours and theme parks. Annual membership from $56.

Go Los Angeles, San Diego and San Francisco Cards and San Francisco Explorer Pass (www.smartdestinations.com; 1-day pass adult/child from $65/49) The Go LA Card and pricier Go San Diego Card include admission to major SoCal theme parks (but not Disneyland). The cheaper Go San Francisco Card covers museums, bicycle rental and a bay cruise. You've got to do a lot of sightseeing over multiple days to make passes come close to paying off. Alternatively, the San Francisco Explorer Pass gives you 30 days to visit three to five attractions (excluding Alcatraz cruises and tours). For discounts, buy online.

International Student Identity, Youth Travel and Teacher Identity Cards (www.isic.org; 12-month card $25) Offers savings on airline fares, travel insurance and local attractions for full-time students (ISIC), for nonstudents 30 years of age or younger (IYTC) and for employed teachers (ITIC). Cards are issued online and by student unions, hosteling organizations and youth-oriented budget travel agencies.

Senior discounts People over the age of 65 (sometimes 50, 55, 60 or 62) often qualify for the same discounts as students; any ID showing your birth date should suffice as proof.

Southern California CityPass (www.citypass.com/southern-california; adult/child from $346/314) If you're visiting SoCal theme parks, CityPass covers three-day admission to Disneyland and Disney California Adventure and one-day admission each to Legoland California and SeaWorld San Diego, with add-ons available for the San Diego Zoo or San Diego Zoo Safari Park. Passes are valid for 14 days from the first day of use.

It's cheapest to buy them online in advance.

Student Advantage Card (📞877-256-4672; www.studentadvantage.com) For international and US students offers 15% savings on Amtrak trains and 10% on Greyhound buses, plus discounts of 10% to 25% on some motels and hotels, rental cars, ride-sharing services and shopping. A 12-month card costs $22.50.

Electricity

Type A
120V/60Hz

Etiquette

Californians are pretty casual by nature, but a few (unspoken) rules still apply.

Bargaining Haggling over the prices of goods usually isn't appropriate, except at outdoor markets and with sidewalk vendors.

Greetings Shaking hands with men and women when meeting for the first time may be a tad formal, but expected for business dealings and by some older adults.

Smoking Don't light up indoors (it's illegal) or anywhere else you don't see others doing it, unless you don't mind lots of dirty looks.

Food & Drink

➡ Lunch is generally served between 11:30am and 2pm, and dinner between 5pm and 9pm daily, though some restaurants stay open later, especially on Friday and Saturday nights.

➡ If breakfast is served, it's usually between 7:30am and 10am. Some diners and cafes keep serving breakfast into the afternoon, or all day. Weekend brunch is a laid-back affair, usually available from 10am until 3pm on Saturday and Sunday.

➡ Like all things Californian, restaurant etiquette tends to be informal. Only a handful of restaurants require more than a dressy shirt, slacks and a decent pair of shoes; most places require far less.

➡ Tipping 18% to 20% is expected anywhere you receive table service.

➡ Smoking is illegal indoors. Some restaurants have patios or sidewalk tables where smoking is tolerated (ask first, or look around for ashtrays), but don't expect your neighbors to be happy about secondhand smoke.

➡ You can bring your own wine to most restaurants; a 'corkage' fee of $15 to $30 usually applies. Lunches rarely include booze, though a glass of wine or beer, while not common everywhere, is socially acceptable.

➡ If you ask the kitchen to divide a plate between two (or more) people, there may be a small split-plate surcharge.

➡ Vegetarians, vegans and travelers with food allergies or other restrictions are in luck – many restaurants are used to catering to specific dietary needs.

EATING PRICE RANGES

The following price ranges refer to an average main course at dinner, unless otherwise stated. These prices don't include taxes or tip. Note the same dishes at lunch will usually be cheaper, even half-price.

$ less than $15

$$ $15 to $25

$$$ more than $25

Health

Healthcare & Insurance

Medical treatment in the USA is of the highest caliber, but the expense could kill you. Many health-care professionals demand payment at the time of service, especially from out-of-towners or international visitors.

Except in the case of medical emergencies (in which case call 📞911 or go to the nearest 24-hour hospital emergency room, or ER), phone around to find a doctor or a walk-in clinic or urgent-care center that will accept your insurance.

Keep all medical receipts and documentation for billing and insurance claims and reimbursement later.

Some health-insurance policies require you to get pre-authorization over the phone for medical treatment before seeking help.

Overseas visitors with travel-health-insurance policies may need to contact a call center for an assessment by phone before getting medical treatment.

Insurance

Getting travel insurance to cover theft, loss and medical problems is highly recommended. Some policies do not cover 'risky' activities such as scuba diving, motorcycling and skiing so read the fine print. Make sure the policy at least covers hospital stays and an emergency flight home.

Paying for your airline ticket or rental car with a credit card may provide limited travel accident insurance. If you already have private health insurance or a homeowners or renters policy, find out what those policies cover and only get supplemental insurance. If you have prepaid a large portion of your vacation, trip-cancellation insurance may be a worthwhile expense.

Worldwide travel insurance is available at www.lonelyplanet.com/travel-insurance. You can buy, extend and claim online anytime – even if you're already on the road.

Legal Matters

Drugs & Alcohol

➡ Possession of up to 1oz of marijuana (if you are 21 years or older) for recreational use is no longer a crime in California, but it is still illegal to use marijuana in public (subject to fines of up to $250, as well as mandatory community-service hours and drug-education classes).

➡ Possession of any other drug or more than an ounce of marijuana is a felony punishable by lengthy jail time. For foreigners, conviction of any drug offense is grounds for deportation.

➡ Police can give roadside sobriety checks to assess if you've been drinking or using drugs. If you fail, they'll require you to take a breath, urine or blood test to determine if your blood alcohol is over the legal limit (0.08%). Refusing to be tested is treated the same as if you had taken and failed the test.

➡ Penalties for driving under the influence (DUI) of drugs or alcohol range from license suspension and fines to jail time.

➡ It's illegal to carry open containers of alcohol inside a vehicle, even if they're empty. Unless they're full and still sealed, store them in the trunk.

➡ Consuming alcohol anywhere other than at a private residence or licensed premises is a no-no, which puts most parks and beaches off-limits (although many campgrounds legally allow it).

➡ Bars, clubs and liquor stores often ask for photo ID to prove you are of legal drinking age (21 years old). Being 'carded' is standard practice, so don't take it personally.

Police & Security

➡ For police, fire and ambulance emergencies, dial ☎911. For nonemergency police assistance, contact the nearest local police station (dial ☎411 for directory assistance).

➡ If you are stopped by the police, be courteous. Don't get out of the car unless asked. Keep your hands where the officer can see them (eg on the steering wheel) at all times.

➡ There is no system of paying fines on the spot. Attempting to pay the fine to the officer may lead to a charge of attempted bribery.

➡ For traffic violations the ticketing officer will explain the options to you. There is usually a 30-day period to pay a fine; most matters can be handled online or by mail.

➡ If you are arrested, you have the right to remain silent and are presumed innocent until proven guilty. Everyone has the right to make one phone call. Foreign travelers who don't have a lawyer, friends or family to help should call their embassy or consulate; the police can provide the number upon request.

➡ Due to security concerns about terrorism, never leave your bags unattended, especially not at airports, bus and train stations or on public transportation.

Smoking

➡ Smoking is generally prohibited inside all public buildings, including airports, shopping malls and train and bus stations.

➡ There is no smoking allowed inside restaurants, although lighting up may be tolerated at outdoor patio or sidewalk tables (ask first).

➡ At hotels, you must specifically request a smoking room, but note some properties are entirely nonsmoking by law.

➡ In some cities and towns, smoking outdoors within a certain distance of any public business is illegal.

LGBTQ Travelers

Coastal California is a magnet for LGBTQ travelers. Hot spots include San Francisco's Castro neighborhood; West Hollywood (WeHo), Silver Lake and Long Beach in LA; the Hillcrest area of San Diego; and Guerneville and Calistoga in Napa Valley.

Same-sex marriage is legal in California. Despite widespread tolerance, homophobic bigotry still exists. In some small towns, especially inland from the coast, tolerance often comes down to a 'don't ask, don't tell' policy.

Helpful Resources

Advocate (www.advocate.com/travel) Online news, gay travel features and destination guides.

Damron (www.damron.com) Classic, advertiser-driven gay travel guides and 'Gay Scout' mobile app.

LGBT National Hotline (☎888-843-4564; www.glbthotline.org) For counseling and referrals of any kind.

Out Traveler (www.outtraveler.com) Free online magazine articles with travel tips, destination guides and hotel reviews.

Purple Roofs (www.purpleroofs.com) Online directory of LGBTQ-friendly accommodations.

Money

➡ California state sales tax (7.5%) is added to the retail price of most goods and services (gasoline and groceries are exceptions). Local and city sales taxes may tack on up to 2.5%.

➡ Tourist lodging taxes vary statewide, but currently average 10.5% to 15.5% in major cities.

➡ No refunds of sales or lodging taxes are available for visitors.

➡ Most ATMs are connected to international networks and offer decent foreign-exchange rates. Expect a minimum surcharge of around $3 per transaction, plus any fees charged by your home bank.

➡ Exchange cash and traveler's checks (the latter have fallen out of use) at major airports, big-city banks and currency-exchange offices such as American Express (www.americanexpress.com) or Travelex (www.travelex.com).

➡ Outside major cities, exchanging money may be a problem, so make sure you have a credit card and sufficient cash. Some businesses refuse to accept bills over $20.

➡ Visa, MasterCard and American Express are the most widely accepted credit cards.

Opening Hours

Businesses, restaurants and shops may close earlier and on additional days during the winter off-season (November to March). Otherwise, standard opening hours are as follows:

Banks 9am–6pm Monday to Friday, some 9am–1pm or later Saturday

Bars 5pm–2am

Business hours (general) 9am–5pm Monday to Friday

Nightclubs 10pm–4am Thursday to Saturday

Post offices 8:30am–5pm Monday to Friday, some 8:30am–noon or later Saturday

Restaurants 7:30am–10am, 11:30am–2pm and 5pm–9pm, some open later Friday and Saturday

Shops 10am–6pm Monday to Saturday, noon–5pm Sunday (malls open later)

Supermarkets 8am–9pm or 10pm, some 24 hours

Public Holidays

On the following national holidays, banks, schools and government offices (including post offices) are closed, and transportation, museums and other services operate on a Sunday schedule. Holidays falling on a weekend are usually observed the following Monday.

New Year's Day January 1

Martin Luther King Jr Day Third Monday in January

Presidents' Day Third Monday in February

Good Friday Friday before Easter in March/April

Memorial Day Last Monday in May

Independence Day July 4

Labor Day First Monday in September

Columbus Day Second Monday in October

Veterans Day November 11

Thanksgiving Day Fourth Thursday in November

Christmas Day December 25

School Holidays

➡ Schools take a one- or two-week 'spring break' around Easter, sometime in March or April. Some hotels and resorts, especially at beaches and near SoCal's theme parks, raise their rates during this time.

➡ School summer vacations run from mid-June until mid-August, making July and August the busiest travel months.

TIPPING

Tipping is *not* optional. Only withhold tips in cases of outrageously bad service.

Airport skycaps & hotel bellhops	$2 to $3 per bag, minimum per cart $5
Bartenders	15% to 20% per round, minimum $1 per drink
Concierges	Nothing for providing simple information, up to $20 for securing last-minute restaurant reservations, sold-out show tickets etc
Housekeepers	$2 to $4 daily, left under the card provided; more if you're messy
Parking valets	At least $2 when handed back your car keys
Restaurant servers & room service	18% to 20%, unless a gratuity is already charged (common for groups of six or more)
Taxi drivers	10% to 15% of metered fare, rounded up to the next dollar

Safe Travel

Despite its seemingly apocalyptic list of dangers – guns, violent crime, riots, earthquakes – California is a reasonably safe place to visit. The greatest danger is posed by car accidents (buckle up – it's the law), while the biggest annoyances are metro-area traffic and crowds. Wildlife poses some small threats, and of course there is the dramatic, albeit unlikely, possibility of a natural disaster. Never feed or approach any wild animals, no matter how harmless they may look.

Telephone

➡ US phone numbers consist of a three-digit area code followed by a seven-digit local number.

➡ When dialing a number within the same area code, only use the seven-digit number (if that doesn't work, try all 10 digits).

➡ For long-distance calls, dial ☎1 plus the area code plus the local number.

➡ Toll-free numbers (eg beginning with ☎800, ☎855, ☎866, ☎877 or ☎888) must be preceded by ☎1.

➡ For direct international calls, dial ☎011 plus the country code plus the area code (usually without the initial '0') plus the local phone number.

➡ If you're calling from abroad, the country code for the US is ☎1 (the same as Canada, but international rates apply between the two countries).

Cell Phones

➡ You'll need a multiband GSM phone in order to make calls in the USA. Popping in a US prepaid rechargeable SIM card is usually cheaper than using your own network.

➡ SIM cards are sold at telecommunications and electronics stores, which also sell inexpensive prepaid phones, including some airtime.

➡ You can rent a cell phone at San Francisco (SFO) International Airport from TripTel (www.triptel.com); pricing plans vary, but typically are expensive.

Pay Phones & Phonecards

➡ Where pay phones still exist, they're usually coin-operated, though some may only accept credit cards (eg in state or national parks). Local calls cost 50¢ minimum.

➡ For long-distance and international calls, prepaid phonecards are sold at convenience stores, supermarkets, newsstands and electronics and convenience stores.

Tourist Information

For pretrip planning, peruse the information-packed website of the **California Travel & Tourism Commission** (Visit California; ☎877-225-4367, 916-444-4429; www.visitcalifornia.com).

The same government agency operates more than a dozen statewide California Welcome Centers (www.visitcwc.com), where staff dispense maps and brochures and may be able to help find accommodations.

Almost every coastal city and town has a local visitor center or a chamber of commerce where you can pick up maps, brochures and information.

Travelers with Disabilities

More populated areas of coastal California are reasonably well-equipped for travelers with disabilities, but facilities in smaller towns and rural areas may be limited.

Download Lonely Planet's free Accessible Travel guide from http://lptravel.to/AccessibleTravel.

Accessibility

➡ Most traffic intersections have dropped curbs and sometimes audible crossing signals.

➡ The Americans with Disabilities Act (ADA) requires public buildings built after 1993 to be wheelchair-accessible, including restrooms.

➡ Motels and hotels built after 1993 must have at least one ADA-compliant accessible room; state your specific needs when making reservations.

➡ For nonpublic buildings built prior to 1993, including hotels, restaurants, museums and theaters, there are no accessibility guarantees; call ahead to find out what to expect.

➡ Most national and many state parks and some other outdoor recreation areas offer paved or boardwalk nature trails that are graded and accessible by wheelchairs.

➡ Many theme parks go out of their way to be accessible to wheelchairs and guests with mobility limitations and other disabilities.

➡ California State Parks' disabled discount pass ($3.50) entitles those with permanent disabilities to 50% off day-use parking and camping fees; for an application, click to www.parks.ca.gov.

Transportation

For wheelchair-accessible van rentals, try **Wheelchair Getaways** (☎800-642-2042; www.wheelchairgetaways.com) or **Mobility Works** (☎877-275-4915; www.mobilityworks.com) in LA and the San Francisco Bay Area.

➡ All major airlines, Greyhound buses and Amtrak trains can

accommodate travelers with disabilities, usually with 48 hours advance notice required.Major car-rental agencies offer hand-controlled vehicles and vans with wheelchair lifts at no extra charge, but you must reserve these well in advance.

➡ Local buses, trains and subway lines usually have wheelchair lifts.

➡ Seeing-eye dogs can accompany passengers on public transportation.

➡ Taxi companies have at least one wheelchair-accessible van, but you'll usually need to call for one and then wait for one.

Helpful Resources

A Wheelchair Rider's Guide to the California Coast (www.wheelingcalscoast.org) Free accessibility information covering beaches, parks and trails, plus downloadable PDF guides to the San Francisco Bay Area and Los Angeles and Orange County coasts.

Access Northern California (www.accessnca.org) Extensive links to accessible-travel resources, including outdoor recreation opportunities, lodgings, tours and transportation.

Access San Francisco Guide (www.sftravel.com) Search the city's official tourism site for this free, downloadable PDF guide – dated, but useful.

Access Santa Cruz County (www.scaccessguide.com) Free online accessible-travel guide for visiting Santa Cruz and around, including restaurants, lodging, beaches, parks and outdoor recreation.

California State Parks (http://access.parks.ca.gov) Searchable online map and database of accessible features at state parks.

Flying Wheels Travel (✆507-451-5005; www.flyingwheelstravel.com) Full-service travel agency for travelers with disabilities, mobility issues and chronic illnesses.

Los Angeles for Disabled Visitors (www.discoverlosangeles.com/search/site/disabled) Tips for accessible sightseeing, entertainment, museums and transportation.

WheelchairTraveling.com (www.wheelchairtraveling.com) Travel articles, lodging and helpful California destination info.

Visas

➡ Visa information is highly subject to change. Depending on your country of origin, the rules for entering the USA keep changing. Double-check current visa requirements *before* arriving.

➡ Currently, under the US Visa Waiver Program (VWP), visas are not required for citizens of 38 countries for stays up to 90 days (no extensions) if you have a machine-readable passport (MRP) that meets current US standards and is valid for six months beyond your intended stay.

➡ Citizens of VWP countries must still register online with the Electronic System for Travel Authorization (ESTA; https://esta.cbp.dhs.gov) at least 72 hours before travel. Once approved, ESTA registration ($14) is valid for up to two years or until your passport expires, whichever comes first.

➡ For most Canadian citizens traveling with Canadian passports that meet current US standards, a visa for short-term visits (usually up to six months) and ESTA registration aren't required.

➡ Citizens from all other countries or whose passports don't meet US standards will need to apply for a visa in their home country. The process costs a nonrefundable fee (minimum $160), involves a personal interview and can take several weeks, so apply as early as possible.

➡ For up-to-date information about entry requirements and eligibility, check the visa section of the US Department of State website (http://travel.state.gov) or contact the nearest USA embassy or consulate in your home country (for a complete list, visit www.usembassy.gov).

Transportation

GETTING THERE & AWAY

Getting to California by air or overland by car, train or bus is easy, although it's not always cheap. Flights, cars and tours can be booked online at lonelyplanet.com/bookings.

Entering the Region

Under the US Department of Homeland Security's Orwellian-sounding Office of Biometric Identity Management, almost all visitors to the USA (excluding, for now, many Canadians, some Mexican citizens, children under age 14 and seniors over age 79) will be digitally photographed and have their electronic (inkless) fingerprints scanned upon arrival.

Regardless of your visa status, immigration officers have absolute authority to refuse entry to the USA. They may ask about your plans and whether you have sufficient funds; it's a good idea to list an itinerary, produce an onward or round-trip ticket and have at least one major credit card. Don't make too much of having friends, relatives or business contacts in the US, because officers may think this makes you more likely to overstay. For more information, visit the US Customs & Border Protection website (www.cbp.gov).

California is an important agricultural state. To prevent the spread of pests and diseases, certain food items (including meats, fresh fruit and vegetables) may not be brought into the state. Bakery items, chocolates and hard-cured cheeses are admissible. If you drive into California across the border from Mexico or from the neighboring states of Oregon, Nevada or Arizona, you may have to stop for a quick questioning and inspection by California Department of Food & Agriculture (www.cdfa.ca.gov) agents.

Passport

- Under the Western Hemisphere Travel Initiative (WHTI), all travelers must have a valid machine-readable passport (MRP) when entering the USA by air, land or sea.
- The only exceptions are for some US, Canadian and Mexican citizens traveling by land who can present other WHTI-compliant documents (eg pre-approved 'trusted traveler' cards). A regular driver's license is *not* sufficient.
- All foreign passports must meet current US standards and be valid for at least six months longer than your intended stay.
- MRPs issued or renewed after October 26, 2006 must be e-passports (ie have a digital photo and integrated chip with biometric data).
- For more information, consult www.cbp.gov/travel.

Air

- To get through airport security checkpoints (30- to 45-minute wait times are standard), you'll need a boarding pass and photo ID.
- Some travelers may be required to undergo a secondary screening, involving hand pat-downs and carry-on-bag searches.
- Airport security measures restrict many common items (eg pocketknives, scissors) from being carried on planes. Check current restrictions with the Transportation Security Administration (TSA; www.tsa.gov).
- Currently, TSA requires that all carry-on liquids and gels be stored in 3oz or smaller bottles placed inside a quart-sized clear plastic zip-top bag. Exceptions, which must be declared to checkpoint security officers, include medications.
- All checked luggage is screened for explosives. TSA may open your suitcase for visual confirmation, breaking the lock if necessary. Leave your bags unlocked or use a TSA-approved lock.

Airports & Airlines

Many domestic and international air carriers offer direct flights to and from California. California's major international airports are in Los Angeles and the San Francisco Bay Area. Smaller regional airports are mainly served by domestic US airlines.

Los Angeles International Airport (LAX; www.lawa.org/welcomeLAX.aspx; 1 World Way) iCalifornia's largest and busiest airport, 20 miles southwest of Downtown LA, near the beaches.

San Francisco International Airport (SFO; www.flysfo.com; S McDonnell Rd) Northern California's major hub. 14 miles south of downtown San Francisco.

Land

Border Crossings

It's relatively easy crossing from the USA into Mexico; it's crossing back into the USA that can pose problems if you haven't brought all of the required documents. Check the ever-changing passport and visa requirements with the US Department of State (http://travel.state.gov) *before* traveling

The US Customs & Border Protection (http://bwt.cbp.gov) tracks current wait times at every US border crossing. On the US–Mexico border between San Diego and Tijuana, San Ysidro is the world's busiest border crossing, with average wait times of an hour or more.

US citizens do not require a visa for stays of 72 hours or less within the Mexican border zone (ie as far south as Ensenada). But to reenter the USA, US citizens need to present a US passport or other WHTI-compliant travel document (see www.cbp.gov/travel); a regular US driver's license is not enough.

BUS

US-based **Greyhound** (☎800-231-2222; www.greyhound.com) and **Greyhound Mexico** (☎01-800-890-6821; www.greyhound.com.mx) have cooperative service, with direct buses between a few major cities in Mexico and California.

Northbound buses from Mexico can take some time to cross the US border, since US immigration may insist on checking every person on board.

CAR & MOTORCYCLE

➡ Unless you're planning an extended stay in Tijuana, driving across the Mexico border is more trouble than it's worth. Instead take the trolley from San Diego or park your car on the US side and walk across.

➡ If you do decide to drive across, you must purchase Mexican car insurance either beforehand or at the border crossing. Bring your vehicle's registration papers, US liability insurance and driver's license.

➡ If you're renting a car, recreational vehicle or motorcycle in the USA, ask if the agency allows its vehicles to be taken across the Mexican border – chances are it doesn't.

➡ Occasionally the authorities of either country decide to search a vehicle *thoroughly*. Remain calm and be polite.

Bus

Greyhound (☎800-231-2222; www.greyhound.com) is the major long-distance bus company, with routes across the USA, including throughout California. It has cut services to many small towns; routes trace major highways and may only stop at larger population centers.

Train

Amtrak (☎800-872-7245; www.amtrak.com) operates a fairly extensive rail system throughout the USA. Trains are comfortable, if a bit slow and occasionally delayed; they're equipped with dining and lounge cars and sometimes wi-fi on long-distance routes. Fares vary according to the type of train and seating (eg coach or business class, sleeping compartments).

Amtrak's major long-distance routes to/from California:

California Zephyr Daily service between Chicago and Emeryville (from $136, 52 hours), near San Francisco, via Denver, Salt Lake City, Reno and Sacramento.

Coast Starlight Travels the West Coast daily from Seattle to LA (from $97, 35½ hours) via Portland, Sacramento, Oakland,

CLIMATE CHANGE & TRAVEL

Every form of transport that relies on carbon-based fuel generates CO_2, the main cause of human-induced climate change. Modern travel is dependent on airplanes, which might use less fuel per mile per person than most cars but travel much greater distances. The altitude at which aircraft emit gases (including CO_2) and particles also contributes to their climate change impact. Many websites offer 'carbon calculators' that allow people to estimate the carbon emissions generated by their journey and, for those who wish to do so, to offset the impact of the greenhouse gases emitted with contributions to portfolios of climate-friendly initiatives throughout the world. Lonely Planet offsets the carbon footprint of all staff and writer travel.

San Jose, San Luis Obispo and Santa Barbara.

Southwest Chief Daily departures from Chicago and LA (from $141, 43 hours) via Kansas City, Albuquerque and Flagstaff.

Sunset Limited Thrice-weekly service between New Orleans and LA (from $136, 46½ hours) via Houston, San Antonio, El Paso and Tucson.

Sea

Several international cruise lines dock along California's coast at piers and cruise-ship terminals in San Diego, Long Beach and San Francisco.

GETTING AROUND

Most people drive themselves around California. You can also fly (it's expensive) or take cheaper long-distance buses or scenic trains. In cities, when distances are too far to walk, hop aboard buses, trains, streetcars, cable cars or trolleys, or grab a taxi.

Air

Several major US carriers fly within California. Flights are often operated by their regional subsidiaries, such as American Eagle, Delta Connection and United Express. Alaska Airlines/Virgin America, Frontier Airlines, Horizon Air and JetBlue serve many regional airports, as do low-cost airlines Southwest and Spirit.

Bicycle

➡ Cycling is a feasible way of getting around smaller cities and beach towns, but it's not much fun in traffic-dense urban areas like LA.

➡ San Francisco, Napa, Arcata and Santa Monica are among California's most bike-friendly communities, as rated by the League of American Bicyclists (www.bikeleague.org).

➡ You can rent bikes by the hour, day or week in most cities and many towns. Rentals start around $10 per day for beach cruisers and go up to $45 or more for mountain bikes (credit-card security deposit normally required).

Although it's a nonpolluting 'green' way to travel, cycling coastal California's roads demands a high level of fitness and the long distances involved make it difficult to cover much ground very fast. Come prepared for weather extremes, from chilly coastal fog and winter rainstorms to intense heat in summer.

Resources

Adventure Cycling Association (☎800-755-2453; www.adventurecycling.org) Online resource for purchasing bicycle-friendly maps and long-distance route guides; also organizes van-supported cycling tours for members (annual membership from $45).

Better World Club (☎866-238-1137; www.betterworldclub.com) Annual membership in the bicycle club (from $40) gets you two 24-hour emergency roadside-assistance calls and transport within a 30-mile radius.

California Bicycle Coalition (http://calbike.org) Links to cycling route maps, events, safety tips, laws, bike-sharing programs and community nonprofit bicycle shops.

Road Rules

➡ Cycling is allowed on all roads and highways – even along freeways if there's no suitable alternative, such as a smaller parallel frontage road; all mandatory exits are marked.

➡ Some cities have designated bicycle lanes, but make sure you have your wits about you in traffic.

➡ Cyclists must follow the same rules of the road as vehicles. Don't expect drivers to always respect your right of way.

➡ Wearing a helmet is mandatory for bicycle riders under 18 years old.

➡ Ensure you have proper lights and reflective gear, especially if you're pedaling at night or in fog.

Transporting Bicycles

➡ Bicycles may be transported on many local buses and trains, sometimes during off-peak, noncommuter hours only.

➡ Greyhound transports bicycles as luggage (surcharge $35 to $45), provided the bicycle is disassembled and placed in a rigid container ($10 box may be available for purchase at some terminals).

➡ Amtrak's *Pacific Surfliner* trains have onboard racks where you can secure your bike unboxed; reserve a spot for your bicycle (no surcharge) when buying tickets.

➡ On Amtrak trains without racks, bikes must be put in a box ($15 at most staffed terminals) and checked as luggage (fee $10 to $20). Not all stations or trains offer checked-baggage service, however.

➡ Before flying, you'll need to disassemble your bike and box it as checked baggage. Contact airlines directly for details, including surcharges ($75 to $150 or more).

Bus

Greyhound (☎800-231-2222; www.greyhound.com) buses are an economical way to travel between major cities and to points along the coast, but won't get you off the beaten path or to national parks or small towns. Frequency of service varies from 'rarely' to 'constantly,' but the main routes have service several times daily.

Greyhound buses are usually clean, comfortable

and reliable. The best seats are typically near the front away from the bathroom. Limited on-board amenities include freezing air-conditioning (bring a sweater) and slightly reclining seats; select buses have electrical outlets and wi-fi. Smoking on board is prohibited. Long-distance buses stop for meal breaks and driver changes.

Bus stations are typically dreary, often in dodgy areas; if you arrive at night, take a taxi into town or to your lodgings. In small towns where there is no bus station, know exactly where and when the bus arrives, be obvious as you flag it down and pay the driver with exact change.

Costs

You may save money by purchasing tickets in advance and by traveling between Monday and Thursday.

Discounts (on unrestricted fares only) are offered to seniors over 62 (5% off), students with a Student Advantage card (10%) and children under 16 years (20%). Tots under two years old ride for free only if they don't require a seat.

Special promotional discounts, such as 50% off companion fares, are often available, though they may come with restrictions or blackout periods. Check the website for current fare specials or ask when buying tickets.

Tickets & Reservations

It's easy to buy tickets online with a credit card, then pick them up (bring photo ID) at the terminal. You can also buy tickets over the phone or in person from a ticket agent. Greyhound terminal ticket agents accept credit and debit cards, traveler's checks (in US dollars) and cash.

General boarding is first-come, first-served. Buying tickets in advance doesn't guarantee a seat on any particular bus unless you also purchase priority boarding, available only on some routes. Otherwise, arrive at least one hour prior to the scheduled departure to get a seat; allow extra time on weekends and holidays.

Car & Motorcycle

California's love affair with cars runs deep for at least one practical reason: the state is so big, public transportation can't cover it. For flexibility and convenience, you'll probably want a car, but rental rates and gas prices can eat up a good chunk of your trip budget.

Automobile Associations

For 24-hour emergency roadside assistance, free maps and discounts on lodging, attractions, entertainment, car rentals and more, consider joining an auto club.

American Automobile Association (AAA; ☎800-922-8228; www.aaa.com) Walk-in offices throughout California, add-on coverage for RVs and motorcycles, and reciprocal agreements with some international auto clubs (eg CAA in Canada, AA in the UK) – bring your membership card from home.

Better World Club (☎866-238-1137; www.betterworldclub.com) Ecofriendly auto club that supports environmental causes and offers add-on or stand-alone emergency roadside assistance for cyclists as well.

Driving Licences

➡ Visitors may legally drive a car in California for up to 12 months with their home driver's license.

➡ If you're from overseas, an International Driving Permit (IDP) will have more credibility with traffic police and simplify the car-rental process, especially if your license doesn't have a photo or isn't written in English.

➡ To drive a motorcycle, you'll need a valid US state motorcycle license or a specially endorsed IDP.

➡ International automobile associations can issue IDPs, valid for one year, for a fee. Always carry your home license together with the IDP.

Fuel

➡ Gas stations in California, nearly all of which are self-service, are ubiquitous, except in national and state parks and some sparsely populated areas.

➡ Gas is sold in gallons (one US gallon equals 3.78L). The cost for midgrade fuel is around $3 a gallon.

Insurance

California law requires liability insurance for all vehicles. When renting a car, check your home auto-insurance policy or your international travel-insurance policy to see if you're already covered. If not, expect to pay around $10 to $20 or more per day.

Insurance against damage to the car itself, called Collision Damage Waiver (CDW) or Loss Damage Waiver (LDW), costs another $20 per day; the deductible may require you to pay the first $100 to $500 for any repairs.

Some credit cards cover CDW/LDW, provided you charge the entire cost of the car rental to the card. Check with your credit-card issuer first to determine the extent of coverage and policy exclusions. If there's an accident you may have to pay the rental-car company first, then seek reimbursement from the credit-card company.

Parking

➡ Parking is usually plentiful and free in small towns and rural areas, but often scarce and/or expensive in cities.

➡ When parking on the street, read all posted regulations and restrictions (eg street-cleaning hours, permit-only residential areas) and pay attention to

ROAD DISTANCES (miles)

	Anaheim	Los Angeles	Mendocino	Monterey	Napa	Sacramento	San Diego	San Francisco	San Luis Obispo
Los Angeles	25								
Mendocino	555	525							
Monterey	375	320	270						
Napa	425	400	140	150					
Sacramento	410	385	200	185	60				
San Diego	95	120	650	440	520	505			
San Francisco	405	380	155	120	50	85	500		
San Luis Obispo	225	200	380	145	275	290	320	230	
Santa Barbara	120	95	480	250	370	395	215	335	105

colored curbs, or you may be ticketed and towed.

➡ You can pay municipal parking meters and sidewalk pay stations with coins (eg quarters) and sometimes credit or debit cards.

➡ Expect to pay $30 to $50 for overnight parking in a city lot or garage.

Rental

CAR

To rent your own wheels, you'll typically need to be at least 25 years old, hold a valid driver's license and have a major credit card, *not* a check or debit card. A few companies may rent to drivers under 25 but over 21 for a hefty surcharge. If you don't have a credit card, large cash deposits are infrequently accepted.

With advance reservations, you can often get an economy-size vehicle with unlimited mileage from around $30 per day, plus insurance, taxes and fees. Weekend and weekly rates are usually the most economical. Airport locations may have cheaper rates but higher add-on fees; if you get a fly-drive package, local taxes may be extra when you pick up the car.

Rates generally include unlimited mileage, but expect surcharges for additional drivers and one-way rentals. Child or infant safety seats are legally required; reserve them when booking for $10 to $15 per day.

If you'd like to minimize your carbon footprint, some major car-rental companies offer 'green' fleets of hybrid or biofueled rental cars, but these fuel-efficient models are in short supply. Reserve those models well in advance and expect to pay significantly higher rates.

To find and compare independent car-rental companies, try **Car Rental Express** (www.carrentalexpress.com).

Avis (☎800-633-3469; www.avis.com)

Budget (☎800-218-7992; www.budget.com)

Dollar (☎800-800-5252; www.dollar.com)

Enterprise (☎855-266-9289; www.enterprise.com)

Fox (☎855-571-8410; www.foxrentacar.com)

Hertz (☎800-654-3131; www.hertz.com)

National (☎877-222-9058; www.nationalcar.com)

Payless (☎800-729-5377; www.paylesscar.com)

Rent-a-Wreck (☎877-877-0700; www.rentawreck.com) Minimum rental age and under-25 driver surcharges vary at six locations, including in LA and the San Francisco Bay Area.

Simply Rent-a-Car (☎323-653-0022; www.simplyrac.com) Rents hybrid, electric and flex-fuel vehicles in LA; ask about free delivery and pickup.

Sixt (☎888-749-8227; www.sixt.com)

Super Cheap! Car Rental (☎310-645-3993; www.supercheapcar.com) No surcharge for drivers ages 21 to 24; nominal daily fee applies for drivers ages 18 to 21 (full-coverage insurance required). Locations in the San Francisco Bay Area, LA and Orange County.

Thrifty (☎800-847-4389; www.thrifty.com)

Zipcar (☎866-494-7227; www.zipcar.com) Currently available in the San Francisco Bay Area, LA, San Diego and Sacramento, this car-sharing club charges usage fees (per hour or day), including free gas, insurance (a damage fee of up to $1000 may apply) and limited mileage. Apply online (foreign drivers accepted); application fee $25, annual membership from $70.

MOTORCYCLE

Depending on the model, renting a motorcycle costs $100 to $250 per day plus taxes and fees, including helmets, unlimited miles and liability insurance; one-way rentals and collision insurance (CDW) cost extra. Discounts may be available for multiday and weekly rentals. Security deposits range up to $2000 (credit card required).

California Motorcycle Adventures (☎800-601-5370, 650-969-6198; www.californiamotorcycleadventures.com; 2554 W Middlefield Rd, Mountain View) Harley-Davidson and BMW rentals in Silicon Valley.

Dubbelju (☎415-495-2774, 866-495-2774; www.dubbelju.com; 274 Shotwell St; per day from $99; ⊙9am-6pm Mon-Sat) Rents Harley-Davidson, Japanese and European imported motorcycles, as well as scooters.

Eagle Rider (☎888-900-9901, 310-321-3180; www.eaglerider.com) Nationwide company with 11 locations in California.

RECREATIONAL VEHICLES

Gas-guzzling recreational vehicles (RVs) remain popular despite fuel prices and being cumbersome to drive. That said, they do solve transportation, accommodation and cooking needs in one fell swoop. It's easy to find RV campgrounds with electricity and water hookups, but in cities, RVs are a nuisance, because there are few places to park or plug them in.

Book RVs as far in advance as possible. Rental costs vary by size and model, but you can expect to pay over $100 per day. Rates often don't include mileage, bedding or kitchen kits, vehicle-prep fees or taxes. If pets are allowed, a surcharge may apply.

Camper USA (☎310-929-5666; www.camperusa.com) Campervan rentals in LA and the San Francisco Bay Area.

Cruise America (☎480-464-7300, 800-671-8042; www.cruiseamerica.com) Nationwide RV-rental company with 20 locations statewide.

El Monte (☎562-483-4985, 888-337-2214; www.elmonterv.com) With over a dozen locations in California, this national RV rental agency offers AAA discounts.

Escape Campervans (☎877-270-8267, 310-672-9909; www.escapecampervans.com) Awesomely painted campervans at economical rates in LA and the San Francisco Bay Area.

Jucy Rentals (☎800-650-4180; www.jucyrentals.com) Campervan rentals in LA and the San Francisco Bay Area.

Road Bear (☎866-491-9853, 818-865-2925; www.roadbearrv.com) RV rentals in LA and the San Francisco Bay Area.

Vintage Surfari Wagons (☎714-585-7565; www.vwsurfari.com) VW campervan rentals in Orange County.

Road Conditions & Hazards

For up-to-date highway conditions, including road closures and construction updates, check with CalTrans (www.dot.ca.gov).

In coastal areas thick fog can often impede driving – slow down and if it's too soupy, get off the road. Along ocean cliffs and on curvy mountain roads, watch out for falling rocks, mudslides and avalanches that could damage or disable your car.

Coastal highways alongside steep, crumbly cliffs may wash out in winter, sometimes for months at a time. When you see signs that read, 'Expect long delays 40 miles ahead' or 'Hwy 1 closed north of Hearst Castle,' heed the warnings, but don't panic. If you have lodging reservations, call ahead and ask about available local detours.

Road Rules

- Drive on the right-hand side of the road.
- Talking, texting or otherwise using a cell (mobile) phone or other mobile electronic device without hands-free technology while driving is illegal.
- The driver and all passengers must use seat belts in a private vehicle. In a taxi or limo, back-seat passengers are not required to buckle up.
- Infant and child safety seats are required for children under eight years old or who are less than 4ft 9in tall.
- All motorcyclists must wear a helmet. Scooters are not allowed on freeways.
- High-occupancy (HOV) lanes marked with a diamond symbol are reserved for cars with multiple occupants, sometimes only during signposted hours.
- Unless otherwise posted, the speed limit is 65mph on freeways, 55mph on two-lane undivided highways, 35mph on major city streets and 25mph in business and residential districts and near schools.
- Except where indicated, turning right at red lights after coming to a full stop is permitted, although intersecting traffic still has the right of way.
- At four-way stop signs, cars proceed in the order in which they arrived; if two cars arrive simultaneously, the one on the right has the right of way. When in doubt, wave the other driver ahead.
- When emergency vehicles (eg ambulances, fire trucks) approach from either direction, carefully pull over to the side of the road.
- Driving under the influence of alcohol or drugs is illegal. It's also illegal to carry open containers of alcohol, even empty ones, inside a vehicle; store them in the trunk.

Local Transportation

California's major coastal cities have relatively cheap local bus, cable-car, trolley, train, light-rail and/or subway systems. Larger coastal towns and counties operate commuter-oriented bus systems, usually with limited evening and weekend services. Public transportation in rural areas and to state and national parks can be sparse.

Taxi

- Taxis are metered, with flag-fall fees of $2.50 to $3.50 to start, plus $2 to $3 per mile. Credit cards may be accepted, but bring cash just in case.

➡ Taxis may charge extra for baggage and airport pickups.

➡ Drivers expect a 10% to 15% tip, rounded up to the next dollar.

➡ Taxis cruise busy urban areas, but elsewhere you may need to call for one.

Train

Amtrak (☎800-872-7245; www.amtrak.com) runs comfortable, if occasionally tardy, trains to major California cities and some towns. Amtrak's Thruway buses provide onward connections from many train stations. Smoking is prohibited aboard trains and buses.

Amtrak routes serving coastal California:

Coast Starlight Chugs roughly north–south almost the entire length of the state. Daily stops include LA, Burbank, Santa Barbara, San Luis Obispo, Paso Robles, Salinas, San Jose, Oakland and Emeryville.

Pacific Surfliner Eight daily trains ply the San Diego–LA route via Orange County, stopping at San Diego's North County beach towns and Orange County's San Juan Capistrano and Anaheim, home of Disneyland. Three trains continue north to Santa Barbara via Burbank, Ventura and Carpinteria, with one going all the way to San Luis Obispo. Trains hug the scenic coastline for much of the route. On-board wi-fi may be available.

Costs

Purchase tickets at train stations, by phone or online (in advance for the cheapest fares). Fares depend on the day of travel, the route, the type of seating etc. They may be slightly higher during peak travel periods (eg summer). Round-trip tickets typically cost the same as two one-way tickets.

Usually seniors over 62 and students ages 13 to 25 with a valid student ID card receive a 15% discount, while up to two children aged two to 12 who are accompanied by an adult get 50% off. AAA members save 10%. Special promotions can become available anytime, so check the website or ask when making reservations.

Reservations

Amtrak reservations can be made up to 11 months prior to departure. In summer and around holidays, trains sell out, so book tickets as early as possible. The cheapest coach fares are usually for unreserved seats; business-class fares come with guaranteed seats.

Travelers with disabilities who need special assistance, wheelchair space, transfer seats or accessible accommodations should call ☎800-872-7245 (TDD/TTY ☎800-523-6590), and also inquire about discounted fares when booking.

Train Passes

Amtrak's California Rail Pass costs $159 ($80 for children ages two to 12) and is valid on all trains (except certain long-distance routes) and most connecting Thruway buses for seven days of travel within a 21-day period. Passholders must reserve each leg of travel in advance and obtain hard-copy tickets prior to boarding.

Behind the Scenes

SEND US YOUR FEEDBACK

We love to hear from travelers – your comments keep us on our toes and help make our books better. Our well-traveled team reads every word on what you loved or loathed about this book. Although we cannot reply individually to your submissions, we always guarantee that your feedback goes straight to the appropriate authors, in time for the next edition. Each person who sends us information is thanked in the next edition – the most useful submissions are rewarded with a selection of digital PDF chapters.

Visit **lonelyplanet.com/contact** to submit your updates and suggestions or to ask for help. Our award-winning website also features inspirational travel stories, news and discussions.

Note: We may edit, reproduce and incorporate your comments in Lonely Planet products such as guidebooks, websites and digital products, so let us know if you don't want your comments reproduced or your name acknowledged. For a copy of our privacy policy visit lonelyplanet.com/privacy.

WRITER THANKS

Nate Cavalieri

Many thanks to my partner Florence, who is always game for a last-minute road trip to Bakersfield. Thanks to Cliff, Daniel, Jane, Diane and the staff Lonely Planet for all the support and to my colleague Alison Bing, who inspired me to get back in the travel- writing game after a long and ill-advised hiatus.

Brett Atkinson

Thanks to everyone who made my exploration of California's Central Coast so enjoyable, especially Christina Glynn in Santa Cruz. In Santa Cruz, thanks also to Margaret Leonard for travel inspiration beyond the borders of Monterey Bay. The staff at the region's visitor centers were all uniformly helpful, and at Lonely Planet, huge thanks to Cliff Wilkinson for the opportunity to return to Big Sur. Across the vast South Pacific in Auckland, thanks to Carol and my family for their support.

Andrew Bender

Thanks to Denise Lengyeltoti, Christie Bacock, Melissa Perez, Jackie Alvarez, Jennifer Tong, Erin Ramsauer, Michael Ramirez, Jenny Wedge, Ashley Johnson and the many information center, hotel and restaurant staffers who gave me way more of their time than I deserved. In house, thanks especially to Clifton Wilkinson, Sarah Stocking, Anita Isalska, Judith Bamber and Kathryn Rowan.

Alison Bing

Thanks to Cliff Wilkinson, Sarah Sung, Lisa Park, DeeAnn Budney, PT Tenenbaum and, above all, Marco Flavio Marinucci, for making a Muni bus ride into the adventure of a lifetime.

Cristian Bonetto

A heartfelt thank you to the many Angelenos (and New Yorkers) who shared their LA secrets and insights with me, especially John-Mark Horton, Michael Amato, Andy Bender, Norge Yip, Calvin Yeung, Douglas Levine, Daphne Barahona, Nicholas Maricich, David Singleman, William J Brockschmidt, Richard Dragisic and Andy Walker. Thanks also to fellow Aussies in SoCal, Mary-ann Gardner and Natalie Yanoulis. At Lonely Planet, much gratitude to Cliff Wilkinson.

Jade Bremner

Thanks to Destination Editor Clifton Wilkinson for his support and endless knowledge about LP. Plus, everyone working their socks off behind the scenes – Cheree Broughton, Dianne, Jane, Neill Coen, Evan Godt and Helen Elfer. Last but not least, thanks to the friendly staff at Fig Tree Cafe for making those marvelous egg Bennies, which often set me up for the day.

Ashley Harrell

Thanks to my coauthors and editors for their diligence and support, the kind people all over Wine Country for their time and recommendations, David Roth and Andy Wright (dumb people) for the endless amusement, Amy Benziger for letting me trash her apartment, Shane Henegan for his glorious Airstream, Paul Stockamore for David Applebaum, Adele Fox for being the best Gumpy, Anne Murphy for sharing her ranch and wise, hilarious opinions, and Andy Lavender for his innumerable contributions and unrelenting care.

Josephine Quintero

Thanks to Cliff Wilkinson for the opportunity to research this fabulous region of California. Also to my road-trip buddy, Robin Chapman, and my good local resident pals who invaluably assisted me: Janice Crowe and Linda Sinclair. Also thanks to the helpful folk in the various visitor centers and, last but not least, those at the SPP help desk when I had a serious technical glitch!

John A Vlahides

Thanks to destination editor Clifton Wilkinson and coauthor Alison Bing, with whom it's always lovely to work. And most of all, thanks to you, dear reader – you make my life so joyful and I'm grateful for the honor of being your guide through the cool gray city of love.

Clifton Wilkinson

Thanks to the Santa Barbara County tourism people (Karna, Danielle, Chrisie) who provided excellent recommendations, including my favorite meal of the whole update. Thanks too to all the inhouse LP team, especially colleagues who listened patiently to all my pre-trip plans. And final thanks to the weather, which mostly played along with my research – except for all the mud on Santa Cruz Channel Island (if anyone finds some sunglasses, they might be the ones I lost falling over).

ACKNOWLEDGMENTS

Climate map data adapted from Peel MC, Finlayson BL & McMahon TA (2007) 'Updated World Map of the Köppen-Geiger Climate Classification', *Hydrology and Earth System Sciences*, 11, pp1633–44.

Cover photograph: Los Angeles, Hero Images/ Getty ©

Illustration on pp66-7 by Michael Weldon.

THIS BOOK

This 6th edition of Lonely Planet's *Coastal California* guidebook was researched and written by Nate Cavalieri, Brett Atkinson, Andrew Bender, Sara Benson, Alison Bing, Cristian Bonetto, Jade Bremner, Ashley Harrell, Josephine Quintero, John A Vlahides and Clifton Wilkinson. Sara, Andrew, Alison and John also wrote the previous edition, alongside Celeste Brash, Beth Kohn and Adam Skolnick. This guidebook was produced by the following:

Destination Editors Sarah Stocking, Clifton Wilkinson

Product Editors Rachel Rawling, Kate Mathews

Senior Cartographer Alison Lyall

Cartographer Valentina Kremenchutskaya

Book Designer Jessica Rose

Assisting Editors Will Allen, Sarah Bailey, Andrew Bain, Judith Bamber, Carolyn Boicos, Andrea Dobbin, Carly Hall, Victoria Harrison, Kate Kiely, Kellie Langdon, Jodie Martire, Charlotte Orr

Cover Researcher Naomi Parker

Thanks to Kate Chapman, Rodrigo Chia, Sasha Drew, Nicholas Colicchia, Jackie Fisher, Amy Luning, Virginia Moreno, Catherine Naghten, Vicky Smith, Lyahna Spencer, Ross Taylor, Regina Wright, Tony Wheeler

Index

Map Pages **000**
Photo Pages **000**

Map Pages **000**
Photo Pages **000**

Map Legend

Sights
- Beach
- Bird Sanctuary
- Buddhist
- Castle/Palace
- Christian
- Confucian
- Hindu
- Islamic
- Jain
- Jewish
- Monument
- Museum/Gallery/Historic Building
- Ruin
- Shinto
- Sikh
- Taoist
- Winery/Vineyard
- Zoo/Wildlife Sanctuary
- Other Sight

Activities, Courses & Tours
- Bodysurfing
- Diving
- Canoeing/Kayaking
- Course/Tour
- Sento Hot Baths/Onsen
- Skiing
- Snorkeling
- Surfing
- Swimming/Pool
- Walking
- Windsurfing
- Other Activity

Sleeping
- Sleeping
- Camping
- Hut/Shelter

Eating
- Eating

Drinking & Nightlife
- Drinking & Nightlife
- Cafe

Entertainment
- Entertainment

Shopping
- Shopping

Information
- Bank
- Embassy/Consulate
- Hospital/Medical
- Internet
- Police
- Post Office
- Telephone
- Toilet
- Tourist Information
- Other Information

Geographic
- Beach
- Gate
- Hut/Shelter
- Lighthouse
- Lookout
- Mountain/Volcano
- Oasis
- Park
- Pass
- Picnic Area
- Waterfall

Population
- Capital (National)
- Capital (State/Province)
- City/Large Town
- Town/Village

Transport
- Airport
- BART station
- Border crossing
- Boston T station
- Bus
- Cable car/Funicular
- Cycling
- Ferry
- Metro/Muni station
- Monorail
- Parking
- Petrol station
- Subway/SkyTrain station
- Taxi
- Train station/Railway
- Tram
- Underground station
- Other Transport

Routes
- Tollway
- Freeway
- Primary
- Secondary
- Tertiary
- Lane
- Unsealed road
- Road under construction
- Plaza/Mall
- Steps
- Tunnel
- Pedestrian overpass
- Walking Tour
- Walking Tour detour
- Path/Walking Trail

Boundaries
- International
- State/Province
- Disputed
- Regional/Suburb
- Marine Park
- Cliff
- Wall

Hydrography
- River, Creek
- Intermittent River
- Canal
- Water
- Dry/Salt/Intermittent Lake
- Reef

Areas
- Airport/Runway
- Beach/Desert
- Cemetery (Christian)
- Cemetery (Other)
- Glacier
- Mudflat
- Park/Forest
- Sight (Building)
- Sportsground
- Swamp/Mangrove

Note: Not all symbols displayed above appear on the maps in this book

Alison Bing

San Francisco Alison has done most things travelers are supposed to do and many you definitely shouldn't, including making room for the chickens, accepting dinner invitations from cults, and trusting the camel to know the way. She has survived to tell tales for Lonely Planet, NPR, BBC Travel, the *Telegraph, New York Times* and other global media.

Cristian Bonetto

Los Angeles Cristian has contributed to over 30 Lonely Planet guides to date, including *New York City*, *Italy*, *Venice & the Veneto*, *Naples & the Amalfi Coast*, *Denmark*, *Copenhagen*, *Sweden* and *Singapore*. Lonely Planet work aside, his musings on travel, food, culture and design appear in numerous publications around the world, including the *Telegraph* (UK) and *Corriere del Mezzogiorno* (Italy). When not on the road, you'll find the reformed playwright and TV scriptwriter slurping espresso in his beloved hometown, Melbourne, Australia. Instagram: rexcat75.

Jade Bremner

San Diego Jade has been a journalist for more than a decade. She has lived in and reported on four different regions. Wherever she goes she finds action sports to try – the weirder the better – and it's no coincidence many of her favorite places have some of the best waves in the world. Jade has edited travel magazines and sections for *Time Out* and Radio Times and has been a correspondent for the *Times*, CNN and the *Independent*. She feels privileged to share tales from this wonderful planet we call home and is always looking for the next adventure.

Ashley Harrell

Napa & Sonoma Wine Country After a brief stint selling day-spa coupons door-to-door in South Florida, Ashley decided she'd rather be a writer. She went to journalism grad school, convinced a newspaper to hire her and starting covering wildlife, crime and tourism, sometimes all in the same story. Fueling her zest for storytelling and the unknown, she traveled widely and moved often, from a tiny NYC apartment to a vast California ranch to a jungle cabin in Costa Rica, where she started writing for Lonely Planet. From there her travels became more exotic and farther flung, and she still laughs when paychecks arrive.

Josephine Quintero

North Coast & Redwoods Josephine first got her taste of not-so-serious travel when she slung a guitar on her back and traveled in Europe in the early '70s. In the mid-'70s Josephine moved to the US and, a U.C. Berkeley (English) degree and two daughters later, launched her journalism career as Assistant Editor for a Napa Valley wine and lifestyle magazine. She was an editor for the now defunct *Go* airlines inflight magazine and still writes two monthly columns (Malaga and Gibraltar) for Easyjet's magazine as well as a bimonthly column on Seville for a Belgian airline. Josephine also writes short stories and has had some minor publishing success.

John A Vlahides

San Francisco John has been a cook in a Parisian bordello, a luxury-hotel concierge, a television host, a safety monitor in a sex club, French–English interpreter and is an experienced and prolific author for Lonely Planet. A native New Yorker living in San Francisco, John has contributed to 18 Lonely Planet guidebooks since 2003, ranging from *California* and *Western USA* to the *Dubai* guide. He is co-host of the TV series *Lonely Planet: Roads Less Travelled* (National Geographic Adventure).

Clifton Wilkinson

Santa Barbara County Clifton has been in love with California since first visiting in 1995. Christmases spent near Sacramento, bike rides across the Golden Gate Bridge and hiking in Yosemite National Park have all reinforced Clifton's opinion that the Golden State is the best state in the whole US, and Santa Barbara is one of its most beautiful corners. Having worked for Lonely Planet for more than 11 years, he's now based in the London office, but hoping for the call back to CA's *Sideways* country and the chance to show that Merlot isn't all that bad.

OUR STORY

A beat-up old car, a few dollars in the pocket and a sense of adventure. In 1972 that's all Tony and Maureen Wheeler needed for the trip of a lifetime – across Europe and Asia overland to Australia. It took several months, and at the end – broke but inspired – they sat at their kitchen table writing and stapling together their first travel guide, *Across Asia on the Cheap*. Within a week they'd sold 1500 copies. Lonely Planet was born.

Today, Lonely Planet has offices in Franklin, London, Melbourne, Oakland, Dublin, Beijing and Delhi, with more than 600 staff and writers. We share Tony's belief that 'a great guidebook should do three things: inform, educate and amuse'.

OUR WRITERS

Nate Cavalieri

Sacramento & the Central Valley Nate is a writer and musician based in Oakland, California and has authored over a dozen titles for Lonely Planet including guides to California, the Caribbean and Latin America. He also married his obsessive interest in cycling and travel as an author of Lonely Planet's *Epic Bike Rides of the World*. In other loosely professional pursuits, Nate has cycled across China and Southern Africa as a guide with Tour d'Afrique, played third chair percussion in an Orlando theme park and accompanied modern dance classes. Nate is fortunate to make his living writing about things he loves: music, travel and social justice.

Brett Atkinson

Central Coast Brett is based in Auckland, New Zealand, but frequently on the road for Lonely Planet. He's a full-time travel and food writer specializing in adventure travel, unusual destinations and surprising angles on more well known destinations. Craft beer and street food are Brett's favorite reasons to explore places and he is featured regularly on the Lonely Planet website and in newspapers, magazines and websites across New Zealand and Australia. Since becoming a Lonely Planet writer in 2005, Brett has covered areas as diverse as Vietnam, Sri Lanka, the Czech Republic, New Zealand, Morocco, California and the South Pacific.

Andrew Bender

Los Angeles; Disneyland & Orange County An award-winning travel and food writer, Andrew has written three dozen Lonely Planet guidebooks (from *Amsterdam* to *Los Angeles*, *Germany* to *Taiwan* and over a dozen titles about Japan), plus numerous articles for lonelyplanet.com. Outside of Lonely Planet, he writes the Seat 1A travel site for Forbes.com and is a frequent contributor to the *Los Angeles Times*, in-flight magazines and more. Andrew has lived in Japan, France and the Netherlands, speaks fluent Japanese and French, reads Korean menus, can follow Italian and Spanish (though not very far) and cannot pronounce a single word correctly in Danish. A native New Englander, he now lives in the Los Angeles area.

Sara Benson

Marin County & the Bay Area After graduating from college in Chicago, Sara jumped on a plane to California with one suitcase and just $100 in her pocket. She landed in San Francisco and today she makes her home in Oakland, just across the Bay. She also spent three years living in Japan, after which she followed her wanderlust around Asia and the Pacific before returning to the USA, where she has worked as a teacher, a journalist, a nurse and a national park ranger. To keep up with Sara's latest travel adventures, read her blog, *The Indie Traveler* (indietraveler.blogspot.com) and follow her on Twitter (@indie_traveler) and Instagram (indietraveler).

OVER PAGE MORE WRITERS

Published by Lonely Planet Global Limited
CRN 554153
6th edition – Mar 2018
ISBN 978 1 78657 360 5

10 9 8 7 6 5 4 3 2 1
Printed in China